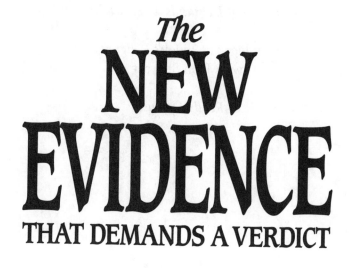

The
NEW
EVIDENCE
THAT DEMANDS A VERDICT

JOSH McDOWELL

The NEW EVIDENCE

THAT DEMANDS A VERDICT

THOMAS NELSON PUBLISHERS

Nashville

Book design and composition by Mark McGarry, Texas Type & Book Works, Dallas, Texas
Set in Minion and Franklin Gothic

Library of Congress Cataloging-in-Publication Data
McDowell, Josh.
    The new evidence that demands a verdict / by Josh McDowell.—Rev., updated, and expanded.
        p. cm.
    "Evidence that demands a verdict, volumes 1 & 2, now together in one volume."
    Includes bibliographical references and indexes.
    ISBN 0-7852-4219-8
1. Bible—Evidences, authority, etc. 2. Apologetics. I. McDowell, Josh. Evidence that demands
a verdict. II. Title.
BS480 .M384 1999
220.6'01—dc21   99-047181

Printed in the United States of America
    12 13 14 — 06

To Dottie:

My sweetheart, my best friend, and my wife.

Without her patience, love, encouragement,
and constructive criticism this project could
never have been completed.

Contents

How a relationship with Jesus Christ transformed the author's life.

Faith built on facts. An intelligent faith. Misconceptions about Christianity. Worldviews behind the misconceptions.

PART ONE: THE CASE FOR THE BIBLE

An intelligent person seeking truth would certainly read and consider a book that has the historical qualifications of the Bible. Unique qualifications that set the Scriptures apart from every other book ever written.

Materials used. Bible divisions. Why just thirty-nine Old Testament books and twenty-seven New Testament books? What about the Apocrypha? Why not other books?

The tests applied to all ancient literature to determine reliability. How does the New Testament compare? Archaeological finds confirming the New Testament.

Bibliographical test. Internal evidence test. Archaeological evidence demonstrating the trustworthiness of the Old Testament.

Foreword

Is Christianity credible?

Is there an intellectual basis for faith in Jesus Christ as the Son of God?

Scholars throughout the centuries, as well as millions of students and older adults, will answer such questions with a resounding, "Yes!" This is what *The NEW Evidence That Demands a Verdict,* by Josh McDowell, is all about.

Since 1964, Josh has served as a traveling representative with Campus Crusade for Christ International. More than seven million students and professors on more than seven hundred campuses in eighty-four countries have been enlightened, encouraged, helped, and challenged by his inspired teaching and witness. His experience speaking to student gatherings—large and small rallies, classroom lectures, and hundreds of counseling sessions and debates—plus a

magna cum laude degree from Talbot Theological Seminary and his extensive research on the historical evidences of the Christian faith, qualify Josh to speak and write with authority on the credibility of Christianity.

A lawyer once asked Jesus: "Sir, which is the most important commandment in the law of Moses?" Jesus replied, "Love the Lord your God with all your heart, soul, and mind. This is the first and greatest commandment" (Matt. 22:37, 38). God created us with the ability to think, to acquire knowledge, and to discern truth. *God wants us to use our minds.*

The apostle Peter admonishes, "Sanctify Christ as Lord in your hearts, always being ready to make a defense to every one who asks you to give an account for the hope that is in you" (1 Pet. 3:15).

For this reason, the ministry of Campus

Crusade for Christ emphasizes the training of Christians to experience and share the abundant, exciting life available to all who place their trust in Jesus Christ. Leadership Training Institutes, Lay Institutes for Evangelism, Institutes of Biblical Studies, and other training programs have prepared hundreds of thousands to give valid, convincing, historical, and documented reasons for their faith in Jesus Christ.

During my fifty-five years of sharing the good news of the Savior with the academic world, I have met very few individuals who have honestly considered the evidence and yet deny that Jesus Christ is the Son of God and the Savior of men. To me, the evidence confirming the deity of the Lord Jesus Christ is overwhelmingly conclusive to any honest, objective seeker after truth. However, not all—not even the majority—of those to whom I have spoken have accepted Him as their Savior and Lord. This is not because they were *unable* to believe—they were simply *unwilling* to believe!

For example, a brilliant but confused psychiatrist came to Arrowhead Springs for counsel. He confessed frankly to me that he had never been willing to consider honestly the claims of Christ in his own life for fear that he would be convinced and, as a result, would have to change his way of life. Other well-known professing atheists, including Aldous Huxley and Bertrand Russell, have refused to come to intellectual grips with the basic historical facts concerning the birth, life, teachings, miracles, death, and resurrection of Jesus of Nazareth. Those who have— C. S. Lewis, C. E. M. Joad, and Malcolm Muggeridge, for example—have found the

evidence so convincing that they have accepted the verdict that Jesus Christ truly is who He claimed to be—the Son of God and their own Savior and Lord.

A careful and prayerful study of the material contained in this book will prepare the reader to make an intelligent and convincing presentation of the good news. One final word of caution and counsel, however: Do not assume that the average person has intellectual doubts about the deity of Jesus Christ. The majority of people in most cultures do not need to be convinced of His deity, nor of their need of Him as Savior. Rather, they need to be told how to receive Him as Savior and follow Him as Lord.

Thus, it is the Christian himself who will derive the greatest benefit from reading *The NEW Evidence That Demands a Verdict*. This book will simultaneously strengthen your own faith in Christ and provide evidence that will enable you to share your faith more effectively with others.

"Then He said to Thomas, 'Reach your finger here, and look at My hands; and reach your hand here, and put it into My side. Do not be unbelieving, but believing.'

"And Thomas answered and said to Him, 'My Lord and my God!'

"Jesus said to him, 'Thomas, because you have seen Me, you have believed. Blessed are those who have not seen and yet have believed'" (John 20:27–29).

William R. Bright
President and Founder
Campus Crusade for Christ International
Arrowhead Springs
San Bernardino, CA 92414

Preface

WHAT? ANOTHER BOOK?

No, this is not a book. It is a compilation of notes prepared for my lecture series, "Christianity: Hoax or History?" There has been a definite shortage of documentation of the historical evidences for the Christian faith. Students, professors, and lay people in the church often ask, "How can we document and use what you and others teach?"

After publishing Volume 1 of *Evidence That Demands a Verdict*, I received many requests from students, professors, and pastors for material dealing with the documentary hypothesis and form criticism. University students often find themselves taking courses under professors who are steeped in one view. Those students, due to their lack of background, find themselves being brainwashed, not educated. Having no basis or sources upon which to base a counter-response to what they are being taught, these students are often intimidated. There has clearly been a need to counteract the "absoluteness" of so many university textbooks on these two subjects. Thus we produced Volume 2 of *Evidence That Demands a Verdict*.

Today the documentary hypothesis and form criticism are out-of-date. But many of the precepts are still parroted by professors in the universities and colleges. Furthermore, these faulty principles are often the starting point for investigations by critics of the Bible, such as those involved in the Jesus Seminar or professors teaching courses that deal with biblical topics. This new edition brings the debate up to date.

WHY THIS REVISED EDITION?

Since the first edition of *Evidence That Demands a Verdict*, published in 1972, and its revision in 1979, significant new discoveries have occurred that further confirm the historical evidence for the Christian faith. For example, new archaeological finds have added additional confirmation to the credibility of both the Old and New Testaments.

Nevertheless, for the past twenty years our culture has been heavily influenced by the philosophical outlook called postmodernism. People today question why evidence for the Christian faith is even necessary or important. There is a skepticism in our land and around the world that has allowed the misguided thinking of such projects as the Jesus Seminar to confuse and disorient people about the true identity of Jesus Christ.

It is my hope that, in providing the most up-to-date information, this third edition of *Evidence That Demands a Verdict* will equip Christians of the twenty-first century with confidence as they seek to understand and defend their faith.

DO WHAT WITH IT?

These notes are intended to help my brothers and sisters in Jesus Christ to write term papers, give speeches, and inject into classroom dialogues or personal conversations with business associates or neighbors their convictions about Christ, the Scriptures, and the relevancy of Christianity to the twenty-first century.

Students have commented on how they have used these lecture notes in their universities.

One wrote: "In my speech class, I used your lecture notes to prepare my three speeches before the class. The first was on the reliability of the Scriptures, the second on Jesus Christ, and the third on the resurrection."

Another student wrote: "Your documentation has encouraged many of us here to speak up in our classes. . . . The boldness of

the Christian is beginning to be evident everywhere."

Still another said: "I used the notes in preparing a speech for an oratory contest. I won, and will be giving the same speech at graduation. Thanks a lot, brother."

From a professor: "Your book provided much of the material I had been looking for to give in my class. Thanks a lot."

A pastor: "The knowledge I gained from reading your book has answered the nagging doubts I had left over from seminary."

A layman: "Your research has helped me to evaluate the Sunday school material I have been asked to teach."

And, finally, from another university student: "If I had had this material last year, I could have intelligently answered almost every negative assertion of the professor in my Old Testament class."

WATCH YOUR ATTITUDE

Our motivation in using these lecture notes is to glorify and magnify Jesus Christ—not to win an argument. *Evidence* is not for proving the Word of God, but rather for providing a basis for faith. One should have a gentle and reverent spirit when using apologetics or evidences: "But sanctify Christ as Lord in your hearts, always being ready to make a defense to every one who asks you to give an account for the hope that is in you, yet *with gentleness and reverence*" (1 Pet. 3:15 NASB, emphasis mine).

These notes, used with a caring attitude, can motivate a person to consider Jesus Christ honestly, and direct him or her back to the central and primary issue—the gospel (such as contained in the Four Spiritual Laws at the end of this book and in 1 Cor. 15:1–4).

When I share Christ with someone who has honest doubts, I always offer enough information to answer his or her questions, then I turn the conversation back to that person's relationship with Christ. The presentation of evidence (apologetics) should never be used as a substitute for sharing the Word of God.

WHY COPYRIGHTED?
These notes are copyrighted, not to limit their use, but to protect against their misuse and to safeguard the rights of the authors and publishers I have quoted and documented.

WHY IN OUTLINE FORM?
Because these notes are in outline form and the transitions between various concepts are not extensively written out, one will make the most effective use of this material by thinking through the individual sections and developing one's own convictions. Thus it becomes your message and not the parroting of someone else's.

GODISNOWHERE . . .

Does this mean GOD IS NO WHERE? or GOD IS NOW HERE? The outline structure of these notes can sometimes lead a person to misunderstand an illustration or concept. Practice caution as you draw conclusions one way or another when you do not clearly understand something. Study it further and investigate other sources.

A LIFETIME INVESTMENT:
I recommend the following books related to Parts One and Two for your library. These are also good books to donate to your university library. (Or, university libraries will often buy books if you fill out a request slip.)

1. Archer, Gleason. *A Survey of Old Testament Introduction.* Moody Press.
2. Bruce, F. F. *The Books and the Parchments.* Fleming Revell.
3. Bruce, F. F. *The New Testament Documents: Are They Reliable?* InterVarsity Press.
4. Geisler, Norman L., and William E. Nix. *A General Introduction to the Bible.* Moody Press.
5. Henry, Carl (ed.). *Revelation and the Bible.* Baker Book House.
6. Kitchen, K. A. *Ancient Orient and Old Testament.* InterVarsity Press.
7. Little, Paul. *Know Why You Believe.* InterVarsity Press.
8. Montgomery, John Warwick. *History and Christianity.* InterVarsity Press.
9. Montgomery, John Warwick. *Shapes of the Past.* Edwards Brothers.
10. Pinnock, Clark. *Set Forth Your Case.* Craig Press.
11. Ramm, Bernard. *Protestant Christian Evidences.* Moody Press.
12. Smith, Wilbur. *Therefore Stand.* Baker Book House.
13. Stoner, Peter. *Science Speaks.* Moody Press.
14. Stott, John R. W. *Basic Christianity.* InterVarsity Press.
15. Thomas, Griffith. *Christianity Is Christ.* Moody Press.

The following books, relating to Part Three, I also recommend:

1. Cassuto, U. *The Documentary Hypothesis.* Magnes Press, The Hebrew University.
2. Free, Joseph P. *Archaeology and Bible History.* Scripture Press.
3. Guthrie, Donald. *New Testament Introduction.* InterVarsity Press.
4. Harrison, R. K. *Introduction to the Old Testament.* Wm. B. Eerdmans Publishing Company.
5. Kistemaker, Simon. *The Gospels in Current Study.* Baker Book House.

6. Ladd, G. E. *The New Testament and Criticism.* Wm. B. Eerdmans Publishing Co.

The following are three excellent books for understanding New Testament criticism:

7. Marshall, Howard I. *Luke: Historian and Theologian.* Zondervan Publishing House.
8. McNight, Edgar V. *What Is Form Criticism?* Fortress Press (any in this series).

9. Perrin, Norman. *What Is Redaction Criticism?* Fortress Press.

The following is an excellent workbook to understand "forms" according to form criticism:

10. Montgomery, Robert M. and Richard W. Stegner. *Auxiliary Studies in the Bible: Forms in the Gospels, 1. The Pronouncement Story.* Abingdon Press.

User's Guide to

THE NEW EVIDENCE THAT DEMANDS A VERDICT

by Bill Wilson, Revision Project Editor

Warning! This is a dangerous book. Digesting its contents may seriously alter your thinking.

Caution! If you expect this book to be a tame, sit-down-by-the-fire-with-a-cup-of-hot-chocolate kind of book, you'd better reconsider. As the ideas begin to flow, you may find yourself looking for a pen and notebook to jot down ideas for that next time you want to share with a friend some compelling evidence for the truth of the good news about Jesus Christ.

"Now wait just a minute," you say. "Me? Share compelling evidence? I only sat down to read a book." Well, you need to know that these are some of Josh McDowell's personal lecture notes, and when you see the force of the arguments, you just might want to do some sharing of your own. One of Josh's greatest motivations for compiling *Evidence That Demands a Verdict, Volumes 1 & 2,* in the first place was to equip others with organized, documented information they can use to share Christ credibly with others. In this revision and update of both volumes—now brought together in one volume—you will find more up-to-date evidence for your faith than ever before.

Here is a vast amount of user-friendly material which could take some time to digest. If you're a person who likes big challenges, and you want to fortify your faith and witness with every fact you can get, by all means start reading and don't look back.

More than likely, though, you will require different information at different times and for different purposes. As a layperson, high school student, college student, or full-time Christian worker, you may have limited time. Possibly, you have not yet entered into a personal relationship with God through faith in Jesus Christ, and are looking for some answers to your own questions. Whatever your situation, a few tips from this User's Guide can save you time in locating the specific material you need.

IF YOU ARE NOT YET A BELIEVER

The section, "He Changed My Life," before the Introduction, will be of great interest to you. Many people today are asking the question, "Can Jesus Christ make a difference in my life right now?" In these opening pages, Josh shares the impact Christ has made on his own life. Christianity is exciting. Jesus not only had a profound effect on people in His own time, as historical evidence shows; He continues to make a life-changing impact on those who trust and follow Him.

FOR ALL READERS

To more thoroughly digest the evidence presented in these volumes, study the Table of Contents pages carefully before proceeding. Part One deals primarily with the trustworthiness of the Bible; Part Two gives the historical evidence and supporting attestations for Jesus' claims to be God.

Part Three addresses primarily two historic challenges to the Christian faith from radical biblical critics: (1) the documentary hypothesis (used by many scholars in the past to deny the accuracy and Mosaic authorship of the first five books of the Old Testament); and (2) form criticism (used by many scholars in the past to deny the accuracy of the Gospel accounts of Jesus—the first four books of the New Testament).

Part Four is an entirely new section devoted to: (1) evidence for the knowability of truth; (2) answers to divergent worldviews; (3) a defense of the existence of miracles; and (4) evidence for the knowability of history. Finally, the Appendix presents four powerful essays regarding cricitism of the Bible.

Any Christian who shares with others his faith in Christ soon learns that certain questions about Christianity surface over and over again. With a little basic preparation you can answer 90 percent of these questions.

Parts One and Two answer some frequently voiced questions and objections:

- The Bible is no different from any other book. [See chapters 1, 3, and 4.]
- How can I trust the Bible when it wasn't officially accepted by the church until 350 years after the crucifixion of Jesus? [See chapters 2, 3, and 4.]
- We don't have the original writings of the Bible authors; so how can we know whether what we have today is authentic? [See chapters 3 and 4.]
- How can I believe in Jesus when all we know about Him comes from biased Christian writers? [See chapter 5.]
- Jesus never claimed to be God. How can Christians claim that He is God? [See chapters 6–10.]
- How can Christians say Jesus rose bodily from the grave? Lots of possible explanations for the resurrection have been suggested. [See chapter 9.]
- What does archaeology say about events recorded in the Bible? [See chapters 3, 4, and 13.]
- If the Bible is true and Jesus is God, what difference can that make to me? [See chapter 11.]

Parts Two, Three, and Four address these questions:

- Many philosophers say that miracles are impossible. What do you say? [See chapters 12 and 39.]
- Many Bible critics say Moses did not write the first five books of the Bible? What do you say? [See Part Three, Section II.]
- My professor says that the Gospels only give us a distorted picture of the vague memories first-century Christians had of Jesus? What do you say? [See Part Three, Section III]
- I keep hearing about the Jesus Seminar, but it doesn't sound all that friendly toward Jesus. What's the deal with it? [See chapter 29.]

Explanation of General Format

Footnotes: For ease in identifying sources used, I have adopted a different method of footnoting. After each quote, the last name of the source author, the first initials of the main words in the title of the work, and the page number(s) appear in parentheses. (Example: Bruce, BP, 21–23). A bibliography at the end of the book provides standard bibliographic information for the works cited.

In cases where a reference is not set off in quotation marks (nor does it appear as a block quote), the material presented is from the work cited, but is not presented in the author's exact words. I want to give credit where credit is due.

Outline: I have chosen not to use the traditional method of outlining. Instead I employ a method that is easy to use for locating specific references in printed notes while lecturing.

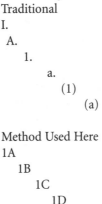

Traditional
I.
 A.
  1.
   a.
    (1)
     (a)

Method Used Here
1A
 1B
  1C
   1D
    1E
     1F

However, since this book is presented in a column format, the following example illustrates how the outline numbering will appear:

1A.
1B.
2B.
2A.

The outline at the beginning of each chapter displays the broad outline of that chapter's contents.

Indexes: Located at the back of the notes are two separate indexes to help you in using these notes: 1. Author Index; 2. Subject Index.

Biographical sketches: At the back of the book is a limited selection of the biographies of various authors. These biographical sketches give the background of some of the authors quoted.

Acknowledgments

Robert Mounce, dean of the Potter College of Arts and Humanities at Western Kentucky University, speaks of the commitment and vision necessary for an endeavor such as this book: "The task of scholarship is in fact a lowly role which demands tremendous dedication. My own personal feeling is that young men with a gift of conceptualization and perception need to be encouraged to really believe that God can be served in the solitude of one's study surrounded by the fruits of scholarly labor."

The publishing of any book requires the efforts of numerous people, many of which play important but behind the scenes roles. And it is especially true of this book, along with its newest revisions. So I would like to acknowledge the following people:

The original research team on *Evidence I* was comprised of eleven students from nine universities. They were: Doug Wilder at Michigan State University; Phil Edwards at Ohio State University; Ron Lutjens at Bowling Green University; Wayne Trout at Virginia Polytechnic Institute; Brent Nelson at Indiana University; David Sheldon at Ohio State University; Frank Dickerson at Ohio State University; Steve Smith at Virginia Polytechnic Institute; James Davis at Louisiana Polytechnic Institute; Linn Smith at North Texas State University; and Stick Ustick at Sacramento State University.

The original research team on *Evidence II* was comprised of fourteen students from fourteen different universities. They were: Ron Lutjens at Bowling Green University; James Davis at Louisiana Polytechnic Institute; Frank Dickerson at Ohio State University; Jay Gary at Georgia Tech; Ray Moran at Baylor University; John Austin at University of Virginia; Richard Beckham at Louisiana State University; Dave Wilson at Trinity Seminary; Terry Shope at University of Arkansas; John Sloan at West Texas State University; Faith Osteen at Arizona State University; Stephanie Ross at North Texas State University; Beth Veazi at University of Arizona; and Nancy Thompson at Chaffey College.

Bill Watkins provided input, design and writing assistance to the *New Evidence* revision.

Dr. James Beverley of Ontario Theological Seminary provided critique and counsel on the design, content, and revision of the *New Evidence*.

Dr. Norm Geisler of Southern Evangelical Seminary in Charlotte, N.C., was the Managing Editor of the *New Evidence* revision along with a team of eighteen seminary students who provided research, writing, and editing to this new volume. They were: Todd B. Vick; Benjamin Hlastan; Steve Bright; Duane Hansen; Sabrina Barnes; D. Scott Henderson; Kenneth Lee Hood; Douglas E. Potter; Scott Matscherz; Gavin T. Head; David L. Johnson; Stephen M. Puryear; Eric F. LaRock; Janis E. Hlastan; Jeff Spencer; Malcolm C. C. Armstrong; Bruce Landon; and Frank Turek. Mrs. Laurel Maugel, Dr. Geisler's secretary, provided the invaluable service of assisting in the typing and coordinating of this project.

Bill Wilson was the Project Editor of the *New Evidence* revision, along with assistant editor Marcus Maranto. Bill's research and writing team was drawn from the Dallas Theological Seminary. They were: Nicholas Alsop; David Hoehner; Ronny Reddy; Mike Svigel; and John Zareva.

My son, Sean McDowell, provided an insightful critique of the entire manuscript and rewrote the chapter on postmodernism.

Dave Bellis, my Resource Development Coordinator for 22 years, orchestrated and facilitated this long revision process through the maze of many details from beginning to end.

Mark Roberts of Thomas Nelson Publishers provided patient guiding, directing, and insight into the revision's design and content.

Lee Hollaway, Thomas Nelson Publishers' reference editor, provided many hours of editing the manuscript and seeing it through the publishing process.

I am grateful to this expert team of over 50 dedicated men and women who labored faithfully to provide a ready defense for the hope that is within us.

JOSH MCDOWELL

He Changed My Life

Thomas Aquinas wrote, "There is within every soul a thirst for happiness and meaning." As a teenager, I exemplified this statement. I wanted to be happy and to find meaning for my life. I wanted the answers to three basic questions: Who am I? Why am I here? Where am I going? These are life's tough questions. I would estimate that 90 percent of people age forty and younger cannot answer these questions. But I was thirsty to know what life was about. So as a young student, I started looking for answers.

Where I grew up, everyone seemed to be into religion. I thought maybe I would find my answers in being religious, so I started attending church. I got into it 150 percent. I went to church morning, afternoon, and evening. But I guess I got into the wrong one, because I felt worse inside the church than I did outside. About the only thing I got

out of my religious experience was seventy-five cents a week: I would put a quarter into the offering plate and take a dollar out so I could buy a milkshake!

I was brought up on a farm in Michigan, and most farmers are very practical. My dad, who was a farmer, taught me, "If something doesn't work, chuck it." So I chucked religion.

Then I thought that education might have the answer to my quest for happiness and meaning. So I enrolled in the university. What a disappointment! I have probably been on more university campuses in my lifetime than anyone else in history. You can find a lot of things in the university, but enrolling there to find truth and meaning in life is virtually a lost cause.

I'm sure I was by far the most unpopular student with the faculty of the first university

I attended. I used to buttonhole professors in their offices, seeking the answers to my questions. When they saw me coming they would turn out the lights, pull down the shades, and lock the door so they wouldn't have to talk to me. I soon realized that the university didn't have the answers I was seeking. Faculty members and my fellow students had just as many problems, frustrations, and unanswered questions about life as I had. A few years ago I saw a student walking around a campus with a sign on his back: "Don't follow me, I'm lost." That's how everyone in the university seemed to me. Education was not the answer!

Prestige must be the way to go, I decided. It just seemed right to find a noble cause, give yourself to it, and become well known. The people with the most prestige in the university, and who also controlled the purse strings, were the student leaders. So I ran for various student offices and got elected. It was great to know everyone on campus, make important decisions, and spend the university's money doing what I wanted to do. But the thrill soon wore off, as with everything else I had tried.

Every Monday morning I would wake up with a headache because of the way I had spent the previous night. My attitude was, *Here we go again, another five boring days.* Happiness for me revolved around those three party-nights: Friday, Saturday, and Sunday. Then the whole boring cycle would start over again. I felt frustrated, even desperate. My goal was to find my identity and purpose in life. But everything I tried left me empty and without answers.

Around this time I noticed a small group of people on campus—eight students and two faculty—and there was something different about them. They seemed to know where they were going in life. And they had a quality I deeply admire in people: conviction. I really like being around people with conviction, even if their convictions are not the same as mine. There is a certain dynamic in the lives of people with deep convictions, and I enjoy that dynamic.

But there was something more about this group that caught my attention. It was love. These students and professors not only loved each other, they loved and cared for people outside their group. They didn't just talk about love; they got involved in loving others. It was something totally foreign to me, and I wanted it. So I decided to make friends with this group of people.

About two weeks later, I was sitting around a table in the student union talking with some members of this group. Soon the conversation got around to the topic of God. I was pretty insecure about this subject, so I put on a big front to cover it up. I leaned back in my chair, acting as if I couldn't care less. "Christianity, ha!" I blustered. "That's for weaklings, not intellectuals." Down deep, I really wanted what they had. But with my pride and my position in the university, I didn't want *them* to know that I wanted what they had. Then I turned to one of the girls in the group and said, "Tell me, what changed your lives? Why are you so different from the other students and faculty?"

She looked me straight in the eye and said two words I had never expected to hear in an intelligent discussion on a university campus: "Jesus Christ."

"Jesus Christ?" I snapped. "Don't give me that kind of garbage. I'm fed up with religion, the Bible, and the church."

She quickly shot back, "Mister, I didn't say 'religion'; I said 'Jesus Christ.'"

Taken aback by the girl's courage and conviction, I apologized for my attitude. "But I'm sick and tired of religion and religious people," I added. "I don't want anything to do with it."

Then my new friends issued me a challenge I couldn't believe. They challenged me, a pre-law student, to examine intellectually the claim that Jesus Christ is God's Son. I thought this was a joke. These Christians were so dumb. How could something as flimsy as Christianity stand up to an intellectual examination? I scoffed at their challenge.

But they didn't let up. They continued to challenge me day after day, and finally they backed me into the corner. I became so irritated at their insistence that I finally accepted their challenge, not to prove anything but to refute them. I decided to write a book that would make an intellectual joke of Christianity. I left the university and traveled throughout the United States and Europe to gather evidence to prove that Christianity is a sham.

One day while I was sitting in a library in London, England, I sensed a voice within me saying, "Josh, you don't have a leg to stand on." I immediately suppressed it. But just about every day after that I heard the same inner voice. The more I researched, the more I heard this voice. I returned to the United States and to the university, but I couldn't sleep at night. I would go to bed at ten o'clock and lie awake until four in the morning, trying to refute the overwhelming evidence I was accumulating that Jesus Christ was God's Son.

I began to realize that I was being intellectually dishonest. My mind told me that the claims of Christ were indeed true, but my will was being pulled another direction. I had placed so much emphasis on finding the truth, but I wasn't willing to follow it once I saw it. I began to sense Christ's personal challenge to me in Revelation 3:20: "Here I am! I stand at the door and knock. If anyone hears my voice and opens the door, I will come in and eat with him, and he with me"

(NIV). But becoming a Christian seemed so ego-shattering to me. I couldn't think of a faster way to ruin all my good times.

I knew I had to resolve this inner conflict because it was driving me crazy. I had always considered myself an open-minded person, so I decided to put Christ's claims to the supreme test. One night at my home in Union City, Michigan, at the end of my second year at the university, I became a Christian. Someone may say, "How do you know you became a Christian?" I was there! I got alone with a Christian friend and prayed four things that established my relationship with God.

First, I said, "Lord Jesus, thank You for dying on the cross for me." I realized that if I were the only person on earth, Christ would have still died for me. You may think it was the irrefutable intellectual evidence that brought me to Christ. No, the evidence was only God's way of getting His foot in the door of my life. What brought me to Christ was the realization that He loved me enough to die for me.

Second, I said, "I confess that I am a sinner." No one had to tell me that. I knew there were things in my life that were incompatible with a holy, just, righteous God. The Bible says, "If we confess our sins, he is faithful and just and will forgive us our sins and purify us from all unrighteousness" (1 John 1:9 NIV). So I said, "Lord, forgive me."

Third, I said, "Right now, in the best way I know how, I open the door of my life and place my trust in You as Savior and Lord. Take over the control of my life. Change me from the inside out. Make me the type of person You created me to be."

The last thing I prayed was, "Thank You for coming into my life."

After I prayed, nothing happened. There was no bolt of lightning. I didn't sprout angel wings. If anything, I actually felt worse after I prayed, almost physically sick. I was afraid I had made an emotional decision that I would later regret intellectually. But more than that, I was afraid of what my friends would say when they found out. I really felt I had gone off the deep end.

But over the next eighteen months my entire life was changed. One of the biggest

> I would sometimes find my mother in the barn, lying in the manure behind the cows where my dad had beaten her with a hose until she couldn't get up. My hatred seethed as I vowed to myself, "When I am strong enough, I'm going to kill him."

changes occurred in how I viewed people. While studying in the university, I had mapped out the next twenty-five years of my life. My ultimate goal had been to become governor of Michigan. I planned to accomplish my goal by using people in order to climb the ladder of political success—I figured people were meant to be used. But after I placed my trust in Christ, my thinking changed. Instead of using others to serve me, I wanted to be used to serve others. Becoming other-centered instead of self-centered was a dramatic change in my life.

Another area that started to change was my bad temper. I used to blow my stack if somebody just looked at me wrong. I still have the scars from almost killing a man during my first year in the university. My bad temper was so ingrained that I didn't consciously seek to change it. But one day, when faced with a crisis that would ordinarily have set me off, I discovered that my bad temper was gone. I'm not perfect in this area, but this change in my life has been significant and dramatic.

Perhaps the most significant change has

been in the area of hatred and bitterness. I grew up filled with hatred, primarily aimed at one man whom I hated more than anyone else on the face of this earth. I despised everything this man stood for. I can remember as a young boy lying in bed at night plotting how I would kill this man without being caught by the police. This man was my father.

While I was growing up, my father was the town drunk. I hardly ever saw him sober. My friends at school would joke about my dad lying in the gutter downtown, making a fool of himself. Their jokes hurt me deeply, but I never let anyone know. I laughed along with them. I kept my pain a secret.

I would sometimes find my mother in the barn, lying in the manure behind the cows where my dad had beaten her with a hose until she couldn't get up. My hatred seethed as I vowed to myself, "When I am strong enough, I'm going to kill him." When Dad was drunk and visitors were coming over, I would grab him around the neck, pull him out to the barn, and tie him up. Then I would park his truck behind the silo and tell everyone he had gone to a meeting, so we wouldn't be embarrassed as a family. When I tied up his hands and feet, I looped part of the rope around his neck. I just hoped he would try to get away and choke himself.

Two months before I graduated from high school, I walked into the house after a date to hear my mother sobbing. I ran into her room, and she sat up in bed. "Son, your father has broken my heart," she said. She put her arms around me and pulled me close. "I have lost the will to live. All I want to do is live until you graduate, then I want to die."

Two months later I graduated, and the following Friday my mother died. I believe she died of a broken heart. I hated my father for that. Had I not left home a few months after the funeral to attend college, I might have killed him.

But after I made a decision to place my trust in Jesus as Savior and Lord, the love of God inundated my life. He took my hatred for my father and turned it upside-down. Five months after becoming a Christian, I found myself looking my dad right in the eye and saying, "Dad, I love you." I did not want to love that man, but I did. God's love had changed my heart.

After I transferred to Wheaton University, I was in a serious car accident, the victim of a drunk driver. I was moved home from the hospital to recover, and my father came to see me. Remarkably, he was sober that day. He seemed uneasy, pacing back and forth in my room. Then he blurted out, "How can you love a father like me?"

I said, "Dad, six months ago I hated you, I despised you. But I have put my trust in Jesus Christ, received God's forgiveness, and He has changed my life. I can't explain it all, Dad. But God has taken away my hatred for you and replaced it with love."

We talked for nearly an hour, then he said, "Son, if God can do in my life what I've seen Him do in yours, then I want to give Him the opportunity." He prayed, "God, if You're really God and Jesus died on the cross to forgive me for what I've done to my family, I need You. If Jesus can do in my life what I've seen Him do in the life of my son, then I want to trust Him as Savior and Lord." Hearing my dad pray this prayer from his heart was one of the greatest joys of my life.

After I trusted Christ, my life was basically changed in six to eighteen months. But my father's life was changed right before my eyes. It was like someone reached down and switched on a light inside him. He touched alcohol only once after that. He got the drink only as far as his lips, and that was it—after forty years of drinking! He didn't need it any more. Fourteen months later, he died from complications of his alcoholism. But in that fourteen-month period over a hundred people in the area around my tiny hometown committed their lives to Jesus Christ because of the change they saw in the town drunk, my dad.

You can laugh at Christianity. You can mock and ridicule it. But it works. If you trust Christ, start watching your attitudes and actions—Jesus Christ is in the business of changing lives.

Christianity is not something to be shoved down your throat or forced on you. You have your life to live and I have mine. All I can do is tell you what I have learned and experienced. After that, what you do with Christ is your decision.

Perhaps the prayer I prayed will help you: "Lord Jesus, I need You. Thank You for dying on the cross for me. Forgive me and cleanse me. Right this moment I trust you as Savior and Lord. Make me the type of person You created me to be. In Christ's name, Amen."

Josh McDowell

INTRODUCTION

1A. TO EVERYONE A REASON

"But sanctify the Lord God in your hearts, and always be ready to give a defense to every one who asks you a reason for the hope that is in you, with meekness and fear" (1 Pet. 3:15).

1B. Apologize . . . for What?

This book of *Evidence* for the validity of the Christian faith is a book of *apologetics*. The word *apologetics* does not mean "to apologize," but to give a defense of what one believes to be true.

The word "defense" (Gk. *apologia*) indicates "a defense of conduct and procedure." Wilbur Smith puts it this way: "a verbal defense, a speech in defense of what one has done or of truth which one believes." (Smith, TS, 45, 481)

"Apologia" (the basic English translation is "apology") was used predominantly in early times, "but it did not convey the idea of excuse, palliation or making amends for some injury done." (Beattie, A, 48)

"Apologia" translated by the English word "defense" is used eight times in the New Testament (including 1 Pet. 3:15 above):

Acts 22:1: "Brethren and fathers, hear my *defense* before you now."

Acts 25:16: "And I answered them that it is not the custom of the Romans to hand over any man before the accused meets his accusers face to face, and has an opportunity to make his *defense* against the charges" (NASB).

1 Corinthians 9:3: "My *defense* to those who examine me is this: . . ."

2 Corinthians 7:11: "For observe this very thing, that you sorrowed in a godly manner: What diligence it produced in you, what clearing of yourselves [*defense*], what indignation, what fear, what vehement desire, what zeal, what vindication! In all things you proved yourselves to be clear in this matter."

Philippians 1:7: "as both in my chains and in the *defense* and confirmation of the gospel, you all are partakers with me of grace."

Philippians 1:17: "the latter [do it] out of love, knowing that I am appointed for the *defense* of the gospel."

2 Timothy 4:16: "At my first *defense* no one stood with me, but all forsook me. May it not be charged against them."

The manner in which the word "defense" is used in 1 Peter 3:15 denotes the kind of defense one would make to a legal inquiry, asking "Why are you a Christian?" A believer is responsible to give an adequate answer to this question.

Paul Little quotes John Stott, saying, "We cannot pander to a man's intellectual arrogance, but we must cater to his intellectual integrity." (Little, KWhyYB, 28)

Beattie concludes that "Christianity is either EVERYTHING for mankind, or NOTHING. It is either the highest certainty or the greatest delusion. . . . But if Christianity be EVERYTHING for mankind, it is important for every man to be able to give a good reason for the hope that is in him in regard to the eternal verities of the Christian faith. To accept these verities in an unthinking way, or to receive them simply on authority, is not enough for an intelligent and stable faith." (Beattie, A, 37, 38)

The basic "apologetic" thesis of these notes is: "There is an infinite, all-wise, all-powerful, all-loving God who has revealed Himself by means natural and supernatural in creation, in the nature of man, in the history of Israel and the Church, in the pages of Holy Scripture, in the incarnation of God in Christ, and in the heart of the believer by the gospel." (Ramm, PCE, 33)

2B. Christianity Is a FACTual Faith

Christianity appeals to history. It appeals to facts of history that are clearly recognizable and accessible by everyone.

J. N. D. Anderson records D. E. Jenkins's remark, "Christianity is based on indisputable facts." (Anderson, WH, 10)

Clark Pinnock defines these types of facts:

"The facts backing the Christian claim are not a special kind of religious fact. They are the cognitive, informational facts upon which all historical, legal, and ordinary decisions are based." (Pinnock, SFYC, 6, 7)

Luke, the first-century Christian historian, demonstrates this truth in his Gospel and in his The Acts of the Apostles. Luke said that he strove to provide an orderly and accurate historical "narrative of those things which are most surely believed among us, just as those, who from the beginning were eyewitnesses and ministers of the word, delivered them to us" (Luke 1:1, 2 NKJV). Among these historical, knowable events was the resurrection of Jesus Christ, an event, Luke says, that was validated by Jesus Himself through "many infallible proofs" over a forty-day period before numerous eyewitnesses (Acts 1:3).

One of the purposes of these "notes on Christian evidences" is to present some of these "indisputable facts," and to determine whether the Christian interpretation of these facts is not by far the most logical. The objective of apologetics is not to convince a man unwittingly, or contrary to his will, to become a Christian. The objective, as Clark Pinnock puts it, "strives at laying the evidence for the Christian gospel before men in an intelligent fashion, so that they can make a meaningful commitment under the convicting power of the Holy Spirit. The heart cannot delight in what the mind rejects as false." (Pinnock, SFYC, 3)

3B. The Best Defense Is . . . a Good Offense

For a philosophical apologetics course in graduate school, I wrote a paper entitled "The Best Defense of Christianity." I found myself constantly putting it off and avoided writing it, not because I didn't have the material but because, in my thinking, I felt I was at odds with what the professor was expecting (an expectation based on the ream of my lecture notes from his class).

Finally I decided to voice my convictions. I began my paper with the phrase, "Some people say the best offense is a good defense, but I say unto you that the best defense is a good offense." I proceeded by explaining that I felt the best defense of Christianity is a "clear, simple presentation of the claims of Christ and who He is, in the power of the Holy Spirit." I then wrote out "The Four Spiritual Laws" and recorded my testimony of how, on December 19, 1959, at 8:30 P.M., during my second year at the university, I placed my trust in Christ as Savior and Lord. I concluded the paper with a presentation of the evidence for the resurrection.

The professor must have pondered it quite laboriously. However, he must have agreed, for he gave me a grade of 96.

William Tyndale was right in saying that "a ploughboy with the Bible would know more of God than the most learned ecclesiastic who ignored it." In other words, an Arkansas farm boy sharing the gospel can be more effective in the long run than a Harvard scholar with his intellectual arguments.

One precaution when using apologetics: God saves—apologetics do not. On the other hand, God often uses apologetics, or evidences, to help clear away obstacles to faith that many people erect, and also to show that faith in Christ is reasonable. The great Princeton theologian and apologist Benjamin Warfield declared:

It certainly is not in the power of all the demonstrations in the world to make a Christian. Paul may plant and Apollos water; it is God alone who gives the increase. . . . [I]t does not in the least follow that the faith that God gives is an irrational faith, that is, a faith without grounds in right reason. . . . We believe in Christ because it is rational to believe in him, not though it be irrational. . . . We are not absurdly arguing that Apologetics has in itself the power to make a man a Christian or to conquer the world to Christ. Only the Spirit of Life can communicate life to a dead soul, or can convict the world in respect of sin, and of righteousness, and of judgment. But we are arguing that faith is, in all its exercises alike, a form of conviction, and is, therefore, necessarily grounded in evidence. (Warfield, A:FA, 24, 25)

Hebrews 4:12: "For the word of God is living and powerful, and sharper than any two-edged sword, piercing even to the division of soul and spirit, and of both joints and marrow, and is a discerner of the thoughts and intents of the heart."

We need a balance of the two above ramifications. We must preach the gospel but also "be ready to give an answer for the hope that is in [us]."

The Holy Spirit will convict men and women of the truth; one does not have to be hit over the head with it. "Now a certain woman named Lydia heard us. She was a seller of purple from the city of Thyatira who worshiped God. The Lord opened her heart to heed the things spoken by Paul" (Acts 16:14).

Pinnock, an able apologist and witness for Christ, appropriately concludes: "An intelligent Christian ought to be able to point up the flaws in a non-Christian position and to present facts and arguments which tell in favor of the gospel. If our apologetic prevents us from explaining the gospel to any person, it is an inadequate apologetic." (Pinnock, SFYC, 7)

2A. CLEARING THE FOG

I used to live in California. On some days in some California cities the fog (okay, smog) was so bad you couldn't see the car directly in front of you. It was dangerous to drive in those conditions.

The point is, if you want to see what's really there, you've got to get rid of what's obscuring your view. In the case of Christianity, many people approach it with such foggy thinking that they can't see what it

> We are not absurdly arguing that Apologetics has in itself the power to make a man a Christian or to conquer the world to Christ. Only the Spirit of Life can communicate life to a dead soul. . . . But we are arguing that faith is, in all its exercises alike, a form of conviction, and is, therefore, necessarily grounded in evidence.
>
> —BENJAMIN WARFIELD,
> PRINCETON UNIVERSITY

really is. Before they look at the evidences for the Christian faith, they need to clear up some misconceptions.

1B. Misconception #1: "Blind Faith"

A rather common accusation sharply aimed at the Christian often goes like this: "You Christians are pitiful! All you have is a 'blind faith.'" This would surely indicate that the accuser seems to think that to become a Christian, one has to commit "intellectual suicide."

Personally, "my heart cannot rejoice in what my mind rejects." My heart and head were created to work and believe together in harmony. Christ commanded us to "love the LORD your God with all your heart, with all your soul, and with all your *mind*" (Matt. 22:37, italics mine).

When Jesus Christ and the apostles called upon a person to exercise faith, it was not a "blind faith" but rather an "intelligent faith." The apostle Paul said, "I *know* whom I have believed" (2 Tim. 1 :12, italics mine). Jesus said, "You shall know [not ignore] the truth, and the truth shall make you free" (John 8:32).

The belief of an individual involves "the *mind,* the emotions, and the will." I like the way F. R. Beattie puts it: "The Holy Spirit does not work a blind and ungrounded faith in the heart." (Beattie, A, 25)

"Faith in Christianity," Paul Little justifiably writes, "is based on evidence. It is reasonable faith. Faith in the Christian sense goes beyond reason but not against it." (Little, KWhyYB, 30) Faith is the assurance of the heart in the adequacy of the evidence.

Often the Christian is accused of taking a blind "leap into the dark." This idea often finds itself rooted in Kierkegaard.

For me, Christianity was not a "leap into the dark," but rather "a step into the light." I took the evidence that I could gather and placed it on the scales. The scales tipped in favor of Christ as the Son of God, resurrected from the dead. The evidence so overwhelmingly leans toward Christ that when I became a Christian, I was "stepping into the light" rather than "leaping into the darkness."

If I had been exercising "blind faith," I would have rejected Jesus Christ and turned my back on all the evidence.

Be careful. I am not saying that I proved beyond a shadow of a doubt that Jesus is the Son of God. What I did was to investigate the evidence and weigh the pros and cons. The results showed that Christ must be who He claimed to be, and I had to make a decision, which I did. The immediate reaction of many is, "You found what you wanted to find." This is not the case. *I confirmed through investigation what I wanted to refute.* I set out to disprove Christianity. I had biases and prejudices not for Christ but contrary to Him.

Hume would say historical evidence is invalid because one cannot establish "absolute truth." I was not looking for absolute truth but rather for "historical probability."

"Without an objective criterion," says John W. Montgomery, "one is at a loss to make a meaningful choice among *a prioris.* The resurrection provides a basis in historical probability for trying the Christian faith. Granted, the basis is only one of probability, not of certainty, but probability is the sole ground on which finite human beings can make any decisions. Only deductive logic and pure mathematics provide 'apodictic certainty,' and they do so because they stem from self-evident formal axioms (e.g., the tautology, if A then A) involving no matter of fact. The moment we enter the realm of fact, we must depend on probability; this

> The Christian faith is faith in *Christ.* Its value or worth is not in the one believing, but in the one believed—not in the one trusting, but in the one trusted.

may be unfortunate, but it is unavoidable." (Montgomery, SP, 141)

At the conclusion of his four articles in *His* magazine, John W. Montgomery writes, concerning history and Christianity, that he has "tried to show that the weight of historical probability lies on the side of the validity of Jesus' claim to be God incarnate, the Savior of man, and the coming Judge of the world. If probability does in fact support these claims (and can we really deny it, having studied the evidence?), then we must act in behalf of them." (Montgomery, HC, 19)

2B. Misconception #2: "Just Be Sincere"

The Christian faith is an objective faith; therefore, it must have an object. The Christian concept of "saving" faith is a faith that establishes one's relationship with Jesus Christ (the object), and is diametrically opposed to the average "philosophical" use of the term faith in the classroom today. We do not accept the cliche, "It doesn't matter what you believe, as long as you believe it enough."

Let me illustrate. I had a debate with the head of the philosophy department of a

Midwestern university. In answering a question, I happened to mention the importance of the resurrection. At this point, my opponent interrupted and rather sarcastically said, "Come on, McDowell, the key issue is not whether the resurrection took place or not; it is 'do you believe it took place?'" What he was hinting at (actually boldly asserting) is that my *believing* was the most important thing. I retorted immediately, "Sir, it does matter what I as a Christian believe, because the value of Christian faith is not in the one believing, but in the one who is believed in, its object." I continued that "if anyone can demonstrate to me that Christ was not raised from the dead, I would not have a justifiable right to my Christian faith." (1 Cor. 15:14)

The Christian faith is faith *in* Christ. Its value or worth is not in the one believing, but in the One believed—not in the one trusting, but in the One trusted.

Immediately following that debate, a Moslem fellow approached me and, during a most edifying conversation, said very sincerely, "I know many Moslems who have more faith in Mohammed than some Christians have in Christ." I said, "That may well be true, but the Christian is 'saved.' You see, it doesn't matter how much faith you have, but rather who is the object of your faith; that is important from the Christian perspective of faith."

I often hear students say, "Some Buddhists are more dedicated and have more faith in Buddha [this showing a misunderstanding of Buddhism] than Christians have in Christ." I can only reply, "Maybe so, but the Christian is saved."

Paul said, "I know *whom* I have believed." This explains why the Christian gospel centers on the person of Jesus Christ.

John Warwick Montgomery writes: "If our 'Christ of faith' deviates at all from the biblical 'Jesus of history,' then to the extent of that deviation, we also lose the genuine Christ of faith. As one of the greatest Christian historians of our time, Herbert Butterfield, has put it: 'It would be a dangerous error to imagine that the characteristics of an historical religion would be maintained if the Christ of the theologians were divorced from the Jesus of history.'" (Montgomery, SP, 145)

In other words, one must avoid the attitude, "Don't confuse me with the facts, my mind is made up!" For the Christian, the historical facts reported in the Scriptures are essential. That is why the apostle Paul said, "If Christ is not risen, then our preaching is empty and your faith is also empty. . . . and if Christ is not risen, your faith is futile; you are still in your sins!" (1 Cor. 15:14, 17).

3B. Misconception #3: "The Bible Is Full of Myths"

Critics sometimes charge, "Events such as the virgin birth, the resurrection and ascension, Jesus' turning water into wine and walking on water didn't really happen. They were inserted to elevate Jesus to the status of a divine figure, though, if he lived at all, he was no more than a mere mortal."

A professor of a world literature class to which I spoke asked the question, "What do you think of Greek mythology?" I answered with another question, "Do you mean, were the events of the life of Jesus, the resurrection, virgin birth, etc., just myth?" He answered, "Yes." I replied that there is an obvious difference between the events recorded about Christ in the Bible and the stories conveyed in Greek mythology that bear a vague similarity. The similar stories, such as resurrections, and others, of Greek mythology were not applied to real flesh-and-blood individuals, but instead to non-historical, fictional, mythological characters. However, when it comes to Christianity, these events are attached to the historic Jesus of Nazareth whom the New Testament writers knew personally. The professor replied, "You're right, I never realized that before."

1C. Eyewitnesses

The writers of the New Testament either wrote as eyewitnesses of the events they described or they recorded eyewitness firsthand accounts of these events. Their personal attachment to the events are clear from statements they made such as the following:

- "For we did not follow cunningly devised fables when we made known to you the power and coming of our Lord Jesus Christ, but were eyewitnesses of His majesty" (2 Pet. 1:16).
- "That which was from the beginning, which we have heard, which we have seen with our eyes, which we have looked upon, and our hands have handled, concerning the Word of life—the life was manifested, and we have seen, and bear witness, and declare to you that eternal life which was with the Father and was manifested to us—that which we have seen and heard we declare to you, that you also may have fellowship with us; and truly our fellowship is with the Father and with His Son Jesus Christ." (1 John 1:1–3).
- "Inasmuch as many have taken in hand to set in order a narrative of those things which have been fulfilled among us, just as those who from the beginning were eyewitnesses and ministers of the word delivered them to us, it seemed good to me also, having had perfect understanding of all things from the very first, to write to you an orderly account, most excellent Theophilus" (Luke 1:1–3).

- "The former account I made, O Theophilus, of all that Jesus began both to do and teach, until the day in which He was taken up, after He through the Holy Spirit had given commandments to the apostles whom He had chosen, to whom He also presented Himself alive, after His suffering by many infallible proofs, being seen by them during forty days and speaking of the things pertaining to the kingdom of God" (Acts 1:1–3).
- "After that He was seen by over five hundred brethren at once, of whom the greater part remain to the present, but some have fallen asleep. After that He was seen by James, then by all the apostles. Then last of all He was seen by me also, as by one born out of due time" (1 Cor. 15: 6–8).
- "And truly Jesus did many other signs in the presence of His disciples, which are not written in this book; but these are written that you may believe that Jesus is the Christ, the Son of God, and that believing you may have life in His name" (John 20:30, 31).
- "And we are witnesses of all the things which He did both in the land of the Jews and in Jerusalem, whom they killed by hanging on a tree. Him God raised up on the third day, and showed Him openly, not to all the people, but to witnesses chosen before by God, even to us who ate and drank with Him after He arose from the dead. And He commanded us to preach to the people, and to testify that this is He who was ordained by God to be Judge of the living and the dead" (Acts 10:39–42).
- "The elders who are among you I exhort, I who am a fellow elder and a witness of the sufferings of Christ, and

also a partaker also of the glory that will be revealed" (1 Pet. 5:1).

- "Now when He had spoken these things, while they watched, He was taken up, and a cloud received Him out of their sight" (Acts 1:9).

- The apostle Peter proclaimed, "Men of Israel, hear these words: Jesus of Nazareth, a Man attested by God to you by miracles, wonders, and signs which God did through Him in your midst, as you yourselves also know" (Acts 2:22).

- "Now as he [Paul] thus made his defense, Festus said with a loud voice, 'Paul, you are beside yourself! Much learning is driving you mad!' But he said, 'I am not mad, most noble Festus, but speak the words of truth and reason. For the king, before whom I also speak freely, knows these things; for I am convinced that none of these things escapes his attention, since this thing was not done in a corner. King Agrippa, do you believe the prophets? I know that you do believe.' Then Agrippa said to Paul, 'You almost persuade me to become a Christian'" (Acts 26:24–28).

2C. Yes You Did: You Knew That . . .

The writers of the New Testament also appealed to the firsthand knowledge of their readers or listeners concerning the facts and evidence about the person of Jesus Christ. The writers not only said "Look, we saw this," or "We heard that," but they turned the tables around and right in front of their most adverse critics said, "You also know about these things. You saw them; you yourselves know about it." One had better be careful when he says to his opposition, "You *know* this also," because if he is not right about the details, his critics will gladly and

quickly expose his error. But this is exactly what the apostles did, and their critics could not refute them.

3C. The Difference between Myth and History

The New Testament writers certainly knew the difference between myth, legend, and reality.

S. Estborn, in *Gripped by Christ*, tells about a man named Anath Nath who was committed to Hinduism. Nath "studied both

> If he [the biblical critic] tells me that something in a Gospel is legend or romance, I want to know how many legends and romances he has read, how well his palate is trained in detecting them by the flavour; not how many years he has spent on that Gospel. . . . I have been reading poems, romances, vision-literature, legends, myths all my life. I know what they are like. I know that not one of them is like this.
>
> —C. S. LEWIS
>
> PROFESSOR OF MEDIEVAL AND RENAISSANCE LITERATURE, CAMBRIDGE UNIVERSITY
>
> AUTHOR OF *THE CHRONICLES OF NARNIA*

the Bible and the *Shastras*. Two biblical themes in particular deeply engaged his mind: first, the reality of the Incarnation, and second, the Atonement for human sin. These doctrines he sought to harmonize with Hindu Scriptures. He found a parallel to Christ's self-sacrifice in Prajapati, the Vedic creator-god. He saw, too, a vital difference. Whereas the Vedic Prajapati is a mythical symbol, which has been applied to several figures, Jesus of Nazareth is an historic person. 'Jesus is the true Prajapati,' he said, 'the true Saviour of the world.'" (Estborn, GBC, 43)

J. B. Phillips, cited by E. M. Blaiklock, states, "'I have read, in Greek and Latin, scores of myths but I did not find the slightest flavour of myth here.' Most people who know their Greek and Latin, whatever their attitude to the New Testament narratives, would agree with him." (Blaiklock, LA, 47)

C. S. Lewis is certainly one scholar of literature who would agree that the biblical narratives are not mythological or legendary. In commenting about the Gospel of John, Lewis chastises those critics who think the Gospel is unhistorical:

> If he [the biblical critic] tells me that something in a Gospel is legend or romance, I want to know how many legends and romances he has read, how well his palate is trained in detecting them by the flavour; not how many years he has spent on that Gospel.... Read the dialogues [in John]: that with the Samaritan woman at the well, or that which follows the healing of the man born blind. Look at its pictures: Jesus (if I may use the word) doodling with his finger in the dust; the unforgettable ἦν δὲ νύξ ["and it was night"] (xiii, 30). I have been reading poems, romances, vision-literature, legends, myths all my life. I know what they are like. I know that not one of them is like this. (Lewis, CR, 154, 155)

4B. Misconception #4: "The Jesus of History Is Unknowable"

"*If* one were to study historically the life of Jesus of Nazareth, he would find a very remarkable man, not the Son of God." It is also sometimes stated to me this way: "Following the 'modern historical' approach one would never discover the resurrection."

Do you know, it is true. Before you jump to a conclusion, let me explain. For many today, the study of history is incorporated with the ideas that there is no God, miracles are not possible, we live in a closed system, and there is no supernatural. With these assumptions or presuppositions they begin their "critical, open, and honest" investigation of history. When they study the life of Christ and read about His miracles or resurrection, they conclude that it was not a miracle or a resurrection because we know (not historically, but philosophically) that there is no God, we live in a closed system, miracles are not possible, and there is no supernatural. Therefore, these things cannot be. What men have done is to rule out the resurrection of Christ even before they start an historical investigation of the resurrection.

These presuppositions are not so much historical biases but, rather, philosophical prejudices. Their approach to history rests on the "rationalistic presupposition" that Christ could not have been raised from the dead. Instead of beginning with the historical data, they preclude them by "metaphysical speculation."

John W. Montgomery writes: "The fact of the resurrection cannot be discounted on *a priori*, philosophical grounds; miracles are impossible only if one so defines them—but such definition rules out proper historical investigation." (Montgomery, SP, 139–144)

I quote Montgomery quite extensively on this issue because he has stimulated my thinking about history. He says: "Kant conclusively showed that all arguments and systems begin with presuppositions; but this does not mean that all presuppositions are equally desirable. It is better to begin, as we have, with presuppositions of method (which will yield truth) rather than with presuppositions of substantive content (which assume a body of truth already). In our modern world we have found that the presuppositions of empirical method best fulfill this condition; but note that we are operating only with the presuppositions of scientific method, not with the rationalistic assumptions of Scientism ('the Religion of Science')." (Montgomery, SP, 144)

Huizenga's comments are cited by Montgomery concerning historical skepticism ("De Historische Idee," in his *Verzamelde Werken*, VII [Haarlem, 1950], 134ff.: quoted in translation in Fritz Stern [ed], *The Varieties of History* [New York: Meridian Books, 1956], p. 302). Huizenga states:

> The strongest argument against historical skepticism . . . is this: the man who doubts the possibility of correct historical evidence and tradition cannot then accept his own evidence, judgment, combination and interpretation. He cannot limit his doubt to his historical criticism, but is required to let it operate on his own life. He discovers at once that he not only lacks conclusive evidence in all sorts of aspects of his own life that he had quite taken for granted, but also that there is no evidence whatever. In short, he finds himself forced to accept a general philosophical skepticism along with his historical skepticism. And general philosophical skepticism is a nice intellectual game, but one cannot live by it. (Montgomery, SP, 139, 140)

Millar Burrows of Yale, the American expert on the Dead Sea Scrolls cited also by Montgomery, writes:

> There is a type of Christian faith . . . rather strongly represented today, [that] regards the affirmations of Christian faith as confessional statements which the individual accepts as a member of the believing community, and which are not dependent on reason or evidence. Those who hold this position will not admit that historical investigation can have anything to say about the uniqueness of Christ. They are often skeptical as to the possibility of knowing anything about the historical Jesus, and seem content to dispense with such knowledge. I cannot share this point of view. I am profoundly convinced that the his-

toric revelation of God in Jesus of Nazareth must be the cornerstone of any faith that is really Christian. Any historical question about the real Jesus who lived in Palestine nineteen centuries ago is therefore fundamentally important. (Montgomery, HC, 15, 16)

Montgomery adds: Historical events are "unique, and the test of their factual character can be only the accepted documentary approach that we have followed here. No historian has a right to a closed system of causation, for, as the Cornell logician Max Black has shown in a recent essay ["Models and Metaphors" (Ithaca: Cornell University Press, 1962), p. 16], the very concept of cause is 'a peculiar, unsystematic, and erratic notion,' and therefore 'any attempt to state a "universal law of causation" must prove futile.'" (Montgomery, HC, 76)

The historian Ethelbert Stauffer gives us some suggestions for our approach to history: "What do we [as historians] do when we experience surprises which run counter to all our expectations, perhaps all our convictions and even our period's whole understanding of truth? We say as one great historian used to say in such instances: 'It is surely possible.' And why not? For the critical historian nothing is impossible." (Montgomery, HC, 76)

The historian Philip Schaff adds to the above: "The purpose of the historian is not to construct a history from preconceived notions and to adjust it to his own liking, but to reproduce it from the best evidence and to let it speak for itself." (Schaff, HCC, 175)

Robert M. Horn helps us to understand people's biases in approaching history:

> To put it at its most obvious, a person who denies God's existence will not subscribe to belief in the Bible. A Muslim, convinced that God cannot beget, will not accept as the Word

of God, a book that teaches that Christ is the only begotten Son of God.

Some believe that God is not personal, but rather the Ultimate, the Ground of Being. Such will be predisposed to reject the Bible as God's personal self-revelation. On their premise, the Bible cannot be the personal word of "I AM WHO I AM" (Exodus 3:14). Others rule out the supernatural. They will not be likely to give credence to the book which teaches that Christ rose from the dead. Still others hold that God cannot communicate His truth undistorted through sinful men; hence they regard the Bible as, at least in parts, no more than human. (Green, RW, 10)

A basic definition of history for me is "a knowledge of the past based on testimony." Some immediately say, "I don't agree." Then I ask, "Do you believe Lincoln lived and was president of the United States?" "Yes," is their usual reply. However, no one I've met has personally seen and observed Lincoln. The only way one knows is by testimony—physical, verbal, and written.

Precaution: When you give history this definition, you have to determine the trustworthiness of your witnesses, a subject covered later in this volume.

5B. Misconception #5: "Loving Christians Should Accept Other Religious Views"

"You Christians seem to think that your way is the only way and that all other views are wrong. How intolerant can you be? Why can't you accept other people and what they believe as also true?"

These criticisms reflect the views of a new definition of the word "tolerance." *Webster's New World Dictionary of English* (third edition) defines "tolerate" as "to recognize and respect [other's beliefs, practices, and so forth] without sharing them," and "to bear or put up with [someone or something not especially liked]." The apostle Paul expressed this concept when he said, "[Love] endures all things" (1 Cor. 13:7).

But today a new definition of tolerance is systematically being foisted upon the minds of all people. As an example, Thomas A. Helmbock, executive vice-president of Lambda Chi Alpha fraternity, states, "The definition of new . . . tolerance is that every individual's beliefs, lifestyle, and perception of truth claims are equal. . . . Your beliefs and my beliefs are equal, and all truth is relative." (Helmbock, IT, 2)

This misconception assumes that truth is inclusive, that it gathers under its wings claims that oppose each other. The fact, however, is that all truth is exclusive—at least to some degree— for it must exclude as false that which is not true.

For instance, it is true that Washington D.C. is the capital city of the United States of America. This means that no other city in the United States is that country's capital. In fact, no other city on planet Earth or anywhere in the universe can lay legitimate claim to being the capital city of the United States. One city and one only fits the bill, and that's Washington D.C.

Simply because just one city is the United States capital does not mean that the people who affirm this truth are therefore intolerant. They may like scores of other cities and even live in different cities themselves. They may even live in different countries and prefer their country to America. Accepting the exclusive truth claim about Washington D.C. does not make a person tolerant or intolerant—it simply makes him or her correct about what the capital city of the United States is.

The same is true about Christianity. If the claims of the Christian faith are true—and many people accept them as true—these people are no more intolerant for their belief than those people who accept Washington

D.C. as the United States capital. They are either correct or mistaken about how God has revealed Himself in the world. If they are right, then there really is no other way to God but through Christ. If they are wrong, then Christianity is false. The question of tolerance isn't the issue. The question of *truth* is.

The misconception of intolerance assumes that a person should always keep his options open, even when the evidence narrows the options to one. Why should we do this? It seems clearly unreasonable, as apologists Norman Geisler and Ron Brooks state:

> Surely, it is good to admit the possibility that one might be wrong and never good to maintain a position no matter what the evidence is against it. Also, one should never make a firm decision without examining all the evidence without prejudice. . . . [But] are we still to remain open-minded when all reason says that there can be only one conclusion? That is the same as the error of the closed mind. . . . What if the absolute view is true? Isn't openness taken to be absolute? In the long run, openness cannot really be true unless it is open to some real absolutes that cannot be denied. Open-mindedness should not be confused with empty-mindedness. One should never remain open to a second alternative when only one can be true. (Geisler, WSA, 259)

It is the person who disbelieves in the face of strong evidence supporting Christianity who is really intolerant and closed-minded.

6B. Misconception #6: "I Have an Intellectual Problem"

The rejection of Christ is often not so much of the "mind," but of the "will"; not so much "I can't," but "I won't."

I have met many people with intellectual excuses, but few (albeit some) with intellectual problems. Excuses can cover a multitude of reasons. I greatly respect one who has taken time to investigate the claims of Christ and concludes he just can't believe. I

I had motives for not wanting the world to have a meaning; consequently [I] assumed that it had none, and was able without any difficulty to find satisfying reasons for this assumption. The philosopher who finds no meaning in the world is not concerned exclusively with a problem in pure metaphysics, he is also concerned to prove that there is no valid reason why he personally should not do as he wants to do, or why his friends should not seize political power and govern in the way that they find most advantageous to themselves. . . . For myself, the philosophy of meaninglessness was essentially an instrument of liberation, sexual and political.

—ALDOUS HUXLEY, AN ATHEIST

have a rapport with a person who knows why he doesn't believe (factually and historically), for I know why I believe (factually and historically). This gives us a common ground (though different conclusions).

I have found that most people reject Christ for one or more of the following reasons:

1. Ignorance: Romans 1:18–23 (often self-imposed), Matthew 22:29
2. Pride: John 5:40–44
3. Moral issues: John 3:19, 20

I once counseled a person who was fed up with Christianity because she believed it was not historical and there was just nothing to it factually. She had convinced everyone that she had searched and, as the result of her university studies, had found profound intellectual problems. One after another had failed to persuade her of the truth about Christ because they approached her intellectually to answer her many accusations.

I listened and then asked several questions. Within thirty minutes she admitted she had fooled everyone and that she developed these intellectual doubts in order to excuse her moral life.

One needs to answer the basic problem or real question—not the surface detour that often manifests itself.

A student in a New England university said he had an intellectual problem with Christianity and therefore just could not accept Christ as Savior. "Why can't you believe?" I asked. He replied, "The New Testament is not reliable." I then asked, "If I demonstrate to you that the New Testament is one of the most reliable pieces of literature of antiquity, will you believe? He retorted, "No!" "You don't have a problem with your mind, but with your will," I answered.

A graduate student at the same university, after a lecture on "The Resurrection: Hoax or History?" bombarded me with questions intermingled with accusations (later I found out he did this with most Christian speakers). Finally, after forty-five minutes of dialogue I asked him, "If I prove to you beyond a shadow of a doubt that Christ was raised from the dead and is the Son of God, will you consider Him?" The immediate and emphatic reply was, "No!"

Michael Green cites Aldous Huxley, the atheist, who has destroyed the beliefs of many and has been hailed as a great intellect. Huxley admits his own biases (*Ends and Means*, pp. 270ff.) when he says:

I had motives for not wanting the world to have a meaning; consequently assumed that it had none, and was able without any difficulty to find satisfying reasons for this assumption. The philosopher who finds no meaning in the world is not concerned exclusively with a problem in pure metaphysics, he is also concerned to prove that there is no valid reason why he personally should not do as he wants to do, or why his friends should not seize political power and govern in the way that they find most advantageous to themselves. . . . For myself, the philosophy of meaninglessness was essentially an instrument of liberation, sexual and political. (Green, RW, 36)

Bertrand Russell is an example of an intelligent atheist who did not give careful examination to the evidence for Christianity. In his essay, *Why I Am Not a Christian*, it is obvious that he has not even considered the evidence of and for the resurrection of Jesus and his remarks cast doubt as to whether he has even glanced at the New Testament. It seems incongruous that a man would not deal with the resurrection in great detail since it is the foundation of Christianity. (Green, RW, 36)

Jesus said: "If anyone wills to do His will, he shall know concerning the doctrine, whether it is from God or whether I speak on My own authority" (John 7:17) .

If any person comes to the claims of Jesus Christ wanting to know if they are true, willing to follow His teachings if they are true, he or she will know. But one cannot come unwilling to accept, and expect to find out.

Pascal, the French philosopher, writes: "The evidence of God's existence and His gift is more than compelling, but those who insist that they have no need of Him or it will always find ways to discount the offer." (Pascal, P, n.p.)

3A. WORLDS IN COLLISION

As amply illustrated in the point above, it will be necessary to honestly deal with one's excuses in order to accurately assess the evidence for the Christian faith. Because many people today are coming from a vastly changed mindset than those of twenty years ago when this book was last revised, I have included a new section of material examining various worldviews. Study these different worlds carefully. They will help you understand the difficulty people trapped in these worldviews often have in understanding what seems, by objective reasoning, to be irrefutable evidence. For a more detailed treatment of these subjects, see the section added to this volume, Part Four: Truth or Consequences.

1B. The Postmodern World

A current trend in philosophy, in the wake of the French philosopher Jacques Derrida, is called deconstructionism, or postmodernism. This view stresses the relativity of all meaning and truth, and denies first principles—that is, the commonly accepted truths (e.g., I exist) that form the starting point for all philosophical enquiry. Though its claims may sound confusing to those without philosophical training, its practical outworking has literally dominated the thinking of most people today. The result is a completely relativistic way of thinking about truth: There are no absolute truths, only truths that are relevant to each individual.

"Christianity may be true for you but it's not true for me." This is the misconception of relativism, a central component of postmodernism. It assumes that Christianity may be true for some people, in some places, and at some times, but it is not true for all people, in all places, and at all times. It is relatively true, not absolutely or universally true.

Carl Henry shows that the seeds for postmodernism were sown in modernity: "The Modern Era sought to liberate humanity from . . . fate or existence in a God-ordered universe. Secular science promised a new freedom for humanity and progress for the planet. The intellectual order of the world was relocated in human reasoning." (Henry, PNS, as cited in Dockery, CP, 36)

Human reasoning thus replaced reliance on God in the modern era. In the postmodern era there is a rejection of the need to be chained even to reason and its resulting responsibilities.

Postmodernism rejects the idea that beliefs can adequately reflect reality. Henry observes, "The one epistemic premise shared by all postmodernists is their rejection of foundationalism, the belief that knowledge consists of sets of beliefs that rest assuredly on still other sets of beliefs and that the whole is supported by irreversible foundational beliefs." (Henry, PNS, as cited in Dockery, CP, 42)

Grenz summarizes, "Postmoderns conclude that all attempts to describe an objective, unifying center—a single real world—behind the flux of experience are doomed; in the end they produce only fictitious creations of the human mind. In detaching human explanation from the notion of an underlying objective world, the postmodern critique of modernism cuts us off from things and leaves us only words." (Grenz, PP, 83, 84)

McCallum summarizes the postmodern position:

But how can we know if the images our senses bring to our minds genuinely match reality outside our minds? Ultimately, the only way to be sure would be to stand outside ourselves and compare our mental images with the real world. But since we can't stand outside ourselves, we have no way to know whether the correspondence is accurate. We are left with skepticism.

This is one reason postmodernists contend that empirical "objectivity" doesn't exist. They raise the problem of representation—how we perceive reality, and whether our perceptions accurately reflect the external world. Postmodernists say they don't. They point out that different people see the same thing differently. (McCallum, DT, 36)

For example, they would say that we can not know what Jesus was really like, we can only construct it out of our own language.

> They are deeply hostile to the thought of anything that in any sense stands in judgment over them. The idea toward which they are most hostile is, of course, the idea of there being a God. But they are almost as hostile to the idea of there being an objective universe that doesn't care what they think and could make their most cherished beliefs false without even consulting them.
>
> —PETER VAN INWAGEN
> AUTHOR, *METAPHYSICS*

Grenz adds, "Postmodern thinkers . . . argue that we do not simply encounter a world that is 'out there' but rather that we construct the world using concepts we bring to it. They contend that we have no fixed vantage point beyond our own structuring of the world from which to gain a purely objective view of whatever reality may be out there." (Grenz, PP, 41)

Rorty maintains, "For the postmodernist, true sentences are not true because they correspond to reality, and so there is no need to worry what sort of reality, if any, a given sentence corresponds to—no need to worry about what 'makes' it true." (Rorty, CP, xvi)

Peter Kreeft and Ronald K. Tacelli of Boston College counter that, "Truth means the correspondence of what you know or say to what is. Truth means 'telling it like it is.'" They continue, "All theories of truth, once they are expressed clearly and simply, presuppose the commonsensical notion of truth that is enshrined in the wisdom of lan-

guage and the tradition of usage, namely the correspondence (or identity) there. For each theory claims that it is really true, that is, that it corresponds to reality, and that the others are really false, that is, that they fail to correspond to reality." (Kreeft, HCA, 365, 366)

McCallum concludes, "So, postmodernists argue, there is no way to know if the laws of language and the laws governing reality are the same. Postmodernism leaves us in an all pervasive skepticism, locked up in what they call the prison house of language. Reality is defined or constructed by culture and language, not discovered by reason and observation." (McCallum, DT, 40, 41)

Henry summarizes, "Texts are declared to be intrinsically incapable of conveying truth about some objective reality. One interpreter's meaning is as proper as another's, however incompatible these may be. There is no original or final textual meaning, no one way to interpret the Bible or any other text." (Cited in Dockery, CP, 36)

Rorty concludes, "In the end, the pragmatists tell us, what matters is our loyalty to other human beings clinging together against the dark, not our hope of getting things right." (Rorty, CP, 166)

Grenz summarizes, "The postmodern worldview operates with a community-based understanding of truth. It affirms that whatever we accept as truth and even the way we envision truth are dependent on the community in which we participate. Further, and far more radically, the postmodern worldview affirms that this relativity extends beyond our perceptions of truth to its essence: there is no absolute truth; rather, truth is relative to the community in which we participate." (Grenz, PP, 8)

That is a scary point of view when you consider what the community of Nazi Germany defined to be true!

Norman Geisler shows the practical implication of postmodern logic: "It would mean that Billy Graham is telling the truth when he says, 'God exists,' and Madalyn Murray O'Hare is also right when she claims, 'God does not exist.' But these two statements cannot both be true. If one is true, then the other is false. And since they exhaust the only possibilities, one of them must be true." (Geisler, BECA, 745)

Geisler also argues that, "If truth is relative, then no one is ever wrong—even when they are. As long as something is true to me, then I'm right even when I'm wrong. The drawback is that I could never learn anything either, because learning is moving from a false belief to a true one—that is, from an absolutely false belief to an absolutely true one." (Geisler, BECA, 745)

Kreeft and Tacelli comment on the popularity of this kind of thinking: "Perhaps the primary origin of subjectivism today, at least in America, is the desire to be accepted, to be 'with it,' fashionable, avant garde, 'in the know,' rather than 'square,' 'hokey' or 'out of it.' We all learn this as children—to be embarrassed is the absolutely primary fear of a teenager—but we put more sophisticated, scholarly disguises on it when we become adults." (Kreeft, HCA, 381)

Another source of subjectivism, according to Kreeft and Tacelli, is the fear of radical change—that is, the fear of conversion, being 'born again,' consecrating one's whole life and will to God's will. Subjectivism is much more comfortable, like a womb, or a dream, or a narcissistic fantasy." (Kreeft, HCA, 381)

Van Inwagen muses on the perplexing fact that some people deny the objectivity of truth:

The most interesting thing about objective truth is that there are people who deny that it exists. One might wonder how anyone could deny that there is such a thing as objective truth. For some people, I am fairly sure, the explanation is something like this. They are deeply hostile to the thought of anything that in any sense stands in judgment over them. The idea toward which they are most hostile is, of course, the idea of there being a God. But they are almost as hostile to the idea of there being an objective universe that doesn't care what they think and could make their most cherished beliefs false without even consulting them. (Van Inwagen, M, 59)

The claims of Christianity stand in marked clarity and contrast to the fuzzy world of postmodern language. Jesus left no doubt that He is man's only cure, his only hope for reconciliation with God. Jesus said, "I am the way, the truth, and the life. No one comes to the Father except through Me" (John 14:6). And the church did not miss the implications of Jesus' words. When the apostle Peter was pressed by the Jewish religious leaders to explain his actions, he said unequivocally: "Let it be known to you all, and to all the people of Israel, that by the name of Jesus Christ of Nazareth, whom you crucified, whom God raised from the dead, by Him this man stands before you whole. This is the 'stone which was rejected by you builders, which has become the chief cornerstone.' Nor is there salvation in any other, for there is no other name under heaven given among men by which we must be saved" (Acts 4:10–12).

When one evaluates the claims of Christianity a clear choice emerges. Jesus Christ is either the answer for all people, at all times, and in all places, or He is the answer for no one, at no time, and in no place. If He is only a psychological crutch for some people, this does not make Him the necessary object of faith for all people. And, conversely, if Jesus is Lord and God, then this fact does not cease to be true simply because someone chooses not to believe it.

Peter van Inwagen explains that "beliefs and assertions are thus related to the world as a map is related to the territory: it is up to the map to get the territory right, and if the map doesn't get the territory right, that's the

> We do not make statements true or false by affirming or denying them. They have truth or falsity regardless of what we think, what opinions we hold, what judgments we make.
>
> —MORTIMER J. ADLER

fault of the map and not the fault of the territory." (van Inwagen, M, 56)

In a real life application, van Inwagen adds: "If your friend Alfred responds to something you have said with the words, 'That may be true for you, but it isn't true for me,' his words can only be regarded as a rather misleading way of saying, 'That may be what you think, but it's not what I think.'" (van Inwagen, M, 56, 57)

Furthermore, according to Mortimer J. Adler, statements such as, "that may have been true in the Middle Ages, but is no longer true," or "That may be true for primitive people, but it is not true for us," are based on two sorts of confusions. Sometimes truth is confused with what a majority of people at a particular time or place think is true, as in the following example: "A portion of the human race some centuries ago held it to be true that the earth is flat. That false opinion has now been generally repudiated. This should not be interpreted to mean that the objective truth has changed—that what once was true is no longer true. What has changed is not the truth of the matter but the prevalence of an opinion that has ceased to be popular." A second sort of confusion results when the spatial or temporal context of a statement is ignored: "The population of

a country changes from time to time, but a statement about the size of a country's population at a given time remains true when, at a later time, it has increased in size. The presence of the date in a statement about the population of the United Stated in a certain year enabled that statement to remain true forever, if it was accurate in the first place." (Adler, SGI, 43)

Even agnostic Bertrand Russell argues that truth is not relative to our minds: "It will be seen that minds do not create truth or falsehood. They create beliefs, but when once the beliefs are created, the mind cannot make them true or false, except in the special case where they concern future things which are within the power of the person believing, such as catching trains. What makes a belief true is a fact, and this fact does not (except in exceptional cases) in any way involve the mind of the person who has the belief." (Russell, PP, 129, 130)

"The truth or falsity of a statement," Adler continues, "derives from its relation to the ascertainable facts, not from its relation to the judgments that human beings make. I may affirm as true a statement that is in fact false. You may deny as false a statement that is in fact true. My affirmation and your denial in no way alter or affect the truth or falsity of the statement that you and I have wrongly judged. We do not make statements true or false by affirming or denying them. They have truth or falsity regardless of what we think, what opinions we hold, what judgments we make." (Adler, SGI, 41)

Dr. William Lane Craig says of postmodernism: "To assert that 'the truth is that there is no truth' is both self-refuting and arbitrary. For if this statement is true, it is not true, since there is no truth. So-called deconstructionism thus cannot be halted from decoding itself. Moreover, there is also no reason for adopting the postmodern perspective rather than, say, the outlooks of

Western capitalism, male chauvinism, white racism and so forth, since postmodernism has no more truth to it than these perspectives." (Craig, PIS, as cited in Phillips, CAPW, 82)

Craig's point shows the danger of postmodern thinking. When there is no objective truth, then there is nothing that is wrong. What most people would consider abhorrent (for example, murder, stealing, and, in the past, lying) must now be accepted because it is acceptable to some people.

James Sire unveils another postmodern inconsistency: "Though ultramodernists (postmodernists) ought to say they never met a narrative they didn't like, it is clear that they have. Christian fundamentalist and evangelical stories are often rejects for their exclusivity." (Sire, BFCIN, as cited in Phillips, CAPW, 120)

McCallum argues,

> Postmodernists hold that since we can't stand outside of ourselves to compare mental images with reality, we are forced to reject the idea that we can know reality in an objective way. We would answer, to the contrary, that our judgments about the world, while not infallibly accurate, are open to revision by further investigation. Just because we lack absolute certainty about the external world doesn't mean we can't know anything about what exists apart from us. We don't have to wallow in postmodern skepticism.
>
> The success of scientific technology is a strong argument that our perceptions of the world are relatively accurate. Countless achievements attest to the reliability of human knowledge. (McCallum, DT, 52)

For example, the calculations of mathematicians to determine what orbits, trajectories, and accelerations would be needed in order to land a man on the moon proved to be accurate. Neil Armstrong actually did set foot on the moon!

A person could neither function nor live very long if he consistently acted as though truth were a matter of perspective rather than an objective reality. He would bounce checks if only "to him" his bank account had money, he'd drink poison if "to him" it was lemonade, he'd fall through the thin ice if it was thick "to him," or get hit by a bus if "to him" it was not moving. To a person who wants to function effectively in the world, the objective correspondence of truth to reality *must matter* in some sense.

Even more dangerous to humanity are those who live by a perceptual view of truth only concerning their moral activities.

Finally, if postmodernism is true, then marriage is impossible. It means a man doesn't have to really listen and understand what his wife is saying. He can put his own meaning on it. And that, most men have found over the years, gets them into a heap of trouble.

2B: The Eastern Mystical World

Since most mystics deny a dualistic worldview such as right versus wrong or truth versus error, the evidence for one's faith is unimportant to the mystic. The danger of an Eastern mystical outlook, then, is the avoidance of information that leads one to a true knowledge of God.

One of the most popular forms of Eastern mysticism in the United States, as well as in other countries of the world, is Zen Buddhism.

Norm Anderson defines mysticism: "In general terms [mysticism] represents the belief that direct knowledge of God, of spiritual truth or ultimate reality, is attainable 'through immediate intuition or insight and in a way different from ordinary sense perception or the use of logical reasoning' (*Webster's New Collegiate Dictionary*)." (Anderson, CWR, 37)

Anderson tells us how Zen reaches this knowledge of ultimate reality: "Zen Buddhists believe that by rigorous self-discipline and a strictly prescribed method of meditation they may attain *satori*, the Japanese term for 'enlightenment'—whether suddenly, as some teach, or gradually, as others hold—by means of a perception which is empirical rather than intellectual." (Anderson, CWR, 88)

D. T. Suzuki states plainly: "Zen does not follow the routine of reasoning, and does not mind contradicting itself or being inconsistent" (Suzuki, LZ, 94). And he also states: "Zen is decidedly not a system founded upon logic and analysis. If anything it is the antipode to logic, by which I mean the dualistic mode of thinking." (Suzuki, IZB, 38)

Suzuki defines satori as completely different than rational knowledge: "Satori may be defined as an intuitive looking into the nature of things in contradistinction to the analytical or logical understanding of it." (Suzuki, EZBI, 230)

As a result, Zen Buddhists and other mystics generally shun the use of logic. The philosopher William Lane Craig examines several logical problems with the claims of mysticism:

Now under the influence of Eastern mysticism, many people today would deny that systematic consistency is a test for truth. They affirm that reality is ultimately illogical or that logical contradictions correspond to reality. They assert in Eastern thought the Absolute or God or the Real transcends the logical categories of human thought. They are apt to interpret the demand for logical consistency as a piece of Western imperialism which ought to be rejected along with other vestiges of colonialism. . . . I am inclined to say frankly that such positions are crazy and unintelligible. To say that God is both good and not good in the same sense or that God neither exists nor does not exist is just incomprehensible to me. In our politically correct age, there is a tendency to vilify all that is Western and to exalt Eastern modes of thinking as at least equally valid if not superior to Western modes of thought. To assert that Eastern thought is seriously deficient in making such claims is to be a sort of epistemological bigot, blinkered by the constraints of the logic-chopping Western mind. (Craig, PIS, as cited in Phillips, CAPW, 78–81)

If one has difficulty accepting the laws of logic, that individual will have problems with the evidence presented in this book. The evidence here brings one to the conclusion, for example, that either Jesus was raised bodily from the grave or He was not. There is a choice. You cannot have both/and reasoning over the question whether or not Jesus was raised from the dead.

Ravi Zacharias tells a story that illuminates the futility of the Eastern mystical *both/and* line of argument:

As the professor waxed eloquent and expounded on the law of non-contradiction, he eventually drew his conclusion: "This [*either/or*] logic is a Western way of looking at reality. The real problem is that you are seeking . . . contradiction as a Westerner when you should be approaching it as an Easterner. The *both/and* is the Eastern way of viewing reality."

After he belabored these two ideas on *either/or* and *both/and* for some time . . . I finally asked if I could interrupt his unpunctuated train of thought and raise one question. . . . I said, "Sir, are you telling me that when I am studying Hinduism I *either* use the *both/and* system of logic or nothing else?"

There was pin-drop silence for what seemed an eternity. I repeated my question: "Are you telling me that when I am studying Hinduism I *either* use the *both/and* logic or nothing else? Have I got that right?"

He threw his head back and said, "The *either/or* does seem to emerge, doesn't it?"

"Indeed, it does emerge," I said. "And as a matter of fact, even in India we look both ways before we cross the street—it is either the bus or me, not both of us."

Do you see the mistake he was making? He was using the *either/or* logic in order to prove the *both/and*. The more you try to hammer the law of non-contradiction, the more it hammers you. (Zacharias, CMLWG, 129)

Zacharias also points out what many do not acknowledge about Eastern philosophy: "The whole method of teaching of the greatest Hindu philosopher Shankara was quite Socratic as he debated ideas not in a dialectical mode, *both/and*, but in a non-contradictory mode, *either/or*. He would challenge his antagonists to prove him wrong, and if not, to surrender to his view. The point, then, is not whether we use an Eastern logic or a Western logic. We use the logic that best reflects reality, and the law of non-contradiction is implicitly or explicitly implied by both the East and the West." (Zacharias, CMLWG, 130)

Ronald Nash adds: "The law of non-contradiction is not simply a law of thought. It is a law of thought because it is first a law of being. Nor is the law something someone can take or leave. The denial of the law of non-contradiction leads to absurdity. It is impossible meaningfully to deny the laws of logic. If the law of non-contradiction is denied, then nothing has meaning. If the laws of logic do not first mean what they say, nothing else can have meaning, including the denial of the laws." (Nash, WVC, 84)

The testimony of ex-Hindu Rabindranath Maharaj illustrates the dilemma facing anyone who adopts the pantheistic mysticism of the East:

My religion made beautiful theory, but I was having serious trouble applying it in everyday life. Nor was it only a matter of my five senses versus my inner visions. It was a matter of reason also.... If there was only one Reality, then Brahman was evil as well as good, death as well as life, hatred as well as love. That made everything meaningless, life an absurdity.... It seemed unreasonable: but I [was reminded] that Reason could not be trusted—it was part of the illusion. If reason also was Maya—as the Vedas taught—then how could I trust any concept, including the idea that all was Maya and only Brahman was real? How could I be sure the Bliss I sought was not also an illusion, if none of my perceptions or reasoning were to be trusted? (Maharaja, DG, 104)

Norman Geisler asks this pointed question: "When we cross a busy street and see three lanes of traffic coming toward us, should we not even worry about it because it is merely an illusion? Indeed, should we even bother to look for cars when we cross the street, if we, the traffic, and the street do not really exist? If pantheists actually lived out their pantheism consistently, would there be any pantheists left?" (Geisler, WA, 102)

Francis Schaeffer tells a story that illustrates the nonviability of denying logical dualism:

One day I was talking to a group of people in the room of a young South African in Cambridge University. Among others, there was present a young Indian who was of Sikh background but a Hindu by religion. He started to speak strongly against Christianity, but did not really understand the problems of his own beliefs. So I said, "Am I not correct in saying that on the basis of your system, cruelty and non-cruelty are ultimately equal, that there is no intrinsic difference between them?" He agreed. The student in whose room we met, who had clearly understood the implications of what the Sikh had admitted, picked up his kettle of boiling water with which he was about to make tea, and stood with it steaming over the Indian's head. The man looked up and asked him what he was doing and he said, with a cold yet gentle finality, "There is no difference between cruelty and non-cruelty." Thereupon the Hindu walked out into the night. (Schaeffer, CWFS, 1:110)

3B. The Atheistic World

The word "atheism" comes from two Greek words. "*A*" meaning "no," and "*theos*," meaning "God." An atheist, then, is one who claims there is no God, which is a most difficult proposition to defend. An atheist, to be consistently assured that his belief is accurate, must also claim to be omniscient, for there always exists the possibility of the existence of God outside his knowledge. And considering the fact that most people would claim to possess only an infinitely small fraction of all the knowledge in the universe, the odds of God existing outside of one's knowledge are extremely high.

Many people I meet have never even heard, much less considered, much of the evidence presented in these notes. I hadn't either until I set out to refute Christianity. And this is why I have pulled this evidence together: to give everyone, especially atheists, an opportunity for a new life based on the truth of Jesus' claims. For if there is truly no God, the future is dim both for society and for the individual. Consider Dostoyevsky's brilliant portrayal of culture without God in *The Brothers Karamazov*: "But what will become of men then? . . . without God and immortal life? All things are lawful then, they can do what they like? Didn't you know?" (Dostoyevsky, BK, 312)

Dostoyevsky continues:

It's God that's worrying me. That's the only thing that's worrying me. What if he doesn't exist? What if Rakitin's right—that it's an idea made up by men? Then if He doesn't exist, man is the chief of the earth, of the universe. Magnificent! Only how is he going to be good

without God? That's the question. I always come back to that. For whom is man going to love then? To whom will he be thankful? To whom will he sing the hymn? Ratkin laughs. Ratikin says that one can love humanity without God. Well, only a sniveling idiot can maintain that. Life's easy for Ratikin. "You'd better think about the extension of civic rights, or even of keeping down the price of meat. You will show your love for humanity more simply and directly by that, than by philosophy." I answered him, "Well, but you, without God, are more likely to raise the price of meat, if it suits you, and make a rouble on every copeck." (Dostoyevsky, BK, 314)

But it is more than just the idea of God that is important. There must be a reality of God and His ability to actually and substantially change a person from the inside out.

If you look at how atheists typically feel at the end of their lives, there is motivation to investigate the possibility that God has revealed Himself to us in Christ.

"Sartre found atheism 'cruel,' Camus 'dreadful,' and Nietzsche 'maddening.' Atheists who consistently try to live without God tend to commit suicide or go insane. Those who are inconsistent live on the ethical or aesthetic shadow of Christian truth while they deny the reality that made the shadow." (Geisler, BECA, 282)

Not long before his death Sartre said, "I do not feel that I am the product of chance, a speck of dust in the universe, but someone who was expected, prepared, prefigured. In short, a being whom only a Creator could put here; and this idea of a creating hand refers to God." (Schwarz, SS, as cited in Varghese, ISOGA, 128)

My prayer is that all who read these notes will come to know the One who has literally "expected, prepared, and prefigured" us for a life of meaning and purpose through Jesus Christ.

4B. The Agnostic World

Because of the difficulty of defending an atheist position, most irreligious people adopt the position of agnosticism.

Once again this term is made up of two Greek terms. "*A*," meaning "no," and "*gnosis*", meaning "knowledge." So the term simply

> The fundamental flaw in Kant's hard agnostic position is his claim to have knowledge of what he declares to be unknowable. In other words, if it were true that reality cannot be known, no one, including Kant, would know it. Kant's hard agnosticism boils down to the claim: "I know that reality is unknowable."
>
> —NORMAN L. GEISLER
> PETER BOCCHINO

means "no knowledge." An agnostic person is not sure if there is a God.

The philosopher's concept of agnosticism is often different from the popular conception of it. Kant and others held that we *can not* know if God exists. Most agnostics would say that they are agnostic because they *do not* know of God's existence. The first group has ruled out the possibility of knowing God altogether. The later is still waiting, knowing only that they do not currently have a knowledge of God. So there are two different ways of defining "no knowledge." The first is that there is no knowledge possible. The second is that there is no knowledge obtained.

Kant's epistemology results in agnosticism, the claim that nothing can be known about reality. Norman Geisler comments: "In its unlimited form [agnosticism] claims that all knowledge about reality (i.e., truth) is impossible. But this itself is offered as truth about reality" (Geisler, CA, 135). Geisler and Peter Bocchino summarize the self-defeating nature of this claim: "The fun-

damental flaw in Kant's hard agnostic position is his claim to have knowledge of what he declares to be unknowable. In other words, if it were true that reality cannot be known, no one, including Kant, would know it. Kant's hard agnosticism boils down to the claim: 'I know that reality is unknowable.'" (Geisler and Bocchino, WSA, n.p.)

Most people, however, limit agnosticism to the belief that you can't know whether God exists, not other forms of reality.

5B. The Scientific World

Oddly enough, of all the worlds in collision today it is the scientific world that is increasingly giving the greatest and most shocking evidence in favor of God's existence.

Over the years the fight between science and religion has been well known. But in recent years the "facts" that science has promoted concerning the origins of the universe as well as human beings has increasingly come under attack, especially from within. Over the years scientists such as Michael Behe have challenged the "facts" of science from a scientific methodology. Works such as Behe's *Darwin's Black Box: The Biochemical Challenge to Evolution,* in which he states evidence from biochemistry that refutes Darwinian evolution, have ushered in a new age of critique of Darwin's theory.

Interestingly, the more science discovers, the more eye-opening the concept of a Creator turns out to be. Concerning DNA, Charles Thaxton states : "A structural identity has been discovered between the genetic message on DNA and the written messages of a human language." (Thaxton, NDA, as cited in CP, 18)

Hupert Yockey explains:

> There is an identity of structure between DNA (and protein) and written linguistic messages. Since we know by experience that intelligence

produces written messages, and no other cause is known, the implication, according to the abductive method, is that intelligent cause produced DNA and protein. The significance of this result lies in the security of it, for it is much stronger than if the structures were merely similar. We are not dealing with anything like a superficial resemblance between DNA and a written text. We are not saying DNA is like a message. Rather, DNA is a message. True design thus returns to biology. (Yockey, JTB, as cited in Thaxton, NDA, 19)

Also William Dembski states: "Within biology, intelligent design is a theory of biological origins and development. Its fundamental claim is that intelligent causes are necessary to explain the complex, information rich structures of biology, and that these causes are empirically detectable." (Dembski, IDM, 24)

Dembski continues: "The world contains events, objects, and structures which exhaust the explanatory resources of undirected natural causes, and which can be adequately explained only by recourse to intelligent causes. Scientists are now in a position to demonstrate this rigorously. Thus what has been a long-standing philosophical intuition is now being cashed out as a scientific research program." (Dembski, IDM, 25)

Chandra Wickramasinghe continues:

I think if you look at the structure of our living system, micro-organisms or ourselves under the microscope, as it were (not literally), if you investigate a living system that is before us, that is accessible to us, one is driven to the conclusion, inescapably, that living systems could not have been generated by random processes, within a finite time-scale, in a finite universe. I think the evidence from life is very hard, a hard fact, from the nature of a living system as you study it in the lab. The information content in the living system that we have on the earth is perhaps the hardest cosmological fact. You can't get away from that, in the sense that the Universe has to in some way discover this arrangement. I would put that datum above the cosmological datum in quality of information. (Wickramasinghe, SDOL, as cited in Varghese, ISOAG, 33)

> We are not dealing with anything like a superficial resemblance between DNA and a written text. We are not saying DNA is like a message. Rather, DNA is a message. True design thus returns to biology.
>
> —HUPERT YOCKEY

Stanley Jaki states:

To speak of purpose may seem, since Darwin, the most reprehensible procedure before the tribunal of science. Bafflingly enough, it is science in its most advanced and comprehensive form, scientific cosmology, which reinstates today references to purpose into scientific discourse. Shortly after the discovery of the 2.7o K radiation, cosmologists began to wonder at the extremely narrow margin allowed for cosmic evolution. The universe began to appear to them more and more as if placed on an extremely narrow track, a track laid down so that ultimately man may appear on the scene. For if that cosmic soup had been slightly different, not only the chemical elements, of which all organic bodies are made, would have failed to be formed. Inert matter would have also been subject to an interaction different from the one required for the coagulation of large lumps of matter, such as protostars and proto-solar systems. . . . At any rate, the emergence of life on earth is, from the purely scientific viewpoint, an outcome of immense improbability. No wonder that in view of this quite a few cosmologists, who are unwilling to sacrifice forever at the alter of blind chance, began to speak of the Anthropic Principle. Recognition of that principle was prompted by the nagging suspicion that the universe may have after all been specifically tailored for the sake of man. (Jaki, FSCC, as cited in Varghese, ISOAG, 71, 72)

Hugh Ross adds, "Astronomers have discovered that the characteristics of the universe, of our galaxy and of our solar system are so finely tuned to support life that the only reasonable explanation for this is the forethought of a personal, intelligent Creator whose involvement explains the degree of finetunedness. It requires power and purpose." (Ross, AEPTG, as cited in Moreland, CH, 160)

Ross records Paul Davies's comment that there "is for me more powerful evidence that there is something going on behind it all. The impression of design is overwhelming." (Davies, CB, 203, as cited in Moreland, CH, 164)

It continues: "The laws of science, as we know them at present, contain many fundamental numbers, like the size of the electric charge of the electron and the ratio of the masses of the proton and the electron. The remarkable fact is that the values of these numbers seem to have been very finely adjusted to make possible the development of life . . . it seems clear that there are relatively few ranges of values for the numbers that would allow the development of any form of intelligent life." (Hawking, BHT, 125)

Hawking adds, "This means that the initial state of the universe must have been very carefully chosen indeed if the hot big bang model was correct right back to the beginning of time. It would be very difficult to explain why the universe should have begun in just this way, except as the act of a God who intended to create beings like us." (Hawking, BHT, 127)

"It is this increasing amazement that has led many astronomers and physicists to change the Anthropic principle somewhat and announce with Sir Fred Hoyle that 'there must be a God.'" (Varghese 1984, vii, 23–27) (Miethe, DGE, 165)

Ross continues: "It is not just the universe that bears evidence for design. The sun and the earth also reveal such evidence. Frank Dake, Carl Sagan, and Josef Shklovskii were among the first astronomers to make this point. They attempted to estimate the number of planets (in the universe) with environments favorable for life support. In the early 1960s they recognized that only a certain kind of star with a planet just the right distance from the star would provide the necessary conditions for life." (Ross, AEPTG, as cited in Moreland, CH, 164)

Ross adds: "Considering that the observable universe contains less than a trillion galaxies, each averaging a hundred billion stars, we can see that not even one planet would be expected, by natural processes alone, to possess the necessary conditions to sustain life. No wonder Robert Rood and James Trefil, among others, have surmised that intelligent physical life exists only on the earth." (Ross, AEPTG, as cited in Moreland, CH, 169, 170)

Ross concludes: "Again we see that a personal, transcendent Creator must have designed the universe. A personal, transcendent Creator must have designed planet Earth. A personal, transcendent Creator must have designed life." (Ross, FG, 138)

Is it possible that simple chance could account for all of this design? "It is hard to believe that the vastness and grandeur of nature is all a matter of chance." (Clark, SC, 154)

Clark continues: "Are the properties of the chemical elements just a matter of chance too—carbon, nitrogen, oxygen, and the rest? Are the remarkable properties of water and carbon dioxide again due to chance?" (Clark, SC, 154)

The fact that these relations [fine-tuned universe] are necessary for our existence is one of the most fascinating discoveries of modern science. . . . All this prompts the question of why, from the infinite range of possible values that nature could have selected for the fundamental constants, and from the very infinite variety of initial conditions that could have characterized the primeval universe, the actual values and conditions conspire to produce the particular range of very special features that we observe. For clearly the universe is a very special place: exceedingly uniform on a large scale, yet not so precisely uniform that galaxies could not form; . . . an expansion rate tuned to the energy content to unbelievable accuracy; values for the strengths of its forces that permit nuclei to exist, yet do not burn up all the cosmic hydrogen, and many more apparent accidents of fortune. (Davies, AU as cited in Plantinga, MN, 111)

Is there purpose in the universe and, if so, what is its relation to the Creator? Henry Margenau answers very definitely, "There my argument is extremely simple. What is the difference between cause and purpose? Cause is determination of future events by the past. Purpose is determination of future events by a vision of the future. You can't have a purpose unless you visualize what you want to do. Therefore, purpose requires a mind." (Margenau, MPBG as cited in Varghese, ISOAG, 42)

4A. CONCLUSION

The skeptic David Hume concluded his famous *Enquiry Concerning Human Understanding* with this challenge: "If we take in hand any volume; of divinity or school metaphysics, for instance; let us ask, 'Does it contain any abstract reasoning concerning quality or number?' No. 'Does it contain any experimental reasoning concerning matters of fact or existence?' No. Commit it to the flames: For it can contain nothing but sophistry and illusion." (Hume, ECHU, 12.2)

Is there any evidence of a compelling nature that can deliver an individual from the futility of skepticism, agnosticism, and atheism? From the contradictions of postmodernism? Or from the deceptive emotions of mysticism? I believe that there certainly is.

B. C. Johnson, in *The Atheist Debater's Handbook*, throws down this challenge: "If God exists, there will be evidence of this; signs will emerge which point to such a conclusion." (Johnson, ADH, 15)

These lecture notes meet the challenges of Hume and Johnson head on. They present evidence, even as Hume has demanded, in terms of quantity and number, and much more beside, to help a reasonable person discover that God has reached out to us in the Person of Jesus Christ.

I agree with Johnson that evidence will exist—in fact has already emerged—that points to God's existence. The evidence has, in fact, emerged in so specific a way that it is clear God wants us to know more than that He simply exists. He wants us to know that we can know Him. Read on to discover EVIDENCE THAT DEMANDS A VERDICT!

Part One

THE CASE FOR THE BIBLE

1
THE UNIQUENESS OF THE BIBLE

INTRODUCTION

Over and over again, like a broken record, people ask me, "Oh, you don't read the Bible, do you?" Sometimes they'll say, "Why, the Bible is just another book; you ought to read . . . ," then they'll mention a few of their favorite books.

There are those who have a Bible in their library. They proudly tell me that it sits on the shelf next to other "greats," such as Homer's *Odyssey* or Shakespeare's *Romeo and Juliet* or Austen's *Pride and Prejudice*. Their Bible may be dusty, not broken in, but they still think of it as one of the classics.

Others make degrading comments about the Bible, even snickering at the thought that anyone might take it seriously enough to spend time reading it. For these folks, having a copy of the Bible in their library is a sign of ignorance.

The above questions and observations bothered me when, as a non-Christian, I tried to refute the Bible as God's Word to humanity. I finally came to the conclusion that these were simply trite phrases from either biased, prejudiced, or simply unread men and women.

The Bible should be on the top shelf all by itself. The Bible is "unique." That's it! The ideas I grappled with to describe the Bible are summed up by the word "unique."

Webster must have had this "Book of books" in mind when he wrote the definition for "unique": "1. one and only; single;

sole. 2. Different from all others; having no like or equal."

Professor M. Montiero-Williams, former Boden professor of Sanskrit, held this perspective. After spending forty-two years studying Eastern books, he compared them with the Bible and said: "Pile them, if you will, on the left side of your study table; but place your own Holy Bible on the right side—all by itself, all alone—and with a wide gap between them. For . . . there is a gulf between it and the so-called sacred books of the East which severs the one from the other utterly, hopelessly, and forever . . . a veritable gulf which cannot be bridged over by any science of religious thought." (Collett, AAB, 314, 315)

The Bible stands alone among all other books. It is unique, "different from all others," in the following ways (plus a multitude more):

1A. UNIQUE IN ITS CONTINUITY

The Bible is the only book that was

1. Written over about a fifteen-hundred-year span.

2. Written by more than forty authors from every walk of life, including kings, military leaders, peasants, philosophers, fishermen, tax collectors, poets, musicians, statesmen, scholars, and shepherds. For example:

   Moses, a political leader and judge, trained in the universities of Egypt;
   David, a king, poet, musician, shepherd, and warrior;
   Amos, a herdsman;
   Joshua, a military general;
   Nehemiah, a cupbearer to a pagan king;
   Daniel, a prime minister;

   Solomon, a king and philosopher;
   Luke, a physician and historian;
   Peter, a fisherman;
   Matthew, a tax collector;
   Paul, a rabbi; and
   Mark, Peter's secretary.

3. Written in different places:

   By Moses in the wilderness,
   Jeremiah in a dungeon,
   Daniel on a hillside and in a palace,
   Paul inside prison walls,
   Luke while traveling,
   John while in exile on the isle of Patmos.

4. Written at different times:

   David in times of war and sacrifice
   Solomon in times of peace and prosperity.

5. Written during different moods:

   Some writing from the heights of joy;
   Others writing from the depths of sorrow and despair;
   Some during times of certainty and conviction;
   Others during days of confusion and doubt.

6. Written on three continents:

   Asia
   Africa
   Europe.

7. Written in three languages:

   Hebrew, the language of the Israelites and practically all of the Old Testament. In 2

Kings 18:26–28 and Nehemiah 13:24, it is called "the language of Judah," and in Isaiah 19:18, "the language of Canaan."

Hebrew is a pictorial language in which the past is not merely described but verbally painted. Not just a landscape is presented but a moving panorama. The course of events is reenacted in the mind's sight. (Note the frequent use of "behold," a Hebraism carried over to the New Testament.) Such common Hebraic expressions as "he arose and went," "he opened his lips and spoke," "he lifted up his eyes and saw," and "he lifted up his voice and wept" illustrate the pictorial strength of the language. (Dockery, FBI, 214)

Aramaic, the "common language" of the Near East until the time of Alexander the Great (sixth century B.C. through the fourth century B.C.). (Albright, AP, 218) Daniel 2 through 7 and most of Ezra 4 through 7 are in Aramaic, as are occasional statements in the New Testament, most notably Jesus' cry from the cross, *"Eli, Eli, lama sabachthani,"* which means "My God, My God, why have You forsaken Me?" (Matt. 27:46 NKJV).

Aramaic is linguistically very close to Hebrew and similar in structure. Aramaic texts in the Bible are written in the same script as Hebrew. In contrast to Hebrew, Aramaic uses a larger vocabulary, including many loan words, and a greater variety of connectives. It also contains an elaborate system of tenses, developed through the use of participles with pronouns or with various forms of the verb "to be." Although Aramaic is less euphonious and poetical than Hebrew, it is probably superior as a vehicle of exact expression.

> *I have found in the Bible words for my inmost thoughts, songs for my joy, utterance for my hidden griefs and pleadings for my shame and feebleness.*
>
> — SAMUEL TAYLOR COLERIDGE, ENGLISH POET AND LITERARY CRITIC

Aramaic has perhaps the longest continuous living history of any language known. It was used during the Bible's patriarchal period and is still spoken by a few people today. Aramaic and its cognate, Syriac, evolved into many dialects in different places and periods. Characterized by simplicity, clarity, and precision, it adapted easily to the various needs of everyday life. It could serve equally well as a language for scholars, pupils, lawyers, or merchants. Some have described it as the Semitic equivalent of English. (Dockery, FBI. 221)

Greek, the language comprising almost all of the New Testament. It was also the international language spoken at the time of Christ, as English is becoming in the modern world.

The Greek script was based on an alphabet presumably borrowed from the Phoenicians and then adapted to the Greek speech sound system and direction of writing. Greek was first written from right to left like the West Semitic languages, then in a back-and-forth pattern, and finally from left to right.

The conquests of Alexander the Great encouraged the spread of Greek language and culture. Regional dialects were largely replaced by "Hellenistic" or "koine" (common) Greek. . . . The koine dialect added many vernacular expressions to Attic Greek, thus making it more cosmopolitan. Simplifying the grammar also better adapted it to a world-wide culture. The new language, reflecting simple, popular speech, became the common language of commerce and diplomacy. The Greek language lost much of its elegance and finely shaded nuance as a result of its evolution from classic to koine. Nevertheless, it retained its distinguishing characteristics of strength, beauty, clarity, and logical rhetorical power.

It is significant that the apostle Paul wrote his letter to Christians in Rome in the Greek language rather than in Latin. The Roman Empire of that time was culturally a Greek world, except for governmental transactions.

The Greek New Testament vocabulary is abundant and sufficient to convey just the shade of meaning the author desires. For example, the New Testament used two different words for "love" (for two kinds of love), two words for "another" (another of the same, or another of a different kind), and several words for various kinds of knowledge. Significantly, some words are omitted, such as *eros* (a third kind of love) and other words commonly employed in the Hellenistic culture of that time. (Dockery, FBI, 224-25, 227)

8. Written in a wide variety of literary styles, including:

> poetry,
> historical narrative,
> song,
> romance,
> didactic treatise,
> personal correspondence,
> memoirs,
> satire,
> biography,
> autobiography,
> law,
> prophecy,
> parable, and
> allegory.

9. The Bible addresses hundreds of controversial subjects, subjects that create opposing opinions when mentioned or discussed. The biblical writers treated hundreds of hot topics (e.g., marriage, divorce and remarriage, homosexuality, adultery, obedience to authority, truth-telling and lying, character development, parenting, the

nature and revelation of God). Yet from Genesis through Revelation these writers addressed them with an amazing degree of harmony.

10. In spite of its diversity, the Bible presents a single unfolding story: God's redemption of human beings. Norman Geisler and William Nix put it this way: "The 'Paradise Lost' of Genesis becomes the 'Paradise Regained' of Revelation. Whereas the gate to the tree of life is closed in Genesis, it is opened forevermore in Revelation." (Geisler/Nix, GIB'86, 28) The unifying thread is salvation from sin and condemnation to a life of complete transformation and unending bliss in the presence of the one, merciful, holy God.

11. Finally, and most important, among all the people described in the Bible, the leading character throughout is the one, true, living God made known through Jesus Christ.

Consider first the Old Testament: The Law provides the "*foundation* for Christ," the historical books show "the *preparation*" for Christ, the poetical works *aspire* to Christ, and the prophecies display an "*expectation*" of Christ. In the New Testament, the "Gospels . . . record the historical *manifestation* of Christ, the Acts relate the *propagation* of Christ, the Epistles give the *interpretation* of Him, and in Revelation is found the *consummation* of all things in Christ." (Geisler/Nix, GIB'86, 29) From cover to cover, the Bible is Christocentric.

Therefore, although the Bible contains many books by many authors, it shows in its continuity that it is also one book. As F. F. Bruce observes, "Any part of the human body can only be properly explained in reference to the whole body. And any part of the Bible can only be properly explained in reference to the whole Bible." (Bruce, BP, 89) Each book is like a chapter in the one book we call the Bible. Bruce concludes:

> The Bible, at first sight, appears to be a collection of literature—mainly Jewish. If we enquire into the circumstances under which the various Biblical documents were written, we find that they were written at intervals over a space of nearly 1400 years. The writers wrote in various lands, from Italy in the west to Mesopotamia and possibly Persia in the east. The writers themselves were a heterogeneous number of people, not only separated from each other by hundreds of years and hundreds of miles, but belonging to the most diverse walks of life. In their ranks we have kings, herdsmen, soldiers, legislators, fishermen, statesmen, courtiers, priests and prophets, a tentmaking Rabbi and a Gentile physician, not to speak of others of whom we know nothing apart from the writings they have left us. The writings themselves belong to a great variety of literary types. They include history, law (civil, criminal, ethical, ritual, sanitary), religious poetry, didactic treatises, lyric poetry, parable and allegory, biography, personal correspondence, personal memoirs and diaries, in addition to the distinctively Biblical types of prophecy and apocalyptic.
>
> For all that, the Bible is not simply an anthology; there is a unity which binds the whole together. An anthology is compiled by an anthologist, but no anthologist compiled the Bible. (Bruce, BP, 88)

Contrast the books of the Bible with the compilation of Western classics called the *Great Books of the Western World*. The *Great Books* contain selections from more than 450 works by close to 100 authors spanning a period of about twenty-five centuries: Homer, Plato, Aristotle, Plotinus, Augustine, Aquinas, Dante, Hobbes, Spinoza, Calvin, Rousseau, Shakespeare, Hume, Kant, Darwin, Tolstoy, Whitehead, and Joyce, to name but a handful. While these individuals are all part of the Western tradition of ideas, they often display an incredible diversity of views on just about every subject. And while their views share some commonalities, they also display numerous conflicting and contradictory positions and perspectives. In fact, they frequently go out of their way to critique and refute key ideas proposed by their predecessors.

A representative of the *Great Books of the Western World* came to my house one day, attempting to recruit salesmen for the series. He spread out a chart describing the series, and spent five minutes talking to my wife and me about it. We then spent an hour and a half talking to him about the Bible, which we presented as the greatest book of all time.

I challenged this representative to take just ten of the authors from the *Great Books* series, all from one walk of life, one generation, one place, one time, one mood, one continent, one language, and all addressing just one controversial subject. I then asked him, "Would the authors agree with one another?"

He paused and then replied, "No."

"What would you have, then?" I retorted.

Immediately he answered, "A conglomeration."

Two days later he committed his life to Christ.

The uniqueness of the Bible as shown above does not *prove* that it is inspired. It does, however, challenge any person sincerely seeking truth to consider seriously its unique quality in terms of its continuity. That *Great Books* representative took this step, and discovered the Savior of the Bible in the process.

2A. UNIQUE IN ITS CIRCULATION

It's not unusual to hear about books that have hit the bestseller list, selling a few hundred thousand copies. It's much rarer to come across books that have sold more than a million copies, and rarer still to find books that have passed the ten-million mark in sales. It staggers the mind, then, to discover that the number of Bibles sold reaches into the billions. That's right, billions! More copies have been produced of its entirety as well as selected portions than any other book in history. Some will argue that in a designated month or year more of a certain book was sold. However, no other book even begins to compare to the Scriptures in terms of its total circulation.

According to the United Bible Societies' *1998 Scripture Distribution Report*, in that year alone member organizations were responsible for distributing 20.8 million complete Bibles and another 20.1 million testaments. When portions of Scripture (i.e., complete books of the Bible) and selections (short extracts on particular themes) are also included, the total distribution of copies of the Bible or portions thereof in 1998 reaches a staggering 585 million—and these numbers only include Bibles distributed by the United Bible Societies!

To put it another way, if you lined up all the people who received Bibles or Scripture selections last year, and handed a Bible to one of them every five seconds, it would take more than ninety-two years to do what just the United Bible Societies accomplished last year alone.

As *The Cambridge History of the Bible* states, "No other book has known anything approaching this constant circulation." (Greenslade, CHB, 479)

The critic is right: "This doesn't prove that the Bible is the Word of God." But it does demonstrate that the Bible is unique.

3A. UNIQUE IN ITS TRANSLATION

The numbers of translations of the Bible are every bit as impressive as its sales numbers. Most books are never translated into another tongue. Among the books that are, most are published in just two or three languages. Far fewer books see translation figures rise into the teens. According to the United Bible Societies, the Bible (or portions of it), has been translated into more than 2,200 languages! Although this is only about one-third of the world's 6,500 known languages, these languages represent the primary vehicle of communication for well over 90 percent of the world's population (www.biblesociety.org). Worldwide, no other book in history has

	Bible	Testaments	Portions	New Reader Portions	Selections	New Reader Selections
Africa	2,436,187	541,915	1,325,206	1,494,911	4,024,764	350,092
Americas	9,869,916	12,743,263	7,074,311	6,277,936	315,468,625	25,120,757
Asia-Pacific	6,213,113	5,368,429	9,007,281	8,262,462	151,042,342	9,765,191
Europe/Mid. East	2,232,299	1,463,020	1,973,054	495,301	2,197,975	275,358
TOTAL 1998	20,751,515	20,116,627	19,379,852	16,530,610	472,733,706	35,511,398

been translated, retranslated, and paraphrased more than the Bible.

The Bible was one of the first major books translated. Around 250 B.C., the Hebrew Old Testament was translated into Greek and given the name Septuagint. (Unger, UBD, 1147) The work was originally produced for Greek-speaking Jews living in Alexandria who could no longer read Hebrew.

Since then translators have actively rendered the Scriptures—both Old Testament and New—into languages that either have or are without a written alphabet. Wycliffe Bible Translators alone has over six thousand people working with more than 850 different languages in fifty countries to produce new or revised versions of the Bible. (Barnes, OCB, 823) Of these, 468 languages are being translated for the first time. According to Ted Bergman at the Summer Institute of Linguistics, at this rate the Bible should be available to almost all language groups between the years 2007 and 2022. This means that we are less than a generation away from witnessing the world's first universally translated text!

No other book in history comes close to comparing with the Bible in its translation activity.

4A. UNIQUE IN ITS SURVIVAL

1B. Through Time

Although it was first written on perishable materials, and had to be copied and recopied for hundreds of years before the invention of the printing press, the Scriptures have never diminished in style or correctness, nor have they ever faced extinction. Compared with other ancient writings, the Bible has more manuscript evidence to support it than any ten pieces of classical literature combined (see Chapter 3).

John Warwick Montgomery observes that "to be skeptical of the resultant text of the New Testament books is to allow all of classical antiquity to slip into obscurity, for no documents of the ancient period are as well attested bibliographically as the New Testament." (Montgomery, HC'71, 29) Similarly, Bruce Metzger, a Princeton professor and one of the world's leading Biblical text critics, comments that in contrast with other ancient texts, "the textual critic of the New Testament is embarrassed by the wealth of his material." (Metzger, TNT, 34)

Bernard Ramm speaks of the accuracy and number of biblical manuscripts: "Jews preserved it as no other manuscript has ever been preserved. With their *massora (parva, magna,* and *finalis)* they kept tabs on every letter, syllable, word and paragraph. They had special classes of men within their culture whose sole duty was to preserve and transmit these documents with practically perfect fidelity—scribes, lawyers, massoretes. Who ever counted the letters and syllables and words of Plato or Aristotle? Cicero or Seneca?" (Ramm, PCE'53, 230–231)

John Lea, in *The Greatest Book in the World,* compares the Bible with Shakespeare's writings:

In an article in the *North American Review,* a writer made some interesting comparisons between the writings of Shakespeare and the Scriptures, which show that much greater care must have been bestowed upon the biblical manuscripts than upon other writings, even when there was so much more opportunity of preserving the correct text by means of printed copies than when all the copies had to be made by hand. He said: "It seems strange that the text of Shakespeare, which has been in existence less than two hundred and eight years, should be far more uncertain and corrupt than that of the New Testament, now over eighteen centuries old, during nearly fifteen of which it existed only in manuscript. . . With perhaps a dozen or twenty exceptions, the text of every verse in the New Testament may be said to be so far settled by general consent of scholars, that any dispute as to its readings must relate rather to the interpretation of the words than to any doubts respecting the words themselves. But in every one of Shakespeare's thirty-seven plays there are probably a hundred readings still in dispute, a large portion of which materially affects the meaning of the passages in which they occur." (Lea, GBW, 15)

2B. Through Persecution

The Bible has withstood vicious attacks by its enemies. Many have tried to burn it, ban it, and "outlaw it from the days of Roman

> The noted French infidel Voltaire, who died in 1778, declared that in one hundred years from his time Christianity would be swept from existence and passed into history.
> Only fifty years after his death, the Geneva Bible Society used Voltaire's press and house to produce stacks of Bibles.
>
> —GEISLER AND NIX

emperors to present-day Communist-dominated countries." (Ramm, *PCE* '53, 232)

In A.D. 303, the Roman emperor Diocletian issued an edict to stop Christians from worshiping and to destroy their Scriptures. "An imperial letter was everywhere promulgated, ordering the razing of the churches to the ground and the destruction by fire of the Scriptures, and proclaiming that those who held high positions would lose all civil rights, while those in households, if they persisted in their profession of Christianity, would be deprived of their liberty." (Greenslade, CHB, 476)

The historic irony of this event is recorded by the fourth-century church historian Eusebius, who wrote that twenty-five years after Diocletian's edict the Roman emperor Constantine issued an edict ordering that fifty copies of the Scriptures should be prepared at the government's expense. (Eusebius, EH, VII, 2, 259)

Many centuries later, Voltaire, the noted French infidel who died in 1778, said that in one hundred years from his time Christianity would be swept from existence and passed into history. But what has happened? Voltaire has passed into history, while the circulation of the Bible continues to increase in almost all parts of the world, carrying blessing wherever it goes. For example, the English Cathedral in Zanzibar is built on the site of the Old Slave Market, and the Communion Table stands on the very spot where the whipping-post once stood! The world abounds with such instances . . . As one has truly said, "We might as well put our shoulder to the burning wheel of the sun, and try to stop it on its flaming course, as attempt to stop the circulation of the Bible." (Collett, AAB, 63)

Concerning Voltaire's prediction of the extinction of Christianity and the Bible in a hundred years, Geisler and Nix point out that "only fifty years after his death the Geneva Bible Society used his press and house to produce stacks of Bibles" (Geisler/Nix, GIB '68, 123, 124)

The Bible's enemies come and go, but the Bible remains. Jesus was right when he said, "Heaven and earth will pass away, but My words will by no means pass away" (Mark 13:31 NKJV).

3B. Through Criticism

H. L. Hastings has forcefully illustrated the unique way in which the Bible has withstood attacks of infidels and skeptics:

Infidels for eighteen hundred years have been refuting and overthrowing this book, and yet it stands today as solid as a rock. Its circulation increases, and it is more loved and cherished and read today than ever before. Infidels, with all their assaults, make about as much impression on this book as a man with a tack hammer would on the Pyramids of Egypt. When the French monarch proposed the persecution of the Christians in his dominion, an old statesman and warrior said to him, "Sire, the Church of God is an anvil that has worn out many hammers." So the hammers of infidels have been pecking away at this book for ages, but the hammers are worn out, and the anvil still endures. If this book had not been the book of God, men would have destroyed it long ago. Emperors and popes, kings and priests, princes and rulers have all tried their hand at it; they die and the book still lives. (Lea, GBW, 17–18)

Bernard Ramm adds:

A thousand times over, the death knell of the Bible has been sounded, the funeral procession formed, the inscription cut on the tombstone, and committal read. But somehow the corpse never stays put.

No other book has been so chopped, knived, sifted, scrutinized, and vilified. What book on philosophy or religion or psychology or *belles lettres* of classical or modern times has been subject to such a mass attack as the Bible? with such venom and skepticism? with such thoroughness and erudition? upon every chapter, line and tenet?

The Bible is still loved by millions, read by millions, and studied by millions. (Ramm, PCE '53, 232–233)

Biblical scholars once deferred to "the assured results of higher criticism." But the results of the higher critics are no longer as assured as we once believed. Take, for example, the "documentary hypothesis." One of the reasons for its development—apart from

the different names used for God in Genesis—was that the Pentateuch could *not* have been written by Moses, as the "assured results of higher criticism" had proven that writing was not in existence at the time of Moses or, if in existence, was used sparingly. Therefore, it was concluded that it had to be of later authorship. The minds of the critics went to work, devising the theory that four writers, designated as J, E, P, and D, had put the Pentateuch together. These critics formulated great structures of criticism, going so far as to attribute the components of one verse to three different authors! (See Part 2 of this book for an in-depth analysis of the documentary hypothesis.)

Then some fellows discovered the "black stele." (Unger, UBD, 444) It had wedge-shaped characters on it and contained the detailed laws of Hammurabi. Was it post-Moses? No! It was pre-Mosaic. Not only that, but it preceded Moses' writings by at least three centuries. (Unger, UBD, 444) Amazingly, it antedated Moses, who is supposed to have been a primitive man lacking an alphabet.

What an irony of history! The documentary hypothesis is still taught, yet much of its original basis ("the assured results of higher criticism") has been shown to be false.

The "assured results of higher criticism" concluded that there were no Hittites at the time of Abraham, as there were no records of their existence apart from the Old Testament. They must be myth. Wrong again. Archaeological research has now uncovered evidence revealing more than 1,200 years of Hittite civilization.

Earl Radmacher, retired president of Western Conservative Baptist Seminary, quotes Nelson Glueck (pronounced Glek), former president of the Jewish Theological Seminary at the Hebrew Union College in Cincinnati, and one of the three greatest archaeologists: "I listened to him [Glueck] when he was at Temple Emmanuel in Dallas, and he got rather red in the face and said, 'I've been accused of teaching the verbal, plenary inspiration of the Scripture. I want it to be understood that I have never taught this. All I have ever said is that in all of my archaeological investigation I have never found one artifact of antiquity that contradicts any statement of the Word of God.'" (Radmacher, PC, 50)

Robert Dick Wilson, a man fluent in more than forty-five languages and dialects, concluded after a lifetime of study in the Old Testament: "I may add that the result of my forty-five years of study of the Bible has led me all the time to a firmer faith that in the Old Testament we have a true historical account of the history of the Israelite people." (Wilson, WB, 42)

The Bible is unique in its ability to stand up to its critics. There is no book in all of literature like it. A person looking for truth would certainly consider a book that bears these qualifications.

5A. UNIQUE IN ITS TEACHINGS

1B. Prophecy

Wilbur Smith, who compiled a personal library of twenty-five thousand volumes, concludes that

whatever one may think of the authority of and the message presented in the book we call the Bible, there is world-wide agreement that in more ways than one it is the most remarkable volume that has ever been produced in

> *Other books claim divine inspiration, such as the Koran, the Book of Mormon, and parts of the [Hindu] Veda. But none of those books contains predictive prophecy.*
>
> —NORMAN GEISLER
> AND WILLIAM NIX

these some five thousand years of writing on the part of the human race.

It is the only volume ever produced by man, or a group of men, in which is to be found a large body of prophecies relating to individual nations, to Israel, to all the peoples of the earth, to certain cities, and to the coming of One who was to be the Messiah. The ancient world had many different devices for determining the future, known as divination, but not in the entire gamut of Greek and Latin literature, even though they use the words prophet and prophecy, can we find any real specific prophecy of a great historic event to come in the distant future, nor any prophecy of a Savior to arise in the human race. . . .

Mohammedanism cannot point to any prophecies of the coming of Mohammed uttered hundreds of years before his birth. Neither can the founders of any cult in this country rightly identify any ancient text specifically foretelling their appearance. (Smith, IB, 9–10)

Geisler and Nix concur. In their book *A General Introduction to the Bible*—an authoritative standard in its own right— they write:

According to Deuteronomy 18, a prophet was false if he made predictions that were never fulfilled. No unconditional prophecy of the Bible about events to the present day has gone unfilled. Hundreds of predictions, some of them given hundreds of years in advance, have been literally fulfilled. The time (Dan. 9), city (Mic. 5:2), and nature (Is. 7:14) of Christ's birth were foretold in the Old Testament, as were dozens of other things about His life, death, and resurrection (see Is. 53). Numerous other prophecies have been fulfilled, including the destruction of Edom (Obad. 1), the curse on Babylon (Is. 13), the destruction of Tyre (Ezek. 26) and Nineveh (Nah. 1—3), and the return of Israel to the Land (Is. 11:11). Other books claim divine inspiration, such as the Koran, the Book of Mormon, and parts of the [Hindu] Veda. But none of those books contains predictive prophecy. As a result, fulfilled prophecy is a strong indication of the unique, divine authority of the Bible. (Geisler/Nix, GIB '86, 196)

2B. History

First Samuel through 2 Chronicles presents approximately five centuries of the history of Israel. *The Cambridge Ancient History* (vol. 1, p. 222) states: "The Israelites certainly manifest a genius for historical construction, and the Old Testament embodies the oldest history writing extant."

The distinguished archaeologist Professor Albright begins his classic essay, "The Biblical Period," with these observations:

Hebrew national tradition excels all others in its clear picture of tribal and family origins. In Egypt and Babylonia, in Assyria and Phoenicia, in Greece and Rome, we look in vain for anything comparable. There is nothing like it in the tradition of the Germanic peoples. Neither India or China can produce anything similar, since their earliest historical memories are literary deposits of distorted dynastic tradition, with no trace of the herdsman or peasant behind the demigod or king with whom their records begin. Neither in the oldest Indic historical writings (the Puranas) nor in the earliest Greek historians is there a hint of the fact that both Indo-Aryans and Hellenes were once nomads who immigrated into their later abodes from the north. The Assyrians, to be sure, remembered vaguely that their earliest rulers, whose names they recalled without any details about their deed, were tent dwellers, but whence they came had long been forgotten. (Finkelstein, JTHCR, 3)

Concerning the reliability of the "Table of Nations" in Genesis 10, Albright concludes: "It stands absolutely alone in ancient literature without a remote parallel even among the Greeks. . . . 'The Table of Nations' remains an astonishingly accurate document. (Albright, RDBL, 70-72)

3B. Character

Lewis S. Chafer, founder and former president of Dallas Theological Seminary, has said, "The Bible is not such a book a man would write if he could, or could write if he would."

The Bible deals very frankly with the sins of its characters, even when those sins reflect badly on God's chosen people, leaders, and the biblical writers themselves. For example:

- The sins of the patriarchs are mentioned (Gen. 12:11–13; 49:5–7).
- The sins of the people are denounced (Deut. 9:24).
- King David's adultery with Bathsheba and his subsequent attempted cover-up is revealed (2 Sam. 11–12).
- The Gospel Evangelists paint their own faults and those of the apostles (Matt. 8:10–26; 26:31–56; Mark 6:52; 8:18; Luke 8:24, 25; 9:40–45; John 10:6; 16:32).
- The disorder within the church is exposed (1 Cor. 1:11; 15:12; 2 Cor. 2:4).

The Bible as a book focuses on reality, not fantasy. It presents the good and bad, the right and wrong, the best and worst, the hope and despair, the joy and pain of life. And so it should, for its ultimate author is God, and "there is no creature hidden from His sight, but all things are naked and open to the eyes of Him to whom we must give account" (Heb. 4:13 NKJV).

6A. UNIQUE IN ITS INFLUENCE ON LITERATURE

Cleland B. McAfee writes in *The Greatest English Classic*: "If every Bible in any considerable city were destroyed, the Book could be restored in all its essential parts from the quotations on the shelves of the city public library. There are works, covering almost all the great literary writers, devoted especially

> An inspired work, the Bible is also a source of inspiration. Its impact has no equal, whether on the social and ethical plane or on that of literary creation. . . . Its characters are dramatic, their dramas timeless, their triumphs and defeats overwhelming. Each cry touches us, each call penetrates us. Texts of another age, the biblical poems are themselves ageless. They call out to us collectively and individually, across and beyond the centuries.
>
> —ELIE WIESEL, NOVELIST, NOBEL PEACE PRIZE

to showing how much the Bible has influenced them." (McAfee, GEC, 134)

Gabriel Sivan writes, "No other document in the possession of mankind offers so much to the reader—ethical and religious instruction, superb poetry, a social program and legal code, an interpretation of history, and all the joys, sorrows, and hopes which well up in men and which Israel's prophets and leaders expressed with matchless force and passion." (Sivan, BC, xiii)

Concerning the Hebrew Bible, he adds,

Since the dawn of civilization no book has inspired as much creative endeavor among writers as the "Old" Testament, the Hebrew Bible. In poetry, drama, and fiction its literary influence has been unrivaled. The German poet Heinrich Heine, writing in 1830, described its significance in lyrical terms:

"Sunrise and sunset, promise and fulfillment, birth and death, the whole human drama, everything is in this book. . . . It is the Book of Books, Biblia." With varying insight, but unvarying consistency, writers in almost every land and culture have for more than a millennium found a matchless treasure house of themes and characters in the Bible. These they have reworked and reinterpreted in the portrayal of eternal motifs—as, for example, God and Man, the conflict of Good and Evil, love, jealousy, and man's struggle for freedom, truth, and justice. (Sivan, BC, 218)

Susan Gallagher and Roger Lundin recognize, "The Bible is one of the most important documents in the history of civilization, not only because of its status as holy inspired Scripture, but also because of its pervasive influence on Western thought. As the predominant world view for at least fourteen centuries, Christianity and its great central text played a major role in the formation of Western culture. Consequently, many literary texts, even those in our post-Christian era, frequently draw on the Bible and the Christian tradition." (Gallagher/Lundin, LTEF, 120)

Elie Wiesel, renowned novelist and Nobel Peace Prize recipient, has observed, "An inspired work, the Bible is also a source of inspiration. Its impact has no equal, whether on the social and ethical plane or on that of literary creation. We forget too often that the Bible pertains equally to the artistic domain. Its characters are dramatic, their dramas timeless, their triumphs and defeats overwhelming. Each cry touches us, each call penetrates us. Texts of another age, the biblical poems are themselves ageless. They call out to us collectively and individually, across and beyond the centuries." (In Epilogue of Liptzen, BTWL, 293)

Harold Fisch, professor emeritus at Bar-Ilan University, has noted: "The Bible has permeated the literature of the Western world to a degree that cannot easily be measured. More than any other single body of writing, ancient or modern, it has provided writers from the Middle Ages on with a store of symbols, ideas, and ways of perceiving reality. This influence can be traced not only in texts that deal directly with biblical characters or topics, but also in a vast number of poems, plays, and other writings that are not overtly biblical in theme but that testify to a biblical view of humankind and the world." (Fisch, HCBD, 136)

In his now classic *Anatomy of Criticism*, world-renowned literary critic Northrop Frye observed that "Western literature has been more influenced by the Bible than any other book." (Frye, AC, 14)

Twenty-five years later, Frye wrote: "I soon realized that a student of English literature who does not know the Bible does not understand a good deal of what is going on in what he reads: The most conscientious student will be continually misconstruing the implications, even the meaning." (Frye, GC, xii)

The historian Philip Schaff (in *The Person of Christ*, American Tract Society, 1913) classically describes the uniqueness of the Bible and the Savior:

This Jesus of Nazareth, without money and arms, conquered more millions than Alexander, Caesar, Mohammed, and Napoleon; without science and learning, He shed more light on things human and divine than all philosophers and scholars combined; without the eloquence of schools, He spoke such words of life as were never spoken before or since, and produced effects which lie beyond the reach of orator or poet; without writing a single line, He set more pens in motion, and furnished themes for more sermons, orations, discussions, learned volumes, works of art, and songs of praise than the whole army of great men of ancient and modern times.

Bernard Ramm adds:

There are complexities of bibliographical studies that are unparalleled in any other science or department of human knowledge. From the Apostolic Fathers dating from A.D. 95 to the modern times is one great literary river inspired by the Bible—Bible dictionaries, Bible encyclopedias, Bible lexicons, Bible atlases, and Bible geographies. These may be taken as a starter. Then at random, we may mention the vast bibliographies around theology, religious education, hymnology, missions, the biblical languages, church history, religious biography, devotional works, commentaries, philosophy of religion, evidences, apologetics, and on and on. There seems to be an endless number....

No other book in all human history has in turn inspired the writing of so many books as the Bible. (Ramm, PCE '53, 239)

7A. UNIQUE IN ITS INFLUENCE ON CIVILIZATION

The Bible is also unique in its impact on civilization. Geisler and Nix succinctly state:

The influence of the Bible and its teaching in the Western world is clear for all who study history. And the influential role of the West in the course of world events is equally clear. Civilization has been influenced more by the Judeo-Christian Scriptures than by any other book or series of books in the world. Indeed, no great moral or religious work in the world exceeds the depth of morality in the principle of Christian love, and none has a more lofty spiritual concept than the biblical view of God. The Bible presents the highest ideals known to men, ideals that have molded civilization. (Geisler, GIB '86, 196–197)

Grady Davis, in *The New Encyclopedia Britannica*, writes, "The Bible brought its view of God, the universe, and mankind into all the leading Western languages and thus into the intellectual processes of Western man." (Davis, EB, 904) He also states, "Since the invention of printing (mid-15th century), the Bible has become more than the translation of an ancient Oriental literature. It has not seemed a foreign book, and it has been the most available, familiar, and dependable source and arbiter of intellectual, moral, and spiritual ideals in the West." (Davis, EB, 905)

Gabriel Sivan observes, "The Bible has given strength to the freedom fighter and new heart to the persecuted, a blueprint to the social reformer and inspiration to the writer and artist." (Sivan, BC, 491)

French philosopher Jean Jacques Rousseau exclaimed: "Behold the works of our philosophers; with all their pompous diction, how mean and contemptible they are by comparison with the Scriptures! Is it possible that a book at once so simple and sublime should be merely the work of man?"

Kenneth L. Woodward points out in *Newsweek* magazine that after "two thousand years . . . the centuries themselves are measured from the birth of Jesus of Nazareth. At the end of this year, calendars in India and China, like those in Europe, America, and the Middle East, will register the dawn of the third millenium." (Woodward, "2000 Years of Jesus," *Newsweek*, March 29, 1999, p. 52)

8A. A REASONABLE CONCLUSION

The evidence presented above does not prove that the Bible is the Word of God. But to me it clearly indicates that it is uniquely superior to any and all other books.

A professor once remarked to me, "If you are an intelligent person, you will read the one book that has drawn more attention than any other, if you are searching for the truth." The Bible certainly qualifies as this one book.

As Theodore Roosevelt once observed, "A thorough knowledge of the Bible is worth more than a college education."

2
HOW WE GOT THE BIBLE

1A. HOW WAS THE BIBLE WRITTEN?

Many people have questions about the background of the Bible, its divisions, and the material used for its production. This section will familiarize you with its construction, and give you a greater appreciation of how it was compiled.

1B. Materials Used

1C. Writing Material

1D. Papyrus

The failure to recover many of the ancient manuscripts (a manuscript is a handwritten copy of the Scriptures) is primarily due to the perishable materials used for writing. "All . . . autographs," writes F. F. Bruce, "have been long lost since. It could not be otherwise, if they were written on papyrus, since . . . it is only in exceptional conditions that papyrus survives for any length of time." (Bruce, BP, 176)

Among the writing materials available in biblical times, the most common was papyrus, which was made from the papyrus plant. This reed grew in the shallow lakes and rivers of Egypt and Syria. Large shipments of papyrus were sent through the Syrian port of Byblos. It is surmised that the Greek word for books *(biblos)* comes from the name of this port. The English word *paper* comes from the Greek word for papyrus *(papyros)*. (Ewert, ATMT, 19–20)

The Cambridge History of the Bible gives

an account of how papyrus was prepared for writing: "The reeds were stripped and cut lengthwise into thin narrow slices before being beaten and pressed together into two layers set at right angles to each other. When dried the whitish surface was polished smooth with a stone or other implement. Pliny refers to several qualities of papyri, and varying thicknesses and surfaces are found before the New Kingdom period when sheets were often very thin and translucent." (Greenslade, CHB, 30)

The oldest papyrus fragment known dates back to 2400 B.C. (Greenslee, INTTC, 19) The earliest manuscripts were written on papyrus, and it was difficult for any to survive except in dry areas such as the sands of Egypt or in caves such as the Qumran caves, where the Dead Sea Scrolls were discovered.

Papyrus enjoyed popular use until about the third century A.D. (Greenlee, INTTC, 20)

2D. Parchment

Parchment is the name given to "prepared skins of sheep, goats, antelope and other animals." These skins were "shaved and scraped" in order to produce a more durable writing material. F. F. Bruce adds that "the word 'parchment' comes from the name of the city of Pergamum in Asia Minor, for the production of this writing material was at one time specially associated with that place." (Bruce, BP, 11)

3D. Vellum

Vellum was the name given to calf skin. Vellum was often dyed purple. In fact, some of the manuscripts we have today are purple vellum. The writing on dyed vellum was usually gold or silver.

J. Harold Greenlee notes that the oldest leather scrolls date from around 1500 B.C. (Greenlee, INTTC, 21)

4D. Other Writing Materials

Ostraca: This unglazed pottery was popular with the common people. The technical name is "potsherd." Ostraca has been found in abundance in Egypt and Palestine. (Job 2:8)

Stones: Archaeologists have found common stones inscribed with an iron pen.

Clay Tablets: Engraved with a sharp instrument and then dried to create a permanent record (Jer. 17:13; Ezek. 4:1), these tablets provided the cheapest and one of the most durable kinds of writing material.

Wax Tablets: A metal stylus was used on a piece of flat wood covered with wax.

2C. Writing Instruments

Chisel: An iron instrument used to engrave stones.

Metal Stylus: "A three-sided instrument with a leveled head, the stylus was used to make incursions into clay and wax tablets." (Geisler, GIB, 228)

Pen: A pointed reed "was fashioned from rushes (*Juncus maritimis*) about 6–16 inches long, the end being cut to a flat chisel-shape to enable thick and thin strokes to be made with the broad or narrow sides. The reed-pen was in use from the early first millennium in Mesopotamia from which it may well have been adopted, while the idea of a quill pen seems to have come from the Greeks in the third century B.C." (Jer. 8:8) (Greenslade, CHB, 31) The pen was used on vellum, parchment, and papyrus.

Ink: The ink in the ancient world was usually a compound of "charcoal, gum and water." (Bruce, BP, 13)

2B. Forms of Ancient Books

Rolls or *scrolls* were made by gluing sheets of papyrus together and then winding the resulting long strips around a stick. The size of the scroll was limited by the difficulty in using it. Writing was usually limited to one side of the scroll. A two-sided scroll is called an "opisthograph" (Rev. 5:1). Some rolls have been known to be 144 feet long. The average scroll, however, was only about twenty to thirty-five feet long.

It is no wonder that Callimachus, a professional cataloguer of books from ancient Alexandria's library, said "a big book is a big nuisance." (Metzger, TNT, 5)

Codex or Book Form: In order to make reading easier and less bulky, the papyrus sheets were assembled in leaf form and written on both sides. Greenlee states that the spread of Christianity was the prime reason for the development of the codex-book form.

3B. Types of Writing

1C. Uncial Writing

According to New Testament scholar Bruce Metzger, "Literary works . . . were written in a more formal style of handwriting, called uncials. This 'book-hand' was characterized by more deliberate and carefully executed letters, each one separate from the others, somewhat like our capital letters." (Metzger, TNT, 9)

Geisler and Nix note that the "most important manuscripts of the New Testament are generally considered to be the great uncial codices that date from the fourth and later centuries. These appeared almost immediately following the conversion of Constantine and the authorization to make multiple copies of the Bible at the Council of Nicea (325)." (Geisler/Nix, GIB, 391)

Probably the two oldest and most significant uncial manuscripts are Codex Vaticanus (about A.D. 325–350) and Codex Sinaiticus (about A.D. 340).

> *When you come, bring . . . the books, especially the parchments.*
>
> —PAUL, 2 TIMOTHY 4:13

2C. Minuscule Writing

Minuscule writing was "a script of smaller letters in a running hand [connected] . . . created for the production of books" around the beginning of the ninth century A.D. (Metzger, TNT, 9)

3C. Spaces and Vowels

The Greek manuscripts were written without any breaks between words, while the Hebrew text was written without vowels until these were added by the Massoretes between the fifth and tenth centuries A.D.

Both practices seem odd and confusing to most modern readers. But to the ancients, for whom Greek or Hebrew was their native tongue, these practices were normal and clearly understood. The Jews did not need vowels written out. As they learned their language they became familiar with how to pronounce and interpret it.

Likewise, Greek-speaking peoples had no trouble reading their language without breaks between words. As Metzger explains: "In that language it is the rule, with very few exceptions, that native Greek words can end only in a vowel (or a diphthong) or in one of three consonants, ν, ρ and ς. Furthermore, it should not be supposed that *scriptio continua* presented exceptional difficulties in reading, for apparently it was customary in antiquity to read aloud, even when one was alone. Thus despite the absence of spaces between words, by pronouncing to oneself what was read, syllable-by-syllable, one soon became used to reading *scriptio continua*." (Metzger, TNT, 13)

4B. Divisions

1C. Books

See material below on "The Canon."

2C. Chapters

1D. Old Testament

The first divisions were made prior to the Babylonian captivity, which began in 586 B.C. The Pentateuch was divided into 154 groupings, called *sedarim*, which "were designed to provide lessons sufficient to cover a three-year cycle of reading." (Geisler, GIB, 339)

During the Babylonian captivity but prior to 536 B.C., the Pentateuch was "divided into fifty-four sections called *parashiyyoth*. . . . These were later subdivided into 669 sections for reference purposes. These sections were utilized for a single-year [reading] cycle." (Geisler, GIB, 339)

Around 165 B.C., the Old Testament books called the Prophets were sectioned.

Finally, "after the Protestant Reformation, the Hebrew Bible for the most part followed the same chapter divisions as the Protestant Old Testament. These divisions were first placed in the margins in 1330." (Geisler, GIB, 339)

2D. New Testament

The Greeks first made paragraph divisions before the Council of Nicea (A.D. 325), perhaps as early as A.D. 250.

The oldest system of chapter division originated about A.D. 350, and appears in the margins of Codex Vaticanus. However, these sections are much smaller than our modern chapter divisions. For example, in our Bible the Gospel of Matthew has twenty-eight chapters, but in Codex Vaticanus, Matthew is divided into 170 sections.

Geisler and Nix write that "it was not until the thirteenth century that those sections were changed, and then only gradually. Stephen Langton, a professor at the University of Paris and afterward Archbishop of Canterbury, divided the Bible into the modern chapter divisions (about 1227). That was prior to the introduction of movable type in printing. Since the Wycliffe Bible (1382) followed that pattern, those basic divisions have been the virtual base upon which the Bible has been printed to this very day." (Geisler, GIB, 340)

3C. Verses

1D. Old Testament

In the Old Testament, the first verse indicators "were merely spaces between words, as the words were run together continuously through a given book. . . . After the Babylonian captivity, for the purpose of public reading and interpretation, space stops were employed, and still later additional markings were added. These 'verse' markings were not regulated, and differed from place to place. It was not until about A.D. 900 that the markings were standardized." (Geisler, GIB, 339)

2D. New Testament

Verse markings similar to what we have in our modern Bibles did not appear in the New Testament until the middle of the sixteenth century. They actually followed the development of chapters, "apparently in an effort to further facilitate cross-references and make public reading easier. The markings first occur in the fourth edition of the Greek New Testament published by Robert Stephanus, a Parisian printer, in 1551. These verses were introduced into the English New Testament by William Whittingham of Oxford in 1557. In 1555, Stephanus introduced his verse divisions into a Latin Vulgate edition, from which they have continued to the present day." (Geisler, GIB, 341)

2A. Who Decided What to Include in the Bible?

The question concerning how it was decided which books would become part of the Bible is the question of *canonicity*. A discerning person would want to know why some books were included in the *canon* while others were excluded.

1B. Meaning of the Word *Canon*

The word *canon* comes from the root word *reed* (English word *cane*, Hebrew form *ganeh*, and Greek form *kanon*). The reed was used as a measuring rod, and came to mean "standard."

The third-century church father Origen used the word "canon to denote what we call the 'rule of faith,' the standard by which we are to measure and evaluate." Later, the term meant a "list" or "index" (Bruce, BP, 95). As applied to Scripture, *canon* means "an officially accepted list of books." (Earle, HWGOB, 31)

It is important to note that the church did not create the canon; it did not determine which books would be called Scripture, the inspired Word of God. Instead, the church recognized, or discovered, which books had been inspired from their inception. Stated another way, "a book is not the Word of God because it is accepted by the people of God. Rather, it was accepted by the people of God because it is the Word of God. That is, God gives the book its divine authority, not the people of God. They merely recognize the divine authority which God gives to it." (Geisler/Nix, GIB, 210) The chart at the bottom of this page is helpful in illustrating this important principle. (Geisler, GIB, 221)

2B. Tests for Inclusion in the Canon

From the writings of biblical and church history we can discern at least five principles that guided the recognition and collection of the true divinely inspired books. Geisler and Nix present the principles as follows (Geisler/Nix, GIB, 223–231):

1. Was the book written by a prophet of God? "If it was written by a spokesman for God, then it was the Word of God."

2. Was the writer confirmed by acts of God? Frequently miracles separated the true prophets from the false ones. "Moses was given miraculous powers to prove his call of God (Ex. 4:1–9). Elijah triumphed over the false prophets of Baal by a supernatural act (1 Kin. 18). Jesus was 'attested to . . . by God with miracles and wonders and signs which God performed through Him' (Acts 2:22). . . . [A] miracle is an act of God to confirm the Word of God given through a prophet of God to the people of God. It is the sign to substantiate his sermon; the miracle to confirm his message."

The Incorrect View	The Correct View
The Church is Determiner of Canon	The Church is the Discoverer of Canon
The Church is Mother of Canon	The Church is Child of Canon
The Church is Magistrate of Canon	The Church is Minister of Canon
The Church is Regulator of Canon	The Church is Recognizer of Canon
The Church is Judge of Canon	The Church is Witness of Canon
The Church is Master of Canon	The Church is Servant of Canon

3. Did the message tell the truth about God? "God cannot contradict Himself (2 Cor. 1:17–18), nor can He utter what is false (Heb. 6:18). Hence, no book with false claims can be the Word of God." For reasons such as these, the church fathers maintained the policy, "if in doubt, throw it out." This enhanced the "validity of their discernment of the canonical books."

4. Does it come with the power of God? "The Fathers believed the Word of God is 'living and active' (Heb. 4:12), and consequently ought to have a transforming force for edification (2 Tim. 3:17) and evangelization (1 Pet. 1:23). If the message of a book did not effect its stated goal, if it did not have the power to change a life, then God was apparently not behind its message." (Geisler, GIB, 228) The presence of God's transforming power was a strong indication that a given book had His stamp of approval.

5. Was it accepted by the people of God? "Paul said of the Thessalonians, 'We also constantly thank God that when you received from us the word of God's message, you accepted it not as the word of men, but for what it really is, the word of God' (1 Thess. 2:13). For whatever subsequent debate there may have been about a book's place in the canon, the people in the best position to know its prophetic credentials were those who knew the prophet who wrote it. Hence, despite all later debate about the canonicity of some books, the definitive evidence is that which attests to its original acceptance by the contemporary believers." (Geisler, GIB, 229) When a book was received, collected, read, and used by the people of God as the Word of God, it was regarded as canonical. This practice is often seen in the Bible itself.

One instance is when the apostle Peter acknowledges Paul's writings as Scripture on par with Old Testament Scripture. (2 Pet. 3:16)

3B. The Christian Canon (New Testament)

1C. Tests for New Testament Canonicity

The basic factor for recognizing a book's canonicity for the New Testament was divine inspiration, and the chief test for this was apostolicity. "In New Testament terminology," write Geisler and Nix, "the church was 'built upon the foundation of the apostles and prophets' (Eph. 2:20) whom Christ had promised to guide into 'all the truth' (John 16:13) by the Holy Spirit. The church at Jerusalem was said to have continued in the 'apostles' teaching' (Acts 2:42). The term *apostolic* as used for the test of canonicity does not necessarily mean 'apostolic authorship,' or 'that which was prepared under the direction of the apostles.'" (Geisler/Nix, GIB, 283)

They go on to state, "It seems much better to agree with Louis Gaussen, B. B. Warfield, Charles Hodge, J. N. D. Kelly, and most Protestants that it is apostolic authority, or apostolic approval, that was the primary test for canonicity, and not merely apostolic authorship." (Geisler/Nix, GIB, 283)

N. B. Stonehouse notes that the apostolic authority "which speaks forth in the New Testament is never detached from the authority of the Lord. In the Epistles there is consistent recognition that in the church there is only one absolute authority, the authority of the Lord himself. Wherever the apostles speak with authority, they do so as exercising the Lord's authority. Thus, for example, where Paul defends his authority as an apostle, he bases his claim solely and directly upon his commission by the Lord

(Gal. 1 and 2); where he assumes the right to regulate the life of the church, he claims for his word the Lord's authority, even when no direct word of the Lord has been handed down (1 Cor. 14:37; cf. 1 Cor. 7:10)." (Stonehouse, ANT, 117–118)

John Murray observes, "The only one who speaks in the New Testament with an authority that is underived and self-authenticating is the Lord." (Murray, AS, 18)

2C. The New Testament Canonical Books

1D. Reasons For Their Collection

> And on the day called Sunday there is a gathering together to one place of all those who live in cities or in the country, and the memoirs of the apostles or the writings of the prophets are read, as long as time permits. Then when the reader has ceased the president presents admonition and invitation to the imitation of these good things.
>
> —JUSTIN MARTYR (A.D. 100–165)

1E. They Were Prophetic

"The initial reason for collecting and preserving the inspired books was that they were prophetic. That is, since they were written by an apostle or prophet of God, they must be valuable, and if valuable, they should be preserved. This reasoning is apparent in apostolic times, by the collection and circulation of Paul's epistles (cf. 2 Peter 3:15–16; Col. 4:16)." (Geisler, GIB, 277)

2E. The Needs of the Early Church

The churches needed to know which books should be read, revered, and applied to their varied and often precarious situations in a generally hostile social and religious environment. They had many problems to address, and they needed assurance regarding which books would serve as their source of authority.

3E. The Rise of Heretics

As early as A.D. 140, the heretic Marcion developed his own incomplete canon and began to propagate it. The church needed to counter his influence by collecting all the books of New Testament Scripture.

4E. The Circulation of Spurious Writings

Many Eastern churches used books in services that were definitely counterfeit. This called for a decision concerning the canon.

5E. Missions

"Christianity had spread rapidly to other countries, and there was the need to translate the Bible into those other languages. . . . As early as the first half of the second century the Bible was translated into Syriac and Old Latin. But because the missionaries could not translate a Bible that did not exist, attention was necessarily drawn to the question of which books really belonged to the authoritative Christian canon." (Geisler, GIB, 278)

6E. Persecution

The edict of Diocletian (A.D. 303) called for the destruction of the sacred books of the Christians. Who would die for a book that was perhaps religious, but not sacred? Christians needed to know which books were truly sacred.

2D. The Canon Recognized

1E. Athanasius of Alexandria

Athanasius (A.D. 367) gave us our earliest list of New Testament books that is exactly like our present New Testament. He provided this list in a festal letter to the churches. As he put it: "Again it is not tedious to speak of the books of the New Testament. These are, the four gospels, according to Matthew, Mark, Luke and John. Afterwards, the Acts of the Apostles and Epistles (called Catholic), seven, viz. of James, one; of Peter, two; of John, three; after these, one of Jude. In addition, there are fourteen Epistles of Paul, written in this order. The first, to the Romans; then two to the Corinthians; after these, to the Galatians; next, to the Ephesians; then to the Philippians; then to the Colossians; after these, two to the Thessalonians, and that to the Hebrews; and again, two to Timothy; one to Titus; and lastly, that to Philemon. And besides, the Revelation of John." (Athanasius, L, 552)

2E. Jerome and Augustine

Shortly after Athanasius circulated his list, Jerome and Augustine followed suit, defining the New Testament canon of twenty-seven books. (Bruce, BP, 112)

3E. Polycarp and His Contemporaries

Polycarp (A.D. 115), Clement of Alexandria (about A.D. 200), and other early church fathers refer to the Old and New Testament books with the phrase "as it is said in these scriptures."

4E. Justin Martyr

Justin Martyr (A.D. 100–165), referring to the Eucharist, writes in his First Apology 1.67: "And on the day called Sunday there is a gathering together to one place of all those who live in cities or in the country, and the memoirs of the apostles or the writings of the prophets are read, as long as time permits. Then when the reader has ceased the president presents admonition and invitation to the imitation of these good things."

He adds in his *Dialogue* with Trypho (pp. 49, 103, 105, 107) the formula "It is written" when he quotes from the Gospels. Both he and Trypho must have known to what "It is written" referred, and that this introduction designated that the Scripture is inspired.

5E. Irenaeus

Concerning the significance of Irenaeus (A.D. 180), F. F. Bruce writes

The importance of evidence lies in his [Irenaeus'] link with the apostolic age and in his ecumenical associations. Brought up in Asia Minor at the feet of Polycarp, the disciple of John, he became Bishop of Lyons in Gaul, A.D. 180. His writings attest the canonical recognition of the fourfold Gospel and Acts, of Rom., 1 and 2 Cor., Gal., Eph., Phil., Col., 1 and 2 Thess., 1 and 2 Tim., and Titus, of 1 Peter and 1 John and of the Revelation. In his treatise, *Against Heresies,* III, ii, 8, it is evident that by A.D. 180 the idea of the fourfold Gospel had become so axiomatic throughout Christendom that it could be referred to as an established fact as obvious and inevitable and natural as the four cardinal points of the compass (as we call them) or the four winds. (Bruce, BP, 109)

6E. Ignatius

Ignatius (A.D. 50–115) wrote, "I do not wish to command you as Peter and Paul; they were apostles." (Trall. 3. 3)

7E. Church Councils

F. F. Bruce states that "when at last a Church Council—The Synod of Hippo in A.D. 393—listed the twenty-seven books of the New Testament, it did not confer upon them any authority which they did not already possess, but simply recorded their previously established canonicity. (The ruling of the Synod of Hippo was re-promulgated four years later by the Third Synod of Carthage.)" (Bruce, BP, 113)

Since this time there has been no serious questioning of the twenty-seven accepted books of the New Testament by Roman Catholics, Protestants, or the Eastern Orthodox Church.

3D. The Canon Classified

The canonical New Testament books were classified as follows:

3C. The New Testament Apocrypha

1D. A List of the Apocrypha

Epistle of Pseudo-Barnabas (A.D. 70–79)
Epistle to the Corinthians (about A.D. 96)
Ancient Homily, or the so-called *Second Epistle of Clement* (about A.D. 120–140)
Shepherd of Hermas (about A.D. 115–140)
Didache, Teaching of the Twelve (about A.D. 100–120)
Apocalypse of Peter (about A.D. 150)
The Acts of Paul and Thecla (A.D. 170)
Epistle to the Laodiceans (fourth century?)

The Gospel According to the Hebrews (A.D. 65–100)
Epistle of Polycarp to the Philippians (about A.D. 108)
The Seven Epistles of Ignatius (about A.D. 100)

This is but a partial list of spurious and rejected writings. (Geisler, BP, 297–316)

2D. Why They Are Rejected

Geisler and Nix sum up the case against the canonical status of these books: "(1) None of them enjoyed any more than a temporary or local recognition. (2) Most of them never did have anything more than a semi-canonical status, being appended to various manuscripts or mentioned in tables of contents. (3) No major canon or church council included them as inspired books of the New Testament. (4) The limited acceptance enjoyed by most of these books is attributable to the fact that they attached themselves to references in canonical books (e.g., Laodiceans to Col. 4:16), because of their alleged

The Gospels	The History	The Epistles (Pauline)	The Epistles (General)	The Prophecy
Matthew, Mark, Luke, John	Acts	Romans, 1 Corinthians 2 Corinthians, Galatians, Ephesians, Philippians, Colossians, 1 Thessalonians, 2 Thessalonians, 1 Timothy, 2 Timothy, Hebrews, Titus, Philemon	James, 1 Peter, 2 Peter, 1 John, 2 John, 3 John, Jude	Revelation

apostolic authorship (e.g., Acts of Paul). Once these issues were clarified, there remained little doubt that these books were not canonical." (Geisler, GIB, 317)

4B. The Old Testament Canon

1C. The Jamnia Theory
Many scholars have theorized that a council of rabbis that convened at Jamnia, near Jaffa, in A.D. 90 finally agreed upon which books would be included in the Hebrew canon and which ones would not. The problem with this theory is that the Jamnia gathering reached neither of these conclusions. The rabbis did not fix the canon, but rather "raised questions about the presence of certain books in the canon. Books that the council refused to admit to the canon had not been there in the first place. The primary concern of the council was the right of certain books to remain in the canon, not the acceptance of new books." (Ewert, ATMT, 71) The rabbis discussed questions surrounding Esther, Proverbs, Ecclesiastes, the Song of Songs, and Ezekiel. "It should be underscored, however, that while questions about these books were raised, there was no thought of removing them from the canon. The discussions at Jamnia dealt not so much 'with acceptance of certain writings into the Canon, but rather with their right to remain there.'" (Ewert, ATMT, 72)

H. H. Rowley writes: "It is, indeed, doubtful how far it is correct to speak of the Council of Jamnia. We know of discussions that took place there amongst the Rabbis, but we know of no formal or binding decisions that were made, and it is probable that the discussions were informal, though none the less helping to crystallize and to fix more firmly the Jewish tradition." (Rowley, GOT, 170)

The fact is that "no human authority and no council of rabbis ever made an [Old Tes-

tament] book authoritative," explains Bible scholar David Ewert. "These books were inspired by God and had the stamp of authority on them from the beginning. Through long usage in the Jewish community their authority was recognized, and in due time they were added to the collection of canonical books." (Ewert, ATMT, 72)

2C. The Recognized Canon
The evidence clearly supports the theory that the Hebrew canon was established well before the late first century A.D., more than likely as early as the fourth century B.C. and certainly no later than 150 B.C. A major reason for this conclusion comes from the Jews themselves, who from the fourth century B.C. onward were convinced that "the voice of God had ceased to speak directly." (Ewert, ATMT, 69) In other words, the prophetic voices had been stilled. No word from God meant no *new* Word of God. Without prophets, there can be no scriptural revelation.

Concerning the Intertestamental Period (approximately four hundred years between the close of the Old Testament and the events of the New Testament) Ewert observes: "In 1 Maccabees 14:41 we read of Simon who is made leader and priest 'until a trustworthy prophet should rise,' and earlier he speaks of the sorrow in Israel such 'as there has not been since the prophets ceased to appear to them.' 'The prophets have fallen asleep,' complains the writer of 2 Baruch (85:3). Books that were written after the prophetic period had closed were thought of as lying outside the realm of Holy Scripture." (Ewert, ATMT, 69–70)

The last books written and recognized as canonical were Malachi (written around 450 to 430 B.C.) and Chronicles (written no later than 400 B.C.) (Walvoord, BKCOT, 589, 1573). These books appear with the rest of the Hebrew canonical books in the Greek translation of the Hebrew canon called the Septuagint (LXX), which was composed around 250 to 150 B.C. (Geisler, GIB, 24; see also Ewert, ATMT, 104–108 and Wurthwein, TOT, 49–53)

F. F. Bruce affirms that, "The books of the Hebrew Bible are traditionally twenty-four in number, arranged in three divisions." (Bruce, CS, 29) The three divisions are the Law, the Prophets, and the Writings. The following is the breakdown of the Hebrew canon found in many books such as the modern editions of the Jewish Old Testament. (Check *The Holy Scriptures*, according to the Massoretic Text, and *Biblia Hebraica*, Rudolph Kittel, Paul Kahle [eds.].)

Although the Christian church has the same Old Testament canon, the number of books differs because we divide Samuel, Kings, Chronicles, and Ezra-Nehemiah into two books each, and we make separate books out of the Minor Prophets rather than combining them into one, as the Jews do under the heading "The Twelve." The church has also altered the order of books, adopting a topical arrangement instead of an official order. (Geisler, GIB, 23)

3C. Christ's Witness to the Old Testament Canon

1D. Luke 24:44. In the upper room, Jesus told the disciples "that all things must be fulfilled, which were written in the law of Moses, and the Prophets, and the Psalms concerning Me" (NASV). With these words "He indicated the three sections into which the Hebrew Bible was divided—the Law, the Prophets, and the 'Writings' (here called 'the Psalms,' probably because the Book of Psalms is the first and longest book in this third section)." (Bruce, BP, 96)

2D. John 10:31–36; Luke 24:44: Jesus disagreed with the oral traditions of the Pharisees (Mark 7, Matthew 15), *not* with their concept of the Hebrew canon. (Bruce, BP, 104) "There is no evidence whatever of any dispute between Him and the Jews as to the canonicity of any Old Testament book." (Young, AOT, 62)

3D. Luke 11:51 (also Matthew 23:35): "From the blood of Abel to the blood of Zechariah." With these words Jesus confirms his witness to the extent of the Old Testament canon. Abel was the first martyr recorded in Scripture (Gen. 4:8), and Zechariah the last martyr to be named in the Hebrew Old Testament order, having been stoned while prophesying to the people "in

The Law (Torah)	Genesis, Exodus, Leviticus, Numbers, Deuteronomy
The Prophets (Nebhim)	Joshua, Judges, Samuel, Kings (Former Prophets)
	Isaiah, Jeremiah, Ezekiel, The Twelve (Latter Prophets)
The Writings (Kethubhim or Hagiographa [GK])	Psalms, Proverbs, Job (Poetical Books)
	Song of Songs, Ruth, Lamentations, Esther, Ecclesiastes (Five Rolls [Megilloth])
	Daniel, Ezra-Nehemiah, Chronicles (Historical Books)

the court of the house of the Lord" (2 Chr. 24:21). Genesis was the first book in the Hebrew canon, and Chronicles the last. So Jesus was basically saying "from Genesis to Chronicles," or, according to our order, "from Genesis to Malachi," thereby confirming the divine authority and inspiration of the entire Hebrew canon. (Bruce, BP, 96)

4C. The Testimonies of Extra-biblical Writers

1D. Prologue to Ecclesiasticus
Possibly the earliest reference to a three-fold division of the Old Testament is in the prologue of the book *Ecclesiasticus* (about 130 B.C.). The prologue, written by the author's grandson, says, "The Law, and the Prophets and the other books of the fathers," indicating three divisions of the Hebrew canon. (Young, AOT, 71)

2D. Philo
"Just after the time of Christ (about A.D. 40), Philo witnessed to a threefold classification, making reference to the Law, the Prophets (or Prophecies), as well as 'hymns and the others which foster and perfect knowledge and piety.'" (Geisler, GIB, 246)

3D. Josephus
The Jewish historian Josephus (end of the first century A.D.) also spoke about the threefold division. And about the entire Hebrew Scriptures, he wrote:

And how firmly we have given credit to those books of our own nation is evident by what we do; for during so many ages as have already passed, no one has been so bold as either to add anything to them or take anything from them, or to make any change in them; but it becomes natural to all Jews, immediately and from their very birth, to esteem those books to contain divine doctrines, and to persist in them, and, if occasion be, willingly to die for them. For it is no new thing for our captives, many of them in number, and frequently in time, to be seen to endure racks and deaths of all kinds upon the theatres, that they may not be obliged to say one word against our laws, and the records that contain them. (Josephus, FJAA, 609)

4D. The Talmud
The Talmud is an ancient "collection of rabbinical laws, law decisions and comments on the laws of Moses" that preserves the oral tradition of the Jewish people (White, T, 589). One compilation of the Talmud was made in Jerusalem circa A.D. 350–425. Another more expanded compilation of the Talmud was made in Babylonia circa A.D. 500. Each compilation is known by the name of its place of compilation—for example, The Jerusalem Talmud and The Babylonian Talmud, respectively.

1E. *Tosefta Yadaim 3:5* says, "The Gospel and the books of the heretics do not make the hands unclean; the books of Ben Sira and whatever books have been written since his time are not canonical." (Pfeiffer, IOT, 63) The reference to a book making the hands unclean meant that the book was divinely inspired and therefore holy. Handlers of the Scriptures were required to wash their hands after touching their holy pages. "By declaring that the Scriptures made the hands unclean, the rabbis protected them from careless and irreverent treatment, since it is obvious that no one would be so apt to handle them heedlessly if he were every time obliged to wash his hands afterward." (Beckwith, OTC, 280) A book that did not do this was not from God. This text is claiming that only the books assembled in the Hebrew canon can lay claim to being God's Word.

2E. *Seder Olam Rabba 30* states, "Until then [the coming of Alexander the Great and the end of the empire of the Persians] the prophets prophesied through the Holy Spirit. From then on, 'incline thine ear and hear the words of the wise.'" (Beckwith, OTC, 370)

3E. Tos. Sotah 13:2: *baraita in Bab. Yoma 9b, Bab. Sotah 48b and Bab. Sanhedrin 11a:* "With the death of Haggai, Zechariah and Malachi the latter prophets, the Holy Spirit ceased out of Israel." (Beckwith, OTC, 370)

5D. Melito, Bishop of Sardis

Melito drew up the first known list of Old Testament books from within Christian circles (about A.D. 170). Eusebius (*Ecclesiastical History IV. 26*) preserves his comments: "Melito said he had obtained the reliable list while traveling in Syria. Melito's comments were in a letter to Anesimius, his friend: 'Their names are these . . . five books of Moses: Genesis, Exodus, Numbers, Leviticus, Deuteronomy. Jesus Naue, Judges, Ruth. Four books of Kingdoms, two of Chronicles, the Psalms of David, Solomon's Proverbs (also called Wisdom), Ecclesiastes, Song of Songs, Job. Of the Prophets: Isaiah, Jeremiah, the Twelve in a single book, Daniel, Ezekiel, Ezra.'"

F. F. Bruce comments: "It is likely that Melito included Lamentations with Jeremiah, and Nehemiah with Ezra (though it is curious to find Ezra counted among the prophets). In that case, his list contains all the books of the Hebrew canon (arranged according to the Septuagint order), with the exception of Esther. Esther may not have been included in the list he received from his informants in Syria." (Bruce, BP, 100)

6D. Mishnah

The threefold division of the present Jewish text (with eleven books in the Writings) is from the Mishnah (Baba Bathra tractate, fifth century A.D.). (Geisler, GIB, 24)

5C. The New Testament Witness to the Old Testament as Sacred Scripture

Matthew 21:42; 22:29; 26:54, 56
Luke 24
John 5:39; 10:35
Acts 17:2, 11; 18:28
Romans 1:2; 4:3; 9:17; 10:11; 11:2; 15:4; 16:26
1 Corinthians 15:3, 4
Galatians 3:8; 3:22; 4:30
1 Timothy 5:18
2 Timothy 3:16
2 Peter 1:20, 21; 3:16

"As the *Scripture* said" (John 7:38) is all the introduction a text needed to indicate the general understanding that a saying, story, or book was the very Word of God from the prophets of God.

6C. Hebrew Apocryphal Literature

The term *apocrypha* comes from the Greek word *apokruphos,* meaning "hidden or concealed."

In the fourth century A.D., Jerome was the first to name this group of literature *Apocrypha.* The Apocrypha consists of the books added to the Old Testament by the Roman Catholic Church. Protestants reject these additions as canonical Scripture.

1D. Why Not Canonical?

Unger's Bible Dictionary, while granting that the Old Testament apocryphal books do have some value, cites four reasons for excluding them from the Hebrew canon:

1. They abound in historical and geographical inaccuracies and anachronisms.
2. They teach doctrines that are false and foster practices that are at variance with inspired Scripture.

3. They resort to literary types and display an artificiality of subject matter and styling out of keeping with inspired Scripture.

4. They lack the distinctive elements that give genuine Scripture its divine character, such as prophetic power and poetic and religious feeling. (Unger, NUBD, 85)

2D. A Summary of the Apocryphal Books

In his excellent study guide *How We Got Our Bible,* Ralph Earle provides brief details of each apocryphal book. Because of its quality, accuracy, and conciseness, I present his outline here in order to give the reader a first-hand feel of the value yet non-canonical nature of these books:

First Esdras (about 150 B.C.) tells of the restoration of the Jews to Palestine after the Babylonian exile. It draws considerably from Chronicles, Ezra, and Nehemiah, but the author has added much legendary material.

The most interesting item is the "Story of the Three Guardsmen." They were debating what was the strongest thing in the world. One said, "'Wine"; another, "the King"; the third, "Woman and Truth." They put these three answers under the king's pillow. When he awoke he required the three men to defend their answers. The unanimous decision was: "Truth is greatly and supremely strong." Because Zerubbabel had given this answer he was allowed, as a reward, to rebuild the Temple at Jerusalem.

Second Esdras (A.D. 100) is an apocalyptic work, containing seven visions. Martin Luther was so confused by these visions that he is said to have thrown the book into the Elbe River.

Tobit (early second century B.C.) is a short novel. Strongly Pharisaic in tone, it emphasizes the Law, clean foods, ceremonial washings, charity, fasting, and prayer. It is clearly unscriptural in its statement that almsgiving atones for sin.

Judith (about the middle of second century B.C.) is also fictitious and Pharisaic. The heroine of this novel is Judith, a beautiful Jewish widow. When her city was besieged she took her maid, together with Jewish clean food, and went out to the tent of the attacking general. He was enamored of her beauty and gave her a place in his tent. Fortunately, he had imbibed too freely and sank into a drunken stupor. Judith took his sword and cut off his head. Then she and her maid left the camp, taking his head in their provision bag. It was hung on the wall of a nearby city, and the leaderless Assyrian army was defeated.

Additions to Esther (about 100 B.C.). Esther stands alone among the books of the Old Testament in that there is no mention of God. We are told that Esther and Mordecai fasted, but not specifically that they prayed. To compensate for this lack, the additions attribute long prayers to these two, together with a couple of letters supposedly written by Artaxerxes.

The Wisdom of Solomon (about A.D. 40) was written to keep the Jews from falling into skepticism, materialism, and idolatry. As in Proverbs, Wisdom is personified. There are many noble sentiments expressed in this book.

Ecclesiasticus, or Wisdom of Sirach (about 180 B.C.), shows a high level of religious wisdom, somewhat like the canonical Book of Proverbs. It also contains much practical advice. For instance, on the subject of after-dinner speeches it says (32:8):

"Speak concisely; say much in few words."

"Act like a man who knows more than he says."

And again (33:4):

"Prepare what you have to say, and then you will be listened to."

In his sermons, John Wesley quotes several times from the Book of Ecclesiasticus. It is still widely used in Anglican circles.

Baruch (about A.D. 100) presents itself as being written by Baruch, the scribe of Jeremiah, in 582 B.C. Actually, it is probably trying to interpret the destruction of Jerusalem in A.D. 70. The book urges the Jews not to revolt again, but to submit to the emperor. In spite of this the Bar-Cochba revolution against Roman rule took place soon after, in A.D. 132–35. The sixth chapter of Baruch contains the so-called "Letter of Jeremiah," which warns strongly against idolatry—probably addressed to Jews in Alexandria, Egypt.

Our Book of Daniel contains twelve chapters. In the first century before Christ a thirteenth chapter was added, the story of *Susanna*. She was the beautiful wife of a leading Jew in Babylon, to whose house the Jewish elders and judges frequently came. Two of these became enamored of her and tried to seduce her. When she cried out, the two elders said they had found her in the arms of a young man. She was brought to trial. Since there were two witnesses who agreed in their testimony, she was convicted and sentenced to death.

But a young man named Daniel interrupted the proceedings and began to cross-examine the witnesses. He asked each one separately under which tree in the garden they had found Susanna with a lover. When they gave different answers they were put to death and Susanna was saved.

Bel and the Dragon was added at about the same time and was called chapter 14 of Daniel. Its main purpose was to show the folly of idolatry. It really contains two stories.

In the first, King Cyrus asked Daniel why he did not worship Bel, since that deity showed his greatness by daily consuming many sheep, together with much flour and oil. So Daniel scattered ashes on the floor of the Temple where the food had been placed that evening. In the morning the king took Daniel in to show him that Bel had eaten all the food during the night. But Daniel showed the king in the ashes on the floor the footprints of the priests and their families who had entered secretly under the table. The priests were slain and the temple destroyed.

The story of the dragon is just as obviously legendary in character. Along with Tobit, Judith, and Susanna, these stories may be clas-sified as purely Jewish fiction. They have little if any religious value.

The Song of the Three Hebrew Children follows Daniel 3:23 in the Septuagint and in the Vulgate. Borrowing heavily from Psalm 148, it is antiphonal, like Psalm 136, repeating thirty-two times the refrain, "Sing praise to him and greatly exalt him forever."

The Prayer of Manasseh was composed in Maccabean times (second century B.C.) as the supposed prayer of Manasseh, the wicked king of Judah. It was clearly suggested by the statement in 2 Chronicles 33:19—"His prayer also, and how God was entreated of him . . . behold, they are written among the sayings of the seers." Since this prayer is not found in the Bible, some scribe had to make up for the deficiency!

First Maccabees (first century B.C.) is perhaps the most valuable book in the Apocrypha. It describes the exploits of the three Maccabean brothers—Judas, Jonathan, and Simon. Along with Josephus, it is our most important source for the history of this crucial and exciting period in Jewish history.

Second Maccabees (same time) is not a sequel to 1 Maccabees, but is a parallel account, treating only the victories of Judas Maccabeus. It is generally thought to be more legendary than 1 Maccabees. (Earle, HWGOB, 37–41)

3D. Historical Testimony of Their Exclusion

Geisler and Nix give ten testimonies of antiquity that argue against recognition of the Apocrypha:

1. Philo, Alexandrian Jewish philosopher (20 B.C.–A.D. 40), quoted the Old Testament prolifically, and even recognized the threefold classification, but he never quoted from the Apocrypha as inspired.

2. Josephus (A.D. 30–100), Jewish historian, explicitly excludes the Apocrypha, numbering the books of the Old Testament as twenty-two. Neither does he quote the apocryphal books as Scripture.

3. Jesus and the New Testament writers never once quote the Apocrypha, although there are hundreds of quotes and references to almost all of the canonical books of the Old Testament.

4. The Jewish scholars of Jamnia (A.D. 90) did not recognize the Apocrypha.

5. No canon or council of the Christian church recognized the Apocrypha as inspired for nearly four centuries.

6. Many of the great Fathers of the early church spoke out against the Apocrypha—for example, Origen, Cyril of Jerusalem, and Athanasius.

7. Jerome (A.D. 340–420), the great scholar and translator of the Latin Vulgate, rejected the Apocrypha as part of the canon. Jerome said that the church reads them "for example of life and instruction of manners," but does not "apply them to establish any doctrine." He disputed with Augustine across the Mediterranean on this point. At first Jerome refused even to translate the apocryphal books into Latin, but later he made a hurried translation of a few of them. After his death and "over his dead body" the apocryphal books were brought into his Latin Vulgate directly from the Old Latin Version.

8. Many Roman Catholic scholars through the Reformation period rejected the Apocrypha.

9. Luther and the Reformers rejected the canonicity of the Apocrypha.

10. Not until A.D. 1546, in a polemical action at the counter-Reformation Council of Trent (1545–63), did the apocryphal books receive full canonical status by the Roman Catholic Church. (Geisler/Nix, GIB, 272–273)

CONCLUSION

David Dockery, Kenneth Matthews, and Robert Sloan, after reviewing the evidence in their recent book, *Foundations for Biblical Interpretation*, conclude concerning the Bible's canon: "No Christian, confident in the providential working of his God and informed about the true nature of canonicity of his Word, should be disturbed about the dependability of the Bible we now possess." (Dockery, FBI, 77, 78)

3

IS THE NEW TESTA-
MENT HISTORICALLY
RELIABLE?

INTRODUCTION: TESTS FOR THE RELIABILITY OF ANCIENT LITERATURE

What we are establishing here is the historical reliability of the Scripture, not its inspiration. The historical reliability of the Scripture should be tested by the same criteria by which all historical documents are tested.

C. Sanders, in *Introduction to Research in English Literary History,* lists and explains the three basic principles of historiography. These are the bibliographical test, the internal evidence test, and the external evidence test. (Sanders, IRE, 143 ff.) This chapter will examine the New Testament portion of the Bible to see how well it does with each test in order to determine its reliability as an accurate source for the historical events it reports.

1A. THE BIBLIOGRAPHICAL TEST FOR THE RELIABILITY OF THE NEW TESTAMENT

The bibliographical test is an examination of the textual transmission by which documents reach us. In other words, since we do not have the original documents, how reliable are the copies we have in regard to the number of manuscripts (MSS) and the time interval between the original and extant (currently existing) copies? (Montgomery, HC, 26)

1B. The Number of Manuscripts and Their Closeness to the Original

F. E. Peters states that "on the basis of manuscript tradition alone, the works that made up the Christians' New Testament were the most frequently copied and widely circulated books of antiquity." (Peters, HH, 50) As a result, the fidelity of the New Testament text rests on a multitude of manuscript evidence. Counting Greek copies alone, the New Testament is preserved in some 5,656 partial and complete manuscript portions that were copied by hand from the second through the fifteenth centuries. (Geisler, GIB, 385)

There are now more than 5,686 known Greek manuscripts of the New Testament. Add over 10,000 Latin Vulgate and at least 9,300 other early versions (MSS), and we have close to, if not more than, 25,000 manuscript copies of portions of the New Testament in existence today. No other document of antiquity even begins to approach such numbers and attestation. In comparison, Homer's *Iliad* is second, with only 643 manuscripts that still survive. The first complete preserved text of Homer dates from the thirteenth century. (Leach, OB, 145)

The following is a breakdown of the number of surviving manuscripts for the New Testament:

Extant Greek Manuscripts:

Uncials	307
Minuscules	2,860
Lectionaries	2,410
Papyri	109
SUBTOTAL	5,686

Manuscripts in Other Languages:

Latin Vulgate	10,000+
Ethiopic	2,000+
Slavic	4,101
Armenian	2,587
Syriac Pashetta	350+
Bohairic	100
Arabic	75
Old Latin	50
Anglo Saxon	7
Gothic	6
Sogdian	3
Old Syriac	2
Persian	2
Frankish	1
SUBTOTAL	19,284+
TOTAL ALL MSS	24,970+

Information for the preceding charts was gathered from the following sources: Michael Welte of the Institute for New Testament Studies in Munster, Germany; Kurt Aland's *Journal of Biblical Literature,* Vol. 87, 1968; Kurt Aland's *Kurzgefasste Liste der Griechischen Handschriften des Neuen Testa-*

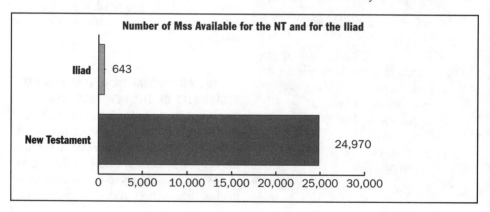

Number of Mss Available for the NT and for the Iliad

Iliad — 643

New Testament — 24,970

0   5,000   10,000   15,000   20,000   25,000   30,000

ments, W. De Gruyter, 1963; Kurt Aland's "Neve Nevtestamentliche Papyri III," *New Testament Studies,* July, 1976; Bruce Metzger's *The Early Versions of the New Testament,* Clarendon Press, 1977; *New Testament Manuscript Studies,* (eds.) Merrill M. Parvis and Allen Wikgren, The University of Chicago Press, 1950; Eroll F. Rhodes's *An Annotated List of Armenian New Testament Manuscripts,* Tokyo, Ikeburo, 1959; *The Bible and Modern Scholarship,* (ed.) J. Phillip Hyatt, Abingdon Press, 1965.

The importance of the sheer number of manuscript copies cannot be overstated. As with other documents of ancient literature, there are no known extant (currently existing) original manuscripts of the Bible. Fortunately, however, the abundance of manuscript copies makes it possible to reconstruct the original with virtually complete accuracy. (Geisler, GIB, 386)

John Warwick Montgomery says that "to be skeptical of the resultant text of the New Testament books is to allow all of classical antiquity to slip into obscurity, for no documents of the ancient period are as well attested bibliographically as the New Testament." (Montgomery, HC, 29)

Sir Frederic G. Kenyon, who was the director and principal librarian of the British Museum and second to none in authority for issuing statements about MSS, states that

> besides number, the manuscripts of the New Testament differ from those of the classical authors. . . . In no other case is the interval of time between the composition of the book and the date of the earliest extant manuscripts so short as in that of the New Testament. The books of the New Testament were written in the latter part of the first century; the earliest extant manuscripts (trifling scraps excepted) are of the fourth century—say from 250 to 300 years later. This may sound a considerable

interval, but it is nothing to that which parts most of the great classical authors from their earliest manuscripts. We believe that we have in all essentials an accurate text of the seven extant plays of Sophocles; yet the earliest substantial manuscript upon which it is based was written more than 1400 years after the poet's death. (Kenyon, HTCNT, 4)

Kenyon continues in *The Bible and Archaeology:* "The interval then between the dates of original composition and the earliest extant evidence becomes so small as to be in fact negligible, and the last foundation for any doubt that the Scriptures have come down to us substantially as they were written has now been removed. Both the authenticity and the general integrity of the books of the New Testament may be regarded as finally established." (Kenyon, BA, 288)

Dockery, Mathews, and Sloan have recently written, "For most of the biblical text a single reading has been transmitted. Elimination of scribal errors and intentional changes leaves only a small percentage of the text about which any questions occur." (Dockery, FBI, 176) They conclude:

> It must be said that the amount of time between the original composition and the next surviving manuscript is far less for the New Testament than for any other work in Greek literature. . . . Although there are certainly differences in many of the New Testament manuscripts, not one fundamental doctrine of the Christian faith rests on a disputed reading. (Dockery, FBI, 182)

F. J. A. Hort rightfully adds that "in the variety and fullness of the evidence on which it rests the text of the New Testament stands absolutely and unapproachably alone among ancient prose writings." (Hort, NTOG, 561)

J. Harold Greenlee states, "The number of

available MSS of the New Testament is overwhelmingly greater than those of any other work of ancient literature. . . . The earliest extant MSS of the NT were written much closer to the date of the original writing than is the case in almost any other piece of ancient literature." (Greenlee, INTTC, 15)

W. F. Albright confidently informs us: "No other work from Graeco-Roman antiquity is so well attested by manuscript tradition as the New Testament. There are many more early manuscripts of the New Testament than there are of any classical author, and the oldest extensive remains of it date only about two centuries after their original composition." (Albright, AP, 238)

Edward Glenny reports that

God has given us 5,656 manuscripts containing all or parts of the Greek NT. It is the most remarkably preserved book in the ancient world. Not only do we have a great number of manuscripts but they are very close in time to the originals they represent. Some partial manuscripts of the NT are from the second century A.D., and many are within four centuries of the originals. These facts are all the more amazing when they are compared with the preservation of other ancient literature. (Glenny, PS, as cited in BVD, .95; see Aland, TNT, 72–84, for a description of the manuscripts of the New Testament. One of the most recent tabulations of NT manuscripts is in Kurt and Barbara Aland, eds. *Kurzgefasste Liste der griechischen Handschriften des Neuen Testaments.* [Aland, KLHNT] (This source lists the extant Greek manuscripts of the NT as 99 papyri, 306 uncials, 2,855 minuscules, and 2,396 Lectionaries, for the total given above.)

Lee Strobel, in a very recent book [published in 1998], reports the latest count of Greek MSS as follows: papyri 99; uncials 306; minuscules 2,856; and lectionaries 2,403, for a total of 5,664. (Strobel, CC, 62–63) (Slight variations in counts may occur, depending on how small fragments were to be considered manuscripts, but the "mountain of evidence" gives the New Testament great historical credibility.)

> To be skeptical of the resultant text of the New Testament books is to allow all of classical antiquity to slip into obscurity, for no documents of the ancient period are as well attested bibliographically as the New Testament.
>
> —JOHN WARWICK MONTGOMERY

Michael Welte of the Institute for New Testament Studies (Westfalische Wilhelms-Universitat, Institut Fur Neutestamentliche Textforschung) in Munster, Germany, has conveyed the latest (as of August 1998) count of Greek MSS as follows: 109 papyri, 307 uncials, 2,860 minuscules, and 2,410 lectionaries, for a total of 5,686.

Glenny continues, citing comparative ancient documents: "No one questions the authenticity of the historical books of antiquity because we do not possess the original copies. Yet we have far fewer manuscripts of these works than we possess of the NT." (Glenny, PS, as cited in BVD, 96)

F. F. Bruce, in *The New Testament Document*, vividly portrays the comparison between the New Testament and ancient historical writings:

Perhaps we can appreciate how wealthy the New Testament is in manuscript attestation if we compare the textual material for other ancient historical works. For Caesar's Gallic Wars (composed between 58 and 50 B.C.) there are several extant MSS, but only nine or ten are good, and the oldest is some 900 years later than Caesar's day. Of the 142 books of the Roman history of Livy (59

B.C.–A.D.17), only 35 survive; these are known to us from not more than 20 MSS of any consequence, only one of which, and that containing fragments of Books III–VI, is as old as the fourth century. Of the 14 books of the Histories of Tacitus (c. A.D. 100) only four and a half survive; of the 16 books of his Annals, 10 survive in full and two in part. The text of these extant portions of his two great historical works depends entirely on two MSS, one of the ninth century and one of the eleventh.

The extant MSS of his minor works (Dialogus de Oratoribus, Agricola, Germania) all descend from a codex of the tenth century. The History of Thucydides (c. 460–400 B.C.) is known to us from eight MSS, the earliest belonging to c. A.D. 900, and a few papyrus scraps, belonging to about the beginning of the Christian era. The same is true of the History of Herodotus (B.C. 488–428). Yet no classical scholar would listen to an argument that the authenticity of Herodotus or Thucydides is in doubt because the earliest MSS of their works which are of any use to us are over 1,300 years later than the originals. (Bruce, NTD, 16,17)

Greenlee writes in *Introduction to New Testament Textual Criticism* about the time gap between the original MS (the autograph) and the extant MS (the oldest surviving copy), saying,

The oldest known MSS of most of the Greek classical authors are dated a thousand years or more after the author's death. The time interval for the Latin authors is somewhat less, varying down to a minimum of three centuries in the case of Virgil. In the case of the N.T., however, two of the most important MSS were written within 300 years after the N.T. was completed, and some virtually complete N.T. books as well as extensive fragmentary MSS of many parts of the N.T. date back to one century from the original writings. (Greenlee, INTTC, 16)

Greenlee adds,

Since scholars accept as generally trustworthy the writings of the ancient classics even though the earliest MSS were written so long after the original writings and the number of extant MSS is in many instances so small, it is clear that the reliability of the text of the N.T. is likewise assured. (Greenlee, INTTC, 16)

Bruce Metzger, in *The Text of the New Testament,* cogently writes of the comparison:

The works of several ancient authors are preserved to us by the thinnest possible thread of transmission. For example, the compendious history of Rome by Velleius Paterculus survived to modern times in only one incomplete manuscript, from which the *editio princeps* was made—and this lone manuscript was lost in the seventeenth century after being copied by Beatus Rhenanus at Amerbach. Even the *Annals* of the famous historian Tacitus is extant, so far as the first six books are concerned, in but a single manuscript, dating from the ninth century. In 1870 the only known manuscript of the *Epistle to Diognetus,* an early Christian composition which editors usually include in the corpus of Apostolic Fathers, perished in a fire at the municipal library in Strasbourg. In contrast with these figures, the textual critic of the New Testament is embarrassed by the wealth of his material. (Metzger, TNT, 34)

F. F. Bruce writes: "There is no body of ancient literature in the world which enjoys such a wealth of good textual attestation as the New Testament." (Bruce, BP, 178)

Compared with nearly 5,700 Greek manuscripts of the NT, the chart on the next page demonstrates the poverty of manuscripts of some other ancient documents. (Geisler, GIB, 408)

No wonder Ravi Zacharias concludes: "In real terms, the New Testament is easily the

AUTHOR	BOOK	DATE WRITTEN	EARLIEST COPIES	TIME GAP	NO. OF COPIES
Homer	*Iliad*	800 B.C.	c. 400 B.C.	c. 400 yrs.	643
Herodotus	*History*	480–425 B.C.	c. A.D. 900	c. 1,350 yrs.	8
Thucydides	*History*	460–400 B.C.	c. A.D. 900	c. 1,300 yrs.	8
Plato		400 B.C.	c. A.D. 900	c. 1,300 yrs.	7
Demosthenes		300 B.C.	c. A.D. 1100	c. 1,400 yrs.	200
Caesar	*Gallic Wars*	100–44 B.C.	c. A.D. 900	c. 1,000 yrs.	10
Livy	*History of Rome*	59 B.C.–A.D. 17	4th cent. (partial) mostly 10th cent.	c. 400 yrs. c. 1,000 yrs.	1 partial 19 copies
Tacitus	*Annals*	A.D. 100	c. A.D. 1100	c. 1,000 yrs.	20
Pliny Secundus	*Natural History*	A.D. 61–113	c. A.D. 850	c. 750 yrs.	7
New Testament		A.D. 50–100	c. 114 (fragment) c. 200 (books) c. 250 (most of N.T.) c. 325 (complete N.T.)	+ 50 yrs. 100 yrs. 150 yrs. 225 yrs.	5366

best attested ancient writing in terms of the sheer number of documents, the time span between the events and the document, and the variety of documents available to sustain or contradict it. There is nothing in ancient manuscript evidence to match such textual availability and integrity." (Zacharias, CMLWG, 162)

2B. Important New Testament Manuscripts

Following is a chronology of some the most important manuscript discoveries. For dating purposes, some of the factors that help determine the age of a MS are:

1. Materials used
2. Letter size and form
3. Punctuation
4. Text divisions
5. Ornamentation
6. The color of the ink
7. The texture and color of parchment (Geisler, GIB, 242–246)

John Rylands's MS (A.D. 130) is located in the John Rylands Library of Manchester, England (oldest extant fragment of the New Testament). "Because of its early date and location (Egypt), some distance from the traditional place of composition (Asia Minor), this portion of the Gospel of John tends to confirm the traditional date of the composition of the Gospel about the end of the 1st century." (Geisler, GIB, 268)

Bruce Metzger speaks of defunct criticism: "Had this little fragment been known during the middle of the past century, that school of New Testament criticism which was inspired by the brilliant Tubingen professor, Ferdinand Christian Baur, could not have argued that the Fourth Gospel was not composed until about the year 160." (Metzger, TNT, 39)

Bodmer Papyrus II (A.D. 150–200) was purchased in the 1950s and 1960s from a dealer in Egypt and is located in the Bodmer Library of World Literature; it contains most of John's Gospel. The most important discovery of New Testament papyri since the Chester Beatty manuscripts (see below) was the acquisition of the Bodmer Collection by the Library of World Literature at Culagny, near Geneva. p66, dating from about A.D. 200 or earlier, contains 104 leaves of John 1:1— 6:11; 6:35b—14:26; and fragments of forty other pages, John 14—21. The text is a mixture of the Alexandrian and Western types, and there are some twenty alterations between the lines that invariably belong to the Western family. (Geisler, GIB, 390) In his article, 'Zur Datierung des Papyrus Bodmer II (P66), 'Anzeiger der osterreichischen Akademie der Wissenschaften, phil.-hist, kl., 1960, Nr. 4, p. 12033, "Herbert Hunger, the director of the papyrological collections in the National Library at Vienna, dates 66 earlier, in the middle if not even in the first half of the second century; see his article." (Metzger, TNT, 39, 40)

"p72., also a part of the collection, is the earliest copy of the epistle of Jude and the two epistles of Peter. p75., still another early Biblical manuscript acquired by M. Bodmer, is a single-quire codex of Luke and John. . . . The editors, Victor Martin and Rodolphe Kaser, date this copy between A.D. 175 and 225. It is thus the earliest known copy of the Gospel according to Luke and one of the earliest of the Gospel according to John." (Metzger, TNT, 41) Thus, Metzger describes it as "the most important discovery of the N.T. manuscripts since the purchase of the Chester Beatty papyri." (Metzger, TNT, 39, 40)

Chester Beatty Papyri (A.D. 200). The manuscripts were purchased in the 1930s from a dealer in Egypt and are located in C.

Beatty Museum in Dublin. Part is owned by the University of Michigan. This collection contains papyrus codices, three of which contain major portions of the New Testament. (Bruce, BP, 182) In *The Bible and Modern Scholarship,* Sir Frederic Kenyon writes, "The net result of this discovery—by far the most important since the discovery of the Sinaiticus—is, in fact, to reduce the gap between the earlier manuscripts and the traditional dates of the New Testament books so far that it becomes negligible in any discussion of their authenticity. No other ancient book has anything like such early and plentiful testimony to its text, and no unbiased scholar would deny that the text that has come down to us is substantially sound." (Kenyon, BMS, 20) (A detailed listing of papyri may be seen in the Greek New Testaments published by United Bible Societies and Nestle-Aland, both printed in Stuttgart.)

Diatessaron means "a harmony of four parts." The Greek *dia Tessaron* literally means "through four." (Bruce, BP, 195) This was a harmony of the Gospels executed by Tatian (about A.D. 160).

Eusebius, in *Ecclesiastical History,* IV, 29 Loeb ed., 1, 397, wrote: "Their former leader Tatian composed in some way a combination and collection of the Gospels, and gave this the name of THE DIATESSARON, and this is still extant in some places." It is believed that Tatian, an Assyrian Christian, was the first to compose a harmony of the Gospels, only a small portion of which is extant today. (Geisler, GIB, 318, 319)

Codex Vaticanus (A.D. 325–350), located in the Vatican Library, contains nearly all of the Bible. After a hundred years of textual criticism, many consider Vaticanus as one of the most trustworthy manuscripts of the New Testament text.

Codex Sinaiticus (A.D. 350) is located in the British Museum. This MS, which contains almost all the New Testament and over half of the Old Testament, was discovered by Dr. Constantin Von Tischendorf in the Mount Sinai Monastery in 1859. It was presented by the monastery to the Russian Czar and bought by the British Government and people from the Soviet Union for 100,000 pounds on Christmas Day, 1933.

The discovery of this manuscript is a fascinating story. Bruce Metzger relates the interesting background leading to its discovery:

> In 1844, when he was not yet thirty years of age, Tischendorf, a *Privatdozent* in the University of Leipzig, began an extensive journey through the Near East in search of Biblical manuscripts. While visiting the monastery of St. Catharine at Mount Sinai, he chanced to see some leaves of parchment in a waste-basket full of papers destined to light the oven of the monastery. On examination these proved to be part of a copy of the Septuagint version of the Old Testament, written in a nearly Greek uncial script. He retrieved from the basket no fewer than forty-three such leaves, and the monk casually remarked that two basket loads of similarly discarded leaves had already been burned up! Later, when Tischendorf was shown other portions of the same codex (containing all of Isaiah and I and II Maccabees), he warned the monks that such things were too valuable to be used to stoke their fires. The forty-three leaves which he was permitted to keep contained portions of I Chronicles, Jeremiah, Nehemiah, and Esther, and upon returning to Europe he deposited them in the university library at Leipzig, where they still remain. In 1846 he published their contents, naming them the codex Frederico-Augustanus (in honour of the King of Saxony, Frederick Augustus, the discoverer's sovereign and patron). (Metzger, TNT, 43)

A second visit to the monastery by Tischendorf in 1853 produced no new manuscripts because the monks were suspicious as a result of the enthusiasm for the MS displayed during his first visit in 1844. He visited a third time in 1859, under the direction of the Czar of Russia, Alexander II. Shortly before leaving, Tischendorf gave the steward of the monastery an edition of the Septuagint that had been published by Tischendorf in Leipzig.

Thereupon the steward remarked that he too had a copy of the Septuagint, and produced from a closet in his cell a manuscript wrapped in a red cloth. There before the astonished scholar's eyes lay the treasure which he had been longing to see. Concealing his feelings, Tischendorf casually asked permission to look at it further that evening. Permission was granted, and upon retiring to his room Tischendorf stayed up all night in the joy of studying the manuscript—for, as he declared in his diary (which as a scholar he kept in Latin), *quippe dormire nefas videbatur* ("it really seemed a sacrilege to sleep!") He soon found that the document contained much more than he had even hoped; for not only was most of the Old Testament there, but also the New Testament was intact and in excellent condition, with the addition of two early Christian works of the second century, the Epistle of Barnabas (previously known only through a very poor Latin translation) and a large portion of the Shepherd of Hermas, hitherto known only by title. (Metzger, TNT, 44)

Codex Alexandrinus (A.D. 400) is located in the British Museum. *Encyclopaedia Britannica* believes it was written in Greek in Egypt. It contains almost the entire Bible.

Codex Ephraemi (A.D. 400s) is located in the Bibliotheque Nationale, Paris. The *Encyclopaedia Britannica* says that "its 5th century origin and the evidence it supplies make it important for the text of certain portions of the New Testament." (EB, Vol. 3, 579; Bruce, BP, 183) Every book is represented in the MS except 2 Thessalonians and 2 John. "This is a fifth century document called a palimpsest. (A palimpsest is a manuscript in which the original writing has been erased and then written over.) Through the use of chemicals and painstaking effort, a scholar can read the original writing underneath the overprinted text." (Comfort, OB, 181)

Codex Bezae (A.D. 450 plus) is located in the Cambridge Library and contains the Gospels and Acts, not only in Greek but also in Latin.

Codex Washingtonensis (or Freericanus) (c. A.D. 450) contains the four Gospels. (Greenlee, INTTC, 39) It is located in the Smithsonian Institution in Washington, D.C.

Codex Claromontanus (A.D. 500s) contains the Pauline Epistles. It is a bilingual MS.

3B. Accuracy of Manuscripts Supported by Various Versions

Another strong support for textual evidence and accuracy is the ancient versions. For the most part, "ancient literature was rarely translated into another language." (Greenlee, INTTC, 45)

From its inception Christianity has been a missionary faith. "The earliest versions of the New Testament were prepared by missionaries to assist in the propagation of the Christian faith among peoples whose native tongue was Syriac, Latin, or Coptic." (Metzger, TNT, 67)

Syriac and Latin versions (translations) of the New Testament were made around A.D. 150. These versions bring us back very near to the time of the originals. There are more than fifteen thousand existing copies of various versions.

1C. Syriac Versions

Old Syriac Version contains four Gospels, copied about the fourth century. It should be explained that "Syriac is the name generally given to Christian Aramaic. It is written in a distinctive variation of the Aramaic alphabet." (Bruce, BP, 193) Theodore of Mopsuestia (fifth century) wrote, "It has been

translated into the tongue of the Syrians." (Bruce, BP, 193)

Syriac Peshitta. The basic meaning is "simple." It was the standard version, produced around A.D. 150–250. There are more than 350 MSS from the 400s extant today. (Geisler, GIB, 317)

Palestinian Syriac. Most scholars date this version at about A.D. 400–450 (fifth century). (Metzger, TNT, 68–71)

Philoxenian (A.D. 508). Polycarp translated a new Syriac New Testament for Philoxenas, bishop of Mabug. (Greenlee, INTTC, 49)

Harkleian Syriac. (A.D. 616) by Thomas of Harkel.

2C. Latin Versions

Old Latin. Testimonies from the fourth century to the thirteenth century relate that in the third century an "old Latin version circulated in North Africa and Europe."

African Old Latin (Codex Babbiensis) (A.D. 400). Metzger writes that "E. A. Lowe shows palaeographical marks of it having been copied from a second century papyrus." (Metzger, TNT, 72–74)

Codex Corbiensis (A.D. 400–500) contains the four Gospels.

Codex Vercellensis (A.D. 360).

Codex Palatinus (fifth century A.D.).

Latin Vulgate (meaning "common or popular"). Jerome was secretary to Damasus, the Bishop of Rome. Jerome fulfilled the bishop's request for a version between A.D. 366–384. (Bruce, BP, 201)

3C. Coptic (or Egyptian) Versions

F. F. Bruce writes that it is probable that the first Egyptian version was translated in the third or fourth century. (Bruce, BP, 214)

Sahidic. Beginning of the third century (Metzger, TNT, 79–80).

Bohairic. The editor, Rodalphe Kasser,

dates it about the fourth century (Greenlee, INTTC, 50).

Middle Egyptian. Fourth or fifth century.

4C. Other early Versions

Armenian (A.D. 400+). Seems to have been translated from a Greek Bible obtained from Constantinople.

Gothic. Fourth century.

Georgian. Fifth century.

Ethiopic. Sixth century.

Nubian. Sixth century.

4B. Accuracy of Manuscripts Supported by Lectionaries

This field is a greatly neglected one, and yet the second largest group of NT Greek MSS is the lectionaries.

Bruce Metzger offers the background of the lectionaries: "Following the custom of the synagogue, according to which portions of the Law and the Prophets were read at divine service each Sabbath day, the Chris-

> The works of several ancient authors are preserved to us by the thinnest possible thread of transmission. . . . In contrast . . . the textual critic of the New Testament is embarrassed by the wealth of his material.
>
> —BRUCE METZGER

tian Church adopted the practice of reading passages from the New Testament books at services of worship. A regular system of lessons from the Gospels and Epistles was developed, and the custom arose of arranging these according to a fixed order of Sundays and other holy days of the Christian year." (Metzger, TNT, 30)

Metzger reports that 2,135 have been catalogued, but as of yet the majority still await critical analysis. (A more recent count is 2,396, as noted previously in this chapter.)

J. Harold Greenlee states that "the earliest lectionary fragments are from the sixth century, while complete MSS date from the eighth century and later." (Greenlee, INTTC, 45)

The lectionaries were usually rather conservative and used older texts, and this makes them very valuable in textual criticism. (Metzger, TNT, 31) It must be admitted, however, that lectionaries are of only secondary value in establishing the New Testament text for at least three reasons:

1. They contain all of the New Testament many times over, with the exception of Revelation and parts of Acts.

2. As a result of recent scholarship on the lectionaries, they are assuming a more significant role in establishing the true text. Lectionary text types are predominantly Byzantine, but there are certain groups that are characterized by Alexandrian and Caesarean readings.

3. Lectionaries have also influenced the understanding of specific passages, for example, John 7:53—8:11 and Mark. 16:9–20. (Geisler, GIB, 418)

   (A detailed listing of lectionaries may be seen in the Greek New Testaments published by United Bible Societies and Nestle-Aland, both printed in Stuttgart.)

5B. Accuracy of Manuscripts Supported by Early Church Fathers

The patristic citations of Scripture are not primary witnesses to the text of the New Testament, but they do serve two very important secondary roles. First, they give overwhelming support to the existence of the twenty-seven authoritative books of the New Testament canon. It is true that their quotations were often loose, although in the case of some Fathers they were very accu-

Early Patristic Quotations of the New Testament

Writer	Gospels	Acts	Pauline Epistles	General Epistles	Revelation	Totals
Justin Martyr	268	10	43	6	3 (266 allusions)	330
Irenaeus	1,038	194	499	23	65	1,819
Clement (Alex.)	1,107	44	1,127	207	11	2,406
Origen	9,231	349	7,778	399	165	17,992
Tertullian	3,822	502	2,609	120	205	7,258
Hippolytus	734	42	387	27	188	1,378
Eusebius	3,258	211	1,592	88	27	5,176
Grand Totals	**19,368**	**1,352**	**14,035**	**870**	**664**	**36,289**

rate, but they do at least reproduce the substantial content of the original text. Second, the quotations are so numerous and widespread that if no manuscripts of the New Testament were extant, the New Testament could be reproduced from the writings of the early Fathers alone. (Geisler, GIB, 430)

In brief, J. Harold Greenlee was right when he wrote, "These quotations are so extensive that the New Testament could virtually be reconstructed from them without the use of New Testament Manuscripts." (Greenlee, INTTC, 54)

Compare, for example, the numerous quotations given in Burgon's index in the case of a few of the earlier and more important writers in the chart above.(Geisler, GIB, 431)

Regarding patristic quotations from the New Testament, Bruce Metzger informs us that: "Besides textual evidence derived from New Testament Greek manuscripts and from early versions, the textual critic has available the numerous scriptural quota-

tions included in the commentaries, sermons, and other treatises written by early Church Fathers. Indeed, so extensive are these citations that if all other sources for our knowledge of the text of the New Testament were destroyed, they would be sufficient alone for the reconstruction of practically the entire New Testament." (Metzger, TNT, 86)

The Encyclopaedia Britannica says: "When the textual scholar has examined the manuscripts and the versions, he still has not exhausted the evidence for the New Testament text. The writings of the early Christian fathers often reflect a form of text differing from that in one or another manuscript . . . their witness to the text, especially as it corroborates the readings that come from other sources, belongs to the testimony that textual critics must consult before forming their conclusions." (EB, Vol 3, 579)

Sir David Dalrymple was wondering about the preponderance of Scripture in early writing when someone asked him, "Suppose that the New Testament had been destroyed, and every copy of it lost by the end of the third century, could it have been collected together again from the writings of the Fathers of the second and third centuries?" After a great deal of investigation Dalrymple concluded: "Look at those books. You remember the question about the New Testament and the Fathers? That question roused my curiosity, and as I possessed all the existing works of the Fathers of the second and third centuries, I commenced to search, and up to this time I have found the entire New Testament, except eleven verses." (Dalrymple, as cited in Leach, OBHWGI, 35, 36)

Joseph Angus, in *The Bible Handbook,* page 56, offers these words of caution concerning the early patristic writings:

1. Quotes are sometimes used without verbal accuracy.
2. Some copyists were prone to mistakes or to intentional alteration.

Some of the most important early witnesses to the New Testament manuscripts among the church fathers were:

Clement of Rome (A.D. 95). Origen, in *De Principus,* Book II, Chapter 3, calls him a disciple of the apostles. (Anderson, BWG, 28)

Tertullian, in *Against Heresies,* Chapter 23, writes that he (Clement) was appointed by Peter.

Irenaeus continues in *Against Heresies,* Book III, Chapter 3, that he "had the preaching of the Apostles still echoing in his ears and their doctrine in front of his eyes."

He quotes from:

Matthew	1 Corinthians
Mark	Titus
Luke	Hebrews
Acts	1 Peter

Ignatius (A.D. 70–110) was Bishop of Antioch and was martyred. He knew well the apostles. His seven epistles contain quotations from:

Matthew	Philippians
John	Colossians
Acts	1 and 2 Thessalonians
Romans	1 and 2 Timothy
1 Corinthians	James
Galatians	1 Peter
Ephesians	

Polycarp (A.D. 70–156), martyred at eighty-six years of age, was Bishop of Smyrna and a disciple of the apostle John. Among others who quoted from the New Testament were Barnabas (c. A.D. 70), Hermas (c. A.D. 95), Tatian (c. A.D. 170), and Irenaeus (c. A.D. 170).

Clement of Alexandria (A.D. 150–212). 2,400 of his quotes are from all but three books of the New Testament.

Tertullian (A.D. 160–220) was a presbyter of the church in Carthage, and quotes the New Testament more than seven thousand times, of which 3,800 are from the Gospels.

Hippolytus (A.D. 170–235) has more than 1,300 references.

Justin Martyr (A.D. 133) battled the heretic Marcion.

Origen (A.D. 185–253 or 254). This vociferous writer compiled more than six thousand works. He lists more than eighteen thousand New Testament quotes. (Geisler, GIB, 353)

Cyprian (died A.D. 258) was bishop of Carthage. Uses approximately 740 Old Testament citations and 1,030 from the New Testament.

Geisler and Nix rightly conclude that "a brief inventory at this point will reveal that there were some 32,000 citations of the New Testament prior to the time of the Council of Nicea (325). These 32,000 quotations are by no means exhaustive, and they do not even include the fourth-century writers. Just adding the number of references used by one other writer, Eusebius, who flourished prior to and contemporary with the Council at Nicea, will bring the total number of citations of the New Testament to over 36,000." (Geisler, GIB, 353, 354)

To all of the above you could add Augustine, Amabius, Laitantius, Chrysostom, Jerome, Gaius Romanus, Athanasius, Ambrose of Milan, Cyril of Alexandria, Ephraem the Syrian, Hilary of Poitiers, Gregory of Nyssa, and so forth.

Leo Jaganay, writing of the patristic quotations of the New Testament, writes: "Of the considerable volumes of unpublished material that Dean Burgon left when he died, of special note is his index of New Testament citations by the church fathers of antiquity. It consists of sixteen thick volumes to be found in the British Museum, and contains 86,489 quotations." (Jaganay, ITCNT, 48)

2A. INTERNAL EVIDENCE TEST FOR THE RELIABILITY OF THE NEW TESTAMENT

1B. Benefit of the Doubt

On this test John Warwick Montgomery writes that literary critics still follow Aristotle's dictum that "the benefit of the doubt is to be given to the document itself, not arrogated by the critic to himself." (Montgomery, EA, 29)

Therefore, "one must listen to the claims of the document under analysis, and not assume fraud or error unless the author disqualified himself by contradictions or known factual inaccuracies." (Montgomery, EA, 29)

Horn amplifies this, saying:

Think for a moment about what needs to be demonstrated concerning a "difficulty" in order to transfer it into the category of a valid argument against doctrine. Certainly much more is required than the mere appearance of

a contradiction. First, we must be certain that we have correctly understood the passage, the sense in which it uses words or numbers. Second, that we possess all available knowledge in this matter. Third, that no further light can possibly be thrown on it by advancing knowledge, textual research, archaeology, etc. . . .

Difficulties do not constitute objections. Unsolved problems are not of necessity errors. This is not to minimize the area of difficulty; it is to see it in perspective. Difficulties are to be grappled with and problems are to drive us to seek clearer light; but until such time as we have total and final light on any issue we are in no position to affirm, "Here is a proven error, an unquestionable objection to an infallible Bible." It is common knowledge that countless 'objections' have been fully resolved since this century began. (Horn, BTSI, 86, 87)

2B. Is the Document Free of Known Contradictions?

He was known around the seminary as the man who had learned over thirty languages, most of them languages of Old Testament times in the Middle Eastern world. Dr. Gleason Archer, who taught for over thirty years at the graduate seminary level in the field of biblical criticism, gives the following modest description of his qualifications to discern the meaning of difficult biblical texts:

As an undergraduate at Harvard, I was fascinated by apologetics and biblical evidences; so I labored to obtain a knowledge of the languages and cultures that have any bearing on biblical scholarship. As a classics major in college, I received training in Latin and Greek, also in French and German. At seminary I majored in Hebrew, Aramaic, and Arabic; and in post-graduate years I became involved in Syriac and Akkadian, to the extent of teaching elective courses in each of these subjects. Earlier, during my final two years of high school, I had acquired a special interest in Middle Kingdom Egyptian studies, which was furthered as I later taught courses in this field. At the Oriental Institute in Chicago, I did specialized study in Eighteenth Dynasty historical records and also studied Coptic and Sumerian. Combined with this work in ancient languages was a full course of training at law school, after which I was admitted to the Massachusetts Bar in 1939. This gave me a thorough grounding in the field of legal evidences.

Dr. Archer, in the forward to his *Encyclopedia of Bible Difficulties*, gives this testimony about the internal consistency of the Bible:

As I have dealt with one apparent discrepancy after another and have studied the alleged contradictions between the biblical record and the evidence of linguistics, archaeology, or science, my confidence in the trustworthiness of Scripture has been repeatedly verified and strengthened by the discovery that almost every problem in Scripture that has ever been discovered by man, from ancient times until now, has been dealt with in a completely satisfactory manner by the biblical text itself—or else by objective archaeological information. The deductions that may be validly drawn from ancient Egyptian, Sumerian, or Akkadian documents all harmonize with the biblical record; and no properly trained evangelical scholar has anything to fear from the hostile arguments and challenges of humanistic rationalists or detractors of any and every persuasion.

Dr. Archer concludes, "There is a good and sufficient answer in Scripture itself to refute every charge that has ever been leveled against it. But this is only to be expected from the kind of book the Bible asserts itself to be, the inscripturation of the infallible, inerrant Word of the Living God." (Archer, EBD, 12)

Students of the Bible are often troubled to find statements in the Bible that appear to contradict other statements in the Bible. For example, one of my associates had always wondered why the books of Matthew and Acts gave conflicting versions of the death of Judas Iscariot. Matthew relates that Judas died by hanging himself. But Acts says that Judas fell headlong in a field, "his body burst open and all his intestines spilled out." My friend was perplexed as to how both accounts could be true. He theorized that Judas must have hanged himself off the side of a cliff, the rope gave way, and he fell headlong into the field below. It would be the only way a fall into a field could burst open a body. Sure enough, several years later on a trip to the Holy Land, my friend was shown the traditional site of Judas's death: a field at the bottom of a cliff outside Jerusalem.

The allegations of error in the Bible are usually based on a failure to recognize basic principles of interpreting ancient literature. The following principles can help one discern whether there is a true error or a contradiction in the literature—in this case, the Bible:

Principle #1: The Unexplained Is Not Necessarily Unexplainable. No informed person would claim to be able to fully explain all Bible difficulties. However, it is a mistake for the critic to assume, therefore, that what has not yet been explained never will be explained. When a scientist comes upon an anomaly in nature, he does not give up further scientific exploration. Rather, he uses the unexplained as a motivation to find an explanation.

Scientists, for example, once had no natural explanation of meteors, eclipses, tornadoes, hurricanes, and earthquakes. Until recently, scientists did not know how the bumblebee could fly. But no scientist throws in the towel and cries "contradiction!" All of these mysteries have yielded their secrets to the relentless patience of science.

Likewise, the Christian scholar approaches the Bible with the same presumption that what is thus far unexplained is not therefore unexplainable. He or she does not assume that discrepancies are contradictions. And when he encounters something for which he has no explanation, he simply continues to do research, believing that one will eventually be found. In fact, if he assumed the opposite he would stop studying. Why pursue an answer when one assumes there is none?

Like his scientific counterpart, the Bible student has been rewarded for his faith and research. Many difficulties for which scholars once had no answer have yielded to the relentless pursuit of answers through history, archaeology, linguistics, and other disciplines. For example, critics once proposed that Moses could not have written the first five books of the Bible because there was no writing in Moses' day. Now we know that writing existed a couple of thousand years or more before Moses. Likewise, critics once believed that the Bible was wrong in speaking of the Hittite people, since they were totally unknown to historians. Now historians know of their existence by way of a Hittite library found in Turkey. This gives us confidence to believe that biblical difficulties not yet explained do have an explanation, and we need not assume that there is a mistake in the Bible.

But when we begin to examine the instances brought forward in support of it (i.e., alleged contradictions in the Bible), they are found to be cases of *difficult,* not of *impossible,* harmony. And it is abundantly plain that it must be shown to be *impossible* to harmonize any two statements on any natural supposition before they can be asserted to be inconsistent. This is a recognized principle of historical investigation, and it is the only reasonable principle possible, unless we are prepared to assert that the two statements necessarily contain all the facts of the case and exclude the possibility of the harmonizing supposition (p. 54, italics theirs). (Geisler, DY, 52)

Principle #2: Fallible Interpretations Do Not Mean Fallible Revelation. Human beings are finite, and finite beings make mistakes. That is why there are erasers on pencils and "delete" keys on computers. As long as imperfect human beings exist, there will be misinterpretations of God's Word and false views about His world. One should not assume that a currently dominant view in science is the final word on the

---

SUMMARY OF PRINCIPLES FOR UNDERSTANDING APPARENT DISCREPANCIES IN THE BIBLE

1. The unexplained is not necessarily unexplainable.
2. Fallible interpretations do not mean fallible revelation.
3. Understand the context of the passage.
4. Interpret difficult passages in the light of clear ones.
5. Don't base teaching on obscure passages.
6. The Bible is a human book with human characteristics.
7. Just because a report is incomplete does not mean it is false.
8. New Testament citations of the Old Testament need not always be exact.
9. The Bible does not necessarily approve of all it records.
10. The Bible uses non-technical, everyday language.
11. The Bible may use round numbers as well as exact numbers.
12. Note when the Bible uses different literary devices.
13. An error in a copy does not equate to an error in the original.
14. General statements don't necessarily mean universal promises.
15. Later revelation supercedes previous revelation.

topic. Prevailing views of science in the past are considered errors by scientists in the present. So, contradictions between popular opinions in science and widely accepted interpretations of the Bible can be expected. But these conflicts fall short of proving there are real contradictions between God's world and God's Word.

Principle #3: Understand the Context of the Passage. Perhaps the most common mistake of critics is to take a text out of its proper context. As the adage goes, "A text out of context is a pretext." One can prove anything from the Bible by this mistaken procedure. The Bible says, "there is no God" (Ps. 14:1). Of course, the context is that "The fool has said in his heart, 'There is no God'" (Ps. 14:1). One may claim that Jesus admonished us to "resist not evil" (Matt. 5:39 KJV), but the anti-retaliatory context in which He cast this statement must not be ignored. Likewise, many fail to understand the context of Jesus' statement "Give to him who asks you." Does this mean that one should give a gun to a small child who asks, or nuclear weapons to Saddam Hussein because he asks? Failure to note the meaning in light of its context is perhaps the chief error of those who find fault with the Bible.

Principle #4: Interpret Difficult Passages in the Light of Clear Ones. Some passages of Scripture are hard to understand. Sometimes the difficulty is due to their obscurity. Sometimes one Scripture teaching appears to contradict another passage of Scripture. For example, James appears to say that salvation is by works (James 2:14–26), whereas Paul taught clearly that salvation is by grace (Rom. 4:5; Titus 3:5–7; Eph. 2:8–9). In this case, James should *not* be construed so as to contradict Paul. Paul is speaking about justification before *God* (which is by faith alone), whereas James is referring to justification

before *men* (who cannot see our faith, but only our works).

Another example is Philippians 2:12 where Paul writes, "work out your own salvation with fear and trembling." On the surface this appears to be saying that salvation is by works. However, this is flatly contradicted by a host of Scriptures that clearly affirm that we are "saved through faith, and that not of yourselves; it is the gift of God, not of works, lest anyone should boast" (Eph. 2:8–9). And, "to him who does not work but believes on Him who justifies the ungodly, his faith is accounted for righteousness" (Rom. 4:5). When this difficult statement about "working out our salvation" is understood in the light of these clear passages, we can see that, whatever it *does* mean, it *does not* mean that we are saved by our works. In fact, what it means is found in the very next verse. We are to work our salvation out because God's grace has worked it in our hearts. In Paul's words, "for it is God who works in you both to will and to do for His good pleasure" (Phil. 2:13).

Principle #5: Don't Base Teaching on Obscure Passages. Some Bible passages are difficult because their meanings are obscure. This is usually because a key word in the text is used only once (or rarely), and so it is difficult to know what the author is saying, unless it can be inferred from the context. For example, one of the best known passages in the Bible contains a word that appears nowhere else in all existing Greek literature up to the time the NT was written. This word appears in what is popularly known as the Lord's Prayer (Matt. 6:11). It is usually translated, "Give us this day our daily bread." The word in question is the one translated "daily"—*epiousion*. Experts in Greek still have not come to any agreement either on its origin or on its precise meaning. Different commentators try to establish links with Greek words that are well-known, and many suggestions have been proposed as to the resulting meaning. Among these suggestions are:

- Give us this day our *continuous bread.*
- Give us this day *our supersubstantial* (or supernatural, from heaven) bread.
- Give us this day bread for *our sustenance.*
- Give us this day our *daily* (what we need for today) bread.

Each proposal has its defenders, each makes sense in the context, and each is based on the limited information available. There does not seem to be any compelling reason to depart from what has become the generally accepted translation. But this example serves to illustrate our point. Some passages of the Bible are difficult to understand because the meaning of some key word appears only once, or very rarely.

At other times, the words may be clear but the meaning is not evident because we are not sure to what they refer. In 1 Corinthians 15:29 Paul speaks of those who were "baptized for the dead." Is he referring to the baptizing of live representatives to ensure salvation for dead believers who were not baptized (as Mormons claim)? Or is he referring to others being baptized into the church to fill the ranks of those who have passed on? Or is he referring to a believer being baptized "for" (i.e., "with a view to") his own death and burial with Christ? Or is he referring to something else?

When we are not sure:

1. We should not build a doctrine on an *obscure* passage. The rule of thumb in Bible interpretation is "the main things are the plain things, and the plain things are the main things." This is called the perspicuity (clearness) of Scripture. If something is important, it will be clearly taught in Scripture, and probably in more than one place.
2. When a given passage is not clear, never conclude that it means something that opposes another plain teaching of Scripture.

Principle #6: The Bible Is a Human Book with Human Characteristics. The Bible claims that God used human personalities to receive and communicate eternal truths. Therefore, expressions of speech (such as when Jesus used exaggeration) should not always be taken literally, then pitted against another portion of Scripture.

Principle #7: Just Because a Report is Incomplete Does Not Mean It Is False. For example, Mark 5:1–20 and Luke 8:26–39 speak of only one demoniac, while Matthew 8:28–34 speaks of two. Mark and Luke, likely using the same firsthand report of the incident, are giving a partial report that focuses on the more prominent of the two demoniacs in the event. The accounts are not contradictory. They are actually complimentary, supplying more information when both are taken together.

Principle #8: New Testament Citations of the Old Testament Need Not Always Be Exact. Just as in our day there is more than one translation of the Bible, early Christians often cited the Septuagint (the Greek translation of the Old Testament), which gave slightly different wording to the same text.

As I have dealt with one apparent discrepancy after another and have studied the alleged contradictions between the biblical record and the evidence of linguistics, archaeology, or science, my confidence in the trustworthiness of Scripture has been repeatedly verified and strengthened.

—DR. GLEASON ARCHER

Principle #9: The Bible Does Not Necessarily Approve of All It Records. It is a mistake to assume that everything contained in the Bible is commended by the Bible. The Bible records some lies—Satan's (Gen. 3:4; cf. John 8:44) and Rahab's (Josh. 2:4), for example. It does not necessarily condone those lies, it simply records accurately and truthfully even the lies and errors of sinful beings. The truth of Scripture is found in what the Bible reveals, not in everything it records. Unless this distinction is maintained, one might incorrectly conclude that the Bible teaches immorality when it narrates David's sin (2 Sam. 11:4), that it promotes polygamy when it records Solomon's many wives (1 Kin. 11:3), or that it affirms atheism when it quotes the fool as saying "there is no God" (Ps. 14:1).

Principle #10: The Bible Uses Non-technical, Everyday Language. Just because a term in the Bible is non-scientific does not necessarily mean that the term is inaccurate. Scientific truths such as the revolving of the earth may be described in language idioms of the time (e.g., the sun running though its circuit).

Principle #11: The Bible May Use Both Round Numbers As Well As Exact Numbers. Round numbers are often used in ancient as well as modern literature. The Bible often contains this same linguistic convention.

Principle #12: Note When the Bible Uses Different Literary Devices. Usually, the context will dictate whether a term should be taken literally or figuratively.

Principle #13: An Error in a Copy Does Not Equate to an Error in the Original. When theologians talk about the inerrancy of the Scriptures, they are referring to the Scriptures as originally written—the autographs—as opposed to a copy or a copy of a copy.

Principle #14: General Statements Don't Necessarily Mean Universal Promises. Critics

often jump to the conclusion that unqualified statements admit of no exceptions. They seize upon verses that offer general truths, and then point with glee to obvious exceptions. In so doing they forget that such statements are only intended to be generalizations.

The Book of Proverbs is a good example. Proverbial sayings by their very nature offer only general guidance, not universal assurance. They are rules for life, but rules that admit of exceptions. Proverbs 16:7 is a case in point. It affirms that "when a man's ways please the Lord, He makes even his enemies to be at peace with him." This statement obviously was not intended to be a universal truth. Paul was pleasing to the Lord, but his enemies stoned him (Acts 14:19). Jesus pleased the Lord, and His enemies crucified Him! Nonetheless, it is generally true that one who acts in a way pleasing to God will often attract his enemy to his side. Just look at how Paul was attracted to Jesus!

Principle #15: Later Revelation Supercedes Previous Revelation. The Bible gives abundant evidence of progressive revelation. That is, God did not reveal everything at once, nor did He always lay down the same conditions for every period of time. Therefore, some of His later revelation supersedes His former statements. Bible critics sometimes interpret a *change* of revelation to mean a mistake.

For example, the fact that a parent allows a very small child to eat with his fingers, only to tell him later to use a spoon, is not a contradiction. Nor does the parent contradict himself when he later insists that the child use a fork, not a spoon, to eat his vegetables. This is progressive revelation, with each command suited to fit the particular circumstance.

There was a period (under the Mosaic Law) when God commanded that animals be sacrificed for people's sin. However, since

Christ has since offered the perfect sacrifice for sin (Heb. 10:11–14), this OT command no longer prevails. Likewise, when God created the human race, He commanded that they eat only fruit and vegetables (Gen. 1:29). Later, when conditions changed after the flood, God commanded that they also eat meat (Gen. 9:3). This change from herbivorous to omnivorous status is an example of progressive revelation, and is not a contradiction. In fact, all these subsequent revelations were simply different commands for different people at different times in God's overall plan of redemption.

A person who takes the Bible seriously, rather than tries to explain it away, may agree with Mark Twain when he said that it was not the part of the Bible he did not understand that bothered him the most, but the parts he did understand! (Geisler and Howe, WCA, 15–26)

3B. Did the Writer Use Primary Sources?

The writers of the New Testament wrote as eyewitnesses or from firsthand information. The books of the New Testament make claims such as the following:

Luke 1:1–3: "Inasmuch as many have undertaken to set in order a narrative of those things which have been fulfilled among us, just as those who from the beginning were eyewitnesses and ministers of the word delivered them to us, it seemed good to me also, having had perfect understanding of all things from the very first, to write to you an orderly account, most excellent Theophilus."

2 Peter 1:16: "For we did not follow cunningly devised fables when we made known to you the power and coming of our Lord Jesus Christ, but were eyewitnesses of His majesty."

1 John 1:3: "That which we have seen and heard we declare to you, that you also may have fellowship with us, and truly our fellowship is with the Father and with His Son Jesus Christ."

Acts 2:22: " 'Men of Israel, hear these words: Jesus of Nazareth, a Man attested by God to you by miracles, wonders, and signs which God did through Him in your midst, as you yourselves also know.'"

John 19:35 "And he who has seen has testified, and his testimony is true; and he knows that he is telling the truth, so that you may believe."

Luke 3:1: "Now in the fifteenth year of the reign of Tiberius Caesar, Pontius Pilate being governor of Judea, Herod being tetrarch of Galilee, his brother Phillip tetrarch of Iturea and the region of Trachonitis, and Lysanias tetrarch of Abilene."

Acts 26:24–26: "Now as he thus made his defense, Festus said with a loud voice, 'Paul, you are beside yourself! Much learning is driving you mad!' But he said, 'I am not mad, most noble Festus, but speak the words of truth and reason. For the king, before whom I also speak freely, knows these things; for I am convinced that none of these things escapes his attention, since this thing was not done in a corner.'"

F. F. Bruce, the former Rylands Professor of Biblical Criticism and Exegesis at the University of Manchester, says, concerning the primary-source value of the New Testament records:

The earliest preachers of the gospel knew the value of . . . first-hand testimony, and appealed to it time and again. "We are witnesses of these things," was their constant and confident assertion. And it can have been by no means so easy as some writers seem to think to invent words and deeds of Jesus in those early years, when so many of His disciples were about, who could remember what had and had not happened.

And it was not only friendly eyewitnesses

that the early preachers had to reckon with; there were others less well disposed who were also conversant with the main facts of the ministry and death of Jesus. The disciples could not afford to risk inaccuracies (not to speak of willful manipulation of the facts), which would at once be exposed by those who would be only too glad to do so. On the contrary, one of the strong points in the original apostolic preaching is the confident appeal to the knowledge of the hearers; they not only said, "We are witnesses of these things," but also, "As you yourselves also know" (Acts 2:22). Had there been any tendency to depart from the facts in any material respect, the possible presence of hostile witnesses in the audience would have served as a further corrective. (Bruce, NTD, 33,44–46)

But some might contend, saying, "Come on, Josh, that's only what the writers claimed. A pseudo-author writing a century or more after the fact can claim anything."

The fact is, however, that the books of the New Testament were not written down a century or more after the events they described, but during the lifetimes of those involved in the accounts themselves. Therefore, the New Testament must be regarded by scholars today as a competent primary source document from the first century. (Montgomery, HC, 34,35)

Figures on the charts on this page are from the following sources: Werner Georg Kümmel's *Introduction to the New Testament,* translated by Howard Clark Kee, Abingdon Press, 1973; Everett Harrison's *Introduction to the New Testament,* William B. Eerdmans Publishing Co., 1971; D. Edmond Hiebert's *Introduction to the New Testament,* Vol. II, Moody Press, 1977; writings and lectures by T. W. Manson and F. C. Baur.

William Foxwell Albright, one of the world's foremost biblical archaeologists, said: "We can already say emphatically that

CONSERVATIVE DATING		
(In some cases [e.g. Matthew's Gospel], now being revised as not conservative enough)		
Paul's Letters	A.D. 50-66	(Hiebert)
Matthew	A.D. 70-80	(Harrison)
Mark	A.D. 50–60	(Harnak)
	A.D. 58–65	(T. W. Manson)
Luke	early 60s	(Harrison)
John	A.D. 80–100	(Harrison)
LIBERAL DATING		
(In some cases, proven to be impossible [e.g. John's Gospel]; in others, rarely accepted by competent scholars today)		
Paul's Letters	A.D. 50–100	(Kümmel)
Matthew	A.D. 80–100	(Kümmel)
Mark	A.D. 70	(Kümmel)
Luke	A.D. 70–90	(Kümmel)
John	A.D. 170	(Baur)
	A.D. 90–100	(Kümmel)

there is no longer any solid basis for dating any book of the New Testament after about A.D. 80, two full generations before the date between 130 and 150 given by the more radical New Testament critics of today." (Albright, RDBL, 136)

He reiterates this point in an interview for *Christianity Today,* 18 Jan. 1963: "In my opinion, every book of the New Testament was written by a baptized Jew between the forties and the eighties of the first century A.D. (very probably some time between about A.D. 50 and 75)."

Albright concludes, "Thanks to the Qumran discoveries, the New Testament proves to be in fact what it was formerly believed to be: the teaching of Christ and his immediate followers between cir. 25 and cir. 80 A.D." (Albright, FSAC, 23)

Many liberal scholars are being forced to consider earlier dates for the New Testament. Dr. John A. T. Robinson, no conservative himself, comes to some startling conclusions in his groundbreaking book *Redating the New Testament*. His research has led to his conviction that the whole of the New Testament was written before the fall of Jerusalem in A.D. 70. (Robinson, RNT)

3A. EXTERNAL EVIDENCE TEST FOR THE RELIABILITY OF THE NEW TESTAMENT

"Do other historical materials confirm or deny the internal testimony provided by the documents themselves?" (Montgomery, HC, 31) In other words, what sources are there—apart from the literature under analysis—that substantiate its accuracy, reliability, and authenticity?

1B. Supporting Evidence of Early Christian Writers Outside the Bible

Eusebius, in his *Ecclesiastical History III.39*, preserves writings of Papias, bishop of Heirapolis (A.D. 130), in which Papius records sayings of "the Elder" (the apostle John):

The Elder used to say this also: "Mark, having been the interpreter of Peter, wrote down accurately all that he (Peter) mentioned, whether sayings or doings of Christ, not, however, in order. For he was neither a hearer nor a companion of the Lord; but afterwards, as I

> *Eighty and six years have I served Him, and He hath done me no wrong. How can I speak evil of my King who saved me?*
>
> —POLYCARP (A DISCIPLE OF JOHN) JUST BEFORE BEING BURNED ALIVE FOR HIS FAITH AT AGE 86

said, he accompanied Peter, who adapted his teachings as necessity required, not as though he were making a compilation of the sayings of the Lord. So then Mark made no mistake writing down in this way some things as he (Peter) mentioned them; for he paid attention to this one thing, not to omit anything that he had heard, not to include any false statement among them."

Papias also comments about the Gospel of Matthew: "Matthew recorded the oracles in the Hebrew (i.e., Aramaic) tongue."

Irenaeus, Bishop of Lyons (A.D. 180), who was a student of Polycarp, Bishop of Smyrna; martyred in A.D. 156 , had been a Christian for eighty-six years, and was a disciple of John the Apostle. He wrote: "So firm is the ground upon which these Gospels rest, that the very heretics themselves bear witness to them, and, starting from these [documents], each one of them endeavours to establish his own particular doctrine." (*Against Heresies III*)

The four Gospels had become so axiomatic in the Christian world that Irenaeus can refer to it [the fourfold Gospel] as an established and recognized fact as obvious as the four cardinal points of the compass:

For as there are four quarters of the world in which we live, and four universal winds, and as the Church is dispersed over all the earth, and the gospel is the pillar and base of the Church and the breath of life, so it is natural that it should have four pillars, breathing immortality from every quarter and kindling the life of men anew. Whence it is manifest that the Word, the architect of all things, who sits upon the cherubim and holds all things together, having been manifested to men, has given us the gospel in fourfold form, but held together by one Spirit.

Matthew published his Gospel among the Hebrews (i.e., Jews) in their own tongue, when Peter and Paul were preaching the gospel in Rome and founding the church there. After their departure (i.e., their death, which strong tradition places at the time of the Neronian persecution in 64), Mark, the disciple and interpreter of Peter, himself handed down to us in writing the substance of Peter's preaching. Luke, the follower of Paul, set down in a book the gospel preached by his teacher. Then John, the disciple of the Lord, who also leaned on His breast (this is a reference to John 13:25 and 21:20), himself produced his Gospel, while he was living at Ephesus in Asia. (Irenaus, AH)

Clement of Rome (c. A.D. 95) uses Scripture as a reliable and authentic source.

Ignatius (A.D. 70–110). This Bishop of Antioch was martyred for his faith in Christ. He knew all the apostles and was a disciple of Polycarp, who was a disciple of the apostle John. (Liplady, TIB, 209)

Elgin Moyer in *Who Was Who in Church History* writes that Ignatius "himself said, I would rather die for Christ than rule the whole earth. Leave me to the beasts that I may by them be partaker of God. He is said to have been thrown to the wild beasts in the colosseum at Rome. His Epistles were written during his journey from Antioch to his martyrdom." (Moyer, WWWCH, 209)

Ignatius gave credence to the Scripture by the way he based his faith on the accuracy of the Bible. He had ample material and witnesses to support the trustworthiness of the Scriptures.

Polycarp (A.D. 70–156) was a disciple of John who succumbed to martyrdom at eighty-six years of age for his relentless devotion to Christ and the Scriptures. Poly-

carp's death demonstrated his trust in the accuracy of the Scripture. "About 155, in the reign of Antoninus Pius, when a local persecution was taking place in Smyrna and several of his members had been martyred, he was singled out as the leader of the Church, and marked for martyrdom. When asked to recant and live, he is reputed to have said, 'Eighty and six years have I served Him, and He hath done me no wrong. How can I speak evil of my King who saved me?' He was burned at the stake, dying a heroic martyr for his faith." (Moyer, WWWCH, 337) Polycarp certainly had ample contacts to verify the truth.

Tatian (c. A.D. 170) organized the Scriptures in order to put them in the first "harmony of the Gospels," the Diatessaron.

2B. Early Non-Christian Confirmation of New Testament History

Negative Bible critics charge or imply that the New Testament documents are unreliable since they were written by disciples of Jesus or later Christians. They note that there is no confirmation of Jesus or New Testament events in non-Christian sources. Not only is this claim false, but, as Geisler notes,

The objection that the writings are partisan involves a significant but false implication that witnesses cannot be reliable if they were close to the one about whom they gave testimony. This is clearly false. Survivors of the Jewish holocaust were close to the events they have described to the world. That very fact puts them in the best position to know what happened. They were there, and it happened to them. The same applies to the court testimony of someone who survived a vicious attack. It applies to the survivors of the Normandy invasion during World War II or the Tet Offensive during the Vietnam War. The New Testament witnesses should not be disqualified because they were close to the events they relate.

Geisler adds,

Suppose there were four eyewitnesses to a murder. There was also one witness who arrived on the scene after the actual killing and saw only the victim's body. Another person heard a secondhand report of the killing. In the trial the defense attorney argues: "Other than the four eyewitnesses, this is a weak case, and the charges should be dismissed for lack of evidence." Others might think that attorney was throwing out a red herring. The judge and jury were being distracted from the strongest evidence to the weakest evidence, and the reasoning was clearly faulty. Since the New Testament witnesses were the only eyewitness and contemporary testimonies to Jesus, it is a fallacy to misdirect attention to the non-Christian secular sources. Nonetheless, it is instructive to show what confirming evidence for Jesus can be gleaned outside the New Testament. (Geisler, BECA, 381)

The references below are discussed in greater detail in my book with Bill Wilson, *He Walked Among Us.* (McDowell, HWAU)

1C. Tacitus

The first-century Roman, Tacitus, is considered one of the more accurate historians of the ancient world. He gives the account of the great fire of Rome, for which some blamed the Emperor Nero:

Consequently, to get rid of the report, Nero fastened the guilt and inflicted the most exquisite tortures on a class hated for their abominations, called Christians by the populace. Christus, from whom the name had its origin, suffered the extreme penalty during the reign of Tiberius at the hands of one of our procurators, Pontius Pilatus, and a most mischievous superstition, thus checked for the moment, again broke out not only in Judea, the first source of the evil, but even in Rome, where all things hideous and shameful from every part of the world find their center

and become popular. (Tacitus, A, 15.44)

The "mischievous superstition" to which Tacitus refers is most likey the resurrection of Jesus. The same is true for one of the references of Suetonius which follows.

2C. Suetonius

Suetonius was chief secretary to Emperor Hadrian (who reigned from A.D. 117–138). He confirms the report in Acts 18:2 that Claudius commanded all Jews (among them Priscilla and Aquila) to leave Rome in A.D. 49. Two references are important:

"As the Jews were making constant disturbances at the instigation of Chrestus, he expelled them from Rome." (Suetonius, *Life of Claudius*, 25.4)

Speaking of the aftermath of the great fire at Rome, Suetonius reports, "Punishment was inflicted on the Christians, a body of people addicted to a novel and mischievous superstition." (Suetonius, *Life of Nero*, 16)

Since Suetonius wrote of these events approximately seventy-five years after their occurrence, he was not in a position to know whether the disturbances were actually instigated by one named Chrestus or because of one by that name. He is probably referring to the dispute between the Jewish people as to the identity of Jesus.

3C. Josephus

Josephus (c. A.D. 37–c. A.D. 100) was a Pharisee of the priestly line and a Jewish historian, though working under Roman authority and with some care as to not offend the Romans. In addition to his autobiography he wrote two major works, *Jewish Wars* (A.D. 77–78) and *Antiquities of the Jews* (c. A.D. 94). He also wrote a minor work, *Against Apion*. He makes many statements that verify, either generally or in specific detail, the historical nature of both the Old and New Testaments of the Bible.

1D. Testimony to the Canon

Josephus supports the Protestant view of the canon of the Old Testament against the Roman Catholic view, which venerates the Old Testament Apocrypha. He even lists the names of the books, which are identical with the thirty-nine books of the Protestant Old Testament. He groups the thirty-nine into twenty-two volumes, to correspond with the number of letters in the Hebrew alphabet: "For we have not an innumerable multitude of books among us, disagreeing from and contradicting one another [as the Greeks have], but only twenty-two books, which contain the records of all the past times; which are justly believed to be divine; and of them, five belong to Moses, which contain his laws. . . . The prophets, who were after Moses, wrote down what was done in their times in thirteen books. The remaining four books contain hymns to God, and precepts for the conduct of human life." (Josephus, AA, 1.8)

Josephus's reference to Daniel the prophet as a sixth-century B.C. writer (Josephus, AJ, 10–12) confirms, as Geisler points out, "the supernatural nature of Daniel's amazing predictions about the course of history after his time. Unlike the later Talmud, Josephus obviously lists Daniel among the prophets, since it is not in Moses or the "hymns to God" section, which would include Psalms, Proverbs, Ecclesiastes, and Song of Solomon. This helps confirm the early date of Daniel." (Geisler, BECA, 254)

2D. Testimony to the New Testament

1E. James the brother of Jesus. Josephus refers to Jesus as the brother of James who was martyred. Referring to the High Priest, Ananias, he writes: " . . . he assembled the Sanhedrin of the judges, and brought before them the brother of Jesus, who was called Christ, whose name was James, and some others, [or some of his companions], and when he had formed an accusation against them as breakers of the law, he delivered them to be stoned." (Josephus, AJ, 20.9.1)

This passage, written in A.D. 93, confirms the New Testament reports that Jesus was a real person in the first century, that he was identified by others as the Christ, and that he had a brother named James who died a martyr's death at the hands of the high priest, Albinus, and his Sanhedrin.

2E. John the Baptist. Josephus also confirmed the existence and martyrdom of John the Baptist, the herald of Jesus. (Ant. XVIII. 5.2) Because of the manner in which this passage is written, there is no ground for suspecting Christian interpolation.

"Now, some of the Jews thought that the destruction of Herod's army came from God, and very justly, as a punishment of what he did against John, who was called the Baptist; for Herod slew him, who was a good man, and commanded the Jews to exercise virtue, both as to righteousness towards one another and piety towards God, and so to come to baptism." (Josephus, AJ, 18.5.2)

The differences between Josephus's account of John the Baptist's baptism and that of the Gospel is that Josephus wrote that John's baptism was not for the remission of sin, while the Bible (Mark 1:4) says it was; and that John was killed for political reasons and not for his denunciation of Herod's marriage to Herodias. As Bruce points out, it is quite possible that Herod believed he could kill two birds with one stone by imprisoning John. In regard to the discrepancy over his baptism, Bruce says that the Gospels give a more probable account from the "religious-historical" point of view and that they are older than Josephus's work and, therefore, more accurate. However, the real point is that the general outline of Josephus' account confirms that of the Gospels. (Bruce, NTD, 107)

3E. Jesus. In a disputed text, Josephus gives a brief description of Jesus and his mission:

> Now there was about this time, Jesus, a wise man, if it be lawful to call him a man, for he was a doer of wonderful works, a teacher of such men as receive the truth with pleasure. He drew over to him both many of the Jews and many of the Gentiles. He was [the] Christ; and when Pilate, at the suggestion of the principal men amongst us, had condemned him to the cross, those that loved him at the first did not forsake him. For he appeared to them alive again the third day, as the divine prophets had foretold these and ten thousand other wonderful things concerning him; and the tribe of Christians, so named from him, are not extinct to this day. (Josephus, AJ, 18.3.3)

This passage was cited by Eusebius (c. A.D. 325) in its present form (*Ecclesiastical History*, 1.11) and the manuscript evidence favors it. It exists in all the extant copies of this text. Still, it is widely considered to be an interpolation, since it is unlikely that Josephus, a Jew, would affirm that Jesus was the Messiah and had been proven so by fulfilled prophecy, miraculous deeds, and the resurrection from the dead. Even "Origin says that Josephus did not believe Jesus to be the Messiah, nor proclaim him as such." (*Contra Celsus* 2.47; 2.13; Bruce, NTD, 108)

F. F Bruce suggests that the phrase "if indeed we should call him a man" may indicate that the text is authentic but that Josephus is writing with tongue in cheek in sarcastic reference to Christian belief that Jesus is the Son of God. (Bruce, NTD, 109)

Other scholars have suggested amending the text in ways that preserve its authenticity without the implication that Josephus personally accepted that Christ was the Messiah. (see Bruce, NTD, 110–111)

It may be that a fourth-century Arabic text (found in a tenth-century Arabic manuscript) reflects the original intent:

> At this time there was a wise man who was called Jesus. And his conduct was good and [he] was known to be virtuous. Many people from among the Jews and other nations became his disciples. Pilate condemned him to be crucified and to die. And those who had become his disciples did not abandon his discipleship. They reported that he had appeared to them three days after his crucifixion and that he was alive; accordingly, he was perhaps the messiah concerning whom the prophets have recounted wonders. (This passage is found in the Arabic manuscript entitled *Kitab Al-Unwan Al-Mukallal Bi-Fadail Al-Hikma Al-Mutawwaj Bi-Anwa Al-Falsafa Al-Manduh Bi-Haqaq Al-Marifa.*)

For Further Study on Josephus:

F. F. Bruce, *The New Testament Documents: Are They Reliable?*

L. H. Feldman, *Studies on Philo and Josephus*

Josephus, *Against Apion*

Josephus, *Antiquities of the Jews*

Josephus, *Jewish Wars*

S. Pines, *An Arabic Version of the Testimonium Flavianum and Its Implications*

R. J. H. Shutt, *Studies in Josephus*

H. St. J. Thackeray, *Josephus the Man and the Historian*

4C. Thallus

Thallus wrote around A.D. 52. None of his works is extant, though a few fragmented citations are preserved by other writers. One such writer is Julius Africanus, who in about A.D. 221 quotes Thallus in a discussion about the darkness that followed the crucifixion of Christ: "On the whole world there pressed a most fearful darkness, and the rocks were rent by an earthquake, and many places in Judea and other districts were thrown down. This darkness Thallus, in the third book of his *History,* calls, as appears to me without reason, an eclipse of the sun." (Julius Africanus, *Chronography,* 18.1 in Roberts, ANF)

Africanus identifies the darkness, which Thallus explained as a solar eclipse, with the darkness at the crucifixion described in Luke 23:44–45. His reason for disagreeing with Thallus is that a solar eclipse can not take place at the time of a full moon, and the account reports that "it was at the season of the paschal full moon that Jesus died."

5C. Pliny the Younger

Ancient government officials often held positions that gave them access to official information not available to the public. Pliny the Younger was a Roman author and administrator. In a letter to the Emperor Trajan in about A.D. 112, Pliny describes the early Christian worship practices:

> They were in the habit of meeting on a certain fixed day before it was light, when they sang in alternate verses a hymn to Christ, as to a god, and bound themselves by a solemn oath, not to do any wicked deeds, but never to commit any fraud, theft or adultery, never to falsify their word, nor deny a trust when they should be called upon to deliver it up; after which it was their custom to separate, and then reassemble to partake of food—but food of an ordinary and innocent kind. (Pliny the Younger, L, 10:96)

This reference provides solid evidence that Jesus Christ was worshipped as God from an early date by Christians who contin-

ued to follow the practice of breaking bread together, as reported in Acts 2:42 and 46.

6C. Emperor Trajan

In reply to Pliny's letter, Emperor Trajan gave the following guidelines for punishing Christians: "No search should be made for these people, when they are denounced and found guilty they must be punished, with the restriction, however, that when the party denies himself to be a Christian, and shall give proof that he is not (that is, by adoring our gods) he shall be pardoned on the ground of repentance even though he may have formerly incurred suspicion." (Pliny the Younger, L, 10:97)

7C. Talmud

Talmudic writings of most value concerning the historical Jesus are those compiled between A.D. 70 and 200 during the so-called *Tannaitic Period.* The most significant text is Sanhedrin 43a: "On the eve of Passover Yeshu was hanged. For forty days before the execution took place, a herald went forth and cried, 'He is going forth to be stoned because he has practiced sorcery and enticed Israel to apostasy. Any one who can say anything in his favour let him come forward and plead on his behalf.' But since nothing was brought forward in his favour he was hanged on the eve of the Passover!" (Babylonian Talmud)

New Testament details confirmed by this passage include the fact and the time of the crucifixion, as well as the intent of the Jewish religious leaders to kill Jesus.

8C. Lucian

Lucian of Samosata was a second-century Greek writer whose works contain sarcastic critiques of Christianity:

> The Christians, you know, worship a man to this day—the distinguished personage who

introduced their novel rites, and was crucified on that account. . . . You see, these misguided creatures start with the general conviction that they are immortal for all time, which explains the contempt of death and voluntary self-devotion which are so common among them; and then it was impressed on them by their original lawgiver that they are all brothers, from the moment that they are converted, and deny the gods of Greece, and worship the crucified sage, and live after his laws. All this they take quite on faith, with the result that they despise all worldly goods alike, regarding them merely as common property. (Lucian of Samosata, DP, 11–13)

Dr. Gary Habermas, a leading researcher and writer on the historical events surrounding Jesus, lists several verified facts that can be ascertained from this text: "Jesus was worshiped by Christians. . . . Jesus introduced new teachings in Palestine. . . . He was crucified because of these teachings. . . . such as all believers are brothers, from the moment that conversion takes place, and after the false gods are denied. . . . [Also] these teachings included worshiping Jesus and living according to his laws. (Habermas, HJ, 206–207)

Habermas adds: "Concerning Christians, we are told that they are followers of Jesus who believe themselves to be immortal. . . . [They] accepted Jesus' teachings by faith and practiced their faith by their disregard for material possessions." (Habermas, HJ, 207)

Dr. Geisler concludes, regarding Lucian, "Despite being one of the church's most vocal critics, Lucian gives one of the most informative accounts of Jesus and early Christianity outside the New Testament." (Geisler, BECA, 383)

9C. Mara Bar-Serapion

A Syrian, Mara Bar-Serapion wrote to his son Serapion sometime between the late first and early third centuries. The letter contains an apparent reference to Jesus:

What advantage did the Athenians gain from putting Socrates to death? Famine and plague came upon them as a judgment for their crime. What advantage did the men of Samon gain from burning Pythagoras? In a moment their land was covered with sand. What advantage did the Jews gain from executing their wise King? It was just after that their kingdom was abolished. God justly avenged these three wise men: the Athenians died of hunger; the Samians were overwhelmed by the sea; the Jews, ruined and driven from their land, live in dispersion. But Socrates did not die for good; he lived on in the statue of Hera. Nor did the wise king die for good; he lived on in the teaching which he had given. (British Museum, Syriac ms, add. 14, 658; cited in Habermas, HJ, 200)

10C. The Gospel of Truth

Immediately after the time of Christ, several non-Christian groups flourished in loose connection with the church. One of the more successful was the gnostics. This second-century book was perhaps written by Valentinus (A.D. 135–160). It confirms that Jesus was a historical person in several passages:

"For when they had seen him and heard him, he granted them to taste him and to smell him and to touch the beloved Son. When he had appeared instructing them about the Father. . . . For he came by means of fleshly appearance." (Robinson, NHL, 30:27–33; 31:4–6)

"Jesus was patient in accepting sufferings since he knows that his death is life for many. . . . He was nailed to a tree; he published the edict of the Father on the cross. . . . He draws himself down to death through life. Having stripped himself of the perishable rags, he put on imperishability, which no one can possibly take away from him." (Robinson, NHL, 20:11–14, 25–34)

11C. The Acts of Pontius Pilate

Beside the extant non-Christian sources for the life of Christ, some documents are hinted at but have not been found. Although a purportedly official document, *The Acts of Pontius Pilate* does not survive; it is referred to by Justin Martyr in about A.D. 150, and by Tertullian in about A.D. 200. Justin writes:

"And the expression, 'They pierced my hands and my Feet,' was used in reference to the nails of the cross which were fixed in his hands and feet. And after he was crucified, they cast lots upon his vesture, and they that crucified him parted it among them. And that these things did happen you can ascertain from the 'Acts' of Pontius Pilate." (Martyr, FA, 35) Justin also claims that the miracles of Jesus can be confirmed in this document. (Martyr, FA, 48)

SUMMARY

Dr. Geisler summarizes:

The primary sources for the life of Christ are the four Gospels. However there are considerable reports from non-Christian sources that supplement and confirm the Gospel accounts. These come largely from Greek, Roman, Jewish, and Samaritan sources of the first century. In brief they inform us that:

(1) Jesus was from Nazareth;

(2) he lived a wise and virtuous life;

(3) he was crucified in Palestine under Pontius Pilate during the reign of Tiberius Caesar at Passover time, being considered the Jewish King;

(4) he was believed by his disciples to have been raised from the dead three days later;

(5) his enemies acknowledged that he performed unusual feats they called 'sorcery';

(6) his small band of disciples multiplied rapidly, spreading even as far as Rome;

(7) his disciples denied polytheism, lived moral lives, and worshiped Christ as Divine.

This picture confirms the view of Christ presented in the New Testament Gospels. (Geisler, BECA, 384–385)

Dr. Habermas concludes that "ancient extrabiblical sources do present a surprisingly large amount of detail concerning both the life of Jesus and the nature of early Christianity." And he adds a point that many overlook: "We should realize that it is quite extraordinary that we could provide a broad outline of most of the major facts of Jesus' life from 'secular' history alone. Such is surely significant." (Habermas, HJ, 224)

F. F. Bruce explains that "it is surprising how few writings, comparatively speaking, have survived from those years of a kind which might be even remotely expected to mention Christ. (I except, for the present, the letters of Paul and several other New Testament writings.)" (Bruce, JCO, 17)

Michael Wilkins and J. P. Moreland conclude that even if we did not have any Christian writings, "we would be able to conclude from such non-Christian writings as Josephus, the *Talmud*, Tacitus, and Pliny the Younger that: (1) Jesus was a Jewish teacher; (2) many people believed that he performed healings and exorcisms; (3) he was rejected by the Jewish leaders; (4) he was crucified under Pontius Pilate in the reign of Tiberius; (5) despite this shameful death, his followers, who believed that he was still alive, spread beyond Palestine so that there were multitudes of them in Rome by A.D. 64; (6) all kinds of people from the cities and countryside—men and women, slave and free—worshiped him as God by the beginning of the second century." (Wilkins, JUF, 222)

For Further Study

J. N. D. Anderson, *Christianity: The Witness of History*

F. F. Bruce, *The New Testament Documents: Are They Reliable?*

F. F. Bruce, *Jesus and Christian Origins Outside the New Testament*

Eusebius, *Ecclesiastical History*, C. F. Cruse, trans.

Flavius Josephus, *Antiquities of the Jews*

Josh McDowell and Bill Wilson, *He Walked Among Us*

G. Habermas, *The Historical Jesus*, chapter 9

Lucian of Samosata, *The Works of Lucian of Samosata*

Origen, *Contra Celsus*

Pliny the Younger, *Letters*. W. Melmoth, trans.

A. Roberts and J. Donaldson, eds., *The Ante-Nicene Fathers*

Suetonius, *Life of Claudius*

Suetonius, *Life of Nero*

Tacitus, *Annals*

3B. The Stones Cry Out: Evidence from Archaeology

Archaeology, a relative newcomer among the physical sciences, has provided exciting and dramatic confirmation of the Bible's accuracy. Whole books are not large enough to contain all the finds that have bolstered confidence in the historical reliability of the Bible. Presented here are some of the findings of eminent archaeologists and their opinions regarding the implications of those finds.

Nelson Glueck, the renowned Jewish archaeologist, wrote: "It may be stated categorically that no archaeological discovery has ever controverted a biblical reference." He continued his assertion of "the almost incredibly accurate historical memory of the Bible, and particularly so when it is fortified by archaeological fact." (Glueck, RDHN, 31)

W. F. Albright adds: "The excessive scepticism shown toward the Bible by important historical schools of the eighteenth- and nineteenth centuries, certain phases of

which still appear periodically, has been progressively discredited. Discovery after discovery has established the accuracy of innumerable details, and has brought

> Luke is a historian of the first rank; not merely are his statements of fact trustworthy . . . this author should be placed along with the very greatest of historians. . . . Luke's history is unsurpassed in respect of its trustworthiness.
>
> —SIR WILLIAM RAMSAY

increased recognition to the value of the Bible as a source of history." (Albright, AP, 127, 128)

He later writes: "Archaeological discoveries of the past generation in Egypt, Syria, and Palestine have gone far to establish the uniqueness of early Christianity as an historical phenomenon." (Albright, AP, 248)

John Warwick Montgomery exposes a typical problem of many scholars today: "[American] Institute [of Holy Land Studies] researcher Thomas Drobena cautioned that where archaeology and the Bible seem to be in tension, the issue is almost always dating, the most shaky area in current archaeology and the one at which scientistic *a priori* and circular reasoning often replace solid empirical analysis." (Montgomery, EA, 47, 48)

Merrill Unger states: "The role which archaeology is performing in New Testament research (as well as that of the Old Testament) in expediting scientific study, balancing critical theory, illustrating, elucidating, supplementing and authenticating historical and cultural backgrounds, constitutes the one bright spot in the future of criticism of the Sacred text." (Unger, AOT, 25, 26)

Millar Burrows of Yale observes: "Archaeology has in many cases refuted the views of modern critics. It has shown in a number of instances that these views rest on false assumptions and unreal, artificial schemes of historical development (AS 1938, p. 182). This is a real contribution, and not to be minimized." (Burrows, WMTS, 291)

F. F. Bruce notes: "Where Luke has been suspected of inaccuracy, and accuracy has been vindicated by some inscriptional evidence, it may be legitimate to say that archaeology has confirmed the New Testament record." (Bruce, ACNT, as cited in Henry, RB, 331)

Bruce adds that "for the most part the service which archaeology has rendered to New Testament studies is the filling in of the contemporary background, against which we can read the record with enhanced comprehension and appreciation. And this background is a first-century background. The New Testament narrative just will not fit into a second century background." (Bruce, ACNT, as cited in Henry, RB, 331)

William Albright continues: "As critical study of the Bible is more and more influenced by the rich new material from the ancient Near East we shall see a steady rise in respect for the historical significance of now neglected or despised passages and details in the Old and New Testament." (Albright, FSAC, 81)

Burrows exposes the cause of much excessive unbelief: "The excessive skepticism of many liberal theologians stems not from a careful evaluation of the available data, but from an enormous predisposition against the supernatural." (Burrows, as cited in Vos, CITB, 176)

The Yale archaeologist adds to his above statement: "On the whole, however, archaeological work has unquestionably strengthened confidence in the reliability of the Scriptural record. More than one archaeologist has found his respect for the Bible increased by the experience of excavation in Palestine." (Burrows, WMTS, 1) "On the whole such evidence as archaeology has afforded thus far, especially by providing additional and older manuscripts of the books of the Bible, strengthens our confidence in the accuracy with which the text

---

JOURNEYS OF A SKEPTICAL ARCHAEOLOGIST

Sir William Ramsay is regarded as one of the greatest archaeologists ever to have lived. He was a student in the German historical school of the mid-19th century. As a result, he believed that the Book of Acts was a product of the mid-second century A.D. He was firmly convinced of this belief. In his research to make a topographical study of Asia Minor, he was compelled to consider the writings of Luke. As a result he was forced to do a complete reversal of his beliefs due to the overwhelming evidence uncovered in his research. He spoke of this when he said: "I may fairly claim to have entered on this investigation without prejudice in favour of the conclusion which I shall now seek to justify to the reader. On the contrary, I began with a mind unfavourable to it, for the ingenuity and apparent completeness of the Tubingen theory had at one time quite convinced me. It did not then lie in my line of life to investigate the subject minutely; but more recently I found myself brought into contact with the Book of Acts as an authority for the topography, antiquities and society of Asia Minor. It was gradually borne upon me that in various details the narrative showed marvelous truth. In fact, beginning with a fixed idea that the work was essentially a second century composition, and never relying on its evidence as trustworthy for first century conditions, I gradually came to find it a useful ally in some obscure and difficult investigations." (Blaiklock, LAENT, 36—quoted from Ramsay's book: *St. Paul the Traveler and the Roman Citizen*)

has been transmitted through the centuries." (Burrows, WMTS, 42)

2C. New Testament Examples

1D. The Incredible Accuracy of Luke

Luke's reliability as an historian is unquestionable. Unger tells us that archaeology has authenticated the Gospel accounts, especially Luke. In Unger's words, "The Acts of the Apostles is now generally agreed in scholarly circles to be the work of Luke, to belong to the first century and to involve the labors of a careful historian who was substantially accurate in his use of sources." (Unger, ANT, 24)

Concerning Luke's ability as a historian, Sir William Ramsay concluded after thirty years of study that "Luke is a historian of the first rank; not merely are his statements of fact trustworthy . . . this author should be placed along with the very greatest of historians." (Ramsay, BRDTNT, 222)

Ramsay adds: "Luke's history is unsurpassed in respect of its trustworthiness." (Ramsay, SPTRC, 81)

What Ramsay had done conclusively and finally was to exclude certain possibilities. As seen in the light of archaeological evidence, the New Testament reflects the conditions of the second half of the first century A.D., and does not reflect the conditions of any later date. Historically it is of the greatest importance that this should have been so effectively established. In all matters of external fact the author of Acts is seen to have been minutely careful and accurate as only a contemporary can be.

It was at one time conceded that Luke had entirely missed the boat in the events he portrayed as surrounding the birth of Jesus (Luke 2:1–3). Critics argued that there was no census, that Quirinius was not governor of Syria at that time, and that everyone did not have to return to his ancestral home. (Elder, PID, 159, 160; Free, ABH, 285)

First of all, archaeological discoveries show that the Romans had a regular enrollment of taxpayers and also held censuses every fourteen years. This procedure was indeed begun under Augustus and the first took place in either 23–22 B.C. or in 9–8 B.C. The latter would be the one to which Luke refers.

Second, we find evidence that Quirinius was governor of Syria around 7 B.C. This assumption is based on an inscription found in Antioch ascribing to Quirinius this post. As a result of this finding, it is now supposed that he was governor twice—once in 7 B.C. and the other time in 6 A.D. (the date ascribed by Josephus). (Elder, PID, 160)

Last, in regard to the practices of enrollment, a papyrus found in Egypt gives directions for the conduct of a census. It reads: "Because of the approaching census it is necessary that all those residing for any cause away from their homes should at once prepare to return to their own governments in order that they may complete the family registration of the enrollment and that the tilled lands may retain those belonging to them." (Elder, PID, 159, 160; Free, ABH, 285)

Dr. Geisler summarizes the problem and its solution in the translation of the Greek text:

Several problems are involved in the statement that Augustus conducted a census of the whole empire during the reign of both Quirinius and Herod. For one, there is no record of such a census, but we now know that regular censuses were taken in Egypt, Gaul, and Cyrene. It is quite likely that Luke's meaning is that censuses were taken throughout the empire at different times, and Augustus started this process. The present tense that Luke uses points strongly toward understanding this as a repeated event. Now Quirinius did take a census, but that was in A.D. 6, too late for Jesus' birth, and Herod died before Quirinius became governor.

Was Luke confused? No; in fact he mentions Quirinius' later census in Acts 5:37. It is most likely that Luke is distinguishing this census in Herod's time from the more well-known census of Quirinius: "This census took place before Quirinius was governor of Syria." There are several New Testament parallels for this translation. (Geisler, BECA, 46–47)

Archaeologists at first believed Luke's implication wrong that Lystra and Derbe were in Lycaonia, and that Iconium was not. (Acts 14:6) They based their belief on the writings of Romans such as Cicero, who indicated that Iconium was in Lycaonia. Thus, archaeologists said the Book of Acts was unreliable. However, in 1910 Sir William Ramsay found a monument that showed that Iconium was a Phrygian city. Later discoveries confirm this. (Free, ABH, 317)

Among other historical references of Luke is that of Lysanias, the Tetrarch of Abilene who ruled in Syria and Palestine (Luke 3:1) at the beginning of John the Baptist's ministry in A.D. 27. The only Lysanias known to ancient historians was one who was killed in 36 B.C. However, an inscription found at Abila near Damascus speaks of "Freedman of Lysanias the Tetrarch," and is dated between A.D. 14 and 29. (Bruce, ACNT, as cited in Henry, RB, 321)

In his Epistle to the Romans, written from Corinth, Paul makes mention of the city treasurer, Erastus (Rom. 16:23). During the excavations of Corinth in 1929, a pavement was found inscribed: ERASTVS PRO:AED:S:P:STRAVIT ("Erastus, curator of public buildings, laid this pavement at his own expense"). According to Bruce, the pavement quite likely existed in the first century A.D., and the donor and the man Paul mentions are probably one and the same. (Bruce, NTD, 95; Vos, CITB, 185)

Also found in Corinth is a fragmentary inscription believed to have borne the words "Synagogue of the Hebrews." Conceivably it stood over the doorway of the synagogue where Paul debated (Acts 18:4–7). Another Corinthian inscription mentions the city "meat market" to which Paul refers in 1 Corinthians 10:25.

Thus, thanks to the many archaeological finds, most of the ancient cities mentioned in the Book of Acts have been identified. The journeys of Paul can now be accurately traced as a result of these finds. (Bruce, NTD, 95; Albright, RDBL, 118)

Geisler reveals, "In all, Luke names thirty-two countries, fifty-four cities and nine islands without an error." (Geisler, BECA, 47)

Luke writes of the riot of Ephesus, and represents a civic assembly (Ecclesia) taking place in a theater (Acts 19:23–29). The facts are that it did meet there, as borne out by an inscription that speaks of silver statues of Artemis ("Diana" in the KJV) to be placed in the "theater during a full session of the *Ecclesia*." The theater, when excavated, proved to

> For Acts the confirmation of historicity is overwhelming. . . . Any attempt to reject its basic historicity must now appear absurd. Roman historians have long taken it for granted.
>
> —ROMAN HISTORIAN A. N. SHERWIN-WHITE

have room for twenty-five thousand people. (Bruce, ACNT, as cited in Henry, RB, 326)

Luke also relates that a riot broke out in Jerusalem because Paul took a Gentile into the temple (Acts 21:28). Inscriptions have been found that read, in Greek and Latin, "No foreigner may enter within the barrier which surrounds the temple and enclosure. Anyone who is caught doing so will be personally responsible for his ensuing death." Luke is proved right again! (Bruce, ACNT, as cited in Henry, RB, 326)

Also in doubt were Luke's usages of certain words. Luke refers to Philippi as a "part" or "district" of Macedonia. He uses the Greek word *meris*, which is translated "part" or "district." F. J. A. Hort believed Luke erred in this usage. He said that *meris* referred to a "portion," not a "district," thus, his grounds for disagreement. Archaeological excavations, however, have shown that this very word, *meris*, was used to describe the divisions of the district. Thus, archaeology has again shown the accuracy of Luke. (Free, ABH, 320)

Other poor word usages were attached to Luke. He was not technically correct for referring to the Philippian rulers as *praetors*. According to the "scholars" two *duumuirs* would have ruled the town. However, as usual, Luke was right. Findings have shown that the title of *praetor* was employed by the magistrates of a Roman colony. (Free, ABH, 321) His choice of the word *proconsul* as the title for Gallio (Acts 18:12) is correct, as evidenced by the Delphi inscription that states in part: "As Lucius Junius Gallio, my friend, and the Proconsul of Achaia. . . ." (Vos, CITB, 180)

The Delphi inscription (A.D. 52) gives us a fixed time period for establishing Paul's ministry of one and a half years in Corinth. We know this by the fact, from other sources, that Gallio took office on July 1, that his proconsulship lasted only one year, and that this year overlapped Paul's work in Corinth. (Bruce, ACNT, as cited in Henry, RB, 324)

Luke gives to Publius, the chief man in Malta, the title "first man of the island" (Acts 28: 7). Inscriptions have been unearthed that do give him the title of "first man." (Bruce, ACNT, as cited in Henry, RB, 325)

Still another case is his usage of *politarchs* to denote the civil authorities of Thessalonica (Acts 17:6). Since *politarch* is not found in the classical literature, Luke was again assumed to be wrong. However, some nineteen inscriptions that make use of the title have been found. Interestingly enough, five of these are in reference to Thessalonica. (Bruce, ACNT, as cited in Henry, RB, 325) One of the inscriptions was discovered in a Roman arch at Thessalonica and in it are found the names of six of that city's politarchs. (360)

Colin Hemer, a noted Roman historian, has catalogued numerous archaeological and historical confirmations of Luke's accuracy in his book *The Book of Acts in the Setting of Hellenistic History*. Following is a partial summary of his voluminous, detailed report (Hemer, BASHH, 104-107):

- Specialized details, which would not have been widely known except to a contemporary researcher such as Luke who traveled widely. These details include exact titles of officials, identification of army units, and information about major routes.

- Details archaeologists know are accurate but can't verify as to the precise time period. Some of these are unlikely to have been known except to a writer who had visited the districts.

- Correlation of dates of known kings and governors with the chronology of the narrative.

- Facts appropriate to the date of Paul or his immediate contemporary in the church but not to a date earlier or later.
- "Undesigned coincidents" between Acts and the Pauline Epistles.
- Internal correlations within Acts.
- Off-hand geographical references that bespeak familiarity with common knowledge.
- Differences in formulation within Acts that indicate the different categories of sources he used.
- Peculiarities in the selection of detail, as in theology, that are explainable in the context of what is now known of first-century church life.
- Materials the "immediacy" of which suggests that the author was recounting a recent experience, rather than shaping or editing a text long after it had been written.
- Cultural or idiomatic items now known to be peculiar to the first-century atmosphere.

Roman historian A. N. Sherwin-White agrees: "For Acts the confirmation of historicity is overwhelming.... Any attempt to reject its basic historicity must now appear absurd. Roman historians have long taken it for granted." (Sherwin-White, RSRLNT, 189)

Is it any wonder that E. M. Blaiklock, professor of classics in Auckland University, concludes that "Luke is a consummate historian, to be ranked in his own right with the great writers of the Greeks." (Blaiklock, AA, 89)

2D. "Earliest Records of Christianity"
In 1945 two ossuaries (receptacles for bones) were found in the vicinity of Jerusalem. These ossuaries exhibited graffiti that their discoverer, Eleazar L. Sukenik, claimed to be "the earliest records of Christianity." These burial receptacles were found in a tomb that was in use before A.D. 50. The writings read *Iesous iou* and *Iesous aloth*. Also present were four crosses. It is likely that the first is a prayer to Jesus for help, and the second, a prayer for resurrection of the person whose bones were contained in the ossuary. (Bruce, ACNT, as cited in Henry, RB, 327, 328)

3D. The Pavement
For centuries there has been no record of the court where Jesus was tried by Pilate (named *Gabbatha*, or the Pavement, John 19:13).

William F. Albright, in *The Archaeology of Palestine*, shows that this court was the court of the Tower of Antonia, the Roman military headquarters in Jerusalem. It was left buried when the city was rebuilt in the time of Hadrian, and was not discovered until recently. (Albright, AP, 141)

4D. The Pool of Bethesda
The Pool of Bethesda, another site with no record except in the New Testament, can now be identified "with a fair measure of certainty in the northeast quarter of the old city (the area called Bezetha, or 'New Lawn') in the first century A.D., where traces of it were discovered in the course of excavations near the Church of St. Anne in 1888." (Bruce, ACNT, as cited in Henry, RB, 329)

5D. The Gospel of John
Archaeology has authenticated the Gospel accounts, including John's. Dr. William Foxwell Albright, a staff person and director for the American School of Oriental Research in Jerusalem for seventeen years, reputably states: "The Dead Sea Scrolls from Qumran have added vital new evidence for the relative antiquity of the Gospel of John." (Albright, AP, 249)

He goes on: "The points of contact in phraseology, symbolism, and conceptual imagery between Essene literature and the

Gospel of St. John are particularly close, though there are also many resemblances between them and nearly all New Testament writers." (Albright, AP, 249)

6D. The Nazareth Decree

Dr. Geisler expounds upon this find:

A slab of stone was found in Nazareth in 1878, inscribed with a decree from Emperor Claudius (A.D. 41–54) that no graves should be disturbed or bodies extracted or moved. This type of decree is not uncommon, but the startling fact is that here "the offender [shall] be sentenced to capital punishment on [the] charge of violation of [a] sepulchre" (Hemer, BASHH, 155). Other notices warned of a fine, but death for disturbing graves? A likely explanation is that Claudius, having heard of the Christian doctrine of resurrection and Jesus' empty tomb while investigating the riots of A.D. 49, decided not to let any such report surface again. This would make sense in light of the Jewish argument that the body had been stolen (Matt. 28:11–15). This is early testimony to the strong and persistent belief that Jesus rose from the dead. (Geisler, BECA, 48)

7D. Yohanan—A Crucifixion Victim

Dr. Geisler explains the importance of this archaeological find:

In 1968, an ancient burial site was uncovered in Jerusalem containing about thirty-five bodies. It was determined that most of these had suffered violent deaths in the Jewish uprising against Rome in A.D. 70. One of these was a man named Yohanan Ben Ha'galgol. He was about twenty-four to twenty-eight years old, had a cleft palate, and a seven-inch nail was driven through both his feet. The feet had been turned outward so that the square nail could be hammered through at the heel, just inside the Achilles tendon. This would have bowed the legs outward as well so that they could not have been used for support on the cross. The nail had gone through a wedge of acacia wood,

then through the heels, then into an olive wood beam. There was also evidence that similar spikes had been put between the two bones of each lower arm. These had caused the upper bones to be worn smooth as the victim repeatedly raised and lowered himself to breathe (breathing is restricted with the arms raised). Crucifixion victims had to lift themselves to free the chest muscles and, when they grew too weak to do so, died by suffocation.

Yohanan's legs were crushed by a blow, consistent with the common use of the Roman *crucifragium* (John 19:31–32). Each of these details confirms the New Testament description of crucifixion. (Geisler, BECA, 48)

8D. The Pilate Inscription

In 1961 an Italian archaeologist, Antonio Frova, discovered an inscription at Caesarea Maritima on a stone slab which at the time of the discovery was being used as a section of steps leading into the Caesarea theater. The inscription in Latin contained four lines, three of which are partially readable. Roughly translated they are as follows:

Tiberium

Pontius Pilate

Prefect of Judea

The inscribed stone was probably used originally in the foundation for a Tiberium (a temple for the worship of the emperor Tiberius) and then reused later in the discovered location. This inscription clarifies the title of Pontius Pilate as "prefect" at least during a time in his rulership. Tacitus and Josephus later referred to him as "procurator." The NT calls him "governor" (Matt. 27:2), a term which incorporates both titles. This inscription is the only archaeological evidence of both Pilate's name and this title. (Dockery, FBI, 360)

9D. The Erastus Inscription

On a slab of limestone which was a part of the pavement near the theater in Corinth, a

Latin inscription was found which translates, "Erastus, in return for the aedileship, laid the pavement at his own expense." In Romans 16:23 Paul (writing from Corinth) mentioned an Erastus and identified him as a city official. It is possible this is the same person. (Dockery, FBI. 361)

10D. New Testament Coins

Three coins mentioned in the Greek NT have been identified with reasonable assurance.

1. The "tribute penny" (Matt. 22:17-21; Mark 12:13-17; Luke 20:20-26). The Greek word for the coin shown to Jesus in these passages is "denarius," a small silver coin which carried the image of Caesar on one side. Its value was equal to one day's wages for an average worker in Palestine.

2. The "thirty pieces of silver" (Matt. 26:14-15). This amount was probably thirty silver shekels. Originally a shekel was a measure of weight equaling approximately two-fifths of an ounce. It later developed into a silver coin of about the same weight.

3. The "widow's mite" (Mark 12:41-44; Luke 21:1-4). The passage in question reads (in NIV): "two very small copper coins, worth only a fraction of a penny." The first words translate the Greek "lepta" which is the smallest Greek copper coin, the second translates the Greek word "quadrans" which is the smallest Roman copper coin. Knowing the minute monetary value of these coins gives even greater meaning to the message of the parable. (Dockery, FBI, 362)

This section can be appropriately summarized by the words of Sir Walter Scott in reference to the Scriptures:

"Within that awful volume lies
The mystery of mysteries
Happiest they of human race

To whom God has granted grace
To read, to fear, to hope, to pray
To lift the latch, and force the way;
And better had they ne'er been born,
Who read to doubt, or read to scorn."
—(Scott, M, 140)

CONCLUSION

After trying to shatter the historicity and validity of the Scripture, I came to the conclusion that it is historically trustworthy. If one discards the Bible as being unreliable, then one must discard almost all literature of antiquity.

One problem I constantly face is the desire on the part of many to apply one standard or test to secular literature and another to the Bible. One must apply the same test, whether the literature under investigation is secular or religious.

Having done this, I believe we can hold the Scriptures in our hands and say, "The Bible is trustworthy and historically reliable."

For Further Study

W. F. Albright, "Retrospect and Prospect in New Testament Archaeology" in E. J. Vardaman, ed., *The Teacher's Yoke*

F. F. Bruce, *The New Testament Documents: Are They Reliable?*

N. Glueck, *Rivers in the Desert*

G. R. Habermas, *The Verdict of History*

C. J. Hemer, *The Book of Acts in the Setting of Hellenistic History*, C. H. Gempf, ed.

J. McRay, *Archaeology and the New Testament*

W. M. Ramsay, *St. Paul the Traveler and the Roman Citizen*

J. A. T. Robinson, *Redating the New Testament*

A. N. Sherwin-White, *Roman Society and Roman Law in the New Testament*

C. A. Wilson, *Rocks, Relics and Biblical Reliability*

E. Yamauchi, *The Stones and the Scriptures*

4

IS THE OLD TESTA-MENT HISTORICALLY RELIABLE?

1A. THE RELIABILITY OF THE OLD TESTAMENT MANUSCRIPTS

This chapter focuses on the historical reliability of the Old Testament (OT), as much of the evidence is different than that for the New Testament (NT). In both chapters 3 and 4 we are dealing with the historical reliability of the Bible, not its inspiration. The inspiration of the Bible is covered in Part 2 of this book.

The Old Testament has been shown to be reliable in at least three major ways: (1) textual transmission (the accuracy of the copying process down through history), (2) the confirmation of the Old Testament by hard evidence uncovered through archaeology, and (3) documentary evidence also uncovered through archaeology.

1B. Textual Transmission: How Accurate Was the Copying Process?

Part of discovering the historical reliability of the Old Testament has to do with examining the textual transmission (the path from the original writings to today's printed copies). As with other literature of antiquity, we do not have the original documents. But the accuracy of the Hebrew copyists is astonishing when comparing the scriptures to other literature of antiquity.

Gleason Archer states,

It should be clearly understood that in this respect [to transmission], the Old Testament differs from all other pre-Christian works of literature of which we have any knowledge. To be sure, we do not possess so many different manuscripts of pagan productions, coming from such widely separated eras, as we do in the case of the Old Testament. But where we do, for example, in the Egyptian Book of the Dead, the variations are of a far more extensive and serious nature. Quite startling differences appear, for example, between chapter 15 contained in the Papyrus of Ani (written in the Eighteenth Dynasty) and the Turin Papyrus (from the Twenty-sixth Dynasty or later). Whole clauses are inserted or left out, and the sense in corresponding columns of text is in some cases altogether different. Apart from divine superintendence of the transmission of the Hebrew text, there is no particular reason why the same phenomenon of divergence and change would not appear between Hebrew manuscripts produced centuries apart. For example, even though the two copies of Isaiah discovered in Qumran Cave 1 near the Dead Sea in 1947 were a thousand years earlier than the oldest dated manuscript previously known (A.D. 980), they proved to be word for word identical with our standard Hebrew Bible in more than 95 percent of the text. The 5 percent of variation consisted chiefly of obvious slips of the pen and variations in spelling. They do not affect the message of revelation in the slightest. (Archer, SOT, 23–25)

Robert Dick Wilson's brilliant observations trace the veracity and trustworthiness of Scriptures back to the surrounding cultures of Old Testament Israel:

The Hebrew Scriptures contain the names of 26 or more foreign kings whose names have been found on documents contemporary with the kings. The names of most of these kings are found to be spelled on their own monuments, or in documents from the time in which they reigned in the same manner that they are spelled in the documents of the Old Testament. The changes in spelling of others are in accordance with the laws of phonetic change as those laws were in operation at the time when the Hebrew documents claim to have been written. In the case of two or three names only are there letters, or spellings, that cannot as yet be explained with certainty; but even in these few cases it cannot be shown that the spelling in the Hebrew text is wrong. Contrariwise, the names of many of the kings of Judah and Israel are found on the Assyrian contemporary documents with the same spelling as that which we find in the present Hebrew text.

In 144 cases of transliteration from Egyptian, Assyrian, Babylonian and Moabite into Hebrew and in 40 cases of the opposite, or 184 in all, the evidence shows that for 2300 to 3900 years the text of the proper names in the Hebrew Bible has been transmitted with the most minute accuracy. That the original scribes should have written them with such close conformity to correct philological principles is a wonderful proof of their thorough care and scholarship; further, that the Hebrew text should have been transmitted by copyists through so many centuries is a phenomenon unequaled in the history of literature. (Wilson, SIOT, 64, 71)

Professor Wilson continues,

For neither the assailants nor the defenders of the Biblical text should assume for one moment that either this accurate rendition or this correct transmission of proper names is an easy or usual thing. And as some of my readers may not have experience in investigating such matters, attention may be called to the names of kings of Egypt as given in Manetho and on the Egyptian monuments. Manetho was a high priest of the idol-temples in Egypt in the time of Ptolemy Philadelphus, i.e., about 280 B.C. He wrote a work on the dynasties of Egyptian kings, of which fragments have been preserved in the works of Josephus, Eusebius, and others. Of the kings of the 31 dynasties, he gives 40 names from 22 dynasties. Of these, 49 appear on the monuments in a form in which every consonant of Manetho's spelling may possibly be recognized, and 28 more may be recognized in part. The other 63 are unrecognizable in any single syllable. If it be true that Manetho himself copied these lists from the original records— and the fact that he is substantially correct in 49 cases corroborates the supposition that he did—the hundreds of variations and corruptions in the 50 or more unrecognizable names must be due either to his fault in copying or to the mistakes of the transmitters of his text. (Wilson, SIOT, 71-72)

Wilson adds that there are about forty of these kings living from 2000 B.C. to 400 B.C. Each appears in chronological order: "With reference to the kings of the same country and with respect to the kings of other countries . . . no stronger evidence for the substantial accuracy of the Old Testament records could possibly be imagined, than this collection of kings." In a footnote he computes the probability of this accuracy occurring by chance. "Mathematically, it is one chance in 750,000,000,000,000,000,000,000 that this accuracy is mere circumstance." (Wilson, SIOT, 74–75)

Because of this evidence Wilson concludes:

> The proof that the copies of the original documents have been handed down with substantial correctness for more than 2,000 years cannot be denied. That the copies in existence 2,000 years ago had been in like manner handed down from the originals is not merely possible, but, as we have shown, is rendered probable by the analogies of Babylonian documents now existing of which we have both

originals and copies, thousands of years apart, and of scores of papyri which show when compared with our modern editions of the classics that only minor changes of the text have taken place in more than 2,000 years and especially by the scientific and demonstrable accuracy with which the proper spelling of the names of kings and of the numerous foreign terms embedded in the Hebrew text has been transmitted to us. (Wilson, SIOT, 85)

F. F. Bruce states that "the consonantal text of the Hebrew Bible which the Masoretes edited had been handed down to their time with conspicuous fidelity over a period of nearly a thousand years." (Bruce, BP, 178)

William Green concludes that "it may safely be said that no other work of antiquity has been so accurately transmitted." (Green, GIOT, 81)

Concerning the accuracy of the transmission of the Hebrew text, Atkinson, who was under-librarian of the library at Cambridge University, says it is "little short of miraculous."

For hundreds of years, Jewish rabbis have guarded the transmission of the Hebrew text with minute precautions. This chapter highlights what has resulted.

1C. Quantity of Manuscripts

Even though the Old Testament does not boast of the same quantity of manuscripts (MSS) as the New Testament, the number of manuscripts available today is quite remarkable. Several reasons have been suggested for the scarcity of early Hebrew manuscripts. The first and most obvious reason is a combination of antiquity and destructibility; two- to three thousand years is a long time to expect ancient documents to last. Nonetheless, several lines of evidence support the conclusion that their quality is very good. First, it is important to establish the quantity of manuscripts available. There are several important collections of Hebrew manuscripts today. The first collection of Hebrew manuscripts, made by Benjamin Kennicott (1776–1780) and published by Oxford, listed 615 manuscripts of the Old Testament. Later, Giovanni de Rossi (1784–1788) published a list of 731 manuscripts. The most important manuscript discoveries in modern times are those of the Cairo Geniza (1890s) and the Dead Sea Scrolls (1947 and following years). In the Cairo synagogue attic, a *geniza*, or storehouse, for old manuscripts was discovered. Two hundred thousand manuscripts and fragments (Kahle, CG, 13, and Wurthwein, TOT, 25), some ten thousand of which are biblical (Goshen-Gottstein, BMUS, 35), were found.

> Near the end of the nineteenth century, many fragments from the six to eighth centuries were found in an old synagogue in Cairo, Egypt, which had been Saint Michael's Church until A.D. 882. They were found there in a *geniza*, a storage room where worn or faulty manuscripts were hidden until they could be disposed of properly. This geniza had apparently been walled off and forgotten until its recent discovery. In this small room, as many as 200,000 fragments were preserved, including biblical texts in Hebrew and Aramaic. The biblical fragments date from the fifth century A.D. (Dockery, FBI, 162–163)

Of the manuscripts found in the Cairo Geniza, about one-half are now housed at Cambridge University. The rest are scattered throughout the world. Cairo Geniza's authority, Paul Kahle, has identified more than 120 rare manuscripts prepared by the "Babylonian" group of Masoretic scribes.

The largest collection of Hebrew Old Testament manuscripts in the world is the Second Firkowitch Collection in Leningrad. It contains 1,582 items of the Bible and Masora on parchment (725 on paper), plus 1,200 additional Hebrew manuscript fragments in the Antonin Collection. (Wurthwein, TOT, 23) Kahle contends also that these Antonin Collection manuscripts and fragments are all from the Cairo Geniza. (Kahle, CG, 7) In the Firkowitch Collection are found fourteen Hebrew Old Testament manuscripts from between the years A.D. 929 and A.D. 1121 that originated in the Cairo Geniza.

Cairo Geniza manuscripts are scattered over the world. Some of the better ones in the United States are in the Enelow Memorial Collection at the Jewish Theological Seminary, New York. (Goshen-Gottstein, BMUS, 44f)

The British Museum catalog lists 161 Hebrew Old Testament manuscripts. At Oxford University, the Bodleian Library catalog lists 146 Old Testament manuscripts, each containing a large number of fragments. (Kahle, CG, 5) Goshen-Gottstein estimates that in the United States alone there are tens of thousands of Semitic manuscript fragments, about 5 percent of which are biblical—more than five hundred manuscripts. (Goshen-Gottstein, BMUS, 30)

The most significant Hebrew Old Testament manuscripts date from between the third century B.C. and the fourteenth century A.D. Of these the most remarkable manuscripts are those of the Dead Sea Scrolls, which date from the third century B.C. to the first century A.D. They include one complete Old Testament book (Isaiah) and thousands of fragments, which together represent every Old Testament book except Esther. (Geisler, BECA, 549) (See the section called "The Dead Sea Scrolls" later in this chapter.)

The Dead Sea Scrolls manuscripts are highly significant because they confirm the accuracy of other manuscripts dated much later. For example, *Cairo Codex* (A.D. 895) is the earliest Masoretic manuscript prior to the Dead Sea Scrolls discoveries. It is now located in the British Museum. Also called *Codex Cairensis*, it was produced by the Masoretic Moses ben Asher family and contains both the latter and former prophets. The rest of the Old Testament is missing from it. (Bruce, BP, 115–16)

Codex of the Prophets of Leningrad (A.D. 916) contains Isaiah, Jeremiah, Ezekiel, and the twelve minor prophets.

The earliest complete MS of the Old Testament is the *Codex Babylonicus Petropalitanus* (A.D. 1008) located in Leningrad. It was prepared from a corrected text of Rabbi Aaron ben Moses ben Asher before A.D. 1000. (Geisler, GIB, 250)

Aleppo Codex (A.D. 900+) is an exceptionally valuable manuscript. It once was thought lost, but in 1958 was rediscovered. It did not, however, escape damage. It was partially destroyed in the 1947 riots in Israel. Aleppo Codex was the oldest complete Masoretic manuscript of the entire Old Testament.

British Museum Codex (A.D. 950) contains part of Genesis through Deuteronomy.

Reuchlin Codex of the Prophets (A.D. 1105). This text was prepared by the Masorete ben Naphtali. This brings up the question of the faithfulness of the transmission of the Bible text. There are numerous types of manuscript error, which the textual critic may discovers in the early manuscripts of the Old Testament. (These will be discussed in a later section of this chapter 4.) Are these of so serious a nature as to corrupt the message itself, or make it impossible to convey the true meaning? If they are, then God's purpose has been frustrated; He could not convey His revelation so that those of later generations could understand it aright-correctly. If He did not exercise a restraining influence over the scribes who wrote out the standard and authoritative copies of the Scriptures, then they corrupted and falsified the message. If the message was falsified, the whole purpose of bestowing a written revelation has come to nothing; for such a corrupted Scripture would be a mere mixture of truth and error, necessarily subject to human judgment (rather than sitting in judgment upon man).

2C. History of the Old Testament Text

Rabbi Aquiba, second century A.D., with a desire to produce an exact text, is credited with saying that "the accurate transmission (Masoreth) of the text is a fence for the Torah." (Harrison, IOT, 211) In Judaism, a succession of scholars was charged with standardizing and preserving the biblical text, fencing out all possible introduction of error:

- The *Sopherim* (from Hebrew meaning "scribes") were Jewish scholars and custodians of the text between the fifth and third centuries B.C.
- The *Zugoth* ("pairs" of textual scholars) were assigned to this task in the second and first centuries B.C.
- The *Tannaim* ("repeaters" or "teachers") were active until A.D. 200. In addition to preserving the Old Testament text, the work of Tannaim can be found in the *Midrash* ("textual interpretation"), *Tosefta* ("addition"), and *Talmud* ("instruction"), the latter of which is divided into *Mishnah* ("repetitions") and *Gemara* ("the matter to be learned"). The Talmud gradually was compiled between A.D. 100 and A.D. 500. It was natural that the Tannaim would preserve the Hebrew Bible, since their work had to do with compiling several centuries of rabbinic teaching based on the biblical text.
- The *Talmudists* (A.D. 100–500)
  Geisler and Nix explain the second scribal

tradition, extending from about 400 B.C. to almost A.D. 1000:

Following the first period of Old Testament scribal tradition, the period of the Sopherim (c. 400 B.C.—c. A.D. 200), there appeared a second, the Talmudic period (c. A.D. 100–c. 500), which was followed by the better-known Masoretic tradition (c. 500–c. 950). Ezra worked with the first of these groups, and they were regarded as the Bible custodians until after the time of Christ. Between A.D. 100 and 500, the Talmud (instruction, teaching) grew up as a body of Hebrew civil and canonical law based on the Torah. The Talmud basically represents the opinions and decisions of Jewish teachers from about 300 B.C. to A.D. 500, and it consists of two main divisions: the Mishnah and the Gemara. (Geisler, GIB, 306)

During this period a great deal of time was spent cataloging Hebrew civil and

> Thus, far from regarding an older copy of the Scriptures as more valuable, the Jewish habit has been to prefer the newer, as being the most perfect and free from damage.
>
> —SIR FREDERIC KENYON

canonical law. The Talmudists had quite an intricate system for transcribing synagogue scrolls.

Samuel Davidson describes some of the disciplines of the Talmudists in regard to the Scriptures. These minute regulations (I am going to use the numbering incorporated by Geisler) are as follows:

[1] A synagogue roll must be written on the skins of clean animals, [2] prepared for the particular use of the synagogue by a Jew. [3] These must be fastened together with strings taken from clean animals. [4] Every skin must contain a certain number of columns, equal throughout the entire codex. [5] The length of each column must not extend over less than 48 or more than 60 lines; and the breadth must consist of thirty letters. [6] The whole copy must be first-lined; and if three words be written without a line, it is worthless. [7] The ink should be black, neither red, green, nor any other colour, and be prepared according to a definite recipe. [8] An authentic copy must be the exemplar, from which the transcriber ought not in the least deviate. [9] No word or letter, not even a yod, must be written from memory, the scribe not having looked at the codex before him. . . . [10] Between every consonant the space of a hair or thread must intervene; [11] between every new parashah, or section, the breadth of nine consonants; [12] between every book, three lines. [13] The fifth book of Moses must terminate exactly with a line; but the rest need not do so. [14] Besides this, the copyist must sit in full Jewish dress, [15] wash his whole body, [16] not begin to write the name of God with a pen newly dipped in ink, [17] and should a king address him while writing that name he must take no notice of him. (Davidson, HTOT, 89)

Davidson adds that "the rolls in which these regulations are not observed are condemned to be buried in the ground or burned; or they are banished to the schools, to be used as reading-books."

The Talmudists were so convinced that when they finished transcribing a MS they had an exact duplicate, that they would give the new copy equal authority.

Frederic Kenyon, in *Our Bible and the Ancient Manuscripts,* expands on the above concerning the destruction of older copies:

The same extreme care which was devoted to the transcription of manuscripts is also at the bottom of the disappearance of the earlier copies. When a manuscript had been copied with the exactitude prescribed by the Talmud, and had been duly verified, it was accepted as authentic and regarded as being of equal value with any other copy. If all were equally correct, *age gave no advantage to a manuscript;* on the contrary age was a positive disadvantage, since a manuscript was liable to become defaced or damaged in the lapse of time. A damaged or imperfect copy was at once condemned as unfit for use.

Attached to each synagogue was a "Gheniza," or lumber cupboard, in which defective manuscripts were laid aside; and from these receptacles some of the oldest manuscripts now extant have in modern times been recovered. Thus, far from regarding an older copy of the Scriptures as more valuable, the Jewish habit has been to prefer the newer, as being the most perfect and free from damage. The older copies, once consigned to the "Gheniza" naturally perished, either from neglect or from being deliberately burned when the "Gheniza" became overcrowded.

The absence of very old copies of the Hebrew Bible need not, therefore, either surprise or disquiet us. If, to the causes already enumerated, we add the repeated persecutions (involving much destruction of property) to which the Jews have been subject, the disappearance of the ancient manuscripts is adequately accounted for, and those which remain may be accepted as preserving that which alone they profess to preserve—namely, the Masoretic text. (Kenyon, OBAM, 43)

"Reverence for the Scriptures and regard for the purity of the sacred text did not first originate after the fall of Jerusalem." (Green, GIOT, 173)

The *Masoretes* were the Jewish scholars who between A.D. 500 and A.D. 950 gave the final form to the text of the Old Testament. The destruction of the temple in A.D. 70, along with the dispersion of the Jews from their land, became a powerful impetus to (1) standardize the consonantal text, and (2) standardize punctuation and the use of vowels to preserve correct vocalization and pronunciation for reading. They were called

Masoretics because they preserved in writing the oral tradition *(masorah)* concerning the correct vowels and accents, and the number of occurrences of rare words of unusual spellings. They received the unpointed (comparable to English without vowels),

> The Masoretes were well disciplined and treated the text "with the greatest imaginable reverence, and devised a complicated system of safeguards against scribal slips. They counted, for example, the number of times each letter of the alphabet occurs in each book; they pointed out the middle letter of the Pentateuch and the middle letter of the whole Hebrew Bible, and made even more detailed calculations than these. 'Everything countable seems to be counted,' says Wheeler Robinson, and they made up mnemonics by which the various totals might be readily remembered."
>
> —F. F. BRUCE

consonantal text of the Sopherim and inserted the vowel points that gave to each word its exact pronunciation and grammatical form. They even engaged in a moderate amount of textual criticism. Wherever they suspected that the word indicated by the consonantal text was erroneous, they corrected it in a very ingenious way. They left the actual consonants undisturbed, as they had received them from the Sopherim. But they inserted the vowel points that belonged to the new word they were substituting for the old, and then inserted the consonants of the new word itself in very small letters in the margin. (Archer, SOT, 63)

There were two major schools or centers of Masoretic activity—each largely independent of the other—the Babylonian and the Palestinian. The most famous

Masoretes were the Jewish scholars living in Tiberias in Galilee, Moses ben Asher (with his son Aaron), and Moses ben Naphtali, in the late ninth and tenth centuries. The ben Asher text is the standard Hebrew text today and is best represented by Codex Leningradensis B19 A (L) and the Aleppo Codex.

The Masoretes (from *masora*, "tradition") accepted the laborious job of editing the text and standardizing it. Their headquarters was in Tiberias. The text that the Masoretes preserved is called the "Masoretic" Text. This resultant text had vowel points added in order to ensure proper pronunciation. This Masoretic Text is the standard Hebrew text today.

The Masoretes were well disciplined and treated the text with the greatest imaginable reverence, and devised a complicated system of safeguards against scribal slips. They counted, for example, the number of times each letter of the alphabet occurs in each book; they pointed out the middle letter of the Pentateuch and the middle letter of the whole Hebrew Bible, and made even more detailed calculations than these. "Everything countable seems to be counted," says Wheeler Robinson, and they made up mnemonics by which the various totals might be readily remembered. (Bruce, BP, 117)

We have given practical proof of our reverence for our own Scriptures. For, although such long ages have now passed, no one has ventured either to add, or to remove, or to alter a syllable; and it is an instinct with every Jew, from the day of his birth, to regard them as the decrees of God, to abide by them, and, if need be, cheerfully to die for them.

—FLAVIUS JOSEPHUS, FIRST-CENTURY HISTORIAN

The scribes could tell if one consonant was left out of say the entire book of Isaiah or the entire Hebrew Bible. They built in so many safeguards that they knew when they finished that they had an exact copy.

Sir Frederic Kenyon says:

Besides recording varieties of reading, tradition, or conjecture, the Masoretes undertook a number of calculations which do not enter into the ordinary sphere of textual criticism. They numbered the verses, words, and letters of every book. They calculated the middle word and the middle letter of each. They enumerated verses which contained all the letters of the alphabet, or a certain number of them. These trivialities, as we may rightly consider them, had yet the effect of securing minute attention to the precise transmission of the text; and they are but an excessive manifestation of a respect for the sacred Scriptures which in itself deserves nothing but praise. The Masoretes were indeed anxious that not one jot nor tittle, not one smallest letter nor one tiny part of a letter, of the Law should pass away or be lost. (Kenyon, OBAM, 38)

A factor that runs throughout the above discussion of the Hebrew manuscript evidence is the Jewish reverence for the Scriptures. With respect to the Jewish Scriptures, however, it was not scribal accuracy alone that guaranteed their product. Rather, it was their almost superstitious reverence for the Bible. According to the Talmud, there were specifications not only for the kind of skins to be used and the size of the columns, but the scribe was even required to perform a religious ritual before writing the name of God. Rules governed the kind of ink used, dictated the spacing of words, and prohibited writing anything from memory. The lines—and even the letters—were counted methodically. If a manuscript was found to contain even one mistake it was discarded and destroyed. This scribal formalism was responsible, at least in part, for the extreme care exercised in copying the Scriptures. It was also for this reason that there were only a few manuscripts (because the rules demanded the destruction of defective copies). (Geisler, BECA, 552)

Flavius Josephus, the Jewish historian writing in the first century A.D., states:

> We have given practical proof of our reverence for our own Scriptures. For, although such long ages have now passed, no one has ventured either to add, or to remove, or to alter a syllable; and it is an instinct with every Jew, from the day of his birth, to regard them as the decrees of God, to abide by them, and, if need be, cheerfully to die for them. Time and again ere now the sight has been witnessed of prisoners enduring tortures and death in every form in the theatres, rather than utter a single word against the laws and the allied documents. (Josephus, FJAA, as cited in JCW, 179, 180)

Josephus continues by making a comparison between the Hebrew respect for Scripture and the Greek regard for their literature:

> What Greek would endure as much for the same cause? Even to save the entire collection of his nation's writings from destruction he would not face the smallest personal injury. For to the Greeks they are mere stories improvised according to the fancy of their authors; and in this estimate even of the older historians they are quite justified, when they see some of their own contemporaries venturing to describe events in which they bore no part, without taking the trouble to seek information from those who know the facts. (Josephus, FJAA, as cited in JCW, 181)

Still, however, the earliest Masoretic manuscripts in existence, dated from about A.D. 1000 and later, awaited confirmation of their accuracy. That confirmation came with an astounding discovery off the shores of Israel's Dead Sea.

3C. The Dead Sea Scrolls

If you had asked any biblical scholar, before the discovery of the Dead Sea Scrolls, what would constitute his dream for a discovery that would greatly verify the reliability of the Old Testament, he or she would have said, "Older witnesses to the original Old Testament manuscripts." The big question was asked first by Sir Frederic Kenyon: "Does this Hebrew text, which we call Masoretic, and which we have shown to descend from a text drawn up about A.D. 100, faithfully represent the Hebrew text as originally written by the authors of the Old Testament books?" (Kenyon, OBAM, 47)

Before the discovery of the Dead Sea Scrolls, the question was, "How accurate are the copies we have today compared to the copies of the first century and earlier?" The earliest complete copy of the Old Testament dates from the tenth century. Thus the big question: "Because the text has been copied over many times, can we trust it?" The Dead Sea Scrolls provide an astounding answer.

1D. What Are the Dead Sea Scrolls?

The scrolls are made up of some forty thousand inscribed fragments. From these fragments more than five hundred books have been reconstructed. Many extrabiblical books and fragments were discovered that shed light on the second century B.C. to first century A.D. religious community of Qumran on the shores of the Dead Sea. Such writings as the "Zadokite documents," a "Rule of the Community," and the "Manual of Discipline" help us to understand the purpose of daily Qumran life. In the various caves are some very helpful commentaries on the Scriptures. But the most important documents of the Dead Sea Scrolls are copies of the Old Testament text dating from more than a century *before* the birth of Christ.

2D. How Were the Dead Sea Scrolls Found?

Ralph Earle gives a vivid and concise answer to how the scrolls were found, by sharing an account showing God's providential care:

The story of this discovery is one of the most fascinating tales of modern times. In February or March of 1947 a Bedouin shepherd boy named Muhammad was searching for a lost goat. He tossed a stone into a hole in a cliff on the west side of the Dead Sea, about eight miles south of Jericho. To his surprise he heard the sound of shattering pottery. Investigating, he discovered an amazing sight. On the floor of the cave were several large jars containing leather scrolls, wrapped in linen cloth. Because the jars were carefully sealed, the scrolls had been preserved in excellent condition for nearly 1,900 years. (They were evidently placed there in A.D. 68.)

Five of the scrolls found in Dead Sea Cave I, as it is now called, were bought by the archbishop of the Syrian Orthodox Monastery at Jerusalem. Meanwhile, three other scrolls were purchased by Professor Sukenik of the Hebrew University there.

When the scrolls were first discovered, no publicity was given to them. In November of 1947, two days after Professor Sukenik purchased three scrolls and two jars from the cave, he wrote in his diary: "It may be that this is one of the greatest finds ever made in Palestine, a find we never so much as hoped for." But these significant words were not published at the time.

Fortunately, in February of 1948, the archbishop, who could not read Hebrew, phoned the American School of Oriental Research in Jerusalem and told about the scrolls. By good providence, the acting director of the school at the moment was a young scholar named John Trever, who was also an excellent amateur photographer. With arduous, dedicated labor

he photographed each column of the great Isaiah scroll, which is 24 feet long and 10 inches high. He developed the plates himself and sent a few prints by airmail to Dr. W. F. Albright of Johns Hopkins University, who was widely recognized as the dean of American biblical archaeologists. By return airmail Albright wrote: "My heartiest congratulations on the greatest manuscript discovery of modern times! . . . What an absolutely incredible find! And there can happily not be the slightest doubt in the world about the genuineness of the manuscript." He dated it about 100 B.C. (Earle, HWGB, 48–49)

3D. The Value of the Scrolls

The oldest complete Hebrew MS we possessed before the Dead Sea Scrolls were from A.D. 900 on. How could we be sure of their accurate transmission since before the time of Christ in the first century A.D.? Thanks to archaeology and the Dead Sea Scrolls, we now know. One of the scrolls in the Dead Sea caves was a complete MS of the Hebrew text of Isaiah. It is dated by paleographers around 125 B.C. This MS is more than one thousand years older than any MS we previously possessed.

The significance of this discovery has to do with the detailed closeness of the Isaiah scroll (125 B.C.) to the Masoretic Text of Isaiah (A.D. 916) one thousand years later. It demonstrates the unusual accuracy of the copyists of the Scripture over a thousand-year period.

Of the 166 *words* in Isaiah 53, there are only seventeen *letters* in question. Ten of these letters are simply a matter of spelling, which does not affect the sense. Four more letters are minor stylistic changes, such as conjunctions. The remaining three letters comprise the word "light," which is added in verse 11, and does not affect the meaning greatly. Furthermore, this word is supported by the LXX and

IQ Is (one of the Isaiah scrolls found in the Dead Sea caves). Thus, in one chapter of 166 words, there is only one word (three letters) in question after a thousand years of transmission—and this word does not significantly change the meaning of the passage. (Burrows, TDSS, 304)

Gleason Archer states that the Isaiah copies of the Qumran community "proved to be word for word identical with our standard Hebrew Bible in more than 95 percent of the text. The 5 percent of variation consisted chiefly of obvious slips of the pen and variations in spelling." (Archer, SOT, 19)

Millar Burrows concludes: "It is a matter of wonder that through something like a thousand years the text underwent so little alteration. As I said in my first article on the scroll, 'Herein lies its chief importance, supporting the fidelity of the Masoretic tradition.'" (Burrows, TDSS, 304)

4D. What Do the Scrolls Contain?

It will not be possible here to survey the more than eight hundred manuscripts represented by the scrolls. The following is a sampling of the texts that have been studied for the last forty years, including most of the older works on which the scrolls were based and the recently published texts from Cave 4. These texts can be grouped in categories: biblical texts, biblical commentaries, sectarian texts, and pseudepigraphical texts, apocalyptic texts, and mystical or ritualistic texts. (Price, SDSS, 86)

Dead Sea Scroll Discoveries. Cave 1 was discovered by the Arab shepherd boy. From it he took seven more-or-less complete scrolls and some fragments:

Isaiah A (IQIs a): St. Mark's Monastery Isaiah Scroll is a popular copy with numerous corrections above the line or in the margin. It is the earliest known copy of any complete book of the Bible.

Isaiah B (IQIs b): The Hebrew University Isaiah is incomplete, but its text agrees more closely with the Masoretic Text than does Isaiah A.

Other Cave 1 Fragments: This cave also yielded fragments of Genesis, Leviticus, Deuteronomy, Judges, Samuel, Isaiah, Ezekiel, Psalms, and some nonbiblical works including Enoch, Sayings of Moses (previously unknown), Book of Jubilee, Book of Noah, Testament of Levi, Tobit, and the Wisdom of Solomon. An interesting fragment of Daniel, containing 2:4 (where the language changes from Hebrew to Aramaic), also comes from this cave. Fragmentary commentaries on the Psalms, Micah, and Zephaniah were also found in Cave 1.

Cave 2: Cave 2 was first discovered and pilfered by the Bedouins. It was excavated in 1952. Fragments of about one hundred manuscripts, including two of Exodus, one of Leviticus, four of Numbers, two or three of Deuteronomy, one each of Jeremiah, Job, and the Psalms, and two of Ruth were found.

Cave 4: Partridge Cave, or Cave 4, after being ransacked by Bedouins, was searched in September 1952, and proved to be the most productive cave of all. Literally thousands of fragments were recovered by purchase from the Bedouins or by the archaeologists sifting the dust on the floor of the cave. These scraps represent hundreds of manuscripts, nearly four hundred of which have been identified. They include one hundred copies of Bible books—all of the Old Testament except Esther.

A fragment of Samuel from Cave 4 (4qsam b) is thought to be the oldest known piece of biblical Hebrew. It dates from the third century B.C. Also found were a few fragments of commentaries of the Psalms, Isaiah, and Nahum. The entire collection of Cave 4 is believed to represent the scope of the Qumran library, and judging from the relative number of books found, their favorite books seemed to be Deuteronomy, Isaiah, the Psalms, the Minor Prophets, and Jeremiah, in that order. In one fragment containing some of Daniel 7:28 and 8:1, the language changes from Aramaic to Hebrew.

Caves 7–10: Caves 7–10, examined in 1955, produced no significant Old Testament manuscripts. Cave 7 did, however; yield some disputed manuscript fragments that have been identified by Jose O'Callahan as New Testament portions. If so, they would be the oldest New Testament manuscript dating from as early as A.D. 50 or 60.

Cave 11: This cave was excavated in early 1956. It produced a well-preserved copy of thirty-six Psalms, plus the apocryphal Psalm 151, previously known only in Greek texts. A very fine scroll of part of Leviticus, some

Qumran Manuscripts of Books of the Old Testament

Canonical Division (According to the Hebrew Bible)	Old Testament Book (According to Order in Hebrew Bible)	Number of Qumran Manuscripts (?=possible fragment)
Pentateuch	Genesis	18+3?
(Torah)	Exodus	18
	Leviticus	17
	Numbers	12
	Deuteronomy	31+3?
Prophets (Nevi'im)	Joshua	2
	Judges	3
Former Prophets	1–2 Samuel	4
	1–2 Kings	3
Latter Prophets	Isaiah	22
	Jeremiah	6
	Ezekiel	7
	Twelve (Minor Prophets)	10+1?
Writings	Psalms	39+2?
	Proverbs	2
	Job	4
The Five Scrolls	Song of Songs	4
	Ruth	4
	Lamentations	4
	Ecclesiastes	3
	Esther	0
	Daniel	8+1?
	Ezra–Nehemiah	1
	1–2 Chronicles	1
Total		223 (233)

large pieces of an Apocalypse of the New Jerusalem, and an Aramaic targum (paraphrase) of Job were discovered.

Several recent studies of the Dead Sea Scrolls provide detailed descriptions and inventories. Gleason L. Archer, Jr., provides an appendix to his *A Survey of Old Testament Introduction.*

Murabba'at Discoveries. Prompted by the profitable finds at Qumran, the Bedouins pursued their search and found caves southeast of Bethlehem that produced self-dated manuscripts and documents from the Second Jewish Revolt (A.D. 132–135). Systematic exploration and excavation of these caves began in January 1952. The later-dated manuscripts helped establish the antiquity of the Dead Sea Scrolls. From these caves came another scroll of the Minor Prophets, the last half of Joel through Haggai, that closely supports the Masoretic Text. The oldest known Semitic papyrus (a palimpsest), inscribed the second time in the ancient Hebrew script (dating from the seventh–eighth centuries B.C.), was found here (see Barthelemy).

The significance of the Qumran documents to textual criticism can be seen in the following perspectives from Old Testament scholars:

First and foremost, the Dead Sea Scrolls take the textual scholar back about one thousand years earlier than previously known Hebrew manuscript evidence. Prior to the Qumran discoveries, the earliest complete copies of Old Testament books dated from about the early tenth century A.D. The earliest complete copy of the entire Old Testament dated from the early eleventh century A.D. The Dead Sea manuscripts thus give much earlier evidence for the text of the Old Testament than anything previously known. (Brotzman, OTTC, 94–95)

Prior to the discovery of the scrolls at Qumran the oldest extant manuscripts were dated from approximately A.D. 900. Some manuscripts of the Dead Sea Scrolls, which included copies of Isaiah, Habakkuk, and others, were dated back to 125 B.C., providing manuscripts one thousand years older than previously available. The major conclusion was that there was no significant difference between the Isaiah scroll at Qumran and the Masoretic Hebrew text dated one thousand years later. This confirmed the reliability of our present Hebrew text. (Enns, MHT, 173)

Together with extant material they [the Dead Sea Scrolls] will do much to extend the frontiers of knowledge in the areas of history, religion, and sacred literature. (Harrison, AOT, 115)

There can be no doubt that the [Dead Sea] scrolls have ushered in a new era of biblical study in which much that was known will be confirmed, and much that was accepted as fact will need to be revised. Not the least benefit will be a movement towards the ultimate reconstruction of a genuine pre-Christian Old Testament text, making the ancient Word of God more intelligible to its modern readers. (Harrison, AOT, 115)

In conclusion, we should accord to the Masoretes the highest praise for their meticulous care in preserving so sedulously the consonantal text of the Sopherim which had been entrusted to them. They, together with the Sopherim themselves, gave the most diligent attention to accurate preservation of the Hebrew Scriptures that has ever been devoted to any ancient literature, secular or religious, in the history of human civilization. So conscientious were they in their stewardship of the holy text that they did not even venture to make the most obvious corrections, so far as the consonants were concerned, but left their *Vorlage* exactly as it had been handed down to them.

Because of their faithfulness, we have today a form of the Hebrew text which in all essentials duplicates the recension which was considered authoritative in the days of Christ and the apostles, if not a century earlier. And this in turn, judging from Qumran evidence, goes back to an authoritative revision of the Old Testament text which was drawn up on the basis of the most reliable manuscripts available for collation from previous centuries. These bring us very close in all essentials to the original autographs themselves, and furnish us with an authentic record of God's revelation. As W. F. Albright has said, "We may rest assured that the consonantal text of the Hebrew Bible, though not infallible, has been preserved with an accuracy perhaps unparalleled in any other Near Eastern literature." (Archer, SOT, 65)

4C. Non-Hebrew Manuscript Evidence

The various ancient translations (called Versions) of the Old Testament provide the textual scholar with valuable witnesses to the text. The Septuagint (LXX), for example, preserves a textual tradition from the third century B.C., and the Samaritan Pentateuchal tradition may date from the fifth century B.C. These and the Masoretic Text provide three Old Testament textual traditions that, when critically evaluated, supply an overwhelming support for the integrity of the Old Testament text. The witness of the Samaritan Pentateuch, and especially that of the LXX with its revisions and recensions, is a major confirmation of the textual integrity.

1D. The Septuagint, or LXX

Just as the Jews had abandoned their native Hebrew tongue for Aramaic in the Near East, so they abandoned the Aramaic in favor of Greek in such Hellenistic centers as Alexandria, Egypt. During the campaigns of Alexander the Great, the Jews were shown considerable favor. In fact, Alexander was sympathetic toward the Jews as a result of their policies toward him in the siege of Tyre

> *[The Septuagint] is uneven, but it is helpful in that it is based on a Hebrew text one thousand years older than our existing Hebrew manuscripts.*
>
> —PAUL ENNS

(332 B.C.). He is even reported to have traveled to Jerusalem to pay homage to their God. As he conquered new lands, he built new cities that frequently included Jewish inhabitants, and often named them Alexandria.

Because the Jews were scattered from their homeland, there was a need for the Scriptures in the common language of that day. The name *Septuagint* (meaning "seventy," and usually abbreviated by use of the Roman numerals LXX) was given to the Greek translation of the Hebrew Scriptures during the reign of King Ptolemy Philadelphia of Egypt. (285–246 B.C.)

F. F. Bruce offers an interesting rendering of the origin of the name for this translation. Concerning a letter purporting to be written around 250 B.C. (more realistically, a short time before 100 B.C.) by Aristeas, a court official of King Ptolemy, to his brother Philocrates, Bruce writes:

Ptolemy was renowned as a patron of literature and it was under him that the great library at Alexandria, one of the world's cultural wonders for 900 years, was inaugurated. The letter describes how Demetrius of Phalerum, said to have been Ptolemy's librarian, aroused the king's interest in the Jewish Law and advised him to send a delegation to the high priest, Eleazar, at Jerusalem. The high priest chose as translators six elders from each of the twelve tribes of Israel and sent them to Alexandria, along with a specially accurate and beautiful parchment of the Torah. The elders were royally dined and wined, and proved their wisdom in debate; then they took up their residence in a house on the island of Pharos (the island otherwise famed for its lighthouse), where in seventy-two days they completed their task of translating the Pentateuch into Greek, presenting an agreed version as the result of conference and comparison. (Bruce, BP, 146, 147)

The Greek Old Testament of the Septuagint differs from the Hebrew canon in the quality of its translation as well as in its contents and arrangement. In addition to the twenty-two books of the Hebrew Old Testament, the LXX contains a number of books that were never part of the Hebrew canon. Apparently those books were circulated in the Greek-speaking world but were never part of the Hebrew canon. The quality of translation in the LXX reflects this situation and provides for several observations: (1) The LXX varies in excellence, ranging from slavishly literal renditions of the Torah to free translations in the Writings (the third division of the Hebrew Scriptures). (See Sir Frederic Kenyon, *The Text of the Greek Bible*, 3d ed., revised and augmented by A. W. Adams, pp. 16–19.) Adams indicates that the text of Job in the original LXX is actually one-sixth shorter than its Hebrew counterpart. There are also large variations in Joshua, 1 Samuel, 1 Kings, Proverbs, Esther, and Jeremiah, as well as lesser variations in other books. The cause of the divergencies is one of the major difficulties of the Septuagint. (2) The LXX was not designed to have the same purpose as the Hebrew text, being used for public services in the synagogues rather than for scholarly or scribal purposes. (3) The LXX was the product of a pioneer venture in transmitting the Old Testament Scriptures, and an excellent example of such an effort. (4) The LXX was generally loyal to the readings of the original Hebrew text, although some have maintained that the translators were not always good Hebrew scholars.

Regarding the Septuagint, Paul Enns notes that "as a translation it is uneven, but it is helpful in that it is based on a Hebrew text one thousand years older than our existing Hebrew manuscripts. Moreover, New Testament writers would at times quote from the Septuagint; this provides us with further insight concerning the Old Testament text. (Enns, MHT, 174)

"As for the influence of the LXX, every page of this lexicon [*A Greek-English Lexicon of the New Testament and Other Early Christian Literature* (Bauer, Arndt, and Gingich)] shows that it outweighs all other influences on our [first century A.D.] literature." (Bauer, GELNT, xxi)

The Septuagint (LXX), the Greek translation of the Old Testament begun c. 250 B.C., ranks next to the Masoretic Text in importance. It was widely used in New Testament times, as may be seen from the fact that the majority of the 250 Old Testament citations in the New Testament are from this version. When the LXX diverged from the Masoretic Text some scholars assumed that the LXX translators had taken liberties with their texts. We now know from Qumran that many of these differences were due to the fact that the translators were following a somewhat different Hebrew text belonging to what we may call the Proto-Septuagint family. (Yamauchi, SS, 130, 131)

The LXX, being very close to the Masoretic Text (A.D. 916) we have today, helps to establish the reliability of its transmission through thirteen hundred years.

The LXX and the scriptural citations found in the apocryphal books of Ecclesiasticus, the Book of Jubilees, and others, give evidence that the Hebrew text today is substantially the same as the text about 300 B.C.

Geisler and Nix give four important contributions of the Septuagint. "[1] It bridged the religious gap between the Hebrew- and Greek-speaking peoples, as it met the needs of the Alexandrian Jews, [2] it bridged the historical gap between the Hebrew Old Testament of the Jews and the Greek-speaking Christians who would use it with their New Testament, [3] it provided a precedent for missionaries to make translations of the

Scriptures into various languages and dialects; and [4] it bridges the textual criticism gap by its substantial agreement with the Hebrew Old Testament text." (Geisler, GIB, 308)

F. F. Bruce gives two reasons why the Jews lost interest in the Septuagint:

1. "From the first century A.D. onwards the Christians adopted it as their version of the Old Testament and used it freely in their propagation and defense of the Christian faith." (Bruce, BP, 150)

2. "About A.D. 100 a revised standard text was established for the Hebrew Bible by Jewish scholars." (Bruce, BP, 151)

What began as a popular Jewish translation of the Old Testament eventually lost much of its appeal to the Jewish people.

2D. Hexapla

The *Hexapla* (meaning sixfold) done by Origen in the second century is inextricably tied to the LXX.

The Hexapla, plus writings of Josephus, Philo, and the Zadokite Documents (Dead Sea Qumran community literature), "bear witness to the existence of a text quite similar to the Masoretic [Text] from A.D. 40 to 100." (Skilton, "The Transmission of the Scripture" in *The Infallible Word* [a symposium], 148)

Origen's Hexapla (c. 240–50). The work of Old Testament translation led to four Greek textual traditions by the third century A.D.: the Septuagint, and versions by Aquila, Theodotion, and Symmachus. This muddled state of affairs set the stage for the first really outstanding attempt at textual criticism, the Hexapla ("sixfold") by Origen of Alexandria (A.D. 185–254). Because of the many divergences between the existing manuscripts of the LXX, the discrepancies between the Hebrew text and the LXX, and the attempts at revising the Old Testament Greek transla-

tions, Origen appears to have settled upon a course that would give the Christian world a satisfactory Greek text or the Old Testament. His work was essentially a recension rather than a version, as he corrected textual corruptions and attempted to unify the Greek text with the Hebrew. Thus his twofold aim was to show the superiority of the various revisions of the Old Testament over the corrupted LXX and to give a comparative view of the correct Hebrew and the divergent LXX. In this he followed the view that the Hebrew Old Testament was a sort of "inerrant transcript" of God's revealed truth to man. . . .

The arrangement of the Hexapla was in six parallel columns. Each column contained the Old Testament in the original Hebrew or a particular version, thus making the manuscript far too bulky to be marketable in ancient times. The six columns were arranged as follows: column one, the Hebrew original; column two, the Hebrew original transliterated into Greek letters; column three, the literal translation of Aquila; column four, the idiomatic revision of Symmachus; column five, Origen's own revision of the LXX; and column six, the Greek revision of Theodotion. (Geisler, GIB, 507–508)

Although the task was of monumental significance, it is well for the modern textual critic to observe the difference between his own and Origen's objectives, as has been so succinctly stated by Kenyon:

For Origen's purpose, which was the production of a Greek version corresponding as closely as possible with the Hebrew text as then settled, this procedure was well enough; but for ours, which is the recovery of the original Septuagint . . . as evidence for what the Hebrew was before the Masoretic text, it was most unfortunate, since there was a natural tendency for his edition to be copied without the critical symbols, and thus for the additions made by him from Theodotion to appear as part of the genuine and original Septuagint. (Kenyon, OBAM, 59)

This unfortunate situation did occur, and "the transcribed Septuagint text without the diacritical markings led to the dissemination of a corrupted Greek Old Testament text, rather than the achievement of a Septuagint version in conformity with the Hebrew text of the day." (Geisler, GIB, 509)

F. F. Bruce writes, "If Origen's *Hexapla* had survived entire, it would be a treasure beyond price." (Bruce, BP, 155)

3D. The Samaritan Pentateuch

The Samaritans separated from the Jews probably during the fifth or fourth century B.C. after a long, bitter religious and cultural struggle. At the time of the schism one would suspect that the Samaritans took with them the Scriptures as they then existed, and prepared their own revised text of the Pentateuch. The Samaritan Pentateuch is not a version in the strict sense, but rather a manuscript portion of the Hebrew text itself. It contains the five books of Moses and is written in an ancient style of Hebrew script. Some of the older biblical manuscripts from Qumran use this script, since it was revived in the second century B.C. during the Maccabean revolt against the Greeks. Textual critic Frank M. Cross, Jr., believes that the Samaritan Pentateuch probably comes from about the Maccabean period.

A form of the Samaritan Pentateuch text seems to have been known to church fathers Eusebius of Caesarea (c. 265–339) and Jerome (c. 345–c. 419). It was not available to modern Western scholars until 1616, when Pietro della Valle discovered a manuscript of the Samaritan Pentateuch in Damascus. A

> *The Samaritan Pentateuch, it is interesting to note, is written in an older form of Hebrew script than that of the Masoretic Bible and Jewish-Hebrew literature in general.*
>
> —F.F. BRUCE

great wave of excitement arose among biblical scholars. The text was regarded as superior to the Masoretic Text until Wilhelm Gesenius in 1815 judged it to be practically worthless for textual criticism. More recently the value of the Samaritan Pentateuch has been reasserted by such scholars as A. Geiger, Kahle, and Kenyon.

No extant manuscript of the Samaritan Pentateuch has been dated before the eleventh century. The Samaritan community claims that one roll was written by Abisha, the great-grandson of Moses, in the thirteenth year after the conquest of Canaan, but the authority is so spurious that the claim may be safely dismissed. The oldest codex of the Samaritan Pentateuch bears a note about its sale in 1149–1150, but the manuscript itself is much older. One manuscript was copied in 1204. Another dated 1211–1212 is now in the John Rylands Library at Manchester. Another, dated c. 1232, is in the New York Public Library.

There are about six thousand deviations of the Samaritan Pentateuch from the Masoretic Text, most considered to be trivial. In about nineteen hundred instances the Samaritan text agrees with the Septuagint against the Masoretic Text. Some of the deviations were deliberately introduced by the Samaritans to preserve their own religious traditions and dialectic. The Masoretic Text perpetuates Judean dialect and traditions.

The Samaritan Pentateuch, it is interesting to note, is written in an older form of Hebrew script than that of the Masoretic Bible and Jewish-Hebrew literature in general. Somewhere about 200 B.C. this older, "paleo-Hebrew" script was superseded among the Jews by the Aramaic or "square" character. Some of the older biblical manuscripts from Qumran still show it. The paleo-Hebrew script is of the same general style as the script found on the Moabite Stone, the Siloam Inscription, and the Lachish Letters, but the script of the Samaritans is a rather more ornamental development of it. (Bruce, BP, 120)

Paul Enns says of the Samaritan Pentateuch that "it is a valuable witness to the text of the Old Testament." (Enns, MHT, 174) This text contains the Pentateuch, and is valuable to determine textual readings. Bruce says that "the variations between the Samaritan Pentateuch and the Masoretic edition [A.D. 916] of these books are quite insignificant by comparison with the area of agreement." (Bruce, BP, 122)

Sir Frederic Kenyon states that when the LXX and the Samaritan Pentateuch agree against the Masoretic Text, "they represent the original reading," but when the LXX and the Masoretic Text are opposed, it is possible that sometimes the one may be right and sometimes the other; but in any case the difference is one of interpretation, not of text.

5C. Other Witnesses to the Old Testament Text

1D. Aramaic Targums

The Targums (copies) appear in written form about A.D. 500.

The basic meaning of the word Targum is "interpretation." Targums are paraphrases of the Old Testament in the Aramaic language.

The origins of the Targums are explained by Geisler and Nix:

There is evidence that the scribes were making oral paraphrases of the Hebrew Scriptures into the Aramaic vernacular as early as the time of Ezra (Neh. 8:1–8). These paraphrases were not strictly translations, but were actu-

ally aids in understanding the archaic language forms of the Torah.... The necessity for such helps arose because Hebrew was becoming less and less familiar to the ordinary people as a spoken language. By the close of the last centuries B.C., this gradual process had continued until almost every book in the Old Testament had its oral paraphrase or interpretation (Targum).

During the early centuries A.D., these Targums were committed to writing, and an official text came to the lore, since the Hebrew canon, text, and interpretation had become well solidified before the rabbinical scholars of Jamnia (c. A.D. 90) and the expulsion of the Jews from Palestine in A.D. 135. The earliest Targums were apparently written in Palestinian Aramaic during the second century A.D.; however, there is evidence of Aramaic Targums from the pre-Christian period. (Geisler, GIB, 304, 305)

Geisler and Nix go into more detail on some of the important Targums:

During the third century A.D., there appeared in Babylonia an Aramaic Targum on the Torah.... It has been traditionally ascribed to Onkelos.... Another Babylonian Aramaic Targum accompanies the Prophets (Former and Latter), and is known as the Targum of Jonathan ben Uzziel. It dates from the fourth century A.D. and is freer and more paraphrastic in its rendering of the text. Both of those Targums were read in the synagogues.... Because the Writings were not read in the synagogues, there was no reason to have official Targums for them, although unofficial copies were used by individuals. During the middle of the seventh century A.D. a Targum of the Pentateuch appeared called the Pseudo-Jonathan Targum.... The Jerusalem Targum also appeared at about 700, but has survived in fragments only. (Geisler, GIB, 304, 305)

After the Jews were taken into captivity, the Chaldean language replaced Hebrew.

Therefore the Jews needed the Scriptures in the spoken language.

F. F. Bruce provides more interesting background on the Targums:

> The practice of accompanying the public reading of the Scriptures in the synagogues by an oral paraphrase in the Aramaic vernacular grew up in the closing centuries B.C. Naturally, when Hebrew was becoming less and less familiar to the ordinary people as a spoken language, it was necessary that they should be provided with an interpretation of the text of Scripture in a language which they did know, if they were to understand what was read. The official charged with giving this oral paraphrase was called a methurgeman (translator or interpreter) and the paraphrase itself was called a targum.
>
> Methurgeman . . . was not allowed to read his interpretation out of a roll, as the congregation might mistakenly think he was reading the original Scriptures. With a view to accuracy, no doubt, it was further laid down that not more than one verse of the Pentateuch and not more than three verses of the Prophets might be translated at one time.
>
> In due course these Targums were committed to writing. (Bruce, BP, 133)

J. Anderson, in *The Bible, the Word of God,* observes: "The great utility of the earlier Targums consists in their vindicating the genuineness of the Hebrew text, by proving that it was the same at the period the Targums were made, as it exists among us at the present day." (Anderson, BWG, 17)

Geisler and Nix conclude that "none of these Targums is important to the textual critic, but they are all rather significant to the study of hermeneutics, as they indicate the manner in which Scripture was interpreted by rabbinical scholars." (Geisler, GIB, 305)

2D. Mishnah

The Mishnah (A.D. 200). "The *Mishnah* (repetition, explanation, teaching) was completed at about A.D. 200, and was a digest of all the oral laws from the time of Moses. It was regarded as the Second Law, the Torah being the First Law. This work was written in Hebrew, and it covered traditions as well as explanations of the oral law." (Geisler, GIB, 502)

The scriptural quotations are very similar to the Masoretic Text and witness to its reliability.

3D. Gemara

The Gemara (Palestinian, A.D. 200; Babylonian, A.D. 500). "The *Gemara* (to complete, accomplish, learn) was written in Aramaic rather than Hebrew, and was basically an expanded commentary on the Mishnah. It was transmitted in two traditions, the Palestinian Gemara (c. A.D. 200), and the larger and more authoritative Babylonian Gemara (c. A.D. 500)." (Geisler, GIB, 502)

These commentaries (written in Aramaic) that grew up around the Mishnah contribute to the textual reliability of the Masoretic Text.

The Mishnah plus the Palestinian Gemara make up the Palestinian Talmud.

The Mishnah plus the Babylonian Gemara make up the Babylonian Talmud.

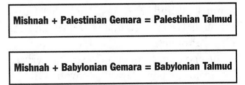

Mishnah + Palestinian Gemara = Palestinian Talmud

Mishnah + Babylonian Gemara = Babylonian Talmud

4D. Midrash

Midrash (100 B.C.–A.D. 300) was made up of doctrinal studies of the Old Testament Hebrew text. The Midrash quotations are substantially Masoretic.

The Midrash (textual study, textual interpretation) was actually a formal doctrinal and homiletical exposition of the Hebrew Scriptures written in Hebrew and Aramaic.

Midrashim (plural) were collected into a body of material between 100 B.C. and A.D. 300. Within the Midrash were two major parts: the *Halakah* (procedure), a further expansion of the Torah only, and the *Haggada* (declaration, explanation), being commentaries on the entire Old Testament. These Midrashim differed from the Targums in that the former were actually commentaries whereas the latter were paraphrases. The Midrashim contain some of the earliest extant synagogue homilies on the Old Testament, including such things as proverbs and parables. (Geisler, GIB, 306)

5D. Other Important Discoveries

Nash Papyri. Among the earliest Old Testament Hebrew manuscripts, there is extant one damaged copy of the Shema (from Deut. 6:4–9) and two fragments of the Decalogue (Ex. 20:2–17; Deut. 5:6–21). The Nash Papyri are dated between the second century B.C. and the first century A.D.

Codex Cairensis. A codex is a manuscript in book form with pages. According to a colophon, or inscription at the end of the book, Codex Cairensis (C) was written and vowel-pointed in A.D. 895 by Moses ben Asher in Tiberias in Palestine. It contains the Former Prophets (Joshua, Judges, 1 and 2 Samuel, 1 and 2 Kings) and the Latter Prophets (Isaiah, Jeremiah, Ezekiel, and the Minor Prophets).

Aleppo Codex. Aleppo Codex was written by Shelomo ben Baya'a (Kenyon, OBAM, 84), but according to a colophon note it was pointed (i.e., the vowel marks were added) by Moses ben Asher (c. A.D. 930). It is a model codex, although it was not permitted to be copied for a long time and was even reported to have been destroyed. (Wurthwein, TOT, 25) It was smuggled from Syria to Israel. It has now been photographed and is the basis of the *New Hebrew Bible* published by Hebrew University. (Goshen-Gottstein, BMUS, 13) It is a sound authority for the ben Asher text.

Codex Leningradensis. According to a colophon note, Codex Leningradensis (L) was copied in Old Cairo by Samuel ben Jacob in 1008 from a manuscript (now lost) written by Aaron ben Moses ben Asher c. 1000. (Kahle, CG, 110) It represents one of the oldest manuscripts of the complete Hebrew Bible.

Babylonian Codex of the Latter Prophets. The Babylonian Codex (V [ar] P) is sometimes called the Leningrad Codex of the Prophets (Kenyon, 85) or the [St.] Petersburg Codex. (Wurthwein, TOT, 26) It contains Isaiah, Jeremiah, and the Twelve. It is dated 916, but its chief significance is that, through it, punctuation added by the Babylonian school of Masoretic scribes was rediscovered. Dated 1105, Reuchlin Codex is now at Karlsruhe. Like the British Museum manuscript (c. A.D. 1150), it contains a recension of Ben Naphtali, a Tiberian Masorete. These have been of great value in establishing the fidelity of the Ben Asher text. (Kenyon, OBAM, 36)

Erfurt Codices. The Erfurt Codices (E1, E2, E3) are listed in the University Library in Tubingen. They represent more or less (more in E3) the text and markings of the Ben Naphtali tradition. E1 is a fourteenth-century manuscript. E2 is probably from the thirteenth century. E3, the oldest, is dated before 1100. (Wurthwein, TOT, 26)

2B. Summary

1C. Rules for Textual Criticism

The list on the facing page has been developed by scholars to give certain criteria for determining which reading is correct or original. Seven are suggested.

2C. Comparison of Duplicate Passages

Another line of evidence for the quality of the Old Testament manuscripts is found in the comparison of the duplicate passages of the Masoretic Text itself. Several psalms occur twice (for example, 14 and 53); much of Isaiah 36–39 is also found in 2 Kings 18—20; Isaiah 2:24 is almost exactly parallel to Micah 4:1–3; Jeremiah 52 is a repeat of 2 Kings 25; and large portions of Chronicles are found in Samuel and Kings. An examination of those passages shows not only a substantial textual agreement but, in some cases, almost word-for-word identity. Therefore it may be concluded that the Old Testament texts have not undergone radical revisions, even if it were assumed that these parallel passages had identical sources.

3C. Support from Archaeology

A substantial proof for the accuracy of the Old Testament text has come from archaeology. Numerous discoveries have confirmed the historical accuracy of the biblical documents, even down to the occasional use of obsolete names of foreign kings. These archaeological confirmations of the accuracy of Scripture have been recorded in numerous books. Archaeologist Nelson Glueck asserts, "It may be stated categorically that no archaeological discovery has ever controverted a biblical reference. Scores of archaeological findings have been made which confirm in clear outline or exact detail historical statements in the Bible." (Glueck, RDHN, 31) (See section 2A of this chapter, "Archaeological and Historical Confirmation of the Old Testament" for more detailed coverage.)

4C. The Septuagint and the Masoretic Text

The Septuagint was the Bible of Jesus and the apostles. Most New Testament quotations are taken from it directly, even when it

> ### GUIDE TO SELECTING A CORRECT READING
>
> 1. An older reading is to be preferred, because it is closer to the original.
> 2. The more difficult reading is to be preferred, because scribes were more apt to smooth out difficult readings.
> 3. The shorter reading is to be preferred, because copyists were more apt to insert new material than omit part of the sacred text.
> 4. The reading that best explains the other variants is to be preferred.
> 5. The reading with the widest geographical support is to be preferred, because such manuscripts or versions are less likely to have influenced each other.
> 6. The reading that is most like the author's usual style is to be preferred.
> 7. The reading that does not reflect a doctrinal bias is to be preferred. (Wurthwein, TOT, 80–81)

differs from the Masoretic Text. On the whole the Septuagint closely parallels the Masoretic Text and is a confirmation of the fidelity of the tenth-century Hebrew text.

If no other evidence were available, the case for the fidelity of the Masoretic Text could be brought to rest with confidence based upon textual comparisons and an understanding of the extraordinary Jewish scribal system. But with the discovery of the Dead Sea Scrolls, beginning in 1947, there is almost overwhelming substantiation of the received Hebrew text of the Masoretes. Critics of the Masoretic Text charged that the manuscripts were few and late. Through the Dead Sea Scrolls, early manuscript fragments provide a check on nearly the whole Old Testament. Those checks date about a thousand years before the Great Masoretic manuscripts of the tenth century. Before the discoveries in the Cairo Geniza and the Dead Sea caves, the Nash Papyrus (a fragment of the Ten Commandments and Shema, Deut. 6:4–9), dated between 150 and 100 B.C., was the only known scrap of the Hebrew text dating from before the Christian era.

5C. Agreement with the Samaritan Pentateuch

Despite the many minor variants between the Samaritan Pentateuch and the Hebrew text of the Old Testament, there is substantial agreement between them. As noted previously, the six thousand variants from the Masoretic Text are mostly differences in spelling and cultural word variation. Nineteen hundred variants agree with the Septuagint (for example, in the ages given for the patriarchs in Genesis 5 and 11). Some Samaritan Pentateuch variants are sectarian, such as the command to build the temple on Mount Gerizim, not at Jerusalem (e.g., after Ex. 20:17). It should be noted, however, that most manuscripts of the Samaritan Pentateuch are late (thirteenth to fourteenth centuries), and none is before the tenth century. (Archer, SOT, 44) But the Samaritan Pentateuch still confirms the general text from which it had diverged many hundreds of years earlier.

6C. Check Against the Dead Sea Scrolls

With the discovery of the Dead Sea Scrolls, scholars have Hebrew manuscripts dated one thousand years earlier than the great Masoretic Text manuscripts, enabling them to check the fidelity of the Hebrew text. There is a word-for-word identity in more than 95 percent of the cases, and the 5-percent variation consists mostly of slips of the pen and spelling. The Isaiah scroll (1QIs a) from Qumran led the Revised Standard Version translators to make only thirteen changes from the Masoretic Text; eight of those were known from ancient versions, and few were significant. (Burrows, WMTS, 30-59) Of the 166 Hebrew words in Isaiah 53, only seventeen Hebrew letters in the Isaiah B scroll differ from the Masoretic Text. Ten letters are a matter of spelling, four are stylistic changes, and the other three compose the word for "light," (added in verse 11), which does not affect the meaning greatly. (Harris, IC, 124) Furthermore that word is also found in the same verse in the Septuagint and in the Isaiah A scroll.

7C. Conclusion

The thousands of Hebrew manuscripts, with their confirmation by the Septuagint and the Samaritan Pentateuch, and the numerous other cross-checks from outside and inside the text provide overwhelming support for the reliability of the Old Testament text. Hence, it is appropriate to conclude with Kenyon's statement, "The Christian can take the whole Bible in his hand and say without fear or hesitation that he holds in it the true word of God, handed down without essential loss from generation to generation throughout the centuries." (Kenyon, OBAM, 23)

Since the Old Testament text is related in important ways to the New Testament, its reliability supports the Christian faith. This is true not only in establishing the dates when supernatural predictions were made of the Messiah, but also in supporting the historicity of the Old Testament that Jesus and New Testament writers affirmed. (Geisler, BECA, 552–553)

For further reading, consult the following sources:

Allegro, I. M. *The Treasure of the Copper Scroll,* 2nd rev. ed.

Archer, G. L., Jr. *A Survey of Old Testament,* Introduction, Appendix 4.

Barthelemy, D. and J. T. Milik. *Ten Years of Discovery in the Judean Wilderness*

Cass, T. S. *Secrets from the Caves.*

Elliger, K. and W. Rudolph, eds. *Biblia Hebraica..*

Geisler, N. L. "Bible Manuscripts." In *Wycliffe Bible Encyclopedia.*

Geisler, N. L. and W. E. Nix. *General Introduction to the Bible.*

Glueck, N. *Rivers in the Desert: A History of the Negev.*

Goshen-Gottstein, M. "Biblical Manuscripts in the United States." *Textus* 3 (1962).

Harris, R. L. *Inspiration and Canonicity.*

Kahle, P. E. *The Cairo Geniza.*

Kenyon, F. G. *Our Bible and the Ancient Manuscripts.*

Kittel, R. and P. Kahle, eds. *Biblia Hebraica*, 7th ed.

Mansoor, M. *The Dead Sea Scrolls.*

Trever, J. C. "The Discovery of the Scrolls." *Biblical Archaeologist* 11 (September 1948).

Vermes, G. trans. *The Dead Sea Scrolls in English.*

Wurthwein, E. *The Text of the Old Testament: An Introduction to the Biblia Hebraica*

2A. ARCHAEOLOGICAL AND HISTORICAL CONFIRMATION OF THE OLD TESTAMENT

1B. Introduction and Definition of Archaeology

The discipline of archaeology has only recently gained relative importance among the physical sciences. However, it has made significant contributions in many areas, including biblical criticism and arguments for the reliability of the biblical text.

The word archaeology is composed of two Greek words: *Archaios,* meaning "old" or "ancient"; and *Logos,* signifying "word, treatise, or study." A literal definition is "the study of antiquity." Webster defines it, "The scientific study of material remains (as fossils, relics, artifacts, and monuments) of past human life and activities." (*Merriam Webster's Collegiate Dictionary*, 10th edition, Springfield, Mass.: Merriam-Webster, Inc., 1997) So the task of the archaeologist is to take what remains from a society and reconstruct what the artifacts tell us.

Archaeology is very different from most of modern science in that it attempts to prove a thesis. The basic premise of an experiment in modern science is that if it is repeatable, then it must be true. Archaeology, on the other hand, cannot possibly repeat its results. It can only give conjectures—not firm conclusions—concerning its finds, unless there is another outside confirmation by means of a text or other report. And this is where biblical archaeology takes on a unique twist.

In the nineteenth and twentieth centuries the Bible took a beating from higher criticism. Critics have sought to destroy the foundations of the historicity of the Bible by showing that the Bible has errors and must be adjusted to fit the "facts" of archaeology. But now the tables are turning. Reformed Jewish scholar Nelson Glueck has observed: "It is worth emphasizing that in all this work no archaeological discovery has ever controverted a single, properly understood biblical statement." (Glueck, as cited in Montgomery, CFTM, 6) Note that this statement was made by a Reformed Jewish scholar. He is not a Christian and yet he sees that archaeology confirms the Bible.

For the purposes of this book, archaeological confirmation is divided into artifact evidence and documentary evidence. Artifact evidence is defined as artifacts of a previous society testifying directly of a biblical event. On the other hand, documentary evidence will be defined as extrabiblical texts (written documents) that confirm Old Testament history directly or indirectly. Both kinds of evidence are archaeological in nature.

2B. A Word of Caution

Even though archaeology has never contradicted the Bible, a word of caution is necessary here. All too often we hear the statement, "Archaeology proves the Bible." Archaeology cannot "prove" the Bible, if by this you mean "proves it to be inspired and revealed by God." But if by "prove" one means "shows some biblical event or passage to be historical," then archaeology does prove the Bible. I believe that archaeology contributes to biblical criticism, not in the area of inspiration or revelation, but as it confirms the historical accuracy and trustworthiness of the events recorded. Let's say the rocks on which the Ten Commandments were written are found. Archaeology could confirm that they were rocks, that the Ten Commandments were written on them, and that they came from the period of Moses; it could not prove that God delivered them to Moses.

Millar Burrows writes that archaeology "can tell us a great deal about the topography of a military campaign. It can tell us nothing about the nature of God." (Burrows, WMTS, 290)

There is one limitation that archaeology has to deal with, and this is the lack of abundant evidence. "Historians of antiquity," writes Edwin Yamauchi, "in using the archaeological evidence have very often failed to realize how slight is the evidence at our disposal. It would not be exaggerating to point out that what we have is but one fraction of a second fraction of a third fraction of a fourth fraction of a fifth fraction of the possible evidence." (Yamauchi, SSS, 9)

Joseph Free, in *Archaeology and Bible History*, addresses the question of archaeology and its relationship to the Bible:

> *In addition to illuminating the Bible, archaeology has confirmed countless passages which have been rejected by critics as unhistorical or contradictory to known facts.*
>
> —JOSEPH FREE

We pointed out that numerous passages of the Bible which long puzzled the commentators have readily yielded up their meaning when new light from archaeological discoveries has been focused on them. In other words, archaeology illuminates the text of the Scriptures and so makes valuable contributions to the fields of biblical interpretation and exegesis. In addition to illuminating the Bible, archaeology has confirmed countless passages which have been rejected by critics as unhistorical or contradictory to known facts. (Free, ABH, 1)

One also needs to realize that archaeology has not completely refuted the "radical critics." These critics have certain presuppositions that bar them from having an objective point of view. Burrows is quite clear on this point: "It is quite untrue to say that all the theories of the critics have been overthrown by archaeological discoveries. It is even more untrue to say that the fundamental attitudes and methods of modern scientific criticism have been refuted." (Burrows, WMTS, 292)

However, as you will see in this chapter, archaeology has shown that many convictions of radical criticism are invalid, and has called into question what have often been taught as "the assured results of higher criticism." Thus it is important when dealing with archaeology not only to seek the facts, but also to examine the presuppositions of those proposing the facts.

For example, Albright comments about the evidence for the extensive reign of Solomon, which had been questioned by the radical critics. He writes: "Once more we find that the radical criticism of the past half-century must be corrected drastically." (Albright, NLEHPC, 22)

Some people will make the unfounded assertion that supernaturalists and non-supernaturalists can never agree on the results of archaeology because they exist in two totally different camps. These will conclude that you interpret archaeological findings according to your own viewpoint.

Joseph Free, in "Archaeology and Higher Criticism," answers this assertion in a very convincing way.

> According to this view, a given archaeological discovery means one thing to a supernaturalist, and something different to a nonsupernaturalist, and therefore archaeology has only an incidental bearing on the whole matter of apologetics.
>
> Actually, this is not the whole picture. To illustrate: in the nineteenth century, the Biblical critic could hold with good reason that there never was a Sargon, that the Hittites either did not exist or were insignificant, that the patriarchal accounts had a late background, that the sevenfold lampstand of the tabernacle was a late concept, that the Davidic Empire was not as extensive as the Bible implied, that Belshazzar never existed, and that a host of other supposed errors and impossibilities existed in the Biblical record.
>
> Archaeological discoveries showed, on the contrary, that Sargon existed and lived in a palatial dwelling some twelve miles north of Nineveh, that the Hittites not only existed but were a significant people, that the background of the patriarchs fits the time indicated in the Bible, that the concept of a sevenfold lamp existed in the Early Iron Age, that a significant city given in the record of David's Empire lies far to the north, that Belshazzar existed and ruled over Babylon, and that a host of other supposed errors and contradictions are not errors at all.
>
> It is of course true that in certain peripheral areas, one's theology will have a bearing on his interpretation of a given fact or a particular archaeological discovery. But in the broad outline as well as in a host of small details, facts are facts whether discovered by a supernaturalist or nonsupernaturalist. The writer knows of no nonsupernaturalist who still argues that Sargon never existed, that there never were any Hittites, or that Belshazzar is still a legend. There are many points on which all candid scholars can agree, regardless of their theology. There are certain areas, however, where the liberal has not taken the evidence, archaeological or otherwise, sufficiently into account. This is true, we believe, in the realm of the documentary theory and in the question of authorship, date, and integrity of the books of the Bible. (Free, AHC, 30, 31)

3B. Interpreting Archaeological Data

The following three points provide helpful guidelines when reviewing archaeological data as it relates to Christianity. First, meaning can only be derived from context. Archaeological evidence is dependent on the context of date, place, materials, and style. How it is understood depends on the interpreter's presuppositions. Therefore, not all interpretations of the evidence will be friendly to Christianity. It is important to make sure that one's presuppositions are accurate before interpreting the data.

Second, archaeology is a special kind of science. Physicists and chemists can do all kinds of experiments to recreate the processes they study and watch them over and over again. Archaeologists cannot. They have only the evidence left from the one and only time that civilization lived. They study past singularities, not present regularities. Because they can't recreate the societies they study, their conclusions can't be tested as can those of other sciences. Archaeology tries to find plausible and probable explanations for the evidence it finds. It cannot make laws as can physics. For this reason, its conclusions are subject to revision. The best interpretation is the one that best explains all the evidence.

Third, the archaeological evidence is fragmentary. It comprises only a tiny fraction of all that occurred. Hence, the discovery of more evidence can change the picture considerably. This is especially true when conclusions have been based on silence—a lack of existing evidence. Many critical views about the Bible have been overturned by archaeological discoveries. For example, it was long believed that the Bible erred when it spoke about Hittites. (Gen. 23:10) But since the discovery of the Hittite library in Turkey (1906) this is no longer the case. (Geisler, BECA, 48, 49)

> With the aid of stratigraphy, scientific analysis, and museum research, the archaeologist can now reconstruct the daily life of ancient peoples with remarkable completeness.
>
> —WILLIAM F. ALBRIGHT

4B. Basic Reasons for the Rapidly Increasing Interest in Archaeology

Why has archaeology received so much more attention in recent years than before? William F. Albright cites four factors for the steady advance in the area of archaeology:

1. "A rapid increase in the number of serious archaeological expeditions from many different countries, including Japan. Museum space and volumes of publication have also kept pace with the field work. So there are not only more digs, but more articles about digs.

2. "An improvement of archaeological method that has been little short of phenomenal. This applies both to the analysis of superimposed layers of occupation (stratigraphy) and to classification and relative dating of objects found (typology).

3. "Use of innumerable new techniques derived from the natural sciences, among them radiocarbon (carbon isotope 14) for dating.

4. "Decipherment and interpretation of the flood of new inscriptions and texts in many scripts and languages, many quite unknown until recent decades. The application of sound linguistic and philological method to well-preserved cuneiform tablets and Egyptian hieratic papyri makes it possible to publish them with speed and accuracy. A new script is deciphered quickly, if there are a few good clues or sufficient material to permit decoding. The number of cuneiform tablets from three millennia preserved under debris of occupation in Western Asia and Egypt seems to be practically unlimited, and new methods of baking and reproduction have reduced losses to a surprisingly low proportion.

"With the aid of stratigraphy, scientific analysis, and museum research, the archaeologist can now reconstruct the daily life of ancient peoples with remarkable completeness." (Albright, ADS, 3)

5B. The Stones Cry Out: Examples of Archaeological Support for the Old Testament Accounts

Archaeology enhances our knowledge of the economic, cultural, social, and political background of biblical passages. Also, archaeology contributes to the understanding of other religions that bordered Israel.

1C. Sodom and Gomorrah

The destruction of Sodom and Gomorrah was thought to be spurious until evidence revealed that all five of the cities mentioned in the Bible were in fact centers of commerce in the area and were geographically situated as the Scriptures describe. The biblical description of their demise seems to be no less accurate. Evidence points to earthquake activity, and that the various layers of the earth were disrupted and hurled high into the air. Bitumen is plentiful there, and an accurate description would be that brimstone (bituminous pitch) was hurled down on those cities that had rejected God. There is evidence that the layers of sedimentary rock have been molded together by intense heat. Evidence of such burning has been found on the top of Jebel Usdum (Mount Sodom). This is permanent evidence of the great conflagration that took place in the long-distant past, possibly when an oil basin beneath the Dead Sea ignited and erupted. Such an explanation in no way subtracts from the miraculous quality of the event, for God controls natural forces. The timing of the event, in the context of warnings and visitation by angels, reveals its overall miraculous nature. (Geisler, BECA, 50, 51)

2C. Jericho

During the excavations of Jericho (1930–1936) Garstang found something so startling that he and two other members of the team prepared and signed a statement describing what was found. In reference to these findings Garstang says: "As to the main fact, then, there remains no doubt: the walls fell outwards so completely that the attackers would be able to clamber up and over their ruins into the city. Why so unusual? Because the walls of cities do not fall outwards, they fall inwards. And yet in Joshua 6:20 we read, 'The wall fell down flat. Then the people went up into the city, every man straight before him, and they took the city.' The walls were made to fall outward." (Garstang, FBHJJ, 146)

Bryant Wood, writing for *Biblical Archaeology Review* (Wood, DICJ, 44–59), includes a list of collaboration between archeological evidence and biblical narrative as follows:

1. The city was strongly fortified (Josh. 2:5, 7, 15; 6:5, 20).
2. The attack occurred just after harvest time in the spring (Josh. 2:1; 3:15; 5:16).
3. The inhabitants had no opportunity to flee with their foodsheds (Josh. 6:1).
4. The siege was short (Josh. 6:15).
5. The walls were leveled, possibly by an earthquake (Josh. 6:20).
6. The city was not plundered (Josh. 6:17, 18).
7. The city was burned (Josh. 6:24).

3C. Saul, David, and Solomon

Saul became the first king of Israel, and his fortress at Gibeah has been excavated. One of the most noteworthy finds was that slingshots were one of the primary weapons of the day. This relates not only to David's victory over Goliath, but to the reference of Judges 20:16 that there were seven hundred expert slingers who "could sling a stone at a hair and not miss."

Upon Saul's death, Samuel tells us that his armor was put in the temple of Ashtaroth (a Canaanite fertility goddess) at Bet She'an, while Chronicles records that his head was put in the temple of Dagon, the Philistine corn god. This was thought to be an error because it seemed unlikely that enemy peoples would have temples in the same place at the same time. However, excavations have revealed that there are two temples at this site that are separated by a hallway: one for Dagon, and the other for Ashtaroth. It appears that the Philistines had adopted the Canaanite goddess.

One of the key accomplishments of David's reign was the capture of Jerusalem. Problematic in the Scripture account was that the Israelites entered the city by way of a tunnel that led to the Pool of Siloam. However, that pool was thought to be *outside* the city walls at that time. But excavations in the 1960s revealed that the wall did indeed extend well past the pool.

The time of Solomon has no less corroboration. The site of Solomon's temple cannot be excavated, because it is near the Muslim holy place, The Dome of the Rock. However, what is known about Philistine temples built in Solomon's time fits well with the design, decoration, and materials described in the Bible. The only piece of evidence from the temple itself is a small ornament, a pomegranate, that sat on the end of a rod and bears the inscription, "Belonging to the Temple of Yahweh." It was first seen in a shop in Jerusalem in 1979, was verified in 1984, and was acquired by the Israel Museum in 1988.

The excavation of Gezer in 1969 ran across a massive layer of ash that covered most of the mound. Sifting through the ash yielded pieces of Hebrew, Egyptian, and Philistine artifacts. Apparently all three cultures had been there at the same time. This puzzled researchers greatly until they realized that the Bible confirms exactly what they found. "Pharaoh king of Egypt had attacked and captured Gezer. He had set it on fire. He killed its Canaanite inhabitants and then gave it as a wedding gift to his daughter, Solomon's wife." (1 Kings 9:16) (Geisler, BECA, 51, 52)

A 1989 article by Alan Millard in *Biblical Archaeology Review,* entitled "Does the Bible exaggerate King Solomon's Wealth?" states, "Those who read the Bible text and make a subjective judgment as to its reliability often conclude—and understandably so—that the descriptions of Solomon's gold are gross exaggerations. The quantity of gold the Bible claims for King Solomon is simply unbelievable, even unimaginable.

"We have not proved that the details in the Bible regarding Solomon's gold are accurate. But by setting the biblical text beside other ancient texts and archeological discoveries we have shown that the biblical narrative is wholly in keeping with the practices of the ancient world, so far as we can ascertain them, not only in the use of gold but also in its records of quantities. While this does not demonstrate that the account in the Bible is accurate, it does show that it is feasible." (Millard, DBEKSW, 20)

4C. David

S. H. Horn, an archaeologist, gives an excellent example of how archaeological evidence helps in biblical study:

Archaeological explorations have shed some interesting light on the capture of Jerusalem by David. The biblical accounts of that capture (II Sam. 5:6–8 and I Chron. 11:6) are rather obscure without the help obtained from archaeological evidence. Take for example II Samuel 5:8, which in the King James Version reads: "And David said on that day, Whosoever getteth up to the gutter, and smiteth the Jebusites, and the lame and the blind, that are hated of David's soul, he shall be chief and captain." Add to this statement First Chronicles 11:6—"So Joab the son of Zeruiah went first up and was chief."

Some years ago I saw a painting of the conquest of Jerusalem in which the artist showed a man climbing up a metal downspout, running on the outside face of the city wall. This picture was absurd, because ancient city walls had neither gutters nor downspouts, although they had weeping holes in the walls to drain water off. The Revised Standard Version, produced after the situation had become clear through archaeological discoveries made on the spot, translates the pertinent passages: "And David said on that day, 'Whoever would smite the Jebusites, let him get up the water shaft to attack the lame and the blind, who are hated by David's soul.' And Joab the son of Zeruiah went up first, so he became chief." What was this water shaft that Joab climbed?

Jerusalem in those days was a small city lying on a single spur of the hills on which the large city eventually stood. Its position was one of great natural strength, because it was surrounded on three sides by deep valleys. This was why the Jebusites boastfully declared that even blind and lame could hold their city against a powerful attacking army. But the water supply of the city was poor; the population was entirely dependent on a spring that lay outside the city on the eastern slope of the hill.

So that they could obtain water without having to go down to where the spring was located, the Jebusites had constructed an elaborate system of tunnels through the rock. First they had dug a horizontal tunnel, beginning at the spring and proceeding toward the center of the city. After digging for ninety feet they hit a natural cave. From the cave they dug a vertical shaft forty-five feet high, and from the end of the shaft a sloping tunnel 135 feet long and a staircase that ended at the surface of their city, 110 feet above the water level of the spring. The spring was then concealed from the outside so that no enemy could detect it. To get water the Jebusite women went down through the upper tunnel and let their water skins down the shaft to draw water from the cave, to which it was brought by natural flow through the horizontal tunnel that connected the cave with the spring.

However, one question remained unanswered. The excavations of R. A. S. Macalister and J. G. Duncan some forty years ago had uncovered a wall and a tower that were thought to be of Jebusite and Davidic origin respectively. This tract of wall ran along the rim of the hill of Ophel, west of the tunnel entrance. Thus the entrance was left outside the protective city wall, exposed to the attacks and interference of enemies. Why hadn't the tunnel been built to end inside the city? This puzzle has now been solved by the recent excavations of Kathleen Kenyon on Ophel. She found that Macalister and Duncan had

given the wall and tower they discovered wrong dates; these things actually originated in the Hellenistic period. She uncovered the real Jebusite wall a little farther down the slope of the hill, east of the tunnel entrance, which now puts the entrance safely in the old city area.

David, a native of Bethlehem, four miles south of Jerusalem, ... made the promise that the first man who entered the city through the water shaft would become his commander-in-chief. Joab, who was already general of the army, did not want to lose that position and therefore led the attack himself. The Israelites apparently went through the tunnel, climbed up the shaft, and were in the city before any of the besieged citizens had any idea that so bold a plan had been conceived. (Horn, RIOT, 15,16)

Avaraham Biram (Biram, BAR, 26) speaks of a new discovery in 1994:

A remarkable inscription from the ninth century BCE that refers to both the [House of David], and to the [King of Israel]. This is the first time that the name of David has been found in any ancient inscription outside the Bible. That the inscription refers not simply to a [David] but to the House of David, the dynasty of the great Israelite king, is even more remarkable . . . this may be the oldest extra-biblical reference to Israel in Semitic script. If this inscription proves anything, it shows that both Israel and Judah, contrary to

> This is the first time that the name of David has been found in any ancient inscription outside the Bible. That the inscription refers not simply to a [David] but to the House of David, the dynasty of the great Israelite king, is even more remarkable . . . this may be the oldest extra-biblical reference to Israel in Semitic script.
>
> —AVARAHAM BIRAM

the claims of some scholarly biblical minimizers, were important kingdoms at this time.

5C. Summary and Conclusions

Henry M. Morris observes: "Problems still exist, of course, in the complete harmonization of archaeological material with the Bible, but none so serious as not to bear real promise of imminent solution through further investigation. It must be extremely significant that, in view of the great mass of corroborative evidence regarding the biblical history of these periods, there exists today not one unquestionable find of archaeology that proves the Bible to be in error at any point." (Morris, BMS, 95)

In every period of Old Testament history, we find that there is good evidence from archaeology that the Scriptures speak the truth. In many instances, the Scriptures even reflect firsthand knowledge of the times and customs it describes. While many have doubted the accuracy of the Bible, time and continued research have consistently demonstrated that the Word of God is better informed than its critics.

In fact, while thousands of finds from the ancient world support in broad outline and often in detail the biblical picture, not one incontrovertible find has ever contradicted the Bible. (Geisler, BECA, 52)

Henry Morris adds:

This great antiquity of the Bible histories in comparison with those of other writings, combined with the evolutionary preconceptions of the 19th century, led many scholars to insist that the Bible histories also were in large part merely legendary. As long as nothing was available, except copies of ancient manuscripts, for the evaluation of ancient histories, such teachings may have been persuasive. Now, however, it is no longer possible to reject the substantial historicity of the Bible, at least as far back as the time of Abraham, because of the remarkable discoveries of archaeology. (Morris, MIP, 300)

6B. Documentary Confirmation of the Old Testament Accounts

1C. The Reliability of the Old Testament History

Not only do we have accurate copies or the Old Testament, but the contents of the manuscripts are historically reliable.

William F. Albright, known for his reputation as one of the great archaeologists, states: "There can be no doubt that archaeology has confirmed the substantial historicity of Old Testament tradition." (Albright, ARI, 176)

Professor H. H. Rowley (cited by Donald F. Wiseman in *Revelation and the Bible*) claims that "it is not because scholars of today begin with more conservative presuppositions than their predecessors that they have a much greater respect for the Patriarchal stories than was formerly common, but because the evidence warrants it." (Rowley, as cited in Wiseman, ACOT, in Henry, RB, 305)

Merrill Unger summarizes: "Old Testament archaeology has rediscovered whole nations, resurrected important peoples, and in a most astonishing manner filled in historical gaps, adding immeasurably to the knowledge of biblical backgrounds." (Unger, AOT, 15)

New discoveries continue to confirm the historical accuracy or the literary antiquity of detail after detail in it [the Pentateuch]. . . . It is, accordingly, sheer hypercriticism to deny the substantially Mosaic character of the Pentateuchal tradition.

—WILLIAM F. ALBRIGHT

Sir Frederic Kenyon says: "It is therefore legitimate to say that, in respect of that part of the Old Testament against which the disintegrating criticism of the last half of the nineteenth century was chiefly directed, the evidence of archaeology has been to re-establish its authority, and likewise to augment its value by rendering it more intelligible through a fuller knowledge of its background and setting. Archaeology has not yet said its last word; but the results already achieved confirm what faith would suggest, that the Bible can do nothing but gain from an increase of knowledge." (Kenyon, BA, 279)

Archaeology has produced an abundance of evidence to substantiate the correctness of our Masoretic Text. Bernard Ramm writes of the Jeremiah Seal:

> *Now, however, it is no longer possible to reject the substantial historicity of the Bible, at least as far back as the time of Abraham, because of the remarkable discoveries of archaeology.*
>
> —HENRY MORRIS

Archaeology has also given us evidence as to the substantial accuracy of our Masoretic text. The Jeremiah Seal, a seal used to stamp the bitumen seals of wine jars, and dated from the first or second century A.D., has Jeremiah 48:11 stamped on it and, in general, conforms to the Masoretic text. This seal ". . . attests the accuracy with which the text was transmitted between the time when the seal was made and the time when the manuscripts were written." Furthermore, the *Roberts Papyrus*, which dates to the second century B.C., and the *Nash Papyrus*, dated by Albright before 100 B.C., confirm our Masoretic text. (Ramm, CITOT, 8–10)

William Albright affirms that "we may rest assured that the consonantal text of the Hebrew Bible, though not infallible, has been preserved with an accuracy perhaps unparalleled in any other Near-Eastern literature. . . . No, the flood of light now being shed on biblical Hebrew poetry of all periods by Ugaritic literature guarantees the relative antiquity of its composition as well as the astonishing accuracy of its transmission." (Albright, OTAAE, as cited in Rowley, OTMS, 25)

Archaeologist Albright writes concerning the accuracy of the Scriptures as the result of archaeology: "The contents of our Pentateuch are, in general, very much older than the date at which they were finally edited; new discoveries continue to confirm the historical accuracy or the literary antiquity of detail after detail in it. . . . It is, accordingly, sheer hypercriticism to deny the substantially Mosaic character of the Pentateuchal tradition." (Dodd, MNTS, 224)

Albright comments on what the critics used to say:

> Until recently it was the fashion among biblical historians to treat the patriarchal sagas of Genesis as though they were artificial creations of Israelite scribes of the Divided Monarchy or tales told by imaginative rhapsodists around Israelite campfires during the centuries following their occupation of the country. Eminent names among scholars can be cited for regarding every item of Gen. 11—50 as reflecting late invention, or at least retrojection of events and conditions under the Monarchy into the remote past, about which nothing was thought to have been really known to the writers of later days. (Albright, BPFAE, 1, 2)

Now it has all been changed, says Albright: "Archaeological discoveries since

1925 have changed all this. Aside from a few die-hards among older scholars, there is scarcely a single biblical historian who has not been impressed by the rapid accumulation of data supporting the substantial historicity of patriarchal tradition. According to the traditions of Genesis the ancestors of Israel were closely related to the semi-nomadic peoples of TransJordan, Syria, the Euphrates basin and North Arabia in the last centuries of the second millennium B.C., and the first centuries of the first millennium." (Albright, BPFAE, 1, 2)

Millar Burrows continues:

To see the situation clearly we must distinguish two kinds of confirmation, general and specific. General confirmation is a matter of compatibility without definite corroboration of particular points. Much of what has already been discussed as explanation and illustration may be regarded also as general confirmation. The picture fits the frame; the melody and the accompaniment are harmonious. The force of such evidence is cumulative. The more we find that items in the picture of the past presented by the Bible, even though not directly attested, are compatible with what we know from archaeology, the stronger is our impression of general authenticity. Mere legend or fiction would inevitably betray itself by anachronisms and incongruities. (Burrows, WMTS, 278)

The University of Chicago professor Raymond A. Bowman denotes that archaeology helps provide a balance between the Bible and critical hypothesis: "The confirmation of the biblical narrative at most points has led to a new respect for biblical tradition and a more conservative conception of biblical history." (Bowman, OTRGW, as cited in Willoughby, SBTT, 30)

Albright, in "Archaeology Confronts Biblical Criticism," says that "archaeological and inscriptional data have established the historicity of innumerable passages and statements of the Old Testament." (Albright, ACBC, 181)

Archaeology does not prove the Bible to be the Word of God. All it can do is confirm the basic historicity or authenticity of a narrative. It can show that a certain incident fits into the time it purports to be from. "We

> The Bible is supported by archaeological evidence again and again. On the whole, there can be no question that the results of excavation have increased the respect of scholars for the Bible as a collection of historical documents.
>
> —MILLAR BURROWS

shall probably never," writes G. E. Wright, "be able to prove that Abram really existed . . . but what we can prove is that his life and times, as reflected in the stories about him, fit perfectly within the early second millennium, but imperfectly within any later period." (Wright, BA, 40)

Millar Burrows of Yale recognized the value of archaeology in confirming the authenticity of the Scriptures:

The Bible is supported by archaeological evidence again and again. On the whole, there can be no question that the results of excavation have increased the respect of scholars for the Bible as a collection of historical documents. The confirmation is both general and specific. The fact that the record can be so often explained or illustrated by archaeological data shows that it fits into the framework of history as only a genuine product of ancient life could do. In addition to this general authentication, however, we find the record verified repeatedly at specific points. Names of places and persons turn up at the right places and in the right periods. (Burrows, HAHSB, 6)

Joseph Free comments that he once "thumbed through the book of Genesis and mentally noted that each of the fifty chapters are either illuminated or confirmed by some archaeological discovery—the same would be true for most of the remaining chapters of the Bible, both Old and New Testaments." (Free, AB, 340)

2C. The Creation

The opening chapters of Genesis (1—11) are typically thought to be mythological explanations derived from earlier versions of the story found in the ancient Near East. But this view chooses only to notice the similarities between Genesis and the creation stories in other ancient cultures. If we can propose derivation of the human race from one family, plus general revelation, some lingering traces of the true historical account would be expected. The differences are more important. Babylonian and Sumerian accounts describe the creation as the product of a conflict among finite gods. When one god is defeated and split in half, the River Euphrates flows from one eye and the Tigris from the other. Humanity is made of the blood of an evil god mixed with clay. These tales display the kind of distortion and embellishment to be expected when a historical account becomes mythologized.

Less likely is that the literary progression would be from this mythology to the unadorned elegance of Genesis 1. The common assumption that the Hebrew account is simply a purged and simplified version of the Babylonian legend is fallacious. In the Ancient Near East, the rule is that simple accounts or traditions give rise (by accretion and embellishment) to elaborate legends, but not the reverse. So the evidence supports the view that Genesis was not myth made into history. Rather the extrabiblical accounts were history turned into myths. (Geisler, BECA, 48, 49)

1D. Tell Mardikh: The Discovery of Ebla

One of the greatest archaeological finds in this century is the discovery of Ebla. In 1964 Professor Paolo Matthiae, archaeologist from the University of Rome, began a systematic excavation of a then unknown city. Due to the determination and foresight of Matthiae, in 1974 and 1975 a great royal palace was uncovered that eventually yielded over fifteen thousand tablets and fragments. Giovanni Pettinato, an epigrapher, had worked closely with Matthiae in helping to determine some of the paleographic significance of the find. At present, only a fraction of the tablets have been translated. It is now certain that upon this ancient site the once prestigious city of Ebla ruled the Near East as the seat of a great empire. Ebla is located near the modern-day city of Aleppo in North Syria.

The zenith of Ebla was principally in the third millennium B.C. (co-terminous with the time of the patriarchs). Although the Ebla texts, at present, do not specifically mention biblical people or events (although there is much debate over this issue) they do provide an abundance of background material and biblical place names for evaluating the biblical narratives. The importance of Ebla for Syrian history is most impressive. The significance of Ebla for biblical studies is phenomenal. So far only the tip of the iceberg has been seen. Although the evidence has taken time to surface, listed here is some of the support for the biblical narratives.

1E. Biblical Towns

In reference to the identification of biblical towns in the Ebla archives, Kitchen notes:

Not a few towns of biblical interest appear in the Ebla tablets, which preserve (in most cases) the earliest-known mention of these in written records.

More useful, potentially, are the Eblaite mentions of familiar Palestinian place-names such as Hazor, Megiddo, Jerusalem, Lachish, Dor, Gaza, Ashtarot (Qarnaim), etc. Several of these places are known archaeologically to have been inhabited towns in the third millennium B.C. (Early Bronze Age III–IV), and these tablets confirm their early importance, possibly as local city states. Finally, Canaan itself now appears as a geographical entity from the later third millennium B.C., long before any other dated external mention so far known to us—it will be interesting to learn what extent is accorded to Canaan in the Ebla texts. (Kitchen, BIW, 53, 54)

2E. Biblical Names

"The most important contributions of the Ebla occurrences of these and other such names are (i) to emphasize once more that these are names used by *real* human individuals (never by gods, or exclusively [if ever] by tribes, or by fairytale figures), and (ii) to indicate the immense antiquity of names of this type, and of these names in particular." (Kitchen, BIW, 53)

Dr. Giovanni Pettinato gives clear Eblaite variations on such Hebrew names as Israel, Ishmael, and Micaiah. (Pettinato, RATME, 50)

3E. Ancient Near-Eastern Tribute

Some consider the tribute received by Solomon at the height of his empire as fanciful exaggeration. But the find at Ebla offers a different interpretation of the accounts.

Imperial Ebla at the height of its power must have had a vast income. From one defeated king of Mari alone, a tribute of 11,000 pounds of silver and 880 pounds of gold was exacted on one occasion. This *ten tons* [sic] of silver and over *one third of a ton* of gold was no mean haul in itself. Yet it was simply one "delectable extra" so far as the treasury-accounts of Ebla were concerned. In such an economic context, the 666 talents (about twenty tons) of gold as Solomon's basic income from his entire "empire" some 15 centuries later (I Kings 10:14; II Chronicles 9:13) loses its air of exaggeration and begins to look quite prosaic as just part of a wider picture of the considerable (if transient) wealth of major kingdoms of the ancient biblical world.

The comparisons just given do *not* prove that Solomon actually did receive 666 talents of gold, or that his kingdom was organized just as Kings describes. But they do indicate clearly (i) that the Old Testament data must be studied in the context of their world and *not* in isolation, and (ii) that the *scale* of activity portrayed in the Old Testament writings is neither impossible nor even improbable when measured by the relevant external standards. (Kitchen, BIW, 51, 52)

4E. Religious Practices

The Ebla texts reveal that many of the Old Testament religious practices are not as "late" as some critical scholars have espoused.

In matters like priests, cult and offerings the records from Ebla so far merely reinforce for Syria-Palestine what we already know for Egypt, Mesopotamia and Anatolia in the third, second and first millennia B.C., and from the records of North-Syrian Qatna and Ugarit for the second millennium B.C. Namely, that well-organized temple cults, sacrifices, full rituals, etc., were a *constant* feature of ancient Near-Eastern religious life at *all* periods from prehistory down to Graeco-Roman times. They have nothing to do with baseless theories of the nineteenth century A.D., whereby such features of religious life can only be a mark of "late sophistication," virtually forbidden to the Hebrews until after the Babylonian exile—alone of *all* the peoples of the ancient East. There is simply no rational basis for the quaint idea that the simple rites of Moses' tabernacle (cf. Leviticus) or of Solomon's temple, both well over 1000 years later than the rituals practiced in half-a-dozen

Eblaite temples, must be the idle invention of idealizing writers as late as the fifth century B.C. (Kitchen, BIW, 54)

Giovanni Pettinato comments on the source of the specifics referred to by Kitchen:

Passing on to the divine cult, we note the existence of the temples of Dagan, Astar, Kamos, Rasap, all attested in the texts from Ebla. Among the offerings are listed bread, drinks, or even animals. Two tablets in particular, TM, 75, G, 1974 and TM, 75, G, 2238, stand out because they record the offerings of various animals to different gods made by all the members of the royal family during a single month. For example, "11 sheep for the god Adad from the en as an offering," "12 sheep for the god Dagan from the en as an offering," "10 sheep for the god Rasap of the city Edani from the en as an offering."

Among the more interesting aspects of the divine cult at Ebla is the presence of diverse categories of priests and priestesses, including two classes of prophets, the *mahhu* and the *nabiutum,* the second of which finds a natural counterpart in the Old Testament. To explain the biblical phenomenon scholars have hitherto looked to Mari for background, but in the future Ebla will also claim their attention. (Pettinato, RATME, 49)

5E. Hebrew Words

K. A. Kitchen speaks of the critical view of Scripture held by many liberal scholars: "Seventy or a hundred years ago, no such vast depth of perspective was possible; and to suit the purely theoretical reconstructions

> The lessons here are—or should be—clear. Set against two thousand years of history and development of the West Semitic dialects, the whole position of the dating of the vocabulary and usages in biblical Hebrew will need to be completely reexamined.
>
> —KENNETH KITCHEN

of Old Testament books and history by German Old Testament scholars in particular, many words in Hebrew were labeled 'late'— 600 B.C. and later, in effect. By this simple means, mere philosophical prejudices could be given the outward appearance of a 'scientific' reconstruction down to the present day." (Kitchen, BIW, 50)

As a reply, he continues:

However, the immense growth in our knowledge of the earlier history of words found in Old Testament Hebrew tends now to alter all this. If a given word is used in Ebla in 2300 B.C., and in Ugarit in 1300 B.C., then it *cannot* by any stretch of the imagination be a "late word" (600 B.C.!), or an "Aramaism" at periods when standard Aramaic had not yet evolved. It becomes instead an *early* word, a part of the ancestral inheritance of biblical Hebrew. More positively, the increased number of contexts that one gains for rarer words can provide useful confirmation—or correction—of our understanding of their meaning. (Kitchen, BIW, 50)

Referring to specific words, Kitchen states:

Thus, to go back to the survey of city officials at Ebla, the term used for those scores of "leaders" was *nase,* the same word as *nasi,* a term in biblical Hebrew used for leaders of the tribes of Israel (e.g., Numbers 1:16, 44, etc.), and applied to other purely human rulers such as Solomon (I Kings 11:34). Old-fashioned biblical criticism declared the word to be "late," a mark of the hypothetical "priestly code" for example.

The word *hetem*, "gold," is in Hebrew a rare and poetic synonym for *zahab*, and is commonly dismissed as "late." Unfortunately for this misdating, the word was borrowed into Egyptian from Canaanite back in the twelfth century B.C., and now—over 1000 years earlier still—recurs as *kutim* in the Paleo-Canaanite of Ebla, 2300 B.C. (Kitchen, BIW, 50)

He continues:

The Hebrew word *tehom*, "deep," was not borrowed from Babylonian, seeing that it is attested not only in Ugaritic as *thmt* (thirteenth century B.C.) but also in Ebla a thousand years earlier *(ti'amatum)*. The term is Common Semitic.

As an example of a rare word confirmed in both existence and meaning, one may cite Hebrew *ereshet*, "desire," which occurs just once in the Bible, in Psalm 21:2 (Heb. 21:3). Besides being found in Ugaritic in the thirteenth century B.C., this word now appears a millennium earlier at Ebla as *irisatum* (Eblaite or Old Akkadian) in the Sumerian/Eblaite vocabulary tablets.

Finally, the supposed "late" verb ha-dash / hiddesh, "be new" "to renew" goes back—again—via Ugaritic (hadath) to Eblaite (h) edash (u). And so on, for many more besides. (Kitchen, BIW, 50, 51)

Kitchen concludes:

The lessons here are—or should be—clear. Set against two thousand years of history and development of the West Semitic dialects, the whole position of the dating of the vocabulary and usages in biblical Hebrew will need to be completely reexamined. The truth appears to be that early West Semitic in the third and second millennia B.C. had in common a vast and rich vocabulary, to which the later dialects such as Canaanite, Hebrew, Phoenician, Aramaic, etc., fell heirs—but in uneven measure. Words that remained in everyday prosaic use in one of these languages lingered on only in high-flown poetry or in traditional expressions in another of the group. Thus, not a few supposed "late words" or "Aramaisms" in Hebrew (especially in poetry) are nothing more than early West-Semitic words that have found less use in Hebrew but have stayed more alive in Aramaic. (Kitchen, BIW, 51)

3C. The Flood of Noah

As with the creation accounts, the flood narrative in Genesis is more realistic and less mythological than other ancient versions, indicating its authenticity. The superficial similarities point toward a historical core of events that gave rise to all accounts, not toward plagiarism by Moses. The names change. Noah is called Ziusudra by the Sumerians and Utnapishtim by the Babylonians. The basic story doesn't. A man is told to build a ship to specific dimensions because God(s) is going to flood the world. He does it, rides out the storm, and offers sacrifice upon exiting the boat. The Deity (-ies) responds with remorse over the destruction of life, and makes a covenant with the man. These core events point to a historical basis.

Similar flood accounts are found all over the world. The flood is told of by the Greeks, the Hindus, the Chinese, the Mexicans, the Algonquins, and the Hawaiians. One list of Sumerian kings treats the flood as a historical reference point. After naming eight kings who lived extraordinarily long lives (tens of thousands of years), this sentence interrupts the list: "[Then] the Flood swept over [the earth] and when kingship was lowered [again] from heaven, kingship was [first] in Kish."

There are good reasons to believe that Genesis gives the original story. The other versions contain elaborations indicating corruption. Only in Genesis is the year of the flood given, as well as dates for the chronology relative to Noah's life. In fact, Genesis reads almost like a diary or ship's log of the events. The cubical Babylonian ship could not have saved anyone. The raging waters would have constantly turned it on every side. However, the biblical ark is rectangular—long, wide, and low—so that it would ride the rough seas well. The length of the rainfall in the pagan accounts (seven days) is not enough time for the devastation they describe. The waters would have to rise at least above most mountains, to a height of above seventeen thousand feet, and it is more reasonable to assume a longer rainfall to do this. The Babylonian idea that all of the flood waters subsided in one day is equally absurd.

Another striking difference between Genesis and the other versions is that in these accounts the hero is granted immortality and exalted. The Bible moves on to Noah's sin. Only a version that seeks to tell the truth would include this realistic admission.

4C. The Tower of Babel

There is now considerable evidence that the world did indeed have a single language at one time. Sumerian literature alludes to this fact several times. Linguists also find this theory helpful in categorizing languages. But what of the tower and the confusion of tongues at the Tower of Babel (Gen. 11)? Archaeology has revealed that Ur-Nammu, king of Ur from about 2044 to 2007 B.C., supposedly received orders to build a great ziggurat (temple tower) as an act of worship to the moon god Nannat. A *stele* (monument) about five feet across and ten feet high reveals Ur-Nammu's activities. One panel has him setting out with a mortar basket to begin construction of the great tower; thus showing his allegiance to the gods by taking his place as a humble workman. Another clay tablet states that the erection of the tower offended the gods, so they threw down what the men had built, scattered them abroad, and made their speech strange. This is remarkably similar to the record in the Bible.

According to Scripture, "The whole earth had one language and one speech" (Gen. 11:1) before the Tower of Babel. After the building of the tower and its destruction, God confounded the language of all the earth (Gen. 11:9). Many modern day philologists attest to the likelihood of such an origin for the world's languages. Alfredo Trombetti says he can trace and prove the common origin of *all* languages. Max Mueller also attests to the common origin. And Otto Jespersen goes so far as to say that language was directly given to the first men by God. (Free, ABH, 47)

5C. The Patriarchs

While the narratives of the lives of Abraham, Isaac, and Jacob do not present the same kinds of difficulties as do the earlier chapters of Genesis, they were long considered legendary because they did not seem to fit with the known evidence of that period. As more has become known, though, these stories are increasingly verified. Legal codes from the time of Abraham show why the patriarch would have been hesitant to throw Hagar out of his camp, for he was legally bound to support her. Only when a higher law came from God was Abraham willing to put her out.

The Mari letters reveal such names as Abamram (Abraham), Jacob-el, and Benjamites. Though these do not refer to the biblical people, they at least show that the names were in use. These letters also support the record of a war in Genesis 14 where five kings fought against four kings. The names of these kings seem to fit with the prominent nations of the day. For example, Genesis 14:1 mentions an Amorite king Arioch; the Mari documents render the king's name

Ariwwuk. All of this evidence leads to the conclusion that the source materials of Genesis were firsthand accounts of someone who lived during Abraham's time. (Geisler, BECA, 50)

In another study done by Kitchen (Kitchen, TPAMH, 48–95), he gives examples of archeological factors for dating the patriarchs during the Middle Bronze Age.

> The Biblical data match objective facts from the ancient world in an almost uncanny way, establishing the general reliability of the Biblical periods.(48)
>
> One important item involves the price of slaves in silver shekels. From Ancient Near Eastern sources we know the price of slaves in some detail for a period lasting about 2000 years, from 2400 B.C. to 400 B.C. . . . These data provide a solid body of evidence that we can compare with the figures in the Bible, in which the price of slaves is mentioned on several occasions (Genesis 37:28; Exodus 20 ff.; Exodus 21:32; 2 Kings 15:20) . . . In each case the Biblical narrative slave price fits the general period to which it relates. (52)

Now, however, there is quietly mounting evidence that the basic inherited outline—from the patriarchs through the Exodus to the Israelites' entry into Canaan, the united monarchy and then the divided kingdoms of Israel and Judah, and the Exile and return—is essentially sound. (94)

1D. Genealogy of Abraham

We find that the genealogy of Abraham is definitely historical. However, there seems to be some question as to whether or not these names represent individuals or ancient cities, although ancient cities often took the name of their founding fathers. The one thing that is certain about Abraham is that he was an individual and that he did exist. As we hear from Burrows: "Everything indicates

that here we have an historical individual. As noted above, he is not mentioned in any known archaeological source, but his name appears in Babylonia as a personal name in the very period to which he belongs." (Burrows, WMTS, 258, 259)

Earlier attempts had been made to move the date of Abraham to the fifteenth or fourteenth century B.C., a time much too late for him. However, Albright points out that because of the data mentioned above and other evidence, we have "a great deal of evidence from personal and place names, almost all of which is against such unwarranted telescoping of traditional data." (Garstang, FBHJJ, 9)

2D. Genealogy of Esau

In the genealogy of Esau, there is mention made of the Horites (Gen. 36:20). It was at one time accepted that these people were "cave-dwellers" because of the similarity between Horite and the Hebrew word for cave—thus the idea that they lived in caves. Now, however, findings have shown that they were a prominent group of warriors living in the Near East in Patriarchal times. (Free, ABH, 72)

3D. Isaac: The Oral Blessing Episode (Genesis 27)

It would seem, indicates Joseph Free, a most unusual event that Isaac did not take his oral blessing back when he discovered Jacob's deception. However, the Nuzi Tablets tell us that such an oral declaration was perfectly legal and binding. Thus he could not retract the oral blessing. One tablet records a lawsuit involving a woman who was to wed a man, but his jealous brothers contested it. The man won the suit because his father had orally promised the woman to him. Oral statements carried a very different weight then than they do today. The Nuzi texts came from a similar culture to that in Genesis. (Free, AL, 322, 323)

G. Ernest Wright explains this serious action: "Oral blessings or death-bed wills were recognized as valid at Nuzi as well as in Patriarchal society. Such blessings were serious matters and were irrevocable. We recall that Isaac was prepared to keep his word even though his blessing had been extorted by Jacob under false pretenses. 'And Isaac trembled with a very great trembling and said: "Whoever it was that hunted game and brought it to me and I ate . . . even he shall be blessed."' (Gen. 27:33)" (Wright, PSBA, as cited in Willoughby, SBTT, 43)

In commenting further on the above Nuzi record, Cyrus Gordon draws three points: "This text conforms with biblical blessings like those of the Patriarchs in that it is (a) an oral will, (b) with legal validity, (c) made to a son by a dying father." (Gordon, BCNT, 8)

Thus a clearer light is thrown on a culture that we know inadequately at best.

4D. Jacob

1E. The Purchase of Esau's Birthright

Gordon provides information on this episode in Genesis 25: "Few incidents in family life seem more peculiar to us than Esau's sale of his birthright to his twin brother, Jacob. It has been pointed out that one of the [Nuzi] tablets . . . portrays a similar event." (Gordon, BCNT, 3, 5)

The tablet to which Gordon refers is explained by Wright: "Esau's sale of his birthright to Jacob is also paralleled in the Nuzi tablets where one brother sells a grove, which he has inherited, for three sheep! This would seem to have been quite as uneven a bargain as that of Esau: 'Esau said to Jacob:

"Give me, I pray, some of that red pottage to eat . . ." And Jacob said: "Sell me first thy birthright." And Esau said: "Behold I am

> In one Nuzi tablet, there is a record of a man named Tupkitilla, who transferred his inheritance rights concerning a grove to his brother, Kurpazah, in exchange for three sheep. Esau used a similar technique in exchanging his inheritance rights to obtain the desired pottage.
>
> —JOSEPH FREE

about to die (of hunger); what is a birthright to me?" And Jacob said: "Swear to me first." And he swore to him and sold his birthright to Jacob. Then Jacob gave Esau bread and a mess of lentils and he ate and drank' (25:30–34)." (Wright, PSBA, as cited in Willoughby, SBTT, 43)

Free explains further. "In one Nuzi tablet, there is a record of a man named Tupkitilla, who transferred his inheritance rights concerning a grove to his brother, Kurpazah, in exchange for three sheep. Esau used a similar technique in exchanging his inheritance rights to obtain the desired pottage." (Free, ABH, 68, 69)

S. H. Horn, in "Recent Illumination of the Old Testament" *(Christianity Today)*, draws a colorful conclusion:

"Esau sold his rights for food in the pot, while Tupkitilla sold his for food still on the hoof." (Horn, RIOT, 14, 15)

2E. The Jacob and Laban Episode (Genesis 29)

Cyrus Gordon claims that we can understand even Genesis 29 by episodes in the Nuzi Tablets: "Laban agrees to give a daughter in marriage to Jacob when he makes him a member of the household; 'It is better that I give her to thee than that I give her to another man. Dwell with me!' (Genesis 29:9). Our thesis that Jacob's joining Laban's household approximates Wullu's [a person mentioned in the Tablets] adoption is borne out by other remarkable resemblances with the Nuzu document." (Gordon, BCNT, 6)

3E. The Stolen Images Episode (Genesis 31)

This event has been explained by other Nuzi discoveries. The following, from J. P. Free's "Archaeology and the Bible" *(His Magazine)*, gives a good explanation not only of the episode, but also of the background on the Nuzi Tablets themselves:

Over 1,000 clay tablets were found in 1925 in the excavation of a Mesopotamian site know today as Yorgan Tepe. Subsequent work brought forth another 3,000 tablets and revealed the ancient site as "Nuzi." The tablets, written about 1500 B.C., illuminate the background of the Biblical patriarchs, Abraham, Isaac, and Jacob. One instance will be cited: When Jacob and Rachel left the home of Laban, Rachel stole Laban's family images or "teraphim." When Laban discovered the theft, he pursued his daughter and son-in-law, and after a long journey overtook them (Genesis 31:19–23). Commentators have long wondered why he would go to such pains to recover images he could have replaced easily in the local shops. The Nuzi tablets record one instance of a son-in-law who possessed the family images having the right to lay legal claim to his father-in-law's property, a fact which explains Laban's anxiety. This and other evidence from the Nuzi tablets fits the background of the Patriarchal accounts into the early period when the patriarchs lived, and does not support the critical view—which holds that the accounts were written 1000 years after their time. (Free, AB, 20)

Thanks to archaeology, we are beginning to understand the actual setting of much of the Bible.

5D. Joseph

1E. Selling into Slavery

K. A. Kitchen brings out in his book, *Ancient Orient and Old Testament,* that Genesis 37:28 gives the correct price for a slave in the eighteenth century B.C.: "The price of twenty shekels of silver paid for Joseph in Genesis 37:28 is the correct average price for a slave in about the eighteenth century B.C.: earlier than this, slaves were cheaper (average, ten to fifteen shekels), and later they became steadily dearer. This is one more little detail true to its period in cultural history." (Kitchen, AOOT, 52–53)

2E. The Visit to Egypt

The possibility of Joseph's visit to Egypt has been questioned by some. Millar Burrows points out: "Accounts of going down to Egypt in times of famine (12:10; 42:1, 2) bring to mind Egyptian references to Asiatics who came to Egypt for this purpose. A picture of visiting Semites may be seen on the wall of a tomb at Beni Hasan which comes from a time not far from that of Abraham." (Burrows, WMTS, 266, 267)

Howard Vos *(Genesis and Archaeology)* also points out the presence of the Hyksos in Egypt.

But we have much more than the pictorial representation from Knumhotep's tomb to support the early entrance of foreigners into Egypt. There are many indications that the Hyksos began to infiltrate the Nile Valley around 1900 B.C. Other contingents came about 1730 and overwhelmed the native Egyptian rulers. So if we take an early date for the entrance of the Hebrews into Egypt, they would have come in during the period of Hyksos infiltration—when many foreigners were apparently entering. If we accept a date of about 1700 or 1650 B.C. for the entrance of the Hebrews, the Hyksos would have been ruling Egypt and likely would have received other foreigners. (Vos, GA, 102)

Vos goes on to draw four connections between the Hyksos tribes and the Bible. One, the Egyptians considered the Hyksos and the Hebrews as different. Two, it is a possibility that the rising Egyptian king who was antagonistic toward Joseph's people (Ex. 1:8) was the nationalistic Egyptian king. Naturally such a fever of nationalism would not be healthy for any foreigners. Three, Genesis 47:17 is the first instance where horses are mentioned in the Bible. The Hyksos introduced horses to Egypt. Four, after the Hyksos expulsion, much land was concentrated in the hands of the monarchs; this fits with the events of the famine that Joseph predicted and through which he strengthened the crown. (Vos, GA, 104)

3E. Joseph's Promotions

The following is a summary of Howard Vos's discussion of the question of Joseph's admittedly unique rise, found in his *Genesis and Archaeology*:

Joseph's being lifted from slavery to prime minister of Egypt has caused some critical eyebrows to rise, but we have some archaeological accounts of similar things happening in the Land of the Nile.

A Canaanite Meri-Ra, became armorbearer to Pharaoh: another Canaanite, Ben-Mat-Ana, was appointed to the high position of interpreter; and a Semite, Yanhamu or Jauhamu, became deputy to Amenhotep III, with charge over the granaries of the delta, a responsibility similar to that of Joseph before and during the famine.

When Pharaoh appointed Joseph prime minister, he was given a ring and a gold chain or a collar which is normal procedure for Egyptian office promotions. (Vos, GA, 106)

E. Campbell, commenting on the Amorna period, further discusses this parallel of Joseph's rise to power:

One figure in the Rib-Adda correspondence constitutes an interesting link both with the princes of the cities in Palestine to the south and with the Bible. He is Yanhamu, whom Rib-Adda at one point describes as the *musallil* of the king. The term means, in all likelihood, the fanbearer of the king, an honorary title referring to one who is very close to the king, presumably sharing in counsels on affairs of state. Yanhamu held, then, a very prominent position in Egyptian affairs. His name appears in correspondence from princes up and down Palestine-Syria. At the beginning of the Rib-Adda period, Yanhamu seems to have been in charge of the issuing of supplies from the Egyptian bread-basket called Yarimuta, and we have already seen that Rib-Adda was apparently constantly in need of his services.

Yanhamu has a Semitic name. This, of course, suggests further parallel to the Joseph narrative in Genesis, beyond the fact that both

> Yanhamu held, then, a very prominent position in Egyptian affairs. His name appears in correspondence from princes up and down Palestine-Syria. At the beginning of the Rib-Adda period, Yanhamu seems to have been in charge of the issuing of supplies from the Egyptian bread-basket called Yarimuta, and we have already seen that Rib-Adda was apparently constantly in need of his services.
>
> —G. E. CAMPBELL

are related to the supplies of food for foreigners. Yanhamu offers an excellent confirmation of the genuinely Egyptian background of the Joseph narrative, but this does not mean, of course, that these men are identical, or that they functioned at the same time. Indeed Joseph may better fit into the preceding period for a number of reasons, although the evidence as yet precludes anything approaching certainty. It is clear that Semites could rise to positions of great authority in Egypt: they may even have been preferred at a time when indigenous leadership got too powerful or too inbred. (Campbell, as cited in Burrows, WMTS, 16, 17)

With regard to Semites rising to power in Egyptian government, Kitchen—with reference to various ancient papyri—comments:

Asiatic slaves in Egypt, attached to the households of officials, are well-known in later Middle-Kingdom Egypt (c. 1850-1700 B.C.) and Semites could rise to high position (even the throne, before the Hyksos period), as did the chancellor Hur. Joseph's career would fall easily enough into the period of the late thirteenth and early fifteenth dynasties. The role of dreams is, of course, well-known at all periods. From Egypt, we have a dream-reader's textbook in a copy of c. 1300 B.C., originating some centuries earlier; such works are known in first-millennium Assyria also. (Kitchen, BW, 74)

4E. Joseph's Tomb

John Elder in his *Prophets, Idols, and Diggers* reveals:

In the last verses of Genesis it is told how Joseph adjured his relatives to take his bones back to Canaan whenever God should restore them to their original home, and in Joshua 24:32 it is told how his body was indeed brought to Palestine and buried at Shechem. For centuries there was a tomb at Shechem

reverenced as the tomb of Joseph. A few years ago the tomb was opened. It was found to contain a body mummified according to the Egyptian custom, and in the tomb, among other things, was a sword of the kind worn by Egyptian officials. (Elder, PID, 54)

6D. Regarding the Patriarchs—Concluding Archaeological Evidence

The Nuzi discoveries have played a central role in illuminating different portions of this section. S. H. Horn lists six areas of influence the texts have exercised:

Other [Nuzi] texts show that a bride was ordinarily chosen for a son by his father, as the patriarchs did; that a man had to pay a dowry to his father-in-law, or to work for his father-in-law if he could not afford the dowry, as poor Jacob had to do; that the orally expressed will of a father could not be changed after it had been pronounced, as in Isaac's refusal to change the blessings pronounced over Jacob even though they had been obtained by deception; that a bride ordinarily received from her father a slave girl as a personal maid, as Leah and Rachel did when they were married to Jacob; that the theft of cult objects or of a god was punishable by death, which was why Jacob consented to the death of the one with whom the stolen gods of his father-in-law were found; that the strange relationship between Judah and his daughter-in-law Tamar is vividly illustrated by the laws of the ancient Assyrians and Hittites. (Horn, RIOT, 14)

Archaeology has indeed had an impact on our knowledge of Bible backgrounds.

6C. The Assyrian Invasion

Much was learned about the Assyrians when twenty-six thousand tablets were found in the palace of Ashurbanipal, son of the Esarhaddon, who took the northern kingdoms into captivity in 722 B.C. These tablets tell of the many conquests of the

Assyrian empire and record the cruel and violent punishments that fell to those who opposed them.

Several of these records confirm the Bible's accuracy. Every reference in the Old Testament to an Assyrian king has been proven correct. Even though Sargon was unknown for some time, when his palace was found and excavated, there was a wall painting of the battle mentioned in Isaiah 20. The Black Obelisk of Shalmaneser adds to our knowledge of biblical figures by showing Jehu (or his emissary) bowing down to the king of Assyria.

Among the most interesting finds is Sennacherib's record of the siege of Jerusalem. Thousands of his men died and the rest scattered when he attempted to take the city and, as Isaiah had foretold, he was unable to conquer it. Since he could not boast about his great victory here, Sennacherib found a way to make himself sound good without admitting defeat (Geisler, BECA, 52):

> As to Hezekiah, the Jew, he did not submit to my yoke. I laid siege to 46 of his strong cities, walled forts, and to the countless small villages in their vicinity. I drove out of them 200,150 people, young and old, male and female, horses, mules, donkeys, camels, big and small cattle beyond counting and considered (them) booty. Himself I made a prisoner in Jerusalem, his royal residence, like a bird in a cage. (Pritchard, ANET, as cited in Geisler, BECA, 52)

7C. The Babylonian Captivity
Various facets of Old Testament history regarding the Babylonian captivity have been confirmed. Records found in Babylon's famous hanging gardens have shown that Jehoiachin and his five sons were given a monthly ration and a place to live and were treated well (2 Kings 25:27–30). The name of Belshazzar caused problems, because there was not only no mention of him, but no room for him in the list of Babylonian kings; however, Nabodonius left a record that he appointed his son, Belshazzar (Daniel 5), to reign for a few years in his absence. Hence, Nabodonius was still king, but Belshazzar ruled in the capital. Also, the edict of Cyrus as recorded by Ezra seemed to fit the picture of Isaiah's prophecies too well to be real, until a cylinder was found that confirmed the decree in all the important details. (Geisler, BECA, 52)

8C. The Lachish Letters

1D. Background to the Find
William F. Albright, in his *Religion in Life* article, "The Bible After Twenty Years of Archaeology," introduces us to this find:

> We mention the new documents from the sixth and fifth centuries B.C. which have come to light since 1935. In 1935 the late J. L. Starkey discovered the Ostraca of Lachish, consisting chiefly of letters written in ink on potsherds. Together with several additional ostraca found in 1938, they form a unique body of Hebrew prose from the time of Jeremiah. Further light on the time of the Exile comes from the ration lists of Nebuchadnezzar, found by the Germans at Babylon and partly published by E. F. Weidner in

> In these letters we find ourselves in exactly the age of Jeremiah, with social and political conditions agreeing perfectly with the picture drawn in the book that bears his name. The Lachish Letters take their place worthily between the Ostraca of Samaria and the Elephantine Papyri as epigraphic monuments of Biblical Hebrew history.
>
> —WILLIAM F. ALBRIGHT

1939.... Somewhat later but of decisive value for our understanding of the history and literature of the Jews in the time of Ezra and Nehemiah are the continuing finds and publications of Aramaic papyri and ostraca from Egypt. Four large groups of this material are being published, and their complete publication will more than double the total bulk of such documents available twenty years ago. (Albright, BATYA, 539)

R. S. Haupert wrote a survey article on these finds, "Lachish—Frontier Fortress of Judah." He goes into the authorship and background of the letters:

Most of the best preserved are letters written by a certain Hoshaiah (a good biblical name: Neh. 12:32; Jer. 42:1; 43:2), apparently a subordinate military officer stationed at an outpost or observation point not far from Lachish, to Yaosh, the commanding officer of Lachish. That the letters were all written within a period of a few days or weeks is indicated by the fact that the pieces of pottery on which they were written were from jars of similar shape and date, and five of the pieces actually fit together as fragments of the same original vessel. The fact that all but two of the letters were found on the floor of the guardroom naturally suggest that they were deposited there by Yaosh himself upon receiving them from Hoshaiah. (Haupert, LFFJ, 30, 31)

2D. Dating and Historical Setting

Albright wrote a special article on this find, "The Oldest Hebrew Letters: Lachish Ostraca," in the *Bulletin of the American Schools of Oriental Research,* in which he deals with the setting of the Letters:

"In the course of this sketch it will have become increasingly evident to the attentive reader that the language of the Lachish documents is perfect classical Hebrew. The divergences from biblical usage are much fewer and less significant than supposed by Torczner. In these letters we find ourselves in

exactly the age of Jeremiah, with social and political conditions agreeing perfectly with the picture drawn in the book that bears his name. The Lachish Letters take their place worthily between the Ostraca of Samaria and the Elephantine Papyri as epigraphic monuments of Biblical Hebrew history." (Albright, OHL, 17)

G. E. Wright, in "The Present State of Biblical Archaeology," dates the letters by internal evidence:

"On Letter XX are the words 'the ninth year,' that is, of King Zedekiah. That is the same year in which Nebuchadnezzar arrived to begin the reduction of Judah: 'in the ninth year . . . , in the tenth month' (II Kings 25:1; this would be about January 588 B.C., the siege of Jerusalem continuing to July 587 B.C.—II Kings 25:2, 3)." (Wright, PSBA, as cited in Willoughby, SBTT, 179)

Millar Burrows *(What Mean These Stones?)* agrees with Wright: "At Lachish evidence of two destructions not far apart has been found; undoubtedly they are to be attributed to Nebuchadnezzar's invasions of 597 and 587 B.C. The now famous Lachish letters were found in the debris from the second of these destructions." (Burrows, WMTS, 107)

Albright sums up the question of the dating of the finds: "Starkey has contributed a useful sketch of the discovery, explaining the archaeological situation in which the ostraca were found and fixing their date just before the final destruction of Lachish at the end of Zedekiah's reign. The facts are so clear that Torczner has surrendered his objections to this date, which is now accepted by all students." (Albright, OHL, 11, 12)

3D. Old Testament Background

Jeremiah 34:6, 7 reads as follows: "Then Jeremiah the prophet spoke all these words to Zedekiah king of Judah in Jerusalem when the king of Babylon's army fought against Jerusalem and all the cities of Judah that were left, against Lachish and Azekah; for only these fortified cities remained of the cities of Judah."

Israel had been in a futile rebellion against Nebuchadnezzar. Judah was not united in this revolt. Jeremiah preached submission, while the Jewish leaders could only speak of resistance—and resist they did, though they were soundly defeated by the powers of Nebuchadnezzar. In the final days of the rebellion, the last vestiges of Hebrew independence were embodied in a pair of outposts, Lachish and Azekah, thirty-five miles southwest of Jerusalem. From Lachish came a series of letters giving a graphic picture of what it was like to be in such a situation. These add greatly to our knowledge of Old Testament background. This discovery is known as the Lachish Letters (or Ostraca).

4D. The Content of the Letters and the Gedaliah Seal

For sake of convenience, each of the letters was labeled with a number. Haupert gives an overview of Letters II through VI: "Throughout this group of letters [Letters II–VI] Hoshaiah is continually defending himself to his superior, although the charges against him are not always clear. It is tempting to think that he is in sympathy with the Jeremiah faction which wanted to submit to the Babylonians instead of rebelling; but, of course, we cannot be sure." (Haupert, LFFJ, 31)

He then touches on several of them:

1E. Letter I

"Letter I . . . though only a list of names, is of striking significance since three of the nine names which occur—Gemariah, Jaazaniah, and Neriah—appear in the Old Testament only in the time of Jeremiah. A fourth

name is Jeremiah, which, however, is not limited in the Old Testament to the prophet Jeremiah, and need not refer to him. A fifth name, likewise not limited to this period, is Mattaniah, which biblical students will recognize as the pre-throne name of King Zedekiah." (Haupert, LFFJ, 31)

2E. Letter III

Haupert continues:

"In Letter III Hoshaiah reports to Yaosh that a royal mission is on the way to Egypt, and that a company of this group has been sent to his outpost (or to Lachish) for provisions, an allusion which points directly to the intrigues of the pro-Egyptian party under Zedekiah. Of unusual interest is the reference in the same letter to 'the prophet.' Some writers have confidently identified this prophet with Jeremiah. This is entirely possible, but we cannot be certain and should be careful about pushing the evidence too far." (Haupert, LFFJ, 32)

3E. Letter IV

J. P. Free (*Archaeology and Bible History*) speaks of Letter IV, an often-mentioned one:

In the days of Jeremiah when the Babylonian army was taking one town after another in

> This letter not only shows us how Nebuchadnezzar's army was tightening its net around the land of Judah, but also evidences the close relationship between Lachish and Azekah which are similarly linked in the book of Jeremiah.
>
> —JOSEPH FREE

Judah (about 589–586 B.C.), we are told in the Bible that, as yet, the two cities of Lachish and Azekah had not fallen (Jer. 34:7). Striking confirmation of the fact that these two cities were among those still holding out is furnished by the Lachish letters. Letter No. 4, written by the army officer at a military outpost to his superior officer at Lachish, says, "We are watching for the signals of Lachish according to all indications which my Lord hath given, for we cannot see Azekah." This letter not only shows us how Nebuchadnezzar's army was tightening its net around the land of Judah, but also evidences the close relationship between Lachish and Azekah which are similarly linked in the book of Jeremiah. (Free, ABH, 223)

Haupert sees it from another angle: "The final statement of Letter IV affords an intimate glimpse into the declining days of the Kingdom of Judah. Hoshaiah concludes: 'Investigate, and (my lord) will know that for the fire-signals of Lachish we are watching, according to all the signs which my lord has given, for we cannot see Azekah.' This statement calls to mind immediately the passage in Jer. 34:7." (Haupert, LFFJ, 32)

Wright adds his view of the reference to not seeing Azekah: "When Hoshaiah says that he 'cannot see Azekah,' he may mean that the latter city has already fallen and is no longer sending signals. At any rate, we here learn that Judah had a signal system, presumably by fire or smoke, and the atmosphere of the letters reflects the worry and disorder of a besieged country. A date in the autumn of 589 (or 588) B.C. has been suggested for the bulk of the letters." (Wright, PSBA, as cited in Willoughby, SBTT, 179)

4E. Letter VI

Joseph Free points out the close relationship between Letter VI and Jeremiah's writings:

J. L. Starkey found (1935) a group of eighteen potsherds bearing on their surface several military messages written by an army officer to his superior officer stationed at Lachish. W. F.

Albright has pointed out ["A Brief History of Judah from the Days of Josiah to Alexander the Great," *Biblical Archaeologist,* Vol. 9, No. 1, February, 1946, p. 4.] that in one of these letters (No. 6) the army officer complains that the royal officials (sarim) had sent out circular letters which "weaken the hands" of the people. The army officer who wrote this Lachish letter used the expression, "weaken the hands," to describe the effect of the over-optimism of the royal officials, whereas the officials, referred to in the book of Jeremiah (38:4), in turn had used the same expression in describing the effect of Jeremiah's realistic prophecy concerning the approaching fall of Jerusalem. The royal officials were deemed guilty of the very action which they sought to ascribe to Jeremiah. (Free, ABH, 222)

5E. Gedaliah Seal

John Elder points out yet another find in addition to the Ostraca, which adds even more weight to the biblical story of Lachish:

The nearby city fortress of Lachish provides clear proof that it had been twice burned over a short period of time, coinciding with the two captures of Jerusalem. In Lachish the imprint of a clay seal was found, its back still shows the fibers of the papyrus to which it had been attached. It reads: "The property of Gedaliah who is over the house." We meet this distinguished individual in II Kings 25:22, where we are told: "And as for the people that remained in the land of Judah, whom Nebuchadnezzar king of Babylon had left, even over them he made Gedaliah ... ruler." (Elder, PID, 108, 109)

5D. Significance of Lachish Findings and Conclusion

Haupert concludes: "The real significance of the Lachish Letters can hardly be exaggerated. No archaeological discovery to date [prior to the Dead Sea Scrolls] has had a more direct bearing upon the Old Testament. The scribes who wrote the letters (for there was more than one) wrote with genuine artistry in classical Hebrew, and we have virtually a new section of Old Testament literature: a supplement to Jeremiah." (Haupert, LFFJ, 32)

Archaeology does not prove the Bible. It does not prove beyond a shadow of a doubt all aspects of the history of the Exile. It does, however, put the one who wishes to maintain the traditional view on at least an equal footing with the skeptics. A person must no longer feel required to believe scholarship like that of Torrey.

Free put a simple closing to his study of the subject thus: "In summary, archaeological discoveries show at point after point that the biblical record is confirmed and commended as trustworthy. This confirmation is not confined to a few general instances." (Free, AHAS, 225)

NOTE: For further study of this area, see either Free, or, better, Albright. These two have done extensive work in this area, as this section indicates:

Free, Joseph P.: *Archaeology and Bible History,* and an article series in *Bibliotheca Sacra* in 1956–57.

Albright, William Foxwell: *Archaeology of Palestine and the Bible,* "King Jehoiachin in Exile," in *Biblical Archaeologist;* and "The Bible After Twenty Years of Archaeology," in *Religion in Life.*

3A. NEW TESTAMENT CONFIRMATION OF THE OLD TESTAMENT

Another area where the Old Testament is confirmed is available from the New Testament. There are numerous remarks by Jesus Himself, the apostles, and various other biblical characters in the New Testament that confirm the truthfulness of the Old Testament narrative.

1B. Jesus' Confirmation

The New Testament records that Jesus believed the Torah to be from Moses:

Mark 7:10; 10:3–5; 12:26

Luke 5:14; 16:29–31; 24:27, 44

John 7:19, 23

Especially in John 5:45–47 Jesus states unequivocally his belief that Moses wrote the Torah:

"Do not think that I shall accuse you to the Father; there is one who accuses you—Moses, in whom you trust.

"For if you believed Moses, you would believe Me; for he wrote about Me.

"But if you do not believe his writings, how will you believe My words?"

Eissfeldt states: "The name used in the New Testament clearly with reference to the whole Pentateuch—the Book of Moses—is certainly to be understood as meaning that Moses was the compiler of the Pentateuch." (Eissfeldt, OTAI, 158)

2B. Biblical Writers' Confirmation

The New Testament writers also held that the Torah or "the Law" came from Moses:

The apostles believed that "Moses wrote for us a law" (Mark 12:19 NASB).

John was confident that "the Law was given through Moses" (John 1:17).

Paul, speaking of a Pentateuchal passage, asserts "Moses writes" (Rom. 10:5).

Other passages asserting this include:

Luke 2:22; 20:28

John 1:45, 8:5; 9:29

Acts 3:22; 6:14; 13:39; 15:1, 21; 26:22; 28:23

1 Corinthians 9:9

2 Corinthians 3:15

Hebrews 9:19

Revelation 15:3

Geisler and Nix provide a helpful list of New Testament references to Old Testament events (see below).

It is my deep conviction, after examining the evidence, that I can hold in my hand the Bible (both Old and New Testaments together) and conclude I have the reliable Word of God.

OLD TESTAMENT EVENT	NEW TESTAMENT REFERENCE
1. Creation of the universe (Gen. 1)	John 1:3; Col. 1:16
2. Creation of Adam and Eve (Gen. 1–2)	1 Tim. 2:13, 14
3. Marriage of Adam and Eve (Gen. 1–2)	1 Tim. 2:13
4. Temptation of the woman (Gen. 3)	1 Tim. 2:14
5. Disobedience and sin of Adam (Gen. 3)	Rom. 5:12; 1 Cor. 15:22
6. Sacrifices of Abel and Cain (Gen. 4)	Heb. 11:4
7. Murder of Abel by Cain (Gen. 4)	1 John 3:12
8. Birth of Seth (Gen. 4)	Luke 3:38
9. Translation of Enoch (Gen. 5)	Heb. 11:5
10. Marriage before the Flood (Gen. 6)	Luke 17:27
11. The Flood and destruction of man (Gen. 7)	Matt. 24:39
12. Preservation of Noah and his family (Gen. 8–9)	2 Pet. 2:5
13. Genealogy of Shem (Gen. 10)	Luke 3:35, 36
14. Birth of Abraham (Gen. 12–13)	Luke 3:34
15. Call of Abraham (Gen. 12–13)	Heb. 11:8
16. Tithes to Melchizedek (Gen. 14)	Heb. 7:1–3
17. Justification of Abraham (Gen. 15)	Rom. 4:3
18. Ishmael (Gen. 16)	Gal. 4:21–24
19. Promise of Isaac (Gen. 17)	Heb. 11:18
20. Lot and Sodom (Gen. 18–19)	Luke 17:29
21. Birth of Isaac (Gen. 21)	Acts 7:9, 10
22. Offering of Isaac (Gen. 22)	Heb. 11:17
23. The burning bush (Ex. 3:6)	Luke 20:32
24. Exodus through the Red Sea (Ex. 14:22)	1 Cor. 10:1, 2
25. Provision of water and manna (Ex. 16:4; 17:6)	1 Cor. 10:3–5
26. Lifting up serpent in wilderness (Num. 21:9)	John 3:14
27. Fall of Jericho (Josh. 6:22–25)	Heb. 11:30
28. Miracles of Elijah (1 Kin. 17:1; 18:1)	James 5:17
29. Jonah in the great fish (Jon. 2)	Matt. 12:40
30. Three Hebrew youths in furnace (Dan. 3)	Heb. 11:34
31. Daniel in lion's den (Dan. 6)	Heb. 11:33
32. Slaying of Zechariah (2 Chr. 24:20–22)	Matt. 23:35

Part Two

THE CASE FOR JESUS

5
JESUS, A MAN OF HISTORY

INTRODUCTION

In his essay "Why I Am Not a Christian," philosopher Bertrand Russell asserts, "Historically it is quite doubtful whether Christ ever existed at all, and if He did we do not know anything about Him." (Russell, WIANC, 16)

One would be hard-pressed to find very many knowledgeable people today who would agree with Russell's radical claim. Many people have raised questions about Jesus Christ, and some have doubted that what the Bible says about Him is true, but the circle of those who claim He never lived at all or that if He did we can know nothing about Him is very small. Even the American revolutionary Thomas Paine, who held Christianity in utter contempt, did not question the historicity of Jesus of Nazareth.

While Paine believed that the biblical statements about Jesus' deity were mythological, he still held that Jesus actually lived. Said Paine, "He [Jesus Christ] was a virtuous and an amiable man. The morality that he preached and practiced was of the most benevolent kind; and though similar systems of morality had been preached by Confucius, and by some of the Greek philosophers, many years before; by the Quakers since; and by many good men in all ages, it has not been exceeded by any." (Paine, CWTP, 9)

Yet, once in a while, I run across someone like Russell who, in spite of the evidence, insists on denying that Jesus ever existed at all. One of these occasions happened during a debate sponsored by the associate students of a midwestern university. My opponent, a congressional candidate for the Progressive Labor Party (Marxist) in New York, said in her opening remarks: "Historians today have fairly well dismissed Jesus as being historical." I couldn't believe my ears. But I was glad she said it, because she gave me the opportunity to show twenty-five hundred students that she had not done her history homework. If she had, she would have discovered what F. F. Bruce, Rylands professor of biblical criticism and exegesis at the University of Manchester, has said: "Some writers may toy with the fancy of a 'Christ-myth,' but they do not do so on the ground of historical evidence. The historicity of Christ is as axiomatic for an unbiased historian as the historicity of Julius Caesar. It is not historians who propagate the 'Christ-myth' theories." (Bruce, NTDATR '72, 119)

Otto Betz is right: "No serious scholar has ventured to postulate the non-historicity of Jesus." (Betz, WDWKAJ, 9)

The historicity of Jesus isn't just a matter of curious interest for the Christian. The Christian faith is grounded in history. New Testament scholar Donald Hagner notes:

> True Christianity, the Christianity of the New Testament documents, is absolutely dependent on history. At the heart of New Testament faith is the assertion that "God was in Christ reconciling the world to Himself" (2 Cor. 5:19 NASB). The incarnation, death, and resurrection of Jesus Christ as a real event in time and space, i.e., as historical realities, are the indispensable foundations of Christian faith. To my mind, then, Christianity is best defined as the recitation of, the celebration of, and the participation in God's acts in history, which as the New Testament writings emphasize have found their culmination in Jesus Christ. (Hagner, NTCI, 73, 74)

This chapter contains evidence from Christian sources, secular authorities, and Jewish references to the life of Christ.

> *No serious scholar has ventured to postulate the non-historicity of Jesus.*
>
> —OTTO BETZ

1A. SECULAR AUTHORITIES ON JESUS' HISTORICITY

By *secular* I mean "pagan"—non-Christian, non-Jewish, and generally anti-Christian. Many ancient secular writers mention Jesus and the movement He birthed. The fact that they are usually antagonistic to Christianity makes them especially good witnesses, since they have nothing to gain by admitting the historicity of the events surrounding a religious leader and His following, which they disdain.

1B. Cornelius Tacitus

According to Habermas, "Cornelius Tacitus (c. A.D. 55–120) was a Roman historian who lived through the reigns of over a half dozen Roman emperors. He has been called the 'greatest historian' of ancient Rome, an individual generally acknowledged among scholars for his moral 'integrity and essential goodness.'" (Habermas, VHCELJ, 87) Tacitus's most acclaimed works are the *Annals* and the *Histories*. "The *Annals* cover the period from Augustus's death in A.D. 14 to that of Nero in A.D. 68, while the *Histories* begin after Nero's death and proceed to that of Domitian in A.D. 96." (Habermas, VHCELJ, 87)

Writing of the reign of Nero, Tacitus alludes to the death of Christ and to the existence of Christians at Rome. His misspelling of Christ—"Christus"—was a common error made by pagan writers. Says Tacitus:

> But not all the relief that could come from man, not all the bounties that the prince could bestow, nor all the atonements which could be presented to the gods, availed to relieve Nero from the infamy of being believed to have ordered the conflagration, the fire of Rome.

Hence to suppress the rumor, he falsely charged with the guilt, and punished with the most exquisite tortures, the persons commonly called Christians, who were hated for their enormities. Christus, the founder of the name, was put to death by Pontius Pilate, procurator of Judea in the reign of Tiberius: but the pernicious superstition, repressed for a time, broke out again, not only through Judea, where the mischief originated, but through the city of Rome also. (Annals XV, 44)

Norman Anderson sees a possible allusion to Jesus' resurrection in this account: "It is distinctly possible, that, when he adds that 'A most mischievous superstition, thus checked for the moment, again broke out,' he is bearing indirect and unconscious testimony to the conviction of the early church that the Christ who had been crucified had risen from the grave." (Anderson, JC, 20)

F. F. Bruce points out another interesting sidelight about this passage from Tacitus: "Pilate is not mentioned in any other pagan document which has come down to us. . . . And it may be regarded as an instance of the irony of history that the only surviving reference to him in a pagan writer mentions him because of the sentence of death which he passed upon Christ. For a moment Tacitus joins hands with the ancient Christian creed: '. . . suffered under Pontius Pilate.'" (Bruce, JCOCNT, 23)

Cambridge lecturer Markus Bockmuehl notes that Tacitus's comments provide us with testimony by the leading Roman historian of his day, "independent confirmation that Jesus lived and was formally executed in Judaea in the reign of Tiberius and during Pontius Pilate's office as procurator (technically still a prefect, A.D. 26–36). That may not seem like much, but it is actually surprisingly useful in discounting two different theories which are still sometimes advanced: first, that Jesus of Nazareth never existed; and secondly, that he did not die by the duly administered Roman death penalty." (Bockmuehl, TJMLM, 10, 11)

2B. Lucian of Samosata

A Greek satirist of the latter half of the second century, Lucian spoke scornfully of Christ and the Christians, never assuming or arguing that they were unreal. As Lucian said: "The Christians, you know, worship a man to this day—the distinguished personage who introduced their novel rites, and was crucified on that account. . . . You see, these misguided creatures start with the general conviction that they are immortal for all time, which explains the contempt of death and voluntary self-devotion which are so common among them; and then it was impressed on them by their original lawgiver that they are all brothers, from the moment that they are converted, and deny the gods of Greece, and worship the crucified sage, and live after his laws. All this they take quite on faith, with the result that they despise all worldly goods alike, regarding them merely as common property." (Lucian, *The Death of Peregrine*, 11–13)

3B. Suetonius

Suetonius, another Roman historian, court official under Hadrian, and annalist of the Imperial House, stated in his *Life of Claudius* 25. 4, "As the Jews were making constant disturbances at the instigation of Chrestus [another spelling of Christus], he [Claudius] expelled them from Rome." Luke refers to this event in Acts 18:2, which took place in A.D. 49.

In another work Suetonius wrote about the fire that swept through Rome in A.D. 64 under the reign of Nero. Suetonius recounts that "Punishment by Nero was inflicted on the Christians, a class of men given to a new and mischievous superstition." (*Lives of the Caesars*, 26. 2)

Assuming Jesus was crucified in the early thirties, Suetonius—no friend of Christianity—places Christians in the imperial city less than twenty years later, and he reports that they were suffering and dying for their conviction that Jesus Christ had really lived, died, and risen from the dead.

4B. Pliny the Younger

Governor of Bithynia in Asia Minor (A.D. 112), Pliny was writing the emperor Trajan to seek counsel as to how to treat the Christians. He explained that he had been killing both men and women, boys and girls. There were so many being put to death that he wondered if he should continue killing anyone who was discovered to be a Christian, or if he should kill only certain ones. He explained that he had made the Christians bow down to the statues of Trajan. Pliny goes on to say that he also "made them curse Christ, which a genuine Christian cannot be induced to do." In the same letter he says of

> The Gospel account of the darkness which fell upon the land during Christ's crucifixion was well known and required a naturalistic explanation from non-Christians. Thallus did not doubt that Jesus had been crucified and that an unusual event had occurred in nature that required an explanation. What occupied his mind was coming up with a different interpretation. The basic facts were not called into question.
>
> —F. F. BRUCE

the people being tried: "They affirmed, however, that the whole of their guilt, or their error, was, that they were in the habit of meeting on a certain fixed day before it was light, when they sang in alternate verse a hymn to Christ as to a god, and bound themselves to a solemn oath, not to do any wicked deeds, but never to commit any fraud, theft, adultery, never to falsify their word, not to deny a trust when they should be called upon to deliver it up." (Epistles X, 96)

5B. Thallus

One of the first secular writers who mentions Christ is Thallus. Dated perhaps around A.D. 52, Thallus "wrote a history of the Eastern Mediterranean world from the Trojan War to his own time." (Habermas, VHCELJ, 93) Unfortunately, his writing now exists only in fragments that have been cited by other writers. One such writer is Julius Africanus, a Christian who penned his work around A.D. 221. One very interesting passage relates to a comment made by Thallus about the darkness that enveloped the land during the late afternoon hours when Jesus died on the cross. As Africanus reports: "Thallus, in the third book of his histories, explains away this darkness as an eclipse of the sun—unreasonably, as it seems to me (unreasonably, of course, because a solar eclipse could not take place at the time of the full moon, and it was at the season of the Paschal full moon that Christ died)." (Julius Africanus, *Chronography*, 18.1)

This reference shows that the Gospel account of the darkness that fell upon the land during Christ's crucifixion was well known and required a naturalistic explanation from non-Christians. Thallus did not doubt that Jesus had been crucified and that an unusual event had occurred in nature that required an explanation. What occupied his mind was the task of coming up with a different interpretation. The basic facts were not called into question. (Bruce, NTDATR, 113)

6B. Phlegon

Another secular authority, Phlegon, wrote a history called *Chronicles*. While this work has been lost, Julius Africanus preserved a small fragment of it in his writing. Like Thallus, Phlegon confirms that darkness came upon the earth at Jesus' crucifixion, and he, too, explains it as the result of a solar eclipse: "During the time of Tiberius Caesar an eclipse of the sun occurred during the full moon." (Africanus, *Chronography*, 18. 1)

Aside from Africanus, Phlegon's reference to this event is also mentioned by the third-century Christian apologist Origen (*Contra Celsum*, 2. 14, 33, 59) and the sixth-century writer Philopon (*De. opif. mund.* II 21). (McDowell/Wilson, HWAU, 36)

7B. Mara Bar-Serapion

Some time after A.D. 70, Mara Bar-Serapion, a Syrian and probably Stoic philosopher, wrote a letter from prison to his son, encouraging him to pursue wisdom. In his letter he compares Jesus to the philosophers Socrates and Pythagoras. He writes:

What advantage did the Athenians gain from putting Socrates to death? Famine and plague came upon them as a judgment for their crime. What advantage did the men of Samos gain from burning Pythagoras? In a moment their land was covered with sand. What advantage did the Jews gain from executing their wise King? It was just after that that their kingdom was abolished. God justly avenged these three wise men: the Athenians died of hunger; the Samians were overwhelmed by the sea; the Jews, ruined and driven from their land, live in complete dispersion. But Socrates did not die for good; he lived on in the teaching of Plato. Pythagoras did not die for good; he lived on in the statue of Hera. Nor did the wise King die for good; He lived on in the teaching which He had given. (Bruce, NTDATR, 114)

This father was certainly not a Christian, since he puts Jesus on equal footing with Socrates and Protagoras; he has Jesus living on in His teaching rather than in His resurrection, and in another place he indicates a belief in polytheism. Nonetheless, his references to Christ indicate that he did not question whether Jesus really lived or not.

2A. JEWISH REFERENCES TO JESUS' HISTORICITY

Scholars have found many reliable references to Jesus, as well as unreliable ones or ones that were once thought to refer to Jesus but do not. (McDowell/Wilson, HWAU, 55–70) I have selected a few of the more important reliable references to focus on here. You can

> Similar to the secular references, the ones found in ancient Jewish sources are unfriendly toward Christianity's founder, followers, and beliefs. For this reason their attestation to events surrounding Jesus' life are valuable testimony to the historicity of these events.

find more citations in chapter 3 of my book *He Walked Among Us: Evidence for the Historical Jesus.*

Similar to the secular references, the ones found in ancient Jewish sources are unfriendly toward Christianity's founder, followers, and beliefs. For this reason their attestation to events surrounding Jesus' life are valuable testimony to the historicity of these events.

1B. The Crucifixion

In the Babylonian Talmud we read: "It has been taught: On the eve of Passover they hanged Yeshu. And an announcer went out, in front of him, for forty days (saying): 'He is going to be stoned, because he practiced sorcery and enticed and led Israel astray. Anyone who knows anything in his favor, let him come and plead in his behalf.' But, not having found anything in his favor, they hanged him on the eve of Passover" (Sanhedrin 43a; cf. t. Sanh. 10:11; y. Sanh. 7:12; Tg. Esther 7:9). Another version of this text says, "Yeshu the Nazarene."

"Yeshu" translates through Greek to English as "Jesus," and the reference to him being a Nazarene makes the link to Jesus Christ even stronger.

Moreover, the word "hanged" is another way of referring to crucifixion (see Luke 23:39; Gal. 3:13). "The Talmud," writes the Jewish scholar Joseph Klausner, "speaks of hanging in place of crucifixion, since this horrible Roman form of death was only known to Jewish scholars from Roman trials, and not from the Jewish legal system. Even Paul the Apostle (Gal. iii. 13) expounds the passage 'for a curse of God is that which is hanged' (Deut. xxi. 23) as applicable to Jesus." (Klausner, JN, 28)

Also, the reference that this crucifixion occurred "on the eve of Passover" agrees with John 19:14 (phrase also found in b. Sanh. 67a; y. Sanh. 7:16).

Therefore, this text clearly affirms the historicity of Jesus and His death. It also affirms that the Jewish authorities were involved in the sentencing, but it tries to justify their actions. In a backhanded way it even attests to Jesus' miracles (see also b. Sanh. 107b; t. Sabb. 11:15; b. Sabb. 104b.; b. Sota 47a), but it attempts to explain them away as the work of a sorcerer or magician, a response mentioned by the Gospel writers (Mark 3:22; Matt. 9:34; 12:24). (Klausner, JN, 23)

Following this Jewish text appears a comment by the late third-century Ammora, 'Ulla, which states: "Would you believe that any defence would have been so zealously sought for him? He was a deceiver, and the All-merciful says: 'You shall not spare him, neither shall you conceal him.' It was different with Jesus, for he

was near to the kingship." This phrase—"near to the kingship"—may refer to Jesus' genealogical descent from Israel's King David, or it may denote Pilate's washing his hands before turning Jesus over to scourging and crucifixion.

2A. Jesus and His Disciples

In a later Talmudic passage on Jesus' crucifixion comes a passage that asserts that "Yeshu had five disciples—Mattai, Nakkai, Netzer, Buni, and Todah." (b. Sanh. 107b). While "Mattai" may be a reference to Matthew, no one is sure that the other names can be identified with any of the other disciples named in the Gospel accounts. The claim that Jesus had five disciples "could be explained by the fact that other teachers in the Talmud, viz. Yohanan ben Zakkai and Akiba, are also described as having five disciples or students." (McDowell/Wilson, HWAU, 65) At any rate, one thing is sure: this text makes it clear that the Jewish tradition accepts the fact that the rabbi Jesus did have followers.

3B. Virgin Born?

In the Talmud, the titles "Ben Pandera (or 'Ben Pantere')" and "Jeshu ben Pandera" are used of Jesus. Many scholars say *pandera* is a play on words, a travesty on the Greek word for virgin, which is *parthenos*. The Jewish scholar Joseph Klausner says, "The Jews constantly heard that the Christians (the majority of whom spoke Greek from the earliest times) called Jesus by the name 'Son of the Virgin,' . . . and so, in mockery, they called him *Ben ha-Pantera*, i.e., 'son of the leopard.'" (Klausner, JN, 23)

In another passage, the Babylonian Talmud states, "R. Shimeon ben Azzai said [concerning Jesus]: 'I found a genealogical roll in Jerusalem wherein was recorded, Such-an-one is a bastard of an adulteress'"

(b. Yebamoth 49a; m. Yebam. 4:13). In yet another passage we find, "His mother was Miriam, a women's hairdresser. As they say . . . 'this one strayed from her husband'" (b. Sabb. 104b). In still another passage we are told that Mary, "who was the descendant of princes and governors, played the harlot with carpenters" (b. Sanh. 106a). This passage is, of course, an attempted explanation for the Christian confession of Jesus' virgin birth (see also b. Sabb. 104b). "Princes and governors" may refer to some of the names in Luke's genealogy, which some of the church fathers assigned as Mary's ancestors back to King David (cf. "Jesus . . . was near to kingship" in b. Sanh. 43a). The allusion to "carpenters" is an obvious reference to Joseph (see also b. Sabb. 104b).

The argument goes like this: If Joseph was not Jesus' father, then Mary was impregnated by another man; therefore she is an adulteress and Jesus was an illegitimate son. The New Testament records that the scribes and Pharisees indirectly leveled this charge at Jesus (John 8:41).

Although the New Testament affirms that this charge is baseless, the accusation does confirm that the Christian account of Jesus' miraculous birth was an early claim of the church that required a response. And notice, the response did not include a denial of Jesus' existence—only a different interpretation of His conception. As Klausner observes, "Current editions of the *Mishnah* add: 'To support the words of R. Yehoshua' (who, in the same *Mishnah*, says: What is a bastard? Everyone whose parents are liable to death by the Beth Din). That Jesus is here referred to seems to be beyond doubt." (Klausner, JN, 35)

4B. The Testimonium of Josephus

"Josephus ben Mattathias (born 37/38 A.D., died after 100 A.D.)," writes professor John P. Meier, was by turns a Jewish aristocrat, a priestly politician, a not-so-eager commander of rebel troops in Galilee during the First Jewish Revolt against Rome (66–73 A.D.), a tricky turncoat, a Jewish historian in the pay of the Flavian emperors, and a supposed Pharisee. Captured by Vespasian in 67, he served the Romans as mediator and interpreter during the rest of the revolt. Brought to Rome, he composed there two great works: *The Jewish War*, written in the early 70s, and the much longer *Jewish Antiquities*, finished about 93, 94. (Meier, BR, 20, 22)

Flavius Josephus became part of the emperor's inner circle. In fact, he was given the emperor's name, Flavius, as his Roman name. Josephus is his Jewish name.

In his *Jewish Antiquities*, a passage occurs that has created heated debate among scholars. This is how it reads:

Now there was about this time Jesus, a wise man, *if it be lawful to call him a man,* for he was a doer of wonderful works, a teacher of such men as receive the truth with pleasure. He drew over to him both many of the Jews, and many of the Gentiles. *He was the Christ,* and when Pilate, at the suggestion of the principal men among us, had condemned him to the cross, those that loved him at the first did not forsake him; *for he appeared to them alive again the third day; as the divine prophets had foretold these and ten thousand other wonderful things concerning him.* And the tribe of Christians so named from him are not extinct at this day. (*Antiquities,* XVIII, 33, italics added)

I won't go into the ins and outs of the positions scholars have taken on this passage, which has come to be known as the Testimonium. For a more detailed discussion of the debate, see my book *He Walked Among Us*, pages 37–45. Instead let me just say here that the passage has raised furor because Josephus, a non-Christian Jew, makes statements about Jesus that an orthodox Jew could not affirm—for instance, he refers to Jesus as the Christ (Messiah) and claims that He rose from the dead as the Hebrew prophets had foretold.

After assessing the evidence for myself, I find myself agreeing with those scholars who see that, while some Christian additions—notably the phrases italicized above—have been made to the text that are clearly foreign to it, the Testimonium contains a good deal of truth that Josephus could have easily affirmed. As Meier states:

Read the Testimonium without the italicized passages and you will see that the flow of thought is clear. Josephus calls Jesus by the generic title "wise man" (*sophos an'r*, perhaps the Hebrew *khakham*). Josephus then proceeds to "unpack" that generic designation (wise man) with two of its main components in the Greco-Roman world: miracle working and effective teaching. This double display of "wisdom" wins Jesus a large following among both Jews and gentiles, and presumably—though no explicit reason is given—it is this huge success that moves the leading men to accuse Jesus before Pilate. Despite Jesus' shameful death on the cross, his earlier adherents do not give up their loyalty to him, and so (note that the transition is much better without the reference to the resurrection in the deleted passage) the tribe of Christians has not yet died out. (Meier, BR, 23)

Following this Testimonium a couple of sections later, Josephus refers to James the brother of Jesus. In *Antiquities* XX, 9. 1 he describes the actions of the high priest Ananus:

But the younger Ananus who, as we said, received the high priesthood, was of a bold disposition and exceptionally daring; he followed the party of the Sadducees, who are severe in judgment above all the Jews, as we have already shown. As therefore Ananus was of such a disposition, he thought he had now

a good opportunity, as Festus was now dead, and Albinus was still on the road; so he assembled a council of judges, and brought before it the brother of Jesus the so-called Christ, whose name was James, together with some others, and having accused them as lawbreakers, he delivered them over to be stoned. (Bruce, NTDATR, 107)

Louis Feldman, professor of classics at Yeshiva University and translator for the Loeb edition of *Antiquities*, states, "Few have doubted the genuineness of this passage." (Josephus, *Antiquities,* Loeb, 496) The passing reference to Jesus as the "so-called Christ" does not make sense unless Josephus has provided a longer discussion about Jesus earlier in his *Antiquities*. This is yet another indication that the earlier and more extensive treatment in *Antiquities* is genuine, excluding the obvious Christian interpolations.

So even the great first-century Jewish historian Josephus, writing just a little more than half a century after Jesus' life and crucifixion, attests to the truth that Jesus was not a figment of the church's imagination but a real historical figure.

3A. CHRISTIAN SOURCES FOR JESUS' HISTORICITY

1B. Pre-New Testament Creedal Confessions

Early Christians often paid with their lives or suffered great persecution for their reports that Jesus had lived, died, risen from the dead, and appeared to many after His resurrection. These early Christians had nothing to gain and everything to lose for their testimony that these things had actually happened. For this reason, their accounts are highly significant historical sources.

Recorded in the pages of the New Testament, biblical scholars have identified what they believe are at least portions of early Christian creedal confessions that were formulated and passed on verbally years before they were recorded in the books of the New Testament. As apologist Gary Habermas explains, these affirmations "preserve some of the earliest reports concerning Jesus from about 30–50 A.D. Therefore, in a real sense, the creeds preserve pre-New Testament material, and are our earliest sources for the life of Jesus." (Habermas, VHCELJ, 119)

In his book *The Verdict of History*, Habermas focuses on several of the creedal affirmations embedded in the New Testament:

- Luke 24:34: " 'The Lord has risen indeed, and has appeared to Simon!' "

  Referring to Joachim Jeremias and his essay "Easter: The Earliest Tradition and the Earliest Interpretation," Habermas writes, "Jeremias holds that Luke's brief mention of Jesus' resurrection appearance to Peter in Luke 24:34 is of even greater antiquity than is 1 Cor. 15:5, which would make this an extremely early witness to these [post-resurrection] appearances." (Habermas, VHCELJ, 122)

- Romans 1:3, 4: "His Son Jesus Christ our Lord, who was born of the seed of David according to the flesh, and declared to be the Son of God with power according to the Spirit of holiness, by the resurrection from the dead." States Habermas:

That Romans 1:3, 4 is an ancient pre-Pauline creed is shown by the parallelism of the clauses, which is especially seen in the contrast between Jesus as both the son of David and the Son of God. The same Jesus who was born in space and time was raised from the dead. This creed proclaims that Jesus was shown to be the Son of God, Christ (or Messiah) and Lord and vindicated as such by his resurrection from the dead. [Oscar] Cullman adds that redemption and Jesus' final exaltation were also included in this significant creedal affirmation. Such an encompassing statement,

including three major Christological titles and implying some of the actions of Jesus, reveals not only one of the earliest formulations of Christ's nature, but also conveys an apologetic motif in relating all of this theology to the vindication provided by Jesus' resurrection (cf. Acts 2:22f). (Habermas, VHCELJ, 123)

- Romans 4:24, 25: "who raised up Jesus our Lord from the dead, who was delivered up because of our offenses, and was raised because of our justification."

  Even the biblical critic Rudolf Bultmann believes this statement "evidently existed before Paul and had been handed down to him" as part of the earliest apostolic Christian tradition. (Bultmann, TNT, 82)

- Romans 10:9, 10: "If you confess with your mouth the Lord Jesus and believe in your heart that God has raised Him from the dead, you will be saved. For with the heart one believes unto righteousness, and with the mouth confession is made unto salvation."

  In the early church, this confession of faith was likely said by believers at their baptism. The confession connects belief in the historical reality of Jesus' resurrection with confessing him as Lord and securing one's salvation. (Habermas, VHCELJ, 123; Martin, WEC, 108; Martin, DPHL, 192)

- 1 Corinthians 11:23–26: "For I received from the Lord that which I also delivered to you: that the Lord Jesus on the same night in which He was betrayed took bread; and when He had given thanks, He broke it and said, 'Take, eat; this is My body which is broken for you; do this in remembrance of Me.' In the same manner He also took the cup after supper, saying, 'This cup is the new covenant in My blood; this do, as often as you drink it, in remembrance of Me.' For as often as you eat this bread and drink this cup, you proclaim the Lord's death till He comes."

Habermas says that

Paul's account in 1 Cor. 11:23ff. presents a fixed tradition that is probably based on material independent of the sources for the synoptic Gospels. Jeremias notes that Paul's words "received" and "delivered" are not Paul's typical terms, but "represent the rabbinical technical terms" for passing on tradition. Additionally, there are other non-Pauline phrases such as "he was betrayed," "when he had given thanks" and "my body" (11:23, 24), which are further indications of the early nature of this report. In fact, Jeremias assets that [t]his material was formulated "in the very earliest period; at any rate before Paul ... a pre-Pauline formula." Paul is actually pointing out "that the chain of tradition goes back unbroken to Jesus himself." (Habermas, VHCELJ, 121)

• 1 Corinthians 15:3–5: "For I delivered to you first of all that which I also received: that Christ died for our sins according to the Scriptures, and that He was buried, and that He rose again on the third day according to the Scriptures, and that He was seen by Cephas, then by the twelve."

Bible scholar Ralph Martin cites several "telltale marks" that "stamp" this passage "as a creedal formula" that predates Paul's writings:

The four-fold "that" introduces each member of the creed (in verses 3, 4, 5). The vocabulary is unusual, containing some rare terms and expressions that Paul never employs again. The preface to the section informs us that Paul "received" what follows in his next sentences as part of the instruction, no doubt, he had known in the early days of his discipleship, possibly through his contacts with the Church

at Jerusalem and Antioch and Damascus. And now in turn, he transmits (using the same technical expressions as in 1 Corinthians xi, 23) to the Corinthian Church what he has received as a sacred tradition. The matter of the suggested background of this passage and its pre-Pauline and creedal origin is clinched by verse 11 of the chapter, where Paul remarks that he has stated what was the common proclamation of the Apostles: "Whether then it was I or they, so we preach and so you believed."

There are certain indications in the text itself that 1 Corinthians xv, 3 ff. is a translation into Greek of a piece of Aramaic. The most obvious points are that Peter's name is given in its Semitic form as Cephas, and that there is a double reference to the Old Testament Scriptures. Professor Jeremias argues, with some cogency, that these verses arose in a Jewish-Christian *milieu*; and more recently still a Scandinavian scholar has submitted that this piece of Christian creed emanated from the earliest Palestinian Church. It represents, he says, "a logos (i.e. statement of belief) fixed by the college of Apostles in Jerusalem." ... If this argument is sound, it is clear that the passage belongs to the very earliest days of the Church and is, as E. Meyer phrased it, "the oldest document of the Christian Church in existence." It goes back to the teaching of the Hebrew-Christian fellowship shortly after the death of Christ, and may well embody the fruit of the post-Resurrection instruction and reflection contained in Luke xxiv, 25–27, 44–47. (Martin, WEC, 57–59)

• Philippians 2:6–11: "Being in the form of God, [He] did not consider it robbery to be equal with God, but made Himself of no reputation, taking the form of a bondservant, and coming in the likeness of men. And being found in appearance as a man, He humbled Himself and became obedient to the point of death, even the death of the cross. Therefore God also has highly exalted Him, and given Him the name which is above every name, that at the name of Jesus every knee should bow, of those in heaven, and of those on earth, and of those under the earth, and that every tongue should confess

It is clear that these pre-New Testament creeds provide the earliest testimony to the church's conviction that Jesus, the sinless God-man, actually lived, died, rose from the dead, and ascended into heaven for the salvation of anyone who would confess Him as Lord and truly believe that God resurrected Him.

that Jesus Christ is Lord, to the glory of God the Father."

Scholars have identified this text as a pre-Pauline hymn that professes belief in a real Jesus who was both human and divine. (Habermas, VHCELJ, 120; Martin, WEC, 49, 50)

- 1 Timothy 3:16: "And without controversy great is the mystery of godliness:

  God was manifested in the flesh,
  Justified in the Spirit,
  Seen by angels,
  Preached among the Gentiles,
  Believed on in the world,
  Received up in glory."

This is another Christological hymn that predates Paul's writings and was probably sung in worship. (Martin, WEC, 48, 49)

- 1 Timothy 6:13: "Christ Jesus, who witnessed the good confession before Pontius Pilate."

According to Habermas, this passage is "also an early tradition, and perhaps even a part of a more extensive oral Christian confession of faith." Habermas also notes that scholar Vernon Neufeld "points out that Jesus' testimony was probably his affirmative answer to Pilate's question as to whether he

was the King of the Jews (see Mark 15:2)." (Habermas, VHCELJ, 122)

- 2 Timothy 2:8: "Remember that Jesus Christ, of the seed of David, was raised from the dead according to my gospel."

"Here Jesus' birth in the lineage of David is contrasted with his resurrection from the dead, again showing the early Christian interest in linking Jesus to history." (Habermas, VHCELJ, 120)

- 1 Peter 3:18: "For Christ also suffered once for sins, the just for the unjust, that He might bring us to God, being put to death in the flesh but made alive by the Spirit."

This ancient piece of tradition connects Jesus' historical death on the cross as the sinless Messiah with His historical resurrection from the dead as the means of bringing sinners to God. (Habermas, VHCELJ, 122)

- 1 John 4:2: "Jesus Christ has come in the flesh."

This is a concise, clear, pre-Johannine affirmation that Jesus the Christ was a historical flesh-and-blood person. (Habermas, VHCELJ, 120)

Reflecting upon these ancient confessions, Habermas notes that they make at least seventeen historical claims about Jesus from his earthly birth to his heavenly ascension and glorification:

Although these early creeds are interested in theological elements of Christology, to be sure, they are also early reports of events in the life of Jesus. We are told (1) that Jesus was really born in human flesh (Phil. 2:6; 1 Tim. 3:16; 1 John 4:2) (2) of the lineage and family of David (Rom. 1:3, 4; 2 Tim. 2:8). We find (3) an implication of his baptism (Rom. 10:9) and (4) that his word was preached, (5) resulting in persons believing his message (1 Tim. 3:16).

In addition to the events of his life, we are further informed that (6) Jesus attended a dinner (7) on the evening of his betrayal. (8) He gave thanks before the meal and (9) shared both bread and drink, (10) which, he declared, represented his imminent atoning sacrifice for sin (1 Cor. 11:23ff.). (11) Later, Jesus stood before Pilate and made a good confession, (12) which very possibly concerned his identity as the King of the Jews (1 Tim. 6:13). (13) Afterward, Jesus was killed for mankind's sins (1 Pet. 3:18; Rom. 4:25; 1 Tim. 2:6), (14) in spite of his righteous life (1 Pet. 3:18). (15) After his death he was resurrected (Luke 24:34; 2 Tim. 2:8). (16) It was asserted that this event validated Jesus' person and message (Rom. 1:3, 4; 10:9, 10). (17) After his resurrection, Jesus ascended to heaven and was glorified and exalted (1 Tim. 3:16; Phil. 2:6ff.). (Habermas, VHCELJ, 121, 123, 124)

It is clear that these pre-New Testament creeds provide the earliest testimony to the church's conviction that Jesus, the sinless God-man, actually lived, died, rose from the dead, and ascended into heaven for the salvation of anyone who would confess Him as Lord and truly believe that God resurrected Him. Furthermore, as noted above, at least some of these creeds can be traced back to Jesus' actual words and the testimony of the apostles themselves. So these creeds are not

The twenty-seven books of the New Testament proclaim, verify, and often assume the historicity of Jesus Christ. Since I have already shown that these books are historically reliable, we can see that their testimony about Jesus provides significant, irrefutable evidence that He really lived and, in fact, still does.

only early but are also based on eyewitness accounts of Jesus' earthly life.

2B. The New Testament Documents

The twenty-seven books of the New Testament proclaim, verify, and often assume the historicity of Jesus Christ. Since I have already shown that these books are historically reliable, we can see that their testimony about Jesus provides significant, irrefutable evidence that He really lived and, in fact, still does.

No wonder historian and legal scholar John Montgomery unequivocally states that the historian can know "first and foremost, that the New Testament documents can be relied upon to give an accurate portrait of Him [Jesus]. And he knows that this portrait cannot be rationalized away by wishful thinking, philosophical presuppositionalism, or literary maneuvering." (Montgomery, HC, 40)

3B. Post-Apostolic Writers

Following the apostles, the next extensive Christian source for the historical nature of Jesus is found in the writings of those people who followed on the heels of the apostles. Some of these writers were church leaders, and others were teachers and apologists. All of them believed Jesus was the incarnate Son of God as revealed in the Scriptures and taught by the apostles.

Below is a good sampling from their writings of the more significant references to the historicity of Jesus Christ.

1C. Clement of Rome

Clement was bishop of the church at Rome toward the end of the first century. He wrote a letter called *Corinthians* to help settle a dispute in the church at Corinth between the church's leaders and laity. In this work, Clement said:

> The Apostles received the Gospel for us from the Lord Jesus Christ; Jesus Christ was sent forth from God. So then Christ is from God, and the Apostles are from Christ. Both therefore came of the will of God in the appointed

order. Having therefore received a charge, and having been fully assured through the resurrection of our Lord Jesus Christ and confirmed in the word of God with full assurance

> Jesus Christ, who was of the race of David, who was the Son of Mary, who was truly born and ate and drank, was truly persecuted under Pontius Pilate, was truly crucified and died in the sight of those in heaven and on earth and those under the earth; who moreover was truly raised from the dead, His Father having raised Him, who in the like fashion will so raise us also who believe on Him.
>
> —IGNATIUS

of the Holy Ghost, they went forth with the glad tidings that the kingdom of God should come. So preaching everywhere in country and town, they appointed their first-fruits, when they had proved them by the Spirit, to be bishops and deacons unto them that should believe. (*Corinthians*, 42)

Among other things, this passage affirms that the gospel message came from the historical Jesus who had been sent by God, and that His message was authenticated by His actual resurrection from the dead.

2C. Ignatius

While on his way to execution in Rome, Ignatius, who was the bishop of Antioch, wrote seven letters—six to different churches and one to his friend Polycarp. Three references Ignatius makes to the Historical Jesus are especially pertinent and characteristic of his other statements:

- "Jesus Christ who was of the race of David, who was the Son of Mary, who was truly born and ate and drank, was

truly persecuted under Pontius Pilate, was truly crucified and died in the sight of those in heaven and on earth and those under the earth; who moreover was truly raised from the dead, His Father having raised Him, who in the like fashion will so raise us also who believe on Him." (*Trallians*, 9)

- "He is truly of the race of David according to the flesh, but Son of God by the Divine will and power, truly born of a virgin and baptized by John that all righteousness might be fulfilled by Him, truly nailed up in the flesh for our sakes under Pontius Pilate and Herod the tetrarch (of which fruit are we—that is, of His most blessed passion); that He might set up an ensign unto all ages through His resurrection." (*Smyrneans*, 1)

- "Be ye fully persuaded concerning the birth and the passion and the resurrection, which took place in the time of the governorship of Pontius Pilate; for these things were truly and certainly done by Jesus Christ our hope." (*Magnesians*, 11)

Ignatius, whom Christian tradition identifies as a disciple of Peter, Paul, and John, was obviously convinced that Jesus really lived and that He was all the apostles said He was. (McDowell/Wilson, HWAU, 79)

3C. Quadratus

A disciple of the apostles and the bishop of the church at Athens, Quadratus was one of the earliest apologists. Church historian Eusebius has preserved the only lines remaining of Quadratus's defense of the faith to the Roman Emperor Hadrian (c. A.D. 125): "The deeds of our Saviour were always before you, for they were true miracles; those that were healed, those that were raised from the dead, who were seen, not only when healed and when raised, but were always present. They remained living a long time, not only whilst our Lord was on earth, but likewise when he had left the earth. So that some of them have also lived to our own times." (Eusebius, IV: III)

Habermas observes that Quadratus affirms the actual existence of Jesus through the historicity of His miracles: "(1) The facticity of Jesus' miracles could be checked by interested persons, since they were done publicly. With regard to the actual types of miracles, (2) some were healed and (3) some were raised from the dead. (4) There were eyewitnesses of these miracles at the time they occurred. (5) Many of those healed or raised were still alive when Jesus 'left the earth' and some were reportedly still alive in Quadratus' own time." (Habermas, VHCELJ, 144)

4C. The Epistle of Barnabas

The authorship of this letter is unknown. The name Barnabas does not occur in the letter, and scholars deny that the New Testament figure called Barnabas penned it. "Dates for this writing have varied widely," Habermas remarks, "often from the late first century to the mid-second century. A commonly accepted date is 130–138 A.D." (Habermas, VHCELJ, 145) This epistle confirms many of the events claimed as facts in the sources already cited. In section 5 of the letter, we read:

He Himself endured that He might destroy and show forth the resurrection of the dead, for that He must needs be manifested in the flesh; that at the same time He might redeem the promise made to the fathers, and by preparing the new people for Himself might show, while He was on earth, that having brought about the resurrection He will Himself exercise judgment. Yea and further, He preached teaching Israel and performing so many wonders and miracles, and He loved him [Israel] exceedingly. And when He chose

His own apostles who were to proclaim His Gospel, who, that He might show that He came not to call the righteous but sinners, were sinners above every sin, then He manifested Himself to be the Son of God." (McDowell/Wilson, HWAU, 82, 83)

In section 7, the author adds, "But moreover when crucified He [Jesus] had vinegar and gall given Him to drink." (McDowell/Wilson, HWAU, 83)

5C. Aristides

Aristides was a second-century Christian apologist and philosopher of Athens. His work was lost until the late nineteenth century when it was discovered in three separate versions—Armenian, Syriac, and Greek. He addressed his defense of Christianity to the Roman Emperor Antonius Pius, who reigned between A.D. 138 and A.D. 161. In part of this treatise, Aristides described Jesus Christ as:

the Son of the most high God, revealed by the Holy Spirit, descended from heaven, born of a Hebrew Virgin. His flesh he received from the Virgin, and he revealed himself in the human nature as the Son of God. In his goodness which brought the glad tidings, he has won the whole world by his life-giving preaching .... He selected twelve apostles and taught the

Accordingly, after He was crucified, even all His acquaintances forsook Him, having denied Him; and afterwards, when He had risen from the dead and appeared to them, and had taught them to read the prophecies in which all these things were foretold as coming to pass, and when they had seen Him ascending into heaven, and had believed, and had received power sent thence by Him upon them, and went to every race of men, they taught these things, and were called apostles.

—JUSTIN MARTYR

whole world by his mediatorial, light-giving truth. And he was crucified, being pierced with nails by the Jews; and he rose from the dead and ascended to heaven. He sent the apostles into all the world and instructed all by divine miracles full of wisdom. Their preaching bears blossoms and fruits to this day, and calls the whole world to illumination. (Carey, "Aristides," NIDCC, 68)

6C. Justin Martyr

"The consensus of scholarly opinion is that Justin [Martyr] is one of the greatest of the early Christian apologists." (Bush, CRCA, 1) He was born around A.D. 100 and was scourged and beheaded for his faith around 167. He was a learned man, well versed in the leading philosophies of his day, including Stoicism, Aristotelianism, Pythagoreanism, and Platonism. (Carey, "Justin Martyr," NIDCC, 558) After his conversion to Christ (c. 132), "Justin became a professor of philosophical Christianity in his own private school in Rome. Since he was a layman, he probably operated the school in his home. He also seems to have traveled considerably throughout the Roman Empire, spending his time in a ministry of teaching and evangelism." (Bush, CRCA, 3)

In his many writings, Justin builds his case for the faith upon the New Testament writings and his independent verification of many of the events they record. Here are some selections from his works concerning the accuracy of the accounts about Jesus Christ:

- "Now there is a village in the land of the Jews, thirty-five stadia from Jerusalem, in which Jesus Christ was born, as you can ascertain also from the registers of the taxing made under *Cyrenius*, your first procurator in Judea." (*First Apology*, 34)
- "For at the time of His birth, Magi who came from Arabia worshiped Him, coming first to Herod, who then was sovereign in your land." (*Dialogue with Trypho*, 77)

- "For when they crucified Him, driving in the nails, they pierced His hands and feet; and those who crucified Him parted His garments among themselves, each casting lots for what he chose to have, and receiving according to the decision of the lot." (*Dialogue with Trypho*, 97)
- "Accordingly, after He was crucified, even all His acquaintances forsook Him, having denied Him; and afterwards, when He had risen from the dead and appeared to them, and had taught them to read the prophecies in which all these things were foretold as coming to pass, and when they had seen Him ascending into heaven, and had believed, and had received power sent thence by Him upon them, and went to every race of men, they taught these things, and were called apostles." (*First Apology*, 50)
- "Christ said amongst you [i.e., the Jews] that He would give the sign of Jonah, exhorting you to repent of your wicked deeds at least after He rose again from the dead . . . yet you not only have not repented, after you learned that He rose from the dead, but, as I said before, you have sent chosen and ordained men throughout all the world to proclaim that a godless and lawless heresy had sprung from one Jesus, a Galilean deceiver, whom we crucified, but His disciples stole him by night from the tomb, where He was laid when unfastened from the cross, and now deceive men by asserting that He has risen from the dead and ascended to heaven." (*Dialogue with Trypho*, 108)

7C. Hegesippus

"Jerome . . . says that Hegesippus lived near the time of the apostles. Eusebius draws the conclusion that Hegesippus was a Jew and says his work comprised five books of

'Memoirs.'" (Williams, NIDCC, 457) Only fragments of these Memoirs have survived in the work of Eusebius. What they show is that Hegesippus traveled extensively and was "intent on determining if the true story [about Jesus] had been passed from the apostles down through their successors." He found it had, even in the troubled church at Corinth. As Eusebius quotes him: "The Corinthian church continued in the true doctrine until Primus became bishop. I mixed with them on my voyage to Rome and spent several days with the Corinthians, during which we were refreshed with the true doctrine. On arrival at Rome I pieced together the succession down to Anicetus, whose deacon was Eleutherus, Anicetus being succeeded by Soter and he by Eleutherus. In every line of bishops and in every city things accord with the preaching of the Law, the Prophets, and the Lord." (Eusebius, *The History of the Church*, 9. 22. 2)

The essential facts about Jesus and His teaching were passed down by the apostles and carefully preserved and faithfully passed on by the churches generation after generation from one location to another. The verdict is in: "The early church writers, both by their lives and words, certified that the historical details of Jesus' life, as present in the gospel accounts, are correct and may be trusted." (McDowell/Wilson, HWAU, 87)

4A. ADDITIONAL HISTORICAL SOURCES FOR CHRISTIANITY

There are additional sources that refer to Christ and Christianity. The following are some additional secular sources that warrant further study:

1B. Trajan, Roman emperor (Pliny the Younger, *Epistles* 10:97). This is a letter from the emperor to Pliny, telling him not to punish those Christians who are forced to retract their beliefs by the Romans. He tells Pliny that anonymous information about the Christians is not to be accepted by the Roman officials.

2B. Macrobius, *Saturnalia*, lib. 2, ch. 4. Pascal *(Pensees)* mentions this quote of Augustus Caesar as an attestation of the slaughter of the babes of Bethlehem.

3B. Hadrian, Roman emperor (Justin Martyr, *The First Apology,* chs. 68, 69). Justin quotes Hadrian's letter to Minucius Fundanus, proconsul of Asia Minor. The letter deals with the accusations of the pagans against the Christians.

4B. Antoninus Pius, Roman emperor (Justin Martyr, *The First Apology,* ch. 70). Justin (or one of his disciples) quotes Antoninus's letter to the general assembly of Asia Minor. The letter basically says that the officials in Asia Minor are getting too upset at the Christians in their province, and that no changes will be made in Antoninus's method of dealing with the Christians there.

5B. Marcus Aurelius, Roman emperor (Justin Martyr, *The First Apology,* ch. 71). This letter from the emperor to the Roman senate was added to the manuscript by one of Justin's disciples. The emperor describes Christians in fighting action in the Roman army.

6B. Juvenal, *Satires,* 1, lines 147–157. Juvenal makes a veiled mention of the tortures of Christians by Nero in Rome.

7B. Seneca, *Epistulae Morales,* Epistle 14, "On the Reasons for Withdrawing from the World," par. 2. Seneca, like Juvenal, describes the cruelties of Nero dealt upon the Christians.

8B. Hierocles (Eusebius, *The Treatise of Eusebius,* ch. 2). This quote by Eusebius preserves some of the text of the lost book of Hierocles, *Philalethes,* or *Lover of Truth.* In this quote, Hierocles condemns Peter and Paul as sorcerers.

9B. In discussing Christ as a man of history, one of the most important collections of material is a volume published in Cambridge in 1923 by C. R. Haines entitled *Heathen Contact with Christianity During Its First Century and a Half.* The subtitle reads as follows: "Being all References to Christianity Recorded in Pagan Writings During That Period."

CONCLUSION

Howard Clark Kee, professor emeritus at Boston University, makes the following conclusions from the sources outside of the New Testament: "The result of the examination of the sources outside the New Testament that bear directly or indirectly on our knowledge of Jesus is to confirm his historical existence, his unusual powers, the devotion of his followers, the continued existence of the movement after his death at the hands of the Roman governor in Jerusalem, and the penetration of Christianity into the upper strata of society in Rome itself by the later first century." (Kee, WCKAJ, 19)

Kee adds: "In spite of this range of ways in which the tradition about Jesus has been transmitted, we have available a clear and remarkably consistent array of evidence about this figure whose life, teachings, and death have continued to have such a profound impact on the subsequent history of the human race." (Kee, WCKAJ, 114)

In the 1974 edition of the *Encyclopaedia Britannica,* the contributor writing about Jesus Christ uses twenty thousand words to describe Him, more space than was given to Aristotle, Cicero, Alexander, Julius Caesar,

> Accordingly, after He was crucified, even all His acquaintances forsook Him, having denied Him; and afterwards, when He had risen from the dead and appeared to them, and had taught them to read the prophecies in which all these things were foretold as coming to pass, and when they had seen Him ascending into heaven, and had believed, and had received power sent thence by Him upon them, and went to every race of men, they taught these things, and were called apostles.
>
> —JUSTIN MARTYR

Buddha, Confucius, Mohammed, or Napoleon Bonaparte. Concerning the testimony of the many independent secular accounts of Jesus of Nazareth, the author resoundingly concludes: "These independent accounts prove that in ancient times even the opponents of Christianity never doubted the historicity of Jesus, which was disputed for the first time and on inadequate grounds by several authors at the end of the 18th, during the 19th, and at the beginning of the 20th centuries." (EB, 145)

To those who would deny the historical existence of Jesus, noted British New Testament scholar I. Howard Marshall comments, "It is not possible to explain the rise of the Christian church or the writing of the Gospels and the stream of tradition that lies behind them without accepting the fact that the Founder of Christianity actually existed." (Marshall, IBHJ, 24)

Though the non-Christian sources do not provide as much detail about Jesus as the New Testament, they do provide corroboration for some of the basic facts of the biblical portrayal of Jesus. Robert Stein, a New Testament professor, states: "The non-Christian sources establish beyond reasonable doubt the following minimum: (1) Jesus was truly a historical person. This may seem silly to stress, but through the years some have denied that Jesus ever lived. The nonbiblical sources put such nonsense to rest. (2) Jesus lived in Palestine in the first century of our era. (3) The Jewish leadership was involved in the death of Jesus. (4) Jesus was crucified by the Romans under the governorship of Pontius Pilate. (5) Jesus' ministry was associated with wonder/ sorcery." (Stein, JM, 49)

R. T. France writes: "Non-Christian evidence therefore substantiates the fact of Jesus' existence, his popular following, his execution and the rough date." (France, NBD, 564)

Edwin Yamauchi, professor of history at Miami University, asserts that we have more and better historical documentation for Jesus than for any other religious founder (e.g., Zoroaster, Buddha, or Mohammed). Of the nonbiblical sources testifying of Christ, Yamauchi concludes:

> Even if we did not have the New Testament of Christian writings, we would be able to conclude from such non-Christian writings as Josephus, the Talmud, Tacitus, and Pliny the Younger that: (1) Jesus was a Jewish teacher; (2) many people believed that he performed healings and exorcisms; (3) he was rejected by the Jewish leaders; (4) he was crucified under Pontius Pilate in the reign of Tiberius; (5) despite this shameful death, his followers, who believed that he was still alive, spread beyond Palestine so that there were multitudes of them in Rome by A.D. 64; (6) all kinds of people from the cities and countryside—men and women, slave and free—worshipped him as God by the beginning of the second century. (Yamauchi, JUF, 221, 222)

The profound and powerful life of Jesus as a historical figure has made a dramatic impact on the rest of history. Noted Yale historian Jaroslav Pelikan writes, "Regardless what anyone may personally think or believe about him, Jesus of Nazareth has been the dominant figure in the history of Western culture for almost twenty centuries. If it were possible, with some sort of supermagnet to pull up out of that history every scrap of metal bearing at least a trace of his name, how much would be left?" (Pelikan, JTC, 1)

His impact on the course of history is without parallel. A *Newsweek* magazine writer observes, "By any secular standard, Jesus is also the dominant figure of Western culture. Like the millennium itself, much of what we now think of as Western ideas, innovations, and values finds its source or inspiration in the religion that worships God in His name. Art and science, the self and society, politics and economics, marriage and family, right and wrong, body and soul—all have been touched and often radically transformed by Christian influence." (Woodward, N, 54)

Upon surveying the historical evidence for the existence of Christ, Gary Habermas notes, "Surprisingly few scholars have asserted that Jesus never existed or have attempted to cast almost total doubt on his life and ministry. When such efforts have occurred, they have been met by rare outcries from the scholarly community. We have seen that these attempts are refuted at almost every turn by the early and eyewitness testimony presented by Paul and others, as well as by the early date of the Gospel." (Habermas, HJ, 46)

The evidence is conclusive. Jesus really lived among us and accomplished powerful works that even hostile, nonChristian sources do not fail to confirm. The skeptics about Jesus' historicity are simply wrong.

6

IF JESUS WASN'T GOD, HE DESERVES AN OSCAR

1A. HIS DIRECT CLAIMS TO DEITY

1B. Introduction: Who Is Jesus?

Best-selling author Tim LaHaye writes, "Almost everyone who has heard of Jesus has developed an opinion about Him. That is to be expected, for He is not only the most famous person in world history, but also the most controversial." (LaHaye, JWH, 59)

Philip Yancey concurs: "It occurs to me that all the contorted theories about Jesus that have been spontaneously generating since the day of his death merely confirm the awesome risk God took when he stretched himself out on the dissection table—a risk he seemed to welcome. Examine me. Test me. You decide." (Yancey, JNK, 21)

The writers of Scripture invite us to examine this person Jesus for ourselves and to conclude for ourselves His significance. But we cannot focus the investigation just on His teaching or works. First and foremost we must focus the investigation on His identity.

"Obviously *who* is Christ, is as important as what He did." (Linton, SV, 11)

"The challenge posed to every succeeding generation by the New Testament witness to Jesus is not so much, 'What did he teach?' but 'Who is he? And what is his relevance for us?'" (McGrath, UJ, 16)

So who is Christ? What type of person is He?

"On the lips of anyone else the claims of Jesus would appear to be evidence of gross egomania, for Jesus clearly implies that the entire world revolves around himself and that the fate of all men is dependent on their acceptance or rejection of him." (Stein, MMJT, 118)

Jesus certainly does not fit the mold of other religious leaders. Thomas Schultz writes: "Not one *recognized* religious leader, not Moses, Paul, Buddha, Mohammed, Confucius, etc., has ever claimed to be God; that is, with the exception of Jesus Christ. Christ is the only religious leader who has ever claimed to be deity and the only individual ever who has convinced a great portion of the world that He is God." (Schultz, DPC, 209)

How could a "man" make others think He was God? We hear first from F. J. Meldau: "His teachings were ultimate, final—above those of Moses and the prophets. He never added any afterthoughts or revisions; He never retracted or changed; He never guessed, 'supposed,' or spoke with any uncertainty. This is all so contrary to human teachers and teachings." (Meldau, PDC, 5)

Add to this the testimony of Foster: "But the reason overshadowing all others, which led directly to the ignominious execution of the Teacher of Galilee, was His incredible claim that He, a simple carpenter's son among the shavings and sawdust of His father's workshop, was in reality God in the flesh!" (Anderson, LH, 49)

One may well say, "Of course Jesus is presented this way in the Bible because it was written by His associates who desired to make an everlasting memorial to Him." However, to disregard the entire Bible is not to disregard all the evidence, as we have seen from historical records that make mention of Jesus, His works, and His teachings. William Robinson states: "If one takes a historically objective approach to the question, it is found that even secular history affirms that Jesus lived on earth and that He was worshiped as God. He founded a church which has worshiped Him for 1,900 years. He changed the course of the world's history." (Robinson, OL, 29)

Consider first, the evidence based upon Jesus' own legal testimony concerning Himself during His trial in a human court.

2B. The Trial

"But He kept silent and answered nothing. Again the high priest asked Him, saying to Him, 'Are You the Christ, the Son of the Blessed?' Jesus said, 'I am. And you will see the Son of Man sitting at the right hand of the Power, and coming with the clouds of heaven.' Then the high priest tore his clothes and said, 'What further need do we have of witnesses? You have heard the blasphemy! What do you think?' And they all condemned Him to be deserving of death" (Mark 14:61–64).

Judge Gaynor, the accomplished jurist of the New York bench, in his address upon the trial of Jesus, maintains that blasphemy was the one charge made against Jesus before the Sanhedrin: "It is plain from each of the gospel narratives, that the alleged crime for which Jesus was tried and convicted was blasphemy: . . . Jesus had been claiming supernatural power, which in a human being was blasphemy" (citing John 10:33). Judge Gaynor's reference is to Jesus' "making Himself God," not to what Jesus said concerning the temple. (Deland, MTJ, 118-19)

Concerning the questions of the Pharisees, A. T. Robertson says, "Jesus accepts the challenge and admits that He claims to be all three (the Messiah, the Son of Man, the Son of God). 'Ye say' (*Humeislegete*), is just a Greek idiom for 'Yes' (compare 'I AM' in Mark 14:62 with 'Thou hast said' in Matthew 26:64)." (Robertson, WPNT, 277)

It was to Jesus' reply that the high priest tore his garments. H. B. Swete explains the significance of this response: "The law forbade the High Priest to rend his garment in private troubles (Lev. x. 6, xxi, 10), but when acting as a judge, he was required by custom to express in this way his horror of any blasphemy uttered in his presence. The relief of the embarrassed judge is manifest. If trustworthy evidence was not forthcoming, the necessity for it had now been superseded: the Prisoner had incriminated Himself." (Swete, GASM, 339)

We begin to see that this is no ordinary trial. Irwin Linton, a lawyer, brings this out when he states, "Unique among criminal trials is this one in which not the actions but the identity of the accused is the issue. The criminal charge laid against Christ, the confession or testimony or, rather, act in presence of the court, on which He was convicted, the interrogation by the Roman governor and the inscription and proclamation on His cross at the time of execution all are concerned with the one question of Christ's real identity and dignity. 'What think ye of Christ? Whose son is he?'" (Linton, SV, 7)

In this same regard the one-time skeptic Frank Morison makes clear that "Jesus of Nazareth was condemned to death, not upon the statements of His accusers, but upon an admission extorted from Him under oath." (Morison, WMS, 25)

> *Unique among criminal trials is this one in which not the actions but the identity of the accused is the issue.*
>
> —IRWIN LINTON

Hilarin Felder adds, "This inspection of the trial of Jesus should be sufficient to give us the invincible conviction that the Saviour confessed His true divinity before His judges." (Felder, CAC, 299-300)

Simon Greenleaf, a one-time Harvard law professor and himself a renowned lawyer, said regarding Jesus' trial, "It is not easy to perceive on what ground His conduct could have been defended before any tribunal unless upon that of His super human character. No lawyer, it is conceived, would think of placing His defense upon any other basis." (Greenleaf, TT, 562)

Even though Jesus' answers to His judges take a different form in each of the Synoptics, we see, as Morison tells us, that they all are equal in meaning: "These answers are really identical. The formulae 'Thou hast said' or 'Ye say that I am,' which to modern ears sound evasive, had no such connotation to the contemporary Jewish mind. 'Thou sayest' was the traditional form in which a cultivated Jew replied to a question of grave or sad import. Courtesy forbade a direct 'yes' or 'no.'" (Morison, WMS, 26)

To be certain that Jesus intended these implications from His answers, C. G. Montefiore analyzes the statement that follows His profession of deity: "The two expressions 'Son of Man' (frequently on his lips) and 'at the right hand of power'. . . (a peculiar Hebrew expression for the Deity) show that the answer is perfectly in accord with Jesus' spirit and manner of speech." (Montefiore, TSG, 360)

Likewise, Craig Blomberg, a noted New Testament scholar and author, writes:

Jesus may even be indicting his interrogators by this way of phrasing things. But he does not stop here. He goes on to add, "and you will see the Son of man sitting at the right hand of Power, and coming with the clouds of heaven" (Mark 14:62b RSV). This reply combines allusions to Daniel 7:13 and Psalm 110:1. In this context, "Son of man" means far more than a simple human being. Jesus is describing himself as the "one like a son of man, coming with the clouds of heaven" who "approached the Ancient of Days and was led into his presence" and given authority and power over all humanity, leading to universal worship and everlasting dominion (Dan. 7:13, 14). This claim to be far more than a mere mortal is probably what elicited the verdict of blasphemy from the Jewish high court. (Blomberg, JG, 341-43)

F. F. Bruce, of the University of Manchester, England, writes: "It is implied, if not expressly stated, that in Daniel's vision this being was enthroned. . . . [Jesus] linked these two scriptures when the high priest of Israel challenged him to declare his identity." (Bruce, RJ, 64-65)

It is perfectly clear then that this is the testimony that Jesus wanted to bear of Himself. We also see that the Jews must have understood His reply as a claim to His being God. There were two alternatives to be faced then; that His assertions were pure blasphemy or that He was God. His judges had to see the issue clearly—so clearly, in fact, that they crucified Him and then taunted Him, saying "He trusted in God . . . for He said, 'I am the Son of God'" (Matt. 27:43). (Stevenson, TTG, 125)

Thus, we see that Jesus was crucified for being who He really was, for being the Son of God. An analysis of His testimony will bear this out. His testimony affirmed that: He was

the Son of the Blessed. He was the one who would sit at the right hand of power. He was the Son of Man who would come on the clouds of heaven.

William Childs Robinson concludes that "each of these [three] affirmations is distinctly Messianic. Their cumulative Messianic effect is 'stunningly significant.'" (Robinson, WSYIA, 65)

Herschel Hobbs comments:

The Sanhedrin caught all three points. They summed them up in one question. "Art thou then the Son of God?" Their question invited an affirmative answer. It was the equivalent of a declarative statement on their part. So Jesus simply replied, "Ye say that I am." Therefore, He made them admit to His identity before they formally found Him guilty of death. It was a clever strategy on Jesus' part. He would die not merely upon His own admission to deity but also upon theirs.

According to them there was need for no other testimony. For they had heard Him themselves. So they condemned Him by the words "of his own mouth." But He also condemned them by their words. They could not say that they did not proclaim the Son of God guilty of death. (Hobbs, AEGL, 322)

Robert Anderson writes: "But no confirmatory evidence is more convincing than that of hostile witnesses, and the fact that the Lord laid claim to Deity is incontestably established by the action of His enemies. We must remember that the Jews were not a tribe of ignorant savages, but a highly cultured and intensely religious people; and it was upon this very charge that, without a dissentient voice, His death was decreed by the Sanhedrin—their great national Council, composed of the most eminent of their religious leaders, including men of the type of Gamaliel and his great pupil, Saul of Tarsus." (Anderson, LH, 5)

Hilarin Felder sheds more light on the

judgment the Pharisees actually impose on themselves: "But since they condemn the Saviour as a blasphemer by reason of his own confession, the judges prove officially and on oath that Jesus confessed not only that he was the theocratical Messiah King and human son of God, but also that he was the divine Messiah and the essential Son of God, and that He on account of this confession was put to death." (Felder, CATC, vol. 1, 306)

As a result of our study, we may then safely conclude that Jesus claimed deity for Himself in a way that all of His accusers could recognize. These claims were regarded as blasphemous by the religious leaders, and according to Hebrew law and custom were punishable by death. They crucified Jesus because "He made Himself out to be the Son of God" (John 19:7 NASB). (Little, KWYB, 45)

3B. Other Claims

1C. Equality with the Father

On a number of occasions Jesus claimed to be equal to God the Father.

1D. John 10:25-33

"Jesus answered, . . . 'I and My Father are one.' Then the Jews took up stones again to stone Him. Jesus answered them, 'Many good works I have shown you from My Father. For which of those works do you stone Me?' The Jews answered Him, saying, 'For a good work we do not stone You, but for blasphemy, and because You, being a Man, make Yourself God.'"

—John 10:25–33

In this account, the Jews clearly understood Jesus' words as a claim to be God. Their response, like that at the trial, shows that they fully understood what He meant by

His words. An interesting and strengthening implication arises when the Greek wording is studied. A. T. Robertson points out: "One *(hen)*. Neuter, no masculine *(heis)*. Not one person (cf. *heis* in Gal. 3:28), but one essence or nature." (Roberston, WPNT, 186)

Biblical commentator J. Carl Laney concurs, stating, "The word 'one' *(hen)* is neuter and speaks of one essence, not one person . . . . The Father and the Son share a oneness of divine essence yet remain two distinct Persons within the godhead." (Laney, JMGC, 195-96)

Robertson goes on to tell us: "This crisp statement is the climax of Christ's claims concerning the relation between the Father and Himself (the Son). They stir the Pharisees to uncontrollable anger." (Robertson, WPNT, 187)

It is evident then that in the minds of those who heard this statement, there was no doubt that Jesus claimed before them that He was God. Thus: "The Jews could regard Jesus' word only as blasphemy, and they proceeded to take the judgment into their own hands. It was laid down in the Law that blasphemy was to be punished by stoning (Lev. 24:16). But these men were not allowing the due processes of law to take their course. They were not preparing an indictment so that the authorities could take the requisite action. In their fury they were preparing to be judges and executioners in one. 'Again' will refer back to their previous attempt at stoning (John 8:59)." (Bruce, NICNT, 524)

Their attempt to stone Jesus for blasphemy shows that they definitely understood His teaching. It also shows that they did not stop to consider whether His claim to deity was true or not!

2D. John 5:17, 18

"But Jesus answered them, 'My Father has been working until now, and I have been

working.' Therefore the Jews sought all the more to kill Him, because He not only broke the Sabbath, but also said that God was His Father, making Himself equal with God."

—John 5:17, 18

Respected biblical scholar Merrill C. Tenney explains, "The Jews were angry because of Jesus' violation of the Sabbath, but they were furious when he was so presumptuous as to claim equality with the Father. This claim of Jesus widened the breach between his critics and himself, for they understood that by it he was asserting his deity. His explanation shows that he did not claim identity with the Father as one person, but he asserted his unity with the Father in a relationship that could be described as sonship." (Tenney, GJ, 64)

A word study from A. T. Robertson's *Word Pictures of the New Testament* gives some interesting insights: "Jesus distinctly says, 'My Father' *(ho pater mou)*. Not 'our Father,' a claim to a peculiar relation to the Father. Worketh even until now *(heos arti ergazetai)*. . . . Jesus put himself on a par with God's activity and thus justifies his healing on the Sabbath." (Robertson, WPNT, 82–83)

It is also noteworthy that the Jews did not refer to God as "My Father." "If they did, they would qualify the statement with "in heaven." However, this Jesus did not do. He made a claim that the Jews could not misinterpret when He called God "My Father." (Morris, GAJ, 309) His claim was to a unique relationship with God as His Father. Just as a human father's son must be fully human, God's Son must be fully God. All that the Father is, the Son is.

Jesus also implies that while God is working, He, the Son, is working too. (Pfeiffer, WBC, 1083) Again, the Jews understood the

implication that He was God's Son. Resulting from this statement, the Jews' hatred intensified. Even though they were seeking mainly to persecute Him, their desire to kill Him began to increase. (Lenski, ISJG, 375)

2C. "I AM"

"Jesus said to them, 'Most assuredly, I say to you, before Abraham was, I AM.'"

—John 8:58

One commentator clarifies this passage well: "He said unto them, 'Verily, verily, I say unto you. . . .' Prefaced by a double Amen— the strongest oath—our Lord claims the incommunicable name of the Divine Being. The Jews recognize His meaning, and, horrified, they seek to stone Him." (Spurr, JIG, 54)

How did the Jews receive this statement? As Henry Alford tells us, "All unbiased exegesis of these words must recognize in them a declaration of the essential pre-existence of Christ." (Alford, GT, 801-02)

Marvin Vincent, in his *Word Studies of the New Testament,* writes that Jesus' statement is "the formula for *absolute,* timeless 'I AM' *(eimi)*." (Vincent, WSNT, vol. 2, 181)

By relying on Old Testament references, we find out that "I AM" refers to the name of God Himself, Yahweh (often translated in English Bibles as "LORD" in all capitals). A. G. Campbell makes this inference for us: "From such Old Testament references as Exodus 3:14, Deuteronomy 32:39, and Isaiah 43:10 it is clear that this is no new idea which Jesus is presenting. The Jews were quite familiar with the idea that the Jehovah of the Old Testament is the eternally existent One. That which is new to the Jews is the identification of this designation with Jesus." (Campbell, GTDC, 12)

From the reactions of the surrounding Jews we have proof that they understood His reference as a claim to absolute deity. Their insights prompted them to set about to fulfill the Mosaic law for blasphemy by stoning Jesus (Lev. 24:13-16). Peter Lewis remarks: "In one single statement the supreme truth about the supreme Man is made known— His pre-existence, His absolute existence." (Lewis, GC, 92)

Campbell explains this point to the non-Jew: "That we must also understand the expression 'I am' *(eimi)* as intended to declare the full deity of Christ is clear from the fact that Jesus did not attempt an explanation. He did not try to convince the Jews that they had misunderstood Him, but rather He repeated the statement several times on various occasions." (Campbell, GTDC, 12–13)

In sum, the renowned biblical scholar Raymond Brown writes in reference to this passage, "No clearer implication of divinity is found in the gospel tradition." (Brown, GAJ, 367)

3C. Jesus Is Due the Same Honor as That Given to God

"That all should honor the Son just as they honor the Father. He who does not honor the Son does not honor the Father who sent him. Most assuredly, I say unto you, he who hears My word and believes in Him who sent Me has everlasting life, and shall not come into judgment, but has passed from death into life."

— John 5:23, 24

In the last part of this verse Jesus thrusts a warning at those who accuse Him of blasphemy. He tells them that by hurling abuse at Him, they are actually hurling it at God, and that it is God who is outraged by their treatment of Jesus. (Godet, CGSJ, vol. 2, 174)

We also see that Jesus claims the right to be worshiped as God. And from this it follows, as previously stated, that to dishonor Jesus is to dishonor God. (Robertston, WPNT, 86)

4C. "To Know Me"

"Then they said to Him, 'Where is Your Father?' Jesus answered, 'You know neither Me nor My Father. If you had known Me, you would have known My Father also.' "

—John 8:19

Jesus claimed that to know and see Him was equivalent to knowing and seeing the Father. Jesus is the perfect and fullest revelation of the Father because He is of the Father's essence and stands in relationship to Him as His Son.

5C. "Believe in Me"

"Let not your heart be troubled; you believe in God, believe also in Me."

— John 14:1

Merrill Tenney explains: "He was doomed to death, the death that overtakes all men. Nevertheless, He had the audacity to demand that they make Him an object of faith. He made Himself the key to the question of destiny, and clearly stated that their future depended on His work. He promised to prepare a place for them, and to return to claim them." (Tenney, JGB, 213)

6C. "He Who Has Seen Me . . ."

"Philip said to Him, 'Lord, show us the Father, and it is sufficient for us.' Jesus said to him, 'Have I been with you so long, and yet you have not known Me, Philip? He who has seen Me has seen the Father; so how can you say, "Show us the Father"?'"

—John 14:8, 9

7C. "I Say to You . . ."

Matthew 5:20, 22, 26, 28, 32, 34, 44

In these scriptures, Jesus teaches and speaks in His own name. By doing so, He elevated the authority of His words directly to heaven. Instead of repeating the prophets by saying, "Thus saith the Lord," Jesus repeated, "but I say to you."

As Karl Scheffrahn and Henry Kreyssler point out: "He never hesitated nor apologized. He had no need to contradict, withdraw or modify anything he said. He spoke the unequivocal words of God (John 3:34). He said, 'Heaven and earth will pass away, but My Words will not pass away'" (Mark 13:31). (Scheffrahn, JN, 11)

4B. Worshiped as God

1C. Worship Reserved for God Only

1D. To fall down in homage is the greatest act of adoration and worship that can be performed for God (John 4:20-22; Acts 8:27).

2D. People Must Worship God in Spirit and in Truth (John 4:24)

3D. "You shall worship the LORD your God, and Him only you shall serve" (Matt. 4:10; Luke 4:8).

2C. Jesus Received Worship as God and Accepted It

1D. "And behold, a leper came and worshiped Him" (Matt. 8:2).

2D. The man born blind, after being healed, falls down and worships Him (John 9:35–39).

3D. The disciples "worshipped him, saying:

'Of a truth thou art the Son of God'" (Matt. 14:33 KJV).

4D. "Then He said to Thomas, 'Reach your finger here, and look at My hands; and reach your hand here, and put it into My side. Do not be unbelieving, but believing.' And Thomas answered and said to Him, 'My Lord and my God!' Jesus said to him, 'Thomas, because you have seen Me, you have believed. Blessed are those who have not seen and yet have believed'" (John 20:27–29).

3C. Jesus Contrasted with Others

1D. The centurion Cornelius fell at the feet of Peter and "worshiped him," and Peter reproved him saying, "Stand up; I myself am also a man" (Acts 10:25, 26).

2D. John fell at the feet of the angel of the Apocalypse to "worship him," but the angel told him that he was a "fellow servant" and that John was to "worship God" (Rev. 19:10).

4C. As we see, Jesus commanded and accepted worship as God. It is this fact that led Thiessen to write: "If He is a deceiver, or is self-deceived, and, in either case, if He is not God He is not good (*Christus si non Deus, non bonus*)." (Thiessen, OLST, 65)

A noted theologian and lecturer at Oxford University, Alister McGrath, adds: "Within the Jewish context in which the first Christians operated, it was God and God alone who was to be worshipped. Paul warned the Christians at Rome that there was a constant danger that humans would worship creatures, when they ought to be worshipping their creator (Romans 1:23). Yet the early Christian church worshiped Christ as God—a practice which is clearly reflected even in the New Testament." (McGrath, CT, 280)

5B. What Others Said

1C. Paul the Apostle

1D. Romans 9:5

"Of whom [the Jewish people] are the fathers and from whom, according to the flesh, Christ came, who is over all, the eternally blessed God. Amen."

—Romans 9:5

The great Princeton theologian and biblical scholar Charles Hodge comments: "Paul . . . declares that Christ, who, he had just said, was, as to his human nature, or as a man, descended from the Israelites, is, in another respect, the supreme God, or God over all, and blessed for ever. . . This passage, therefore, shows that Christ is God in the highest sense of the word." (Hodge, CF, 300, 302)

Dr. Murray J. Harris, a well-known New Testament scholar, after discussing this passage of Romans at great length in the original Greek, concludes, "What the apostle is affirming at the end of 9:1–5 is this: As opposed to the indignity of rejection accorded him by most of his fellow Israelites, the Messiah, Jesus Christ, is in fact exalted over the whole universe, animate and inanimate, including the Jews who reject him, in that he is God by nature, eternally the object of worship." (Harris, JG, 172)

2D. Philippians 2:6–11

"Who, being in very nature God, did not consider equality with God something to be grasped, but made himself nothing, taking the very nature of a servant, being made in human likeness. And being found in appearance as a man, he humbled himself and became obedient to death—even death on a cross! Therefore God exalted him to the highest place and gave him the name that is above every name, that at the name of Jesus every knee should bow, in heaven and on earth and under the earth, and every tongue confess that Jesus Christ is Lord, to the glory of God the Father."

—Philippians 2:6–11 NIV

Verses 6 through 8 describe the exalted Christ as having two natures: the nature of God (2:6) and the nature of a servant (2:7). This passage presents Jesus as fully God and fully human by nature. As Peter Toon writes: "The contrast of the heavenly and earthly existence suggests that *morphe* [used in both v. 6 and v. 7 and translated "form" or "nature" of God and of a servant or bondservant] points to a participation in God which is real, just as partaking in human life and history was real for Jesus." (Toon, OTG, 168)

Verses 9 through 11 equate Christ with God. F. F. Bruce writes:

The hymn includes echoes of Isaiah 52:13 . . . and also of Isaiah 45:23, where the one true God swears by Himself: "To me every knee shall bend, every tongue make solemn confession." But in the Christ-hymn it is this same God who decrees that every knee shall bend at Jesus' name and every tongue confess that Jesus Christ is Lord. . . . It is sometimes asked whether "the name above every name" in the Christ-hymn is "Jesus" or "Lord." It is both, because by divine decree the name "Jesus" henceforth has the value of the name "Lord" in the highest sense which that name can bear—the sense of the Hebrew Yahweh. (Bruce, RJ, 202)

So, in two ways Philippians 2:6–11 demonstrates the deity of Christ: by His dual nature and by equating Him with the exclusive name of God (LORD, Yahweh) of the Old Testament.

3D. Colossians 1:15–17

"He is the image of the invisible God, the firstborn over all creation. For by Him all things were created that are in heaven and that are on earth, visible and invisible, whether thrones or dominions or principalities or powers. All things were created through Him and for Him. And He is before all things, and in Him all things consist."

—Colossians 1:15–17

In verse 15, Christ is called "the image of the invisible God." Peter Lewis remarks: "What He images He must also possess; He images God's real being precisely because He shares that real being. As the image of God, Jesus Christ is God's equivalent in the world of men (John 14:9)." (Lewis, GC, 259–60)

F. F. Bruce adds, "The words he spoke, the works he performed, the life he led, the person he was—all disclosed the unseen Father. He is, in Paul's words, the visible 'image of the invisible God.'" (Bruce, RJ, 158)

The term "firstborn" over all creation means that as the eternal Son, He is the heir of all things. (Ryrie, RSB, 1831) This is also shown to us in the fact that He is the Creator of all things (verses 16, 17). Who else could Jesus be but God?

4D. Colossians 2:9

"For in Him dwells all the fullness of the Godhead bodily."

—Colossians 2:9

This simple statement points us to who Jesus is and why He should be important to us. Carl F. H. Henry comments: "The belief that gives the Christian confession its singularly unique character, that in Jesus Christ dwelt 'all the fullness of the Godhead bodily' (Col. 2:9), is an integral and definitive aspect of the New Testament teaching; it is affirmed and reiterated by the apostles who were contemporaries of Jesus." (Henry, IJ, 53)

5D. Titus 2:13

"Looking for the blessed hope and glorious appearing of our great God and Savior Jesus Christ."

—Titus 2:13

In our English translations, this verse reads as if two Persons are in view here: God and Jesus Christ. However, the Greek construction suggests that both titles, "great God" and "Savior," refer to one Person: Jesus Christ. (Harris, JG, 173-85)

2C. John the Baptist

"And the Holy Spirit descended in bodily form like a dove upon Him, and a voice came from heaven which said, 'You are My beloved Son; in You I am well pleased.'"

—Luke 3:22

In John 1:29, 34, John the Baptist proclaims: "'Behold! The Lamb of God who takes away the sin of the world! . . . I have seen and testified that this is the Son of God.'"

3C. Peter the Apostle

1D. Probably Peter's most famous affirmation is found in Matthew 16:15–17: "He said to them, 'But who do you say that I am?' Simon Peter answered and said, 'You are the Christ, the Son of the living God.' Jesus answered and said to him, 'Blessed are you, Simon Bar-Jonah, for flesh and blood has not revealed this to you, but My Father who is in heaven.'"

Concerning this statement, Scheffrahn and Kreyssler write that "instead of rebuking for his brashness (as Jesus always did when confronted by error), Jesus blesses Peter for his confession of faith. Throughout His ministry Jesus accepted prayers and worship as rightfully belonging to Himself." (Scheffrahn, JN, 10)

2D. Peter again affirms his belief in Acts 2:36: "'Therefore let all the house of Israel know assuredly that God has made this Jesus, whom you crucified, both Lord and Christ.'"

3D. In one of his letters, the apostle Peter writes, "Simon Peter, a bondservant and apostle of Jesus Christ, to those who have obtained like precious faith with us by the righteousness of our God and Savior Jesus Christ" (2 Pet. 1:1).

Murray J. Harris, after discussing the passage in the original Greek, concludes: "The conclusion seems inescapable that in 2 Peter 1:1 the title [our God and Savior] . . . is applied to Jesus Christ." (Harris, JG, 238)

4C. Thomas the Apostle

"The Doubter" bears the following witness found in John 20:28: "And Thomas answered and said to Him, 'My Lord and my God.'"

John Stott, in *Basic Christianity*, expounds on Thomas's exclamation: "The Sunday following Easter Day, incredulous Thomas is with the other disciples in the upper room when Jesus appears. He invites Thomas to feel His wounds, and Thomas, overwhelmed with wonder, cries out, 'My Lord and my God!' (John 20:26–29). Jesus accepts the designation. He rebukes Thomas for his unbelief, but not for his worship." (Stott, BC, 28)

As noted above, when men or angels were worshiped they immediately rebuked the worshipers and told them to worship God (Acts 10:25, 26; Rev. 19:10). Jesus not only accepts this worship from Thomas, but encourages his statement of faith.

5C. The Writer of Hebrews

1D. Hebrews 1:3

"Who being the brightness of His glory and the express image of His person, and upholding all things by the word of His power . . ."

—Hebrews 1:3

F. F. Bruce comments on the word "express image": "Just as the image and superscription on a coin exactly corresponds to the device on the die, so the Son of God 'bears the very stamp of his nature' (RSV). The Greek word *charakter*, occurring here only in the New Testament, expresses this truth even more emphatically than *eikon*, which is used elsewhere to denote Christ as the 'image' of God (2 Cor. 4:4; Col. 1:15). . . . What God essentially is, is made manifest in Christ." (Bruce, EH, 48)

2D. Hebrews 1:8

"But to the Son He says: 'Your throne, O God, is forever and ever; a scepter of righteousness is the scepter of Your kingdom.'"

—Hebrews 1:8

Thomas Schultz writes that "the vocative . . . in 'thy throne, O God' is preferred to the nominative where it would be translated 'God is thy throne' or 'thy throne is God.' Once again the evidence is conclusive— Jesus Christ is called God in the Scriptures." (Schultz, DPC, 180)

6C. John the Apostle

1D. John 1:1, 14

"In the beginning was the Word, and the Word was with God, and the Word was God. . . . And the Word became flesh and dwelt among us, and we beheld His glory, the glory as of the only begotten of the Father, full of grace and truth."

—John 1:1, 14

Teacher and respected theologian R. C. Sproul comments on John 1:1 with reference to the Word (Gk. *Logos*): "In this remarkable passage the *Logos* is both distinguished from God ('was with God') and identified with God ('was God'). This paradox had great influence on the development of the doctrine of the Trinity, whereby the *Logos* is seen as the Second Person of the Trinity. He differs in person from the Father, but is one in essence with the Father." (Sproul, ETCF, 105)

J. Carl Laney also notes that John 1 affirms "the eternal existence (v. 1a), personal distinctiveness (v. 1b), and divine nature of the Logos [Word] (v. 1c)." (Laney, J, 37–38) The Greek scholar and grammarian Dr. Daniel B. Wallace comments on the significance of the Greek construction here: "The construction the evangelist chose to express this idea was the most *concise* way he could have stated that the Word was God and yet was distinct from the Father." (Wallace, GGBB, 269)

2D. 1 John 5:20

"And we know that the Son of God has come and has given us an understanding, that we may know Him who is true; and we are in Him who is true, in His Son Jesus Christ. This is the true God and eternal life."

—1 John 5:20

JESUS IS JEHOVAH		
Of Jehovah	**Mutual Title or Act**	**Of Jesus**
Is. 40:28	Creator	John 1:3
Is. 45:22; 43:11	Savior	John 4:42
1 Sam. 2:6	Raise dead	John 5:21
Joel 3:12	Judge	John 5:27, cf. Matt. 25:31-46
Is. 60:19, 20	Light	John 8:12
Ex. 3:14	I Am	John 8:58, cf. 18:5, 6
Ps. 23:1	Shepherd	John 10:11
Is. 42:8; cf. 48:11	Glory of God	John 17:1, 5
Is. 41:4; 44:6	First and Last	Rev. 1:17; 2:8
Hosea 13:14	Redeemer	Rev. 5:9
Is. 62:5; Hosea 2:16	Bridegroom	Rev. 21:2, cf. Matt. 25:1ff.
Ps. 18:2	Rock	1 Cor. 10:4
Jer. 31:34	Forgiver of Sins	Mark 2:7, 10
Ps. 148:2	Worshiped by Angels	Heb. 1:6
Throughout O. T.	Addressed in Prayer	Acts 7:59
Ps. 148:5	Creator of Angels	Col. 1:16
Is. 45:23	Confessed as Lord	Phil. 2:11

Again, John, who is an eyewitness of Jesus Christ, makes no hesitation in calling Him "God."

6B. Conclusion: Jesus Is God

William Biederwolf draws from the evidence a very apt comparison: "A man who can read the New Testament and not see that Christ claims to be more than a man, can look all over the sky at high noon on a cloudless day and not see the sun." (Mead, ERQ, 50)

The "Beloved Apostle" John states this conclusion: "And many other signs truly did Jesus in the presence of His disciples, which are not written in this book: But these are written, that ye might believe that Jesus is the Christ, the Son of God; and that believing ye might have life through His name" (John 20:30, 31 KJV).

2A. HIS INDIRECT CLAIMS TO DEITY

Jesus, in many cases, made known His deity indirectly by both His words and His actions. Listed below are many of these references, with a few direct claims as well.

Some of the above claims require further explanation, as given below:

1B. He Forgave Sins

"When Jesus saw their faith, He said to the paralytic, 'Son, your sins are forgiven you.' But some of the scribes were sitting there and reasoning in their hearts, 'Why does this Man speak blasphemies like this? Who can forgive sins but God alone?'"

—Mark 2:5–7

To the Jewish mind, trained in the Law of God, the idea that a man could forgive sins against God is inconceivable. Forgiveness is a prerogative of God alone. John Stott, renowned Bible scholar and theologian, writes, "We may forgive the injuries which others do to us; but the sins we commit against God only God himself can." (Stott, BC, 29)

Some may question whether Jesus really had the divine authority to forgive sins. Jesus knew His audience had doubts about this, so He proved His authority to them: "'Which is easier, to say to the paralytic, "Your sins are forgiven you," or to say, "Arise, take up your bed and walk?" But that you may know that the Son of Man has power on earth to forgive sins'—He said to the paralytic, 'I say to you, arise, take up your bed, and go to your house.' Immediately he arose, took up the bed, and went out in the presence of them all, so that all were amazed and glorified God, saying, 'We never saw anything like this!'" (Mark 2:9–12).

In this event, Jesus asks which would be easier, to say "your sins are forgiven" or to say "rise and walk." According to the Wycliffe Commentary this is "an unanswerable question. The statements are equally simple to pronounce; but to say either, with accompanying performance, requires divine power. An imposter, of course, in seeking to avoid detection, would find the former easier. Jesus proceeded to heal the illness that men might *know* that He had *authority* to deal with its cause." (Pfeiffer, WBC, 944)

At this He was accused of blasphemy by the scribes and Pharisees. "The charge by the scribes and Pharisees . . . condemned Him for taking to Himself the prerogatives of God." (Pfeiffer, WBC, 943)

C. E. Jefferson states that "He forgave sins, He spoke as one having authority. Even the worst sinners when penitent at His feet received from Him authoritative assurance of forgiveness." (Jefferson, CJ, 330)

Lewis Sperry Chafer points out that "none on earth has either authority or right to forgive sin. None could forgive sin save the One against whom all have sinned. When Christ forgave sin, as He certainly did,

He was not exercising a human prerogative. Since none but God can forgive sins, it is conclusively demonstrated that Christ, since He forgave sins, is God, and being God, is from everlasting." (Chafer, ST, vol. 5, 21)

2B. Jesus Claimed to Be "Life"

In John 14:6 Jesus claims, "I am the way, the truth, and the life." In analyzing this statement, Merrill Tenney tells us that "He did not say He knew the way, the truth, and the life, nor that He taught them. He did not make Himself the exponent of a new system; He declared Himself to be the final key to all mysteries." (Tenney, JGB, 215)

3B. In Him Is Life

"And this is the testimony: that God has given us eternal life, and this life is in His Son. He who has the Son has life; he who does not have the Son of God does not have life."

—1 John 5:11, 12

Speaking of this life, John Stott writes: "He likened His followers' dependence on Him to the sustenance derived from the vine by its branches. He stated that God had given Him authority over all flesh, that He should give life to as many as God gave Him." (Stott, BC, 29)

4B. Jesus Has Authority

The Old Testament is clear that God is the judge over all of creation (Gen. 18:25; Pss. 50:4-6; 96:13). Yet, in the New Testament this authority to judge is handed over by the Father to the Son: "And He [God] gave Him [Jesus] authority to execute judgment, because He [Jesus] is the Son of Man" (John 5:27 NASB).

In claiming that He will judge the world, Jesus will Himself arouse the dead, He will gather the nations before Himself, He will sit on a throne of glory and He shall judge the world. Some, on the basis of His judgment, will inherit heaven—others, hell.

John Stott adds: "Not only will Jesus be the judge, but the criterion of judgement will be men's attitude to him as shown in their treatment of his 'brethren' or their response to his word. . . . It is hard to exaggerate the magnitude of this claim. Imagine a minister addressing his congregation in these terms today: 'Listen attentively to my words. Your eternal destiny depends on it. I shall return at the end of the world to judge you, and your fate will be settled according to your obedience to me.' Such a preacher would not long escape the attention of the police or the psychiatrists." (Stott, BC, 31–32)

3A. TITLES OF DEITY

1B. YHWH—LORD

Many English translations of the Bible translate the name of God as "LORD" (all capitals) or "Jehovah." The word in the original Hebrew is made up of four consonants: YHWH. The more literal translation of YHWH is *Yahweh*.

1C. Sacred to the Jews

"The precise meaning," writes Herbert F. Stevenson, "of the name is obscure. In the Hebrew, it was originally composed of four consonants YHWH—known to theologians as 'the tetragrammaton'—to which the vowels of *Adonai* were afterwards added (except when the name is joined to *Adonai*: then the vowels of *Elohim* are used). The Jews came to regard the name as too sacred to pronounce, however, and in the public reading of the Scriptures they substituted *Adonai* for it—Jehovah was indeed to them 'the incommunicable name.'" (Stevenson, TTG, 20)

Dr. Peter Toon, the noted author and theologian, writes: "As this name was treated with ever more and more reverence, the Jews ceased to pronounce it during the latter part of the Old Testament period." (Toon, OTG, 96)

L. S. Chafer notes: "The avoidance of the actual pronouncement of this name may be judged as mere superstition; but plainly it was an attempt at reverence however much misguided, and doubtless this practice, with all its confusing results, did serve to create a deep impression on all as to the ineffable character of God." (Chafer, ST, vol. 1, 264)

The *Jewish Encyclopedia* (ed., Isidore Singer, Funk and Wagnalls, vol. 1, 1904) indicates that the translation of YHWH by the word "Lord" can be traced to the Septuagint. "About the pronunciation of the Shem ha Metorash, the 'distinctive name' YHWH, there is no authentic information." Beginning from the Hellenistic period, the name was reserved for use in the temple: "From Sifre to Num. vi. 27, Mishnah Tamid, vii. 2, and Sotah vii. 6 it appears that the priests were allowed to pronounce the name at the benediction only in the Temple; elsewhere they were obliged to use the appellative name *(kinnuy)* 'Adonai.'"

The *Jewish Encyclopedia* goes on to quote from the Jewish historians Philo and Josephus:

Philo: "The four letters may be mentioned or heard only by holy men whose ears and tongues are purified by wisdom, and by no others in any place whatsoever." ("Life of Moses," iii, 41)

Josephus: "Moses besought God to impart to him the knowledge of His name and its pronunciation so that he might be able to invoke Him by name at the sacred acts, whereupon God communicated His name, hitherto unknown to any man; and it would be a sin for me to mention it." (Antiquities. ii 12, par. 4)

2C. The Meaning of the Name

The content of Exodus 3:14, as well as recent scholarly research, indicate that YHWH is to be taken as a form of the verb *haya*, "to be." In the light of this it is appropriate to see two meanings arising out of this name. First of all, from Exodus 3:14, 15, YHWH as a name is a positive assurance of God's acting, aiding, and communing presence. The "I AM" will be always with his covenant people. He who is now will be also. In the second place, and based on the declarations of Deuteronomy 4:39, 1 Kings 8:60, and Isaiah 45:21, 22, YHWH is the one and only deity, who is both above and within his creation; all other gods are but creatures or the projections of human imagination. (Toon, OTG, 97)

3C. Christ Speaks of Himself as Jehovah

Scotchmer, cited by W. C. Robinson: "The identification of our Lord Jesus Christ with the Lord of the Old Testament results in an explicit doctrine of His Deity." (Robinson, WSYTIA, 118)

Kreyssler and Scheffrahn write:

He claimed the covenant of YHWH—or Jehovah. In the 8th Chapter of John's Gospel we find: "Unless you believe that I AM, you shall die in your sins." v. 24; "When you lift up (i.e., on the cross) the Son of Man, then you will know that I AM. . . . " v. 28; "Truly, truly, I say to you, before Abraham was, I AM," v. 58. His use of the I AM connects with Exodus 3:14 where God reveals Himself to Moses: "I AM Who I AM." And He said, "Say this to the people of Israel, I AM has sent me to you." Thus the name of God in Hebrew is YHWH or I AM. (Scheffrahn, JN, 11)

In Matthew 13:14, 15, Christ identifies Himself with the "Lord" (Adonai) of the Old Testament (Isaiah 6:8–10). (Meldau, PDD, 15)

Clark Pinnock, in *Set Forth Your Case*, says that "His teachings rang with the great I AM statements which are divine claims in structure and content (Exodus 3:14; John 4:26; 6:35; 8:12; 10:9; 11:25)." (Pinnock, SFYC, 60)

John 12:41 describes Christ as the one seen by Isaiah in Isaiah 6:1. "Isaiah also writes," says William C. Robinson, "of the forerunner of Jehovah: 'Prepare ye the way of the Lord' (Isaiah 40:3 KJV). Christ endorsed the claim of the Samaritans who said, 'We . . . know that this is indeed the Christ, the Saviour of the world' (John 4:42 KJV). From the Old Testament this can only designate the Jehovah-God. Hosea 13:4 declares: 'I am the Lord thy God . . . thou shalt know no god but Me: for there is no saviour besides Me' (KJV)." (Robinson, WSY, 117–18)

2B. Son of God

The noted theologian and Bible teacher Charles Ryrie writes concerning the title "Son of God": "What does it mean? Though the phrase 'son of' can mean 'offspring of,' it also carries the meaning, 'of the order of.' Thus in the Old Testament 'sons of the prophets' meant of the order of prophets (1 Kings 20:35), and 'sons of the singers' meant of the order of the singers (Neh. 12:28). The designation 'Son of God' when used of our Lord means of the order of God and is a strong and clear claim to full Deity." (Ryrie, BT, 248)

H. F. Stevenson comments that "it is true that the term 'sons of God' is used of men (Hosea 1:10) and of angels, in the Old Testament (Gen. 6:2; Job 1:6; 38:7). But in the New Testament, the title 'Son of God' is used

of, and by, our Lord in quite a different way. In every instance the term implies that He is the one, only-begotten Son; co-equal, co-eternal with the Father." (Stevenson, TTG, 123)

The repeated uses of the term "Son" in juxtaposition to "the Father" declare Jesus'

> As often as Jesus speaks of His relations with His Father He uses constantly and without exception the expression "My Father"; and as often as He calls the attention of the disciples to their childlike relation to God, there is the equally definite characterization, "Your Father." Never does He associate Himself with the disciples and with men by the natural form of speech, "Our Father."
>
> —HILARIN FELDER

explicit claim to equality with the Father and formulate the truth of the Trinity (Matt. 23:9, 10; Mark 13:32; John 3:35; 5:19-27; 6:27; 10:33-38; 14:13).

At Caesarea Philippi Jesus complimented Peter on his recognition of Him as the Son of God: "Simon Peter answered and said, 'You are the Christ, the Son of the living God.' Jesus answered and said to him, 'Blessed are you, Simon Bar-Jonah, for flesh and blood has not revealed this to you, but My Father who is in heaven'" (Matthew 16:16, 17).

Felder writes on Christ's concept of God being His Father: "As often as Jesus speaks of His relations with His Father He uses constantly and without exception the expression 'My Father'; and as often as He calls the attention of the disciples to their childlike relation to God, there is the equally definite characterization, 'Your Father.' Never does He associate Himself with the disciples and with men by the natural form of speech, 'Our Father.'"

Felder continues:

Even on those occasions in which Jesus unites Himself with the disciples before God, and when therefore it would be certainly expected that He would use the collective expression, "Our Father," there stands, on the contrary, "My Father": "I will not drink henceforth of this fruit of the vine until that day when I shall drink it with *you* new in the kingdom of *My Father*" (Matt. xxvi, 29). "And I send the promise of *My Father* upon *you*" (Luke xxiv, 49). "Come, ye blessed of *My Father,* possess you the kingdom prepared for *you* from the foundation of the world" (Matt. xxv, 34). Thus and similarly does Jesus distinguish unequivocally between His divine sonship and that of the disciples and men in general. (Felder, CAC, 268-69).

3B. Son of Man

Jesus makes use of the title "Son of Man" in three distinctive ways:

1. Concerning His earthly ministry:
   - Matthew 8:20
   - Matthew 9:6
   - Matthew 11:19
   - Matthew 16:13
   - Luke 19:10
   - Luke 22:48

2. When foretelling His passion:
   - Matthew 12:40
   - Matthew 17:9, 22
   - Matthew 20:18

3. In His teaching regarding His coming again:
   - Matthew 13:41
   - Matthew 24:27, 30
   - Matthew 25:31
   - Luke 18:8
   - Luke 21:36

Stevenson attaches a special significance to the title "Son of man," "because this was the designation which our Lord habitually used concerning Himself. It is not found in the New Testament on any other lips than His own—except when His questioners

quoted His words (John 12:34), and in the one instance of Stephen's ecstatic exclamation in the moment of his martyrdom, 'Behold, I see the heavens opened, and the Son of man standing on the right hand of God' (Acts 7:56 KJV). It is clearly a Messianic title, as the Jews recognized." (John 12:34) (Stevenson, TTG, 120)

Kreyssler and Scheffrahn write that "Jesus clearly believed Himself to be the fulfillment of the Old Testament prophecies of the Messiah. In referring to Himself He continually used the title 'The Son of Man' from Daniel's vision" (Daniel 7:13, 14). (Scheffrahn, JN, 9–10)

In Mark 14:61–64 Jesus applies Daniel 17:13, 14 and, alongside of it, Psalm 110:1 to Himself as something that is going to transpire before their eyes. C. G. Montefiore points out that: "If Jesus said these words we can hardly think that He distinguished between Himself, the Son of man, and the Messiah. The Son of man must be the Messiah, and both must be Himself." (Montefiore, SG, 361)

4B. Abba—Father

Michael Green, in his book *Runaway World,* writes that Christ

asserted that He had a relationship with God which no one had ever claimed before. It comes out in the Aramaic word *Abba* which He was so fond of using, especially in prayer. Nobody before Him in all the history of Israel had addressed God by this word. . . . To be sure, Jews were accustomed to praying to God as Father: but the word they used was *Abhinu,* a form of address which was essentially an appeal to God for mercy and forgiveness. There is no appeal to God for mercy in Jesus' mode of address, *Abba.* It is the familiar word of closest intimacy. That is why He differentiated between His own relationship with God as Father and that of other people. (Green, RW, 99-100)

It is interesting that even David, with his closeness to the Father, did not speak to God as Father but said that "like as a father . . . so the Lord" (Psalm 103:13 KJV). In contrast, Jesus used the word "Father" often in prayer. "The Pharisees, of course, realized the implications of it, and charged Him with blasphemy (John 5:18) '. . . but [He] also called God His Father, making Himself equal with God' (RSV). And indeed unless He were equal with God His words were blasphemous." (Stevenson, TTG, 97)

7
SIGNIFICANCE OF DEITY: THE TRILEMMA— LORD, LIAR, OR LUNATIC?

1A. WHO IS JESUS OF NAZARETH?

Throughout history, people have given a variety of answers to the question, "Who is Jesus of Nazareth?" Whatever their answer, no one can escape the fact that Jesus really lived and that His life radically altered human history forever. The world-renowned historian Jaroslav Pelikan makes this clear: "Regardless of what anyone may personally think or believe about him, Jesus of Nazareth has been the dominant figure in the history of Western culture for almost twenty centuries. If it were possible, with some sort of supermagnet, to pull up out of that history every scrap of metal bearing at least a trace of his name, how much would be left? It is from his birth that most of the human race dates its calendars, it is by his name that millions curse and in his name that millions pray." (Pelikan, JTTC, 1)

How influential has Jesus been? In their book *What If Jesus Had Never Been Born?*, D. James Kennedy and Jerry Newcombe attempt to answer this question, at least partially. They begin with the assumption that the church—the body of Christ—is Jesus' primary legacy to the world. Then they examine what has happened in history that displays the influence of the church. Here are "a few highlights" they cite:

- Hospitals, which essentially began during the Middle Ages.
- Universities, which also began during the Middle Ages. In addition, most of the world's greatest universities were started by Christians for Christian purposes.
- Literacy and education of the masses.
- Representative government, particularly as it has been seen in the American experiment.
- The separation of political powers.
- Civil liberties.
- The abolition of slavery, both in antiquity and in modern times.
- Modern science.
- The discovery of the New World by Columbus.
- Benevolence and charity; the Good Samaritan ethic.
- Higher standards of justice.
- The elevation of the common man.
- The high regard for human life.
- The civilizing of many barbarian and primitive cultures.
- The codifying and setting to writing of many of the world's languages.
- The greater development of art and music. The inspiration for the greatest works of art.
- The countless changed lives transformed from liabilities into assets to society because of the gospel.
- The eternal salvation of countless souls! (Kennedy, WIJ, 3, 4)

Anyone who has studied church history knows that the church has had its share of leaders and sects who have abused the lofty ideals established by Jesus and brought shame to His name. Often it has been those of one sect or another within recognized Christendom who have propagated policies and practices completely at odds with the love of Christ. The persecutions of one supposedly Christian body against another stand as a sad example. And too often the church has lagged behind when some in the secular arena have advanced needed change. Civil rights for African Americans is one such example, although it must be added that the Christian faith was one of the primary motivations of the giants, the champions of racial freedom, such as Abraham Lincoln and Martin Luther King Jr.

On balance, it is the followers of Jesus who have taken the great sacrificing steps to lift others out of the dregs of life. Jesus of Nazareth has been transforming lives for almost two millennia, and in the process He has been rewriting the progress and outcome of human history.

In the nineteenth century Charles Bradlaugh, a prominent atheist, challenged a Christian man to debate the validity of the claims of Christianity. The Christian, Hugh Price Hughes, was an active soul-winner who worked among the poor in the slums of London. Hughes told Bradlaugh he would agree to the debate on one condition.

Hughes said, "I propose to you that we each bring some concrete evidences of the validity of our beliefs in the form of men and women who have been redeemed from the lives of sin and shame by the influence of our teaching. I will bring 100 such men and women, and I challenge you to do the same."

Hughes then said that if Bradlaugh couldn't bring 100, then he could bring 50; if he couldn't bring 50, then he could bring 20. He finally whittled the number down to one. All Bradlaugh had to do was to find one person whose life was improved by atheism and Hughes—who would bring 100 people improved by Christ—would agree to debate him. Bradlaugh withdrew! (Kennedy, WIJ,189)

When we consider the basic facts about Jesus' life, the vast impact He has had is nothing short of incredible. A nineteenth-century writer put it this way:

He [Jesus] was born in an obscure village, the child of a peasant woman. He grew up in another village, where He worked in a carpenter shop until He was thirty. Then for three years He was an itinerant preacher. He never wrote a book. He never held an office. He never had a family or owned a home. He didn't go to college. He never visited a big city. He never traveled two hundred miles from the place where He was born. He did none of the things that usually accompany greatness. He had no credentials but Himself.

He was only thirty-three when the tide of public opinion turned against Him. His friends ran away. One of them denied Him. He was turned over to His enemies and went through the mockery of a trial. He was nailed to a cross between two thieves.

While He was dying, His executioners gambled for His garments, the only property He had on earth. When He was dead, He was laid in a borrowed grave through the pity of a friend. Nineteen centuries have come and gone, and today He is the central figure of the human race.

All the armies that ever marched, all the navies that ever sailed, all the parliaments that ever sat, all the kings that ever reigned, put together, have not affected the life of man on this earth as much as that one solitary life. (Kennedy, WIJ, 7, 8)

So what did Jesus believe about Himself? How did others perceive Him? Who was this solitary figure? Who is Jesus of Nazareth?

Jesus thought it was fundamentally important what others believed about Him. It was not a subject that allowed for neutrality or a less than honest appraisal of the evidence. C. S. Lewis, a professor of English literature at Cambridge University and a former agnostic, captured this truth in his book *Mere Christianity*. After surveying some of the evidence regarding Jesus' identity, Lewis writes:

I am trying here to prevent anyone saying the really foolish thing that people often say about Him: "I'm ready to accept Jesus as a great moral teacher, but I don't accept His claim to be God." That is the one thing we must not say. A man who was merely a man and said the sort of things Jesus said would not be a great moral teacher. He would either be a lunatic— on a level with the man who says he is a poached egg—or else he would be the Devil of Hell. You must make your choice. Either this man was, and is, the Son of God: or else a mad man or something worse. You can shut Him up for a fool, you can spit at Him and kill Him as a demon; or you can fall at His feet and call Him Lord and God. But let us not come up with any patronizing nonsense about His being a great human teacher. He has not left that open to us. He did not intend to. (Lewis, MC'52, 40, 41)

F. J. A. Hort points out that whatever we think about Jesus, we cannot divorce His identity from what He said: "His words were so completely parts and utterances of Himself, that they had no meaning as abstract statements of truth uttered by Him as a Divine oracle or prophet. Take away Himself as the primary (though not the ultimate) subject of every statement and they all fall to pieces." (Hort, WTL, 207)

Kenneth Scott Latourette, the late great historian of Christianity at Yale University, echoes Hort's observation when he states: "It is not His teachings which make Jesus so remarkable, although these would be enough to give Him distinction. It is a combination of the teachings with the man Himself. The two cannot be separated." (Latourette, AHC, 44) To which he added a bit later: "It must be obvious to any thoughtful reader of the Gospel records that Jesus regarded Himself and His message as inseparable. He was a great teacher, but He was more. His teachings about the kingdom of God, about human conduct, and about God

We have already seen that the New Testament books are historically accurate and reliable; so reliable, in fact, that Jesus cannot be dismissed as a mere legend. The Gospel

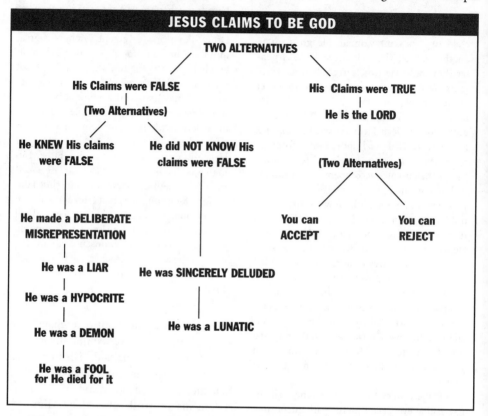

were important, but they could not be divorced from Him without, from His standpoint, being vitiated." (Latourette, AHC, 48)

2A. THREE ALTERNATIVES

Some people believe Jesus is God because they believe the Bible is inspired by God, and since it teaches that Jesus is God, well then He must be God. Now even though I too believe that the Bible is the wholly inspired word of God, I do not think one needs to hold that belief in order to arrive at the conclusion that Jesus is God. Here's why:

accounts preserve an accurate record of the things He did, the places He visited, and the words He spoke. And Jesus definitely claimed to be God (see below and in Chapter 6). So every person must answer the question: Is His claim to deity true or false? This question deserves a most serious consideration.

In the first century, when people were giving a number of answers about Jesus' identity, Jesus asked His disciples, "But who do you say that I am?" to which Peter responded, "You are the Christ, the Son of the living God" (Matt. 16:15, 16 NIV). Not everyone accepts Peter's answer, but no one should avoid Jesus' question.

Jesus' claim to be God must be either true or false. If Jesus' claims are true, then He is the Lord, and we must either accept or reject His lordship. We are "without excuse."

If Jesus' claims to be God were false, then there are just two options: He either knew His claims were false, or He did not know they were false. We will consider each alternative separately and then consider the evidence.

1B. Was He a Liar?

If, when Jesus made His claims, He knew He was not God, then He was lying. But if He was a liar, then He was also a hypocrite, because He told others to be honest, whatever the cost, while He, at the same time, was teaching and living a colossal lie.

More than that, He was a demon, because He deliberately told others to trust Him for their eternal destiny. If He could not back up His claims and knew they were false, then He was unspeakably evil.

Last, He would also be a fool, because it was His claims to deity that led to His crucifixion.

• Mark 14:61-64: "But He kept silent, and made no answer. Again the high priest was questioning Him, and saying to Him, 'Are You the Christ, the Son of the Blessed *One?*'

"And Jesus said, 'I am; and you shall see the SON OF MAN SITTING AT THE RIGHT HAND OF POWER, and COMING WITH THE CLOUDS OF HEAVEN.'

"And tearing his clothes, the high priest said, 'What further need do we have of witnesses? You have heard the blasphemy; how does it seem to you?'

"And they all condemned Him to be deserving of death." (NASV)

• John 19:7: "The Jews answered him, 'We have a law, and by that law He ought to die because He made Himself out *to be* the Son of God.'" (NASV)

If Jesus was a liar, a con man, and therefore an evil, foolish man, then how can we explain the fact that He left us with the most profound moral instruction and powerful moral example that anyone ever has left? Could a deceiver—an imposter of monstrous proportions—teach such unselfish ethical truths and live such a morally exemplary life as Jesus did? The very notion is incredulous.

John Stuart Mill, the philosopher, skeptic, and antagonist of Christianity, admitted that Jesus was a first-rate ethicist supremely worthy of our attention and emulation. As Mill expressed it:

About the life and sayings of Jesus there is a stamp of personal originality combined with profundity of insight in the very first rank of men of sublime genius of whom our species can boast. When this pre-eminent genius is combined with the qualities of probably the greatest moral reformer and martyr to that mission who ever existed upon earth, religion cannot be said to have made a bad choice in pitching upon this man as the ideal representative and guide of humanity; nor even now would it be easy, even for an unbeliever, to find a better translation of the rule of virtue from the abstract into the concrete than to endeavour to live so that Christ would approve of our life. (Grounds, RFOH, 34)

Throughout history Jesus Christ has captured the hearts and minds of millions who have strived to order their lives after His. Even William Lecky, one of Great Britain's most noted historians and a dedicated opponent of organized Christianity, noted this in his *History of European Morals from Augustus to Charlemagne*:

It was reserved for Christianity to present to the world an ideal character which through all the changes of eighteen centuries has inspired the hearts of men with an impassioned love; has shown itself capable of acting on all ages, nations, temperaments and conditions; has been not only the highest pattern of virtue, but the strongest incentive to its practice.... The simple record of [Jesus'] these three short years of active life has done more to regenerate and soften mankind than all the disquisitions of philosophers and all the exhortations of moralists. (Lecky, HEMFAC, 8; Grounds, RFOH, 34)

> *It would take more than a Jesus to invent a Jesus.*
>
> —HISTORIAN PHILLIP SCHAFF

When the church historian Philip Schaff considered the evidence for Jesus' deity, especially in light of what Jesus taught and the kind of life He led, Schaff was struck by the absurdity of the explanations designed to escape the logical implications of this evidence. Stated Schaff:

This testimony, if not true, must be down right blasphemy or madness. The former hypothesis cannot stand a moment before the moral purity and dignity of Jesus, revealed in His every word and work, and acknowledged by universal consent. Self-deception in a matter so momentous, and with an intellect in all respects so clear and so sound, is equally out of the question. How could He be an enthusiast or a madman who never lost the even balance of His mind, who sailed serenely over all the troubles and persecutions, as the sun above the clouds, who always returned the wisest answer to tempting questions, who calmly and deliberately predicted His death on the cross, His resurrection on the third day, the outpouring of the Holy Spirit, the founding of His Church, the destruction of Jerusalem—predictions which have been literally fulfilled? A character so original, so complete, so uniformly consistent, so perfect, so human and yet so high above all human greatness, can be neither a fraud nor a fiction. The poet, as has been well said, would in this case be greater than the hero. It would take more than a Jesus to invent a Jesus. (Schaff, HCC, 109)

In his work *The Person of Christ*, Schaff revisits the theory that Jesus was a deceiver, and mounts a convicting attack against it:

The hypothesis of imposture is so revolting to moral as well as common sense, that its mere statement is its condemnation. . . . [N]o scholar of any decency and self-respect would now dare to profess it openly. How, in the name of logic, common sense, and experience, could an impostor—that is a deceitful, selfish, depraved man—have invented, and consistently maintained from the beginning to end, the purest and noblest character known in history with the most perfect air of truth and reality? How could he have conceived and successfully carried out a plan of unparalleled beneficence, moral magnitude, and sublimity, and sacrificed his own life for it, in the face of the strongest prejudices of his people and ages? (Schaff, TPOC, 94, 95)

The answer, of course, is that Jesus could not have! Someone who lived as Jesus lived, taught as Jesus taught, and died as Jesus died could not have been a liar.

So what are the other alternatives?

2B. Was He a Lunatic?

If it is inconceivable for Jesus to have been a liar, then could He have thought He was God but have been mistaken? After all, it is possible to be both sincere and wrong.

But we must remember that for someone to think he was God, especially in a culture that was fiercely monotheistic, and then to tell others that their eternal destiny depends on believing in him, was no slight flight of fantasy but the thoughts of a lunatic in the fullest sense. Was Jesus Christ such a person?

Christian philosopher Peter Kreeft presents this option, then shows why we must reject it:

A measure of your insanity is the size of the gap between what you think you are and what you really are. If I think I am the greatest philosopher in America, I am only an arrogant fool; if I think I am Napoleon, I am probably over the edge; if I think I am a butterfly, I am fully embarked from the sunny shores of sanity. But if I think I am God, I am even more insane because the gap between anything finite and the infinite God is even greater than the gap between any two finite things, even a man and a butterfly.

Well, then, why [was not Jesus a] liar or lunatic? . . . [A]lmost no one who has read the Gospels can honestly and seriously consider that option. The savviness, the canniness, the human wisdom, the attractiveness of Jesus emerge from the Gospels with unavoidable force to any but the most hardened and prejudiced reader. . . . Compare Jesus with liars . . . or lunatics like the dying Nietzsche. Jesus has in abundance precisely those three qualities that liars and lunatics most conspicuously lack: (1) his practical wisdom, his ability to read human hearts; (2) his deep and winning love, his passionate compassion, his ability to attract people and make them feel at home and forgiven, his authority, "not as the scribes"; (3) his ability to astonish, his unpredictability, his creativity. Liars and lunatics are all so dull and predictable! No one who knows both the Gospels and human beings can seriously entertain the possibility that Jesus was a liar or a lunatic, a bad man. (Kreeft, FOTF, 60, 61)

Here . . . rests the blueprint for successful human life with optimism, mental health, and contentment.

—J. T. FISCHER, PSYCHIATRIST

Even Napoleon Bonaparte went on record as saying:

I know men; and I tell you that Jesus Christ is not a man. Superficial minds see a resemblance between Christ and the founders of empires, and the gods of other religions. That resemblance does not exist. There is between Christianity and whatever other religions the distance of infinity. . . . Everything in Christ astonishes me. His spirit overawes me, and His will confounds me. Between Him and whoever else in the world, there is no possible term of comparison. He is truly a being by Himself. His ideas and sentiments, the truth which He announces, His manner of convincing, are not explained either by human organization or by the nature of things. . . . The nearer I approach, the more carefully I examine, everything is above me— everything remains grand, of a grandeur which overpowers. His religion is a revelation from an intelligence which certainly is not that of man. . . . One can absolutely find nowhere, but in Him alone, the imitation or the example of His life. . . . I search in vain in history to find the similar to Jesus Christ, or anything which can approach the gospel. Neither history, nor humanity, nor the ages, nor nature, offer me anything with which I am able to compare it or to explain it. Here everything is extraordinary. (Grounds, ROH, 37)

William Channing, although a nineteenth-century Unitarian and humanist, rejected the lunatic theory as a completely unsatisfactory explanation of Jesus' identity:

The charge of an extravagant, self-deluding enthusiasm is the last to be fastened on Jesus. Where can we find the traces of it in His history? Do we detect them in the calm authority of His precepts? in the mild, practical and beneficent spirit of His religion; in the unlabored simplicity of the language with which He unfolds His high powers and the sublime truths of religion; or in the good sense, the knowledge of human nature, which He always discovers in His estimate and treatment of the different classes of men with whom He acted? Do we discover this enthusiasm in the singular fact, that whilst He claimed power in the future world, and always turned men's minds to heaven, He never indulged His own imagination, or stimulated that of His disciples, by giving vivid pictures or any minute description of that unseen state? The truth is, that, remarkable as was the character of Jesus, it was distinguished by nothing more than by calmness and self-possession. This trait pervades His other excellences. How calm was His piety! Point me, if you can, to one vehement, passionate expression of His religious feelings. Does the Lord's Prayer breathe a feverish enthusiasm? . . . His benevolence, too, though singularly earnest and deep, was composed and serene. He never lost the possession of Himself in His sympathy with others; was never hurried into the impatient and rash enterprises of an enthusiastic philanthropy; but did good with the tranquility and constancy which mark the providence of God. (Schaff, TPOC, 98, 99)

Philip Schaff, the noted historian, wrote: "Is such an intellect—clear as the sky, bracing as the mountain air, sharp and penetrating as a sword, thoroughly healthy and vigorous, always ready and always self-possessed—liable to a radical and most serious delusion concerning His own character and mission? Preposterous imagination!" (Schaff, TPOC, 97, 98)

The truth is, Jesus was not only sane, but the counsel He provided gives us the most concise and accurate formula for peace of mind and heart. I like the way psychiatrist J. T. Fisher brings this out:

If you were to take the sum total of all authoritative articles ever written by the most quali-

fied of psychologists and psychiatrists on the subject of mental hygiene—if you were to combine them and refine them and cleave out the excess verbiage—if you were to take the whole of the meat and none of the parsley, and if you were to have these unadulterated bits of pure scientific knowledge concisely expressed by the most capable of living poets, you would have an awkward and incomplete summation of the Sermon on the Mount. And it would suffer immeasurably through comparison. For nearly two thousand years the Christian world has been holding in its hands the complete answer to its [humankind's] restless and fruitless yearnings. Here . . . rests the blueprint for successful human life with optimism, mental health, and contentment. (Fisher, AFBM, 273)

No lunatic could be the source of such perceptive and effective psychological insight. C. S. Lewis is right. No other explanation but the Christian one will do: "The historical difficulty of giving for the life, sayings and influence of Jesus any explanation that is not harder than the Christian explanation is very great. The discrepancy between the depth and sanity and (let me add) *shrewdness* of His moral teaching and the rampant megalomania which must lie behind His theological teaching unless He is indeed God, has never been satisfactorily got over. Hence the non-Christian hypotheses succeed one another with the restless fertility of bewilderment." (Lewis, MAPS, 113)

3B. He Is Lord!

If Jesus of Nazareth is not a liar or a lunatic, then He must be Lord.

- "Thou art the Christ, the Son of the living God," Peter proclaimed (Matt. 16:18 NASV).
- "Yes, Lord, I believe that You are the Christ, the Son of God, who is to come into the world," confessed Martha of

Bethany, Lazarus' sister (John 11:27 NKJV).

- "My Lord and my God!" Thomas exclaimed after seeing the resurrected Jesus standing before him (John 20:28 NKJV).
- "The beginning of the gospel of Jesus Christ, the Son of God," Mark wrote as the opening line of the New Testament book bearing his name (Mark 1:1 NKJV).
- "He [Jesus] is the radiance of His [God's] glory and the exact representation of His nature, and upholds all things by the word of His power," stated the author of Hebrews (Heb. 1:3 NASB).

Other self-proclaimed gods and saviors have come and gone upon history's stage, but Jesus is still here, standing head-and-shoulders above them all. The modern historian Arnold J. Toynbee spent page after page discussing the exploits of history's so-called "saviours of society"—those who have tried to prevent some social calamity or cultural disintegration by heralding the past, or pointing people toward the future, or waging war or bartering for peace, or claiming wisdom or divinity. After covering such individuals for some eighty pages in the sixth volume of his magnum opus *Study of History*, Toynbee finally comes to Jesus Christ and finds there is no comparison:

When we first set out on this quest we found ourselves moving in the midst of a mighty marching host; but as we have pressed forward on our way the marchers, company by company, have been falling out of the race. The first to fail were the swordsmen, the next the archaists, the next the futurists, the next the philosophers, until at length there were no more human competitors left in the running. In the last stage of all, our motley host of would-be saviours, human and divine, has dwindled to a single company of none but gods; and now the strain has been testing the staying-power of these last remaining runners, notwithstanding their superhuman strength. At the final ordeal of death, few, even of these would-be saviour-gods, have dared to put their title to the test by plunging into the icy river. And now as we stand and gaze with our eyes fixed upon the farther shore, a single figure rises from the flood, and straightway fills the whole horizon. There is the Saviour; "and the pleasure of the Lord shall prosper in his hand; he shall see of the travail of his soul and shall be satisfied." (Toynbee, SOH, 278)

Who you decide Jesus Christ is must not be an idle intellectual exercise. You cannot put Him on the shelf as a great moral teacher. That is not a valid option. He is either a liar, a lunatic, or the Lord. You must make a choice. "But," as the apostle John wrote, "these have been written that you may believe that Jesus is the Christ, the Son of God"; and more important, "that believing you may have life in His name" (John 20:31 NASB).

The evidence is clearly in favor of Jesus as Lord. However, some people reject the clear evidence because of the moral implications involved. There needs to be a moral honesty in the above consideration of Jesus as either liar, lunatic, or Lord and God.

[1]How did they treat liars back in the first century? See the text about Beelzebub in the Gospels. This was their way of dealing with liars and lunatics.

[2]What evidence is there for this? Look at Keener, *The IVP Bible Background Commentary: New Testament,* (Intervarsity, 1993) and the other volume by Ferguson, Everett, *Backgrounds of Christianity.*

8
Support of Deity: Old Testament Prophecies Fulfilled in Jesus Christ

Throughout the New Testament the apostles appealed to two areas of the life of Jesus of Nazareth to establish His messiahship. One was the resurrection and the other was fulfilled messianic prophecy. The Old Testament, written over a one-thousand-year period, contains nearly three hundred references to the coming Messiah. All of these were fulfilled in Jesus Christ, and they establish a solid confirmation of His credentials as the Messiah.

1A. INTRODUCTION

1B. Purpose of Messianic Prophecy

1C. God Is the Only True God

His knowledge is infinite and His word is never broken.

"God is not a man, that He should lie,
Nor a son of man, that He should repent.
Has He said, and will He not do?
Or has He spoken, and will He not make it good?" (Num. 23:19).

2C. All Things Are Subject to God's Divine Will

"Remember the former things of old,
For I am God, and there is no other;
I am God, and there is none like Me,
Declaring the end from the beginning,
And from ancient times things that are not yet done,
Saying, 'My counsel shall stand,
And I will do all My pleasure'" (Is. 46:9, 10).

3C. Messiah Will Be Absolutely Known, Based upon His Credentials

"I have declared the former things from the beginning;
They went forth from My mouth, and I caused them to hear it.
Suddenly I did them, and they came to pass.
Even from the beginning I have declared it to you;
Before it came to pass I proclaimed it to you,
Lest you should say, 'My idol has done them,
And my carved image and my molded image
Have commanded them'" (Is. 48:3, 5).

"Which He promised before through His prophets in the Holy Scriptures, concerning His Son Jesus Christ our Lord, who was born of the seed of David according to the flesh, and declared to be the Son of God with power according to the Spirit of holiness, by the resurrection from the dead" (Rom. 1:2–4).

2B. Appeal to Messianic Prophecy

1C. Jesus

"Do not think that I came to destroy the Law or the Prophets. I did not come to destroy but to fulfill" (Matt. 5:17).

"And beginning at Moses and all the Prophets, He expounded to them in all the Scriptures the things concerning Himself" (Luke 24:27).

"Then He said to them, 'These are the words which I spoke to you while I was still with you, that all things must be fulfilled which were written in the Law of Moses and the Prophets and the Psalms concerning Me'" (Luke 24:44).

"You search the Scriptures, for in them you think you have eternal life; and these are they which testify of Me. But you are not willing to come to Me that you may have life. For if you believed Moses, you would believe Me; for he wrote about Me. But if you do not believe his writings, how will you believe My words?" (John 5:39, 40, 46, 47).

"And in them the prophecy of Isaiah is fulfilled, which says: 'Hearing you will hear and shall not understand, and seeing you will see and not perceive'" (Matt.13:14 [on parables]).

"This is the one about whom it was written, 'Behold, I send My messenger before Your face, Who will prepare Your way before You'"(Matt. 11:10 [on John the Baptist]).

"Jesus said to them, 'Have you never read the Scriptures: "The stone which the builders rejected has become the chief cornerstone"?'" (Matt. 21:42).

"But all this was done that the Scriptures of the prophets might be fulfilled" (Matt. 26:56).

"Then they will see the Son of Man coming in the clouds with great power and glory" (Mark 13:26 [refers to Dan. 7:13, 14]).

"Then He closed the book, and gave it back to the attendant and sat down. And the eyes of all who were in the synagogue were fixed on Him. And He began to say to them, 'Today this Scripture is fulfilled in your hearing'" (Luke 4:20, 21).

"For I say to you that this which is written must still be accomplished in Me: 'And He was numbered with the transgressors.' For the things concerning Me have an end" (Luke 22:37).

"But this happened that the word might be fulfilled which is written in their law, 'They hated Me without a cause'" (John 15:25).

2C. New Testament Writers Appeal to Prophecies Fulfilled in Jesus

"But those things which God foretold by the mouth of all His prophets, that the Christ would suffer, He has thus fulfilled" (Acts 3:18).

"To Him all the prophets witness that, through His name, whoever believes in Him will receive remission of sins" (Acts 10:43).

"Now when they had fulfilled all that was written concerning Him, they took Him down from the tree and laid Him in a tomb" (Acts 13:29).

"Then Paul, as his custom was, went in to them, and for three Sabbaths reasoned with them from the Scriptures, explaining and demonstrating that the Christ had to suffer and rise again from the dead, and saying, 'This Jesus whom I preach to you is the Christ'" (Acts 17:2, 3).

"For I delivered to you first of all that which I also received: that Christ died for our sins according to the Scriptures, and that He was buried, and that He rose again the third day according to the Scriptures" (1 Cor. 15:3, 4).

"Which He promised before through His prophets in the Holy Scriptures" (Rom. 1:2).

"You also, as living stones, are being built up a spiritual house, a holy priesthood, to offer up spiritual sacrifices acceptable to God through Jesus Christ. Therefore it is also contained in the Scripture, 'Behold, I lay in Zion a chief cornerstone, elect, precious, and he who believes on Him will by no means be put to shame'" (1 Pet. 2: 5, 6).

"And when he had gathered all the chief priests and scribes of the people together, he inquired of them where the Christ was to be born. So they said to him, 'In Bethlehem of Judea, thus it is written by the prophet: "But you, Bethlehem, in the land of Judah, are not the least among the rulers of Judah; for out of you shall come a Ruler, who will shepherd My people Israel"'" (Matt. 2:4–6).

3C. In the Work and Person of Christ There Is a Fulfillment of the Levitical Feasts (Geisler, CTB, 41)

The Feast (Lev. 23)	The Fulfillment in Christ
Passover (April)	Death of Christ (1 Cor. 5:7)
Unleavened Bread (April)	Holy Walk (1 Cor. 5:8)
First Fruits (April)	Resurrection (1 Cor. 15:23)
Pentecost (June)	Outpouring of Spirit (Acts 1:5; 2:4)
Trumpets (Sept.)	Israel's Regathering (Matt. 24:31)
Atonement (Sept.)	Cleansing by Christ (Rom. 11:26)
Tabernacles (Sept.)	Rest and Reunion with Christ (Zech. 14:16–18)

3B. Significance of Predictive Prophecy

1C. Concludes That There Is a Divine Intellect Behind the Old and New Testaments

2C. Establishes the Fact of God

3C. Authenticates the Deity of Jesus

4C. Demonstrates the Inspiration of the Bible

2A. THE BREADTH OF PREDICTIVE PROPHECY

The Old Testament contains over three hundred references to the Messiah that were fulfilled in Jesus.

1B. Objection

The prophecies were written at or after the time of Jesus, and therefore fulfill themselves.

2B. Answer

If you are not satisfied with 450 B.C. as the historic date for the completion of the Old Testament (and all the prophecies about Christ contained in it), take into consideration the following: The Septuagint—the Greek translation of the Hebrew Scriptures—was initiated in the reign of Ptolemy Philadelphus (285–246 B.C.). It is rather obvious that if you have a Greek translation initiated in 250 B.C., then you had to have the Hebrew text from which it was written. This will suffice to indicate that there was *at least* a 250-year gap between the prophecies being written down and their fulfillment in the person of Christ.

3A. CREDENTIALS OF JESUS AS THE MESSIAH THROUGH FULFILLED PROPHECY

1B. Prophecies Concerning His Birth

1. Born of the Seed of Woman

PROPHECY

"And I will put enmity
between you and the woman
and between your seed and her Seed;
He shall bruise your head,
and you shall bruise His heel."
—Genesis 3:15

FULFILLMENT

"But when the fullness of the time had
come, God sent forth His Son,
born of a woman, born under the law."
—Galatians 4:4 (See also Matt. 1:20.)

Jewish source: *Targum Onkelos* on Genesis 3:15 says, "And I will put enmity between thee and between the woman, and between thy son and her son. He will remember thee, what thou didst to him (at) from the beginning, and thou shalt be observant unto him at the end." (Ethridge, TOJ, 41)

Jewish source: *Targum Pseudo Jonathanon* Genesis 3:15 states, "And I will put enmity between thee and the woman, and between the seed of your offspring and the seed of her offspring; and it shall be that when the offspring of the woman keep the commandments of the Law, they will aim right (at you) and they will smite you on the head; but when they abandon the commandments of the Law, you will aim right (at them), and you will wound them in the heel. However, for them there will be a remedy, but for you there will be none, and in the future they will make peace with the heel in the days of the king, Messiah." (Bowker, TRL, 122)

David L. Cooper makes an interesting observation:

> In Gen. 3:15 we find the first prediction relative to the Saviour of the world, called "the seed of the women." In the original oracle God foretold the age-long conflict which would be waged between "the seed of the woman" and "the seed of the serpent" and which will eventually be won by the former. This primitive promise indicates a struggle between the Messiah of Israel, the Saviour of the world, on one hand, and Satan, the adversary of the human soul, on the other. It foretells complete victory eventually for the Messiah. Some commentators believe that an echo of this promise and Eve's understanding of it is found in Genesis 4:1—the statement of Eve when Cain, her first son, was born. "I have gotten a man even Jehovah." She correctly understood this primitive prediction but misapplied it in her interpreting it as being fulfilled in Cain, her son. It is clear that Eve believed that the child of promise would be Jehovah Himself. Some old Jewish commentators used to interpolate the word "angel" in this passage and say that Eve claimed that her son was "the angel of Jehovah." There is no ground for this assertion. (Cooper, GM, 8, 9)

The New American Standard Bible renders Genesis 4:1: "She said, 'I have gotten a man child with *the help of* the LORD.'"

2. Born of a Virgin

PROPHECY	FULFILLMENT
"Therefore the Lord Himself will give you a sign: Behold, the virgin shall conceive and bear a Son, and shall call His name Immanuel." —Isaiah 7:14	"She was found with child of the Holy Spirit. . . . Then Joseph . . . did not know her till she had brought forth her firstborn Son. And he called His name JESUS." —Matthew 1:18, 24, 25 (See also Luke 1:26–35.)

In Hebrew the word "virgin" is denoted by two words:

1. *bethulah:* The proper meaning denotes a virgin maiden (Gen. 24:16; Lev. 21:13; Deut. 22:14, 23, 28; Judg. 11:37; 1 Kin. 1:2). Joel 1:8 is, according to Unger, not an exception because here it "refers to the loss of one betrothed, not married."

2. *almah* (veiled): A young woman of marriageable age. This word is used in Isaiah 7:14. "The Holy Spirit through Isaiah did not use *bethulah,* because both the ideas of virginity and marriageable age had to be combined in one word to meet the immediate historical situation and the prophetic aspect centering in a virgin-born Messiah." (Unger, UBD, 1159)

"Virgin" is denoted in Greek by the word *parthenos:* a virgin, marriageable maiden, or young married woman, pure virgin (Matt. 1: 23; 25:1, 7, 11; Luke 1:27; Acts 21:9; 1 Cor. 7:25, 28, 33; 2 Cor. 11:2). (Unger, UBD, 1159)

When the translators of the Septuagint translated Isaiah 7:14 into Greek they used the Greek word *parthenos*. To them Isaiah 7:14 denoted that the Messiah would be born of a virgin.

3. Son of God

PROPHECY

"I will declare the decree: The LORD has said to Me, 'You are My Son, today I have begotten You.'"
—Psalm 2:7 (See also 1 Chr. 17:11–14; 2 Sam. 7:12–16.)

FULFILLMENT

"And suddenly a voice came from heaven, saying, 'This is My beloved Son, in whom I am well pleased.'"
—Matthew 3:17 (See also Matt.16:16; Mark 9:7; Luke 9:35; 22:70; Acts 13:30–33; John 1:34, 49.)

Mark 3:11: The demons realized His Sonship.

Matthew 26:63: Even the high priest realized His Sonship.

E. W. Hengstenberg writes: "It is an undoubted fact, and unanimously admitted even by the recent opposers of its reference to Him, that the Psalm (Psalm 2) was universally regarded by the ancient Jews as foretelling the Messiah." (Hengstenberg, COT, 43)

"At the incarnation the First-begotten was brought into the world (Heb. 1:6). But it was only at and by His resurrection that His Divinity, as the Only-begotten of the Father, was manifested and openly attested by God. 'Made of the seed of David according to the flesh,' He was then 'declared to be the Son of God with power, according to the spirit of holiness, by the resurrection from the dead' (Rom. 1:3, 4 KJV)." (Fausset, CCEP, 107)

4. Seed of Abraham

PROPHECY

"In your seed all the nations of the earth shall be blessed, because you have obeyed My voice."
—Genesis 22:18 (See also Gen. 12:2, 3.)

FULFILLMENT

"The book of the genealogy of Jesus Christ, the Son of David, the Son of Abraham."
—Matthew 1:1

"Now to Abraham and his Seed were the promises made. He does not say, 'And the seeds,' as of many, but as of one, 'And to your Seed,' who is Christ."
—Galatians 3:16

The importance of this event in Genesis 22:18 is established when we realize that it is the only time that God swears by Himself in His relationship with the patriarchs.

Matthew Henry says about Genesis 22:18, "In thy Seed, one particular person that shall descend from thee (for he speaks not of many, but of one, as the apostle observes [Gal. 3:16]), shall all the nations of the earth be blessed, or shall bless themselves, as the phrase is, Isa. 65:16." (Henry, MHCWB, 82)

The above passage determines that the Messiah would come from the Hebrew race.

5. Son of Isaac

PROPHECY

"But God said to Abraham . . . in Isaac your seed shall be called."
—Genesis 21:12

FULFILLMENT

"Jesus, . . . the son of Isaac."
—Luke 3:23, 34 (See also Matt. 1:2.)

Abraham had two sons: Isaac and Ishmael. Now God eliminates one-half of the lineage of Abraham.

6. Son of Jacob

PROPHECY

"I see him, but not now;
I behold Him, but not near;
A Star shall come out of Jacob,
A Scepter shall rise out of Israel,
And batter the brow of Moab,
And destroy all the sons of tumult."
—Numbers 24:17
(See also Gen. 35:10–12.)

FULFILLMENT

"Jesus, . . . the son of Jacob."
—Luke 3:23, 34
(See also Matt. 1:2 and Luke 1:33.)

Jewish source: *Targum Jonathan* on Genesis 35:11, 12 says, "And the Lord said to him, I am El Shaddai: spread forth and multiply; a holy people, and a congregation of prophets and priests, shall be from thy sons whom thou hast begotten, and two kings shall yet from thee go forth. And the land which I gave to Abraham and to Izhak will I give unto thee, and to thy sons after thee will I give the land." (Ethridge, TOJ, 279)

Jewish source: *Targum Onkelos* on Numbers 24:17 states, "I see him, but not now; I behold him, but not nigh. When a king shall arise out of Jakob, and the Meshiha be anointed from Israel." (Ethridge, TOJ, 309)

In the above *Targums* we can see that the Jews gave Messianic import to these passages. Likewise, the *Midrash Bamidbar Rabbah* gives a Messianic meaning to this text. Paul Heinisch relates that "at the time of Hadrian (A.D. 132) the Jews revolted against the Roman yoke, they called their leader Barkochba, 'The Son of the Star.' For they believed that Balaam's oracle on the star from Jacob was then being fulfilled and that through him God would utterly destroy the Romans." (Heinisch, CP, 44, 45)

Hengstenberg, in his *Christology of the Old Testament,* points out that "by this Ruler, the Jews from the earliest times have understood the Messiah, either exclusively, or else principally, with a secondary reference to David. Either its exclusive relation to the Messiah was maintained, or it was allowed to refer indeed, in the first instance, to David; but then both himself and his temporal victories were regarded as typical of Christ, and His spiritual triumphs, which (according to this exposition) the prophet had especially in view." (Hengstenberg, COT, 34)

Isaac had two sons: Jacob and Esau. Now God eliminates one-half of the lineage of Isaac.

7. Tribe of Judah

PROPHECY	FULFILLMENT
"The scepter shall not depart from Judah, Nor a lawgiver from between his feet, Until Shiloh comes; And to Him shall be the obedience of the People." —Genesis 49:10 (See also Mic. 5:2.)	"Jesus, . . . the son of Judah." — Luke 3:23, 33 (See also Matt. 1:2 and Heb. 7:14.)

Jewish source: *Targum Jonathan* on Genesis 49:10, 11 says, "Kings shall not cease, nor rulers, from the house of Jehuda, nor sapherim teaching the law from his seed, till the time that the King, the Meshiha, shall come, the youngest of his sons; and on account of him shall the peoples flow together. How beauteous is the King, and Meshiha who will arise from the house of Jehuda!" (Ethridge, TOJ, 331)

Jewish source: *Targum Pseudo Jonathanon* Genesis 49:11 states, "How noble is the King, Messiah, who is going to rise from the house of Judah." (Bowker, TRL, 278)

Jacob had twelve sons out of which developed the twelve tribes of the Hebrew nation. Now God eliminates eleven-twelfths of the tribes of Israel. Joseph had no tribe named after him, but his two sons Ephraim and Manasseh did become heads of tribes.

8. Family Line of Jesse

PROPHECY	FULFILLMENT
"There shall come forth a Rod from the stem of Jesse, And a Branch shall grow out of his roots." —Isaiah 11:1 (See also Is. 1:10.)	"Jesus, . . . the son of Jesse." —Luke 3:23, 32 (See also Matt. 1:6.)

Jewish source: *Targum Isaiah* states, "And a King shall come forth from the sons of Jesse, and an Anointed One (or Messiah) from his son's sons shall grow up. And there shall rest upon him a spirit from before the Lord, the spirit of wisdom and understanding, the spirit of counsel and might, the spirit of knowledge, and of the fear of the Lord." (Stenning, TI, 40)

Delitzsch comments, "Out of the stumps of Jesse, i.e., out of the remnant of the chosen royal family which has sunk down to the insignificance of the house from which it sprang, there comes forth a twig *(choter)*, which promises to supply the place of the trunk and crown; and down below, in the roots covered with earth, and only rising a little above it, there shows itself a netzer, i.e., a fresh green shoot (from natzer, to shine or blossom). In the historical account of the fulfillment, even the ring of the words of the prophecy is noticed: the *netzer*, at first so humble and insignificant, was a poor despised Nazarene" (Matt. 2:23). (Delitzsch, BCPI, 281, 282)

9. House of David

PROPHECY

" 'Behold, the days are coming,' says the LORD, 'That I will raise to David a Branch of righteousness; A king shall reign and prosper, and execute judgment and righteousness in the land.' "
—Jeremiah 23:5

FULFILLMENT

"Jesus, . . . the son of David. . . ."
—Luke 3:23, 31
(See also Matt. 1:1; 9:27; 15:22; 20:30, 31; 21:9, 15; 22:41–46; Mark 9:10; 10:47, 48; Luke 18:38, 39; Acts 13:22, 23; Rev. 22:16.)

Jewish source: The Messiah as being referred to as the "Son of David" is scattered throughout the Talmuds.

Driver says about 2 Samuel 17:11, "Here Nathan comes to the main subject of his prophecy—the promise relating not to David himself, but to his posterity, and the declaration that it is not David who will build a house for Yahweh, but Yahweh who will build a house (i.e., a family) for David." (Driver, NHT, 275)

Jacob Minkin, in his book titled *The World of Moses Maimonides,* gives the view of this learned Jewish scholar: "Dismissing the mystical speculations concerning the Messiah, his origin, activity, and the marvelous superhuman powers ascribed to him, Maimonides insisted that he must be regarded as a mortal human being, differing from his fellow-men only in the fact that he will be greater, wiser, and more resplendent than they. He must be a descendant of the House of David and like him, occupy himself with the Study of the Torah and observance of its commandments." (Minkin, WMM, 63)

"Behold, the days are coming" is a common expression used in reference to the entrance of the Messianic era (see Jer. 31:27–34). (Laetsch, BCJ, 189)

Jesse had *at least* eight sons (see 1 Sam. 16:10, 11). Now God eliminates all of Jesse's sons except one: David.

10. Born at Bethlehem

PROPHECY

"But you, Bethlehem Ephrathah, Though you are little among the

FULFILLMENT

"Jesus was born in Bethlehem of Judea."
—Matthew 2:1

Thousands of Judah,
Yet out of you shall come forth to Me
The One to be Ruler in Israel,
Whose goings forth are from of old,
From everlasting."
—Micah 5:2

(See also Matt. 2:4; Luke 2:4–7; John 7:42.)

In Matthew 2:6 the scribes told Herod with great assurance that the Christ would be born in Bethlehem. It was well known among the Jews that the Christ would come from Bethlehem (see John 7:42). It is only fitting that Bethlehem, meaning the house of bread, should be the birthplace of the one who is the Bread of Life. (Henry, MHC, 1414)

God now eliminates all the cities in the world, save one, for the entrance of His incarnate Son.

11. Presented with Gifts

PROPHECY

"The kings of Tarshish and of the isles
will bring presents;
the kings of Sheba and Seba
will offer gifts."
—Psalm 72:10 (See also Is. 60:6.)

FULFILLMENT

"Wise men from the East came to
Jerusalem . . . and fell down and
worshiped Him. And when they
had opened their treasures,
they presented gifts to Him."
—Matthew 2:1, 11

The historic application of this passage is to Solomon. The messianic application is amplified in verses 12 through 15 (Ps. 72).

The inhabitants of Seba and Sheba, the Sabeans, lived in Arabia. (Nezikin, BT, 941, 1006) Matthew Henry says about Matthew 2, verses 1 and 11, that the wise men were "men of the east, who were noted for their soothsaying (Isa. 2:6). Arabia is called the land of the east (Gen. 25:6) and the Arabians are called, Men of the east (Judg. 6:3). The presents they brought were the products of that country." (Henry, MHC, 16)

12. Herod Kills Children

PROPHECY

"Thus says the LORD:
'A voice was heard in Ramah,
Lamentation and bitter weeping,
Rachel weeping for her children,
Refusing to be comforted for her
    Children,

FULFILLMENT

"Then Herod, when he saw that he was
deceived by the wise men, was exceedingly
angry; and he sent forth and put to death
all the male children who were in
Bethlehem and in all its districts, from
two years old and under, according

Because they are no more.'"
—Jeremiah 31:15

to the time which he had determined
from the wise men."
—Matthew 2:16

The dispersion and extermination of Israel is spoken of in Jeremiah 31:17, 18. What does Herod murdering the infants of Bethlehem have to do with the deportation? Was Matthew mistaken when he viewed Jeremiah's prophecy as fulfilled in Herod's atrocities (Matt. 2:17, 18) or the murder of the innocents as a type of the destruction of Israel or Judah? Laetsch says

No. Certainly not. The entire context of ch. 31, beginning ch. 30:20 and continuing to ch. 33:26, is Messianic. The four chapters speak of the approach of the Lord's salvation, of the coming of Messiah to re-establish the Kingdom of David in the form of a new covenant, of which forgiveness of sins is to be the foundation (ch. 31:31-34); a kingdom in which every weary and sorrowful soul shall be fully comforted (vv. 12–14, 25). As an example of this comfort the Lord introduces the consolation to be extended to mothers who had suffered great loss for the sake of Christ, the cruel murder of their infant sons. (Laetsch, BCJ, 250)

2B. Prophecies Concerning His Nature

13. His Pre-Existence

PROPHECY

"But you, Bethlehem Ephrathah,
Though you are little among the
    Thousands of Judah,
Yet out of you shall come to Me
The One to be Ruler in Israel,
Whose goings forth are from of old,
From everlasting."
—Micah 5:2

FULFILLMENT

"And He is before [or, has existed prior to] all things, and in Him all things consist."
—Colossians 1:17 (See also John 17:5, 24; Rev.1:1, 2; 1:17; 2:8; 8:58; 22:13.)

Jewish source: *Targum Isaiah* says, "The prophet saith to the house of David, A child has been born to us, a son has been given to us; and He has taken the law upon Himself to keep it, and His name has been called from of old, Wonderful counselor, Mighty God, He who lives forever, the Anointed one (or Messiah), in whose days peace shall increase upon us" (Is. 9:6). (Stenning, TI, 32)

Jewish source: *Targum Isaiah* states, "Thus saith the Lord, the King of Israel, and his saviour the Lord of hosts; I am He, I am He that is from of old; yea, the everlasting ages are mine, and beside me there is no God" (Is. 44:6). (Stenning, TI, 148)

Hengstenberg says about Micah 5:2, "The existence of the Messiah in general, before His temporal birth at Bethlehem, is asserted; and then His eternity in contrast with all time is mentioned here." (Hengstenberg, COT, 573)

14. He Shall Be Called Lord

PROPHECY

"The LORD said to my Lord,
'Sit at My right hand,
Till I make Your enemies Your
footstool.'"
—Psalm 110:1 (See also Jer. 23:6.)

FULFILLMENT

"For there is born to you this day in the
city of David a Savior, who is Christ
the Lord."
—Luke 2:11

"He said to them, 'How then does David in
the Spirit call Him "Lord," saying:
"The LORD said to my Lord,
'Sit at My right hand,
Till I make Your enemies Your
footstool'"?
If David then calls Him "Lord," how is He
his Son?'"
—Matthew 22:43–45

Jewish source: *The Midrash Tehillim,* commentary on the Psalms, A.D. 200–500, on Psalm 21:1 says: "God calls King Messiah by His own name. But what is His name? Answer: Jehovah is a man of war" (Ex. 15:3). (Laetsch, BCJ, 193)

Jewish source: *Echa Rabbathi,* A.D. 200–500 (Lamentations in Large Commentary on the Pentateuch and Five Scrolls), on Lamentations 1:16: "'What is the name of Messiah?' R. Abba ben Cahana (A.D. 200–300) has said: Jehovah is His name, and this is proved by 'This is His name'" (Jer. 23:6). (Laetsch, BCJ, 193)

"The Lord said unto my Lord. 'Jehovah said unto Adonai,' or 'my Lord,'—i.e., the Lord of David, not in his merely personal capacity, but as representative of Israel, literal and spiritual. It is because he addresses Him as Israel's and the Church's Lord, that Christ in the three Gospels quotes it. 'David calls Him Lord,' not 'His Lord.'" (Fausset, CCE, 346)

15. Shall Be Immanuel (God with Us)

PROPHECY

"Therefore the Lord Himself will give
you a sign: Behold, a virgin shall conceive
and bear a Son, and shall call His
name Immanuel."
—Isaiah 7:14

FULFILLMENT

"'Behold, the virgin shall be with child,
and bear a Son, and they shall call His
name Immanuel,' which is translated,
'God with us.'"
—Matthew 1:23 (See also Luke 7:16.)

Jewish source: *Targum Isaiah* on Isaiah 7:14 says, "Therefore the Lord himself shall give you a sign; Behold a damsel is with child, and shall bear a son, and shall call His name Immanuel." (Stenning, TI, 24)

Delitzsch says about Isaiah 9:6, "There is no reason why we should take El in this name of the Messiah in any other sense than in Immanu-El; not to mention the fact that El in Isaiah is always a name of God, and that the prophet was ever strongly conscious of the antithesis between El and Adam, as ch. 31:3 (cf. Hosea 11:9) clearly shows." (Delitzsch, BCPI, 252)

16. Shall Be a Prophet

PROPHECY

"I will raise up for them a Prophet like you from among their brethren, and will put My words in His mouth, and He shall speak to them all that I command Him."
—Deuteronomy 18:18

FULFILLMENT

"So the multitudes said, 'This is Jesus, the prophet from Nazareth of Galilee.' "
—Matthew 21:11
(See also Luke 7:16; John 4:19; 6:14; 7:40.)

Jewish source: The Jewish scholar Maimonides, in a letter to the community of Yemen, denounces a purporter of the Messiahship by writing: "The Messiah will be a very great Prophet, greater than all the Prophets with the exception of Moses our teacher. . . . His status will be higher than that of the Prophets and more honourable, Moses alone excepted. The Creator, blessed be He, will single him out with features wherewith He had not singled out Moses; for it is said with reference to him, 'And his delight shall be in the fear of the Lord; and he shall not judge after the sight of his eyes, neither decide after the hearing of his ears'" (Is. 11:3). (Cohen, TM, 221)

Christ compared to Moses:
1. He was delivered from a violent death in His infancy.
2. He was willing to become Redeemer of His people (Ex.3:10).
3. He worked as mediator between Yahweh and Israel (Ex. 19:16; 20:18).
4. He made intercession on behalf of sinful people (Ex. 32:7–14, 33; Num. 14:11–20).
"Sir, I perceive that You are a prophet" (John 4:19).

Kligerman says, "The use of the term 'prophet' by the Jews of Jesus' day shows not only that they expected the Messiah to be a prophet in accordance with the promise in Deuteronomy eighteen, but also that He who performed these miracles was indeed the Promised Prophet." (Kligerman, MPOT, 22, 23)

"For the law was given through Moses; but grace and truth came through Jesus Christ" (John 1:17).

17. Priest

PROPHECY

"The LORD has sworn and will not relent, 'You are a priest forever according to the order of Melchizedek.'"
—Psalm 110:4

FULFILLMENT

"Therefore, holy brethren, partakers of the heavenly calling, consider the Apostle and High Priest of our confession, Christ Jesus."
—Hebrews 3:1

"So also Christ did not glorify Himself to become a High Priest, but it was He who said to Him, 'You are My Son, today I have begotten You.' As He also says in another place, 'You are a priest forever according to the order of Melchizedek.'"
—Hebrews 5:5, 6

The final victory of Messiah's people over the world and Satan is . . . certain. The oath of God did not accompany the Aaronic priesthood, as it does our Melchizedek-like Priest, who "is made not after the law of a carnal commandment, but after the power of an endless life." "After the order of Melchizedek" is explained, Heb. 7:15, "after the similitude of Melchizedek." The oath of covenant on the part of the Father to the Son is for the comfort of Messiah's people. Uzziah's punishment for his usurpation of the functions of priest shows that David cannot be the King-Priest here described (II Chron. 26:16–21). The extraordinary oath of God shows that the King-Priesthood here is something unparalleled. David died, but this Melchizedek-like Priest lives forever. Zech. 6:9–15, especially 13, similarly describes Messiah "He shall sit and rule upon His throne, and He shall be a Priest upon His throne." (Fausset, CCE, 347)

18. Judge

PROPHECY

"For the LORD is our Judge, the LORD is our Lawgiver, the LORD is our King; He will Save us."
—Isaiah 33:22

FULFILLMENT

"I can of Myself do nothing. As I hear, I judge; and My judgment is righteous, because I do not seek My own will but the will of the Father who sent Me."
—John 5:30 (See also 2 Tim. 4:1.)

Jewish source: *Targum Isaiah* on Isaiah 33:22 says, "For the Lord is our judge, who brought us out of Egypt by his might; the Lord is our teacher, who gave us the instruction of his law from Sinai; the Lord is our King, he shall deliver us, and execute a righteous vengeance for us on the armies of Gog." (Stenning, TI, 110)

"Judge . . . Lawgiver . . . King—perfect ideal of the theocracy, to be realized under Messiah alone: the judicial, legislative, and administrative functions as King, to be exercised by Him in person (Isaiah 11:4; 32: 1; James. 4:12)." (Fausset, CCE, 666)

19. King

PROPHECY

"Yet I have set My King on My holy hill of Zion."
—Psalm 2:6 (See also Jer.23:5; Zech. 9:9.)

FULFILLMENT

"And they put up over His head the accusation written against Him: THIS IS JESUS THE KING OF THE JEWS."
—Matthew 27:37
(See also Matt. 21:5; John 18:33–38.)

20. Special Anointing of Holy Spirit

PROPHECY

"The Spirit of the LORD shall rest upon Him, the Spirit of wisdom and understanding, the Spirit of counsel and might, the Spirit of knowledge and of the fear of the LORD."
—Isaiah 11:2
(See also Ps. 45:7; Is. 42:1; 61:1, 2.)

FULFILLMENT

"When He had been baptized, Jesus came up immediately from the water; and behold, the heavens were opened to Him, and He saw the Spirit of God descending like a dove and alighting upon Him. And suddenly a voice came from heaven, saying, 'This is My beloved Son, in whom I am well pleased.'"
—Matthew 3:16, 17 (See also Matt. 12:17–21; Mark 1:10, 11; Luke 4:15–21, 43; John 1:32.)

Jewish source: *Targum Isaiah* on Isaiah 11:1–4 says, "And a king shall come forth from the sons of Jesse, and an Anointed One (or Messiah) from his sons' sons shall grow up. And there shall rest upon him a spirit from before the Lord, the spirit of wisdom and understanding, the spirit of counsel and might, the spirit of knowledge, and of the fear of the Lord: and the Lord shall bring him to his fear: and not according to the sight of his eyes shall he judge, nor exercise judgement according to the hearing of his ears. But he shall judge with truth the poor, and adjudge with faithfulness the needy among the people." (Stenning, TI, 40)

Jewish source: In the *Babylonian Talmud,* the *Sanhedrin II* says, "The Messiah—as it is written, And the spirit of the Lord shall rest upon him, the spirit of wisdom and understanding, the spirit of counsel and might, the spirit of knowledge of the fear of the Lord. And shall make him of quick understanding [*wa-hariho*] in the fear of the Lord. R. Alexandri said: This teaches that he loaded him with good deeds and suffering as a mill [is laden]." (Nezikin, BT, 626, 627)

21. His Zeal for God

PROPHECY

"Because zeal for Your house has eaten me up, and the reproaches of those who reproach You have fallen on me."
—Psalm 69:9

FULFILLMENT

"When He had made a whip of cords, He drove them all out of the temple. . . . And He said, . . . 'Take these things away! Do not make My Father's house a house of merchandise!'"
—John 2:15, 16

A. R. Fausset writes: "For the zeal of thine house hath eaten me up—-consumes me like a flame with its very intensity (Ps. 119:139). The expansion of 'for thy sake' (Ps. 69:7): cf.

John 2:17 as a specimen of Messiah's zeal for the honour of the house of God. And the reproaches of them that reproached thee are fallen upon me—in consequence of my glowing 'zeal' for thine honour, the reproaches aimed at thee fall upon me." (Fausset, CCE, 245)

3B. Prophecies Concerning His Ministry

22. Preceded by Messenger

PROPHECY

"A voice of one crying in the wilderness: 'Prepare the way of the LORD; Make straight in the desert a highway for our God.'"
—Isaiah 40:3 (See also Mal. 3:1.)

FULFILLMENT

"John the Baptist came preaching in the wilderness of Judea, and saying, 'Repent, for the kingdom of heaven is at hand!'"
—Matthew 3:1, 2 (See also Matt. 3:3; 11:10; John 1:23; Luke 1:17.)

Jewish source: *Targum Isaiah* on Isaiah 40:3 says, "The voice of one that crieth, Prepare ye a way in the wilderness before the people of the Lord, tread down paths in the desert before the congregation of our God." (Stenning, TI, 130)

23. Ministry to Begin in Galilee

PROPHECY

"Nevertheless the gloom will not be upon her who is distressed, as when at first He lightly esteemed the land of Zebulun and the land of Naphtali, and afterward more heavily oppressed her, by the way of the sea, beyond the Jordan, in Galilee of the Gentiles."
—Isaiah 9:1

FULFILLMENT

"Now when Jesus heard that John had been put into prison, He departed to Galilee. And leaving Nazareth, He came and dwelt in Capernaum, which is by the sea, in the regions of Zebulun and Naphtali. From that time Jesus began to preach and to say, 'Repent, for the kingdom of heaven is at hand.'"
—Matthew 4:12, 13, 17

24. Ministry of Miracles

PROPHECY

"Then the eyes of the blind will be opened, And the ears of the deaf will be unstopped. Then the lame will leap like a deer, And the tongue of the dumb will sing For joy."
—Isaiah 35:5, 6 (See also Is. 32:3, 4.)

FULFILLMENT

"And Jesus was going about all the cities and the villages, teaching in their synagogues, and proclaiming the gospel of the kingdom, and healing every kind of disease and every kind of sickness."
—Matthew 9:35 (See also Matt.9:32, 33; 11:4–6; Mark 7:33–35; John 5:5–9; 9:6–11; 11:43, 44, 47.)

25. Teacher of Parables

PROPHECY

"I will open my mouth in a parable;
I will utter dark sayings of old."
—Psalm 78:2

FULFILLMENT

"All these things Jesus spoke to the
multitude in parables; and without a
parable He did not speak to them."
—Matthew 13:34

26. He Was to Enter the Temple

PROPHECY

"And the Lord, whom you seek, will
suddenly come to His temple."
—Malachi 3:1

FULFILLMENT

"Then Jesus went into the temple of God
and drove out all those who bought and
old in the temple."
—Matthew 21:12
(See also John 1:14; 2:19–21.)

27. He Was to Enter Jerusalem on a Donkey

PROPHECY

"Rejoice greatly, O daughter of Zion!
Shout, O daughter of Jerusalem!
Behold, your King is coming to you;
He is just and having salvation, humble,
lowly and riding on a donkey, a colt,
the foal of a donkey."
—Zechariah 9:9

FULFILLMENT

"And they brought him to Jesus. And they
threw their own clothes on the colt,
and they set Jesus on him. And as
He went, many spread their clothes on the
road. Then, as He was now drawing
near the descent of the Mount of Olives."
—Luke 19:35–37 (See also Matt. 21:6–11.)

28. "Stone of Stumbling" to Jews

PROPHECY

"The stone which the builders rejected
has become the chief cornerstone."
—Psalm 118:22 (See also Is. 8:14, 28:1.)

FULFILLMENT

"Therefore, to you who believe, He is
precious; but to those who are
disobedient, 'The stone which the
builders rejected has become the cheif
cornerstone.'"
—1 Peter 2:7 (See also Rom. 9:32, 33.)

Jewish source: *Targum Isaiah* on Isaiah 8:13–15 says, "The Lord of hosts, him shall ye call holy; and let him be your fear and let him be your strength. And if ye will not hearken, his Memra shall be amongst you for vengeance and for a stone of smiting, and for a rock of offence to the two houses of the princes of Israel, for a breaking, and for a stumbling, because the house of Israel hath been separated from them of the house of Judah who dwell in Jerusalem. And many shall stumble against them, and shall fall, and be broken and be snared, and be taken." (Stenning, TI, 28)

29. "Light" to Gentiles

PROPHECY

"The Gentiles shall come to your light,
And kings to the brightness of
your rising."
—Isaiah 60:3 (See also Is. 49:6.)

FULFILLMENT

"For so the Lord has commanded us, 'I
have set you as a light to the Gentiles,
that you should be for salvation to the
ends of the earth.' Now when the Gentiles
heard this, they were glad and glorified
the word of the Lord."
—Acts 13:47, 48
(See also Acts 26:23; 28:28.)

4B. Prophecies Concerning Events after His Burial

30. Resurrection

PROPHECY

"For You will not leave my soul in Sheol;
nor will You allow Your Holy One to see
corruption."
—Psalm 16:10

FULFILLMENT

"His soul was not left in Hades, nor
did His flesh see corruption."
—Acts 2:31
(See also Matt. 28:6; Mark 16:6;
Luke 24:46; Acts 13:33.)

Jewish source: Friedlaender says, "Ibn Ezra frequently takes occasion to assert his firm belief in the resurrection of the dead." (Friedlaender, EWA, 100)

Jewish source: The *Sanhedrin II, Babylonian Talmud* states the following: "Mishnah. All Israel have a portion in the world to come, for it is written, 'Thy people are all righteous; they shall inherit the land forever, the branch of My planting, the work of My hands, that I may be glorified.' But the following have noportion there-in: He who maintains that resurrection is not a biblical doctrine, the Torah was not divinely revealed." (Nezikin, BT, 601)

31. Ascension

PROPHECY

"You have ascended on high."
—Psalm 68:18

FULFILLMENT

"He was taken up, and a cloud received Him out of their sight."
—Acts 1:9

32. Seated at the Right Hand of God

PROPHECY

"The LORD said to my Lord, 'Sit at My right hand, till I make Your enemies Your footstool.'"
—Psalm 110:1

FULFILLMENT

"When He had by Himself purged our sins, [He] sat down at the right hand of the Majesty on high."
—Hebrews 1:3
(See also Mark 16:19; Acts 2:34, 35.)

5B. Prophecies Fulfilled in One Day

The following twenty-nine prophecies from the Old Testament, which speak of the betrayal, trial, defeat, and burial of our Lord Jesus Christ, were spoken at various times by many different voices during the five centuries from 1000–500 B.C. Yet all of them were literally fulfilled in Jesus in one twenty-four-hour period of time.

33. Betrayed by a Friend

PROPHECY

"Even my familiar friend in whom I trusted,who ate my bread, has lifted up his heel against me."
—Psalm 41:9
(See also Psalm 55:12–14.)

FULFILLMENT

"Judas Iscariot, who also betrayed Him."
—Matthew 10:4
(See also Matt. 26:49, 50; John 13:21.)

Psalm 41:9: "Lit., 'the man of my peace'; he who saluted me with the kiss of peace, as Judas did" (Matthew 26:49: cf. the type, Jeremiah 20:10). (Fausset, CCE, 191)

34. Sold for Thirty Pieces of Silver

PROPHECY

"Then I said to them, 'If it is agreeable to you, give me my wages; and if not, refrain.' So they weighed out for my wages thirty pieces of silver."
—Zechariah 11:12

FULFILLMENT

"'What are you willing to give me if I deliver Him to you?' And they counted out to him thirty pieces of silver."
—Matthew 26:15 (See also Matt. 27:3.)

35. Money to Be Thrown into God's House

PROPHECY

"So I took the thirty pieces of silver and threw them into the house of the LORD for the potter."
—Zechariah 11:13

FULFILLMENT

"Then he threw down the pieces of silver in the temple and departed."
—Matthew 27:5

36. Price Given for Potter's Field

PROPHECY

"So I took the thirty pieces of silver and threw them into the house of the LORD for the potter."
—Zechariah 11:13

FULFILLMENT

"And they consulted together and bought with them the potter's field, to bury strangers in."
—Matthew 27:7

In the previous four prophecies we find both prophecied and fulfilled:
1. Betrayal
2. By a friend
3. For thirty pieces (not twenty-nine)
4. Of silver (not gold)
5. Thrown down (not placed)
6. In the house of the LORD
7. Money used to buy potter's field

37. Forsaken by His Disciples

PROPHECY

"Strike the Shepherd, and the sheep will be scattered."
—Zechariah 13:7

FULFILLMENT

"Then they all forsook Him and fled."
—Mark 14:50
(See also Matt. 26:31; Mark 14:27.)

Laetsch writes that Zechariah 13:7 is "a clear prophecy of the offense taken by the disciples when Christ was smitten. So Christ Himself interprets these words (Matthew 26:31; Mark 14:27). They were fulfilled (see Matthew 26:56; Mark 14:50 ff.). Yet the Lord would not forsake the sheep. The Lord Himself, acting in and through the person of His 'Fellow' (John 5:19f., 30), will turn His hand upon (Gr. N.), come to the aid of the little ones (Gr. N.), His despondent, terrified disciples (Luke 24:4f., 11, 17ff., 37; John 20:2, 11ff., 19, 26). These weaklings and deserters became the courageous, invincible heralds of the Messiah's kingdom." (Laetsch, BCMP, 491, 492)

38. Accused by False Witnesses

PROPHECY

"Fierce witnesses rise up; they ask me things that I do not know."
—Psalm 35:11

FULFILLMENT

"Now the chief priests, the elders, and all the council sought false testimony against Jesus to put Him to death, but found none. Even though many false witnesses came forward, they found none."
—Matthew 26:59, 60

39. Silent before Accusers

PROPHECY

"He was oppressed and He was afflicted, Yet He opened not His mouth."
—Isaiah 53:7

FULFILLMENT

"And while He was being accused by the chief priests and elders, He answered nothing."
—Matthew 27:12

40. Wounded and Bruised

PROPHECY

"But He was wounded for our transgressions, He was bruised for our iniquities; the chastisement for our peace was upon Him, and by His stripes we are healed."
—Isaiah 53:5 (See also Zech. 13:6.)

FULFILLMENT

"Then he released Barabbas to them; and when he had scourged Jesus, he delivered Him to be crucified."
—Matthew 27:26

"A bodily wound: not mere mental sorrow; *mecholal*, from *chalal*—literally pierced; minutely appropriate to Messiah, whose hands, feet, and side were pierced (Psalm 22:16)." (Fausset, CCE, 730)

"But from the crown of the head, which was crowned with thorns, to the soles of his feet, which were nailed to the cross, nothing appeared but wounds and bruises." (Henry, MHC, 826)

41. Smitten and Spit Upon

PROPHECY

"I gave My back to those who struck Me, and My cheeks to those who plucked out the beard; I did not hide My face from shame and spitting."
—Isaiah 50:6 (See also Mic. 5:1.)

FULFILLMENT

"Then they spat in His face and beat Him; and others struck Him with the palms of their hands.
—Matthew 26:67
(See also Luke 22:63.)

Jewish source: *Targum Isaiah* on Isaiah 50:6 says, "I gave my back to the smiters, and my cheeks to them that pluck out the hair; I hid not my face from humiliation and spitting." (Stenning, TI, 170)

Henry states, "In this submission, He resigned Himself, (1.) To be scourged; . . . (2.) To be buffeted; . . . (3.) To be spit upon; . . . All this Christ underwent for us, and voluntarily, to convince us of His willingness to save us." (Henry, MHC, 816)

42. Mocked

PROPHECY

"All who see Me ridicule Me; They shoot out the lip, they shake the head, saying, 'He trusted in the LORD; let Him rescue Him; let Him deliver Him, since He delights in Him!'"
—Psalm 22:7, 8

FULFILLMENT

"When they had twisted a crown of horns, they put it on His head, and a reed in His right hand; and they bowed the knee before Him and mocked Him, saying, 'Hail, King of the Jews!'"
—Matthew 27:29
(See also Matt. 27:41–43.)

43. Fell under the Cross

PROPHECY

"My knees are weak through fasting; and my flesh is feeble from lack of fatness. I also have become a reproach to them; when they look at me, they shake their heads."
—Psalm 109:24, 25

FULFILLMENT

"And He, bearing His cross, went out to a place called the Place of a Skull, which is called in Hebrew, Golgotha."
—John 19:17

"Now as they led Him away, they laid hold of a certain man, Simon a Cyrenian, who was coming from the country, and on him they laid the cross that he might bear it after Jesus."
—Luke 23:26 (See also Matt.27:31, 32.)

Evidently Jesus was so weak that, under the weight of the heavy cross, His knees were giving way, so they had to place it on another.

44. Hands and Feet Pierced

PROPHECY

"They pierced My hands and My feet."
—Psalm 22:16
(See also Zech. 12:10.)

FULFILLMENT

"And when they had come to the place called Calvary, there they crucified Him."
—Luke 23:33 (See also John 20:25.)

Jesus was crucified in the usual Roman manner: The hands and feet were pierced by large, dull spikes that attached the body to the wooden cross or stake.

45. Crucified with Thieves

PROPHECY

"Because He poured out His soul unto death, and He was numbered with the transgressors."
—Isaiah 53:12

FULFILLMENT

"Then the two robbers were crucified with Him, one on the right and another on the left."
—Matthew 27:38 (See also Mark 15:27, 28.)

Blinzler states, "Crucifixion was unknown in Jewish criminal law. The hanging on a gibbet, which was prescribed by Jewish law for idolaters and blasphemers who had been stoned, was not a death penalty, but an additional punishment after death designed to brand the executed person as one accursed of God, in accordance with Deut. 21:23 (LXX): 'For he is accursed of God that hangeth on a tree.' The Jews applied these words also to one who had been crucified. If crucifixion was the most shameful and degrading death penalty even in the eyes of the pagan world, the Jews in the time of Jesus regarded a person so executed as being, over and above, accursed of God." (Blinzler, TJ, 247, 248)

The Encyclopedia Americana records: "The history of crucifixion as a mode of punishment for crime must be studied as a part of the Roman system of jurisprudence. . . . The Hebrews, for example, adopted or accepted it only under Roman compulsion: under their own system, before Palestine became Roman territory, they inflicted the death penalty by stoning." (EA, 8:253)

"In 63 B.C., Pompey's legions cut their way into the Judean capital. Palestine became a Roman province, though nominally a puppet Jewish dynasty survived" (Wilson, DDWD, 262).

Thus, the type of death pictured in Isaiah 53 and Psalm 22 did not come into practice under the Jewish system until hundreds of years after the account was written.

46. Made Intercession for His Persecutors

PROPHECY

"And He bore the sin of many, and made intercession for the transgressors."
—Isaiah 53:12

FULFILLMENT

"Father, forgive them, for they do not know what they do."
—Luke 23:34

"This office He began on the cross (Luke 23:34), and now continues in heaven (Heb. 9:24; 1 John 2:1)." (Fausset, CCE, 733)

47. Rejected by His Own People

PROPHECY

"He is despised and rejected by men, a Man of sorrows and acquainted

FULFILLMENT

"For even His brothers did not believe in Him. 'Have any of the rulers or the

with grief. And we hid, as it were, our faces from Him; He was despised, and we did not esteem Him."
—Isaiah 53:3
(See also Pss. 69:8; 118:22.)

Pharisees believed in Him?'"
—John 7:5, 48
(See also Matt. 21:42, 43; John 1:11.)

"This was fulfilled in Christ, whose brethren did not believe on Him (John 7:5), who came to His own, and His own received Him not (John 1:11), and who was forsaken by His disciples, whom He had been free with as His brethren." (Henry, MHC, 292)

NOTE: Further confirmation of the predictive nature of Isaiah 53 is that it was common for Jewish interpreters before the time of Christ to teach that here Isaiah spoke of the Jewish Messiah (see S. R. Driver, et al., trans., *The Fifty-Third Chapter of Isaiah According to Jewish Interpreters*). Only after early Christians began using the text apologetically with great force did it become in rabbinical teaching an expression of the suffering Jewish nation. This view is implausible in the context of Isaiah's standard references to the Jewish people in the first-person plural ("our" or "we,") whereas he always refers to the Messiah in the third-person singular, as in Isaiah 53 ("he" and "his" and "him"). (Geisler, BECA, 612)

48. Hated Without a Cause

PROPHECY

"Those who hate me without a cause are more than the hairs of my head."
—Psalm 69:4
(See also Is. 49:7.)

FULFILLMENT

"But this happened that the word might be fulfilled which is written in their law, 'They hated Me without a cause.'"
—John 15:25

49. Friends Stood Afar Off

PROPHECY

"My loved ones and my friends stand aloof from my plague, and my relatives stand afar off."
—Psalm 38:11

FULFILLMENT

"But all His acquaintances, and the women who followed Him from Galilee, stood at a distance, watching these things."
—Luke 23:49
(See also Matt. 27:55, 56; Mark 15:40.)

"At the very time when my affliction would have required them to stand nearer and more steadily by me than ever, they are afraid of the danger that they would incur by seeming to take part with me. While the enemies are near, the friends are far. So in the case of Messiah" (Matt. 26:56; 27:55; Luke 23:49; John 16:32). (Fausset, CCE, 184)

50. People Shook Their Heads

PROPHECY

"I also have become a reproach to them; When they look at me, they shake their heads."
—Psalm 109:25 (See also Ps. 22:7.)

FULFILLMENT

"And those who passed by blasphemed Him, wagging their heads."
—Matthew 27:39

"A gesture implying that there is no hope for the sufferer, at whom they contemptuously sneer" (Job 16:4; Ps. 44:14). (Ethridge, TOJ, 148)

"As though it was all over with me: and I and my cause were irretrievably ruined" (Ps. 22:7; Matt. 27:39). (Ethridge, TOJ, 345)

51. Stared Upon

PROPHECY

"I can count all My bones. They look and stare at Me."
—Psalm 22:17

FULFILLMENT

"And the people stood looking on."
—Luke 23:35

52. Garments Parted and Lots Cast

PROPHECY

"They divide My garments among them, and for My clothing they cast lots."
—Psalm 22:18

FULFILLMENT

"The soldiers, when they had crucified Jesus, took His garments and made four parts, to each soldier a part, and also the tunic. Now the tunic was without seam, woven from the top in one piece. They said . . . 'Let us not tear it, but cast lots for it, whose it shall be.'"
—John 19:23, 24

The Old Testament statement in Psalm 22 almost seems to be contradictory until we look at the account at the scene of the cross. The garments were parted among the soldiers, but the vesture was awarded to one by the casting of lots.

53. To Suffer Thirst

PROPHECY

"And for my thirst they gave me vinegar to drink."
—Psalm 69:21

FULFILLMENT

"After this, Jesus . . . said, 'I thirst!'"
—John 19:28

54. Gall and Vinegar Offered to Him

PROPHECY

"They also gave me gall for my food,
and for my thirst they gave me vinegar
to drink."
—Psalm 69:21

FULFILLMENT

"They gave Him sour wine mingled with
gall to drink. But when He had tasted it,
He would not drink."
—Matthew 27:34
(See also John 19:28, 29.)

A. R. Fausset writes: "His bitter sufferings might have been expected to soften even His enemies, who had caused those sufferings; but instead of cordials, they gave Him gall and vinegar. Twice vinegar was offered to the Saviour on the cross—first vinegar mixed with gall (Matthew 27:34), and myrrh (Mark 15:23); but when He had tasted it, He would not drink it; for He would not meet His sufferings in a state of stupefaction, which is the effect of myrrh. As given to criminals, it was a kindness; as given to the righteous Sin-bearer, it was an insult. Next, in order to fulfill this Scripture, He cried 'I thirst,' and vinegar was given Him to drink" (John 19:28; Matt. 27:48). (Fausset, CCE, 246)

55. His Forsaken Cry

PROPHECY

"My God, My God, why have You
forsaken Me?"
—Psalm 22:1

FULFILLMENT

"And about the ninth hour Jesus cried out
with a loud voice, saying, 'Eli, Eli, lama
sabachthani?' that is, 'My God, My God,
why have You forsaken Me?'"
—Matthew 27:46

Psalm 22: "The expressive repetition twice (v. 1) of the cry, 'my God,' implies that the Sufferer clung firmly to this truth, that God was still His God, in spite of all appearances to the contrary. This was His antidote to despair, and the pledge that God would yet interpose as His Deliverer." (Fausset, CCE, 148)

This cry turned the attention of the people back to Psalm 22. Christ was quoting the first verse of the psalm, and that psalm is a clear prophecy of the crucifixion.

56. Committed Himself to God

PROPHECY

"Into Your hand I commit my spirit."
—Psalm 31:5

FULFILLMENT

"And when Jesus had cried out with a
loud voice, He said, 'Father, "into Your
hands I commit My spirit."'"
—Luke 23:46

57. Bones Not Broken

PROPHECY

"He guards all his bones; not one of them is broken."
—Psalm 34:20

FULFILLMENT

"But when they came to Jesus and saw that He was already dead, they did not break His legs."
—John 19:33

Although not stated in Scripture, there are two other prophecies that concern His bones that undoubtedly had an exact fulfillment.
1. "And all My bones are out of joint" (Ps. 22:14). The disjointing of bones while hanging on the cross by the hands and feet could easily come about, especially when we note that His body was attached to the cross while it was lying on the ground.
2. "I can count all My bones. They look and stare at me" (Ps. 22:17). All His bones could easily be seen while He was left hanging on the cross. The extension of His body during crucifixion would tend to make the bones more prominent than usual.

58. Heartbroken

PROPHECY

"My heart is like wax; it has melted within Me."
—Psalm 22:14

FULFILLMENT

But one of the soldiers pierced His side with a spear, and immediately blood and water came out."
—John 19:34

The blood and water that came forth from His pierced side are evidence that the heart had literally burst.

59. His Side Pierced

PROPHECY

"They will look on Me whom they pierced."
—Zechariah 12:10

FULFILLMENT

"But one of the soldiers pierced His side with a spear."
—John 19:34

Theodore Laetsch writes: "Now a remarkable statement is added. The Lord Jehovah speaks of Himself as having been pierced by men who shall look upon Him and shall mourn for Him.

"The word pierce—thrust through—occurs nine times as a thrust by a sword or spear (Num. 25:8; Judg. 9:54; 1 Sam. 31:4; 1 Chron. 10:4; Is. 13:15; Jer. 37:10, 'wounded'; 51:4; Zech. 12:10; 13:3); it occurs once as pierced by pangs of hunger described as more painful than a sword thrust" (Lam. 4:9). (Laetsch, BCMP, 483)

60. Darkness over the Land

PROPHECY

"'And it shall come to pass in that day,' says the Lord GOD, 'That I will make the sun go down at noon, and I will darken the earth in broad daylight.'"
—Amos 8:9

FULFILLMENT

"Now from the sixth hour until the ninth hour there was darkness over all the land."
—Matthew 27:45

Because the Jews reckoned twelve hours from sunrise to sunset, it would make the sixth hour near noon and the ninth hour about three o'clock.

61. Buried in a Rich Man's Tomb

PROPHECY

"And they made His grave with the wicked—but with the rich at His death."
—Isaiah 53:9

FULFILLMENT

"There came a rich man from Arimathea, named Joseph. . . and [he] asked for the body of Jesus. . . . When Joseph had taken the body, he wrapped it in a clean linen cloth, and laid it in his new tomb."
—Matthew 27:57–60

4A. CONFIRMATION OF JESUS AS THE MESSIAH, THROUGH FULFILLED PROPHECIES

1B. Objection: Fulfilled Prophecy in Jesus Was Deliberately Engineered by Him

In *The Passover Plot*, radical New Testament scholar H. J. Schonfield proposes that Jesus was an innocent messianic pretender who connived to "fulfill" prophecy in order to substantiate His claims. (Schonfield, H.J., 35–38)

First of all, this was contrary to Jesus' honest character as noted above. It assumes He was one of the greatest deceivers of all time. It presupposes that He was not even a good person, to say nothing of the perfect man the Gospels affirm Him to be. There are several lines of evidence that combine to demonstrate that this is a completely implausible thesis.

Second, there is no way Jesus could have controlled many events necessary for the fulfillment of Old Testament prophecies about the Messiah. For example, He had no control over where He would be born (Mic. 5:2), how He would be born of a virgin (Is. 7:14), when He would die (Dan. 9:25), what tribe (Gen. 49:10) and lineage He would be from (2 Sam. 7:12), or other facts about His life that have corresponded to prophecy.

Third, there is no way short of being supernatural that Jesus could have manipulated the events and people in His life to respond in exactly the way necessary for it to appear that He was fulfilling all these prophecies, including John's heralding Him (Matt. 3), His accuser's reactions (Matt. 27:12), how the soldiers cast lots for His garments (John 19:23, 24), and how they would pierce His side with a spear (John 19:34).

Indeed even Schonfield admits that the plot failed when the Romans actually pierced Christ. The fact is that anyone with all this power would have to be divine—the very thing the Passover hypothesis attempts to avoid. In short, it takes a bigger miracle to believe the *Passover Plot* than to accept these prophecies as supernatural. (Geisler, BECA, 585)

Answer: The above objection might seem plausible until we realize that many of the prophecies concerning the Messiah were totally beyond the human control of Jesus:

1. Place of birth (Mic. 5:2)
2. Time of birth (Dan. 9:25; Gen. 49:10)
3. Manner of birth (Is. 7:14)
4. Betrayal
5. Manner of death (Ps. 22:16)
6. People's reactions (mocking, spitting, staring, etc.)
7. Piercing
8. Burial

2B. Objection: Fulfilled Prophecy in Jesus Was Coincidental—an Accident

"Why, you could find some of these prophecies fulfilled in the deaths of Kennedy, King, Nasser, and other great figures," replies the critic.

Answer: Yes, one could possibly find one or two prophecies fulfilled in the lives of other men, but not all sixty-one major prophecies! In fact, for years, if you could have found someone other than Jesus, living or dead, who fulfilled half of the predictions concerning Messiah, as listed in *Messiah in Both Testaments* by Fred John Meldau, the Christian Victory Publishing Company of Denver offered to give you a one-thousand-dollar reward. There are a lot of men in the universities who could have used this extra cash!

H. Harold Hartzler, of the American Scientific Affiliation, Goshen College, in the foreword of Peter Stoner's book writes: "The manuscript for *Science Speaks* has been carefully reviewed by a committee of the American Scientific Affiliation members and by the Executive Council of the same group and has been found, in general, to be dependable and accurate in regard to the scientific material presented. The mathematical analysis included is based upon principles of probability which are thoroughly sound and Professor Stoner has applied these principles in a proper and convincing way." (Hartzler, "F," as cited in Stoner, SS)

The following probabilities are taken from Stoner in *Science Speaks* to show that coincidence is ruled out by the science of probability. Stoner says that by using the modern science of probability in reference to eight prophecies (*1.*—No. 10; *2.*—No. 22; *3.*—No. 27; *4.*—Nos. 33 & 44; *5.*—No. 34; *6.*—Nos. 35 & 36; *7.*—No. 39; *8.*—Nos. 44 & 45 [crucified]),

We find that the chance that any man might have lived down to the present time and fulfilled all eight prophecies is 1 in 10^{17} [(10 to the 17th power). That would be 1 in 100,000,000,000,000,000 (17 zeros after the one). In order to help us comprehend this staggering probability, Stoner illustrates it by supposing that] we take 10^{17} silver dollars and lay them on the face of Texas. They will cover all of the state two feet deep. Now mark one of these silver dollars and stir the whole mass thoroughly, all over the state. Blindfold a man and tell him that he can travel as far as he wishes, but he must pick up one silver dollar and say that this is the right one. What chance would he have of getting the right one? Just the same chance that the prophets would have had of writing these eight prophecies and having them all come true in any one man, from their day to the present time, providing they wrote them according to their own wisdom.

Now these prophecies were either given by inspiration of God or the prophets just wrote them as they thought they should be. In such a case the prophets had just one chance in 10^{17} of having them come true in any man, but they all came true in Christ. This means that the fulfillment of these eight prophecies alone proves that God inspired the writing of those prophecies to a definiteness which lacks only one chance in 10^{17} of being absolute. (Stoner, SS, 100–107)

Stoner considers forty-eight prophecies and reports,

We find the chance that any one man fulfilled all 48 prophecies to be 1 in 10^{157}. This is really a large number and it represents an extremely small chance. Let us try to visualize it. The silver dollar, which we have been using, is entirely too large. We must select a smaller object. The electron is about as small an object as we know of. It is so small that it will take 2.5 times 10^{15} of them laid side by side to make a line, single file, one inch long. If we were going to count the electrons in this line one inch long, and counted 250 each minute, and if we counted day and night, it would take us 19,000,000 years to count just the one-inch line of electrons. If we had a cubic inch of these electrons and we tried to count them it would take us, counting steadily 250 each minute, 19,000,000 times 19,000,000 times 19,000,000 years or 6.9 times 10^{21} years.

With this introduction, let us go back to our chance of 1 in 10^{157}. Let us suppose that

The highly reputed "predictions" of Nostradamus were not that amazing at all. Contrary to popular belief, he never predicted either the place or the year of a great California earthquake. Most of his "famous" predictions, such as the rise of Hitler, were vague. As other psychics, he was frequently wrong, a false prophet by biblical standards.

—GEISLER, BECA, 615

we are taking this number of electrons, marking one, and thoroughly stirring it into the whole mass, then blindfolding a man and letting him try to find the right one. What chance has he of finding the right one? What

kind of a pile will this number of electrons make? They make an inconceivably large volume. (Stoner, SS, 109, 110)

Such is the chance of any individual fulfilling forty-eight prophecies.

3B. Objection: Psychics Have Made Predictions Like the Bible's

Contemporary critics of biblical prophecy nominate psychic predictions for equality with Scripture. There is another quantum leap between every psychic and the unerring prophets of Scripture (see *Miracle and Magic*). Indeed, one test of a prophet was whether they ever uttered predictions that did not come to pass (Deut. 18:22). Those whose prophecies failed were stoned (18:20)—a practice that no doubt gave pause to any who were not absolutely sure their messages were from God. Amid hundreds of prophecies, biblical prophets are not known to have made a single error. A study of prophecies made by psychics in 1975 and observed until 1981 showed that of the seventy-two predictions, only six were fulfilled in any way. Two of these were vague and two others were hardly surprising—the United States and Russia would remain leading powers and there would be no world wars. *The People's Almanac* (1976) did a study of the predictions of twenty-five top psychics. The results: Of the total seventy-two predictions, sixty-six (92 percent) were totally wrong. (Kole, MM, 69) An accuracy rate around 8 percent could easily be explained by chance and general knowledge of circumstances. In 1993 the psychics missed every major unexpected news story, including Michael Jordan's retirement, the Midwest flooding, and the Israel-PLO peace treaty. Among their false prophecies were the prediction that the Queen of England would become a nun, and that Kathy Lee Gifford would replace Jay Leno as host of *The Tonight Show. (Charlotte Observer* 12/30/93)

Likewise, the highly reputed "predictions" of Nostradamus were not that amazing at all. Contrary to popular belief, he never predicted either the place or the year of a great California earthquake. Most of his "famous" predictions, such as the rise of Hitler, were vague. As other psychics, he was frequently wrong, a false prophet by biblical standards. (Geisler, BECA, 615)

4B. The Time of Messiah's Coming

1C. The Removal of the Scepter:

"The scepter shall not depart from Judah,
    Nor a lawgiver from between his feet,
    Until Shiloh comes,
    And to Him shall be the obedience of the people" (Gen. 49:10).

The word that is best translated "scepter" in this passage means a "tribal staff." Each of the twelve tribes of Israel had its own particular "staff" with its name inscribed on it. Therefore, the "tribal staff" or "tribal identity" of Judah was not to pass away before Shiloh came. For centuries Jewish and Christian commentators alike have taken the word "Shiloh" to be a name of the Messiah.

We remember that Judah was deprived of its national sovereignty during the seventy-year period of the Babylonian captivity; however, it never lost its "tribal staff" or "national identity" during that time. They still possessed their own lawgivers or judges even while in captivity (see Ezra 1:5, 8).

Thus, according to this Scripture and the Jews of their time, two signs were to take place soon after the advent of the Messiah:

1. Removal of the scepter or identity of Judah.
2. Suppression of the judicial power.

The first visible sign of the beginning of the removal of the scepter from Judah came about when Herod the Great, who had no Jewish blood, succeeded the Maccabean princes, who belonged to the tribe of Levi and who were the last Jewish kings to have their reign in Jerusalem. (Sanhedrin, folio 97, verso.) (*Maccabees,* Book 2)

Le Mann, in his book *Jesus before the Sanhedrin,* titles his second chapter: "The legal power of the Sanhedrin is restricted twenty-three years before the trial of Christ." This restriction involved the loss of the power to pass the death sentence.

This occurred after the deposition of Archelaus, the son and successor of Herod, A.D. 11, or 7 V.E. (Josephus, AJ, Book 17, Chap. 13, 1–5) The procurators, who administered in the Augustus name, took the supreme power of the Sanhedrin away so they could exercise the *jus gladii* themselves; that is, the sovereign right over life and death sentences. All the nations that were subdued by the Roman Empire were deprived of their ability to pronounce capital sentences. Tacitus writes, "The Romans reserved to themselves the right of the sword, and neglected all else."

The Sanhedrin, however, retained certain rights:

1. Excommunication (John 9:22)
2. Imprisonment (Acts 5:17, 18)
3. Corporal punishment (Acts 16:22)

The Talmud itself admits that "a little more than forty years before the destruction of the Temple, the power of pronouncing capital sentences was taken away from the Jews." (*Talmud,* Jerusalem, Sanhedrin, fol. 24, recto.) However, it hardly seems possible that the *jus gladii* remained in the Jewish hands until that time. It probably had ceased at the time of Coponius, 7 A.D. (*Essai sur l'histoire et la geographie de la Palestine, d'apres les Talmuds et la geographie de la Palestine, d'apres les Talmuds et les autres sources Rabbinique,* p. 90: Paris, 1867.) Rabbi

Once the judicial power was suppressed, the Sanhedrin ceased to be. Yes, the scepter was removed and Judah lost its royal or legal power. And the Jews knew it themselves! "Woe unto us, for the scepter has been taken from Judah, and the Messiah has not appeared!"

—THE TALMUD

Rachmon says, "When the members of the Sanhedrin found themselves deprived of their right over life and death, a general consternation took possession of them; they covered their heads with ashes, and their bodies with sackcloth, exclaiming: 'Woe unto us, for the scepter has departed from Judah, and the Messiah has not come!'" (LeMann, JBS, 28–30)

Josephus, who was an eyewitness of this decadent process, wrote, "After the death of the procurator Festus, when Albinus was about to succeed him, the high-priest Ananus considered it a favorable opportunity to assemble the Sanhedrin. He therefore caused James the brother of Jesus, who was called Christ, and several others, to appear before this hastily assembled council, and pronounced upon them the sentence of death by stoning. All the wise men and strict observers of the law who were at Jerusalem expressed their disapprobation of this act. . . . Some even went to Albinus himself, who had departed to Alexandria, to bring this breach of the law under his observation, and to inform him that Ananus had acted illegally in assembling the Sanhedrin without the Roman authority." (Josephus, AJ, Book 20, Chap. 9, Section 1)

The Jews, in order to save face, made up various reasons for eliminating the death penalty. For example, the Talmud (Bab., *Aboda Zarah,* or *Of Idolatry,* fol. 8, recto.) states, "The members of the Sanhedrin, hav-

ing noticed that the number of murderers had increased to such an extent in Israel that it became impossible to condemn them all to death, they concluded among themselves [and said], 'It will be advantageous for us to change our ordinary place of meeting for another, so that we may avoid the passing of capital sentences.'" To this, Maimonides adds in the *Const. Sanhedrin,* Chap. 14, that "forty years before the destruction of the second Temple criminal sentences ceased in Israel, although the Temple was still standing. This was due to the fact that the members of the Sanhedrin quitted the Hall Of Hewn Stones and held their sessions there no longer." (LeMann, JBS, 30–33)

Lightfoot, in *Evangelium Matthaei, horoe hebraicoe,* pp. 275, 276, Cambridge, 1658, adds that

the members of the Sanhedrin . . . had taken the resolution not to pass capital sentences as long as the land of Israel remained under the government of the Romans, and the lives of the children of Israel were menaced by them. To condemn to death a son of Abraham at a time when Judea is invaded on all sides, and is trembling under the march of the Roman legions, would it not be to insult the ancient blood of the patriarchs? Is not the least of the Israelites, by the very fact that he is a descendant of Abraham, a superior being to the Gentiles? Let us, therefore, quit the hall of hewn stones, outside of which no one can be condemned to death, and in protestation of which let us show by our voluntary exile and by the silence of justice that Rome, although ruling the world, is nevertheless mistress over neither the lives nor the laws of Judea. (Lightfoot, EM, as cited in LeMann, JBS, 33, 34, 38)

The Talmud (Bab., Sanhedrin, Chap. 4, fol. 51b) states, "Since the Sanhedrin no longer had jurisdiction in capital offenses, there is no practical utility in this ruling, which can become effective only in the days of the Messiah." (Nezikin, BT, 346)

Once the judicial power was suppressed, the Sanhedrin ceased to be. Yes, the scepter was removed and Judah lost its royal or legal power. And the Jews knew it themselves! "Woe unto us, for the scepter has been taken from Judah, and the Messiah has not appeared!" (Talmud, Bab., Sanhedrin, Chap. 4, fol. 37, recto.). Little did they realize their Messiah was a young Nazarene walking in the midst of them.

2C. The Destruction of the Temple

"And the Lord, whom you seek, will suddenly come to His temple" (Mal. 3:1).

This verse, along with four others (Ps.118:26; Dan. 9:26; Hag. 2:7–9; Zech. 11:13), demands that the Messiah come while the temple at Jerusalem is still standing. This is of great significance when we realize that the temple was destroyed in A.D. 70 and has *never* been rebuilt!

"And after the sixty-two weeks Messiah shall be cut off, but not for Himself; and the people of the prince who is to come shall destroy the city and the sanctuary" (Dan. 9:26).

This is a remarkable statement! Chronologically:

1. Messiah comes (assumed)
2. Messiah cut off (dies)
3. Destruction of city (Jerusalem) and sanctuary (the temple)

The temple and city were destroyed by Titus and his army in A.D. 70; therefore, either Messiah had already come or this prophecy was false.

3C. Fulfilled to the Day

In Daniel 9:24-27, a prophecy is given in three specific parts concerning the Messiah; it includes seventy sevens (of years), or 490 years. The first part states that at the end of sixty-nine "weeks" (or sevens), the Messiah will come to Jerusalem. (The seven and sixty-two sevens are understood as sixty-nine seven-year periods by contrast with the "seventy years" [Dan. 9:2] in the context.) The starting point of the sixty-nine weeks multiplied by seven years equals 483 years is the decree to restore and rebuild Jerusalem found in verse 25.

The second part states that after the Messiah comes, He will be cut off (idiom for His death). Then the prince to come will destroy Jerusalem and the temple and complete the seventy-times-seven, or 490, years with a final seven-year period.

All of the above, according to Daniel 19:24–26, take place after the sixty-nine weeks of years. But Daniel 19:24 mentions seventy weeks (7+62+1), not just sixty-nine. The final week is described in 9:27. Many scholars believe 9:27 discusses a different person and time than that of 9:26. Even though the author refers to the prince, the reference is probably to another prince who is to come later in history. (Double references are somewhat common in prophecy. For example, a reference may refer to King David and also later to Christ.) This is supported by their actions: The prince in 9:27 forces Jewish temple practices to stop, but the prince in 9:26 has just destroyed the temple! So this prince probably comes later after the temple is rebuilt, which has yet to occur. No matter which way one interprets the seventieth week (the last seven years of the prophecy), the first two parts of the prophecy still can be examined historically. For further study on this prophecy in Daniel, see *Chronological Aspects of the Life of Christ.* (Hoehner, CALC, 17)

1D. The Text

Seventy weeks are determined for your people and for your holy city, to finish the transgression, to make an end of sins, to make reconciliation for iniquity, to bring in everlasting righteousness, to seal up vision and prophecy, and to anoint the Most Holy.

Know therefore and understand, that from the going forth of the command to restore and build Jerusalem until Messiah the Prince, there shall be seven weeks and sixty-two weeks; the street shall be built again, and the wall, even in troublesome times.

And after the sixty-two weeks Messiah shall be cut off, but not for Himself; and the people of the prince who is to come shall destroy the city and the sanctuary. The end of it shall be with a flood, and till the end of the war desolations are determined.

Then he shall confirm a covenant with many for one week; but in the middle of the week he shall bring an end to sacrifice and offering. And on the wing of abominations shall be one who makes desolate, even until the consummation, which is determined, is poured out on the desolate. (Dan. 9:24–27)

2D. Interpretation of the Prophecy

1E. Main Features of this Prophecy

(Taken from Dr. James Rosscup's class notes, Talbot Theological Seminary, California)

Concerns Daniel's people, Israel, and Daniel's city, Jerusalem (v. 24)

Two princes mentioned:

1. Messiah (v. 25)
2. Prince to come (v. 26)

Time period of seventy weeks (v. 24)

1. As a unit (v. 24)
2. As a division of three periods: seven weeks, sixty-two weeks, and one week (vs. 25, 27)

Specified beginning of the seventy weeks (v. 25)

Messiah appears at end of sixty-nine weeks (v. 25)

Destruction of city and sanctuary by people of prince to come (v. 26)

Covenant made between Israel and the coming prince at the beginning of last week

(v. 27); this covenant is broken mid-week (v. 27).

At end of the seventy weeks, Israel will have everlasting righteousness (v. 24).

2E. Time Measure Indicated by Seventy Weeks:

Jewish concept of week

1. The Hebrew word for "week" is *shabua,* which literally means a "seven." (We should disassociate any English concept of week with the concept intended by Gabriel.) Then, in Hebrew, the idea of seventy weeks is "seventy sevens."
2. The Jews were familiar with a "seven" of both days and years. "It was, in certain respects, even more important." (McClain, DPSW, 13)
3. Leviticus 25:2–4 illustrates the above fact. Leviticus 25:8 shows that there was a multiple of a week of years.

Remembering what has been said previously, there are several reasons to believe that the seventy weeks mentioned in Daniel are seventy sevens of years.

1. Daniel had been thinking in terms of years and multiples of seven earlier in the chapter (Dan. 9:1, 2).
2. Daniel knew that the Babylonian captivity was based on violation of the Sabbatic year, and since they were in captivity for seventy years, evidently the Sabbatic year was violated 490 years (Lev. 26:32–35; 2 Chr.36:21; and Dan. 9:24).
3. The context is consistent and makes sense when we understand the seventy weeks as years.
4. *Shabua* is found in Daniel 10:2, 3. Context demands it to mean "weeks" of days. It is literally "three sevens of days." If Daniel meant days in 9:24–27, why don't we find the same form of expres-

sion as that in chapter 10? Obviously, years are meant in chapter 9.

3E. Length of Prophetic Year

The calendar year used in the Scriptures must be determined from the Scriptures themselves.

1. Historically: Compare Genesis 7:11 with Genesis 8:4, and the two of these with Genesis 7:24 and Genesis 8:3.
2. Prophetically: Many Scriptures refer to the great tribulation under various terms, but all have the common denominator of a 360-day year.

Daniel 19:27: "Midst" of the seventieth

> This decree then is the "commandment to restore and rebuild Jerusalem." There is no other decree authorizing the restoration of the city. This decree authorizes the restoration and the book of Nehemiah tells how the work was carried on.
>
> —J.D. WILSON

week (obviously 3 1/2 years) (KJV)

Daniel 7:24, 25: "a time and times and the dividing of time" (KJV) (literally 3 1/2 times)

Revelation 13:4–7: "forty and two months" (3 1/2 years) (KJV)

Revelation 12:13, 14: "a time, and times, and half a time" (KJV)

Revelation 12:6: "a thousand, two hundred and three score days" (KJV) (1,260 days or 3 1/2 years)

4E. Beginning of Seventy Weeks

There are several commandments or decrees in Israel's history that have been suggested as the *terminus a quo* (beginning) of the seventy weeks. These are:

1. The decree of Cyrus, 539 B.C. (Ezra 1:1–4).
2. The decree of Darius, 519 B.C. (Ezra 5:3–7).
3. The decree of Artaxerxes to Ezra, 457 B.C. (Ezra 7:11–16).
4. The decree of Artaxerxes to Nehemiah, 444 B.C. (Neh. 2:1–8). (Hoehner, CALC, 131)

However, the only one that appears to fit the data accurately is item four, the decree of Artaxerxes to Nehemiah.

J. D. Wilson comments on the starting point of the prophecy:

> The . . . decree is referred to in Neh. ii. It was in the twentieth year of Artaxerxes. The words of the decree are not given, but its subject matter can easily be determined. Nehemiah hears of the desolate condition of Jerusalem. He is deeply grieved. The King asks the reason. Nehemiah replies, "the city, the place of my fathers' sepulchres, lieth waste, and the gates thereof are consumed with fire." The King bids him make request. He does so promptly, asking an order from the King that "I be sent to the city that I may build it." And, as we read, he was sent, and he rebuilt Jerusalem.
>
> This decree then is the "commandment to restore and rebuild Jerusalem." There is no other decree authorizing the restoration of the city. This decree authorizes the restoration and the book of Nehemiah tells how the work was carried on. The exigencies of their various theories have led men to take some other decree for the *terminus a quo* of their calculations, but it is not apparent how any could have done so without misgivings. This decree of Neh. ii is the commandment to restore and rebuild Jerusalem; no other decree gives any permission to restore the city. All other decrees refer to the building of the temple and the temple only. (Wilson, DDWD, 141, 42)

This decree was given in 444 B.C., based on the following:

1. "In the month Nisan, in the twentieth year of King Artaxerxes" (Neh. 2:1).
2. Artaxerxes' accession was in 465 B.C.
3. There is no date specified, so according to the Jewish custom the date is understood as the first day of the month, which would be Nisan 1, 444 B.C.
4. March 5, 444 B.C. is our corresponding calendar date.

5E. End of First Seven Weeks of Years

1. It took forty-nine years to restore the city (v. 25).
2. The close of Hebrew prophecy and of the Old Testament canon in Malachi is noteworthy, marked forty-nine years after 444 B.C.

If Daniel is correct, the time from the edict to restore and rebuild Jerusalem (Nisan 1444 B.C.) to the coming of the Messiah to Jerusalem is 483 years (sixty-nine times seven), each year equaling the Jewish prophetic year of 360 days (173,880 days).

The terminal event of the sixty-nine weeks is the presentation of Christ Himself to Israel as the Messiah, as predicted in Zechariah 9:9. Harold Hoehner, who has thoroughly researched this prophecy in Daniel and the corresponding dates, calculates the date of this event:

Multiplying the sixty-nine weeks by seven years for each week by 360 days gives a total of 173,880 days. The difference between 444 B.C. and A.D. 33 then is 476 solar years. By multiplying 476 by 365.24219879 or by 365 days, 5 hours, 48 minutes, 45.975 seconds [there are 365 1/4 days in a year], one comes to 173,855 days, 6 hours, 52 minutes, 44 seconds, or 173,855 days. This leaves only 25 days to be accounted for between 444 B.C. and A.D. 33. By adding the 25 days to March 5 (of 444 B.C.), one comes to March 30 (or A.D. 33) which was Nisan 10 in A.D. 33. This is the triumphal entry of Jesus into Jerusalem. (Hoehner, CALC, 138)

6E. Interval between Weeks Sixty-nine and Seventy

After the termination of the sixty-nine weeks and before the commencement of the seventieth week, two events had to occur:

1. The "cutting off" of the Messiah (Dan. 9:26).

   Christ was crucified April 3, A.D. 33, the Friday following His triumphal entry into Jerusalem.
2. The destruction of Jerusalem and the temple (Dan. 9:26).

Wilson discusses this part of the prophecy:

After that, the Roman prince [Titus] sent an army which utterly destroyed the city and temple of Jerusalem. That destruction was complete. The temple was not simply polluted, as it was by Antiochus Epiphanes—it was destroyed. It has not been reared in Jerusalem since. The Jewish ritual was ended. It has never been restored, and it never can be. It has had no priesthood since Jerusalem fell; for every son of Aaron was slain. There can be no more priestly sacrifices, nor atonement by high priest; for in that dire disaster, the older covenant passed away. Its vitality and validity had ceased when the Lamb of God was offered upon Calvary; but for forty years the outward shell remained. That shell was removed in the destruction of Jerusalem, 70 A.D. (Wilson, DDWD, 148, 149)

3D. Summary

So Daniel prophesied accurately concerning the Messiah in his prophecy of the seventy weeks. Even if the 165 B.C. date of authorship is correct, all these events took place at least two hundred years later.

They include:

Timeline

March 4, 444 B.C.   March 30, A.D. 33
(Neh. 2:1–8)   (Zech. 9:9;
    Luke 19:28–40)   A.D. 70   (Dan. 9:27)

- - - - 69 weeks - - - -   April 3,   - - - - 1 week - - - -
(7 weeks + 62 weeks)   A.D. 33   (70th week)

        3-1/2 | 3-1/2

Weeks: 69   7 years
Years: 69 x 7 = 483
Days: 483 x 360 + 173, 880

        Destruction of
    Crucifixion   Jerusalem
- - - - 173,880 days - - - -

Decree of   Triumphal entry
Artaxerxes   into Jerusalem

1. The coming of the Messiah.
2. The death of the Messiah.
3. The destruction of Jerusalem and the temple.

The third part of the prophecy pertaining to the seventieth week is yet to occur.

5A. SUMMARY OF OLD TESTAMENT PREDICTIONS LITERALLY FULFILLED IN CHRIST

Floyd Hamilton, in *The Basis of Christian Faith* (a modern defense of the Christian religion), writes: "Canon Liddon is authority for the statement that there are in the Old Testament 332 distinct predictions which were literally fulfilled in Christ" (Hamilton, BCF, 160). Payne lists 191 in his *Encyclopedia of Biblical Prophecy.* (Payne, EBP, 665–670)

1B. His First Advent

The fact: Genesis 3:15; Deuteronomy 18:15; Psalm 89:20; Isaiah 9:6; 28:16; 32:1; 35:4; 42:6; 49:1; 55:4; Ezekiel 34:24; Daniel 2:44; Micah 4:1; Zechariah 3:8.

The time: Genesis 49:10; Numbers 24:17; Daniel 9:24; Malachi 3:1.

His divinity: Psalms 2:7, 11; 45:6, 7, 11; 72:8; 89:26, 27; 102:24–27; 110:1; Isaiah 9:6; 25:9; 40:10; Jeremiah 23:6; Micah 5:2; Malachi 3:1.

Human generation: Genesis 12:3; 18:18; 21:12; 22:18; 26:4; 28:14; 49:10; 2 Samuel 7:14; Psalms 18:4–6, 50; 22:22, 23; 29:36; 89:4; 132:11; Isaiah 11:1; Jeremiah 23:5; 33:15.

2B. His Forerunner: Isaiah 40:3; Malachi 3:1; 4:5

3B. His Nativity and Early Years

The fact: Genesis 3:15; Isaiah 7:14; Jeremiah 31:22.

The place: Numbers 24:17, 19; Micah 5:2.

Adoration by Magi: Psalm 72:10,15; Isaiah 60:3, 6.

Descent into Egypt: Hosea 11:1.

Massacre of innocents: Jeremiah 31:15.

4B. His Mission and Office

Mission: Genesis 12:3; 49:10; Numbers 24:19; Deuteronomy 18:18, 19; Psalm 21:1; Isaiah 59:20; Jeremiah 33:16.

Priest like Melchizedek: Psalm 110:4.

Prophet like Moses: Deuteronomy 18:15.

Conversion of Gentiles: Isaiah 11:10; Deuteronomy 32:43; Psalms 18:49; 19:4; 117:1; Isaiah 42:1; 45:23; 49:6; Hosea 1:10; 2:23; Joel 2:32.

Ministry in Galilee: Isaiah 9:1, 2.

Miracles: Isaiah 35:5, 6; 42:7; 53:4.

Spiritual graces: Psalm 45:7; Isaiah 11:2; 42:1; 53:9; 61:1, 2.

Preaching: Psalms 2:7; 78:2; Isaiah 2:3; 61:1; Micah 4:2.

Purification of the temple: Psalm 69:9.

5B. His Passion

Rejection by Jews and Gentiles: Psalms 2:1; 22:12, 41:5; 56:5; 69:8; 118:22, 23; Isaiah 6:9, 10; 8:14; 29:13; 53:1; 65:2.

Persecution: Psalms 22:6; 35:7, 12; 56:5; 71:10; 109:2; Isaiah 49:7; 53:3.

Triumphal entry into Jerusalem: Psalms 8:2; 118:25, 26; Zechariah 9:9.

Betrayal by own friend: Psalms 41:9; 55:13; Zechariah 13:6.

Betrayal for thirty pieces of silver: Zechariah 11:12.

Betrayer's death: Psalms 55:15, 23; 109:17.

Purchase of Potter's Field: Zechariah 11:13.

Desertion by disciples: Zechariah 13:7.

False accusation: Psalms 2:1, 2; 27:12; 35:11; 109:2.

Silence under accusation: Psalm 38:13; Isaiah 53:7.

Mocking: Psalms 22:7, 8, 16; 109:25.

Insults, buffeting, spitting, scourging: Psalm 35:15, 21; Isaiah 50:6.

Patience under suffering: Isaiah 53:7–9.

Crucifixion: Psalm 22:14, 17.

Offer of gall and vinegar: Psalm 69:21.

Prayer for enemies: Psalm 109:4.

Cries upon the Cross: Psalms 22:1; 31:5.

Death in prime of life: Psalms 89:45; 102:24.

Death with malefactors: Isaiah 53:9, 12.

Death attested by convulsions of nature: Amos 5:20; Zechariah 14:4–6.

Casting lots for garments: Psalm 22:18.

Bones not to be broken: Psalm 34:20.

Piercing: Psalm 22:16; Zechariah 12:10; 13:6.

Voluntary death: Psalm 40:6–8.

Vicarious suffering: Isaiah 53:4–6, 12; Daniel 9:26.

Burial with the rich: Isaiah 53:9.

6B. His Resurrection: Psalms 2:7; 16:8–10; 30:3; 41:10; 118:17

7B. His Ascension: Psalms 16:11; 24:7; 68:18; 110:1; 118:19

8B. His Second Advent: Psalm 50:3–6; Isaiah 9:6, 7; 66:18; Daniel 7:13, 14; Zechariah 12:10; 14:4–8

Dominion universal and everlasting: 1 Chronicles 17:11–14; Psalms 2:6–8; 8:6; 45:6-7; 72:8; 110:1–3; Isaiah 9:7; Daniel 7:14.

9

SUPPORT OF DEITY: THE RESURRECTION— HOAX OR HISTORY?

1A. INTRODUCTION

After more than seven hundred hours of studying this subject and thoroughly investigating its foundation, I have came to the conclusion that the resurrection of Jesus Christ is one of the *most wicked, vicious, heartless hoaxes ever foisted upon the minds of men,* OR it is the most fantastic fact of history.

Jesus has three basic credentials: (1) The impact of His life, through His miracles and teachings, upon history; (2) Fulfilled prophecy in His life; and (3) His resurrection. The resurrection of Jesus Christ and Christianity stand or fall together. A student at the University of Uruguay once said to me: "Professor McDowell, why can't you refute

Christianity?" I answered: "For a very simple reason: I am not able to explain away an event in history—the resurrection of Jesus."

The Resurrection as Recorded in Matthew 28:1–11 (see also Mark 16; Luke 24; John 20, 21)

1. Now after the Sabbath, as the first day of the week began to dawn, Mary Magdalene and the other Mary came to see the tomb.

2. And behold, there was a great earthquake; for an angel of the Lord descended from heaven, and came and rolled back the stone from the door, and sat on it.

3. His countenance was like lightning, and his clothing as white as snow.

4. And the guards shook for fear of him, and became like dead men.

5. But the angel answered and said to the women, "Do not be afraid; for I know that you seek Jesus who was crucified.

6. "He is not here; for He has risen, just as He said. Come, see the place where the Lord lay.

7. "And go quickly and tell His disciples that He is risen from the dead, and indeed He is going before you into Galilee, there you will see Him. Behold, I have told you."

8. So they went out quickly from the tomb with fear and great joy, and ran to bring His disciples word.

9. And as they went to tell His disciples, behold, Jesus met them, saying, "Rejoice!" So they came and held Him by the feet and worshiped Him.

10. Then Jesus said to them, "Do not be afraid. Go and tell My brethren to go to Galilee, and there they will see Me."

11. Now while they were going, behold, some of the guards came into the city and reported to the chief priests all the things that had happened.

2A. THE IMPORTANCE OF THE PHYSICAL RESURRECTION OF CHRIST

Since Jesus Himself pointed to the physical nature of His resurrection body as evidence that He had risen from the dead, and since

> Without the belief in the resurrection the Christian faith could not have come into being. The disciples would have remained crushed and defeated men. Even had they continued to remember Jesus as their beloved teacher, his crucifixion would have forever silenced any hopes of his being the Messiah. The cross would have remained the sad and shameful end of his career. The origin of Christianity therefore hinges on the belief of the early disciples that God had raised Jesus from the dead.
>
> —WILLIAM LANE CRAIG

by implication this proved His claims to be God incarnate, the assertion by critics that His body was merely immaterial undermines the deity of Christ. The empty tomb does not, by itself, prove the resurrection of Jesus any more than a body missing from a morgue proves that someone has been resurrected. The truth of Christianity is based on the bodily resurrection of Christ.

As Dr. Norman Geisler puts it, "If Christ did not rise in the same physical body that was placed in the tomb, then the resurrection loses its value as an evidential proof of His claim to be God (John 8:58; 10:30). The resurrection cannot verify Jesus' claim to be God unless He was resurrected in the body in which He was crucified. That body was a literal, physical body. Unless Jesus rose in a material body, there is no way to verify His resurrection. It loses its historically persuasive value." (Geisler, BR, 36)

3A. THE SIGNIFICANCE OF THE RESURRECTION

All but four of the major world religions are based on mere philosophical propositions. Of the four that are based on personalities rather than on a philosophical system, only Christianity claims an empty tomb for its founder. Abraham, the father of Judaism, died about 1900 B.C., but no resurrection was ever claimed for him.

Wilbur M. Smith says in *Therefore Stand:* "The original accounts of Buddha never ascribe to him any such thing as a resurrection; in fact, in the earliest accounts of his death, namely, the *Mahaparinibbana Sutta,* we read that when Buddha died it was 'with that utter passing away in which nothing whatever remains behind.'" (Smith, TS, 385)

"Professor Childers says, 'There is no trace in the *Pali* scriptures or commentaries (or so far as I know in any Pali book) of Sakya Muni having existed after his death or appearing to his disciples.' Mohammed died June 8, 632 A.D., at the age of sixty-one, at Medina, where his tomb is annually visited by thousands of devout Mohammedans. All the millions and millions of Jews, Buddhists, and Mohammedans agree that their founders have never come up out of the dust of the earth in resurrection." (Childers, as cited in Smith, TS, 385)

William Lane Craig writes: "Without the belief in the resurrection the Christian faith could not have come into being. The disciples would have remained crushed and defeated men. Even had they continued to remember Jesus as their beloved teacher, his crucifixion would have forever silenced any hopes of his being the Messiah. The cross would have remained the sad and shameful end of his career. The origin of Christianity therefore hinges on the belief of the early disciples that God had raised Jesus from the dead." (Craig, KTR, 116–17)

Theodosus Harnack says: "Where you stand with regard to the fact of the Resurrection is in my eyes no longer Christian theology. To me Christianity stands or falls with the Resurrection." (Harnack, as cited in Smith, TS, 437)

William Milligan states: "While speaking of the positive evidence of the Resurrection of our Lord, it may be further urged that the fact, if true, harmonizes all the other facts of His history." (Milligan, RL, 71)

Wilbur M. Smith concludes: "If our Lord said, frequently, with great definiteness and detail, that after He went up to Jerusalem He would be put to death, but on the third day He would rise again from the grave, and this prediction came to pass, then it has always seemed to me that everything else that our Lord ever said must also be true." (Smith, TS, 419)

It is further stated by W. J. Sparrow-Simpson:

If it be asked how the resurrection of Christ is a proof of His being the Son of God, it may be answered, first, because He rose by His own power. He had power to lay down His life, and He had power to take it again, John x.18. This is not inconsistent with the fact taught in so many other passages, that He was raised by the power of the Father, because what the Father does the Son does likewise; creation, and all other external works, are ascribed indifferently to the Father, Son and Spirit. But in the second place, as Christ had openly declared Himself to be the Son of God, His rising from the dead was the seal of God to the truth of that declaration. Had He continued under the power of death, God would thereby have disallowed His claim to be His Son; but as He raised Him from the dead, He publicly acknowledged Him; saying, "Thou art My Son, this day have I declared Thee such." (Sparrow-Simpson, RCF, 287–88)

Also, Peter's sermon on the day of Pentecost is

wholly and entirely founded on the Resurrection. Not merely is the Resurrection its principal theme, but if that doctrine were removed there would be no doctrine left. For the Resurrection is propounded as being (1) the explanation of Jesus' death; (2) prophetically anticipated as the Messianic experience; (3) apostolically witnessed; (4) the cause of the outpouring of the Spirit, and thus accounting for religious phenomena otherwise inexplicable; and (5) certifying the Messianic and Kingly position of Jesus of Nazareth. Thus the whole series of arguments and conclusions depends for stability entirely upon the Resurrection. Without the Resurrection the Messianic and Kingly position of Jesus could not be convincingly established. Without it the new outpouring of the Spirit would continue a mystery unexplained. Without it the substance of the apostolic witness would have disappeared. All that would be left of this instruction would be the Messianic exposition of Psalm xvi.; and that, only as a future experience of a Messiah who had not yet appeared. The Divine Approval of Jesus as certified by His works would also remain; but apparently as an approval extended only to His life; a life ending like that of any other prophet whom the nation refused to tolerate any longer. Thus the first Christian sermon is founded on the position of Jesus as determined by His Resurrection. (Smith, TS, 230)

Even Adolf Harnack, who rejects the church's belief in the resurrection, admits: "The firm confidence of the disciples in Jesus was rooted in the belief that He did not abide in death, but was raised by God. That Christ was risen was, in virtue of what they had experienced in Him, certainly only after they had seen Him, just as sure as the fact of His death, and became the main article of their preaching about Him." (Harnack, HD, as cited in Day, ER, 3)

H. P. Liddon says: "Faith in the resurrection is the very keystone of the arch of Christian faith, and, when it is removed, all must inevitably crumble into ruin." (Liddon, as cited in Smith, TS, 577)

Douglas Groothuis declares:

The New Testament reverberates and glistens with the reality of Jesus' resurrection. The Gospels record Jesus' teaching that he must be betrayed, killed, and rise again. Then they all testify that his tomb was empty and that he appeared to his disciples as he said. The book of Acts records the preaching of the resurrected Christ as its central fact. The various

> If the Resurrection is not historic fact, then the power of death remains unbroken, and with it the effect of sin; and the significance of Christ's Death remains uncertified, and accordingly believers are yet in their sins, precisely where they were before they heard of Jesus' name.
>
> —W. J. SPARROW-SIMPSON

New Testament letters and the book of Revelation would melt into nothingness without a resurrected Jesus. The resurrection is attested to by four separate Gospels, the history of the early church (Acts), by the letters of Paul, Peter, John, James, Jude, and the letter to the Hebrews. There is a diversity of credible witnesses. Since the New Testament volumes show considerable fitness in terms of historical reliability, . . . this is a good initial reason to accept the resurrection as an objective reality. (Groothuis, JAC, 273)

The resurrection of Christ has categorically always been the central tenet of the church. As Wilbur Smith states:

From the first day of its divinely bestowed life, the Christian church has unitedly borne testimony to its faith in the Resurrection of Christ. It is what we may call one of the great fundamental doctrines and convictions of the church, and so penetrates the literature of the New Testament, that if you lifted out every passage in which a reference is made to the Resurrection, you would have a collection of writings so mutilated that what remained could not be understood. The Resurrection entered intimately into the life of the earliest Christians; the fact of it appears on their tombs, and in the drawings found on the walls of the catacombs; it entered deeply into Christian hymnology; it became one of the most vital themes of the great apologetic writings of the first four centuries; it was the theme constantly dwelt upon in the preaching of the ante-Nicene and post-Nicene period. It entered at once into the creedal formulae of the church; it is in our Apostles' Creed; it is in all the great creeds that followed.

All evidence of the New Testament goes to show that the burden of the good news or gospel was not "Follow this Teacher and do your best," but, "Jesus and the Resurrection." You cannot take that away from Christianity without radically altering its character and destroying its very identity. (Smith, TS, 369–70)

Professor Milligan says: "It thus appears that from the dawn of her history the Christian Church not only believed in the Resurrection of her Lord, but that her belief upon the point was interwoven with her whole existence." (Milligan, RL, 170)

W. Robertson Nicoll quotes Pressensé as saying: "The empty tomb of Christ has been the cradle of the Church." (Smith, TS, 580)

W. J. Sparrow-Simpson says: "If the Resurrection is not historic fact, then the power of death remains unbroken, and with it the effect of sin; and the significance of Christ's Death remains uncertified, and accordingly believers are yet in their sins, precisely where they were before they heard of Jesus' name." (Sparrow-Simpson, as cited in Hastings, DCG, 514)

R. M'Cheyne Edgar, in his work *The Gospel of a Risen Saviour*, has said:

Here is a teacher of religion and He calmly professes to stake His entire claims upon His ability, after having been done to death, to rise again from the grave. We may safely assume that there never was, before or since, such a proposal made. To talk of this extraordinary test being *invented* by mystic students of the prophecies, and inserted in the way it has been into the gospel narratives, is to lay too great a burden on our credulity. He who was ready to stake everything on His ability to come back from the tomb stands before us as the most original of all teachers, one who shines in His own self-evidencing life! (Edgar, GRS, as cited in Smith, TS, 364)

William Lane Craig points out what the resurrection meant to the disciples:

It is difficult to exaggerate what a devastating effect the crucifixion must have had on the disciples. They had no conception of a dying, much less a rising, Messiah, for the Messiah would reign forever (cf. John 12:34). Without prior belief in the resurrection, belief in Jesus as Messiah would have been impossible in light of his death. The resurrection turned catastrophe into victory. Because God raised Jesus from the dead, he could be proclaimed as Messiah after all (Acts 2:32, 36). Similarly for the significance of the cross—it was his resurrection that enabled Jesus' shameful death to be interpreted in salvific terms. Without it, Jesus' death would have meant only humiliation and accursedness by God; but in view of the resurrection it could be seen to be the event by which forgiveness of sins was obtained. Without the resurrection, the Christian Way could never have come into being. Even if the disciples had continued to remember Jesus as their beloved teacher, they could not have believed in him as Messiah, much less deity. (Craig, DJRD, as cited in Wilkins, JUF, 159)

The following is found in the *Dictionary of the Apostolic Church*:

D. F. Strauss, e.g., the most trenchant and remorseless of her [the church's] critics in dealing with the Resurrection, acknowledges that it is the "touchstone not of lives of Jesus only, but of Christianity itself," that it "touches all Christianity to the quick," and is "decisive for the whole view of Christianity" (*New Life of Jesus*, Eng. tr., 2 vols., London, 1865, i. 41, 397). If this goes, all that is vital and essential in Christianity goes; if this remains, all else remains. And so through the centuries, from Celsus onwards, the Resurrection has been the storm centre of the attack upon the Christian faith. (Hastings, DAC, 330)

"Christ Himself," as B. B. Warfield puts it, "deliberately staked His whole claim to the credit of men upon His resurrection. When asked for a sign He pointed to this sign as His single and sufficient credential." (Warfield, as cited in Anderson, CWH, 103)

Ernest Kevan says of the famous Swiss theologian, Frederick Godet: "In his *Lectures in Defence of the Christian Faith* [1883, p. 41], [he] speaks of the importance of the resurrection of Christ, and points out that it was this miracle, and this alone, to which Christ referred as the attestation of His claims and authority." (Kevan, RC, 3)

Michael Green makes the point well:

Christianity does not hold the resurrection to be one among many tenets of belief. Without faith in the resurrection *there would be no Christianity at all*. The Christian church would never have begun; the Jesus-movement would have fizzled out like a damp squib with His execution. Christianity stands or falls with the truth of the resurrection. Once disprove it, and you have disposed of Christianity.

Christianity is a historical religion. It claims that God has taken the risk of involving Himself in human history, and the facts are there for you to examine with the utmost rigour. They will stand any amount of critical investigation." (Green, MA, 61)

John Locke, the famous British philosopher, said concerning Christ's resurrection: "Our Saviour's resurrection . . . is truly of great importance in Christianity; so great that His being or not being the Messiah stands or falls with it: so that these two important articles are inseparable and in effect make one. For since that time, believe one and you believe both; deny one of them, and you can believe neither." (Smith, TS, 423)

As Philip Schaff, the church historian, concludes: "The resurrection of Christ is therefore emphatically a test question upon which depends the truth or falsehood of the Christian religion. It is either the greatest miracle or the greatest delusion which history records." (Schaff, HCC, 173)

Wilbur M. Smith, noted scholar and teacher, says: "No weapon has ever been forged, and . . . none ever will be, to destroy rational confidence in the historical records of this epochal and predicted event. The resurrection of Christ is the very citadel of the Christian faith. This is the doctrine that turned the world upside down in the first century, that lifted Christianity preeminently above Judaism and the pagan religions of the Mediterranean world. If this goes, so must almost everything else that is vital and unique in the Gospel of the Lord Jesus Christ: 'If Christ be not risen, then is your faith vain'" (1 Cor. 15:17). (Smith, SR, 22)

Peter Kreeft and Ronald K. Tacelli describe the incredible impact of the resurrection:

The resurrection is of crucial practical importance because it completes our salvation. Jesus came to save us from sin and its consequence, death (Rom. 6:23). The resurrection also sharply distinguishes Jesus from all other religious founders. The bones of Abraham and Muhammad and Buddha and Confucius and Lao-Tzu and Zoroaster are still here on earth. Jesus' tomb is empty.

The existential consequences of the resurrection are incomparable. It is the concrete, factual, empirical proof that: life has hope and meaning; "love is stronger than death"; goodness and power are ultimately allies, not enemies; life wins in the end; God has touched us right here where we are and has defeated our last enemy; we are not cosmic orphans, as our modern secular worldview would make us. And these existential consequences of the resurrection can be seen by comparing the disciples before and after. Before, they ran away, denied their Master and huddled behind locked doors in fear and confusion. After, they were transformed from scared rabbits into confident saints, world-changing missionar-

> But when He said that He himself would rise again from the dead, the third day after He was crucified, He said something that only a fool would dare say, if he expected longer the devotion of any disciples—unless He was sure He was going to rise. No founder of any world religion known to men ever dared say a thing like that!
>
> —WILBUR SMITH

ies, courageous martyrs and joy-filled touring ambassadors for Christ. (Kreeft, HC, 177)

4A. THE CLAIMS OF CHRIST THAT HE WOULD BE RAISED FROM THE DEAD

1B. The Importance of the Claims
Wilbur M. Smith asserts:

It was this same Jesus, the Christ who, among many other remarkable things, said and repeated something which, proceeding from any other being would have condemned him at once as either a bloated egotist or a dangerously unbalanced person. That Jesus said He was going up to Jerusalem to die is not so remarkable, though all the details He gave

about that death, weeks and months before He died, are together a prophetic phenomenon. But when He said that He himself *would rise again from the dead,* the third day after He was crucified, He said something that only a fool would dare say, if he expected longer the devotion of any disciples—unless He was sure He was going to rise. No founder of any world religion known to men ever dared say a thing like that! (Smith, GCWC, 10–11)

Christ predicted His resurrection in an unmistakable and straightforward manner. While His disciples simply couldn't understand it, the Jews took His assertions quite seriously.

Concerning the above point, J. N. D. Anderson makes the following observation:

Not so very long ago there was in England a young man barrister, or what you would call a trial lawyer, by the name of Frank Morison. He was an unbeliever. For years he promised himself that one day he would write a book to disprove the resurrection finally and forever. At last he got the leisure. He was an honest man and he did the necessary study.

Eventually [after accepting Christ] he wrote a book that you can buy as a paperback, *Who Moved the Stone?* Starting from the most critical possible approach to the New Testament documents he concludes *inter alia* that you can explain the trial and the conviction of Jesus only on the basis that He Himself had foretold His death and resurrection. (Anderson, RJC, 9)

Smith says further:

If you or I should say to any group of friends that we expected to die, either by violence or naturally, at a certain time, but that, three days after death, we would rise again, we would be quietly taken away by friends, and confined to an institution, until our minds became clear and sound again. This would be right, for only a foolish man would go around talking about rising from the dead on the third day, only a foolish man, unless he knew that this was going to take place, and no one in the world has ever known that about himself except One Christ, the Son of God. (Smith, TS, 364)

Bernard Ramm remarks: "Taking the Gospel record as faithful history there can be no doubt that Christ Himself anticipated His death and resurrection, and plainly declared it to His disciples. . . . The gospel writers are quite frank to admit that such predictions really did not penetrate their minds till the resurrection was a fact (John 20:9). But the evidence is there from the mouth of our Lord that He would come back from the dead after three days. He told them that He would be put to death violently, through the cause of hatred, and would rise the third day. All this came to pass." (Ramm, PCE, 191)

John R. W. Stott writes: "Jesus Himself never predicted His death without adding that He would rise, and described His coming resurrection as a 'sign.' Paul, at the beginning of his letter to the Romans, wrote that Jesus was 'designated Son of God in power . . . by His resurrection from the dead,' and the earliest sermons of the apostles recorded in the Acts repeatedly assert that by the resurrection God has reversed man's sentence and vindicated His Son." (Stott, BC, 47)

Jesus' Predictions of His Resurrection

Matthew 12:38–40; 16:21; 17:9; 17:22, 23; 20:18, 19; 26:32; 27:63

Mark 8:31–9:1; 9:10; 9:31; 10:32–34; 14:28, 58

Luke 9:22–27

John 2:18–22; 12:34; chapters 14–16

2B. The Claims as Given by Jesus

Jesus not only predicted His resurrection but also emphasized that His rising from the dead would be the "sign" to authenticate His claims to be the Messiah (Matt. 12; John 2).

Matthew 16:21—"From that time Jesus Christ began to show to His disciples that He must go to Jerusalem, and suffer many things from the elders and chief priests and scribes, and be killed, and be raised the third day."

Matthew 17:9—"Now as they came down from the mountain, Jesus commanded them, saying, 'Tell the vision to no one until the Son of Man is risen from the dead.' "

Matthew 17:22, 23—"Now while they were staying in Galilee, Jesus said to them, 'The Son of Man is about to be betrayed into the hands of men, and they will kill Him, and the third day He will be raised up.' And they were exceedingly sorrowful."

Matthew 20:18, 19—"Behold, we are going up to Jerusalem; and the Son of Man will be betrayed to the chief priests and to the scribes; and they will condemn Him to death, and deliver Him up to the Gentiles to mock and to scourge and to crucify. And the third day He will rise again."

Matthew 26:32—"But after I have been raised, I will go before you to Galilee."

Mark 9:10—"So they kept this word to themselves, questioning what the rising from the dead meant."

Luke 9:22–27—"'The Son of Man must suffer many things, and be rejected by the elders and chief priests and scribes, and be killed, and be raised the third day.' Then He said to them all, 'If anyone desires to come after Me, let him deny himself, and take up his cross daily, and follow Me. For whoever desires to save his life will lose it, but whoever loses his life for My sake will save it. For what profit is it to a man if he gains the whole world, and is himself destroyed or lost? For whoever is ashamed of Me and My words, of him the Son of Man will be ashamed when He comes in His own glory, and in His Father's, and of the holy angels. But I tell you truly, there are some standing here who shall not taste death until they see the kingdom of God.'"

John 2:18–22—"The Jews answered and said to Him, 'What sign do You show to us, since You do these things?' Jesus answered and said to them, 'Destroy this temple, and in three days I will raise it up.' Then the Jews said, 'It has taken forty-six years to build this temple, and will You raise it up in three days?' But He was speaking of the temple of His body. Therefore, when He had risen from the dead, His disciples remembered that He had said this to them; and they believed the Scripture, and the word which Jesus had said."

5A. THE HISTORICAL APPROACH

1B. The Resurrection of Christ as a Time-Space Dimension Event in History

The resurrection of Christ is an event in history wherein God acted in a definite time-space dimension. Concerning this, Wilbur Smith says,

The *meaning* of the resurrection is a theological matter, but the fact of the resurrection is a historical matter; the nature of the resurrection body of Jesus may be a mystery, but the fact that the body disappeared from the tomb is a matter to be decided upon by historical evidence.

The place is of geographical definiteness, the man who owned the tomb was a man living in the first half of the first century; that tomb was made out of rock in a hillside near Jerusalem, and was not composed of some mythological gossamer, or cloud-dust, but is something which has geographical significance. The guards put before that tomb were not aerial beings from Mt. Olympus; the Sanhedrin was a body of men meeting frequently in Jerusalem. As a vast mass of literature tells us, this person, Jesus, was a living person, a man among men, whatever else He was, and

the disciples who went out to preach the risen Lord were men among men, men who ate, drank, slept, suffered, worked, died. What is there "doctrinal" about this? This is a historical problem. (Smith, TS, 386)

Ignatius (A.D. c. 50–115), bishop of Antioch, a native of Syria and pupil of the apostle John, is said to have "been thrown to the

> Let it simply be said that we know more about the details of the hours immediately before and the actual death of Jesus, in and near Jerusalem, than we know about the death of any other one man in all the ancient world.
>
> —WILBUR SMITH

wild beasts in the colosseum at Rome. His epistles were written during his journey from Antioch to his martyrdom" (Moyer, WWCH, 209). At a time when he would undoubtedly have been very sober of mind, he says of Christ:

He was crucified and died under Pontius Pilate. He really, and not merely in appearance, was crucified, and died, in the sight of beings in heaven, and on earth, and under the earth.

He also rose again in three days.... On the day of the preparation, then, at the third hour, He received the sentence from Pilate, the Father permitting that to happen; at the sixth hour He was crucified; at the ninth hour He gave up the ghost; and before sunset He was buried.

During the Sabbath He continued under the earth in the tomb in which Joseph of Arimathaea had laid Him.

He was carried in the womb, even as we are, for the usual period of time; and was really born, as we also are; and was in reality nourished with milk, and partook of common meat and drink, even as we do. And when He had lived among men for thirty years, He was baptized by John, really and not in appearance; and when He had preached the gospel three years, and done signs and wonders, He who was Himself the Judge was judged by the Jews, falsely so called, and by Pilate the governor; was scourged, was smitten on the cheek, was spit upon; He wore a crown of thorns and a purple robe; He was condemned: He was crucified in reality, and not in appearance, not in imagination, not in deceit. He really died, and was buried, and rose from the dead. (Ignatius, IET, as cited in Roberts, ANCL, 199–203)

The brilliant historian Alfred Edersheim speaks of the particular time of Christ's death and resurrection:

The brief spring-day was verging towards the "evening of the Sabbath." In general, the Law ordered that the body of a criminal should not be left hanging unburied overnight. Perhaps in ordinary circumstances the Jews might not have appealed so confidently to Pilate as actually to ask him to shorten the sufferings of those on the Cross, since the punishment of crucifixion often lasted not only for hours but days, ere death ensued. But here was a special occasion. The Sabbath about to open was a "high-day"—it was both a Sabbath and the second Paschal Day, which was regarded as in every respect equally sacred with the first—nay, more so, since the so-called Wavesheaf was then offered to the Lord. (Edersheim, LTJM, 612–13)

As Wilbur Smith put it: "Let it simply be said that we know more about the details of the hours immediately before and the actual death of Jesus, in and near Jerusalem, than we know about the death of any other one man in all the ancient world." (Smith, TS, 360)

"Justin Martyr (c. 100–165) philosopher, martyr, apologist. . . . Being an eager seeker for truth, knocked successively at the doors of Stoicism, Aristotelianism, Pythagoreanism and Platonism, but hated Epicureanism. . . . This zealous Platonist became a believing Christian. He said 'I found this philosophy alone to be safe and profitable.'" (Moyer, WWCH, 227)

Indeed, Justin Martyr came to realize that while the philosophical systems of the world offered intellectual propositions, Christianity alone offered God Himself intervening in time and space through Jesus Christ. In a very straightforward manner he asserts: "Christ was born one hundred and fifty years ago under Cyrenius, and subsequently, in the time of Pontius Pilate." (Martyr, as cited in Roberts, ANCL, 46)

Tertullian (c. 160–220) of Carthage, North Africa, wrote: "But the Jews were so exasperated by His teaching, by which their rulers and chiefs were convicted of the truth, chiefly because so many turned aside to Him, that at last they brought Him before Pontius Pilate, at the time Roman governor of Syria, and, by the violence of their outcries against Him, extorted a sentence giving Him up to them to be crucified." (Tertullian, WQSFT, as cited in Roberts, ANCL, 94)

Of Christ's ascension Tertullian reported: It is "a fact more certain far than the assertions of your Proculi concerning Romulus" [Proculus was a Roman senator, who affirmed that Romulus had appeared to him after his death].

All these things Pilate did to Christ: and now

in fact a Christian in his own convictions, he sent word of Him to the reigning Caesar, who was at the time Tiberius. Yes, and the Caesars too would have believed on Christ, if either the Caesars had not been necessary for the world, or if Christians could have been Caesars. His disciples also spreading over the world, did as their Divine Master bade them; and after suffering greatly themselves from the persecutions of the Jews, and with no unwilling heart, as having faith undoubting in the truth, at last by Nero's cruel sword sowed the seed of Christian blood at Rome. (Tertullian, WQSFT, as cited in Roberts, ANCL, 95)

Josephus, a Jewish historian writing at the end of the first century A.D. has this fascinating passage in *Antiquities*, 18.3.3:

Now there was about this time Jesus, a wise man, if it be lawful to call him man; for he was a doer of wonderful works, a teacher of such men as receive the truth with pleasure. He drew over to him many Jews, and also many of the Greeks. This man was the Christ. And when Pilate had condemned him to the cross, upon his impeachment by the principal man among us, those who had loved him from the first did not forsake him, for he appeared to them alive on the third day, the divine prophets having spoken these and thousands of other wonderful things about him. And even now, the race of Christians, so named from him, has not died out. (Josephus, AJ, 18.3.3).

Attempts have been made to show that Josephus could not have written this (see

> The letters addressed to the Galatians, the Corinthians, and the Romans, about the authenticity and date of which there is very little dispute, belong to the time of Paul's missionary journeys, and may be dated in the period A.D. 55–58. This brings the evidence of the resurrection of Christ still nearer to the event: the interval is the short span of twenty-five years.
>
> —ERNEST KEVAN

page 127). However "this passage," writes Michael Green in *Man Alive*, "was in the text of Josephus used by Eusebius in the fourth century." Also, it is "reiterated by the most

recent Loeb edition of his works. And it is all the more remarkable when we remember that, so far from being sympathetic to Christians, Josephus was a Jew writing to please the Romans. This story would not have pleased them in the slightest. He would hardly have included it if it were not true." (Green, MA, 35–36)

Leaney says concerning the historical nature of the faith of the early church:

The New Testament itself allows absolutely no escape from putting the matter as follows: Jesus was crucified and buried. His followers were utterly dejected. A very short time afterwards they were extremely elated and showed such reassurance as carried them by a sustained life of devotion through to a martyr's death. If we ask them through the proxy of writings dependent upon them, what caused this change, they do not answer, "the gradual conviction that we were marked out by death but the crucified and buried one was alive" but "Jesus who was dead appeared to some of us alive after his death and the rest of us believed their witness." It may be worth noting that this way of putting the matter is a historical statement, like the historical statement, "The Lord is risen indeed," which has influenced men and women toward belief. (Leaney, as cited in Hanson, A., VEHBC, 108)

Speaking of the forensic nature of the New Testament narratives, Bernard Ramm writes: "In Acts 1, Luke tells us that Jesus showed Himself alive by many infallible proofs *(en pollois tekmeriois)*, an expression indicating the strongest type of legal evidence." (Ramm, PCE, 192)

Clark Pinnock also states:

The certainty of the apostles was founded on their experiences in the factual realm. To them Jesus showed Himself alive "by many infallible proofs" (Acts 1:3). The term Luke uses is *tekmerion*, which indicates a demonstrable proof.

The disciples came to their Easter faith through inescapable empirical evidence available to them, and available to us through their written testimony. It is important for us, in an age that calls for evidence to sustain the Christian claim, to answer the call with appropriate historical considerations. For the resurrection stands within the realm of historical factuality, and constitutes excellent motivation for a person to trust Christ as Saviour. (Anderson, DCR, 11)

Ernest Kevan further establishes the evidential quality of these witnesses:

The Book of the *Acts of the Apostles* was written by Luke sometime between A.D. 63 and the fall of Jerusalem in A.D. 70. He explains in the preface to his Gospel that he gathered his information from eye-witnesses, and this, it may be concluded, was also the way in which he prepared the Book of the *Acts*. Further as certain sections in the history show, by the use of the pronoun "we," Luke was himself a participator in some of the events which he narrates. He was in the midst of the early preaching, and took a share in the great happenings of the early days. Luke is, therefore, a contemporary and first-hand witness. . . . It is impossible to suppose that the Early Church did not know its own history; and the very fact of the acceptance by the Church of this book is evidence of its accuracy. (Kevan, RC, 4–5)

Quoting a noted Christian scholar, Kevan points out: "As the Church is too holy for a foundation of rottenness, so she is too real for a foundation of myth." (Kevan, RC, 4–5)

"For the establishment of an alleged historical fact no documents are esteemed to be more valuable than contemporary letters." (Kevan, RC, 6)

Professor Kevan says of the epistles of the New Testament, "There is the unimpeachable evidence of the contemporary letters of Paul the Apostle. These epistles constitute historical evidence of the highest kind. The letters addressed to the *Galatians,* the *Corinthians,* and the *Romans,* about the authenticity and date of which there is very little dispute, belong to the time of Paul's missionary journeys, and may be dated in the period A.D. 55–58. This brings the evidence of the resurrection of Christ still nearer to the event: the interval is the short span of twenty-five years. Since Paul himself makes it plain that the subject of his letter was the same as that about which he had spoken to them when he was with them, this really brings back the evidence to a still earlier time. (Kevan, RC, 6)

Bernard Ramm says that even "the most cursory reading of the Gospels reveals the fact that the Gospels deal with the death and resurrection of Christ in far greater detail than any other part of the ministry of Christ. The details of the resurrection must not be artificially severed from the passion account." (Ramm, PCE, 191–92)

Christ made many appearances after His resurrection. These appearances occurred at specific times in the lives of specific individuals and were further restricted to specific places.

Wolfhart Pannenberg, "professor of systematic theology at the University of Munich, Germany, studied under Barth and Jaspers, and has been concerned primarily with questions of the relation between faith and history. With a small group of dynamic theologians at Heidelberg, he has been forging a theology that considers its primary task the scrutiny of the historical data of the origins of Christianity." (Anderson, DCR, 9) This brilliant scholar says, "Whether the resurrection of Jesus took place or not is a historical question, and the historical question at this point is inescapable. And so the question has to be decided on the level of historical argument." (Anderson, DCR, 10)

The New Testament scholar C. H Dodd writes, "The resurrection remains an event within history." (Straton, BLR, 3)

J. N. D. Anderson, citing Cambridge professor C. F. D. Moule, asserts,

From the very first the conviction that Jesus had been raised from death has been that by which their very existence has stood or fallen. There was no other motive to account for them, to explain them. . . . At no point within the New Testament is there any evidence that the Christians stood for an original philosophy of life or an original ethic. Their sole function is to bear witness to what they claim as an event—the raising of Jesus from among the dead. . . . The one really distinctive thing for which the Christians stood was their declaration that Jesus had been raised from the dead according to God's design, and the consequent estimate of Him as in a unique sense Son of God and representative man, and the resulting conception of the way to reconciliation. (Anderson, CWH, 100–101)

J. Sparrow-Simpson says:

The Resurrection of Christ is *the foundation of Apostolic Christianity,* and this for dogmatic just as truly as for evidential reasons. . . . Their consciousness of its basal character is shown in the position it occupies in their witness. An Apostle is ordained to be a witness of the Resurrection (Acts 1:22). The content of St. Paul's Christianity is thought at Athens to be "Jesus and the resurrection" (17:18). The early sections in the Acts reiterate the statement, "This Jesus hath God raised up, whereof we all are witnesses." (Anderson, CWH, 32)

As a historic fact, it has been His Resurrection that has enabled men to believe in His official exaltation over humanity. It is not a mere question of the moral influence of His character, example, and teaching. It is that their present surrender to Him as their Redeemer has been promoted by this belief, and could not be justified without it. Indeed, those who deny His Resurrection consistently deny as a rule His Divinity and His redemptive work in any sense that St. Paul would have acknowledged. (Sparrow-Simpson, as cited in Hastings, DCG, 513–14)

2B. The Testimony of History and Law

When an event takes place in history and there are enough people alive who were eyewitnesses of it or had participated in the event, and when the information is published, one is able to verify the validity of an historical event (circumstantial evidences).

William Lyon Phelps, for more than forty years Yale's distinguished professor of English literature, author of some twenty volumes of literary studies, and a public orator of Yale, says:

In the whole story of Jesus Christ, the most important event is the resurrection. Christian faith depends on this. It is encouraging to know that it is explicitly given by all four evangelists and told also by Paul. The names of those who saw Him after His triumph over death are recorded; and it may be said that the historical evidence for the resurrection is stronger than for any other miracle anywhere narrated; for as Paul said, if Christ is not risen from the dead then is our preaching in vain, and your faith is also vain. (Phelps, as cited in Smith, GCWC, 18)

Ambrose Fleming, emeritus professor of Electrical Engineering at the University of London, was an honorary fellow of St. John's College, Cambridge, recipient of the Faraday medal in 1928, and one of England's outstanding scientists. He says of the New Testament documents:

We must take this evidence of experts as to the age and authenticity of this writing, just as we take the facts of astronomy on the evidence of astronomers who do not contradict each other. This being so, we can ask ourselves whether it is probable that such a book, describing events that occurred about thirty or forty years previously, could have been

> I have been used for many years to study the histories of other times, and to examine and weigh the evidence of those who have written about them, and I know of no one fact in the history of mankind which is proved by better and fuller evidence of every sort, to the understanding of a fair inquirer, than the great sign which God hath given us that Christ died and rose again from the dead.
>
> —THOMAS ARNOLD,
> OXFORD UNIVERSITY

accepted and cherished if the stories of abnormal events in it were false or mythical. It is impossible, because the memory of all elderly persons regarding events of thirty or forty years before is perfectly clear.

No one could now issue a biography of Queen Victoria, who died thirty-one years ago, full of anecdotes which were quite untrue. They would be contradicted at once. They would certainly not be generally accepted and passed on as true. Hence, there is a great improbability that the account of the resurrection given by Mark, which agrees substantially with that given in the other Gospels, is a pure invention. This mythical theory has had to be abandoned because it will not bear close scrutiny. (Fleming, as cited in Smith, TS, 427–28)

Ambrose Fleming asserts that there is nothing in the Gospels that would cause a man of science to have problems with the miracles contained therein, and concludes with a challenge to intellectual honesty, asserting that if such a "study is pursued with what eminent lawyers have called a

willing mind, it will engender a deep assurance that the Christian Church is not founded on fictions, or nourished on delusions, or, as St. Peter calls them, 'cunningly devised fables,' but on historical and actual events, which, however strange they may be, are indeed the greatest events which have ever happened in the history of the world." (Fleming, as cited in Smith, TS, 427–28)

In his book that has become a bestseller, *Who Moved the Stone?*, Frank Morison, a lawyer,

tells us how he had been brought up in a rationalistic environment, and had come to the opinion that the resurrection was nothing but a fairy tale happy ending which spoiled the matchless story of Jesus. Therefore, he planned to write an account of the last tragic days of Jesus, allowing the full horror of the crime and the full heroism of Jesus to shine through. He would, of course, omit any suspicion of the miraculous, and would utterly discount the resurrection. But when he came to study the facts with care, he had to change his mind, and he wrote his book on the other side. His first chapter is significantly called, "The Book that Refused to Be Written," and the rest of his volume consists of one of the shrewdest and most attractively written assessments I have ever read. (Morison, WMS, as cited in Green, MA, 54–55)

The noted scholar, Edwin Gordon Selwyn, says: "The fact that Christ rose from the dead on the third day in full continuity of body and soul—that fact seems as secure as historical evidence can make it." (Selwyn, as cited in Smith, GCWC, 14)

Thomas Arnold, cited by Wilbur Smith, was for fourteen years the famous headmaster of Rugby, author of the famous three-volume *History of Rome,* appointed to the chair of modern history at Oxford, and certainly a man well acquainted with the value of evidence in determining historical facts. This great scholar said:

> The evidence for our Lord's life and death and resurrection may be, and often has been, shown to be satisfactory; it is good according to the common rules for distinguishing good evidence from bad. Thousands and tens of thousands of persons have gone through it piece by piece, as carefully as every judge summing up on a most important cause. I have myself done it many times over, not to persuade others but to satisfy myself. I have been used for many years to study the histories of other times, and to examine and weigh the evidence of those who have written about them, and I know of no one fact in the history of mankind which is proved by better and fuller evidence of every sort, to the understanding of a fair inquirer, than the great sign which God hath given us that Christ died and rose again from the dead. (Arnold, as cited in Smith, TS, 425–26)

Simon Greenleaf (1783–1853) was the famous Royall Professor of Law at Harvard University and succeeded Justice Joseph Story as the Dane Professor of Law in the same university upon Story's death in 1846.

H. W. H. Knott says of this great authority in jurisprudence: "To the efforts of Story and Greenleaf is to be ascribed the rise of the Harvard Law School to its eminent position among the legal schools of the United States." (Knott, as cited in Smith, TS, 423)

Greenleaf produced a famous work entitled *A Treatise on the Law of Evidence* that "is still considered the greatest single authority on evidence in the entire literature of legal procedure." (Smith, TS, 423)

In 1846, while still professor of law at Harvard, Greenleaf wrote a volume entitled *An Examination of the Testimony of the Four Evangelists by the Rules of Evidence Administered in the Courts of Justice.* In this classic work the author examines the value of the testimony of the apostles to the resurrection of Christ. The following are this brilliant jurist's critical observations:

> The great truths which the apostles declared, were, that Christ had risen from the dead, and that only through repentance from sin, and faith in Him, could men hope for salvation. This doctrine they asserted with one voice, everywhere, not only under the greatest discouragements, but in the face of the most appalling errors that can be presented to the mind of man. Their master had recently perished as a malefactor, by the sentence of a public tribunal. His religion sought to overthrow the religions of the whole world. The laws of every country were against the teachings of His disciples. The interests and passions of all the rulers and great men in the world were against them. The fashion of the world was against them.
>
> Propagating this new faith, even in the most inoffensive and peaceful manner, they could expect nothing but contempt, opposition, revilings, bitter persecutions, stripes, imprisonments, torments, and cruel deaths. Yet this faith they zealously did propagate; and all these miseries they endured undismayed, nay, rejoicing. As one after another was put to a miserable death, the survivors only prosecuted their work with increased vigor and resolution. The annals of military warfare afford scarcely an example of the like heroic constancy, patience, and unblenching courage. They had every possible motive to review carefully the grounds of their faith, and the evidences of the great facts and truths which they asserted; and these motives were pressed upon their attention with the most melancholy and terrific frequency.
>
> It was therefore impossible that they could have persisted in affirming the truths they have narrated, had not Jesus actually risen from the dead, and had they not known this fact as certainly as they knew any other fact. If it were morally possible for them to have been

deceived in this matter, every human motive operated to lead them to discover and avow their error. To have persisted in so gross a falsehood, after it was known to them, was not only to encounter, for life, all the evils which man could inflict, from without, but to endure also the pangs of inward and conscious guilt; with no hope of future peace, no testimony of a good conscience, no expectation of honor or esteem among men, no hope of happiness in this life, or in the world to come.

Such conduct in the apostles would moreover have been utterly irreconcilable with the fact that they possessed the ordinary constitution of our common nature. Yet their lives do show them to have been men like all others of our race; swayed by the same motives, animated by the same hopes, affected by the same joys, subdued by the same sorrows, agitated by the same fears, and subject to the same passions, temptations, and infirmities, as ourselves. And their writings show them to have been men of vigorous understandings. If then their testimony was not true, there was no possible motive for its fabrication. (Greenleaf, TE, 28–30)

John Locke was probably the greatest philosopher of his century. In his work, *A Second Vindication of the Reasonableness of Christianity, Works,* this British scholar writes:

There are some particulars in the history of our Saviour, allowed to be so peculiarly appropriated to the Messiah, such innumerable marks of Him, that to believe them of Jesus of Nazareth was in effect the same as to believe Him to be the Messiah, and so are put to express it. The principal of these is His Resurrection from the dead; which being the great and demonstrative proof of His being the Messiah, it is not at all strange that those believing His Resurrection should be put forth for believing Him to be the Messiah; since the declaring His Resurrection was declaring Him to be the Messiah. (Locke, SVRC, as cited in Smith, TS, 422–23)

Brooke Foss Westcott (1825–1901), English scholar who was appointed regius professor at Cambridge in 1870, said; "Indeed, taking all the evidence together, it is not too much to say that there is no historic incident better or more variously supported than the resurrection of Christ. Nothing but the antecedent assumption that it must be false could have suggested the idea of deficiency in the proof of it." (Little, KWhyB, 70)

Clifford Herschel Moore, professor at Harvard University, well said, "Christianity knew its Saviour and Redeemer not as some god whose history was contained in a mythical faith, with rude, primitive, and even offensive elements. . . . Jesus was a historical not a mythical being. No remote or foul myth obtruded itself of the Christian believer; his faith was founded on positive, historical, and acceptable facts." (Moore, as cited in Smith, GCWC, 48)

Benjamin Warfield of Princeton expressed in his article, "The Resurrection of Christ an Historical Fact, Evinced by Eye-Witnesses": "The Incarnation of an Eternal God is Necessarily a Dogma; no human eye could witness His stooping to man's estate, no human tongue could bear witness to it as a fact and yet, if it be not a fact, our faith is vain, we are yet in our sins. On the other hand the Resurrection of Christ is a fact, an external occurrence within the cognizance of man, to be established by other testimonies and yet which is the cardinal doctrine of our system: on it all other doctrines hang." (Warfield, RCHF, as cited in Smith, TS, 361–62)

Wilbur Smith introduces an outstanding scholar of this century:

One of the greatest physiologists of our generation is Dr. A. C. Ivy, of the Department of Chemical Science of the University of Illinois (Chicago Campus), who served as head of the Division of Physiology in Chicago Professional Colleges, 1946–1953. President of the American Physiological Society from 1939–1949 and author of many scientific articles, his words are wholesome: "I believe in the bodily resurrection of Jesus Christ. As you say, this is a 'personal matter,' but I am not ashamed to let the world know what I believe, and that I can intellectually defend my belief. . . . I cannot prove this belief as I can prove certain scientific facts in my library which one hundred years ago were almost as mysterious as the resurrection of Jesus Christ. On the basis of historical evidence of existing biological knowledge, the scientist who is true to the philosophy of science can doubt the bodily resurrection of Jesus Christ, but he cannot deny it. Because to do so means that he can prove that it *did not* occur. I can only say that present-day biological science cannot resurrect a body that has been dead and entombed for three days. To deny the resurrection of Jesus Christ on the basis of what biology now knows is to manifest an unscientific attitude according to my philosophy of the true scientific attitude." (Ivy, as cited in Smith, SR, 6, 22)

Armand Nicholi of Harvard Medical School speaks of J. N. D. Anderson as "a scholar of international repute and one eminently qualified to deal with the subject of evidence. He is one of the world's leading authorities on Islamic law. . . . He is dean of the faculty of law in the University of London, chairman of the department of Oriental law at the School of Oriental and African Studies, and director of the Institute of Advanced Legal Studies in the University of London." (Nicholi, as cited in Anderson, RJC, 4)

This outstanding British scholar who is today influential in the field of international jurisprudence says: "The evidence for the historical basis of the Christian faith, for the essential validity of the New Testament witness to the person and teaching of Christ Himself, for the fact and significance of His atoning death, and for the historicity of the empty tomb and the apostolic testimony to the resurrection, is such as to provide an adequate foundation for the venture of faith." (Anderson, CWH, 106)

Two able young men, Gilbert West and Lord Lyttleton, went up to Oxford. They were friends of Dr. Johnson and Alexander Pope, in the swim of society. They were determined to attack the very basis of the Christian faith. So Lyttleton settled down to prove that Saul of Tarsus was never converted to Christianity, and West to demonstrate that Jesus never rose from the tomb.

Some time later, they met to discuss their findings. Both were a little sheepish. For they had come independently to similar and disturbing conclusions. Lyttleton found, on examination, that Saul of Tarsus *did* become a radically new man through his conversion to Christianity; and West found that the evidence pointed unmistakably to the fact that Jesus did rise from the dead. You may still find his book in a large library. It is entitled *Observations on the History and Evidences of the Resurrection of Jesus Christ,* and was published in 1747. On the fly-leaf he has had printed his telling quotation from Ecclesiasticus 11:7, which might be adopted with profit by any modern agnostic: *"Blame not before thou hast examined the truth."* (Green, MA, 55–56)

The evidence points unmistakably to the fact that on the third day Jesus rose. This was the conclusion to which a former Chief Justice of England, Lord Darling, came. At a private dinner party the talk turned to the truth of Christianity, and particularly to a certain book dealing with the resurrection. Placing his fingertips together, assuming a judicial attitude, and speaking with a quiet emphasis that was extraordinarily impressive, he said, "We, as Christians, are asked to take a very great deal on trust; the teachings, for example, and the miracles of Jesus. If we had to take all on trust, I, for one, should be sceptical. The crux of the problem of whether Jesus was, or was not, what He proclaimed Himself to be, must surely depend upon the truth or otherwise of the resurrection. On that greatest point we are not merely asked to have faith. In its favour as living truth there exists such overwhelming evidence, positive and negative, factual and circumstantial, that no intelligent jury in the world could fail to bring in a verdict that the resurrection story is true." (Green, MA, 53–54)

3B. The Testimony of the Early Church Fathers

W. J. Sparrow-Simpson says that "next to Christology, the Resurrection is undoubtedly the doctrine which held the chief place in early Christian literature. The sub-apostolic age presents many references, but the second century yields treatises exclusively devoted to it; as, for instance, Athenagoras, and the work ascribed to Justin Martyr." (Sparrow-Simpson, RCF, 339)

Bernard Ramm comments: "In both ecclesiastical history and creedal history the resurrection is affirmed from the earliest times. It is mentioned in Clement of Rome, *Epistle to the Corinthians* (A.D. 95), the earliest document of church history and so continuously throughout all of the patristic period. It appears in all forms of the *Apostles' Creed* and is never debated." (Ramm, PCE, 192)

Sparrow-Simpson says:

> The substance of Ignatius' Gospel [c. 5–c. 115] is Jesus Christ, and the Christian religion consists in "faith in Him and love toward Him, in His Passion and Resurrection." He enjoins upon Christians to "be fully convinced of the birth and passion and resurrection." Jesus Christ is described as "our hope through the Resurrection." The Resurrection of Jesus is the promise of our Resurrection also. (Sparrow-Simpson, RCF, 339)

Sparrow-Simpson adds: "In the Epistle of S. Polycarp to the Philippians (about A.D. 110) the writer speaks of our Lord Jesus Christ having 'endured to come so far as to death for our sins, whom God raised, having loosed the pains of death.' He says that God 'raised our Lord Jesus Christ from the dead and gave Him glory and a throne on His right hand, to Whom were subjected all things in heaven and on earth.' The Risen Jesus 'is coming as Judge of quick and dead.'

And 'He that raised Him from the dead will raise us also, if we do His will and walk in His commandments.'

"To S. Polycarp the exalted Jesus is 'the Eternal High Priest.' And the saintly bishop's final prayer before his martyrdom was that he 'might take a portion in the number of the martyrs in the cup of Christ, to the resurrection of eternal life both of soul and body in the incorruption of the Holy Ghost.'" (Sparrow-Simpson, RCF, 341)

Professor Sparrow-Simpson says of Justin Martyr's treatise on the resurrection (c. 100–165): It "deals with distinctively Christian doctrine. Contemporary opposition to the faith asserted that the Resurrection was impossible; undesirable, since the flesh is the cause of sins; inconceivable, since there can be no meaning in the survival of existing organs. They further maintained that the Resurrection of Christ was only in physical appearance and not in physical reality. To these objections and difficulties Justin . . . [made reply]." (Sparrow-Simpson, RCF, 342)

Elgin Moyer, in *Who Was Who in Church History*, mentions another church father, Quintus Septimius Florens Tertullian: "(c. 160–220) Latin church father and apologist, born in Carthage, North Africa. . . . Thorough education prepared him for successful writing in both Greek and Latin, as well as for politics, the practice of law, and forensic eloquence. For thirty or forty years lived in licentiousness. In about 190 he embraced Christianity with deep conviction. The rest of his life faithfully devoted to defending the Christian faith against heathen, Jew, and heretic. He was . . . a strong defender of the faith." (Moyer, WWCH, 401)

Bernard Ramm concludes: "Unbelief has to deny all the testimony of the Fathers. . . . It must assume that these men either did not have the motivation or the historical standards to really investigate the resurrection of Christ. The Fathers, considered by the Eastern Orthodox Catholic Church and by the Roman Catholic Church and Anglican Church as authoritative or highly authoritative, respected by the Reformers, and given due weight by all theologians, *are written off the record by unbelief.* They are deemed trustworthy for data about apostolic or near-apostolic theology, yet in matters of fact they are not granted a shred of evidential testimony. But this must be, or unbelief cannot make its case stick." (Ramm, PCE, 206)

6A. THE RESURRECTION SCENE

1B. The Pre-Resurrection Scene

1C. Jesus Was Dead

The whipping of a victim prior to crucifixion is described by John Mattingly: "The

> And wishing to satisfy the multitude, Pilate released Barabbas for them, and after having Jesus scourged, he delivered Him over to be crucified. And the soldiers took Him away into the palace (that is, the Praetorium), and they called together the whole Roman cohort. And they dressed Him up in purple, and after weaving a crown of thorns, they put it on Him; and they began to acclaim Him, "Hail, King of the Jews!" And they kept beating His head with a reed, and spitting at Him, and kneeling and bowing before Him. And after they had mocked Him, they took the purple off Him, and put His garments on Him. And they led Him out to crucify Him. —Mark 15:15–20

adjudged criminal was usually first forcefully stripped of his clothes, and then tied to a post or pillar in the tribunal. Then the awful and cruel scourging was administered by the lictors or scourgers. Although the Hebrews limited by their law the number of strokes in a scourging to forty, the Romans set no such limitation; and the victim was at the mercy of his scourgers."

The brutal instrument used to scourge the victim was called a flagrum. Of this device Mattingly comments: "It can readily be seen that the long, lashing pieces of bone and metal would greatly lacerate human flesh." (Mattingly, COAC, 21)

Bishop Eusebius of Caesarea, the church historian of the third century, said *(Epistle of the Church in Smyrna)* concerning the Roman scourging inflicted on those to be executed: the sufferer's "veins were laid bare, and . . . the very muscles, sinews, and bowels of the victim were open to exposure." (Mattingly, COAC, 73)

John Mattingly, citing John Peter Lange, says of Christ's sufferings: "It has been conjectured that [His] scourging even surpassed the severity of the normal one. Although the normal scourging was administered by lictors, Lange concludes that since there were no lictors at Pilate's disposal, he used the soldiers. Thus, from the very character of these low, vile soldiers, it may be supposed that they exceeded the brutality meted out by the lictors." (Mattingly, COAC, 33)

After suffering the most intense forms of physical punishment, Christ also had to endure the journey to the place of crucifixion—Golgotha. Of this stage of Christ's sufferings Mattingly relates:

1. Even the preparation for the journey must have been a source of acute agony. Matthew 27:31 reads: "And when they had mocked Him, they took the robe off from Him and put His own raiment on Him, and led Him away to crucify Him." The rude stripping of the mock royal garments and the replacing of His own garments, undoubtedly on contact with the cut and bruised skin from the

scourging, resulted in great pain. (Mattingly, COAC, 35)

2. The phrase "And they bring him unto the place Golgotha" (Mark 15:22a) would also indicate that Christ, unable to walk under His own power, had to be literally brought or borne along to the place of execution. Thus, the revolting and horrifying pre-cross sufferings were brought to a close, and the actual act of crucifying began. (Mattingly, COAC, 36)

Of the crucifixion itself, Mattingly says: "It cannot be overemphasized that the sufferings endured on the cross were extremely intense and severe. The abominableness of this torture was realized by Rome's most famous orator, Marcus Tullius Cicero, who said, 'Even the mere word, cross, must remain far not only from the lips of the citizens of Rome, but also from their thoughts, their eyes, their ears' [Marcus Tullius Cicero, *Pro Rabirio*, V, 16]." (Mattingly, COAC, 26)

Michael Green says of Jesus' physical sufferings: "After a sleepless night, in which He was given no food, endured the mockery of two trials, and had His back lacerated with the cruel Roman cat-o'-nine-tails, He was led out to execution by crucifixion. This was an excruciatingly painful death, in which every nerve in the body cried aloud in anguish." (Green, MA, 32)

Frederick Farrar gives a vivid description of death by crucifixion:

For indeed a death by crucifixion seems to include all that pain and death *can* have of horrible and ghastly—dizziness, cramp, thirst, starvation, sleeplessness, traumatic fever, tetanus, shame, publicity of shame, long continuance of torment, horror of anticipation, mortification of untended wounds—all intensified just up to the point at which they can be endured at all, but all stopping just short of the point which would give to the sufferer the relief of unconsciousness.

The unnatural position made every movement painful; the lacerated veins and crushed tendons throbbed with incessant anguish; the wounds, inflamed by exposure, gradually gangrened; the arteries—especially at the head and stomach—became swollen and oppressed

And they brought Him to the place Golgotha, which is translated, Place of a Skull. Then they gave Him wine mingled with myrrh to drink; but He did not take it. And when they crucified Him, they divided His garments, casting lots for them to determine what every man should take. Now it was the third hour, and they crucified Him. And the inscription of His accusation was written above: THE KING OF THE JEWS. With Him they also crucified two robbers, one on His right and the other on His left. And those who passed by blasphemed Him, wagging their heads and saying, "Aha! You who destroy the temple and build it in three days, save Yourself, and come down from the cross!" Likewise the chief priests also, mocking among themselves with the scribes, said, "He saved others; Himself He cannot save. Let the Christ, the King of Israel, descend now from the cross, that we may see and believe." Even those who were crucified with Him reviled Him. Now when the sixth hour had come, there was darkness over the whole land until the ninth hour. And at the ninth hour Jesus cried out with a loud voice, saying, "Eloi, Eloi, lama sabachthani?" which is translated, "My God, My God, why have You forsaken me?" Some of those who stood by, when they heard that, said, "Look, He is calling for Elijah!" Then someone ran and filled a sponge full of sour wine, put it on a reed, and offered it to Him to drink, saying, "Let Him alone; let us see if Elijah will come to take Him down." And Jesus cried out with a loud voice, and breathed His last. Then the veil of the temple was torn in two from top to bottom. So when the centurion, who stood opposite Him, saw that He cried out like this and breathed His last, he said, "Truly this man was the Son of God!'" (Mark 15:22–27, 29–39) with surcharged blood; and while each variety of misery went on gradually increasing, there was added to them the intolerable pang of a burning and raging thirst; and all these physical complications caused an internal excitement and anxiety, which made the prospect of death itself—of death, the unknown enemy, at whose approach man usually shudders most—bear the aspect of a delicious and exquisite release. (Farrar, LC, 440)

E. H. Day relates: "It is St. Mark who lays stress upon Pilate's wonder at hearing that Christ was already dead, and upon his personal questioning of the centurion before he

> Clearly, the weight of historical and medical evidence indicates that Jesus was dead before the wound to His side was inflicted and supports the traditional view that the spear, thrust between His right ribs, probably perforated not only the right lung but also the pericardium and heart and thereby ensured His death. Accordingly, interpretations based on the assumption that Jesus did not die on the cross appear to be at odds with modern medical knowledge.
>
> —WILLIAM D. EDWARDS, M.D.

would give leave for the removal of the body from the Cross. The Roman soldiers were not unfamiliar with the evidences of death, or with the sight of death following upon crucifixion." (Day, ER, 46–48)

As Michael Green points out, crucifixions were "not uncommon in Palestine." (Green, MA, 32)

Pilate required certification of Christ's death. Of this Green remarks: "Four executioners came to examine him, before a friend, Joseph of Arimathea, was allowed to take away the body for burial." (Green, MA, 32)

Green says of these four specialists who were accustomed to dealing with death:

"They knew a dead man when they saw one—and their commanding officer had heard the condemned man's death cry himself and certified the death to the governor, Pontius Pilate." [And when the centurion, who was standing right in front of Him, saw the way He breathed His last, he said, 'Truly this man was the Son of God' (Mark 15:39)! "And Pilate wondered if He was dead by this time, and summoning the centurion, he questioned him as to whether He was already dead (Mark 15:44)."] (Green, MA, 32–33)

John R. W. Stott writes: "Pilate was indeed surprised that Jesus was already dead, but he was sufficiently convinced by the centurion's assurance to give Joseph permission to remove the body from the cross." (Stott, BC, 49)

Day observes that "the account in St. Matthew's Gospel of the guarding of the sepulchre is clear evidence that the Jews, for their part, believed that Jesus was dead." (Day, ER, 46–48)

Day further points out that none "of those who were occupied with the taking down of the body, and its laying in the grave, [had] any suspicion that life remained." (Day, ER, 46–48)

Professor Day, speaking of the volume *The Physical Cause of the Death of Christ*, says that its author, James Thompson, "demonstrates that the death of Christ was due, not to physical exhaustion, or to the pains of crucifixion, but to agony of mind producing rupture of the heart. His energy of mind and body in the act of dissolution proves beyond contradiction that His death was not the result of exhaustion; the soldier's spear was the means to exhibiting to the world that His death was due to a cardiac rupture." (Day, ER, 48–49)

An article in the *Journal of the American Medical Association* concluded from the Gospel accounts that Jesus certainly had died before He was removed from the cross: "Clearly, the weight of historical and medical evidence indicates that Jesus was dead before the wound to His side was inflicted and supports the traditional view that the spear, thrust between His right ribs, probably perforated not only the right lung but also the pericardium and heart and thereby ensured His death. Accordingly, interpretations based on the assumption that Jesus did not die on the cross appear to be at odds with modern medical knowledge." (Edwards, PDJC, 1463)

Samuel Houghton, M.D., the great physiologist from the University of Dublin, relates his view on the physical cause of Christ's death:

When the soldier pierced with his spear the side of Christ, He was already dead; and the flow of blood and water that followed was either a natural phenomenon explicable by natural causes or it was a miracle. That St. John thought it, if not to be miraculous, at least to be unusual, appears plainly from the comment he makes upon it, and from the emphatic manner in which he solemnly declares his accuracy in narrating it.

Repeated observations and experiments made upon men and animals have led me to the following results—When the left side is freely pierced after death by a large knife, comparable in size with a Roman spear, three distinct cases may be noted:

1st. No flow of any kind follows the wound, except a slight trickling of blood.

2nd. A copious flow of blood only follows the wound.

3rd. A flow of water only, succeeded by a few drops of blood, follows the wound.

Of these three cases, the first is that which usually occurs; the second is found in cases of death by drowning and by strychnia, and may be demonstrated by destroying an animal with that poison, and it can be proved to be the natural case of a crucified person; and the third is found in cases of death from pleurisy, pericarditis, and rupture of the heart. With the foregoing cases most anatomists who have devoted their attention to this subject are familiar; but the two following cases, although readily explicable on physiological principles, are not recorded in the books (except by St. John). Nor have I been fortunate enough to meet with them.

4th. A copious flow of water, succeeded by a copious flow of blood, follows the wound.

5th. A copious flow of blood, succeeded by a copious flow of water, follows the wound.

Death by crucifixion causes a condition of blood in the lungs similar to that produced by drowning and strychnia; the fourth case would occur in a crucified person who had previously to crucifixion suffered from pleuritic effusion; and the fifth case would occur in a crucified person, who had died upon the cross from rupture of the heart. The history of the days preceding our Lord's crucifixion effectually excludes the supposition of pleurisy, which is also out of the question if blood first and water afterwards followed the wound. There remains, therefore, no supposition possible to explain the recorded phenomenon except *the combination of the crucifixion and rupture of the heart.*

That rupture of the heart was the cause of

The remarkable Circumstance of wrapping up the dead Body in Spices, by Joseph and Nicodemus, according to the Manner of the Jews in burying, is full Proof that Jesus was dead, and known to be dead. Had there indeed been any Remains of Life in Him, when taken down from the Cross, the pungent Nature of the Myrrh and Aloes, their strong Smell, their Bitterness, their being wrapped round His Body in Linens with a Roller, and over His Head and Face with a Napkin, as was the Custom of the Jews to bury, must have entirely extinguished them.

—SAMUEL CHANDLER

the death of Christ is ably maintained by Dr. William Stroud; and that rupture of the heart actually occurred I firmly believe." (Houghton, as cited in Cook, CHB, 349–50)

The apostle John records a minutely detailed description of his observations at Golgotha. Houghton concludes: "The importance of this is obvious. It [shows] that the narrative in St. John xix. could never have been invented; that the facts recorded must have been seen by an eyewitness; and that the eyewitness was so astonished that he apparently thought the phenomenon miraculous." (Houghton, as cited in Cook, CHB, 349–50)

Michael Green writes of Christ's death:

> We are told on eyewitness authority that "blood and water" came out of the pierced side of Jesus (John 19:34, 35). The eyewitness clearly attached great importance to this. Had Jesus been alive when the spear pierced His side, strong spouts of blood would have emerged with every heart beat. Instead, the observer noticed semi-solid dark red clot seeping out, distinct and separate from the accompanying watery serum. This is evidence of massive clotting of the blood in the main arteries, and is exceptionally strong medical proof of death. It is all the more impressive because the evangelist could not possibly have realized its significance to a pathologist. The "blood and water" from the spear-thrust is proof positive that Jesus was already dead. (Green, MA, 33)

Samuel Chandler says: "All the Evangelists agree, that Joseph had begged the body of Jesus off Pilate; who finding from the Centurion, who guarded the Cross, that He had been . . . sometime dead, gave it to him." (Chandler, RJC, 62–63)

Chandler then asserts that "the remarkable Circumstance of wrapping up the dead Body in Spices, by Joseph and Nicodemus, according to the Manner of the Jews in burying, is full Proof that Jesus was dead, and known to be dead. Had there indeed been any Remains of Life in Him, when taken down from the Cross, the pungent Nature of the Myrrh and Aloes, their strong Smell, their Bitterness, their being wrapped round His Body in Linens with a Roller, and over His Head and Face with a Napkin, as was the Custom of the Jews to bury, must have entirely extinguished them." (Chandler, RJC, 62–63)

As Professor Albert Roper puts it, "Jesus was crucified by Roman soldiers, crucified according to the laws of Rome, which the soldiers had to the very last degree faithfully carried out." (Roper, JRD, 33)

In conclusion, we can agree with the statement made by the apostle John concerning his observations of Christ's death as he validated his testimony of the event: "He who has seen has born witness, and his witness is true; and he knows that he is telling the truth" (John 19:35).

2C. The Tomb

Wilbur M. Smith observes that "the word for *tomb* or *sepulcher* occurs thirty-two times in these four Gospel records of the resurrection." (Smith, IFET, 38)

The tomb of Joseph of Arimathea on Easter morning was indeed a subject of much interest to the Gospel writers.

Concerning the burial given Christ, W. J. Sparrow-Simpson makes the following observation:

> The Roman practice was to leave the victim of crucifixion hanging on the cross to become the prey of birds and beasts. But who would dream of saying that there were no exceptions to this rule? Josephus [*Autobiography*, ch. 75; *Wars of the Jews*, IV, v.2] induced the Emperor

Titus to take down from the cross three crucified persons while still alive. Would any one argue that this cannot be historic because the rule was otherwise? The Jewish practice, no doubt, was the burial of the condemned. This was the Jewish law. But Josephus assures us that even the Jews themselves broke the law of burial at times. In the "Wars of the Jews," he writes: "They proceeded to that degree of impiety as to cast away their dead bodies without burial, although the Jews used to take so much care of the burial of men, that they took down those that were condemned and crucified, and buried them before the going down of the sun."

Loisy thinks that relatives might obtain permission for burial of one condemned. No relative, however, obtained it for Jesus' body: nor any of the Twelve. The three crucified men whom Josephus induced the imperial authority to take down from the cross were not relatives; they were only friends. He "remembered them as his former acquaintances." A strong case might be made out against the likelihood of Josephus' request, still more of its being granted. No one, however, appears to doubt the facts. They are constantly quoted as if they were true. Why should not Joseph of Arimathea make a similar request to Pilate? (Sparrow-Simpson, RCF, 21–22)

Henry Latham, in *The Risen Master*, gives the following information concerning Jesus' burial. He first cites

the description of the Sepulchre of our Lord when it was supposed to have been newly discovered by the Empress Helena. The account is that of Eusebius of Caesarea—the father of Church History. It is taken from his *Theophania*—a work recovered during this century, and of which a translation was published by Dr. Lee at Cambridge in 1843.

The grave itself was a cave which had evidently been hewn out; a cave that had now been cut out in the rock, and which had experienced (the reception of) no other body. For it was necessary that it, which was itself a

wonder, should have the care of that corpse only. For it is astonishing to see even this rock, standing out erect, and alone on a level land, and having only one cavern within it; lest had there been many, the miracle of Him who overcame death should have been obscured. (Latham, RM, 87–88)

Guignebert, in his work, *Jesus,* page 500, makes the following utterly unfounded statement: "The truth is that we do not know, and in all probability the disciples knew no better, where the body of Jesus had

"Now when evening had come, there came a rich man from Arimathea, named Joseph, who himself had also become a disciple of Jesus. This man went to Pilate and asked for the body of Jesus. Then Pilate commanded the body to be given to him" (Matt. 27:57, 58).

"Now when evening had come, because it was the Preparation Day, that is, the day before the Sabbath, Joseph of Arimathea, a prominent council member, who was himself waiting for the kingdom of God, coming and taking courage, went in to Pilate and asked for the body of Jesus. Pilate marveled that He was already dead; and summoning the centurion, he asked him if He had been dead for some time. So when he found out from the centurion, he granted the body to Joseph" (Mark 15:42–45).

"Now behold, there was a man named Joseph, a council member, a good and just man. He had not consented to their decision and deed. He was from Arimathea, a city of the Jews, who himself was also waiting for the kingdom of God. This man went to Pilate and asked for the body of Jesus" (Luke 23:50–52).

"And this, Joseph of Arimathea, being a disciple of Jesus, but secretly, for fear of the Jews, asked Pilate that he might take away the body of Jesus; and Pilate gave him permission. So he came and took the body of Jesus" (John 19:38).

been thrown after it had been removed from the cross, probably by the executioners. It is more likely to have been cast into the *pit* for the executed than laid in a new *tomb*." (Guignebert, J, as cited in Smith, TS, 372)

1D. Professor Guignebert makes these assertions with absolutely no supporting evidence for his claims.

2D. He totally disregards the testimony to the events as preserved in the secular and ecclesiastical literature of the first three centuries.

3D. He completely ignores the perfectly straightforward narrative of the Gospel records:

1E. Why are the following accounts given if Christ's body was not actually taken by Joseph of Arimathea?

The records speak for themselves; the body of Christ was anything but thrown into a pit for the executed!

2E. And also what about the accounts of the burial preparations?

Why are these accounts recorded if such preparations did not take place?

3E. What of the women who watched while Joseph of Arimathea and Nicodemus prepared and entombed Jesus' body?

They had "followed after, and they observed the tomb" (Luke 23:55), and were "sitting opposite the tomb" (Matt. 27:61), and they "observed where He was laid" (Mark 15:47).

These women surely knew there was a tomb. The records make this point very clear.

4E. How can one ignore the observations recorded concerning the tomb itself?

"When Joseph had taken the body . . . and

laid it in his new tomb" (Matt.27:59, 60), "which had been hewn out of the rock" (Mark 15:46), "where no one had ever lain before" (Luke 23:53), which was located "in the place where He was crucified . . . in the garden" (John 19:41).

Henry Alford, the Greek scholar, states his observations concerning the evidence contained in the Gospel accounts: "Matthew alone relates that it was Joseph's *own* tomb. John, that it was *in a garden,* and *in the place where he was crucified.* All, except Mark, notice the *newness* of the tomb. John does not mention that it *belonged to Joseph.*" (Alford, GTCRT, 298–99)

Of Joseph of Arimathea, he writes: "His reason for the body being laid there is that *it was near,* and the preparation rendered haste necessary." (Alford, GTCRT, 298–99)

Concluding from Alford's comments, then, the evidence "that we can determine respecting the sepulchre from the data here furnished, is (1) That it was not a *natural* cave, but an *artificial excavation in the rock.*

"When Joseph had taken the body, he wrapped it in a clean linen cloth" (Matt. 27:59).

"Then he bought fine linen, took Him down, and wrapped Him in the linen" (Mark 15:46).

"Now when the Sabbath was past, Mary Magdalene, Mary the mother of James, and Salome bought spices, that they might come and anoint Him" (Mark 16:1).

"Then they [the women who had come with Him out of Galilee] returned and prepared spices and fragrant oils" (Luke 23:56).

"He [Joseph of Arimathea] came . . . and Nicodemus . . . also came . . . bringing a mixture of myrrh and aloes, about a hundred pounds. Then they took the body of Jesus, and bound it in strips of linen with the spices, as the custom of the Jews is to bury" (John 19:38–40).

(2) That it was not cut *downwards,* after the manner of a grave with us, but *horizontally or nearly so,* into the face of the rock." (Alford, GTCRT, 298–99)

5E. Why did the Jews ask Pilate to place a guard at Christ's tomb, if no such sepulchre existed?

"On the next day, which followed the Day of Preparation, the chief priests and Pharisees gathered together to Pilate, saying, 'Sir, we remember, while He was still alive, how that deceiver said, "After three days I will rise." Therefore command that the tomb be made secure until the third day, lest His disciples come by night and steal Him away, and say to the people, "He has risen from the dead." So the last deception will be worse than the first.' Pilate said to them, 'You have a guard; go your way, make it as secure as you know how.' So they went and made the tomb secure, sealing the stone and setting the guard" (Matt. 27:62–66).

Indeed, the truth of the matter is plain, as Major so clearly puts it: "Had the body of Christ merely been thrown into a common grave and left unattended, there would have been no possible reason for the anxiety of His enemies to spread the report that the body had been stolen." (Major, as cited in Smith, TS, 578)

6E. What are we to think of the visit of the women to the tomb after the Sabbath?

"Now after the Sabbath, as the first day of the week began to dawn, Mary Magdalene and the other Mary came to see the tomb" (Matt. 28:1).

"Very early in the morning, on the first day of the week, they came to the tomb when the sun had risen" (Mark 16:2).

"Now on the first day of the week, very early in the morning, they [the women who had come with Him out of Galilee], and certain other women with them, came to the tomb bringing the spices which they had prepared" (Luke 24:1).

"Now on the first day of the week Mary Magdalene went to the tomb early, while it was still dark, and saw that the stone had been taken away from the tomb" (John 20:1).

If Jesus hadn't actually been entombed in Joseph's grave, records of such a visit would not appear in the Gospel narratives.

7E. What are we to think of Peter's and John's visit to the tomb after their hearing the women's report?

"But Peter arose and ran to the tomb; and stooping down, he saw the linen cloths lying by themselves; and he departed, marveling to himself at what had happened" (Luke 24:12).

"Peter therefore went out, and the other disciple [John], and were going to the tomb. So they both ran together; and the other disciple outran Peter and came to the tomb first. And he, stooping down and looking in, saw the linen cloths lying there; yet he did not go in. Then Simon Peter came, following him, and went into the tomb; and he saw the linen cloths lying there, and the handkerchief that had been around His head, not lying with the linen cloths, but folded together in a place by itself. Then the other disciple, who came to the tomb first, went in also; and he saw and believed" (John 20:3–8).

The evidence of this narrative is likewise ignored.

8E. Wilbur M. Smith makes the following statement concerning Guignebert's hypothesis: "He denies the fact which the four Gospels clearly set forth, that the body of Jesus was placed in the tomb of Joseph of Arimathea. Denying this he presents no evidence to contradict it, but makes a statement which proceeds out of his own imagination. In fact, one would say his statement about the body of Jesus proceeds not alone from his imagination, but from his preconceived [philosophical, not historical, prejudice] determination." (Smith, TS, 372)

The evidence clearly speaks for itself, but Professor Guignebert refuses to acknowledge the evidence because it does not agree with his worldview that the miraculous is not possible. The French professor draws his conclusions in spite of the evidence, not because of it. Indeed, as Smith says of his theory: "We dismiss it, as being utterly without historical foundation, and for this reason not deserving further consideration, in studying the four *historical* documents we have in front of us, known as the Gospels." (Smith, TS, 372)

3C. The Burial

In discussing the records of Jesus' entombment in Joseph of Arimathea's sepulchre, Wilbur Smith writes:

> We know more about the burial of the Lord Jesus than we know of the burial of any single character in all of ancient history. We know infinitely more about His burial than we do the burial of any Old Testament character, of any king of Babylon, Pharaoh of Egypt, any philosopher of Greece, or triumphant Caesar. We know who took His body from the cross; we know something of the wrapping of the body in spices, and burial clothes; we know the very tomb in which this body was placed, the name of the man who owned it, Joseph, of a town known as Arimathaea. We know even where this tomb was located, in a garden nigh to the place where He was crucified, outside the city walls. We have four records of this burial of our Lord, all of them in amazing agreement, the record of Matthew, a disciple of Christ who was there when Jesus was crucified; the record of Mark, which some say was written within ten years of our Lord's ascension; the record of Luke, a companion of the apostle Paul, and a great historian; and the record of John, who was the last to leave the

cross, and, with Peter, the first of the Twelve on Easter to behold the empty tomb. (Smith, TS, 370–71)

The historian Alfred Edersheim gives these details of the burial customs of the Jews:

> Not only the rich, but even those moderately well-to-do, had tombs of their own, which probably were acquired and prepared long before they were needed, and treated and inherited as private and personal property. In such caves, or rock-hewn tombs, the bodies were laid, having been anointed with many spices, with myrtle, aloes, and, at a later period, also with hyssop, rose-oil, and rose-water. The body was dressed and, at a later period, wrapped, if possible, in the worn cloths in which originally a Roll of the Law had been held. The "tombs" were either "rock-hewn," or natural "caves" or else large walled vaults, with niches along the sides. (Edersheim, LTJM, 318–19)

Of Christ's burial, Edersheim writes:

> The proximity of the holy Sabbath, and the consequent need of haste, may have suggested or determined the proposal of Joseph to lay the Body of Jesus in his own rock-hewn new tomb, wherein no one had yet been laid. . . .
>
> The Cross was lowered and laid on the ground; the cruel nails drawn out, and the ropes unloosed. Joseph, with those who attended him, "wrapped" the Sacred Body "in a clean linen cloth," and rapidly carried It to the rock-hewn tomb in the garden close by. Such a rock-hewn tomb or cave *(Meartha)* had niches *(Kukhin)*, where the dead were laid. It will be remembered, that at the entrance to "the tomb"—and within "the rock"—there was "a court," nine feet square, where ordinarily the bier was deposited, and its bearers gathered to do the last offices for the Dead. (Edersheim, LTJM, 617)

Edersheim next mentions: "that other Sanhedrist, Nicodemus . . . now came, bringing 'a roll' of myrrh and aloes, in the fragrant mixture well known to the Jews for purposes of anointing or burying.

"It was in 'the court' of the tomb that the hasty embalmment—if such it may be called—took place." (Edersheim, LTJM, 617)

It was customary in Christ's time to use great quantities of spices for embalming the dead, especially for those held in high esteem.

Michael Green relates the following concerning the burial preparation given Jesus' remains: "The body was placed on a stone ledge, wound tightly in strips of cloth, and covered with spices. St. John's Gospel tells us that some seventy pounds were used, and that is likely enough. Joseph was a rich man, and no doubt wanted to make up for his cowardliness during the lifetime of Jesus by giving him a splendid funeral. The amount, though

> No one can affirm the historicity of the burial story and plausibly deny the historicity of the empty tomb.
>
> —WILLIAM LANE CRAIG

great, has plenty of parallels. Rabbi Gamaliel, a contemporary of Jesus, was buried with eighty pounds of spices when he died." (Green, MA, 33)

Flavius Josephus, the Jewish historian of the first century, mentions the funeral of Aristobulus, who was "murdered, being not eighteen years old, and having kept the high priesthood one year only." (Josephus, AJ, XV, iii, 3)

At his funeral Herod "took care [that it] should be very magnificent, by making great preparation for a sepulchre to lay his [Aristobulus's] body in, and providing a great quantity of spices, and burying many ornaments together with him." (Josephus, AJ, XVII, viii, 3)

James Hastings says concerning the grave clothes found in Christ's empty tomb: "As far back as Chrysostom's time [the fourth century A.D.] attention was called to the fact that the myrrh was a drug which adheres so closely to the body that the grave clothes would not easily be removed" (Joan. Hom. 85). (Hastings, DCG, 507)

Merrill Tenney explains the grave clothes as follows:

> In preparing a body for burial according to Jewish custom, it was usually washed and straightened, and then bandaged tightly from the armpits to the ankles in strips of linen about a foot wide. Aromatic spices, often of a gummy consistency, were placed between the wrappings or folds. They served partially as a preservative and partially as a cement to glue the cloth wrappings into a solid covering. . . . John's term "bound" (Gr. *edesan*) is in perfect accord with the language of Lk. 23:53, where the writer says that the body was *wrapped* . . . in linen. . . . On the morning of the first day

---

In preparing a body for burial according to Jewish custom, it was usually washed and straightened, and then bandaged tightly from the armpits to the ankles in strips of linen about a foot wide. Aromatic spices, often of a gummy consistency, were placed between the wrappings or folds. They served partially as a preservative and partially as a cement to glue the cloth wrappings into a solid covering. . . . John's term "bound" (Gr. *edesan*) is in perfect accord with the language of Lk. 23:53, where the writer says that the body was wrapped . . . in linen. . . . On the morning of the first day of the week the body of Jesus had vanished, but the graveclothes were still there.

—MERRILL TENNEY

of the week the body of Jesus had vanished, but the graveclothes were still there. (Tenney, RR, 117)

George B. Eager, in *The International Standard Bible Encyclopedia,* says of Christ's burial:

It was in strict accordance with such customs and the provision of the Mosaic law (Deut. 21:23) ["His corpse shall not hang all night on the tree, but you shall surely bury him on the same day (for he who is hanged is accursed of God), so that you do not defile your land which the Lord your God gives you as an inheritance."] (cf. Gal. 3:13) ["Christ redeemed us from the curse of the Law, having become a curse for us—for it is written, 'CURSED IS EVERYONE WHO HANGS ON A TREE'"], as well as in compliance with the impulses of true humanity, that Joseph of Arimathea went to Pilate and begged the body of Jesus for burial on the very day of the crucifixion (Matthew 27:58ff.). (Eager, as cited in Orr, ISBE, 529)

Eager further observes:

Missionaries and natives of Syria tell us that it is still customary to wash the body (cf. John 12:7; 19:90; Mark 16:1; Luke 24:1), swathe hands and feet in gravebands, usually of linen (John 19:40), and cover the face or bind it about with a napkin or handkerchief (John 11:44b). It is still common to place in the wrappings of the body aromatic spices and other preparations to retard decomposition . . . we are . . . told that after the burial of Jesus, Nicodemus brought "a mixture of myrrh and aloes, about a hundred pounds," and that they "took the body of Jesus, and bound it in linen wrappings with the spices, as the custom of the Jews is to bury," and that Mary Magdalene and two other women brought spices for the same purpose (Mark 16:1; Luke 23:56). (Eager, as cited in Orr, ISBE, 529)

William Lane Craig, on the careful preservation of graves of Jewish holy men:

During Jesus' time there was an extraordinary interest in the graves of Jewish martyrs and holy men, and these were scrupulously cared for and honored. This suggests that the grave of Jesus would also have been noted. The disciples had no inkling of any resurrection prior to the general resurrection at the end of the world, and they would therefore not have allowed the burial site of the Teacher to go unnoted. This interest also makes plausible the women's lingering to watch the burial and their subsequent intention to anoint Jesus' body with spices and perfumes (Luke 23:55, 56). (Craig, DJRD, as cited in Wilkins, JUF, 148–49)

Craig comments further concerning the relation of the burial to the empty tomb:

If the burial story is basically reliable, then the inference that Jesus' tomb was found empty lies close at hand. For if the burial story is fundamentally accurate, the site of Jesus' tomb would have been known to Jew and Christian alike. But in that case, it would have been impossible for the resurrection faith to survive in the face of a tomb containing the corpse of Jesus. The disciples could not have believed in Jesus' resurrection; even if they had, scarcely anyone else would have believed them as they preached Jesus' resurrection; and their Jewish opponents could have exposed the whole affair, perhaps even by displaying the body, as the medieval Jewish polemic portrays them doing (*Toledot Yeshu*). . . . No one can affirm the historicity of the burial story and plausibly deny the historicity of the empty tomb. (Craig, DJRD, as cited in Wilkins, JUF, 146–47)

4C. The Stone

Concerning that which covered the opening of Jesus' tomb, A. B. Bruce says: "The Jews called the stone *golel.*" (Bruce, EGNT, 334)

H. W. Holloman, citing G. M. Mackie, says: "The opening to the central chamber was guarded by a large and heavy disc of rock which could roll along a groove slightly depressed at the centre, in front of the tomb entrance." (Holloman, EPR, 38)

T. J. Thorburn mentions that this stone was used "as a protection against both men and beasts." He further observes: "This stone is often mentioned by the Talmudists. According to Maimonides, a structure *ex lingo, alia Materia* was also used." Of the enormous size of such a stone Dr. Thorburn comments: "It usually required several men to remove it." Since the one rolled to the entrance of Jesus' tomb was intended to prevent an expected theft, it was probably even larger than what would normally have been used! (Thorburn, RNMC, 97–98)

Indeed, concerning the tremendous weight of the rock, Thorburn remarks: "A gloss in Cod. Bez. [a phrase written in parenthesis, within the text of Mark 16:4 as found in a (fourth) century manuscript (Codex Bezae in the Cambridge Library)] adds, 'And when he was laid there, he (Joseph) put against the tomb a stone which twenty men could not roll away.'" The significance of Dr. Thorburn's observation is realized when one considers the rules for transcribing manuscripts. It was the custom that if a copier was emphasizing his own interpretation, he would write his thought in the margin and not include it within the text. One might conclude, therefore, that the insert in the text was copied from a text even closer to the time of Christ, perhaps a first century manuscript. The phrase, then, could have been recorded by an eye-witness who was impressed with the enormity of the stone that was rolled against Jesus' sepulchre. Gilbert West of Oxford also brings out the importance of this portion of the Bezae Codex on pages 37 and 38 of his work,

---

What Is the Shroud of Turin?

The Shroud of Turin is a linen cloth that measures 14.25 feet by 3.58 feet *(Biblical Archaeology Review* [1986]: 26) and is housed in Turin, Italy. There is a double, head-to-head image of a man on the material, revealing the front and back of his body.

The Shroud has been known to exist since 1354, but many believe it is much older. In 1978, the Shroud was subjected to extensive scientific investigation. No sign of paint or dye that could account for the image was on it. The image was thought to be three-dimensional and was found only on the surface of the cloth.

However in 1988, three independent laboratories made carbon-dating tests of threads of the Shroud. They all gave it a late medieval date. Proponents of the Shroud objected that the sample was too fragmentary and was from a contaminated section of the Shroud that reflected a medieval church fire.

Is the Shroud authentic? The authenticity of the Shroud is hotly debated. Those favoring it stress its unique features. Those against it point to the lack of historical evidence and the scientific dating evidence against it. (Geisler, BECA, 706)

Observations on the History and Evidences of the Resurrection of Jesus Christ. (Thorburn, RNMC, 1–2)

Samuel Chandler says: "The Witnesses here all agree, that when the Women came, *they found the Stone rolled or* taken away. The Women could not do it, the Stone being *too large* for them to move." (Chandler, RJC, 33)

Alfred Edersheim, the Hebrew-Christian who is an exceptionally good source for the historical background of the New Testament times, relates the following concerning Jesus' burial:

"And so they laid Him to rest in the niche of the rock-hewn new tomb. And as they went out, they rolled, as was the custom, a 'great stone'—the *Golel*—to close the entrance to the tomb, probably leaning against it for support, as was the practice, a smaller stone—the so-called *Dopheg*. It would be where the one stone was laid against the other, that on the next day, the Sabbath though it was, the Jewish authorities would have affixed the seal, so that the slightest disturbance might become apparent." (Edersheim, LTJM, 618)

Frank Morison, commenting on the visit of Mary and her friends to Jesus' tomb that early Sunday morning, says:

> The question as to how they were to remove this stone must of necessity have been a source of considerable perplexity to the women. Two of them at least had witnessed the interment and knew roughly how things stood. The stone, which is known to have been large and of considerable weight, was their great difficulty. When, therefore, we find in the earliest record, the Gospel of St. Mark, the words: "Who shall roll us away the stone from the door of the tomb?" we can hardly avoid feeling that this preoccupation of the women with the question of the stone is not only a psychological necessity of the problem, but a definitely historical element in the situation right up to the moment of their arrival at the grave. (Morison, WMS, 76)

Morison calls the stone at Jesus' tomb

the one silent and infallible witness in the whole episode—and there are certain facts about this stone which call for very careful study and investigation.

Let us begin by considering first its size and probable character. . . . No doubt . . . the stone was large and consequently very heavy. This fact is asserted or implied by all the writers who refer to it. St. Mark says it was "exceeding great." St. Matthew speaks of it as "a great stone." Peter says, "for the stone was great." Additional testimony on this point is furnished by the reported anxiety of the

women as to how they should move it. If the stone had not been of considerable weight the combined strength of three women should have been capable of moving it. We receive, therefore, a very definite impression that it was at least too weighty for the women to remove unaided. All this has a very definite bearing upon the case. (Morison, WMS, 147)

5C. The Seal

Matthew 27:66 states: "So they went and made the tomb secure, sealing the stone and setting the guard."

A. T. Robertson says that the method of sealing the stone at Jesus' tomb was

> probably by a cord stretched across the stone and sealed at each end as in Dan. 6:17 ["And a stone was brought and laid over the mouth of the den; and the king sealed it with his own signet ring and with the signets of his nobles, so that nothing might be changed in regard to Daniel"]. The sealing was done in the presence of the Roman guards who were left in charge to protect this stamp of Roman authority and power. They did their best to prevent theft and the resurrection (Bruce), but they overreached themselves and provided additional witness to the fact of the empty tomb and the resurrection of Jesus (Plummer). (Robertson, WPNT, 239)

A. B. Bruce observed that "the participial clause [sealing the stone] is a parenthesis pointing to an additional precaution, sealing the stone, with a thread over it and sealed to the tomb at either end. The worthy men did their best to prevent theft, and—the resurrection!" (Bruce, EGNT, 335)

Henry Sumner Maine, "member of the Supreme Council of India; formerly Reader on Jurisprudence and the Civil Law at the Middle Temple, and Regius Professor of the Civil Law in the University of Cambridge," speaks of the legal authority attached to the Roman seal. He points out that it was actually "considered as a mode of authentication." (Maine, as cited in Lewis, M, 203)

> See, at any rate, these words bearing witness to every one of these facts. "We remember," these are the words, "that that deceiver said, when He was yet alive," (He was therefore now dead), "After three days I rise again. Command therefore that the sepulchre be sealed," (He was therefore buried), "lest His disciples come and steal Him away." So that if the sepulchre be sealed, there will be no unfair dealing. For there could not be. So then the proof of His resurrection has become incontrovertible by what ye have put forward. For because it was sealed, there was no unfair dealing. But if there was no unfair dealing, and the sepulchre was found empty, it is manifest that He is risen, plainly and incontrovertibly. Seest thou, how even against their will they contend for the proof of the truth?
>
> —JOHN CHRYSOSTOM

In the area of jurisprudence, Maine continues, "We may observe, that the seals of Roman Wills and other documents of importance did not only serve as the index of the presence or assent of the signatory, but were also literally fastenings which had to be broken before the writing could be inspected." (Maine, AL, 203–04)

Considering in like manner the securing of Jesus' tomb, the Roman seal affixed thereon was meant to prevent any attempted vandalizing of the sepulchre. Anyone trying to move the stone from the tomb's entrance would have broken the seal and thus incurred the wrath of Roman law.

Henry Alford says, "The sealing was by means of a cord or string passing across the stone at the mouth of the sepulchre, and fas-

tened at either end to the rock by sealing-clay." (Alford, GTCRT, 301)

Marvin Vincent comments: "The idea is that they sealed the stone in the presence of the guard, and then left them to keep watch. It would be important that the guard should witness the sealing. The sealing was performed by stretching a cord across the stone and fastening it to the rock at either end by means of sealing clay. Or, if the stone at the door happened to be fastened with a cross beam, this latter was sealed to the rock." (Vincent, WSNT, 147)

D. D. Whedon says: "The door could not be opened, therefore, without breaking the seal; which was a crime against the authority of the proprietor of the seal. The guard was to prevent the duplicity of the disciples; the seal was to secure against the collusion of the guard. So in Dan. vi, 17; 'A stone was brought, and laid upon the mouth of the den; and the king sealed it with his own signet and with the signet of his lord.'" (Whedon, CGM, 343)

John Chrysostom, archbishop of Constantinople in the fourth century, records the following observations concerning the security measures taken at Jesus' tomb:

See, at any rate, these words bearing witness to every one of these facts. "We remember," these are the words, "that that deceiver said, when He was yet alive," (He was therefore now dead), "After three days I rise again. Command therefore that the sepulchre be sealed," (He was therefore buried), "lest His disciples come and steal Him away." So that if the sepulchre be sealed, there will be no unfair dealing. For there could not be. So then the proof of His resurrection has become incontrovertible by what ye have put forward. For because it was sealed, there was no unfair dealing. But if there was no unfair dealing, and the sepulchre was found empty, it is manifest that He is risen, plainly and incontrovertibly. Seest thou, how even against their will they contend for the proof of the truth? (Chrysostom, HGSM, as cited in Schaff, SLNPNF, 525)

"On the next day, which followed the Day of Preparation, the chief priests and Pharisees gathered together to Pilate, saying, 'Sir, we remember while He was still alive, how that deceiver said, "After three days I will rise." Therefore command that the tomb be made secure until the third day, lest His disciples come by night and steal Him away, and say to the people, "He has risen from the dead." So the last deception will be worse than the first.' Pilate said to them. 'You have a guard; go your way, make it as secure as you know how.' So they went and made the tomb secure, sealing the stone and setting the guard." (Matt. 27:62–66)

6C. The Guard at the Tomb

1D. The Fact of the Guard

Commenting on this passage, Albert Roper in *Did Jesus Rise from the Dead?* makes the following observations:

Led by Annas and Caiaphas, their chief priests, a deputation of Jewish leaders sought out Pilate, to request that the tomb wherein Jesus was buried be sealed and that a Roman guard be stationed around it, giving as their motive their fear that the friends of Jesus might come stealthily by night and steal His body in order to make it appear that a resurrection had taken place.

To this request the acquiescent Pilate responded: "Ye shall have a guard; go your way; make it secure according to your wish." They went their way, attended by a guard of Roman soldiers numbering from ten to thirty who, under their direction, sealed the tomb of Joseph of Arimathaea with the Imperial Seals

of Rome, affixing thereto in wax the official stamp of the procurator himself which it would be a high crime even to deface. Thus did these zealous enemies of Jesus unwittingly prepare in advance an unanswerable challenge to their subsequent explanation of the resurrection—an explanation which did not, and could not, in the very nature of things explain [it]. (Roper, DJRD, 23–24)

Professor Roper continues:

Commanding the guard was a centurion designated by Pilate, presumably one in which he had full confidence, whose name according to tradition was Petronius. It is, therefore, reasonable to assume that these representatives of the Emperor could have been trusted to perform their duty to guard a tomb quite as strictly and as faithfully as they had executed a crucifixion. They had not the slightest interest in the task to which they were assigned. Their sole purpose and obligation was rigidly to perform their duty as soldiers of the empire of Rome to which they had dedicated their allegiance. The Roman seal affixed to the stone before Joseph's tomb was far more sacred to them than all the philosophy of Israel or the sanctity of her ancient creed. Soldiers coldblooded enough to gamble over a dying victim's cloak are not the kind of men to be hoodwinked by timid Galileans or to jeopardize their Roman necks by sleeping on their post. (Roper, DJRD, 33)

2D. The Identity of the Guard

There has been much discussion concerning the phrase in Matthew 27:65, "You have a guard." The question is whether this term speaks of the "temple police" or a "Roman guard."

Concerning this Henry Alford says that the phrase can be translated "either (1) indicative, *Ye have:*—but then the question arises, *What guard* had they? and if they had one, why go to Pilate? Perhaps we must understand some detachment placed at their disposal during the feast—but there does not seem to be any record of such a practice ... or (2) ... imperative; ... and the sense ... would be, *Take a body of men for a guard.*" (Alford, GTCRT, 301)

E. Le Camus writes:

Some think that Pilate here means ministers of the Temple whom the chief priests had in their service, and whom they might employ with advantage in guarding a tomb. It would be easier to explain the corruption of the latter than that of Roman soldiers in inducing them to declare that they had slept when they should have kept watch. Nevertheless, the word ... [*koustodia*] borrowed from the Latin, would seem to indicate a *Roman* guard, and the mention of the captain ... (St. Matt. xxviii, 14) ought to make this opinion prevail. (Le Camus, LC, 392)

A. T. Robertson, the noted Greek scholar, says that the phrase " 'Have a guard' *(echete koustodian)* [is] present imperative [and refers to] a guard of Roman soldiers, not mere temple police." (Robertson, WPNT, 239)

Robertson further observes that "the Latin term *koustodia* occurs in an Oxyrhynchus papyrus of A.D. 22." (Robertson, WPNT, 239)

T. J. Thorburn remarks: "It is generally assumed that Matthew means it to be understood that the guard referred to consisted of *Roman* soldiers. ... However ... the priests had a Jewish Temple guard, which would probably not be allowed by the Romans to discharge any duties outside those precincts. Pilate's reply, therefore, which may read either, 'Take a guard,' or 'Ye have a guard' (a polite form of refusal, if the request was for Roman soldiers), may be understood in either sense. If the guard were Jewish it would explain the fact that Pilate overlooked the negligence. Ver. 14 [And if this should

come to the governor's ears, we will win him over and keep you out of trouble.'], however, seems against this view." (Thorburn, RNMC, 179–82)

A. B. Bruce says that the phrase "You have" is "probably imperative, not indicative—have your watch, the ready assent of a man who thinks there is not likely to be much need for it, but has no objections to gratify their wish in a small matter." (Bruce, EGNT, 335)

Arndt and Gingrich (*A Greek-English Lexicon of the New Testament*, University of Chicago Press, 1952) cite the following sources wherein the word for guard, *koustodia*, is found:

"POxy. 294,20 [22 ad]; PRyl. 189,2; BGU 341,3; cf. Hahn 233,6; 234,7 w. lit. Lat. loanw., custodia, also in rabb.)." (Arndt, GEL, 448)

They define it as being *"a guard* composed of soldiers" (Matt. 27:66; 28:11), ... *"take a guard"* (Matt. 27:65). (Arndt, GEL, 448)

Harold Smith, in *A Dictionary of Christ and the Gospels,* gives the following information on the Roman guard: *"GUARD.*—1. RV rendering of [koustodia] (Lat. *custodia*), Mt. 27:65, 66; 28:11, AV 'watch'; obtained by the chief priests and Pharisees from Pilate to guard the sepulchre. The need of Pilate's authorization and the risk of punishment from him (Mt. 28:14) show that this guard must have consisted, not of the Jewish Temple police, but of soldiers from the Roman cohort at Jerusalem; possibly, though not probably, the same as had guarded the cross. ... [You have] is probably imperative, 'have (take) a guard.'" (Smith, as cited in Hastings, DCG, 694)

Lewis and Short record the following in their Latin dictionary: *"Custodia,* ae. f. [id], *a watching, watch, guard, care, protection.* 1. Usu in *plur.* and in milit. lang., *persons who serve as guards, a guard, watch, sentinel.*" (Lewis, LD, 504–05)

The context of Matthew 27 and 28 seems to corroborate the view that it was a "Roman guard" that was used to secure Jesus' tomb. If Pilate had told them to use the "temple

> The punishment for quitting post was death, according to the laws (Dion. Hal, *Antiq. Rom.* VIII.79). The most famous discourse on the strictness of camp discipline is that of Polybius VI.37, 38 which indicates that the fear of punishments produced faultless attention to duty, especially in the night watches. It carries weight from the prestige of the author, who was describing what he had an opportunity to see with his own eyes.
>
> —GEORGE CURRIE

police" just to get rid of them, then the guard would have been responsible to the chief priests only and not to Pilate. However, if Pilate gave them a "Roman guard" to protect the tomb, then the guard would have been responsible to Pilate and not to the chief priests. The key lies in verses 11 and 14 of chapter 28.

Verse 11 records that the guard came and reported to the chief priests. At first glance it seems that they were responsible to the chief priests. But if some of the guards had reported to Pilate they would have been put to death immediately, as will be explained below. Verse 14 confirms the view that they were a Roman guard and directly responsible to Pilate.

"And if this should come to the governor's ears, we will win him over and keep you out of trouble" (NASB). If they were the "temple police," why worry about Pilate hearing about it? There is no indication that he would have had jurisdiction over them. The writer feels this is what happened: They were

a "Roman guard" to which Pilate had given instructions to secure the grave in order to satisfy and keep peace with the religious hierarchy. The chief priests had cautiously sought a "Roman guard": "Therefore command that the tomb be made secure" (Matt. 27:64).

If the priests had wanted to post temple police at the tomb, they would not have needed the orders of the governor to do it. As it happened, the Roman soldiers came to the chief priests for protection, because they knew that they would have influence over Pilate and would keep them from being executed: "We will win him [the governor, Pilate] over and keep you out of trouble" (Matt. 28:14).

3D. The Military Discipline of the Romans

George Currie says, "The punishment for quitting post was death, according to the laws (Dion. Hal, *Antiq. Rom.* VIII.79). The most famous discourse on the strictness of camp discipline is that of Polybius VI. 37, 38, which indicates that the fear of punishments produced faultless attention to duty, especially in the night watches. It carries weight from the prestige of the author, who was describing what he had an opportunity to see with his own eyes. His statements are duplicated in a general way by others." (Currie, MDR, 41–43)

Citing Polybius, Currie writes: "Running a gauntlet [sica] of cudgels . . . is referred to as punishment for faulty night watches, stealing, false witnessing, and injuring one's own body; decimation for desertion of the ranks because of cowardice is also mentioned." (Currie, MDR, 43–44)

Currie continues, "Vegetius speaks of daily attention to strictness of discipline by the prefect of the legion (*Military Institutes* 11.9). And Vegetius certainly maintains (*Military Institutes* 1.21) that the earlier

Romans [at the time of Christ] disciplined more strictly than those of his day." (Currie, MDR, 43–44)

Currie, in speaking of Vegetius's comments on the Roman army, says: "The system he described provided for the severest punishment. The classicum was the signal blown on the trumpet to announce an execution (11.22). Daily attention to strictness of discipline was the duty of the prefect of the legion (11.9)." (Currie, MDR, 49–50)

Currie also points out:

In the various writers of [Justinian's] Digest 49.16, eighteen offenses of soldiers are mentioned punishable by death. They are as follows: a scout remaining with the enemy (-3.4), desertion (-3.11; -5. 1-3), losing or disposing of one's arms (-3.13), disobedience in war time (-3.15), going over the wall or rampart (-3.17), starting a mutiny (-3.19), refusing to protect an officer or deserting one's post (-3.22), a drafted man hiding from service (-4.2), murder (-4.5), laying hands on a superior or insult to a general (-6.1), leading flight when the example would influence others (-6.3), betraying plans to the enemy (-6.4; -7), wounding a fellow soldier with a sword (-6.6), disabling self or attempting suicide without reasonable excuse (-6.7), leaving the night watch (-10.1), breaking the centurion's staff or striking him when being punished (-13.4), escaping guard house (-13.5), and disturbing the peace (-16.1). (Currie, MDR, 49–50)

Currie documents the following examples from the annals of Roman military history that reflect the type of disciplinary measures employed in the Roman army: "In 418, standard bearer lagging in battle, slain by general's own hand; in 390, asleep on duty, hurled from the cliff of the Capitolium [Dig. 49.16.3.6.; -10.1], in 252, negligence, beaten and rank reduced; in 218, negligence, punished; in 195, lagging, struck with

weapon; . . . The types of punishment above mentioned would justify the word 'strict' as descriptive of them." (Currie, MDR, 33)

Currie further comments: "Since the death penalty was assessed in 40 cases out of 102 where the punishment is mentioned, it is clear that punishment in the Roman army was severe in comparison with that in modern armies." Currie speaks of the Roman army as "an instrument for conquest and domination" and, concerning its strict discipline, writes: "Valerius Maximus . . . refers to sharp observation of camp discipline and military theory (11.8 intro.; 11.9 intro.) [as being the primary reasons for] the extensive conquests and power of Rome." (Currie, MDR, 33, 38, 43–44)

T. G. Tucker gives the following vivid description of the weaponry a Roman soldier would carry:

In his right hand he will carry the famous Roman pike. This is a stout weapon, over 6 feet in length, consisting of a sharp iron head fixed in a wooden shaft, and the soldier may either charge with it as with a bayonet, or he may hurl it like a javelin and then fight at close quarters with his sword. On the left arm is a large shield, which may be of various shapes. One common form is curved inward at the sides like a portion of a cylinder some 4 feet in length by 2 1/2 in width: another is six-sided—a diamond pattern, but with the points of the diamond squared away. Sometimes it is oval. In construction it is of wicker-work or wood, covered with leather, and embossed with a blazon in metalwork, one particularly well known being that of a thunderbolt. The shield is not only carried by means of a handle, but may be supported by a belt over the right shoulder. In order to be out of the way of the shield, the sword—a thrusting rather than a slashing weapon, approaching 3 feet in length—is hung at the right side by a belt passing over the left shoulder. Though this arrangement may seem awkward to us, it is to be remembered that the sword is not required until the right hand is free of the pike, and that then, before drawing, the weapon can easily be swung around to the left by means of the suspending belt. On the left side the soldier wears a dagger at his girdle. (Tucker, LRW, 342–44)

4D. What Was a Roman Guard?

When it comes to the topic of the Roman guard, William Smith, in the *Dictionary of Greek and Roman Antiquities,* gives us some information about the number of men in a Roman "guard." According to Dr. Smith, the maniple (a subdivision of the Roman legion) consisting of either 120 or 60 men "furnished . . . for the tribune to whom it was specially attached . . . two guards . . . of four men each, who kept watch, some in front of the tent and some behind, among the horses. We may remark in passing, that four was the regular number for a Roman guard . . . of these one always acted as a sentinel, while the others enjoyed a certain degree of repose, ready, however, to start up at the first alarm." (Smith, William, DGRA, 250–51)

Harold Smith relates: "A watch usually consisted of four men (Polyb. vi.33), each of whom watched in turn, while the others rested beside him so as to be roused by the least alarm; but in this case the guards may have been more numerous." (Smith, as cited in Hastings, DCG, 694)

Professor Whedon says of a watch: "Probably a guard of four soldiers. Such certainly was the number who watched the crucifixion. John xix, 23." (Whedon, CGM, 343)

5D. What Was the Temple Guard?

Specifically in regards to the identity of the temple guard the Jewish historian, Alfred Edersheim, gives us the following information: "At night guards were placed in twenty-four stations about the gates and courts. Of these twenty-one were occupied by Levites alone; the other innermost three jointly by priests and Levites. Each guard consisted of

> During the night the "captain of the Temple" made his rounds. On his approach the guards had to rise and salute him in a particular manner. Any guard found asleep when on duty was beaten, or his garments were set on fire—a punishment, as we know, actually awarded [Rev. 16:15].
>
> —ALFRED EDERSHEIM

ten men; so that all two hundred and forty Levites and thirty priests were on duty every night. The Temple guards were relieved by day, but not during the night, which the Romans divided into four, but the Jews, properly, into three watches, the fourth being really the morning watch." (Edersheim, TMS, 147–49)

The Mishnah (translated by Herbert Danby, Oxford University Press, 1933) relates the following concerning the temple guard: "The priests kept watch at three places in the Temple: at the Chamber of Abtinas, at the Chamber of the Flame, and at the Chamber of the Hearth; and the Levites at twenty-one places: five at the five gates of the Temple Mount, four at its four corners inside, five at five of the gates of the Temple Court, four at its four corners outside, and one at the Chamber of Offerings, and one at the Chamber of the Curtain, and one behind the place of the Mercy Seat." (*The Mishnah,* Middoth, 1.1)

P. Henderson Aitken records: "The duty of this 'captain of the mount of the Temple' was to keep order in the Temple, visit the stations of the guard during the night, and see that the sentries were duly posted and alert.

He and his immediate subalterns are supposed to be intended by the 'rulers' mentioned in Ezra 9:2 and Nehemiah." (Aitken, as cited in Hastings, DCG, 271)

6D. The Military Discipline of the Temple Guard

Alfred Edersheim gives us this description of the tight discipline under which the temple guard worked: "During the night the 'captain of the Temple' made his rounds. On his approach the guards had to rise and salute him in a particular manner. Any guard found asleep when on duty was beaten, or his garments were set on fire—a punishment, as we know, actually awarded. Hence the admonition to us who, as it were, are here on Temple guard, 'Blessed is he that watcheth, and keepeth his garments' [Rev. 16:15]." (Edersheim, TMS, 147–49)

The Mishnah shows the treatment given anyone found asleep during the watch:

The officer of the Temple Mount used to go round to every watch with lighted torches before him, and if any watch did not stand up and say to him, "O officer of the Temple Mount, peace be to thee!" and it was manifest that he was asleep, he would beat him with his staff, and he had the right to burn his raiment. And they would say, "What is the noise in the Temple Court?" "The noise of some levite that is being beaten and having his raiment burnt because he went to sleep during his watch." R. Eliezer b. Jacob said: "They once found my mother's brother asleep and burnt his raiment." (*The Mishnah*, Middoth, 1.2)

The Jewish Encyclopedia comments concerning "the sacred premises within [the temple]," those who were on watch therein "were not allowed to sit down, much less to sleep. The captain of the guard saw that every man was alert, chastising a priest if found asleep at his post, and sometimes even punishing him by burning his shirt upon him, as a warning to others (Mid. k.I)." (*The Jewish Encyclopedia*, 81)

7D. Conclusions

E. LeCamus says in reference to the tight security measures taken at Jesus' sepulchre: "Never had a criminal given so much worry after his execution. Above all never had a crucified man had the honour of being guarded by a squad of soldiers." (Le Camus, LC, 396–97)

G. W. Clark concludes: "So everything was done that human policy and prudence could, to prevent a Resurrection, which these very precautions had the most direct tendency to indicate and establish (Matt. 27:35)." (Clark, GM)

7C. The Disciples Went Their Own Way

In his Gospel, Matthew shows us the cowardice of the disciples (26:56). Jesus had been arrested in the garden of Gethsemane and "then all the disciples forsook Him and fled."

Mark writes in his Gospel (14:50): "Then they all forsook Him and fled."

George Hanson remarks: "They were not naturally either very brave or large-minded. In the most cowardly fashion, when their

> This scared, frightened band of the apostles, which was just about to throw away everything in order to flee in despair to Galilee; when these peasants, shepherds, and fishermen, who betrayed and denied their master and then failed him miserably, suddenly could be changed overnight into a confident mission society, convinced of salvation and able to work with much more success after Easter than before Easter, then no vision or hallucination is sufficient to explain such a revolutionary transformation.
>
> —JEWISH RABBI PINCHAS LAPIDE

Master was arrested, they 'all forsook Him' and fled, leaving Him to face His fate alone." (Hanson, RL, 24–26)

Albert Roper speaks of Simon Peter's "cringing under the taunt of a maid in the court of the high priests and denying with a curse that he knew 'this man of whom ye speak.'" (Roper, JRD, 50)

He asserts that "fear, abject fear for his own personal safety, brought Peter to reject the Man he truly loved. Fear, craven fear, made him recreant to the One who had called him from his nets to become a fisher of men." (Roper, JRD, 52)

Concerning the character of the disciples, Roper comments:

> They are Galileans, for the most part fisherfolk, all of them more or less strangers to cities and to the ways of city life. One by one, they had become adherents of the young Teacher from Nazareth and devoted to His way of life. They had followed Him gladly and reverently until the hour of crisis came. When He was arrested on the outskirts of the Garden of Gethsemane, they all fell back and away, awed by the torches and the clamor and the rattling sabers.
>
> [The disciples] secreted themselves in their lodgings and nothing is heard of them until the startling news is brought to them by the Magdalene on the morning of the third day. Thereupon, two—and two only—have the temerity to venture forth to learn for themselves if the news brought to them by Mary could be as reported by her or was as they themselves believed, just "idle talk." The whole demeanor of the disciples is one of abject fright and self-preservation. (Roper, JRD, 34–35)

Jewish rabbi *Pinchas Lapide* on the transformation of the disciples:

> This scared, frightened band of the apostles which was just about to throw away every-

thing in order to flee in despair to Galilee; when these peasants, shepherds, and fishermen, who betrayed and denied their master and then failed him miserably, suddenly could be changed overnight into a confident mission society, convinced of salvation and able to work with much more success after Easter than before Easter, then no vision or hallucination is sufficient to explain such a revolutionary transformation. For a sect or school or an order, perhaps a single vision would have been sufficient—but not for a world religion which was able to conquer the Occident thanks to the Easter faith. (Lapide, RJ, 125)

Douglas Groothuis, on the disciples' reaction to the resurrected Christ: "The resurrected Jesus elicited the faith of his doubting disciple Thomas when he appeared and said, 'Put your finger here; see my hands. Reach out your hand and put it into my side. Stop doubting and believe' (John 20:27). Thomas then exclaimed, 'My Lord and my God!' (verse 28). Jesus was demonstrated to be God in the flesh, crucified as the Christ had to be, but now risen from the dead as Lord." (Groothuis, JAC, 256)

Alfred Edersheim asks: "What thoughts concerning the Dead Christ filled the minds of Joseph of Arimathea, of Nicodemus, and of the other disciples of Jesus, as well as of the Apostles and of the pious women?" (Edersheim, LTJM, 623)

To this question he answers: "They believed Him to be dead, and they did not expect Him to rise again from the dead—at least, in our accepted sense of it. Of this there is abundant evidence from the moment of His Death, in the burial-spices brought by Nicodemus, in those prepared by the women (both of which were intended as against corruption), in the sorrow of the women at the empty tomb, in their supposition that the Body had been removed, in the perplexity and bearing of the Apostles, in the doubts of so many, and indeed in the express statement: 'For as yet they knew not the Scripture, that He must rise again from the dead.'" (Edersheim, LTJM, 623)

J. P. Moreland on the women's testimony:

In first-century Judaism, a woman's testimony was virtually worthless. A woman was not

> The disciples had nothing to gain by lying and starting a new religion. They faced hardship, ridicule, hostility, and martyr's deaths. In light of this, they could have never sustained such unwavering motivation if they knew what they were preaching was a lie. The disciples were not fools and Paul was a cool-headed intellectual of the first rank. There would have been several opportunities over three to four decades of ministry to reconsider and renounce the lie.
>
> —J. P. MORELAND

allowed to give testimony in a court of law except on rare occasions. No one would have invented a story and made women the first witnesses to the empty tomb. The presence of women was an embarrassment; this probably explains why the women are not mentioned in 1 Corinthians 15 and the speeches in Acts, since these speeches were evangelistic. There was no reason to include in evangelistic messages an incidental detail which would cause the audience to stumble and not deal with the main point. The fact is included in the Gospels because the Gospels are attempting to describe what actually happened. No other explanation can adequately account for the inclusion of this fact. (Moreland, SSC, 168)

J. P. Moreland on the likelihood of the disciples inventing Christianity:

For one thing, the disciples had nothing to gain by lying and starting a new religion. They

faced hardship, ridicule, hostility, and martyr's deaths. In light of this, they could have never sustained such unwavering motivation if they knew what they were preaching was a lie. The disciples were not fools and Paul was a cool-headed intellectual of the first rank. There would have been several opportunities over three to four decades of ministry to reconsider and renounce the lie. Religion had its rewards for them, but those rewards came from a sincere belief that what they were living for was true. (Moreland, SSC, 171–72)

John Ankerberg and John Weldon on what brought about the birth of the church:

Could the Christian Church ever have come into existence as a result of what had become, after Jesus' crucifixion and death, a group of disheartened, frightened, skeptical apostles? Not a chance.

Only the resurrection of Christ from the dead can account for motivating the disciples to give their lives to preach about Christ and nurture the Christian Church the Lord had founded. It can hardly be overestimated how devastating the crucifixion was to the apostles. They had sacrificed everything for Jesus, including their jobs, their homes, and their families (Matthew 19:27). Everything of value was pinned squarely on Jesus: all their hopes, their entire lives, everything. But now He was dead, publicly branded a criminal.

The apostles were dejected and depressed in their conclusion that Christ was not their expected Messiah (Luke 24:21). In such a condition, they can hardly be considered the subjects of hopeful visions and hallucinations. These were not men ready to believe. The very fact that Jesus rebuked them for their unbelief indicates that Thomas was not the only one who was a hardheaded skeptic. At one time or another Jesus rebuked all of the eleven apostles for their unbelief in His resurrection (Matthew 28:17; Luke 24:25–27, 38, 41; John 20:24–27). This proves they were finally convinced against their will.

As the Gospels show, they rejected the first

reports of Jesus' resurrection. It was only after Jesus appeared to them again and again, talking with them, encouraging them to touch Him, to see that He had a physical body, showing them the wounds in His hands and His side, that they became convinced (John 29:20, 27). If they *had* expected a resurrection, they would have been waiting for it. But they weren't, *and* they needed a lot of convincing when it did happen (Acts 1:3). (Ankerberg, RWA, 82)

2B. The Post-Resurrection Scene

1C. The Empty Tomb

Winfried Corduan writes on the certainty of the empty tomb:

If ever a fact of ancient history may count as indisputable, it should be the empty tomb. From Easter Sunday on there must have been a tomb, clearly known as the tomb of Jesus, that did not contain His body. This much is

> When therefore the disciples began to preach the resurrection in Jerusalem and people responded, and when religious authorities stood helplessly by, the tomb must have been empty. The simple fact that the Christian fellowship, founded on belief in Jesus' resurrection, came into existence and flourished in the very city where he was executed and buried is powerful evidence for the historicity of the empty tomb.
>
> —WILLIAM LANE CRAIG

beyond dispute: Christian teaching from the very beginning promoted a living, resurrected Savior. The Jewish authorities strongly opposed this teaching and were prepared to go to any lengths in order to suppress it. Their job would have been easy if they could have invited potential converts for a quick stroll to the tomb and there produced Christ's body. That would have been the end of the Christian

message. The fact that a church centering around the risen Christ could come about demonstrates that there must have been an empty tomb. (Corduan, NDA, 222)

William Lane Craig on the importance of the empty tomb:

The empty tomb is a *sine qua non* of the resurrection. The notion that Jesus rose from the dead with a new body while his old body still lay in the grave is a modern conception. Jewish mentality would never have accepted a division of two bodies. Even if the disciples failed to check the empty tomb, the Jewish authorities could have been guilty of no such oversight. When therefore the disciples began to preach the resurrection in Jerusalem and people responded, and when religious authorities stood helplessly by, the tomb must have been empty. The simple fact that the Christian fellowship, founded on belief in Jesus' resurrection, came into existence and flourished in the very city where he was executed and buried is powerful evidence for the historicity of the empty tomb. (Craig, DJRD, as cited in Wilkins, JUF, 151–52)

W. J. Sparrow-Simpson points out that the empty tomb by itself did not cause the disciples to believe. Of John it is said: "he saw and believed" (John 20:8). This, however, was probably because he remembered that Christ had foretold His resurrection. Neither Mary Magdalene, nor the women, nor even Peter were brought to believe by the testimony of the empty tomb. (Sparrow-Simpson, as cited in Hastings, DCG, 506)

It was Christ's post-resurrection appearances that assured His followers that He had actually risen from the dead. The empty tomb stood as a historical fact, verifying the appearances as being nothing less than Jesus of Nazareth, resurrected in flesh and blood. (Hastings, DCG, 506)

J. N. D. Anderson, lawyer and professor of

oriental law at the University of London, asks: "Have you noticed that the references to the empty tomb all come in the Gospels, which were written to give the Christian community the facts they wanted to know? In the public preaching to those who were not believers, as recorded in the Acts of the Apostles, there is an enormous emphasis on the fact of the resurrection but not a single reference to the empty tomb. Now, why? To me there is only one answer: There was no point in arguing about the empty tomb. Everyone, friend and opponent, knew that it was empty. The only questions worth arguing about were why it was empty and what its emptiness proved." (Anderson, RJC, 4–9)

In other writings, Anderson says:

The empty tomb stands, a veritable rock, as an essential element in the evidence for the resurrection. To suggest that it was not in fact empty at all, as some have done, seems to me ridiculous. It is a matter of history that the apostles from the very beginning made many converts in Jerusalem, hostile as it was, by proclaiming the glad news that Christ had risen from the grave—and they did it within a short walk from the sepulchre. Any one of their hearers could have visited the tomb and come back again between lunch and whatever may have been the equivalent of afternoon tea. Is it conceivable, then, that the apostles would have had this success if the body of the one they proclaimed as risen Lord was all the time decomposing in Joseph's tomb? Would a great company of the priests and many hard-headed Pharisees have been impressed with the proclamation of a resurrection which was in fact no resurrection at all, but a mere message of spiritual survival couched in the misleading terms of a literal rising from the grave? (Anderson, CWH, 95–96)

Paul Althus, cited by Wolfhart Pannenberg, says: " 'In Jerusalem, the place of Jesus' execution and grave, it was proclaimed not long after his death that he had been raised. The situation *demands* that within the circle of the first community one had a reliable testimony for the fact that the grave had been found empty.' The resurrection Kerygma [proclamation] 'could have not been maintained in Jerusalem for a single day, for a single hour, if the emptiness of the tomb had not been established as a fact for all concerned.'" (Althus, as cited in Pannenberg, JGM, 100)

E. H. Day comments: "If it be asserted that the tomb was in fact not found to be empty, several difficulties confront the critic. He has to meet, for example, the problem of the rapid rise of the very definite tradition, never seriously questioned, the problem of the circumstantial nature of the accounts in which the tradition is embodied, the problem of the failure of the Jews to prove that the Resurrection had not taken place by producing the body of Christ, or by an official examination of the sepulchre, a proof which it was to their greatest interest to exhibit." (Edersheim, LTJM, 25–26)

English barrister Frank Morison comments: "In all the fragments and echoes of this far-off controversy which have come down to us we are nowhere told that any responsible person asserted that the body of Jesus was still in the tomb. We are only given reasons why it was not there. Running all through these ancient documents is the persistent assumption that the tomb of Christ was vacant. Can we fly in the face of this cumulative and mutually corroborative evidence? Personally, I do not think we can. The sequence of coincidences is too strong." (Morison, WMS, 115)

Michael Green cites a secular source of early origin that bears testimony to Jesus' empty tomb. This piece of evidence "is called the Nazareth Inscription, after the town where it was found. It is an imperial edict, belonging either to the reign of Tiberius (A.D. 14–37) or of Claudius (A.D. 41–54). And it is an invective, backed with heavy sanctions, against meddling around with tombs and graves! It looks very much as if the news of the empty tomb had got back to Rome in a garbled form (Pilate would have had to report: and he would obviously have said that the tomb had been rifled). This edict, it seems, is the imperial reaction." (Green, MA, 36)

Green concludes: "There can be no doubt that the tomb of Jesus was, in fact, empty on the first Easter day." (Green, MA, 36)

Matthew 28:11–15 records the attempt of the Jewish authorities to bribe the Roman guard to say the disciples stole Jesus' body. *The Dictionary of the Apostolic Church* comments: "This fraudulent transaction proceeds upon the admission by the enemies of Christianity that the grave was empty—an admission which is enough to show that the evidence for the empty grave was 'too notorious to be denied.'" (Hastings, DAC, 340)

J. P. Moreland concludes: "In sum, the absence of explicit mention of the empty tomb in the speeches in Acts is best explained by noting that the fact of the empty tomb was not in dispute and thus it was not at issue. The main debate was over why it was empty, not whether it was empty. . . . No need existed for the early Christian preachers to make a major issue of the empty tomb. It was common knowledge which could be easily verified if such verification was needed." (Moreland, SSC, 163)

W. J. Sparrow-Simpson writes: "The emptiness of the grave is acknowledged by *opponents* as well as affirmed by disciples. The narrative of the guards attempts to account for the fact as a fraudulent transaction (Matthew 28:11–15). 'But this Jewish accusation against the Apostles takes for granted that the grave was empty. What was

needed was an explanation.' . . . This acknowledgment by the Jews that the grave was vacated extends to all subsequent Jewish comments on the point." (Sparrow-Simpson, as cited in Hastings, DCG, 507–08)

Sparrow-Simpson supports this point by citing as an example: "A 12th century version of the empty grave circulated by the Jewish anti-Christian propaganda. The story is that when the queen heard that the elders had slain Jesus and had buried Him, and that He was risen again, she ordered them within three days to produce the body or forfeit their lives. 'Then spake Judas, "Come and I will show you the man whom ye seek: for it was I who took the fatherless from his grave. For I feared lest his disciples should steal him away, and I have hidden him in my garden and led a waterbrook over the place."' And the story explains how the body was produced." (Sparrow-Simpson, as cited in Hastings, DCG, 507–08)

Sparrow-Simpson concludes: "It is needless to remark that this daring assertion of the actual production of the body is a mediaeval fabrication, but it is an assertion very necessary to account for facts, when the emptiness of the grave was admitted and yet the Resurrection denied." (Sparrow-Simpson, as cited in Hastings, DCG, 507–08)

Ernest Kevan cites as evidence what he describes as "the indisputable fact of the *empty tomb*. The tomb was empty; and the foes of Christ were unable to deny it." (Kevan, RC, 14)

He asserts, "The fact of the empty tomb deals a mortal blow to all the hypotheses which are set up against the Christian testimony. This is the stone over which all specious theories stumble, and it is therefore not surprising to discover that reference to the empty tomb is studiously avoided by many of the counter-arguments which are brought forward." (Kevan, RC, 14)

W. J. Sparrow-Simpson, citing Julius Wellhausen, the famous German scholar noted for his higher criticism of the Old Testament, gives this testimony concerning the resurrection of Christ: "It is admitted that with the Resurrection the body of Jesus also had vanished from the grave, and it will be impossible to account for this on natural grounds." (Sparrow-Simpson, as cited in Hastings, DCG, 508)

Why did Jesus' sepulchre not become an object of veneration? J. N. D. Anderson comments that "it is also significant that no suggestion has come down to us that the tomb became a place of reverence or pilgrimage in the days of the early church. Even if those who were convinced Christians might have been deflected from visiting the sepulchre by their assurance that their Master had risen from the dead, what of all those who had heard His teaching, and even known the miracle of His healing touch, without joining the Christian community? They, too, it would seem, knew that His body was not there, and must have concluded that a visit to the tomb would be pointless." (Anderson, CWH, 97)

Frank Morison in his book *Who Moved the Stone?* makes an interesting observation:

Consider first the small but highly significant fact that not a trace exists in the Acts, or the Missionary Epistles or in any apocryphal document of indisputably early date, of anyone going to pay homage at the shrine of Jesus Christ. It is remarkable—this absolutely unbroken silence concerning the most sacred place in Christian memory. Would no woman, to whom the Master's form was a hallowed recollection, ever wish to spend a few moments at that holy site? Would Peter and John and Andrew never feel the call of a sanctuary that held all that was mortal of the Great Master? Would Saul himself, recalling his earlier arrogance and self-assurance, not have made one solitary journey and shed hot tears

of repentance for his denial of the Name? If these people really knew that the Lord was buried there, it is very, very strange.

To a critic of the resurrection, this extraordinary silence of antiquity concerning the later history of the grave of Jesus produces, I'm sure, a feeling of profound disquiet and unrest. (Morison, WMS, 137)

2C. The Grave Clothes

In the following narrative, John shows the significance of the grave clothes as evidence for the resurrection:

Peter therefore went out, and the other disciple, and were going to the tomb. So they both ran together; and the other disciple outran Peter and came to the tomb first. And he, stooping down and looking in, saw the linen cloths lying there; yet he did not go in. Then Simon Peter came, following him, and went into the tomb; and he saw the linen cloths lying there; and the handkerchief that had been around His head, not lying with the linen cloths, but folded together in a place by itself. Then the other disciple, who came to the tomb first, went in also; and he saw and believed. For as yet they did not know the Scripture, that He must rise again from the dead (John 20:3–9).

Commenting on John's narrative, J. N. D. Anderson says of the empty tomb:

It seems that it wasn't really empty. You remember the account in John's Gospel of how Mary Magdalene ran and called Peter and John and how the two men set out to the tomb. John, the younger, ran on quicker than Peter and came first to the tomb. He stooped down, "peeped" inside (which I believe is the literal meaning of the Greek), and saw the linen clothes and the napkin that had been about the head. And then Simon Peter came along and, characteristically, blundered straight in, followed by John; and they took note of the linen clothes and the napkin, which was not lying with the linen clothes but was apart, wrapped into one place. The Greek there seems to suggest that the linen clothes were lying, not strewn about the tomb, but where the body had been, and that there was a gap where the neck of Christ had lain—and that the napkin which had been about His head was not with the linen clothes but apart and wrapped in its own place, which I suppose means still done up, as though the body had simply withdrawn itself. We are told that when John saw that, he needed no further testimony from man or angel; he saw and believed, and his testimony has come down to us. (Anderson, RJC, 7–8)

E. H. Day says of John's narrative:

It is characterized throughout by the personal touch, it has all the marks of the evidence not only of an eyewitness, but of a careful observer.... The running of the disciples, the order of their arrival at the sepulchre and their entry, the fact that St. John first stooped down and looking through the low doorway saw the linen clothes lying, while St. Peter, more bold, was the first to enter; the exact word, ... [*theorei*], which is used for St. Peter's careful observation (even examination may perhaps be implied in it) of the grave-clothes; the description of the position of the linen clothes and the napkin, a description not laboured, but minutely careful in its choice of words; the subsequent entry of St. John, and the belief which followed upon the sight of the grave-clothes—this can surely be nothing else than the description of one who actually *saw,* upon whose memory the scene is still impressed, to whom the sight of the empty grave and the relinquished grave-clothes was a critical point in faith and life. (Day, ER, 16–17)

Latham writes of the face cloth that had covered Jesus' head:

The words "not lying with the linen cloths" yield me something; ... they tell me inciden-

tally that the linen cloths were all in one place. If they were lying, as I take them to have done, all upon the lower part of the ledge, the expression is perfectly clear; but if the linen cloths had been lying, one here and one there, as though they had been thrown hastily aside, there would have been no meaning in saying that the napkin was "not lying with the linen cloths," for the "linen cloths" would not have defined any particular spot. We again note the introduction of the word "lying" when it is not absolutely required. The napkin was not lying flat, as the linen cloths were, and S. John, perhaps, marks the difference. (Latham, RM, 44)

Latham continues: "The napkin, which had been twisted round the top of the head, would remain on . . . [the] elevated slab; there it would be found 'rolled up in a place by itself.'" (Latham, RM, 36)

Latham says that the phrase " 'rolled up' is ambiguous, the twisted napkin I suppose formed a ring like the roll of a turban loosened, without the central part." (Latham, RM, 36)

He concludes:

There lie the clothes—they are fallen a little together, but are still wrapped fold over fold, and no grain of spice is displaced. The napkin, too, is lying on the low step which serves as a pillow for the head of the corpse; it is twisted into a sort of wig, and is all by itself. The very quietude of the scene makes it seem to have something to say. It spoke to those who saw it, and it speaks to me when I conjure it before my mind's eye, with the morning light from the open doorway streaming in.

What it says, I make out to be this: "All that was Jesus of Nazareth has suffered its change and is gone. We,—grave-clothes, and spices, and napkin,—belong to the earth and remain." (Latham, RM, 11)

3C. The Seal

A. T. Robertson comments: "The sealing was done in the presence of the Roman guard who were left in charge to protect this stamp of Roman authority and power." (Robertson, WPNT, 239)

D. D. Whedon says: "The door could not be opened, therefore, without breaking the seal; which was a crime against the authority of the proprietor of the seal." (Whedon, CGM, 343)

The seal was broken when the stone was rolled away. The person or persons who were responsible for breaking the seal would have the provincial governor and his agencies to answer to. Indeed, at the time of Christ's resurrection everyone feared the breaking of the Roman seal.

4C. The Roman Guard

Understanding who these guards were makes the narrative of Matthew 28 very impressive. The sight which coincided with Jesus' resurrection was frightening enough to cause rugged soldiers to "become like dead men" (Matt. 28:4).

> "And behold, there was a great earthquake; for an angel of the Lord descended from heaven and came and rolled back the stone from the door, and sat on it. His countenance was like lightning, and his clothing as white as snow. And the guards shook for fear of him, and became like dead men.
>
> "Now while they were going, behold, some of the guard came into the city and reported to the chief priests all the things that had happened. When they had assembled with the elders and consulted together, they gave a large sum of money to the soldiers, saying, 'Tell them, "His disciples came at night and stole Him away while we slept." And if this comes to the governor's ears, we will appease him and make you secure.' So they took the money and did as they were instructed; and this saying is commonly reported among the Jews until this day" (Matt. 28:2–4, 11–15).

Roper gives this description of the guard: "They had not the slightest interest in the task to which they were assigned. Their sole purpose and obligation was rigidly to perform their duty as soldiers of the empire of Rome to which they had dedicated their allegiance. The Roman seal affixed to the stone before Joseph's tomb was far more sacred to them than all the philosophy of Israel or the sanctity of her ancient creed. [They were] . . . cold-blooded enough to gamble over a dying victim's *cloak*." (Roper, JRD, 33)

T. G. Tucker describes in great detail the armor and weapons a centurion would have worn. The picture he gives is of a human fighting machine. (Tucker, LRW, 342–44)

Thomas Thorburn tells us that the guard that had kept the watch was in dire straits. After the stone had been rolled away and the seal broken, they were as good as court-martialed. Thorburn writes: "The soldiers cannot have alleged they were asleep, for they well knew that the penalty of sleeping upon a watch was death—always rigorously enforced." (Thorburn, RNMC, 179–82)

Thorburn continues: "Here the soldiers would have practically no other alternative than to trust to the good offices of the priests. The body (we will suppose) was *gone*, and their negligence in *any* case would (under ordinary circumstances) be punishable by death (cp. Acts xii. 19)." (Thorburn, RNMC, 179–82)

5C. Jesus Was Alive, as His Appearances Demonstrated

1D. Importance of the Appearances

C. S. Lewis, in speaking of the importance of Christ's post-resurrection appearances, writes: "The first fact in the history of Christendom is a number of people who say they have seen the Resurrection. If they had died without making anyone else believe this 'gospel' no gospels would ever have been written." (Lewis, M, 149)

J. P. Moreland on the reports of Jesus' appearances: "Finally, the resurrection appearances are reported with extreme reserve. When one compares them with the

> In 56 A.D. Paul wrote that over 500 people had seen the risen Jesus and that most of them were still alive (1 Corinthians 15:6 ff.). It passes the bounds of credibility that the early Christians could have manufactured such a tale and then preached it among those who might easily have refuted it simply by producing the body of Jesus.
>
> —JOHN WARWICK MONTGOMERY

reports in the apocryphal gospels (second century on), the difference is startling. In the Apocrypha, detailed explanations are given about how the resurrection took place. Gross details are added. For example, the Gospel of Peter (mid-second century) reports a cross coming out of the tomb after Jesus, and Jesus is so tall he extends above the clouds." (Moreland, SSC, 175)

William Lane Craig on the factual nature of appearances: "Since the apostles were the guardians of the Jesus tradition and directed the Christian community, it would have been difficult for fictitious appearance stories incompatible with the apostles' own experience to arise and flourish so long as they were alive. Discrepancies in secondary details could exist, and the theology of the Evangelists could affect the traditions, but the basic traditions themselves could not have been legendary. The substantially unhistorical accounts of Jesus did not rise until the second century, and even then they were universally rejected by the church." (Craig, DJRD, as cited in Wilkins, JUF, 155)

J. N. D. Anderson writes of the testimony of the appearances:

The most drastic way of dismissing the evidence would be to say that these stories were mere fabrications, that they were pure lies. But, so far as I know, not a single critic today would take such an attitude. In fact, it would really be an impossible position. Think of the number of witnesses, over 500. Think of the character of the witnesses, men and women who gave the world the highest ethical teaching it has ever known, and who even on the testimony of their enemies lived it out in their lives. Think of the psychological absurdity of picturing a little band of defeated cowards cowering in an upper room one day and a few days later transformed into a company that no persecution could silence—and then attempting to attribute this dramatic change to nothing more convincing than a miserable fabrication they were trying to foist upon the world. That simply wouldn't make sense. (Anderson, RJC, 5–6)

John Warwick Montgomery comments:

Note that when the disciples of Jesus proclaimed the resurrection, they did so as eyewitnesses and they did so while people were still alive who had had contact with the events they spoke of. In 56 A.D. Paul wrote that over 500 people had seen the risen Jesus and that most of them were still alive (1 Corinthians 15:6 ff.). It passes the bounds of credibility that the early Christians could have manufactured such a tale and then preached it among those who might easily have refuted it simply by producing the body of Jesus. (Montgomery, HC, 78)

Bernard Ramm writes: "If there were no resurrection it must be admitted by radical critics that Paul deceived the apostles of an actual appearance of Christ to him, and they in turn deceived Paul about the appearances of a risen Christ to them. How difficult it is to impugn the evidence of the Epistles at this point when they have such strong validation as authentic!" (Ramm, PCE, 203)

The Appearance of Christ in the Lives of Individuals

1. To Mary Magdalene: Mark 16:9, John 20:14
2. To women returning from the tomb: Matthew 28:9, 10
3. To Peter later in the day: Luke 24:34; 1 Corinthians 15:5
4. To the Emmaus disciples: Luke 24:13–33
5. To the apostles without Thomas: Luke 24:36–43; John 20:19–24
6. To the apostles with Thomas present: John 20:26–29
7. To the seven by the Lake of Tiberias: John 21:1–23
8. To a multitude of 500-plus believers on a Galilean mountain: 1 Corinthians 15:6
9. To James: 1 Corinthians 15:7
10. To the eleven: Matthew 28:16–20; Mark 16:14–20; Luke 24:33–52; Acts 1:3–12
11. At the ascension: Acts 1:3–12
12. To Paul: Acts 9:3–6; 1 Corinthians 15:8
13. To Stephen: Acts 7:55
14. To Paul in the temple: Acts 22:17–21; 23:11
15. To John on Patmos: Revelation 1:10–19

J. P. Moreland, on the nature of Jesus' resurrection body: "First, the writers of the Gospels and Paul are agreed the Jesus appeared in bodily form. It should be granted that Jesus now had a spiritual body which was not entirely the same as his earthly body. But Jesus still had a spiritual *body*, and neither Paul nor the Gospel writers understand this to mean a purely spiritual being who can be seen only in the mind. This body could be seen and touched, and had continuity with the body laid in the tomb. The risen Christ was capable of eating (see Luke 24:41–43)." (Moreland, SSC, 82)

William Lane Craig, on the nature of the resurrection body:

But while it is true that Paul teaches that our resurrection bodies will be modeled after Jesus' body and that they will be spiritual, it does not follow that these bodies will be nonphysical. Such an interpretation is not supported by an exegesis of Paul's teaching. If by *soma pneumatikon* ("spiritual body") one understands a body that is intangible, unextended, or immaterial, then it is false to assert that Paul taught that we shall have *that* kind of resurrection body. New Testament commentators agree that a *pneumatikos* means "spiri-

tual" in the sense of orientation, not substance (cf. 1 Cor. 2:15; 10:4). The transformation of the earthly body to a *soma pneumatikon* accordingly does not rescue it from materiality, but from mortality.

A *soma* ("body") that is unextended and intangible would have been a contradiction in terms for the apostle. The resurrection body will be an immortal, powerful, glorious, Spirit-directed body, suitable for inhabiting a renewed creation. All commentators agree that Paul did not teach the immortality of the soul alone; but his affirmation of the resurrection of the body becomes vacuous and indistinguishable from such a doctrine unless it means the tangible, physical resurrection. The exegetical evidence does not, therefore, support a bifurcation between Paul and the Evangelists with regard to the nature of the resurrection body. (Craig, DJRD, as cited in Wilkins, JUF, 157)

6C. The Enemies of Christ Gave No Refutation of the Resurrection

1D. They Were Silent

In Acts 2, Luke records Peter's sermon on the day of Pentecost. There was no refutation given by the Jews to his bold proclamation of

Christ's resurrection. Why? Because the evidence of the empty tomb was there for anyone to examine if they wanted to disclaim it. However, everyone knew that the grave no longer held the body of Jesus Christ.

In Acts 25, we see Paul imprisoned in Caesarea. Festus, "sitting on the judgment seat, . . . commanded Paul to be brought. When he had come, the Jews who had come down from Jerusalem stood about and laid many serious complaints against Paul, which they could not prove" (vv. 6, 7). Just what was it about Paul's gospel that so irritated the Jews? What point did they totally avoid in making their accusations? Festus, in explaining the case to King Agrippa, describes the central issue as concerning "a certain Jesus, who had died, whom Paul affirmed to be alive" (Acts 25:19). The Jews could not explain the empty tomb.

They made all kinds of personal attacks on Paul, but avoided the objective evidence for the resurrection. They were reduced to subjective name-calling and avoided discussing the silent witness of the empty grave.

The silence of the Jews speaks louder than the voice of the Christians, or, as Fairbairn notes: "The silence of the Jews is as significant as the speech of the Christians." (Fairbairn, SLC, 357)

Professor Day says, "The simple disproof, the effective challenging, of the fact of the Resurrection would have dealt a death-blow to Christianity. And they had every opportunity of disproof, if it were possible." (Day, ER, 33–35)

W. Pannenberg, cited by J. N. D. Anderson, states: "The early Jewish polemic against the Christian message about Jesus' resurrection, traces of which have already been left in the Gospels, does not offer any suggestion that Jesus' grave had remained untouched. The Jewish polemic would have had to have every interest in the preservation of such a report. However, quite to the contrary, it

shared the conviction with its Christian opponents that Jesus' grave was empty. It limited itself to explaining this fact in its own way." (Pannenberg, as cited in Anderson, CWH, 96)

The church was founded on the resurrection, and disproving it would have destroyed the whole Christian movement. However, instead of any such disproof, throughout the first century, Christians were threatened, beaten, flogged, and killed because of their faith. It would have been much simpler to have silenced them by producing Jesus' body, but this was never done.

As John R. W. Stott has well said, the silence of Christ's enemies "is as eloquent a proof of the resurrection as the apostles' witness." (Stott, BC, 51)

2D. They Mocked

1E. In Athens

When Paul spoke to the Athenians about Christ, they had no answer for his claims: "And when they heard of the resurrection of the dead, some mocked" (Acts 17:32). They merely laughed it off, because they could not understand how a man could rise from the dead. They did not even attempt to defend their position. In essence, they said: "Don't confuse me with the facts, my mind is already made up."

Why did Paul encounter such unbelief in Greece, and not in Jerusalem? Because while in Jerusalem the fact of the empty tomb was indisputable (it was right there for people to examine), in Athens the evidence was far away, so that the emptiness of the tomb was not common knowledge. Paul's hearers had not checked the story out for themselves, and rather than go to any trouble to investigate, they were satisfied to jest in ignorance. Intellectual suicide best describes their stand.

2E. Before Agrippa and Festus in Caesarea

Paul told Agrippa and everyone in the court that Christ "would be the first to rise from the dead, and would proclaim light to the Jewish people and to the Gentiles" (Acts 26:23). And while Paul was saying this in his defense, Festus said in a loud voice,

> "Paul, you are beside yourself! Much learning is driving you mad" But he [Paul] said, "I am not mad, most noble Festus, but speak the words of truth and reason. For the king [Agrippa], before whom I also speak freely, knows these things; for I am convinced that none of these things escapes his attention, since this thing was not done in a corner. King Agrippa, do you believe the prophets? I know that you do believe." Then Agrippa said to Paul, "You almost persuade me to become a Christian" (Acts 26:24–28).

Again, just as in Athens, Paul met with unbelief. His message was that Christ is risen from the dead (Acts 26:23), and again no evidence to the contrary was presented in rebuttal. Only vain mockery came from Festus. Paul's defense was uttered in words "of sober truth" [marginal reading of truth and reason] (Acts 26:25, compare NASB and NKJV).

Paul stressed the empirical nature of his case saying, "This thing was not done in a corner" (Acts 26:26). He challenged Agrippa and Festus with the evidence, but Festus, like the Athenians, only laughed it off. This incident took place in Caesarea, where it would not have been known by everyone that the tomb was empty. A trip to Jerusalem would have confirmed the fact.

3B. Established Historical Fact

The empty tomb, the silent testimony to the resurrection of Christ, has never been refuted. The Romans and Jews could not produce Christ's body or explain where it went. Nevertheless they refused to believe. Men and women still reject the resurrection, not because of the insufficiency of evidence but in spite of its sufficiency.

E. H. Day writes: "In that empty tomb Christendom has always discerned an important witness to the reasonableness of belief. Christians have never doubted that as a matter of fact it was found empty on the third day; the Gospel narratives agree in emphasizing it; it [the burden of proof] . . . rests not upon those who hold the tradition, but upon those who either deny that the tomb was found empty, or explain the absence of the Lord's body by some rationalistic theory." (Day, ER, 25)

James Denney, cited by Smith, says: "The empty grave is not the product of a naive apologetic spirit, a spirit not content with the evidence for the Resurrection contained in the fact that the Lord had appeared to His own and had quickened them unto new victorious life; . . . it is an original, independent and unmotived part of the apostolic testimony." (Denney, as cited in Smith, TS, 374).

4B. Established Psychological Facts

1C. The Transformed Lives of the Disciples

John R . W. Stott says: "Perhaps the transformation of the disciples of Jesus is the greatest evidence of all for the resurrection." (Stott, BC, 58–59)

Simon Greenleaf, a Harvard attorney,

> Are these men, who helped transform the moral structure of society, consummate liars or deluded madmen? These alternatives are harder to believe than the fact of the Resurrection, and there is no shred of evidence to support them.
>
> —PAUL LITTLE

says of the disciples: "It was therefore impossible that they could have persisted in affirming the truths they have narrated, had not Jesus actually risen from the dead, and had they not known this fact as certainly as they knew any other fact.

"The annals of military warfare afford scarcely an example of the like heroic constancy, patience, and unflinching courage. They had every possible motive to review carefully the grounds of their faith, and the evidences of the great facts and truths which they asserted." (Greenleaf, TE, 29)

Paul Little asks: "Are these men, who helped transform the moral structure of society, consummate liars or deluded madmen? These alternatives are harder to believe than the fact of the Resurrection, and there is no shred of evidence to support them." (Little, KWhyB, 63)

Look at the changed life of James, the brother of Jesus. Before the resurrection he despised all that his brother stood for. He thought Christ's claims were blatant pretention and served only to ruin the family name. After the resurrection, though, James is found with the other disciples preaching the gospel of their Lord. His epistle describes well the new relationship that he had with Christ. He describes himself as "a bondservant of God and of the Lord Jesus Christ" (James 1:1). The only explanation for this change in his life is that which Paul gives: "After that He [Jesus] was seen by James" (1 Cor. 15:7).

George Matheson says that

the scepticism of Thomas comes out in the belief that the death of Jesus would be the death of His kingdom. "Let us go, that we may die with Him." The man who uttered these words had, at the time when he uttered them, no hope of Christ's resurrection. No man would propose to die with another if he expected to see him again in a few hours.

Thomas, at that moment, had given up all intellectual belief. He saw no chance for Jesus. He did not believe in His physical power. He had made up his mind that the forces of the outer world would be too strong for Him, would crush Him. (Matheson, RMNT, 140)

However, Jesus made Himself known to Thomas also. The result was recorded in John's Gospel where Thomas exclaimed: "My Lord and my God!" (John 20:28). Thomas made an about-face after seeing his Lord risen from the grave. He went on to die a martyr's death.

2C. Transformed Lives through Almost Two-Thousand Years of History

Just as Jesus Christ transformed the lives of His disciples, so the lives of men and women throughout the past nineteen hundred years have also been transformed. For further evidence concerning the witness of transformed lives, see chapter 12: "The Uniqueness of the Christian Experience."

3C. The Verdict

The established psychological fact of changed lives, then, is a credible reason for believing in the resurrection. It is subjective evidence bearing witness to the objective fact that Jesus Christ arose on the third day. For only a risen Christ could have such transforming power in a person's life.

5B. Established Sociological Fact

1C. An Institution: the Christian Church

1D. A basic foundation for the establishment of the church was the preaching of Christ's resurrection.

Acts 1:21, 22: "Therefore all these men who have accompanied us all the time that the Lord Jesus went in and out among us,

On the day of the crucifixion they were filled with sadness; on the first day of the week with gladness. At the crucifixion they were hopeless; on the first day of the week their hearts glowed with certainty and hope. When the message of the resurrection first came they were incredulous and hard to be convinced, but once they became assured they never doubted again. What could account for the astonishing change in these men in so short a time? The mere removal of the body from the grave could never have transformed their spirits, and characters. Three days are not enough for a legend to spring up which would so affect them. Time is needed for a process of legendary growth. It is a psychological fact that demands a full explanation.

Think of the character of the witnesses, men and women who gave the world the highest ethical teaching it has ever known, and who even on the testimony of their enemies lived it out in their lives. Think of the psychological absurdity of picturing a little band of defeated cowards cowering in an upper room one day and a few days later transformed into a company that no persecution could silence—and then attempting to attribute this dramatic change to nothing more convincing than a miserable fabrication they were trying to foist upon the world. That simply wouldn't make sense. (Anderson, RJC, 5–6)

beginning from the baptism of John to that day when He was taken up from us, one of these must become a witness with us of His resurrection."

Acts 2:23, 24: "Him, being delivered by the determined purpose and foreknowledge of God, you have taken by lawless hands, have crucified, and put to death; whom God raised up, having loosed the pains of death, because it was not possible that He should be held by it."

Acts 2:31, 32: "He, foreseeing this, spoke concerning the resurrection of the Christ, that His soul was not left in Hades, nor did His flesh see corruption. This Jesus God has raised up, of which we are all witnesses."

Acts 3:14, 15: "But you denied the Holy One and the Just, and asked for a murderer to be granted to you, and killed the Prince of life, whom God raised from the dead, of which we are witnesses."

Acts 3:26: "To you first, God, having raised up His Servant Jesus, sent Him to bless you, in turning every one of you from your iniquities."

Acts 4:10: "Let it be known to you all, and to all the people of Israel, that by the name of Jesus Christ of Nazareth, whom you crucified, whom God raised from the dead, by Him this man stands here before you whole."

Acts 5:30: "The God of our fathers raised up Jesus whom you murdered by hanging on a tree."

Acts 10:39–41: "And we are witnesses of all things which He did both in the land of the Jews and in Jerusalem, whom they killed by hanging on a tree. Him God raised up on the third day, and showed Him openly, not to all the people, but to witnesses chosen before by God, even to us who ate and drank with Him after He arose from the dead."

Acts 13:29–39: "Now when they had fulfilled all that was written concerning Him, they took Him down from the tree and laid Him in a tomb. But God raised Him from the dead. He was seen for many days by those who came up with Him from Galilee to Jerusalem, who are His witnesses to the people. And we declare to you glad tidings—that promise which was made to the fathers. God has fulfilled this for us their children, in that He raised up Jesus. As it is also written in the second Psalm: 'You are My Son, Today I have begotten You.' And that He raised Him from the dead, no more to return to corruption, He has spoken thus: 'I will give you the sure mercies of David.' Therefore He also says in another Psalm: 'You will not allow Your Holy One to see corruption.' For David, after he had served his own generation by the will of God, fell asleep, was buried with his fathers, and saw corruption; but He whom God raised up saw no corruption. Therefore let it be known to you, brethren, that through this Man is preached to you the forgiveness of sins; and by Him everyone who believes is justified from all things, from which you could not be justified by the law of Moses."

Acts 17:30, 31: "Truly, these times of ignorance God overlooked, but now commands all men everywhere to repent, because He has appointed a day on which He will judge the world in righteousness by the Man whom He has ordained. He has given assurance of this to all by raising Him from the dead."

Acts 26:22, 23: "Therefore, having obtained help from God, to this day I stand, witnessing both to small and great, saying no other things than those which the prophets and Moses said would come—that the Christ would suffer, that He would be the first to rise from the dead, and would proclaim light to the Jewish people and to the Gentiles."

2D. The church is a fact of history. The explanation for the existence of the church is its faith in the resurrection. Throughout its early years, this institution suffered much persecution from the Jews and Romans. Individuals suffered torture and death for their Lord only because they knew that He had risen from the grave.

Wilbur Smith points out that even the rationalist Dr. Guignebert is forced to the following admission:

There would have been no Christianity if the

belief in the resurrection had not been founded and systematized. . . . The whole of the soteriology and the essential teaching of Christianity rests on the belief of the Resurrection, and on the first page of any account of Christian dogma must be written as a motto, Paul's declaration: "And if Christ be not risen,

> Had the crucifixion of Jesus ended His disciples' experience of Him, it is hard to see how the Christian church could have come into existence. That church was founded on faith in the Messiahship of Jesus. A crucified messiah was no messiah at all. He was one rejected by Judaism and accursed of God.
>
> —H. D. A. MAJOR

then is our preaching vain, and your faith is also vain." From the strictly historical point of view, the importance of the belief in the resurrection is scarcely less. . . . By means of that belief, faith in Jesus and in His mission became the fundamental element of a new religion which, after separating from, became the opponent of Judaism, and set out to conquer the world. (Smith, GCWC, 20–21)

Paul Little points out that the church, which was founded around A.D. 32, did not just happen, but had a definite cause. It was said of the Christians at Antioch in the early days of the church that they turned the world upside down (Acts 17:6). The cause of this influence was the resurrection. (Little, KWhyB, 62)

H. D. A. Major, principal of Ripon Hall, Oxford, (cited by Smith) says: "Had the crucifixion of Jesus ended His disciples' experience of Him, it is hard to see how the Christian church could have come into existence. That church was founded on faith in the Messiahship of Jesus. A crucified messiah was no messiah at all. He was one rejected by Judaism and accursed of God. It was the Resurrection of Jesus, as St. Paul declares in Romans 1:4, which proclaimed him to be the Son of God with power." (Major, as cited in Smith, TS, 368)

Kenneth S. Latourette, cited by Straton, says: "It was the conviction of the resurrection of Jesus which lifted His followers out of the despair into which His death had cast them and which led to the perpetuation of the movement begun by Him. But for their profound belief that the crucified had risen from the dead and that they had seen Him and talked with Him, the death of Jesus and even Jesus Himself would probably have been all but forgotten." (Latourette, as cited in Straton, BLR, 3)

2C. The Phenomenon of the Christian Sunday

The Jews' original day of rest and worship was Saturday because it was said that God had finished His creation and rested on the seventh day. This was written into their holy laws. The Sabbath is one of the supporting columns of Judaism. One of the most reverent things in the life of a Jew was the keeping of the Sabbath. The Christians met for worship on the first day of the Jewish week in acknowledgment of the resurrection of Jesus. These Christians actually succeeded in moving to Sunday this age-old and theologically-backed day of rest and worship. Yet remember, THEY WERE JEWS THEMSELVES! Keeping in mind what they thought would happen if they were wrong, we must recognize that this was probably one of the biggest decisions any religious body of men have ever made!! How are we to explain the change from Saturday to Sunday worship without the resurrection? (Green, MA, 51)

J. N. D. Anderson observes that the majority of the first Christians were of Jewish background and had been fanatically attached to their Sabbath. It took, therefore, something extremely significant to change this habit; it took the resurrection to do it! (Anderson, RJC, 9)

3C. The Phenomenon of Christian Sacraments

1D. Communion

[See Acts 2:46; John 6; Matthew 26:26; Mark 14:22; Luke 22:19; 1 Corinthians 11:23, 24.]

The Lord's Supper is a remembrance of His death, but we read in Acts 2:46 that it was a time of joy. Now, if there was not a resurrection, how could there be joy? The memory of the meal that led directly to the betrayal and crucifixion of Jesus, their Lord, would have been an unbearable pain. What changed the anguish of the Last Supper into a communion of joy the world over?

Michael Green comments:

They *met* Him in this sacrament. He was not dead and gone, but risen and alive. And they would celebrate this death of His, in the consciousness of His risen presence, until His longed for return at the end of history (1 Corinthians 11:26). We possess a short eucharistic prayer from the earliest Christian community, from the original Aramaic-speaking church (1 Corinthians 16:22 and *Didache*, 10). Here it is. *Maranatha!* It means, "Our Lord, come!" How that could have been the attitude of the early Christians as they met

They were Jews, and Jews have a tenacity in clinging to their religious customs. Yet these men observed the Lord's day, a weekly memorial of the resurrection, instead of the Sabbath.

—L. L. MORRIS, CITED BY J. D. DOUGLAS

to celebrate the Lord's Supper among themselves is quite inexplicable, unless He did indeed rise from the dead on the third day. (Green, MA, 53)

2D. Baptism

[See Colossians 2:12; Romans 6:1–6.]

The Christians had an initiation ceremony—baptism. This is where they dared to depart again from Judaism. The Jews continued to circumcise, while the Christians followed their Lord's command concerning baptism. A person was called to repent of his or her sins, believe in the risen Lord, and be baptized.

Now, what did baptism symbolize? There is little doubt about this! Paul explains that in baptism a believer is united to Christ in His death and resurrection. When he enters the water he dies to his old sin nature, and he rises out of the water to share a new resurrected life of Christ. There is nothing in Christianity older than the sacraments, and yet they are directly linked to the death and resurrection of Christ. How is one to account for the meaning of Christian baptism if the resurrection never took place?

4C. The Historical Phenomenon of the Church

The institution of the church, then, is a historical phenomenon explained only by Jesus' resurrection. Those sacraments that Christianity observes serve also as a continual evidence of the church's origin.

Concerning the first believers who witnessed Christ's resurrection, L. L. Morris comments:

They were Jews, and Jews have a tenacity in clinging to their religious customs. Yet these men observed the Lord's day, a weekly memorial of the resurrection, instead of the Sabbath.

> *Of making many books there is no end.*
>
> —ECCLESIASTES 12:12

On that Lord's day they celebrated the holy communion, which was not a commemoration of a dead Christ, but a thankful remembrance of the blessings conveyed by a living and triumphant Lord. Their other sacrament, baptism, was a reminder that believers were buried with Christ and raised with Him (Colossians 2:12). The resurrection gave significance to all that they did. (Morris, as cited in Douglas, NBD, 1088)

7A. INADEQUATE THEORIES ABOUT THE RESURRECTION

Winfried Corduan comments on the alternative theories to the resurrection en masse: "Non-miraculous explanations of what happened at the empty tomb have to face a cruel choice: either they have to rewrite the evidence in order to suit themselves or they have to accept the fact that they are not consistent with present evidence. The only hypothesis that fits the evidence is that Jesus was really resurrected. Could the Man who predicted His death and resurrection, only to have it come to pass exactly as He had said, be anything but God?" (Corduan, NDA, 227).

Listed on the next few pages is a compilation of the most popular theoretical explanations that have been put forth to explain away the resurrection of Christ. Each theory will be considered in turn with its corresponding refutation. J. N. D. Anderson, the British attorney, is quite aware of the importance of good evidence in judging a case's veracity. Concerning the testimony that history gives to the resurrection, he writes:

A point which needs stressing is that the evidence must be considered as a whole. It is comparatively easy to find an alternative explanation for one or another of the different strands which make up this testimony. But such explanations are valueless unless they fit the other strands in the testimony as well. A number of different theories, each of which might conceivably be applicable to part of the evidence but which do not themselves cohere into an intelligible pattern, can provide no alternative to the one interpretation which fits the whole. (Anderson, DCR, 105)

Such will be the approa ch taken in considering the following theories.

1B. The Swo-o-o-n Theory

1C. The View
This view holds that Christ never actually died on the cross, but only *swooned*. When He was placed in the tomb of Joseph of Arimathea, He was still alive. After several hours, He was revived by the cool air of the tomb, arose, and departed.

J. N. D. Anderson says of this theory that it was "first put forward by a man named Venturini a couple of centuries or so ago. It has been resuscitated in recent years in a slightly different form by a heterodox group of Muslims called the Ahmadiya, who used to have their main headquarters at a place called Qadian and who have their English headquarters in a part of London called Putney.

Their explanation runs like this: Christ was indeed nailed to the cross. He suffered terribly from shock, loss of blood, and pain, and He swooned away; but He didn't actually die. Medical knowledge was not very great at that time, and the apostles thought He was dead. We are told, are we not, that Pilate was surprised that He was dead already. The explanation assertedly is that He was taken down from the cross in a state of swoon by those who wrongly believed Him to be dead, and laid in the sepulchre. And the cool restfulness of the sepulchre so far revived Him that He

was eventually able to issue forth from the grave. His ignorant disciples couldn't believe that this was a mere resuscitation. They insisted it was a resurrection from the dead. (Anderson, CWH, 7)

Professor Kevan says of the swoon theory that also responsible for Christ's resuscitation were the "reviving effects of the spices with which He had been embalmed." (Kevan, RC, 9)

2C. The Refutation
Anderson comes to the conclusion: "This theory does not stand up to investigation." (Anderson, DCR, 95)

W. J. Sparrow-Simpson says that it is "now quite obsolete." (Fallow, PCBE, 510)

I am confident that the following points will show why these men came to such conclusions.

1D. Christ did die on the cross, according to the judgment of the soldiers, Joseph, and Nicodemus.

Paul Little writes in reference to the swoon theory: "It is significant that not a suggestion of this kind has come down from antiquity among all the violent attacks which have been made on Christianity. All of the earliest records are emphatic about Jesus' *death.*" (Little, KWhyB, 65)

T. J. Thorburn mentions the following as what Christ suffered at the hands of Pilate: "The Agony in the Garden, the arrest at midnight, the brutal treatment in the hall of the High Priest's palace and at the praetorium of Pilate, the exhausting journeys backwards and forwards between Pilate and Herod, the terrible Roman scourging, the journey to Calvary, during which He fell exhausted by the strain upon His powers, the agonizing torture of the Crucifixion, and the thirst and feverishness which followed." (Thorburn, RNMC, 183–85)

Thorburn observes: "It would be difficult to imagine even the most powerful of men, after enduring all these, not succumbing to death. Moreover, it is recorded that the victims of crucifixion seldom recovered, even under the most favourable circumstances." (Thorburn, RNMC, 183–85)

He concludes: "We cannot state the insuperable objections to this theory better than in . . . [these] words. . . . 'Then,' says Keim, 'there is the most impossible thing of all; the poor, weak Jesus, with difficulty holding Himself erect, in hiding, disguised, and finally dying—this Jesus an object of faith, of exalted emotion, of the triumph of His adherents, a risen conqueror, and Son of God! Here, in fact, the theory begins to grow paltry, absurd, worthy only of rejection.'" (Thorburn, RNMC, 183–85)

J. N. D. Anderson remarks on the hypothesis that Jesus did not die:

Well . . . it's very ingenious. But it won't stand up to investigation. To begin with, steps were taken—it seems—to make quite sure that Jesus was dead; that surely is the meaning of the spear-thrust in His side. But suppose for argument's sake that He was not quite dead. Do you really believe that lying for hour after hour with no medical attention in a rock-hewn tomb in Palestine at Easter, when it's quite cold at night, would so far have revived Him, instead of proving the inevitable end to His flickering life, that He would have been able to loose Himself from yards of grave-clothes weighted with pounds of spices, roll away a stone that three women felt incapable of tackling, and walk miles on wounded feet? (Anderson, RJC, 7)

As John R. W. Stott asks, are we to believe

that after the rigours and pains of trial, mockery, flogging and crucifixion He could survive thirty-six hours in a stone sepulchre with neither warmth nor food nor medical care? That He could then rally sufficiently to perform the superhuman feat of shifting the boulder which secured the mouth of the tomb, and this without disturbing the Roman guard? That then, weak and sickly and hungry, He could appear to the disciples in such a way as to give them the impression that He had vanquished death? That He could go on to claim that He had died and risen, could send them into all the world and promise to be with them unto the end of time? That He could live somewhere in hiding for forty days, making occasional surprise appearances, and then finally disappear without any explanation? Such credulity is more incredible than Thomas' unbelief. (Stott, BC, 48–49)

Of modern rationalists who deny the resurrection of Christ, E. Le Camus writes:

Jesus, before His crucifixion, had already suffered much, both in body and soul. He had passed through the anticipation of His death in Gethsemane. He had undergone the frightful pain of a Roman scourging, which left deep scars on the back of the sufferer, and which is almost equivalent to capital punishment. Then they had pierced His hands and feet with nails. The small amount of strength which He might still have had left had been worn away by the six hours of frightful suffering which He had already passed through. Consumed with thirst and completely exhausted, He had at last breathed out His soul in that last cry recorded by the evangelists. Again, a Roman soldier had pierced His heart with a spear. With no food or drink, with no one to dress His wounds or alleviate His suffering in any way, He had passed a whole day and two nights in the cave in which He was laid. And yet, on the morning of the third day behold Him reappearing, active and radiant!

—F. GODET, AS CITED BY E. F. KEVAN

They say: "If He is risen, He was not dead, or if He died, He is not risen."

Two facts, one as certain as the other, throw light on this dilemma. The first is that on Friday evening Jesus was dead; and the second, that He appeared full of life on Sunday and on the days that followed.

That He was dead on Friday evening no one has doubted; neither in the Sanhedrin, nor in the Praetorium, nor on Calvary. Pilate alone was astonished that He had so soon given up the ghost, but his astonishment only called forth new testimony corroborating the assertion of those who asked for His body.

Therefore, friends and enemies, looking on the Crucified, saw clearly that He was no more. To prove it the better, the centurion pierced Him with his lance, and the corpse made no motion. From the wound came forth a mixture of water and of blood, which revealed a rapid decomposition of the vital elements. Bleeding, they say, is fatal in syncope. Here it has not killed Him Who is already dead. For the circumstances in which it occurred prove that Jesus had ceased to live some moments before. And it does not occur to the most intelligent of His enemies, such as the chief priests, to cast a doubt on the reality of His death. All that they fear is fraud on the part of the disciples, who may remove the body, but not on the part of Jesus Whom they have seen expire. He was taken down from the cross, and just as He had shown no sign of life at the stroke of the soldier's spear, so now He lies still and cold in the loving arms that lift Him up, take Him away, embalm, enshroud, and lay Him in the tomb, after covering Him with proofs of their desolation and their love. Can we imagine a more complete swoon than this or one more suitably timed? Let us add that this would indeed be a most fortuitous ending of a life already, in itself, so prodigious in its sanctity and so fecund in its influence. This were an impossible coincidence! It were more miraculous even than the Resurrection itself! (Le Camus, LC, 485–86)

2D. Jesus' disciples did not perceive Him as having merely revived from a swoon.

Skeptic David Friedrich Strauss—himself certainly no believer in the resurrection—gave the deathblow to any thought that Jesus revived from a swoon:

> It is impossible that a being who had stolen half-dead out of the sepulchre, who crept about weak and ill, wanting medical treatment, who required bandaging, strengthening and indulgence, and who still at last yielded to his sufferings, could have given to the disciples the impression that he was a Conqueror over death and the grave, the Prince of Life, an impression which lay at the bottom of their future ministry. Such a resuscitation could only have weakened the impression which he had made upon them in life and in death, at the most could only have given it an elegiac voice, but could by no possibility have changed their sorrow into enthusiasm, have elevated their reverence into worship. (Strauss, LJP, 412)

William Milligan, in describing Jesus' appearances to His disciples, says they were "not those of a sick chamber, but of health and strength and busy preparation for a great work to be immediately engaged in." He continues: "Despondency has given place

> Those who hold this theory have to say that Christ, in a weakened condition, was able to roll back the stone at the entrance of the tomb—a feat which historians say would take several men—step out of the sepulchre without awaking any one of the soldiers (if we assume for argument's sake that they were asleep, and we know they were certainly not!), step over the soldiers and escape.
>
> —JAMES ROSSCUP

to hope, despair to triumph, prostration of all energy to sustained and vigorous exertion." (Milligan, RL, 76–77)

He continues: "When the first fears of the disciples were dispelled, it was one of joy, of boldness, and of enthusiasm; we see none of those feelings of pity, of sympathy with suffering, of desire to render help, that must have been called forth by the appearance of a person who had swooned away through weariness and agony, who had continued in unconsciousness from Friday afternoon to Sunday morning, and who was now only in the first moments of recovery." (Milligan, RL, 76–77)

E. H. Day says: "In the narratives of the various appearances of the risen Christ there is no hint of any such physical weakness as would have been inevitable if Christ had revived from apparent death. The disciples in fact saw in their risen Master not One recovering against all expectation from acute sufferings, but One Who was the Lord of life and the Conqueror of death, and Who was no longer fettered as they had known Him to be in the days of His ministry, by physical limitations." (Day, ER, 49–50)

3D. Those who propose the swoon theory would also have to say that Jesus, once He had revived, was able to perform the miracle of wiggling out of the grave clothes that were wound tightly about all the curves of His body, and leave without at all disarranging these.

Merrill C. Tenney explains the grave clothes:

In preparing a body for burial according to Jewish custom, it was usually washed and straightened, and then bandaged tightly from the armpits to the ankles in strips of linen about a foot wide. Aromatic spices, often of a gummy consistency, were placed between the wrappings or folds. They served partially as a preservative and partially as a cement to glue the cloth wrappings into a solid covering. . . . John's term "bound" (Gr. *edesan*), is in perfect accord with the language of Luke 23:53, where the writer says that the body was *rolled . . . in linen*. . . .

On the morning of the first day of the week the body of Jesus had vanished, but the graveclothes were still there. . . .

The wrappings were in position where the head had been, separated from the others by the distance from armpits to neck. The shape of the body was still apparent in them, but the flesh and bone had disappeared. . . . How was the corpse extricated from the wrappings, since they would not slip over the curves of the body when tightly wound around it? (Tenney, as cited in Smith, TS, 116–17)

4D. "Those who hold this theory," writes James Rosscup, "have to say that Christ, in a weakened condition, was able to roll back the stone at the entrance of the tomb—a feat which historians say would take several men—step out of the sepulchre without awaking any one of the soldiers (if we assume for argument's sake that they were asleep, and we know they were certainly not!), step over the soldiers and escape." (Rosscup, CN, 3)

E. H. Day comments on this point: "The physical improbabilities of the supposition are indeed overwhelming. Even if we were to reject the account of the guarding of the sepulchre (in obedience to the dictates of a criticism which finds in it an inconvenient incident) there remains the difficulty of supposing that One but just recovered from a swoon could have rolled away the stone from the door of the sepulchre, 'for it was very great.'" (Day, ER, 48–49)

It is absurd to suppose that Jesus could

have fought off the Roman guard even if He had managed to roll away the stone. Such men as would have kept the watch should scarcely have had difficulty in dealing with "a being who had stolen half-dead out of the sepulchre," as Strauss described Jesus. Also, the punishment for falling asleep while on watch was death, so the guard would have been wide awake.

5D. If Jesus had merely revived from a swoon, the long walk "to a village named Emmaus, which was about seven miles from Jerusalem" (Luke 24:13), would have been impossible.

Professor Day observes, "A long walk, followed by the appearance to the disciples at Jerusalem, is inconceivable in the case of one recovered from a swoon caused by wounds and exhaustion." (Day, ER, 48–49)

E. F. Kevan makes the following comments on this point:

On His feet, which had been pierced through and through only two days back, He walks without difficulty the two leagues between Emmaus and Jerusalem. He is so active, that during the repast He disappears suddenly out of sight of His fellow-travelers, and when they return to the capital to announce the good news to the apostles, they find Him there again! He has overtaken them. With the same quickness which characterizes all His movements, He presents Himself suddenly in the room in which the disciples are assembled.... Are these the actions of a man who had just been taken down half-dead from the cross, and who has been laid in a grave in a condition of complete exhaustion? No. (Kevan, RC, 9–10)

6D. If Jesus had merely revived from a deathlike swoon, He would have explained His condition to the disciples. Remaining silent, He would have been a liar and deceiver, allowing His followers to spread a resurrection proclamation that was really a resurrection fairy tale.

E. Le Camus writes:

Let us say, moreover, that if Jesus had only swooned, He could not, without injury to His character, allow any one to believe that He had been dead. Instead of presenting Himself as one *risen again*, He should have said simply *preserved* by chance. In fact, here as every where else in the Gospel, we encounter this insurmountable dilemma: either Jesus was the Just One, the Man of God, or among men He is the greatest of criminals. If He presented Himself as one from the dead, whereas He was not such, He is guilty of falsehood, and must be denied even the most common honesty. (Le Camus, LC, 485–86)

Paul Little comments that such a theory requires us to believe that "Christ Himself was involved in flagrant lies. His disciples believed and preached that He was dead but became alive again. Jesus did nothing to dispel this belief, but rather encouraged it." (Little, KWhyB, 66)

John Knox, the New Testament scholar, is quoted by Straton: "It was not the fact that a

> In fact, here as every where else in the Gospel, we encounter this insurmountable dilemma: either Jesus was the Just One, the Man of God, or among men He is the greatest of criminals. If He presented Himself as one from the dead, whereas He was not such, He is guilty of falsehood, and must be denied even the most common honesty.
>
> —E. LE CAMUS

man had risen from the dead but that a particular man had done so which launched the Christian movement. . . . The character of Jesus was its deeper cause." (Knox, as cited in Straton, BLR, 3)

Jesus would have had no part in perpetrating the lie that He had risen from the grave if He had not. Such an allegation is unreservedly impugned as one examines His spotless character.

7D. If Christ did not die at this time, then when did He die, and under what circumstances?

E. H. Day asserts: "If the swoon-theory be accepted, it is necessary to eliminate from the Gospels and the Acts the whole of the Ascension narrative, and to account for the sudden cessation of Christ's appearances by the supposition that He withdrew Himself from them completely, to live and die in absolute seclusion, leaving them with a whole series of false impressions concerning His Own Person, and their mission from Him to the world." (Day, ER, 50)

William Milligan writes that if Christ merely swooned on the cross and later revived,

> He must have retired to some solitary retreat unknown even to the most attached of His disciples. While His Church was rising around Him, shaking the old world to its foundations, and introducing everywhere amid many difficulties a new order of things—while it was torn by controversies, surrounded by temptations, exposed to trials, placed in short in the very circumstances that made it most dependent on His aid—He was absent from it, and spending the remainder of His days, whether few or many, in what we can describe by no other term than ignoble solitude. And then at last He must have died—no one can say either where, or when, or how! There is not a ray of light to penetrate the darkness; and these early Christians, so fertile, we are told, in legends, have not a single legend to give us help. (Milligan, RL, 79)

3C. Conclusion

With George Hanson, one can honestly say of the swoon theory: "It is hard to believe that this was the favourite explanation of eighteenth-century rationalism." The evidence speaks so much to the contrary of such a hypothesis that it is now obsolete. (Hanson, G., RL, 19)

2B. The Theft Theory

1C. The View
In this view it is understood that the disciples came during the night and stole the body from the tomb.

1D. Matthew records the following as being the prevailing theory of his time to explain away the resurrection of Christ:

> Now while they were going, behold, some of the guard came into the city and reported to the chief priests all the things that had happened. When they had assembled with the elders and consulted together, they gave a large sum of money to the soldiers, saying, "Tell them, 'His disciples came at night and stole Him away while we slept.' And if this comes to the governor's ears, we will appease him and make you secure." So they took the money and did as they were instructed; and this saying is commonly reported among the Jews until this day (Matt. 28:11–15).

2D. That the theft theory as recorded in Matthew was popular among the Jews for some time is seen in the writings of Justin Martyr, Tertullian, and others.

Professor Thorburn observes:

> In Justin's *Dialogue Against Trypho* 108, the Jew speaks of "one Jesus, a Galilean deceiver, whom we crucified; but his disciples stole him by night from the tomb, where he was laid when unfastened from the cross, and now deceive men by asserting that he has risen from the dead and ascended into heaven."
>
> So also Tertullian (*Apology* 21) says: "The grave was found empty of all but the clothes of

THERE ARE ONLY *TWO* EXPLANATIONS FOR THE EMPTY TOMB	
A Human Work	*A Divine Work*
Removed by Enemies—No Motive Removed by Friends—No Power	Most Logical Explanation

the buried one. But, nevertheless, the leaders of the Jews, whom it nearly concerned both to spread abroad a lie, and keep back a people tributary and submissive to them from the faith, gave it out that the body of Christ had been stolen by his followers." And, again, with a fine scorn he says [*De Spectaca* 30.], "This is he whom his disciples secretly stole away that it might be said that he had risen again, or the gardener had taken away, in order that his lettuces might not be damaged by the crowds of visitors!"

This statement we find repeated in Jewish mediaeval literature [Jewish book in Eisenmenger, i. pp. 189 ff., etca]. Reimarus repeats the same story: "The disciples of Jesus," he says, "purloined the body of Jesus before it had been buried twenty-four hours, played at the burial-place the comedy of the empty grave, and delayed the public announcement of the resurrection until the fiftieth day, when the decay of the body had become complete."

The statements and arguments of this very old theory were fully answered by Origen [*Cont. Cels.*]. (Thorburn, RNMC, 191–92)

3D. John Chrysostom of Antioch (A.D. 347–407) said of the theft theory:

"For indeed even this establishes the resurrection, the fact I mean of their saying, that the disciples stole Him. For this is the language of men confessing, that the body was not there. When therefore they confess the body was not there, but the stealing it is shown to be false and incredible, by their watching by it, and by the seals, and by the timidity of the disciples, the proof of the resurrection even hence appears incontro-

vertible." (Chrysostom, as cited in Clark, GM, 531)

2C. The Refutation

1D. The Empty Tomb Has to Be Explained Somehow

E. F. Kevan says that while the empty tomb does not necessarily prove the resurrection, it does present two distinct alternatives: "The empty tomb was either a Divine work or a human one." Both of these choices must be objectively considered and the one with the highest probability of being true must be accepted. (Kevan, RC, 14)

Kevan continues: "No difficulty presents itself, however, when the decision has to be made between such alternatives as these. The enemies of Jesus had no motive for removing the body; the friends of Jesus had no power to do so. It would have been to the advantage of the authorities that the body should remain where it was; and the view that the disciples stole the body is impossible. The power that removed the body of the Saviour from the tomb must therefore have been Divine." (Kevan, RC, 14)

Le Camus puts it this way:

If Jesus, who had been laid in the tomb on Friday, was not there on Sunday, either He was removed or He came forth by His own power. There is no other alternative. Was He removed? By whom? By friends or by enemies? The latter had set a squad of soldiers to guard Him, therefore they had no intention of causing Him to disappear. Moreover, their prudence could not counsel this. This would have made the way too easy for stories of the resurrection which the disciples might invent. The wisest course was for them to guard Him as a proof. Thus they could reply to every pretension that might arise: "Here is the corpse, He is not risen."

As for His friends, they had neither the intention nor the power to remove Him. (Le Camus, LC, 482)

Wilbur Smith writes: "These soldiers did not know how to explain the empty tomb; they were told what to say by the Sanhedrin and bribed that they might repeat in fear this quickly concocted tale." (Smith, GCWC, 22–23)

A. B. Bruce comments: "The report to be sent abroad assumes that there is a fact to be explained, the disappearance of the body. And it is implied that the statement to be given out as to that was known by the soldiers to be false." (Bruce, EGNT, 337–38)

2D. That the disciples stole Christ's body is not a reasonable explanation for the empty tomb.

1E. The guard's testimony was not questioned. Matthew records that "some of the guard came into the city and reported to the chief priests all the things that had happened" (Matt. 28:11).

R. C. H. Lenski remarks that the message of Jesus' resurrection was delivered to the high priests through their own witnesses, "the soldiers they themselves had posted, the most unimpeachable witnesses possible." The testimony of the guard was accepted as being entirely true; they knew the guard had no reason to lie. (Lenski, IMG, 1161–62)

Wilbur M. Smith writes: "It should be noticed first of all that the Jewish authorities never questioned the report of the guards.

They did not themselves go out to see if the tomb was empty, because they knew it was empty. The guards would never have come back with such a story as this on their lips, unless they were reporting actual, indisputable occurrences, as far as they were able to apprehend them. The story which the Jewish authorities told the soldiers to repeat was a story to explain how the tomb became empty." (Smith, TS, 375–76)

Albert Roper, speaking of Annas and Caiaphas, says: "Their hypocritical explanation of the absence of the body of Jesus from the tomb proclaims the falsity of their allegation, else why should they have sought to suborn the perjured testimony of the soldiers?" (Roper, JRD, 37)

The Jews, then, by not questioning the veracity of the guard's testimony, give tacit assent to the emptiness of Christ's tomb. Their concocted tale that the disciples stole Jesus' body is only a lame excuse, put forth for lack of anything better.

2E. Much precaution was taken in securing the tomb against the theft. To the disciples, such measures would have been an insurmountable obstacle in any plan of grave robbery.

Albert Roper says:

Let us be fair. We are confronted with an explanation which to reasonable minds cannot and does not explain; a solution which does not solve. When the chief priests induced Pilate to "command . . . that the sepulchre be made sure until the third day," the factual record justifies the conclusion that the sepulchre was in very truth made "sure." Reasoning, therefore, from that record, we are inescapably faced with the conclusion that the measures taken to prevent the friends of Jesus from stealing His body now constitute unimpeachable proof that they could not and did not steal it. (Roper, JRD, 34)

John Chrysostom, in speaking of the women who came early Sunday morning to Jesus' tomb, writes: "They considered that no man could have taken Him when so many soldiers were sitting by Him, unless He raised up Himself." (Chrysostom, HGSM, as cited in Schaff, SLNPNF, 527)

3E. The depression and cowardice of the disciples is a hard-hitting argument that they could not have suddenly become so brave and daring as to face a detachment of soldiers at the tomb and steal the body. They were in no mood to try anything like that.

Wilbur M. Smith says: "The disciples who had fled from Jesus when He was being tried, neither had the courage nor the physical power to go up against a group of soldiers." (Smith, GCWC, 22–23)

Smith continues:

These disciples were in no mood to go out and face Roman soldiers, subdue the entire guard, and snatch that body out of the tomb. I think, myself, if they had attempted it, they would have been killed, but they certainly were in no mood even to try it. On Thursday night of that week Peter had proved himself such a coward, when a maid twitted him in the lower hall of the palace of the high priest, accusing him of belonging to the condemned Nazarene, that, to save his own skin, he denied his Lord, and cursed and swore. What could have happened to Peter within those few hours to change him from such a coward to a man rushing out to fight Roman soldiers? (Smith, TS, 376–77)

Concerning the theft theory, Fallow writes in his encyclopedia:

It is probable they would not, and it is next to certain they [the disciples] could not [rob Jesus' grave].

How could they have undertaken to remove the body? Frail and timorous creatures, who fled as soon as they saw Him taken

into custody; even Peter, the most courageous, trembled at the voice of a servant girl, and three times denied that he knew Him. People of this character, would they have dared to resist the authority of the governor? Would they have undertaken to oppose the determi-

> If Jesus Christ were not risen again (I speak the language of unbelievers), He had deceived His disciples with vain hopes of His resurrection. How came the disciples not to discover the imposter?
>
> —WILBUR SMITH

nation of the Sanhedrin, to force a guard, and to elude or overcome soldiers armed and aware of danger? If Jesus Christ were not risen again (I speak the language of unbelievers), He had deceived His disciples with vain hopes of His resurrection. How came the disciples not to discover the imposter? Would they have hazarded themselves by undertaking an enterprise so perilous in favor of a man who had so cruelly imposed on their credulity? But were we to grant that they formed the design of removing the body, how could they have executed it? (Fallow, PCBE, 1452)

A. Roper writes: "There is not one of that little band of disciples who would have dared to violate that sealed tomb even if there were no Roman soldiers guarding it. The thought that one of them could accomplish such an undertaking in the face of the preventive measures which had been adopted is utterly fantastic." (Roper, JRD, 37)

4E. If the soldiers were sleeping, how could they say the disciples stole the body?

The following commentary on the theft theory appears in *Fallow's Encyclopedia:* "'Either,' says St. Augustine, 'they were asleep or awake; if they were awake, why should they suffer the body to be taken away? If asleep, how could they know that the disciples took it away? How dare they then depose that it was stolen?'" (Fallow, PCBE, 1452)

A. B. Bruce says of the Roman guard: "They were perfectly aware that they had not fallen asleep at their post and that no theft had taken place. The lie for which the priests paid so much money is suicidal; one half destroys the other. Sleeping sentinels could not know what happened." (Bruce, EGNT, 337–38)

David Brown remarks: "If anything were needed to complete the proof of the reality of Christ's resurrection, it would be the silliness of the explanation which the guards were bribed to give of it. That a whole guard should go to sleep on their watch at all, was not very likely; that they should do it in a case like this, where there was such anxiety on the part of the authorities that the grave should remain undisturbed, was in the last degree improbable." (Jamieson, CCEP, 133)

Paul Little says of the theory concocted by the Jews: "They gave the soldiers money and told them to explain that the disciples had come at night and stolen the body while they were asleep. That story is so obviously false that Matthew does not even bother to refute it! What judge would listen to you if you said that while you were asleep, your neighbor came into your house and stole your television set? Who knows what goes on while he's asleep? Testimony like this would be laughed out of any court." (Little, KWhyB, 63–64).

5E. The soldiers would not have fallen asleep while on watch—to do so would have meant death from their superior officers.

A. B. Bruce writes: "The ordinary punishment for falling asleep on the watch was death. Could the soldiers be persuaded by any amount of money to run such a risk? Of course they might take the money and go away laughing at the donors, meaning to tell their general the truth. Could the priests

expect anything else? If not, could they propose the project seriously? The story has its difficulties." (Bruce, EGNT, 337–38)

Edward Gordon Selwyn, cited by Wilbur Smith, comments on the possibility of the guards' falling asleep:

That without an exception *all* should have fallen asleep when they were stationed there for so extraordinary a purpose, to see that the body was not stolen . . . is not credible: especially when it is considered that these guards were subjected to the severest discipline in the world. It was death for a Roman sentinel to sleep at his post. Yet these guards were not executed; nor were they deemed culpable even by the rules, woefully chagrined and exasperated as they must have been by failure of their plan for securing the body. . . . That the Jewish rulers did not believe what they instructed and bribed the soldiers to say, is almost self-evident. If they did, why were not the disciples at once arrested and examined? For such an act as was imputed to them involved a serious offence against the existent authorities. Why were they not compelled to give up the body? Or, in the event of their being unable to exculpate themselves from the charge, why were they not punished for their crime? . . . It is nowhere intimated that the rulers even attempted to substantiate the charge. (Selwyn, as cited in Smith, TS, 578–79)

William Paley, the English theologian and philosopher, writes: "It has been rightly, I think, observed by Dr. Townshend (Dis. upon the Res. p. 126), that the story of the guards carried collusion upon the fact of it:—'His disciples came by night, and stole him away, while we slept.' Men in their circumstances would not have made such an acknowledgment of their negligence, without previous assurances of protection and impunity." (Paley, VEC, 196)

6E. The stone at the tomb was extremely large. Even if the soldiers were asleep and the disciples did try to steal the body, the noise caused while moving such a rock would surely have awakened them.

Wilbur Smith says: "Surely these soldiers would have been awakened by the rolling back of a heavy stone, and the taking out of the body of Jesus." (Smith, GCWC, 22–23)

David Brown writes: "But—even if it could be supposed that so many disciples should come to the grave as would suffice to break the seal, roll back the huge stone, and carry off the body—that the guards should all sleep soundly enough and long enough to admit of all this tedious and noisy work being gone through at their very side without being awoke." (Jamieson, CCEP, 133)

7E. The grave clothes give a silent testimony to the impossibility of theft.

Merrill Tenney remarks: "No robbers would ever have rewound the wrappings in their original shape, for there would not have been time to do so. They would have flung the cloths down in disorder and fled with the body. Fear of detection would have made them act as hastily as possible." (Tenney, RR, 119)

Albert Roper says:

Such orderliness is inconsistent with grave desecration and body-snatching. One brash enough to undertake such a mission, if one could have been found, would assuredly not have practiced such orderliness, such leisureliness, such calm. It is certainly not in keeping with similar felonious acts with which we are familiar that criminals practice such studious care to leave in a meticulously neat and tidy condition premises which they have looted or vandalized. On the contrary, disorder and disarray are the earmarks of a prowling visitor. Such acts, in the very nature of things, are not performed in a leisurely manner. Their perpetration calls for haste in which tidiness plays no part. The very orderliness of the tomb, tes-

tified to by John, proclaims the absurdity of the charge that the body of Jesus was stolen by His disciples. (Roper, JRD, 35–37)

Gregory of Nyssa, writing fifteen hundred years ago, observes "that the disposition of

> The disposition of the clothes in the sepulchre, the napkin that was about our Saviour's head, not lying with the linen clothes, but wrapped together in a place by itself, did not bespeak the terror and hurry of thieves, and, therefore, refutes the story of the body being stolen.
>
> —GREGORY OF NYSSA

the clothes in the sepulchre, the napkin that was about our Saviour's head, not lying with the linen clothes, but wrapped together in a place by itself, did not bespeak the terror and hurry of thieves, and, therefore, refutes the story of the body being stolen." (Whitworth, LHP, 64–65)

Chrysostom, also a fourth century author, writes in like manner:

And what mean also the napkins that were stuck on with the myrrh; for Peter saw these lying. For if they had been disposed to steal, they would not have stolen the body naked, not because of dishonoring it only, but in order not to delay and lose time in stripping it, and not to give them that were so disposed opportunity to awake and seize them. Especially when it was myrrh, a drug that adheres so to the body, and cleaves to the clothes, whence it was not easy to take the clothes off the body, but they that did this needed much time, so that from this again, the tale of the theft is improbable.

What? did they not know the rage of the Jews? and that they would vent their anger on them? And what profit was it at all to them, if He had not risen again? (Chrysostom,

HGSM, as cited in Schaff, SLNPNF, 530–31).

Simon Greenleaf, the famous Harvard professor of law, says:

The grave-clothes lying orderly in their place, and the napkin folded together by itself, made it evident that the sepulchre had not been rifled nor the body stolen by violent hands; for these garments and spices would have been of more value to thieves, than merely a naked corpse; at least, they would not have taken the trouble thus to fold them together. The same circumstances showed also that the body had not been removed by friends; for they would not thus have left the grave-clothes behind. All these considerations produce in the mind of John the germ of a belief that Jesus was risen from the dead. (Greenleaf, TE, 542)

Henry Latham, who gives a good description of the grave clothes, remarks that they were in one spot, and makes further observations on

the hundred pounds' weight of spice. This spice was dry; the quantity mentioned is large; and if the clothes had been unwrapped, the powdered myrrh and aloes would have fallen on the slab, or on the floor, in a very conspicuous heap. Peter, when from the inside of the tomb he described to John, with great particularity, what he saw, would certainly have not passed this by. Mr. Beard bears the spice in mind, and speaks of it as weighing down the grave-clothes, but he misses the point—to me so significant—that if the clothes had been unfolded the spice would have dropped out and made a show. That nothing is said about the spice favours the supposition that it remained between the wrappers where it was originally laid, and consequently was out of sight. (Latham, RM, 9)

8E. The disciples would not have moved Christ's body.

Wilbur Smith comments:

The disciples had absolutely no reason for taking away the body, which had been honorably buried. They could do no more for the body of their Lord than had been done. Joseph of Arimathea never told them to remove the body from its first burial place; it was not suggested by anyone else; and therefore, if they *had* undertaken such a task, it would only be, not for the honor of the Lord, or for their own preservation, but for the purpose of deceiving others; in other words, to foist a lie concerning Jesus upon the people of Palestine. Now whatever else these disciples were, who had followed the Lord for three years, they were not liars, with the exception of Judas, who was already dead. They were not mean men given to deceit. It is inconceivable that the eleven, after having companioned with the Holy Son of God who, Himself, condemned falsehood and ever exalted the truth, after hearing Him preach a gospel of more exalted righteousness than had ever been heard anywhere in the world before, it is inconceivable that these eleven disciples should all suddenly agree to enter into such a vile conspiracy as this. (Smith, TS, 377)

9E. The disciples did not realize the truth of the resurrection as yet and so would not have been seeking to make it come true (see Luke 24).

As John F. Whitworth observes, "They did not seem to understand that He was to rise the third day; they certainly were surprised when they found that He had risen. These circumstances negate the thought that they would even contemplate stealing the body to create the impression that He had risen." (Whitworth, LHP, 64)

A. B. Bruce writes:

The disciples, even if capable of such a theft, so far as scruples of conscience were concerned, were not in a state of mind to think of it, or to attempt it. They had not spirit left for such a daring action. Sorrow lay like a weight of lead on their hearts, and made them almost as inanimate as the corpse they are supposed to have stolen. Then the motive for the theft is one which could not have influenced them then. Steal the body to propagate a belief in the resurrection! What interest had they in propagating a belief which they did not entertain themselves? "As yet they knew not the Scriptures, that He must rise again from the dead": nor did they remember aught that their Master had said on this subject before His decease. (Bruce, TT, 494)

10E. "The disciples were men of honor," says James Rosscup, "and could not have foisted a lie upon the people. They spent the rest of their lives proclaiming the message of the resurrection, as cowards transformed into men of courage. They were willing to face arrest, imprisonment, beating, and horrible deaths, and not one them ever denied the Lord and recanted of his belief that Christ had risen." (Rosscup, CN, 4)

Paul Little, in discussing the theft theory, remarks: "Furthermore, we are faced with a psychological and ethical impossibility. Stealing the body of Christ is something totally foreign to the character of the disciples and all that we know of them. It would mean that they were perpetrators of a deliberate lie which was responsible for the misleading and ultimate death of thousands of people. It is inconceivable that, even if a few of the disciples had conspired and pulled off this theft, they would never have told the others." (Little, KWhyB, 63–64)

J. N. D. Anderson, the British lawyer, in commenting on the idea that the disciples stole Christ's body, says: "This would run totally contrary to all we know of them: their ethical teaching, the quality of their lives,

> *The historian must acknowledge that the disciples firmly believed that Jesus was risen.*
>
> —DAVID STRAUSS, 19TH-CENTURY SKEPTIC

their steadfastness in suffering and persecution. Nor would it begin to explain their dramatic transformation from dejected and dispirited escapists into witnesses whom no opposition could muzzle." (Anderson, CWH, 92)

Concerning the theft theory, Kevan writes: "It is here that even the opponents of the Christian view come to its help, for Strauss [1808–1874], the skeptic, rejects the hypothesis of imposture on the part of the disciples as morally impossible. 'The historian,' says Strauss, 'must acknowledge that the disciples firmly believed that Jesus was risen'" (*Leben Jesu,* 1864, p. 289). (Kevan, RC, 9)

Wilbur Smith says, "Even many orthodox Jewish scholars today utterly repudiate this story, including Klausner himself, who will have none of it, and who himself admits that the disciples were too honorable to perform any piece of deception like this" (*Jesus of Nazareth; His Life, Times, and Teaching,* New

"Then Peter, filled with the Holy Spirit, said to them, 'Rulers of the people and elders of Israel: If we are judged for a good deed done to a helpless man, by what means he has been made well, let it be known to you all, and to all the people of Israel, that by the name of Jesus Christ of Nazareth, whom you crucified, whom God raised from the dead, by Him this man stands here before you whole. This is the "stone which was rejected by you builders, which has become the chief cornerstone." Nor is there salvation in any other, for there is no other name under heaven given among men by which we must be saved.'" (Acts 4:8–12)

York, 1925, p. 414). (Smith, GCWC, 22–23)

Was it a "stolen body" that gave Peter boldness in his refutation in Acts 4:8?

Wilbur Smith explains:

> The power of God so came down upon Peter on the day of Pentecost that on that one day, in a sermon occupied, for the most part, with the truth of the Resurrection of Christ, three thousand souls were won to the Lord. One thing is true: *Peter was at least preaching what he believed:* that God had raised Christ from the dead. You cannot conscientiously preach lies with power like this. The disciples went on preaching the Resurrection, until the whole world was turned upside down by faith in this glorious truth. No, the disciples did not and could not have stolen the body of our Lord. (Smith, TS, 377–78)

Each of the disciples, except John, died a martyr's death. They were persecuted because they tenaciously clung to their beliefs and statements. As Paul Little writes: "Men will die for what they *believe* to be true, though it may actually be false: They do not, however, die for what they *know* is a lie." (Little, KWhyB, 173) If the disciples had stolen Jesus' body, they would have known that their resurrection proclamation was false. However, they "constantly referred to the Resurrection as the basis for their teaching, preaching, living and—significantly—dying." The theory that the disciples stole the body, then, is utterly absurd! (Lewis and Short, LD, 62–64)

I agree with John R. W. Stott: The theory that the disciples stole Christ's body "simply does not ring true. It is so unlikely as to be virtually impossible. If anything is clear from the Gospels and the Acts, it is that the apostles were sincere. They may have been deceived, if you like, but they were not deceivers. Hypocrites and martyrs are not made of the same stuff." (Stott, BC, 50)

3D. The theory that the Jews, the Romans, or Joseph of Arimathea moved Christ's body is no more reasonable an explanation for the empty tomb than theft by the disciples.

1E. Did the Jews move the body? J. N. D. Anderson observes,

> Within seven short weeks [after Christ's resurrection]—if the records are to be believed at all, and I cannot see any possible reason for Christian writers to have invented that difficult gap of seven weeks—within seven short weeks Jerusalem was seething with the preaching of the resurrection. The apostles were preaching it up and down the city. The chief priests were very much upset about it. They said that the apostles were trying to bring this man's blood upon them. They were being accused of having crucified the Lord of glory. And they were prepared to go to almost any lengths to nip this dangerous heresy in the bud. (Anderson, RJC, 6)

If the Jews had issued on official order to have the body moved, why, when the apostles were preaching the resurrection in Jerusalem, didn't they explain: "Wait! We moved the body—Christ didn't rise from the grave."

If such a rebuttal failed, why didn't they explain exactly where His body lay?

If this failed, why didn't they recover the corpse, put it on a cart, and wheel it through the center of Jerusalem? Such an action would have destroyed Christianity—not in the cradle, but in the womb!

William Paley, the English theologian and philosopher, writes, "It is evident that, if His body could have been found, the Jews would have produced it, as the shortest and completest answer possible to the whole story. For, notwithstanding their precaution, and although thus prepared and forewarned; when the story of the resurrection of Christ came forth, as it immediately did; when it was publicly asserted by His disciples, and made the ground and basis of their preaching in His name, and collecting followers to His religion; the Jews had not the body to produce." (Paley, VEC, 196–98)

John Whitworth writes of the Jews' silence as to the whereabouts of Jesus' body:

"While this story [of the theft] was afterwards commonly reported among the Jews, yet, as Dr. Gilmore observes, 'not once is it adverted to on those trials of the Apostles which soon took place at Jerusalem, on account of their bold and open proclamation of their Master's resurrection.' Though the Apostles were cited before that very body who had given currency to the report of the disciples' theft, they are not even once taxed with the crime; not even a whisper escapes the lips of the Sanhedrin on the subject; and the story was soon abandoned as untenable and absurd." (Whitworth, LHP, 66)

2E. Did the Romans move the body?

It would have been to the governor's advantage to keep the body in its grave. Pilate's main interest was to keep things peaceful. Moving the body would have caused unwanted agitation to arise from the Jews and the Christians.

J. N. D. Anderson says of Pilate: "He . . . was upset about this strange teaching. If he had had the body moved, it seems incredible that he wouldn't have informed the chief priests when they were so upset." (Anderson, RJC, 6)

Pilate merely wanted peace.

3E. Did Joseph of Arimathea move the body?

Joseph was a secret disciple and as such would not have moved the body without consulting the other disciples first.

If Joseph had ventured to move Christ's body without consulting the rest, he surely would have told the other disciples afterward, when the resurrection message was being published, what he had done.

> The simple faith of the Christian who believes in the Resurrection is nothing compared to the credulity of the sceptic who will accept the wildest and most improbable romances rather than admit the plain witness of historical certainties. The difficulties of belief may be great; the absurdities of unbelief are greater.
>
> —GEORGE HANSON

4E. In conclusion, the facts of the case speak loudly against the theory that Christ's body was moved.

As George Hanson says: "The simple faith of the Christian who believes in the Resurrection is nothing compared to the credulity of the sceptic who will accept the wildest and most improbable romances rather than admit the plain witness of historical certainties. *The difficulties of belief may be great; the absurdities of unbelief are greater.*" (Hanson, G., RL, 24)

3B. The Hallucination Theory

1C. The View

All of Christ's post-resurrection appearances were really only supposed appearances. What really happened was this—people had hallucinations.

> The Hallucination theory "means that if there had been a good neurologist for Peter and the others to consult, there never would have been a Christian Church."
>
> —GRESHAM MACHEN

2C. The Refutation

1D. Were Christ's Appearances That Important?

C. S. Lewis writes:

In the earliest days of Christianity an "apostle" was first and foremost a man who claimed to be an eyewitness of the Resurrection. Only a few days after the Crucifixion when two candidates were nominated for the vacancy created by the treachery of Judas, their qualification was that they had known Jesus personally both before and after His death and could offer first-hand evidence of the Resurrection in addressing the outer world (Acts 1:22). A few days later St. Peter, preaching the first Christian sermon, makes the same claim—"God raised Jesus, of which we all (we Christians) are witnesses" (Acts 2:32). In the first *Letter to the Corinthians* St. Paul bases his claim to apostleship on the same ground— "Am I not an apostle? Have I not seen the Lord Jesus?" (Lewis, M, 148)

2D. Would It Matter If Christ's Post-Resurrection Appearances Were Visions?

Considering Lewis' definition, if the view that regards all of Christ's appearances to have been mere hallucinations were true, then the value of the apostolic office would be nil.

If true, it means, in Gresham Machen's words, "that the Christian Church is founded upon a pathological experience of certain persons in the first century of our era. It means that if there had been a good neurologist for Peter and the others to consult, there never would have been a Christian Church." (Kevan, RC, 10–11)

J. N. D. Anderson, in speaking of "the credibility of the apostolic witness," says that it will either "stand or fall by the validity of their testimony." (Anderson, DCR, 100)

3D. What Is a Vision?

Wilbur Smith says,

The most satisfying *definition* of a vision I have seen is the one by Weiss: "The scientific meaning of this term is that an apparent act of vision takes place for which there is no corresponding external object. The optic nerve has not been stimulated by any outward waves of light or vibrations of the ether, but has been excited by a purely inner physiological cause. At the same time the sense-impression of sight is accepted by the one who experiences the vision as completely as if it were wholly 'objective'; he fully believes the object of his vision to be actually before him." (Smith, TS, 581)

4D. Were Christ's Post-Resurrection Appearances Visions?

Mere visions were not the experience of the disciples; the testimony of the New Testament totally opposes such a hypothesis.

As Hillyer Straton has said: "Men who are subject to hallucinations never become moral heroes. The effect of the resurrection of Jesus in transformed lives was continuous, and most of these early witnesses went to their deaths for proclaiming this truth." (Straton, BLR, 4)

5D. The hallucination theory is not plausible because it contradicts certain laws and principles to which psychiatrists say visions must conform.

1E. Generally, only particular kinds of people have hallucinations. (Anderson, RJC, 4–9); (Little, KWhyB, 67–69); (Peru, OPC, 97–99)

They are those whom one would describe as "high-strung," highly imaginative and very nervous.

The appearances that Christ made were not restricted to persons of any particular psychological make-up.

John R. W. Stott says:

"There was a variety in mood. . . .
"Mary Magdalene was weeping; . . .
"the women were afraid and astonished; . . .
"Peter was full of remorse, . . .
". . . and Thomas of incredulity.
"The Emmaus pair were distracted by the events of the week . . .
". . . and the disciples in Galilee by their fishing."

"It is impossible to dismiss these revelations of the divine Lord as hallucinations of deranged minds." (Stott, BC, 57)

2E. Hallucinations are linked in an individual's subconscious to his particular past experiences. (Anderson, RJC, 4–9); (Little, KWhyB, 67–69); (Peru, OPC, 97–99)

1F. They are very individualistic and extremely subjective.

Heinrich Kluerer in *Psychopathology of Perception,* cites a famous neurobiologist: "[Raoul] Mourgue, in his fundamental treatise on the neurobiology of hallucinations, reached the conclusion that variability and inconstancy represent the most constant features of hallucinatory and related phenomena. For him the hallucination is not a static phenomenon but essentially a dynamic process, the instability of which reflects the very instability of the factors and conditions associated with its origin." (Kleurer, as cited in Hoch, PP, 18)

It is extremely unlikely, then, that two persons would have the same hallucination at the same time.

2F. The appearances that Christ made were seen by many people.

Thomas J. Thorburn asserts:

It is absolutely inconceivable that as many as (say) five hundred persons, of average soundness of mind and temperament, in various numbers, at all sorts of times, and in divers situations, should experience all kinds of sensuous impressions—visual, auditory, tactual—and that all these manifold experiences should rest entirely upon subjective hallucination. We say that this is incredible, because if such a theory were applied to any other than a "supernatural" event in history, it would be dismissed forthwith as a ridiculously insufficient explanation. (Thorburn, RNMC, 158–59)

Theodore Christlieb, cited by Wilbur Smith, says:

We do not deny that science can tell us of cases in which visions were seen by whole assemblies at once; but where this is the case, it has always been accompanied by a *morbid excitement of the mental life,* as well as by a morbid bodily condition, especially by nervous affections. Now, even if one or several of the disciples had been in this morbid state, we should by no means be justified in concluding that all were so. They were surely men of most varied temperament and constitution. And yet, one after another is supposed to have fallen into this morbid condition; not only the excited women, but even Peter, that strong and hardy fisherman who was assuredly as far from nervousness as any one, James, the two on their way to Emmaus, and so on down to the sober, doubting Thomas, aye, and all eleven at once, and even *more than five hundred brethren together.* All of these are supposed to have fallen suddenly into some self-deception, and that, be it noticed, at the most different times and places, and during the most varied occupations (in the morning by the grave; in conversation by the wayside; in the confidential circle of friends at work on the lake); in which their frames of mind most assuredly have been very varied and their internal tendency to visions most uneven. And could they, all of them, have agreed to announce these visions to the world as bodily appearances of the risen Christ? Or had they done so, could it have been pure self-deception and intentional deceit? Surely, some one or other of them must afterwards seriously have asked himself whether the image he had seen was a reality. Schleiermacher says most truly, "Who ever supposes that the disciples deceived themselves and mistook the internal for the external, accuses them of such mental weakness as must invalidate their entire testimony concerning Christ and make it appear as though Christ Himself, when He chose such witnesses, did not know what was in man. Or, if He Himself had willed and ordained that they should mistake inward appearances for outward perceptions, He would have been the author of error, and all moral ideas would be confounded if this were compatible with His high dignity." (Christlieb, as cited in Smith, TS, 396–97)

3E. According to two noted psychiatrists, L. E. Hinsie and J. Shatsky, "[An illusion is] an erroneous perception, a false response to a sense-stimulation. . . . But in a normal individual this false belief usually brings the desire to check often another sense or other senses may come to the rescue and satisfy him that it is merely an illusion." (Hinsie, PD, 280)

The appearances that Christ made could not have been "erroneous" perceptions:

Wilbur Smith writes of Luke's observations. He describes him as "a man accustomed to scientifically considering any subject which he is studying. Luke says at the beginning of his second book, the Acts of the Apostles, that our Lord showed Himself alive after His Passion 'by many infallible proofs,' or more literally, 'in many proofs.'" (Smith, TS, 400)

Smith continues:

The very kind of evidence which modern science, and even psychologists, are so insistent upon for determining the reality of any object under consideration is the kind of evidence that we have presented to us in the Gospels regarding the Resurrection of the Lord Jesus, namely, the things that are seen with the human eye, touched with the human hand, and heard by the human ear. This is what we call empirical evidence. (Smith, TS, 389–90)

W. J. Sparrow-Simpson writes that "the Appearances of the Risen Master may be analyzed according to the human senses to which they appealed, whether the sense of sight, or of hearing, or of touch. The different phenomena may be conveniently grouped together under these divisions." (Sparrow-Simpson, RCF, 83)

Sparrow-Simpson continues: "And first as to the sense of sight. This is naturally first, as the initial form of gaining their attention. It is described in the Gospels by various expressions: "Jesus met them" (Matt. 28:9).

"They saw Him" (Matt. 28:17).

"They knew Him" (Luke 24:31).

"They . . . supposed that they beheld a spirit" (Luke 24:37).

"See . . . My hands and My feet, that it is I Myself; handle Me and see, for a spirit hath not flesh and bones as ye behold . . . Me having. And when He had said this He shewed unto them . . . His hands and His feet" (Luke 24:39, 40).

Similarly also in the fourth Evangelist: "I have seen the Lord" (John 20:18).

"He shewed unto them His hands and His side" (John 20:20).

"They saw the Lord" (John 20:20).

"Except I shall see in His hands the print of the nails" (John 20:25).

"Because thou hast seen Me" (John 20:29).

"And none of His disciples durst inquire of Him, Who art Thou? knowing that it was the Lord" (John 21:12).

"Appearing unto them by the space of forty days" (Acts 1:3).

Appeal is made by the Risen Lord in these

Appearances to the marks of the wounds inflicted in the Passion: St. Luke speaks of the hands and the feet [Luke 24:29–40]. . . . St. Matthew mentions neither. St. John mentions "His hands and His side" (John 20:20–25, 27). (Sparrow-Simpson, RCF, 183–84)

"The appearances of the risen Christ are reported also as appeals to the sense of touch. . . . By far the most emphatic words in this respect are those in St. Luke: 'Handle Me and see; for a spirit hath not flesh and bones, as ye behold Me having'" (Luke 24:39).

"And they gave Him a piece of a broiled fish. And He took it, and did eat before them" (Luke 24:42, 43). (Sparrow-Simpson, RCF, 92–93)

Thomas Thorburn writes: "The 'hallucinatory' vision at the tomb in Mark has an *auditory* experience: the angel tells the women to go and announce the fact to the disciples. (Mark 16:5–7)"

Thorburn continues, "Similarly in Matthew (who drew largely from the same sources as Mark) the women both see *and* hear Jesus, and *also touch* Him (Matthew 28:9–10)." (Thorburn, RNMC, 133)

4E. Hallucinations are usually restricted in terms of when and where they occur. (Anderson, RJC, 4–9); (Little, KWhyB, 67–69); (Peru, OPC, 97–99)

Hallucinations usually are experienced:

* In a place with a nostalgic atmosphere, or
* At a time that particularly brings the person to a reminiscing mood.

The times of Christ's appearances and their locations did not conduce the witnesses to hallucinate. No fancied events were dreamed up because of familiar surroundings.

John R. W. Stott observes that "the outwardly favourable circumstances were missing." (Stott, BC, 57)

Stott continues: "If the appearances had all taken place in one or two particularly sacred places, which had been hallowed by memories of Jesus," and if "their mood had been expectant," then "our suspicions might well be aroused." (Stott, BC, 57)

Stott concludes:

> If we had only the story of the appearances in the upper room, we should have cause to doubt and question. If the eleven had been gathered in that special place where Jesus had spent with them some of His last earthly hours, and they had kept His place vacant, and were sentimentalizing over the magic days of the past, and had remembered His promises to return, and had begun to wonder if He might return and to hope that He would, until the ardour of their expectation was consummated by His sudden appearance, we might indeed fear that they had been mocked by a cruel delusion. (Stott, BC, 57)

W. Robertson Nicoll, cited by Kevan, says: "Let it be remembered that the disciples thought not only that they saw Christ, but that they conversed with Him, that the interviews were held in various circumstances, and that there were many witnesses." (Nicoll, as cited in Kevan, RC, 10)

James Orr considers the time factor, noting that the appearances "were not fleeting glimpses of Christ but 'prolonged interviews'" (Orr, RJ, as cited in Ramm, PCE, 186)

Consider the wide variety of times and places:

Matthew 28:9, 10: The early morning appearance to the women at the tomb.

Luke 24:13–33: The appearance on the road to Emmaus one afternoon.

Luke 24:34; 1 Corinthians 15:7: A couple of private interviews in broad daylight.

John 21:1–23: By the lake, early one morning.

1 Corinthians 15:6: On a Galilean mountain by five-hundred-plus believers.

Indeed, there is almost a studied variety

in the times and places of Christ's appearances—a variance that defies the hypothesis that these were mere visions.

5E. Hallucinations require of people an anticipating spirit of hopeful expectancy that causes their wish to become father to the thought. (Anderson, RJC, 4–9); (Little, KWB, 67–69); (Peru, OPC, 97–99)

1F. The following principles are characteristic of hallucinations:

William Milligan states that the subject of the vision must be characterized by "belief in the idea that it expresses, and excited expectation that the idea will somehow be realized." (Milligan, RL, 93–95)

1G. "In order to have an experience like this, one must so intensely want to believe that he projects something that really isn't there and attaches reality to his imagination." (Little, KWhyB, 68).

2G. E. H. Day observes that "the seeing of visions, the perception of exceptional phenomena subjectively by large numbers of persons at the same time, necessitates a certain amount of 'psychological preparation,' extending over an appreciably long period." (Day, ER, 51–53)

3G. Paul Little writes: "For instance, a mother who has lost a son in the war remembers how he used to come home from work every evening at 5:30 o'clock. She sits in her rocking chair every afternoon musing and meditating. Finally, she thinks she sees him come through the door, and has a conversation with him. At this point she has lost contact with reality." (Little, KWhyB, 68)

2F. In the case of His post-resurrection appearances, Christ's followers were caused to believe against their wills.

W. J. Sparrow-Simpson writes: "The phenomena, therefore, suggest that the Appearances were rather forced upon the mind's attention from without rather than created from within." (Sparrow-Simpson, RCF, 88)

Alfred Edersheim says that "such visions presuppose a previous expectancy of the event, which, as we know, is the opposite of the fact." (Edersheim, LTJM, 626)

E. H. Day writes in objection to the hallucination theory: "We may recognize the slowness with which the disciples arrive at a conviction to which only the inexorable logic of facts led them." (Day, ER, 53–54)

Concerning the absence of "psychological preparation," Day observes:

The first appearance of the Lord found the various disciples in very various mental attitudes, but the states of expectancy, anticipation, or preparedness to see Him are conspicuously absent from the category....

The faith of all had been shaken by the catastrophe of the shameful death, a death recalling so vividly the word of the Jewish Law, "He that is hanged is accursed of God" (Deut. xxi. 23). The theory of subjective visions might seem a plausible one if there had been among the disciples a refusal to believe the worst. But the hopes of the disciples were so far shattered that recovery was very slow. (Edersheim, LTJM, 53–54)

Paul Little explains that the general disposition of Christ's followers was not like what one would find in victims of an hallucinatory

> Any theory of hallucination breaks down on the fact (and if it is invention it is the oddest invention that ever entered the mind of man) that on three separate occasions this hallucination was not immediately recognized as Jesus.
>
> —C. S. LEWIS

experience: "Mary came to the tomb on the first Easter Sunday morning with spices in her hands. Why? To anoint the dead body of the Lord she loved. She was obviously not expecting to find Him risen from the dead. In fact, when she first saw Him she mistook Him for the gardener! When the Lord finally appeared to the disciples, they were frightened and thought they were seeing a ghost!" (Little, KWhyB, 68–69)

Alfred Edersheim comments: "Such a narrative as that recorded by St. Luke seems almost designed to render the 'Vision-hypothesis' impossible. We are expressly told, that the appearance of the Risen Christ, so far from meeting their anticipations, had affrighted them, and that they had thought it spectral, on which Christ had reassured them, and bidden them handle Him, for 'a spirit hath not flesh and bones, as ye behold Me having.'" (Edersheim, LTJM, 628)

Continuing, Edersheim says: "*Reuss* well remarks, that if this fundamental dogma of the Church had been the outcome of invention, care would have been taken that the accounts of it should be in the strictest and most literal agreement." (Edersheim, LTJM, 628)

C. S. Lewis says that

> any theory of hallucination breaks down on the fact (and if it is invention it is the oddest invention that ever entered the mind of man) that on three separate occasions this hallucination was not immediately recognized as Jesus (Luke xxiv. 13–31; John xx. 15, xxi. 4). Even granting that God sent a holy hallucination to teach truths already widely believed without it, and far more easily taught by other methods, and certain to be completely obscured by this, might we not at least hope that He would get the fact of the hallucination right? Is He who made all faces such a bungler that He cannot even work up a recognizable likeness of the Man who was Himself? (Lewis, M, 153)

Writing of Jesus' manifestation to His disciples, T. J. Thorburn remarks, "If it had been mere subjective imagination, originating a similar train of equally unreal conceptions in the others, tradition would surely have given us a more highly elaborated account of it." (Thorburn, RNMC, 29–31)

6E. Hallucinations usually tend to recur over a long period of time with noticeable regularity. (Anderson, RJC, 4–9); (Little, KWB, 67–69); (Peru, OPC, 97–99)

They either recur more frequently until a point of crisis is reached, or they occur less frequently until they fade away.

Notice the following observations concerning Christ's appearances:

C. S. Lewis writes: "All the accounts suggest that the appearances of the Risen Body came to an end; some describe an abrupt end six weeks after the death. . . . A phantom can just fade away, but an objective entity must go somewhere—something must happen to it." (Lewis, M, 153–54)

He concludes: "If it were a vision then it was the most systematically deceptive and lying vision on record. But if it were real, then something happened to it after it ceased to appear. You cannot take away the Ascension without putting something else in its place." (Lewis, M, 154)

Hastings' *Dictionary of the Apostolic Church* records that "the theory is inconsistent with the fact that the visions came so suddenly to an end. After the forty days no appearance of the Risen Lord is recorded, except that to St. Paul, the circumstances and object of which were altogether exceptional. It is not thus that imagination works. As Keim says, 'The spirits that men call up are not so quickly laid.'" (Hastings, DAC, 360)

Kevan asks, "But if the visions of the risen Saviour were hallucinations, why did they stop so suddenly? Why, after the Ascension, does one not find others still seeing the coveted vision? By the law of development, says Dr. Mullins, 'hallucinations should have become chronic after five hundred had been brought under their sway. But now hallucination gives place to a definite and conquering programme of evangelisation.'" (Kevan, RC, 11)

3C. What Conclusions Can We Draw?

Winfried Corduan summarizes the hallucination theory:

> The problem with this theory is that, in the case of the Resurrection appearances, everything we know about hallucinations is violated. The appearances did not follow the patterns always present in hallucinations, for hallucinations are private and arise out of a state of extreme emotional instability in which the hallucination functions as a sort of wish-fulfillment. What occurred after the Resurrection was very different. The disciples had little trouble accepting Christ's departure; they decided to go back to their fishing. The appearances came as surprises while the disciples were intent on other things. Most importantly, the appearances came to *groups* of people, with each member seeing the same thing. That is simply not how hallucinations work. Thus the Resurrection appearances could not have been hallucinations. (Corduan, NDA, 221)

John R. W. Stott writes: "The disciples were not gullible, but rather cautious, sceptical and 'slow of heart to believe.' They were not susceptible to hallucinations. Nor would strange visions have satisfied them. Their faith was grounded upon the hard facts of verifiable experience." (Stott, BC, 57)

Hallucinations have never, writes T. J. Thorburn, "stimulated people to undertake a work of enormous magnitude, and, while carrying it out, to lead lives of the most rigid and consistent self-denial, and even suffering. In a word, . . . we are constrained to agree with Dr. Sanday, who says, 'No apparition, no mere hallucination of the senses, ever yet moved the world.'" (Thorburn, RNMC, 136)

4B. That the Women, and Subsequently Everyone Else, Went to the Wrong Tomb

1C. The View

Professor Kirsopp Lake writes:

> It is seriously a matter for doubt whether the women were really in a position to be quite certain that the tomb which they visited was that in which they had seen Joseph of Arimathea bury the Lord's body. The neighborhood of Jerusalem is full of rock tombs, and it would not be easy to distinguish one from another without careful notes. . . . It is very doubtful if they were close to the tomb at the moment of burial. . . . It is likely that they were watching from a distance, and that Joseph of Arimathea was a representative of the Jews

> [Hallucinations have never] stimulated people to undertake a work of enormous magnitude, and, while carrying it out, to lead lives of the most rigid and consistent self-denial, and even suffering. In a word, . . . we are constrained to agree with Dr. Sanday, who says, "No apparition, no mere hallucination of the senses, ever yet moved the world."
>
> —J. T. THORBURN

rather than of the disciples. If so, they would have had but a limited power to distinguish between one rock tomb and another close to it. The possibility, therefore, that they came to the wrong tomb is to be reckoned with, and it is important because it supplies the natural explanation of the fact that whereas they had seen the tomb closed, they found it open. . . .

If it were not the same, the circumstances all seem to fall into line. The women came in the early morning to a tomb which they thought was the one in which they had seen the Lord buried. They expected to find a closed tomb, but they found an open one; and a young man . . . guessed their errand, tried to tell them that they had made a mistake in the place "He is not here," said he, "see the place where they laid him," and probably pointed to the next tomb. But the women were frightened at the detection of their errand, and fled. (Lake, HERJC, 250, 251, 252)

2C. The Refutation

The women's visit to the empty tomb on Sunday morning is one of the best attested events in the New Testament narratives. Kirsopp Lake's theory assumes its historicity.

Frank Morison comments, "The story of the women's adventure is in the earliest authentic document we possess, the Gospel of St. Mark. It is repeated by St. Matthew and St. Luke, it is confirmed so far as Mary Magdalene herself is concerned by St. John, it is in the Apocryphal Gospel of Peter; and, perhaps even more significantly, it is in that very ancient and independent fragment, preserved by St. Luke in chapter xxiv., verses 13–34, the journey to Emmaus." (Morison, WMS, 98)

Lake accepts the visit as historical, but he is wrong in his speculations as to what happened at the tomb.

1D. These women had carefully noted where the body of Jesus was interred less than seventy-two hours before:

"And Mary Magdalene was there, and the other Mary, sitting opposite the tomb" (Matt. 27:61).

"And Mary Magdalene and Mary the mother of Joses observed where He was laid" (Mark 15:47).

"And the women who had come with Him from Galilee followed after, and they observed the tomb and how His body was laid" (Luke 23:55).

Do you think that you or I or these women or any other rational person would forget so quickly the place where a dearly loved one was laid to rest just seventy-two hours earlier?

2D. The women reported to the disciples what they had experienced, and later Peter and John also found the tomb empty.

Then she ran and came to Simon Peter, and to the other disciple, whom Jesus loved, and said to them, "They have taken away the Lord out of the tomb, and we do not know where they have laid Him." Peter therefore went out, and the other disciple, and were going to the tomb. So they both ran together, and the other disciple outran Peter and came to the tomb first. And he, stooping down and looking in, saw the linen cloths lying there; yet he did not go in. Then Simon Peter came, following him, and went into the tomb; and he saw the linen cloths lying there, and the handkerchief that had been around His head, not lying with the linen cloths, but folded together in a place by itself. Then the other disciple, who came to the tomb first, went in also; and he saw and believed (John 20:2–8).

> Even if the women, the disciples, the Romans and the Jews all went to the wrong tomb, one thing is sure: "Certainly Joseph of Arimathea, owner of the tomb, would have solved the problem."
>
> —PAUL LITTLE

Is it to be argued that Peter and John also went to the wrong tomb?

Paul Little remarks, "It is inconceivable

that Peter and John would succumb to the same mistake." (Little, KWhyB, 65)

3D. Furthermore an angel, sitting there on a stone, said, "Come, see the place where the Lord lay" (Matt. 28:6). Are we to believe that the angel was also mistaken?

Wilbur Smith says, "Someone has suggested, in trying to force this theory of the mistaken tomb, that the angel's words really meant, 'You are in the wrong place, come over here to see where the Lord's body was placed.'

"Well, in nineteen hundred years of the study of the New Testament, it took our modern, sophisticated age to find *that* in the Gospel records, and no trustworthy commentary on any of the Gospels entertains such a foolish interpretation as that." (Smith, TS, 381–82)

4D. If the women went to the wrong tomb (an empty sepulchre), then the Sanhedrin could have gone to the right tomb and produced the body (if Jesus did not rise). This would have silenced the disciples forever!

The high priests and the other enemies of Christ would certainly have gone to the right tomb!

5D. Even if the women, the disciples, the Romans and the Jews all went to the wrong tomb, one thing is sure, as Paul Little points out: "Certainly Joseph of Arimathea, owner of the tomb, would have solved the problem." (Little, KWhyB, 65)

6D. The narrative in Mark reads:

"And entering the tomb, they saw a young man clothed in a white robe sitting on the right side; and they were alarmed. But he said to them, 'Do not be alarmed. You seek Jesus of Nazareth, who was crucified. He has

risen! He is not here. See the place where they laid Him'" (Mark 16:5, 6).

Professor Lake's citing of Mark 16:6 is incomplete. He quotes only part of what the young man said and ignores the key part of the narration. The phrase, "He has risen," is conspicuously absent in Lake's citing of the verse. Notice the following comparison with the NASB:

LAKE'S VERSION

"He is not here, see the place where they laid Him."

ACTUAL VERSION

"He has risen; He is not here; behold, here is the place where they laid Him."

J. N. D. Anderson says of Lake's misquote: "For [it] I can see no scholarly justification whatever." (Anderson, RJC, 7)

If the text is quoted correctly, then Lake's theory cannot stand!

7D. Anderson points out another problem for those who hold to the Lake theory:

"When the women went back to the disciples, these men would have done one of two things: They would have gone to the tomb to verify the women's report; or they would have immediately begun proclaiming the resurrection." (Anderson, RJC, 7)

Such preaching, however, did not begin until seven weeks later.

Anderson writes: "I cannot see any possible motive for Christian writers to have invented that seven-week gap. So we're asked to believe that the women didn't tell the apostles this story for quite a long time. Why not? Because the apostles had supposedly run away to Galilee." (Anderson, RJC, 7)

Concerning this point, Frank Morison says that the

interdependence of the women upon the men very seriously embarrasses Prof. Lake's theory at its most vital point. . . . Prof. Lake is compelled to keep the women in Jerusalem until Sunday morning, because he firmly believes that they really went to the tomb. He is also compelled to get the disciples out of Jerusalem before sunrise on Sunday because he holds that the women kept silence.

Finally, to harmonize this with the fact that they did subsequently tell the story, with all its inevitable and logical results, he finds it necessary to keep the women in Jerusalem for several weeks while the disciples returned to their homes, had certain experiences, and came back to the capital. (Morison, WMS, 10)

8D. John R. W. Stott mentions the attitude of the women. They were not blinded by tears of remorse, but had a practical purpose for their early morning visit.

He writes: "They had bought spices and were going to complete the anointing of their Lord's body, since the approach of the sabbath had made the work so hasty two days previously. These devoted and business-like women were not the kind to be easily deceived or to give up the task they had come to do." (Stott, BC, 48)

9D. This was not a public cemetery, but a private burying ground. No other tomb there would allow them to make such a mistake. Wilbur Smith, in commenting on this point, says: "The whole idea is so utterly fantastic that Professor A. E. J. Rawlinson, no conservative, in his epochal commentary on St. Mark's Gospel, felt compelled to say of Lake's suggestion, 'That the women went by mistake to the wrong tomb, and that the attempt of a bystander to direct them to the right one was misunderstood, is rationalization which is utterly foreign to the spirit of the narrative.'" (Smith, TS, 382)

10D. Merrill Tenney writes, "Lake fails to explain why the 'young man' [Mark 16:5] would have been present either in a public cemetery or in a private garden at such an early hour." (Tenney, RR, 115–16)

He asks, "What conceivable motive would have drawn a stranger there? If He were not a stranger, but one of the disciples making an independent investigation, why should his presence have frightened the women?" (Tenney, RR, 115–16)

Tenney further comments that "Mark's account, on which Lake relies, states that he was seated *inside* the tomb [vs. 5], so that he could scarcely have meant that they were at the wrong place, . . . but that Jesus was no longer there; they could see where He had been laid, but the body had vanished." (Tenney, RR, 115–16)

11D. Some identify the "young man" as a gardener. Frank Morison, however, says that

this theory, despite its appearance of rationality, has one peculiar weakness. If it was so dark that the women accidentally went to the wrong tomb, it is exceedingly improbable that the gardener would have been at work. If it was late enough and light enough for the gardener to be at work, it is improbable that the women would have been mistaken. The theory just rests upon the synchronization of two very doubtful contingencies. This is, however, only part of the improbability and intellectual difficulty which gathers around it. (Morison, WMS, 97)

Also, if the "young man" was the gardener, as some people assert, why didn't the priests secure his testimony as evidence that Christ's body was still in the grave? (Morison, WMS, 101–2)

He was not the gardener, but was an angel from heaven (Matt. 28:1–10).

Everyone *knew* that Christ's grave was

empty—the real issue was *how* did it get that way?

12D. What are we to think of Professor Lake's theory that the people went to the wrong tomb?

George Hanson says: "If I had any doubts about the Resurrection, Professor Lake's book would provide a most salutary counteractive to my scepticism. After reading it I am more than ever of the opinion expressed by De Wette in his 'Historical Criticism of the Evangelical History' (p. 229): 'The *fact* of the Resurrection, although a darkness which cannot be dissipated rests on the way and manner of it, cannot be doubted.'" (Hanson, G., RL, 8)

Wilbur Smith cites the verdict of the British scholar, Professor Morse: "Their theory that the women were approaching the wrong tomb arises, not from any evidence, but from disbelief in the possibility of the supernatural emptying of our Lord's tomb." (Smith, TS, 382).

8A. CONCLUSION: HE IS RISEN, HE IS RISEN INDEED!

John Warwick Montgomery writes:

> The earliest records we have of the life and ministry of Jesus give the overwhelming impression that this man went around not so much "doing good" but making a decided nuisance of Himself.
>
> The parallel with Socrates in this regard is strong: Both men infuriated their contemporaries to such an extent that they were eventually put to death. But where Socrates played the gad fly on the collective Athenian rump by demanding that his hearers "know themselves"—examine their unexamined lives—Jesus alienated His contemporaries by continually forcing them to think through their attitude to Him personally. "Who do men say that I the Son of man am? . . . Who do

> Let the witnesses be compared with themselves, with each other, and with surrounding facts and circumstances; and let their testimony be sifted, as if it were given in a court of justice, on the side of the adverse party, the witness being subjected to rigorous cross-examination. The result, it is confidently believed, will be an undoubting conviction of their integrity, ability, and truth.
>
> —SIMON GREENLEAF,
> HARVARD PROFESSOR OF LAW

you say that I am?"; "What do you think of Christ? Whose son is He?" These were the questions Jesus asked. (Montgomery, HC, 12)

Christ made it very clear who He was. He told Thomas: "I am the way, the truth, and the life; no one comes to the Father except through Me" (John 14:6).

The apostle Paul said that Christ was "declared to be the Son of God with power according to the Spirit of holiness, by the resurrection from the dead" (Rom. 1:4).

Simon Greenleaf, the famous Harvard professor of law, says:

> All that Christianity asks of men . . . is, that they would be consistent with themselves; that they would treat its evidences as they treat the evidence of other things; and that they would try and judge its actors and witnesses, as they deal with their fellow men, when testifying to human affairs and actions, in human tribunals. Let the witnesses be compared with themselves, with each other, and with surrounding facts and circumstances; and let their testimony be sifted, as if it were given in a court of justice, on the side of the adverse party, the witness being subjected to rigorous cross-examination. The result, it is confidently believed, will be an undoubting conviction of their integrity, ability, and truth. (Greenleaf, TE, 46)

As G. B. Hardy has said, "Here is the complete record:

Confucius's tomb:	occupied
Buddha's tomb:	occupied
Mohammed's tomb:	occupied
Jesus' tomb:	EMPTY."

(Hardy, C)

The verdict is in. The decision is clear. The evidence speaks for itself. It says very clearly:

CHRIST IS RISEN INDEED!

10
SUPPORT OF DEITY: THE GREAT PROPOSITION

1A. INTRODUCTION

"If God became man, then WHAT would He be like?"

or

"Did Jesus possess the attributes of God?"

To answer these questions, it will be helpful to answer another question:

"Why would God become a man?"

One reason would be to communicate with us more effectively. Imagine you are watching a farmer plow a field. You notice that an ant hill will be plowed under by the farmer on his next time around. Because you love ants, you run to the ant hill to warn its tiny inhabitants. First you shout to them the impending danger, but they continue their work. You then try many other forms of communication, but nothing seems to get through to the imperiled ants. You soon realize that the only way you can really reach them is by becoming one of them.

Throughout human history, God has used numerous means of communication to reach humankind with His message. He finally sent His Son into the world. The opening verses of Hebrews state, "God, who at various times and in various ways spoke in time past to the fathers by the prophets, has in these last days spoken to us by His Son" (Heb. 1:1, 2). John writes in his Gospel, "And the Word became flesh and dwelt among us, and we beheld His glory, the glory as of the only begotten of the Father, full of grace and truth. . . . No one has seen God at any time. The only begotten Son, who is in the bosom of the Father, He has declared Him" (John 1:14, 18).

The prophets gave us God's words. But Jesus is the very Word of God in human form, revealing God to us in person, not just in verbal statements. He gave us God Himself in a form we could touch, hear, and see. Jesus brought God to our level and lifted us up with Him in the process.

Not only did God want to communicate with us, He wanted to demonstrate to us just how much He loves us. "For God so loved the world," Jesus said, "that He gave His only begotten Son, that whoever believes in Him should not perish but have everlasting life. For God did not send His Son into the world to condemn the world, but that the world through Him might be saved" (John 3:16, 17). The apostle John echoed Jesus' words: "In this the love of God was manifested toward us, that God has sent His only begotten Son into the world, that we might live through Him. In this is love, not that we loved God, but that He loved us and sent His Son to be the propitiation for our sins" (1 John 4:9, 10).

In his book *The Jesus I Never Knew*, Philip Yancey captures this idea in a memorable way:

[T]he Jews associated fear with worship. . . . God made a surprise appearance as a baby in a manger. What can be less scary than a newborn with his limbs wrapped tight against his body? In Jesus, God found a way of relating to human beings that did not involve fear. I learned about incarnation when I kept a salt-water aquarium. . . .

Every time my shadow loomed above the tank [the fish] dove for cover into the nearest shell. They showed me one "emotion" only: fear. Although I opened the lid and dropped in food on a regular schedule, three times a day, they responded to each visit as a sure sign of my designs to torture them. I could not convince them of my true concern. . . .

To change their perceptions, I began to see, would require a form of incarnation. I would have to become a fish and "speak" to them in a language they could understand.

A human being becoming a fish is nothing compared to God becoming a baby. And yet according to the Gospels that is what happened at Bethlehem. The God who created matter took shape within it, as an artist might become a spot on a painting or a playwright a character within his own play. God wrote a story, only using real characters, on the pages of real history. The Word became flesh. (Yancey, JNK, 37–39)

But how would humanity know that some man claiming to be God really was God? One way is through fulfilled prophecy. God could speak to people in their language, in their thoughts, telling them what to look for—far in advance of His actually becoming a man. Then, when He became a man and fulfilled those predictions, the world would know it was He who had been speaking. This is just what God did.

The prophet Isaiah had predicted that the Messiah-God would come (Is. 9:6; compare Pss. 45:6; 110:1). The Bible said of His mission many times: "That it might be fulfilled" (see Matt. 2:15, 17, 23; 13:14).

So, if God entered human history and walked among us as a man, what traces of His presence would we expect to find? How would we know that He had really been here in human form? I suggest we would find at least eight telltale signs of His historical presence:

IF GOD BECAME A MAN, THEN WE WOULD EXPECT HIM TO:

1. Have an utterly unique entrance into human history.
2. Be without sin.
3. Manifest His supernatural presence in the form of supernatural acts—that is, miracles.
4. Live more perfectly than any human who has ever lived.
5. Speak the greatest words ever spoken.
6. Have a lasting and universal influence.
7. Satisfy the spiritual hunger in humanity.
8. Overcome humanity's most pervasive and feared enemy—death.

It is my contention that only in Jesus Christ's life can we find all eight of these signs clearly exhibited. He gave us no reason to doubt that He is God become man. It is clearly evident that He satisfied these eight expectations of God's presence in human history.

2A. AN UTTERLY UNIQUE ENTRANCE INTO HUMAN HISTORY

Mohammed, Confucius, Buddha, and all other human beings were conceived by natural means: a male human sperm fertilizing a female human egg. Not so with Jesus Christ. His mother conceived Him while she was yet a virgin. He had no paternal father. The virgin conception and birth of Christ is utterly unique in human history.

1B. Biblical Testimony for the Virgin Birth

The main body of testimony concerning the virgin birth occurs in the Gospels of Matthew and Luke. However, the Old Testament predicted the Messiah's unusual conception hundreds of years before Matthew and Luke ever wrote their Gospels. The concept of the virgin birth of Jesus must concur with the prescribed mode of entrance granted the Messiah in the Old Testament. The key Old Testament text is Isaiah 7:14. There may also be an allusion to the virgin conception in Genesis 3:15.

1C. Genesis 3:15

The first prophecy concerning Christ's first coming appears in Genesis 3:15. Here God promised that the seed of the woman would crush the head of the serpent.

Claus Westermann, the Old Testament scholar, states: "From the time of Irenaeus, Christian tradition has understood the passage as a prophecy about Christ (and Mary). The 'seed of the woman' referred to one individual descendant who crushed the head of the serpent, whose seed was also an individual in the person of the devil (Satan), who is locked in deadly struggle with 'the seed of the woman,' and who eventually succumbs to it. This explanation runs from Irenaeus right through the history of exegesis in both Catholic and evangelical tradition." (Westermann, GAC, 260)

John Walvoord, one of America's longtime leading evangelical biblical theologians, agrees. In his book *Jesus Christ Our Lord*, he says: "The reference to the seed of the woman is a prophecy of the birth of the Son of God. This is the point of Luke's genealogy (cf. Gal. 4:4). The coming Saviour was to be the seed of the woman—human; and yet in the fact that He is not called the seed of man, we have the foreshadowing of the virgin birth (Isa. 7:14; Matt. 1:21, 22). To Adam it was made very plain that his hope lay in this future Child of the woman, that through this Child salvation would come from God." (Walvoord, JCOL, 57)

Karlheinz Rabast, a German Lutheran minister writing in the mid-twentieth century, also accepts the traditional view of Genesis 3:15. "The seed of the woman ... has its ultimate and deepest meaning in that it refers to the Virgin Mary and her Seed, Christ." (Rabast, GADES, 120)

Edward Young, a distinguished Old Testament scholar, states: "That there is a reference to Christ, however, is not to be rejected. Nevertheless, it is also true that the way in which man will vanquish Satan is that there will be born of woman One, even Jesus Christ, who will obtain the victory. It is the seed of the woman as comprehended in the Redeemer that will deliver the fatal blow." (Rabast, GADES, 120)

The ultimate fulfillment of Genesis 3:15 is found in the coming of the Messiah, Jesus Christ, who was, in fact, conceived by "the seed of the woman," the virgin Mary—not by the seed of any man.

2C. Isaiah 7:14

A clearer prophecy occurs in Isaiah 7:14: "Therefore the Lord Himself will give you a sign: Behold, the virgin shall conceive and bear a Son, and shall call His name Immanuel."

Two key questions go far in opening up interpretation of this passage. The first is, what is the meaning of *'almah*, the Hebrew word translated "virgin"? The second is, to whom does "the virgin" refer?

1D. What Does *'Almah* Mean?

A word's meaning is settled by its context. For instance, the word *trunk* means the storage area in the back end of a car in the sentence "She put the suitcases in the trunk of her four-door sedan," or the long nose of an elephant in the sentence "The elephant raised his trunk over the fence and grabbed the peanuts out of the child's hand." Similarly, we must consult the context to learn what *'almah* means in that context.

In the Old Testament, *'almah* is used seven times to refer to a young woman (Gen. 24:43; Ex. 2:8; Ps. 68:25; Prov. 30:19; Song 1:3; 6:8; Is. 7:14). Edward Hindson states, "Though it is true that *'almah* is not the common word for virgin, its employment always denotes a virgin." Moreover, "Biblical usage of *'almah* is clearly never that of a married woman, but always of an unmarried one." (Hindson, II, 7) This is seen from the Bible passages in which the word occurs.

1E. Genesis 24:43

In Genesis 24, after Eliezer arrives in Nahor, he prays to God, asking for help in finding the right woman for Abraham's son. Verse 16 describes Rebekah as a "young woman" who was "very beautiful to behold, a virgin [*betulah*]; no man had known her." Later Eliezer refers to her as "the virgin [*'almah*]" (v. 43).

2E. Exodus 2:8

Regarding this passage, Richard Niessen writes:

> Exodus 2 relates the incident of the infant Moses being rescued from the river by Pharaoh's daughter. Moses' sister, Miriam, stood by watching and ran to Pharaoh's daughter to suggest that she could find a Hebrew woman (her mother) to nurse the infant. "And Pharaoh's daughter said to her, Go. And the maiden ['almah] went and called the child's mother" (Exod. 2:8).
>
> The way Miriam is introduced in 2:4

> It appears from this passage that any element of biological virginity in the term ['almah] is subsumed under the term's connotation of age. Miriam was a teenager who was also a virgin.
>
> —RICHARD NIESSEN

implies that she was not much older than Moses, and this is confirmed by the fact that she was still living in her mother's house at the time.

It appears from this passage that any element of biological virginity in the term ['almah] is subsumed under the term's connotation of age. Miriam was a teenager who was also a virgin. (Niessen, V, 137)

Albert Myers agrees, stating that Moses' sister Miriam "was undoubtedly a virgin (Ex. 2:8)." (Myers, UAOT, 139)

3E. Psalm 68:25

In this passage "the maidens ['almah] playing timbrels" are part of a procession that accompanies the divine King "into the sanctuary." In his comments on this text, Niessen states that the maidens "are certainly not harlots or impure women, but are chaste servants of God; hence they would be virgins.

Moreover, according to Semitic custom, single women generally participated in bridal processions and other festive occasions. One may therefore conclude that the young women who participated were, according to custom, virgins." (Niessen, V, 138)

4E. Proverbs 30:19

The writer of this passage mentions four things that are "too wonderful" for him: "the way of an eagle in the air; the way of a serpent upon a rock; the way of a ship in the midst of the sea; and the way of a man with a 'almah. In verse 20 he then contrasts the evil woman to the virtuous maiden." (Hindson, II, 7)

Hindson, presenting an interpretation of Proverbs 30:19, points out, "The juxtaposition of the next verses by the compiler provides a contrast between the natural blessing of the virtuous maiden and the evil of the adulterous woman. Therefore, the picture here should be interpreted as that of a virgin maid." (Hindson, II, 7)

Niessen understands the passage similarly: "What is being described here is the courtship and infatuation of youthful love between a young man and his young girl friend. While the passage does not specifically make a point about the girl's virginity, it may be presumed." (Niessen, V, 140)

5E. Song of Solomon 1:3

In this poetic portion of Solomon's love song, the bride says of her groom, "Because of the fragrance of your good ointments, / Your name is ointment poured forth; / Therefore the virgins ['almah] love you." "A person's name," Jack Deere explains, "represented his character or reputation (cf. 2 Sam. 7:9). So comparing Solomon's name to perfume meant that his *character* was pleasing and attractive to the beloved. For this reason, she said, many were attracted to him" (Deere, SS, 1011, 1012). The other women attracted to the beloved because of his character were "not married women but maidens who have desired a husband but failed to acquire him. The word ['almah] here implies the idea of virginity. (Niessen, V, 140–41)

6E. Song of Solomon 6:8

This passage mentions three categories of women that comprised the king's court: queens, concubines, and maidens ['almah]. Niessen observes that the

queens were quite obviously married, and the concubines were like the common-law wives of today. The [maidens] are apparently in contrast to these two groups of wives, and as such would be unmarried women. They were in the service of the queens and destined to be chosen eventually as wives by the king. Thus it would be quite natural to expect them to be virgins. This is confirmed by the events in Esther 2. King Xerxes had gathered together a great number of virgins for the purpose of selecting a new queen (2:1–4). Purity was so essential that the women were to go through a process of ceremonial purification for an entire year (2:12, 13) before going into the king's chamber. Their biological virginity was not open to question; it was assumed. (Niessen, V, 141)

7E. Isaiah 7:14

After studying the uses of 'almah in the Hebrew Scriptures, R. Dick Wilson draws two conclusions: "first, that 'almah, so far as known, never meant 'young married woman'; and secondly since the presump-

> There is no place among the seven occurrences of 'almah in the Old Testament where the word is clearly used of a woman who was not a virgin.
>
> —GRESHAM MACHEN

tion in common law and usage was and is, that every 'almah is virgin and virtuous, until she is proven not to be, we have a right to assume that Rebecca and the 'almah of Is. vii. 14 and all other 'almahs were virgin, until and unless it shall be proven that they were not." (Wilson, M'AI, 316)

Erudite scholar J. Gresham Machen, in *The Virgin Birth of Christ*, comes to the same conclusion: "There is no place among the seven occurrences of 'almah in the Old Testament where the word is clearly used of a woman who was not a virgin. It may readily be admitted that 'almah does not actually indicate virginity, as does *bethulah*; it means rather 'a young woman of marriageable age.' But on the other hand one may well doubt, in view of the usage, whether it was a natural word to use of anyone who was not in point of fact a virgin." (Machen, VBC, 288)

Willis J. Beecher, in his classic essay "The Prophecy of the Virgin Mother," shares the same assessment: "The Hebrew lexicons tell us that the word *almah*, here [i.e., in Is. 7:14] translated virgin, may denote any mature young woman, whether a virgin or not. So far as its derivation is concerned, this is undoubtedly the case; but in biblical usage, the word denotes a virgin in every case where its meaning can be determined." (Beecher, PVM, 179–80)

In other words, since 'almah includes virginity in the context of the other biblical passages in which the term appears, it should be assumed that 'almah includes virginity in Isaiah 7:14. The context of this passage provides further confirmation that the prophetic 'almah must be a virgin.

1F. The Historical Setting

The sign of the virgin birth came at a traumatic time in the history of Judah. According to Isaiah 7:1, "Rezin king of Syria and

Pekah the son of Remaliah, king of Israel," were waging war against Jerusalem and had so far failed to overtake the city. Ahaz, who was the king of Judah at the time, panicked and seriously considered asking for military assistance from Assyria in order to stop and defeat the assaulting armies. The problem with this option, as Niessen points out, was that "Assyria was a selfish, conquering power; and an alliance with them could have been purchased only at the price of Judah's independence. It would not have been long before Jehovah would have been swept from His own Temple and the gods of Assyria installed in His place." Niessen continues,

> Isaiah met Ahaz to assure him that God would deliver Jerusalem and to warn him against a disastrous entanglement with Assyria. Isaiah's message was twofold: (a) The two invading kings were nothing more than "smoking firebrands"—the smoldering ends of an expired torch—and were therefore nothing to be concerned about (7:3–9). (b) As proof that Isaiah was not a false prophet and that God actually had the power to deliver Judah, Ahaz was told to ask for a confirmatory sign—anything he could conceive of from heaven above to Sheol below (7:10, 11)—and yet he refused (7:12).
>
> Ahaz knew that he had been presented with a dilemma by Isaiah. Had he accepted the sign he would have been prohibited by his own honor and by public opinion from calling in the Assyrians, which he was determined to do anyway. . . . Ahaz refused the sign because of political considerations and because of an unbelieving heart. . . . After rebuking Ahaz, Isaiah continued his message. "Therefore the Lord . . . himself will give you [plural] a sign: behold a [lit., the] *'almah* shall conceive, and bear a son, and shall call his name Immanuel (7:13)." (Niessen, V, 142–43)

2F. The Nature of the Sign

In this context the sign should be understood as a highly unusual event, something only God could do, a miracle. As John Martin notes, the sign here was to be "an attesting miracle that would confirm God's word." (Martin, I, 1047) A. Barnes concurs, stating that the sign in this context is "a miracle wrought in attestation of a Divine promise or message." (Feinberg, VBOTI, 253)

Since Ahaz refused to come up with a sign for God to perform, God Himself tells what the sign will be. It's reasonable to conclude that when God comes up with His own sign, that it would be miraculous as well. J. A. Alexander is contextually justified when he reasons that "it seems very improbable that after such an offer [by God to Ahaz], the sign [God finally] bestowed would be merely a thing of every day occurrence, or at most the application of a symbolical name. This presumption is strengthened by the solemnity with which the Prophet speaks of the predicted birth, not as a usual and natural event, but as something which excites his own astonishment, as he beholds it in prophetic vision." (Feinberg, VBOTI, 254)

"It is also important to notice," Hindson says, "that the sign [God proposes himself] is directed to 'you' (plural) and is not evidently directed to Ahaz who rejected the first offer. In v. 13, Isaiah had said: 'Hear ye now, O house of David' and it is apparent that the plural 'you' in v. 14, is to be connected to its antecedent 'ye' in v. 13. Since the context tells us that the dynasty of David is what is at stake in the impending invasion, it would seem proper to interpret the plural 'you' as the 'house of David' which is the recipient of the sign." (Hindson, II, 6)

Now a woman becoming pregnant through natural means could not possibly fit the criteria for a supernatural sign. The great Protestant reformer John Calvin hits the mark when he says,

> What wonderful thing did the prophet say, if he spoke of a young woman who conceived through intercourse with a man? It would certainly have been absurd to hold this out as a *sign* or a miracle. Let us suppose that it denotes a young woman who should become pregnant in the ordinary course of nature; everybody sees that it would have been silly and contemptible for the prophet, after having said that he was about to speak about something strange and uncommon to add "a young woman shall conceive." It is, therefore, plain enough that he speaks of a virgin who should conceive, not by the ordinary course of nature, but by the gracious influence of the Holy Spirit. (Calvin, CBPI, 248)

A closer examination of some key words in Isaiah 7:14 bears out Calvin's observation. The Hebrew word *h~r~h*, which is translated "conceive" in Isaiah 7:14, is "neither a verb nor a participle, but a feminine adjective connected with an active participle

> The hardest sign God could give that was relevant to the occasion was a true biological impossibility—the miraculous conception of a son by a woman who was a virgin in the biological sense of the word.
>
> —RICHARD NIESSEN

('bearing') and denotes that the scene is present to the prophet's view" (Hindson, II, 8). This means that the word and tense usage are similar to what the Angel of the Lord told Hagar in the wilderness centuries earlier: "Behold, you are with child, / And you shall bear a son" (Gen. 16:11). In short, Isaiah 7:14

would be better translated, "Behold, the virgin is pregnant and will bear a Son." Edward Hindson comments:

> It is quite obvious that the verbal time [of *h~r~h*] indicated here should be taken as a present tense. . . . . . The concept of the time element involved is very important to the interpretation of the passage. If the word *'almah* means "virgin" and if this *'almah* is already pregnant and about to bear a son, then, the girl is still a virgin, even though she is a mother. Consider the contradiction if this passage is not referring to the only virgin birth in history—that of Jesus Christ. The *virgin* is *pregnant!* How can she still be a virgin and be pregnant at the same time? The implication is that this child is to be miraculously born without a father and despite the pregnancy, the mother is still considered to be a virgin. The word *'almah* ("virgin") implies a present state of virginity just as the word *h~r~h* implies a present state of pregnancy. If the verbal action were in the future tense there would be no guarantee that the virgin who would (in the future) bear a son, would still be a virgin, and not a wife. But if a "virgin" "is with child" and is obviously both a virgin and a mother, we cannot escape the conclusion that this is a picture of the virgin birth. (Hindson, II, 8)

Niessen concludes, "The sign in Isaiah 7:14 was therefore something which exceeded the natural processes of nature. It was not a meaningless display, but a sign appropriate to the occasion and relevant to the continuance of the Davidic line which was being threatened with extinction. The hardest sign God could give that was relevant to the occasion was a true biological impossibility—the miraculous conception of a son by a woman who was a virgin in the biological sense of the word." (Niessen, V'aI, 144)

3F. Additional Translation Evidence

The Greek word for virgin is *parthenos*, the Latin word is *virgo*, and one of the Hebrew words frequently used is *betfl~h* (though whether *betfl~h* means "virgin" or not must be determined by the context in which it appears). R. Dick Wilson observes that

the LXX version of Is. vii. 14, made about 200 B.C., Matthew i. 23, from the first century A.D., the Syriac Peshitto, from the second century A.D., and Jerome's Latin Vulgate, from about A.D. 400, all render *'almah* by *parthenos* (virgin) or its equivalents *bethula* and *virgo*. . . . Since the LXX version was made in the case of . . . Isaiah 200 years B.C., it is to be presumed that their rendering of *'almah* by *parthenos* in . . . Is. vii. 14 was in their minds a justifiable rendering. So far as we have any evidence, the citation of Is. vii 14 in Matt. i. 23 is thus justified by the Jewish interpretation up to the time when Matthew was written. (Wilson, M'AI, 310–15)

Or, as Henry Morris states it, "The scholars who translated the Old Testament into the Greek Septuagint version used the standard Greek word for 'virgin' in translating Isaiah 7:14. So did Matthew when he quoted this prophecy (Matt. 1:23) as being fulfilled in the virgin birth of Christ." (Morris, BHA, 36)

B. Witherington III agrees, stating, "It is probably correct to say that if *'almah* did not normally have overtones of virginity, it is difficult if not impossible to see why the translators of the LXX used *parthenos* as the Greek equivalent." (Witherington III, BJ, 64)

The evidence, therefore, supporting the view that the *'almah* in Isaiah's prophecy is a young virgin woman is definitive and conclusive. No other understanding does justice to the word or its literary, social, or historical context.

2D. Who Is the *'Almah?*

Since we have determined that the *'almah* of Isaiah 7:14 is a young virgin woman of marriageable age who becomes pregnant through supernatural means, we can safely conclude that the only woman in history who fits this criterion is the virgin Mary, the

> Within the larger context of Isaiah 6–12, the Immanuel child to come from the womb of the virgin had to be a God-man, not simply a man (see Is. 9:6, 7; 11:1–16). No other person in history could fill this bill except Jesus of Nazareth.

mother of Jesus Christ. Hindson is right: "Only Mary the mother of Jesus can meet the qualifications to fulfill this prophecy. The virgin is not the prophet's [i.e., Isaiah's] wife, the wife of Ahaz, the wife of Hezekiah, nor some unknown by-stander. She is the only Virgin-Mother history or Scripture has ever recorded." (Witherington III, BJ, 9)

Some Bible scholars have countered this conclusion, arguing that Isaiah's prophecy "was to be a sign from God to King Ahaz indicating the nearness of the conquest of both the Northern and the Southern kingdoms by the king of Assyria. Since the birth of this child was to be a sign to Ahaz, it is only logical to conclude that the birth took place during the lifetime and reign of Ahaz. This would, therefore, necessitate an immediate, partial fulfilment of the prophecy of Isaiah 7:14." (Mueller, VSC, 205–6) While this view seems reasonable to some, I think it flounders on several key points.

First, to be successful this position must adopt an understanding of *'almah* that does not require it to include virginity in Isaiah 7:14. Otherwise, the advocates of this position would have to find the impossible: *two virgin births in history*—one during Ahaz's time and the other identified with Jesus' mother, Mary. But we have already seen the abundant evidence for arriving at the opposite conclusion: The evidence clearly shows that 'almah in Isaiah's prophecy means a young *virgin* woman of marriageable age, not simply a young woman. Isaiah's 'almah is definitely a virgin who is pregnant.

Second, the immediate-fulfillment view does not take seriously enough the tenses of Isaiah 7:14, which support the conclusion that the 'almah is at the same time a virgin and pregnant.

Third, the nature of the sign in Isaiah 7:14 is supernatural, not natural. A woman conceiving a child through sexual intercourse with a man would be insufficient in authenticating God's word. A miracle is required, and a virgin birth is that miracle.

Fourth, within the larger context of Isaiah 6–12, the Immanuel child to come from the womb of the virgin had to be a God-man, not simply a man (see Is. 9:6, 7; 11:1–16). No other person in history could fill this bill except Jesus of Nazareth.

And finally, Isaiah's prophetic utterance in 7:14 is directed to Ahaz as the temporary head of David's kingly line and to the Davidic kings who would follow him. In part, the prophecy was designed to demonstrate to Ahaz and his descendants that the Davidic line would survive them. This supports a far-fulfillment perspective rather than a near-fulfillment view. Bible scholar Charles Feinberg makes this point well:

Ahaz and his courtiers were fearful of the extinction of the Davidic dynasty and the displacement of the king by a Syrian pretender. However, the longer the time needed to fulfill the promise to the Davidic house, the longer that dynasty would be in existence to witness the realization of the prediction. It is well stated by Alexander: " . . . The assurance that Christ was to be born in Judah, of its royal family, might be a *sign* to Ahaz, that the kingdom should not perish in his day; and so far was the remoteness of the sign in this case

from making it absurd or inappropriate, that the further off it was, the stronger the promise of continuance of Judah, which it guaranteed." The conclusion, then, is inescapable that " . . . there is no ground, grammatical, historical, or logical, for doubt as to the main point, that the Church in all ages has been right in regarding this passage as a signal and explicit prediction of the miraculous conception and nativity of Jesus Christ." (Feinberg, VBOTI, 258)

We can therefore see that the doctrine of the virgin birth of Jesus Christ presented in the New Testament is in accord with the teachings and messianic prophecies of the Old Testament.

3C. The Gospels of Matthew and Luke

The first two chapters of the Gospels of Matthew and Luke relate the Virgin's miraculous conception to Jesus' birth. Matthew's account of these events emphasizes Jesus' legal father, Joseph, while Luke's account focuses on Jesus' mother, Mary. Theologian James Buswell suggests that one reason for the different emphases is that the accounts may be based on different sources, Matthew deriving his information from Joseph, and Luke getting his details from Mary:

The record of the virgin birth is found in the first and third gospels. Matthew's account (Matthew 1:18–25) is given from the point of view of Joseph, the husband of Mary. . . . Orr suggests that Matthew's account of the birth and the infancy of Christ might well have been derived by Matthew directly from the personal testimony of Joseph.

Luke's account (Luke 1:26–38; 2:1–7), on the other hand, is given from the point of view of Mary. . . . She may have been one of the "eye witnesses" (Luke 1:2) to which Luke refers as his sources. (Buswell, STCR, vol. 2, 41)

Witherington III concludes:

One must not underestimate either the Jewish flavor of both birth narratives or the skill with which the Evangelists have integrated their source material into moving and meaningful presentations about the good news that is and has come in Jesus. The shape of their presentations strikingly differs—even when they use many of the same elements. This in itself demonstrates that the First and Third Evangelists were not rigid editors of their sources, but creative shapers of their material who used their sources to highlight their own theological emphases and successfully integrated this material into the larger schemas of their respective Gospels. (Witherington III, BJ, 63)

Granting the different emphases, the Gospels of Matthew and Luke contain remarkable similarities, showing that they agree on the essential details of the virgin conception and birth. In his book *The Virgin Birth of Christ*, James Orr lists twelve points of agreement between the two Gospel accounts (see below).

If something is true, those bearing an accurate witness of it must agree in their testimonies. In regard to the accounts of Matthew and Luke, Orr states that although they are told from different points of view and may originate from different sources, they agree on several critical facts, including the one most essential of all, "that Jesus, conceived by the Holy Ghost, was born of Mary, a Virgin betrothed to Joseph, with his full knowledge of the cause." (Orr, VBC, 35)

The evidence strongly suggests that the birth narratives in Matthew and Luke are built on the firsthand testimony of Jesus' own family members, which further support the conclusion that Jesus' conception and birth were indeed the fulfillment of Isaiah's ancient prophecy. As Matthew wrote: "Now all this was done that it might be fulfilled which was spoken by the Lord through the prophet, saying: 'Behold, a virgin shall be with child, and bear a Son, and they shall call His name Immanuel,' which is translated 'God with us.'" (Matt. 1:22, 23)

While many scholars have thought that Mark was the first Gospel written, it is instructive to go back to the words of Irenaeus, bishop of Lyons in A.D. 180 and a student of Polycarp, a disciple of the apostle John. Irenaeus gives us the background of the writing of the four Gospel accounts and

1. Jesus was born in the last days of Herod (Matt. 2:1, 13; Luke 1:5).
2. He was conceived by the Holy Ghost (Matt. 1:18, 20; Luke 1:35).
3. His mother was a virgin (Matt. 1:18, 20, 23; Luke 1:27, 34).
4. She was betrothed to Joseph (Matt. 1:18; Luke 1:27; 2:5).
5. Joseph was of the house and lineage of David (Matt. 1:16, 20; Luke 1:27; 2:4).
6. Jesus was born at Bethlehem (Matt. 2:1; Luke 2:4, 6).
7. By divine direction He was called Jesus (Matt. 1:21; Luke 1:31).
8. He was declared to be a Savior (Matt. 1:21; Luke 2:11).
9. Joseph knew beforehand of Mary's condition and its cause (Matt. 1:18–20; Luke 2:5).
10. Nevertheless, he took Mary as wife and assumed full paternal responsibilities for her child (Matt. 1:20, 24, 25; Luke 2:5 ff.).
11. The annunciation and birth were attended by revelations and visions (Matt. 1:20, etc.; Luke 1:26, 27, etc.).
12. After the birth of Jesus, Joseph and Mary dwelt in Nazareth (Matt. 2:23; Luke 2:39). (Orr, VBC, 36–37)

attests to the fact that Matthew, the Gospel first containing an account of the virgin birth, was written earliest of all the Gospels:

> Matthew published his gospel among the Hebrews [i.e., Jews] in their own tongue, when Peter and Paul were preaching the gospel in Rome and founding the church there. After their departure [i.e., death, which strong tradition places at the time of the Neronian persecution in 64], Mark, the disciple and interpreter of Peter, himself handed down to us in writing the substance of Peter's preaching. Luke, the follower of Paul, set down in a book the gospel preached by his teacher. Then John, the disciple of the Lord, who also leaned on his breast [this is a reference to John 13:25 and 21:20], himself produced his gospel, while he was living at Ephesus in Asia. (Irenaeus, AH, 3.1.1)

Matthew, the former tax collector, a man accustomed to keeping accurate records, was probably now in his sixties and feeling the need, near the end of his life, to leave behind an orderly account of all that he had collected and written down about the life of Jesus. He begins his account with a listing of Jesus' ancestors and a detailed account of Jesus' miraculous conception in the womb of a virgin:

> This is how the birth of Jesus Christ came about: His mother Mary was pledged to be married to Joseph, but before they came together, she was found to be with child through the Holy Spirit. Because Joseph her husband was a righteous man and did not want to expose her to public disgrace, he had in mind to divorce her quietly. But after he had considered this, an angel of the Lord appeared to him in a dream and said, "Joseph son of David, do not be afraid to take Mary home as your wife, because what is conceived in her is from the Holy Spirit. She will give birth to a son, and you are to give him the name Jesus, because he will save his people from their sins."

> All this took place to fulfill what the Lord had said through the prophet: "the virgin will be with child and will give birth to a son, and they will call him Immanuel"—which means, "God with us." When Joseph woke up, he did what the angel of the Lord had commanded him and took Mary home as his wife. But he had no union with her until she gave birth to a son. And he gave him the name Jesus (Matthew 1:18–25 NIV).

1D. Answers to Objections

Some critics have argued against the historical accuracy of the birth narratives in Matthew and Luke, raising what they think are clear factual mistakes or unresolvable contradictions. The most frequently cited objections concern the genealogies of the two Gospels and Luke's mention of Quirinius and a certain census (addressed in chapter 3).

Concerning contradictory genealogies, Matthew records "the genealogy of Jesus Christ, the son of David" (Matt. 1:1), and Luke provides another genealogy of Jesus, "being (as was supposed) the son of Joseph" (Luke 3:23). James Montgomery Boice explains the problem well:

> Matthew's genealogy begins with Abraham and moves forward in history to Christ. It traces Abraham's descendants through fourteen generations to David, David's descendants through fourteen generations to the Babylonian captivity, then the later descendants through fourteen more generations up to "Jacob the father of Joseph, the husband of Mary, of whom was born Jesus, who is called Christ." Luke, on the other hand, moves backward. He begins with Joseph and goes back through David, to Abraham—and then even back beyond Abraham to Adam, who, he says, was the son of God.

> Two of Luke's sections present no problem. His final section—from Abraham to Adam—does not occur in Matthew. So there is no

basis for comparison. His second section—from David to Abraham—is also free of problems because it corresponds to the genealogy we find in Matthew.

The difficulty comes in Luke's first section. For Luke traces Joseph's descendants back to David through Nathan, one of David's sons, while Matthew traces what is apparently the same line of descent through Solomon, another of David's sons. Consequently, in this section of the genealogies all the names are different.

The fact that these are two separate lines is no problem. We can understand how two different sons of David would give birth to two different family trees. The difficulty is that Matthew and Luke both claim Joseph as a descendant of their particular trees. Luke says that Joseph was the son of Heli (3:23), Matthew says that Joseph was the son of Jacob (1:16), and both apparently cannot be true. (Boice, CC, 40–41)

Scholars have proposed a number of solutions to this problem.

1E. Adoptive vs Physical Descent

The oldest solution was proposed by Africanus, and has come down to us through the ancient church historian Eusebius. New Testament scholar I. Howard Marshall says of this theory:

Africanus (Eusebius, HE 1:7) utilised the ideas of adoptive and physical descent, and employed the device of levirate marriage to harmonise the two genealogies. According to information which he claimed to have received from the descendants of James, the brother of Jesus, Africanus stated that Matthan (Mt. 1:15) married a certain Estha, by whom he had a son, Jacob; when Matthan died, his widow married Malchi (Lk. 3:24) and had a son Eli (Lk. 3:23; note that Africanus did not apparently know of Levi and Matthat who come between Malchi and Eli in Luke's list). The second of these two

half-brothers, Eli, married, but died without issue; his half-brother Jacob took his wife in levirate marriage, so that his physical son, Joseph, was regarded as the legal son of Eli. (Marshall, GL, 158)

The custom of levirate marriage is described in Scripture (Deut. 25:5, 6; Gen. 38:8–10; the book of Ruth). In a levirate marriage, explains Bible commentator Walter Liefeld,

The widow of a childless man could marry his brother so that a child of the second marriage could legally be considered as the son of the deceased man in order to perpetuate his name. In a genealogy the child could be listed under his natural or his legal father. Joseph is listed as the son of Heli in Luke but as the son of Jacob in Matthew. On the levirate marriage theory, Heli and Jacob may have been half-brothers, with the same mother but fathers of different names. Perhaps Heli died and Jacob married his widow. (Liefeld, L, 861)

Marshall contends that this theory "is not impossible . . . , but it is improbable, especially if we accept the usual text of Luke." (Marshall, GL, 158).

2E. Father vs Grandfather

A theory advanced by R. P. Nettelhorst is that "the genealogy in Luke is through Joseph's father and that the one in Matthew is through Joseph's maternal grandfather." Nettelhorst adds:

That Matthew should skip Joseph's mother in the genealogical listing is not peculiar since it is readily apparent that Matthew skips a number of people in his genealogy. For instance in Matthew1:8 he writes: "Joram the father of Uzziah." But when his statement is compared with 1 Chronicles 3:10–12, it is evident that three people have been left out of Matthew's genealogy: Ahaziah, Joash, and Amaziah.

Matthew left names out in order to arrive at the structural symmetry he desired: "Thus there were fourteen generations in all from Abraham to David, fourteen from David to the exile to Babylon, and fourteen from the exile to Christ" (Matt. 1:17).

Therefore it would not be unreasonable to suppose that Matthew might leave out the name of Joseph's mother so that he could get the structural format he needed. Furthermore, his genealogy lists four women—Tamar, Rahab, Ruth, and Bathsheba—a fact that lends support to the idea that it might be a woman's genealogy. (Nettelhorst, GJ, 171–72)

While this view could be right, it seems odd that Matthew would name four women in his genealogy and yet leave out the name of the woman who is supposedly the centerpiece of the genealogy. If he were going to leave out a name for the sake of maintaining symmetry, why drop one of the most important names of all—that of Joseph's mother?

3E. Joseph vs Joseph

J. Gresham Machen advanced a solution proposed by Lord A. Hervey, a "theory which has gained [the] most support in modern times" (Marshall, GL, 158). As Boice summarizes it, Machen argued that the genealogies in Matthew and Luke "are indeed both genealogies of Joseph but that Matthew gives what Machen calls the 'legal' descendants of David, that is, the line that actually sat upon the throne or would have, had it continued, and that Luke gives the actual 'paternal' line that produced Joseph." (Boice, CC, 41)

This proposal has some merits, but, as Marshall says, the "solution depends upon conjecture, and there is no way of knowing whether the conjectures correspond to reality." (Marshall, GL, 159) Witherington agrees, concluding, "unfortunately there is no way either to prove or disprove this theory." (Witherington III, BJ, 65)

4E. Joseph vs Mary

Perhaps the best solution is one of the oldest ones. "Since at least the time of Annius of Viterbo in A.D. 1490," Witherington notes,

it has been traditional to assume that Matthew's genealogy traces Jesus' lineage through Joseph (his legal genealogy), whereas Luke's genealogy traces his lineage through

> Luke does not say that he is giving Jesus' genealogy through Joseph. Rather, he notes that Jesus was "as was supposed" (Luke 3:23) the son of Joseph, while He was actually the son of Mary.
>
> —NORMAN GEISLER

Mary (his natural genealogy). [This solution finds] support from the fact that the Matthean birth narrative focuses more on the role of Joseph than of Mary, while Luke's narrative makes Mary the more central figure in the drama. It also comports with the ancient conjecture that Joseph is ultimately the source of much of the Matthean birth narratives, while Mary is the source for most of Luke's material. (Witherington III, BJ, 65)

Geisler and Howe adopt this position as their solution to the differences between the two genealogies. Their articulation of the position and their reasons for accepting it add some significant points to Witherington's observations:

[The genealogies in Matthew and Luke] are two different lines of ancestors, one traced through His [Jesus'] legal father, Joseph and the other through His actual mother, Mary. Matthew gives the official line, since he addresses Jesus' genealogy to Jewish concerns for the Jewish Messiah's credentials which required that Messiah come from the seed of Abraham and the line of David (cf. Matt. 1:1).

Luke, with a broader *Greek* audience in view, addresses himself to their interest in Jesus as the *Perfect Man* (which was the quest of Greek thought). Thus, he traces Jesus back to the first man, Adam (Luke 3:38).

That Matthew gives Jesus' paternal genealogy and Luke his maternal genealogy is further supported by several facts. First of all, while both lines trace Christ to David, each is through a different son of David. Matthew traces Jesus through Joseph (his *legal father*) to David's son, *Solomon* the king, by whom Christ rightfully inherited the throne of David (cf. 2 Sam. 7:12ff). Luke's purpose, on the other hand, is to show Christ as an actual human. So he traces Christ to David's son, *Nathan*, through his *actual mother*, Mary, through whom He can rightfully claim to be fully human, the redeemer of humanity.

Further, Luke does not say that he is giving Jesus' genealogy through Joseph. Rather, he notes that Jesus was "as was supposed" (Luke 3:23) the son of Joseph, while He was actually the son of Mary. Also, that Luke would record Mary's genealogy fits with his interest as a doctor in mothers and birth and with his emphasis on women in his Gospel which has been called "the Gospel for Women."

Finally, the fact that the two genealogies have some names in common (such as Shealtiel and Zerubbabel, Matt. 1:12; cf. Luke 3:27) does not prove they are the same genealogy for two reasons. One, these are not uncommon names. Further, even the same genealogy (Luke's) has a repeat of the names Joseph and Judah (3:26, 30). (Geisler, WCA, 385–86)

Biblical scholar Gleason Archer accepts this solution as well, and adds more lines of support:

Matthew 1:1–16 gives the genealogy of Jesus through Joseph, who was himself a descendant of King David. As Joseph's adopted Son, Jesus became his legal heir, so far as his inheritance was concerned. Notice carefully the wording of v. 16: "And Jacob begat Joseph the husband of Mary, of whom was born Jesus,

who is called Christ" (NASB). This stands in contrast to the format followed in the preceding verses of the succession of Joseph's ancestors: "Abraham begat [*egennʾsen*] Isaac, and

> But the greatest proof of all lies in one of the names in the account of Matthew: the name Jechonias. It is that name that furnishes the reason for the inclusion of the genealogy of Jesus' step-father, for it proves that Joseph could not have been the father of Jesus, or if he had been, that Jesus could not have been the Messiah.
>
> —DONALD GREY BARNHOUSE

Isaac begat Jacob, etc." Joseph is not said to have begotten Jesus; rather he is referred to as "the husband of Mary, of whom [feminine genitive] Jesus was born."

Luke 3:23–38, on the other hand, seems to record the genealogical line of Mary herself, carried all the way back beyond the time of Abraham to Adam and the commencement of the human race. This seems to be implied by the wording of v. 23: "Jesus . . . being (as was supposed) the son of Joseph." This "as was supposed" indicates that Jesus was not really the biological son of Joseph, even though this was commonly assumed by the public. It further calls attention to the mother, Mary, who must of necessity have been the sole human parent through whom Jesus could have descended from a line of ancestors. Her genealogy is thereupon listed, starting with Heli, who was actually Joseph's father-in-law, in contradistinction to Joseph's own father, Jacob (Matt. 1:16). Mary's line of descent came through Nathan, a son of Bathsheba (or "Bathshua," according to 1 Chron. 3:5), the wife of David. Therefore, Jesus was descended from David naturally through Nathan and legally through Solomon. (Archer, EBD, 316)

Still more evidence for this view comes from Bible expositor Donald Grey Barnhouse:

There [are] two genealogies. The lines run parallel from Abraham to David, but then Matthew comes down to Jesus by way of Solomon the son of David, while Luke comes down to Jesus by way of Nathan the son of David. In other words, the two genealogies are the lines of two brothers and the children become cousins. When I state that Luke's genealogy is that of the Virgin Mary and Matthew's genealogy is that of Joseph, I am not merely following the persistent tradition of the earthly church, as Dr. James Orr states it, but I am setting forth the only explanation that will fit the facts. The whole point of the difference is that Solomon's line was the royal line and Nathan's line was the legal line. . . .

But the greatest proof of all lies in one of the names in the account of Matthew: the name Jechonias. It is that name that furnishes the reason for the inclusion of the genealogy of Jesus' step-father, for it proves that Joseph could not have been the father of Jesus, or if he had been, that Jesus could not have been the Messiah. In the use of that name is conclusive evidence that Jesus is the son of Mary and not the son of Joseph. Jechonias was accursed of God with a curse that took the throne away from any of his descendants.

"Thus saith the Lord," we read in Jeremiah 22:30, "write ye this man childless, a man that shall not prosper in his days: for no man of his seed shall prosper, sitting upon the throne of David, and ruling any more in Judah." Not one of the seven sons (1 Chron. 3:17, 18) of this man ever possessed the throne. No carnal son of this man could have been king because of the curse of God. If Jesus had been the son of Joseph, He would have been accursed and could never have been the Messiah.

On the other hand, the line of Nathan was not the royal line. A son of Heli would have faced the fact that there was a regal line that would have contested any claim that came from the line of Nathan. How was the dilemma solved? It was solved in a manner that is so simple that it is the utter confusion of the agnostics who seek to tear the Bible to pieces. The answer is this: The line that had no

curse upon it produced Heli and his daughter the Virgin Mary and her Son Jesus Christ. He is therefore eligible by the line of Nathan and exhausts that line. The line that had a curse on it produced Joseph, exhausts the line of Solomon, for Joseph's other children now have an older brother who, legally, by adoption, is the royal heir. How can the title be free in any case? A curse on one line and the lack of reigning royalty in the other.

But when God the Holy Spirit begat the Lord Jesus in the womb of the Virgin without any use of a human father, the child that was born was the seed of David according to the flesh. And when Joseph married Mary and took the unborn child under his protecting care, giving Him the title that had come down to Him through His ancestor Solomon, the Lord Jesus became the legal Messiah, the royal Messiah, the uncursed Messiah, the true Messiah, the only possible Messiah. The lines are exhausted. Any man that ever comes into this world professing to fulfill the conditions will be a liar and the child of the Devil. (Barnhouse, MR, 45–47)

Liefeld concludes: "We possess not a poverty but a plethora of possibilities. Therefore the lack of certainty due to incomplete information need not imply error in either genealogy." (Liefeld, L, 861–62)

There may not be enough information yet to resolve with certainty the differences between Matthew's genealogy and Luke's, but there certainly is enough information to know that the differences are not insoluble, therefore they do not pose a genuine contradiction to the biblical account of Jesus' virgin birth.

4C. The Witnesses of Mark, John, and Paul

Critics often argue that since there is no reference in the New Testament to the virgin birth except in Matthew and Luke, the doctrine was not vital to the message of the New Testament church. I believe these critics are shortsighted, and that there is reference elsewhere in the New Testament to the virgin birth (see below). But first, some faulty logic in their arguments needs to be revealed.

William Childs Robinson, emeritus professor of historical theology at Columbia Theological Seminary, points out that "what is explicit in Matthew and Luke is implicit in Paul and John." (Robinson, WSYTIA, n.p.)

Robert Gromacki writes that

it is not tenable to argue from silence to disbelief or from silence to an ignorance of the doctrine. The apostles did not record everything that they taught or knew (cf. John 20:30). In fact, the so-called silence argument of the liberal can boomerang on him. Since Paul did not mention any human father for the person Jesus, does that mean that he believed that Jesus had no human father? Most regard silence as assent. If Paul and the others did not believe in the virgin birth, should they not have corrected the earlier birth narratives? The argument of silence can be used both ways. Actually, no confession or denial should ever be based upon the argument from silence. (Gromacki, VB, 183)

Clement Rogers wrote that

while it is true that it [the account of the virgin birth] appears at the beginning of both the first and third Gospels, it is absent from that of St. Mark, or, as it is commonly put, St. Mark "knows nothing about it," though his was the first to be written and was used by the other two. St. Mark's Gospel, we have it on good authority, was his account of what he had heard St. Peter preach. He was his "interpreter." It represents what St. Peter found useful or necessary in preaching in public, just as St. Paul preached on the Areopagus at Athens, or at Jerusalem, Antioch, and Rome.

Now, for obvious reasons, the question of our Lord's birth would not have been a subject to be discussed on such occasions, especially so long as His Mother was still alive, and was, possibly, personally known to those listening. The main appeal was to be teaching that Christ gave, the signs that He had wrought, and, above all, as we see from the place it occupies, the events of His Passion. (Rogers, CM, 99–101)

On the other hand, Millard Erickson states,

There is, indeed, one item in Mark's Gospel that some see as a hint that the author did know about the virgin birth. That occurs in 6:3. In the parallel passage Matthew reports that the people of Nazareth asked, "Is not this the carpenter's son?" (Matt. 13:55); and Luke has, "Is not this Joseph's son?" (4:22). However, the report in Mark reads, "Is not this the carpenter; the son of Mary and brother of James and Joses and Judas and Simon, and are not his sisters here with us?" It is as if Mark is taking pains to avoid referring to Jesus as the son of Joseph. Unlike Matthew's and Luke's readers, who had been made aware of the virgin birth in the opening chapter of each of those Gospels, Mark's readers would have no way of knowing about it. So he chose his words very carefully in order not to give the wrong impression. The crucial point for us is that Mark's account gives no basis whatsoever for concluding that Joseph was the father of Jesus. Thus, although Mark does not tell us of the virgin birth, he certainly does not contradict it either. (Erickson, CT, vol. 2, 750–51)

> Jesus repeatedly referred to Himself as God's "only begotten Son." Now the word "begat" is a word of human genealogies, a term referring to the male part in procreating or generating a child. It refers to the physical birth. Jesus insisted that He was not begotten of Joseph but was begotten of God. The same word, *monogenes,* is used six times in the New Testament about Jesus as the only-begotten of God, and twice Jesus Himself used it about Himself!
>
> —JOHN R. RICE

Actually, I believe the apostle John does refer to a miraculous birth of Jesus by his use of the word *begotten* in John 3:16. Bible expositor John R. Rice takes this view:

> Jesus repeatedly referred to Himself as God's "only begotten Son." Now the word "begat" is a word of human genealogies, a term referring to the male part in procreating or generating a child. It refers to the physical birth. Jesus insisted that He was not begotten of Joseph but was begotten of God. The same word, *monogenes,* is used six times in the New Testament about Jesus as the only-begotten of God, and twice Jesus Himself used it about Himself! Note that Jesus does not claim to be simply one who is begotten of God. Rather, He claims to be the only one ever born who was so begotten. He is the *only* begotten Son of God. No one else was ever born of a virgin. In a spiritual sense, it may be said that Christians are "begotten . . . again unto a lively hope" (I Peter 1:3), but in the sense in which Jesus was begotten of God, no one else ever was. Clearly Jesus was claiming that He was physically begotten of God and not by any human father. (Rice, IJG, 22–23)

The apostle John's genealogy is essentially "in the beginning," from the standpoint of divine eternity, and therefore doesn't deal with the virgin birth: "In the beginning was the Word . . . and the Word became flesh" (John 1:1, 14).

Likewise, in regard to Paul: "St. Paul knew St. Luke quite well. He was his companion for a long time in his travels, and was with him at Rome, and St. Luke is our chief authority for the story of our Lord's birth. St. Paul must have known it, and it is quite natural that, knowing it, he should have spoken of our Lord as he does when he says: 'God sent forth His Son born of a woman'" (Rogers, CM, 101), not of a man.

Isn't it interesting how many people celebrate Christmas every year without being fully aware of the uniqueness of the event they celebrate: a baby born to a woman who was a virgin! Not even the tabloids could have thought of that one.

2B. Extra-biblical Evidence for the Virgin Birth

1C. Time

An important consideration concerning the Gospel accounts is the time they were written. Due to the early dating of the Gospel writings, there was insufficient time for the growth of a myth around the birth of Christ. Thus, we should see evidence of the teaching of the virgin birth in the early church. Two questions arise in relation to this fact: How did the concept of a virgin birth arise so soon if it was not based on fact? If the Gospels were not historical, how were they accepted so universally at such an early date?

In regard to the early church belief in the virgin birth, Gresham Machen writes: "Even . . . if there were not a word about the subject in the New Testament, the second-century testimony would show that the belief in the virgin birth must have arisen, to say the least, well before the first century was over." (Machen, VBC, 44)

The Apostles' Creed was one of the earliest creedal statements of belief in the early church. Concerning the virgin birth it says that Jesus "was conceived by the power of the Holy Spirit and born of the Virgin Mary." Regarding this universally accepted creed of the church, Erickson writes:

> The form [of the Apostles' Creed] which we now use was produced in Gaul in the fifth or sixth century, but its roots go back much further. It actually is based upon an old Roman baptismal confession. The virgin birth is affirmed in the earlier as well as the later form. Shortly after the middle of the second century

the early form was already in use, not only in Rome, but by Tertullian in North Africa and Irenaeus in Gaul and Asia Minor. The presence of the doctrine of the virgin birth in an early confession of the important church of Rome is highly significant, especially since such a creed would not have incorporated any new doctrine. (Erickson, CT, vol. 2, 747)

In the early church, there were a few who rejected the virgin birth. Some of these heretics belonged to a Jewish Christian sect called the Ebionites. While some Ebionites accepted the virgin birth, others did not. Among those who denied the virgin birth were those who objected to the church's use of the passage in Isaiah concerning the virgin bearing a son (Is. 7:14). They said that the verse should be translated "a young woman." (Rogers, CM, 105) But with the exception of these Ebionites and a handful of others, the rest of the church upheld the virgin birth of Christ and passed it on as part of orthodox doctrine. James Orr writes: "Apart from the Ebionites . . . and a few Gnostic sects, nobody of Christians in early times is known to have existed who did not accept as part of their faith the birth of Jesus from the Virgin Mary; . . . we have the amplest evidence that *this belief was part of the general faith of the Church.*" (Orr, VBC, 138)

In speaking of the early church, Aristides says, "Everything that we know of the dogmatics of the early part of the second century agrees with the belief that at that period the virginity of Mary was a part of the formulated Christian belief." (Aristides, AA, 25)

2C. The Witness of Early Church Fathers

Very important in the history of the early church's belief in the virgin birth is the testimony of its early fathers. In A.D. 110, Ignatius, bishop of Syrian Antioch, wrote in his *Epistle to the Ephesians,* "For our God

Jesus Christ was . . . conceived in the womb of Mary . . . by the Holy Ghost." (GEAF, 18:2) He also wrote, "Now the virginity of Mary, and He who was born of her . . . are the mys-

> Justin Martyr in A.D. 150 gives ample evidence for the concept of Jesus' miraculous birth. "Our Teacher Jesus Christ, who is the first-begotten of God the Father, was not born as a result of sexual relations. . . . The power of God descending upon the virgin overshadowed her, and caused her, while still a virgin, to conceive. . . . For, by God's power He was conceived by a virgin."

teries most spoken of throughout the world, yet done in secret by God." (Wells, OH, 19:1) Ignatius received his information from his teacher, John the apostle.

Erickson points out that Ignatius was arguing against a group called Docetists. The Docetists denied that Jesus had a real human nature and that He could undergo birth and suffering. To them Jesus was divine but not human. Ignatius challenged this heresy by producing "a summary of the chief facts about Christ." Among these facts was "a reference to the virginity of Mary as one of the 'mysteries to be shouted about.'"

According to Erickson:

Several observations make this reference the more impressive: (1) inasmuch as Ignatius was writing against Docetism, the expression "born of woman" (as in Gal. 4:4) would have been more to his purpose than was "born of a virgin"; (2) it was written not by a novice, but by the bishop of the mother church of Gentile Christianity; (3) it was written no later than 117. As J. Gresham Machen has observed, "when we find [Ignatius] attesting the virgin birth not as a novelty but altogether as a matter of course, as one of the accepted facts about Christ, it becomes evident that the belief in the virgin birth must have been prevalent long before the close of the first century." (Erickson, CT, vol. 2, 747–48)

"We have further evidence," writes Clement F. Rogers, "which shows that the belief in Ignatius' time was no new one. For we know that the belief of Christians in the Virgin Birth was attacked by those outside. Cerinthus, for example, was the contemporary and opponent of St. John. It was said that the Evangelist, meeting him in the public baths, cried out, 'Let us flee lest the bath fall in while Cerinthus, the enemy of the truth, is here.' He [Cerinthus] taught, Irenaeus tells us, that our Lord was born of Joseph and Mary like other men." (Rogers, CM, 105)

Another of the post-apostolic writers, Aristides, in A.D. 125 spoke of the virgin birth: "He is Himself Son of God on high, who was manifested of the Holy Spirit, came down from heaven, and being born of a Hebrew virgin took on His flesh from the virgin. . . . He it is who was according to the flesh born of the race of Hebrews, by the God-bearing virgin Miriam." (Aristides, AA, 32)

Justin Martyr in A.D. 150 gives ample evidence to the concept of Jesus' miraculous birth. "Our Teacher Jesus Christ, who is the first-begotten of God the Father, was not born as a result of sexual relations . . . the power of God descending upon the virgin overshadowed her, and caused her, while still a virgin, to conceive. . . . For, by God's power He was conceived by a virgin . . . in accordance with the will of God, Jesus Christ, His Son, has been born of the Virgin Mary." (*Apology* 1:21–33; *Dialogue with Trypho the Jew*)

"The first great Latin-speaking Christian was the converted lawyer Tertullian. He tells us that not only there was in his days (c. A.D. 200) a definite Christian creed on which all churches agree, but he also tells us, its technical name was a *tessera*. Now things only get technical names when they have been established for some time. He quotes this creed four times. It includes the words '*ex virgine Maria*' (of the Virgin Mary)." (Rogers, CM, 103)

3C. The Early Jewish Witness

As should be expected, there are negative arguments concerning the virgin birth also. These were largely raised by some Jews. Our purpose here is to show that in the very early days of the church there was external controversy concerning the birth of Jesus, and that for this controversy to have originated, the church must have been teaching Christ's miraculous birth.

Ethelbert Stauffer says that "In a genealogical table dating from before A.D. 70 Jesus is listed as 'the bastard of a wedded wife.' Evidently the Evangelist Matthew was familiar with such lists and was warring against them. Later rabbis bluntly called Jesus the son of an adulteress. They also claimed to know precisely the 'unknown father's name: Panthera.' In old rabbinical texts we find frequent mention of Jesus ben Panthera, and the eclectic Platonist. Celsus around 160 details all sorts of gossipy anecdotes about Mary and the legionary Panthera." (Stauffer, JHS, 17)

In the *Toldoth Jeschu,* a fifth century (or later) fictitious tale about Christ, it is taught that Jesus is of "illegitimate origin, through the union of his mother with a soldier named Panthera." (Orr, VBC, 146)

Hugh Schonfield, the Jewish skeptic, writes: "R. Shimeon ben Azzai said: 'I found a genealogical scroll in Jerusalem, and therein was written, "so-and-so, bastard son of an adulteress."'" (Schaff, HCC, 139) R. Shimeon lived at the end of the first and beginning of the second century A.D.

According to Schonfield this scroll must have been in existence at the time of the capture of Jerusalem in A.D. 70. In the older Jewish records, Jesus' name is represented by the

> The Jews had strict rules governing name-giving. A Jew was named after his father (Jochanan ben Sakkai, for example) even if his father had died before his birth. He was named after his mother only when the father was unknown.
>
> —ETHELBERT STAUFFER

phrase "so and so." Schonfield then goes on to say that "there would be no object in making [the scroll] unless the Christian original (genealogy) made some claim that the birth of Jesus was not normal" (Schonfield, AH, 139, 140). Due to the reference of R. Shimeon, Schonfield says that the charge against Jesus "that he was the bastard son of an adulteress, goes back to an early date." (Schonfield, AH, 140)

Origen (c. A.D. 185–c. A.D. 254) in his *Contra Celsum* writes:

Let us return, however, to the words put into the mouth of the Jew, where the mother of Jesus is described as having been turned out by the carpenter who was betrothed to her, as she had been convicted of adultery and had a child by a certain soldier named Panthera. Let us consider whether those who fabricated the myth that the virgin and Panthera committed adultery and that the carpenter turned her out, were not blind when they concocted all this to get rid of the miraculous conception by the Holy Spirit. For on account of its highly miraculous character they could have falsified the story in other ways without, as it were, unintentionally admitting that Jesus was not born of an ordinary marriage. It was inevitable that those who did not accept the miraculous birth of Jesus would have invented

some lie. But the fact that they did not do this convincingly, but kept as part of the story that the virgin did not conceive Jesus by Joseph, makes the lie obvious to people who can see through fictitious stories and show them up. Is it reasonable that a man who ventured to do such great things for mankind in order that, so far as in the universe, should have had, not a miraculous birth, but a birth more illegitimate and disgraceful than any? . . . It is therefore probable that this soul, which lived a more useful life on earth than many men (to avoid appearing to beg the question by saying "all" men), needed a body which was not only distinguished among human bodies, but was also superior to all others. (Origen, CC, 1:32–33).

This controversy is brought out even in the Gospels: "'Is this not the carpenter, the Son of Mary, and brother of James, Joses, Judas, and Simon? And are not His sisters here with us?' So they were offended at Him" (Mark 6:3). "This account," writes Ethelbert Stauffer, "which appears only in Mark does full justice to the situation. The Jews had strict rules governing name-giving. A Jew was named after his father (Jochanan ben Sakkai, for example) even if his father had died before his birth. He was named after his mother only when the father was unknown." (Schonfield, AH, 16)

Moreover,

In the *Logia* we learn that Jesus was berated for being a "glutton and drunkard." There must have been some grounds for this charge. For it fits in with all that we know about the attitude of Jesus and about his Pharisaical groups' reaction to it. Now, among Palestinian Jews this particular insult would be flung at a person born of an illegitimate connection who betrayed by his mode of life and his religious conduct the stain of his birth. This was the sense in which the Pharisees and their followers employed the phrase against Jesus. Their meaning was: "he is a bastard." (Schonfield, AH, 16)

The early Jewish allusions to the supposed illegitimacy of Christ (before A.D. 70) demonstrate that there was doubt as to His parentage. This is evidence that the very early Christian church, at most forty years after His death, must have been teaching something unusual about His birth—namely, that He was born of a virgin.

4C. The Koran

In the Koran we find Jesus referred to regularly as Isaibn Maryam—Jesus, the son of Mary. Stauffer writes, "Abdullahal-Baidawi, the classical commentator on the Koran, remarks with full understanding of the Semitic practice in nomenclature: The name of the mother is borne when the father is unknown. But this name and explanation are here intended in a thoroughly positive sense. In Islam Jesus is regarded as the Son of the Virgin Mary who was begotten by the creative Word of God." (Schonfield, AH, 17–18)

The Koran refers explicitly to Jesus' virgin conception in Mary, v. 20. According to this passage, when it was announced to Mary that she would bear a son, she replied, "How can this be, for I am a virgin and no mortal has ever touched me." The account goes on to say that "it is easy for Me (the Lord)." He then "breathed on her His Spirit." (Box, MC, 6)

3B. Summation by Various Writers

On the basis of the available evidence, it is important to see what some of the world's authors say about Jesus' unusual entrance into human history.

W. H. Griffith Thomas writes, "The chief support for the doctrine [of the virgin birth] is the necessity of accounting for the uniqueness of the life of Jesus." (Griffith Thomas, CIC, 125)

Henry Morris states:

It is altogether fitting that the One who performed many miracles during His life, who offered Himself on the cross as an atoning sacrifice for the sins of men, and who then rose bodily from the dead in vindication of all His claims, should have begun such a unique life by a unique entrance into that life. . . .

If He is truly our Savior, He must be far more than a mere man, though also He is truly the Son of man. To die for our sins, He must Himself be free from any sin of His own. To be sinless in practice, He must first be sinless in nature. He could not have inherited a human nature, bound under the Curse and the bondage of sin as it must have been, as do all other sons of men. His birth, therefore, must have been a miraculous birth. The "seed of the woman" was implanted in the virgin's womb when, as the angel said: "The Holy Ghost shall come upon thee, and the power of the Highest shall overshadow thee; therefore also that holy thing which shall be born of thee shall be called the Son of God" (Luke 1:35). . . .

Not only is the Virgin Birth true because it is clearly taught in the Bible, but also because it is the only type of birth consistent with the character and mission of Jesus Christ and with God's great plan of salvation for a lost world. . . .

To say that such a miracle is impossible is to deny the existence of God or else to deny that He can control His creation. (Morris, BHA, 38)

In summing up the evidence of Jesus' birth, J. Gresham Machen states, "Thus there is good ground, we think, to hold that the reason why the Christian Church came to believe in the birth of Jesus without a human father was simply that He was as a matter of fact so born." (Machen, VBC, 269)

Clement Rogers concludes that "All the evidence there is goes to prove the miraculous birth of Christ." (Rogers, CM, 115)

Jesus Christ did indeed have an utterly unique entrance into human history.

3A. IF GOD BECAME A MAN, THEN WE WOULD EXPECT HIM TO BE WITHOUT SIN

1B. Jesus' View of Himself

Jesus once asked a hostile crowd, "Which of you convicts Me of sin?" (John 8:46). He received no answer. When He invited them to accuse Him, He stayed and bore their scrutiny and was found innocent. He could encourage such a public examination because He was without sin.

He also said "I always do those things that please Him" (John 8:29)—namely, His heav-

> It is highly significant that in one as sensitive morally as was Jesus and who taught His followers to ask for the forgiveness of their sins there is no hint of any need of forgiveness for Himself, no asking of pardon, either from those about Him or of God.
>
> —KENNETH SCOTT LATOURETTE

enly Father. Jesus apparently lived in unbroken communion with God.

Christ's self-conscious purity is astonishing. It is totally unlike the experience of other believers in God. Every Christian knows that the nearer he approaches God, the more aware he becomes of his sin. However, with Christ this was not the case. Jesus lived more closely to God than anyone else and yet was free from all sense of sin.

Along this same line of thought, we are told of the temptations of Jesus (Luke 4) but never of His sins. We never hear of Him confessing or asking forgiveness of any wrongdoing of His own, although He tells His

disciples to do so. It appears that He had no sense of guilt that accompanies a sin nature resident in the rest of the members of the human race.

"The best reason we have for believing in the sinlessness of Jesus," writes C. E. Jefferson,

is the fact that He allowed His dearest friends to think that He was. There is in all His talk no trace of regret or hint of compunction or suggestion of sorrow for shortcoming, or slightest vestige of remorse. He taught other men to think of themselves as sinners, He asserted plainly that the human heart is evil, He told His disciples that every time they prayed they were to pray to be forgiven, but He never speaks or acts as though He Himself has the faintest consciousness of having ever done anything other than what was pleasing to God. (Jefferson, CJ, 225)

In this regard Philip Schaff states: "It is an indisputable fact, then, both from His mission and uniform conduct, and His express dedication, that Christ knew Himself free from sin and guilt. The only rational explanation of this fact is that Christ *was* no sinner." (Schaff, PC, 40)

Another testimony is that of A. E. Garvie: "If there were any secret sin in Him, or even the memory of sins in the past, this would show a moral insensibility in irreconcilable contrast with the moral discernment His teaching shows." (Garvie, HCA, 97)

C. E. Jefferson adds, "There is nothing in Jesus' consciousness which indicates that He was guilty of any sin." (Jefferson, CJ, 328)

Jesus' personality betrayed his thoughts and beliefs. As John Stott tells us, "It is clear then that Jesus believed Himself to be sinless, as He believed Himself to be the Messiah and the Son of God." (Stott, BC, 39)

Kenneth Scott Latourette, the famous historian, testifies: "Another quality which has often been remarked was the absence of any sense of having committed sin or of a basic corruption of Himself. . . . It is highly significant that in one as sensitive morally as was Jesus and who taught His followers to ask for the forgiveness of their sins there is no hint of any need of forgiveness for Himself, no asking of pardon, either from those about Him or of God." (Latourette, HC, 47)

2B. The Witness of His Friends

Throughout the Bible, the inconsistencies of all persons are revealed. None of the great Jewish heroes are presented without blemish, not even David, Israel's greatest king, or Moses, the Hebrews' greatest deliverer. Even in the New Testament the shortcomings of the apostles are written about in almost every book, and yet nowhere do we find mention of one sin in Christ's life. This is even more incredible when we realize that Jesus had disciples around Him most of the time every day of His three-and-a-half-year ministry. When we consider that His disciples lived in close contact with Jesus during this time, and that their Jewish heritage emphasized human sinfulness and the need for God's redemptive work, it's even more incredible that they would not find a single fault with their Master. Surely they would have noticed at least one misstep while serving under Jesus, but their testimony is that none occurred.

In their close contact with Him, they never saw in Him the sins they saw in themselves. They got on one another's nerves, they grumbled and argued, but never did they see these things in Jesus. Because of their strict Jewish background, they would be hard set to say that Jesus was without sin unless He really was.

Jesus' closest associates, Peter and John, attest to His being without sin:

- 1 Peter 1:19: "but with the precious blood of Christ, as of a lamb without blemish and without spot."
- 1 Peter 2:22: "who committed no sin, nor was guile found in His mouth."
- 1 John 3:5: "And you know that He was manifested to take away our sins, and in Him there is no sin."

John went so far as to say that if anyone declares himself to be without sin, he is a liar and he is calling God a liar also. However, John also gave testimony to the sinless character of Jesus when he said that in Christ "there is no sin" (1 John 3:5).

Even the one responsible for Jesus' death recognized Jesus' innocence and piety. Judas, after betraying Jesus, recognized the Lord's righteousness and fell into deep remorse, confessing, "I have sinned by betraying innocent blood" (Matt. 27:3, 4).

The apostle Paul also bore witness of Jesus' sinlessness, stating, "For He [God] made Him [Jesus Christ] who knew no sin to be sin for us, that we might become the righteousness of God in Him" (2 Cor. 5:21). Commenting on this passage, Murray Harris writes:

[I]t seems Paul's intent [was] to say more than that Christ was made a sin-offering and yet less than that Christ became a sinner. So complete was the identification of the sinless Christ with the sin of the sinner, including its dire guilt and its dread consequence of separation from God, that Paul could say profoundly, "God made him . . . to be sin for us."

Paul's declaration of Christ's sinlessness may be compared with the statements of Peter (1 Peter 2:22, quoting Isa 53:9), John (1 John 3:5), and the author of Hebrews (Heb 4:15; 7:26). Just as "the righteousness of God" is extrinsic to us, so the sin with which Christ totally identified himself was extrinsic to him. He was without any acquaintance with sin that might have come through his ever having a sinful attitude or doing a sinful act. (Harris, 2C, vol. 10, 354)

The writer of Hebrews adds his voice to this chorus, saying, "For we do not have a High Priest [Jesus Christ] who cannot sympathize with our weaknesses, but was in all points tempted as we are, yet without sin" (Heb. 4:15). New Testament scholar Philip Hughes brings out the meaning and implications of this passage with particular clarity and force:

Temptation itself is neutral: to be tempted indicates neither virtue nor sinfulness; for the proper connotation of temptation is testing, or proving, and virtue is in the resistance and overcoming of temptation, whereas sin is in yielding and capitulation. Our high priest's experience of temptation corresponded *in every respect* to ours. From first to last he was being put to the test, whether by enticements to self-concern, popular acclaim, and ambition for power when assailed by Satan in the wilderness (Mt. 4:1ff.), or by the temptation in the garden to draw back rather than go through the dreadful ordeal that lay before him (Mt. 26:38ff.), or by the taunt hurled at him even as he hung in agony on the cross: "If you are the Son of God, come down from the cross" (Mt. 27:40ff.). . . . His whole life on earth was one of testing and proving: thus he spoke of the members of the intimate circle of the apostles, when Calvary was approaching, as those who had continued with him in his temptations (Lk. 22:28). And not only was he led to victory through temptation, but in doing so he has also gained the profoundest fellow feeling for our weaknesses, at the same time demonstrating that our human frailty is the opportunity for the power of God and for the triumph of his grace (2 Cor. 12:9f.).

That our high priest did not merely survive the severe testing through which he passed but was in fact completely victorious over every single temptation is made plain by the addition of the phrase *yet without sinning*. The implications of this qualification are highly significant. For one thing, had Jesus fallen into sin by giving way to temptation he would himself have been in need of atonement, and thus at no higher level than the high priests of old for whom a sacrifice was first necessary in expiation of their own sins (Heb. 7:27), and no more competent than they were to procure eternal redemption for others. For another thing, for him, who by the offering up of himself was to be the sacrifice as well as the sacrificer, to have been stained by sin, would have incapacitated him to serve as God's Lamb without blemish or spot and rendered his offering unacceptable (cf. Jn. 1:29; 1 Pet. 1:19; Eph. 5:2). (Hughes, CEH, 172–73)

3B. The Witness of His Enemies

One of the men crucified with Jesus testified to His sinlessness. In Luke 23:41, one thief rebuked the other one, saying, "This Man has done nothing wrong."

Pilate also found Jesus innocent of wrongdoing. After interrogating Him and considering the false charges against Him, Pilate told the religious leaders and the rest of the people, "You have brought this Man to me, as one who misleads the people. And indeed, having examined Him in your presence, I have found no fault in this Man concerning those things of which you accuse Him" (Luke 23:14). Even after the angry crowd cried out for Jesus' death, Pilate asked, incredulous, "Why, what evil has He done? I have found no reason for death in Him" (Luke 23:22).

The Roman centurion standing near Jesus' cross proclaimed, "Certainly this man was innocent" (Luke 23:47 NASB).

Jesus' enemies frequently brought accusations against Him in an attempt to convict Him of wrong. But they never succeeded in making their case (Mark 14:55, 56). Mark tells us about four of these criticisms (Mark 2:1—3:6).

First, Jesus' enemies accused Him of blasphemy because He had forgiven a man's sins. However, if Jesus was divine He had the authority and the power to grant forgiveness.

Second, they were appalled by Jesus' associations with the 'unclean'—sinners, publicans, prostitutes, and the like. Many of the religious leaders thought righteous people should avoid contact with such wicked people. Jesus answered this charge by referring to Himself as a physician come to heal sinners (Mark 2:17).

Third, Jesus was accused of practicing a watered-down version of Judaism because He and his disciples did not fast like the Pharisees did. Jesus responded by saying that as long as He was with His disciples, there was no need for them to fast. But once He was gone, fasting would become one of their practices.

Last, Jesus' critics tried to find fault with Him because He broke their traditions against working on the Sabbath when He healed people and picked grain on that holy day. Jesus, however, defended His actions by pointing out the fallacies of His critics' traditions. Jesus was certainly submissive to the law of God. On the other hand, because He was "Lord of the Sabbath," He chose to disobey human traditions that actually undermined the true interpretation and intent of God's law.

1C. The Assessment of History

Jesus' faultless life has drawn men and women for two millennia now. It has stood up to critical scrutiny and captured the minds and hearts of human beings from all walks of life and from a variety of religious traditions. For example, in the world religion of Islam, Jesus is viewed as sinless. According to the Koran (Mary, V. 19), the angel Gabriel came to Mary and told her that her son, Jesus, would be "without fault," that is, free of all sin.

Church historian Philip Schaff assures us that in respect to Christ, "Here is the Holy of Holies of humanity." (Schaff, HCC, 107) "There never lived a more harmless being on earth. He injured nobody, He took advan-

> This utter disregard of self in the service of God and man is what the Bible calls love. There is no self-interest in love. The essence of love is self-sacrifice. The worst of men is adorned by an occasional flash of such nobility, but the life of Jesus irradiated it with a never-fading incandescent glow. Jesus was sinless because He was selfless. Such selflessness is love. And God is love.
>
> —JOHN STOTT

tage of nobody. He never spoke an improper word, He never committed a wrong action." (Schaff, PC, 36–37)

"The first impression which we receive from the life of Jesus is that of perfect innocency and sinlessness in the midst of a sinful world. He, and He alone, carried the spotless purity of childhood untarnished through His youth and manhood. Hence the lamb and the dove are His appropriate symbols." (Schaff, PC, 35)

"It is, in one word, the absolute perfection which raises His character high above the reach of all other men and makes it an exception to a universal rule, a moral miracle in history." (Schaff, HCC, 107) "He is the living incarnation of the ideal standard of virtue and holiness, and the highest model for all that is pure and good and noble in the sight of God and man." (Schaff, PC, 44)

"Such was the Jesus of Nazareth, a true man in body, soul, and spirit, yet differing from all men; a character unique and original from tender childhood to ripe manhood, moving in unbroken union with God, overflowing with love to man, free from every sin and error, innocent and holy, devoted to the noblest ends, teaching and practicing all virtues in perfect harmony, sealing the purest life with the sublimest death, and ever acknowledged since as the one and only perfect model of goodness and holiness." (Schaff, PC, 73)

John Stott adds: "This utter disregard of self in the service of God and man is what the Bible calls love. There is no self-interest in love. The essence of love is self-sacrifice. The worst of men is adorned by an occasional flash of such nobility, but the life of Jesus irradiated it with a never-fading incandescent glow. Jesus was sinless because He was selfless. Such selflessness is love. And God is love." (Stott, BC, 44–45)

Scholar Wilbur Smith, states, "The outstanding characteristic of Jesus in His earthly life was the one in which all of us acknowledge we fall so short, and yet which at the same time all men recognize as the most priceless characteristic any man can have, namely, *absolute* goodness, or, to phrase it otherwise, perfect purity, genuine *holiness*, and in the case of Jesus, nothing less than sinlessness." (Smith, HYCH, 7)

Living a sinless life was no small task, and yet Jesus did it. As Wilbur Smith observes: "Fifteen million minutes of life on this earth, in the midst of a wicked and corrupt generation—every thought, every deed, every purpose, every work, privately and publicly, from the time He opened His baby eyes until He expired on the cross, were all approved of God. Never once did our Lord have to confess any sin, for He had no sin." (Smith, HYCH, 8–9)

In the case of Jesus' most famous and praised sermon, Thomas Wright astutely observes: "The Sermon on the Mount is Christ's biography. Every syllable He had already written down in deeds. The sermon merely translated His life into language." (Mead, ERQ, 60)

Bernard Ramm says, "Jesus led the one perfect life of piety and personal holiness on the sole consideration that He was God incarnate." (Ramm, PCE, 169) This is important, for as Henry Morris points out, "If God Himself, incarnate in His only Son, could not measure up to the standard of His own holiness, then it is utterly futile to search elsewhere for meaning and salvation in the universe." (Morris, BHA, 34)

However, Griffith Thomas is right when he says that in Jesus we do have the divine standard perfectly met: "Not for a single instant did the faintest shadow come between Him and His heavenly Father. He was without sin. . . . If Christ's own life had not been sinless, it is obvious that He could not be the Redeemer of mankind from sin." (Griffith Thomas, CIC, 17)

From Philip Schaff we read: "The better and holier a man is, the more he feels his need of pardon, and how far he falls short of his own imperfect standard of excellence. But Jesus, with the same nature as ours and tempted as we are, never yielded to temptation; never had cause for regretting any thought, word, or action; He never needed pardon, or conversion, or reform; He never fell out of harmony with His heavenly Father. His whole life was one unbroken act of self-consecration to the glory of God and the eternal welfare of His fellow-men." (Schaff, HCC, 107)

"I know of no sincere enduring good," says William Ellery Channing, "but the moral excellency which shines forth in Jesus Christ." (Mead, ERQ, 51) That is the resounding conclusion of history on the life of the God-man, Jesus Christ.

2C. Testimonies of Some of the World's Most Renowned Skeptics

The French deist Jacques Rousseau stated, "When Plato describes his imaginary righteous man, loaded with all the punishments of guilt, yet meriting the highest rewards of virtue, he describes exactly the character of Jesus Christ." (Schaff, PC, 134)

The famous philosopher and educator John Stuart Mill asked, "But who among his disciples or among their proselytes was capable of inventing the saying ascribed to Jesus, or imagining the life and character revealed in the Gospels?" (Schaff, PC, 145) The

> Even David Strauss, the bitterest of all opponents of the supernatural elements of the Gospels, whose works did more to destroy faith in Christ than the writings of any other man in modern times—even Strauss, with all his slashing, brilliant, vicious criticisms and his sweeping denials of everything partaking of the miraculous, was forced to confess, toward the end of his life, that in Jesus there is moral perfection. "This Christ . . . is historical, not mythical; is an individual, no mere symbol. . . . He remains the highest model of religion within the reach of our thought; and no perfect piety is possible without His presence in the heart"
>
> —WILBUR SMITH

expected answer, of course, is no one. The Jesus of the Gospels is the Jesus of history.

"Jesus is the most perfect of all men that have yet appeared," exclaimed Ralph Waldo Emerson. (Mead, ERQ, 52)

The historian William Lecky states, "He [Jesus] . . . has been not only the highest pattern of virtue, but the strongest incentive to its practice." (Lecky, HEMAC, 8)

"Even David Strauss," writes Wilbur Smith,

the bitterest of all opponents of the supernatural elements of the Gospels, whose works did more to destroy faith in Christ than the writings of any other man in modern times—even Strauss, with all his slashing, brilliant, vicious criticisms and his sweeping denials of everything partaking of the miraculous, was forced to confess, toward the end of his life, that in Jesus there is moral perfection. "This Christ . . . is *historical,* not mythical; is an individual, no mere symbol. . . . He remains the highest model of religion within the reach of our thought; and no perfect piety is possible without His presence in the heart." (Smith, HYCH, 11)

To conclude, Bernard Ramm writes: "Sinless perfection and perfect sinlessness is what we would expect of God-incarnate, and this we do find in Jesus Christ. The hypothesis and the facts concur." (Ramm, PCE, 169)

4A. IF GOD BECAME A MAN, THEN WE WOULD EXPECT HIM TO MANIFEST HIS SUPERNATURAL PRESENCE IN THE FORM OF SUPERNATURAL ACTS—MIRACLES

1B. The Scriptural Witness

Jesus said, "Go and tell John the things you have seen and heard: the blind see, the lame walk, the lepers are cleansed, the deaf hear, the dead are raised, the poor have the gospel preached to them" (Luke 7:22). Jesus' miracles demonstrated a great variety of power: power over nature, power over disease, power over demons, powers of creation, and power over death. What He did also fulfilled prophecy and pointed to Him as the Messiah predicted in the Hebrew Scriptures.

Among the many supernatural acts He performed were (Stott, BC, 500):

Miracles of Physical Healing

—A leper (Matt. 8:2–4; Mark 1:40–45; Luke 5:12–15)

—A paralytic (Matt. 9:2–8; Mark 2:3–12; Luke 5:18–26)

—Peter's mother-in-law (Matt. 8:14–17; Mark 1:29–31)

—A nobleman's son (John 4:46–53)

—Physical infirmity (John 5:1–9)

—A withered hand (Matt. 12:9–13; Mark 3:1–6; Luke 6:6–11)

—Deafness and dumbness (Mark 7:31–37)

—Blindness at Bethsaida (Mark 8:22–25); in Jerusalem (John 9); Bartimaeus (Mark 10:46–52)

—Ten lepers (Luke 17:11–19)

—Malchus's severed ear (Luke 22:47–51)

—Hemorrhage (Matt. 9:20–22; Mark 5:25–34; Luke 8:43–48)

—Dropsy (Luke 14:24)

Miracles in the Natural Realm

—Water converted to wine at Cana (John 2:1–11)

—Stilling of a storm (Matt. 8:23–27; Mark 4:35–41; Luke 8:22–25)

—Supernatural catch of fish (Luke 5:1–11; John 21:6)

—Multiplying food: 5,000 fed (Matt. 14:15–21; Mark 6:34–44; Luke 9:11–17; John 6:1–14); 4,000 fed (Matt. 15:32–39; Mark 8:1–9)

—Walking on water (Matt. 14:22, 23; Mark 6:45–52; John 6:19)

—Money from a fish (Matt. 17:24–27)

—Fig tree dried up (Matt. 21:18–22; Mark 11:12–14)

Miracles of Raising the Dead

—Jairus's daughter (Matt. 9:18–26; Mark 5:35–43; Luke 8:41–56)

—Widow's son (Luke 7:11–15)

—Lazarus of Bethany (John 11:144)

2B. Comments on His Miracles

Paul Little states simply, "Christ demonstrated a power over natural forces that could belong only to God, the author of these forces." (Little, KWYB, 56)

Philip Schaff states that Christ's miracles were "in striking contrast with deceptive juggler works and the useless and absurd miracles of apocryphal fiction. They were performed without any ostentation, with such simplicity and ease as to be called simply His." (Schaff, HCC, 105)

Continuing this thought, Griffith Thomas relates: "It is noteworthy that one of the words very frequently used of these miracles in the Gospels is the ordinary term, works (*erga*). They were the natural and necessary outcome of His life, the expression in act of what He Himself was" (Thomas, CIC, 50). To this Thomas adds: "The inquiry resolves itself simply into this: granted such a supernatural Person, were supernatural deeds congruous with His life? The character of the works attributed to Him, their beneficence, the restraint under which they were worked, the comparatively insignificant place they occupied in His ministry, and the constant stress laid by

> For us today the Person of Christ is the great miracle, and the true line of thought is to argue from Christ to miracles rather than from miracles to Christ.
>
> —GRIFFITH THOMAS

Him on spiritual kinship as primary—these are all entirely congruous with the manifestation and working of so miraculous and superhuman a Person as Jesus is seen to be." (Thomas, CIC, 54)

Philip Schaff agrees with this assessment: "All His miracles are but natural manifestations of His person, and hence they were performed with the same ease with which we perform our ordinary daily works." (Schaff, PC, 76–77) "His miracles were, without exception, prompted by the purest motives and aimed at the glory of God and the benefit of men; they are miracles of love and mercy, full of instruction and significance and in harmony with His character and mission." (Schaff, PC, 91)

F. H. Chase states:

The motive and scope of the Lord's miracles recorded in the Gospels are ever the same. The notices of the miracles are scattered up and down over the Gospels. But when they are considered in relation to each other, we discover in them an undesigned unity. Together they cover the whole ground of our Lord's work as the Saviour, renewing each element in man's complex being and restoring peace in the physical order. They are not presented in the Gospels as primarily designed to enhance His dignity and His power. If they had been the invention of pious fancy, yearning to illustrate by imposing stories of His greatness and His glory, it is a moral impossibility that this subtle unity of purpose should have been so consistently and so unobtrusively observed. (Rice, IJG, 404)

"The miracles," writes A. E. Garvie, "are harmonious with the character and consciousness of Jesus; they are not external confirmations but internal constituents of the revelation of the Heavenly Father's love, mercy, and grace, given in Him, the beloved Son of God, and the compassionate Brother of men." (Rice, IJG, 51–52)

Thomas concludes, "For us today the Person of Christ is the great miracle, and the true line of thought is to argue from Christ to miracles rather than from miracles to Christ." (Thomas, CIC, 49)

Islam even recognizes Jesus' ability to perform miracles. The Koran (the *Table* V. 110) bears reference to them. It speaks of Jesus healing the blind and the lepers and raising the dead.

3B. The Early Jewish Witness

"We find many references to Jesus' miracles in the Jewish law books and histories," writes Ethelbert Stauffer in *Jesus and His Story.* "Around A.D. 95 Rabbi Eliezer ben Hyrcanus of Lydda speaks of Jesus' magic arts." (Stauffer, JHS, 9) "Around the same period (A.D. 95–110) we encounter the ritual denunciation: 'Jesus practiced magic and led Israel astray'" (Sanhedrin 43a). (Stauffer, JHS, 10) "Around 110 we hear of a controversy among Palestinian Jews centering upon the question of whether it is permissible to heal in the name of Jesus. . . . Now, miraculous healings in the name of Jesus imply that Jesus Himself performed such miracles." (Stauffer, JHS, 10)

We also have a roundabout reference from Julian the Apostate, Roman Emperor from A.D. 361–363, who was one of the most gifted of the ancient adversaries to Christianity. In his work against Christianity, he states: "Jesus . . . has now been celebrated about three hundred years; having done nothing in his lifetime worthy of fame, unless anyone thinks it a very great work to heal lame and blind people and exorcise demoniacs in the villages of Bethsaida and Bethany." (Schaff, PC, 133) Julian thus unwittingly ascribes to Christ the power to perform miracles.

4B. To Silence the Critic

"If miracles," writes Bernard Ramm, "are capable of sensory perception, they can be made matters of testimony. If they are adequately testified to, then the recorded testimony has the same validity for evidence as the experiences of beholding the events." (Ramm, PCE, 140) This certainly holds true of Jesus' miracles, for they were performed before the public and therefore were open to scrutiny and investigation by anyone, including skeptics.

Let's consider, for example, the biblical account of Jesus raising Lazarus from the dead. Bernard Ramm observes, "If the raising of Lazarus was actually witnessed by John and recorded faithfully by him when still in soundness of faculties and memory, for purposes of evidence it is the same as if we were there and saw it." (Ramm, PCE, 140–41)

It is also significant that Christ's adversaries did not deny the miracle of raising Lazarus, but instead tried to kill Jesus before all the people believed in Him (John 11:48).

Thus, Jesus' contemporaries, His enemies included, attested to His ability to perform miracles.

However, His enemies attributed this power to Satan, while His friends understood that the power came from God (Matt. 12:24). In answer to the charge that His miracle-working ability was demonic, Jesus said, "Any kingdom divided against itself is laid waste; and any city or house divided against itself shall not stand. And if Satan casts out Satan, he is divided against himself: how then shall his kingdom stand?" (Matt. 12:25, 26 NASB).

On the basis of the evidence and testimonies available, we see that the Gospel miracles cannot be discounted just because pagan miracle accounts are extravagant and clearly superstitious. The fact that some miracles are counterfeit is not proof that all are fraudulent.

Nor can we reject Jesus' miracles and still hold on to some semblance of Christianity. As C. S. Lewis makes clear: "All the essentials of Hinduism would, I think, remain unimpaired if you subtracted the miraculous, and the same is almost true of Muhammadanism, but you cannot do that with Christianity. It is precisely the story of a great Miracle. A naturalistic Christianity leaves out all that is specifically Christian." (Lewis, M, 83)

In Christianity, miracles are not an addendum that can be removed without losing anything of importance. Bernard Ramm is right when he says: "Miracles are believed in non-Christian religions because the religion is already believed, but in the BIBLICAL religion, miracles are part of the means of establishing the true religion. This distinction is of immense importance. Israel was brought into existence by a series of miracles, the law was given surrounded by supernatural wonders, and many of the prophets were identified as God's spokesmen by their power to perform miracles. Jesus came not only preaching but performing miracles, and the apostles from time to time worked wonders. It was the miracle authenticating the religion at every point." (Ramm, PCE, 142–43)

Therefore, as John A. Broadus notes, we must "take the Gospels as they stand . . . and if Jesus of Nazareth did not perform supernatural works, He many times spoke falsely. Either He who spake as never man spake, and in whose character no criticism can discern a fault . . . either He did perform supernatural works or He spoke falsely." (Broadus, JN, 72) A. E. Garvie concurs, stating, "A Christ who being Son of God, and seeking to become Saviour of men, (and) wrought no miracle, would be less intelligible and credible than the Jesus whom the Gospel records so consistently present to us." (Garvie, HCA, 73)

Jesus was a miracle-worker because the power of God resided in Him as the very Son of God.

5A. IF GOD BECAME A MAN, THEN WE WOULD EXPECT HIM TO LIVE MORE PERFECTLY THAN ANY HUMAN WHO HAS EVER LIVED

1B. What His Friends Say

"Jesus, in every respect, was truly human and also more than human." (Scott, JMSH, 27)

A. M. Fairbairn, in *Philosophy of the Christian Religion,* writes: "Jesus, in a word, was Deity manifested in humanity and under the conditions of time. Now this is in itself an extraordinary conception, and it is made more extraordinary by the marvelous way in which it is embodied in a personal history. There never was a loftier idea." (Fairbairn, PCR, 326)

"His life was holy; His word was true; His whole character was the embodiment of truth. There never has been a more real or genuine man than Jesus of Nazareth." (Thomas, CIC, 11)

Hausrath, cited by Frank Ballard, states that "There is no other noble life known to human record encumbered with so little that

His zeal never degenerated into passion, nor His constancy into obstinacy, nor His benevolence into weakness, nor His tenderness into sentimentality. His unworldliness was free from indifference and unsociability, His dignity from pride and presumption, His affectibility from undue familiarity, His self-denial from moroseness, His temperance from austerity. He combined child-like innocency with manly strength, absorbing devotion to God with untiring interest in the welfare of man, tender love to the sinner with uncompromising severity against sin, commanding dignity with winning humility, fearless courage with wise caution, unyielding firmness with sweet gentleness.

—HISTORIAN PHILIP SCHAFF

is earthy, transitory, local; no other that can be put to purposes so high and universal." (Ballard, MU, 252)

John Young, in *Christ of History,* asks: "How it has come to pass, that of all men He alone has risen to spiritual perfection? What God did for piety and virtue on the earth at one time and in one case, God certainly could have done at other times and in other cases. If Jesus was man only, God could have raised up, in successive ages, many such living examples of sanctified humanity as He was, to correct, instruct, and quicken the world. But He did not." (Young, CH, 243)

Carnegie Simpson wrote:

Instinctively we do not class Him with others. When one reads His name in a list beginning with Confucius and ending with Goethe we feel it is an offense less against orthodoxy than against decency. Jesus is not one of the group of the world's great. Talk about Alexander the Great and Charles the Great and Napoleon the Great if you will . . . Jesus is apart. He is not the Great; He is the Only. He is simply Jesus. Nothing could add to that . . . He is beyond our analyses. He confounds our canons of human nature. He compels our criticism to overleap itself. He awes our spirits. There is a saying of Charles Lamb . . . that "if Shakespeare was to come into this room we should all rise up to meet him, but if that Person [i.e., Jesus] was to come into it, we should all fall down and try to kiss the hem of his garment." (Quoted in Stott, BC, 36)

Griffith Thomas states, "He [Jesus] represents a definite, divine intervention on behalf of man, at a particular moment of time in the world's history, and on this great miracle of the Person of Christ we take our stand." (Thomas, CIC, 53) "He embraces all the good elements which mark other men, and it is not too much to say that there is no element missing which men think desirable in the human character." (Thomas, CIC, 11)

"His zeal never degenerated into passion," observes Philip Schaff,

nor His constancy into obstinacy, nor His benevolence into weakness, nor His tenderness into sentimentality. His unworldliness was free from indifference and unsociability, His dignity from pride and presumption, His affectibility from undue familiarity, His self-denial from moroseness, His temperance from austerity. He combined child-like innocency with manly strength, absorbing devotion to God with untiring interest in the welfare of man, tender love to the sinner with uncompromising severity against sin, commanding dignity with winning humility, fearless courage with wise caution, unyielding firmness with sweet gentleness. (Schaff, PC, 63)

Klausner, a Jewish scholar, says, "Jesus was the most Jewish of Jews; even more Jewish than Hillel." (Klausner, YH, 1249)

"It is universally admitted . . . that Christ taught the purest and sublimest system of ethics, one which throws the moral precepts and maxims of the wisest men of antiquity far into the shade." (Schaff, PC, 44)

Joseph Parker writes in *Ecce Deus,* "Only a Christ could have conceived a Christ." (Martin, CC, 57)

Johann Gottfried Von Herder declares, "Jesus Christ is in the noblest and most perfect sense the realized ideal of humanity." (Mead, ERQ, 53)

G. A. Ross goes so far as to say:

Have we ever thought of the peculiar position occupied by Jesus with respect to the ideals of the sexes? No man has ever dared to call Jesus, in any opprobrious sense, sexless: yet in character He stands above, and if one may use the term, midway between the sexes—His comprehensive humanity a veritable storehouse of the ideals we associate with both the sexes. No woman has ever had any more difficulty than men have had in finding in Him the realized ideal. Whatever there is in men of strength, justice, and wisdom, whatever there is in women of sensibility, purity, and insight, is in Christ without the conditions which hinder among us the development of contrasted virtues in one person. (Ross, UJ, 23)

W. R. Gregg affirms that "Jesus had one of those gifted natures rarely met with, never in equal perfection, the purity and absolute harmony of whose mental and moral elements confer a clearness of vision which almost rises to the quality of prophecy." (Ballard, MU, 152)

Napoleon Bonaparte has said: "I know men and I tell you that Jesus Christ is no mere man. Between Him and every other person in the world there is no possible term of comparison. Alexander, Caesar, Charlemagne, and I have founded empires. But on what did we rest the creations of our genius? Upon force. Jesus Christ founded His empire upon love; and at this hour millions of men would die for Him." (Mead, ERQ, 56)

Theodore Parker, a famous Unitarian, avows that "Christ unites in Himself the sublimest principles and divinest practices, thus more than realizing the dream of prophets and sages, rises free from all prejudices of his age, nation, or sect, and pours out a doctrine beautiful as the light, sublime as heaven, and true as God. Eighteen centuries have passed since the sun of humanity rose so high in Jesus. What man, what sect has mastered His thought, comprehended His method, and fully applied it to life?" (Ballard, MU, 252)

Jesus' influence has been such that most people when confronted with it have either had to stand for Him or stand against Him. Though many may appear indifferent, it is not a logical position to take.

In the Koran (Al-Imran, V. 45) Jesus is referred to as "the greatest above all in this world and in the world to come."

Pascal asked, "Who has taught the

evangelists the qualities of a perfectly heroic soul, that they paint it so perfectly in Jesus Christ?" (Wolff, SMIJCU, 29)

Channing, cited by Frank Ballard in *The Miracles of Unbelief*, stated, "I know not what can be added to heighten the wonder, reverence, and the love which are due to Jesus." (Ballard, MU, 252)

"Jesus Christ as the God-man is the greatest *personality* that ever lived," wrote Bernard Ramm, "and therefore His personal impact is the greatest of any man that ever lived." (Ballard, MU, 173)

Perhaps Phillips Brooks summarizes all of these thoughts the most succinctly: "Jesus Christ, the condescension of divinity, and the exaltation of humanity." (Mead, ERQ, 56)

2B. What Antagonists Say

"Goethe," cites historian Philip Schaff, "another commanding genius, of very different character, but equally above suspicion of partiality for religion, looking in the last years of his life over the vast field of history, was constrained to confess that 'if ever the Divine appeared on earth, it was in the Person of Christ,' and that 'the human mind, no matter how far it may advance in every other department, will never transcend the height and moral culture of Christianity as it shines and glows in the Gospels.'" (Schaff, HCC, 110)

"I esteem the Gospels to be thoroughly genuine, for there shines forth from them the reflected splendour of a sublimity, proceeding from the person of Jesus Christ, and of as Divine a kind as was ever manifested upon earth." (Ballard, MU, 251)

H. G. Wells, the noted historian, wrote a fascinating testimony to Jesus Christ:

He was too great for his disciples. And in view of what he plainly said, is it any wonder that all who were rich and prosperous felt a horror of strange things, a swimming of their world

at his teaching? Perhaps the priests and the rulers and the rich men understood him better than his followers. He was dragging out all the little private reservations they had made from social service into the light of a universal religious life. He was like some terrible moral huntsman digging mankind out of the snug burrows in which they had lived hitherto. In the white blaze of this kingdom of his there was to be no property, no privilege, no pride and precedence; no motive indeed and no reward but love. Is it any wonder that men were dazzled and blinded and cried out against him? Even his disciples cried out when he would not spare them the light. Is it any wonder that the priests realized that between this man and themselves there was no choice but that he or the priestcraft should perish? Is it any wonder that the Roman soldiers, confronted and amazed by something soaring over their comprehension and threatening all their disciplines, should take refuge in wild laughter, and crown him with thorns and robe him in purple and make a mock Caesar of him? For to take him seriously was to enter upon a strange and alarming life, to abandon habits, to control instincts and impulses, to essay an incredible happiness. . . .

Is it any wonder that to this day this Galilean is too much for our small hearts? (Wells, OH, 535–36)

When Wells was asked which person has left the most permanent impression on history, he replied that, judging a person's greatness by historical standards, "By this test Jesus stands first." (Ramm, PCE, 163)

"Whatever may be the surprises of the future, Jesus will never be surpassed," assessed Ernest Renan. (Ross, UJ, 146)

Thomas Carlyle refers to Jesus as "our divinest symbol. Higher has the human thought not yet reached. A symbol of quite perennial, infinite character; whose significance will ever demand to be anew inquired into, and anew made manifest." (Schaff, PC, 139)

Rousseau asks, "Can the Person whose history the Gospels relate be Himself a man? What sweetness, what purity in His manners! What affecting goodness in His instructions! What sublimity in His maxims! What profound wisdom in His discourses! What presence of mind, what ingenuity of justice in His replies! Yes, if the life and death of Socrates are those of a philosopher, the life and death of Jesus Christ are those of a God." (Ballard, MU, 251)

6A. IF GOD BECAME A MAN, THEN CERTAINLY HE WOULD SPEAK THE GREATEST WORDS EVER SPOKEN

1B. What the New Testament Records

Jesus said about his own words, "Heaven and earth will pass away, but My words will by no means pass away" (Luke 21:33).

It was common for the crowds who heard Him to be "astonished at His teaching" (Luke 4:32). Even a Roman officer exclaimed, "No one ever spoke like this Man!" (John 7:46).

2B. The Greatest Words

Sholem Ash wrote: "Jesus Christ is the outstanding personality of all time. . . . No other teacher—Jewish, Christian, Buddhist, Mohammedan—is *still* a teacher whose teaching is such a guidepost for the world we live in. Other teachers may have something basic for an Oriental, an Arab, or an Occidental; but every act and word of Jesus has value for all of us. He became the Light of the World. Why shouldn't I, a Jew, be proud of that?" (Mead, ERQ, 49)

G. J. Romanes writes:

For when we consider what a large number of sayings are recorded of—or at least attributed to—Him, it becomes most remarkable that in literal truth there is no reason why any of His

words should ever pass away in the sense of becoming obsolete. . . . Contrast Jesus Christ in this respect with other thinkers of like antiquity. Even Plato, who, though some four hundred years before Christ in point of time, was greatly in advance of Him in respect of philosophic thought, is nowhere in this respect as compared with Christ. Read the *Dialogues,* and see how enormous is the contrast with the Gospels in respect of errors of all kinds, reaching even to absurdity in respect of reason, and to sayings shocking to the moral sense. Yet this is confessedly the highest level of human reason on the lines of spirituality when unaided by alleged revelation. (Ross, UJ, 157)

Joseph Parker states, "After reading the doctrines of Plato, Socrates or Aristotle, we feel the specific difference between their words and Christ's is the difference between an inquiry and a revelation." (Mead, ERQ, 57)

"For two thousand years, He [Jesus] *has* been the Light of the World, and His words have not passed away." (Morris, BHA, 28)

From F. J. A. Hort: "His [Jesus'] words were so completely parts and utterances of Himself, that they had no meaning as abstract statements of truth uttered by Him as a Divine oracle or prophet. Take away Himself as the primary (though not the ultimate) subject of every statement and they all fall to pieces." (Hort, WTL, 207)

"But Jesus' words and acts are impressively integral, and we trust those sayings we judge to be authentically His as revelatory of His person. When Jesus uses the personal pronoun, 'I' ('But I say to you,' 'Amen, I say to you'), He stands in back of every word with personal fidelity and personal intentionality. If His words and acts are messianic in character, it is because He intends them to be, and if He intends them to be, He is thinking of Himself in messianic terms." (Gruenler, JPKG, 97)

"Christ's words are of permanent value

because of His person; they endure because He endures." (Thomas, CIC, 44)

In the words of Bernard Ramm:

Statistically speaking, the Gospels are the greatest literature ever written. They are read by more people, quoted by more authors, translated into more tongues, represented in more art, set to more music, than any other book or books written by any man in any century in any land. But the words of Christ are not great on the grounds that they have such a statistical edge over anybody else's words. They are read more, quoted more, loved more, believed more, and translated more because they are the greatest words ever spoken. And where is their greatness? Their greatness lies in the pure, lucid spirituality in dealing clearly, definitively, and *authoritatively* with the greatest problems that throb in the human breast; namely, Who is God? Does He love Me? What should I do to please Him? How does He look at my sin? How can I be forgiven? Where will I go when I die? How must I treat others? No other man's words have the appeal of Jesus' words because no other man can answer these fundamental human questions as Jesus answered them. They are the kind of words and the kind of answers we would expect God to give, and we who believe in Jesus' deity have no problem as to why these words came from His mouth. (Ramm, PCE, 170–71)

"Never did the Speaker seem to stand more utterly alone than when He uttered this majestic utterance. Never did it seem more improbable that it should be fulfilled. But as we look across the centuries we see how it has been realized. His words have passed into law, they have passed into doctrines, they have passed into proverbs, they have passed into consolations, but they have *never* 'passed away.' What human teacher ever dared to claim an eternity for his words?" (Maclean, CBS, 149)

"Systems of human wisdom will come and go, kingdoms and empires will rise and

fall, but for all time to come Christ will remain 'the Way, the Truth, and the Life.'" (Schaff, HCC, 111)

Christ's teachings are complete in every point, from the regulation of thought to

> How was it that a carpenter, of no special training, ignorant of the culture and learning of the Greeks, born of a people whose great teachers were narrow, sour, intolerant, pedantic legalists, was the supreme religious Teacher the world has known, whose supremacy here makes Him the most important figure in the world's history?

control of the will. In this light Griffith Thomas points out that Christ's message is "inexhaustible." Each generation finds it new and exciting. (Thomas, CIC, 36)

Mark Hopkins affirms, "No revolution that has ever taken place in society can be compared to that which has been produced by the words of Jesus Christ." (Mead, ERQ, 53)

W. S. Peake fully agrees:

It is sometimes said, "Everything that Jesus said has been said before Him by others." Let us grant that it is true, what then? Originality may or may not be a merit. If the truth has already been uttered, the merit lies in repeating it, and giving it new and fuller application. But there are other considerations to be borne in mind. We have no other teacher who so completely eliminated the trivial, the temporal, the false from his system, no one who selected just the eternal and the universal, and combined them in a teaching where all these great truths found their congenial home. These parallels from the teaching of others to that of Christ are brought together from this quarter and from that; how is it that none of these teachers furnishes us with any parallel to the teachings of Christ? As a whole, while each of them gives us such truths as He expresses mingled with a mass of what is trivial and absurd? How was it that a carpenter, of no special training, ignorant of the culture and learning of the Greeks, born of a people whose great teachers were narrow, sour, intolerant, pedantic legalists, was the supreme religious Teacher the world has known, whose supremacy here makes Him the most important figure in the world's history? (Peake, CNT, 226–27)

Griffith Thomas concludes:

[T]hough without formal rabbinical training, He showed no timidity or self-consciousness, no hesitation as to what He felt to be truth. Without any thought of Himself or His audience, He spoke out fearlessly on every occasion, utterly heedless of the consequences to Himself, and only concerned for truth and the delivery of His Father's message. The power of His teaching was also deeply felt. "His word was with power" (Luke 4:32). The spiritual force of His personality expressed itself in His utterances and held His hearers in its enthralling grasp. And so we are not surprised to read of the impression of uniqueness made by Him. "Never man spake like this man" (John 7:46). The simplicity and charm and yet the depth, the directness, the universality, and the truth of His teaching made a deep mark on His hearers, and elicited the conviction that they were in the presence of a Teacher such as man had never known before. And thus the large proportion of teaching in the Gospels, and the impressions evidently created by the Teacher Himself, are such that we are not at all surprised that years afterward the great Apostle of the Gentiles should recall these things and say, "Remember the words of the Lord Jesus" (Acts 20:35). The same impression has been made in every age since the days of Christ and His immediate followers, and in any full consideration of His Person as the substance of Christianity great attention must necessarily be paid to His teaching. (Thomas, CIC, 32)

7A. IF GOD BECAME A MAN, THEN WE WOULD EXPECT HIM TO HAVE A LASTING AND UNIVERSAL INFLUENCE

To be sure, the personality of Jesus Christ has made such an impact on humanity that even after two thousand years the impact has not worn off. Each day, there are persons who have revolutionary experiences with Jesus.

The great historian Kenneth Scott Latourette said: "As the centuries pass the evidence is accumulating that, measured by His effect of history, *Jesus is the most influential life ever lived on this planet.* That influence appears to be mounting." (Latourette, AHR, 272)

Philip Schaff adds:

This Jesus of Nazareth, without money and arms, conquered more millions than Alexander, Caesar, Mohammed, and Napoleon; without science and learning, He shed more light on things human and divine than all philosophers and scholars combined; without the eloquence of schools, He spoke such words of life as were never spoken before or since and produced effects which lie beyond the reach of orator or poet; without writing a single line, He set more pens in motion, and furnished themes for more sermons, orations, discussions, learned volumes, works of art, and songs of praise, than the whole army of great men of ancient and modern times. (Schaff, PC, 33)

"The influence of Jesus on mankind is today as strong as it was when He dwelt among men." (Scott, JMSH, 29)

"That ministry [of Jesus] lasted only three years—and yet in these three years is condensed the deepest meaning of the history of religion. No great life ever passed so swiftly, so quietly, so humbly, so far removed from the noise and commotion of the world; and no great life after its close excited such universal and lasting interest." (Schaff, HCC, 103)

"When Jesus Christ left this earth," Griffith Thomas writes,

He told His disciples that after His departure they should do greater works than He had done, and the centuries of Christianity have borne out the truth of this statement. Works greater in kind have been done—are being done. Jesus Christ is doing more wonderful

> It was reserved for Christianity to present to the world an ideal character, which through all the changes of eighteen centuries has inspired the hearts of men with an impassioned love; has shown itself capable of acting on all ages, nations, temperaments, and conditions; has been not only the highest pattern of virtue, but the strongest incentive to its practice; and has exercised so deep an influence that it may be truly said that the simple record of three short years of active life has done more to regenerate and soften mankind than all the disquisitions of philosophers and all the exhortations of moralists.
>
> —WILLIAM LECKY, SKEPTIC

things today than ever He did when on earth, redeeming souls, changing lives, transforming characters, exalting ideals, inspiring philanthropies, and making for the best, truest, and highest in human life and progress. . . . We are therefore justified in calling attention to the influence of Christ through the ages as one of the greatest, most direct, and most self-evident proofs that Christianity is Christ, and that Christ has to be accounted for. It is impossible to consider this question solely as one of history; it touches life at every point today. (Thomas, CIC, 121)

William Lecky, the skeptic, states in *History of European Morals from Augustus to Charlemagne:*

The Platonist exhorted men to imitate God; the Stoic, to follow reason; the Christian, to

the love of Christ. The later Stoics had often united their notions of excellence in an ideal sage, and Epictetus had even urged his disciples to set before them some man of surpassing excellence, and to imagine him continually near them; but the utmost the Stoic ideal could become was a model for imitation, and the admiration it inspired could never deepen into affection. It was reserved for Christianity to present to the world an ideal character, which through all the changes of eighteen centuries has inspired the hearts of men with an impassioned love; has shown itself capable of acting on all ages, nations, temperaments, and conditions; has been not only the highest pattern of virtue, but the strongest incentive to its practice; and has exercised so deep an influence that it may be truly said that the simple record of three short years of active life has done more to regenerate and soften mankind than all the disquisitions of philosophers and all the exhortations of moralists. This has indeed been the wellspring of whatever is best and purest in the Christian life. Amid all the sins and failings, amid all the priestcraft and persecution and fanaticism that have defaced the Church, it has preserved in the character and example of its Founder, an enduring principle of regeneration. (Lecky, HEMAC, 8)

"He is the greatest influence in the world today," exclaims Griffith Thomas. "There is, as it has been well said, a fifth Gospel being written—the work of Jesus Christ in the hearts and lives of men and nations." (Thomas, CIC, 117)

Napoleon said:

Christ alone has succeeded in so raising the mind of man towards the unseen that it becomes insensible to the barriers of time and space. Across the chasm of eighteen hundred years Jesus Christ makes a demand which is beyond all others difficult to satisfy. He asks for that which a philosophy may often seek in vain at the hands of his friends, or a father of his children, or a bride of her spouse, or a man of his brother. He asks for the human heart; He will have it entirely to Himself; He demands it unconditionally, and forthwith His demand is granted. Its powers and faculties become an annexation to the empire of Christ. All who sincerely believe in Him experience that supernatural love towards Him. This phenomenon is unaccountable, it is altogether beyond the scope of man's creative powers. Time, the great destroyer, can neither exhaust its strength nor put a limit to its range. (Ballard, MU, 265)

Again from Napoleon: "The nature of Christ's existence is mysterious, I admit; but this mystery meets the wants of man—reject it and the world is an inexplicable riddle; believe it, and the history of our race is satisfactorily explained." (Mead, ERQ, 56)

One cannot "fail to see . . . that since the days of Christ, in spite of all the progress of thought, not a single new ethical ideal has been given to the world." (Hunter, WWJ, 35)

R. G. Gruenler says: "The kerygma of the community is the proclamation that Jesus is of universal relevance. Wherever and whenever He is proclaimed, men are confronted by His concreteness, His humanness, and are brought into the presence of God." (Hort, WTL, 25)

Other religions have had their ethical ideal of duty, opportunity, and even of love, but nowhere have they approached those of Christ, either in reality or in attractiveness or in power. Christ's message is remarkable for its universal adaptation. Its appeal is universal; it is adapted to all men from the adult down to the child; it makes its appeal to all times and not merely to the age in which it was first given. And the reason is that it emphasizes a threefold ethical attitude toward God and man which makes a universal appeal as nothing else does or perhaps can do. Christ calls for repentance, trust and love. (Thomas, CIC, 35)

"The most marvelous and astonishing thing in nineteen centuries of history is the power of His life over the members of the Christian Church." (Thomas, CIC, 104)

"It is true that there have been other religions with millions of adherents, but it is also true that the existence and progress of the Church is something unique in history to say nothing of the fact that Christianity has attracted to itself the profoundest thinkers of the human race, and is in no way hindered by the ever-advancing tide of human knowledge." (Thomas, CIC, 103)

A. M. Fairbairn has said: "The most remarkable fact in the history of His religion is the continuous and ubiquitous activity of His person. He has been the permanent and efficient fact or in its extension and progress. Under all its forms, in all its periods, and through all its divisions, the one principle alike of reality and unity has been and is devotion to Him." (Fairbairn, CMT, 380)

George Bancroft flatly stated, "I find the name of Jesus Christ written on the top of every page of modern history." (Mead, ERQ, 50)

Even after almost two millennia, David Strauss was forced to admit, "He [Jesus] remains the highest model of religion within the reach of our thought; and no perfect piety is possible without His presence in the heart." (Schaff, PC, 142)

William E. Channing put it this way: "The sages and heroes of history are receding from us, and history contracts the record of their deeds into a narrower and narrower page. But time has no power over the name and deeds and words of Jesus Christ." (Mead, ERQ, 51)

From Ernest Renan we have the following two quotes: "Jesus was the greatest religious genius that ever lived. His beauty is eternal, and His reign shall never end. Jesus is in every respect unique, and nothing can be compared with Him." (Mead, ERQ, 57) "All history is incomprehensible without Christ." (Mead, ERQ, 57)

"That a Galilean carpenter should so claim to be the Light of the world, and be so recognized after so many centuries, is best explained on the ground of His divinity," concludes Bernard Ramm. (Ramm, PCE, 177)

In a *Life* magazine article, George Buttrick wrote: "Jesus gave history a new beginning. In every land He is at home: everywhere men think His face is like their best face—and like God's face. His birthday is kept across the world. His death-day has set a gallows against every city skyline." (Mead, ERQ, 51)

The famous essay "One Solitary Life" is reprinted in the box at right:

In "The Incomparable Christ," another vivid essay, we read:

More than nineteen hundred years ago there was a Man born contrary to the laws of life. This Man lived in poverty and was reared in obscurity. He did not travel extensively. Only once did He cross the boundary of the country in which He lived; that was during His exile in childhood.

He possessed neither wealth nor influence. His relatives were inconspicuous, and had neither training nor formal education. In infancy He startled a king; in childhood He puzzled doctors; in manhood He ruled the course of nature, walked upon the billows as if pavements, and hushed the sea to sleep. He healed the multitudes without medicine and made no charge for His service.

He never wrote a book, and yet all the libraries of the country could not hold the books that have been written about Him. He never wrote a song, and yet He has furnished the theme for more songs than all the songwriters combined.

He never founded a college, but all the schools put together cannot boast of having as many students.

He never marshaled an army, nor drafted a soldier, nor fired a gun; and yet no leader ever had more volunteers who have, under His orders, made more rebels stack arms and surrender without a shot fired.

He never practiced psychiatry, and yet He has healed more broken hearts than all the doctors far and near. Once each week the wheels of commerce cease their turning and multitudes wend their way to worshipping assemblies to pay homage and respect to Him.

The names of the past proud statesmen of Greece and Rome have come and gone. The names of the past scientists, philosophers, and

---

Here is a man who was born in an obscure village, the child of a peasant woman. He grew up in another village. He worked in a carpenter shop until He was thirty, and then for three years He was an itinerant preacher. He never owned a home. He never wrote a book. He never held an office. He never had a family. He never went to college. He never put his foot inside a big city. He never traveled two hundred miles from the place where He was born. He never did one of the things that usually accompany greatness. He had no credentials but Himself. . . . While still a young man, the tide of popular opinion turned against Him. His friends ran away. One of them denied Him. He was turned over to His enemies. He went through the mockery of a trial. He was nailed upon a cross between two thieves. While He was dying His executioners gambled for the only piece of property He had on earth—His coat. When He was dead, He was taken down and laid in a borrowed grave through the pity of a friend.

Nineteen long centuries have come and gone, and today He is the centerpiece of the human race and the leader of the column of progress. I am far within the mark when I say that all the armies that ever marched, all the navies that ever were built, all the parliaments that ever sat and all the kings that ever reigned, put together, have not affected the life of man upon this earth as powerfully as has that one solitary life.

—ANONYMOUS

theologians have come and gone; but the name of this Man abounds more and more. Though time has spread nineteen hundred years between the people of this generation and the scene of His crucifixion, yet He still lives. Herod could not destroy Him, and the grave could not hold Him.

He stands forth upon the highest pinnacle of heavenly glory, proclaimed of God, acknowledged by angels, adored by saints, and feared by devils, as the living, personal Christ, our Lord and Saviour. —*Anonymous*

8A. IF GOD BECAME A MAN, THEN WE WOULD EXPECT HIM TO SATISFY THE SPIRITUAL HUNGER IN HUMANITY

Otto Rauk, in *Beyond Psychology*, says that "man needs to be in touch with something more than himself."

The major religions testify to humanity's need. The pyramids of Mexico and the shrines of India are examples of mankind's spiritual search.

Mark Twain said this about human emptiness: "From his cradle to his grave a man never does a single thing which has any first and foremost objective save one—to secure peace of mind—spiritual comfort for himself."

Fisher, the historian, said, "There is a cry in the soul, to which no response comes from the world."

Thomas Aquinas exclaimed, "The soul's restless thirst [is] for happiness, yet it is a thirst to be satisfied in God alone."

"Yet thousands and millions today, as in all ages, are testifying to the power and glory of Christianity in dealing with their sin and wickedness. These are facts which stand the test of examination and carry their own conclusion to all who are willing to learn." (Thomas, CIC, 119)

Bernard Ramm states that the "Christian experience alone provides man with an experience commensurate with his nature as free spirit. . . . Anything less than God leaves the spirit of man thirsty, hungry, restless, frustrated, and incomplete." (Ramm, PCE, 215)

From Philip Schaff we read: "He [Jesus] rose above the prejudices of party and sect, above the superstitions of His age and nation. He addressed the naked heart of man and touched the quick of the conscience." (Schaff, HCC, 104–5)

George Schweitzer, in his personal testi-

"Blessed are those who hunger and thirst for righteousness, for they shall be filled" (Matt. 5:6).

"If any one thirsts, let Him come to Me and drink" (John 7:37).

"But whoever drinks of the water that I shall give him will never thirst" (John 4:14).

"Peace I leave with you; My peace I give to you, not as the world gives do I give to you. Let not your heart be troubled, neither let it be afraid" (John 14:27).

"I am the bread of life. He who comes to Me shall never hunger, and he who believes in Me shall never thirst" (John 6:35).

"Come to Me, all you who labor and are heavy laden, and I will give you rest" (Matt. 11:28).

"I have come that they may have life, and that they may have it more abundantly" (John 10:10).

mony in *Ten Scientists Look at Life*, says:

Man has changed his world in a remarkable way, but has not been able to alter himself. Since this problem is basically a spiritual one, and since man is naturally bent toward evil (as history attests), the sole way that man can be changed is by God. Only if a man commits himself to Christ Jesus and submits himself to the Holy Spirit for guidance can he be changed. Only in this miraculous transformation rests hope for the atom-awed, radio-activity-ruffled world of our day and its inhabitants. (Schweitzer, TSLL, n.p.)

The director of scientific relations at Abbott Laboratories, E. J. Matson, stated, "No matter how exacting, how tiring my life as scientist, business man, citizen, husband or father, I had only to return to this center to meet Jesus Christ, demonstrating His keeping power as well as His saving power." (Schweitzer, TSLL, n.p.)

A student at the University of Pittsburgh says, "Whatever joys and gladness, all put together of my past experience, these can never equal that special joy and peace that the Lord Jesus Christ has given me since that time when He entered into my life to rule and to guide." (Ordonez, IWBBNIS, n.p.)

From R. L. Mixter, professor of zoology at Wheaton College: "When he follows the creed of his profession, a scientist believes what he does because of the evidence he can find. I became a Christian because I found in myself a need which could be satisfied only by Jesus Christ. I needed forgiveness and He gave it. I needed companionship and He was a Friend. I needed encouragement and He provided it." (Schweitzer, TSLL, n.p.)

Paul H. Johnson: "God has shaped a peculiar vacuum inside us—a vacuum shaped like God. Nothing satisfies that vacuum except God Himself. You can put money, homes, wealth, power, fame, or anything you want into the vacuum, but it doesn't fit. Only God fills it, fits it and satisfies it." (Johnson, MP, n.p.)

Walter Hearn of Ohio State College, "Often I am absorbed in a kind of philosophical quest . . . knowing Christ means life itself to me, but a new kind of life, the 'abundant life' He promised." (Schweitzer, TSLL, n.p.)

A public relations and advertising man, Frank Allnutt relates: "Then I asked Jesus to come into my life and dwell there. For the first time in my life I experienced complete peace. The lifetime of emptiness I had known was removed, and I have never felt alone since." (Allnutt, C, 22)

J. C. Martin, former major league baseball catcher, says, "I have found happiness and the fulfillment of all I have desired in Jesus Christ." (Martin, CC, n.p.)

9A. IF GOD BECAME A MAN, THEN WE WOULD EXPECT HIM TO OVERCOME HUMANITY'S MOST PERVASIVE AND FEARED ENEMY—DEATH

1B. His Death

Jesus was not forced to give up His life. As evidenced in Matthew 26:53, 54, He had the power available to Him to do whatever He pleased. John 10:18 affirms this: "No one takes it (My life) away from Me, but I lay it down of Myself. I have power to lay it down, and I have power to take it again. This command I have received from My Father." We see that Christ willingly died for the sins of all human beings.

W. H. Griffith Thomas attests that Jesus' death "was not the death of a suicide, for did He not say, 'I lay down My life of Myself.' The death was purely voluntary. We have to suffer: He need not have suffered. A word from Him might have saved His life. Nor was it an accidental death, for the obvious reason that it was foreseen, foretold, and prepared for in a variety of ways. Again, it was certainly not the death of a criminal, for no two witnesses could be found to agree together as to the charge against Him. Pilate declared that he found no fault in Him, and even Herod had not a word to say against Him. This, then, was no ordinary execution." (Thomas, CIC, 61)

Another important fact of His death is related by W. C. Robinson: "For no mere man in all history has ever had the power to dismiss his spirit of his own volition as did our Lord Jesus (Luke 23:46). . . . Luke and John use verbs which can only be interpreted as meaning that Jesus miraculously . . . handed over His spirit to God when He had paid the full price for sin. There was a miracle on Calvary on Friday as well as a miracle in the garden on Easter morning." (Robinson, WSYTIA, 85–86)

2B. His Burial

"And when evening had come, there came a rich man from Arimathea, named Joseph, who himself had also become a disciple of Jesus. This man went to Pilate and asked for the body of Jesus. Then Pilate commanded the body to be given over to him" (Matt. 27:57, 58).

"And Nicodemus, who had first came to Jesus by night, also came, bringing a mixture of myrrh and aloes, about a hundred pounds" (John 19:39).

"Then he bought fine linen, took Him down, and wrapped Him in the linen. And he laid Him in a tomb which had been hewn out in the rock; and rolled a stone against the door of the tomb. And Mary Magdalene and Mary the mother of Jesus observed where He was laid" (Mark 15:46, 47).

"And they returned and prepared spices and fragrant oils. And they rested on the Sabbath according to the commandment" (Luke 23:56).

"So they [the Pharisees' guard] went and made the tomb secure, sealing the stone and setting the guard" (Matt. 27:66).

3B. His Resurrection

"Indeed, taking all the evidence together," B. F. Westcott writes, "it is not too much to say that there is no historic incident better or more variously supported than the resurrection of Christ. Nothing but the antecedent assumption that it must be false could have suggested the idea of deficiency in the proof of it." (Westcott, GR, 4–6)

From Henry Morris we read, "The fact of His resurrection is the most important event of history and therefore, appropriately, is one of the most certain facts in all history." (Morris, BHA, 46)

Jesus not only predicted His death, but He also predicted His bodily resurrection. He said, "Destroy this temple, and in three days I will raise it up" (John 2:19). Here, *temple* refers to His body.

Again Morris writes: "He alone, of all men who ever lived, conquered death itself. By all rules of evidence, His bodily resurrection from the grave can be adjudged the best-proved fact of all history. 'I am the resurrection and the life,' He said. 'Because I live, ye shall live also'" (John 11:25; 14:19). (Morris, BHA, 28)

"The resurrection of Christ is *the seal of our resurrection*. The healing of sick people does not warrant us in believing that Christ will heal each of us today, nor did the resuscitation of Lazarus guarantee our immortality. It is the resurrection of Christ as *firstfruits* which alone opens the grave—in anticipation—to the believer and unto life eternal. Because He arose, we shall arise" (Rom. 8:11). (Ramm, PCE, 185–86)

After Jesus' resurrection, the apostles were able to raise the dead through His power (Acts 9:40, 41). Thus, He gave life to others after His death.

The evidence showsthat Jesus is alive (Heb. 13:8) and that "this same Jesus, who was taken up from you into heaven, will so come in like manner as you saw Him go into heaven" (Acts 1:11).

"But Jesus Christ, the eternal Son of God and the world's promised Redeemer, has conquered death." (Morris, BHA, 46)

Part Three

THE CASE FOR AND AGAINST CHRISTIANITY

SECTION I

INTRODUCTION

11

IS THE BIBLE FROM GOD?

Part Three of this book is designed to address both critics of the Bible and those who hold to its inspiration and authority. Therefore, it is necessary to begin this section of *Evidence* with a discussion of what it is that the critics seem intent on undermining: the unerring communication of a perfect God to fallen humanity.

In Part One of this book, I presented evidence that leads to the conclusion that the Bible is historically accurate, and remarkably so at that. But as I cautioned in that section, the fact that it is historically accurate does not necessarily mean that the Bible is inspired by God. The box score in this morning's sports pages is historically accurate, but this doesn't mean it is inspired by God.

The Bible, on the other hand, does claim to be the Word of God.

1A. WHAT THE BIBLE CLAIMS

In many places the Bible claims to be the "Word of God." But just what exactly does this mean? And if it is God's Word, then just how did God communicate it to humanity?

Paul tells us that: "All Scripture is God-breathed and is useful for teaching, rebuking, correcting and training in righteousness" (2 Tim. 3:16 NIV). This passage is the key text for the doctrine of inspiration. The Greek word *theopneustos* is usually translated "inspiration." In other words the Bible is "inspired" by God. The term simply means, as the New International Version translates it, "God-breathed." The Bible is from the breath of God.

Inspiration can be defined as the mysterious process by which God worked through human writers, employing their individual personalities and styles to produce divinely authoritative and inerrant writings. (Geisler, GIB, 39)

It is important to be careful in how we use the term "inspiration." This word is part of our everyday vocabulary. "That artist was inspired," we say, or "That music was certainly inspired." This is a very general use of the term and it is understood today as meaning something that is well done or of great value. But when we apply this word to the Bible we intend a different meaning. The Bible was not inspired the same way in which a singer or artist may be inspired. The Bible has been breathed by God. The Bible claims to be His very Word; it has come from His very mouth.

1B. Old Testament Claims to Inspiration

Many books of the Old Testament claim that they are from God. Throughout time this part of the Bible has been considered "God's Word." The Old Testament can be divided in many different ways. In the New Testament it was divided into a twofold arrangement (Matt. 5:17; 7:12) and also a threefold arrangement (Luke 24:44). In this section we will examine the twofold arrangement of the Old Testament—The Law and The Prophets—in terms of their claims to inspiration. We will discuss as well the sections that do not make a specific claim to inspiration.

1C. Inspiration of the Law

The first five books of the Old Testament are often referred to as "The Law;" "The Torah," which is the Hebrew term for law; or "The Pentateuch." These books—Genesis, Exodus, Leviticus, Numbers, and Deuteronomy—are traditionally understood as being the works of Moses.

The books of Exodus (32:16), Leviticus (1:1), Numbers (1:1), and Deuteronomy (31:24–26) all make explicit claim to inspiration. Genesis alone makes no such direct claim. However, Genesis too was considered to be part of the "Book of Moses" (see 2 Chr. 35:12; Neh. 13:1), and by virtue of this association carries the same divine authority. Whatever holds true for one book holds true for all of them. In other words, a claim by or for one book in this canonical section is a claim for all of them since they were all unified under one title: the Book, or Law, of Moses.

Throughout the remainder of the Old Testament, in an unbroken succession, the Law of Moses was enjoined on the people as the Law of God; Moses' voice was heeded as God's. Joshua began his ministry as Moses' successor with the statement, "This Book of the Law shall not depart from your mouth, . . . that you may observe to do according to all that is written in it" (Josh. 1:8). God tested the people of Israel to know whether they "would obey the commandments of the LORD, which He had commanded their fathers by the hand of Moses" (Judg. 3:4). "Then Samuel said to the people, 'It is the LORD who raised up Moses and Aaron, and who brought your fathers up from the land of Egypt. . . . [But] they forgot the LORD their God'" (1 Sam. 12:6, 9). In Josiah's day, "Hilkiah the priest found the Book of the Law of the LORD given by Moses" (2 Chr.

34:14). While in exile, Daniel recognized Moses' Law as God's Word, saying, "The curse and the oath written in the law of Moses the servant of God have been poured out on us, because we have sinned against Him. And He has confirmed His words which He spoke against us" (Dan. 9:11, 12). Even in post-exilic times, the revival under Nehemiah came as a result of obedience to Moses' law (see Ezra 6:18; Neh. 13:1). (Geisler, GIB, 71)

2C. Inspiration of the Prophets

The second division of the Old Testament is called "The Prophets." Now this can be tricky, as some of us think of the Prophets as the books of Isaiah, Jeremiah, and the like. But the section of the Old Testament known as The Prophets as it is sometimes used not only refers to the writing prophets, but to all of the Old Testament, excluding the first five books known as The Law.

Some references in some of the later prophets reveal a high regard for the utterances of earlier prophets. God spoke to Daniel through the writings of Jeremiah (compare Dan. 9:2 with Jer. 25:11). Ezra likewise recognized the divine authority of Jeremiah's writings (Ezra 1:1), as well as those of Haggai and Zechariah (Ezra 5:1). One of the strongest passages in this regard is found in one of the last of the Old Testament prophets, Zechariah. He speaks of "the law and the words which the LORD of hosts had sent by His Spirit through the former prophets" (Zech. 7:12). In a similar passage in the last historical book of the Old Testament, Nehemiah writes, "For many years You [God] had patience with them, and tes-

tified against them by your Spirit in Your prophets" (Neh. 9:30). These examples confirm the high regard that the latter prophets had for the writings of their predecessors; they considered them to be the Word of God, given by the Spirit of God for the good of Israel.

The characteristic prophetic introduction "thus says the LORD" and similar expressions are found here and in other parts of the Old Testament hundreds of times. (see Thomas, NASECB, 1055–65)

A sample survey finds Isaiah proclaiming, "Hear O heavens, and give ear, O earth! For the LORD has spoken" (Is. 1:2). Jeremiah proclaimed, "The word of the LORD came to me, saying . . ." (Jer. 1:11). "The word of the LORD came expressly to Ezekiel" (Ezek. 1:3). Similar statements are found throughout the twelve "minor" prophets (see Hos. 1:1–2; Joel 1:1).

> *The characteristic "thus says the LORD" and similar expressions are found here and in other parts of the Old Testament hundreds of times.*

The books of the prophets later sectioned off as "Writings" are automatically included in the overall claim for the prophets of which they were a part. Even the book of Psalms (part of the "Writings"), which Jesus singled out for its messianic importance (Luke 24:44), was part of the Law and the Prophets that Jesus said constituted "all the Scriptures" (Luke 24:27). Josephus placed Daniel (which comes later in the "Writings") in the "Prophets" section of his day (*Against Apion* 1. 8). So whatever alternate (or later) manner of arranging the Old Testament books into three sections may have existed, it is clear that the early arrangement was a twofold division of Law and Prophets (which included the books later to be known as "Writings") from late Old Testament times through the "Intertestamental" period and on into the New Testament era. (Geisler, GIB, 72)

The prophets were the voice of God not only in what they *said* but also in what they *wrote*. God commanded Moses, "Write these words" (Ex. 34:27). The Lord ordered Jeremiah to "take yet another scroll, and write on it all the former words that were in the first scroll" (Jer. 36:28). Isaiah testified that the Lord said to him: "Take a large scroll, and write on it" (Is. 8: 1). And again God told him: "Now go, write it before them on a tablet, and note it on a scroll, that it may be for time to come, forever and ever" (Is. 30:8). A similar command was given to Habakkuk: "Write the vision and make it plain on tablets, that he may run who reads it" (Hab. 2:2).

3C. Inspiration of All of the Books?

The vast majority of the books of the Old Testament (about eighteen of twenty-four) explicitly claim that they are God's words to men. But some do not make such clear statements concerning their origin. Several reasons are here provided:

1D. They Are All Part of a Given Section

Every book is considered part of a section—either The Law or The Prophets—in which there is a distinct and indisputable claim to inspiration. This claim covers every book within that section. As a result, each individual book need not state its own case; the claim has already been made for it by the claim made for the section as a whole, and is confirmed by the fact that later biblical books refer to the authority of that section as a whole.

2D. The Nature of Historic and Poetic Books

The historic and poetic books alone do not contain direct statements concerning their divine origin. All of the didactic books do make the claim "thus says the LORD." The reason that the historic and poetic books do not is that they present "what God showed" (history) rather than "what God said" (law and prophets). Nonetheless, the implicit didactic, "thus says the Lord," is present even in the historic and poetic books. History is what God said in the concrete events of national life. Poetry is what God said in the hearts and aspirations of individuals within the nation. Both are what God said, just as much so as the explicit record He spoke through the Law and the other didactic writings.

3D. The Writers of the Books Were Men Accredited of God

Solomon, credited by Jewish tradition with writing the Song of Solomon, Proverbs, and Ecclesiastes, possessed God-given wisdom (1 Kin. 4:29). Furthermore, he fulfilled the qualification for a prophet laid down in Numbers 12:6: one to whom God spoke in visions or dreams (see 1 Kin. 11:9). David is credited with writing nearly half of the psalms. And although the psalms themselves do not lay direct claim to divine inspiration, David's testimony of his own ministry is recorded in 2 Samuel 23:2: "The Spirit of the LORD spoke by me, and His word was on my tongue." Jeremiah, the traditional author of 1 and 2 Kings, has well-known prophetic credentials (see Jer. 1:4, 17). Chronicles and Ezra-Nehemiah are attributed to Ezra the priest, who functioned with all the authority of a prophet, interpreting the law of Moses and instituting civil and religious reforms thereupon (see Jer. 1:10, 13). So then, either the books of the Old Testament testify for themselves, or the men who are believed to have written them, almost without exception, claim them to be the authoritative word of God. (Geisler, GIB, 69–70)

2B. New Testament Claims to Inspiration

The New Testament also claims to be the "Word of God." From the very time it was

> "God, after He spoke long ago to the fathers in the prophets in many portions and in many ways, in these last days has spoken to us in His Son, whom He appointed heir of all things, through whom also He made the world.
>
> "After it was at the first spoken through the Lord, it was confirmed to us by those who heard."
>
> —HEBREWS 1:1, 2; 2:3 NASB

being written the people of God knew that the writings were special.

In a real sense, Christ is the key to the inspiration and canonization of the Scriptures. It was He who confirmed the inspiration of the Hebrew canon of the Old Testament; and it was He who promised that the Holy Spirit would direct the apostles into "all truth," the fulfillment resulting in the New Testament. (Geisler, GIB, 89)

Remembering how highly esteemed the Old Testament prophets were and how divinely authoritative their writings were considered to be, to compare the New Testament message to the Old Testament Scrip-

tures amounts to a claim to the same authority and inspiration. Such is confirmed in Hebrews 1:1–2: "God, who at various times and in various ways spoke in time past to the fathers by the prophets, has in these last days spoken to us by His Son," and the message was "at the first . . . spoken by the Lord, and was confirmed to us by those who heard Him" (Heb. 2:3). In other words, the message of Christ as given by His disciples is God's voice today just as much as the message of the prophets was in time past.

According to Ephesians 2:20 the church is "built on the foundation of the apostles and prophets." The word "apostle" should not be limited to the twelve apostles. Paul was an apostle (Gal. 1; 2 Cor. 12), as was Barnabas (Acts 14:14). James wrote with divine authority (James 1:1), and there were others with prophetic gifts (for example Agabus in Acts 11:28). The gift of either an apostle or a prophet would qualify one to receive a revelation (see Eph. 2:20), and several New Testament writers qualify as "prophets" (for example, Mark, Luke, James, and Jude).

Acts 2:42 records that the believers "continued steadfastly in the apostles' doctrine and fellowship." The authority of apostolic teaching, then, is seen not only by virtue of its equality with the prophets but by its fundamentality to the church. What the apostles taught is the authoritative foundation of the

> "Do not think that I came to abolish the Law or the Prophets; I did not come to abolish, but to fulfill. For truly I say to you, until heaven and earth pass away, not the smallest letter or stroke shall pass away from the Law, until all is accomplished."
>
> —MATTHEW 5:17, 18 NASB

> "But the Helper, the Holy Spirit, whom the Father will send in My name, He will teach you all things, and bring to your remembrance all that I said to you."
>
> —JOHN 14:26 NASB

church. Therefore the New Testament is the authoritative foundation of the church. (Geisler, GIB, 92)

Peter refers to Paul's writings as "Scripture" (2 Pet. 3:16), and 1 Timothy 5:18 draws from both Luke 10:7 and Deuteronomy 25:4 in applying the phrase "for the Scripture says." If the writings of Luke, who was not an apostle, are quoted as Scripture, and Peter, who incidentally was rebuked by Paul (Gal. 2:11), considered Paul's books to be Scripture, then it follows that the New Testament as a whole should be regarded as Scripture. It would be included in the statement "All Scripture is inspired by God" (2 Tim. 3:16).

3B. Is God's Word Inerrant?

The Bible claims to be inspired by God. And if it is from God, then we can logically assume that the Bible is without error, or inerrant. The words "inspired" and "inerrant" are usually linked together. In order to understand inerrancy let us consider the following issues: God's character, what inerrancy means, and what inerrancy doesn't mean.

1C. God's Character

A proper understanding of the inspiration of Scripture must include its inerrancy. The Bible is the Word of God . . . and God cannot err (Heb. 6:18; Titus 1:12). To deny the inerrancy of Scripture is to impugn either the integrity of God or the identity of the Bible as God's Word.

The character of God demands inerrancy. If every utterance in the Bible is from God and God is a God of truth, as the Bible declares Him to be, then the Bible must be wholly truthful, or inerrant. Jesus said of God's utterances, "Your word is truth" (John 17:17). The Psalmist wrote, "The entirety of Your word is truth" (Ps. 119:160). Solomon declared, "Every word of God is pure" (Prov. 30:5). Paul wrote to Titus, "God . . . cannot lie" (Titus 1:2). The author of Hebrews declared, "It is impossible for God to lie" (Heb. 6:18). In the final analysis, then, an attack on the inerrancy of the Bible is an attack on the character of God. Every true Christian will join with Paul in saying, "Let God be true but every man a liar" (Rom. 3:4).

2C. What Is Inerrancy?

Inerrancy means that when all the facts are known, the Scriptures in their original autographs, properly interpreted, will be shown to be wholly true in everything they affirm, whether this has to do with doctrine or morality or with the social, physical, or life sciences.

The bottom line is that the Bible has been breathed by God. He used men to write out exactly what He wanted them to write. He kept them free from error but at the same time used their unique personalities and styles to convey exactly what He wanted.

Peter tells us that "holy men of God spoke as they were moved by the Holy Spirit" (2 Pet. 1:21). The idea conveyed is that just as the wind controls the sails of a boat, so also the breath of God controlled the writers of the Bible. The end result was exactly what God intended.

1D. God Used a Variety of Expressions

Inerrancy does not mean that every word in the Bible is the same. Because God is creative (He is the Creator), He said the same thing in different ways, from different viewpoints, and at different times. Inspiration does not exclude diversity of expression. The four Gospels relate the same story in different ways to different groups of people. They sometimes even quote Christ as saying the same thing, but using different words.

Compare, for example, Peter's famous confession at Caesarea Philippi:

Matthew records it: "You are the Christ, the Son of the living God" (16:16).

Mark records it: "You are the Christ" (8:29).

Luke records it: "The Christ of God" (9:20).

Even the Decalogue is recorded in a variety of ways: "Written by the finger of God" (Deut. 9:10), is stated differently the second time that God gave it (compare Ex. 20:8–11 with Deut. 5:12–15). For example, Exodus cites creation as the reason that Israel is called to rest on the Sabbath, while Deuteronomy gives redemption as the reason. (see Archer, EBD, 191–92)

If such important utterances as Peter's confession of Christ and the inscription on the cross (see Matt. 27:37; Mark 15:26; Luke 23:38; and John 19:19), and such permanent and special laws as the one "written with the finger of God" can be stated in different ways, then there should be no problem extending the concept of inerrancy to the diversity of expression in the rest of Scripture.

2D. God Used Different Personalities and Styles

Inspiration can also include God's use of different personalities—with their own literary styles and idiosyncrasies—to record His word. One need only compare the powerful style of Isaiah with the mournful tone of Jeremiah in the Old Testament. In the New Testament, Luke manifests a marked medical interest, while James is distinctly practical, Paul is theological and polemical, and John writes with simplicity. God has communicated through a multiplicity of human personalities, each having unique literary characteristics.

The traditional biblical authors include a lawgiver (Moses), a general (Joshua), prophets (Samuel, Isaiah, et al.), kings (David and Solomon), a musician (Asaph), a herdsman (Amos), a prince and statesman (Daniel), a priest (Ezra), a tax collector (Matthew), a physician (Luke), a scholar (Paul), and fishermen (Peter and John). God used the variety of occupations and circumstances represented by biblical writers, as well as their unique personal interests and character traits, to reflect His timeless truths.

3D. God Sometimes Used Non-biblical Sources

Undoubtedly the doctrine of inspiration does not exclude the use of human documents as a source of divine truth. Such use is exactly what the Bible does claim. Luke's

"Inasmuch as many have taken in hand to set in order a narrative of those things which have been fulfilled among us, just as those who from the beginning were eyewitnesses and ministers of the word delivered them to us, it seemed good to me also, having had perfect understanding of all things from the very first, to write to you an orderly account, most excellent Theophilus, that you may know the certainty of those things in which you were instructed."

—LUKE 1:1–4

Gospel was based on research he had done using written sources of his day (see Luke 1:1–4). The writer of Joshua used the Book of Jasher for his famous quotation about the sun's standing still (Josh. 10:13). (see Nix, J, as cited in Criswell, CSB, 267–96) The apostle Paul quoted freely from a heathen poet (Acts 17:28) in his well-known Mars Hill address. Jude cited a noncanonical saying about the prophecy of Enoch (v. 14).

The use of nonbiblical sources should not be thought incongruous with inspiration—it is to be remembered that "all truth is

God's truth." The God who commanded "light to shine out of darkness" (2 Cor. 4:6) is able to speak truth through a pagan prophet (Num. 24:17), an unwitting high priest (John 11:50), and even a stubborn donkey (Num. 22:28).

3C. What Inerrancy Is Not

1D. Not Strict Grammar

Inerrancy is defined in terms of truth, and truth is a property of words organized in sentences. Therefore, a modern grammatical error does not preclude an inerrant Bible. This is as it should be. The rules of grammar merely represent normal usage of language. Every day skilled writers break these rules in the interest of superior communication. Why should we deny the writers of Scripture this privilege? (Feinberg, MI, as cited in Geisler, I, 299)

2D. Figures of Speech Are Present

We should not assume that an "inspired" book must have been written in one—and only one—literary mold. Humankind is not limited in our modes of expression; there is no reason to suppose that God is limited to one style or literary genre in His communication to man.

The Bible reveals a number of literary devices. Several whole books are written in the poetic style (e.g., Job, Psalms, Proverbs). The synoptic Gospels are filled with parables. In Galatians 4, Paul uses allegory. The New Testament abounds with metaphors (2 Cor. 3:2–3; James 3:6) and similes (Matt. 20:1; James 1:6); hyperboles may also be found (Col. 1:23; John 21:25; 2 Cor. 3:2). Jesus Himself on occasion used satire (compare Matt. 19:24 with 23:24).

The claim for inspiration, as understood in the light of the character of the inspired record itself, reveals that "inspiration" must not be viewed as a mechanical or wooden process. It is a dynamic and personal process that results in a divinely authoritative and inerrant product—the written Word of God. (Geisler, GIB, 58)

3D. Historical Precision?

It is often asserted that the doctrine of inerrancy cannot be accepted because the Bible does not reflect the canons of historical and linguistic precision recognized and required in the modern world. Like so many words used in the debate between inerrantists and errantists, the definition of precision is ambiguous. To some, imprecision implies error. This surely need not be so. As some of the wise men of past ages put it, all that is necessary is that statements be adequate. I interpret this in terms of truth. Almost any statement could be expressed more precisely than it appears. Any historiography, even a detailed chronicle, is still only an approximation.

Let me illustrate. If we record an event as having transpired in 1978, we could obviously have said it more precisely—in the month of May, on the fifteenth day, at the hour of 10 P.M., and so on. But the original, simpler statement would still be true. The essential criterion, as I see it, for inerrancy is this: Is the sentence as stated true? If so, there is no problem for the doctrine. Why should the modern criterion of precision be absolutized? Should we not expect Scripture to reflect the standards of its day? Is it not arrogant to think that our standards are right and theirs wrong? (Feinberg, MI, as cited in Geisler, I, 299–300)

4D. The Bible Uses Nonscientific Language

Inspiration certainly does not require the use of scholarly, technical, or scientific language. The Bible is written for the common people of every generation, and it therefore uses common, everyday language. The use of observational, nonscientific language is not unscientific; it is merely prescientific.

The Scriptures were recorded in *ancient* times using ancient standards. It would be anachronistic to superimpose modern scientific standards upon the biblical texts. It is no more unscientific to speak of the sun standing still (Josh. 10:12) than it is to refer to the sun rising. (Josh. 1:16). (Nix, J, 267–96) Contemporary meteorologists still speak daily of the times of "sunrise" and "sunset." The Scriptures say that the Queen of Sheba "came from the ends of the earth" (Matt. 12:42). Since "the ends of the earth" was only several hundred miles away, in Arabia (Kraeling, RMBA, 231, map IV), it appears that this is observational language. In like manner, the Scripture records that on the Day of Pentecost there were people "from every nation under heaven" (Acts 2:5). These nations are identified in Acts 2:9–11, and they do not literally include all the world (e.g., North and South America are excluded).

Thus, universal language is used in a *geographical* sense and is to be taken generally to mean "the then-known world." The Bible was written for a nonscientific people in a prescientific age. It is not reasonable for one to say the Bible is scientifically *incorrect*; it simply does not use modern scientific vernacular. But, in sacrificing scientific jargon, the Bible has gained a perfection in view of its universality and its simplicity of style.

The Bible also uses round numbers (see 1 Chr. 19:18; 21:5). It may be imprecise from the standpoint of a contemporary technological society to speak of the number 3.14159265 as the number three, but this is not incorrect for an ancient nontechnological people. Three and fourteen-hundredths can be rounded off to three. This is sufficient for a "cast bronze sea" (2 Chr. 4:2) in an

ancient Hebrew temple, even though it would not suffice for a computer in a rocket. But one should not expect scientific precision in a prescientific age.

The Bible speaks in the language of its day, in the mode that the people of that day will understand. It must be judged by the very nature of the divine revelation. The revelation came from God through men speaking human language and living in a cultural context.

To be meaningful, it had to come in the language of the prophets and apostles and employ the cultural background of figures, illustrations, analogies, and other elements generally associated with linguistic communication. No artificial or abstract theory of inerrancy that imposes modem scientific or technical precision upon the Scriptures is warranted. (Geisler, GIB, 57)

5D. Exact Words?

Inerrancy does not demand that the *logia jesu* (the sayings of Jesus) contain the *ipsissima verba* (the exact words) of Jesus, only the *ipsissima vox* (the exact voice). This point is closely akin to the one just made about historical precision. When a New Testament writer cites the sayings of Jesus, it is not nec-

> The writers of the New Testament did not have available to them the linguistic conventions that we have today. Thus it is impossible for us to know which of the sayings are direct quotes, which are indirect discourse, and which are even freer renderings.

essary that Jesus used those exact words. Undoubtedly the exact words of Jesus are to be found in the New Testament, but they need not be exact in every instance.

Many of Jesus' sayings were spoken in

Aramaic and therefore had to be translated into Greek. Moreover, as mentioned above, the writers of the New Testament did not have available to them the linguistic conventions that we apply today. Thus it is impossible for us to know which of the sayings are direct quotes, which are indirect discourse, and which are even freer renderings. (Osborne, RCGC, 83–85) With regard to the sayings of Jesus, what, in light of these facts, would count against inerrancy? If the sense of the words attributed to Jesus by the writers was not intended by Jesus, or if the exact words of Jesus are so construed that they have a sense never intended by Him, then inerrancy would be threatened.

An example of God's desire to communicate an accurate *meaning* to us (rather than just mechanically precise words) is the fact that He gave us four Gospels. The slight variations in Jesus' words actually help us capture the accurate meaning He intended. Had each writer simply parroted the others, the text might be precise but the meaning might be misconstrued.

6D. Comprehensive Accounts?

Inerrancy does not guarantee the exhaustive comprehensiveness of any single account or of combined accounts where those are involved. This point is also somewhat related to the earlier statement on precision. It must be remembered that from the standpoint of any discipline, even theology, the Scriptures are partial. The word "partial" is often taken to mean incorrect or false. But this idea is false. The Bible is a complete revelation of all that man needs for faith and practice. That is, there are many things we might like to know but that God has not seen fit to reveal. It is also true that God has not seen fit to record every detail of every account.

I think that this point has implications also for the Gospel accounts. The problems in the Gospels (some of which are covered in Section Three: Form Criticism) can often be resolved when one realizes that none of the evangelists was obligated to give an exhaustive account of any one event. He had the right to record an event in light of his purposes in writing his Gospel. Moreover, it must be remembered that the accounts of all four Gospel writers together do not exhaust the details of any one event. There may be some unknown bit of information that would resolve seeming conflicts. All that is required is that the sentences used by each writer be true. (Feinberg, MI, as cited in Geisler, I, 300–2)

7D. The Autographs

Inerrancy does not apply to every copy, only to the original text. The view that has persisted throughout the centuries and is common among evangelicals today is that inerrancy (or infallibility, inspiration) of the Scriptures pertains only to the text of the original autographs.

In a letter to Jerome (Letter 82) concerning anything he found in the biblical books that seemed contrary to the truth, Augustine wrote: "I decide that either the text is corrupt, or the translator did not follow what was really said, or that I failed to understand it." (Bahnsen, IA, as cited in Geisler, I, 155–56)

Scripture has scattered indications of interest in or recognition of copies and translations of God's Word in distinction from the original manuscripts. We can also draw useful inferences from various passages that tell us something of the scriptural attitude toward the then-existing copies and subsequent translations. What we primarily learn is that these nonautographical manuscripts were deemed adequate to perform the purposes for which God originally gave the Scriptures. King Solomon possessed a copy of the original Mosaic law (see Deut.

17:18), and yet it was considered to contain, truly and genuinely, "the charge of Jehovah . . . according to that which was written in the law of Moses" (1 Kin. 2:3). (Payne, PB, 16–18)

The law of God that was in the hand of Ezra was clearly a copy, but nevertheless it functioned as authoritative in his ministry (Ezra 7:14). When Ezra read from this law to the people so that divine guidance might be given for their lives, he apparently read to them by way of translation so they could understand the sense in the Aramaic to which they had become accustomed in exile: "And they read in the book, in the law of God, distinctly [with interpretation]; and they gave the sense, so that they understood the reading" (Neh. 8:8). (Berkouwer, HS, 217) In all of these examples the secondary text performs the work of God's written Word and shares its original authority in a practical sense.

It needs to be reiterated quite unambiguously that evangelical restriction of inerrancy to the autographs (1) is a restriction to the autographic text, thereby guarding the uniqueness of God's verbal message, and (2) does not imply that present Bibles, because they are not fully inerrant, fail to be the Word of God. The evangelical view does not mean that the inerrancy, or inspiration, of present Bibles is an all-or-nothing matter. (Bahnsen, IA, as cited in Geisler, I, 173)

So if only the autographs are inspired, what about the translations? If only the errorless autographs were God-breathed, and the translators were not preserved from error, how can there be certainty about any passage of Scripture? Perhaps the very passage that comes under question is a mistaken transcription or copy. The scholarly procedure of textual criticism treats this problem by showing the accuracy of the copies of the originals. To borrow this conclusion in advance, the copies are known to be accurate and sufficient in all matters except possibly minor details. The resulting situation exists, then, that although only the autographs are inspired, it may be said nevertheless that all good copies or translations are adequate. Although no one in modern times has ever seen an infallible original, it is also true that no one has ever seen a fallible one.

Just why God did not see fit to preserve the autographs is unknown, although man's tendency to worship religious relics is certainly a possible determining factor (2 Kin. 18:4).

Others have noted that God could have avoided the worship of the originals by simply preserving a perfect copy. (Bahnsen, IA, as cited in Geisler, I, 172–73) But He has not seen fit to do even this. It seems more likely that God did not preserve the originals so no one could tamper with them. It is practically impossible for anyone to make changes in the thousands of existing copies.

In seeking to avoid the two extremes of either an unattainable original or a fallible one, it must be asserted that a good copy or translation of the autographs is for all practical purposes the inspired Word of God. (Geisler, GIB, 42–44)

2A. OBJECTIONS TO THE CLAIMS

The Bible certainly claims to be the inspired Word of God. But some people object to the idea that the Bible is the Word of God and that it is inerrant. In this section some of the major objections to inspiration and inerrancy will be addressed.

1B. Arguing in Circles

Some assert that to believe in inerrancy you have to argue in circles. "You believe in inerrancy because you believe the Bible teaches it, but you believe the Bible because you believe in inerrancy," some will say.

But this is not the case. A logical presentation of the case for inerrancy is not circular.

The Bible is a reliable and trustworthy document. This is established by treating it as any other historical record, as, for instance, the works of Josephus or the accounts of war by Julius Caesar.

On the basis of the history recorded by the Bible, we have sufficient grounds for believing that the central character of the Bible, Jesus Christ, did what He is claimed to have done and therefore is who He claimed to be. He claimed to be the unique Son of God—in fact, God in human flesh. As the unique Son of God, the Lord Jesus Christ is an infallible authority.

Jesus Christ not only assumed the authority of the Bible existing in His day, the Old Testament; He taught it, going so far as to say that the Scriptures are entirely without error and eternal, being the Word of God.

If the Scriptures are the Word of God, as Jesus taught, they must for this reason alone be entirely trustworthy and inerrant, for God is a God of truth.

Therefore, on the basis of the teaching of Jesus Christ, the infallible Son of God, the church believes the Bible also to be infallible.

This argument begins with the nature of the Bible in general, proceeds to the person and teaching of Jesus Christ, and concludes by adopting His teaching concerning the nature of the Bible.

2B. Inerrancy Is Not Taught in the Bible

"Inerrancy is not taught in the Bible" is the claim by those opposed to inerrancy. They say that the Bible does not teach its own inerrancy, but only teaches that it is inspired.

This claim is as incorrect as saying the Bible does not teach the doctrine of the Trinity. True, nowhere does the Bible say in so many words, "there are three persons in one God: Father, Son, and Holy Spirit." But

despite this fact, the doctrine of the Trinity is clearly and emphatically taught in Scripture. How does one arrive at this? By a logical deduction from two principles that are

> Like the doctrine of the Trinity, nowhere do the Scriptures explicitly say, "The Bible is inerrant in all that it affirms." Nevertheless, the Bible does clearly and emphatically teach two truths from which this conclusion is inevitable.

clearly taught in Scripture: (1) there are three persons who are called God: Father, Son, and Holy Spirit; and (2) there is only one God. Simple logic demands that from these two truths only one conclusion follows, a conclusion that no orthodox Christian fails to draw: There are three persons in the one God.

Now, by this same logic the Bible also teaches its own inerrancy. Like the doctrine of the Trinity, nowhere do the Scriptures explicitly say, "The Bible is inerrant in all that it affirms." Nevertheless, the Bible does clearly and emphatically teach two truths from which this conclusion is inevitable: First, the very words of Scripture, all of them, are the revelation of God. Paul wrote, "All Scripture is given by inspiration of God" (2 Tim. 3:16). The word "scripture" means "writings." Over and over the biblical prophets were commanded to record the very "words" of God (Ex. 24:4; Rev. 22:19). David confessed on his deathbed, "the Spirit of the LORD spoke by me, and His word was on my tongue" (2 Sam. 23:2). Jeremiah was told "Do not diminish a word" of God's prophecy (Jer. 26:2). The apostle Paul claimed to teach "words . . . which the Holy Spirit teaches" (1 Cor. 2:13).

Second, the Bible emphatically teaches

that everything that God utters is true and completely without error. Jesus said to the Father, "Your word is truth" (John 17:17). The psalmist declared, "Your word is truth" (Ps. 119:160). The writer of Hebrews stated emphatically, "It is impossible for God to lie" (Heb. 6:18). Paul told Titus that "God . . . cannot lie" (1:2). Proverbs assures us that "every word of God proves true" (30:5 RSV). In short, the very character of God as true demands that when He speaks He must speak the truth. At the same time, the Scriptures are the very utterance of God. Hence, from these two clearly taught truths of Scripture one and only one conclusion logically follows: Everything the Bible teaches is the unerring truth of God.

Thus it is that inerrancy follows logically from inspiration. If the Bible is God's Word, then it must be without error. Christians have often summarized the doctrine of inerrancy this way: "What the Bible says, God says." Indeed the words "God" and "Scripture" are often used interchangeably in this regard. For example, Hebrews 3:7 declares "the Holy Spirit says" with a reference to the Old Testament Scripture (Ps. 95:7). This pattern is repeated elsewhere (see Acts 2:17; Gal. 3:8; Heb. 9:8).

The Bible does indeed claim its own inerrancy as surely as it teaches that God is a Trinity.

3B. Inerrancy Is Not Important

"Inerrancy is not important" is the cry of some. They believe that the Bible does not have to be without error to be authoritative.

This objection raised by the opponents of inerrancy is easily dismissed in view of the point just made. They argue that inerrancy is not an important doctrine. Inspiration is important, they claim, but not inerrancy. But if whatever the Bible teaches clearly and emphatically is important, and the Bible does teach its own inerrancy clearly and emphatically, it follows that inerrancy is important.

To say that inerrancy is not important is like claiming that it is not important whether or not God utters only the truth. The Lord Jesus taught that the Bible was true right down to the smallest part: "Till heaven and earth pass away, one jot or one tittle will by no means pass from the law till all is fulfilled" (Matt. 5:18). Elsewhere Jesus declared, "The Scripture cannot be broken" (John 10:35). Hence, inerrancy will be important as long as Jesus is Lord!

4B. Inerrancy Is a Recent Invention

Those denying inerrancy often claim that inerrancy is a recent invention. Some say it originated with B. B. Warfield at Princeton in the late 1800s. Other, such as Jack Rogers of Fuller, trace it back to the Lutheran theologian Turretin just after the Reformation.

Both of these views are mistaken. Inerrancy was taught in the Bible long before Luther or Calvin. And there is evidence that the earliest church fathers held to the doctrine of inerrancy. Augustine said, "I have teamed to yield this respect and honor only to the canonical books of Scripture. Of these alone do I most firmly believe that the authors were completely free from error." (Letters, LXXXII)

The great medieval theologian Thomas Aquinas said, "Nothing false can underlie the literal sense of Scripture." *(Summa Theologica, 1,* 1, 10, ad 3) The great Reformer Martin Luther repeated over and over, "The Scriptures have never erred" and "The Scriptures cannot err." *(Works of Luther,* XV:1481; XIX: 1073) John Calvin clearly endorsed the inerrancy of Scripture in his *Institutes* when he wrote, "Error never can be eradicated from the heart of man until the true knowledge of God [through Scripture] has been implanted in it." (Book I, Chapter 6) John Wesley, the founder of Methodism, was emphatic about the inerrancy of Scripture. He wrote, "Nay, if there be any mistakes in the Bible there may as well be a thousand. If there is one falsehood in that book it did not come from the God of truth." (Journal VI, 117)

These clear statements of the church fathers and Reformers clearly indicate that inerrancy was not a late invention of the post-Reformation period or of nineteenth-century American theologians.

5B. There Are Errors in the Bible

Some claim that we must give up the belief in inerrancy because there are errors in the Bible. Davis offers as an example of error God's command to Joshua to kill the Canaanites. What is his basis for calling this an error? Davis answers very clearly: "I speak for no one except myself, but I believe that killing innocent people is morally wrong." (Davis, DAB, 96)

But Davis forgets several points. First, the Canaanites were far from innocent (Lev. 18:25; Deut. 9:5). The practices of child sacrifice and other inhumane behavior were rampant in their land. Second, this command was unique. It is not a biblical doctrine meant for all times, but was a specific command for a specific occasion at a unique time in history. Third, God is sovereign over all of life. He gave life and He has the right to take it away (Job 1:21; Deut. 32:39).

There is an error here, but it is not in God's action or His Word to Joshua. The mistake is in using human reason or sentiment as the basis for determining what is true in the Word of God and what is not. As God spoke in Isaiah 55:8, "For My thoughts are not your thoughts, nor are your ways My ways, says the LORD."

Some alleged errors turn out to be discrepancies introduced by the copyists who made handwritten copies of Bible manuscripts. An example is the age of Ahaziah when he began to reign (age 22 according to 2 Kin. 8:26, but age 42 according to 2 Chr. 22:2). Other supposed "errors" are *divergent* but not contradictory accounts. Luke records that there were two angels at the tomb after the resurrection (24:4), but Matthew mentions only one (28:2). This is, of course, divergent, but it would be contradictory only if Matthew had said there was *only* one angel at the tomb at *one and the same time* that Luke declared two to be present.

Such alleged contradictions are not new. They have been recognized by biblical scholars down through the centuries. And yet one gets the impression from reading current scholars who deny inerrancy that some recent factual finds have forced them to the conclusion that they must now give up inerrancy. Just the contrary is true. More of the Bible stands confirmed today and more problems are explainable than has been the case in centuries. Discoveries from the Dead Sea, from Sumeria, from Nag Hammadi, and more recently from Ebla provide more support than ever before for the positions that evangelicals have long held.

> One gets the impression from reading current scholars who deny inerrancy that some recent factual finds have forced them to the conclusion that they must now give up inerrancy. Just the contrary is true. More of the Bible stands confirmed today and more problems are explainable than has been the case for centuries. Discoveries from the Dead Sea, from Sumeria, from Nag Hammadi, and more recently from Ebla provide more support than ever before for the positions that evangelicals have long held.

Why, then, is the impression left that "facts" are just now leading men to give up this crucial doctrine of the Christian faith? I am convinced that it is not a *factual* matter at all; it is *a philosophical* issue. Paul warned, "Beware lest any man cheat you through philosophy and empty deceit" (Col. 2:8). What has happened, I suggest, is that many of these fine Christian scholars have been seduced by philosophical presuppositions, often adopted unconsciously during their graduate studies, so that their conclusions are determined in part by rationalistic and existential thinking rather than by the Word of God.

Davis unwittingly analyzed the problem of those who deny inerrancy when he wrote, "What leads them to liberalism . . . is their acceptance of certain philosophical or scientific assumptions that are inimical to evangelical theology—e.g., assumptions about what is 'believable to modern people.'" (Davis, DAB, 139, as cited in Geisler, ID, 2)

6B. Limited Scope

Another objection to inerrancy is the claim that inspiration covers only the doctrinal or moral areas of Scripture, but not necessarily the historical and the scientific areas. "All Scripture is given by inspiration of God, and is profitable for doctrine" (2 Tim. 3:16).

There are several serious flaws in the view of "limited inspiration." First, the Bible makes no such distinction between doctrinal and historical matters. *Everything* affirmed in the Bible is true. Secondly, in many biblical teachings there is no way to separate the spiritual from the physical or historical. For instance, Jesus' teaching about divorce is inseparable from His affirmation that God created a literal Adam and Eve (Matt. 19:4). And how can one separate the spiritual and the historical in the Cross or the Resurrection?

Thirdly, this false dichotomy between the spiritual and historical shows no awareness of our Lord's statement to Nicodemus, "If I have told you earthly things and you do not believe, how will you believe if I tell you heavenly things?" (John 3:12). That is, if we cannot trust the Bible and our Lord when they speak of historical events, how can we trust them when they speak of spiritual matters?

Finally, those evangelicals who deny inerrancy of the Bible do not limit their denial to purely scientific, chronological, and historical matters. Paul Jewett denied the truthfulness of Paul's teaching on women. Davis denied the validity of God's command to drive out the Canaanites—a moral matter. To allow for an errant Bible is to allow anyone and everyone to choose which parts of God's commands they are willing to accept, and which they will reject.

7B. Nonexistent Originals

This objection contends that evangelicals who believe in inerrancy retreat into an unfalsifiable position that rests in nonexistent originals. Since only the original manuscripts were inspired by God, and since there are no original manuscripts around today, there is no way to prove an error in them.

In response, we do have highly accurate copies that are perfectly adequate for Christian teaching and life. In fact, no major (or even minor) biblical doctrine is undermined by any copyist's mistakes.

The Bible contains very little that evangelicals would say is in error due to copyist mistakes. There is plenty in the Bible for which critics are able to blast Christians!

In short, the originals are not nonexistent for all practical purposes. All essential teachings are preserved in the copies we possess. Just as no American's liberties would be jeopardized were the original constitution to be destroyed—as long as we possess good copies of it—so no Christian need fear because we don't have the original texts of Scripture.

8B. Does God Care?

Some claim that if God did not provide error-free copies, He could hardly be concerned that the originals are flawless. If copies are adequate, even with their minor scribal errors, then why is it so important that the originals were without error? Or else, why did not God either keep the errorless originals from disappearing, or keep the copyists from making any errors?

The answer to the first part of this question has to do with consistency in God's nature. Because God is perfect, whatever comes directly from His hand must be perfect. An original Bible with errors would imply that God can err. This would be like saying that God created Adam in an imperfect state. The second part of the question can be answered with another question: Why did God not preserve Adam from sinning? Humankind tends to corrupt what we touch, whether the Bible or ourselves. Of course, God preserved both "originals," the Bible and humankind, from becoming distorted beyond recognition. Man is still substantially in God's image (though imperfect), and the Bible is essentially God's Word (though there are minor errors in the copies).

There are important reasons why God did not preserve the original manuscripts. First humankind has a propensity to worship the creature rather than the Creator (Rom. 1:25). Remember the brazen serpent God appointed for Israel's deliverance? It was later worshiped (2 Kin. 18:4). How much more would we worship the very original words from God appointed for our salvation? Furthermore, by not preserving the

originals there is no way for sinful people to tamper with their contents.

9B. Too Many Qualifications

A final claim is that defenders of inerrancy place so many limitations on the doctrine that it dies the "death by a thousand qualifications."

This point is very much overstated. Basically there are only two qualifications to inerrancy: first, only the *original manuscripts* are inerrant, not the copies; second, only what the Bible *affirms* is inerrant, not everything it contains.

To be sure, many complicated issues are involved in determining precisely what the Bible affirms in any given passage, including meaning, context, and literary form. This, however, is not a question of inspiration but of interpretation. All would agree, for example, that the Bible contains lies, including Satan's lies. But the Bible does not affirm that these lies are true. All inerrancy claims is that *the record* of these lies is true.

Not everyone would agree, on the other hand, that everything contained in the book of Ecclesiastes is true. Many Christian interpreters of Ecclesiastes view the statements in the middle of the book as simply *a true record of the false views* of natural man "under the sun."

There seems to be room for difference of opinion here and in other like situations (the speeches of Job's friends, for example). Christians may differ as to what the Bible actually affirms in a given passage and what it merely records, but there should be no disagreement among us that what the Bible does affirm is inerrant. God cannot err.

Along with the question of how to interpret Scripture there is nothing in the doctrine of inerrancy that dictates, as has sometimes been charged, that every passage be taken literally. It is surely wrong to take an allegory as literal (Gal. 4:24, 25). Likewise, the Bible no doubt speaks in round numbers at times. But imprecision is not error. Math teachers do not consider their students in error simply

> Basically there are only two qualifications to inerrancy: first, only the original manuscripts are inerrant, not the copies; second, only what the Bible affirms is inerrant, not everything it contains.

because they used 22/7 or 3.1416 as the value of π. But both are imprecise.

Also, biblical authors spoke in the same manner in which people speak today—even scientists—that is, in observational language. It appears as though the sun "sets," and even a scientist will say, "look at the beautiful sunset." But these are questions of interpretation, not of inspiration. The real crux of the inerrancy issue is this: Is it the case or is it not that *whatever* the Bible affirms is without error? Is the biblical teaching without error whether or not God created Adam and Eve, a flood destroyed the world in Noah's day, Jonah was three days in a great fish, or Jesus rose from the dead? (Geisler, ID, 1–4)

3A. CONCLUSION

What does the above discussion mean for the average person today? Do I or do I not have a Bible that is the inspired and inerrant Word of God? Can I be confident that what I read in the Bible is truly from God?

The answer is a hearty "Yes!" The Bible that we have today is the inspired Word of God. Recent archaeological discoveries (see chapters 3, 4, and 14 on archaeology) have confirmed that the Bibles we have today are accurate transmissions of what existed two thousand years ago. We simply have a translation in our current language of the God-breathed Scriptures that were originally written in Aramaic, Hebrew, and Greek.

Remember that the doctrine of inerrancy applies only to the original copies of the Bible. Until the printing press was invented the Bible had to be copied by hand for at least one thousand years. It is therefore possible that some transmissional errors crept into the text. The abundance of manuscripts, however, along with archaeological finds, textual notes, and other devices, have all helped to ensure an accurate translation of the inerrant Word of God.

"You can trust your Bible, for it is the inspired word of God. The pollution which intruded in the transmission and translation of the Bible is minor, under control, and diminishing. Therefore, your Bible is trustworthy." (Goodrick, IMBIWG, 113)

In the remainder of Part Three, a discussion of the attacks by critics of the Bible will reveal attempts to erode confidence that God has surely spoken to us throughout the Scriptures. Before an answer can be given in response to these critics, though, it is important to understand a common misconception and faulty mind-set held by most antagonists of the Bible: the presupposition of anti-supernaturalism.

12

THE PRESUPPOSITION OF ANTI-SUPERNATURALISM

Before beginning our study of the documentary hypothesis and form criticism, there is a very crucial and often misunderstood topic that we should deal with—anti-supernaturalism.

If there is any subject in which ignorance abounds, it is this. Many sincere students and laymen are led astray because of conclusions allegedly based on objective historical or literary investigation and method. In reality these conclusions are the result of a subjective worldview.

1A. PRESUPPOSITION

1B. Definition
A presupposition is something assumed or supposed in advance. A good definition is "to require or involve necessarily as an antecedent condition." One could say that to "presuppose" is to conclude something before the investigation is commenced.

2B. Synonyms
Prejudgement, assumption of something as true, prejudice, forejudgement, preconceived opinion, fixed conclusion, preconceived notion, premature conclusion.

3B. Unavoidable
Presuppositions are to a degree inevitable. Thomas Whitelaw of Great Britain cites the German theologian Biedermann, (Christliche Dogmatik), as saying that it is

> not true but sand in the eyes, if one asserts that genuinely scientific and historic criticism can and should proceed without dogmatic presuppositions. In the last instance the consideration of the so-called purely historic grounds always reaches the point where it can and will decide concerning this, whether it can or cannot hold some particular thing in and of itself to be possible. . . . Some sort of boundary definitions, be they ever so elastically held, of what is historically possible, every student brings with him to historical investigations; and these are for that student dogmatic presuppositions. (Whitelaw, OTC, 172)

"It is perfectly true," continues James Orr, "that it is impossible in any inquiry to dispense with guiding principles of investigation, and with presuppositions of some

kind, and there is no criticism on earth that does so. . . . Only these should not be allowed to warp or distort the facts, or be applied to support a preconceived conclusion. The scientist also finds it incumbent on him to 'anticipate nature' with his interrogations and tentative hypotheses, which, however, have to be brought to the test . . . of experimental verification." (Orr, TPOT, 14)

Commenting on the need for presuppositions, John Warwick Montgomery observes: "First, though Kant was quite right that all arguments begin with *a prioris,* it does not follow that one presupposition is as good as another." (Carlson, SS, 388)

Thomas Whitelaw writes that both radical and conservative critics presuppose too much:

> So long as Higher Critics believe in a God, they have no right to postulate His noninterference with the ordinary line of causation or to assume beforehand that "miracles do not happen," or that "prediction" in the sense of foretelling future events "is impossible." Admitting that it would be a violation of sound reasoning to make the contrary suppositions, viz. that in God's providential government of the world and revelation of Himself miracles and predictions must occur, one has ground to contend that the argumentation is equally unfair—is a virtual begging of the question—which starts from the premise, No supernatural except within the lines and limits of the natural. Impartial inquirers will severely restrict themselves to investigating the reality or non-reality of so-called facts, *i.e.* to examining and proving phenomena with a view to ascertaining their true character, whether they are natural or not. (Whitelaw, OTC, 178)

In all fairness to the radical critic, it should be realized that "sometimes professedly conservative writers take great liberties with the simple facts of Scripture and put forward conclusions which are quite as baseless as the conclusions of radical criticism." (Allis, TFBM, 339)

Oswald Allis observes prejudices on both sides:

> The "scientific scholar" is, generally speaking, quite as dogmatic in rejecting the authority of the Old Testament, as the conservative is in accepting and defending it. He is just as insistent on fitting the Old Testament into a world view which rejects the redemptive supernaturalism of the Bible and the uniqueness of its history, religion and cultus, as the Bible defender is in insisting on the uniqueness of Old Testament history and the supernaturalism which pervades it. . . . To charge an opponent with bias and dogmatism, is an easy way of avoiding the issue. (Allis, TFBM, 338)

4B. Do We Have a Right?

One must be constantly and consciously aware of his presuppositions. I have to ask myself, "Do I have a right to my presuppositions?" A key question is, "Do my presuppositions coincide with reality, with what really is? Is there sufficient evidence to support them?"

2A. ANTI-SUPERNATURALISM

Since this concept of anti-supernaturalism is prevalent among the radical proponents of both the documentary hypothesis and form criticism schools, I have decided to deal with it here rather than in their respective sections.

1B. Definition

For our purposes we will define anti-supernaturalism as disbelief either in God's existence or in His intervention in the natural order of the universe. In the Pentateuch it is explicitly stated no less than 235 times that either God "spoke" to Moses, or God "commanded" Moses to do something (*Strong's Exhaustive Concordance of the Bible*). Prior to his investigation, a critic with an anti-supernaturalism bias (presupposition) would immediately reject these accounts as unhistorical.

A. J. Carlson, in *Science and the Supernatural,* defines the supernatural as "information, theories, beliefs and practices claiming origins other than verifiable experience and thinking, or events contrary to known processes in nature." (Carlson, SS, 5–8)

2B. Explanation

1C. Statement of Position

Since we purportedly live in a *closed* system or universe, there can be no interference or intrusion from the outside by an alleged God. This closed system or continuum means that every event has its cause within the system. To put it plainly, every event or happening has a natural explanation. Therefore, any reference to a divine act or event is futile, since it is presumed there has to be a natural explanation for all phenomena.

2C. Basic Tenets

It is difficult to summarize the tenets of those holding to an anti-supernatural viewpoint because they vary among themselves. The following are held by many:

1D. We live in a closed system (every cause has its natural effect).

2D. There is no God. (For many critics it would be more appropriate to state: "For all practical purposes, there is no God.")

3D. There is no supernatural.

4D. Miracles are not possible.

3B. Some Illustrations

1C. A Story about My First Book

A group of students gave my first book to a professor, who was head of the history department of a large, well-known university. They asked him to read *Evidence That Demands A Verdict* and to give them his opinion.

Several months later one of the students returned to his office to inquire about his progress. The professor replied that he had finished the book. He continued that it contained some of the most persuasive arguments that he had read and that he didn't know how anyone could refute them. At this point he added, "However, I do not accept Mr. McDowell's conclusions." The student, slightly baffled, asked, "Why?" The head of the history department answered, "Because of my worldview!"

His final rejection was not based upon the evidence, but was maintained in spite of the evidence. The motivating factor for his refusing to acknowledge the evidence was his presupposition about the supernatural, not an investigation of the historical.

2C. At Another University

At another university I was lecturing in a philosophy class. Upon my conclusion the professor immediately began to badger me with questions about the validity of the Resurrection. After several minutes the discussion almost became obnoxious.

Finally a student asked the professor what he believed took place that first Easter morning. After a brief pause, the professor honestly replied: "To tell you the truth, I really don't know." Then he immediately added rather forcefully, "But it wasn't the Resurrection!"

After a short period of interrogation he reluctantly admitted that he held this view because of his world outlook and bias against the notion that God acts within the realm of history.

3C. During Another Class Lecture

During another class lecture in which I was spoke on Christianity and philosophy, the professor interrupted me and said, "This is all ridiculous. We all know that there has to be some other explanation for the empty tomb."

4C. The Reason for My Introductory Statement on History

The above examples are the reason why I often make the statement in history classes that "following the modern historical approach I would never come to believe in the resurrection of Jesus as Savior and Lord." Most Christians at this point look askance at me because they know I teach that Christianity is a historical faith. I then point out that I qualified my statement with the words "following the modern historical approach." I could not justify my examination of history if I were to adhere to the "modern approach." The reason is that the modern historical approach presupposes certain conclusions before an investigation is commenced. The average "modern" historian rules out any reference to the supernatural as being unhistorical, or to use a hackneyed expression, as "myth."

They approach history with a preconceived notion, and then adjust the evidence accordingly. In other words, before they even begin their historical examination they have already determined the content of their results.

Many historians approach history with certain presuppositions. These presuppositions are not historical biases but rather philosophical prejudices. Their historical perspective is rooted within a philosophical framework, and their metaphysical convic-

> The conclusion is not therefore purely a result of open-minded study of the supernatural, but a conclusion dictated dogmatically by an antisupernatural metaphysics. On what other basis could critics *completely* rule out the supernatural in a document that admittedly has historical value?
>
> —BERNARD RAMM

tion usually determines the "historical" content and results. The "modern" researcher, when presented with the historical evidence for the Resurrection, will usually reject it, but not on the basis of his or her historical examination.

The response will often be: "Because we know there is no God"; or "The supernatural is not possible"; or, "We live in a closed system"; or "Miracles are not possible"; and so forth *ad infinitum*. I usually reply, "Did you come to this conclusion by studying the historical evidence or did you think it up philosophically?" All too often their conclusion is the offshoot of *philosophical speculation,* not historical homework.

The professors mentioned previously rejected my contentions, not because of any weakness in the material itself but because they were confirmed naturalists.

Clark Pinnock clearly describes the problem: "Until he (the naturalist) will admit the possibility of a theistic world, no amount of evidence will convince modern man that the Resurrection is not absurd." (Pinnock, SFYC, 6–7)

Bernard Ramm clarifies the naturalistic approach and its effect upon the results of one's study: "If the issue is over the existence of the supernatural, very obviously such an approach has made the conclusion its major premise. In short, before the criticism actually begins, the supernatural is ruled out. All of it must go. The conclusion is not therefore purely a result of open-minded study of the supernatural, but a conclusion dictated dogmatically by an antisupernatural metaphysics. On what other basis could critics *completely* rule out the supernatural in a document that admittedly has historical value?" (Ramm, PCE, 204)

5C. A Vivid Example of a Commitment to a Presupposed Conclusion

For many years I have shared an anecdote, told by J. Warwick Montgomery, that illustrates a presuppositional viewpoint:

Once upon a time there was a man who thought he was dead. His concerned wife and friends sent him to the friendly neighborhood psychiatrist. The psychiatrist determined to cure him by convincing him of one fact that contradicted his belief that he was dead. The psychiatrist decided to use the simple truth that dead men do not bleed. He put his patient to work reading medical texts, observing autopsies, etc. After weeks of effort the patient finally said, "All right, all right! You've convinced me. Dead men do not bleed." Whereupon the psychiatrist stuck him in the arm with a needle, and the blood flowed. The man looked down with a contorted, ashen face and cried: "Good Lord! Dead men bleed after all!"

Montgomery comments:

This parable illustrates that if you hold unsound presuppositions with sufficient tenacity, facts will make no difference at all, and you will be able to create a world of your own, totally unrelated to reality and totally incapable of being touched by reality. Such a condition (which the philosophers call solipsistic, psychiatrists call autistically psychotic, and lawyers call insane) is tantamount to death because connection with the living world is severed. The man in the parable not only thought he was dead, but in a very real sense, he *was* dead because facts no longer meant anything to him. (Montgomery, TAMD, 21–22)

4B. Examples of Proponents

This section will deal basically with those who advocate either the documentary hypothesis or form criticism.

1C. The Documentary Hypothesis

The German scholar Frank (*Geshichte und Kritik der Neuren Theologie*, p. 289) gives this exact summary of the presuppositions maintained by the documentary hypothesis: "The representation of a course of history is *a priori* to be regarded as untrue and unhistorical if supernatural factors interpose in it. Everything must be naturalised and likened to the course of natural history."

In his work *De Profeten en de Profetie onder Israel* (Vol. I, pp. 5, 585), A. Kuenen states his anti-supernaturalist position:

"So long as we attribute a part of Israel's religious life directly to God and allow supernatural or immediate revelation to intervene even in one instance, just so long does our view of the whole remain inexact, and we see ourselves obliged to do violence here or there to the well-assured content of the historical accounts. It is only the assumption of a natural development that takes account of all the phenomena."

In *De Godsdienst van Israel* (Vol. I, p. 111), Kuenen confesses that "the familiar intercourse of the divinity with the patriarchs constitutes for me one of the determining considerations against the historical character of the narratives."

The idea that there was no supernatural intervention on the part of God in the affairs of the Israelites has not been abandoned.

Langdon B. Gilkey, formerly of Vanderbilt University, now with the University of Chicago, describes the biblical account of the Exodus-Sinai experience as "the acts Hebrews believed God might have done and the words he might have said had he done and said them—but of course we recognize he did not." (Gilkey, COTBL, 148)

Julius Wellhausen, in his *Israelitische und Juedische Geschichte* (p. 12), ridicules the account of the miracles that occurred at Sinai when God gave Moses the law, saying "Who can seriously believe all that?"

Referring to the Hebrews' crossing of the Red Sea, Gilkey writes: "We deny the miraculous character of the event and say its cause was merely an East wind, and then we point to the unusual response of Hebrew faith." (Gilkey, COTBL, 150)

In contrast to these anti-supernaturalist views, W. H. Green concludes that "we cannot intelligently nor safely overlook the palpable bias against the supernatural which has infected the critical theories. . . . All the acknowledged leaders of the movement have, without exception, scouted the reality of miracles and prophecy and immediate divine revelation in their genuine and evangelical sense. Their theories are all inwrought with naturalistic presuppositions, which cannot be disentangled from them without their falling to pieces." (Green, THCP, 157)

J. Orr, speaking of the nineteenth century documentation scholarship (very much applicable to the twentieth century), states that "for now the fact becomes apparent, there is, indeed, not the least attempt to disguise it—that, to a large and influential school of critical inquirers—those, moreover, who have had the most to do with the shaping of the current critical theories—this question of a supernatural origin for the religion of Israel is already foreclosed; is ruled out at the start as a 'a priori' inadmissible." (Orr, TPOT, 12)

2C. Form Criticism

Rudolph Bultmann, one of the foremost proponents of form criticism, lays the initial groundwork for his discipline:

The historical method includes the presupposition that history is a unity in the sense of a closed continuum of effects in which individual events are connected by the succession of cause and effect. This does not mean that the process of history is determined by the causal law and that there are no free decisions of men whose actions determine the course of historical happenings. But even a free decision does not happen without cause, without a motive; and the task of the historian is to come to know the motives of actions. All decisions and all deeds have their causes and consequences; and the historical method presupposes that it is possible in principle to exhibit these and their connection and thus to understand the whole historical process as a closed unity.

This closedness means that the continuum of historical happenings cannot be rent by the interference of supernatural, transcendent powers and that therefore there is no "miracle" in this sense of the word. Such a miracle would be an event whose cause did not lie within history. . . . It is in accordance with such a method as this that the science of history goes to work on all historical documents. And there cannot be any exceptions in the case of biblical texts if the latter are at all to be understood historically. (Bultmann, KM, 291–92)

Bultmann presupposes that twentieth-century people take it for granted that the events of nature and history are nowhere interrupted by the intervention of supernat-

> *An historical fact which involves a resurrection from the dead is utterly inconceivable.*
>
> —RUDOLPH BULTMANN

ural powers. According to Bultmann, "an historical fact which involves a resurrection from the dead is utterly inconceivable." (Bultmann, KM, 39)

Norman Perrin, in *The Promise of Bultmann*, states that "perhaps most important of all for Bultmann is the fact that not only are there no unique events in history, but also that history which historians investigate is a closed chain of cause and effect. The idea of God as a force intervening in history as an effective cause is one which a historian cannot contemplate." (Perrin, TPB, 38)

"It follows," adds Perrin, "from what we have said that God cannot be the effective cause of an event within history; only a man or a people's faith in God can be that. Moreover, since the process of history is uniform and not random—if it were random any kind of historical existence would become impossible—then it follows that there never has been and there never will be an event within history (that is, world history) of which God has been or will be the effective cause." (Perrin, TPB, 90–91)

Bultmann rejects the possibility of "miracles." Writing in *Jesus Christ and Mythology*, he says that "modern man acknowledges as reality only such phenomena or events as are comprehensible within the framework of the rational order of the universe. He does not acknowledge miracles because they do not fit into this lawful order." (Bultmann, JCM, 37–38)

Bultmann continues his argument in *Kerygma and Myth*:

It is not at all relevant for critics to point out that the world-picture of natural science today is no longer that of the nineteenth century, and it is naive to seek to use the relativization of the causal law to refurbish the belief in miracle, as if by this relativization the door had been opened for the intrusion of transcendent powers. Does science today renounce experiment? So long as it does not, it stands in the tradition of thought that began in Greece with the question of the cause, and the demand that a reason be given for things. (Bultmann, KM, 120–21)

Writing on anti-supernaturalism and Bultmann, Herman Ridderbos comments:

It is inconceivable to a modern thinker that it is possible for one who is dead to be brought again into physical existence; for modern man has learned to understand the organization of the human body. Modern man can conceive of God's action only as an event which intervenes and transforms the reality of his own "essential" life; that is to say, an event in the reality of his existence as spirit. He cannot conceive of the acts of redemption insofar as they are concerned with man as a natural reality and with the natural reality of the whole cosmos. It is at the same time implied that the conception of Christ, as a pre-existent heavenly being, and of the removal of man into a heavenly world of light, and the clothing of man in a heavenly body, is not only rationally unthinkable but also is meaningless; it says nothing. (Ridderbos, B, 18)

Pierre Benoit, after analyzing the method of form criticism concludes:

Behind all these relatively new methods, new at least in their technical application, we discover one fundamental thesis which is not itself new at all. This is the denial of the supernatural which we are so accustomed to meeting in works of modern rationalist criticism. It is a thesis which, once it is stripped of its various masks, literary, historical or sociological analysis, reveals its true identity—it is a philosophical one. (Benoit, JG, Vol. I, 39)

3C. Other Proponents

W. J. Sparrow-Simpson points out that David Strauss

long ago fully admitted that "the origin of that faith in the disciples is fully accounted for if we look upon the Resurrection of Jesus, as the Evangelists describe it, as an external miraculous occurrence" (New Life, i, 399). Nothing can be more genuine than Strauss' acknowledgment that he was controlled by *a priori* considerations, to which the fact of a resurrection was inadmissible:

"Here, then, we stand on that decisive point where, in the presence of the accounts of the miraculous Resurrection of Jesus, we either acknowledge the inadmissibility of the natural and historical view of the life of Jesus, and must consequently retract all that precedes and give up our whole undertaking, or pledge ourselves to make out the possibility of the results of these accounts, *i.e.* the origin of the belief in the Resurrection of Jesus without any correspondingly miraculous fact."

This is his conscious, deliberate undertaking—to give an explanation of the evidence on the presupposition of a certain view of the universe. It invariably amounts to this. At the grave in Joseph's garden two antagonistic world-theories confront each other (cf. Ihmels, *Auferstehung*, p. 27; Luthardt, *Glaubenslehre*).

The ultimate reasons for rejecting the Resurrection evidence are not historical. As Sabatier truly says, "Even if the differences were perfectly reconciled, or even did not exist at all, men who will not admit the miraculous would none the less decisively reject the witness. As Zeller frankly acknowledges, their rejection is based on a philosophic theory, and not on historic considerations" (*L'Apôtre* Paul, p. 42). (Sparrow-Simpson, RC, 511)

Schubert Ogden, a form critic, cites Glauben and Verstehn ("The Problem of Miracles," *Religion in Life*, I, Winter,

1957–58, p. 63): "The idea of miracle has become impossible for us today because we understand nature as a lawful occurrence and must therefore understand miracle as an event that breaks this lawful continuum. Such an idea is no longer acceptable to us." (Ogden, CWM, 33)

F. C. Burkitt, in *Jesus Christ*, acknowledges the following: "I confess that I see no way to treat the Feeding of the Five Thousand except by a process of frank rationalization. . . . The solution which alone appeals to me is that Jesus told the disciples to distribute their scanty store, and that their example made those who were well provided share with those who had little." (Burkitt, JC, 32)

Ernst Käsemann vividly expresses the opinion of the anti-supernaturalist. He writes about the words and deeds of Jesus in the Gospels as "an unbroken series of divine revelations and mighty acts, which have no common basis of comparison with any other human life and thus can no longer be comprehended within the category of the historical." (Käsemann, ENTT, 30)

3A. SCIENCE AND MIRACLES

1B. Definition of Miracles
"The first step in this, as in all other discussions, is to come to a clear understanding as to the meaning of the terms employed. Argumentation about whether miracles are

> Subtract miracles from Islam, Buddhism, Confucianism, or Taoism, and you have essentially the same religion left. Subtract miracles from Christianity, and you have nothing but the cliches and platitudes most American Christians get weekly (and weakly) from their pulpits.
>
> —PETER KREEFT

possible and, if possible, credible, is mere beating the air until the arguers have agreed what they mean by the word 'miracle.'" (Huxley, WTHH, 153)

We are defining miracles as special acts of God in the world. Since miracles are special acts of God, they can only exist where there is a God who can perform such acts.

2B. Miracles in a Christian Framework
Peter Kreeft observes that the role of miracles in Christianity is unique among the world's religions:

> The clinching argument for the importance of miracles is that God thought they were important enough to use them to found and perpetuate his Church.
>
> In fact, all the essential and distinctive elements of Christianity are miracles: creation, revelation (first to the Jews), the giving of the law, prophesies, the Incarnation, the Resurrection, the Ascension and the Second Coming and Last Judgment.
>
> Subtract miracles from Islam, Buddhism, Confucianism, or Taoism, and you have essentially the same religion left. Subtract miracles from Christianity, and you have nothing but the cliches and platitudes most American Christians get weekly (and weakly) from their pulpits. Nothing distinctive, no reason to be a Christian rather than something else. (Kreeft, CMP, 273)

Sproul, Gerstner, and Lindsley argue that miracles are also indispensable to the demonstration of the case for Christianity: "Technically . . . miracles are visible and external and perceivable by both converted and unconverted alike, carrying with them the power to convince, if not to convert. Certainly, as far as apologetics is concerned, the visible miracle is indispensable to the case for Christianity which case would thereby be demonstrated sound whether anyone believed it or not, whether anyone was converted or not, whether anyone experienced an internal 'miracle' or not. The proof would be demonstrative even if all people willfully refused to acquiesce in it." (Sproul, CA, 145)

3B. The Limitations of Science in the Realm of Miracles and the Supernatural

J. W. N. Sullivan, in his book *The Limitations of Science*, shows that since the publication of Einstein's *Special Theory of Relativity* (1905) and Planck's endeavors with "black-body radiation," scientists are faced with "the vicissitudes of so-called natural law in an uncharted and unobstructed universe." (Sullivan, TLS, 79)

Sullivan writes: "What is called the modern 'revolution in science' consists in the fact that the Newtonian outlook which dominated the scientific world for nearly two hundred years, has been found insufficient. It is in process of being replaced by a different outlook, and, although the reconstruction is by no means complete, it is already apparent that the philosophical implications of the new outlook are very different from those of the old one." (Sullivan, TLS, 138)

James R. Moore, in *Christianity for the Tough Minded* (edited by John Warwick Montgomery), adds that "today scientists will admit that no one knows enough about 'natural law' to say that any event is necessarily a violation of it. They agree that an individual's non-statistical sample of time and space is hardly sufficient ground on which to base immutable generalizations concerning the nature of the entire universe. Today what we commonly term 'natural law' is in fact only our *inductive and statistical descriptions of natural phenomena*." (Moore, SC: TPC, 79)

John Montgomery denotes that the anti-supernatural position is both "philosophically and scientifically irresponsible." First of all, philosophically: "because no one below the status of a god could know the universe so well as to eliminate miracles *a priori*." Secondly, scientifically: "because in the age of Einsteinian physics (so different from the world of Newtonian absolutes in which Hume formulated his classic anti-miraculous argument) the universe has opened up to all possibilities, 'any attempt to state a "universal law of causation" must prove futile' (Max Black, *Models and Metaphor*), and only a careful consideration of the empirical testimony for a miraculous event can determine whether in fact it has or has not occurred." (Montgomery, CFTM, 32)

The discussion continues in *History and Christianity*:

> But can the modern man accept a "miracle" such as the resurrection? The answer is a surprising one: The resurrection has to be accepted by us just because we are modern men, men living in the Einstein relativistic age. For us, unlike people of the Newtonian epoch, the universe is no longer a tight safe, predictable playing-field in which we know all the rules. Since Einstein no modern has had the right to rule out the possibility of events because of prior knowledge of "natural law."
>
> The only way we can know whether an event can occur is to see whether in fact it has occurred. The problem of "miracles," then, must be solved in the realm of historical investigation, not in the realm of philosophical speculation. (Montgomery, HC, 75–76)

"And note," continues Montgomery, "that a historian, in facing an alleged 'miracle,' is really facing nothing new. All historical events are unique, and the test of their factual character can be only the accepted documentary approach that we have followed here. No historian has a right to a closed system of natural causation, for, as the Cornell logician Max Black has shown in a recent essay, the very concept of cause is 'a peculiar, unsystematic, and erratic notion'

(*Models and Metaphors,* p. 169)." (Montgomery, HC, 75–76)

Vincent Taylor, a prominent form critic, warns against too great a dogmatism with regard to the miraculous:

It is far too late today to dismiss the question by saying that "miracles are impossible"; that stage of the discussion is definitely past. Science takes a much humbler and truer view of natural law than was characteristic of former times; we now know that the "laws of Nature" are convenient summaries of existing knowledge. Nature is not a "closed system," and miracles are not "intrusions" into an "established order." In the last fifty years we have been staggered too often by discoveries which at one time were pronounced impossible. We have lived to hear of the breaking up of the atom, and to find scientists themselves speaking of the universe as "more like a great thought than like a great machine." This change of view does not, of course, accredit the miraculous; but it does mean that, given the right conditions, miracles are not impossible; no scientific or philosophic dogma stands in the way. (Taylor, TFGT, 13)

4B. Hume's Philosophical Argument

1C. Hume's Position

A miracle is a violation of the laws of nature; and as a firm and unalterable experience has established these laws, the proof against a miracle, from the very nature of the fact, is as entire as any argument from experience can possibly be imagined. . . . Nothing is esteemed a miracle if it ever happens in the common course of nature. It is no miracle that a man, seemingly in good health, should die on a sudden; . . . But it is a miracle that a dead man should come to life; because that has never been observed in any age or country. There must, therefore, be a uniform experience against every miraculous event, otherwise the

event would not merit that appellation. (Hume, ECHU, 126–27)

2C. Rebuttals

Instead of weighing the evidence in favor of miracles, Hume simply plays statistical games. Geisler puts it this way:

Hume does not really weigh evidence for miracles; rather, he adds evidence against them. Since death occurs over and over again and resurrection occurs only on rare occasions at best, Hume simply adds up all the deaths against the very few alleged resurrections and rejects the latter. . . . But this does not involve weighing evidence to determine whether or not a given person, say Jesus of Nazareth . . . has been raised from the dead. It is simply adding up the evidence of all other occasions where people have died and have not been raised and using it to overwhelm any possible evidence that some person who died was brought back to life. . . . Second, this argument equates quantity of evidence and probability. It says, in effect, that we should always believe what is most probable (in the sense of "enjoying the highest odds"). But this is silly. On

> But this is silly. On these grounds a dice player should not believe the dice show three sixes on the first roll, since the odds against it are 1,635,013,559,600 to 1! What Hume seems to overlook is that wise people base their beliefs on facts, not simply on odds. Sometimes the "odds" against an event are high (based on past observation), but the evidence for the event is otherwise very good (based on current observation or reliable testimony).
>
> —NORMAN GEISLER

these grounds a dice player should not believe the dice show three sixes on the first roll, since the odds against it are 1,635,013,559,600 to 1! What Hume seems to overlook is that wise people base their beliefs on facts, not simply on odds. Sometimes the "odds" against an event are high (based on past observation), but the evidence for the event is otherwise very good (based on current observation or reliable testimony). Hume's argument confuses quantity of evidence with the quality of evidence. Evidence should be weighed, not added. (Geisler, MMM, as cited in Geivett, IDM, 78–79)

Moreover, Hume confuses the probability of historical events with the way in which scientists employ probability to formulate scientific law. As Nash explains:

Critics of Hume have complained that his argument is based on a defective view of probability. For one thing, Hume treats the probability of events in history like miracles in the same way he treats the probability of the recurring events that give rise to the formulation of scientific laws. In the case of scientific laws, probability is tied to the frequency of occurrence; the more times scientists observe similar occurrences under similar conditions, the greater the probability that their formulation of a law is correct. But historical events including miracles are different; the events of history are unique and nonrepeatable. Therefore, treating historical events including miracles with the same notion of probability the scientist uses in formulating his laws ignore a fundamental difference between the two subject matters. (Nash, FR, 234)

Another strong rebuttal against Hume's position that "nothing is esteemed a miracle if it ever happens in the common course of nature" is made by C. S. Lewis. Lewis cogently answers Hume's assertion: "Now of course we must agree with Hume that if there is absolutely 'uniform experience' against miracles, if in other words they have never happened, why then they never have. Unfortunately, we know the experience against them to be uniform only if we know

that all the reports of them are false. And we can know all the reports of them to be false only if we know already that miracles have never occurred. In fact, we are arguing in a circle." (Lewis, M, 105)

"The critical historian, confronted with some story of a miracle, will usually dismiss it out of hand . . . to justify his procedure, he will have to appeal to precisely the principle which Hume advanced: the 'absolute impossibility of miraculous nature' or the events attested must, 'in the eyes of all reasonable people . . . alone be regarded as a sufficient refutation.'" (Flew, M, as cited in Edwards, EP, 351–52) In other words, it is a circular argument: If miracles are impossible, then the report of any miraculous event must be false, and therefore, miracles are impossible.

Merald Westphal, in his review of "The Historian and the Believer," writes:

If God exists, miracles are not merely logically possible, but really and genuinely possible at every moment. The only condition hindering the actualisation of this possibility lies in the divine will. (For the theologian to say that scientific knowledge has rendered belief in miracles intellectually irresponsible is to affirm that scientific knowledge provides us with knowledge of limits within which the divine will always operates.) Since the question of morality has been introduced, one may perhaps be permitted to inquire about the intellectual integrity of such an affirmation. Is peace with one's age to be purchased at any cost? (Westphal, THB, 280)

4A. A PROPER APPROACH TO HISTORY

Before we are able to give a proper approach to history, it is necessary that we give a rebuttal to the relativist's argument.

1B. Rebuttal to the Relativist's Arguments

1C. History Is Not Directly Observable.

While the historian does not have direct access to the past, the residue of the past, things that have really existed, is directly accessible to him. . . . For example, archaeological data furnish direct access to the objects of the historian's investigation.

—WILLIAM LANE CRAIG

Geisler explains what must be meant by objective: "If by 'objective' one means *absolute* knowledge, then of course no human historian can be objective. This we will grant. On the other hand, if 'objective' means a *fair but revisable* presentation that reasonable men should accept, then the door is still open to the possibility of objectivity." (Geisler, CA, 290, emphasis his)

In response to the relativist claim that the historian is disadvantaged in comparison to the scientist, Craig writes:

First, it is naive to think that the scientist always has direct access to his objects of study. Not only is the scientist largely dependent on the reports of others' research (which, interestingly, constitute for him historical documents) for his own work, but furthermore, the objects of the scientist's research are often only indirectly accessible, especially in the highly theoretical fields like physics.

Second, while the historian does not have direct access to the past, the residue of the past, things that have really existed, is directly accessible to him. . . . For example, archaeological data furnish direct access to the objects of the historian's investigation. (Craig, RF, 176)

Hence, "the historian, no less than the scientist, has the tools for determining what really happened in the past. The lack of direct access to the original facts or events does not hinder the one more than the other." (Geisler, CA, 291)

2C. The Fragmentary Nature of Historical Accounts

Fischer points out the error in this argument: "Relativism mistakenly argues that because all historical accounts must be partial, in the sense of incomplete, that they must also be partial in the sense of false. An incomplete account can be an objectively true account; it cannot be the whole truth." (Fischer, HF, 42)

Geisler adds:

The fact that accounts of history are fragmentary does not destroy its objectivity . . . history need be no less objective than geology simply because it depends on fragmentary accounts. Scientific knowledge is also partial and depends on assumptions and an overall framework which may prove to be inadequate upon the discovery of more facts.

Whatever difficulty there may be, from a strictly scientific point of view, in filling in the gaps between the facts, once one has assumed a philosophical stance toward the world, the problem of objectivity in general is resolved. If there is a God, then the overall picture is already drawn; the facts of history will merely fill in the details of its meaning. (Geisler, CA, 292–93)

3C. The Selective Nature of Historical Methodology and Interpretive Structuring of the Facts of History

"The fact that the historian must select his materials does not automatically make history purely subjective. Jurors make judgments 'beyond reasonable doubt' without having all the evidence. If the historian has the relevant and crucial evidence, it will be sufficient to attain objectivity. One need not know everything in order to know something." (Geisler, CA, 293)

4C. The Historian Cannot Avoid Value Judgments

It should be noted that: "This by no means makes historical objectivity impossible. Objectivity means to be fair in dealing with the facts. It means to present *what* happened as correctly as possible. Further, objectivity means that when one interprets *why* these events occurred, the language of the historian should ascribe to these events the value which they really had in their original context. . . . Once the world view has been determined, value judgments are not undesirable or merely subjective; they are in fact essential and objectively demanded." (Geisler, CA, 295–96, emphasis his)

5C. Every Historian Is a Product of His or Her Time and Worldview

While it is true that every historian is a product of his or her time, as Geisler notes, "it does not follow that because the *historian* is a product of his time that his *history* is also a product of the time. . . . The criticism confuses the *content* of knowledge and the *process* of attaining it. It confuses the *formation* of a view with its *verification*. Where one derives a hypothesis is not essentially related to how he can establish its truth." (Geisler, CA, 296–97, emphasis his)

Fischer similarly notes "there is a confusion between the way knowledge is acquired and the validity of that knowledge. An American historian may chauvinistically assert that the United States declared its independence from England in 1776. That statement is true, no matter what the motives of its maker may have been. On the other hand, an English historian may patriotically insist that England declared its independence from the Unites States in 1776. That assertion is false, and always will be." (Fischer, HF, 42)

6C. The Selection and Arrangement of Materials Is Subject to the Historian

Concerning the possibility of prejudice, bias, or passion obscuring the objectivity of history, philosopher of history W. H. Walsh has noted "It is doubtful, all the same, whether we should regard bias of this kind as a serious obstacle to the attainment of objective truth in history. It is doubtful for the simple reason that we all know from our own experience that this kind of bias can be corrected or at any rate allowed for. . . . And we do hold that historians ought to be free from personal prejudice and condemn those historians who are not." (Walsh, IPH, 101)

Even Van A. Harvey notes that "it can be questioned, however, whether passion and objectivity are mutually exclusive, if by objectivity one means the capacity to withhold judgment until one has good reason for making it. Might not a judge who is also the father of a son accused of a crime be even more objective in his search for the truth than one who was less interested?" (Harvey, HB, 212)

7C. Conclusion: What Can History Establish?

We conclude: "Absolute objectivity is possible only for an infinite Mind. Finite minds must be content with systematic consistence, that is, fair but revisable attempts to reconstruct the past based on an established framework of reference which comprehensively and consistently incorporates all the facts into the overall sketch provided by the frame of reference." (Geisler, CA, 298)

"Unless one can settle the question as to whether this is a theistic or nontheistic world on grounds independent of the mere facts themselves, there is no way to determine the objective meaning of history. If, on the other hand, there are good reasons to believe that this is a theistic universe, . . . then objectivity in history is a possibility. For once the overall viewpoint is established, it is simply a matter of finding the view of history that is most consistent with that overall system. That is, systematic consistence is the test for objectivity in historical matters as well as in scientific matters." (Geisler, CA, 298)

2B. A Critical Method

The Erlangen historian Ethelbert Stauffer gives us some suggestions for how to approach history:

What do we [as historians] when we experience surprises which run counter to all our expectations, perhaps all our convictions and even our period's whole understanding of

> The purpose of the historian is not to construct a history from preconceived notions and to adjust it to his own liking, but to reproduce it from the best evidence and to let it speak for itself.
>
> —PHILIP SCHAFF

truth? We say as one great historian used to say in such instances: "It is surely possible." And why not? For the critical historian nothing is impossible. (Stauffer, JHS, 17)

1C. Schaff

The historian Philip Schaff adds to the above:

The purpose of the historian is not to construct a history from preconceived notions and to adjust it to his own liking, but to reproduce it from the best evidence and to let it speak for itself. (Schaff, HCC, Vol. I., 175)

2C. Sider

Ronald Sider, professor of history at the Messiah College campus at Temple University, details how a historian should deal with presuppositions:

What does the critical historian do when his evidence points very strongly to the reality of an event which contradicts his expectations and goes against the naturalistic view of reality? I submit that he must follow his critically analyzed sources. It is unscientific to begin with the philosophical presupposition that miracles cannot occur. Unless we avoid such one-sided presuppositions, historical interpretation becomes mere propaganda.

We have a right to demand good evidence for an alleged event which we have not experienced, but we dare not judge reality by our limited experience. (Sider, ACE, 31)

3C. Montgomery Concludes

Montgomery concludes that

we have no right to begin with the presupposition that Jesus can be no more than a man. For then, obviously, our conclusions may simply reflect our preconceptions instead of representing the actual content of the documents. We must, in other words, objectively try to discover the picture Jesus and his contemporaries had of him whether we agree with it or not. The question for us is not whether Jesus is pictured as a man. Virtually no one today would question this, for the records tell us that he was hungry and tired, that he wept, that he suffered and died, in short, that he was human.

The question we face today is whether he was depicted as no more than a man. (Montgomery, HC, 48–49)

3B. An Appropriate Investigation

A critical historian should "decide the historicity of alleged miracles on the basis of the evidence that can be adduced for each individual case." (Sider, THTMPNM, 313)

The application of the above historical inquiry is greatly enhanced with the scientific knowledge we have today. "The scientific description," comments Professor Sider, "of the observed regularity of nature was a very significant factor in the development of a more critical attitude toward reports of unusual events of all kinds. The fact that an alleged event is not what one would expect on the basis of observed regularity in a given scientific field 'activates a warning light' [Harvey, "The Historian and the Believer," p. 225]." (Sider, THTMPNM, 314)

At this point one must proceed with caution and carefully examine the data about the alleged event.

For example—the resurrection of Jesus: A critical historian would want to check out the witnesses, confirm the fact of death by crucifixion, go over the burial procedures, and confirm the reports that Jesus was alive on the third day and that the tomb was empty. Then one would consider every possible explanation of the above data. At this stage one would want to peruse other corroborative evidence and from this draw an appropriate conclusion.

The historian cannot prove that the resurrection and the subsequent empty tomb was a direct intervention by God. Ronald Sider states that

the historian *qua* historian of course could never prove that an unusual event was inexplicable in terms of natural causes, much less that it was due to direct divine activity. (At best the historian could say that the evidence for the event was strong enough to warrant his affirming its historicity even though the event was inexplicable in terms of present scientific knowledge.) But he could never rule out the possibility that future scientific knowledge would be able to explain the event as one instance of a regularly recurring pattern. [See Patrick Nowell-Smith, "Miracles," in *New Essays in Philosophical Theology*, ed. A. Flew and A. MacIntyre (Macmillan, New York, 1964), pp. 243–53, and especially p. 245.] But the historian's inability to prove that the unusual event is a "miracle" does not preclude his ruling on its facticity. In the case of the alleged resurrection of Jesus of Nazareth, the historian *qua* historian could never demonstrate that *God* raised Jesus, but he might, if he found the evidence adequate, conclude that Jesus was probably alive on the third day. (Sider, THTMPNM, 317–18)

One's conclusion could be reached only after sufficient evidence indicates that "Jesus probably was alive on the third day."

Orr warns us that "whatever our personal convictions—and of these, of course, we cannot divest ourselves—we must, in conducting our argument, place ourselves in as

> Faith does not, however, mean a leap in the dark, an irrational credulity, a believing against evidences and against reason. It means believing in the light of historical facts, consistent with evidences, on the basis of witnesses. It would be impossible to believe in the resurrection of Jesus apart from the historical facts of His death, His burial, and the witness of the disciples.
>
> —GEORGE E. LADD

absolutely neutral an attitude of mind as we can. We must try to see the facts exactly as they are. If differences emerge, let them be noted. If the facts are such as to compel us to assume a special origin for this religion, let that come to light in the course of the inquiry." (Orr, TPOT, 14)

"The ultimate test," continues Orr, "in either case is fitness to meet the facts." (Orr, TPOT, 14)

George E. Ladd, speaking of the inability

to recount the Resurrection in natural terms, writes that the Christian faith affirms that

in the resurrection of Christ an event occurred in history, in time and in space, among men which is without historical explanation or causality, but is a direct unmediated act of God. Indeed, *when the historian can explain the resurrection of Jesus in purely human terms,* those who hold anything like an evangelical faith will be faced with a problem of shattering dimensions. Faith does not, however, mean a leap in the dark, an irrational credulity, a believing against evidences and against reason. It means believing in the light of historical facts, consistent with evidences, on the basis of witnesses. It would be impossible to believe in the resurrection of Jesus apart from the historical facts of His death, His burial, and the witness of the disciples. (Ladd, TNTC, 187, emphasis his)

"If historical criticism," concludes Ladd, "could establish that the great events of redemptive history did not occur, any evangelical faith would be impossible. If the historical critic could prove that Jesus never rose from the tomb, Christian faith would be shattered. Scripture itself affirms as much (1 Corinthians 15:12–19)." (Ladd, TNTC, 86)

The very story of Christianity is that God has intervened in history, and these acts or interventions are beyond natural explanation when it comes to analyzing their cause. The author firmly believes that a living God who acts within history would obviously be beyond "natural human explanation."

What men have done today is to rule God out by a narrow naturalistic definition of history. "If historical study," advises Wolfhart Pannenberg, "keeps itself free from the dogmatic postulate that all events are of the same kind, and at the same time remains critical toward its own procedure, there does not have to be any impossibility *in principle*

in asserting the historicity of the resurrection of Jesus." (Pannenberg, RAH, 264–65, emphasis his)

Robert M. Horn *(The Book That Speaks for Itself,* used by permission of InterVarsity Press, Downers Grove, Ill.) is very helpful in exploring people's biases in approaching history:

To put it at its most obvious, a person who denies God's existence will not subscribe to belief in the Bible.

A Muslim, convinced that God cannot beget, will not accept as the Word of God, a book that teaches that Christ is the only begotten Son of God.

Some believe that God is not personal, but rather the Ultimate, the Ground of Being. Such will be predisposed to reject the Bible as God's personal self-revelation. On their premise, the Bible cannot be the personal word of "I AM WHO I AM" (Ex. 3:14).

Others rule out the supernatural. They will not be likely to give credence to the book which teaches that Christ rose from the dead.

Still others hold that God cannot communicate His truth undistorted through sinful men; hence they regard the Bible as, at least in parts, no more than human. (Horn, TBTSI, 10)

Gerhardus Vos is very explicit in his analysis of the anti-supernaturalist approach:

Historical study has become a powerful instrument in the service of the anti-supernaturalistic spirit of the modern age. Professing to be strictly neutral and to seek nothing but the truth it has in point of fact directed its assault along the whole line against the outstanding miraculous events of Sacred History. It has rewritten this history so as to make the supernatural elements disappear from its record. It has called into question the historicity of one after the other of the great redemptive acts of God. We need not say here that the apologetic answer to these attacks has been able and fully satisfactory to every intelligent believer. But the Christian public at large is not always able to distinguish between well-authenticated facts as such and historical constructions in which the facts have been manipulated and their interpretation shaped by *a priori* philosophical principles. People are accustomed to look upon history as the realm of facts *par excellence,* second only to pure science in the absolute certainty of its concrete results. They do not as easily detect in historical argumentation as they would in philosophic reasoning the naturalistic premises which predetermine the conclusions. It is not difficult, therefore, to give the popular mind the impression that it is confronted with an irrefutable array of evidence discrediting the Bible facts, whereas in reality it is asked to accept a certain philosophy of the facts made to discredit the Bible. Hence there has arisen in many quarters a feeling of uneasiness and concern with regard to the historical basis of facts on which Christianity has hitherto been supposed to rest. (Vos, BTONT, 293)

Bultmann, one of the more radical form critics, speaks about the need for objectivity and the need for a freedom from presuppositions:

And just for this reason the demand for freedom from presuppositions, for an unprejudiced approach, which is valid for all science, is also valid for historical research. The historian is certainly not allowed to presuppose the results of his research, and he is obliged to keep back, to reduce to silence, his personal desires with regard to these results. (Bultmann, HE, 122)

Bultmann continues this thought in *Existence and Faith:* "The question whether exegesis without presuppositions is possible must be answered affirmatively if 'without presuppositions' means 'without presupposing the results of the exegesis.' In this sense,

exegesis without presuppositions is not only possible but demanded."

Bultmann qualifies this by saying that in another sense there is no such thing as presuppositionless research. He asserts: "However the one presupposition that cannot be

> If there was no record of miracles in the Old and New Testaments, it may be questioned whether so much zeal would have been displayed in endeavouring to throw doubt on the authenticity of their contents.
>
> —A.H. SAYCE

dismissed is the historical method of interrogating the text." (Bultmann, EF, 289–90)

With regard to presuppositionless scholarship, Swedish scholar Seth Erlandsson states:

But at the same time that this is maintained it is often said that we must presuppose that the Bible is of the same nature as any other human literature. By this assertion it is not merely meant that the Bible was written in human language and contains the literary finesses or expressions found in human literature. It is presupposed that the Bible "like all other products of human activity contains mistakes and inaccuracies" and that all that is related in it including its ideological content, is altogether conditioned by human forces and has a complete explanation in this—worldly factors. If an other-worldly factor has intervened, then it cannot be analyzed historically, and for this reason we must presuppose that such an other-worldly factor, if it exists, has only made use of this-worldly causes, (so that what happened can be fully explained in terms of these latter, that is, this-worldly causes). (Sullivan, TLS, 8–9)

Erlandsson's point is that even those who

advocate no presuppositions still approach the Scriptures with them.

I contend that by using the historical method, as Bultmann defines it, as a closed continuum of effects—closed to transcendental intervention—the presuppositions will inevitably presuppose the results.

Orr correctly concludes that "to assume beforehand, in an inquiry which turns on this very point, that the religion of Israel presents no features but such as are explicable out of natural causes—that no higher factors are needed to account for it—is to prejudge the whole question." (Orr, TPOT, 13)

To the radical critic, the presence of the miraculous is sufficient evidence for rejecting its historicity, or at least sufficient reason to reject the "credibility of its witnesses."

One would wonder, along with A. H. Sayce: "if there was no record of miracles in the Old and New Testaments, it may be questioned whether so much zeal would have been displayed in endeavouring to throw doubt on the authenticity of their contents." (Sayce, MFHCF, 126)

The Christian should not permit the "modern historians" or "radical critics" to determine the "limits of its discipline. . . . On the contrary," writes Ladd, "Christian theology must recognize that the critical-historical method is a child of rationalism and as such is based on a naturalistic world view." (Ladd, TNTC, 190)

The radical critics are not lacking when it comes to ability and scholarship. The problem is not their lack of knowledge of the evidence but rather their hermeneutics or approach to biblical criticism based upon their worldview.

Birger Gerhardsson has appropriately remarked that, "the validity of its results depends on the validity of its first principles." (Gerhardsson, TTEC, 6)

5A. IN SUMMARY

1B. Anti-Supernaturalist Presuppositions
The anti-supernaturalist bases his thinking on the *presupposition* that God has not intervened in history. Therefore he rejects evidence indicating the supernatural no matter how convincing.

2B. Both conservative and radical critics must beware of prejudices.

3B. Modern science no longer views nature as a "closed system," and therefore cannot insist that miracles do not exist.

4B. The historian should draw his conclusions from the facts at his disposal, not force the facts to conform to his presuppositions.

13
ARCHAEOLOGY AND BIBLICAL CRITICISM

Before considering the positions of negative biblical criticism, it will be helpful to know how the young science of archaeology has contributed to the field of biblical criticism. The positions of some critics can be discounted from the beginning, simply because certain archaeological discoveries have ruled out their theories.

1A. BASIC CONTRIBUTIONS TO BIBLICAL CRITICISM

Following are just a few of the contributions that the science of archaeology has made to the field of biblical criticism:

1B. Archaeology Enhances the "Scientific Study" of the Text

Archaeological discoveries have contributed to the analysis of manuscripts, the understanding of technical words, and the development of more dependable lexicons.

2B. Archaeology Acts as a Check in the Area of Critical Studies (Radical and Conservative)

H. M. Orlinsky, in *Ancient Israel,* discusses a new attitude that has developed regarding the negative results of radical criticism: "More and more the older view that the biblical data were suspect and even likely to be false, unless corroborated by extra-biblical facts, is giving way to one which holds that, by and large, the biblical accounts are more likely to be true than false, unless clear cut evidence from sources outside the Bible demonstrates the reverse." (Orlinsky, AI, 6)

Reformed Jewish scholar Nelson Glueck has affirmed: "It is worth emphasizing that in all this work no archaeological discovery has ever controverted a single, properly understood Biblical statement." (Glueck, as cited in Montgomery, CFTM, 6)

L. H. Grollenberg adds that archaeological research greatly illumines the biblical background of many passages: "The views (of the older documentary critics) proceeded from a rather hasty application of the evolutionary pattern and were based too exclusively upon textual criticism. Thanks to the work of the archaeologist, the modern scholar is in closer contact with the actual world in which Israel had its roots.... Today ... many scholars feel a renewed confidence

in the skillful narrators of chapters 12–50 of Genesis, ... the stories of the patriarchs must be based on historical memories." (Grollenberg, AB, 35)

University of Chicago professor Raymond A. Bowman notes that archaeology helps provide a balance between the Bible and critical hypothesis: "The confirmation of the biblical narrative at most points has led to a new respect for biblical tradition and a more conservative conception of biblical history." (Bowman, OTRGW, as cited in Willoughby, SBTT, 30)

A. T. Olmstead, in "History, Ancient World, and the Bible," speaks about the unfolding of the documentary hypothesis: "While Old Testament Higher Critics spun out their increasingly minute dissections, and more and more took an agnostic attitude toward the recorded facts, this attitude was sharply challenged by exciting discoveries in the Near East." (Olmstead, HAWB, 13)

Albright, in "Archaeology Confronts Biblical Criticism," writes that "archaeological and inscriptional data have established the historicity of innumerable passages and statements of the Old Testament." (Albright, ACBC, 181)

Archaeology does not prove the Bible to be the Word of God. All it can do is confirm the basic historicity or authenticity of a narrative. It can show that a certain incident fits into the time it purports to be from. "We shall probably never," writes G. E. Wright, "be able to prove that Abram really existed ... but what we can prove is that his life and times, as reflected in the stories about him, fit perfectly within the early second millennium, but imperfectly within any later period." (Wright, BA, 40)

Millar Burrows of Yale recognized the value of archaeology in confirming the authenticity of the Scriptures:

The Bible is supported by archaeological evidence again and again. On the whole, there can be no question that the results of excavation have increased the respect of scholars for the Bible as a collection of historical documents. The confirmation is both general and specific. The fact that the record can be so often explained or illustrated by archaeological data shows that it fits into the framework of history as only a genuine product of ancient life could do. In addition to this general authentication, however, we find the record verified repeatedly at specific points. Names of places and persons turn up at the right places and in the right periods. (Burrows, HAHSB, 6)

Joseph Free comments that he once "thumbed through the book of Genesis and mentally noted that each of the fifty chapters are either illuminated or confirmed by some archaeological discovery—the same would be true for most of the remaining chapters of the Bible, both Old and New Testaments." (Free, AB, 340)

3B. Archaeology Helps to Illustrate and Explain Various Biblical Passages

Archaeology enhances our knowledge of the economic, cultural, social, and political background of biblical passages. It also contributes to the understanding of other religions that bordered Israel.

S. H. Horn, an archaeologist, gives an excellent example of how archaeological evidence helps in biblical study:

Archaeological explorations have shed some interesting light on the capture of Jerusalem by David. The biblical accounts of that capture (II Sam. 5:6–8 and I Chron. 11:6) are rather obscure without the help obtained from archaeological evidence. Take for example Second Samuel 5:8, which in the King James Version reads: "And David said on that

day, Whosoever getteth up to the gutter, and smiteth the Jebusites, and the lame and the blind, that are hated of David's soul, he shall be chief and captain." Add to this statement First Chronicles 11:6: "—So Joab the son of Zeruiah went first up and was chief."

Some years ago I saw a painting of the conquest of Jerusalem in which the artist showed a man climbing up a metal downspout, running on the outside face of the city wall. This picture was absurd, because ancient city walls had neither gutters nor downspouts, although they had weeping holes in the walls to drain water off. The Revised Standard Version, produced after the situation had become clear through archaeological discoveries made on the spot, translates 2 Samuel 5:8 as "And David said on that day, 'Whoever would smite the Jebusites, let him get up the water shaft to attack the lame and the blind, who are hated by David's soul.'"

Jerusalem in those days was a small city lying on a single spur of the hills on which the large city eventually stood. Its position was one of great natural strength, because it was surrounded on three sides by deep valleys. This was why the Jebusites boastfully declared that even blind and lame could hold their city against a powerful attacking army. But the water supply of the city was poor; the population was entirely dependent on a spring that lay outside the city on the eastern slope of the hill.

So that they could obtain water without having to go down to where the spring was located, the Jebusites had constructed an elaborate system of tunnels through the rock. First they had dug a horizontal tunnel, beginning at the spring and proceeding toward the center of the city. After digging for ninety feet they hit a natural cave. From the cave they dug a vertical shaft forty-five feet high, and from the end of the shaft a sloping tunnel 135 feet long and a staircase that ended at the surface of their city, 110 feet above the water level of the spring. The spring was then concealed from the outside so that no enemy could detect it.

To get water the Jebusite woman went down through the upper tunnel and let their water skins down the shaft to draw water from the cave, to which it was brought by natural flow through the horizontal tunnel that connected the cave with the spring.

However, one question remained unanswered. The excavations of R. A. S. Macalister and J. G. Duncan some forty years ago had uncovered a wall and a tower that were thought to be of Jebusite and Davidic origin respectively. This tract of wall ran along the rim of the hill of Ophel, west of the tunnel entrance. Thus the entrance was left outside the protective city wall, exposed to the attacks and interference of enemies. Why hadn't the tunnel been built to end inside the city? This puzzle has now been solved by the recent excavations of Kathleen Kenyon on Ophel. She found that Macalister and Duncan had given the wall and tower they discovered wrong dates; these things actually originated in the Hellenistic period. She uncovered the real Jebusite wall a little farther down the slope of the hill, east of the tunnel entrance, which now puts the entrance safely in the old city area. (Horn, RIOT, 15–16)

One also needs to realize that archaeology has not completely refuted the "radical critics." Burrows is quite clear on this point: "It is even more untrue to say that the fundamental attitudes and methods of modern scientific criticism have been refuted." (Burrows, WMTS, 292)

However, archaeology has shown that many tenets of radical criticism are invalid, and has called into question what has often been received as the "assured results of higher criticism."

Albright comments about the evidence for the extensive reign of Solomon, which was

> *Once more we find that the radical criticism of the past half-century must be corrected drastically.*
>
> —WILLIAM F. ALBRIGHT

questioned by the radical critics. He writes: "Once more we find that the radical criticism of the past half-century must be corrected drastically." (Albright, NLEHPC, 22)

Some people will make the unfounded assertion that supernaturalists and the non-supernaturalists can never agree on the results of archaeology because they exist in two totally different planes. Therefore, some conclude that we interpret archaeological findings according to our own viewpoints.

In summary we can conclude that (1) archaeology does not prove the Bible; it confirms its historicity and explains various passages. And (2) archaeology has not totally refuted the radical critics, but has challenged many of their presuppositions.

2A. THE RELIABILITY OF THE OLD TESTAMENT HISTORY

Not only do we have accurate copies of the Old Testament, but the contents of the manuscripts are historically reliable.

1B. Archaeological Confirmation of the Old Testament

William F. Albright, reputed to be one of the great archaeologists, states: "There can be no doubt that archaeology has confirmed the substantial historicity of Old Testament tradition." (Albright, ARI, 176)

Professor H. H. Rowley (cited by Donald F. Wiseman in *Revelation and the Bible*) claims that "it is not because scholars of today begin with more conservative presuppositions than their predecessors that they have a much greater respect for the Patriarchal stories than was formerly common, but because the evidence warrants it." (Rowley, as cited in Wiseman, ACOT, in Henry, RB, 305)

Merrill Unger summarizes: "Old Testament archaeology has rediscovered whole nations, resurrected important peoples, and in a most astonishing manner filled in historical gaps, adding immeasurably to the knowledge of biblical backgrounds." (Unger, AOT, 15)

Sir Frederic Kenyon says: "It is therefore legitimate to say that, in respect of that part of the Old Testament against which the disintegrating criticism of the last half of the nineteenth century was chiefly directed, the evidence of archaeology has been to reestablish its authority, and likewise to augment its value by rendering it more intelligible through a fuller knowledge of its background and setting. Archaeology has not yet said its last word; but the results already achieved confirm what faith would suggest, that the Bible can do nothing but gain from an increase of knowledge." (Kenyon, BA, 279)

Archaeology has produced an abundance of evidence to substantiate the correctness of our Hebrew text.

Bernard Ramm writes of the Jeremiah Seal:

Archaeology has also given us evidence as to the substantial accuracy of our Massoretic text. The Jeremiah Seal, a seal used to stamp the bitumen seals of wine jars, and dated from the first or second century A.D., has Jeremiah 48:11 stamped on it and, in general, conforms to the Massoretic text. This seal " . . . attests the accuracy with which the text was transmitted between the time when the seal was made and the time when the manuscripts were written." Furthermore, the *Roberts Papyrus,* which dates to the second century B.C., and the *Nash Papyrus,* dated by Albright before 100 B.C., confirm our Massoretic text. (Ramm, CITOT, 8–10)

William Albright affirms that "we may rest assured that the consonantal text of the Hebrew Bible, though not infallible, has been preserved with an accuracy perhaps unparalleled in any other Near-Eastern literature. . . . No, the flood of light now being shed on biblical Hebrew poetry of all periods by Ugaritic literature guarantees the relative antiquity of its composition as well as the astonishing accuracy of its transmission." (Albright, OTAAE, as cited in Rowley, OTMS, 25)

Archaeologist Albright writes concerning the accuracy of the Scriptures as the result of archaeology: "The contents of our Pentateuch are, in general, very much older than the date at which they were finally edited; new discoveries continue to confirm the historical accuracy or the literary antiquity of detail after detail in it. . . . It is, accordingly, sheer hypercriticism to deny the substantially Mosaic character of the Pentateuchal tradition." (Dodd, MNTS, 224)

Albright comments on what the critics used to say:

Until recently it was the fashion among biblical historians to treat the patriarchal sagas of Genesis as though they were artificial cre-

> The more we find that items in the picture of the past presented by the Bible, even though not directly attested, are compatible with what we know from archaeology, the stronger is our impression of general authenticity.
>
> —MILLAR BURROWS

ations of Israelite scribes of the Divided Monarchy or tales told by imaginative rhapsodists around Israelite campfires during the centuries following their occupation of the country. Eminent names among scholars can be cited for regarding every item of Gen.

11–50 as reflecting late invention, or at least retrojection of events and conditions under the Monarchy into the remote past, about which nothing was thought to have been really known to the writers of later days. (Albright, BPFAE, 1–2)

Now it has all been changed, writes Albright: "Archaeological discoveries since 1925 have changed all this. Aside from a few die-hards among older scholars, there is scarcely a single biblical historian who has not been impressed by the rapid accumulation of data supporting the substantial historicity of patriarchal tradition. According to the traditions of Genesis the ancestors of Israel were closely related to the semi-nomadic peoples of TransJordan, Syria, the Euphrates basin and North Arabia in the last centuries of the second millennium B.C., and the first centuries of the first millennium." (Albright, BPFAE, 1–2)

Millar Burrows comments:

To see the situation clearly we must distinguish two kinds of confirmation, general and specific. General confirmation is a matter of compatibility without definite corroboration of particular points. Much of what has already been discussed as explanation and illustration may be regarded also as general confirmation. The picture fits the frame; the melody and the accompaniment are harmonious. The force of such evidence is cumulative. The more we find that items in the picture of the past presented by the Bible, even though not directly attested, are compatible with what we know from archaeology, the stronger is our impression of general authenticity. Mere legend or fiction would inevitably betray itself by anachronisms and incongruities. (Burrows, WMTS, 278)

2B. Archaeology Helps to Supplement Areas Not Dealt with in the Bible

A good example here is the intertestamental period, kings, military campaigns, and empires not mentioned in the Scriptures.

But a word of caution must be issued. All too often we hear the phrase, "Archaeology proves the Bible." Archaeology cannot "prove" the Bible, if by this you mean "prove it to be inspired and revealed by God." If by prove, one means "showing some biblical event or passage to be historical," then this would be an accurate statement.

I believe archaeology contributes to biblical criticism, not in the area of inspiration or revelation, but in confirming the historical accuracy and trustworthiness of the events recorded. Let's say the rocks on which the Ten Commandments were written are found. Archaeology could confirm that they were rocks, that the Ten Commandments were written on them, and that they came from the period of Moses. It could not prove that God was their source.

Millar Burrows writes that archaeology "can tell us a great deal about the topography of a military campaign. It can tell us nothing about the nature of God." (Burrows, WMTS, 290)

One limitation of archaeology is the paucity of evidence. "Historians of antiquity," writes Edwin Yamauchi, "in using the archaeological evidence have very often failed to realize how slight is the evidence at our disposal. It would not be exaggerating to point out that what we have is but one fraction of a second fraction of a third fraction of a fourth fraction of a fifth fraction of the possible evidence." (Yamauchi, SSS, 9)

Joseph Free, in *Archaeology and Bible History,* addresses the question of archaeology and its relationship to the Bible: "We pointed out that numerous passages of the Bible which long puzzled the commentators have readily yielded up their meaning when new light from archaeological discoveries has been focused on them. In other words, archaeology illuminates the text of the

Scriptures and so makes valuable contributions to the fields of Biblical interpretation and exegesis. In addition to illuminating the Bible, archaeology has confirmed countless passages which have been rejected by critics as unhistorical or contradictory to known facts." (Free, ABH, 1)

3A. ARCHAEOLOGY SUPPORTS THE OLD TESTAMENT ACCOUNTS

1B. The Creation—The Ebla Tablets

The opening chapters of Genesis (1–11) are typically thought to be mythological explanations derived from earlier versions of the story found in the ancient Near East. But this view chooses only to notice the similarities between Genesis and the creation stories in other ancient cultures. If we can propose derivation of the human race from one family, plus general revelation, some lingering traces of the true historical account would be expected. The differences are more important. Babylonian and Sumerian accounts describe the creation as the product of a conflict among finite gods. When one god is defeated and split in half, the River Euphrates flows from one eye and the Tigris from the other. Humanity is made of the blood of an evil god mixed with clay. These tales display the kind of distortion and embellishment to be expected when a historical account becomes mythologized.

Less likely is the notion that the literary progression would be from this mythology to the unadorned elegance of Genesis 1. The common assumption that the Hebrew account is simply a purged and simplified version of the Babylonian legend is fallacious. In the Ancient Near East, the rule is that simple accounts or traditions give rise (by accretion and embellishment) to elaborate legends, but not the reverse. So the evidence supports the view that Genesis was not myth made into history. Rather, the extrabiblical accounts were history turned into myths.

The recent discoveries of creation accounts at Ebla add evidence for this fact. This library of sixteen thousand clay tablets predates the Babylonian account by about six hundred years. The creation tablet is strikingly close to Genesis, speaking of one being who created the heavens, moon, stars, and earth. The people at Ebla believed in creation out of nothing. The Bible contains the ancient, less embellished version of the story and transmits the facts without the

> Proponents of the "documentary hypothesis" have taught in the past that the period described in the Mosaic narrative (1400 B.C., a thousand years after the Ebla Kingdom) was a time prior to all knowledge of writing. . . . But Ebla shows that a thousand years before Moses, laws, customs and events were recorded in writing in the same area of the world in which Moses and the patriarchs lived.
>
> —MILLAR BURROWS

corruption of the mythological renderings. (Geisler, BECA, 48–49)

An archaeological find that impacts biblical criticism is the recently discovered Ebla tablets. This discovery was made in northern Syria by two professors from the University of Rome, Dr. Paolo Matthiae, an archaeologist; and Dr. Giovanni Pettinato, an epigrapher. The excavation of the site, Tell Mardikh, began in 1964; in 1968 they uncovered a statue of King Ibbit-Lim. The inscription refers to Ishtar, the goddess who "shines brightly in Ebla." Ebla, at its height of power in 2300 B.C., had a population of 260,000 people. It was destroyed in 2250

B.C. by Naram-Sin, the grandson of Sargon the Great.

The aplogetic importance of the Ebla tablets is that they parallel and confirm early chapters of Genesis. Although clouded by subsequent political pressure and denials, the published reports in reputable journals offer several possible lines of support for the biblical record.

Tablets contain the names of the cities Ur, Sodom, and Gomorrah, and such pagan gods mentioned in the Bible as Baal. (Ostling, "New Groundings for the Bible," in T, 76–77) The Ebla tablets reportedly contain references to names found in the book of Genesis, including Adam, Eve, and Noah. (Dahood, AETRBR, 55–56)

Of great importance is the discovery of the oldest known creation accounts outside the Bible. Ebla's version predates the Babylonian account by some six hundred years. The creation tablet is strikingly close to that of Genesis, speaking of one being who created the heavens, moon, stars, and earth. Parallel accounts show that the Bible contains the older, less embellished version of the story and transmits the facts without the corruption of the mythological renderings. The tablets report belief in creation out of nothing, declaring: "Lord of heaven and earth; the earth was not, you created it, the light of day was not, you created it, the morning light you had not [yet] made exist." *(Ebla Archives, 259)*

One very significant implication in the Ebla archives is that they destroy the critical belief in the evolution of monotheism from supposed earlier polytheism and henotheism. This evolution of religion hypothesis has been popular from the time of Charles Darwin (1809–1882) and Julius Wellhausen (1844–1918). Now monotheism is known to be earlier. Also, the force of the Ebla evidence supports the view that the earliest chapters

of Genesis are history, not mythology. (Geisler, BECA, 208)

Another significant outcome of the Ebla discovery delivered a crushing blow to the documentary supposition that Moses could not have written the Pentateuch because writing was nonexistent in his day. The proponents of the documentary hypothesis have claimed that the period described in the Mosaic narrative (1400 B.C., a thousand years after the Ebla kingdom) was prior to all knowledge of writing. But the findings from Ebla demonstrate that a thousand years before Moses, laws, customs, and events were recorded in writing in the same area of the world in which Moses and the patriarchs lived.

The higher critics have taught not only that this was a time prior to writing but also that the priestly code and legislation recorded in the Pentateuch were too far developed to have been written by Moses. They alleged that the Israelites were too primitive at that time to have written them and that it wasn't until about the first half of the Persian period (538–331 B.C.) that such detailed legislation was recorded.

However, the tablets containing the law codes of Ebla have demonstrated elaborate judicial proceedings and case law. Many are very similar to the Deuteronomic law code (example: Deuteronomy 22:22–30), to which critics attribute a very late date.

An additional example of the contribution of the Ebla discovery relates to Genesis 14, which for years has been considered historically unreliable. Abraham's victory over Chedolaomer and the Mesopotamian kings has been described as fictitious, and the five Cities of the Plain (Sodom, Gomorrah, Admah, Zeboiim and Zoar) legendary.

Yet the Ebla archives refer to all five Cities of the Plain, and on one tablet the Cities are listed in the exact same sequence as appears in Genesis 14. The milieu of the tablets reflect the culture of the patriarchal period and depict that before the catastrophe recorded in Genesis 14 the area was a flourishing region, prosperous and successful, as recorded in Genesis.

2B. The Flood of Noah

As with the creation accounts, the flood narrative in Genesis is more realistic and less mythological than other ancient versions, indicating its authenticity. The superficial similarities point toward a historical core of events that gave rise to all of these renditions. The names change: Noah is called Ziusudra by the Sumerians and Utnapishtim by the Babylonians. The basic story doesn't: A man is told to build a ship to specific dimensions because God(s) is going to flood the world. He obeys, rides out the storm, and offers sacrifice upon exiting the boat. The Deity (-ies) responds with remorse over the destruction of life, and makes a covenant with the man. These core events point to a historical basis.

Similar flood accounts are found all over the world. The flood story is told by the Greeks, the Hindus, the Chinese, the Mexicans, the Algonquins, and the Hawaiians. One list of Sumerian kings treats the flood as a historical reference point. After naming eight kings who lived extraordinarily long lives (tens of thousands of years), this sentence interrupts the list: "[Then] the Flood swept over [the earth] and when kingship was lowered [again] from heaven, kingship was [first] in Kish."

There are good reasons to believe that Genesis relates the original story. The other versions contain elaborations, indicating corruption. Only in Genesis is the year of the flood given, as well as dates for the chronology relative to Noah's life. In fact, Genesis reads almost like a diary or ship's log of the events. The cubical Babylonian ship could not have saved anyone. The raging waters would have constantly turned it on every side. However, the biblical ark is rectangular—long, wide, and low—so that it would ride well on rough seas. The length of the rainfall in the pagan accounts (seven days) is not enough time for the devastation they describe. The waters would have to rise at least above most mountains, to a height of over seventeen thousand feet, and it is more reasonable to assume a longer rainfall to do this. The Babylonian idea that all of the flood waters subsided in one day is equally absurd. Another striking difference between Genesis and the other versions is that in these accounts the hero is granted immortality and exalted. The Bible moves on to describe Noah's sin. Only a version that seeks to tell the truth would include such realistic admission.

Some have suggested that this was a severe but localized flood. However there is geological evidence to support a worldwide flood. Partial skeletons of recent animals are found in deep fissures in several parts of the world, and the flood seems to be the best explanation for these. This would explain how these fissures occur even in hills of considerable height, which extend from 140 feet to 300 feet. Since no skeleton is complete, it is safe to conclude that none of these animals (mammoths, bears, wolves, oxen, hyenas, rhinoceri, aurochs, deer, and smaller mammals) fell into these fissures alive, nor were they rolled there by streams. Yet the calcite cementing these diverse bones together indicates that they must have been deposited under water. Such fissures have been discovered in various places around the world. This evidence shows what a brief but violent episode of this sort would be expected to cause within the short span of one year. (Geisler, BECA, 49–50)

3B. The Tower of Babel

There is considerable evidence now that the world did indeed have a single language at one time. Sumerian literature alludes to this several times. Linguists also find this theory helpful in categorizing languages. But what of the tower and the confusion of tongues at the tower of Babel (Gen. 11)? Archaeology has revealed that Ur-Nammu, King of Ur from about 2044 to 2007 B.C., supposedly received orders to build a great ziggurat (temple tower) as an act of worship to the moon god Nannat. A stele (monument) about five feet across and ten feet high reveals Ur-Nammu's activities. One panel shows him setting out with a mortar basket to begin construction of the great tower; thus showing his allegiance to the gods as he takes his place as a humble workman.

Another clay tablet states that the erection of the tower offended the gods, so they threw down what the men had built, scattered them abroad, and made their speech strange. This is remarkably similar to the record in the Bible.

Conservative scholars believe Moses wrote these early chapters of Genesis. But how could he, since these events occurred long before his birth? There are two possibilities. First, God could have revealed the accounts to Moses supernaturally. Just as God can reveal the future by prophetic revelation, he can also reveal the past by retrospective revelation. The second possibility is more likely, namely, that Moses compiled and edited earlier records of these events. This does not contradict biblical practice. Luke did this in his Gospel (Luke 1:1–4). P. J. Wiseman argues convincingly that the history of Genesis was originally written on clay tablets and passed on from one generation to the next, with each "clan leader" responsible for keeping them edited and up to date. Wiseman cites, as a main clue in the Bible, the periodic repetition of words and phrases— especially the phrase "This is the generation of" (see Gen. 2:4; 6:9; 10:1; 11:10).

Many ancient tablets were kept in order by making the first words of a new tablet a repetition of the last words of the previous stone. A literary evaluation of Genesis compared to other ancient literature indicates that it was compiled no later than the time of Moses. It is quite possible that Genesis is a family history recorded by the patriarchs and edited into its final form by Moses. (Geisler, BECA, 50)

4B. The Patriarchs

While the narratives of the lives of Abraham, Isaac, and Jacob do not present the same kinds of difficulties as do the earlier chapters of Genesis, they were long considered legendary because they did not seem to fit with the known evidence of that period. As more has become known, though, these stories are increasingly verified. Legal codes from the time of Abraham show why the patriarch would have been hesitant to throw Hagar out of his camp, for he was legally bound to support her. Only when a higher law came from God was Abraham willing to put her out.

The Mari letters reveal such names as Abamram (Abraham), Jacob-el, and Benjamites. Though these do not refer to the biblical people, they at least show that these names were in use. These letters also support the record of a war in Genesis 14 where five kings fought against four kings. The names of these kings seem to fit with the prominent nations of the day. For example, Genesis 14:1 mentions an Amorite king Arioch; the Mari documents render the king's name Ariwwuk. All of this evidence supports the conclusion that the source materials for Genesis were firsthand accounts of someone who lived during Abraham's time. (Geisler, BECA, 50)

5B. Sodom and Gomorrah

The destruction of Sodom and Gomorrah was thought to be spurious until evidence revealed that all five of the cities mentioned in the Bible were in fact centers of commerce in the area and were geographically situated as the Scriptures describe. The biblical description of their demise seems to be no less accurate. Evidence points to earthquake activity, and that the various layers of the earth were disrupted and hurled high into the air. Bitumen is plentiful there, and an accurate description would be that brimstone (bituminous pitch) was hurled down on those cities that had rejected God. There is evidence that the layers of sedimentary rock have been molded together by intense heat. Evidence of such burning has been found on the top of Jebel Usdum (Mount Sodom). This is permanent evidence of the great conflagration that took place in the long-distant past, possibly when an oil basin beneath the Dead Sea ignited and erupted. Such an explanation in no way subtracts from the miraculous quality of the event, for God controls natural forces. The timing of the event, in the context of warnings and visitation by angels, reveals its overall miraculous nature. (Geisler, BECA, 50–51)

6B. The Dating of the Exodus

One of several questions concerning Israel's relationship with Egypt is when the Exodus into Palestine took place. There is even an official "Generally Accepted Date" (GAD) for the Israelites' entrance into Canaan: about 1230–1220 B.C. The Scriptures, on the other hand, teach in three different texts (1 Kin. 6:1; Judg. 11:26; Acts 13:19–20) that the Exodus occurred in the 1400s B.C., and the entrance into Canaan forty years later. While the debate rages on, there is no longer any reason to accept the 1200 date.

Assumptions have been made that the city "Rameses" in Exodus 1:11 was named after Rameses the Great, that there were no building projects in the Nile Delta before 1300, and that there was no great civilization in Canaan from the nineteenth to the thirteenth centuries. However, the name Rameses is common in Egyptian history. Rameses the Great is Ramses II. Nothing is known about Rameses I. Also, the name might not refer to a city but to an area. In Genesis 47:11, the name Rameses describes the Nile Delta area where Jacob and his sons settled.

Some scholars now suggest that reinterpretation of the data requires moving the date of the Middle Bronze (MB) age. If this is done, it would show that several cities of Canaan that have been uncovered were destroyed by the Israelites. Recent digs have uncovered evidence that the last phase of the MB period involves more time than originally thought, so that its end is closer to 1400 B.C. than 1550 B.C. This realignment would bring together two events previously thought to have been separated by centuries: the fall of Canaan's MB II cities and the conquest.

Another change may be warranted in the traditional view of Egyptian history. The chronology of the whole ancient world is based on the order and dates of the Egyptian kings, which were generally thought to have been fixed. However, Velikovsky and Courville assert that six hundred extra years in that chronology throw off these dates for events all around the Near East. Courville has shown that the lists of Egyptian kings should not be understood to be completely consecutive. He argues that some "kings" listed were not pharaohs, but high officials. Historians had assumed that each dynasty followed the one before it. Instead, many dynasties list subrulers who lived at the same time as the preceding dynasty. Working out this new chronology places the Exodus at about 1450 B.C., and would make the other periods of Israelite history fall in line with the Egyptian kings mentioned. The evidence is not definitive, but there is no longer any reason to demand a late-date Exodus. (Geisler, BECA, 51)

7B. Saul, David, and Solomon

Saul became the first king of Israel, and his fortress at Gibeah has been excavated. One of the most noteworthy finds was that sling-shots were one of the most important weapons of the day. This relates not to David's victory over Goliath, but to the reference of Judges 20:16 that there were seven hundred expert slingers who "could sling a stone at a hair and not miss."

Upon Saul's death, Samuel tells us that his armor was put in the temple of Ashtaroth (a Canaanite fertility goddess) at Bet She'an, while Chronicles records that his head was put in the temple of Dagon, the Philistine

> The excavation of Gezer in 1969 ran across a massive layer of ash that covered most of the mound. Sifting through the ash yielded pieces of Hebrew, Egyptian, and Philistine artifacts. Apparently all three cultures had been there at the same time. This puzzled researchers greatly until they realized that the Bible told them exactly what they had found. "Pharaoh king of Egypt had attacked and captured Gezer. He had set it on fire. He killed its Canaanite inhabitants and then gave it as a wedding gift to his daughter; Solomon's wife" (1 Kings 9:16).
>
> —NORMAN GEISLER

corn god. This was thought to be an error because it seemed unlikely that enemy peoples would have temples in the same place at the same time. However, excavations have found two temples at this site that are separated by a hallway: one for Dagon, the other

for Ashtaroth. It appears that the Philistines had adopted the Canaanite goddess.

One of the key accomplishments of David's reign was the capture of Jerusalem. Problematic in the Scripture account was that the Israelites entered the city by way of a tunnel that led to the Pool of Siloam. However, that pool was thought to be *outside* the city walls at that time. Excavations in the 1960s finally revealed that the wall did indeed extend well past the pool.

The psalms attributed to David are often said to have been written much later because their inscriptions suggest that there were musician's guilds (for example, the sons of Korah). Such organization leads many to think that these hymns should be dated to about the time of the Maccabeans in the second century B.C. Following excavations at Ras Shamra it is now known that there were such guilds in Syria and Palestine in David's time.

The time of Solomon has strong archaeological corroboration as well. The site of Solomon's temple cannot be excavated because it is near the Muslim holy place, The Dome of the Rock. However, what is known about Philistine temples built in Solomon's time fits well with the design, decoration, and materials described in the Bible. The only piece of evidence from the temple itself is a small ornament, a pomegranate, that sat on the end of a rod and bears the inscription, "Belonging to the Temple of Yahweh." It was first seen in a shop in Jerusalem in 1979, was verified in 1984, and was acquired by the Israel Museum in 1988.

The excavation of Gezer in 1969 ran across a massive layer of ash that covered most of the mound. Sifting through the ash yielded pieces of Hebrew, Egyptian, and Philistine artifacts. Apparently all three cultures had been there at the same time. This puzzled researchers greatly until they realized that the Bible told them exactly what they had found. "Pharaoh king of Egypt had attacked and captured Gezer. He had set it on fire. He killed its Canaanite inhabitants and then gave it as a wedding gift to his daughter; Solomon's wife" (1 Kings 9:16). (Geisler, BECA, 51–52)

8B. The Assyrian Invasion

Much was learned about the Assyrians when twenty-six thousand tablets were found in the palace of Ashurbanipal, son of the Esarhaddon, who took the northern kingdoms into captivity in 722 B.C. These tablets tell of the many conquests of the Assyrian empire and record with honor the cruel and violent punishments dealt those who opposed them.

Several of these records confirm the Bible's accuracy. Every reference in the Old Testament to an Assyrian king has proven correct. Even though Sargon was unknown for some time, when his palace was found and excavated a wall painting of the battle mentioned in Isaiah 20 was found. The Black Obelisk of Shalmaneser adds to our knowledge of biblical figures by showing Jehu (or his emissary) bowing down to the king of Assyria.

Among the most interesting finds is Sennacherib's record of the siege of Jerusalem. Thousands of his men died and the rest scattered when he attempted to take the city and, as Isaiah had foretold, he was unable to conquer it. Since he could not boast about his great victory here, Sennacherib found a way to make himself sound good without admitting defeat (Geisler, BECA, 52): "As to Hezekiah, the Jew, he did not submit to my yoke. I laid siege to 46 of his strong cities, walled forts, and to the countless small villages in their vicinity. I drove out of them 200,150 people, young and old, male and female, horses, mules, donkeys, camels, big

and small cattle beyond counting and considered (them) booty. Himself I made a prisoner in Jerusalem, his royal residence, like a bird in a cage." (Pritchard, ANET, as cited in Geisler, BECA, 52)

9B. The Captivity

Various facets of the Old Testament history regarding the captivity have been confirmed. Records found in Babylon's famous hanging gardens have shown that Jehoiachin and his five sons were given a monthly ration and a place to live, and were treated well (2 Kin. 25:27–30). The name "Belshazzar" caused problems because there was not only no mention of him, but no room for him in the list of Babylonian kings. However, Nabodonius left a record that he appointed his son, Belshazzar (Dan. 5), to reign for a few years in his absence. Hence, Nabodonius was still king, but Belshazzar ruled in the capital. Also, the edict of Cyrus as recorded by Ezra seemed to fit the picture of Isaiah's prophecies too well to be real, until a cylinder was found that confirmed this decree in all the important details. (Geisler, BECA, 52)

4A. OLD TESTAMENT EXAMPLES OF ARCHAEOLOGICAL CONFIRMATION

It is this fact with which archaeological findings concur. Albright says that it is "beyond reasonable doubt that Hebrew tradition was correct in tracing the patriarchs directly back to the Balikh Valley in northwestern Mesopotamia." The evidence is based on the coincidence of biblical and archaeological findings tracing the movement of these people out of the land of Mesopotamia. (Albright, BPFAE, 2)

According to Scripture, "The whole earth was of one language and one speech" (Gen.11:1) before the Tower of Babel. After the building of the tower and its destruction,

God confounded the language of all the earth (Gen. 11:9). Many modern-day philologists attest to the likelihood of such an origin for the world's languages. Alfredo Trombetti states that he can trace and prove

> The discoveries found thus far have led scholars, no matter what their religious opinion, to affirm the historical nature of the narratives related to the Patriarchs.
>
> —DONALD F. WISEMAN.

the common origin of *all* languages. Max Mueller also attests to the common origin. And Otto Jespersen goes so far as to say that language was directly given to the first men by God. (Free, ABH, 47)

In the genealogy of Esau, mention is made of the Horites (Gen. 36:20). It was at one time accepted that these people were "cave-dwellers" because of the similarity between the name "Horite" and the Hebrew word for cave. Now, however, findings have shown that they were a prominent group of warriors living in the Near East in patriarchal times. (Free, ABH, 72)

During the excavations of Jericho (1930–1936) Garstang found something so startling that a statement of what was found was prepared and signed by himself and two other members of the team. In reference to these findings Garstang writes: "As to the main fact, then, there remains no doubt: the walls fell outwards so completely that the attackers would be able to clamber up and over their ruins into the city." Why so unusual? Because the walls of cities do not fall outwards, they fall inwards. And yet in Joshua 6:20 we read "The wall fell down flat, so that the people went up into the city every man straight ahead, and they took the city." The walls were made to fall outward. (Garstang, FBHJJ, 146)

We find that the genealogy of Abraham is definitely historical. However, there seems to be some question as to whether or not these names represent individuals or ancient cities. One thing is certain about Abraham: He was an individual and he did exist. As Burrows writes: "Everything indicates that here we have an historical individual. As noted above, he is not mentioned in any known archaeological source, but his name appears in Babylonia as a personal name in the very period to which he belongs." (Burrows, WMTS, 258–259)

Earlier attempts were made to move the date of Abraham to the fifteenth or fourteenth century B.C., a time much too late. However Albright points out that because of the data mentioned above and other findings, we have "a great deal of evidence from personal and place names, almost all of which is against such unwarranted telescoping of traditional data." (Garstang, FBHJJ, 9)

Although specific archaeological evidence for the stories of the patriarchs may not be forthcoming, the social customs of the stories fit the period and region of the patriarchs. (Burrows, WMTS, 278–79)

Much of this evidence has come from excavations at Nuzu and Mari. Light was shed on Hebrew poetry and language from work at Augured. Mosaic legislation was seen in Hittite, Assyrian, Sumerian, and Achene codes. Through these discoveries we are able to see the life of the Hebrew in relation to the surrounding world. As Albright says, "This is a contribution before which everything else must fade into insignificance." (Albright, OTAAE, as cited in Rowley, OTMS, 28)

The discoveries found thus far have led scholars, no matter what their religious opinion, to affirm the historical nature of the narratives related to the patriarchs. (Wiseman, ACOT, as cited in Henry, RB, 305)

Julius Wellhausen, a well-known biblical critic of the nineteenth century, believed that the record of the laver made of brass mirrors was not an original entry into the priestly code. In stating this he places the record of the tabernacle much too late for the time of Moses. However there is no valid reason for employing this late dating (500 B.C.). There is specific archaeological evidence of such bronze mirrors in what is known as the Empire Period of Egypt's history (1500–1400 B.C.). Thus we see that this period is contemporary with Moses and the Exodus (1500–1400 B.C.). (Free, ABH, 108)

Henry M. Morris observes: "Problems still exist, of course, in the complete harmonization of archaeological material with the Bible, but none so serious as not to bear real promise of imminent solution through further investigation. It must be extremely significant that, in view of the great mass of corroborative evidence regarding the Biblical history of these periods, there exists today not one unquestionable find of archaeology that proves the Bible to be in error at any point." (Morris, BMS, 95)

Geisler concludes by saying, "In every period of Old Testament history, we find that

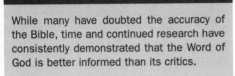

While many have doubted the accuracy of the Bible, time and continued research have consistently demonstrated that the Word of God is better informed than its critics.

—NORMAN GEISLER

there is good evidence from archaeology that the Scriptures speak the truth. In many instances, the Scriptures even reflect firsthand knowledge of the times and customs it describes. While many have doubted the accuracy of the Bible, time and continued research have consistently demonstrated that

the Word of God is better informed than its critics. In fact, while thousands of finds from the ancient world support in broad outline and often in detail the biblical picture, not one incontrovertible find has ever contradicted the Bible." (Geisler, BECA, 52)

Henry Morris adds: "This great antiquity of the Bible histories in comparison with those of other writings, combined with the evolutionary preconceptions of the 19th century, led many scholars to insist that the Bible histories also were in large part merely legendary. As long as nothing was available, except copies of ancient manuscripts, for the evaluation of ancient histories, such teachings may have been persuasive. Now, however, it is no longer possible to reject the substantial historicity of the Bible, at least as far back as the time of Abraham, because of the remarkable discoveries of archaeology." (Morris, MP, 300)

5A. ARCHAEOLOGICAL EVIDENCE FOR THE MOSAIC AUTHORSHIP OF THE PENTATEUCH

1B. Antiquity of the Pentateuch—Internal Evidence

Optimum objectivity in dating any written document may be achieved through examining internal evidence. Clues may be discovered in allusions to current events, geographical or climatic conditions, prevalent flora and fauna, and eyewitness involvement. And from these clues can be established a reasonably accurate estimate of the place and date of the origin of the document. (Archer, SOT, 101)

There is substantial internal evidence that the Pentateuch, both in its form and content, is very much older than the ninth-through-fifth-centuries-B.C. dating scheme assigned it by the critics.

Following are a few examples of the internal details that indicate the antiquity of the Pentateuch:

1C. The Desert Setting of Exodus–Numbers

Exodus, Leviticus, and Numbers are quite obviously aimed at a people wandering in the desert, not a nation of farmers settled for centuries in their promised land. Otherwise, the frequent and detailed descriptions of the portable tabernacle would be absurd. The meticulous instructions for encampment (Num. 2:1–31) and for marching (Num. 10:14–20) would be irrelevant for a settled nation, but were eminently practical for the desert experience. Desert references are abundant, including sanitary instructions for desert life (Deut. 23:12, 13) and the sending of the scapegoat into the desert (Lev. 16:10). (Archer, SOT, 106–108)

2C. Egyptian Influence in Portions of the Pentateuch

Much of the material in Genesis and Exodus has an obvious Egyptian background. We would expect this if it was written by Moses (reared in an Egyptian court) shortly after the Israelites' Exodus from Egypt. But it would hardly be explainable had it been written, as the documentarians claim, more than four hundred years after the Hebrews left Egypt. [See Abraham Yahuda's *The Language of the Pentateuch in Its Relationship to Egyptian* (1933), an ambitious work discussing the Egyptian background of the stories of Moses and Joseph in Egypt.]

This Egyptian influence is manifest in at least these different areas:

1D. Geography

The geography of Egypt and Sinai is familiar to the author of these narratives (Gen. 37—Num. 10). Many authentic locales that have been confirmed by modern archaeology are referred to by the author. Conversely, this author knows little of the Palestinian geography, except by patriarchal tradition. For example, in Genesis 13, when the author wants to convey a picture of the land of Canaan he compares it with Egypt (v. 10). Similarly, in a P passage the author refers to Hebron by its preexilic name Kirjath-arba (Gen. 23:2). And its founding is explained by the author in Numbers 13:22, in which the author refers to the building of Zoan in Egypt. The reference to Shalem, "a city of Shechem, which is in the land of Canaan," is improbable for a writer whose people had dwelt in Canaan for centuries. The writer of the Pentateuch generally regards Palestine as a new country that the Israelites will enter in the future. (Archer, SOT, 106)

This intimacy with Egyptian geography is especially apparent in the case of the second book.

The writer of Exodus had a thorough knowledge of Egyptian territory. He knew the Egyptian papyrus (Ex. 2:3), the character of the Nile bank, and was well acquainted with the sandy desert (Ex. 2:12). He knew of such places as Rameses, Succoth (Ex. 12:37), Etham (Ex.13:20), and Pi-Hahiroth (Ex. 14:2). The mention in Exodus 14:3 that "the wilderness had shut them in" shows an intimate knowledge of the geography of Egypt. In fact, chapter 14 cannot be understood without knowledge of Egyptian geography. (Raven, OTI, 109)

2D. Diction

Archer observes that

He [the author of Genesis and Exodus] uses a greater percentage of Egyptian words than elsewhere in the Old Testament. For example: (a) the expression *abrek* (Gen. 41:43—translated "bow the knee") is apparently the Egyptian *'b rk* ("O heart, bow down!"), although many other explanations have been offered for this; (b) weights and measures, such as *zeret* ("a span") from *drt*–"*hand*"; *'ephah* ("tenth of a homer") from *'pt;hin* (about five quarts volume) from *hnw;* (c) *gome'* ("papyrus") from *kmyt;* (d) *qemah* ("flour") from *kmhw* (a type of bread); (e) *ses* ("fine linen") from *ss* ("linen"); (f) *y⁶or* ("Nile," "river") from *'trw* "river" (which becomes *eioor* in Coptic). (Archer, SOT, 102–03)

This author also makes use of numerous distinctively Egyptian names. These include:

Potipherah (Gen. 41:45; 46:20) and its shorter form.

Potiphar (Gen. 37:36; 39:1) meaning "whom Ra (the Sun-God) gave."

Zaphnath-paaneah (Gen. 41:45), whom Pharaoh named Joseph. The LXX interprets this to mean "savior of the world"—a fitting title for the one who delivered Egypt from famine.

Asenath (Gen. 41:45, 50), Joseph's wife.

On (Gen. 41:45, 50; 46:20), the ancient Egyptian name for Heliopolis.

Rameses (Gen. 47:11; Ex. 1:11; 12:37; Num. 33:3, 5).

Pithom (Ex. 1:11), likely the Egyptian Pi-Tum first mentioned in the nineteenth dynasty monuments, just as Exodus here records it. (Raven, OTI, 107–8)

3D. Names of Egyptian Kings

A few Egyptologists committed to the position of radical criticism have argued that an early author would certainly have mentioned the names of the contemporary Egyptian kings. In fact, the absence of such names in Hebrew literature until the time of Solomon actually supports early authorship. The custom of the New Kingdom Egyptian official language was to refer to the king simply as "Pharaoh," without connecting his name with the title. While the Israelites were in Egypt, they conformed to this practice. (Archer, SOT, 105)

It is here also worthy of note that the antiquity of the Old Testament is supported in the mention of royalty wearing a signet ring and a chain of gold as a token of authority (Gen. 41:42; Esth. 3:10, 12; 8:2, 8, 10; Dan. 5:29). This was unknown to Israel but existed in ancient Egypt, Persia, and Babylon.

3C. Archaisms in Language

Certain words and phrases used in the Pentateuch are known to have become obsolete after the Mosaic age.

Concerning chapter 15 of Genesis, Albright writes:

The account of the covenant between Yahweh and Abraham . . . is replete with archaisms; its antiquity has been established by E. A. Speiser. Here we have an example of the central place held in early Hebrew religion by the special god of a man with whom he made a solemn compact, according to the terms of which the god would protect him and his family in return for an oath of allegiance. This is a primitive form of the suzerainty treaty. . . . In the Late Bronze Age the word *beritu*, Hebrew *berit*, "compact," appears in Syria and Egypt

> Judging therefore by the internal evidences of the Pentateuchal text, we are driven to the conclusion that the author must have been originally a resident of Egypt (not of Palestine), a contemporary eyewitness of the Exodus and wilderness wandering, and possessed of a very high degree of education, learning and literary skill.
>
> —GLEASON ARCHER

(where it was a Semitic loanword) in connection with contract labor and contractual hiring of persons listed in a given document. (Albright, BPFAE, 8)

Archer gives other examples of archaisms: "The word for the pronoun 'she' is frequently spelled *HW'* instead of the regular *HY'*. We also meet with *N'R* instead of the feminine form *N'RH* for 'young girl.' Occasionally (i.e., twice in Genesis) *HLZH (hallazeh)* appears for demonstrative 'that' instead of *hallaz*, the form in use in Judges, Samuel and thereafter. The verb 'laugh' is spelled *SHQ* (in Genesis and Exodus) instead of *ŚHQ*; 'lamb' is *KŚB* instead of the later *KBŚ (kebes)*." (Archer, SOT, 107)

This body of evidence also includes the fact that there are places in the Old Testament where trivial details are mentioned that a later author would be unlikely to include. For example, when Joseph and the Egyptians were separated from Joseph's brothers at the table, an explanatory note is inserted: "The Egyptians could not eat bread with the Hebrews, for that is loathsome to the Egyptians" (Gen. 43:32). Would a later writer have included this? (Raven, OTI, 109)

On the basis of the above evidence, Archer makes this final evaluation: "Judging therefore by the internal evidences of the Pentateuchal text we are driven to the conclusion that the author must have been originally a resident of Egypt (not of Palestine), a contemporary eyewitness of the Exodus and wilderness wandering, and possessed of a very high degree of education, learning and literary skill." (Archer, SOT, 101)

2B. Other Archaeological Evidence for Mosaic Authorship

1C. Early Hebrew Literature

The traditional destructive higher critical view that Hebrew literature was, for the most part, comparatively late, still prevails today as can be seen from this statement by J. L. McKenzie: "It is generally accepted that no Israelite literature was written extensively

before the reign of David." (McKenzie, as cited in Laymon, IOVCB, 1073)

But, because of the recently discovered evidence for the literacy of the ancient Near East, we are able to assign an earlier date to the Pentateuch than was previously suggested. The scribes of antiquity recorded events at the time of their occurrence or shortly thereafter, thus reducing the time of oral transmission of the material before it was written down. It is now known that oral transmission was used to disseminate the material to the people and not primarily to preserve the material, since they had written records in existence.

That the majority of the Old Testament is of great antiquity is without question. (Harrison, OTT, 18–19)

2C. Early Parallels In Pentateuchal Laws

Numerous discoveries of parallel laws in other Mesopotamian cultures now show that many of the laws and legal procedures recorded in the Pentateuch are much older than was formerly assumed.

We cite three specific examples:

1D. The Covenant Code

Mendenhall says:

It is hard to conceive of a law code which could be more at variance from what we know of Canaanite culture than the Covenant Code (Exod. 21—23—JE). . . . The Canaanite cities were predominantly commercial, rigidly stratified in social structure. . . . The Covenant Code shows no social stratification, for the slaves mentioned are not members of the community, with the single exception of the daughter who is sold as an *amah* or slave-wife (who is herself strongly protected by law). . . . The laws of the Covenant Code reflect the customs, morality and religious obligations of the Israelite community (or perhaps some specific Israelite community of the North) before the monarchy . . . since it exhibits just that mixture of case law and apodictic law (technique and policy respectively) which we find in

> New discoveries continue to confirm the historical accuracy or the literary antiquity of detail after detail in [the Pentateuch].
>
> —WILLIAM F. ALBRIGHT

covenants from the Hittite sources and in Mesopotamian codes as well; any study which assumes that it is a later, artificial composite from originally independent literary sources may be assigned rather to rational ingenuity than to historical fact. (Mendenhall, LCIANE, 13–14)

Albright also establishes the antiquity of the Covenant Code:

> Moreover, the Eshnunna Code, which is nearly two centuries older than the Code of Hammurabi, contains the first exact parallel to an early biblical law (Ex. xxi. 35, dealing with the division of oxen after a fatal combat between the animals). Since the Code of Eshnunna is on any rational theory at least five centuries earlier than the Book of the Covenant, this parallel becomes particularly interesting. Of course, it is now becoming a truism that the cultural background of the Book of the Covenant lies in the Bronze Age, not in the Iron; i.e., it must go back substantially to the Mosaic Age. (Albright, OTAP, as cited in Rowley, OTMS, 39)

2D. Land Transaction Recorded in Genesis 23

Archer discusses the antiquity of this particular procedure. Genesis 23 describes Abraham's reluctance in purchasing an entire tract of land from Ephron the Hittite, rather desiring only the cave of Machpelah itself and the immediate grounds. The discovery of

the Hittite Legal Code (dating from 1300 B.C.) provides amazing parallels, and explains that the owner of an entire parcel must carry out the duties of feudal service, including pagan religious observances. Thus Abraham plainly refused to purchase any more than a portion of the tract so as to avoid any involvement with gods other than Yahweh. This narrative reflects such a grasp of Hittite procedure as to make it highly probable that it preceded the fall of the Hittites in the thirteenth century B.C. (Archer, SOT, 161)

3D. Three Customs Referred to in Genesis

Archer points out that the antiquity of three customs referred to in Genesis (chapters 16, 27, and 31 respectively) has been established by archaeology. Many of the ancient customs of Genesis are proven to have been common in the second millennium B.C., but not in the first millennium B.C. Nuzi yielded numerous fifteenth century B.C. legal documents that speak of siring legitimate children by handmaidens (such as Abraham by Hagar); an oral deathbed will as binding (such as Isaac's to Jacob); and the need for having the family teraphim (such as Rachel took from Laban) to claim inheritance rights. (Archer, SOT, 107)

3C. Conclusion

It should be clear at this point that archaeology has done much not only to undermine the documentary hypothesis, but also to, in fact, support the Mosaic authorship of the Pentateuch.

About the Pentateuch Albright writes: "New discoveries continue to confirm the historical accuracy or the literary antiquity of detail after detail in it." (Albright, AP, 225)

Bright makes this statement about the patriarchal narratives: "No evidence has come to light contradicting any item in the tradition."

Albright warns: "It is . . . sheer hypercriticism to deny the substantial Mosaic character of the Pentateuchal tradition." (Albright, AP, 224)

Meredith Kline gives an appropriate conclusion: "The story of twentieth century Biblical archaeology is the story of the silencing of the clamorous voice of the modern western Wellhausen by the voiceless witnesses emerging from ancient eastern mounds. The plot of the story would be clearer were it not for the reluctance of critical scholars to part with their traditional teachings. But all are now obliged to admit that far from the Biblical narratives of patriarchal and Mosaic days being alien to the second millennium B.C. where the Biblical chronology locates them, they would be completely out of place in the first millennium B.C. The Biblical sequence of Law and Prophets has been vindicated." (Kline, CITMB, 139)

SECTION II

DOCUMENTARY HYPOTHESIS

14
INTRODUCTION TO THE DOCUMENTARY HYPOTHESIS

Those adhering to the documentary hypothesis teach that the first five books of the Bible were written close to one thousand years after Moses' death and were the result of a process of writing, rewriting, editing, and compiling by various anonymous editors or redactors.

Here we will examine the discipline of literary criticism as applied to the Pentateuch, along with evidence for Mosaic authorship.

Julius Wellhausen in 1895 added the finishing touches to a hypothesis that is prevalent in modern biblical circles. This hypothesis is known as the documentary hypothesis (or JEDP hypothesis). Using literary criticism as its basis for argument, this hypothesis sets forth the theory that the Pentateuch (Genesis through Deuteronomy) was not written by Moses, as the Bible claims, but was completed years after Moses died.

Those adhering to the documentary hypothesis teach that the first five books of the Bible were written close to one thousand years after Moses' death and were the result of a process of writing, rewriting, editing, and compiling by various anonymous editors or redactors.

Citing literary variations within the text (divine names, doublets, repetition of accounts), style, and diction, the documentarians assert that there are four different documents—J, E, D, and P—that make up the Pentateuch. The J stands for the divine name YHWH, the name for God characteristically used by the anonymous J writer. This writer used a flowing style and a peculiar vocabulary. E denotes the Elohist document, known for its use of the name "Elohim" for God. J and E are often difficult to separate within the text, so are often referred to as one source, "JE." The letter D describes the Deuteronomic code, found in 621 B.C. Finally, P represents the Priestly writer. This writer was the last compiler to work with the Old Testament. He put the finishing touches on it. P is characterized by its use of the name Elohim for God and its acrid style. "Its language is that of a jurist, rather than a historian." (Driver, ILOT, 12) P is not to be confused with the Elohist document that has a fresh, flowing style.

Chronologically these were written in the same order as the letters are given: J, E, D, P. The following is an excellent description of the background and purpose of each writer:

J, or the Yahwist, was the first writer to bring together the legends, myths, poems even well-known stories from other peoples, such as the Babylonians, into one great history of God's people. Some of the sources J used were oral traditions; some were already in written form. This anonymous writer lived about the time of David or Solomon. He was concerned to save the old traditions when Israel was becoming a nation and, as a world power, was coming into contact with other nations and ideas. In planning his work, J seems to have used the old confessions of faith or creeds about what God had done for his people. As an example see *Deut. 26:5-10.* Around this basic outline of creeds, he grouped the narratives. This writer is called the Yahwist because he used Yahweh as the name for God. German scholars, who first discovered this writer, spell Yahweh with a "J."

E, or the Elohist, was the second writer to gather all the traditions into one history. He wrote about 700 B.C., perhaps when the Northern Kingdom, Israel, was threatened by enemies. E used traditions that had been passed down among northern tribes. Some of these were the same as those used by J: others were different. E used the name Elohim for

God in stories before the time of Moses. He believed that the name Yahweh was revealed to Moses. E gave special emphasis to Moses. See his description in *Deut. 34:10-12.* E was a good writer of stories, for example, the story of Joseph.

JE. The works of these two writers were put together into one history by an unknown editor after Jerusalem was destroyed. Sometimes the editor kept both J's and E's telling of a story, even when they differed in details. Other times he would use one as the basic material and add details from the other. In *Ex., ch. 14,* the basic material is from J; very little from E is used. Occasionally the editor added sentences of his own.

P may have been a priest or a group of priests who lived during the exile in Babylon. They worked out a code of holiness for the people, that is, the ways of worship and the laws that ought to be observed. This Priestly Code was at first a separate book. Sometime in the fourth century B.C. it was worked into parts of the JE book. It was "as if someone were to take a stirring account of American history and insert into it at key points the American Constitution or legislation of Congress." Usually the P material is not so lively as the JE parts. The P writers were interested in details of worship and sacrifice, in laws, in genealogies, in specific locations and dates, in exact descriptions and measurements, and the like. When they added to the stories of J and E, they were likely to emphasize and even overemphasize the intervention of God and to make some actions almost magical. (Pederson, ILC, 11–14)

The D, or Deuteronomy, document has as its purpose reform in religious practices. J, E, and P were not yet united into a single work when D was composed.

"It was a great manifesto," writes Driver,

against the dominant tendencies of the time. It laid down the lines of a great religious reform. Whether written in the dark days of Manasseh, or during the brighter years which followed the accession of Josiah, it was a nobly-conceived endeavour to provide in anticipation a spiritual rallying-point, round which, when circumstances favoured, the disorganized forces of the national religion might range themselves again. It was an emphatic reaffirmation of the fundamental principles which Moses had long ago insisted on, loyalty to Jehovah and repudiation of all false gods: it was an endeavour to realize in practice the ideals of the prophets, especially of Hosea and Isaiah, to transform the Judah demoralized by Manasseh into the "holy nation" pictured in Isaiah's vision, and to awaken in it that devotion to God, and love for man, which Hosea had declared to be the first of human duties. (Driver, ILOT, 89)

"Throughout the discourses the author's aim is to provide motives, by which to secure loyalty to Him. . . . Deuteronomy may be described as the *prophetic re-formulation, and adaptation to new needs, of an older legislation.* It is highly probable that . . . the bulk of the laws contained in Dt. is undoubtedly far more ancient than the time of the author himself: and in dealing with them as he has done, in combining them into a manual for the guidance of the people, and providing them with hortatory introductions and comments." (Driver, ILOT, 91, emphasis mine)

Herbert Livingston gives an excellent summary of the dates of the four documents of Wellhausen's theory:

How then did the Wellhausen theory date the four documents? Since the D document was declared to be written in the seventh century and made public in Josiah's reform of 621 B.C., that document became the keystone for the procedure. It was decided that D knew about the contents of J and E, but not of the contents of P; hence, J and E were written before 621 B.C., and P, at a later date.

Dialectically, the J document, with its naive concepts, could be dated before E, and the early phases of the divided kingdom seemed to provide a good historical setting. It could be argued that J was the kingdom of Judah's reaction against the establishment of the kingdom of north Israel. The purpose of J, then, was to provide Judah with a "historical" document that would justify Judah's and Jerusalem's claim to be the governmental center of all Israel. Likewise, E would be the antithetical production of the kingdom of north Israel, led by the tribe of Ephraim, to show that there were historical antecedents in the Patriarchs and in Joshua for the governmental center to be located in the north.

The theory continued to conclude that after the destruction of the northern kingdom of Israel, in 721 B.C., broadminded men during the reign of Manasseh (first half of seventh century B.C.) felt that the E document was too valuable to lose, so they blended it with the J document. This new JE document became a new thesis and the D document its antithesis. The thinking of the D document is said to have triumphed, substantially, during the Exile in Babylon and colored the composition of the historical books Joshua through II Kings. However, the "Holiness Code," tied with Ezekiel, arose as another antithesis to D; and slowly, for perhaps a century, the priests in exile and then in Jerusalem put together the P document and made it the framework of a grand synthesis, the Pentateuch.

In summary, the J document is dated a bit later than 900 B.C., and the E document somewhat later in the ninth century B.C. The two were put together about 650 B.C., and were written about that same time and made public in 621 B.C. The P document appeared in the fifth century and the Pentateuch composed in approximately its present form about 400 B.C. (Livingston, PCE, 228–29)

As a result of the above assertions, those adhering to the documentary hypothesis reject the Mosaic authorship of the Pentateuch.

Moses, who may be dated around 1400 B.C., purports to have written the Pentateuch.

The documentarians reject this date and say it was not completed until sometime between the eighth and fifth centuries B.C.

The documentary hypothesis calls into question the credibility of the entire Old Testament. One would have to conclude, if their assertions are correct, that the Old Testament is a gigantic literary fraud. Either God did speak to and through Moses or we have to acknowledge that we possess a *belles-lettres* hoax.

The primary issue is not the "unity of the Pentateuch," but "how did this unity come about?" In other words, the literary section consisting of Genesis through Deuteronomy is one continuous narrative. The question posed here is, "How did this continuous narrative come into existence?" Was it, as traditional Christianity asserts and the Bible teaches, written by Moses, or was it compiled years later? This whole issue calls into question the trustworthiness of Jesus, the accuracy of both the Old and New Testament writers, and the integrity of Moses himself.

Livingston makes this acute observation:

Almost every book that promotes the theory has a listing of chapters and verses originally belonging to the independent documents. All isolated fragments that are left over are attributed, much too easily, to redactors or compilers. It should be understood, however, that there are no literary references, no extant manuscripts of any kind, which mention the J, E, D, or P documents, either singly or as a group. They have been created by separating them, with the aid of the above mentioned criteria, from the extant text of the Pentateuch. (Livingston, PCE, 227)

He goes on to cite the consequences of an adherence to the theory of the documentary hypothesis:

(a) Mosaic authorship is rejected, with only bits of the Pentateuch attributed to the Mosaic period; (b) for many of the scholars who accept the Wellhausen view, the men and women of the Pentateuch were not actual human beings—at best they were idealized heroes; (c) the Pentateuch does not give us a true history of ancient times but it reflects instead the history of the divided kingdom through the early part of the postexilic period; (d) none of the people in the Pentateuch were monotheistic, and it was the postexilic priests who made them look like believers in one God; (e) God never spoke to any individuals in ancient times, but again, it was the work of the priests that gives that impression; (f) very few of the laws in the Pentateuch were prekingdom in origin; (g) very few of the cultic practices recorded in the Pentateuch were prekingdom, and many were postexilic; (h) the early Israelites never had a tabernacle such as described in Exodus; (i) all claims in the Pentateuch that God acted redemptively and miraculously in behalf of Israel are erroneous; (j) any concept that the present structural unity of the five books was original with Moses is erroneous, and, finally; (k) the skepticism inherent in the theory creates a credibility gap with the ordinary layman to the extent that the Pentateuch becomes practically useless to him. (Livingston, PCE, 229)

The following chapters will (1) present the evidence for Mosaic authorship; (2) clarify the assertions of those who advocate and propagate the documentary hypothesis; and (3) provide some basic answers to the documentarian assumptions.

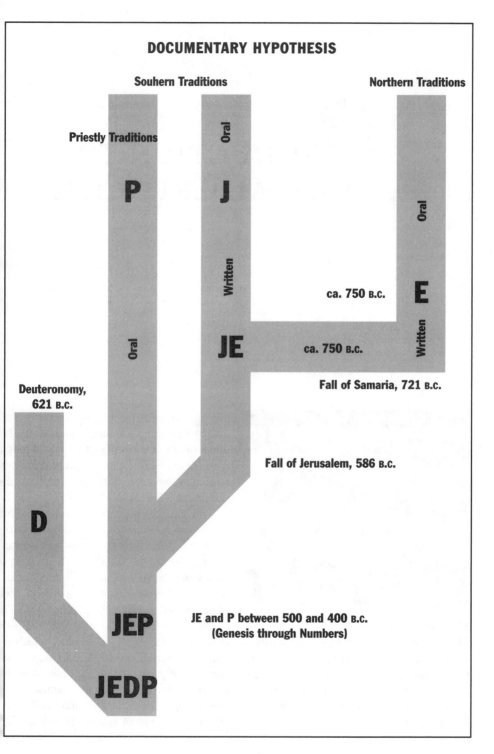

DOCUMENTARY HYPOTHESIS

Souhern Traditions

Northern Traditions

Priestly Traditions

Oral

P

J

Oral

E

Written

ca. 750 B.C.

Oral

JE

ca. 750 B.C.

Written

Fall of Samaria, 721 B.C.

Deuteronomy,
621 B.C.

Fall of Jerusalem, 586 B.C.

D

JEP

JE and P between 500 and 400 B.C.
(Genesis through Numbers)

JEDP

15
INTRODUCTION TO BIBLICAL CRITICISM

1A. DEFINITIONS

"The word *criticism* denotes, primarily, a judgment, or an act of judging; its derivation from a Greek verb (. . . [*krino*]) meaning *to discern,* or *to try,* or *to pass judgment upon,* or *to determine,* gives it this signification. As applied to literary matters, it conveys the idea, not of fault-finding, but of fairly and justly estimating both merits and defects. In other words, it is simply an impartial judgment, or as nearly such as the given critic can render, on whatever question is under consideration." (Selleck, NAB, 70–71)

This kind of study can be applied to the Bible, and is therefore called biblical criticism. It is defined by the *Christian Cyclopedia* as: "the science by which we arrive at a satisfactory acquaintance with the origin, history, and present state of the original text of Scripture." (Gardner, CC, 206)

Biblical criticism has been divided into two kinds: (1) Lower criticism, "which is more of a verbal and historical nature, and confined to the words, or the collocation of the words, as they stand in the manuscript or printed texts, the ancient versions, and other legitimate sources of appeal." (Gardner, CC,

206) Lower criticism is also known as textual criticism. (2) Higher criticism "consists in the exercise of the judgment in reference to the text, on grounds taken from the nature, form, method, subject, or arguments of the different books; the nature and connection of the context; the relation of passages to each other; the known circumstances of the writers, and those of the persons for whose immediate use they wrote." (Gardner, CC, 206)

1B. Higher Criticism

The questions posed by higher criticism are questions concerning the integrity, authenticity, credibility, and literary forms of the various writings that make up the Bible.

The term "higher criticism" is not, in and of itself, a negative term. James Orr, former professor of apologetics and systematic theology at the United Free Church College in Glasgow, Scotland, states it this way:

The truth is, and the fact has to be faced, that no one who studies the Old Testament in the light of modern knowledge can help being, to some extent, a "Higher Critic," nor is it desirable he should. The name has unfortunately come to be associated all but exclusively with a method yielding a certain class of results; but it has no necessary connection with these results. "Higher Criticism," rightly understood, is simply the careful scrutiny, on the principles which it is customary to apply to all literature, of the actual phenomena of the Bible, with a view to deduce from these such conclusions as may be warranted regarding the age, authorship, mode of composition, sources, etc., of the different books; and everyone who engages in such inquiries, with whatever aim, is a "Higher Critic," and cannot help himself. (Orr, POT, 9)

Green adds that higher criticism in its modern implication has a negative connotation, but in fact it properly means an inquiry into the origin and character of the writings to which it is applied. By using all available materials the higher critic seeks to ascertain the author of a work, the period in which it was written, the circumstances surrounding the writing, and the design with which the writing was produced. Investigations conducted in such a manner will prove most important in understanding and appreciating the writing. (Gilkey, COTBL, 6)

Higher criticism should remain as objective as possible. Orr states: "The age, authorship, and simple or composite character of a book are matters for investigation, to be determined solely by evidence, and it is justly claimed that criticism, in its investigation of such subjects, must be untrammelled: That faith cannot be bound up with results of purely literary judgments." (Orr, POT, 16)

This includes faith in theories and presuppositions as well as "religious" faith.

2B. History of Higher Criticism

Although higher criticism as an exacting science was applied to some classical literature before the nineteenth century, J. G. Eichhorn, a German rationalist of the late 1700s, was the first to apply the term to the study of the Bible. He introduced the second edition of his *Einleitung in das Alte Testament* (Old Testament Introduction) in 1787 with the words:

"I have been obliged to bestow the greatest amount of labor on a hitherto entirely unworked field, the investigation of the inner constitution of the particular writings of the Old Testament, by the Higher Criticism (a new name to no humanist)." (Chapman, IP, 19)

Eichhorn has thus been called the "Father of Old Testament Criticism."

Although the term "higher criticism" was not associated with biblical studies until

Eichhorn, it was Jean Astruc's treatise on Genesis in 1753 that actually marked the beginning of higher critical methodology as applied to the Old Testament. While Astruc defended Moses as the author of Genesis, he concluded that there were independent sources woven together throughout the book. Subsequently the entire Pentateuch (Genesis through Deuteronomy) was subjected to extensive source analysis. Higher criticism therefore may be said to have been spawned and developed in Pentateuchal analysis. It was the highly complex conclusions regarding the authorship and dating of the Pentateuch (the documentary hypothesis) by European (especially German) higher critics, promulgated primarily during the 1800s, that established the foundation for most subsequent critical inquiry into the Old Testament. Therefore, an investigation of modern Old Testament higher criticism in general will have to consider, first of all, past Pentateuchal analysis. It is the key to a proper evaluation of all higher criticism of the Old Testament since Astruc.

Unfortunately, the higher critical school that grew up out of German scholarship in the last century employed some faulty methodology and tenaciously held to some questionable presuppositions. This seriously

> Because of its wholesale reconstruction of Israelite literature, and its radical remaking of Hebrew history, this school, which has dominated Old Testament studies since its inception, together with the methodology that achieved these drastic results, came to be known in some circles as "destructive higher criticism."

undermined the validity of many of their conclusions. Entire books were rent into numerous "sources"; most of the books in the Old Testament were dated later—by almost a thousand years in some cases—than the actual witness of the documents themselves would allow. The biblical account of the early Hebrews' history was replaced by a complicated and well-thought-out theory in contradiction to Israel's own account of her history in almost every major point.

Because of its wholesale reconstruction of Israelite literature and its radical remaking of Hebrew history, this school, which has dominated Old Testament studies since its inception, together with the methodology that achieved these drastic results, came to be known in some circles as "destructive higher criticism."

2A. THREE SCHOOLS OF RADICAL PENTATEUCHAL CRITICISM

1B. Documentary Hypothesis: Statement of Theory

The Pentateuch, although traditionally ascribed to Moses, was actually a compilation of four basic documents written by independent authors over a period of approximately four hundred years, beginning about 850 B.C., and gradually combined by unknown redactors who put it in its basic form by about 400 B.C. The main criterion for this theory was a close analysis of the text itself through which it was thought the actual documents could be isolated. The classic expression of this theory came from German scholar Julius Wellhausen in 1878. (Harrison, IOT, 19–27)

2B. Form Criticism (Formgeschichte)

The form critical school likewise held that the Pentateuch was the product of a compilation process and not the work of Moses. But it differed from the documentary hypothesis in that it held that the individual documents were themselves compilations developed from early oral tradition and placed in writing only during or after the exilic period (586 B.C.). Very little could be known about the literary development of these documents and it was clear to this school that the neat isolation of documents achieved by the documentary school was impossible. The only practical approach was to go behind the sources in their written form and examine the types of categories to which the original material belonged in its oral state, then to follow the probable course of development of each one of these oral units until it finally reached its written form. Great emphasis was placed upon the *Sitz im Leben* (life situation) of these different categories in determining through what kind of process they evolved into their written form. Herman Gunkel and Hugo Gressmann, two German scholars, have been credited with founding this school at the beginning of the twentieth century. (Gunkel's *Die Sagen der Genesis,* 1901; *Die Schriften des Alten Testaments,* 1911; Gressmann's *Die Alteste Geschichtsschreibung und Prophetie Israels,* 1910) (Harrison, IOT, 35–38)

3B. Oral Traditionists ("Uppsala School")

Similar to the form critical school, the oral traditionists held that the Pentateuch is not Mosaic in origin but is rather a collection of material compiled over centuries and com-

mitted to writing not before the Exile. Totally rejecting the documentary hypothesis as an occidental solution to a literary problem of the vastly different ancient Near East, this Scandinavian school placed even more emphasis on oral tradition than Gunkel and the form critics. Some even claimed that oral tradition was more important than writing in the transmission of material in the ancient Orient. It is not written documents that must be dealt with but rather units of oral tradition, circles of tradition, and various "schools" within these traditionist circles.

They seek to classify the material into literary categories such as narratives, legal, prose, poetry, and especially subdivided types called *Gattungen.* These subdivided types are given "laws" as to how they develop in "life situations" *(Sitz im Leben).*

There are two basic sources of tradition in the Pentateuch: one extends from Genesis through Numbers and points to a P (priestly) type school of tradition. The other is a D (Deuteronomy through 2 Kings) work that exhibits a different style than P and points to a D circle of traditionists. Largely responsible for this most recent trend in Pentateuchal analysis were Johannes Pedersen (*Die Auffassung vom Alten Testament,* 1931) and Ivan Engnell (*Gamla Testamentet en Traditionshistorisk Inledning,* 1945). (Harrison, IOT, 66–69)

16

INTRODUCTION TO THE PENTATEUCH

1A. WHAT IS THE PENTATEUCH?

As noted earlier, the first five books of the Old Testament—Genesis, Exodus, Leviticus, Numbers, and Deuteronomy—are known as the Pentateuch. The word *Pentateuch* is derived from the Greek word *pentateuchos*, meaning "a compilation of five" or "five-volumed [book]." (Aalders, ASIP, 13; NBD, 957) Jewish tradition has called these five books the Torah (deriving from the Hebrew word *tôrâ*, meaning "instruction"), or, the

Book of the Law, the Law of Moses, or, simply, the Law. (Albright, ACBC, 903) Origen, a third-century church father, was the first to give the name Pentateuch to these five books of Moses. (Harrison, IOT, 495)

2A. WHAT DOES IT CONTAIN?

Harrison breaks down the contents of the Pentateuch as follows:

1. Primeval History with a Mesopotamian Background: Genesis 1—11
2. History of the Patriarchs: Genesis 12—50
3. The Oppression of Israel and Preparations for the Exodus: Exodus 1—9
4. The Exodus, Passover, and the Arrival at Sinai: Exodus 10—19
5. The Decalogue and the Covenant at Sinai: Exodus 20—24
6. Legislation Relating to the Tabernacle

and Aaronic Priesthood: Exodus 25—31

7. The Idolatrous Violation of the Covenant: Exodus 32—34

8. The Implementation of Regulations Concerning the Tabernacle: Exodus 35—40

9. The Law of Offerings: Leviticus 1—7

10. The Consecration of the Priests and Initial Offerings: Leviticus 8—10

11. The Laws of Cleanliness: Leviticus 11—15

12. The Day of Atonement: Leviticus 16

13. Laws Concerning Morality and Cleanliness: Leviticus 17—26

14. Vows and Tithes: Leviticus 27

15. Numberings and Laws: Numbers 1—9

16. The Journey from Sinai to Kadesh: Numbers 10—20

17. Wanderings to Moab: Numbers 21—36

18. Historical Retrospect to the Wilderness Period: Deuteronomy 1—4

19. Second Speech, with a Hortatory Introduction: Deuteronomy 5—11

20. Collected Statutes and Rights: Deuteronomy 12—26

21. Cursing and Blessing: Deuteronomy 27—30

22. The Accession of Joshua and Death of Moses: Deuteronomy 31—34 (Harrison, IOT, 496)

3A. PURPOSE AND IMPORTANCE OF THE PENTATEUCH

The Bible is history, but of a very special kind. It is the history of God's redemption of mankind, and the Pentateuch is chapter one of that history. (Unger, IGOT, 187–88)

Unger elaborates:

The author of the Pentateuch had a definite plan. He did not apply himself to recording the story of human history. His task was rather to give an account of God's gracious provisions for man's salvation. The Pentateuch, accordingly, is history with a motive behind it, a deep, religious motive, which imbues the whole. The religious principle underlying it, on the other hand, does not ren-

> The Pentateuch testifies to the saving acts of God, who is sovereign Lord of history and nature. The central act of God in the Pentateuch (and indeed the Old Testament) is the Exodus from Egypt. Here God broke in upon the consciousness of the Israelites and revealed Himself as the redeeming God.
>
> —D. A. HUBBARD

der the events recounted any less historical. It merely gives them a permanent importance far transcending the times in which and about which they were written and far out-reaching in importance their application to any one nation or people, investing them with an inestimable and abiding value for all mankind.…

Failure to comprehend the precise character and purpose of the Pentateuch has led many critics to deny its historicity altogether or to adopt low views of its reliability. If, for instance, the account of the Egyptian sojourn, the miraculous deliverance and the wilderness wanderings were fictitious, its vital connection not only with Hebrew history but with the whole Biblical plan of salvation raises the insoluable [sic] problem of how this extraordinary record could ever have been fabricated. (Unger, IGOT, 188–89)

D. A. Hubbard speaks of the prime importance of the Pentateuch in understanding Israel's relationship with God:

A record of revelation and response, the Pentateuch testifies to the saving acts of God who is sovereign Lord of history and nature. The central act of God in the Pentateuch (and indeed the Old Testament) is the Exodus from Egypt. Here God broke in upon the consciousness of the Israelites and revealed

Himself as the redeeming God. Insights gained from this revelation enabled them under Moses' leadership to reevaluate the traditions of their ancestors and see in them the budding of God's dealings which had bloomed so brilliantly in the liberation from Egypt. (Hubbard, NBD, 963)

Even Langdon B. Gilkey, hardly a conservative scholar, calls the Exodus-Sinai experience "the pivotal point of biblical religion." (Gilkey, COTBL, 147)

Therefore, the Pentateuch occupies an important place in the Christian view of the universe since it records God's initial revealing of Himself to mankind.

As Gilkey puts it: "The Exodus event has a confessional as well as a historical interest for us. The question of what God did at Sinai is, in other words, not only a question for the scholar of Semitic religion and theology, it is even more a question for the contemporary believer who wishes to make his witness today to the acts of God in history." (Gilkey, COTBL, 147)

4A. ORIGIN AND HISTORY OF NON-MOSAIC AUTHORSHIP THEORY

According to John of Damascus, the Nazarites, a sect of Christians of Jewish birth living during the second century, denied that Moses wrote the Pentateuch. (Young, IOT, 113) The Clementine Homilies, a collection of ancient writings somewhat later than the second century, stated that the Pentateuch was written by seventy wise men after Moses' death. (For a study of the unreliability of these writings and the invalid methodology of the historical and biblical interpretation they employed, see E. J. Young's *An Introduction to the Old Testament,* pp. 118–19.) (Young, IOT, 112)

Although there were several groups and individuals from the first two centuries A.D. who denied the essential Mosaic authorship of the Pentateuch, the following passage from Young should be noted:

During the first two centuries of the Christian era there is no recorded instance of criticism that is hostile to the Bible among the Church fathers or in the orthodox Church itself. The Apostolic Fathers and the subsequent Ante-Nicene Fathers, in so far as they expressed themselves on the subject, believed Moses to be the author of the Pentateuch, and the Old Testament to be a divine book. . . .

Such instances of hostile criticism as are extant from this period come either from groups that were considered to be heretical or from the external pagan world. Furthermore, this criticism reflected certain philosophical presuppositions and is of a decidedly biased and unscientific character. (Young, IOT, 113–14)

The allegation that Moses was not the author of the Pentateuch thus had its beginning during the first two centuries A.D. The primary basis upon which this charge rested was the presence of passages supposedly written after Moses' time.

Though there was some minor activity in the questioning of Mosaic authorship during the following centuries, it was not until the eighteenth century, when the argument moved to a new foundation—that of literary criticism—that the theory of non-Mosaic authorship was extensively developed. (For a survey of the developments from the third century to the 1700s, see E. J. Young, *An Introduction to the Old Testament.*) (Young, IOT, 116–20)

17
DEVELOPMENT OF THE DOCUMENTARY HYPOTHESIS

1A. IMPORTANCE OF THE DOCUMENTARY HYPOTHESIS IN RADICAL HIGHER CRITICISM

We have already referred to the important role that the documentary hypothesis has played in the establishment of a whole school of higher critical scholarship that has undeniably undermined the literary and historical integrity of the Old Testament. The radical conclusions reached by this school therefore necessitate a careful and searching investigation of its position by all serious students of the Old Testament. Any such investigation must start with the analysis of the Pentateuch as set forth in the documentary hypothesis. Whether this radical higher criticial position is indeed a valid one or whether it ought to be discarded in favor of one that is better suited to the facts at hand will be determined largely by an objective assessment of the classic documentary hypothesis and its subsequent revisions.

2A. HISTORY OF ITS DEVELOPMENT

1B. First Documentary Theory

As far as is known, a Protestant priest, H. B. Witter, in the early part of the eighteenth century, was the first to assert that there were two parallel accounts of creation and that they were distinguishable by the use of the different divine names. He was also the first to suggest the divine names as criteria for distinguishing the different documents. (See his *Jura Israelitarum in Palestina,* 1711.) (Cassuto, DH, 9; Young, IOT, 118)

The first significant treatment of the documentary theory was set forth in 1753 by the French physician Jean Astruc in his book *Conjectures Concerning the Original Memoranda Which It Appears Moses Used to Compose the Book of Genesis.*

Astruc held that there were distinct documents in Genesis, discernible primarily by the unique usage of the divine names Elohim and Jehovah in the opening chapters. Astruc realized that the divine name phenomenon could not be used as a criterion for testing any portions of the Pentateuch beyond Genesis. Alleged repetition of events (for example, the creation and flood stories) and chronological inaccuracies were also cited by Astruc as evidence for underlying sources. Although he developed a documentary theory, Astruc defended Moses as being the compiler of the documents. (Young, IOT, 118–21)

The first to introduce Astruc's theory to Germany was J. G. Eichhorn. In his three-volume introduction to the Old Testament, *Einleitung in das Alte Testament* (1780–1783),

Eichhorn suggested that criteria for source analysis in the Pentateuch should include literary considerations (such as diversity in style, words peculiar to previously isolated documents, and so forth) in addition to Astruc's divine name criterion. (Harrison, IOT, 14)

2B. Fragmentary Hypothesis

1C. The Theory

In 1800 a Scottish Roman Catholic priest, A. Geddes, called Astruc's two-document theory a "work of fancy." He held that there is a mass of fragments, large and small (not actual documents), that were pieced together by a redactor about five hundred years after Moses' death. From 1802 through 1805 the German Johann Vater developed Geddes's theory. He tried to demonstrate the gradual growth of the Pentateuch from individual fragments. He held that there were at least thirty-eight different fragment sources. Although some of the particular fragments were from Moses' time, the Pentateuch as we now have it was compiled about the time of the Jewish Exile (586 B.C.). This theory was developed more fully in 1831 by the German scholar A. T. Hartmann. (Young, IOT, 123–27)

2C. Essential Difference from Astruc's Documentary Theory

Those who hold this theory believe there are no continuous documents, but rather a mass of fragments of documents that are impossible to isolate.

3B. Supplementary Theory

1C. The Theory

In 1823 Heinrich Ewald dealt the "death blow" to the fragmentary hypothesis in his book *Die Komposition der Genesis Kritisch Untersucht,* in which he defended the unity of Genesis. By 1830 he had developed a new theory that held that the basis of the first six books of the Bible lay in an Elohistic writing, but that later a parallel document that used the divine name "Jehovah" arose. Still later, an editor took excerpts from this J document and inserted them into the initial E document. Numerous versions of this basic hypothesis subsequently developed, with some, such as De Wette (1840) and Lengerke (1844), holding not to one supplementation but to three. (Young, IOT, 127–29)

2C. Essential Difference from Fragmentary Hypothesis

According to this theory, there is not a hodgepodge of sources but rather a unity with one basic document (E) running throughout Genesis, while supplements (J) were added later.

4B. Crystallization Theory

1C. The Theory

By 1845 Ewald had rejected his own supplementary theory. In its place he suggested that instead of one supplementer there were five narrators who wrote various parts of the Pentateuch at different times over a period of seven hundred years. The fifth narrator, supposedly a Judean of the time of King Uzziah, constantly used the name Jehovah and was the final editor. He completed the Pentateuch between about 790 and 740 B.C. Ewald also held that Deuteronomy was an independent work added around 500 B.C. Others who held to a simpler form of this theory were August Knobel (1861) and E. Schraeder (1869). (Young, IOT, 129–30)

2C. Essential Difference from Supplementary Theory

This theory holds that there is not one supplementer but rather five different narrators who wrote different parts of the Pentateuch at various times.

5B. Modified Documentary Theory

1C. The Theory

In 1853 Herman Hupfeld sought to show:

(a) that the J sections in Genesis were not supplements but rather formed a continuous document.

(b) that the basic E document (supplementary theory) was not one continuous document but rather a composite of two separate documents (which he called P and E).

(c) that these three documents were put into their present form by a redactor.

(d) that Deuteronomy was an entirely separate document, added last (designated by D).

Thus, Hupfeld held that there were actually four distinct documents woven into the fabric of the Pentateuchal narrative: P (early Elohist), E, J, and D. (Young, IOT, 130–31)

2C. Essential Difference from Crystallization Theory

Not five narrators but one redactor combined three documents: the J document, the early Elohist P document, and the late Elohist E document.

6B. Development Hypothesis (Revised Documentary Theory)

Wellhausen restated the documentary hypothesis (later to be called the Graf-Wellhausen hypothesis) in terms of the evolutionary view of history that prevailed in philosophical circles at that time.

1C. The Theory (today most commonly called the "Documentary Hypothesis")

Whereas Hupfeld had established the chronological order of the documents as being P E J D, during the 1860s, Karl H. Graf reversed the order to J E D P, holding that the basic document (first Elohist or P) was not the earliest portion of the Pentateuch but the last. Graf's theory was strengthened by Abraham Kuenen's book *Die Godsdienst van Israel* (1869–1870).

Julius Wellhausen (*Die Komposition des Hexateuchs,* 1876, and *Prolegomena zur Geschichte Israels,* 1878) skillfully and eloquently formulated Graf's and Kuenen's revised documentary theory and gave it the classic expression that brought it to prominence in most European (and later American) scholarly circles. Wellhausen restated the documentary hypothesis (later to be called the Graf-Wellhausen hypothesis) in terms of the evolutionary view of history that prevailed in philosophical circles at that time.

Wellhausen held that:

(1) The earliest part of the Pentateuch came from two originally independent documents, the Jehovist (850 B.C.) and the Elohist (750 B.C.).

(2) From these the Jehovist compiled a narrative work (650 B.C.).

(3) Deuteronomy was written in Josiah's time and its author incorporated this into the Jehovist's work.

(4) The priestly legislation in the Elohist document was largely the work of Ezra and is referred to as the Priestly document. A later editor(s) revised and edited the conglomeration of documents by about 200 B.C. to form the Pentateuch we have today.

In England, W. Robertson Smith (*The Old Testament in the Jewish Church,* 1881) interpreted and propounded the writings of Wellhausen.

But it was Samuel R. Driver who, in his *Introduction to the Literature of the Old Testament* (1891), gave Wellhausenism its classic presentation to the English-speaking world. The most notable early advocate of the Wellhausen school in America was Charles A. Briggs (*The Higher Criticism of the Hexateuch,* 1893). (Archer, SOTI, 79; Young, IOT, 136–38)

2C. Essential Difference from Modified Documentary Theory

P is not the earliest document but the latest JEDP sequence as worked out on a systematic evolutionary pattern.

7B. The Development and Modern Revisions of the Documentary Hypothesis Since Wellhausen

1C. Rudolph Smend (*Die Erzählung des Hexateuchs auf Ihre Quellen Untersucht,* 1912):
Not one J document but two: J1 and J2. (Archer, SOTI, 91)

2C. Otto Eissfeldt (*Hexateuchsynopse,* 1922): L document within J document, written in 860 B.C. (Archer, SOTI, 91)

3C. R. H. Kennett in *Deuteronomy and the Decalogue* (1920); Gustav Hölscher in *Komposition und Ursprung des Deuteronomiums* (The Composition and Origin of Deuteronomy) (1922). Both held that: "Deuteronomy was later than the Josiah period. Thus, the 'book of the law' found in the temple in 621 B.C. was not Deuteronomy." (Archer, SOTI, 100–1)

4C. Martin Kegel, in *Die Kultusreformation des Josias* (Josiah's Reformation of the Cultus) (1919), Adam C. Welch, in *The Code of Deuteronomy* (1924), Edward Robertson, in *Bulletin of John Rylands Library* (1936, 1941, 1942, 1944), all concluded that Deuteronomy was written much earlier than Josiah's time (621 B.C.). (Archer, SOTI, 101–2)

5C. Max Löhr, in his *Der Priestercodex in der Genesis* (The Priestly Code in Genesis) (1924), asserted that:

1. An independent P source never existed.
2. The Pentateuch was composed by Ezra, who drew upon preexilic written materials.
3. These written materials could not be identified with any specific documents (such as J, E, and so forth). (Archer, SOTI, 97)

6C. Julius Morgenstern (*The Oldest Document of the Hexateuch,* 1927): Concluded that a K document (somewhat similar to Eissfeldt's L) was present in J. (Archer, SOTI, 91)

7C. Paul Volz and Wilhelm Rudolph, in their *Der Elohist als Erzähler: Ein Irrweg der Penta-teuchkritik?* (The Elohist as a Narrator: a Mistake in Pentateuchal Criticism?) (1933), concluded:

1. There were no grounds for the existence of a separate E document.
2. Only one person wrote the whole book of Genesis, with a few additions made by a later editor. (Archer, SOTI, 100)

8C. Robert Pfeiffer (*Introduction to the Old Testament,* 1941): Claimed that an S document is found in the J and E sections of Genesis 1—11 and 14—8, dated 950 B.C. (Archer, SOTI, 91)

18
GROUND RULES

The ancient oriental environment of the Old
Testament provides many very close literary
parallels. And while many ignore it, no one
can well deny that principles found to be
valid in studying ancient oriental history and
literature should be applied to the Old Testament history and literature. Likewise principles that are decidedly false when applied to
ancient Near Eastern literature and history
should not be applied to Old Testament literature and history. (Kitchen, AOOT, 28)

Three elementary principles should permeate this investigation:

1A. APPROACH THE HEBREW SCRIPTURES AS OTHER ANCIENT LITERATURE—HARMONISTICALLY

The literary genius and critic Coleridge
established long ago this basic rule for literature: "When we meet an apparent error in a
good author, we are to presume ourselves
ignorant of his understanding, until we are
certain that we *understand his ignorance.*"
(Cited by Allis, FBM, 125, emphasis his)

Historian John Warwick Montgomery
states that in determining the essential historicity of an ancient document "historical
and literary scholarship continues to follow
Aristotle's dictum [*De Arte Poetica,*
14606–14616] that the benefit of the doubt

is to be given to the document itself, not arrogated [unjustly assumed] by the critic to himself." (Montgomery, HC, 29)

Kitchen has more recently emphasized the necessity of this principle in Old Testament studies as well as in Egyptology: "It is normal practice to assume the general reliability of statements in our sources, unless there is good, explicit evidence to the contrary. . . . The basic harmony that ultimately underlies extant records should be sought out, even despite apparent discrepancy. Throughout ancient history, our existing sources are incomplete and elliptical." (Kitchen, AOOT, 28–33)

Allis labels this approach the "harmonistic method," and elaborates on its application to the Hebrew writings:

> It has two obvious advantages. The one is that it does justice to the intelligence and common sense of the writers of the Bible. To claim that the writers compilers, editors of the biblical records would introduce or combine conflicting accounts of the same event into a narrative is to challenge their intelligence, or their honesty, or their competence to deal with the data which they record. The second is that it is the biblical method of interpretation. The many times and various ways in which the biblical writers quote or refer to one another implies their confidence in the sources quoted. Their method is a harmonistic method. Most important of all, this method of interpretation is the only one which is consistent with the high claims of the Bible to be the Word of God. (Allis, OTCC, 35)

2A. EXERCISE AN OPEN MIND

Bewer, a firm defendant of the documentary position, has provided an outstanding exposition of this principle: "A truly scientific criticism never stops. No question is ever closed for it. When new facts appear or a new way of understanding old facts is shown, the critic is ready to reexamine, to modify or to overthrow his theory, if it does not account for all the facts in the most satisfactory way. For he is interested in the truth of his theory, and indifferent to the label, old or new, orthodox or heterodox, conservative, liberal or radical, that others may place upon it." (Bewer, PDS, 305)

Another radical critic, W. R. Harper, heartily agrees: "It should be remembered that, after all, it is not a question of opinion, but of fact. It matters not what any particular critic may think or say. It is the duty of every man who studies this question to take up one by one the points suggested, and to decide for himself whether or not they are true." (Harper, PQ, 7)

R. K. Harrison is likewise insistent upon such an attitude: "As the result of the impact of what T. H. Huxley once called 'one ugly little fact,' the truly scientific investigator will make whatever changes are demanded by the situation, even if he is compelled to begin his research *de novo* to all intents and purposes." (Harrison, IOT, 508)

The direction in which the facts lead may not be palatable, but it must be followed. Kitchen reasons that even if "some of the results reached here approximate to a traditional view or seem to agree with theological orthodoxy, then this is simply because the tradition in question or that orthodoxy are that much closer to the real facts than is commonly realized. While one must indeed never prefer mere orthodoxy to truth, it is also perverse to deny that orthodox views can be true." (Kitchen, AOOT, 173)

The highly respected Jewish scholar Cyrus Gordon, formerly of Brandeis University and New York University, concludes that "a commitment to any hypothetical source structure like JEDP is out of keeping with what I consider the only tenable position for a critical scholar: *to go wherever the evidence leads him.*" (Gordon, HCFF, 3, emphasis his)

3A. SUBMIT TO EXTERNAL, OBJECTIVE CONTROLS

These all-important facts to which our minds must necessarily remain open are discovered by an archaeological examination of the ancient Orient. Cassuto exhorts us "to conduct our investigation without prejudgment or anticipatory fear, but to rely on the

> Priority must always be given to tangible, objective data, and to external evidence, over subjective theory or speculative opinions. Facts must control theory, not vice versa.
>
> —KENNETH KITCHEN

objective examination of the texts themselves and the help afforded by our knowledge of the ancient East, in the cultural environment of which the children of Israel lived when the Torah was written. Let us not approach the Scriptural passages with the literary and aesthetic criteria of our time, but let us apply to them the standards obtaining in the ancient East generally and among the people of Israel particularly." (Cassuto, DH, 12)

Kitchen establishes this principle as an axiom: "Priority must always be given to tangible, objective data, and to external evidence, over subjective theory or speculative opinions. Facts must control theory, not vice versa." (Kitchen, AOOT, 28–33)

Certainly Cassuto is to be commended for attributing much respect to the documentarians because of their labor. There should be no attempt to belittle them, but we do have the right to examine rigidly the

hypothesis they put forth and their method of obtaining their evidence for this hypothesis. Since a tremendous amount of archaeological evidence today suggests that these documentarians were lacking when they constructed their theories, we may discover something they missed or solve a problem that left them perplexed. (Cassuto, DH, 13)

"In view of the grave shortcomings," writes Harrison, "of the Graf-Wellhausen approach to the problems of the Pentateuch, and to the Old Testament in general, any new study will need to be based firmly upon an accredited methodology that will utilize the vast quantities of control material now available to scholars throughout the world, and will argue inductively from the known to the unknown instead of making pronouncements from a purely theoretical standpoint that bears only a slight relation to some of the known facts." (Harrison, IOT, 533)

Elsewhere, Harrison affirms that "it is only when criticism is properly established upon an assured basis of ancient Near Eastern life rather than upon occidental philosophical or methodological speculations that Old Testament scholarship can expect to reflect something of the vitality, dignity, and spiritual richness of the law, prophecy, and the sacred writings." (Harrison, IOT, 82)

Kyle very effectively epitomizes this principle: "Theory must always give way to fact. In the settlement of disputes, facts are final. Even so staunch a defender of the rights and function of criticism as Dr. Driver (*Authority and Archaeology*, p. 143) recognized this principle, *at least in theory.* For he says: 'Where the testimony of archaeology is direct, it is of the highest possible value, and, as a rule, determines the question decisively: even where it is indirect, if it is sufficiently circumstantial and precise, it makes a settlement highly probable.'" (Kyle, DVMBC, 32)

4A. CONCLUSION

These principles are implicit in ancient Near Eastern studies. A positive approach does not exclude critical study of material. It does, however, avoid the distortions that hypercriticism brings. If positive studies had been pursued, the modern critical school would have a different position, and many of the supposed problems would be in correct proportion. (Kitchen, AOOT, 34)

The present condition in Old Testament criticism is summed up by Kitchen:

> Through the impact of the Ancient Orient upon the Old Testament and upon Old Testament studies a new tension is being set up while an older one is being reduced. For the comparative material from the Ancient Near East is tending to agree with the extant structure of Old Testament documents as actually transmitted to us, rather than with the reconstructions of nineteenth-century Old Testament scholarship—or with its twentieth-century prolongation and developments to the present day.
>
> Some examples may illustrate this point. The valid and close parallels to the social customs of the Patriarchs come from documents of the nineteenth to fifteenth centuries B.C. (agreeing with an early-second-millennium origin for this material in Genesis), and not from Assyro-Babylonian data of the tenth to sixth centuries B.C. (possible period of the supposed "J," "E" sources). Likewise for Genesis 23, the closest parallel comes from the Hittite laws which passed into oblivion with the fall of the Hittite Empire about 1200 B.C. The covenant-forms which appear in Exodus, Deuteronomy and Joshua follow the model of those current in the thirteenth century B.C.— the period of Moses and Joshua—and *not* those of the first millennium B.C. (Kitchen, AOOT, 25)

Instead of beginning our biblical studies with the presupposition that the Old Testament has error throughout, many contradictions, historical inaccuracies, and gross textual errors, our study should include a meticulous examination of the Hebrew text in light of modern archaeology and existing knowledge of cultures of the ancient Near East in the third millennium B.C. (Harrison, IOT, 532)

Orlinsky remarks that the modern flow of thinking is going in this direction: "More and more the older view that the Biblical data were suspect and even likely to be false, unless corroborated by extra-biblical facts, is giving way to one which holds that, by and large, the Biblical accounts are more likely to be true than false, unless clear-cut evidence from sources outside the Bible demonstrates the reverse." (Orlinsky, AI, 81)

19
DOCUMENTARY
PRESUPPOSITIONS

1A. INTRODUCTION

Some very important presuppositions underly much radical higher critical methodology. This is not necessarily objectionable, and is to a degree inevitable. Orr cites the German theologian Biedermann *(Christliche Dogmatik)*: It is

not true but sand in the eyes, if one asserts that genuinely scientific and historic criticism can and should proceed without dogmatic presuppositions. In the last instance the consideration of the so-called purely historic grounds always reaches the point where it can and will decide concerning this, whether it can or cannot hold some particular thing in and of itself to be possible. . . . Some sort of boundary definitions, be they ever so elastically held, of what is historically possible, every student brings with him to historical investigations; and these are for that student dogmatic presuppositions. (Orr, POT, 172)

The radical critics are not lacking when it comes to ability and scholarship. The problem is not their lack of knowledge of the evidence but rather their hermeneutics or approach to biblical criticism based upon their worldview.

Gerhardsson has appropriately said, "The validity of its results depends on the validity of its first principles." (Gerhardsson, TTEC, 6)

So often discussion in the area of biblical criticism is carried out on the level of conclusions or answers, rather than at the level of presuppositions or our basis of thinking.

Talking at the level of presuppositions reveals whether people have the right to come to a logical conclusion. If a person has reasonable presuppositions in light of known evidence, his logical conclusions may well be correct. But if his presuppositions are faulty, his logical conclusions will only magnify original errors as an argument is extended.

In the study of the Bible there have always been various philosophical presuppositions. Evaluating these is beyond the scope of this work. But archaeology has given us much to consider today in the objective realm. Any presuppositions regarding the Bible must consider this as well.

One of the first steps in this study is to harmonize presuppositions with the objec-

tive data available, before serious discussion on other points begins.

Concerning the work of documentarians, we must ask the question, "What were their presuppositions, and were they admissible?"

The most basic presupposition of the majority of radical critics is an antisupernaturalistic worldview. We addressed this presupposition in chapter 12.

2A. PRIORITY OF SOURCE ANALYSIS OVER ARCHAEOLOGY

One of the major weaknesses of the radical higher critical school was that in much of their analysis and isolation of alleged documents their conclusions were based almost exclusively upon their own subjective theories regarding the history of Israel and the probable development and compilation process of the supposed sources. They failed to refer adequately to the more objective and verifiable information provided by archaeology.

The methodological parallels that continue between Pentateuchal and Homeric studies are due to reciprocal influence and also to mutual profit from the progress made in general techniques of research.

"Undoubtedly," writes Cassuto,

it is affected also by the opinions and concepts, the trends and demands, the character and idiosyncrasies of each age. This being so, it may well be that we have not before us an objective discovery of what is actually to be found in the ancient books, but the result of the subjective impression that these writings have on the people of a given environment. If among peoples so different from one another . . . scholars find literary phenomena so complex and yet so similar, and precisely one trend in one epoch and another trend in another, and yet a third period, the suspicion naturally arises that the investigators' conceptions are not based on purely objective facts but that they were appreciably motivated by the subjective characteristics of the researchers themselves. (Cassuto, DH, 12)

Harrison points out:

Whatever else may be adduced in criticism of Wellhausen and his school, it is quite evident that his theory of Pentateuchal origins would have been vastly different (if, indeed, it had

> Wellhausen took almost no note whatever of the progress in the field of oriental scholarship, and once having arrived at his conclusions, he never troubled to revise his opinion in the light of subsequent research in the general field.
>
> —R. K. HARRISON

been formulated at all) had Wellhausen chosen to take account of the archaeological material available for study in his day, and had he subordinated his philosophical and theoretical considerations to a sober and rational assessment of the factual evidence as a whole. While he and his followers drew to some extent upon the philological discoveries of the day and manifested a degree of interest in the origins of late Arabic culture in relation to Semitic presursors, they depended almost exclusively upon their own view of the culture and religious history of the Hebrews for purposes of Biblical interpretation. (Harrison, IOT, 509)

Harrison continues: "Wellhausen took almost no note whatever of the progress in the field of oriental scholarship, and once having arrived at his conclusions, he never troubled to revise his opinion in the light of subsequent research in the general field." (Harrison, IOT, 509)

Even as late as 1931 some critics were still claiming that analyzing alleged sources was

the most accurate method for determining the historical background of the Pentateuch. J. Pedersen, a Swedish scholar and one of the pioneers of the oral tradition school, made the following statement ("Die Auffassung vom Alten Testament" in *Zeitschrift fur die Alttestamentliche Wissenschaft*, 1931, Vol. 49, p. 179) here cited by C. R. North: "All the sources of the Pentateuch are both pre-exilic and post-exilic. When we work with them and the other sources, we have no other means than that of intrinsic appraisement *(innere Schatzung)*; in every single case the character of the material must be examined and the supposed background be inferred from that." (North, PC, 62)

Such dependence upon so subjective a methodology as source analysis has been criticized by many scholars.

Mendenhall writes: "The value of literary analysis for history and its success in convincing the scholarly world today depends upon the isolation of more adequate criteria for judgment than has evidently so far been produced by its adherents. The results, consequently, must be judged to fall in the category of hypotheses, not of historical fact. For the reconstruction of history itself, something more than literary analysis is needed, valuable and necessary as hypotheses are." (Mendenhall, BHT, 34)

"Literary criticism," cautions Wright,

is an indispensable tool for the introductory study of written documents, but it is not in itself the key to *historical* reconstruction. As Mendenhall has expressed it, "The isolation of a source in the Pentateuch or elsewhere could give no more historical information other than the fact that it was reduced to written form, at some more or less fixed chronological period, by a person with a particular view of Israel's past. It could not produce criteria for the evaluation of the sources it isolated, beyond a possible demonstration that a later source used an earlier" ("Biblical History in Transition"). Consequently, external criteria are needed, and these are precisely what the archaeologist has provided in abundance. (Wright, AOTS, 46)

A. H. Sayce adds that: "Time after time the most positive assertions of a skeptical criticism have been disproved by archaeological discovery, events and personages that were confidently pronounced to be mythical have been shown to be historical, and the older writers have turned out to have been better acquainted with what they were describing than the modern critic who has flouted them." (Sayce, MFHCF, 23)

G. E. Wright warns that "we must attempt to reconstruct the history of Israel, as historians do that of other early peoples, by the use of every tool available, and that by no means permits the neglect of archaeology." (Wright, AOTS, 51)

Similarly Albright calls for verifiable methods: "The ultimate historicity of a given datum is never conclusively established nor disproved by the literary framework in which it is imbedded: there must always be external evidence." (Albright, ICCLA, 12)

The following statement by Mendenhall is well worth noting: "It is significant that most of the important new results in historical studies have little to do with literary analysis." (Mendenhall, BHT, 50)

Wright, speaking of external data to check hypercriticism (which leads to hyperskepticism), says that:

When the basic attitudes of higher criticism were being formed in the last century, there was an insufficient amount of extra-biblical data to serve as a check to hyperskepticism. Consequently, passage after passage was challenged as being a literary forgery, and the possibility of "pious fraud" in the compilation of written documents was exaggerated beyond the limits

even of common sense. When such a critical attitude is established, constructive work becomes increasingly difficult, since emotional as well as rational actors are involved in the general negativism. (Wright, PSBA, 80)

Albright comments with regard to the historicity of the Old Testament: "Archaeological and inscriptional data have established the historicity of innumerable passages and statements of the Old Testament; the number of such cases is many times greater than those where the reverse has been proved or has been made probable." (Albright, RDBL, 181)

Albright further states: "Wellhausen still ranks in our eyes as the greatest Biblical scholar of the nineteenth century. But his standpoint is antiquated and his picture of the evolution of Israel is sadly distorted." (Albright, RDBL, 185)

3A. NATURAL VIEW OF ISRAEL'S RELIGION AND HISTORY (EVOLUTIONARY)

Concomitant with Hegel's evolutionary concept applied to history is its application to religion, especially to the Old Testament. Rationalistic critics hypothesized that religious development went through an evolutionary process that commenced with "a belief in spirits in the days of primitive man, and then went through various stages, which included manism or ancestor worship; fetishism or belief in objects indwelt by spirits; totemism or the belief in a tribal god and a tribal animal related to the members of the tribe; mana, or the idea of an indwelling power; magic, the control of the supernatural. Finally man conceived of clear-cut deities (polytheism) and later elevated one deity above the others, a stage called henotheism." (Free, AL, 332)

G. E. Wright explains the view of Wellhausen and many other radical critics:

The Graf-Wellhausen reconstruction of the history of Israel's religion was, in effect, an assertion that within the pages of the Old Testament we have a perfect example of the evolution of religion from animism in patriarchal times through henotheism to monotheism. The last was first achieved in pure form during the sixth and fifth centuries. The patriarchs worshipped the spirits in trees, stones, springs, mountains, etc. The God of pre-prophetic Israel was a tribal deity, limited in his power to the land of Palestine. Under the influence of Baalism, he even became a fertility god and sufficiently tolerant to allow the early religion of Israel to be distinguished from that of Canaan. It was the prophets who were the true innovators and who produced most, if not all, of that which was truly distinctive in Israel, the grand culmination coming with the universalism of II Isaiah. Thus we have animism, or polydemonism, a limited tribal deity, implicit ethical monotheism, and finally, explicit and universal monotheism. (Wright, PSBA, 89–90)

Orr says that

if, on impartial consideration, it can be shown that the religion of Israel admits of explanation on purely natural principles, then the historian will be justified in his verdict that it stands, in this respect, on the same footing as other religions. If, on the other hand, fair investigation brings out a different result,—if it demonstrates that this religion has features which place it in a different category from all others, and compel us to postulate for it a different and higher origin,—then that fact must be frankly recognized as part of the scientific result, and the nature and extent of this higher element must be made the subject of inquiry. It will not do to override the facts—if facts they are—by *a priori* dogmatic assumptions on the one side any more than on the other. Thus far we agree with Kuenen, that we must *begin* by treating the religion of Israel exactly as we would treat any other religion. (Orr, POT, 14)

Orr continues: "First, and perhaps deepest, of the reasons for this rejection is the *a priori* one, that such a conception of God as the Old Testament attributes to the patriarchs and to Moses was *impossible* for them at that stage of history. It is too elevated and spiritual for their minds to have entertained. The idea of the unity of God has for its correlates the ideas of the world and of humanity, and neither of these ideas, it is asserted, was possessed by ancient Israel." (Orr, POT, 127–28)

Wellhausen, speaking on the creation of the world, says that "in a youthful people such a theological abstraction is unheard of, and so with the Hebrew we find both the word and the notion only coming into use after the Babylonian exile." (Wellhausen, PHI, 305)

Wellhausen adds that "the religious notion of *humanity* underlying Gen. ix. 6 is not ancient with the Hebrews any more than with other nations." (Wellhausen, PHI, 312)

The Dutch scholar Kuenen stated this position in the chapter entitled, "Our Standpoint," in his book, *The Religion of Israel.* He lays down the principle that no distinction can be made between the religion of Israel and other religions. Kuenen says, "For us the Israelitish religion is one of those religions;

An evolutionary understanding of history and an anthropocentric view of religion dominated the nineteenth century. The prevailing thinkers viewed religion as devoid of any divine intervention, explaining it as a natural development produced by man's subjective needs. Their verdict was that the Hebrew religion, as its neighbor religions, certainly must have begun with animism and then evolved through the stages of polydemonism, polytheism, menolatry, and finally monotheism.

nothing less, but also nothing more." (Kuenen, RI, n.p.)

Orr's evaluation of this position is well taken: "To assume beforehand, in an inquiry which turns on this very point, that the religion of Israel presents no features but such as are explicable out of natural causes—that no higher factors are needed to account for it—is to prejudge the whole question." (Orr, POT, 13)

Here we see the critics' actual interpretation of Israel's history. Gleason Archer, a graduate of Harvard University, Suffolk Law School, Princeton Theological Seminary, and then chairman of the department of Old Testament at Trinity Evangelical Divinity School, introduces us to this point.

An evolutionary understanding of history and an anthropocentric view of religion dominated the nineteenth century. The prevailing thinkers viewed religion as devoid of any divine intervention, explaining it as a natural development produced by man's subjective needs. Their verdict was that the Hebrew religion, as its neighbor religions, certainly must have begun with animism and then evolved through the stages of polydemonism, polytheism, menolatry, and finally monotheism. (Archer, SOTI, 132–33)

That the then-current evolutionary philosophy of Hegel had a significant effect on Old Testament studies is clearly attested to by Herbert Hahn:

The conception of historical development was the chief contribution of the liberal critics to the exegesis of the Old Testament. It is true, of course, that this conception did not grow merely from an objective reading of the sources. In a larger sense, it was a reflection of the intellectual temper of the times. The genetic conception of Old Testament history fitted in with the evolutionary principle of interpretation prevailing in contemporary science and philosophy. In the natural sciences,

the influence of Darwin had made the theory of evolution the predominant hypothesis affecting research. In the historical sciences and in the areas of religious and philosophical thought, the evolutionary concept had begun to exercise a powerful influence after Hegel had substituted the notion of "becoming" for the idea of "being." He had arrived at the notion by *a priori* reasoning without testing it by scientific application to observable fact, but Hegel was none the less the intellectual progenitor of the modern point of view. In every department of historical investigation the conception of development was being used to explain the history of man's thought, his institutions, and even his religious faiths. It was not strange that the same principle should be applied to the explanation of Old Testament history. In every age exegesis has conformed to the thought forms of the time, and in the latter half of the nineteenth century thought was dominated by the scientific methods and an evolutionary view of history. (Hahn, OTMR, 9–10)

Paul Feinberg writes of Hegel's historical approach:

Hegel believed that the problem of philosophy was to find the meaning of history. From this fundamental presupposition he attempted to explain the whole of human history. The history of Israel covering nearly two millennia was a likely starting place. In his *Philosophy of Religion*, Hegel assigns the Hebrew religion a defined and necessary place in the evolutionary development of Christianity, the absolute religion. Hegel's view of Hebrew religion and his general schematization of history offered an irresistible framework in which Hegelians would attempt to interpret the Old Testament. (Feinberg, DGP, 3)

The *Encyclopedia Britannica* summarizes Hegel's philosophy: "Hegel presupposes that the whole of human history is a process through which mankind has been making spiritual and moral progress; it is what human mind has done in the course of its advance to self-knowledge. . . . The first step was to make the transition from a natural life of savagery to a state of order and law." (EB, 1969, 202–3)

Hegel's influence on nineteenth-century Old Testament scholars is reflected in a statement of Kuenen (*Religion of Israel,* p. 225) cited by Orr: "To what we might call the universal, or at least the common rule, that religion begins with fetishism, then develops into polytheism, and then, but not before, ascends to monotheism—that is to say, if this highest stage be reached—to this rule the Israelites are no exception." (Orr, POT, 47)

Such a position either ignores or discredits Israel's own account of her history as we have it in the Old Testament.

The Wellhausen school approached the Hebrew religion with the preconceived notion that it was a mere product of evolution, untouched by the supernatural. This approach completely ignored the fact that *only* the Hebrew religion and its branches have produced a genuine monotheism, and that the singular message throughout the entirety of the Hebrew Scriptures is monotheism. Thus, the accounts of the Israelite fathers such as Abraham, Isaac, Jacob, and Moses have been re-examined with intent to show that their early polytheism was camouflaged by the later Deuteronomic and Priestly writers. (Archer, SOTI, 98)

That this whole presupposition—the evolutionary view of Israel's history and religion—was crucial to the entire documentary hypothesis is stated in this summary of the foundations of the theory found in *The Interpreter's Dictionary of the Bible*:

In its standard form the documentary hypothesis rested upon arguments of two kinds: those based upon literary and linguistic evidence, which resulted in the division of the Pentateuchal material into various written sources; and those based upon historical evidence for the evolution of religious institutions and ideas in Israel, which produced an analytical description of the interrelationships among the documents, and a chronological arrangement to account for them. (IDB, 713)

W. F. Albright, W. W. Spence Professor of Semitic Languages from 1929 until 1958 at Johns Hopkins University and a sometime director of the American Schools of Oriental Research in Jerusalem, was, until his death in 1971, considered by many to be the foremost biblical archaeologist in the world. His work has forced many critics to completely reassess their conclusions regarding the history of Israel. About Wellhausen's application of Hegel's philosophical theories to the history of Israel, Albright writes:

He tried, by means of Hegelian analogy with pre-Islamic and Islamic Arabia, to build a system for the development of Israel's history, religion, and literature which would fit his critical analysis. Wellhausen's structure was so brilliant and afforded such a simple, apparently uniform interpretation that it was adopted almost universally by liberal Protestant scholars, and even largely by Catholic and Jewish scholars. There were, of course, some exceptions, but in nearly all places where men were thoroughly schooled by learning Hebrew and Greek and absorbing the critical method, they also learned Wellhausenian principles. Unfortunately all of this was developed in the infancy of archaeology, and was of very little value in interpreting history. (Albright, AHAEBT, 15)

Critics have often restricted advanced theological concepts to Israel's later history, concluding that early concepts must have been primitive.

Kitchen has conclusively demonstrated that many such "advanced concepts" were common property of the ancient Orient as early as the third millennium B.C. Their

> Many have attributed the personification of wisdom in Proverbs eight and nine to influence of the third and fourth century B.C. Greeks. But exactly the same type of personification of truth, justice, understanding, etc. is found as early as the third millennium B.C. in Egypt and Mesopotamia, as well as in the second millennium B.C. in Hittite, Hurrian, and Canaanite literature.
>
> —KENNETH KITCHEN

widespread presence in so many written documents makes the familiarity of these ideas to the Hebrews likely at any point of their history. For example, many have attributed the personification of wisdom in Proverbs eight and nine to influence of the third and fourth century B.C. Greeks. But exactly the same type of personification of truth, justice, understanding, etc. is found as early as the third millennium B.C. in Egypt and Mesopotamia, as well as in the second millennium B.C. in Hittite, Hurrian, and Canaanite literature. The concept of a universal God was demonstrated as early as 1940 to be widespread during the third millennium B.C., yet some radical critics are still insistent upon attributing this biblical idea (as seen in Psalm 67) to "relatively late times." (Kitchen, AOOT, 126–27)

John Mackay, former president of Princeton Seminary, reflects this language of the evolutionary school when he says, concerning the Old Testament: "The narrative, taken as a whole, aims at conveying the idea that, first under the lowly form of a *tribal deity,* the one universal God, the 'god of the whole earth,' manifested himself in the life of Israel" *(History and Destiny,* p. 17). (Cited by Free, ANO, 131)

Albright sums up this view when he states: "The entire school of Wellhausen has agreed on a refusal to admit Mosaic monotheism, and a conviction that Israelite monotheism was the result of a gradual process, which did not culminate until the eighth century B.C." (Albright, APB, 163)

The radical critics are here expressing the obvious results or conclusions of their anti-supernatural presuppositions applied to the religion of Israel in the Old Testament. Since a direct revelation from God is ruled out, their monotheism must have developed through regular evolutionary channels like other religions.

Therefore, the radical critics conclude that a piece of literature can be dated by its stage of religious teaching. One is supposed to deduce that the earlier the literary source, the more primitive the religious concepts.

When monotheism appears in a book purporting to be dated at the time of Moses (c. 1400 B.C.) it is immediately rejected by many radical critics because the "roots of monotheism," writes Pfeiffer, "were not planted until the time of Amos." (Pfeiffer, IOT, 580)

Following are a few of the assumptions made by those who advocate the evolutionary presupposition:

1B. Monotheism

1C. Documentary Assumption

It was not until the time of Amos—definitely not during the Mosaic age (c. 1400 B.C.)—that monotheism found a beginning in Israel's religion. As Harrison says, "Wellhausen rejected the idea that the Torah as a whole was the starting point for the history of Israel as a community of the Faith." (Harrison, IOT, 352)

Concerning monotheism, Wellhausen writes: "It is extremely doubtful whether the actual monotheism, which is undoubtedly presupposed in the universal moral precepts of the Decalogue, could have formed the foundation of a national religion at the downfall of the nation, and thereupon kept its hold upon the people in an artificial manner by means of the idea of a covenant formed by the God of the universe with, in the first instance, Israel alone." (Wellhausen, SHIJ, 20–21)

Monotheism was not considered to have been present in the Mosaic age. It was, rather, considered to have been a result of the purifying effects of the Babylonian exile, and not characteristic of Israel until after the sixth century B.C.

"The Hebrews," Kuenen agrees, "were undoubtedly polytheists. This is shown, not only by the sequel of their history, but also by positive evidence of later date, it is true, but still admissible, because it is not contradicted by a single account of former times." (Kuenen, RI, 270)

Kuenen continues: "At first the religion of Israel was polytheism. During the eighth century B.C. the great majority of the people still acknowledged the existence of many gods, and, what is more, they worshipped them. And we can add that during the seventh century, and down to the beginning of the Babylonish exile (586 B.C.), this state of things remained unaltered." (Kuenen, RI, 223–24)

Kuenen explains his reasons for evolution of religion, "To what one might call the universal, or at least the common rule, that religion begins with fetishism, then develops into polytheism, and then, but not before, ascends to monotheism—that is to say, if this highest stage be reached—to this rule the Semites are no exception." (Kuenen, RI, 225)

Kuenen summarizes his theory:

The lowest conception of religion will no doubt have had most adherents. This we know as fetishism, which continues to exist even where less childish ideas have already arisen and, for instance, the adoration of the heavenly bodies, of the sun, moon, and planets, has been introduced. Therefore we certainly shall not err if we assume that the worship of trees and especially of stones, which for some reason or other were held to be abodes of the deity, was very common among the Hebrews. The Old Testament still contains many reminiscences of that stone-worship, which was by no means limited to the land of Goshen, but was continued in Canaan also. When Jahveh was afterwards acknowledged by many as the only god, these holy stones were brought into connection with him in various ways. It is here worthy of note, that most of them are said to have been set up by the patriarchs during their wanderings through Canaan, either as altars in honor of Jahveh or as memorials of his presence: this is easily accounted for, if the worship of stones had really been common in former times. (Kuenen, RI, 270–71)

Pfeiffer concludes: "Amos, without discrimination of race or nation, planted the roots of a universal religion, from which were to grow the great monotheistic religions of salvation, Judaism, Christianity, and Islam." (Pfeiffer, IOT, 580)

2C. Basic Answer

William F. Albright says that "it is precisely between 1500 and 1200 B.C., i.e., in the Mosaic age, that we find the closest approach to monotheism in the ancient Gentile world before the Persian period." (Albright, ARI, 178)

Joseph Free continues that an

examination of the archeological inscriptional material shows that a monotheistic type of worship of the god Aton came into Egypt in the period between 1400 and 1350 B.C. Monotheistic tendencies in Babylonia are evidenced in the period 1500–1200 B.C. in a famous Babylonian text which identifies all

> It is an incontestable fact of history that no other nation (apart from those influenced by the Hebrew faith) ever did develop a true monotheistic religion which commanded the general allegiance of its people.
>
> —GLEASON ARCHER

important Babylonian deities with some aspect of the great god Marduk; Zababa is Marduk of battle, Sin is Marduk as illuminer of night, Adad is Marduk of rain. There is one great god, with various functions. Monotheistic tendencies also appear in Syria and Canaan in this same period of the fourteenth century B.C. Certain names were given to gods worshiped in many different places, all of whom were considered as variant forms of one great deity: there was a Teshup of Nirik, a Teshup of Khalab (Aleppo), a Teshup of Shamukha; it seems that finally Teshup was thought of as the great and sole god, who manifested himself in many places. (Free, AL, 334–35)

Albright writes that he had "gathered archaeological data from many quarters for the purpose of filling in the historical background of religious syncretism and conflict against which the prophets fulfilled their mission. Thanks to archaeology we can see more clearly that the prophets of Israel were neither pagan ecstatics or religious innovators." (Albright, ARI, 178)

Albright not only concludes that Amos "was no religious innovator, much less the earliest monotheistic teacher of Israel," but that "orthodox Yahwism remained the same from Moses to Ezra." (Albright, FSAC, 313)

G. E. Wright observes that "we can assert with confidence that by the time of the patriarchs the religion of all parts of the Near East was a long distance removed from the animistic stage, if the latter in any approved textbook form ever existed at all." (Wright, PSBA, 90)

"It is an incontestable fact of history," concludes Archer, "that no other nation (apart from those influenced by the Hebrew faith) ever did develop a true monotheistic religion which commanded the general allegiance of its people. Isolated figures may be pointed out like *Akhnaton* and *Xenophanes* (both of whom also spoke of 'gods' in the plural number), but it remains incontrovertible that neither the Egyptians nor the Babylonians nor the Greeks ever embraced a monotheistic faith on a national basis." (Archer, SOTI, 134)

James Orr observes that the monotheism of the Israelites is one of the first characteristics to be noted when studying the Old Testament. This is quite a feat in itself, in view of the fact that polytheism and idolatry were the modern trend. The religions of the Babylonians, the Assyrians, the Egyptians, and even Israel's Palestinian neighbors were incorrigibly corrupt and polytheistic. Only in Judah was God known. (Orr, POT, 40–41)

Thus Wellhausen's theory of unilinear evolutionary development on a simple, one-dimensional time line from the "simple" to the "complex" has come to be regarded by most archaeologists as erroneous.

Kitchen concludes:

> Unilinear evolution is a fallacy. It is valid only within a small field of reference for a limited segment of time and not for whole cultures over long periods of time. One thinks of Egypt's thrice repeated rise and fall in and after the Old, Middle and New Kingdoms respectively, or of the successive flowerings of Sumerian civilization, Old Babylonian culture

and the Assyro-Babylonian kingdoms in Mesopotamia. This oscillation and mutation applies to all aspects of civilization: artistic standards, literary output and abilities, political institutions, the state of society, economics, and not least religious belief and practice. Intertwined with the multicolored fabric of change are lines of continuity in usage that show remarkable consistency from early epochs . (Kitchen, AOOT, 113–14)

Ronald Youngblood adds that "it cannot be shown that there is a universal tendency on the part of polytheistic religions to gradually reduce the number of deities until finally arriving at one deity. In some instances, in fact, such a religion may even add *more* deities as its adherents become aware of more and more natural phenomena to deify! At any rate, the Old Testament teaches that monotheism, far from having evolved through the centuries of Israel's history, is one of the inspired insights revealed to the covenant people by the one true God Himself." (Youngblood, HOT, 9)

Here it is appropriate to ask, "Was Moses a monotheist?"

"If by 'monotheist,'" writes Albright,

is meant a thinker with views specifically like those of Philo Judaeus or Rabbi Aquiba, of St. Paul or St. Augustine, of Mohammed or Maimonides, of St. Thomas or Calvin, of Mordecai Kaplan or H. N. Wieman, Moses was not one. If, on the other hand, the term "monotheist" means one who teaches the existence of only one God, the creator of everything, the source of justice, who is equally powerful in Egypt, in the desert, and in Palestine, who has no sexuality and no mythology, who is human in form but cannot be seen by human eye and cannot be represented in any form—then the founder of Yahwism was certainly a monotheist. (Albright, FSAC, 271–72)

The degree to which Moses can be considered a true monotheist has been a topic of much scholarly discussion. However, R. K. Harrison believes that there is little "justification for not attributing monotheism to Moses, although care should be taken not to understand that concept in a speculative Hellenic sense. A more accurate designation of the situation might well be framed in terms of an empirical ethical monotheism." (Harrison, IOT, 403)

2B. Environmental Conditioning

1C. Documentary Assumption

A natural evolutionary process through conditioning by environmental and geographical conditions produced the Israelite religion. Basically, the religious tenets were borrowed by Israel from the pagan religions surrounding Israel.

2C. Basic Answers

"The faith of Israel," writes G. E. Wright, "even in its earliest and basic forms is so utterly different from that of the contemporary polytheisms that one simply cannot explain it fully by evolutionary or environmental categories. Such a contention runs somewhat counter to the habits of thought and the methodological assumptions of many leading scholars of the last two generations. Yet it is difficult to see how any other conclusion is justified by the facts as we now know them from the vast accumulation of knowledge about the Biblical world." (Wright, OTAE, 7)

W. F. Albright points out that it is impossible that the Israelite religion could be accounted for by saying it was borrowed from the adjacent religions: "Every new publication of North-Canaanite inscriptions or literary documents will thus add to our knowledge of the literary background of the Old Testament. On the other hand, every fresh publication of Canaanite mythological texts makes the gulf between the religions of Canaan and of Israel increasingly clear. A common geographical environment, a common material culture, and a common language were not enough to quench the glowing spark of Israelite faith in the God of Moses or to assimilate the cult of Yahweh to that of Baal." (Albright, RPNCR, 24)

The Israelites were able to resist the pressure of syncretism with the pagan religions that surrounded them.

Alexander Heidel describes the differences between the contemporary Babylonian polytheism and Israelite monotheism:

The Babylonian creation stories are permeated with a crude polytheism. They speak not only of successive generations of gods and goddesses proceeding from Apsû and Tiâmat, with all of them in need of physical nourishment, since all consist of matter as well as of spirit, but they speak also of different creators.

> It is increasingly realized today that the attempt to make of the Old Testament a source book for the evolution of religion from very primitive to highly advanced concepts has been made possible only by means of a radical misinterpretation of the literature.
>
> —G. E. WRIGHT

Against all of this, the opening chapters of Genesis as well as the Old Testament in general refer to only one Creator and Maintainer of all things, one God who created and transcends all cosmic matter. In the entire Old Testament, there is not a trace of a theogony [battle of the gods], such as we find, for example in Enûma elish and in Hesiod. To this faith the Babylonians never attained. (Heidel, BG, 96–97)

The danger of environmental corruption is indicated by Merrill Unger: "The patriarchs, sojourning in the midst of polytheism with its divination and other forms of occultism, were constantly in danger of corruption. The teraphim of Rachel (Gen. 31:19), 'the strange gods' which Jacob ordered put away from his household (Gen. 35:2) and hid under an oak in Shechem (v. 4), are indicative of contamination. However, the patriarchs were remarkably free from the divinatory methods of surrounding pagan peoples." (Unger, AOT, 127)

One of the many major differences is the duality of pagan religion in terms of sex.

"For some reason," writes G. E. Wright,

perhaps in part because of the historical nature of God's revelation, the Israelite did not combine the complementary forces of nature by means of a duality expressed in terms of sex. While the category of personality is, of course, applied to Yahweh and while the pronouns used are in their masculine gender, there is no complementary feminine. The duality of male and female is to be found only in the created world; it is not a part of the Godhead, which is essentially sexless. Biblical Hebrew has no word for goddess. Equally phenomenal is the preservation of God's mystery and holiness by the prohibition of images, either of God himself or of any other spiritual being in heaven or on earth, a prohibition preserved in the oldest law which the Old Testament contains. (Wright, OTAE, 23)

Albright concludes: "This is not the place to describe the total breakdown of Wellhausenism under the impact of our new knowledge of antiquity; suffice it to say that no arguments have been brought against early Israelite monotheism that would not apply equally well (with appropriate changes in specific evidence) to postexilic Judaism. Nothing can alter the now certain fact that the gulf between the religions of Israel and of Canaan was as great as the resemblance between their material cultures and their poetic literatures." (Albright, BATYE, 545)

Wright adds, "It is increasingly realized today that the attempt to make of the Old Testament a source book for the evolution of religion from very primitive to highly advanced concepts has been made possible only by means of a radical misinterpretation of the literature." (Wright, OTAE, 12)

3B. The Second Commandment

1C. Documentary Assumption

The second commandment, though attributed to Moses, could not have been a part of the early Israelite religions because of its prohibition of images. The radical critics reject Mosaic authorship and early dating of the decalogue because it is believed that they in fact did worship images. Julius Wellhausen states that "the prohibition of images was during the older period quite unknown." (Wellhausen, PHI, 439) Wellhausen says this is one of the main reasons for rejecting the authenticity of Mosaic authorship.

R. W. Smith writes: "Even the principle of the second commandment, that Jehovah is not to be worshipped by images . . . cannot, in the light of history, be regarded as having so fundamental a place in the religion of early Israel." (Smith, PI, 63)

2C. Basic Answer

It becomes clear that, if the prohibition of image worship was a late addition to the Pentateuch, and the Israelites worshiped images, then one should find images of Jehovah.

However this has not been the case. G. E. Wright records that the excavation of Megiddo by the University of Chicago failed to turn up images of Jehovah. "Tremendous amounts of debris were moved from the first five town levels (all Israelite), and not a single example has been found as far as this writer is aware." (Wright, TOTRS, 413)

Wright continues:

There is no image of deity ever mentioned in Patriarchal worship, nor in connection with the incitation of the Tabernacle which served as the central shrine of the tribal amphicty-ony, nor in the Temple of Solomon. On the other hand, we know from archaeology that Israelites possessed small plaques or figures of the Canaanite fertility and mother goddesses in great number. This indicates the widespread syncretism which went on in early Israel, precisely as the literature frankly testi-fies. When the Aramaeans and Philistines set-tled in Canaanite territory, they adopted Canaanite customs. When the Amorites set-tled in Mesopotamia, they took over Sumerian religion, adjusting their own religious pan-theon to it. Similarly, the people of Israel were tempted to adopt the customs of their envi-ronment. Yet in the vast mass of debris dug out of Israelite towns there is yet to be found an image of a male deity. (Wright, OTAE, 24)

Many of the misunderstandings are the result of failure to discern between the "offi-cial doctrines" of Israel's religion and the "actual practices" of some of the common people.

Wright concludes that "the evidence is vividly clear that the prohibition against images of Yahweh was so deeply fixed in early Israel, that even the unenlightened and the tolerant understood that Yahweh was simply not to be honored in this way." (Wright, OTAE, 24–25)

He adds: "The basic character and antiq-uity of the second commandment thus receives as strong a support as archeology will probably ever be able to produce for it." (Wright, PSBA, 93)

4B. Moral Level

1C. Documentary Assumption

The laws, moral tone, and social level ascribed to Moses are too lofty to be found so early in Israel's development.

2C. Basic Answer

Various archaeological discoveries have discouraged the continuation of this assumption. Millar Burrows writes: "The standards represented by the ancient law codes of the Babylonians, Assyrians, and Hittites, as well as the high ideals found in the Egyptian Book of the Dead and the early Wisdom Literature

> Archaeological evidence, on the contrary, shows that there is no valid reason for dating the Levitical sacrificial laws late, for they appear in the Ugaritic material from the fourteenth century B.C.
>
> —JOSEPH P. FREE

of the Egyptians, have effectively refuted this assumption." (Burrows, WMTS, 46)

Speaking of the Israelites, of the conquest of Canaan, and of the pagan worship encountered by Israel, Albright says that their gross mythology and worship "were replaced by Israel, with its nomadic [although they were not nomads] simplicity and purity of life, its lofty monotheism, and its severe code of ethics." (Albright, FSAC, 214)

5B. The Priestly Code

1C. Documentary Assumption

"The Priestly Code," writes Pfeiffer, "like all legislation, notwithstanding its deliberate timelessness and fictitious Mosaic background, bears the earmarks of its age, the first half of the Persian period (538–331 B.C.)." (Pfeiffer, IOT, 257)

Joseph P. Free, in "Archaeology and Higher Criticism," further explains the situation when he states that

> another body of supposedly very late material in the Pentateuch is the record of the Levitical sacrificial laws, assigned to the P document. . . . If the bulk of much of the Pentateuch, assigned to the P document, is to be dated 500 B.C., the Mosaicity of the Pentateuch is definitely set aside.
>
> Archaeological evidence, on the contrary, shows that there is no valid reason for dating the Levitical sacrificial laws late, for they appear in the Ugaritic material from the fourteenth century B.C. (Free, AHC, 33)

2C. Basic Answer

1D. Tenure in Egypt

Apparently the skeptics of the early dating believe that the Israelites were simply too primitive in Moses' day to write such a law. Archer disagrees: "It can hardly be objected that the Israelites were too primitive to be governed by laws such as these back in Moses' time, since according to their own explicit record they had been living in the midst of one of the most advanced civilizations of ancient times for over four hundred years, and would naturally have entertained more advanced concepts of jurisprudence than tribes indigenous to the desert." (Archer, SOTI, 162)

2D. Code of Hammurabi

Also, it seems that the other half of the skepticism comes from the belief that no primitive civilization could have written such a work as the code we have today. J. P. Free, in *Archaeology and Bible History,* takes issue with this:

Archaeological discoveries, however, have shown that the advanced laws of Deuteronomy and the rest of the Pentateuch do not have to be dated late in accordance with the supposition of the critical school. The Code of Hammurabi (written within the period 2000–1700 B.C.) was found by a French archaeological expedition under the direction of M. Jacques de Morgan in 1901–1902 at the site of ancient Susa, to the east of the region of Mesopotamia. The code was written on a piece of black diorite, nearly eight feet high, and contained two hundred eighty-two sections or paragraphs.

The Code of Hammurabi was written several hundred years before the time of Moses (c. 1500–1400 B.C.), and yet it contains some laws which are similar to those recorded by Moses. In the light of this, the liberal has no right to say that the laws of Moses are too advanced for his time, and could not have been written by him. (Free, ABH, 121)

Meredith G. Kline, in a chapter entitled "Is the History of the Old Testament Accurate?" of *Can I Trust the Bible?* (edited by Howard Vos) adds:

Archaeology speaks decisively against Wellhausen's notion that Pentateuchal legislation is too complex and its cultic provisions too elaborate for so early a time as that of Moses, to whom the authorship of the Pentateuch is attributed in both Old and New Testaments. As evidence of the antiquity of codified law, there are Assyrian and Hittite law codes from approximately the time of Moses, the Code of Hammurabi some three centuries before Moses, and the more recently discovered fragments of other Babylonian and Sumerian predecessors of Hammurabi's Code, dating back to Abraham's day. (Vos, CTB, 146)

A. H. Sayce (*Monument Fact and Higher Critical Fancies*) answers Pfeiffer soundly: "In other words, the Mosaic code must belong to the age to which tradition assigns it, and presupposes the historical conditions which the Biblical narrative describes. Not only has the code of Khammu-rabi [i.e. Hammurabi] proved that the legislation of Moses was possible, it has also shown that the social and political circumstances under which it claims to have arisen are the only ones under which it could have been compiled." (Sayce, MFHCF, 82)

If the equal caliber of the codes is not enough to support the possibility of the early date, Archer points out that the "Babylonian Code of Hammurabi . . . shows numerous similarities to the provisions in Exodus, Leviticus and Numbers relative to the punishment of crimes and the imposition of damages for torts and breaches of contract." (Archer, SOTI, 161)

Not only is the quality comparable, but even some of the laws are similar. Free sums this up:

The Code of Hammurabi was found in 1901–2 by a French expedition at the site of ancient Susa, east of Mesopotamia. On the surface of this monument some 282 laws were recorded, comprising the legislation of the Babylonian king Hammurabi, who lived within the period of 2000–1700 B.C. . . . Some critics held that the laws of Moses (1500–1400 B.C.) were too advanced for his day and assigned them to a much later period (800–400 B.C.). The discovery of Hammurabi's code, which precedes Moses by several centuries, effectively answered this objection. (Free, AB, 20)

3C. Counter Assumption

Unfortunately this has led to an assumption by the documentarians:

"Then it was suggested," Free continues, "that Moses borrowed his laws from the Code of Hammurabi. A comparison of the two over a period of years, however, has convinced most critics that there are essential differences and that the laws of the Old Testament are in no essential way dependent upon the Babylonian." (Free, AB, 20)

Sayce explains the issue at hand: "Certain German Assyriologists have been at great pains to discover similarities between the codes of Khammu-rabi and Moses, and to infer from this a connection between them. And there are cases in which the similarity is striking." (Sayce, MFHCF, 71)

Merrill Unger writes: "Again, higher critical views which have placed the origin of many of the laws ascribed to Moses in the ninth, eighth, or seventh century B.C., or even later, have had to be drastically revised or entirely rejected. On the other hand, the discovery of the early extra-Biblical legal material has led many to adopt an equally faulty view that Hebrew legislation is merely a selection and adaptation of Babylonian law." (Unger, AOT, 154–55)

4C. Further Answers

1D. Contrast of the Codes

Archer explains that "it should be understood, of course, that the differences between the Torah and the Code of Hammurabi are far more striking than the resemblances. But the differences proceed largely from the entirely different ideology to which each of the two cultures adhered." (Archer, SOTI, 162)

And again: "The Babylonian code is alleged to have been received by Hammurabi from the sun god, Shamash. Moses received his laws directly from God. Hammurabi, despite his purported reception from Shamash, takes credit for them in both the prologue and epilogue of the Code. He, not Shamash, established order and equity throughout the land. Moses, in contrast, is only an instrument. The legislation is, 'Thus saith Yahweh.'" (Unger, AOT, 156)

Further, "in the Hebrew laws a greater value is set upon human life, a stricter regard for the honor of womanhood is discernible, and a more humane treatment of slaves is enjoined. Moreover, the Babylonian Code has nothing in it corresponding to that twofold golden thread running through the Mosaic legislation—love to God and love to one's neighbor (Matt. 22:37–40)." (Unger, AOT, 157)

Unger goes on to say that "Hammurabi's laws are adapted to the irrigation-culture and the highly commercialized urban society of Mesopotamia. The Mosaic injunctions, on the other hand, suit a simple agricultural, pastoral people of a dry land like Palestine, much less advanced in social and commercial development, but keenly conscious in all phases of their living of their divine calling." (Unger, AOT, 156)

And, finally, "the Hebrew Code contains many purely religious injunctions and ritual regulations. The Code of Hammurabi is civil. However, the priestly laws of Leviticus contain many points of contact with corresponding priestly ritual and practice in Western Asia, whether in Canaan and Phoenicia or in Mesopotamia." (Unger, AOT, 156)

Free finds "no real connection between the Mosaic laws and the Code of Hammurabi. Such an acknowledgment was made by G.A. Barton, a liberal professor at the University of Pennsylvania, who said, 'A comparison of the Code of Hammurabi as a whole with the Pentateuchal laws as a whole, while it reveals certain similarities, convinces the student that the laws of the Old Testament

> A comparison of the Code of Hammurabi as a whole with the Pentateuchal laws as a whole, while it reveals certain similarities, convinces the student that the laws of the Old Testament are in no essential way dependent upon the Babylonian laws.
>
> — G.A. BARTON, A LIBERAL PROFESSOR

are in no essential way dependent upon the Babylonian laws.' The Code contains many laws peculiar to itself, including those relating to soldiers, tax-collectors, and wine-merchants." (Free, ABH, 121)

Sayce, an Assyriologist, concludes that "the difference between the two codes in this last particular is characteristic of a difference which runs through the whole of them, and makes the contrast between them far greater and more striking than any agreement that can be pointed out." (Sayce, MFHCF, 72)

2D. Ugarit (Ras Shamra) Discoveries

It seems that this section thus far indicates the only evidence available is the Hammurabi Code. This is not true, as we will now see how the Priestly Code compares with another archaeological find.

To begin with, Joseph P. Free points out that "the fact that the Ras Shamra Tablets [Ras Shamra is a Canaanite city located on the Syro-Palestinian coast just opposite the tip of Cyprus.], dating back to about 1400 B.C. record several laws similar to those of Leviticus, shows that the liberal has no right to deny the possibility of such a code of sacrificial laws as early as the time of Moses." (Free, ABH, 112)

Millar Burrows, in *What Mean These Stones?*, goes further to explain that "texts from Ras Shamrah name many kinds of sacrificial animals, including some that were used also in the Hebrew religion and some which were excluded by the laws of the Old Testament. Several of the terms employed in the Hebrew Old Testament for the various types of offering also have appeared in the Ras Shamrah tablets, for example the burnt offering, the whole burnt offering, the guilt offering, and the peace offering." (Burrows, WMTS, 234)

Would not mutual sacrifices mean Moses used Ras Shamra as a source? Free con-

cludes: "We believe that there are at least two possible answers. In the first place, they may have been diffused from Israel at the time they were revealed to Moses (about 1450 B.C.) and have come into the practices of the Canaanites and people of Syria, being reflected in the Ras Shamra tablets (1400–1350 B.C.). The second possibility is that the laws and statutes revealed by the Lord at a much earlier time (and later given to Moses) were handed down among various peoples and appear in a modified and often corrupted form among such people as those of Ras Shamra." (Free, ABH, 112)

3D. Lipit-Ishtar Law Code

Briefly, the Lipit-Ishtar Code is another discovery. Francis Steele, in "Lipit-Ishtar Law Code" *(American Journal of Archeology)*, explains: "The importance of the Lipit-Ishtar law code can scarcely be overemphasized. Its discovery extends the history of codified law by nearly two centuries and thereby paves the way for a comparative study of law almost four thousand years old." (Steele, LILC, 164)

4D. The Laws of Eshnunna

The same can be said of the Eshnunna law code of the old Babylon period (1830–1550 B.C.). Hammurabi apparently incorporated some of this code into his own system. Two tablets found in 1945 and 1947 near Baghdad contain these ancient laws.

Reunen Yaron points out that archaeology confirms that these tablets could not be dated after the reign of King Dadusha. The last year of Dadusha's reign is set in the seventh year of Hammurabi. However archaeology cannot set the date of its composition. The usual date given to the Eshnunna Law Codes is about two hundred years before Hammurabi. (Yaron, LE, 1–2)

The kingdom of Eshnunna "fell . . .

victim to the expansionist policies pursued with success by Hammurabi of Babylon, during the fourth decade of his reign." (Yaron, LE, 1)

The discovery of the above two tablets adds additional evidence that the Hammurabi Codes were not the only source of an early codified law.

The Laws of Eshnunna: "The code, written during the twentieth century B.C. in the Akkadian language, contains sixty paragraphs of law dealing with such subjects as the price of commodities, the hire of wagons and boats, the wages of laborers, marriage, divorce and adultery, assault and battery, and the placing of responsibility for the ox that gores a man and the mad dog that bites a man (*Biblical World*, 1966, p. 232)." (Albright, AP, 1)

6B. Additional Comments

Albright writes that Wellhausen's "standpoint is antiquated and its picture of the early evolution of Israel is sadly distorted." (Albright, ACBC, 185)

Wright, speaking of Albright, says that he "has amassed archeological fact upon fact in his review of the Bible's setting in the world in order to show that Wellhausen's developmental scheme, ultimately drawn from the idealistic philosophy of Hegel, no longer fits the facts as they are now known." (Wright, AOTS, 45)

Ira Maurice Price, in *The Monuments and the Old Testament*, writes that "the critical views of the origin of many of the laws ascribed to Moses locating them in the ninth, eighth, and seventh centuries, and even later B.C., must not only be modified, but in some cases, entirely rejected." (Price, MOT, 219)

M. J. Lagrange ("L' Authenticité Mosaïque de la Genése et la Théorie des Documents"), a man who was involved in biblical and

archaeological endeavors in Jerusalem for nearly forty years, concludes: "It is a fact that the historical work of Wellhausen is more than compromised. The evolution which starts from fetishism to rise to monolatry and then to monotheism, or from a very rudimentary rustic worship to complicated

> It is a fact that the historical work of Wellhausen is more than compromised. The evolution which starts from fetishism to rise to monolatry and then to monotheism, or from a very rudimentary rustic worship to complicated social and sacerdotal institutions, cannot be maintained in face of the evidence of the facts revealed by the recent discoveries.
>
> —M. J. LAGRANGE, BIBLICAL AND ARCHAEOLOGICAL SCHOLAR

social and sacerdotal institutions, cannot be maintained in face of the evidence of the facts revealed by the recent discoveries." (Cited by Stearns, BAHC, 312–13)

Where did this archaeological evidence come from?

George Mendenhall of the University of Michigan, speaking of the actual excavations that have led archaeologists to the preceding conclusion, writes:

> The starting point was the introduction of new evidence from Ras Shamra and Mari, which excluded from the realm of probability certain theories about the Patriarchal narratives previously held, and which, together with many details from other sources, called for a new theory to account for the new evidence. . . . If those who made up the twelve tribes of Israel included some at least who had first been in contact with Mesopotamian civilization, then for a period of centuries lived in a land surrounded by a cosmopolitan complex

of many cultures in process of amalgamation, then it follows that they can hardly have been childlike, cultureless, traditionless barbarians. It follows that the earliest stages of the religion of Israel need not have been as primitive as earlier scholars had thought—not on the grounds of evidence, but on the basis of an a priori theory of how religion must evolve. (Mendenhall, BHT, 40)

So Albright had taught:

History is not a meaningless record of chance happenings, or even a mere chain of related occurrences; it is a complex web of interacting patterns, each of which has its own structure, however difficult it may be to dissect the structure and to identify its characteristic elements. Moreover, the web is itself constantly changing, and by comparing successive states which it exhibits to the trained eye of the historian we can detect the direction in which it is changing—in other words, its evolution. We also emphasized the fact that the evolution of historical patterns is highly complex and variable; it may move in any direction and it cannot be detected by a priori hypotheses nor can it be explained by any deterministic theory. We also pointed out that this organismic nature of history makes unilinear "historicism" unsuitable as a clue to the complexities of the history of religion. For this reason Wellhausen's Hegelian method was utterly unsuited to become the master-key with which scholars might enter the sanctuary of Israelite religion and acquire a satisfying understanding of it. (Albright, ARI, 3)

Albright's conclusion seems final: "In the light of the ancient orient nothing seems more artificial and contrary to analogy than the postulated evolution of Hebrew religion within the limits of time and circumstance allowed by the school of Wellhausen." (Albright, ACBC, 182)

7B. Implications

These conclusions seriously undermine the entire documentary hypothesis both in its classical form and in its present state of flux, since current Pentateuchal analysis is, for the most part, still solidly based on the classical documentary theory.

Kitchen's conclusion is justified: "As extended unilinear development is, therefore, an invalid assumption, there is no reason whatever to date supposed literary fragments or sources by the imaginary level of their concepts on a scale from 'primitive' to 'advanced.'" (Kitchen, AOOT, 114)

4A. NO WRITING IN ISRAEL AT MOSES' TIME (c. 1500–1400 B.C.)

1B. Documentary Assumption

Writing was virtually unknown in Israel during Moses' time; consequently Moses could not have written the Pentateuch.

Wellhausen himself said: "Ancient Israel was certainly not without God-given bases for the ordering of human life; only they were not fixed in writing." (Wellhausen, PHI, 393)

Schultz, in 1893, stated in his book *Old Testament Theology*:

Of the legendary character of the pre-Mosaic narrators, the time of which they treat is a sufficient proof. It was a time prior to all knowledge of writing, a time separated by an interval of more than four hundred years, of which there is absolutely no history, from the nearest period of which Israel had some dim historical recollection, a time when in civilized countries writing was only beginning to be used for the most important matters of State. Now wandering herdsmen have invariably an instinctive dislike to writing. In fact, at the present day, it is considered a disgrace among many Bedouin tribes in the peninsula of Sinai to be able to write. It is therefore impossible that such men could hand down their family histories, in themselves quite unimportant, in any other way than orally, to wit, in legends. And even when writing had come into use, in the time, that is, between Moses and David, it would be but sparingly used, and much that happened to the people must still have been handed down simply as legend. (Schultz, OTH, 25–26)

There is every reason to believe that in the time of Moses language was highly usable as a vehicle of literary expression, and most likely had been so for centuries. Concerning this point, Driver contends, "It is not denied that the patriarchs possessed the art of writing" but the use of documents from the patriarchal age is "a mere hypothesis, for the truth of which no positive grounds can be alleged." (Driver, BG, xlii)

Speaking of hypothesis, Orr reminds us that the critical view itself is surely

built on hypothesis. The value of a hypothesis is the degree in which it explains facts, and, in the silence of the Book of Genesis, we can only reason from general probabilities. But the probabilities, derived from the state of culture at the time, from the fixed and circumstantial character of the tradition, and from the archaeological notices embedded in the book, are, we think, strong, that the Hebrews, even in the patriarchal age, were to some extent acquainted with books and writing. If so, we may believe that at an early period, in Egypt under Joseph, if not before, attempts would be made to set down things in writing. (Orr, POT, 375)

When it was believed that Israel's beginnings dated to the early dawn of civilization, the position was more tenable that the Hebrews were unacquainted with writing. It was likewise respectable to doubt their capacity to conceive such lofty ideas as expressed in Moses' laws or David's psalms.

2B. Basic Answer

1C. Evaluation and Cultural Climate

The British Assyriologist A. H. Sayce evaluates this theory of a late date of writing. He claims that

this supposed late use of writing for literary purposes was merely an assumption, with nothing more solid to rest upon than the critic's own theories and presuppositions. And as soon as it could be tested by solid fact it crumbled into dust. First Egyptology, then Assyriology, showed that the art of writing in the ancient East, so far from being of modern growth, was of vast antiquity, and that the two great powers which divided the civilized world between them were each emphatically a nation of scribes and readers. Centuries before Abraham was born, Egypt and Babylonia were alike full of schools and libraries, of teachers and pupils, of poets and prose-writers, and of the literary works which they had composed. (Sayce, MFHCF, 28–29)

Sayce cites Crete as another example.

A. J. Evans found evidence of pre-Mosaic writing on Crete. Not only were Egypt and Babylon writing in hieroglyphic and

The excavations at Ugarit have revealed a high material and literary culture in Canaan prior to the emergence of the Hebrews. Prose and poetry were already fully developed. The educational system was so advanced that dictionaries in four languages were compiled for the use of scribes, and the individual words were listed in their Ugaritic, Babylonian, Sumerian, and Hurrian equivalents.

—CYRUS GORDON,
CHAIR OF THE DEPARTMENT OF MEDITERRANEAN
STUDIES, BRANDEIS UNIVERSITY

cuneiform respectively, but Crete had three, perhaps four, systems, i.e. pictographs, linear symbols, and so forth. (Sayce, MFHCF, 41)

Albright, speaking of the various writing systems that existed in the ancient Orient even during pre-Mosaic patriarchal times, says:

> In this connection it may be said that writing was well known in Palestine and Syria throughout the Patriarchal Age (Middle Bronze, 2100–1500 B.C.). No fewer than five scripts are known to have been in use: Egyptian hieroglyphs, used for personal and place names by the Canaanites; Accadian cuneiform; the hieroglyphiform syllabary of Phoenicia, used from the 23rd century or earlier (as known since 1935); the linear alphabet of Sinai, three inscriptions in which are now known from Palestine (this script seems to be the direct progenitor of our own); the cuneiform alphabet of Ugarit (used also a little later in Palestine), which was discovered in 1929. This means that Hebrew historical traditions need not have been handed down through oral transmission alone. (Albright, ACBC, 186)

Cyrus Gordon, former professor of Near Eastern studies and chairman of the Department of Mediterranean Studies at Brandeis University, and an authority on the tablets discovered at Ugarit, concludes similarly:

> The excavations at Ugarit have revealed a high material and literary culture in Canaan prior to the emergence of the Hebrews. Prose and poetry were already fully developed. The educational system was so advanced that dictionaries in four languages were compiled for the use of scribes, and the individual words were listed in their Ugaritic, Babylonian, Sumerian, and Hurrian equivalents. The beginnings of Israel are rooted in a highly cultural Canaan where the contributions of several talented peoples (including the Mesopotamians, Egyptians, and branches of the Indo-Europeans)

had converged and blended. The notion that early Israelite religion and society were primitive is completely false. Canaan in the days of the Patriarchs was the hub of a great international culture. The Bible, hailing from such a time and place, cannot be devoid of sources. But let us study them by taking the Bible on its own terms and against its own authentic background. (Gordon, HCFF, 133–34)

The archaeological evidence serves not only to refute the older critics' antiquated theory but also serves as positive evidence to support the probability that Moses kept written records.

Sayce makes a shuddering conclusion: "The Babylonia of the age of Abraham was a more highly educated country than the England of George III." (Sayce, MFHCF, 35)

Why can archaeologists make such statements? Several archaeological finds support this conclusion. We will look at four.

2C. Ugarit (Ras Shamra)

William F. Albright explains the Ugarit discoveries. The cuneiform writing of Ugarit is a system completely native to Syria-Palestine and was recovered in 1929 by C. F. A. Schaeffer on the Syrian north coast. The most prominent deposits of tablets with this writing are at Ugarit and Ras Shamra. Artifacts with this script are dated as early as 1400 B.C., though the alphabet itself is probably older. (Albright, AP, 187; Archer, SOTI, 157)

Albright writes: "It is difficult to exaggerate the importance of the Canaanite alphabetic tablets from Ugarit, north of Canaan proper. Thanks to them, we have a vast body of texts from the age of Moses (fourteenth and thirteenth centuries B.C.). They are partly in local prose dialect of Ugarit at that time, but mostly in a generalized poetic dialect that corresponds closely to such early Hebrew poetic language as the Song of Miriam (thirteenth century B.C.) and the Son of Deborah (twelfth century), as well as to many of the early Psalms. They have enormously widened our knowledge of biblical Hebrew vocabulary and grammar." (Albright, ADS, 3–4)

3C. Egyptian Letters

Sayce noted that Egypt was a very literate nation. During the reign of Ikhnaton (or Amenhotep IV), who tried to change the entire religious system of Egypt from about 1375 to 1358 B.C., great amounts of correspondence, called the Amarna tablets, were exchanged between Egypt, Syria, Palestine, and Babylon. Many of these have been discovered at Amarna since 1887. Not only do these show writing to have been in use, but further, they are not in hieroglyphics but Babylonian cuneiform. This indicates a close contact between the two, so much so that a standard diplomatic language of the day appears to have been used. The art of writing was well entrenched by this time. (Sayce, MFHCF, 38–39)

4C. Mt. Sinai Inscriptions

S. H. Horn explains yet another find: "In 1917 Alan Gardiner, noted British Egyptologist, made the first decipherment of the Proto-Semitic inscriptions found at Mt. Sinai by Flinders Petrie more than ten years earlier. These inscriptions, written in a pictorial script by Canaanites before the middle of the second millennium B.C., prove that alphabetic writing existed before the time of Moses." (Horn, RIOT, 14)

5C. Gezer Calendar

The Gezer Calendar, written in 925 B.C. (found by Macalister in the 1900s), is obviously an exercise performed by a child. It proves that writing was well established in society at that time even to the point of being taught to children. (Archer, SOTI, 157)

Look at Judges 8:14, where a youth picked at random from the town of Succoth was able to "write down" for Gideon the names of the seventy-seven elders.

Albright shows the importance of this definitely Semitic writing: "The oldest important Israelite inscription is the Gezer Calendar, a schoolboy's exercise tablet of soft limestone, on which he had awkwardly scratched the text of a ditty giving the order of the chief agricultural operations through the year. It dates from the late tenth century, if we may judge from the agreement of the evidence for forms of letters from contemporary Byblus with the stratigraphic context in which it was discovered." (Albright, AP, 132)

6C. Conclusion: Critics Criticized

This issue constitutes a major upset for skeptics of Bible history. Sayce said it well when he asserted: "As late as 1862, Sir George Cornwall Lewis denied it [writing in Moses'

> This contention is now rendered impossible by the discovery of the extraordinary light of civilization which shone in the Tigro-Euphrates valley, and in the valley of the Nile, millenniums before Abraham left Ur of the Chaldees, or Moses led his people out of Egypt. The transformation of opinion is revolutionary.
>
> —JAMES ORR

day], and as late as 1871 the eminent Semitic scholar Professor Noldeke declared that the results of Assyriology in both linguistic and historical matters had 'a highly suspicious air.' It was subjective theory against objective fact, and in accordance with the usual 'critical' method fact had to give way to theory." (Sayce, MFHCF, 35–36)

He then concludes, "Moses not only could

have written the Pentateuch, but it would have been little short of a miracle had he not been a scribe." (Sayce, MFHCF, 42–43)

James Orr, in *The Problem the Old Testament,* explains the transformation of modern thought in the following manner:

> Formerly Israel was looked upon as a people belonging to the dim dawn of history at a period when, except in Egypt, civilization had hardly begun. It was possible then to argue that the art of writing did not exist among the Hebrews, and that they had not the capacity for the exalted religious ideas which the narratives of their early history implies. Moses could not have given the laws, nor David have written the psalms, which the history ascribes to them. This contention is now rendered impossible by the discovery of the extraordinary light of civilization which shone in the Tigro-Euphrates valley, and in the valley of the Nile, millenniums before Abraham left Ur of the Chaldees, or Moses led his people out of Egypt. The transformation of opinion is revolutionary. (Orr, POT, 396–97)

5A. THE LEGENDARY VIEW OF PATRIARCHAL NARRATIVES

1B. Documentary Assumption

The question of the historicity of the Abraham accounts has been a favorite battleground between believer and skeptic. It is difficult to remain neutral on this issue if we consider the Bible important for humankind today. Merrill Unger, in his *Archaeology and the Old Testament,* shows that the historicity of Abraham is no mean issue, but is vital to New Testament faith: "The figure of Abraham emerges from the ancient Mesopotamian world of his time with such remarkable vividness and assumes a role of such importance in the history of redemption that he is not overshadowed by even Moses, the great emancipator and lawgiver

of Israel. Throughout the Old Testament and especially the New Testament the name of Abraham stands for the representative man of faith (cf. Rom. 4:1–25)." (Unger, AOT, 105)

Therefore we can turn to Gleason Archer, in *A Survey of Old Testament Introduction,* for a phrasing of the allegation. He explains that the documentarians believe "the Genesis accounts of the career of Abraham and his descendants are untrustworthy and often unhistorical. Noldeke even went so far as to deny the historical existence of Abraham altogether." (Archer, SOTI, 158)

From the pen of noted critics we have explanatory material. Julius Wellhausen writes: "From the patriarchal narratives it is impossible to obtain any historical information with regard to the patriarchs; we can only learn something about the time in which the stories about them were first told by the Israelite people. This later period, with all its essential and superficial characteristics, was unintentionally projected back into hoary antiquity and is reflected there like a transfigured mirage." (Wellhausen, PHI, 331)

Wellhausen viewed Abraham as "a free creation of unconscious art." (Wellhausen, PHI, 320)

Hermann Schultz says:

> The result may be given in outline as follows: Genesis is the book of sacred legend, with a mythical introduction. The first three chapters of it, in particular, present us with revelation myths of the most important kind, and the following eight with mythical elements that have been recast more in the form of legend. From Abraham to Moses we have national legend pure and simple, mixed with a variety of mythical elements which have become almost unrecognisable. From Moses to David we have history still mixed with a great deal of the legendary, and even partly with mythical ele-

ments that are no longer distinguishable. From David onwards we have history, with no more legendary elements in it than are everywhere present in history as written by the ancients. (Schultz, OTH, 31)

And finally, from Robert H. Pfeiffer: "Our sharp distinction between story and history, fancy and fact, seems meaningless when applied to the body of Old Testament narratives which present all the gradations between pure fiction (as in the stories about Adam, Noah, Samson) and genuine history (as in the ancient biography of David and in the Memoirs of Nehemiah). Only in the recital of events on the part of an eyewitness (unless he be lying as in I Sam. 22:10a and II Sam. 1:7–10) may exact historicity be expected in the Old Testament narratives. Their credibility decreases in the ratio of their distance in time from the narrator." (Pfeiffer, IOT, 27)

2B. Basic Answer

In the next few pages we will examine what we know about the patriarchal period and show that archaeology has played a big part in increasing this knowledge. G. Ernest Wright points out: "There are numerous illustrations of the service which archaeology has rendered along this line. Perhaps the most noteworthy is the partial 'recovery' of the patriarchal period of biblical history." (Wright, PSBA, 80)

1C. Inscriptional Material

Under this heading we will investigate certain finds; in 2C we will see how these finds have contributed to our understanding of patriarchal culture. Unger has struck a balance between the two: "As a result of archaeological research, particularly that of the last three decades, a large quantity of inscriptional material is now available to scholars,

which has an important bearing on the patriarchal age. This material is of the greatest importance." (Unger, AOT, 120–21)

He goes on to add that, though much is yet unpublished, it has been crippling to skeptical theories, and analysis of the material has raised the standing of the Old Testament history. It does not establish such accounts as inviolate, but "it does mean that it has furnished a great deal of indirect evidence showing that the stories fit into the background of the age, as that age can now be recovered from the new sources of knowledge available, and that customs which

> I am here to inform you that recent archaeological discoveries have proved to be directly pertinent to the question of the historicity of the patriarchal traditions, as they are preserved in the Genesis narratives. Generally they confirm or at least support the basic positions maintained by giants like Albright and Speiser, while effectively undercutting the prevailing skepticism and sophistry of the larger contingent representative of continental and American scholarship.
>
> —DAVID NOEL FREEDMAN, DIRECTOR OF AN ARCHAEOLOGICAL RESEARCH INSTITUTION

appear in the stories prevailed in the world in which the patriarchs are set." (Unger, AOT, 120–21)

Professor David Noel Freedman of the University of Michigan, director of the William F. Albright School for Archaeological Research in Jerusalem, makes this statement regarding the historicity of the patriarchs:

> In the same mood, that is the search for truth, I now bring you word, not about Moses and his generation, the historicity of which continues to be questioned by many leading scholars, but about an earlier generation still,

that of the patriarchs, and to be more specific, the father of them and of us all, that is by faith if not in fact—Abraham or Abram. Even to talk about the possible historicity of the stories of Genesis and the figures who play leading roles in them is to jeopardize one's standing in the profession and to lay oneself open to the charges of pseudoscholarship.

Nevertheless, there have been outstanding scholars in the past who held these peculiar notions, and I do not hesitate to identify myself with this viewpoint and as an adherent of that school of thought. I recall an interesting and remarkable ultimate ancestor, for the members of the three great monotheistic faiths—Judaism. Christianity and Islam—all trace their descent from Abraham himself, which makes the subject of his historicity of something more than academic interest. Professor W.F. Albright whom we all acknowledge as an Abrahamic figure in the scholarship of our day, and the father-professor of a legion of us, his followers and disciples, was quite circumspect about a historical reconstruction of the Genesis narratives and about precise circumstances and activities of the patriarchs, as well as their beliefs. At the same time, the illustrious cuneiformist at the University of Pennsylvania, E. Speiser, who unlike Albright did not profess a personal religion, had hardly any reservations at all; he did not merely assert the historicity of Abraham and his extensive family, but insisted on his monotheistic faith. Together these eminent scholars were an island fortress of conservative, almost traditional views, in an age of skepticism, but, of the two, Speiser was the more outspoken and direct, while Albright was more reticent and nuanced. Now that vindication is on its way, it is clear that Speiser was closer to historical reality, but even the presently known facts go far beyond what either of these great thinkers could have imagined.

I am here to inform you that recent archaeological discoveries have proved to be directly pertinent to the question of the historicity of the patriarchal traditions, as they are preserved in the Genesis narratives. Generally they confirm or at least support the basic positions maintained by giants like Albright and Speiser, while effectively undercutting the prevailing skepticism and sophistry of the larger contingent representative of continental and American scholarship. (Freedman, RSET, 144)

1D. The Mari Tablets

William F. Albright, in his *From the Stone Age to Christianity,* comments,

> The latest discoveries at Mari on the Middle Euphrates . . . have strikingly confirmed the Israelite traditions according to which their Hebrew forefathers came to Palestine from the region of Harran in northwestern Mesopotamia. (Albright, FSAC, 197)

In his article "The Bible After Twenty Years of Archaeology," Albright goes further: "The excavation of Mari began in 1933, under the direction of Andre Parrot. Situated on the Middle Euphrates, Mari was one of the most important centers of the Northwest Semitic life of Patriarchal times. In 1936, M. Parrot unearthed many thousands of cuneiform tablets dating mostly from about 1700 B.C., which are now in course of being studied and published. These tablets throw direct light on the background of the Patriarchal traditions of Genesis." (Albright, BATYA, 538)

He goes on to explain the impact of the Mari Tablets: "Now we can speak even more emphatically, and with a wealth of additional detail. For example, the 'city of Nahor' which plays a role next to Harran in the Patriarchal stories (Gen. 24:10) turns up frequently along with Harran in the Mari documents about 1700 B.C. The name of a prince of Mari, Arriyuk, is evidently the same as the Arioch of Genesis 14. 'Benjamin' often appears as a tribal name at Mari." (Albright, BATYA, 541–42)

In the 1950 edition of *The Archaeology of Palestine,* one senses the impact of these tablets by noting the following:

> Dossin and Jean are editing the thousands of tablets from Mari; every new publication of theirs helps us better to understand the life and times of the Hebrew Patriarchs. Abraham, Isaac, and Jacob no longer seem isolated figures, much less reflections of later Israelite history; they now appear as true children of their age, bearing the same names, moving about over the same territory, visiting the same towns (especially Harran and Nahor), practicing the same customs as their contemporaries. In other words, the patriarchal narratives have a historical nucleus throughout, though it is likely that long oral transmission of the original poems and later prose sagas which underlie the present text of Genesis has considerably refracted the original events. (Albright, AP, 236)

2D. The Law Codes

We have come to understand many of the actions of the patriarchs through the law codes of the Hittites, who exerted a strong influence on culture at that time. Archer notes the findings of one archaeologist: "As Manfred Lehmann brings out [*Bulletin of the American Schools of Oriental Research,* No. 129, Feb. 1953, p. 18], the account in Genesis 23 exhibits such an intimate knowledge of Hittite procedure as to make it certain that the episode antedated the destruction of the Hittite power in the thirteenth century B.C." (Archer, SOTI, 161)

Henry T. Frank, in *Bible, Archaeology, and Faith,* elucidates an Abrahamic episode:

> Similarly, a number of once puzzling incidents associated with the patriarchs are also shown by archaeological discoveries to have been commonplace in the early second millennium. We have already seen that Abraham's haggling with Ephron concerning the purchase of the Cave of Machpelah was in accordance with common ancient practice. Apparently Abraham wished to purchase only the cave itself in which to bury his wife, Sarah. Yet governed by Hittite practice he had to buy not only the cave but the land and the arbors associated with it. This assumption of feudal obligation described in Genesis 23:1–20 is exactly in accord with the recovered Hittite documents from Boghazköy in which such details are stressed. (Frank, BAF, 74)

3D. The Egyptian Execration Texts

Unger explains these denunciatory artifacts:

> The so-called "Execration Texts" add their evidence to attest the authentic background of the patriarchs as presented in Genesis. These curious documents are statuettes and vases inscribed in Egyptian hieratic script with the names of potential enemies of the Pharaoh. If threatened by rebellion the Egyptian king had only to break the fragile objects on which were written the names and accompanying formulae, to the accompaniment of a magical ceremony, and forthwith the rebels would somehow come to grief. The group of vases from Berlin, published by Kurt Sethe (1926), probably date from the end of the twentieth century B.C., while the collection of statuettes from Brussels, published by G. Posener (1940), date from the late nineteenth century. (Unger, AOT, 127)

4D. The Nuzi Tablets

S. H. Horn, in his *Christianity Today* article "Recent Illumination of the Old Testament," introduces the Nuzi Tablets: "The discovery of a whole archive of legal and social texts at Nuzi, a small place in northeastern Iraq, has revealed that the social and legal background of the patriarchal age is reflected accurately and in great detail in the Old Testament patriarchal narratives." (Horn, RIOT, 14)

G. E. Wright, in his "Present State of Biblical Archaeology" (1947) in *The Study of the Bible Today and Tomorrow*, and Cyrus Gordon, in "Biblical Customs and the Nuzu Tablets" *(The Biblical Archaeologist)*, provide good background material. Wright includes certain key points: Nuzi (or Nuzu) is located southeast of Nineveh. Some of the patriarchal episodes seem unusual, even to the later Israelites but this find at Nuzu clears the picture. The Nuzians were Hurrians (biblical Horites), formerly thought of as "cave dwellers," and are now understood as Armenoid, non-Indo-Europeans of North Mesopotamia, who flourished in the 1500 and 1400s B.C. (Wright, PSBA, 43)

Gordon follows up by explaining that though the patriarchs were not Nuzians, the cultures of the two were alike due to similar time and place. Therefore the Nuzi Tablets help us to understand Abraham, Isaac, and Jacob. (Gordon, BCNT, 2)

Wright points out that the "Nuzi tablets elucidate many a custom typical of the patriarchal age in the second millennium, but not of Israelite life in the first." (Wright, PSBA, 87)

Cyrus Gordon contends: "Thanks to the

> The cuneiform contracts from Nuzu have demonstrated that the social institutions of the patriarchs are genuine and pre-Mosaic. They cannot have been invented by any post-Mosaic. They cannot have been invented by any post-Mosaic J, E, D or P.
>
> —CYRUS GORDON

Nuzu texts we may feel confident that the social institutions have come down to us authentically." (Gordon, BCNT, 9)

What are some specific instances in which the Nuzi Tablets help us to understand Genesis? Horn writes:

First, in the patriarchal stories we find several strange accounts of a barren wife who asked her husband to produce a child for her by her maid servant. Sarah did this, and later also Jacob's two wives, Rachel and Leah. Today we know that this practice was not unusual during the patriarchal age. The laws of that period as well as ancient marriage contracts mention it. For example, in a marriage contract from Nuzi, the bride Kelim-ninu promises in written form to procure for her husband Shennima a slave girl as a second wife, if she fails to bear him children. She also promises that she will not drive out the offspring of such a union. In no other period besides the patriarchal age do we find this strange custom. (Horn, RIOT, 14)

Gordon in another article refers to the documentary hypothesis: "The cuneiform contracts from Nuzu have demonstrated that the social institutions of the patriarchs are genuine and pre-Mosaic. They cannot have been invented by any post-Mosaic. They cannot have been invented by any post-Mosaic J, E, D or P." (Gordon, PA, 241)

In Gordon's "Biblical Customs and the Nuzu Tablets," we find yet another custom explained: "It was a custom at Nuzu for childless people to adopt a son to serve them as long as they lived and to bury and mourn for them when they died. In exchange for these services the adopted son was designated as heir. If, however, the adopter should beget a son after the adoption, the adopted must yield to the real son the right of being the chief heir. . . . Once we know of this proviso, we have the legal meaning of God's reply in Genesis 15:4: 'This (slave) shall not inherit thee, but he that shall come out of thine inwards shall inherit thee.'" (Gordon, BCNT, 2–3)

Albright emphasizes the value of the Nuzi Tablets: "When we add the fact that our present knowledge of social institutions and customs in another part of northern

Mesopotamia in the fifteenth century (Nuzi) has brilliantly illuminated many details in the patriarchal stories which do not fit into the post-Mosaic tradition at all, our case for the substantial historicity of the tradition of the Patriarchs is clinched." (Albright, BPAE, 4–5)

5D. The Ebla Tablets

The tremendous archaeological discovery at Tell Mardikh of the ancient city of Ebla reveals a wealth of new light on the patriarchal narratives. Although very little has been published yet, the evidence points to exciting new gains and significant inroads for Near Eastern studies of the third millennium B.C., especially as related to the Old Testament accounts.

Referring to the patriarchal narratives, with general reference at first to Ebla and then specifically to a tablet that has been uncovered, David Noel Freedman states: "Nevertheless, in spite of the bad examples from the past and the ample warnings by those associated with the Ebla finds, I believe firmly that there is a link between the Ebla tablets and the Bible, not only of the general linguistic and literary type already mentioned, which is almost inevitable, or even in terms of a common pool of names of persons and places, but much more direct in terms of history, chronology and fact." (Freedman, RSET, 148)

Some of the specifics that Dr. Freedman mentions with regard to history, chronology, and fact center on a tablet, the exact translation of which is now a clouded issue. Some of the information first released to Dr. Freedman has been revised (as he himself mentions in his article [Eichrodt, E, 143–64].) Hopefully with its publication the evidence will support the original reading of the tablet. But while this is pending, Dr. Freedman also pointed out that there is still

a link between Ebla and the Bible, and that time should reveal to what extent.

2C. The Living Conditions

All these finds and more are combined to give us a picture of the culture of Middle Bronze Age Palestine (2000–1500 B.C.). For convenience, the following discussion is broken into the social-cultural setting and the geographical setting.

1D. The Social-Cultural Setting

Millar Burrows introduces this area: "Specific archaeological evidence that this or that event in the stories of the patriarchs actually occurred may not be forthcoming, but the social customs reflected by the stories fit the patriarchal period; they also fit the region from which the patriarchs are said to have come." (Burrows, WMTS, 278–79)

Albright is even stronger: "The picture of movements in the hill country of Palestine, of seasonal migration between the Negreb and central Palestine, and of easy travel to Mesopotamia and Egypt is, accordingly, so perfectly in accord with conditions in the Middle Bronze Age that historical skepticism is quite unwarranted." (Albright, BPAE, 4)

For some specific instances, Fred H. Wight mentions the question of travel.

Men who have doubted the historic character of the patriarchs have questioned the migration of Abraham from Ur of the Chaldees to the land of Canaan, and also the military expedition from Babylonia to Palestine as indicated in Genesis 14, because they have insisted that extensive travel was not known in that day. But Babylonian excavators [at Mari] have uncovered a tablet that shows there was much travel between these two lands in those days. This tablet is dated in the era of Abraham, and it was a wagon contract. The owner of the wagon leased it to a man for a year on condition that it not be driven to Kittim (i.e., the coast land of the Mediterranean Sea). Evidently, it was quite customary for men to drive their wagons over this route from Babylonia to Canaan or vicinity, and this owner stipulated that this should not be done with his wagon. This is clear evidence of wide travel between these two sections of the ancient world. (Wight, HABL, 61–62)

Joseph P. Free even mentions the custom of heavy doors during Lot's time. He cites Genesis 19:9, where the evil men of Sodom could not get through Lot's doorway. Keil and Albright studied Tell Beit Mirsim, which is Kirjath-Sepher of the Bible, and found walls and doors of the time between 2200 and 1600 B.C. to have been heavy and strong. At the 900 through 600 B.C. level homes most likely had archways or curtains, but no doors were found. In Lot's day, the police force was not so strong, so forbidding doors were needed. But with stronger law and order, such doors were no longer needed for protection. (Free, ABH, 62)

Free then takes the offensive: "Lot's heavy door fits precisely in this period. The critics, however, date the writing of the accounts of Abraham in the ninth and eighth centuries B.C. How did the writer know the conditions a thousand years or more before his time?" (Albright, FSAC, 63)

Concerning the name of Abraham, John Elder explains: "It is not to be expected that the histories which kings of those times have left will contain mention of such a man as Abraham. But a tablet found in Babylonia bears the name Abarama and records that he paid his rent. At the least it shows that Abraham was one of the names used in that period." (Elder, PID, 50)

To summarize, Albright sets forth a broad analysis: "Numerous recent excavations in sites of this period in Palestine, supplemented by finds made in Egypt and Syria, give us a remarkably precise idea of patriarchal Palestine, fitting well into the picture handed down in Genesis." (Albright, BPAE, 3)

2D. The Geographical-Topographical Setting

Unger speaks of the topographical accuracy of Genesis and shows that "it is significant, too, in this connection that the topographical allusions in the patriarchal stories fit the archaeological indications of the Middle Bronze Age (200–1500 B.C.) extremely well." (Unger, AOT, 114)

And further, "The five cities of the plain (circle) of the Jordan, Sodom, Gomorrah, Admah, Zeboiim and Zoar, also belong to

> Practically all of the towns mentioned in connection with Abraham (such as Shechem, Ai, Bethel) have been excavated, and the findings show that these go back to Abraham's time.
>
> —JOSEPH P. FREE

the early patriarchal age. The Biblical notices that the district of the Jordan, where these cities were located, was exceedingly fertile and well-peopled around 2065 B.C. but that not long afterwards was abandoned, are in full accord with the archaeological facts." (Unger, AOT, 114)

Earlier scholars maintained that the Jordan Valley was hardly populated in Abraham's day. Archer, however, shows that "Nelson Glueck has in recent decades uncovered more than seventy sites in the Jordan Valley, some of them as ancient as 3000 B.C." (Archer, SOTI, 159)

Archer continues that "as for Abraham's career in Palestine, the excavations at Shechem and Bethel show that they were inhabited in Abraham's time." (Archer, SOTI, 159)

Joseph Free speaks of Shechem, Ai, and Bethel: "When Abraham came into Canaan, he dwelt for a time near Shechem (Shichem, Gen. 12:6), about thirty miles north of Jerusalem, in a plain within the central mountain ridge of Palestine. Later he moved a few miles to the south and pitched his tent between Bethel and Ai (Gen. 12:8), some twelve miles north of Jerusalem (ISBE, article on 'Bethel'). Here he built an altar to the Lord and worshipped." (Free, ABH, 53)

He goes on to say that "practically all of the towns mentioned in connection with Abraham (such as Shechem, Ai, Bethel) have been excavated, and the findings show that these go back to Abraham's time." (Free, ABH, 53)

Concerning the "Table of Nations" in Genesis 10, and the listings in Genesis 11, Burrows comments that the lists of Genesis 10 and 11 have been enlightened by archaeology, since many names remained lost to outside sources until recent material was discovered. (Burrows, WMTS, 258)

Free, in his article "Archaeology and the Historical Accuracy of Scripture," refers to Albright:

Archaeological monuments, however, have yielded the names of peoples and countries mentioned in this record [Gen. 10]. Many of them were unknown until discovered in ancient archaeological records. W. F. Albright, in his 1955 revision of the article, "Recent Discoveries in Bible Lands," pointed out what he had said earlier, that this chapter stands absolutely alone in ancient literature (*Young's Analytical Concordance to the Bible*, p. 30). We find that the monuments attest:

Tubal in the form Tabal
Meshech as Mushke
Ashkenaz as Ashkunz
Togarmah as Tegarama
Elishah as Alashi (Alashiyah)
Tarshish as Tarsisi (Assyrian Tarshish)

Cush as Kusi (pronounced Kush in Assyrian)
Phut as Putu
Dedan as Ddn
Accad as Akkadu
Shinar as Shanghar

Many other parallels appear in the monuments, and this evidence leads Dr. Albright to conclude that The Table of Nations remains an astonishingly accurate document. (Free, AHAS, 215)

Summing up, in his *Archaeology and Bible History* Free concludes: "The fact, however, that the cities mentioned in connection with Abraham are shown by archaeological discoveries to have existed in his time constitutes a definite argument for the accuracy of the background of the Abrahamic accounts in the Scriptures." (Free, ABH, 53)

3C. The Counter-issue: Abraham in Egypt

Before moving to a conclusion, we must deal with one final point: Some critics will maintain that Abraham could not have visited Egypt due to a closed-door policy. This issue is addressed by Edgar Banks: "Frequently it has been asserted that neither Abraham nor any other of his people and age was ever down in Egypt, and that it would have been impossible for him or for any other stranger to enter the country from which all strangers were excluded." (Banks, BS, 58)

This question has been brought to my attention by Joseph Free in his *Archaeology and Bible History*. He explains the situation: "Popular books on archaeology frequently allude to the critical view that strangers could not have come into Egypt in earlier times, and often refer the basis of such an idea back to the first century historians Strabo or Diodorus, but ordinarily no further documentation is given." (Free, ABH, 54)

Free also cites Millar Neatby: "Neatby says that the critic could quote Strabo, the

Greek geographer and historian, who stated shortly before the time of Christ that 'Not till the time of Psammetichus (654 B.C.) did Egypt open its ports to strangers or grant security to foreign traders' (T. Millar Neatby, *Confirming the Scriptures*, (London: Marshall, Morgan and Scott, n.d.), Vol. II, pp. 114–15." (Free, ABH, 54)

"A detailed examination of the writings of Strabo and Diodorus has shown, however, that such an implication is given by Strabo, and a point blank statement is made by Diodorus." (Free, ABH, 54)

Strabo: "Now the earlier kings of the Egyptians, being content with what they had and not wanting foreign imports at all, and being prejudiced against all who sailed the seas, and particularly against the Greeks (for owing to scarcity of land of their own the Greeks were ravagers and coveters of that of others), set a guard over this region and ordered it to keep away any who should approach." (Strabo, GS, 27)

Diodorus: "Psammetichus . . . regularly treated with kindness any foreigners who sojourned in Egypt of their own free will . . . and, speaking generally, he was the first Egyptian king to open to other nations the trading-places through the rest of Egypt and to offer a large measure of security to strangers from across the seas. For his predecessors in power had consistently closed Egypt to strangers, either killing or enslaving any who touched its shores." (Diodorus, DS, 235)

There is only one problem. Archaeology has shown the Old Testament to be the accurate record—not the first-century historians:

Archaeological discoveries, however, show that people from the region of Palestine and Syria were coming to Egypt in the period of Abraham. This is clearly indicated by a tomb painting at Beni Hassan, dating a little after

2000 B.C. It shows Asiatic Semites who have come to Egypt. . . . Furthermore, the archaeological and historical indications of the coming of the Hyksos into Egypt c. 1900 B.C. provides another piece of evidence showing that strangers could come into that land. Their entrance was almost contemporary with that of Abraham. The Bible is correct in this indication and Diodorus was wrong. (Albright, FSAC, 54–55)

4C. Conclusion

G. E. Wright gives the story behind a most rare extra-biblical reference to Abraham:

The first great disaster since the reign of Saul descended upon the two kingdoms about 918 B.C. Our books of Kings give us scant information about it: "And it came to pass in the fifth year of King Rehoboam that Shishak, king of Egypt came up against Jerusalem. And he took away the treasures of the house (Temple) of the Lord, and the treasures of the king's house. . . . And he took away all the shields of gold which Solomon had made (I Kings 14:25–6)."

This king of Egypt thought more highly of his campaign, however, and on the walls of the great temple of Karnak in Upper Egypt he had his artists carve a picture of himself smiting the Asiatics in the presence of the god Amon, who with a goddess is depicted as presenting to him ten lines of captives. Each captive symbolized a town or locality, the name of which was inscribed below. From these names we can gather the extent of his campaign. The biblical account implies that only Judah was affected, but all of Palestine apparently suffered, for the list includes cities in the Esdraelon, Transjordan, the hill country of both Israel and Judah, and even Edom. There is an interesting reference to the Field of Abram, presumably the Hebron area, and this is the first time that a source outside the Bible confirms that Patriarch's connection with a locality in Palestine. (Wright, PSBA, 148)

W. F. Albright writes that "so many corroborations of details have been discovered in recent years that most competent scholars have given up the old critical theory according to which the stories of the Patriarchs are mostly retrojections from the time of the Dual Monarchy (ninth–eighth centuries B.C.)." (Albright, FSAC, 183)

Albright concludes that "as a whole the picture in Genesis is historical, and there is no reason to doubt the general accuracy of the biographical details and the sketches of personality which make the Patriarchs come alive with a vividness unknown to a single extrabiblical character in the whole vast literature of the ancient Near East." (Albright, BPAE, 5)

Millar Burrows says: "No longer can we think of Abraham as a lonely figure moving across uninhabited wastes to an almost unoccupied land, and taking possession of it as an arctic explorer claims the wastes of the north for his nation." (Burrows, WMTS, 92)

J. P. Free, citing Gordon, writes that "in regard to the background of the patriarchal narratives Cyrus Gordon, writing on the Nuzi tablets, points out that they show us

> So many corroborations of details have been discovered in recent years that most competent scholars have given up the old critical theory according to which the stories of the Patriarchs are mostly retrojections from the time of the Dual Monarchy (ninth–eighth centuries B.C.).
>
> —WILLIAM F. ALBRIGHT

that the picture of patriarchal society has come down to us authentically *(Biblical Archaeologist,* 3:1:9, January, 1940)." (Free, ABH, 34)

Even W. A. Irwin of Southern Methodist University, not a conservative in his views,

writes in his article "The Modern Approach to the Old Testament": "An extreme skepticism in regard to the patriarchal stories has given place to recognition that they preserve valid reminiscences of historic movements and social conditions." (Irwin, MAOT, 14)

W. F. Albright concludes:

> Turning to Israel, I defend the substantial historicity of patriarchal tradition, without any appreciable change in my point of view, and insist, just as in 1940–46, on the primacy of oral tradition over written literature. I have not surrendered a single position with regard to early Israelite monotheism but, on the contrary, consider the Mosaic tradition as even more reliable than I did then. Without altering my general view of the growth of the social and political institutions of Israel, I now recognize that Israelite law and religious institutions tend to be old and more continuous than I had supposed—in other words, I have grown more conservative in my attitude to Moasic tradition. (Albright, FSAC, 2)

J. Bright states: "We can assert with full confidence that Abraham, Isaac, and Jacob were actual historical individuals." (Bright, HI, 82)

Any discussion of the historicity of the patriarchs will have to consider Bright's recommendation: "The only safe and proper course lies in a balanced examination of the traditions against the background of the world of the day and, in the light of that, making such positive statements as the evidence allows. Hypothetical reconstructions, plausible though these may be, are to be eschewed. Much must remain obscure. But enough can be said to make it certain that the patriarchal traditions are firmly anchored in history." (Bright, HI, 69)

3B. Genesis 14—An Additional Example

One area that has been continuously criticized in regard to its historicity is the abstruse chapter 14 of Genesis. This chapter narrates Abraham's victory over Chedorlaomer and the Mesopotamian kings.

The first person to apply the "German rationalistic criticism" to Genesis 14 was Theodore Noldeke (1826–1930). He wrote a pamphlet titled "The Unhistorical Character of Genesis 14," in which he labels it a forgery and describes the expedition as "ficititous."

Julius Wellhausen writes of its "historical unreliability": "That 'at the time of Abraham' four Kings from the Persian Gulf made a razzia (or raid) as far as the peninsula of Sinai; that they, on that occasion, surprised and captured five city-princes who reigned in the Dead Sea; that finally Abraham, at the head of 318 servants, fell upon the departing victors, and recaptured what they had robbed, —these are simply impossibilities." (Wellhausen, DCH, 312)

Wellhausen continues: "From the patriarchal narratives it is impossible to obtain any historical information with regard to the Patriarchs. We can only learn something about the time in which the stories about them were first told by the Israelite people. This later period, with all its essential and superficial characteristics, was unintentionally projected backward into hoary antiquity, and is reflected there like a transfigured mirage." (Wellhausen, DCH, 331)

William F. Albright in 1918 wrote an article entitled "Historical and Mythical Elements in the Story of Joseph." He concluded that chapter 14 "must be regarded, with Asmussen . . . and Haupt . . . as a political pamphlet, designed (so Haupt) to strengthen the hands of the patriotic Jews who were supporting the rebellion of Zerubbabel

> *As a result of his own archaeological discoveries in 1929, Albright had his skeptical views radically changed.*

against the Persian monarch." (Albright, HMESJ, 136)

Albright concludes that "the Hebrew material was either borrowed from extant legends like the saga of the cities of the plain and the legend of Melchizedek, or invented by use of haggadic processes." (Albright, HMESJ, 136)

However, as a result of his own archaeological discoveries in 1929, Albright had his skeptical views radically changed and concluded that

this account represents the invading host as marching down from Hauran through eastern Gilead and Moab to the southeastern part of Palestine. Formerly the writer considered this extraordinary line of march as being the best proof of the essentially legendary character of the narrative. In 1929 however, he discovered a line of Early and Middle Bronze Age mounds, some of great size running down along the eastern edge of Gilead, between the desert and the forest of Gilead. Moreover, the cities of Hauran (Bashan) with which the account of the campaign opens, Ashtaroth and Karnaim, were both occupied in this period, as shown by archaeological examination of their sites. The same is true of eastern Moab, where the writer discovered an Early Middle-Bronze city at Ader in 1924. This route called "The Way of the King," in later Israelite tradition, does not appear to have ever been employed by invading armies in the Iron Age. (Albright, APB, 142–43)

The following indicates Albright's change in view when he asserts that Genesis 14 "can no longer be considered as unhistorical, in view of the many confirmations of details which we owe to recent finds." (Albright, OTA, 140)

Joseph Free lists several specific accusations made by the radical critics against the historicity of Genesis 14. We shall treat these briefly.

1C. The Mesopotamian Kings

1D. Documentary Assumption

The Mesopotamian kings' names were said to be fictitious or unhistorical.

2D. Basic Answer

The Mari tablets (eighteenth century B.C.) discovered in 1933 contain the name Arriyuk (or Arriwuk), identified with the name Arioch of Genesis 14. (Albright, BATYE, 542)

K. A. Kitchen points out: "Tid'al is a Tidkhalia, a Hittite name known from the nineteenth century B.C. onwards, and borne by four or five Hittite kings in the eighteenth to the thirteenth centuries B.C. Chedorla'-omer is typically Elamite . . . of the Old Babylonian period (2000–1700 B.C.) and later. . . . The individuals themselves have not yet been identified in extra-biblical documents, but this is not surprising when one considers the gaps in our knowledge of the period." (Kitchen, AOOT, 44)

Howard Vos concludes: "For a long time the names of the four kings of the East were thought to be unhistorical, but most scholars now find some means of identifying them with known persons or at least identifying them as historical name forms." (Vos, GA, 68–69)

Nahum Sarna recognizes that events in Genesis 14 are based upon documents of great antiquity. He writes that

the prose style has preserved indications of an archaic substratum in verse form. For instance, the names of the Canaanite Kings are arranged in two alliterative pairs, Bera-Birsha and Shinab-Shemeber. The language contains

some unique or very rare words and phrases. One such, *hanikh* (v. 14), meaning "an armed-retainer," appears but this once in the Bible, but it is found in the Egyptian execration texts of the nineteenth through eighteenth centuries B.C.E. and in a fifteenth-century B.C.E. cuneiform inscription from Taanach, Israel.

It will be noticed that only four of the local monarchs are mentioned by name, the fifth being called simply, "the king of Bela" (v. 2). Had the whole episode no historical foundation, the writer would surely not have been at a loss for a name. (Sarna, UG, 111)

2C. The Extensive Travel

1D. Documentary Assumption

There could not have been "extensive travel" such as the military campaign in Genesis 14.

2D. Basic Answer

Vos states that "the assertion made formerly that travel was not so extensive in the patriarchal period as indicated in this chapter and that military control of Palestine by Mesopotamian kings did not exist at that time must now be discarded. The expedition of kings of Elam and Babylonia appears in different light when we learn, for instance, that as early as 2300 B.C. Sargon of Akkad (near Babylon) made raids on the Amorites of Syria and Palestine." (Vos, GA, 70–71)

Another example of extensive travel as implied in Genesis 14 is given by G. A. Barton. The paragraph is entitled: "Travel between Babylonia and Palestine." Barton translates a document from a Babylonian clay tablet containing a wagon contract. He writes:

The date of the above interesting document has not been identified with certainty. It is thought by some to belong to the reign of Shamsuiluna, the successor of Hammurabi. The writing clearly shows that at any rate it comes from the period of this dynasty . . .

Kittim in the contract is the word used in the Hebrew of Jeremiah 2:10 and Ezekiel 27:6 for the coast lands of the Mediterranean. It undoubtedly has that meaning here. This contract was written in Sippar, the Agade of earlier times, a town on the Euphrates a little to the north of Babylon. It reveals the fact that at the time the document was written there was so much travel between Babylonia and the Mediterranean coast that a man could not lease a wagon for a year without danger that it might be driven over the long route to Syria or Palestine. (Barton, AB, 347)

Joseph Free relates that "other implication of long-distance travel is found in one of the Mari Tablets, which indicated that the King of ancient Ugarit on the Mediterranean coast planned to visit the King of Mari on the Euphrates. Such discoveries do not support the idea of limited travel, but rather the implication of the extensive travel involved in the campaign of the four kings of the east." (Free, AHAS, 217–18)

3C. The Route of the March

1D. Documentary Assumption
It is not reasonable that the route of the march would have followed the geographical lines as indicated.

2D. Basic Answer
Fred Wight states that "archaeological discoveries have compelled an increasing recognition of the value of this Scripture from the historical viewpoint." (Wight, HABL, 105)

William F. Albright confesses that "the underlying account of the campaign waged by the Eastern kings appears to be historical. This account represents the invading host as marching down from Hauran through eastern Gilead and Moab to the southeastern part of Palestine." (Albright, APB, 142)

However, Albright did not always attest to the historicity of the campaign. For a long time he "considered this extraordinary line of march as being the best proof of the essentially legendary character of the narrative." (Albright, APB, 142)

He retracted this legendary view when he

> In the light of all this, it is not unreasonable to assume that the story of the battle of the Kings in the Book of Genesis preserves an authentic echo of a great military expedition which put an end to the Middle Bronze I settlements. The annals recording the catastrophic events may well have furnished the basis for the biblical account.
>
> —NAHUM SARNA

wrote (also a quote previously used): "In 1929, however, he [Dr. Albright referring to himself] discovered a line of Early and middle Bronze Age mounds, some of great size, running down along the eastern edge of Gilead, between the desert and the forests of Gilead. Moreover, the cities of Hauran (Bashan) with which the account of the campaign opens, Ashtaroth and Karnaim, were both occupied in this period, as shown by archaeological examination of their sites. The same is true of eastern Moab, where the writer discovered an Early Middle Bronze city at Ader in 1924." (Albright, APB, 142)

If the account of the invasion is historical, there would be various areas of developed regions of permanent sedentary occupation existing very early along the route followed.

Nahum Sarna writes that

> extensive archaeological surveys of Transjordan and the Negeb have indeed shown this to have been the case during what is known as the Middle Bronze I period, i.e. between the

twenty-first and nineteenth centuries B.C.E. A civilization of a high order of achievement flourished throughout this period, and a truly amazing number of settlements has been discovered. Strangely enough, there occurs a complete and sudden interruption in settled life in Transjordan and the Negeb just at the end of the period, apparently as a result of some historic catastrophic invasion that systematically wiped out everything in its path. For the next six hundred years, Transjordan remained desolate until the founding of the Kingdoms of Edom and Moab in the thirteenth century B.C.E. In the Negeb, the break in civilization lasted nearly a thousand years.

In the light of all this, it is not unreasonable to assume that the story of the battle of the Kings in the Book of Genesis preserves an authentic echo of a great military expedition which put an end to the Middle Bronze I settlements. The annals recording the catastrophic events may well have furnished the basis for the biblical account. (Sarna, UG, 113–15)

The evidence has caused Albright to conclude that "Genesis 14 can no longer be considered as unhistorical, in view of the many confirmations of details which we owe to recent finds." (Albright, OTA, 140)

4C. Authority Over Canaan

1D. Documentary Assumption
The Mesopotamian kings had no sovereignty over Canaan.

2D. Basic Answer
Joseph Free writes concerning their control over Canaan: "Archaeological evidence of their control or attempt at control over the region of Canaan was found in an inscription in which the King of Elam (Persia) called himself 'the prince of the Land of Amurru' (M. G. Kyle, *Deciding Voice of the Monuments*, p. 133). Amurru, the land of the Amorites, included Syria and Canaan." (Free, AHAS, 218–19)

5C. Some Additional Comments
Kenneth Kitchen contends that "the system of power-alliances (four kings against five) is typical in Mesopotamian politics within the period c. 2000–1750 B.C., but not before or after this general period when different political patterns prevailed." (Kitchen, AOOT, 44)

Millar Burrows: "According to the fourteenth chapter of Genesis, eastern Palestine was invaded by a coalition of kings in the time of Abraham. The route taken by the invading armies led from the region of Damascus southward along the eastern edge of Gilead and Moab. The explorations of Albright and Glueck have shown that there was a line of important cities along this route before 2000 B.C. and for a century or two thereafter, but not in later periods." (Burrows, WMTS, 71)

Howard Vos: "As we continue to investigate the historicity of Genesis 14, we might well ask if any of the towns mentioned in verses 5 through 7 have yet been identified. At least three have been." (Vos, GA, 72)

S. L. Caiger states that "there seems no reason to question a factual basis of Genesis 14." (Caiger, BS, 34)

William Albright: "A generation ago most critical scholars regarded this chapter as very late and as quite unhistorical. Now we cannot accept such an easy way out of the difficulties which the chapter presents, since some of its allusions are exceedingly early, carrying us directly back into the Middle Bronze Age." (Albright, APB, 237)

6A. CONCLUSION REGARDING PRESUPPOSITIONS OF DOCUMENTARY HYPOTHESIS

1B. Presuppositions as the Basis

George Mendenhall brings out the importance of presuppositions in the formulation of the documentary hypothesis when he writes: "Wellhausen's theory of the history of Israelite religion was very largely based on a Hegelian philosophy of history, not upon his literary analysis. It was an *a priori* evolutionary scheme which guided him in the utilization of his sources." (Mendenhall, BHT, 36)

That the founders of the documentary theory were not as scientifically objective in their handling of the material as modern critics would have us believe (Hahn, OTMR,

> At last, in the course of a casual visit in Gottingen in the summer of 1867, I learned through Ritschl that Karl Heinrich Craf placed the Law later than the Prophets, and, almost without knowing his reasons for the hypothesis, I was prepared to accept it; I readily acknowledged to myself the possibility of understanding Hebrew antiquity without the book of the Torah.
>
> —JULIUS WELLHAUSEN

17) is supported by two statements made by Wellhausen. Here he reveals a careless and subjective methodology as well as the priority he gave to *a priori* theories over the textual evidence itself: "At last, in the course of a casual visit in Gottingen in the summer of 1867, I learned through Ritschl that Karl Heinrich Craf placed the Law later than the Prophets, and, almost without knowing his reasons for the hypothesis, I was prepared to accept it; I readily acknowledged to myself the possibility of understanding Hebrew antiquity without the book of the Torah." (Wellhausen, PHI, 3–4)

"Almost more important to me than the phenomena themselves, are the presupposi-

tions which lie behind them." (Wellhausen, PHI, 368)

Whitelaw's criticism is certainly justified:

It is not questioned that hypothesis as a tentative method of proof is perfectly legitimate. Frequently no other means of arriving at the solution of hard problems in science and philosophy is possible than by testing the applicability of first one supposition and then another.... In this way Grotefend, Rawlinson, and other Assyriologists deciphered the cuneiform inscriptions which have so wondrously enriched our knowledge of antiquity. Hence no real objection can be taken to the adoption by Biblical scholars of the same plan when confronted by knotty questions which cannot otherwise be answered. What is complained of is the making of *a priori* assumptions which rather raise difficulties than remove them, and holding these assumptions as demonstrated truths without having previously established them by convincing argument. (Whitelaw, OTC, 188–89)

Hence, we must regard all six of the documentarian presuppositions we have examined as invalid. Anti-supernaturalism must be rejected on the grounds that it claims to have absolute truth regarding the existence of God or the extent and nature of His intervention in the natural order of the universe, i.e., either His existence or His divine intervention is ruled out as an *impossibility* on an *a priori* basis.

Another of these presuppositions (an *a priori* distrust of the Old Testament record) must be rejected because it flies in the face of an accepted cannon of criticism that has stood the test of time, having guided literary and historical scholars since the time of Aristotle.

The remaining four presuppositions (the evolutionary view of Israel's history; the priority given to source analysis over verifiable methodology; the legendary view of patriarchal narratives; and the assumption that there was no writing in Israel during the Mosaic age) have all been soundly refuted by archaeological discoveries.

2B. Presuppositions and Contemporary Biblical Criticism

Some students of the Bible assume that in the field of biblical study the age of "the *a priori* assumption" has been rendered obsolete, having been replaced by "the conclusion that is reached only after the application of the totally objective scientific method in an analysis of the data." If preconceived positions are held, it is the conservative "fundamentalists" who hold them, not the unbiased adherents of higher liberal criticism whose interest in the Bible is not hampered by "dogmatic religious beliefs." Indeed, the term "liberal" connotes in many minds one who is less biased than the "conservative."

Such conclusions are at best wishful thinking. Although of a decidedly different nature, modern liberal critics, like conservatives, maintain certain preconceived positions. This important fact cannot be overstressed and failure to recognize it invites the serious charge of intellectual dishonesty.

Langdon Gilkey, himself a documentarian, concludes his article, "Cosmology, Ontology, and the Travail of Biblical Language," with this reminder to the entire school of liberal biblical criticism to which he belongs: "And for all of us, a contemporary understanding of ancient Scriptures depends as much on a careful analysis of our present presuppositions as it does on being learned in the religion and faith of the past." (Gilkey, COTBL, 154)

20
CONSEQUENCES OF RADICAL HIGHER CRITICISM

To accept the conclusions of radical higher criticism, one must embrace the following consequences:

1A. THE OLD TESTAMENT IS ESSENTIALLY UNHISTORICAL

For most adherents of the radical higher critical schools, the Old Testament does not contain an accurate history of Israel. It records, to be sure, isolated events that in themselves may be considered historical, but when viewed as a whole it gives a false picture of Israelite chronological history. Working from this premise, the critics have constructed their own account of early Hebrew history that, as can be seen from the table on the next page, contradicts the Old Testament record on many major points.

Walther Eichrodt comments on the critics' treatment of the book of Ezekiel, pointing out the difficulties of constructing theories that contradict the actual text:

This unsatisfactory fluctuation in the theories is no mere matter of chance; it is the necessary result of all the difficulties encountered by any attempt to work out such a fundamental theory on the basis of a text which states the exact opposite. Whenever they do not fit in with the theory, the established pieces of information about dates and geographical locations must now be accepted, and again dismissed as doubtful, without any reliable methodological basis for the conclusions. There is also a readiness to take those elements of the tradition that are difficult to accommodate to this interpretation, and either make them mean something else or else try to eliminate them by critical methods. (Eichrodt, E, 8–9)

The following chart compares the Hebrew's account of their own history (some of the major events) with that of the modern higher critics. This chart represents only the general trend in radical higher criticism; it does not represent the view of every critic. However, the general outline is prominent in most destructive higher critical circles today. In passing, it should also be noted that Wellhausen's reconstruction of early Hebrew history was even more radical than the view represented here.

Old Testament Record		Documentarian View	
1445–1405 B.C.	Moses gives the Law, and writes Genesis, Exodus, Leviticus, Numbers, Deuteronomy	1400 B.C.	Covenant Code (Material in Exodus 20–23)
1000	David's reign	1000	David's reign
960	Solomon's temple	960	Solomon's temple
850(?)	Obadiah—first writing prophet	950	J document
		930	Kingdom divides
850–550	Golden Age of the Prophets	850	E document
		750	Amos—first writing prophet
		750–550	Golden Age of the Prophets
722	End of northern kingdom	722	End of northern kingdom (Israel)
		622	Deuteronomic Code
586	Jerusalem falls; Exile	586	Jerusalem falls; exile
		575	H (Holiness) Code (Leviticus 17–20)
		550	Deuteronomic circle edits Deuteronomy—II Kings
539	Restoration of Israel	539	Restoration of Israel
450	Ezra reforms second Jewish Commonwealth on basis of the Law (Torah)	450	P document written for the purpose of instituting Second Jewish Commonwealth
		450–400	P circle compiles Tetrateuch (Genesis–Numbers); Deuteronomy added later to form Pentateuch

We see that the biblical sequence of the Law—given early and *followed* by the prophets—has been exactly reversed; for, according to the critics, the Law, comprised of the Deuteronomic Code, the Holiness Code, and the Priestly Code (the bulk of the legislative material in the Pentateuch) did not come into existence until long after the prophets. And yet it is clear from the text that many of the prophets appealed to a body of law that was already in existence in their time and that was authoritatively binding upon the people. Amos even refers to this law as "the *Torah* ['Law'] of Yahweh" (Amos 2:4).

Thus the critics have created a crucial and irreconcilable contradiction regarding both the chronology and the theological development of Israel's history.

This contradiction leaves us with an insurpassable gulf between an authoritative Word of God, on the one hand, and what someone has called "a tattered miscellany of half-mythical and historically unreliable literary fragments" on the other. And even more fundamentally, we are left with extreme tension between the scriptural portrayal of Israelite history and the reconstruction of the radical critics.

> It does not put the matter too strongly to say that, to the more radical school of critics, the Old Testament is in the main *unhistorical*. Not necessarily, of course, that there is not in parts—some would acknowledge in considerable parts—a historical substratum. Everyone may not go so far, at one end of the history, as Stade, who doubts whether Israel as a people was ever in Egypt at all; or, at the other end, as Kosters, who denies the return from the exile at Babylon under Zerubbabel. But the books as they stand are, for all that, held not to be, at least till the days of the kings, and even then only very partially, genuine history. (Orr, POT, 56)

This implies that the clear picture we see in the Old Testament of the development of a coherent and unified divine plan (teleological element) in Israel's history beginning in Genesis with Adam, and to be culminated in the promised Messiah as witnessed to by the prophets, was contrived.

Kautzsch, of Halle, in his lecture "*The Abiding Value of the Old Testament*" cited by Orr, writes: "The abiding value of the Old Testament lies above all in this, that it guarantees to us with absolute certainty the fact and the process of a divine plan and way of salvation, which found its conclusion and fulfillment in the new covenant, in the Person and work of Jesus Christ." (Orr, POT, 61)

Orr says that the reply that

> comes from the side of the criticism that seeks to get rid of the teleological element in the history is, that the Biblical representation is an unreal and artificial one: not a development in accordance with the actual history, but an *imaginary* development, the result of a reading back into the primitive legends of the ideas of the prophetic age. The appearance of development is superimposed on the historical tradition by the manner in which its materials are manipulated. Grant, it is said, the critical scheme—its analysis and partition of documents—and the illusion of teleology in the Old Testament story disappears; so far at least as any extraordinary cause is required to account for it. In the words of Professor Robertson: "What they maintain is, that the scheme of the Biblical writers is an afterthought, which by a process of manipulation of older documents, and by a systematic representation of earlier events in the light of much later times, has been made to appear as if it were the original and genuine development." (Orr, POT, 61–62)

2A. ISRAEL'S RELIGION IS TOTALLY NATURAL, NOT SUPERNATURAL IN ORIGIN AND DEVELOPMENT

(In other words, God did not *really* act in Israel's history; the Hebrews only *thought* He did.)

How is this theory derived from the literary analysis of the Pentateuch? Orr explains:

Nothing, it may be plausibly argued, depends, for the decision of the supernatural origin of the religion, on whether the Pentateuch, as we have it, is from the pen of Moses, or is made up of three or four documents, put together at a late date; or at what period the Levitical law as finally codified; or whether the Book of Isaiah is the work of one, or two, or of ten authors; or whether the Psalms are pre-exilic, or post-exilic, in origin. Yet, as will be seen more fully later, the dependence of the literary criticism on the religious theory is really very close. For, if it be true, as every fair mind must admit, that there are many scholars who succeed, to their own satisfaction, in combining the acceptance of the main results of the critical hypothesis of the Old Testament, even in its advanced form, with firm belief in the reality of supernatural revelation in Israel it is equally true that, in the case of others, and these pre-eminently, in Dr. Cheyne's phrase, "The Founders of Criticism," the decisions arrived at on purely literary questions,—the date of a psalm, e.g., the genuineness of a passage, or the integrity of a book,—are largely controlled by the view taken of the origin and course of development of the religion; and, with a different theory on these subjects, the judgments passed on the age, relations and historical value, of particular writings, would be different also. This dependence of many of the conclusions of criticism—by no means, of course, all—on the religious and historical standpoint is practically admitted by Wellhausen, [Wellhausen, PHI, 12] when he declares that "it is only within the region of religious antiquities and dominant religious ideas—the region which Vatke in his *Biblische Theologie* had occupied in its full breadth, and

where the real battle first kindled—that the controversy can be brought to a definite issue." (Orr, POT, 4–5)

Gilkey, an honest spokesman for this view, states it quite unequivocally:

Now this assumption of a causal order among phenomenal events, and therefore of the

> The difference between this view of the Bible as a parable illustrative of Hebrew religious faith and the view of the Bible as a direct narrative of God's actual deeds and words is so vast that it scarcely needs comment.
>
> —LANGDON GILKEY

authority of the scientific interpretation of observable events, makes a great difference to the validity one assigns to biblical narratives and so to the way one understands their meaning. Suddenly a vast panoply of divine deeds and events recorded in Scripture are no longer regarded as having actually happened. Not only, for example, do the six days of creation, the historical fall in Eden, and the flood seem to us historically untrue, but even more the majority of divine deeds in the biblical history of the Hebrew people become what we choose to call symbols rather than plain old historical facts. To mention only a few: Abraham's unexpected child; the many divine visitations; the words and directions to the patriarchs; the plagues visited on the Egyptians; the pillar of fire; the parting of the seas; the verbal deliverance of covenantal law on Sinai; the strategic and logistic help in the conquest; the audible voice heard by the prophets; and so on—all these "acts" vanish from the plane of historical reality and enter the never-never land of "religious interpretation" by the Hebrew people. Therefore when we read what the Old Testament seems to say God did, or what precritical commentators said God did (see Calvin), and then look at a modern interpretation of what God did in biblical times, we find a tremendous difference: the wonder events and the verbal divine commentaries, commands, and promises are gone. Whatever the Hebrews believed, *we* believe that the biblical people lived in the same causal continuum of space and time in which we live, and so one in which no divine wonders transpire and no divine voices were heard. (Gilkey, COTBL, 144–45)

Gilkey brings this view to its logical conclusion:

The vast panoply of wonder and voice events that preceded the Exodus-covenant event, in effect the patriarchal narratives, are now taken to be Hebrew interpretations of their own historical past based on the faith gained at the Exodus. For us then, these narratives represent not so much *histories* of what God actually did and said as *parables* expressive of the faith the post-Exodus Jews had, namely, belief in a God who was active, did deeds, spoke promises and commands, and so on. Third, the biblical accounts of the post-Exodus life—for example, the proclamation and codification of the law, the conquest, and the prophetic movement—are understood as the covenant people's interpretation through their Exodus faith of their continuing life and history. For modern biblical theology the Bible is no longer so much a book containing a description of God's actual acts and words as it is a book containing Hebrew interpretations, "creative interpretations" as we call them, which, like the parable of Jonah, tell stories of God's deeds and man's responses to express the theological beliefs of Hebrew religion. Thus the Bible is a book descriptive not of the acts of God but of Hebrew religion. (Gilkey, COTBL, 146)

The radical nature of this position is realized by Gilkey when he admits: "The difference between this view of the Bible as a parable illustrative of Hebrew religious faith and the view of the Bible as a direct narrative of God's actual deeds and words is so vast that it scarcely needs comment." (Gilkey, COTBL, 146)

3A. THE HISTORY AND RELIGION OF ISRAEL ARE BASICALLY FRAUDULENT

It is clear upon reading the Hebrews' account of their own history and religion as laid out before us in the Old Testament that they *intended* the account to be accepted by readers as truly historical. The sequence of Moses giving the Law and then later the prophets judging the people by harking back to the Mosaic Law was meant to be an account of what really happened—and the precise order in which it happened.

Unger makes a similar point: "Again, Deuteronomy if not published till 621 B.C., yet professing to be from Moses' mouth and pen, cannot be cleared of the suspicion of pious forgery. The same may be said of the Priestly Code, not completed till about 500 B.C., but repeatedly professing to be directly and divinely commanded to Moses. Under these circumstances the honesty and integrity of the redactors can scarcely be unchallenged." (Unger, IGOT, 231)

Whoever wrote the Old Testament books and canonized them wanted us to think that the history depicted in them was indeed the real history of Israel. If the documentarians are right, the historians of the Old Testament are wrong, and there does not seem to be any reasonable way of getting around the implications of a "contrived" history.

21
EVIDENCE FOR MOSAIC AUTHORSHIP

1A. INTERNAL EVIDENCE

1B. Witness of the Pentateuch

The Pentateuch itself clearly states that these portions of its contents were written by Moses:

1C. Book of the Covenant (Ex. 20:22—23:33)

"And Moses wrote all the words of the LORD. Then he arose early in the morning, and built an altar at the foot of the mountain, and twelve pillars according to the twelve tribes of

Israel. . . . Then he took the Book of the Covenant and read in the hearing of the people. And they said, 'All that the LORD has said we will do, and be obedient'" (Ex. 24:4, 7).

2C. Renewal of the Covenant (Ex. 34:10–26)

"Then the LORD said to Moses: 'Write these words, for according to the tenor of these words I have made a covenant with you and with Israel'" (Ex. 34:27).

3C. Deuteronomic Code (Deut. 5—30)

"So Moses wrote this law and delivered it to the priests, the sons of Levi, who bore the ark of the covenant of the LORD, and to all the elders of Israel" (Deut. 31:9).

"So it was, when Moses had completed writing the words of this law in a book, when they were finished, that Moses commanded the Levites, who bore the ark of the covenant of the LORD, saying: 'Take this Book of the Law, and put it beside the ark of the covenant of the LORD'" (Deut. 31:24–26).

Such a passage cannot be used to prove that Moses wrote the Pentateuch; but it does presuppose a considerable book that at least refers to Deuteronomy 5 through 26, and indicates a large amount of literary activity by Moses. (Raven, OTI, 86)

4C. God's Judgment of Amalek

"Then the LORD said to Moses, 'Write this for a memorial in the book, and recount it in the hearing of Joshua, that I will utterly blot out the remembrance of Amalek from under heaven'" (Ex. 17:14).

5C. Itinerary of Israelites from Ramses to Moab

"Now Moses wrote down the starting points of their journeys at the command of the LORD. And these are their journeys according to their starting points" (Num. 33:2).

6C. The Song of Moses in Deuteronomy 32

"Now therefore, write down this song for yourselves, and teach it to the children of Israel; put it in their mouths, that this song may be a witness for Me against the children of Israel.

"When I have brought them to the land flowing with milk and honey, of which I swore to their fathers, and they have eaten and filled themselves and grown fat, then they will turn to other gods and serve them; and they will provoke Me and break My covenant.

"Then it shall be, when many evils and troubles have come upon them, that this song will testify against them as a witness; for it will not be forgotten in the mouths of their descendants, for I know the inclination of their behavior today, even before I have brought them to the land of which I swore to give them" (vv. 19–21).

7C. The Use of Scribes

When we speak of Moses as having "written" the Pentateuch or being its "author," it should be noted, as has previously been pointed out, that quite in accord with ancient Mesopotamian practice, this does not necessarily mean that he himself wrote the words with his own hand, although such may have been the case. It is quite possible that the bulk of the Pentateuch was, like Hammurabi's Law Code, dictated to scribes. This in no way undermines the essential Mosaic authorship of the contents of the Pentateuch.

8C. The Legal Documents in These Passages Attribute Their Authorship to Moses in Either the Superscription or Subscription:

Exodus: 12:1–28; 20—24; 25—31; 34
Leviticus: 1—7; 8; 13; 16; 17—26; 27
Numbers: 1; 2; 4; 6:1–21; 8:1–4; 8:5–22; 15; 19; 27:6–23; 28; 29; 30; 35
Deuteronomy: 1—33

9C. Moses Certainly Was in a Position to Write the Pentateuch

He grew up in Pharoah's house and was, as Stephen said, "learned in all the wisdom of the Egyptians" (Acts 7:22). All now agree that this learning would have included the ability to write.

Moses had the information necessary for the project. It is likely that records of pre-Mosaic history existed, and had they been in the possession of the Hebrews they would have certainly have been accessible to Moses, the champion of his people. Had they been kept in the Egyptian archives from Joseph's time, they would still have been available to Moses during his early adulthood.

Moses also had the time to record this history. He spent forty years in Egypt and forty years in Midian, and there was plenty of time in both of these periods to author Genesis. (Raven, OTI, 93–94)

That Moses was preeminently prepared to author a work such as the Pentateuch is witnessed by the following qualifications:

(a) Education: Moses was trained in the highly developed academic disciplines of the royal Egyptian court. This without a doubt included a knowledge of writing, for even the women's toilet articles of the time were inscribed.

(b) Tradition: He undoubtedly received the traditions of the early Hebrew history and their encounters with God.

(c) Geographical familiarity: Moses possessed an intimate knowledge of the climate and geography of Egypt and Sinai as displayed in the Pentateuch.

(d) Motivation: As the founder of the Commonwealth of Israel, he had more than adequate incentive to provide the nation with concrete moral and religious foundations.

(e) Time: Forty long years of wandering in the Sinai wilderness provided ample opportunity to write this work.

At a time when even uneducated slaves working at the Egyptian turquoise mines were inscribing their records on the tunnel walls, it is inconceivable that a man of Moses' background would fail to record the details of one of history's most significant epochs.

Kurt Sethe, one of this century's greatest authorities on ancient Egypt, in attempting to find the father of one of the greatest contributions to the literary progress of civilization, the North Semitic script, mentions Moses as a possibility [*Vom Bilde Zum Buchstaben*, (1939), p. 56]. (Martin, SCAP, 23)

2B. Witness of the Other Old Testament Books

These Old Testament verses record that the Torah or "Law," was from Moses:

Joshua 8:32 speaks of "the Law of Moses, which he had written." (The following verses marked by an asterisk refer to the actual written "Law of Moses," not simply to an oral tradition):

Joshua 1:7, 8*; 8:31*, 34*; 23:6*
1 Kings 2:3*
2 Kings 14:6*; 23:25

> At a time when even uneducated slaves working at the Egyptian turquoise mines were inscribing their records on the tunnel walls, it is inconceivable that a man of Moses' background would fail to record the details of one of history's most significant epochs.

1 Chronicles 22:13

2 Chronicles 5:10; 23:18*; 25:4*; 30:16; 33:8; 34:14; 35:12*

Ezra 3:2; 6:18*; 7:6

Nehemiah 1:7, 8; 8:1*, 14*; 9:14; 10:29; 13:1*

Daniel 19:11, 13

Malachi 4:4

3B. Witness of the New Testament

The New Testament writers also held that the Torah, or "Law," came from Moses. The apostles believed that "Moses wrote for us a law" (Mark 12:19 NASB).

John was confident that "the law was given through Moses" (John 1:17).

Paul, speaking of a Pentateuchal passage, asserts "Moses writes" (Rom. 10:5).

Other passages that insist on this include:

Luke 2:22; 20:28

John 1:45; 8:5; 9:29

Acts 3:22; 6:14; 13:39; 15:1, 21; 26:22; 28:23

1 Corinthians 9:9

2 Corinthians 3:15

Hebrews 9:19

Revelation 15:3

These passages also testify that Jesus believed the Torah to be from Moses:

Mark 7:10; 10:3–5; 12:26

Luke 5:14; 16:29–31; 24:27, 44

John 7:19, 23

John records that Jesus expressed unequivocally his belief that Moses wrote the Torah:

"Do not think that I shall accuse you to the Father; there is one who accuses you—Moses, in whom you trust.

"For if you believed Moses, you would believe Me; for he wrote about Me.

"But if you do not believe his writings, how will you believe My words?" (John 5:45–47).

Eissfeldt states: "The name used in the New Testament clearly with reference to the whole Pentateuch—the Book of Moses—is certainly to be understood as meaning that Moses was the compiler of the Pentateuch." (Eissfeldt, OTI, 158)

2A. EXTERNAL EVIDENCE

1B. Jewish Tradition

R. H. Pfeiffer writes: "There is no reason to doubt that the Pentateuch was considered the divine revelation to Moses when it was canonized about 400 B.C." (Pfeiffer, IOT, 133)

1C. Ecclesiasticus, one of the books of the Apocrypha, written about 180 B.C., gives this witness: "All this is the covenant-book of God Most High, the law which Moses enacted to be the heritage of the assemblies of Jacob" (Ecclesiasticus 24:23 NEB).

2C. The Talmud, (*Baba Bathra,* 146), a Jewish commentary on the Law *(Torah)* dating from about 200 B.C., and the Mishnah *(Pirqe Aboth,* I, 1), a rabbinic interpretation and legislation dating from about 100 B.C., both attribute the *Torah* to Moses.

3C. Likewise, Philo, the Jewish philosopher theologian born approximately A.D. 20, held Mosaic authorship: "But I will . . . tell the story of Moses as I have learned it, both from the sacred books, the wonderful monuments of his wisdom which he has left behind him, and from some of the elders of the nation." (Philo, WP, 279)

4C. The first century A.D. Jewish historian Flavius Josephus writes in his *Josephus*

Against Apion (11:8): "For we have not an innumerable multitude of books among us, disagreeing from and contradicting one another (as the Greeks have) but only 22 books [our present 39], which are justly believed to be divine; and of them, five belong to Moses, which contain his laws, and the traditions of the origin of mankind till his death." (Josephus, WFJ, 609)

2B. Early Christian Tradition

1C. Junilius, an imperial official in the court of Justinian I, Byzantine emperor A.D. 527–565, held to the Mosaic authorship of the Pentateuch as can be seen from this dialogue between himself and one of his disciples, recorded in *De Partibus Divinae Legis:*

Concerning The Writers of The Divine Books
    Disciple: How do you know who are the writers of the divine books?
    Master: In three ways. Either from the titles and prefaces ... or from the titles alone ... or from the tradition of the ancients, as Moses is believed to have written the first 5 books of the History; although the title does not say so, nor does he himself write, "the Lord spake

All this is the covenant-book of God Most High, the law which Moses enacted to be the heritage of the assemblies of Jacob.

—ECCLESIASTICUS, 180 B.C.

unto me," but as of another, "the Lord spake unto Moses." (Gray, OTCm, 44–45)

2C. Leontius of Byzantium (sixth century A.D.) wrote in his treatise *Contra Mestorianos:*

"As for these five books, all bear witness that they are (the work) of Moses." (Gray, OTCM, 45)

3C. Other Church Fathers attributing the Pentateuch to Moses in their lists of the Old Testament canon:

1. Melito, Bishop of Sardi (A.D. 175)
2. Cyril of Jerusalem (A.D. 348–386)
3. Hilary (A.D. 366)
4. Rufinus (A.D. 410)
5. Augustine (A.D. 430)

4C. The Pentateuch is ascribed to Moses also in the following canonical lists of the early church:

1D. Dialogue of Timothy and Aquila

2D. The Synopsis (revised by Lagarde)

3D. List of the Apostolic Canons

4D. Innocent I (A.D. 417)

3B. Covenant-Form Analysis

1C. Introduction
In 1954 George Mendenhall published an epochal article in which he described the ancient suzerainty treaties established between victorious Near Eastern kings and their vanquished subjects. He pointed out striking similarities between these treaties and certain treaty forms in the Hebrew scriptures. Meredith Kline took this work further by demonstrating the correlation of these treaties to the Book of Deuteronomy as a whole.

    The renowned archaeologist G. Ernest Wright introduces us to Mendenhall's study:

Another major discovery within the realm of law which I venture to predict will stand the test of time is George E. Mendenhall's pioneer work on the formal background of the Mosaic covenant. This background, he has shown, is not to be found in the covenants of Bedouin society, as Johannes Pedersen had supposed. Instead it is to be found in the realm of international law, specifically in the suzerainty treaties of the Late Bronze Age found among the Hittite archives. This discovery has meant a number of things, of which I can mention only one. For the first time, we can gain a clearer perception of the way Deity was conceived in Israel and of the reason why certain types of language were permissible when used of him and others were not. The God of Israel was not the head of a pantheon which represented the primary powers of the natural world. He was first and foremost a suzerain, not a king among kings but the Emperor, the "King of kings and Lord of lords" who had no equal. Consequently, the Hebrew term, *melek*, rarely used of God before the time of David, was not strictly applicable to him because it had received its primary political definition from the rival Bronze Age dynasts of Syro-Palestinian city-states. The suzerainty of Israel's God concerned the whole world, and the focus of attention was not on the life of nature but on the administration of a vast empire. The language was thus closely geared to history and historical perspectives. (Wright, BAT, 150)

2C. Deuteronomy and the Form of Hittite Suzerainty Treaties of the Second Millennium B.C.

K. A. Kitchen reveals the following elements of Hittite suzerainty treaties of the fourteenth to thirteenth centuries:

(1) *Preamble or title*, identifying the author of the covenant.

(2) *Historical prologue* or retrospect, mentioning previous relations between the two parties involved; past benefactions by the suzerain are a basis for the vassal's gratitude and future obedience.

(3) *Stipulations* basic and detailed; the obligations laid upon the vassal by the sovereign.

(4) (a) *Deposition* of a copy of the covenant in the vassal's sanctuary and

(b) *Periodic public reading* of the covenant terms to the people.

(5) *Witnesses*, a long list of gods invoked to witness the covenant.

(6) (a) *Curses*, invoked upon the vassal if he breaks the covenant and,

(b) *Blessings*, invoked upon the vassal if he keeps the covenant.

Nearly all the known treaties of the fourteenth to thirteenth centuries B.C. follow this pattern closely. Sometimes some elements are omitted, but the order of them is almost invariable, whenever the original texts are sufficiently well preserved to be analyzed. This is, therefore, a stable form in the period concerned. Earlier than this, the pattern was apparently somewhat different. (Kitchen, AOOT, 92–93)

Form of Deuteronomic Covenant

Sinai Covenant in Deuteronomy

(1) Preamble: 1:1–5

(2) Historical prologue: 1:6—3:29

(3) Stipulations: 4—11 (basic); 12—26 (detailed)

(4) (a) Deposition of text: 31:9, 24–26

(b) Public reading: 31:10–12

(5) Witnesses: since pagan gods are excluded here, ancient oriental godlists are absent. Moses' song could have been the witness (31:16–30; 32:1–47), as Kitchen suggests.

(6) Curses and Blessings: 28:1–14 (blessings); 28:15–68 (curses); the sequence here is blessings—curses—witness as opposed to the witness—curses—blessings sequence of ancient oriental treaties, possibly due to the different nature of the witness here in Deuteronomy. (Kitchen, AOOT, 96–97)

> In the light of the evidence now surveyed, it would seem indisputable that the Book of Deuteronomy, not in the form of some imaginary original core but precisely in the integrity of its present form, the only one for which there is any objective evidence, exhibits the structure of the ancient suzerainty treaties in the unity and completeness of their classic pattern.
>
> —MEREDITH G. KLINE

The close correspondence between the two has led Kitchen to observe that "there can be no serious doubt (on present evidence) that the greater bulk of Deuteronomy coincides very closely indeed with the fourteenth- and thirteenth-century treaties, even more strikingly than do Exodus and Joshua. The essential difference in literary nature is that the Near Eastern documents are formal legal documents of the covenants concerned, whereas Deuteronomy is cast as the report of an actual ceremony of renewing a covenant in acts and speech." (Kitchen, AODOT, 3)

Kline displays equal confidence: "In the light of the evidence now surveyed, it would seem indisputable that the Book of Deuteronomy, not in the form of some imaginary original core but precisely in the integrity of its present form, the only one for which there is any objective evidence, exhibits the structure of the ancient suzerainty treaties in the unity and completeness of their classic pattern." (Kline, DC, 41)

But Kline and Kitchen are not alone in their observations. D. J. McCarthy has produced the most thorough examination of the ancient treaties in his scholarly *Treaty and Covenant.* Although he identifies more readily with the radical critics, he finds the comparison unavoidable: "Is there, therefore, a text in the Old Testament which exemplifies with sufficient fullness the treaty form? For an affirmative answer we need only look at the basic elements of the Book of Deuteronomy." (McCarthy, TC, 110)

McCarthy goes on to assert that Deuteronomy's basic components "present an organic structure which is that of the treaty." (McCarthy, TC, 110)

Elsewhere he emphatically states that "there can be no doubt that Deuteronomy does show some kind of relationship to the literary forms of these treaties." (McCarthy, COT, 230)

Even G. von Rad, the form critic who dates Deuteronomy sometime after 701 B.C., admits: "Comparison of the ancient Near Eastern treaties, especially those made by the Hittites in the fourteenth and thirteenth centuries B.C., with passages in the Old Testament has revealed so many things in common between the two, particularly in the matter of the form, that there must be some connection between these suzerainty treaties and the exposition of the details of Jahweh's covenant with Israel given in certain passages in the Old Testament." (von Rad, OTT, 132)

The most recent extensive study of this issue has been undertaken by Weinfeld. While he goes to great length to maintain a late date for Deuteronomy, he is forced to acknowledge:

"The major sections of the Hittite state treaties . . . are all found in the book of Deuteronomy." (Weinfeld, DDS, 61)

3C. Deuteronomy and the First Millennium B.C. Treaties

If we find no appreciable differences between the treaty forms of the first and second millennia B.C., then there is no reason on the basis of this particular investigation to assign to Deuteronomy the traditional early date as opposed to the sixth to seventh century B.C. date given by the radical critics. But this is not the case.

As early as 1954, Mendenhall recognized that the covenant type which is found in the second millennium B.C. in Deuteronomy "cannot be proven to have survived the downfall of the great empires of the late second millennium B.C. When empires again arose, notably Assyria, the structure of the covenant by which they bound their vassals is entirely different. Even in Israel, the writer submits that the older form of covenant was no longer widely known after the united monarchy." (Mendenhall, LCIANE, 30)

The quite conspicuous differences to which Mendenhall refers can be detailed as follows:

(1) Order

(a) The earlier form almost invariably places divine witnesses between stipulations and curses; this is *never* found in later treaties. (Kitchen, AOOT, 95)

(b) The highly consistent order of the earlier treaties is replaced by more randomness. (Kitchen, AOOT, 96)

(2) Content

(a) The customary historical prologue of the second millennium B.C. is totally absent in the later treaties. (Kitchen, AOOT, 95; Kline, DC, 43; Mendenhall, LCIANE, 56; Huffmon, ESC, 84)

(b) The first millennium B.C. treaties are also lacking in the earlier usage of blessings in conjunction with the cursings. (Kitchen, AOOT, 96; Kline, DC, 42)

What are the immediate implications of this?

Kline says:

The implications of the new evidence for the questions of the antiquity and authenticity of Deuteronomy must not be suppressed. Though the tradition of the suzerainty form is

attested down into the first millennium B.C., the full classic pattern is documented only in the Syro-Anatolian treaties of the fourteenth-thirteenth centuries B.C. Accordingly, the customary higher critical view of Deuteronomy's origins can be maintained only by scholars able to persuade themselves that a process of accretion in the first millennium B.C., with more or less of a conscious editorial assist, managed to reproduce exactly a complex legal pattern belonging to the second millennium B.C. To preserve any semblance of plausibility the hypothesis of these scholars must be so drastically modified in the direction of a greater antiquity for so much more of Deuteronomy as to leave practically meaningless any persistent insistence on a final seventh century B.C. edition of the book. (Kline, DC, 15)

The Old Testament covenant form demonstrates an amazing correspondence to the pattern of the late-second-millennium treaties as opposed to the pattern of the first-millennium treaties. The Sinai covenant and its renewals *must* be classified with the former, for with the latter it shares only the essential common core (title, stipulation, witnesses, and curses). Recent evidence has only buttressed Mendenhall's original view that the Sinai covenant closely parallels the late-second-millennium treaties and not those of the first millennium. (Kitchen, AOOT, 98)

4C. Conclusion

Even if we may conclude with confidence that Deuteronomy uniquely reflects the covenant form of the second millennium B.C., does this give us reason to conclude that it was necessarily authored then? Kitchen answers with a resounding *yes,* reasoning that if Deuteronomy and the other passages displaying this form "first took fixed literary forms only in the ninth to sixth centuries

> The present writer cannot see any legitimate way of escape from the crystal-clear evidence of the correspondence of Deuteronomy with the remarkably stable treaty or covenant form of the fourteenth-thirteenth centuries B.C.
>
> —KENNETH A. KITCHEN

B.C. and onward, why and how should their writers (or redactors) so easily be able to reproduce covenant-forms that had fallen out of customary use 300 to 600 years earlier (*i.e.*, after about 1200 B.C.), and entirely fail to reflect the first-millennium covenant-forms that were commonly used in their own day?" (Kitchen, AOOT, 100)

In a recent article, Kitchen presents a forceful summary of the body of evidence we have considered:

> The present writer cannot see any legitimate way of escape from the crystal-clear evidence of the correspondence of Deuteronomy with the remarkably stable treaty or covenant form of the fourteenth–thirteenth centuries B.C. Two points follow here. First, the basic structure of Deuteronomy and much of the content that gives specific character to that structure *must* constitute a recognizable literary entity; second, this is a literary entity *not* of the eighth or seventh century B.C. but rather from ca. 1200 B.C. *at latest.* Those who so choose may wish to claim that this or that individual "law" or concept appears to be of later date than the late thirteenth century B.C.; but it is no longer methodologically permissible gaily to remove essential features of the covenant-form on a mere preconception (especially if of nineteenth century [A.D.] vintage) of what is merely thought—not proven—to be late. (Kitchen, AODOT, 4)

Kline concludes: "Accordingly, while it is necessary to recognize a substantial continu-ity in pattern between the earlier and later treaties, it is proper to distinguish the Hittite treaties of the second millennium B.C. as the 'classic' form. And without any doubt the Book of Deuteronomy belongs to the classic stage in this documentary evolution. Here then is significant confirmation of the prima facie case for the Mosaic origin of the Deuteronomic treaty of the great King." (Kline, DC, 43)

Many scholars will allow that archaeology has demonstrated the "essential reliability" of many historical facts within the biblical record, but they still contend that these facts, along with legend and myth, were passed "orally" for a millennium or more. But Deuteronomy's form demonstrates that it had to be written in the middle of the second millennium B.C. Otherwise no account can be given for its literary format.

3A. THE ANTIQUITY OF THE ALLEGED D SOURCE

1B. Introduction

The crucial role Deuteronomy plays in the entire documentary scheme is recognized by all. Radical critic George Dahl acknowledges this fact:

> By unanimous consent this book is accorded a central and pivotal position in the study of Old Testament history, literature and religion. The epochal reconstruction of the course of Hebrew history, which it has been the supreme service and merit of critical Biblical scholarship to mediate, depends for its validity first of all upon the essential correctness of our dating of Deuteronomy. In particular, the identification of the so-called Fifth Book of Moses with the book of the law mentioned in 2 Kings 22f. is generally regarded as the very keystone of the arch of Old Testament research. (Bewer, PDS, 360)

"The Code of Deuteronomy," Rowley concurs, "is . . . of vital importance in Pentateuchal criticism, since it is primarily by relation to it that the other documents are dated." (Rowley, GOT, 29)

There is also little disagreement among scholars of all positions that the book discovered in the temple in 621 B.C., sparking the reforms of King Josiah (2 Kin. 22 and 23), was essentially the book we now call Deuteronomy. But there is much disagreement over the date of its original authorship: the radical critics assign it to a time not long before the 621 discovery, while others insist that it must be dated from the time of Moses.

2B. Statements

1C. Frequently Recurring Statements

Von Rad, speaking of Deuteronomy, tells us that the most frequent phrases show the most important thoughts.

Research into the most common phrases reveals the following groupings:

(a) memories of the past in Egypt

(b) Yahweh's covenant for protection from Canaanite influence in the land

(c) entry into the land

(d) national unity (with no mention of the split kingdom of the seventh century B.C.)

(e) sin and cleansing (all of an exceedingly different nature from the eighth century B.C. denunciations for moral evils)

(f) blessings when the land will be entered (Manley, BL, 28–36)

Pederson describes the purpose of the entire book: "The main object of the book, in its present shape, is to protect the Israelite community against Canaanite influence." (Pederson, ILC, 27)

These theme ideas sharply contrast with any period in the first millennium B.C., but harmonize perfectly with the period the book claims for itself—that immediately preceding the entrance into Canaan in the second millennium B.C.

2C. Geographical Statements

Manley quite aptly summarizes the geographical attestations for the antiquity of this book: "When we review the geographical data as a whole," he observes,

> the details appear to be much too accurate to be due either to chance or to oral tradition. The account of the journeyings in chapters i–iii is altogether realistic and quite unlike an introduction prefixed to a collection of old laws; it bears every sign of originality. The views described and the features of the Moabite country reproduced must have been seen by human eyes; the antiquarian notes also belong to the period and are not the result of archaeological research.
>
> The omissions also are significant: there is no hint of Jerusalem, nor of Ramah, dear to Samuel's heart, not even of Shiloh, where the tabernacle came to rest. Everything points to its historical character and early date. (Manley, BL, 64)

3B. Style

Radical critic Norman Habel succinctly phrases this accusation that the D writing is different from the rest of the Pentateuch: "The style and jargon of Deuteronomy are very obvious. They stand in sharp contrast

But the alleged differences in style and elements of distinction between Deuteronomy and the rest of the Pentateuch are mainly caused by their respective standpoints. Leviticus, for example is a codified law book that the priests are to use, while Deuteronomy is made up of popular addresses.

to the literary characteristics of the rest of the Pentateuch. When compared with Genesis through Numbers, Deuteronomy presents a new world of terms, thought patterns, groups of expressions, and stereotype idioms." (Habel, LCOT, 12)

Dahl mentions another distinctive aspect of this book's style: "The developed oratorical style of Deuteronomy, smooth, flowing and sustained, presupposes a long literary history behind it." (Bewer, PDS, 372)

But the alleged differences in style and elements of distinction between Deuteronomy and the rest of the Pentateuch are mainly caused by their respective standpoints. Leviticus, for example is a codified law book that the priests are to use, while Deuteronomy is made up of popular addresses. Therefore, we are not surprised to find that in Deuteronomy Moses uses an oratorical style, edits details, emphasizes practical issues, and often includes directions regarding the entrance of the Israelites into Canaan. (Raven, OTI, 113)

And to say with Dahl (as do many scholars) that the oratorical style indicates a long period of development is so irresponsible as to barely merit a response. It would seem probable that a book recording the speeches of a great orator would display a "developed oratorical style" without needing a long period of evolution. Besides this, examples abound of literature, with no longer a period of development, having a smooth and developed style.

A final stylistic point is emphasized by Manley: "The same style can to some extent be perceived in some of the earlier speeches of Moses recorded in the Pentateuch." (Manley, BL, 27)

4B. Antiquity of Legislation

The radical argument for a late date based on legislative consideration is competently related by Dahl: "In general, . . . it would appear that the relationship of Deuteronomy lies in the general direction of expansion and development of the earlier laws. Its code reflects a distinctly more advanced and complicated community life than that underlying Ex. 21–23 (34)." (Bewer, PDS, 367)

G. T. Manley, a respected British Old Testament scholar, conducted a detailed and thorough study of each of the Pentateuchal laws to discover if this bold claim were indeed true. His startling conclusions are as follows:

It has to be admitted that the Wellhausen scheme breaks down upon a close examination of the laws.

1. The absolute dating has no foundation. There is nothing specific to connect the laws of JE with the early monarchy, those of Deuteronomy with 621 B.C., nor those of P with the exile.

On the contrary, laws of great antiquity are found in all these, and some are peculiar to each—rather they bear the appearance of contemporary layers of material.

2. The statement that Deuteronomy xii–xxvi is an "expansion" of the JE code is misleading. A few of the old laws and precepts are repeated, more of the same type are omitted; where a law is modified there is no sign that it has been adapted to the needs of the seventh century. The material peculiar to Deuteronomy includes much that is demonstrably old, and nothing manifestly of a late origin.

The two groups of laws appear to be complementary and roughly contemporary.

3. The argument for the chronological sequence JE, D, P, fares no better: it cannot rightly be said that Deuteronomy shows dependence on JE and ignorance of P; it has some elements in common with both, rather more with the latter.

The laws of Lv. xi concerning food reappear in Dt. xiv in a different form, but one which shows no difference of period.

Deuteronomy asserts the existence of a priestly law concerning leprosy, and assumes the existence of laws of sacrifice, such as are found in P.

4. The laws of Dt. xii–xxvi follow naturally upon the preceding discourse in chapters v–xi and appear quite suitable to the place and occasion stated in iv. 44–49. The parenetic additions also, where they occur, belong to the period when the deliverance from the bondage of Egypt was a living memory, and are quite different from the exhortations which Isaiah addressed to a disillusioned and sophisticated people. (Manley, BL, 94–95)

Later in the same monograph (*The Book of the Law*), Manley adds these observations:

If the author be a reformer addressing the people of Judah groaning under the evils of Manasseh's rule, he is wonderfully successful in concealing the fact. He encumbers his programme of reform with a number of obsolete, impracticable and irrelevant laws; he betrays no hint of the divided kingdom, or of the promises to David; and whilst the possibility of a king is envisaged, the civil law entirely ignores his existence.

The author of Deuteronomy issues laws which he expects to be obeyed; this is not the attitude of the reforming prophets, who call upon Israel to repent over laws that have been broken. This contrast with the prophetic utterances goes down to the very heart of the book, and colours the legislation throughout.

From this aspect also the only time which provides a suitable background for the legislation is the pre-prophetic period. (Manley, BL, 121)

5B. Statements Alleged to Oppose Mosaic Authorship and Antiquity of D

Proponents of the documentary hypothesis point to certain statements within the book of Deuteronomy as evidence against Mosaic authorship and for a late date for its formation:

(a) The phrase "beyond the Jordan" to refer to the region east of the Jordan. It is contended that since Deuteronomy claims to have been written in that region, "beyond the Jordan" could only refer to Canaan proper, on the western side. However, it has been adequately demonstrated that this phrase was simply a technical term for that region, even as it was known as Paraea ("The Other-side Land") during the New Testament times and has more recently been known as Transjordania (even to its inhabitants). (Archer, SOTI, 244; Manley, BL, 49)

(b) The phrase "until this day." Here it is urged that this indicates a great lapse of time since the event mentioned. Yet in each instance of its usage it is highly appropriate that Moses use this phrase in light of only the previous forty-year period, to indicate that a situation has persisted until these final days of his life. (Archer, SOTI, 243)

(c) The account of Moses' death in Deuteronomy 34. But it is quite reasonable to assume that Joshua included this account, just as often an obituary is added to the final work of a man of great letters. (Archer, SOTI, 244) And it is worthy of note here that the other events of the book cover all of Moses' life, and never transgress that limit. (Manley, BL, 172)

6B. Centralized Worship

1C. Documentary Assumption

The adherents to the documentary hypothesis assume that at the time of Moses there was a plurality of sanctuaries that were permitted or legitimate. Then at the time of Josiah (621 B.C.) there was a religious revival and the major reform was the establishment of a central sanctuary in Jerusalem.

The main function of the Code of Deuteronomy, found in the temple at the time of Josiah, was to put an end to the various places of worship.

It is held that Exodus 20:24 is an "old law" that commanded the building of altars in various parts of the land. (Driver, D, 136–138) These locations of worship were appropriate, and the Israelites were to worship Yahweh at these sanctuaries. Then, at the publication of Deuteronomy, the worship was to be permitted only at the central sanctuary in Jerusalem, while worship at the multiplicity of sanctuaries was forbidden.

2C. Basic Answer

1D. "An altar of earth you shall make for Me, and you shall sacrifice on it your burnt offerings and your peace offerings, your sheep and your oxen. In every place where I record

> The statement that when Deuteronomy was composed the old law "was revoked, and worship centralized in Jerusalem" is also contrary to the facts and inconsistent with the theory itself. Would any author engaged on an "expansion" of the JE code revoke an important element in it without a word of explanation?
>
> —G. T. MANLEY

My name I will come to you, and I will bless you" (Ex. 20:24).

Nowhere does this verse speak of sanctuaries. It mentions only altars. Since this is the first legal directive about worship in the Pentateuch (except for the second commandment), it is to be connected with the patriarchal and Mosaic period. Thus the phrase "in every place where I record My name" refers to such places as the plain of Moreh (Gen. 12:16), Mount Moriah (Gen. 22:2), Beersheba (Gen. 26:23), Bethel

(Gen. 35:1), and Rephidim (Ex. 17:8, 15).

To this G. T. Manley adds that the statement that "when Deuteronomy was composed the old law 'was revoked, and worship centralized in Jerusalem' is also contrary to the facts and inconsistent with the theory itself. Would any author engaged on an 'expansion' of the JE code revoke an important element in it without a word of explanation?" (Manley, BL, 131)

"If the legislator," writes G. A. Aalders, "was thinking of sanctuaries, of which no mention whatever had been made previously, he undoubtedly would have indicated it more clearly. So the text certainly does not mean a plurality of sanctuaries; at most it refers to a multiplicity of altars." (Aalders, ASIP, 72)

2D. To the above, one could say that a plurality of altars speaks of a multiplicity of sanctuaries. The phrase "in every place where I record My name" does not necessarily mean that this is done simultaneously.

Aalders points out that

> as a rule the Hebrew noun *kol*, when combined with another noun provided with the definite article, as is the case here, indicates rather a number of persons or things in *succession*, especially when the noun added is singular. We point to the well-known *kol hayom* of which "always" is the ordinary sense, that is to say: "all successive days"; to Ex. i. 22 where "every son" and "every daughter" naturally refers to all children born successively; to Gn. xx. 13 where "every place whither we shall come" cannot but indicate a number of places reached by Abraham and Sarah in succession; and to Dt. xi. 24; I Sa. iii. 17, etc. It is therefore incorrect to state that the expression "in all places where I record my name" *must* be understood of a number of places of worship existing at the same time. (Aalders, ASIP, 73)

3D. It is interesting that the exhortation chapters (5—11) of Deuteronomy do not once mention the place of worship. Deuteronomy 12 demands, not the unification of worship, but its purification. The worship itself needed to be protected from pagan and idolatrous influence and cleansed from the idols and abominations that had defiled it.

4D. Deuteronomy 12, verses 13 and 14 warn about the central sanctuary: "Take heed to yourself that you do not offer your burnt offerings in every place that you see; but in the place which the LORD chooses, in one of your tribes, there you shall offer your burnt offerings, and there you shall do all that I command you."

The documentary assumption is that "in every place that you see" refers to the previous multiple sanctuaries that are now forbidden. However, 12:15 must give it another connotation: "However, you may slaughter and eat meat within all your gates, whatever your heart desires, according to the blessin of the LORD your God which He has given you; the unclean and the clean may eat of it, of the gazelle and the deer alike."

Verses 13 and 14 are limited by the word "however" in 15. Verse 13 is speaking of "burnt offerings" that are to be presented in a sanctuary the existence of which is presupposed. But the phrase "in every place" in verse 13 does not refer to a condemnation of previous altars, but is taken synonymously with the phrase "within all your gates" in verse 15. Therefore verses 13 through 15 mean that cattle can be slaughtered anywhere, but burnt offerings are not to be presented everywhere.

Contrary to the documentary assumption, verse 13 does not "require that there should be a concentration of worship in contrast to a previous time when various cult-places were legitimate, but it simply cautions the Israelite not to offer burnt offerings

wherever he might wish, and limits these offerings to the one sanctuary whose existence is presupposed." (Aalders, ASIP, 75)

5D. There are many situations that presuppose a central sanctuary prior to Josiah's reformation in 621 B.C.; for example, "the house of God" (Judg. 18:31) and "the temple of the Lord" (1 Sam. 1:9; 3:3).

The following references refer to a simple sanctuary: 1 Samuel 1:3; Exodus 23:17, 19; 34:23, 26 (compare Deut. 16:16). These are directly connected with the sanctuary: 1 Samuel 21:4; Exodus 25:30; Leviticus 24:5; 1 Samuel 21:9 (compare Ex. 28:6).

6D. First Kings 8:4 records that the elders and priests brought the ark and all the holy vessels to the tabernacle. Aalders writes that it is difficult

to understand how anyone can imagine that even at that time a multiplicity of sanctuaries existed and was deemed legitimate. The beautiful temple with its glorious wealth and grandeur must naturally have occupied such a prominent place in the religious life of the people that it is utterly inconceivable how it could have had a number of rival sanctuaries. This is confirmed by the proceedings of Jeroboam, the first ruler of the Northern Kingdom, who feared lest the heart of the people might turn again unto Rehoboam, the king of Judah, if they went up to sacrifice in the house of the Lord at Jerusalem (I Ki. xii. 27). He therefore instituted two places of worship, one in Beth-el and the other in Dan (verses 28 f.). This proves that in his days the people were accustomed to bring their offerings to the temple, and that the temple was the central sanctuary for the whole people of Israel. It could not therefore have been necessary in the days of King Josiah to concentrate the cult at the temple, since the temple had been the uncontested centre of worship from its foundation. (Aalders, ASIP, 79–80)

7D. The text of 2 Kings 22:8–13 beseeches us to conclude that the "book of the law" that was found was an old book. The phrase "our fathers have not listened to the words of this book" (2 Kin. 22:13), and this being the cause of the wrath of God, indicate its antiquity.

G. T. Manley says: "It was at once recognized as the 'book of the law,' which suggests that such a book was known to have existed, but had been lost or forgotten. These things could not have been if the book were known by some to be the work of men still living." (Manley, BL, 125)

8D. There is no apparent close connection between Deuteronomy and the events surrounding Josiah. They agree in their

> There are many commands in Deuteronomy, such as the destruction of the Amalekites and the assigning of the cities of refuge, which are not mentioned as part of Josiah's reform, and would have been anachronisms at that time.
>
> —G. T. MANLEY

denouncing of the sins of wizardry and idolatry, but these same sins are also denounced in other parts of the Pentateuch. "But certain evils of the time," writes Manley, "such as the *kemārîm* ('idolatrous priests'), though known to Hosea (x. 5) and Zephaniah (i. 4, 5), and put down by Josiah (II Ki. xxiii. 5), are ignored in Deuteronomy. The same is true of the burning of incense to Baal (Ho. ii. 13, xii. 2; II Ki. xxiii. 5), and of the 'sun-images' (Is. xvii. 8, xxvii. 9; II Ch. xxxiv. 4)." (Manley, BL, 125)

"On the other hand," continues Manley, "there are many commands in Deuteronomy, such as the destruction of the Amalekites and the assigning of the cities of

refuge, which are not mentioned as part of Josiah's reform, and would have been anachronisms at that time." (Manley, BL, 125)

9D. Deuteronomy 27:1–8

One of the most formidable barriers to the documentary assumption of centralization is the command in Deuteronomy 27:1–8 in which Moses is told to build an altar on Mount Ebal. This passage uses the same words as Exodus 20:24 about an altar that Deuteronomy was supposed to forbid or revoke.

The construction of this altar, commanded by Yahweh (Deut. 27) is accomplished in Joshua 8:30, 31. It is no wonder that S. R. Driver recognizes that this passage produces "considerable critical difficulties" and that "it stands in a most unsuitable place." (Driver, D, 294)

10D. Sacrifices at "Altars" and "High Places"

The writer is indebted to the publisher and author of *The Book of the Law* for allowing the generous quoting of the following treatment of the Hebrew *bamah*—"high places."

Local Sanctuaries

The term "local sanctuaries" is somewhat vague, and if used loosely apt to mix together things which differ, and which need separate treatment. The information at our disposal concerning local altars is scanty, and the shortage of facts encourages speculation. It is tempting to group together every place of sacred memories or where a sacrifice is recorded, and to reckon them all as permanent sanctuaries, each with a complement of sacrificing priests who followed a particular ritual and built up its own body of traditions. The wiser course, however, is to adhere as closely as possible to the record and to observe certain obvious distinctions, such as between acts on the one hand which claimed divine sanction and, on the other, cases where the people "did evil in the sight of the Lord."

We shall begin with a brief survey of what is recorded of sacrifices, (1) at altars and (2) at high places, in the books of Joshua to 2 Samuel, that is, before the temple was built.

In these books there are seven instances of an "altar" being erected, two in connection with theophanies (Jdg. vi. 26–28, xiii. 20), and five on other occasions (Jos. viii. 30; Jdg. xxi. 2–4; I Sa. vii. 17, xiv. 35; 2 Sa. xxiv. 25). Moreover there is the statement in Jos. ix. 27 concerning the Gibeonites serving the "altar of the Lord," presumably at the tabernacle, and the story of the "altar of witness" in Jos. xxii.

It is a curious fact, and may be only a coincidence, that both in these books and in the legislation of Deuteronomy, the plural "altars" occurs only once, and then in each case in reference to those of the Canaanites (Jdg. ii. 2; Dt. xii. 2).

We read also of sacrifices at Bethlehem (I Sa. xvi. 5, xx. 29) and Gilgal (I Sa. xiii. 8) and by the men of Beth-shemesh in the presence of the ark (I Sa. vi. 15).

Gideon's altar was still standing when the story was written, and that at Shechem at the time of Joshua's death (Jos. xxiv. 26); the site of David's altar was used for the temple. The others fade into oblivion.

The "high place" *(bāmāh)* is not the same as the "altar." The two words differ in origin and meaning and call for separate treatment.

The word *bāmāh* is absent from Joshua and Judges, but in I Samuel two are mentioned.

There was one at Ramah to which Samuel "went up" (I Sa. ix. 13), and one nearby the "hill of God," from which a band of musical prophets came "down" (I Sa. x. 5). On the former was a "guest chamber" where Samuel entertained thirty persons at a sacrificial feast. The language employed shows that these *bāmôth* were, or were situated upon, eminences.

This ends our information about sacrifices offered to Yahweh, which are authorized and approved. When under the judges the people "forsook the Lord and served Baal and Ashtaroth" (Jdg. ii. 13), this was something quite different, and was condemned.

A new phase is introduced with the building of the temple; the tone changes, and the word *bāmāh* begins to acquire a new and evil connotation. A transition can be seen in I Ki. iii. 1–4, where the writer tells us that "the people still sacrificed in high places because there was no house built to the name of the Lord until those days"; this practice on the part of "the people" is deprecated rather than condemned.

We next read that Solomon walked "in the statutes of David his father; only he sacrificed and burned incense in high places," which also involves a tone of disapproval. The writer adds: "The king went to Gibeon to sacrifice there; for that was the great high place" (I Ki. iii. 4).

Here the LXX translates ὑψηλοτάτη καὶ μεγάλη (transliterated *hūpsālátatā, kai, mágelā*; translated *highest and great*), as if its lofty elevation was in mind (Gibeon being the highest point in the region); but possibly the reference is to the presence of the tabernacle there (cf. II Ch. i. 1–3). Up to this point the notion of height lingers about the word *bāmāh*; it now disappears, and it comes to represent some kind of structure which can be "built" (I Ki. xiv. 23), and destroyed and rebuilt II Ki. xxi. 3), in a city or in a gateway (II Ki. xxiii. 8).

The continued existence of the *bāmôth* is considered a blot on the record of otherwise good kings; the building of them by the people is condemned outright (I Ki. xiv. 22–24), a condemnation passed equally upon the *bēth-bāmôth*, whatever their exact nature may have been (I Ki. xii. 31; II Ki. xvii. 29, xxiii. 19).

This disapproval cannot be attributed

merely to the Deuteronomic bias of the author, for it is expressed with great vigour by the prophets also (Ho. viii. 11, x. 1; Am. iii. 14, iv. 4–6, v. 4–6; Mi. i. 7; Is. ii. 8).

The ground of objection has no relevance to a centralizing law, but is to the idolatry and corruption introduced by syncretism with the Canaanite religion, against which stern warnings had been given not only in Dt. xii. 29–32, but earlier in Ex. xxxiv. 12–16 (J).

In the northern kingdom the pure religion of Yahweh was threatened with extinction by the royal patronage of the Phoenician Ba'al worship under Ahab and Jezebel. This was fiercely contested by Elijah; the altars of Yahweh to which he referred (I Ki. xix. 10) may have been erected by pious Israelites who were prevented from going up to Jerusalem to worship, or were possibly some of more ancient origin.

Archaeology has little to add to this picture. Canaanite shrines which have been discovered at Gezer and elsewhere belong to the pre-Israelite period, and "it still requires explanation why no Hebrew high place or other shrine for worship, whether of Yahweh or of some 'strange god,' is known from the period of Hebrew domination and the area of Hebrew occupation in Palestine."

This is the historical background, cleared of conjecture, against which Wellhausen's interpretations must be judged. (Manley, BL, 128–31)

11D. Aalders concludes: "The advocates of the documentary theory criticize it as 'subjective history'; but such a verdict is not scientific. On the contrary, we must apply the accusation to the theory itself, which having forced an interpretation upon the Pentateuchal code which has absolutely no foundation in the wording of the law, rewrites history in order to bring the facts in harmony with this interpretation; and finally assigns all historical evidence discordant with its supposition to a 'deuteronomic' redactor! Against such a method the most energetic protest must be raised." (Aalders, ASIP, 81)

NOTE: See the following section for information on the antiquity of P and the tabernacle.

7B. Conclusion

On the basis of the internal evidence, we are left with a number of extremely difficult problems if we tenaciously retain the late-date position for D. Besides the problems mentioned above, we must ask other questions of those holding to a seventh-century

> Many persons in Judah . . . had powerful motives for exposing this forgery if it was one. The wicked people whom the book condemned would have seized the opportunity of condemning it as a forgery.
>
> —JOHN HOWARD RAVEN

B.C. date. Since the author was clearly a preacher of distinction and of power (even founding a "Deuteronomic" school of writers, according to the documentarians), why are we left with no trace of his name or person in the mid-first millennium B.C.? If he is such an effective reformer, why does he only denounce the sins of his ancestors? If his code of rules is intended to revoke an old Mosaic law, why does he ascribe them to Moses himself? If his purpose is to centralize worship in Jerusalem, why does he never show a knowledge of its existence? And why would he hide his book in the temple? (Manley, BL, 142)

Moreover, given that it is of a late date and

thus a forgery, Raven has discussed the "many persons in Judah who had powerful motives for exposing this forgery if it was one. The wicked people whom the book condemned would have seized the opportunity of condemning it as a forgery." (Raven, OTI, 112)

4A. THE ANTIQUITY OF THE ALLEGED P SOURCE

1B. Documentary Assumption

Driver has asserted: "The pre-Exilic period shows no indications of P being in operation." (Driver, BG, 136)

And Wellhausen has confidently affirmed: "To any one who knows anything about history it is not necessary to prove that the so-called Mosaic theocracy, which nowhere suits the circumstances of the earlier periods, and of which the prophets, even in their most ideal delineations of the Israelite state as it ought to be have not the faintest shadow of an idea, is, so to speak, a perfect fit for post-exilian Judaism, and had its actuality only there." (Wellhausen, PHI, 151)

2B. Basic Answer

1C. Comparing P to the Prophets

We may determine whether the Priestly writing is indeed a "perfect fit" for the postexilic period by testing P in light of the writings of Ezra, Nehemiah, Esther, Haggai, Zechariah, and Malachi. If its ideas are shown to be harmonious with these writers and contradictory to the earlier ones, the radical claim will be strengthened.

1D. Features Present in P, but Absent from the Postexilic Period:

tabernacle
ark
Ten Commandments
Urim and Thummim
Day of Atonement
cities of refuge
test of adultery by ordeal
wave offerings
Korban

2D. Features Present in P and in the Pre-exilic Period, but Absent from the Postexilic Period:

circumcision (heavily emphasized in pre-exilic Joshua and 1 and 2 Samuel)
significance of blood
leprosy
Nazarites
various offerings

3D. Features Present in P and in Both Periods:

Sabbath
Passover
Feast of Unleavened Bread
Feast of Tabernacles

4D. Features Absent from P, yet Prominent in Postexilic Period:

divine name "Yahweh of hosts" (86 occurences in postexilic authors)
singing and music as central in worship
scribes
use of sackcloth
designation of central sanctuary as the "temple"
mention of legislation concerning the postexilic industrial revolution (Kelso, AOOTC, 39)
city of Jerusalem (Allis, FBM, 196–99)

The radical critics have failed to adequately deal with any of these astonishing discrepancies when assigning to P a date in the sixth century B.C. O. T. Allis is forced to conclude: "The claim that the Priest Code fits the post-exilic period like a glove is as little justified as the claim that it does not fit the pre-exilic period." (Allis, FBM, 201)

2C. Internal Evidence and P's Relation to the Other Sources

If P is the last source to be recorded, it follows that no other sources would show a knowledge of P. Many such statements have been issued, such as the declaration by Driver, "nor is the legislation of P presupposed in Deuteronomy." (Driver, ILOT, 137)

However, the following facts make it difficult to honestly conclude that P was unknown until the sixth century B.C.

1D. Material dealing with Aaron is usually assigned to document P. According to Brightman, "Aaron is missing from J and only incidental in E." This is accomplished by deleting all thirteen occurrences in J. (Brightman, SH, 459)

2D. Deuteronomy 14:3–20: This passage is almost identical to one in Leviticus, forcing Driver to observe "that it is borrowed by D from P—or at least from a priestly collection of *toroth*—rather than conversely, appears from certain features of style which connect it with P and not with Deuteronomy. . . . If so, however, one part of P was in existence when Deuteronomy was written." (Driver, ILOT, 137–38)

3D. The following list substantiates the antiquity of the law and shows that P was known in the preexilic times.

Deuteronomy 15:1—the year of release (Lev. 25:2)

Deuteronomy 23:9, 10—ceremonial impurity (Lev. 15)

Deuteronomy 24:8—a law of leprosy given to the priests (Lev. 1 and 14)

Amos 2:11, 12—Nazarites forbidden wine (Num. 6:1–21 [P])

Amos 4:5—proscription of leaven in sacrifices (Lev. 2:11)

Amos 5:22—burnt, meat, and peace offerings (Lev. 7 and 8)

Amos 4:5—free-will offering (Lev. 7, etc.)

Amos 5:21—solemn assembly (Lev. 23, etc.)

Hosea 12:9—dwelling in booths (Lev. 23:42) (Kitchen, AOOT, 150–51)

The list could be extended but the point has been established. We must decide with Archer that "already in 755 B.C. there was a written body of law, including both P and D, and labeled by the prophet himself as the Torah of Yahweh (Amos 2:4), and accepted by his public as an authentic and authoritative body of legislation binding upon them." (Archer, SOTI, 151)

And Allis effectively expresses this conclusion: "When the critics reject those statements in the record which indicate that the law was ancient, they are not only guilty of tampering with the evidence, but they also make the denunciations uttered by Israel's historians and prophets of her failure to keep the law both farcical and cruel. For these teachers of Israel insisted that all of Israel's sufferings were due to the failure of the people to keep a law which, if the critics are correct, was unknown to them." (Allis, FBM, 202)

3C. Genesis 17

Samuel R. Külling in "The Dating of the So-Called 'P-sections' in Genesis," an abstract of his book published under the title *Zur Datierung Der "Genesis-P-Stucke" Namentlich Des Kapitels Genesis XVII*, writing about Genesis 17 and circumcision, says that the form, style and content of Genesis 17 belong to the 2nd millenium [sic] B.C. and have nothing to do with post-exilic writers. As Mendenhall (Law and Covenant, 1955), Baltzer (Das Bundesformular, 1960), M. G. Kline (Treaty of the Great King, 1963), have done, and previous to this Wiener (Studies in Biblical Law, 1904), among others, I draw a parallel to the Vassal Treaties and show how Genesis 17, as to construction and style, is similar to these treaties of the middle of the 2nd millenium [sic] B.C., which no longer exist in this form after the year 1200 B.C. There is, moreover, no motive for reproducing the chapter in this form later in view of the fact that the structure of the treaties of later periods is different. (Külling, DSCPSG, 68)

4C. Genesis 9

This section attributed to the P source is said to be late and is a reference to the Persian period. The critic often contends that the eating and spilling of blood are a rejection of the holy war.

Külling concludes that the same reasons for

rejecting a priestly tendency writing for the exilic-postexilic period, also applies to a Persian period: "Just why an exilic-postexilic priest should select from the food laws one that allows the eating of meat without blood is quite unexplainable, especially because no particular reason is given by the writer. For the exilic-postexilic period it appears superfluous to grant a general permission to eat meat (Genesis 9:3). In this period a law differentiating between prohibited and non-prohibited meats would be more understandable. It is just verse 3 which indicates that there is no exilic-postexilic priestly interest involved and that the levitical legislation is not yet in existence.

"A priestly tendency cannot be recognized. If there had been any special danger of an undue consumption of blood in the exilic-postexilic period it would then not have been

necessary to first permit meat to be eaten and after this to forbid the eating of blood. However, the so-called exilic-postexilic sources indicate no such danger and I Samuel 14:32–34 presumes such a prohibition." (Külling, DSCPSG, 75)

5C. The Tabernacle

1D. Documentarian Assumption

Usually the documentarian passes off the tabernacle in Exodus as a "pure fantasy." The entire Exodus account is attributed to the P document and is considered late and unreliable. The structure is thought to be too elaborate for the time of Moses. It is alleged to be the pure creation of the postexilic imagination. It has been proposed that the Hebrews of Moses' age did not have the skills necessary to construct such an *elaborate* tabernacle or tent.

Wellhausen writes: "The temple, the focus to which the worship was concentrated, and which was not built until Solomon's time, is by this document regarded as so indispensable even for the troubled days of the wanderings before the settlement, that it is made portable, and in the form of a tabernacle set up in the very beginning of things. For the truth is, that the tabernacle is the copy, not the prototype, of the temple at Jerusalem." (Wellhausen, PHI, 36–37)

Wellhausen continues that "the tabernacle rests on an historical fiction . . . at the outset its very possibility is doubtful." (Wellhausen, PHI, 39)

A. Bentzen asserts that the tabernacle is "quite unrealistic." (Bentzen, IOT, 34)

"The Tabernacle, *as described by P,* represents, not a historical structure, which once actually existed, but an ideal,—an ideal, based indeed upon a historical reality, but far transcending it, and designed as the embodiment of certain spiritual ideas." (Driver, BE, 426)

2D. Basic Answer

Kenneth Kitchen, in "Some Egyptian Background to the Old Testament," enumerates the various archaeological discoveries that give the general background of portable structures very close in most essentials to the Mosaic tabernacle.

The first is dated about 2600 B.C. and is the prefabricated, portable bed canopy of Queen Hetepheres I, the mother of Kheops, who constructed the great pyramid.

> In view of this evidence there seems to be no adequate reason for denying the existence of a structure such as the Tabernacle to the Hebrews of the Mosaic period.
>
> —R. K. HARRISON

"This remarkable structure," writes Kitchen, "is a framework of long beams along top and bottom separated by vertical rods and corner-posts on three sides of a rectangle, with a lintel beam and other horizontal 'roof-beams' across the top. The entire structure was of wood, was throughout overlaid with gold, had hooks for curtains all round, and consisted entirely of beams and rods fitting together with tenons in sockets for rapid and customary erection and dismantling, just like the Hebrew Tabernacle thirteen centuries later." (Kitchen, SEBOT, 9)

There are various prefabricated structures from the Archaic and Old Kingdom periods (c. 2850–2200). G. A. Reisner and W. S. Smith describe other structures that were depicted on the walls of tombs of the fourth through sixth dynasties (c. 2600–2200 B.C.). (Reisner, HGN, 14–15)

Another form of prefabricated structures dating back to the third millennium B.C. is described by Kitchen. He writes about "the Tent of Purification *(ibw)* to which the corpses of royal and exalted personages were borne for the rituals of purification both before and after embalmment. From pictures in Old Kingdom tombs, it is clear that these portable 'tents' were sizeable structures having hangings of cloth (like curtaining) upon a framework of vertical poles or pillars linked along the top by horizontal bars and beams—again, directly reminiscent of the Tabernacle (B. Grdseloff, *Das Aegyptische Reinigungszelt,* 1941, plus E. Drioton, *Annales du Service des Antiquités de l'Égypte,* 40, (1940), 1008. Good pictures of "Tent of Purification" showing construction in Blackman, *Rock Tombs ol Meir,* V, 1952, Pls. 42–43)." (Kitchen, SEBOT, 9–10)

The relics of several of these "tents" have been discovered. See Kitchen (Kitchen, SEBOT, 10) and Reisner and Smith (Reisner, HGN, 13–17) for further descriptions of these.

Kitchen indicates that "clearer evidence of the practicality and actual use at a remote age of the very constructional techniques exemplified by the Tabernacle could hardly be wished for." (Kitchen, SEBOT, 9)

R. K. Harrison concludes: "In view of this evidence there seems to be no adequate reason for denying the existence of a structure such as the Tabernacle to the Hebrews of the Mosaic period." (Harrison, IOT, 405)

Kitchen adds: "Hitherto-neglected Egyptian evidence for prefabricated structures for religious and other uses definitively refutes the charge of late fantasy with very early examples of the constructional techniques so airily dismissed." (Kitchen, SEBOT, 9)

To this Kitchen says that "it is now entirely unnecessary to dismiss either the concept or construction of the Tabernacle of Ex. xxvi, xxxvi as fantasy or free idealisation. The Egyptian data here adduced cannot of course directly prove the early existence of that Tabernacle, but it does create a very strong presumption in favour of the reasonableness and veracity of the straightforward Biblical account." (Kitchen, SEBOT, 11)

Against the objection that the Hebrews at the time of Moses did not possess the necessary ability to construct such an elaborate structure, R.K. Harrison writes that "it need only be remarked that the Egyptians placed a high value upon Semitic craftsmanship in precious metals when it came to exacting tribute from subjugated areas of Syria and Palestine, as illustrated by a number of tomb-scenes." (Harrison, IOT, 405)

Kitchen concludes that "it is sometimes objected that as a subject-race before the Exodus, the Hebrews would have no skills such as the work of the Tabernacle required, and could hardly have obtained the necessary materials even from spoiling the Egyptians. However, this is far from being necessarily the case . . . amply sufficient skills to furnish a Bezalel and an Oholiab, and from the Egyptians in the E. Delta at that particular epoch spoils (Ex. xii, 35–36) amply sufficient for the work of the Tabernacle." (Kitchen, SEBOT, 12–13)

G.T. Manley writes: "It is true that the unity of the nation and the one-ness of Yahweh called for one sanctuary round which the people could gather. But this was no discovery of later times, it went back to the covenant in Horeb (Ex. xxxiv. 23; Dt. v. 2, 6, vi. 2). The simple fact is that from Joshua onwards there always existed a national cen-

tre for worship, first the tabernacle, then the temple." (Manley, BL, 127)

For further information on the tabernacle, see three excellent chapters in *The Unity of the Pentateuch* by A. H. Finn on its antiquity.

Concerning the belief that there were two different representations of the "Tent of Meeting," one in the early JE passages and another in the late P passages, see A. H. Finn, above, and also James Orr's *The Problem of the Old Testament*.

> *Archaeology has recently provided us with two powerful supports for the early dating of the priestly writings.*

6C. See the preceding section for information on the antiquity of D and centralized worship.

7C. External Evidence

Archaeology has recently provided us with two powerful supports for the early dating of the priestly writings.

Kitchen describes the first find: "Certain difficult expressions and passages in Leviticus could be solved only with cuneiform data of the eighteenth to fifteenth centuries B.C. . . . These were archaic and obscure by the postexilic period." (Kitchen, AOOT, 129)

The Ras Shamra tablets (1400 B.C.), which contain a large amount of Ugaritic literature, render the Wellhausen postexilic concept void. Many of the technical sacrificial terms of Leviticus were discovered in far-removed Canaanite-speaking Ugarit (1400 B.C.). Such P terms include:

(1) *ishsheh:* "offering made by fire"
(2) *kālîl:* "whole burnt offering"
(3) *shelāmîn:* "peace offering"
(4) *āshām* (?): "guilt offering"

Archer correctly concludes that "these terms were already current in Palestine at the time of Moses and the conquest, and that the whole line of reasoning which made out the terminology of the Levitical cultus to be late is devoid of foundation." (Archer, SOTI, 149–50)

3B. External Evidence

See 2A., 3B. of this chapter regarding covenant-form analysis.

5A. Archaeology

See 5A. of chapter 13 for numerous examples of archaeological evidence supporting Mosaic authorship of the Pentateuch.

22

THE PHENOMENON OF DIVINE NAMES

Otto Eissfeldt names four main foundations of the documentary hypothesis:

(1) Change in divine names

(2) Linguistic usage: (a) persons, places, objects are designated by different names,

(b) words, expressions, and stylistic peculiarities are said to be characteristic of different documents

(3) Diversity of ideas: religious, moral, legal, political; also, the difference in the contemporary conditions and events that they presuppose

(4) Literary phenomena: double accounts, interruption of a continuous narrative by extraneous material, and so forth. (Eissfeldt, OTI, 182–88)

1A. INTRODUCTION

The name "Elohim" occurs thirty-three times in the first thirty-four verses of Genesis. The name "Jehovah (YHWH) Elohim" occurs twenty times in the next forty-five verses, and the name "Jehovah" (YHWH) appears ten times in the following twenty-five verses. It would seem that such selective usage of divine names is more than coincidental. (Allis, FBM, 23)

2A. DOCUMENTARY ASSUMPTION

Critics have held that the isolated use of various divine names [i.e., Jehovah (English pronunciation) or Yahweh (Hebrew pronunciation) and Elohim] indicates that there

> Each divine name bore a special significance, and they were not necessarily synonymous. The author used Jehovah, Elohim, or Jehovah-Elohim according to the context of the passage. Therefore there is a real purpose behind the isolated usage of divine names, and not a random choosing.

was more than one author. This is what initially led Astruc to the conclusion that various sources lay intertwined and combined in the Pentateuch. Notice this statement in his *Conjectures,* cited by *The Encyclopedia of Religion and Ethics:*

In the Hebrew text of Genesis, God is designated by two different names. The first is Elohim, for, while this name has other meanings in Hebrew, it is especially applied to the Supreme Being. The other is Jehovah, יהוה, the great name of God, expressing his essence. Now one might suppose that the two names were used indiscriminately as synonymous terms, merely to lend variety to the style. This, however, would be an error. The names are never intermixed; there are whole chapters, or large parts of chapters, in which God is always called Elohim, and others, at least as numerous, in which he is always named Jehovah. If Moses were the author of Genesis, we should have to ascribe this strange and harsh variation to himself. But can we conceive such negligence in the composition of so short a book

as Genesis? Shall we impute to Moses a fault such as no other writer has committed? Is it not more natural to explain this variation by supposing that Genesis was composed of two or three memoirs, the authors of which gave different names to God, one using that of Elohim, another that of Jehovah or Jehovah Elohim? (ERE, 315)

While it is often claimed that this criterion is no longer employed by the critics, the following statement by A. Bentzen shows how important it still remains to modern critics:

If we are to distinguish between the traditions we must look for "constants" along this line. The first "constant" which was noticed was the peculiar changes in the use of the Divine names. The change in the use of the Divine names is however more than a simply linguistic "constant." It is a *material "constant."* We know that its use, at least in Gen. and in the beginning of Exodus follows a definite plan. . . . Accordingly, in the parts of the Pentateuch from Gen. 1 to Exodus 6 we must be entitled to use the criterion of the Divine names to distinguish between different traditions. (Bentzen, IOT, vol. II 27,–28)

3A. BASIC ANSWER

1B. Specific Uses of Various Divine Names

Each divine name bore a special significance, and they were not necessarily synonymous. The author used Jehovah, Elohim, or Jehovah-Elohim according to the context of the passage. Therefore there is a real purpose behind the isolated usage of divine names, and not a random choosing.

In the twelfth century R. Jehuda Halevi wrote a book called *Cosri* in which he explained the etymology of each of the divine names. His conclusions are paraphrased here by E. W. Hengstenberg, professor of theology at the University of Berlin during the middle of the nineteenth century:

[Elohim] is the most general name of the Deity; it distinguishes him only in his fullness of power without reference to his personality or moral qualities—to any special relation in which he stands to men—either as to the benefits he bestows, or to the requirements he makes. On this account, where God has witnessed of himself and is truly known, another name is added to *Elohim*—this is the name *Jehovah,* peculiar to the people who received his revelation and his covenant. . . . The name Jehovah is unintelligible to all who are not acquainted with that development of the Divine essence which is represented by it; while Elohim distinguishing him as God in those respects which are known to all men, is universally intelligible. . . . The name *Jehovah* is the *nomen proprium* [proper name] of God, and being one that expresses the inmost nucleus of his essence, is only intelligible where God has come forth, laid open the recesses of his heart, and has permitted his creatures to behold them, so that, instead of an obscure undefined being, of whom thus much only is known and affirmed, that he is powerful, that he is immense—he here exhibits himself the most personal of all persons, the most characteristic of all characters. (Hengstenberg, DGP, 216–17)

Umberto Cassuto, the Jewish scholar and late professor at the Hebrew University, continues:

First consider the characters of the two Names. They are not of the same type. The designation *'Elohim* was originally a common noun, an appellative, that was applied both to the One God of Israel and to the heathen gods (so, too, was the name *'El*). On the other hand the name YHWH is a proper noun, the specific name of Israel's God, the God whom the Israelites acknowledged as the Sovereign of the universe and as the Divinity who chose them as His people. Let me cite a parallel by way of illustration. A certain city may be called *Jerusalem* or simply *city.* The appellation *city* is common to her and to all other cities; the name *Jerusalem* belongs to her alone. When the ancestors of the Jewish people realized that there is but One God, and that only "YHWH, He is *'Elohim*" (I Kings xviii 39), then the common substantive *'Elohim* also acquired for them the signification of a proper noun, and became synonymous with the name YHWH. If Jerusalem had been the sole city in the world of those who spoke Hebrew, then of course the word *city* would have become a proper name, synonymous with *Jerusalem.* (Cassuto, DH, 18)

Cassuto sets forth the rules below as an explanation for the use of divine names:

YHWH	ELOHIM
(1) "It selected the name YHWH when the text reflects the Israelite conception of God, which is embodied in the portrayal of YHWH and finds expression in the attributes traditionally ascribed to Him by Israel, particularly in His ethical character."	(1) "It preferred the name Elohim when the passage implies the abstract idea of the Deity prevalent in the international circles of 'wise men'—God conceived as the Creator of the physical universe, as the Ruler of nature, as the Source of life.
(2) YHWH "is used, when expression is given to the direct intuitive notion of God, which characterizes the simple faith of the multitude or the ardour of the prophetic spirit.	(2) "The name Elohim when the concept of thinkers who mediate on the lofty problems connected with the existence of the world and humanity is to be conveyed.

(3) "The name YHWH occurs when the context depicts the Divine attributes in relatively lucid and, as it were, palpable terms, a clear picture being conveyed."

(4) YHWH "is found when the Torah seeks to arouse in the soul of the reader or the listener the feeling of the sublimity of the Divine Presence in all its majesty and glory.

(5) "The name YHWH is employed when God is presented to us in His personal character and in direct relationship to people or nature."

(6) YHWH "appears when the reference is to the God of Israel relative to His people or to their ancestors.

(7) "YHWH is mentioned when the theme concerns Israel's tradition."

(3) "Elohim, when the portrayal is more general, superficial and hazy, leaving an impression of obscurity."

(4) "Elohim, when it wishes to mention God in an ordinary manner or when the expression or thought may not, out of reverence, be associated directly with the Holiest name.

(5) "Elohim, when the Deity is alluded to as a Transcendental Being who exists completely outside and above the physical universe.

(6) "Elohim, when He is spoken of in relation to one who is not a member of the Chosen people.

(7) "Elohim, when the subject-matter appertains to the universal tradition."

Sometimes, of course, it happens that two opposite rules apply together and come in conflict with each other; then, as logic demands, the rule that is more material to the primary purport of the relevant passage prevails. (Cassuto, DH, 30–41)

These rules apply to certain types of literature in different ways:

PROPHETIC. The prophets of the Old Testament consistently used the divine name YHWH instead of Elohim. Jonah is an exception, employing the title Elohim for the God of Israel a number of times. But this exception only proves the rule, for Jonah actually belongs to the narrative literature because of its viewpoint. Isaiah is another exception; he replaces Yahweh, not with Elohim but with El, a name for God that was originally a common noun. (Cassuto, DH, 20)

LEGAL. Yahweh the only personal name of God employed throughout the legal literature of the Pentateuch and Ezekiel. (Cassuto, DH, 20)

POETIC. The literature classified as poetic normally uses YHWH. Some poems that belong to the wisdom literature or that have been influenced by it are an exception. In the second and third books, known as the Elohistic books, the use of El or Elohim are of the majority. (Cassuto, DH, 20)

WISDOM. Wisdom literature is unique in that it is a universal literary style. Similar writings may be discovered throughout the ancient Orient. An investigation of the similar literature among Israel's neighbors should prove quite beneficial.

But as one begins to study these books "we are struck by an amazing phenomenon. The wisdom books of the ancient East, irrespective of the people from which they emanated or the language in which they were written, usually refer to the Godhead by an appellative rather than by the proper names of the various divinities." (Cassuto, DH, 21)

NARRATIVE. Narrative literature, as is found throughout the Pentateuch, the Earlier Prophets, Job, Jonah, and so forth, frequently uses both Yahweh and Elohim in close proximity. (Cassuto, DH, 21)

CHARACTERISTICALLY JEWISH PASSAGES. Umberto Cassuto, the late professor at the Hebrew University, in explaining the use of Yahweh states that in "those categories that have a purely Israelite character, only the Tetragrammaton [Yahweh] occurs, this being the national name of God, expressing the personal conception of the Deity exclusive to Israel." (Cassuto, DH, 23)

ANCIENT HEBREW. Ancient Hebrew letters found at Lachish illustrate the usage of Yahweh in daily life. It is employed not only in greetings and in oaths, but throughout the entire letter. Elohim never appears. A parallel is seen in the consistent use of Yahweh on scriptural greetings (Judg. 6:12; Ps. 129:8; Ruth 2:4) and in the actual rabbinical dictum that required the use of Yahweh in greeting another. (Cassuto, DH, 24)

MODERN HEBREW. Even in modern Hebrew, Cassuto says, "We are exact in our choice of words, we employ the Tetragrammaton [Yahweh] when we have in mind the traditional Jewish idea of the Deity, and the name Elohim when we wish to express the philosophic or universal concept of the Godhead." (Cassuto, DH, 30)

The following is a brief application of these rules to Genesis: In Genesis chapter 1, God appears as Creator of the physical universe and as Lord of the world who has dominion over everything. Everything that exists does so because of His fiat alone, without direct contact between Him and nature. Thus the rules apply here that Elohim should be used. (Cassuto, DH, 32)

In the story of the Garden of Eden we find God as a moral ruler because He imposes certain rules on man. Also, a personal side of God is shown as He relates directly to man. Yahweh fits easily here as would be expected. The only place the name Elohim is used is when the serpent speaks and when the woman is talking to the serpent. The name Yahweh is avoided out of reverence to the national God of Israel. (Cassuto, DH, 33)

In the same passage we find Yahweh linked with Elohim, because the Scriptures now wish to identify Elohim with Yahweh: "In other words that the God of the ethical world is none other than the God of the physical world, that the God of Israel is God of the entire universe, that the names YHWH and Elohim point only to two different aspects of His activity, or to two different ways in which He reveals Himself to the children of men." (Cassuto, DH, 33) This explains the double usage, and in subsequent chapters the names are used individually according to context.

Cassuto explains:

In the story of the Generation of Division (xi 1–9) YHWH appears. The reason is clear: in this narrative only the place of the occurrence is outside the Land of Israel; the story itself is wholly Israelite in character, and it contains not an iota of foreign material. Unlike the accounts of the Creation and the Flood, it has no cosmopolitan tradition as its background to serve as the basis of the Torah's portrayal; on the contrary, here we find the Israelite spirit in complete opposition to the attitude and aspirations of the proud heathen peoples, who dominate the world. Thus the Israelite conception of the relationship between man and God is conveyed by the Israelite name of the Deity. (Cassuto, DH, 37)

In chapter 12 of Genesis, the story of Abraham starts. It seems fitting that the Israelite name for the Godhead should be used.

Archer applied this to the early chapters

of Genesis. A careful study of the use of Yahweh and Elohim in the book of Genesis will reveal the purpose that the writer had in

> Why did J prefer the name Jehovah, and E and P the name Elohim? To this important question the divisive hypothesis gives no satisfactory answer. If the Pentateuch however be the work of one author, the use of these names is sufficiently clear.
>
> —JOHN R. RAVEN

mind. Elohim (which is perhaps derived from a root meaning "powerful," "strong," or "foremost") refers to God as being the almighty Creator and Lord of the universe. Thus Elohim is appropriate for Genesis 1 because God is in the role of the almighty Creator, whereas Yahweh is the name of God when He is in the covenant engagement. Thus in Genesis 2 Yahweh is almost exclusively used because God is dealing with Adam and Eve in a covenant relationship. In Genesis 3, when Satan appears, the name for God changes back to Elohim because God is in no way related to Satan in a covenant relationship. Thus, both the serpent and Eve refer to Him as Elohim. The name changes back to Jehovah as He calls out to Adam (3:9) and reproves Eve (3:13) and it is the covenant God that puts the curse on the serpent (3:14). (Archer, SOTI, 112)

John H. Raven argues similarly:

This argument ignores the etymology of the names of God and conceives of them as used interchangeably merely as a matter of habit. It is not claimed by the critics that J was ignorant of the name Elohim or P and E of the name Jehovah, but that each preferred one of these names. But if so, the question remains, why did J prefer the name Jehovah, and E and P the name Elohim? To this important question the divisive hypothesis gives no satisfac-

tory answer. If the Pentateuch however be the work of one author, the use of these names is sufficiently clear. It is precisely that which the so-called characteristics of P, J and E require. P is said to be cold, formal, systematic, logical; but it is precisely in such passages that one would expect Elohim, the general name for God, the name which has no special relation to Israel but is used many times in reference to the deities of the Gentiles. J on the other hand is said to be naïve, anthropomorphic in his conception of God; but these evidences of religious fervor would lead us to expect the proper national name of God, the name which emphasized his covenant relations with Israel. (Raven, OTI, 118–19)

Even Kuenen, one of the founders of the classic documentary hypothesis, admitted the uncertainty of this criterion: "The original distinction between Jahweh [another spelling] and Elohim very often accounts for the use of one of these appellations in preference to the other." (Kuenen, HCIOCH, 56)

"The history of critical investigation," continues Kuenen, "has shown that far too much weight has often been laid on agreement in the use of the divine names. . . . It is well, therefore, to utter a warning against laying an exaggerated stress on this one phenomenon." (Kuenen, HCIOCH, 61)

More recently, the oral traditionalist Engnell has charged that source division on the basis of differing usages is totally unwarranted (*Swedish Bible Dictionary: Svenskt Bibliskt Uppslagsverk,* ii). He is cited by North as saying:

In so far as a certain "constant" change of divine names is really to be found, a closer examination shows that this does not rest upon change of documents but upon a conscious stylistic practice of the traditionist, something which is bound up with the fact that the different divine names have different ideological associations and therewith different import. Thus, Yahweh is readily used when it is a question of Israel's national God, indicated as such over against foreign gods, and where the history of the fathers is concerned, &c., while on the other hand Elohim, "God," gives more expression to a "theological" and abstract-cosmic picture of God, and is therefore used in larger and more moving contexts. . . . So, then, it is the traditionist, the *same* traditionist, who varies in the choice of divine names, not the "documents." (North, PC, 66–67)

Cassuto boldly proclaims that there

is no reason, therefore, to feel surprise that the use of these Names varies in the Torah. On the contrary, we should be surprised if they were not changed about. The position is of necessity what it is. It is not a case of disparity between different documents, or of mechanical amalgamation of separate texts; every Hebrew author was compelled to write thus and to use the two Names in this manner, because their primary signification, the general literary tradition of the ancient East, and the rules governing the use in the Divine Names throughout the entire range of Hebrew literature, demanded this. (Cassuto, DH, 41)

Archaeology provides an answer for the use of the compound name Yahweh-Elohim.

One of the major assumptions of the JEDP hypothesis is that the use of Jehovah is typical of a J document and Elohim of an E document. The combination of these two documents is the ground used by the radical critics to account for the compound name Yahweh-Elohim. Cyrus Gordon cites his personal discoveries regarding this subject, "All this is admirably logical and for years I never questioned it. But my Ugaritic studies destroyed this kind of logic with relevant facts." (Gordon, HCFF, 132) At Ugarit, deities were found with compound names. For example: Qadish-Amrar is the name of one, and Ibb-Nikkal another. Most of the

time "and" was put between the two parts, but the conjunction can be omitted.

Thus it was common to use compound names for a god. Amon-Re, the most famous god with a compound name, was a deity that resulted from the Egyptian conquest under the eighteenth dynasty. Amon was the god of the city of Thebes where the political power existed, while Re was the universal sun god. These two gods were combined because of the political leadership in Thebes and the universalism of Re. But Amon-Re is one god. This sheds light on the combination of Yahweh-Elohim. Yahweh refers to the specifics of the deity, while Elohim is more of a general or universal designation of the deity. This consolidation of Yahweh-Elohim may demonstrate that Yahweh equals Elohim, which can be restated "Yahweh is God." Yet the documentarians tell us that Yahweh-Elohim is the result of combining the two documents J and E. This is as unfounded as using an A document and R document to explain the compound deity Amon-Re. (Gordon, HCFF, 132–33)

Kitchen adds:

For multiple terms for deity, compare the use of three names, a fixed epithet, and common noun "god" for the god Osiris on the Berlin stela of Ikhernofret: Osiris, Wennofer, Khentamentiu, "Lord of Abydos" *(Neb-'Abdju)*, and *nuter*, "god" (cf. *'Elohim* in Hebrew). But no Egyptologist bothers to invent "Osirist," "Wennofrist," "Khentamentist," Neb-'Abdjuist and Nuterist sources to match the Yahwist and Elohist of Old Testament studies. Ikhernofret shows what could be taken as "prolixity" of expression, but it is certain that this commemorative inscription was composed (as one unit), carved and set up within weeks, or possibly even days, of the events to which it chiefly relates, and has no literary "pre-history" of several centuries of "hands," redactors and conflation. This applies to other texts, a few cited here and many more not. Alongside

Egypt, multiple divine names occur in Mesopotamia. We might cite Enlil also called Nunamnir in the prologue to the Lipit-Ishtar laws, and in the prologue to Hammurapi's laws we have Inanna/Ishtar/Telitum, and Nintu/Mama. (Kitchen, AOOT, 121)

Raven, in the material cited previously, introduces a difficulty in using divine names as evidence for multiple authors: "It is not claimed by the critics that J was ignorant of the name Elohim or P and E of the name Jehovah, but that each preferred one of these names. But if so, the question remains, why did J prefer the name Jehovah, and E and P the name Elohim? To this important question the divisive hypothesis gives no satisfactory answer. If the Pentateuch however be the work of one author, the use of these names is sufficiently clear." (Raven, OTI, 118)

"The great innovation on the part of the Israelites," Cassuto observes,

consists in the fact that, while the writings of the pagans give expression, on the one hand, to the abstract and general notion of Divinity, and, on the other, make mention of some particular god, in Hebrew literature the concept of the specific God of Israel is completely identified with that of the God of the whole earth. YHWH, whom the children of Israel recognize and before whom they prostrate themselves, is none other than 'Elohim, of whose dominion over them all men are more or less clearly conscious, and whom they are destined to acknowledge fully in time to come. This is the sublime thought to which the Biblical poets give expression through the variation of the Names. (Cassuto, DH, 25)

2B. Exegesis of Exodus 6:3

1C. Documentary Assumption

This verse is taken by the critics to mean that the name Jehovah (Yahweh, YHWH) was not known in Israel until God revealed it to Moses at Sinai. Therefore, all the passages in Genesis and in Exodus before this one where "Jehovah" is used must have been written by a hand other than the one who wrote this Exodus passage; otherwise (if there is only one author) he would be guilty of an obvious contradiction: having the patriarchs use "Jehovah" throughout Genesis but then stating that the name was unknown until it was revealed to Moses.

This view is stated by the British scholar, H. H. Rowley:

Exodus 6:2f. says: "I am Jehovah, and I appeared unto Abraham, unto Isaac, and unto Jacob as El Shaddai, but by my name Jehovah I was not known to them." Yet there are several passages in the book of Genesis which declare that God was known to the patriarchs by the name Jehovah. The name is known to Abram (Genesis 15:2, 8), to Sarai (16:2), to Laban (24:31); it is used by angelic visitors in conversation with Abraham (18:14) and with Lot (19:13); and God is represented as saying "I am Jehovah" to Abram (14:7) and to Jacob (28:13). (Rowley, GOT, 20–21) (See also Fohrer, IOT, 115)

2C. Basic Answer

The word "to know" in the Old Testament generally includes the idea of apprehension and the expression "to know the name of Jehovah" is used many times in this fuller sense of apprehending the divine attributes (I Kings 8:43; Psalms 9:11, 91:14; Isaiah 52:6, 64:1; Jeremiah 16:21; Ezekiel 39:6, 7). All this shows the meaning to be that Abraham, Isaac and Jacob knew God as a God of power but not as the God of the covenant.

—JOHN H. RAVEN

Correct exegesis of Exodus 6:3: This verse does not mean that the name "Jehovah" was literally unknown to the Israelites before Moses' time (i.e., that it did not *exist*), but rather that they didn't have the relationship with God that the name "Jehovah" implied. In other words, they knew God by His *name* "Jehovah" but not by his *character* "Jehovah."

W. J. Martin, in his book *Stylistic Criteria and the Analysis of the Pentateuch,* said: "It might have been possible, of course, to have denied the implications by drawing attention to the full sense of the Hebrew word for 'name.' The field of meaning of this word covers not only that of 'name,' that is, a verbal deputy, a label for a thing, but also denotes the attributes of the thing named. It may stand for reputation, character, honour, name and fame. Hence the reference would not be so much to nomenclature as to the nature of the reality for which the name stood." (Martin, SCAP, 17–18)

J. H. Hertz, former chief rabbi in London, England, in his commentary on the Pentateuch and Haftorahs writes:

Exodus 6:3 is the focal point of critical scholarship. According to them, God here first reveals his name as YHWH to Moses. Thus all chapters in Genesis and Exodus where the name Yahweh appears are from another source. This is used as decisive proof of the multiple document hypothesis of the Pentateuch, and is proclaimed by all radical critics as the clue to the JEDP hypothesis.

The current Critical explanation of this verse, however, rests on a total misunderstanding of Hebrew idiom. When Scripture states that Israel, or the nations, or Pharaoh, "shall know that God is Adonay"—this does *not* mean that they shall be informed that His Name is Y H W H (Adonay), as the Critics would have it; but that they shall come to witness His power and comprehend those attributes of the Divine nature which that Name denotes. Thus, Jer. xvi, 21, "I will cause

them to know my hand and my might, and they shall know that my name is Adonay." [Orthodox Jews do not pronounce YHWH's name lest they break the third commandment and thus substitute Adonay which means "Lord."] In Ezekiel the phrase, "they shall know that I am Adonay," occurs more than sixty times. Nowhere does it mean, they will know Him by the four letters of His Name. Every time it means, they will know Him by His acts and the fulfillment of His promise. (Hertz, PH, 104)

"The word 'to know' in the Old Testament" states Raven, "generally includes the idea of apprehension and the expression 'to know the name of Jehovah' is used many times in this fuller sense of apprehending the divine attributes (I Kings 8:43; Psalms 9:11, 91:14; Isaiah 52:6, 64:1; Jeremiah 16:21; Ezekiel 39:6, 7). All this shows the meaning to be that Abraham, Isaac and Jacob knew God as a God of power but not as the God of the covenant." (Raven, OTI, 121)

Archer argues similarly that the radical critics reject the method of founding Christian doctrine on proof-text but yet they found one of their primary doctrines upon this very method. This method seeks a literal interpretation of two verses without considering context or the analogy of other scriptural teaching. This instance is found in Exodus 6:2, 3. ("I am YHWH and I appeared to Abraham, to Isaac and Jacob, as El Shaddai, but by My name, YHWH, I did not make Myself known to them.") The documentarians hold that this is the first time the name Yahweh was revealed to Moses in the E document. However, J did not know about this and assumed Yahweh was a suitable name for the pre-Mosaic era. Yet, with a proper understanding both of the verb "to know" *yadra*) and of the implications in Hebrew of knowing someone's name, it becomes clear that the meaning is not literal. All ten plagues were surely not for the mere purpose that the Egyptians might know that the God of the Israelites was named Yahweh (Ex. 14:4, ". . . and the Egyptians will know that I am Yahweh.") Rather, the intent of the plagues is that the Egyptians might witness the covenant faithfulness of God to His people and thus know Him by experience as Yahweh, the covenant God. (See also Ex. 6:7: "You shall know that I am Yahweh your God, who brought you out from under the burdens of the Egyptians.") "Hebrew usage therefore indicates clearly enough that Exodus 6:3 teaches that God, who in earlier generations had revealed Himself as El Shaddai (God Almighty) by deeds of power and mercy, would now in Moses' generation reveal Himself as the covenant-keeping Jehovah by His marvelous deliverance of the whole nation of Israel." (Archer, SOTI, 122)

"The context of the passage," continues Raven, "and the *usus loquendi* of the expression, 'to know the name' show clearly that the meaning is to have an experimental knowledge of the attributes emphasized by the name." (Raven, OTI, 121)

G. T. Manley makes this observation concerning the Hebrew verbs involved: "Where a name is made known for the first time the verb commonly used is *nāghadh* (hiph), as in Genesis 32:29. Here [Exodus 6:3] it is *yādra,* the same as is found in I Sam. 2:12 and 3:7, where the persons concerned were familiar with the name Yahweh but not with all that the name implied." (Manley, BL, 47)

The critics use this verse as the basis for their division of the J document, which uses the name Jehovah, from the E document, which uses Elohim. But this verse distinguishes not Elohim from Jehovah, but El Shaddai from Jehovah, as Merrill Unger points out:

That this supposition regarding the meaning of Exodus 6:2, 3 is totally unwarranted and has

no foundation outside the exigencies of the critical hypothesis is apparent *first, because of the clear distinction indicated in the passage itself:* "God spake unto Moses, and said unto him, I am the Lord: and I appeared unto Abraham, unto Isaac, and unto Jacob, by the name of God Almighty (El Shaddai); but by my name Jehovah was I not known to them." Significantly, the reference does not distinguish Jehovah from Elohim (occurring over 200 times in Genesis) but from El Shaddai (occurring five times in Genesis), the name denoting the particular character in which God revealed Himself to be the patriarchs (Genesis 17:1; 28:3; 35:11; 43:14; 48:3). (Unger, IGOT, 251, emphasis his)

Another important issue often overlooked in regard to Exodus 6:2, 3 is what is referred to in Hebrew as the *Beth Essential.*

The revised version renders this passage as follows: "I appeared . . . *as* El Shaddai, but *by* my name Yahweh."

This translation does not indicate that although there is a preposition (prefix *Beth*) in the original for "as," which governs "El Shaddai," there is no corresponding preposition for the word "by" which here governs "my name Yahweh." Grammatically there needs to be a preposition "by" or "as" in English.

Gesenius gives an excellent basis for the use of the preposition "as" in relationship to "my name Yahweh."

This would carry the meaning of "character or inner condition, as distinct from outer circumstances or designation." (Motyer, RDN, 14)

Gesenius writes that "in poetic parallelism the governing power of a preposition is sometimes extended to the corresponding substantive of the second member [Gesenius-Kautzsch, *Hebrew Grammar*, Para. 119 hh, 1910]." (Motyer, RDN, 14)

Isaiah is an excellent example of this "poetic parallelism": "For my name's sake I defer my anger, for the sake of my praise I restrain it for you" (RSV). Although English demands two uses of "for the sake of," Hebrew allows only one (here used before the first noun).

In this case, as in others, "the preposition extends to the second word exactly the same [meaning] which it exercises over the first." (Motyer, RDN, 14)

There is no reason why Exodus 6:2, 3 should not be governed by the same principle. "My name Yahweh" should be governed the same way as the *Beth Essential* governs "El Shaddai."

Motyer, in *The Revelation of the Divine Name*, gives an excellent treatment of the meaning of the *Beth Essential*:

In this verse [Exodus 6:3] the *Beth Essential* is appropriately translated "as," that is to say, it is used with a view to concentrating attention on character or inner condition, as distinct from outer circumstances or designation. When God revealed Himself "as" El Shaddai, it was not with a view to providing the patriarchs with a title by which they could address Him, but to give them an insight into His character such as that title aptly conveyed. Likewise, in Exodus iii. 2, "the angel of Yahweh appeared . . . *as* a flame of fire. . . ." The outward circumstances may have served in the first instance to attract Moses' attention—though this is not necessary, for his attention was, in point of fact, caught by the continued existence of the bush in spite of the flame. The flame was the appropriate characterization of God Himself, designed to provide a suitable revelation of the divine Nature to Moses at that particular juncture of his career. When we carry this force over to the nouns "my name Yahweh" we reach a conclusion in accordance with the translation we are seeking to justify: "I showed myself . . . in the character of El Shaddai, but in the character expressed by my name Yahweh I did not make myself known." (Motyer, RDN, 14)

Motyer continues:

The accuracy of the proposed translation is further established by its suitability to its context. (The place of the verse in the scheme of revelation, as we see it, is this: not that now for the first time the name as a sound is declared, but that now for the first time the essential significance of the name is to be made known). The patriarchs called God Yahweh, but knew Him as El Shaddai; their descendants will both call Him and know Him by His name Yahweh. This is certainly the burden of Exodus vi.. 6ff. where Moses receives the message he is to impart to Israel. The message opens and closes with the seal of the divine authority, "I am Yahweh," and on the basis of this authority it declares the saving acts which, it is specifically stated, will be a revelation of Yahweh's nature, for, as a result of what He will do, Israel "know that I am Yahweh," but, in point of fact, their knowledge will be, not the name merely, but also the character of Israel's God. This meaning of the phrase is consistent throughout the Bible. (Motyer, RDN, 14)

Given the documentarians' interpretation of this passage, we are left with a most difficult question: Why did not one of the many redactors involved in the compilation of the Pentateuch reconcile the obvious contradiction between the use of the name Jehovah by the patriarchs in Genesis and the statement in Exodus 6:3 that the name was first revealed to Moses at Sinai?

Unger says that, besides the problems both of the context and of the true meaning of the words, the radical critics' position on Exodus 6:2, 3 is further weakened by the common sense implication of their own hypothesis. The redactor to whom they attribute these accounts clearly did not understand the passage as they do, for he saw here no contradiction with the frequent usage of "Yahweh" throughout Genesis. Had he seen a contradiction, he surely would have either altered the verse or deleted the earlier occurrences of the name "Yahweh." (Unger, IGOT, 252)

"The redactor of the Pentateuch, if such there were," Raven notes, "could not have considered the statement of Exodus 6:3 inconsistent with the frequent use of the name Jehovah by the patriarchs. Otherwise he would either have changed the statement in Exodus or the name Jehovah in Genesis. The many generations of Jews and Christians who were ignorant of the composite authorship of Genesis also saw nothing difficult in Exodus 6:3." (Raven, OTI, 121)

It is also possible that the passage has been incorrectly translated into English. Martin explains:

There is, however, another possible translation which would eliminate all conflict with the remote context. The phrase, "but by my name the LORD I did not make myself known to them" could be taken in Hebrew as an elliptical interrogative. The translation of the whole verse would then run: "I suffered myself to appear *(Niph'al)* to Abraham, to Isaac, and to Jacob, as El-Shaddai, for did I not let myself be known to them by my name YHWH?" Hebrew possesses an interrogative particle but on a number of occasions it is as here omitted: a good example is in Genesis xviii. 12. It is possible that in the spoken language the intonation was usually sufficient to indicate a question, as is still the case in living Semitic languages. Intonation has been described as the subjective stratum in languages in contrast to words, the objective stratum. Writing can never be a full, but only to a greater or less degree a partial representation of the spoken word. No ancient script attempted to indicate intonation, and even at the present day with all our typographical aids no completely satisfactory system has been devised. It should not be a cause for surprise that, in the transference of speech to writing, such meagre aids as there were should on occasion, possibly because unexpressed in speech, be omitted altogether. Commentators have not always reckoned with the possibility. For instance, in Job xxiii. 17, "For have I not been cut off on account of the darkness?" which is a parallel case to the one under discussion, Bick quite unashamedly deletes the negative.

No objection could be taken to this translation of Exodus vi. 3 in the light of Semitic usage, even if it had only the context to commend it. There is, however, strong support forthcoming from the grammatical structure of the following sentence. This is introduced by the words "and also." Now in Hebrew common syntactical practice demands that where "and also" is preceded by a negative it also introduces a negative clause and vice versa, otherwise we would be faced with a *non sequitur*. In this instance the clause after "and also" is positive, hence one would expect to find the preceding clause a positive one. The translation of the clause as an interrogative would thus remove any illogicality. A perfectly good reason can be given for the use of an interrogative form here: it is a well-known method of giving a phrase an asseverative character. A translation of "and also" in this context by "but" would be highly unsatisfactory if not altogether inadmissible on the ground that the next clause again is introduced by "and also." This makes it extremely hard to avoid drawing the conclusion that we are here dealing with a series of positive statements, the first couched for the sake of emphasis in an interrogative form, and the two subsequent ones introduced by "and also" to bring them into logical co-ordination. (Martin, SCAP, 18–19)

> The Koran provides a helpful parallel to the irregular distribution of the divine names on the Pentateuch. No one questions the single authorship of these Arabic scriptures. Yet they display the same phenomenon as their Hebrew relative.

Finally, it should be noted that the divine name criterion cannot be applied to any material after Exodus 6:3 since from that point on, according to the critics, E and P, like J, are free to use Jehovah. Even Eissfeldt admits this: "Admittedly the difference of divine names may only be used in the analysis of Genesis and the beginning of Exodus. For the two sources we now call E and P avoid the name Yahweh at first and only use it from the moment when God makes this known as his name to Moses—E from Exodus 3:15 and P from Exodus 6:6 on." (Eissfeldt, OTI, 183)

Yet many critics have attempted to show composite authorship for the remaining portions of the Pentateuch on the basis of divine names. It should be obvious that all such attempts have no logical foundation and are therefore invalid.

3B. Similar Use of Divine Names in the Koran

The Koran provides a helpful parallel to the irregular distribution of the divine names on the Pentateuch. No one questions the single authorship of these Arabic scriptures. Yet they display the same phenomenon as their Hebrew relative. The name Allahu parallels with Elohim, and Rabbu ("lord") corresponds to Adonay ("lord"), which the Jews used later to refer to Yahweh. In some suras (chapters) the names are intermingled, but in others only one or the other appears. For example, the name Rabbu never occurs in the following suras: 4, 9, 24, 33, 48, 49, 57, 59, 61, 62, 63, 64, 86, 88, 95, 101, 102, 103, 104, 107, 109, 111, 112; while the name Allahu is never used in these suras: 15, 32, 54, 55, 56, 68, 75, 78, 83, 87, 89, 92, 93, 94, 99, 100, 105, 106, 108, 113, 114.

This is conclusive evidence that ancient Semitic literature was capable of using two names for God, yet with one author. (Archer, SOTI, 111)

4B. Difficulties with the Documentarians' Manipulation of Divine Names

1C. Inconsistency

According to the documentarians, the divine name Yahweh indicates J source, Elohim indicates E source, and P source used Elohim up to Exodus 6:3 but thereafter used Jehovah also.

The following sample passages contain divine names that do not correspond with the right source from which the passage is supposed to come:

a. Elohim occurs in these J source passages:
(1) Genesis 31:50
(2) Genesis 33:5, 11

b. Yahweh occurs in these P source passages before Exodus 6:3:
(1) Genesis 17:1
(2) Genesis 21:1

c. Yahweh occurs in these E source passages:
(1) Genesis 21:33
(2) Genesis 22:4, 11
(3) Genesis 28:21
(4) Exodus 18:1, 8, 9, 10, 11

2C. Appeal to Redactors

The critics' answer to these obvious contradictions is that the redactors (those who

> It is to be noted, therefore, that every appeal to the redactor is a tacit admission on the part of the critics that their theory breaks down at that point.
>
> —OSWALD T. ALLIS

compiled and edited the documents) either made a mistake by copying in the wrong name or took the liberty to arbitrarily inter-change the names here and there. The sec-ond explanation is, of course, appealed to more than the first.

H. H. Rowley is an example:

We need not, therefore, be surprised that the compiler of the Pentateuch should have extracted material from older sources, or should have worked material from more than one source into a continuous narrative, or should have felt himself free to make slight alterations in what he took over, or have com-posed the joins in his narratives. These alter-ations and joins are usually attributed to the Redactor, and it should occasion no surprise that the compiler or redactor has left some traces of his own work. (Rowley, GOT, 25) (See also R. H. Pfeiffer, *Introduction to the Old Testament*, (1941), pp. 282–89.)

Oswald T. Allis comments on such an assumption:

Finally, it is to be noted that what cannot but be regarded as a major defect of the critical analysis appears already quite plainly in con-nection with the use of the divine names: it cannot be carried through without appeal to a redactor or redactors. This means that where simple, even if hairsplitting, partitioning of the text will not give the source analysis desired by the critics, it is alleged that a redactor has altered or edited the sources. If JEHOVAH is regarded as the name of Deity characteristic of J, the addition of ELOHIM in the title Jehovah Elohim in Genesis 2:4b–3:24 has to be attributed to a redactor. (Allis, FBM, 38–39)

Raven points out the fallacious circular reasoning of the critics' appeal to redactors:

Sometimes they sweep aside difficulties by asserting that R altered the name, at others that the text is evidently corrupt. Neither of these suppositions however has any basis out-side of the exigencies of the hypothesis. The

hypothesis is said to be derived from the phe-nomena of the text, as we have it; but if those phenomena do not suit the hypothesis, they are rejected as worthless. May we not reason-ably ask: If the text is corrupt how can we trust the hypothesis which is derived from it? The very existence of R and several R's is a baseless assumption made necessary by the difficulties of the divisive hypothesis. (Raven, OTI, 120)

The implication of all this is well stated by Allis when he concludes: "It is to be noted, therefore, that every appeal to the redactor is a tacit admission on the part of the critics that their theory breaks down at that point." (Allis, FBM, 39)

3C. Extent of Source Division

Even single verses are chopped up into "sources." For example, Genesis 21:1, 2:

(1) "And the LORD [Yahweh] visited Sarah as He had said, and the LORD [Yahweh] did for Sarah as He had spoken.

(2) For Sarah conceived and bore Abraham a son in his old age, at the set time of which God [Elohim] had spoken to him."

Now, according to the critics, "Then the Lord [Yahweh] took note of Sarah as He had said" is assigned to J; "and the Lord [Yahweh] did for Sarah as He had spoken" is assigned to P (in spite of the documentarians' insis-tence that P didn't use "Yahweh" before Exo-dus 6:3); "So Sarah conceived and bore Abraham a son in his old age" is assigned to J; and "at the set time of which God [Elohim] had spoken to him" is assigned to P.

Throughout this discussion we refer to the lists found in *The Interpreter's One-Volume Commentary on the Bible* (IOVCB, 2, 34, 85) in which all the passages in Genesis, Exodus, and Numbers are assigned to their respective sources. These lists are found on pages: 2 (Genesis), 34 (Exodus), and 85 (Numbers).

Nearly one hundred verses in Genesis,

Genesis:

2:4	21:1, 2, 6	41:46
7:16, 17	25:11, 26	42:28
8:2, 3, 13	31:18	45:1, 5
10:1	32:13	46:1
12:4	33:18	47:5, 6, 27
13:11, 12	35:22	48:9, 10
16:1	37:25, 28	49:1, 28
19:30		

Exodus:

1:20	12:27	25:18
2:23	13:3	31:18
3:4	14:9, 19, 20, 21, 27	32:8, 34, 35
4:20	15:21, 22, 25	33:5, 19
7:15, 17, 20, 21	16:13, 15	34:1, 11, 14
8:15	17:1, 2, 7	
9:23, 24, 35	19:2, 3, 9, 11, 13	
10:1, 13, 15	24:12, 15, 18	

Numbers:

13:17, 26	16:1, 2, 26, 27
14:1	20:22

Exodus, and Numbers (listed above) are likewise divided up into at least two sources by the documentarians.

Professor F. Dornseiff of Germany, a student of Greek philology during the 1930s, drew parallels between Greek and Old Testament literature. His comments on the implausibility of the above conclusions (*Zeitschrift für die Alttestamentliche Wissenschaft*, 1934, pp. 57–75) are cited by Aalders: "Who can picture the genesis of a first-rate literary work like the Greek Homer or the Pentateuch by 'redactors' cutting 'sources' into small pieces, and compacting these separate sentences into a new unit, and that in following out such a method they met with a great literary success?" (Aalders, ASIP, 28)

5B. Divine Name Variation in the LXX (Septuagint)

There is much more variation in the use of divine names in the LXX than there is in the Masoretic Text (MT). Documentarians have traditionally used the MT as the basis for their source division, holding that it is by far the more reliable of the two, and have consequently almost totally ignored divine name usage in the LXX.

Archer points out that the usage of divine names as a means of separating documents was first rejected by A. Klostermann (*Der Pentateuch*, 1893), who insisted that the Hebrew text has not been accurately transmitted through the centuries. Johannes Dahse (Dahse, TBAP, n.p.) was the first to come up with a scholarly investigation of the relationship of the MT to the LXX when he showed that the LXX had no less than 180 instances of non-corresponding names (e.g., *theos* for Yahweh or *kyrios* for Elohim). This gives pause to the assumption that the MT is sufficiently well known in all of its variants so that we may autonomically prefer the MT reading in every case over the LXX. Many of these decisions were made before the Dead Sea Scrolls were found, and need to be re-evaluated.

In 1914 J. Skinner replied to Dahse in a book called *The Divine Names in Genesis*, in which he showed that the agreement of divine names in the Masoretic Text and the Samaritan texts (earlier than the LXX) extends to over three hundred cases, while there were only eight or nine differences. Critics have assumed that Skinner's "crushing reply" (Albright, OTAP, 79) to Dahse was final on the issue of divine names and the LXX. But as a result of the findings of the Dead Sea Scrolls, scholars are now quite confident that there were at least three separate families of manuscripts existing before the Masoretic period. Therefore the close agreement of the Masoretic Text with the Samaritan texts probably means nothing more than that they came from the same manuscript tradition. It does not prove that the MT is closer to the original text than the LXX.

In 1908, in his *Die Komposition der Genesis*, B. D. Eerdmans, Kuenen's successor at the University of Leiden, also admitted that this argument based on Septuagintal data was a powerful one and asserted that it was impossible to use the divine names as evidence for separate documents. (Archer, SOTI, 84–85)

Wellhausen himself admitted (in a private letter to J. Dahse, published in 1912) that the argument against using the divine names as a criterion in light of the variations in usage in the LXX had "touched the weak point of his theory." (Aalders, ASIP, 21)

Harrison speaks of how the Dead Sea Scrolls have strengthened the opinion that there was possibly more variation of divine names in the original text than the MT allows:

That there were at least three distinct families of Hebrew manuscripts in existence in the pre-Massoretic period has been demonstrated convincingly as a result of the manuscript discoveries at Qumran, and in particular from the fragments recovered from 4Q, thereby confirming the opinion that there was considerably more variety in the text of early Pentateuchal manuscripts than was the case with the MT itself. Since the latter has traditionally been used as the basis of documentary analysis in view of the fact that it was regarded as the "fixed" text, it is interesting to speculate as to what might have happened to the entire Graf-Wellhausen theory had one or more pre-Massoretic texts been available for the use of nineteenth-century literary critics. The answer has in fact been supplied to a large extent by Albright, who, as mentioned above, has stated that the fragmentary manuscripts recovered from 4Q have already seriously undermined the foundations of detailed literary criticism. (Harrison, IOT, 518)

Harrison speaks about some of the textual evidence at Qumran "which shows that it was eminently possible for the translators of the LXX version to have had several manuscript families of the Pentateuch at their disposal, whose nature and contents were by no means identical in all respects with those of the Massoretic tradition." (Harrison, IOT, 518)

23
THE REPETITION OF ACCOUNTS AND ALLEGED CONTRADICTIONS

1A. REPETITION OF ACCOUNTS

1B. Introduction

Certain stories in the Pentateuch are said to be repeated twice. Other stories are said to have contradictory details (i.e., Creation: Gen. 1–2:4a-P; 2:4b–25-J; Flood: Gen. 6:1–8; 7:1–5, 7–10, 12, 16b, 17b, 22–23; 8:2b–3a, 6–12, 13b, 20–22-J; Gen. 6:9–22; 7:6, 11, 13–16a, 17a [except "forty days"], 18–21, 24; 8:1-2a, 3b–5, 13a, 14–19-P). (Bright, HI, 159)

2B. Documentary Assumption

Since no author would have reason to repeat the same story twice, the repetition of certain narratives (parallel accounts) indicates more than one author at work. Also, since one author could hardly be charged with giving us obviously contradictory details, those stories in which such discrepancies occur are the work of a redactor or editor who wove together two different accounts of the same story (interwoven accounts).

Rollin Walker speaks for this view (*A Study of Genesis and Exodus*, p. 24), as cited by O. T. Allis: "Toward the question of the precise historical accuracy of the stories of the books of Genesis and Exodus we ought to take somewhat the same attitude that the editor of the books took when he gave us parallel and conflicting accounts of the same event, and thereby confessed that he was not sure which of the two was exactly right." (Allis, FBM, 123)

Otto Eissfeldt lists no less than nineteen allegedly repetitious or contradictory accounts. (Eissfeldt, OTI, 189–90)

3B. Basic Answer

Supposed double and triple accounts of the same story are actually different stories with similar details.

Concerning the dual accounts of certain stories in the Pentateuch, Raven notes that "these accounts are not really parallel. Some

> The supposed contradictory details in certain stories are in fact supplementary details and are seen as being contradictory only when the stories are misinterpreted.

of them are merely similar events, as the two instances in which Abraham lied concerning his wife and the same action later taken by Isaac. The redactor must have considered these quite distinct. In other cases there is a repetition from a different standpoint, as the account of the creation in Genesis 2 is from the standpoint of the God of revelation and providence. Sometimes the repetition is a characteristic of Hebrew style, which often

makes a general statement by way of introduction and then enlarges upon it." (Raven, OTI, 124–25)

The supposed contradictory details in certain stories are in fact supplementary details and are seen as being contradictory only when the stories are misinterpreted.

1C. The Creation Story

H. H. Rowley says: "For instance, between the two accounts of the Creation there is a disagreement as to the sequence of creation, a difference in the usage of the divine names, a difference in the conception of God, and a difference of style." (Rowley, GOT, 24) (See also Driver, BG, 35–36)

Attacking this position, Kitchen points out that two lines of argument have been drawn in favor of a double narrative of the creation accounts: theological and stylistic differences between Genesis 1 and 2 and a seemingly different order of creation. The style differences have no weight as an argument and simply reflect changes in subject matter; and the understanding of a transcendent God in Genesis 1 as opposed to an anthropomorphic God in Genesis 2 is "vastly overdrawn and frankly, illusory." (Kitchen, AOOT, 118)

E. J. Young illustrates this: "The anthropomorphic God of Genesis 2 'fashions,' 'breathes,' 'plants,' 'places,' 'takes,' 'sets,' 'brings,' 'closes up,' 'builds,' 'walks.' But the critics have quite a superficial argument. Man in his finite mind cannot express ideas about God in anything but anthropomorphisms. Chapter 1 of Genesis expresses God in such equally anthropomorphic terms as, 'called,' 'saw,' 'blessed,' 'deliberated' (verse 26 'let us make'), God 'worked' for six days then He 'rested.'" (Young, IT, 51)

Kitchen continues: "The same may be said of the order of events. In Genesis 2:19, there is no explicit warrant in the text for assuming that the creation of animals here happened immediately before their naming (*i.e.*, after man's creation); this is eisegesis, not exegesis. The proper equivalent in English for the first verb in Genesis 2:19 is the pluperfect ('. . . had formed . . .'). Thus the artificial difficulty over the order of events disappears." (Kitchen, AOOT, 118)

An essential difference in the two accounts must be appreciated: Genesis 1 describes the creation of the world, while Genesis 2 details and further describes the specific creation of Adam and of his immediate environment in the Garden of Eden. This is highlighted by the introductory phrase in Genesis 2:4, "These are the generations of the heavens and of the earth when they were created, in the day that Yahweh Elohim made the earth and the heavens." Throughout Genesis the phrase "these are the generations" occurs nine other times, each time introducing an account of the offspring descended from a specific ancestor. This would then indicate that in the verses following Genesis 2:4, we will find an account of the offspring of the heavens and earth after the initial creation has taken place. And that is just what we find here in the case of Adam and Eve (v. 7: "Yahweh Elohim formed man of *dust from the ground*"). (Archer, SOTI, 118)

It must be emphasized that we do not have here an example of incompatible repetition. We have an example of a skeletal outline of creation as a whole, followed by a detailed focus on the final point of the outline—man. Lack of recognition of this common Hebrew literary device, in the words of Kitchen, "borders on obscurantism." (Kitchen, AOOT, 116–17)

Kitchen then shows how archaeology has brought this type of literary pattern to light. Just such a literary pattern is commonplace in other texts of the ancient Near East. On the Karnak Poetical Stela from Egypt, the address of Amun to King Tuthmosis III breaks down thus:

> Paragraph One: expressing his general supremacy (Would the diversified style indicate a J source?)
>
> Paragraph Two: more precise poetical expression of supremacy (Would the rigidity indicate a P source?)

The Gebel Barker Stela is similar:

> Paragraph One: general royal supremacy (J source?)
>
> Paragraph Two: specific triumphs in Syria-Palestine (P source?)

Several of the royal inscriptions of Urartu are likewise enlightening:

> Paragraph One: victory over specified lands ascribed to the chariot of the god Haldi (Would an "H" source be indicated by the brief, rigid style?)
>
> Paragraph Two: detailed repetition of description of these victories, this time as achieved by the king (Is a "K" source indicated by this detailed, varied style?)

Just as an assignment of the various portions of these Egyptian texts to different documents is unheard of in scholarly circles, so is it absurd to practice a dissection of sources in their contemporary literature found in Genesis one and two. (Kitchen, AOOT, 117)

> Just as an assignment of the various portions of these Egyptian texts to different documents is unheard of in scholarly circles, so is it absurd to practice a dissection of sources in their contemporary literature found in Genesis one and two.

Orr explains it this way:

To the *beginnings of things,* how constantly is it alleged that "we have two contradictory accounts of the *creation.*" It is certain that the narratives in Gen. i.–ii. 4 and chap. ii. 4 ff. are quite different in character and style, and view the work of creation from different standpoints. But they are not "contradictory"; they are, in fact, bound together in the closest manner as complementary. The second narrative, taken by itself, begins abruptly, with manifest reference to the first: "In the day that Jehovah Elohim made earth and heaven" (ver. 4). It is, in truth a misnomer to speak of chap. ii. as an account of the "creation" at all, in the same sense as chap. i. It contains no account of the creation of either earth or heaven, or of the general world of vegetation; its interest centers in the making of man and woman, and everything in the narrative is regarded from that point of view. (Orr, POT, 346–47)

2C. The Naming of Isaac

It is theorized that the accounts of three different documents regarding the naming of Isaac have been included in Genesis (Gen. 17:17 from P, 18:12 from J, and 21:6 from E). But is it unreasonable to assume that both Abraham and Sarah laughed with disbelief when they were individually told that Isaac would be born, and that they later laughed with joy at his birth?

3C. Abraham's Deceit

The critics allege that the two occurrences of Abraham passing Sarah off as his sister are merely variations of the same event. It is naive to assume that men never make the same mistake twice nor yield to the same temptation more than once. In this case, the weakness of the assumption is magnified by the consideration that Abraham profited financially on both occasions. (Archer, SOTI, 120)

4C. Isaac's Deceit

When Isaac allowed his wife to be regarded as his sister while Abimelech was king of the Philistines in Gerar (Gen. 26:6–11), he provided striking similarities to the E account of Abraham and Sarah in Genesis 20. If these are to be understood as differing versions of the same event that have been incorporated into Genesis by the redactor, several very difficult assumptions must be made: (1) that sons never follow the bad example of the parents, (2) that the sexual habits of the people of Gerar had changed for the better by the time of Isaac, (3) that the Philistine dynasties never handed down the same name from ruler to ruler, (i.e., Abimelech I, Abimelech II, and so forth), even though in Egypt the twelfth dynasty practiced the exact same thing (Amenemhat I, II, and III, and also Senwosret I, II, and III). The same practice occurred in Phoenicia. A series of Hirams or Ahirams ruled in Tyre and Byblos. It is noteworthy that the account of Abraham's first deception concerning his relationship to Sarah (Gen. 12) is assigned to J along with the similar Genesis 26 account of Isaac and Rebekah. Another instance of "repetitive" accounts being allowed by the critics to stand as genuinely separate events

> [In] the royal inscriptions at Urartu, . . . one paragraph attributes victory over specified nations to the chariot of the god Haldi and the next paragraph repeats the same victories in more detail as accomplished by the king. No scholar would think of dividing this account into various sources upon such grounds.

is seen in the assigning to E of both of Jacob's visits to Bethel (Gen. 35:1–8 and Gen. 28:18–22). (Archer, SOTI, 120–21)

5C. The Naming of the Well at Beersheba

In Genesis we discover two stories of the naming of the well at Beersheba—first by Abraham in Genesis 21:31 (assigned to E) and then by Isaac in Genesis 26:33 (attributed to P). But there is no evidence that these are actually two (J and P) versions of the same original episode. In light of the nomadic habits of Abraham and Isaac, it is more likely that the well was stopped up by Abraham's enemies upon his departure, only to be reopened by Isaac when he returned to his father's old rangeland. And it is reasonable to see Isaac reviving the old name and reconfirming the treaty which gave him the right to the well. (Archer, SOTI, 121)

6C. Jacob's Flocks Prosper

Driver divides Genesis 30:25 through 31:18 into two sections: Genesis 30:25–31, which comes mainly from the J source; and Genesis 31:2–18, taken mainly from the E source. He confirms:

"The two sources give a different account of the arrangement between Jacob and Laban, and of the manner in which, nevertheless, Jacob prospered. The success which in 30, 35 ff. is attributed to Jacob's stratagem, with the effect of the striped rods upon the ewes in the flock, is in 31:7–12 attributed to the frustration by Providence of Laban's attempt, by repeatedly altering his terms, to overreach Jacob, and to the fact that only the striped he-goats leaped upon the ewes." (Driver, ILOT, 15)

When these two chapters are heard for what they are saying and are evaluated in light of the rest of Scripture as well as the ancient Near East, they neither contain any discrepancy nor require divergent sources. Chapter 30 contains the author's objective description of the selective breeding that Jacob practiced in this situation. In chapter 31 the author relates the event from Jacob's perspective (by dialogue) as Jacob, speaking to his wives, ascribes to the all-provident God the credit for both his knowledge and success in the venture. Jacob had to acknowledge in the end that it was not any prenatal influence stratagem at work (does it at all work?) but only God! So Genesis 30 *reports* what Jacob did and hoped for, but Genesis 31 *teaches* what was actually so, and even Jacob had to agree. In the process, Jacob relates complementary but not contradictory details.

Numerous examples of an event being described from both the human and the divine perspective may be found in Scripture (Judg. 7:7, 21–23; Ex. 14:21; Gen. 4:1).

This may also be found in other ancient Near Eastern cultures. Kitchen cites the royal inscriptions at Urartu, in which one paragraph attributes victory over specified nations to the chariot of the god Haldi and the next paragraph repeats the same victories in more detail as accomplished by the king. No scholar would think of dividing this account into various sources upon such grounds. (Kitchen, AOOT, 117)

7C. The Continuity of Isolated Documents

Eissfeldt states that one of the characteristic features of the Pentateuchal narratives is "the interweaving of compiled parallels, which are therefore incomplete." (Eissfeldt, OTI, 189) (See also Driver, ILOT, 8 and Chapman, IP, 76–77)

One of the destructive higher critics' reasons for holding that there are various sources interwoven in certain narratives is the argument that when these sources are isolated and all the J passages put together and all the P passages put together, there are formed two separate continuous and coherent stories.

In his book *The Higher Criticism of the Pentateuch,* the late William H. Green gave a brilliant illustration of the arbitrary nature of this argument. He took the New Testament parable of the prodigal son and subjected it to the same treatment to which the documentarians were subjecting some of the Pentateuchal narratives. Here are his results (phrases in parentheses Green attributes to a "redactor"):

The Prodigal Son, Luke 15:11–32

A	B
11. A certain man had two sons: 12. and the younger of them said to his father, Father, give me the portion of thy substance that falleth to me. . . .	(A certain man had two sons:) 12b. and he divided unto them his living.
13. And not many days after the younger son gathered all together, . . . and there he wasted his substance with riotous living. . . .	13b. And (one of them) took his journey into a far country. . . . 14. And when he had spent all, there arose a mighty famine in that country. . . . 15. And he went and joined himself to one of the citizens of that country; and he sent him into his fields to feed swine. 16. And he would fain have been filled with the husks that the swine did eat. . . . 17. But when he came to himself he said, How many hired servants of my father's have bread enough and to spare, and I perish here with hunger! 18. I will arise and go to my father, and will say unto him, Father, I have sinned against heaven, and in thy sight: 19. I am no more worthy to be called thy son: make me as one of thy hired servants. . . . 20b. But while he was yet afar off, his father saw him, and was moved with compassion: . . . 23. and (said) Bring the fatted calf, and kill it, and let us eat, and make merry. . . . 24b. he was lost, and is found. . . . 25b. (And the other son) heard music and dancing. 26. And he called to him one of the servants, and inquired what these things might be. 27. And he said unto him, Thy brother is come; and thy father hath killed the fatted calf, because he hath received him safe and sound . . . 32b. and he was lost and is found. (Green, HCP, 119–20)

14b. and he began to be in want.

16b. And no man gave unto him.

20. And he arose, and came to his father; . . . and he ran, and fell on his neck, and kissed him. 21. And the son said unto him, Father, I have sinned against heaven, and in thy sight: I am no more worthy to be called thy son. 22. But the father said to his servants, Bring forth quickly the best robe, and put it on him; and put a ring on his hand, and shoes on his feet: . . . 24. for this my son was dead, and is alive again. . . . And they began to be merry. 25. Now his elder son was in the field: and as he came and drew nigh to the house, . . . 28. he was angry, and would not go in: and his father came out, and entreated him. 29. But he answered and said to his father, Lo, these many years do I serve thee, and I never transgressed a commandment of thine: and yet thou never gavest me a kid, that I might make merry with my friends: 30. but when this thy son came, which hath devoured thy living with harlots, thou killedst for him the fatted calf. 31. And he said unto him, Son, thou art ever with me, and all that is mine is thine. 32. But it was meet to make merry and be glad: for this thy brother was dead, and is alive again.

Although these two stories were arbitrarily manufactured by Green out of the one story, each has unique characteristics which, by someone unfamiliar with Green's clever scheme, might be induced as evidence for composite authorship:

A and B agree that there were two sons, one of whom received a portion of his father's property, and by his own fault was reduced to great destitution, in consequence of which he returned penitently to his father, and addressed him in language which is nearly identical in both accounts. The father received him with great tenderness and demonstrations of joy, which attracted the attention of the other son.

The differences are quite as striking as the points of agreement. A distinguishes the sons as elder and younger; B makes no mention of their relative ages. In A the younger obtained his portion by solicitation, and the father retained the remainder in his own possession; in B the father divided his property between both of his sons of his own motion. In A the prodigal remained in his father's neighborhood, and reduced himself to penury by riotous living; in B he went to a distant country and spent all his property, but there is no intimation that he indulged in unseemly excesses. It would rather appear that he was injudicious; and to crown his misfortunes there occurred a severe famine. His fault seems to have consisted in having gone so far away from his father and from the holy land, and in engaging in the unclean occupation of tending swine. In A the destitution seems to have been chiefly want of clothing; in B want of food. Hence in A the father directed the best robe and ring and shoes to be brought for him; in B the fatted calf was killed. In B the son came from a distant land, and the father saw him afar off, in A he came from the neighborhood, and the father ran at once and fell on his neck and kissed him. In B he had been engaged in a menial occupation, and so bethought himself of his father's hired servants, and asked to be made a servant himself; in A he had been living luxuriously, and while confessing his unworthiness makes no request to be put on the footing of a servant. In A the father speaks of his son having been dead because of his profligate life; in B of his having been lost because of his absence in a distant land. In A, but not in B, the other son was displeased at the reception given to the prodigal. And here it would appear that R has slightly altered the text. The elder son must have said to his father in A, "When this thy son came, which hath devoured thy substance with harlots, thou didst put on him the best robe." The redactor has here substituted the B word "living" for "substance," which is used by A; and with the view of making a better contrast with "kid" he has introduced the B phrase, "thou killedst for him the fatted calf." (Green, HCP, 121–22)

Green points out another similar experiment, a work entitled "Romans Dissected" by E. D. McRealsham, the pseudonym of Professor C. M. Mead, formerly of Hartford Theological Seminary. Green comments: "The result of his ingenious and scholarly discussion is to demonstrate that as plausible an argument can be made from diction, style, and doctrinal contents for the fourfold division of the Epistle to the Romans as for the composite character of the Pentateuch." (Green, HCP, 125)

1D. The Flood Story
Rowley writes:

Again in the story of the Flood we find that according to Gen. vi. 19f. Noah is commanded to take a single pair of every species into the Ark, whereas according to Gen. vii. 2 he is bidden to take seven pairs of clean beasts and a single pair of unclean. Gen. vii. 8f. emphasizes this contradiction with its specific statement that of clean and unclean a single pair went into the Ark, though it is possible that the emphasis on the contradiction is not original. Similarly there is disagreement in the duration of the Flood. According to Gen. vii. 12 the rains lasted forty days, after which, according to vii. 6ff., Noah waited for certain periods of seven days before the waters were abated, whereas according to Gen. vii. 24 the waters prevailed for a hundred and fifty days, and were not finally abated until a year and ten days after the beginning of the Flood (vii. 14; cf. vii.). (Rowley, GOT, 18)

Kitchen argues:

It has often been claimed, for example, that Genesis 7 to 8 gives two different estimates for the duration of the Flood, but in fact these are purely the invention of the theory. The biblical text as it stands is wholly consistent in giving a year and ten days (eleven, if first and last are both counted) as the total duration of the Flood episode, as clearly pointed out by Aalders, Heidel and others long ago. Likewise, the supposed clash between Genesis 6:19, 20 (cf. Gn. 7:8, 9) and Genesis 7:2, 3 over "two by two" or "seven pairs" is imaginary. In Genesis 6:20 *shenayim*, "pair," is probably being used as a collective for "pairs," seeing that one cannot form a plural of a dual word in Hebrew (no *shenayimim!*); Genesis 6:19, 20 and 7:8, 9 are general statements while Genesis 7:2, 3 (clearly twos and sevens) is specific. (Kitchen, AOOT, 120)

Alexander Heidel provides us with a thorough investigation concerning the biblical account of the duration of the Flood:

Modern biblical criticism, as is well known, sees in the Genesis account of the deluge a blending of two main, in several respects irreconcilably contradictory, sources put together by a redactor. According to the one source, called P (or the Priestly Code), the flood began on the seventeenth day of the second month (7:11) and ended on the twenty-seventh day of the second month of the following year (8:13-14), the whole occurrence thus extending over a period of one year and eleven days. But according to the other source, called J (or the Yahwistic Narrative), it rained for forty days and forty nights (7:12), at the end of which Noah opened the window of the ark and sent forth four birds at intervals of three successive periods of seven days (8:6–12), whereupon he removed the covering of the ark and found that the face of the ground was dry (vs. 13 *b*); accordingly, the duration of the flood was only sixty-one days.

With this view I cannot agree. However, this is not the place to enter upon a detailed discussion of the problems involved; a few words will have to suffice. I do by no means deny that a number of different documents may have been utilized in the composition of the biblical flood story, for the Scriptures themselves indicate unmistakably that the sacred penmen employed written records and the like in the preparation of their books. But, in spite of the claims that have been made, I am not at all convinced that the biblical material can be resolved into its constituent elements with any degree of certainty. Moreover, I am not in sympathy with the common practice of treating the alleged remnants of each supposed document as if it constituted the whole, with the result that the Genesis account of the deluge, with which alone we are at present concerned, fairly teems with discrepancies. It must be apparent to every unprejudiced reader that the Genesis version of the flood, as divided by modern biblical criticism, shows several important gaps in the portions assigned to J and P. Therefore, if we had access to the complete text of the supposed documents denominated J and P (assuming, for the sake of argument, that such documents ever existed), we might see at once that there were no discrepancies at all between the two. But even without such access, it has

> It has been demonstrated repeatedly that the alleged contradictions in the Genesis narrative are capable of a simple and reasonable solution if the story is left as we find it in the Hebrew text.
>
> —ALEXANDER HEIDEL

been demonstrated repeatedly that the alleged contradictions in the Genesis narrative are capable of a simple and reasonable solution if the story is left as we find it in the Hebrew text.

A good illustration of this we have in the point under examination—the duration of the flood. If we leave the biblical text as it stands and treat the story as one whole, the numerical data on the duration of the deluge are in perfect harmony, as shown by the following.

According to 7:11, the flood began in the six hundredth year of Noah's life, on the seventeenth day of the second month, coming seven days after Noah had received the command to enter the ark (7:1–4, 10). For forty days and forty nights it rained upon the earth (vs. 12). It is not said anywhere that after this period the downpour stopped *altogether*. On the contrary, the rain and the gushing-forth of the subterranean springs continued; for it is clearly stated that the fountains of the deep and the windows of heaven were not closed and that the rain from heaven was not stopped . . . until the end of the one hundred and fiftieth day after the outbreak of the flood, for which reason the waters kept rising or maintained their maximum height during all this time (7:24–8:2). But while the flow of the subterranean waters may have continued with great force even after the first forty days, the uninterrupted and unrestrained torrential downpour from heaven must have ceased and the rain must have continued much more moderately, for we read in 7:12: "The rain came upon the earth forty days and forty nights," and in verse 17: "The flood *(mabbûl)* came upon the earth forty days." As pointed out before, the term *mabbûl* in verse 17 undoubtedly describes the unprecedented stream of rain from above, which made the waters mount on the surface of the earth. From this it seems quite obvious that it was the unchecked torrential rain or the sheets of water from the sky which ceased after the first forty days.

At the end of the 150 days the waters began to decrease (8:3), and on the seventeenth day of the seventh month the ark rested on one of the mountains of Ararat (vs. 4). This was exactly five months and 1 day from the beginning of the flood (cf. 7:11). The obvious conclusion appears to be that the 150 days constituted 5 months and that each month, consequently, consisted of 30 days. On the day that the waters began to abate, i.e., on the one hundred and fifty-first day from the commencement of the flood, the ark grounded. The waters continued to decrease until, on the first day of the tenth month, the tops of the mountains became visible (8:5). If a month is reckoned at 30 days, this gives us 74 additional days, yielding a total of 225 days. At the end of 40 days from this date, i.e., the first of the tenth month, Noah opened the window of the ark and sent forth four birds at intervals of three successive periods of 7 days (vss. 6–12). Since the first bird was released on the forty-first day, these figures add up to 62 more days and bring the total up to 287 days. The last bird was sent forth on the two hundred and eighty-seventh day from the beginning of the deluge, or (adding the 46 days of the year which elapsed before the outbreak of the flood) on the three hundred and thirty-third day of the year. We have, accordingly, arrived at the third day of the twelfth month. Twenty-eight days later, on the first day of the following year, in the six hundred and first year of Noah's life, the waters were dried up from off the earth (but the surface of the ground was not yet fully dry) and Noah removed the covering of the ark (vs. 13). A month and 26 days after that, on the twenty-seventh of the second month, the earth was again dry and firm, and Noah left the ark (vss. 14 ff.). These two periods amount to 84 days. Adding these days to the 287, we gain a grand total of 371 days, or 1 year and 11 days, beginning with the outbreak of the flood. There is here no discrepancy whatever. (Heidel, GEOTP, 245–47)

Not only are the alleged discrepancies nonexistent, but the two accounts are organically dependent upon one another and thus already form a unit. Raven demonstrates this:

The critics have been unable to extract two records of the flood even tolerably complete. The beginning of chapter seven is assigned to J. If so, we are told by J that God commanded Noah to come with all his house into the ark, without telling a word about the building of the ark or the members of Noah's family. Chapter seven needs precisely the statement of Chap. 6:9–22 to make it complete or comprehensible. Gen. 8:13 says: "And Noah removed the covering of the ark and looked and behold the face of the ground was dry—" This is assigned to J but not another word of J is recorded till verse 20 where we read: "And Noah builded an altar unto the Lord." This serious gap is bridged by the intervening statements which the critics assigned to P. Furthermore Gen. 9:1–17 (P) is not a useless repetition of Gen. 8:12–22 (J) but an enlargement of God's covenant with Noah after he had built the altar to Jehovah and recommenced his life upon earth. (Raven, OTI, 125)

2D. Abraham's Journey

The critics also have "discovered" two interwoven stories in chapters 11 through 13 of Genesis, which Orr describes and answers thus:

After many variations of opinion, the critics have settled down to give Gen. xi. 28–30 to J, and ver. 27, 31, and 32 to P; beyond this only chaps. xii. 4b, 5, and xiii. 6, 11b, 12 are assigned to P in chaps. xii., xiii. But this yields some remarkable results. In chap. xi. 28, the J story begins quite abruptly, without telling us who Terah, Haran, Abram, and Nahor are; *i.e.,* it needs ver. 27 for its explanation. The residence of the family is placed by J in Ur of the Chaldees (elsewhere given as a P mark), and nothing is related of the migration to Haran (cf. P, vers. 31, 32). Yet this migration is apparently assumed in the call to Abraham in Gen. xii. 1. In ver. 6, Abraham is said to have "passed through the land into the place of Sichem," but we are not told *what* land. It is P alone who tells of his departure from Haran, and

coming to the land of Canaan (ver. 4b, 5). But this very fragment in P assumes the departure from Haran as a thing known (ver. 4b), and so needs the first part of the verse, given to J. In other words, the story, as it stands, is a unity; divided, its connection is destroyed. (Orr, POT, 351)

3D. Isaac's Blessing

Genesis 27 has likewise failed to escape the scalpel of the critics. The chapter opens with the account of Isaac's preparations to bestow his blessing upon Esau. The first four verses provide an excellent example of arbitrary methods by the critics in dissecting passages.

Verse one reads "Now it came to pass, when Isaac was old and his eyes were so dim that he could not see, that he called Esau his older son and said to him, 'My son.' And he answered, 'Here I am.'" Because this passage is given to J, the final phrase "and said to him, 'My son.' And he answered, 'Here I am'" is deleted as a feature unique to E. But certainly such a basic formula cannot be reasonably assigned to one author and excluded from all others. This is not even supported by the text, for Genesis 22:11 records the words, "But the Angel of the LORD [Yahweh] called to him from heaven and said, 'Abraham, Abraham!' So he said, 'Here I am.'" Not only do the critics here replace Yahweh with Elohim, but they go on to assign to E every passage containing the formula but no divine name. This is a blatant example of arguing in a circle. And further, if in Genesis 27:1 the formula were removed, we would expect verse two to read, "And Isaac said *to him*." But this word is missing from the Hebrew text and confirms that this sentence is not the conversation opener.

Verses 2 through 4 continue, "Then he [Isaac] said, 'Behold now, I am old. I do not know the day of my death. Now therefore, please take your weapons, your quiver and your bow, and go out to the field and hunt game for me. And make me savory food, such as I love, and bring it to me that I may eat, that my soul may bless you before I die.'" Claiming that the words "and make me savory food . . . that I may eat," represent a variant motif of the same story, the phrase is deleted and assigned to E. The other variant of this motif, majoring on "game" as opposed to the "savory food," goes to J. Thus J reads, "Now then, please take your quiver . . . and hunt game for me, so that my soul may bless you before I die." Yet this totally eliminates the crucial point that Esau return with the game and serve it to his father. On the other hand, J reads, "And make me savory food such as I love . . . so that my soul may bless you before I die." Here our story is further twisted so that Esau, the valiant hunter, is relegated to the more mundane role of cook.

Taken as we have it, this passage is clearly a sensible, lucid unit; dissected, it is meaningless. (Cassuto, DH, 87–97)

4D. The Story of Joseph
Rowley speaks of contradictions in this story also: "In Gen. xxxvi. 27 Judah proposes that Joseph should be sold to some Ishmaelites, and the following verse states that this was done, while Gen. xxxix. 1 says the Ishmaelites sold him to an Egyptian. But Gen. xxxvii. 28a introduces Midianites who passed by and kidnaped Joseph from the pit, without the knowledge of his brethren (29f.), and who later sold Joseph to Potiphar (xxxvii. 36)." (Rowley, GOT, 18–19)

Kitchen again answers the charge:

It is also often asserted that Genesis 37 contains parts of two irreconcilable accounts of how Joseph was sold into Egypt: (a) by his brothers to the Ishmaelites and so into Egypt (Gn. 37:25, 28b; cf. 45:4, 5), and (b) by the

Midianites who took him from the pit (Gn. 37:28a, 36; cf. 40:14, 15). The truth is much simpler.

First, the terms "Ishmaelites/Midianites" overlap, and refer to the same group in whole or in part (cf. Jdg. 8:24).

Secondly, the pronoun "they" in Genesis 37:28 refers back to Joseph's brothers, not to the Midianites. In Hebrew, the antecedent of a pronoun is not always the last preceding noun. If this were not so the phrase "he has brought an evil name . . ." in Deuteronomy 22:19 would refer to the innocent father; likewise the pronouns "his" and "he" in Deuteronomy 22:29 go back to an erring other man; and so elsewhere in Hebrew. In Egypt, after talking to Tuthmosis II, Ineni mentions the accession of "his (Tuthmosis II's) son," Tuthmosis II, and then the real rule of "his sister, . . . Hatshepsut." But "his" here refers back to Tuthmosis II, not to his son.

Thirdly, in private conversation Joseph could be blunt with his own brothers (Gn. 45:4, 5, "you sold . . ."), but in seeking a favour from the royal butler, an alien, he could not very well reveal the humiliating fact that his own blood brothers wanted to be rid of him (Gn. 40: 14, 15)—however unjustly, what kind of impression would that admission have made on the butler? (Kitchen, AOOT, 119–20)

(It should be noted that this reference to being "kidnapped" in Genesis 40:14, 15 is totally accurate since Joseph was literally kidnapped from his father by his brothers and it was ultimately because of them that he was taken out of "the land of the Hebrews.")

Lamenting a critical attack upon a passage much like the instances described above, Cassuto appropriately remarks that the passage "affords a classic example of outstandingly beautiful narrative art, and by dismembering it we only destroy a wonderful literary work, the like of which it is hard to find." (Cassuto, DH, 96)

8C. Other Evidence Explaining Repetitious Accounts

Hebrew style is marked by three distinctive traits that illuminate the problem of repetitious accounts:

1D. Paratactic sentence structure is the practice, writes Archer, "by which subordinate or interdependent ideas are linked

> The Bible is a very emphatic book. Its aim is to impress upon the hearer or reader the great importance of the themes of which it treats. The most natural way of securing emphasis in a narrative is by amplification or reiteration. Consequently the Biblical style is often decidedly diffuse and characterized by elaborateness of detail and by repetition.
>
> —OSWALD T. ALLIS

together by the simple connective "and" (Heb. *We*)." (Archer, SOTI, 122) This word thus may be used to convey the meaning of "in order that," "when," "while," "then," "even," or "that is to say"—a versatility acknowledged by all Hebrew grammarians.

Allis elaborates further:

The Hebrew not infrequently uses dependent clauses as the English does. But very often coordinates clauses by "and" where we would subordinate one to the other. . . . It is to be noted, therefore, that this tendency to join complete sentences together loosely by "and" may make it appear that the writer is repeating himself; and these loosely connected sentences which all refer to the same event or topic may seem more or less repetitious and to be lacking in strictly logical or chronological sequence. And the very simplicity of the syntax makes it a relatively easy matter to cut apart such sentences, to assert that they describe the same event from different and even conflicting viewpoints and must be assigned to different sources. Were the Biblical narratives written in complicated periodic sentences in the style of an Addison, such analysis would be far more difficult if not impossible. (Allis, FBM, 96–97)

A misunderstanding of this basic principle allows many to assume that a late editor clumsily glued his sources together with the word "and." But a similar dissection would be impossible in languages which are more precise in this respect, such as classical Greek and Latin. (Archer, SOTI, 122)

2D. Repetition for emphasis is seen in the "tendency to repeat in slightly varied form those elements of the narrative which are of special importance," states Archer. (Archer, SOTI, 122)

Allis develops this idea, explaining that "the Bible is a very emphatic book. Its aim is to impress upon the hearer or reader the great importance of the themes of which it treats. The most natural way of securing emphasis in a narrative is by amplification or reiteration. Consequently the Biblical style is often decidedly diffuse and characterized by elaborateness of detail and by repetition." (Allis, FBM, 97)

The account of the ten plagues (Ex. 7—11) provides an excellent example of this. Some of the plagues are described in as many as five steps: threat, command, enaction, prayer for removal, and termination. By misunderstanding the emphatic nature of this repetition, the radical critics have given seven plagues to J, five plagues to E, and only four to P (not including a fifth which is threatened but not executed). This leaves us with three incomplete accounts, each needing the material in the others to form a sensible entity. (Archer, SOTI, 122–23)

3D. Poetic parallelism, in Archer's words, is the "balanced structure of paired clauses which is employed so extensively in Hebrew verse." (Archer, SOTI, 123)

Again, Allis provides a clear statement of the issue:

In dealing with the question of repetitions, it is important to note that repetition or parallelism in phraseology and content (*parallelismus membrorum*) is a characteristic feature of Hebrew poetry. This is so obvious that proof is unnecessary. A familiar illustration of practically synonymous parallelism is as follows:

"The law of Jehovah is perfect, restoring the soul,
     The testimony of Jehovah is sure, making wise the simple"
(Ps. xix. 7). (Allis, FBM, 108)

In demonstrating the role of such parallelism beyond the boundaries of poetry, Allis expresses that "it has been clearly shown that the dividing line between prose and poetry is not fixed and sharply defined but that elevated or impassioned prose may approximate very closely to poetry, balanced repetition or parallelism." (Allis, FBM, 108–9)

When the divine names are alternated in such a parallel fashion, it should clearly be attributed to the poetic style, not to divergent sources. Verses 23 and 24 of Genesis 30 illustrate this: "*Elohim* has taken away (*'asaf'*) my reproach. . . . May *Yahweh* add (*'yosef'*) to me another son."

To divide this passage into E and J due to the divine names (as the critics do) is to fail to recognize the poetic purpose of the alternation of the names and to violate the clear poetic parallelism of "asaf" and "yosef." (Archer, SOTI, 122–23)

4D. Gordon correlates the Hebrew style with other ancient oriental styles:

One of the commonest grounds for positing differences of authorship are the repetitions, with variants, in the Bible. But such repetitions are typical of ancient Near East literature: Babylonian, Ugaritic, and even Greek. Moreover, the tastes of the Bible world called for duplication. Joseph and later Pharaoh, each had prophetic dreams in duplicate. In Jonah 4, the Prophet's chagrin is described at two stages, each accompanied by God's asking "Are you good and angry?" (vv. 4, 9). Would anyone insist that such duplicates stem from different pens? (Gordon, HCFF, 132)

5D. The Critics' Inconsistency

Allis points out also the inconsistency of the documentarians in not identifying as repetitious the references to Moses' and Aaron's deaths:

Three statements are made in Numbers regarding the death of Moses and Aaron. (1) Chap. xx. 24 declares that Aaron is to die because Moses and Aaron sinned, but says nothing of Moses' death; (2) chap. xxvi. 13 says that Moses shall die as Aaron did and for the same reason; (3) chap. xxxi. 2 declares that Moses shall die, but gives no reason of any kind. It would be easy to assert that the first passage belongs to a source which knew only of Aaron's death as a punishment for their joint act of disobedience, that the third knew of Moses' death but of no reason for it unless it be that his work was finished. But all are given to P. This is especially noteworthy because the critics cite as proof that Num. xiii.—xiv. is composite the fact that xiii. 30 and xiv. 24 do not mention Joshua along with Caleb, while xiv. 6, 39, do mention him. So they assign these passages to JE and P respectively. (Allis, FBM, 94)

2A. ALLEGED CONTRADICTIONS

1B. Introduction

Upon a casual reading of the text, certain contradictions regarding nomenclature, geography, legislation, customs, ethics, and so forth seem to appear.

> The admission of a final redactor is fatal to the assertion of irreconcilable contradictions in the Pentateuch. A man of such marvelous ability as he must have possessed would have seen the contradictions if they were as patent as they are said to be, and would have removed them.
>
> —JOHN H. RAVEN

2B. Documentary Assumption

The contradictions are, in fact, real. This is further evidence that there are different authors from different backgrounds writing at different times. Rather than try to correct the contradictions by deciding which one was right and rejecting the other, the redactors incorporated both accounts into the work.

3B. Basic Answer

Upon careful analysis of the text, the Hebrew language, and the ancient oriental cultural background in which the Israelites lived, one finds that these alleged contradictions can be justly harmonized and do in fact, in many cases, disappear.

This finding is tacitly acknowledged by the critics, as Raven perceptively notes: "The admission of a final redactor is fatal to the assertion of irreconcilable contradictions in the Pentateuch. A man of such marvelous ability as he must have possessed would have seen the contradictions if they were as patent as they are said to be, and would have removed them." (Raven, OTI, 127)

1C. Nomenclature

The critics hold that different names given to the same person or place is an indication that there is more than one author. (See Driver, BG, 13; Bentzen, IT, 47; Eissfeldt, OTI, 182–88)

Examples:

(1) *Amorite* is used in Genesis 10:16 and Deuteronomy 2:24, but *Canaanite* in Genesis 10:18 and Deuteronomy 1:7.

(2) *Horeb* is used in Exodus 33:6 and 17:6, but *Sinai* in Exodus 34:2 and 16:1.

(3) *Jethro* is used in Exodus 3:1 and 4:18, but *Reuel* in Genesis 36:17 and Exodus 2:18.

R. K. Harrison offers a much more plausible and verifiable alternative, making it clear that such a criterion involves utter disregard for its only possible source of objective verification—the evidence from the ancient Near East. The hundreds of examples from Egypt include such personal name variations as Sebekkhu, a military commander, likewise referred to as Djaa. (Harrison, IT, 521)

K. A. Kitchen has provided us with many other helpful instances:

In Egypt, many people had double names like the Israel/Jacob or Jethro/Reuel of the Old Testament, *e.g.*, Sebek-khu called Djaa whose stela in Manchester University Museum exemplifies the use of three names for one Palestinian populace: Mentiu-Setet ("Asiatic Beduin"), Retenu ("Syrians") and "Amu" ("Asiatics")—just like the Ishmaelites/Midianites or Canaanites/Amorites of the Old Testament. For personal and group names elsewhere, *cf.* in Mesopotamia the sage Ahiqar (or Ahuqar) who is Aba'-enlil-dari (not to mention Tiglathpileser III = Pul, and Shalmaneser V = Ululai). In the Hittite Empire, a series of kings had double names, while "Mitanni" and "Hanigalbat" and "Mitanni" and "Hurrians" occur as double designations of the state and people of Mitanni.

For place-names like Sinai/Horeb, compare in the text of Merenptah's "Israel Stela" two names for Egypt (Kemit, Tameri) and five names and variants for Memphis (Mennefer;

Ineb-hedj, Inbu, Ineb-heqa, Hatkup-tah). Similarly, examples can be found elsewhere. (Kitchen, AOOT, 123–24)

The two alleged accounts of Aaron's death at Mount Hor (Num. 20:22; 21:4; 33:33; Deut. 32:50) and at Moserah (Deut. 10:6) provide good evidence for the multiple document theory, or so a documentarian would say. But a careful scrutiny of the passages will show that in fact there is no contradiction and thus no ground for a multiple source conclusion. The word "Moserah" in Deuteronomy 10:6 means "chastisement" and designates the *event* of Aaron's death, not the *place*. This makes it clear that his death on Mount Hor was a reproof, a chastisement for his sin at Meribah (Num. 20:24; Deut. 32:51). He received the same recompense for his rebellion that Moses received: never to enter the Promised Land. The two accounts are thus in harmony and preserve the fact that Aaron did die at Mount Hor while the people were camped below. Moses marked the sad occasion by naming the camp site Moseroth (Num. 33:31; Deut. 10:6). (Harrison, IT, 510–11)

2C. Legislation

Critics have consistently held that certain laws contained in the Pentateuch are contradictory and that others are identically repeated. Hahn points out: "The theory that separate groups of cultic regulations originated at the local shrines raises the possibility that the duplications and inconsistencies in the Pentateuchal law may have been due to independent, parallel developments rather than successive stages in the history of the law." (Hahn, OTMR, 32)

These differences in and repetitions of some of the legislative material are held to be evidence of composite authorship, since one writer could hardly have been guilty of such obvious inconsistency. Harrison supplies a feasible solution:

Thus it is quite possible that in the post-Mosaic period some of the enactments were altered somewhat to suit changing circumstances, a process that is perfectly legitimate in any culture, and which does not in any sense vitiate the provenance of the original legislation. No doubt some of the duplications and inconsistencies in Pentateuchal law of which Hahn speaks were due, not to the rise of separate though parallel cultic regulations, as he and many other liberal writers suppose, but to the deliberate attempt on the part of the responsible authorities, whether priestly or other, to adapt the traditional legislation to the point where new conditions of life would be properly accommodated. This doubtless underlies the situation whereby the provisions of Numbers 26:52–56 relating to inheritance were modified by the circumstances detailed in Numbers 27:1–11 and Numbers 36:1–9, or where the regulations for an offering to cover sins of ignorance or inadvertence (Lev. 4:2–21) were changed by the provisions of Numbers 15:22–29. Again, it is of importance to note the witness of the text to the fact that some later additions were made to the Book of the Covenant in the time of Joshua (Josh. 24:26). (Harrison, IT, 539–40)

3C. Customs

In examining the customs of naming the children, the negative critics cite a proof for multiple documents. They say that in the P document the father names the children, while the mother has this privilege in J and E documents. Thus the conclusion that each of these documents originated in separate environments.

Looking at the cases in J and E, one finds that there are nineteen or twenty examples that conform to the rule; but there are also fourteen exceptions. The number of exceptions is enough to arouse suspicion, especially since every instance connected with Jacob is counted as one instance. This weakens the credibility of the case, especially in the light of the fact that two of these instances are classified as P simply because the father names the son. A third instance is unclear as to whether the father named the son or not, which leaves only one instance; and this is nothing on which to base a hypothesis.

The Torah informs us why there is a difference in the naming of children. Usually the reason for naming a child is etymological and concerns the circumstances at birth. When the circumstance concerns the father he names it, and the same with the mother. This rule is simple and logical, and is valid in every case. When the circumstances apply to the son only or in the rare event that etymological explanation is given, the rule does not apply; in these instances it is once the father, once the mother, and otherwise indefinite. (Cassuto, DH, 66)

4C. Ethics

J and E are said to have a defect in their moral sensitivity, while P is alert and sensitive. One evidence for this is cited from the story in which Jacob tricks Isaac into giving him Esau's blessing. The moral character of the story must be judged by what attitude the text takes toward the transgressors. In narratives of this nature it is fundamental that the text does not express its judgment explicitly and subjectively, but it relates the story objectively and allows the reader to learn the moral from the way the events unfold.

It is a fact that Jacob and Rebekah sinned in tricking Isaac, but what did they receive? Jacob was exploited by Laban in the same manner that he exploited his father, and Scripture makes it clear that Jacob received the wrong wife, Leah, as a punishment.

Rebekah, too, received her heartache when she had to send away the son she loved so much. She once asked him to obey her in the deceitful plot, and again she had to ask him to obey her in leaving. Thus, the moral ethic of the Torah is preserved and source division is again shown to be without grounds.

P is void of a single passage that requires close examination in order to learn its moral. P's complete silence concerning the transgressions of the patriarchs, however, does not necessitate a divergence of sources. For it is significant to note that only *two* narratives concerning the patriarchs are assigned to P (the cave of Machpelah and the circumcision). On the other hand, P abounds with dry reports, chronologies, and genealogies. Certainly the point on ethics is meaningless when applied to material with *no* didactic content and no relevant narratives. (Cassuto, DH, 63–65)

3A. ANACHRONISMS—LATE WORDS

1B. Introduction

Certain words used in the Pentateuch seem to have come from a later time period. There are also words that occur only a few times in the Old Testament and then reappear only much later in other Jewish writings.

2B. Documentary Assumption

The occurrence of such anachronistic words shows that the Pentateuch was written at a time much later than Moses.

3B. Basic Answer

Some of these words can be attributed to later scribal glosses. Others are, in fact, early and not late words, and with still others it is difficult to tell whether they are early or late.

1C. Scribal Glosses

Three examples of words that obviously came (that is, to radical critics) from a period of history later than the Mosaic age:

1. "Philistines" (Ex. 13:17)
2. "Dan" (Gen. 14:14; Deut. 34:1)
3. Canaan, called "land of the Hebrews" (Gen. 40:15) (See Driver, BG, 15; Rowley, GOT, 17)

Harrison suggests that such supposed anachronisms may be successive scribal revisions that brought the text up-to-date in some areas.

Other examples include the description of Moses as a prophet of Israel (Deut. 34:10), as well as the various scribal glosses that give later forms of earlier names (Gen. 14:8, 15, 17; 17:14; 23:2; 35:6). Weiser alleges that the reference to a king in Deuteronomy 17:14 is anachronistic; but this shows lack of perception because the passage is foretelling events to take place, and is not recording the present situation. (Harrison, IT, 524)

Harrison continues: "Along with revisions of spelling and the inclusion of glosses on the text, the scribes of antiquity frequently replaced an earlier proper name by its later form. This latter phenomenon may well account for such apparent anachronisms as the mention in the Pentateuch of the 'way of the land of the Philistines' (Exod. 13:17), at a time when the Philistines had yet to occupy the Palestinian coastal region in any strength." (Harrison, IT, 523)

2C. Rare Words

Archer paraphrases the critics' argument regarding rare words: "If a word occurring less than three or four times in the Old Testament recurs only in later Hebrew literature (the Talmud and Midrash), then the word is of late origin, and the Old Testament pas-sage must be of late composition." (Archer, SOTI, 125)

This is invariably the interpretation offered by Old Testament scholars; but there are in fact *three* viable explanations:

(1) as stated previously, that the "early" occurrence is actually within a body of writing that had a later origin;

(2) that the "early" occurrence provides evidence that the word was actually in common usage at the earlier date;

(3) that a truly "late" word may only demonstrate that the word itself was originated in the text (having been substituted for an obsolete, offensive, or obscure word), and shows nothing as to the date of the body of writing.

While most scholars ignore the last two principles, the validity of the principles may be proven by an examination of literary remains of the ancient Orient that are objectively dated.

An example of (2) presents itself in the well-known phenomenon of the sporadic occurrence of words in, for instance, the Pyramid Texts of 2400 B.C. The word may then totally disappear, only to be found twenty-one centuries later (about 300–30 B.C.) in the writings of the Greco-Roman period. To compact more than two millennia of Egyptian history into a two-and-a-half-century period is, of course, absurd. Yet a wholesale application of this criterion leads scholars to just such absurdities with Hebrew literature. (Kitchen, AOOT, 141–42)

Likewise, Ecclesiasticus 50:3, dated second century B.C., provided the earliest occurrence of *swh* ("reservoir"), leading to the conclusion that it was a late word. But the more recent surprise discovery of the same word on the Moabite Stone added a sudden seven centuries to its age. (Archer, SOTI, 126–27)

One of many examples of (3) is seen in the Ashmolean text of the story of Sinuhe, which is definitely dated in the twentieth century B.C. due to internal statements. However, the occurrence of *yam* for "sea" and the Late-Egyptian *bw* for "no" point to a date of 1500 B.C., according to principle (1). Manuscripts from about 1800 B.C. provide

> It is obvious that a kind of proof that will prove almost everything to be late, and especially the parts considered late to be early, is absurd and inadmissible as evidence in a case designed to prove that some documents are later than others because they contain words of this kind. For it is certain that if all are late, then none are early.
>
> —ROBERT DICK WILSON

us with the answer—that the two words were actually substituted for early forms. The future discovery of very ancient Old Testament manuscripts may show the same truth in the Hebrew Scriptures. (Kitchen, AOOT, 141–43)

Further, the Old Testament provides only a bare representation of the entire Hebrew literary output. Three thousand Old Testament words appear less than six times; fifteen hundred occur but once. Certainly a greater knowledge of Hebrew literature and conversation would establish many of these as everyday Hebrew terms. Similarly, no one would argue that words like "invasion" (1 Sam. 30:14), "jumping" (Nah. 3:2) and "lance" (Jer. 50:42) are rare in English, yet they are found only once in the English Bible. (Archer, SOTI, 126–27)

Robert Dick Wilson has done an excellent study of the words used five or fewer times in the Old Testament. He has shown that

a large part of the words that are produced as evidence [by the critics] of the late date of

documents containing them cannot themselves be proved to be late. For, first, no one can maintain that because a word occurs only in a late document the word itself is therefore late; for in this case, if a late document was the only survival of a once numerous body of literature, every word in it would be late; which is absurd. Nor, secondly, can one maintain that a document is late merely because it contains words which do not occur in earlier ones, which are known to us. Every new find of Egyptian Aramaic papyri gives us words not known before, except, if at all, in documents written hundreds of years later. Nor, thirdly, is a word to be considered as evidence of the lateness of a document in which it occurs simply because it occurs again in documents known to be late, such as the Hebrew parts of the Talmud. And yet, this is frequently affirmed by the critics. . . . it is obvious that a kind of proof that will prove almost everything to be late, and especially the parts considered late to be early, is absurd and inadmissible as evidence in a case designed to prove that some documents are later than others because they contain words of this kind. For it is certain that if all are late, then none are early—a conclusion which would overthrow the position of all critics, radical as well as conservative; and since this conclusion is desired and maintained by none, it must be dismissed as *absurd.*

In proof, however, that such words are found in every book, and in almost every part of every book, of the Old Testament we subjoin the following tables. These tables are based on special concordances of every book and of every part of every book of the Old Testament, prepared by and now in the possession of the writer of this article. In accordance with the laws of evidence, that "witnesses must give evidence of facts," and "an expert may state general facts which are the result of scientific knowledge, and that an expert may give an account of experiments [hence, also of investigations] performed by him for the purpose of forming his opinion," it may add force and clearness to the evidence about to be presented, if an account is first given of the way in which the facts upon which the tables are based were collected. One whole summer was spent in gathering from a Hebrew concordance all the words in the Old Testament that occur there five times or less, giving also the places where the words occur. A second summer sufficed for making from this general concordance a special concordance for each book. In the third summer, special concordances were made for J, E. D, H, and P, for each of the five books of the Psalter and for each of the psalms; for each of the

parts of Proverbs, and of the alleged parts of Isaiah, Micah, Zechariah, Chronicles, Ezra, Nehemiah; and for such parts as Gen. xiv and the poems contained in Gen. xlix, Ex. xv, Deut. xxxii, xxxiii and Judges v. Then, each of the words of this kind was sought for in the Aramaic and in the Hebrew of the post-biblical Jewish writers. The evidence of the facts collected is manifest, and we think conclusive.

A study of these percentages should convince everyone that the presence of such words in a document is no proof of its relative lateness.*

	Number of words occurring in O.T. five time or less	Percentage of these words in Talmud
Psalms lxxix	3	00.0
Prov. xxxi. 1–9	0	00.0
Isaiah xxiv—xxvii	0	00.0
Obadiah	7	14.3
Isaiah xxxvi—ix	7	14.3
Judges—Ruth	107	15.8
Nahum	36	16.7
Ezra i—vi	6	16.7
Micah ii	11	18.2
Isaiah xxxiv–v	5	20.0
Isaiah xiii–xiv	10	20.0
Isaiah (1st pt.)	121	22.3
Malachi	13	23.1
Ezekiel	335	24.9
Lamentation	56	25.0
Haggai	4	25.0
Ezra vii—x	8	25.0
Zechariah ii	16	25.0
Isaiah xl—lxvi	62	25.8
Proverbs i—ix	69	27.5
Daniel	47	29.8
Zecharia [sic] i	22	30.8

*In explanation of these tables it may be said that they are prepared with special reference to the critical analysis of the O.T. Thus the Pentateuch is arranged according to the documents, J, E, D, H and P; and the Proverbs are divided into seven portions (following LOT). The first column of the tables gives for each book or part of a book the number of words occurring five times or less in the Old Testament that are found in it; and the second column the percentage of these words that are to be found in the same sense in the Hebrew of the Talmud.

	Number of words occurring in O.T. five time or less	Percentage of these words in Talmud
Zecharia [sic] iii	12	30.8
Micah i	22	31.8
Job	374	31.0
Jeremiah	278	32.1
Psalms	514	33.1
Book I	123	35.8
Book II	135	31.1
Book III	76	30.3
Book IV	61	31.1
Book V	118	34.7
Micah iii	15	33.3
Proverbs x—xxii. 16	80	33.8
Proverbs xxii. 17–xxiv	30	36.7
Samuel—Kings	356	37.2
Habakkuk	34	38.2
Joel	28	39.3
Jonah	15	40.0
Hosea	65	41.5
Jehovist (J)	162	44.4
Zephaniah	31	45.2
Amos	50	46.0
Elohist (E)	119	48.7
Proverbs xxxi. 10–31	6	50.0
Holiness Code (H)	48	50.0
Chronicles	144	51.5
Proverbs xxv—xxix	52	51.9
Esther	57	52.6
Priest Code (P)	192	53.1
Deuteronomist (D)	154	53.2
Proverbs xxx	15	53.5
Song of Songs	99	54.6
Nehemiah	48	56.3
Ecclesiastes	77	57.1
Memoirs of Nehemiah	27	59.3

A careful reading of this table will justify the statement made above that a "kind of proof that will prove almost everything to be late, and especially the parts considered late to be early, is absurd and inadmissible as evidence in a case designed to prove that some documents are later than others because they contain words of this kind." This kind of evidence would simply prove almost all the documents of the Old Testament to be late. If admitted as valid, it would militate as much against the views of the radicals as it would against those of the conservatives.

Take, for example, the number of these words occurring in the alleged documents of the Pentateuch. J and E together have 281 words in about 2,170 verses (one in less than every 7.7 verses) and about 46 percent of these words are found in the Talmud; D has 154 words in about 1,000 verses (or one in every 6.5 verses) and about 53 percent of them in the Talmud, and PH 201 words in 2,340 verses (or one in every 8.6 verses) and about 52 percent of the words in the Talmud. Surely, no unbiased judge of literature would attempt to settle the dates of documents on such slight variations as these from one word in 6.5 to one in 8.6 and from 46 to 53 percent in the Talmud! Besides, in regard to the relative proportion in verses the order is PH, JE, D and in percentages in the Talmud JE, PH, D; but according to the Wellhausians, it should in both cases be JE, D, PH. The slight variations in both cases point to unity of authorship and likeness of date. (Wilson, SIOT, 131–36)

3C. Aramaisms

The Babylonian Captivity (607–538 B.C.) marked the beginning of the Jews' abandonment of their ancestral Hebrew language in favor of the more widely spoken Aramaic language. Therefore, the critics held that the presence of an Aramaic word in the biblical text was evidence that the passage had a postexilic origin. They asserted that many such "Aramaisms" do in fact appear in the Pentateuch. This supports their theory of a late origin for their written sources (J, E, D, P, and so forth).

But Archer offers this philological evidence:

> A great number of Hebrew words which they [documentarians] have classified as Aramaisms turn out, on closer examination, to have a very good claim to the status of authentic Hebrew words, or else to be derivable from Phoenician, Babylonian or Arabic dialects, rather than from Aramaic. For example, many critics have carelessly assumed that Hebrew nouns ending in -on are necessarily Aramaic because the -an ending is so common in Aramaic. Yet the fact of the matter is that this ending is also found with fair frequency in Babylonian and Arabic, and further proof is necessary to demonstrate that it could not have been native in Hebrew from Canaanite times. (Archer, SOTI, 129)

The Jewish scholar M. H. Segal concludes similarly: "It has been the fashion among writers on the subject to brand as an Aramaism any infrequent Hebrew word which happens to be found more or less frequently in Aramaic dialects. Most of the Aramaisms are as native in Hebrew as they are in Aramaic. Many of them are also found in other Semitic languages." (Segal, GMH, 8)

Kautzsch *(Die Aramaismen im Alten Testamente)* has listed about 350 words as being possibly of Aramaic origin. On this basis, over fifteen hundred Old Testament verses in which the words occur are assigned a late date. Yet the thorough scholarship of R. D. Wilson has revealed the following information:

(a) 150 of these 350 words are *never* found in an Aramaic dialect.

(b) 235 of these 350 words are *never* found in Aramaic literature before the second century A.D.

(c) Only 40 of those found earlier than the second century A.D. are unique to Aramaic among the Near Eastern languages.

(d) Only 50 of the list of 350 words are found in the Pentateuch.

(e) More than two-thirds of these 50 "Aramaic" words in the Pentateuch had to be replaced by an genuinely Aramaic word to make them intelligible in the Aramaic translations.

(f) Most of the words that were *not* replaced in the Aramaic translations are still not unique to Aramaic among the Near Eastern Languages.

Even using the dating of the radical critics, we find that a full 120 of these alleged 350 "Aramaic words" are used by Old Testament writers as much as seven hundred years before they are found in any Aramaic documents. While it is easy to understand these as Hebrew words that were incorporated into Aramaic as more and more Jews made the transition, it is difficult to believe that the biblical writers borrowed so many Aramaic words that are apparently not used until seven centuries later. (Wilson, SIOT, 155–63)

24
INCONGRUITIES

1A. INTRODUCTION

The Pentateuch was supposed to have been written by Moses, yet many passages regarding Moses are written in the third person, rather than in the first. Also, if the Pentateuch was written by Moses, how could it contain the account of his death?

2A. DOCUMENTARY ASSUMPTION

Such incongruities are an indication that in reality Moses did not write the Pentateuch.

3A. BASIC ANSWER

There are two very plausible alternatives to the critics' third-person argument. And the account of Moses' death need not necessarily be attributed to Moses.

1B. Third-person Phenomenon

1C. Possibly Dictated

Moses may have dictated his work to scribes.

Harrison suggests: "Equally uncertain is the actual extent to which Moses recorded personally the written material credited to him. It may well be that the presence of third-person pronouns in various sections of the Mosaic enactments indicate that these sections were dictated. Quite possibly many of the small or isolated sections in the Hebrew text were committed initially to the priests for safekeeping, and only at a later period were the manuscript pieces assembled into some sort of mosaic and joined together into a roll." (Harrison, IOT, 538)

This would be quite consistent with ancient oriental practice. R. D. Wilson argues:

Is one to allege, then, that Hammurabi cannot be called the author of the code named after him, unless, forsooth, he inscribed it with his own hand? And yet the monument expressly ascribes itself to Hammurabi in the words of the epilogue (Col. Li. 59–67): "In the days that are yet to come, for all future times, may the king who is in the land observe the words of righteousness which I have written upon my monument. . . ." Are we to suppose that Moses cannot have recorded his thought and words and deeds just in the same way that his predecessors, contemporaries, and successors did? (Wilson, SIOT, 24–25)

2C. Possibly Written by Moses in Third Person

Moses may have actually written in the third person. This does not seem too unreasonable in light of the fact that the following authors of antiquity wrote about themselves, either in part or in full, in the third person:

Josephus, *The Wars of the Jews* (first century A.D.)

Xenophon, *Anabasis* (fifth century B.C.)

Julius Caesar, *Gallic War* (first century B.C.) (Kim, MAP, 23–24; Unger, IGOT, 265)

2B. Moses' Death

The account of Moses' death was a later addition.

The Talmud [*Baba Bathra* 146] attributes this section relating to Moses' death to Joshua. (Harrison, IOT, 661)

Archer says this about Deuteronomy: "Chapter 34 is demonstrably post-Mosaic, since it contains a short account of Moses' decease. But this does not endanger in the slightest the Mosaic authenticity of the other thirty-three chapters, for the closing chapter furnishes only that type of obituary which is often appended to the final work of great men of letters." (Archer, SOTI, 224)

G. Aalders, in his book, A *Short Introduction to the Pentateuch,* treats the various views on the death of Moses recorded in chapter 34 of Deuteronomy. (Aalders, ASIP, 105–10)

25
INTERNAL DIVERSITY

1A. INTRODUCTION

There is considerable diversity in the Pentateuch as to subject matter, style, and diction.

2A. DOCUMENTARY ASSUMPTION

This internal diversity highly suggests that the Pentateuch was written by different men at different times, each of whom had his own individual point of view and technique. This is much more plausible than believing that only one man is responsible for a work characterized by such diversity as the Pentateuch.

3A. BASIC ANSWER

Diversity of subject matter, style, and diction can be legitimately accounted for without resorting to composite authorship as an explanation.

1B. Subject Matter

Regarding the ancient Orientals' ability to write different subject matter, Harrison says:

> The concentration in one man of the ability to write historical narrative, to compose poetry,

and to collate legal material is by no means as unique as earlier critical writers were wont to assume. As Kitchen has pointed out, an illustration of this kind of ability from ancient Egypt at a period some seven centuries prior to the time of Moses has been furnished in all probability by Khety (or Akhtoy), son of Duauf, a writer who lived in the time of the pharaoh Amenemhat I (*ca.* 1991–1962 B.C.). This versatile individual apparently combined the functions of educator, poet, and political propagandist, and wrote the *Satire of the Trades* as a text for use by students in the scribal schools. He was probably commissioned to give literary form to the *Teaching of Amenemhat I,* which was a political pamphlet popular in the Eighteenth to Twentieth Dynasties as an exercise to be copied by schoolboys. In addition, he may have been the author of a popular *Hymn to the Nile,* which with the foregoing works was also frequently copied out by scribes. Quite clearly, then, it is by no means inherently impossible for a talented individual to have engaged during the Amarna period in the kind of literary activity traditionally ascribed to Moses. (Harrison, IOT, 538)

2B. Style

Driver states, "If the parts assigned to P be read attentively, even in a translation, and compared with the rest of the narrative, the peculiarities of style will be apparent." (Driver, ILOT, 20) (See the quote by Driver in the Diction section.)

Raven deals well with this phenomenon as it occurs in passages relating specifically to God:

P is said to be cold, formal, systematic, logical but it is precisely in such passages that one would expect Elohim, the general name for God, the name which has no special relation to Israel but is used many times in reference to the deities of the Gentiles. J on the other hand is said to be naive, anthropomorphic in his conception of God; but these evidences of

religious fervor would lead us to expect the proper national name of God, the name which emphasized his covenant relations with Israel. There are passages in which we cannot explain why one name of the deity is used rather than another; but in the great majority of cases, any other name would be inappropriate. (Raven, OTI, 119)

Dante's *Divine Comedy* provides a helpful example of a work that has only one author but divergent styles in presenting God's nature. Many passages colorfully depict the

> The supposed consistency of criteria over a large body of writing is contrived and deceptive (especially on vocabulary, for example), and will hold for "style" only if one in the first place picks out everything of a particular kind, then proclaims it as all belonging to one document separate from the rest, and finally appeals to its remarkable consistency—a consistency obtained by deliberate selection in the first place, and hence attained by circular reasoning.
>
> —KENNETH A. KITCHEN

intervention of God into human affairs (as J and E), while immediately beside them are passages rich in systematic doctrine (as P). Yet here we have one author and one document—no more. (Cassuto, DH, 59)

Indeed, it cannot be contested that in the P document one finds a cold, dry atmosphere that has an affinity for details and a fondness of stereotyped phrases. In contrast to P, J, and E are marked by their vividness, color, and vitality. But let us not be deceived by appearances. The reason P is dull and dry is because the material attributed to it is that way by nature. How is it possible to give vitality and charm to a genealogical record? But the few narratives given to P contain vividness and grace of diction, just as the genealogies assigned to J are frigid, insipid, and schematic. Thus one finds, notes Cassuto, that "change of style depends on change of subject matter, not on different sources." (Cassuto, DH, 53–54)

Raven further develops this central issue: "The claim of a distinct vocabulary for P and JE can be maintained only by mutilating the record. If an expression usually found in P occurs in a JE section, the chapter and sometimes even the verse is divided. If narratives were left entire except in case of an expression which might be a later gloss, the argument would be much weakened. By this method any literary work could be divided into several sources, more or less complete." (Raven, OTI, 124)

Kitchen very aptly drives home this weakness in the critics' methodology, stating that

the supposed consistency of criteria over a large body of writing is contrived and deceptive (especially on vocabulary, for example), and will hold for "style" only if one in the first place picks out everything of a particular kind, then proclaims it as all belonging to one document separate from the rest, and finally appeals to its remarkable consistency—a consistency obtained by deliberate selection in the first place, and hence attained by circular reasoning. "P" owes its existence mainly to this kind of procedure, and was not even recognized to have existed for the one hundred years from Astruc in 1753 until Hupfeld in 1853. (Kitchen, AOOT, 115–16)

Many radical critics are confident that a difference in style within the same subject matter would tend to indicate different authors. But any one author may use different styles for different emphases, even within similar subject matter. A lawyer, for example, will use a different style in a letter to his mother than in a brief he has prepared, even though his subject matter is investment protection in each. Here again a clergyman uses a different style talking to his children in the morning than he does in his benediction, even though his subject matter in both situations may be God's faithfulness. A physician will only use a prescription style of writing when writing a prescription, but have a very different "bedside manner." In the same vein, the technical description of the ark in Genesis is no more evidence of different authorship from the surrounding narrative than a naval architect's style of describing a vessel makes him a different author than the same architect writing a love letter to his fiancée. (Gordon, HCFF, 132)

Finally, archaeological data indicate that the existence of stylistic differences in a literary work was characteristic of much of the ancient Orient. Kitchen has described the inscription of Uni, an Egyptian official (2400 B.C.), which contains a flowing narrative (J, E?), summary statements (P?), a victory hymn (H), and two different refrains (R1, R2?) that are repeated often. Yet the fact remains that there is no question of different documents in the monumental inscription that was engraved in stone at the request of the one it commemorates. (Kitchen, AOOT, 125–26)

Another helpful parallel is discovered in the royal inscriptions of the kings of Urartu. There is a set formula for the going forth of the god Haldi (P?), a triple formula for the going forth of the king (K1, K2, K3?), a compact statement of success (S?) or first personal narrative (N?), and every so often there are statistics of the Urartian army or of the spoils they have taken (P again?). As a document this is unquestioned because it has no prehistory or rival proto-author, and its style has lasted a century. (Kitchen, AOOT, 125–26)

3B. Diction

Certain words are considered to be unique to the J document, others to the P document, and so on. Driver has compiled an extensive list of those words and phrases said to indicate composite authorship. (see Driver, ILOT, 131–35)

About Genesis, Driver writes: "In short, the Book of Genesis presents two groups of sections, distinguished from each other by differences of phraseology and style." (Driver, BG, IV)

Even allowing that there was no other plausible explanation for this phenomenon, W. J. Martin points out that inducing composite authorship from a variation in vocabulary is groundless:

> When the inner meaning of the words is sought and the passage is not looked at mechanically, the underlying principles become clear.

The invalidity of such criteria has long been recognized by classical scholars, and no one would now think of attaching any significance to, say, the fact that beans are mentioned in the Iliad but not in the Odyssey; that the Iliad is rich in words for wounds and wounding, whereas such words are rare in, or absent from, the Odyssey; that the words for grasshopper, crane, eel, maggots, snow, sparrow, and donkey occur only in the Iliad, palmtree only in the Odyssey. In fact the Iliad uses 1,500 words none of which occur in the Odyssey. Or again, no deductions of any kind could be made from the fact that in the works of Shakespeare the word 'pious' is found only in Hamlet and subsequent plays. Even inconsistencies may occur in one and the same author; Virgil in a single book makes the wooden horse of fir in one passage, of maplewood in another, and of oak in yet another. (Martin, SCAP, 13)

Cassuto establishes the following ground rules for the proper handling of linguistic diversity:

> (a) we must not rely upon the differences in language in order to determine the origin of the sections, which we shall subsequently use to decide the linguistic characteristics of the sources, for in that case we shall indeed fall into the snare of reasoning in a circle; (b) nor emend the texts in order to make them conform to our theory; (c) nor consider words and forms mechanically, as though they were divorced from their context and the latter could have no bearing on their use. As we shall soon see, the exponents of the documentary hypothesis were not always careful to avoid all these pitfalls. (Cassuto, DH, 44)

While it is readily admitted that there is considerable variation of vocabulary in the Pentateuch (i.e., that different words denote the same thing, that certain phrases and words appear in some sections but not in others, and so forth), the evidence for the existence of unique diction in each "source" is the result of the critics' circular reasoning. They compile a list of all the passages that contain certain words, labeling these passages as being from a particular "source," and then announce that since these words do not appear elsewhere in the text outside that "source" they are, in fact, characteristic of that "source" only. Thus, the phenomenon is created by the hypothesis itself. (See Kitchen's first quote on variation in style above.)

Here is one example: There are two words in Hebrew for "female slave," one being *amah* and the other *shiphah*. Critics have assigned *amah* to the Elohist as being the word he used for "female slave" and *shiphah* to the Yahwist as being his term for the same thing. (Archer, SOTI, 111)

Some critics assert that when speaking of a female slave the Yahwist *invariably* uses the Hebrew word *shiphah* and the Elohist *always* uses *amah*. Driver quite prudently concedes that E's use of *amah* is not invariable, only preferable. Yet even this is strong. E uses *amah* six times in Genesis (20:17; 21:10, 12, 13; 30:3; 31:33), yet *shiphah* occurs almost as often in E or in solidly unified contexts (assigned to E: Gen. 20:14; 29:24, 29; assigned to P: 30:4, 7, 18.)

Orr reacts harshly to the methodology practiced here, retorting: "It is pure arbitrariness and circular reasoning to change this single word in chap. xx. 14 and xxx. 18, on the ground that 'the regular word for women slaves in E is *Amah*,' and that 'J on the other hand always employs *Shiphah*'— the very point in dispute. In chap. xxix. 24, 29, the verses are cut out and given to P; chap. xxx. 4, 7 are similarly cut out and given to J." (Orr, POT, 231)

Genesis 20 furnishes the first substantial E portion in Genesis; yet *shiphah* (the J word) appears in verse 14, then followed by *amah* (the E word) in v. 17. Holzingar, asserting that "E does not use the word," deletes *shiphah*, as he also does in Genesis 30:18. To presuppose that E uses this word and to then attribute every exception to J's insertion or to the redactor's blunder is to simply build one's conclusion into his premise. Such a method is logically fallacious, unscientific, and would allow one to prove anything he likes. (Archer, SOTI, 111)

Cassuto provides us with another very beneficial example. He believes that a lack of scholarship is shown when the proponents of the theory deal with the Hebrew words *beterem* and *terem*. Each place *beterem* appears is ascribed to E and where *terem* is

found, it is ascribed to J. Unfortunately for the documentarians, these words are not synonyms. They are two totally different words; *beterem* means "before" and *terem* means "not only." It is apparent since these words mean two different things that their usage would be different. There is no question here of different sources. (Cassuto, DH, 51)

Diversity of diction is also the issue when the documentarians argue that the use of the words "to bring up from Egypt" (employed by the E document) and "to bring forth from Egypt" (employed by the J document) are proof of multiple documents.

But in understanding the meaning of each phrase we reach a different conclusion. When the phrase "to bring up from Egypt" is used, it means they came from Egypt and entered into the Promised Land, while "to bring forth from Egypt" simply means to leave Egypt. In Genesis 46:4, God tells Jacob "I will also surely bring you up." This means He will bring him back to the Promised Land. On the other hand, in Genesis 15:14, we read, "and afterwards they will come out with many possessions." When read within the context this clearly shows that the Exodus is being talked about. When the inner meaning of the words is sought and the passage is looked at carefully, the underlying principles become clear. (Cassuto, DH, 48)

We find a further example in the fact that the Pentateuch records numbers in two different ways: ascending order, such as the number "twenty and a hundred," and descending order, "a hundred and twenty." The critics postulate that J, E, and D employ the descending order, and that ascending order is characteristic of P.

A more logical explanation can be found in the fact that the ascending order is consistently associated with technical or statistical dates. On the other hand, solitary numbers are almost always in descending order, except in a few cases where special circumstances operate. Examples of this rule are seen when Moses was addressing the children of Israel, saying, "I am one hundred and twenty years old" (Deut. 31:2), and in the passage concerning the offering of princes, where it states, "all the gold of the dishes being twenty and a hundred shekels" (Num. 7:86 RSV).

In the light of this explanation one may ask how it is possible to explain the fact that the ascending order is to be found only in the P sections. The answer is simple: P is formulated on the basis of its assumed constituency of all chronological and genealogical tables, all statistical records, all technical descriptions of services and the like. Thus, it is obvious that the ascending order will occur more often in the supposed P document. (Cassuto, DH, 51-54)

A final example is supplied by the word *yalad*. This Hebrew word for "beget" is alternately used in its causative form and in its regular form (but with causative meaning). Critics explain this by assigning the former to P and the latter to J. Their reasons? Apparently so that in passages of doubtful source, a precedent may now be established for assigning to J those that use the regular form with a causative meaning and to P those that use the strictly causative form. (Cassuto, DH, 43)

1C. Subject Matter

In answer to the argument that words peculiar to the supposed documents are evidence for the documentary theory, Raven points out that the real reason for word variation is a difference in subject matter: "Of course the argument has no weight unless the words or expression is one which both writers had occasion to use. Many of the words in Driver's list are confined to P because nei-

ther J, E, nor D had occasion to use them." (Raven, OTI, 122)

This should be obvious. We would expect the vocabulary used in a systematic genealogy (for example, Gen. 10) to be somewhat different from the vocabulary used in a flowing narrative (Gen. 8—9, for example). Upon investigation we find that it is not because it was written by two different persons but because one is a genealogy and one is a narrative.

2C. Variety

It is essential to remember that a single author will utilize variety to attain vividness or emphasis. A helpful example is seen in the Exodus account of Pharaoh's refusal to release the Israelites from Egypt. His obstinacy in the face of the plagues is referred to by three verbs meaning "to make strong or bold" (assigned to P and E), "to make hard" (assigned to P), and "to make heavy and insensible" (given to J). But an examination of the sequence of their usage yields the recognition of a natural psychological order—from boldness, to hardness, to insensibility. This is clearly due to the design of the author, not to the mingling of documents. (Archer, SOTI, 116)

3C. Our Possession of Only a Fraction of the Archaeological Evidence that Could Shed Much Light on Ancient Hebrew Usage of Certain Words

The radical critics have traditionally held that the longer form of the pronoun "I" (*anoki*) is earlier in usage than the shorter form (*ani*). This distinction is employed as a criterion for source division, even though an investigation of the text shows that the alternation of the two forms is frequently due to cliché. "I (*ani*) am Yahweh" is obviously a conventional phrase regularly found in contexts that freely use the longer form *anoki*.

The entire argument has recently been proven a fabrication by the discovery of fifteenth-century-B.C. inscriptions at Ras Shamra in which *both* forms of the pronoun are seen side by side.

Another example: Two Hebrew words for "window" are used in the Flood story. *Arub-*

> Such archaeological discoveries have seriously undermined the arguments of the documentary hypothesis and there is every reason to believe that further excavations will continue to provide us with verifiable data regarding the *real* literary techniques of the ancient Hebrews.

bah is used in Genesis 7:11 and 8:2. But in 8:6 the word for "window" is *challon*. (Allis, FBM, 78–79) The documentarians hold that *arubbah* is the word that the P author used for "window," and consequently Genesis 7:11 and the first part of 8:2 are part of the P document. *Challon* is the word that the J author used for "window," so Genesis 8:6 is part of the J document.

Is there another way to account for the use of both these words that seem to denote the very same thing in so short a narrative as the Flood story?

The answer is yes. Although we do not yet know why both these terms were used in such close proximity to each other, archaeological excavations at Ras Shamra uncovered a tablet on which *both* of these words appear, thus rendering it highly untenable that the same usage in Genesis must mean two authors.

Such archaeological discoveries have seriously undermined the arguments of the documentary hypothesis and there is every reason to believe that further excavations will continue to provide us with verifiable data regarding the *real* literary techniques of the ancient Hebrews.

While archaeology has already done much to defend the integrity of Israelite literature, it should be realized that it has barely even scratched the surface. Edwin Yamauchi, formerly of Rutgers University and now of Miami University (Ohio), points out:

"If one could by an overly optimistic estimate reckon that 1/4 of our materials and inscriptions survived, that 1/4 of the available sites have been excavated, that 1/4 of the excavated sites have been examined, and that 1/4 of the materials and inscriptions excavated have been published, one would still have less than 1/1000 of the possible evidence (1/4x1/4x1/4x1/4). Realistically speaking the percentage is no doubt even smaller." (Yamauchi, SSS, 12)

4B. The Unity of the Pentateuch

The entire Pentateuch is founded upon a unity of arrangement and is linked together into an organic whole, with only rare overlapping and restatement due to the progressive nature of God's revelation to Moses. Even the critics acknowledge this unity when they introduce the hypothetical redactor to account for the Pentateuch's present order and harmony. (Archer, SOTI, 108)

An example of such a concession is provided by Edward Riehm *(Einleitung in das Alte Testament,* 1889, I, p. 202), cited here by Archer:

Most of the laws of the middle books of the Pentateuch form essentially a homogeneous whole. They do not indeed all come from one hand, and have not been written at one and the same time. . . . However, they are all ruled by the same principles and ideas, have the same setting, the like form of representation, and the same mode of expression. A multitude of definite terms appear again and again. In manifold ways also the laws refer to one another. Apart from isolated subordinate differences, they agree with one another, and so supplement each other as to give the impression of a single whole, worked out with a marvelous consistency in its details. (Archer, SOTI, 108)

W. W. J. Martin states:

Genesis possesses all the characteristics of a homogeneous work: articulation, the unwitting use of forms and syntactical patterns which indicate the linguistic and geographical milieu of the writer, the function of particles, and in particular the definite article passing through the stages from demonstrative to definitive, as well as here the fluid state of grammatical gender. The writer of Genesis was a man of such pre-eminent literary gifts, as almost to suggest a facility and preoccupation with models in another literary medium. He has all the characteristics of genius: variety and diversity, multiplicity of alternatives, wide range of colours, a full gamut of notes exploited with masterly skill. No man now would dream of deducing from diversity of style diversity of authorship; diversity is part of the very texture of genius. It is not in the uniformity of diction or style but in the uniformity of quality that unity is discerned. It is easier to believe in a single genius than to believe that there existed a group of men possessing such preeminent gifts, so self-effacing, who could have produced such a work. (Martin, SCAP, 22)

26
CONCLUSION TO THE DOCUMENTARY HYPOTHESIS

1A. SUGGESTED STRENGTHS

1B. Collective Force of the Hypothesis

Critics readily admit that each criterion by which the Pentateuch has been divided into sources is not, by itself, a convincing argument. When taken collectively, however, these criteria do in fact present a powerful case for composite authorship.

Along these lines the British documentarian A. T. Chapman writes: "The strength of the critical position is mainly due to the fact that the same conclusions are reached by independent lines of argument." (Chapman, IP, 39) Hence they appeal to the cumulative effect of these "independent lines of argument" (criteria).

But as Kitchen points out: "It is a waste of time to talk about the 'cumulative force' of arguments that are each invalid; 0 + 0 + 0 + 0 = 0 on any reckoning. The supposed concordance of assorted criteria whose independence is more apparent than real has had to be rejected . . . on evidence far too bulky to include in this book." (Kitchen, AOOT, 125)

2B. The Reason for the Widespread Acceptance of the Theory

Why, it may be asked, if the documentary hypothesis is as invalid as this investigation has attempted to show, was it so eagerly received and defended in most scholarly circles throughout continental Europe, Great Britain, and the United States?

W. H. Green answers this way:

> A large number of eminent scholars accept the critical partition of the Pentateuch in general, if not in all its details. It has its fascinations, which sufficiently account for its popularity. The learning, ability, and patient toil which have been expended upon its elaboration, the specious arguments arrayed in its support, and the skill with which it has been adapted to the phenomena of the Pentateuch and of the Old Testament generally, have given to it the appearance of great plausibility. The novel lines of inquiry which it opens make it attractive to those of a speculative turn of mind, who see in it the opportunity for original and fruitful research in the reproduction of ancient documents, long buried unsuspected in the existing text, which they antedate by centuries. The boldness and seeming success with which it undertakes to revolutionize traditional opinion and give a new respect to the origin and history of the religion of the Old Testament, and its alliance with the doctrine of development, which has found such wide application in other fields of investigation, have largely contributed to its popularity. (Green, HCP, 131–32)

Green adds: "Its failure is not from the lack of ingenuity or learning, or persevering

> It is very doubtful whether the Wellhausen hypothesis is entitled to the status of scientific respectability. There is so much of special pleading, circular reasoning, questionable deductions from unsubstantiated premises that it is absolutely certain that its methodology would never stand up in a court of law.
>
> —GLEASON ARCHER

effort on the part of its advocates, not from the want of using the utmost latitude of conjecture, but simply from the impossibility of accomplishing the end proposed." (Green, HCP, 132)

2A. FATAL METHODOLOGICAL WEAKNESSES

Gleason Archer, a graduate of Suffolk Law School, sums up the fallacious methodology in this way:

> It is very doubtful whether the Wellhausen hypothesis is entitled to the status of scientific respectability. There is so much of special pleading, circular reasoning, questionable deductions from unsubstantiated premises that it is absolutely certain that its methodology would never stand up in a court of law. Scarcely any of the laws of evidence respected in legal proceedings are honored by the architects of this Documentary Theory. Any attorney who attempted to interpret a will or statute or deed of conveyance in the bizarre and irresponsible fashion of the source-critics of the Pentateuch would find his case thrown out of the court without delay. (Archer, SOTI, 99)

Some specific examples of these weaknesses are outlined below.

1B. The Imposition of a Modern Occidental View on Ancient Oriental Literature

The radical critics' approach is highly questionable when it is assumed that (1) the date of composition of each document can be confidently fixed, even with *no* other contemporary Hebrew literature available for comparison, and that, (2) unexpected or rare words in the Masoretic Text can be readily replaced by a more suitable word.

These practices are especially doubtful in light of Archer's observation:

As foreigners living in an entirely different age and culture, they have felt themselves competent to discard or reshuffle phrases or even entire verses whenever their Occidental concepts of consistency or style have been offended.

They have also assumed that scholars living more than 3,400 years after the event can (largely on the basis of philosophical theories) more reliably reconstruct the way things really happened than could the ancient authors themselves (who were removed from the events in question by no more than 600 or 1000 years even by the critic's own dating). (Archer, SOTI, 99)

2B. The Lack of Objective Evidence

Even the most dogmatic documentarian must admit that there is no objective evidence for the existence or the history of the J, E, or any of the documents alleged to make up the Torah. There is no manuscript of any portion of the Old Testament dating from earlier than the third century B.C. (Kitchen, AOOT, 2)

W. H. Green's comment on this point (in Chambers, *Moses and His Recent Critics*, pp. 104–5), cited by Torrey, is well taken: "All tradition and all historical testimony as to the origin of the Pentateuch are against them. The burden of proof is wholly upon the critics. And this proof should be clear and convincing in proportion to the gravity and the revolutionary character of the consequences which it is proposed to base upon it." (Torrey, HCNT, 74)

Bruce K. Waltke, Ph.D., Harvard University and Fellow of the Hebrew University in Jerusalem, states firmly: "Though one who has read only the popular literature advancing the conclusions of the literary analytical approach might not realize it, even the most ardent advocate of the theory must admit that we have as yet not a single scrap of tangible, external evidence for either the existence or the history of the sources J, E, D, P." (Albright, AP, 2)

3B. Substitution of Disintegrative Approach for Harmonistic Approach

The harmonistic approach is the standard methodology in the study both of literature and of ancient documents. Anytime it is abandoned for an attempt to find contradictions, literature will yield such "contradictions" by virtue of its inherent diversity. The same is true of biblical studies.

Allis has aptly noted: "Disintegration must result inevitably from the application of the disintegrative method of interpretation, whether the variations or differences appealed to are found in the form or in the content of the document to which it is applied." (Allis, FBM, 126)

Kyle draws a similar conclusion: "Criticism is not faultfinding, but it very easily becomes so. And when it sets out on a course of reconstruction which questions the integrity and trustworthiness of the documents to which it is applied, the disposition to find fault, to look for discord, is irresistible; indeed, it is essential to the process. But it is a fallacious method which is very apt to nullify processes of thought." (Kyle, DVMBC, 178)

One of the most painful features of this weakness is its tendency to fabricate problems normally not there. "Some of the alleged difficulties," avers Kitchen, "are merely the illegitimate product of the literary theory itself. Theories which artificially *create* difficulties that were previously nonexistent are obviously wrong and should therefore be discarded." (Kitchen, AOOT, 114)

The fallacy of this approach is epitomized by O. T. Allis's illustration:

It is to be noted, therefore, that the quest for such differences is a relatively simple and easy one. It would be a simple matter to break a crystal ball into a number of fragments and then to fill a volume with an elaborate description and discussion of the marked differences between the fragments thus obtained, and to argue that these fragments must have all come from different globes. The only conclusive refutation would be the proof that when fitted together they form once more a single globe. After all is said it is the unity and

> The logical fallacy committed by the radical critics is variously referred to as *petitio principii*, begging the question or arguing in a circle. Putting it simply, this is the practice of building one's desired conclusions into his premises so as to assure that said conclusions will result.

harmony of the Biblical narratives as they appear in the Scriptures which is the best refutation of the theory that these self-consistent narratives have resulted from the combining of several more or less diverse and contradictory sources. (Allis, FBM, 121)

4B. The Number of "Original Documents" Is Unlimited

Due to the disintegrative nature of the methodology and the absence of any objective controls, any consistent analysis of the text becomes ridiculous.

North has described some early instances of such effects.

Baentsch, it may be remembered, in his Leviticus Commentary (1900), worked with no less than seven P-sigla: P, Ps, Pss, Ph (xvii–xxvi), Po (i–vii), Pr (xi–xv), and Rp. Any one of the secondary sources might have a second (Ph5, Pr5) or third (Pr55) hand, together with redactors (Rpo, Rph) and even secondary redactors (Rp5). We even meet with refinements like Po1, Po2, Po5, Po25. This is surely the *reductio ad absurdum* of the analytical method. (North, PC, 56)

Recent analysis has fared no better; new sources such as J1, J2, L, K, and S have abounded. This has led North, a prominent spokesman for the radical critics, to a logical conclusion: "It seems likely that with sufficient analytical ingenuity it would be possible to sort out more such documents." (Cited by Albright, OTAP, 55)

Green clearly perceives the reasoning behind such boundless fragmentation. "It is," he notes, "the inevitable nemesis of the hypothesis reacting upon itself. The very principles and methods which are employed in dividing the Pentateuch into different documents, can be applied with like success and quite as much cogency in the division and subdivision of each of the documents to any assignable extent." (Harper, PQ, 164)

Equally perceptive is Allis, who points out that "if consistently applied the principles and methods of the higher criticism would lead to the complete disintegration of the Pentateuch and . . . it is only the failure on the part of the critics to apply them in thoroughgoing fashion which prevents this fiasco from occurring." (Allis, FBM, 89)

Alan Cole rings the death knell: "The old and tidy 'documentary hypothesis' has largely failed by its own success, with ever smaller and smaller units, or unconnected fragments postulated by scholars, instead of major and continuous written sources." (Cole, E, 13)

5B. Irresponsible Logic

The logical fallacy committed by the radical critics is variously referred to as *petitio principii*, begging the question or arguing in a circle. Putting it simply, this is the practice of building one's desired conclusions into his premises so as to assure that said conclusions will result. At least two blatant occurrences of this may be found.

1C. The Formulation of Documents J, E, D, and P

In the construction of the four primary documents, the characteristics of each document were predetermined. Then each passage containing the appropriate characteristics was assigned to the corresponding document.

S. R. Driver writes that "Elohim is not here accompanied by the other criteria of P's style, [that] forbids our assigning the sections thus characterized to that source." (Driver, ILOT, 13)

The result is four documents, each containing material having distinctive traits. But to then triumphantly assert that this demonstrates the original existence of these four documents is logically untenable, for the resulting "sources" are only the product of a predetermined purpose, totally devoid of any objective evidence or any parallel occurence in the world of literature. And so the argument spins in its unverifiable and meaningless circle.

2C. The Utter Dependence upon Redactors

With the introduction of the redactor, the radical critics add another example of a solution that originates in their construction

and not in fact. The redactor stretches their logic even thinner, for his presence ensures that any evidence that arises can, at least hypothetically, be falsified by material drawn from the arenas of logic and speculation, which thus is unsupportable.

Allis contends that

> in assigning to the redactor the role of editor and making him responsible for all the cases where the analysis does not work out as they think it should, the critics resort to a device which is destructive of their whole position. For the critics to blame the failure of the analysis to work out satisfactorily on an unknown redactor who has changed the text of his sources is equivalent to changing the actual text which the critics have before them in the interest of their theory as to what the text originally was. To put it bluntly, it is what is called "doctoring the evidence." By such means any theory can be proved or disproved. (Allis, FBM, 60)

And he elsewhere reminds us that "every appeal to the redactor is a tacit admission on the part of the critics that their theory breaks down at that point." (Allis, FBM, 39)

The renowned Jewish novelist Herman Wouk undertook a searching investigation of the documentary hypothesis. His reaction to the idea of a redactor deserves close attention. "With the discovery of the interpolater," writes Wouk, "Wellhausen's difficulties were at an end. As a tool of controversial logic this figure is wonderful. . . . When all else fails Wellhausen—grammar, continuity, divine names or outright falsifying of the plain sense of the Hebrew—he works [in] an interpolater." He declares that Engnell "dealt the death blow to the *Prolegomena* by analysing Wellhausen's villainous ghost, the interpolater, and driving it from the field with a polite scholarly horse laugh." (Wouk, TMG, 315–17)

3A. ULTIMATE FAILURE OF THE HYPOTHESIS

In his book *The Documentary Hypothesis,* the

> Wellhausen's arguments complemented each other nicely, and offered what seemed to be a solid foundation upon which to build the house of biblical criticism. Since then, however, both the evidence and the arguments supporting this structure have been called into question and, to some extent, even rejected. Yet biblical scholarship, while admitting that the grounds have crumbled away, nevertheless continues to adhere to the conclusions.
>
> —YEHEZKEL KAUFMAN

late Umberto Cassuto devotes six entire chapters to investigate the five most significant criteria the documentarians offer as evidence that Moses did not write the Pentateuch. He compares these five basic objections to pillars that hold up a house. (Naturally, these objections to Mosaic authorship are also supports for the documentary hypothesis.) About these supports or "pillars" of the documentary hypothesis, Cassuto writes in his concluding chapter: "I did not prove that the pillars were weak or that each one failed to give decisive support, but I established that they were not pillars at all, that they did not exist, that they were purely imaginary. In view of this, my final conclusion that the documentary hypothesis is null and void is justified." (Cassuto, DH, 100–1)

Another Jewish scholar, M. H. Segal, after investigating the Pentateuchal problem in his book *The Pentateuch—Its Composition and Its Authorship,* concludes:

> The preceding pages have made it clear why we must reject the Documentary Theory as an

explanation of the composition of the Pentateuch. The Theory is complicated, artificial and anomalous. It is based on unproved assumptions. It uses unreliable criteria for the separation of the text into component documents.

To these defects may be added other serious faults. It carries its work of analysis to absurd lengths, and neglects the synthetic study of the Pentateuch as a literary whole. By an abnormal use of the analytical method, the Theory has reduced the Pentateuch to a mass of incoherent fragments, historical and legalistic, to a collection of late legends and of traditions of doubtful origin, all strung together by late compilers on an artificial chronological thread. This is a fundamentally false evaluation of the Pentateuch. Even a cursory reading of the Pentateuch is sufficient to show that the events recorded therein are set out in logical sequence, that there is some plan combining its various parts and some purpose unifying all its contents, and that this plan and purpose find their realization in the conclusion of the Pentateuch which is also the end of the Mosaic age. (Segal, PCA, 22)

Thus, Wellhausen's documentary hypothesis must, in the final analysis, be regarded as unsuccessful in attempting to substantiate its denial of Mosaic authorship in favor of the JEDP source theory.

4A. SOME CLOSING COMMENTS

1B. The Jewish scholar, Yehezkel Kaufmann, describes the present state of affairs:

> Wellhausen's arguments complemented each other nicely, and offered what seemed to be a solid foundation upon which to build the house of biblical criticism. Since then, however, both the evidence and the arguments supporting this structure have been called into question and, to some extent, even rejected. Yet biblical scholarship, while

admitting that the grounds have crumbled away, nevertheless continues to adhere to the conclusions. (Kaufman, RI, 1)

2B. Mendenhall speaks of the continued acceptance of the documentarian evolutionary religious development: "It is at least a justified suspicion that a scholarly piety toward the past, rather than historical evidence, is the main foundation for their position." (Mendenhall, BHT, 36)

3B. Bright adds that even today the "documentary hypothesis still commands general acceptance, and must be the starting point of any discussion." (Bright, HI, 62)

4B. The renowned Jewish scholar Cyrus Gordon relates the almost blind adherence of many critics to the documentary theory: "When I speak of a 'commitment' to JEDP, I mean it in the deepest sense of the word. I have heard professors of Old Testament refer to the integrity of JEDP as their 'conviction.' They are willing to countenance modifications in detail. They permit you to subdivide (D1, D2, D3, and so forth) or combine (JE) or add a new document designated by another capital letter but they will not tolerate any questioning of the basic JEDP structure." (Gordon, HCFF, 131)

Gordon concludes: "I am at a loss to explain this kind of 'conviction' on any grounds other than intellectual laziness or inability to reappraise." (Gordon, HCFF, 131)

5B. The British scholar H. H. Rowley will not reject the theory simply because he sees nothing better to replace it with: "That it [the Graf-Wellhausen theory] is widely rejected in whole or in part is doubtless true, but there is no view to put in its place that would not be more widely and emphatically

rejected. . . . The Graf-Wellhausen view is only a working hypothesis, which can be abandoned with alacrity when a more satisfying view is found, but which cannot with profit be abandoned until then." (Rowley, GOT, 46)

According to this view it is better to hold to an invalid theory than to have to admit to not holding one at all.

6B. Cyrus Gordon, concluding an article in which he uncompromisingly criticizes the entire Wellhausen theory, gives a striking example of this unquestioned allegiance to the documentary hypothesis: "A professor of Bible in a leading university once asked me to give him the facts on JEDP. I told him essentially what I have written above. He replied: 'I am convinced by what you say but I shall go on teaching the old system.' When I asked him why, he answered: 'Because what you have told me means I should have to unlearn as well as study afresh and rethink. It is easier to go on with the accepted system of higher criticism for which we have standard textbooks.'" (Gordon, HCFF, 134)

7B. Such a statement would seem to justify Mendenhall's suspicion of many modern biblical critics: "It is much easier to follow the accepted pattern of the 19th century, especially since it has received some academic respectability, mostly through default, and to be content with pointing out a few inadequacies here and there which will show that one is keeping up to date." (Mendenhall, BHT, 38)

8B. Herman Wouk, the Jewish author and playwright, while not a professional biblical scholar as such, nevertheless provides some honest suggestions as to why there remains a general basic acceptance of the theories propounded by Wellhausen and his followers. In his book, *This Is My God,* Wouk offers this poignant evaluation: "It is a hard thing for men who have given their lives to a theory, and taught it to younger men, to see it fall apart." (Wouk, TMG, 318)

To this Wouk adds:

What the scholars had found out at long last, of course, was that literary analysis is not a scientific method. Literary style is a fluid, shifting thing, at best, a palimpsest or a pot-pourri. The hand of Shakespeare is in the pages of Dickens; Scott wrote chapters of Mark Twain; Spinoza is full of Hobbes and Descartes. Shakespeare was the greatest echoer of all, and the greatest stylist of all. Literary analysis has been used for generations by obsessive men to prove that everybody but Shakespeare wrote Shakespeare. I believe literary analysis could be used to prove that I wrote both *David Copperfield* and *A Farewell to Arms*. I wish it were sound. (Wouk, TMG, 317)

Section III

BIBLICAL CRITICISM
AND THE NEW TESTAMENT

27
INTRODUCTION TO
NEW TESTAMENT
FORM CRITICISM

The basic tenets of form criticism are examined. Practical answers are given to the basic assumptions and conclusions.

Source criticism can only take a person back to the written sources for the life of Christ, which appeared no earlier than twenty-five years after the events they recorded. The material was passed by word of mouth until it was written down in the form of the Gospels. Form criticism tries to fill in this gap of oral transmission.

The form critics assume that the Gospels are composed of small independent units or episodes. These small single units (pericopes) were circulated independently. The critics teach that the units gradually took on the form of various types of folk literature, such as legends, tales, myths, and parables.

According to form criticism, the formation and preservation of the units were basically determined by the needs of the Christian community *(Sitz im Leben)*. In other words, when the community had a problem, they either created or preserved a saying or episode of Jesus to meet the needs of that particular problem. Therefore, these units are not basically witnesses to the life of Christ but rather are considered to be the beliefs and practices of the early church.

This criticism proposes that the evangelists were not so much the writers as the editors of the four Gospels. They took the small units and put them in an artificial framework to aid in preaching and teaching. Phrases such as "again," "immediately," "after a few days," "while on the way" and "after this" are not historical. Instead, they provide a fictitious framework for gluing together the separate units or episodes. These chronological phrases serve as connectives for the various literary units.

The task of form criticism was to discover the "laws of tradition" which governed the collection, development, and writing down of the isolated units. Then with the removal of the artificial (editorial) framework of chronology provided by the evangelists, form criticism attempts to recover the original form of the units (pericopes) and determine for what practical purpose *(Sitz im Leben)* the early Christians preserved them.

By this method it was thought that one could "pierce back beyond written sources into the period of oral transmission and account for the rise of the different types of episodes which eventually became a part of the Gospels." (Fitzmyer, MMOTGT, 445)

Form criticism eventually became more than a literary analysis. It developed into a historical analysis and began to pass judgment on the historicity of various passages or units.

1A. DEFINITIONS

1B. Form criticism is basically the translation of the German word *Formgeschichte.* Its literal translation is "history of form."

Form criticism is the study of forms of literature and "documents that preserve earlier tradition. Its basic assumption is that the earlier, oral use of the tradition shaped the material and resulted in the variety of literary forms found in the final written record. Study of these forms, therefore, throws light on the life and thinking of the people who thus preserved tradition." (Filson, FC, 436)

2B. Robert Spivey and D. Moody Smith, in *The Anatomy of the New Testament,* further define the method of form criticism as "the classification of the 'forms' in which the tradition, especially the Gospel tradition, circulated before being written down and the attempt to determine the 'setting of life' of the church which they reflect." (Spivey, ANT, 463)

3B. As E. B. Redlich, a form critic, observes:

Form Criticism is a method of study and investigation which deals with the pre-literary stage of the Gospel tradition, when the material was handed down orally. It seeks to discover the origins and history of the material, that is to say, of the narratives and sayings which make up the Gospels, and to explain how the original narratives and sayings assumed their present form in the Gospels. It is concerned with the processes that led to the formation of the Gospels. (Redlich, FC, 9)

Laurence J. McGinley lists five basic principles of form criticism:

1. "The synoptic Gospels are popular, subliterary compositions.
2. "They depict the faith of the primitive Christians who created them, not the historical Jesus.
3. "They are artificial collections of isolated units of tradition.
4. "These units originally had a definite literary form which can still be detected.
5. "This form was created by a definite social situation." (McGinley, FCSHN, 4)

4B. G. E. Ladd defines form criticism by concluding that

the designation "form criticism" refers to the various literary forms which the oral tradition assumed as it was passed from mouth to mouth. Back of this study was the assumption that certain laws of oral tradition when applied to the Gospels will lead to the recovery of the earliest form of the tradition. A close study of these forms led to the critical conclusion that in its earliest stages, the material in the Gospels was passed on orally as a series of disconnected units, anecdotes, stories, sayings, teachings, parables, and so on. Each unit of tradition had its own history in the church. The historical outline of Jesus' career as it is found in Mark and largely embodied in Matthew and Luke is no part of this tradition, but is the creation of the author of the Second Gospel, who collected many of these units of tradition, created a historical outline for Jesus' career, and used this outline as a narrative thread upon which to string the disconnected beads of independent traditions. This means that the indications in the Gospels of sequence, time, place, and the like are quite unhistorical and untrustworthy and must therefore be ignored by serious Gospel criticism. As a result, we have no "life" or "biography"of Jesus, but only a series of detached anecdotes and teachings artificially and unhistorically strung together. (Ladd, NTC, 144, 145)

5B. Rudolf Bultmann, a radical form critic, explains the form critical approach by saying:

For over forty years now, students of the New Testament have been aware of the existence of a school of gospel research known as Form Criticism–or, more accurately, *Formgeschichte,* Form History. Its attention has been devoted to the component units into which the tradition underlying the Synoptic Gospels may be analyzed. It endeavors to study the oral tradition at a stage prior to its crystallization in gospels, or even in sources underlying the gospels, whether written documents or cycles of fixed tradition–such as Q, the pre-Marcan outline of Jesus' ministry, the sequences in the narratives and discourse material, the Passion Narrative, and so on. (Bultmann, FC, vii)

He continues his explanation:

Form Criticism begins with the realization that the tradition contained in the Synoptic Gospels originally consisted of separate units, which were joined together editorially by the evangelists. Form Criticism is therefore concerned to distinguish these units of tradition, and to discover their earliest form and origin in the life of the early Christian community. It views the gospels as essentially compilations of this older material. But it also studies them as finished works, in order to evaluate the literary activity of the evangelists, and to discover the theological motives that guided them. (Bultmann, FC, 3, 4)

2A. PURPOSES OF FORM CRITICISM

R. H. Lightfoot summarizes the precepts of form criticism:

They remind us that the early church is by no means likely to have expressed itself at once in a literary way, and they believe, first, that in the earliest years memories and traditions of the words and deeds of Jesus were only handed on from mouth to mouth, and secondly, that they were valued, not so much (as we might have expected) in and for themselves, as for their importance in solving problems connected with the life and needs of the young churches. These needs, they think, would be chiefly concerned with mission preaching, catechetical teaching, demonstration of the content and meaning of the Christian life, refutation of Jewish and other objections, and, perhaps above all, worship. They believe, further, that these memories and traditions would circulate at first chiefly in two forms: on the one hand, that of little, separate stories, and, on the other that of sayings of the Lord, whether in isolation or in small collections. Both would gradually assume a more or less fixed shape, through constant repetition in the churches; and, whatever may be true about the sayings, the stories would tend to form themselves upon the model of similar stories about teachers and leaders in the Jewish or the Hellenistic world. And, finally, they suggest that many of these pre-literary traditions are still discernible in our written gospels, especially St. Mark, and that to some extent they can be classified according to their type or form; whence the name of the new study. (Lightfoot, HIG, 30, 31)

Martin Dibelius provides an explanation: "It tries to bridge the gap in the New Testament by setting forth the common basis upon which both the doctrine of Jesus Christ and the narrative of Jesus of Nazareth rests." (Dibelius, GCC, 18)

He continues by citing one of the objectives of the form critical method: "In the first place, by reconstruction and analysis, it seeks to explain the origin of the tradition about Jesus, and thus to penetrate into a period previous to that in which our Gospels and their written sources were recorded." (Dibelius, FTG, Preface)

Dibelius adds that "it seeks to make clear the intention and real interest of the earliest tradition. We must show with what objective the first churches recounted stories about Jesus, passed them from mouth to mouth as independent narratives, or copied them from papyrus to papyrus. In the same manner we must examine the sayings of Jesus and ask with what intention these churches collected them, learnt them by heart, and wrote them down." (Dibelius, FTG, Preface)

Rudolf Bultmann has asserted, "The central principle of Form Criticism has been fully established, viz. that the earliest gospel traditions circulated orally within the church, whose religious needs they served, and were only gradually gathered together into groups, blocks, or sequences and finally gospels." (Bultmann, FC, ix)

He explains that form criticism has developed into "an attempt to apply to them [the Gospels] the *methods of form-criticism* which H. Gunkel and his disciples had already applied to the Old Testament. This involved discovering what the original units of the synoptics were, both sayings and stories, to try to establish what their historical setting was, whether they belonged to a primary or secondary tradition or whether they were the product of editorial activity." (Bultmann, HST, 2–3)

3A. METHODOLOGY

Vincent Taylor notes the steps taken in form criticism:

1. Classification of material by form.
2. Recovering of original form.
3. Search for *Sitz im Leben* (life-situation) (Taylor, FGT, 22)

Robert Mounce, in an informal interview,

has summarized the form critical procedure in the following manner:

The form critic first lists the various types of forms into which the Bible narratives may be divided. Then he tries to determine the *Sitz im Leben,* the situation in life, of the early church that accounts for the development of each of the pericopes which are placed in the categories. Was it fear of persecution? Was it the movement of the Gentile church out of the Jewish setting? Was it heresy? Etc.

After determination of the *Sitz im Leben,* one can account for the changes that have taken place and peel off the layers that have been added to the sayings of Jesus. The result is the return of the Gospel sayings, to their original or pure state. (Mounce, I)

4A. BACKGROUND AND HISTORY

1B. Background

Form criticism originated in Germany in the years after the close of the War of 1914–1918. (Redlich, FC, 16)

Floyd V. Filson explains the early history of form criticism of the synoptic Gospels:

It appeared as a clear-cut method in works by K. L. Schmidt (1919), M. Dibelius (1919), and R. Bultmann (1921), the three scholars whose work still dominates this field of study. It built upon many forerunners: Olrick's studies of folk tales; Gunkel's identification of oral traditions embedded in the Old Testament; Wellhausen's critical attention to the individual items of the gospel tradition and to the early stages of that tradition; Norden's study of prose style and mission discourses, etc. It built

> *What actually happens . . . to stories when they are passed from mouth to mouth in an unliterary community?*
>
> —C. F. D. MOULE

upon the concept that identification of written sources could not fully bridge the gap between Jesus and the written Gospels. A period of oral tradition had intervened and called for study. (Filson, FC, 436)

The outstanding scholars of the immediate pre-war age in Germany include Bernard Weiss, Holtzmann, Wrede, Johannes Weiss, Wellhausen, Gunkel, and Wendland. (Redlich, FC, 16)

In the field of form criticism, Easton parallels some main authors and their works: "Their authors are respectively, Martin Albertz, Rudolf Bultmann, Martin Dibelius and Karl Ludwig Schmidt. While their results are very diverse, all have in common the essential quality of endeavoring to define sharply the nature of the first Gospel tradition, and to determine something of the laws that governed its formation and transmission." (Easton, CG, 28–29)

Among other notable form critics are D. E. Nineham and R. H. Lightfoot.

Some of the less radical form critics include Frederick Grant, C. H. Dodd, B. S. Easton, and Vincent Taylor. They have been influenced by Bultmann and his followers, as evidenced in their writings and their use of the same or similar terminology. (Gundry, IFAFC, 2)

Rudolf Pesch continues to trace the early development of form criticism as he relates that

at the beginning of the present century, J. Weiss declared explicitly that the investigation of the literary forms of the gospels and of the individual groupings of material in them was one of the "tasks for contemporary scientific research into the N.T." (*Aufgaben der neutestamentlichen Wissenschaft in der Gegenwart* [1908], p. 35). But his predecessor, J. G. Herder, had already "recognized for the first time the problems involved in form-critical research into the gospels" (W. G. Kümmel, p. 98). Another predecessor toward the end of the previous century was F. Overbeck, who had called for "a history of the forms" of "the primitive literature of Christianity" (*Historische Zeitschrift* 48 [1882], p. 423). Before the First World War two classical scholars, P. Wendland (*Die urchristlichen Literaturformen* [1912]) and E. Norden (*Agnosthos Theos. Untersuchungen zur Formengeschichte religiöser Rede* [1913]), set in motion form-critical researches into the N.T. in certain important directions. After the War, the period of the form-critical approach really began. (Pesch, FC, 337–338)

C. F. D. Moule remarks that

the new impetus seems to have come at first from work on folklore, especially in the Old Testament, by scholars in Scandinavia and Germany, who claimed attention for the investigation of the laws of oral transmission. What actually happens, they asked, to stories when they are passed from mouth to mouth in an unliterary community? Gradually, at least two important principles formulated themselves in reply. First, that, by examining a sufficiently wide range of examples, one might become familiar enough with the standard "shapes" or "forms" assumed by stories in successive stages of transmission to be able, with some degree of accuracy, to strip the latest form of a given story down, by a kind of onion-peeling process, to its most primitive, original shape. And secondly, that it is a mistake to treat the sort of written documents which are now under discussion as though they were "literary," since the collective influence of communities was generally more important than any one individual in shaping a story, and even in molding a whole document. (Moule, FCPS, 87)

E. V. McKnight, in his short but thorough study of form criticism, *What Is Form Criticism?*, provides further background information concerning the positions arrived at through source criticism:

By the early part of the twentieth century the critical study of the Synoptic Gospels had arrived at the following positions: (1) The "two document" hypothesis was accepted. Mark and Q served as sources for Matthew and Luke. (2) Both Mark and Q, as well as Matthew and Luke, were influenced by the

> We hoped to be able to test the trustworthiness of the tradition of the life of Jesus by the employment of new and less subjective criteria, to escape in this way from the arbitrary judgments of the psychological treatment of the life of Jesus, and finally in some measure to establish more firmly the knowledge of the words and deeds of Jesus.
>
> —MARTIN DIBELIUS

theological views of the early church. (3) Mark and Q contained not only early authentic materials but also materials of a later date. (McKnight, WFC, 9,10)

2B. History

Bob E. Patterson, in an article entitled "The Influence of Form Criticism on Christology," has set forth a complete history of form criticism. (*Encounter*, Winter, 1970)

Donald Guthrie has observed that there has been a noticeable rise in the acceptance of form criticism. He notes that many influences have helped to produce and maintain this movement. Among these influences are:

(1) Weak points in the theory of source criticism. Being a literary criticism, source

criticism limited itself to the available documents. And, when studying Matthew and Luke, the source critic failed to deal with the twenty- to thirty-year span which came between the death of Jesus and the point in time when the written sources appeared. The form critics attempt to account for this time span.

(2) A general questioning of the historical accuracy of Mark. Wilhelm Wrede started this trend with his "Messianic Secret" theory, which stated that Mark wrote his Gospel with the purpose of conveying the unfolding revelation of Jesus' messiahship (or the conveyance of the "Messianic Secret").

Later, Julius Wellhausen put forth the idea that the original or first tradition in Mark was interlaced with added material from the Gospel writers and heavily dependent on the Christian thinking of that day.

(3) The desire to update the Gospels. Because the first-century view of the world is no longer relevant, according to form critics, an avid wish arose among these theologians to bring the Gospels into the world of the twentieth century.

(4) The attempt to position the literary materials in their original situation, life setting or *Sitz im Leben*. This thrust was readily observed in the form critics' appeal to the Gospel backgrounds. (Guthrie, NTI, 188, 195)

5A. MAJOR PROPONENTS OF FORM CRITICISM

1B. Martin Dibelius

Martin Dibelius, author of *From Tradition to Gospel, A Fresh Approach to the New Testament and Early Christian Literature, Gospel Criticism and Christology, Jesus,* and other major works, was one of the first renowned form critics. A summary presentation of his approach to form criticism follows.

Initially, he comments that "in prosecuting a research in the history of the Form of the Gospels, we must concern ourselves first of all and most of all with only one section of primitive Christian literature, namely the synoptic Gospels." (Dibelius, FTG, 2)

He continues: "The literary understanding of the synoptics begins with the recognition that they are collections of material. The composers are only to the smallest extent authors. They are principally collectors, vehicles of tradition, editors. Before all else their labor consists in handing down, grouping, and working over the material which has come to them." (Dibelius, FTG, 3)

Dibelius announces his personal goal in form criticism: "We hoped to be able to test the trustworthiness of the tradition of the life of Jesus by the employment of new and less subjective criteria, to escape in this way from the arbitrary judgments of the psychological treatment of the life of Jesus, and finally in some measure to establish more firmly the knowledge of the words and deeds of Jesus." (Dibelius, CGNTS, 42)

He interprets that "the first understanding afforded by the standpoint of *Formgeschichte* is that there never was a 'purely' historical witness to Jesus. Whatever was told of Jesus' words and deeds was always a testimony of faith as formulated for preaching and exhortation in order to convert unbelievers and confirm the faithful. What founded Christianity was not knowledge about a historical process, but the confidence that the content of the story was salvation: the decisive beginning of the End." (Dibelius, FTG, 295)

Another theological goal of *Formgeschichte*, as Dibelius puts it, is to undertake to depict a comprehension of the story of

Jesus, by which the frameworks of the material are dominated. (Dibelius, FTG, 295)

Dibelius alleges that the Gospels did not

> Bultmann's program has had a tremendous influence. . . . Nearly all leading theologians in Germany today are former students of his, or at least have been strongly influenced by his way of thinking. In the United States, similar but even more radical ideas have been advocated by Paul Tillich, and again we must say that many of the leading theologians belong to this school. Some go even so far as to say that the traditional idea of God, based on the Bible, is dead.
>
> —KLAAS RUNIA

intend to portray the person of Jesus Christ. With this being the case, we should not question the tradition preserved in the Gospels. But, if we did search them for information concerning the character or qualities of Christ, none would be found. By using secular interrogation and finding no answers, we must conclude that the tradition was not literary. (Dibelius, FTG, 300)

The fortune of primitive Christianity is reflected in the various forms of Gospel tradition. The form was "determined by ecclesiastical requirements arising in the course of missionary labor and of preaching." (Dibelius, FTG, 287)

The early church was a missionary church, and the "missionary purpose was the cause and preaching was the means of spreading abroad that which the disciples of Jesus possessed as recollections." (Dibelius, FTG, 13)

What drove the early Christians to such a propagation of the tradition "was the work of proselytizing to which they felt themselves bound, i.e. the missionary purpose." (Dibelius, FTG, 13)

When Dibelius speaks of preaching, "all possible forms of Christian propaganda are included: mission preaching, preaching during worship, and catechumen instruction. The mission of Christendom in the world was the originative cause of all these different activities." (Dibelius, FTG, 15)

There is only one complete connected narrative about a portion of the life of Christ and that is the "Passion story." (Dibelius, FTG, 23, 178) The main purpose of the "Passion story," according to Dibelius, was not to confirm the story but "to make clear what in the Passion took place by God's will." (Dibelius, FTG, 186)

All the other traditional units existed without any connection to other units.

In conclusion, Dibelius speaks of the formation of the Gospel tradition: "When, however, we trace the tradition back to its initial stage we find no description of the life of Jesus, but short paragraphs or pericopae. This is the fundamental hypothesis of the method of Form Criticism (formgeschichtliche Methode) as a representative of which I am speaking here." (Dibelius, GCC, 27)

2B. Rudolf Bultmann

Rudolf Bultmann, a former professor of New Testament studies at Breslau, Giessen, and Marburg, retired from his professorship in 1951. But he has continued to have a worldwide impact due to his outstanding contribution to contemporary New Testament critical scholarship. Bultmann has authored many books expressing the form critical viewpoint. Some of these are The History of the Synoptic Tradition, Jesus and the Word, Theology of the New Testament, and Jesus Christ and Mythology.

1C. The following represents a collection of statements about and by Bultmann:

Klaas Runia comments on the impact that Bultmann has made on the world:

Bultmann's program has had a tremendous influence upon postwar theology. Nearly all leading theologians in Germany today are former students of his, or at least have been strongly influenced by his way of thinking. In the United States, similar but even more radical ideas have been advocated by Paul Tillich, and again we must say that many of the leading theologians belong to this school. Some go even so far as to say that the traditional idea of God, based on the Bible, is dead. (Runia, MDAB, 13)

Rudolf Pesch continues: "R. Bultmann, whose approach is more strongly influenced by comparative religion and historical criticism, formulated the truth 'that the literature in which the life of a given community, even the primitive Christian community, is reflected, springs out of quite definite social conditions and needs, which produce a quite definite style and quite specific forms and categories.'" (Pesch, FC, 338)

H. N. Ridderbos observes that Bultmann's approach to the New Testament is to compare it to non-Christian religions and their development. This approach is called the method of the history of religion *(Religiongeschichte)*. (Ridderbos, B, 12)

Bultmann has been noted for his skeptical approach to the Gospels. It is his conclusion that "one can only emphasize the uncertainty of our knowledge of the person and work of the historical Jesus and likewise of the origin of Christianity." (Bultmann, FC, 20)

Bultmann describes the development of form criticism by stating that "the forms of the literary tradition must be used to establish the influences operating in the life of the community, and the life of the community must be used to render the forms themselves intelligible." (Bultmann, HST, 5)

Bultmann discusses his method: "The first step is to distinguish between the tradition material which the evangelists used and their editorial additions." (Bultmann, FC, 25)

2C. A Few Comments and Criticisms

G. E. Ladd points out that one of Bultmann's fundamental methods for reconstructing the early history of Christian thought and establishing the historicity of Jesus is the "comparative religious method."

"This is a method developed in German scholarship which assumes that any given religious phenomenon must be understood in terms of its religious environment." (Ladd, NTC, 8)

Schubert Ogden, in his book *Christ Without Myth*, has observed:

The first step in an imminent criticism of Bultmann's proposal is to show that its entire meaning may be reduced to two fundamental propositions: (1) Christian faith is to be interpreted exhaustively and without remainder as man's original possibility of authentic historical *(geschichtlich)* existence as this is more or less adequately clarified and conceptualized by an appropriate philosophical analysis. (2) Christian faith is actually realizable, or is a 'possibility in fact,' only because of the particular historical *(historisch)* event Jesus of Nazareth, which is the originative event of the church and its distinctive word and sacraments. The second step in the criticism is to demonstrate that, as Barth and Buri and many others have held, these two propositions are mutually incompatible. (Ogden, CWM, 111–112)

Edward Ellwein interprets Bultmann's view of what we can know of Jesus in this way:

Who is the man Jesus? He is a man like ourselves, not a mythical figure; he is without messianic radiance, a real man–but merely a man, a teacher and a prophet, who worked for a brief time, who prophesied the imminent end of the world and the breaking in of the rule of God, who renewed and radicalized the protest of the great Old Testament prophets against legalism and cultic worship of God, and who was delivered up by the Jews to the Romans and was crucified. Everything else is uncertain and legendary. (Ellwein, RBIK, 34)

Donald Guthrie, in his *New Testament Introduction,* identifies the underlying cause of Bultmann's theology:

Bultmann's disillusionment led him to seek an approach to the Gospels which would emancipate him from the need for historical demonstration. Only so could the simplest, in his opinion, ever come to faith. He was further prompted to this non-historical approach by his commitment to existential philosophy. Deeply influenced by Heidegger, Bultmann maintained that the most important element in Christian faith was an existential encounter with Christ. (Guthrie, NTI, 93–94)

In conclusion, Martin E. Marty from the University of Chicago states the different reactions toward Bultmann:

Rudolf Bultmann has been the greatest New Testament scholar of the twentieth century. So say many of his colleagues and rivals. No, Bultmann has muddied theological waters by tying himself to the tortured philosophy of his fellow Marburger, Martin Heidegger. So say most anti-Heideggerians, and their number is legion. Another voice, from a large Lutheran party in Germany, about their fellow Lutheran: Rudolf Bultmann is the archheretic of the century. (Marty, F, 10)

> *Bultmann maintained that the most important element in Christian faith was an existential encounter with Christ.*
>
> —DONALD GUTHRIE

3B. Vincent Taylor

Vincent Taylor, one of the major form critics, has actually been quite critical of the study that he supports. Taylor's primary work dealing with the area of form criticism has been *The Formation of the Gospel Tradition* that was first copyrighted in 1935. In this work he comments on what he concludes to be the major strengths and weaknesses of form criticism. Taylor does not possess the historical skepticism of Bultmann.

Initially, Taylor concurs with the form critics concerning their basic assumption:

It remains for us to consider the fundamental assumption of Form-Criticism, that, in the main, the earliest tradition consisted of small isolated units without local or temporal connections; and further, since the two questions are inseparable, to ask what place is to be given to the recollections of eyewitnesses. With the Gospel of Mark before us it is impossible to deny that the earliest tradition was largely a mass of fragments. (Taylor, FGT, 38–39)

Concerning the oral tradition as presented by Dibelius and Bultmann, Taylor tends to agree with both:

Form Criticism operates on the principle that the materials of the written Gospels can be divided into groups on the basis of differences in structure and form, and that these differences give us clues to the ways in which they developed in the pre-literary period. The differences grew out of the ways in which the elements of the Gospels were used in the day to day life of the Church, as material for preaching, for teaching, and for missionary propaganda. (Taylor, MGT, 470–71)

In reference to the crucial issue of community creativity and biographical interest, Taylor makes this assumption:

> Several reasons can be suggested for the want of a biographical interest. First, the early Christians were men of humble origin and attainments; they were not a literary people, and so did not face the problems which confront the chronicler. Further, their eyes were on the New Heaven and the New Earth which they believed Christ would soon bring. They did not know that nineteen centuries later we should still lack the consummation: nothing would have astonished them more. Their hopes were on the future; what need was there to record the past? Again, the formation of Jesus-tradition was largely a communal process. Stories had survival-value, not so much because they had interest for the individual, but because they ministered to the needs of

> In seeking parallels for the Gospel stories, Dibelius frequently refers to the rabbinic writings. Despite the relatively late redaction of this literature, he believes that the anecdotes themselves are of comparatively early origin and satisfactorily illustrate the synoptic narratives.
>
> —LAURENCE J. MCGINLEY

Christians who met together in religious fellowship. Had the first Christians a biographical interest?

So far as the Evangelists are concerned, somewhat different answers must be given. None of them aims at producing a biography in the modern sense of the term, although all wish to tell the Story of Jesus. In the Fourth Gospel the dominant aims are religious and doctrinal, but the material is presented in a historical framework. In Mark there is present a desire to sketch in outline the course of the

Ministry of Jesus, and the same outline is followed in Matthew, although here it is subordinated to didactic and ecclesiastical interests. In Luke the sixfold date of iii. 1f., and the terms of the Preface (i. 1–4) indicate an intention to tell the Story in orderly succession, although we cannot assume that chronological succession is meant, or still less is achieved. (Taylor, FGT, 143–144)

4B. Summary

To summarize these major proponents of form criticism, it is necessary to consider some of the similarities and differences among them.

1C. Similarities Between Dibelius And Bultmann

Although Bultmann and Dibelius classify the traditional material differently, that is, they see different forms with different life situations, they are in basic agreement about their fundamental assumption. That assumption is twofold. They agree that the traditional material first existed as brief, rounded units, having the early community as their *Sitz im Leben,* and that all historical contexts in the Gospels (with the exception of the Passion story) are to be regarded as the editorial work of the evangelists. (Gundry, IFAFC, 24–25)

E. V. McKnight continues to note the similarities between Dibelius and Bultmann: They "assume that the materials can be classified as to form and that the form enables the students to reconstruct the history of the tradition." (McKnight, WFC, 20)

L. J. McGinley approaches Dibelius and Bultmann in a slightly different manner. He points out that they have agreed on style, disagreed on terminology, agreed on material, disagreed on the growth of the tradition, disagreed on the *Sitz im Leben* and finally agreed with a complete denial of the historical value of their categories. (McGinley, FCSHN, 45–46)

McGinley continues:

Bultmann and Dibelius agree that the description and classification of forms is but one part of the task undertaken by form-criticism. They maintain that since there exists a relationship between the different literary species produced in a community and the various functions of the community life, this relationship can be detected and the historico-social situation which created a definite form to satisfy a definite need can be determined. (McGinley, FCSHN, 18,19)

McGinley observes that "in seeking parallels for the Gospel stories, Dibelius frequently refers to the rabbinic writings.

Form Criticism sounds like a scientific method. If it were, you would find consistency of interpretation. But the interpretations of a single saying vary widely. Not only are interpretations widespread but form critics often can't agree whether a pericopae is a miracle story or a pronouncement story—the two can be woven together. One would expect consistency in historical reconstruction if Form Criticism were a true science.

—ROBERT MOUNCE

Despite the relatively late redaction of this literature, he believes that the anecdotes themselves are of comparatively early origin and satisfactorily illustrate the synoptic narratives." (McGinley, FCSHN, 96)

McGinley adds that

Bultmann also makes abundant use of illustrations and analogies from the rabbinic tradition. He believes, however, that the process that led to its fixation was more complicated

than that which occurred with regard to the synoptic tradition. In the Gospels the forms were preserved more purely than in the rabbinic literature, where the formation was more conscious and where the motifs were artistically varied and individual units reshaped. (McGinley, FCSHN, 97)

2C. Some Basic Criticism

One of the most basic differences between Bultmann and Dibelius is their concept of the "controlling motive" in the formation of the units.

(1) Bultmann: The alleged debates between the early community and Judaism were the motive. (Bultmann, SSG, 39–44; Kenyon, BMS, 350–351)

(2) Dibelius: "Missionary goal" was the actual motive and "preaching" was the means of propagation. (Dibelius, FTG, 13)

Vincent Taylor provides a criticism of Bultmann when he claims that

Bultmann's tests of genuineness are much too subjective. Can we get very far by selecting a few characteristic features in the sayings of Jesus, and by making these a touchstone by which we decide the genuineness of the tradition as a whole? To decide what is characteristic is not easy, and, even if we can do this, the test must often fail because even the greatest of teachers often say familiar things. Great teachers refuse to be true to type, even their own type. (Taylor, FGT, 107–108)

Bultmann, who follows Martin Dibelius in the chronological development of form criticism, states that "in distinction from Dibelius I am indeed convinced that form-criticism, just because literary forms are related to the life and history of the primitive Church not only presupposes judgements of facts alongside judgements of literary criticism, but must also lead to judgements about facts (the genuineness of a saying, the historicity of a report and the like)." (Bultmann, HST, 5)

Alfred Wikenhauser presents a serious criticism against the major form critics:

> The ascription to the primitive Christian community of a really creative power is a serious defect in Form Criticism as it is applied by many of its exponents—notably by Bultmann and Bertram, and, less radically, by Dibelius; they maintain that certain parts of the synoptic Gospels were free creations of the community, or that motifs for their forming—especially for miracle stores or *Novellen,* and legends—were borrowed from Judaism and more particularly from Hellenism. (Wikenhauser, NTI, 276)

One of the major accusations against the form critics has been in the area of subjectivity. Robert Mounce, in an interview, has commented on this particular problem as he says: "Form Criticism sounds like a scientific method. If it were, you would find consistency of interpretation. But the interpretations of a single saying vary widely. Not only are interpretations widespread but form critics often can't agree whether a pericopae is a miracle story or a pronouncement story—the two can be woven together. One would expect consistency in historical reconstruction if Form Criticism were a true science." (Mounce, 144)

I. J. Peritz, also commenting on the area of subjectivity of the form critics, has concluded:

> Form Criticism thus brings face to face with the obligation either to acquiesce in its faulty method and conclusions or to combat them. What is involved, however, is not the alternative between an uncritical attitude and criticism, but between criticism and hypercriticism. A critical view of the Gospels does not claim strict objectivity. It is hard to tell

sometimes where poetry ends and history begins. It is highly probable that there is no underlying strictly chronological or topographical scheme; and that they are not biography in "our sense." But this is far from admitting that we have no reliable testimony from eyewitnesses: that the Church from its

> Bultmann's tests of genuineness are much too subjective. Can we get very far by selecting a few characteristic features in the sayings of Jesus, and by making these a touchstone by which we decide the genuineness of the tradition as a whole? To decide what is characteristic is not easy, and, even if we can do this, the test must often fail because even the greatest of teachers often say familiar things. Great teachers refuse to be true to type, even their own type.
>
> —VINCENT TAYLOR

Christ of faith created the Jesus of history, instead of from the Jesus of history its Christ of faith. (Peritz, FCE, 205)

He adds: "The great fault of Form Criticism is its imaginative subjectivity in evaluating tradition." (Peritz, FCE, 205)

In a recent periodical Peritz sums up the views of form critics by stating that "it is only in one thing they all agree, namely, that the earliest disciples of Jesus were too ignorant in literary method or too indifferent to biography or history to make an effort to perpetuate the memory of their Master." (Peritz, FCE, 202)

6A. IN SUMMARY

1B. Form criticism seeks to discover the original literary forms in which the traditions of Jesus were written down.

2B. The form critics hope by discovering the original forms to be able to identify the needs of the early church that prompted their creation.

3B. The form critical method involves dividing the Gospels as to literary form, then seeking the life situation that brought them into being. They seek to reduce the Gospels to their original pure state.

4B. Form criticism was born in Germany following World War I.

5B. Among its major proponents are Martin Dibelius, Rudolf Bultmann, and Vincent Taylor.

28
HISTORICAL
SKEPTICISM

1A. BASIC ASSUMPTION

The New Testament writings do not portray a historical picture of Jesus.

Rudolf Bultmann quotes Julius Wellhausen as saying: "The spirit of Jesus undoubtedly breathes in the utterances derived from the community at Jerusalem; but we do not derive a historical picture of Jesus himself from the conception of Jesus which prevailed in the community." (Bultmann, NASP, 341)

In order to establish a principle for historical research of Jesus, Wellhausen goes on to say: "We must recognize that a literary work or a fragment of tradition is a primary source for the historical situation out of which it arose, and is only a secondary source for the historical details concerning which it gives information." (Bultmann, NASP, 341)

This assertion leads us to view the Gospels as a secondary source for the facts concerning Jesus. J. Martin concurs: "Gospels must be taken as reliable renderings of *what the Church believed at the time of writing* concerning the facts on which its faith was founded." (Martin, RG, 44)

Therefore, R. H. Lightfoot, a noted critic, infers: "It seems, then, that the form of the earthly no less than of the heavenly Christ is for the most part hidden from us. For all the inestimable value of the gospels, they yield us little more than a whisper of his voice; we trace in them but the outskirts of his ways." (Lightfoot, HIG, 225)

1B. The Opinion of Albert Schweitzer

The search for a historical Jesus, a Jesus whose existence could be concretely proven (outside the Bible and Christian experience), was led by critic Albert Schweitzer. He writes: "The Jesus of Nazareth who came forward as the Messiah, who preached the ethic of the Kingdom of God, who founded the Kingdom of Heaven upon earth, and died to give His work its final consecration, never had any existence. He is a figure designed by rationalism, endowed with life by liberalism, and clothed by modern theology in an historical garb." (Schweitzer, PSJ, 396)

Schweitzer continues with an observation about the problem of our study of a historical Jesus, which itself, he claims, has had erratic background:

The study of the Life of Jesus has had a curious history. It set out in quest of the historical Jesus, believing that when it had found Him it could bring Him straight into our time as a Teacher and Savior. It loosed the bands by which He had been riveted for centuries to the stony rocks of ecclesiastical doctrine, and rejoiced to see life and movement coming into the figure once more, and the historical Jesus

advancing, as it seemed, to meet it. But He does not stay; He passes by our time and returns to His own. (Schweitzer, PSJ, 397)

2B. The Opinion of Martin Dibelius

Martin Dibelius doubts any historical interest in Jesus: "The first Christians had no interest in reporting the life and passion of Jesus objectively to mankind, *sine ira et studio.* They wanted nothing else than to win as many as possible to salvation in the last hour just before the end of the world, which they believed to be at hand. Those early Christians were not interested in history." (Dibelius, GCC, 16)

Attacking the objectivity of biblical events, Dibelius elaborates on the aspect of Christian "propaganda" clouding the true historical picture: "A further limitation of the historicity of the tradition is entailed by this concentration of interest on its missionary application. The stories are couched in a certain style, that is to say, they are told in a way calculated to edify believers and to win over unbelievers. They are not objective accounts of events." (Dibelius, GCC, 76)

3B. The Opinion of Rudolf Bultmann

The skepticism of the historical truth of Jesus' life often surfaces in Bultmann's theology: "I do indeed think that we can now know almost nothing concerning the life and personality of Jesus, since the early Christian sources show no interest in either, are moreover fragmentary and legendary; and other sources about Jesus do not exist." (Bultmann, JW, 8)

He proclaims "the *character* of Jesus, the vivid picture of his personality and his life, cannot now be clearly made out." (Bultmann, FC, 61)

Bultmann comments on a historical method of searching the Scriptures, and his view of how an event, such as a miracle,

> [The consequence of employing the historical skepticism of the form critics is that the] Son of God incarnate in Jesus of Nazareth becomes a product rather than the creator of Christian faith.
>
> —GEORGE E. LADD

should be interpreted (actually ruled out):

The historical method includes the presupposition that history is a unity in the sense of a closed continuum of effects in which individual events are connected by the succession of cause and effect. This does not mean that the process of history is determined by the causal law and that there are no free decisions of men whose actions determine the course of historical happenings. But even a free decision does not happen without cause, without a motive; and the task of the historian is to come to know the motives of actions. All decisions and all deeds have their causes and consequences; and the historical method presupposes that it is possible in principle to exhibit these and their connection and thus to understand the whole historical process as a closed unity.

This closedness means that the continuum of historical happenings cannot be rent by the interference of supernatural, transcendent powers and that therefore there is no "miracle" in this sense of the word. Such a miracle would be an event whose cause did not lie within history.... It is in accordance with such a method as this that the science of history goes to work on all historical documents. And there cannot be any exceptions in the case of biblical texts if the latter are at all to be understood [as] historical. (Bultmann, EF, 291–292)

He adds: "All this goes to show that the interest of the gospels is absolutely different from that of the modern historian. The historian can make progress toward the recovery of the life of Jesus only through the process of critical analysis. The gospels, on the other hand, proclaim Jesus Christ, and were meant to be read as proclamations." (Bultmann, FC, 70)

It is not the existence of Jesus that Bultmann questions; rather, he questions how objective the Gospel writers were.

Bultmann concludes that "the doubt as to whether Jesus really existed is unfounded and not worth refutation. No sane person can doubt that Jesus stands as founder behind the historical movement whose first distinct stage is represented by the oldest Palestinian community. But how far that community preserved an objectively true picture of him and his message is another question." (Bultmann, JW, 13)

Fuller sums up Bultmann's view: "All we know, he says, is that Jesus was executed by the Romans as a political criminal. But what we can reconstruct does not take us very far." (Fuller, NTCS, 14)

The extreme skepticism of Bultmann is not adhered to by Dibelius. He admits that some of the earliest pieces of tradition possess "authentic memories" conveyed by eyewitnesses.

4B. The Opinion of Ernst Käsemann

A former student of Rudolf Bultmann, Ernst Käsemann holds that "it was not historical but kerygmatic interest which handed them [the individual units of Gospel tradition] on. From this standpoint it becomes comprehensible that this tradition, or at least the overwhelming mass of it, cannot be called authentic. Only a few words of the Sermon on the Mount and of the conflict with the Pharisees, a number of parables and some scattered material of various kinds go back with any degree of probability to the Jesus of history himself. Of his deeds, we know only that he had the reputation of being a miracle-worker, that he himself referred to his power of exorcism and that he was finally crucified under Pontius Pilate. The preaching about him has almost entirely supplanted his own preaching, as can be seen most clearly of all in the completely unhistorical Gospel of John." (Käsemann, ENT, 59–60)

In approaching the problem of historical revision of the Gospel material by the community, Käsemann maintains: "To state the paradox as sharply as possible: the community takes so much trouble to maintain historical continuity with him who once trod this earth that it allows the historical events of this earthly life to pass for the most part into oblivion and replaces them by its own message." (Käsemann, ENT, 20)

His fixation on one's existential identification with the cross, instead of a historically based faith, leads him to conclude that "for this reason the historical element in the story of Jesus has, in these other writings, shrunk almost to vanishing point." (Käsemann, ENT, 21)

2A. REBUTTAL

The consequence of employing the historical skepticism of the form critics is exposed by Ladd: "The Son of God incarnate in Jesus of Nazareth becomes a product rather than the creator of Christian faith. He is no longer seen as the Saviour of the Christian community." (Ladd, NTC, 147)

1B. The Result of Following Bultmann

What remains after Bultmann and his followers have eliminated from tradition most of the Gospel material as historically inaccurate and as creations of the community?

Peter G. Duncker cites P. Benoit concerning what would be left:

Very little; a quite inoffensive residue: Jesus of Galilee, who thought himself to be a prophet, who must have spoken and acted accordingly, without our being able to say exactly what he spoke and how he acted, who eventually died in a lamentable way. All the rest: his divine origin, his mission of salvation, the proof he gave for these by his words and miracles, finally the resurrection which set a seal on his work, all this is pure fiction, proceeding from faith and cult, and clothed with a legendary tradition, which was formed in the course of the preachings and the disputes of the primitive community [Benoit, Pierre. *Exégèse of Théologie.* (p. 46, Vol. I) Paris: Editions du Cerf. 1961]. (Duncker, BC, 28)

One author, David Cairns, has made this conclusion about Bultmann's form of theology, which runs away from the historical toward the existential: "Our provisional conclusion in this chapter must be that none of the justifications urged by Bultmann in support of his flight from history carries conviction. The whole enterprise resembles too much the remedy of decapitation as a cure for a headache." (Cairns, GWM, 149)

A frightening aspect of Bultmann's approach to the New Testament is observed by Ellwein when he notes Bultmann's existential basis: "Is it not a disturbing feature of Bultmann's interpretation of the New Testament message when the historical reality of the historical Jesus of Nazareth becomes a 'relative X'? This means that the occurrence of God's revelation which has assumed bodily and historical form in Jesus evaporates and is, so to speak, placed within parentheses." (Ellwein, RBIK, 42)

Ellwein continues: "All that remains is the punctual event of preaching, a kind of 'mathematical point' which lacks any extension just because this very extension would illicitly render the 'other-worldly' into something 'this-worldly.'" (Ellwein, RBIK, 42)

Bultmann's desire to exclude historical framework and analysis "leaves a mangled text, of interest neither to the primitive Christian nor the modern exegete." (McGinley, FCSHN, 70)

2B. The Historical Accounts of the Disciples

Peritz cites the purpose of the disciples to be the recording of the Gospels. He claims: "To declare, as Form Critics do, that the early disciples of Jesus expected the end of the age and had no interest in history, may be true of a small group; but it was not true of all. If it were true of all, we should have no gospel records whatever; and Luke's 'many' who had attempted gospel accounts could not have existed." (Peritz, FCE, 205)

A. N. Sherwin-White makes a comparison between the methods of writing history used by the Roman writers and the Gospel

> For all their effort to create a conviction about that person, and to testify to the divine power that operated through him, they are essentially reporters, not free to invent or falsify the data which the tradition of their churches presented as having happened in Galilee and Judaea a generation earlier.
>
> —E.C. BLACKMAN

writer. He concludes that "it can be maintained that those who had a passionate interest in the story of Christ, even if their interest in events was parabolical and didactic rather than historical, would not be led by that very fact to pervert and utterly destroy the historical kernel of their material." (Sherwin-White, RSRLNT, 191)

F. F. Bruce comments on the historical accuracy of Luke: "A man whose accuracy can be demonstrated in matters where we are able to test it is likely to be accurate even where the means for testing him are not available. Accuracy is a habit of mind, and we know from happy (or unhappy) experience that some people are habitually accurate just as others can be depended upon to be inaccurate. Luke's record entitles him to

be regarded as a writer of habitual accuracy." (Bruce, NTDATR, 90)

Blackman notes the dependability of the Gospel writers as he indicates that

> Luke's awareness that the salvation-history concerning Jesus of Nazareth is a part of history as a whole. In this Luke is not to be completely differentiated from his fellow evangelists. All of them are conscious of being reporters of real events played out by a real historical person. For all their effort to create a conviction about that person, and to testify to the divine power that operated through him, they are essentially reporters, not free to invent or falsify the data which the tradition of their churches presented as having happened in Galilee and Judaea a generation earlier. (Blackman, JCY, 27)

3B. The Unique Character of Jesus

Regarding the unique character of Jesus as the foundation of the authenticity of the New Testament, E. F. Scott makes an observation about the attack of the critics: "(Their) evidence would hardly be challenged if they were concerned with some other hero of antiquity, and it is only because they recount the life of Jesus that they are viewed suspiciously." (Scott, VGR, 1)

If one is to judge the historicity of Jesus, then He ought to be judged as impartially as any other figure in history. F. F. Bruce testifies that "the historicity of Christ is as axiomatic for an unbiased historian as the historicity of Julius Caesar. It is not historians who propagate the 'Christ-myth' theories." (Bruce, NTDATR, 119)

> The earliest propagators of Christianity welcomed the fullest examination of the credentials of their message. The events which they proclaimed were, as Paul said to King Agrippa, not done in a corner, and were well able to bear all the light that could be thrown on

them. The spirit of these early Christians ought to animate their modern descendants. For by an acquaintance with the relevant evidence they will not only be able to give to everyone who asks them a reason for the hope that is in them, but they themselves, like Theophilus, will thus know more accurately how secure is the basis of the faith which they have been taught. (Bruce, NTDATR, 119–120)

The claims by the New Testament writers about the character of the historical Jesus are not seen to be a problem by Montgomery:

However, the inability to distinguish Jesus' claims for himself from the New Testament writers' claims for him should cause no dismay, since (1) the situation exactly parallels that for all historical personages who have not themselves chosen to write (e.g., Alexander the Great, Augustus Caesar, Charlemagne). We would hardly claim that in these cases we can achieve no adequate historical portraits. Also, (2) the New Testament writers, as we saw in the previous chapter, record eyewitness testimony concerning Jesus and can therefore be trusted to convey an accurate historical picture of him. (Montgomery, HC, 48)

4B. Ancient Historiography

J. P. Moreland presents the main issue: "Were ancient historians able to distinguish fact from fiction? Is there any evidence that they desired to do so? The works of Greek, Roman and Jewish historians all probably influenced the New Testament writers." (Barrett, MNT, 87)

Thus, a major objection often penned against the Gospels as ancient documents is that their authors (as well as authors of other ancient documents) lived in a different historical arena where factual accuracy was not important.

Moreland continues by discussing some of the evidence:

Among Greek writers, many discussed the importance of giving an accurate account of what happened. Herodotus emphasizes the role of eyewitnesses in historical reporting. The historian must, however, evaluate and verify their reports using common sense. Reports of superhuman and miraculous occurrence should be regarded with suspicion. Thucydides also attempted to evaluate the accuracy of reports that came to him. In *History of the Peloponnesian War,* 1.22.1, he does admit that on occasion he did invent speeches. But in those cases he attempted to be consistent with what was known of the speaker. In any case, he did not feel free to invent narrative. Polybsius held very exacting standards. He advocated examination of sources, objectivity, and castigated superstition and a 'womanish love of the miraculous.' He also advocated the questioning of reliable eyewitnesses. (Barrett, MNT, 88)

A. W. Mosely concludes his article, "Historical Reporting in the Ancient World," with the following summation: "The survey shows clearly, then, that the question, 'Did it happen in this way?' was a question which made sense to the people living at that time, and was a question which was often asked. People living then knew that there was a difference between fact and fiction."

Mosely further states:

Generally it was easier to be inaccurate when a writer was dealing with events that had happened a long time before. Writers who were dealing with events of the recent past—eyewitnesses being still alive—seem generally to have tried to be as accurate as possible and to get the information from the eyewitnesses. They knew they could not get away with inventing freely stories of events and personalities of the recent past. We note that Josephus accused Justus of holding back publication of his history until eyewitnesses were no longer available and this is strongly condemned. We have seen that these historians (e.g., Lucian, Dionysius, Polybius, Ephorus, Cicero, Josephus and Tacitus) were quick to criticize their fellow writers if they gave inaccurate accounts. A person who gave an inaccurate account of something that had happened was regarded as having—in some measure at least—failed. We would expect to find that such charges were brought against the New Testament writers if they had failed in this way. (Mosely, HRAW, 26)

Our survey has not proven anything conclusive about the attitude of the New Testament writers to the historicity of the traditions they received and passed on about the historical Jesus, but it would suggest that we should not assume from the start that they could not have been interested in the question of authenticity. It is quite possible that people were concerned to distinguish which reports were factually true, and that this influenced the development of the Christian tradition, both in the period where

> The Christians may not have been interested in "history"; but they were certainly interested in the "historical." The preachers of the new faith may not have wanted to narrate *everything* about Jesus, but they certainly did not want to relate anything that was not real.
>
> —PIERRE BENOIT

reports were passed on orally, and later when the tradition came to be written down. (Bowman, FSB, 26)

5B. The View of the Critics—Is It Truly Impartial?

Objecting to form critics' personal opinions, Redlich writes: "Historical Criticism must not be identified, as Form Critics often do, with the critic's own personal opinion of

the historical truth of a narrative or saying. This latter is a historical value-judgment. It has no connection with laws of the tradition or with formal characteristics." (Redlich, FC, 11)

McNeile believes that the form critics have gone too far in passing judgment on the contents of the Gospels, for their method is a literary one—not historical. (McNeile, ISNT, 54)

G. E. Ladd reasons: "It must be recognized that modern biblical criticism was not the product of a believing scholarship concerned with a better understanding of the Bible as the Word of God in its historical setting, but of scholarship which rejected the Bible's claim to be the supernaturally inspired Word of God." (Ladd, NTC, 38)

6B. Conclusion

"The Christians," concludes Pierre Benoit, "may not have been interested in 'history'; but they were certainly interested in the 'historical.' The preachers of the new faith may not have wanted to narrate *everything* about Jesus, but they certainly did not want to relate anything that was not real." (Benoit, JG, 32)

Benoit poses the following question: "Is it credible that the converts accepted so novel a faith, which demanded so much of them, on the strength of mere gossip-sessions, at which Dibelius and Bultmann's preachers invented sayings and actions which Jesus never uttered and never performed merely to suit themselves?" (Benoit, JG, 32)

Filson notes the ultimate result of extending the form critic's historical skepticism:

As may readily be seen, if the Gospels thus reflect the life and thought of the primitive Church, the problem of the reliability of the material for the study of Jesus' life arises. This is frankly recognized by the form critic, and when an element of the tradition shows a developed church interest, or a Hellenistic character, it is rejected from the fund of usable data for the life of Jesus. Since all the material preserved was used by the Church, this skepticism may go so far as practically to deny that we have any dependable data left with which to picture the historical Jesus. (Filson, OG, 99)

Emphasizing the need for external evidence, Albright holds that "the ultimate historicity of a given datum is never conclusively established nor disproved by the literary framework in which it is imbedded; there must always be external evidence." (Albright, ICCLA, 12)

Albright adds: "From the standpoint of the objective historian data cannot be disproved by criticism of the accidental literary framework in which they occur, unless there are solid independent reasons for rejecting the historicity of an appreciable number of other data found in the same framework." (Albright, FSAC, 293–294)

Finally, the testimony of contemporary historians of Jesus' day should be acknowledged. Laurence J. McGinley confirms:

In any study of the Synoptic Gospels, whether it's Dibelius' concentration on transmission and composition or Bultmann's historical portrayal of the synoptic tradition from origin to crystallization, something should be said for historical testimony. But, it's not! [H. Dieckmann, *"Die Formgeschichtliche Methode und ihre Anwendung auf die Auferstehungs Berichte,"* Scholastik, I, 1926, p. 389] External testimony such as Irenaeus, Tertullian, and Origen is noticeably not referred to. Justin's observation that the Gospels are merely apostolic memoirs [Apologia, I, 66] is mentioned only to be rejected as misleading [Bultmann, *Die Erforschung der Synoptischen Evangelien, The New Approach,* p. 397]. Papias' testimony [Eusebius, *Ecclesiastical History,* III, 39 (MP6,

xx, 296–300) pp. 22, 23] of Matthew and Mark fares no better. Bultmann refers to Papias' reference to Mark as the interpreter of Peter—as an error; Dibelius refers to Papias' testimony on the authorship of Matthew and Mark but concludes that he has been mislead by thinking that the evangelists were really authors [Bultmann, *Zur Formgeschichte der Evangelien,* Theol. Rund. N.F.I. 1929, p. 10]. This neglect of historical testimony seems to show a lack of completeness and perspective.

As De Grandmaison remarks, "It is the wisest method in these matters to prefer an ounce of ancient information which is authentic to a bookful of learned conjectures" [De Grandmaison, *Jesus Christ,* I, 1935, p. 115]. (McGinley, FCSHN, 22–23)

Norman Pittenger declares: "Let us take it for granted that all attempts to deny the historicity of Jesus have failed." (Pittenger, PHJ, 89–90)

3A. IN SUMMARY

1B. Form criticism assumes the New Testament portrays what the church *believed* to be true of Jesus, rather than what *was* true.

2B. The answer—Bultmann's conclusions concerning the historical inaccuracy of the Gospels are unsound, for not even the Christian would be interested in the end product of a Gospel taken out of its historical framework.

1C. Luke proved himself to be habitually accurate.

2C. No other historical figure is attacked as Jesus is. Critics' views are not impartial.

3C. Attempts to deny the historicity of Jesus have failed.

29
JESUS UNDER FIRE

1A. THE HISTORICAL QUESTS FOR JESUS

Over the past few centuries many doctrines of the historical, orthodox Christian faith have been challenged by liberal thinkers all over the world. None has been more harmful for the church than the seemingly never-ending quest for the historical Jesus.

In Walter Elwell's *Evangelical Dictionary of Theology*, R. H. Stein gives the history of the quest for the historical Jesus:

> The beginning of the quest for the historical Jesus can be dated to 1774–78 when the poet Lessing published posthumously the lecture notes of Hermann Samuel Reimarus. These notes challenged the traditional portrait of Jesus found in the NT and the church.
>
> For Reimarus, Jesus never made any messianic claim, never instituted any sacraments, never predicted his death nor rose from the dead. The story of Jesus was in fact a deliberate imposture of the disciples. In so portraying Jesus, Reimarus raised the question, "What was Jesus of Nazareth really like?" And so the

quest to find the "real" Jesus arose. (Stein, JC, as cited in Elwell, EDT, 584)

This quest for the Jesus of history has continued throughout the past two centuries, taking on many different shapes and forms. In fact, the past two centuries have seen "three" different quests for the historical Jesus. Before looking at each one individually, it may help to see the quests in chart form as proposed. (Horrell, T, 30)

1B. The First Quest

"During the earliest part of the nineteenth century, the dominating method of research in the quest was rationalism, and attempts were made to explain 'rationally' the life of Christ (cf. K. H. Venturini's *A Non-Supernatural History of the Great Prophet of Nazareth*). A major turning point came when D. F Strauss's *The Life of Christ* was published in 1835, for Strauss in pointing out the futility of the rationalistic approach argued that the miraculous in the Gospels was to be understood as nonhistorical 'myths.' This new approach was in turn succeeded by the liberal interpretation of the life of Jesus, which minimized and neglected the miraculous dimension of the Gospels and viewed it as 'husk' which had to be eliminated in order to concentrate on the teachings of Jesus. Not surprisingly, this approach found in the teachings of Jesus such liberal doctrines as the fatherhood of God, the brotherhood of man, and the infinite value of the human soul." (Stein, JC, as cited in Elwell, EDT, 584)

Gary Habermas states: "There have been many popular attempts to discredit the Jesus of the Gospels. Even in the eighteenth and nineteenth centuries these attempts were prevalent. While they have been rejected almost unanimously by careful scholars, especially those who remember similar attempts disproven long ago, they still receive widespread attention among lay people." (Habermas, HJ, 98).

Stein cites several reasons for the temporary demise of the Quest:

For one, it became apparent, through the work of Albert Schweitzer; that the liberal Jesus never existed but was simply a creation of liberal wishfulness. Another factor that

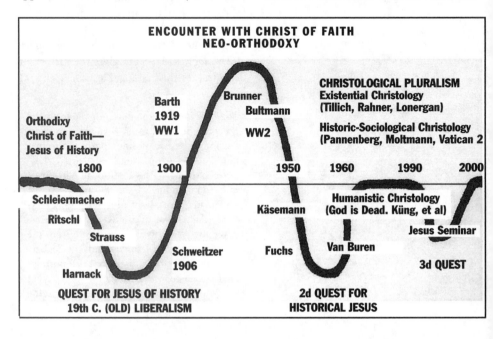

ENCOUNTER WITH CHRIST OF FAITH
NEO-ORTHODOXY

Barth
1919
WW1

Brunner
Bultmann
WW2

CHRISTOLOGICAL PLURALISM
Existential Christology
(Tillich, Rahner, Lonergan)

Historic-Sociological Christology
(Pannenberg, Moltmann, Vatican 2

Orthodixy
Christ of Faith—
Jesus of History

| 1800 | 1900 | 1950 | 1960 | 1990 | 2000 |

Schleiermacher

Ritschl

Strauss

Harnack

Schweitzer
1906

Käsemann

Fuchs

Van Buren

Humanistic Christology
(God is Dead. Küng, et al)

Jesus Seminar

3d QUEST

QUEST FOR JESUS OF HISTORY
19th C. (OLD) LIBERALISM

2d QUEST FOR
HISTORICAL JESUS

helped end the quest was the realization that the Gospels were not simple objective biographies which could easily be mined for historical information. This was the result of the work of William Wrede and the form critics. Still another reason for the death of the quest was the realization that the object of faith for the church throughout the centuries had never been the historical Jesus of theological liberalism but the Christ of faith, i.e., the supernatural Christ proclaimed in the Scriptures. Martin Kahler was especially influential in this regard. (Stein, JC, as cited in Elwell, EDT, 585)

2B. The Second Quest

During the period between the two World Wars, the quest lay dormant for the most part due to disinterest and doubt as to its possibility. In 1953 a new quest arose at the instigation of Ernst Käsemann. Käsemann feared that the discontinuity in both theory and practice between the Jesus of history and the Christ of faith was very much like the early docetic heresy, which denied the humanity of the Son of God. As a result he argued that it was necessary to establish a continuity between the historical Jesus and the Christ of faith. Furthermore, he pointed out that the present historical skepticism about the historical Jesus was unwarranted because some historical data were available and undeniable. The results of this new quest have been somewhat disappointing, and the enthusiasm that greeted it can be said, for the most part, to have disappeared. New tools have been honed during this period, however; which can assist in this historical task. (Stein, JC, as cited in Elwell, EDT, 584–585)

> The Jesus Seminar and its friends do not reflect any consensus of scholars except for those on the "radical fringe" of the field. Its methodology is seriously flawed and its conclusions unnecessarily skeptical.
>
> —CRAIG BLOMBERG

3B. The Third Quest

Dr. Geisler explains the latest quest:

The most recent research into the historical Jesus is largely a reaction to the "new quest." It is multifaceted, including some from the radical tradition, a new perspective tradition, and conservatives. In the "conservative" category are I. Howard Marshall, D. F. D. Moule, and G. R. Beasley-Murray. They reject the idea that the picture of the New Testament Jesus was somehow painted by Hellenic Savior cults.

The new perspective group places Jesus in his first-century Jewish setting. This group includes F. P. Sanders, Ben F Meyer, Geza Vermes, Bruce Chilton, and James H. Charlesworth. The radical tradition is exemplified by the Jesus Seminar and their interest in the *Gospel of Thomas* and the Q document. The Jesus Seminar uses many of the methods of Strauss and Bultmann, but unlike the latter, the group is optimistic about recovering the historical individual. Their results to date, however, have yielded very different views, based on a small fragment of New Testament sayings they believe to be authentic. (Geisler, BECA, 385–386)

Craig Blomberg adds: "The Jesus Seminar and its friends do not reflect any consensus of scholars except for those on the 'radical fringe' of the field. Its methodology is seriously flawed and its conclusions unnecessarily skeptical. Far more worthy of a claim to a responsible, historical interpretation of the available data is the third quest for the historical Jesus. Yet even here scholars often stop a little short of historic, Christian orthodoxy." (Blomberg, WDWSSJ, as cited in Wilkins, JUF, 43)

4B. Conclusion

Stein goes on to point out the problem with the critical definition of "historical."

The major problem that faces any attempt to arrive at the "historical Jesus" involves the definition of the term "historical." In critical circles the term is generally understood as "the product of the historical-critical method."

This method for many assumes a closed continuum of time and space in which divine intervention, i.e., the miraculous, cannot intrude. Such a definition will, of course, always have a problem seeking to find continuity between the supernatural Christ and the Jesus of history, who by such a definition cannot be supernatural. If "historical" means non-supernatural, there can never be a real continuity between the Jesus of historical research and the Christ of faith. It is becoming clear, therefore, that this definition of "historical" must be challenged, and even in Germany spokesmen are arising who speak of the need for the historical-critical method to assume an openness to transcendence, i.e., openness to the possibility of the miraculous. Only in this way can there ever be hope of establishing a continuity between the Jesus of historical research and the Christ of faith. (Stein, JC, as cited in Elwell, EDT, 585)

2A. THE JESUS SEMINAR

Over the past few years, one of the most radical quests for the historical Jesus has shown itself in the so-called Jesus Seminar. Any reading of the major newsmagazines, especially around the holiday seasons, will encounter the conclusions of these so-called "scholars."

1B. What Is the Jesus Seminar?

The Jesus Seminar is a consortium of New Testament scholars, directed by, Robert W. Funk, which was organized in 1985 under the auspices of the Estar Institute of Santa Rosa, California. Seventy-plus scholars meet twice a year to make pronouncements about the authenticity of the words and deeds of Christ.

> *Truth is not determined by majority vote.*
>
> —NORMAN GEISLER

The Seminar is comprised of liberal Catholics and Protestants, Jews, and atheists. Most are male professors, though their number includes a pastor, a filmmaker and three women. About half are graduates of Harvard, Claremont, or Vanderbilt divinity schools. (Geisler, BECA, 386)

2B. The Aims of the Seminar

Dr. Geisler goes on to explain the stated goals of the Seminar:

While Seminar members produce critical works, from its inception the Jesus Seminar has sought to make its views available to the general public, rather than just the scholarly community: "We are going to try to carry out our work in full public view; we will not only honor the freedom of information, we will insist on the public disclosure of our work" (Funk, Forum, 1.1). To this end the Seminar has sought publicity from every possible source. A TV summit, many articles, interviews with the press, tapes, and even a possible movie are part of this public information campaign for anti-supernatural theology. Funk frankly confessed the radical nature of the work when he said, "We are probing what is most sacred to millions, and hence we will constantly border on blasphemy" (ibid., 8). This is an honest and accurate disclosure of what has happened. (Geisler, BECA, 387)

3B. Voting on Jesus?

The Jesus Seminar votes on the accuracy of Jesus' sayings by using colored beads. Dr. Geisler explains: "The group has used colored beads to vote on the accuracy of Jesus' sayings. A red bead means words that Jesus probably spoke. Pink indicates words that could probably be attributed to Jesus. Gray represents words that probably, though not certainly, came from later sources. Black indicates words that Jesus almost certainly did not speak."

The vote was based on a variety of Christian writings other than the four canonical Gospels, including the fragmentary *Gospel of Peter,* the supposed but not extant Q or *Quelle* ("source") document, the second-century *Gospel of Thomas,* and the non-extant *Secret Mark. Thomas* is usually treated as a fifth gospel, on a par with the four canonical books.

The result of their work is the conclusion that only fifteen sayings (2 percent) can absolutely be regarded as Jesus' actual words. About 82 percent of what the canonical Gospels ascribe to Jesus are not authentic. Another 16 percent of the words are of doubtful authenticity.

4B. Conclusions of the Seminar

Geisler points out the radical conclusions of the seminar that affect the historic orthodox Christian faith:

1. The "old" Jesus and "old Christianity" are no longer relevant.
2. There is no agreement about who Jesus was: a cynic, a sage, a Jewish reformer, a feminist, a prophet-teacher, a radical social prophet, or an eschatological prophet.
3. Jesus did not rise from the dead. One member, Crossan, theorizes that Jesus' corpse was buried in a shallow grave, dug up, and eaten by dogs.
4. The canonical Gospels are late and cannot be trusted.
5. The authentic words of Jesus can be reconstructed from the so-called "Q document," *The Gospel of Thomas, Secret Mark,* and *The Gospel of Peter.* (Geisler, BECA, 387)

5B. The Jesus Seminar Employs . . .

1C. A Radical Fringe of Scholarship

"Truth is not determined by majority vote." (Geisler, BECA, 387)

"Most of the proofs they offer . . . are uncompelling and often nonexistent except for quotations from one another and other liberal scholars." (Geisler, BECA, 388)

2C. Unjustified Anti-supernaturalism

"The radical conclusions of the group are based on radical presuppositions, one of which is an unjustified rejection of any miraculous intervention in history by God." (Geisler, BECA, 388)

Regarding the Jesus Seminar, Gary Habermas notes that: "They are honest enough to state at the outset their aversion to the supernatural, including the deity and resurrection of Jesus, preferring to think that the modern scientific worldview simply rules out such matters." (Habermas, HJ, 124)

Habermas continues: "Although the Jesus Seminar has received much attention from its treatment of the historical Jesus, their conclusions must be apportioned to the data. As a result, their basic rejection of the supernatural events in Jesus' life is unwarranted." (Habermas, HJ, 139)

3C. Unfounded Acceptance of Late Dates

By positing and accepting late dates, "they can create enough time between the events and the recording for eyewitnesses to die off and a mythology to develop around the founder of Christianity." (Geisler, BECA, 388)

4C. Logical Fallacies

"The reasoning process of the Jesus Seminar is a sophisticated form of the logical fallacy known as *Petitio Principii,* or begging the question. Its circular reasoning begins with a desupernaturalized view of a first-century religious figure and concludes at the same point." (Geisler, BECA, 388).

"Another point of logic concerns the Seminar's commission of the genetic fallacy,

> Another point of logic concerns the Seminar's commission of the genetic fallacy, which occurs when one challenges the origin of an idea without actually addressing its facticity. In other words, if it is thought that merely attributing a Gospel report to the author's style, or to other ancient parallels, or to a pre-modern mindset thereby explains it away, this is a logical mistake. These charges do not preclude historicity.
>
> —GARY HABERMAS

which occurs when one challenges the origin of an idea without actually addressing its facticity. In other words, if it is thought that merely attributing a Gospel report to the author's style, or to other ancient parallels, or to a pre-modern mindset thereby explains it away, this is a logical mistake. These charges do not preclude historicity." (Habermas, HJ, 125).

6B. Conclusion

"Despite their desire and achievements for drawing wide publicity, nothing is new in the Jesus Seminar's radical conclusions. They offer only another example of unsubstantiated negative Bible criticism. Their conclusions are contrary to the overwhelming evidence for the historicity of the New Testament and the reliability of the New Testament witnesses. They are based on an unsubstantiated antisupernatural bias." (Geisler, BECA, 388)

Edwin Yamauchi adds: "In spite of what some modern scholars claim, the extrabiblical evidence will not sustain their eccentric pictures of Jesus that attract such widespread media attention because of their novelty. In contrast to these idiosyncratic and ephemeral revisions, the orthodox view of Jesus still stands as the most credible portrait when all of the evidence is considered, including the corroboration offered by ancient sources outside the New Testament." (Yamauchi, as cited in Wilkins, JUF, 222)

3A. THE CHRIST OF FAITH OR THE JESUS OF HISTORY?

Through all of the historical quests for Jesus, many different views have surfaced. Some see a difference between the Jesus of history and the Messiah of faith. They say that it doesn't really matter what the historical Jesus did or said. It is the Christ of our faith that is important.

1B. Development of the Dichotomy

Some biblical critics have undermined the historicity of Jesus by making a separation or dichotomy between a Christ of faith and a Christ of history. This disjunction can be traced back to the original gapthat Gotthold Lessing made between history and faith. *"Accidental truths of history can never become the proof of necessary truths of reason."* (Lessing, LTW, 53, emphasis his)

Lessing writes,

It is said: "The Christ of whom on historical grounds you must allow that he raised the dead, that he himself rose from the dead, . . ." This would be quite excellent! if only it were not the case that it is not more than historically certain that Christ said this. If you press me still further and say: "Oh yes! This is more than historically certain. For it is asserted by inspired historians who cannot make a mistake." . . . That, then, is the ugly, broad ditch which I cannot get across, however often and however earnestly I have tried to make the leap. (Lessing, LTW, 55)

Immanuel Kant also found it necessary to make a dichotomy in philosophy and religion: "I therefore had to annul *knowledge* in order to make room for *faith*." (Kant, CPR, 31)

Concerning Jesus, Kant creates a chasm between the historical Jesus and personified ideal man: "Now it is our universal duty as men to *elevate* ourselves to this ideal of moral perfection, that is, to this archetype of the moral disposition in all its purity—and this idea itself, which reason presents to us for our zealous emulation, can give us power." (Kant, RLRA, 54)

"We need, therefore, no empirical example to make the idea of a person morally well-pleasing to God our archetype; this idea as an archetype is already present in our reason." (Kant, RLRA, 56)

Søren Kierkegaard diminished the need for a historical Jesus and emphasized a leap of faith:

If Christianity is viewed as a historical document, the important thing is to obtain a completely reliable report of what the Christian doctrine really is. If the inquiring subject were infinitely interested in his relation to this truth, he would here despair at once, because nothing is easier to perceive than this, that with regard to the historical the greatest certainty is only an *approximation,* and an approximation is too little to build his happiness on and is so unlike an eternal happiness that no result can ensure. (Kierkegaard, CUPPF, 23)

Even if the contemporary generation had not left anything behind except these words, "We have believed that in such and such a year the god appeared in the humble form of a servant, lived and taught among us, and

then died"—this is more than enough. (Kierkegaard, PF, 104)

Martin Kahler follows, "For historical facts which first have to be established by science cannot *as such* become experiences of faith. Therefore, Christian faith and a history of Jesus repel each other like oil and water." (Kahler, SHJHBC, 74, emphasis his)

Kahler thus goes on to distinguish between the historical and the historic Christ. Kahler asks of the historical Christ of the scholars: "How can Jesus Christ be the authentic object of faith of all Christians if the questions what and who he really was can be established only by ingenious investigation and if it is solely the scholarship of our time which proves itself equal to the task?" (Kahler, SHJHBC, 102)

Kahler says that the real historic Christ "*is the Christ who is preached.*" And, "the Christ who is preached . . . is precisely the Christ of faith." (Kahler, SHJHBC, 66, emphasis his)

"Thus every part of our Scriptures contributes its own share in fully portraying

> I believe that the best rebuttal to those that make a disjunction between the Christ of faith and the Jesus of history is first a rebuttal to the philosophical presuppositions and then a strong presentation on the historical reliability of the New Testament accounts of Jesus.

Jesus the Christ to us . . . In reality, therefore, we are not able to separate Christ and the Bible." (Kahler, SHJHBC, 86)

2B. Modern Assumptions and Dichotomies

One modern assumption is that the New Testament writings do not portray a historical picture of Jesus.

Rudolf Bultmann cites Julius Wellhausen as saying: "We must recognize that a literary work or a fragment of tradition is a primary source for the historical situation out of which it arose, and is only a secondary source for the historical details concerning which it gives information." (Bultmann, NASP, 341)

This assertion leads these scholars to view the Gospels as a secondary source for the facts concerning Jesus. J. Martin concurs: "The Gospels must be taken as reliable renderings of *what the Church believed at the time of writing* concerning the facts on which its faith was founded." (Martin, RG, 44)

Therefore, R. H. Lightfoot, a noted critic, infers: "It seems, then, that the form of the earthly no less than of the heavenly Christ is for the most part hidden from us. For all the inestimable value of the gospels, they yield us little more than a whisper of his voice; we trace in them but the outskirts of his ways." (Lightfoot, HIG, 255)

1C. Albert Schweitzer

"The Jesus of Nazareth who came forward as the Messiah, who preached the ethic of the Kingdom of God, who founded the Kingdom of heaven upon earth, and died to give His work its final consecration, never had any existence. He is a figure designed by rationalism, endowed with life by liberalism, and clothed by modern theology in an historical garb." (Schweitzer, PSJ, 396)

Schweitzer's *Quest for the Historical Jesus* assumes a dichotomy from the very start of Christianity:

It is only at first sight that the absolute indifference of early Christianity toward the life of the historical Jesus is disconcerting. When Paul, representing those who recognize the signs of the times, did not desire to know Christ after the flesh, that was the first expression of the impulse of self-preservation by which Christianity continued to be guided for centuries. It felt that with the introduction of

the historic Jesus into its faith, there would arise something new, something which had not been foreseen in the thoughts of the Master Himself, and that thereby contradiction would be brought to light, the solution of which would constitute one of the greatest problems of the world. (Schweitzer, QHJ, 2)

After presenting his study of the progress for the historical Jesus, Schweitzer concluded it by saying, "But the truth is, it is not Jesus as historically known, but Jesus as spiritually arisen within men, who is significant for our time and can help it. Not the historical Jesus, but the spirit which goes forth from Him and in the spirits of men strives for new influence and rule, is that which overcomes the world." (Schweitzer, QHJ, 401) How does he know this spirit of Jesus is anything more than a figment of one's imagination, unless there is some evidence in time and space on earth that the spirit of Jesus actually manifested Himself, the Spirit of Jesus, in some demonstrably apparent manner?

"Jesus as a concrete historical personality remains a stranger to our time, but His spirit, which lies hidden in His words, is known in simplicity, and its influence is direct. Every saying contains in its own way the whole Jesus. The very strangeness and unconditionedness in which He stands before us makes it easier for individuals to find their own personal standpoint in regard to Him." (Schweitzer, QHJ, 401) Schweitzer's very words are a dodge of real experience.

2C. Rudolf Bultmann

"I do indeed think that we can now know almost nothing concerning the life and personality of Jesus, since the early Christian sources show no interest in either, are moreover fragmentary and legendary; and other sources about Jesus do not exist." (Bultmann, JW, 8)

Rudolf Bultmann, while admitting the historicity of Jesus, expresses skepticism concerning the objectivity of the biblical accounts:

Of course the doubt as to whether Jesus really existed is unfounded and not worth refutation. No sane person can doubt that Jesus stands as founder behind the historical movement whose first distinct stage is represented by the oldest Palestinian community. But how far that community preserved an objectively true picture of him and his message is another question. For those whose interest is in the personality of Jesus, this situation is depressing or destructive; for our purpose it has no particular significance. (Bultmann, JW, 13–14)

3B. Philosophical Objections Answered

I believe that the best rebuttal to those who make a disjunction between the Christ of faith and the Jesus of history is first a rebuttal to the philosophical presuppositions and then a strong presentation of the historical reliability of the New Testament accounts of Jesus.

Concerning this, Geisler, in response to Kant, says, "Kant's assumption that one can separate fact from value is clearly false, as is evident in the impossibility of separating the fact of Christ's death from its value. There is no spiritual significance in the virgin birth unless it is a biological fact. Nor can one separate the fact of human life from its value; a murderer inescapably attacks the individual's value as a human by taking the person's life." (Geisler, BECA, 386)

4B. Historical Objections Answered

In specific response to Bultmann, David Cairns has made this conclusion about Bultmann's form of theology, which runs away from the historical toward the existential:

"Our provisional conclusion in this chapter must be that none of the justifications urged by Bultmann, in support of his flight from history, carries conviction. The whole enterprise resembles too much the remedy of decapitation as a cure for a headache." (Cairns, GWM, 149)

A frightening aspect of Bultmann's approach to the New Testament is observed by Ellwein when he notes Bultmann's existential basis: "Is it not a disturbing feature of Bultmann's interpretation of the New Nazareth that it becomes a 'relative X'? This means that the occurrence of God's revelation which has assumed bodily and historical form in Jesus evaporates and is, so to speak, placed within parentheses." (Ellwein, RBIK, as cited in Kegley, TRB, 42)

As Geisler asserts, scholars who search for the historical Jesus "assume, without proof, that the Gospels are not historical and that they do not set out the historical person of Jesus." (Geisler, BECA, 386)

The New Testament writers make essential a belief that involves a unity of the Christ of faith and the Jesus of history.

Paul said,

And if Christ is not risen, then our preaching is empty and your faith is also empty. Yes, and we are found false witnesses of God, because we have testified of God that He raised up Christ, whom He did not raise up—if in fact the dead do not rise. For if the dead do not rise, then Christ is not risen. And if Christ is not risen, your faith is futile; you are still in your sins! Then also those who have fallen asleep in Christ have perished. If in this life only we have hope in Christ, we are of all men the most pitiable (1 Cor. 15:14–19 NKJV).

For all practical purposes, to construct a "Christ of faith" which ignores the historical life of Jesus on earth comes dangerously close to denying that Jesus has come in the flesh at all. John warned, "Every spirit that does not confesses that Jesus Christ has come in the flesh is not of God. And this is the spirit of the Antichrist, which you have heard was coming, and is now already in the world" (1 John 4:3 NKJV).

Luke explained his research techniques as a historian:

> Inasmuch as many have taken in hand to set in order a narrative of those things which have been fulfilled among us, just as those who from the beginning were eyewitnesses and ministers of the word delivered them to us, it seemed good to me also, having had perfect understanding of all things from the very first, to write to you an orderly account, most excellent Theophilus, that you may know the certainty of those things in which you were instructed (Luke 1:1–3 NKJV).

Historian A. N. Sherwin-White makes a comparison between the methods of writing history used by the Roman writers and the Gospel writers. He concludes that "it can be maintained that those who had a passionate interest in the story of Christ, even if their interest in events was parabolical and didactic rather than historical, would not be led by that very fact to pervert and utterly destroy the historical kernel of their material." (Sherwin-White, RSRLNT, 191)

The research of a number of scholars (e.g., F. F. Bruce, W. M. Ramsay) has shown Luke-Acts to be historically reliable, or more accurately, historically precise. Most recently, noted Roman historian Colin Hemer concluded after considering the knowledge displayed in the Book of Acts:

> We discovered a wealth of material suggesting an author of sources familiar with the particular locations and at the times in question. Many of these connections have only recently come to light with the publication of new collections of papyri and inscriptions. We con-

sidered these details from various, often overlapping, perspectives, risking repetitiveness, since our interest was not primarily in the details themselves, but rather in the way that they supported and confirmed different ways of reading the text—various levels in the relationship of the narrative with the history it purports to describe. By and large, these perspectives all converged to support the general reliability of the narrative, through the details so intricately yet often unintentionally woven into the narrative. (Hemer, BASHH, 412)

Finally, such a "separation of historical Jesus from historic Christ is based on a false dichotomy of fact and faith . . . The historic significance of Christ cannot be separated from his historicity. If he did not live, teach, die, and rise from the dead as the New Testament claims, then he has no saving significance today." (Geisler, BECA, 142).

4A. THE JESUS IN THE FIRE

In Daniel, chapter 3, Daniel's three friends, Shadrach, Meshach, and Abed-nego, get thrown into a fire but don't get burned. And a fourth person, many scholars believe, the pre-incarnate Christ, is seen walking around in the fire with Daniel's friends. King Nebuchadnezzar himself described this one, saying, "the form of the fourth is like the Son of God." (Dan. 3:25). The fourth was undoubtedly the Son of God, and He never gets burned!

Erudite scholars in ivory towers may construct a "Christ of faith" to their own liking. This Christ is much easier to accept. He performs no supernatural feats. He is not all that different from the various leaders of different philosophical or thought systems. He has no hard sayings that incite controversy or challenge the souls of men and women. He does not cause great concern with warnings of eternal consequences for our rejection of him. He fits rather nicely, actually, into each individual's personal outlook on life. And this view is the great problem with the quest for the historical Jesus which ends in the discovery of a Jesus who is so divorced from history. The problem is that a Jesus who can be imagined, dreamed up like any other fairy tale or legend, is a Jesus who has no more power to change lives than does a Johnny Appleseed or a Paul Bunyan.

Almost two thousand years ago, real men with dirt under their fingernails met a real Jesus who challenged them to follow Him. Real women and real children also met and followed this Jesus. Many lost their lives for following Christ and refusing to recant their testimony of what this Jesus had done and said when He walked among them.

There is a great contrast here, and one must choose whom they will believe. I have a great respect for solid scholarship. That should be obvious from all I have researched and written. But at times scholars can use their great learning to justify their own prej-udices. I believe that is what has happened in the quests for the historical Jesus. An antisu-pernatural bias has turned the quest for the historical Jesus into a presentation of a ficti-tious and powerless Jesus.

Now the verdict must be delivered. Every individual must decide whom to believe: the erudite philosopher centuries removed from the Jesus who walked on earth, or those who walked with Him and died for Him.

The verdict of millions throughout the ages, whether simple peasants or brilliant, unbiased professors, has been that Jesus lived, died, and lives again to change the lives of those who will accept Him as He really is. Will you accept Him? Will you follow Him? You have the evidence. What is your verdict? If you have never put your trust in Him to be your Savior from sin and the Master of your life, the short article on "The Four Spiritual Laws" at the end of this book can help you commit your life to Christ.

30

CONCLUSION TO
FORM CRITICISM

CHAPTER OVERVIEW

Contributions of Form Criticism
Limitations of Form Criticism

Every critical method or study has its pros and cons, its contributions and shortcomings. This section gives some of the contributions and limitations of the "form critical" approach.

1A. CONTRIBUTIONS OF FORM CRITICISM

B. S. Easton highlights a contribution made through the form critical study when he concludes: "Form-study brings us into contact with the earliest Christian pedagogy, and so should prove a fruitful field of study,

particularly in the light it will throw on the early Palestinian Christian interests. This is reason enough to give the new discipline our full attention." (Easton, GBG, 77)

Barker, Lane, and Michaels establish the following contributions of form criticism:

1. It helps immeasurably in the appreciation of the distinctive style and structure of synoptic tradition. The form of the written Gospels essentially mirrors that of the oral tradition which preceded them.

2. It is neither possible nor necessary to demand a complete harmonization of the chronologies of the different Gospels. Consequently the Gospel narratives are grouped according to a variety of patterns.

3. Form criticism helps explain some otherwise perplexing variations in parallel accounts of the same incident. A detail omit-

ted by one evangelist may be included by another because it carries for him a certain relevance with respect to the situation out of which he writes. (Barker, NTS, 70)

Some other results are noted by Floyd Filson:

It is true that the gospel tradition was orally preserved for a time. It is also true that this early period was of the greatest importance for the dependability of all later forms of the tradition, and therefore merits our closest scrutiny.

It is true that small units of tradition, whether teaching tradition or narrative material, were known and utilized for practical purposes as occasion demanded. It may also be accepted as reasonable that typical incidents or utterances were preserved, and in some cases these units may have been composite.

Beyond question it is true that the surviving gospel material is but a very small portion of the total amount that might have been preserved. It is likewise true that the selection of what was to survive was governed largely by practical interests connected with the faith and life of the Church. Just as a preacher in our day will remember particularly those features of an address or book which affect his own life, thinking, and preaching, so the memory of those early Christians was much governed by their needs and interests.

It is also true that the needs of guidance, instruction, worship, and controversy were prominent influences in this whole process, and that the attitude of those who transmitted the tradition was not that of the research fellow or detached biographer. And this means that to some extent even a careful and cautious critical study of the Gospels will see reflected in them the life of the primitive Church, for the interests and problems of the early Christians can be inferred from them. (Filson, OG, 103–105)

Another important aspect, as New Testament scholar Harold W. Hochner has pointed out, is that form criticism has focused our attention on the oral period. (Barr, BEJ, n.p.)

Steven Travis agrees: "Form criticism has helped us, however tentatively, to penetrate into the 'tunnel period' between A.D. 30 and 50, before any of our New Testament documents were written down. For instance, it has given us clues about methods of preaching and teaching among the early Christians, and about their debates with Jewish opponents." (Barnes, GCFC, 161)

One important conclusion of form critical study is contributed by Mounce: "Form Criticism is a good reminder of the nature of Jesus' teaching: its conciseness and its wide applicability. What we have in the Gospels is a select body of teaching capable of universal application." (Mounce, INTHA, 144)

Two important conclusions of form criticism are revealed by Redlich:

1. Form Criticism by admitting that collections of saying were made early has pointed to the possibility that the *ipsissima verba* ["exact words"] of our Lord were treasured as oracles to guide and control the destinies of individuals and of the Church.

2. Form Criticism has stimulated the study of Gospel origins, and its method of research and investigation may lead to a wider scientific study in the future. (Redlich, FC, 79)

2A. LIMITATIONS OF FORM CRITICISM

Basil Redlich summarizes the limitations of the form critical technique:

(1) Classification should be according to form and nothing else, as in Apothegm-Stories, Miracle-Stories and Parables. Where forms do not exist, classification according to contents is not Form Criticism.

(2) Form-less groups should not be given historical value-judgments before investigation. Also where a type or form does not exist,

no historical valuation can be justified. Form Criticism should investigate the forms of the tradition, explain the forms, and attempts to trace the development of forms and of forms only.

(3) Form Criticism has not made adequate use of the results of Literary Criticism of the Gospels, e.g., the dating of the documentary sources of the synoptic gospels, and the connection of these sources with the great centers of Christendom.

(4) Form Criticism in stressing the influence of the primitive community is blind to the influence of Jesus as a Rabbi and a prophet. On the one hand, it makes the community a creative body, of which there is little or no trace in the New Testament. The primitive Christians were not all Rabbis nor all Solomons. On the other hand, it is not recognized that Jesus was not a teacher who perpetually repeated the same maxims or memorized addresses which He delivered without variation. He is likely to have repeated the same saying in different form and constantly varied His discourses. Also, variations in the Gospels may have been due to fuller information. Matthew and Luke and John, who composed their Gospels after Mark would have been able to revise the narrative from further knowledge.

(5) Form Criticism neglects far too much the presence of eyewitnesses in the formative period and their ability to check the tradition and to safeguard it.

(6) Form Criticism neglects the evidence of second-century and later writers.

(7) Form Criticism has not clearly defined the extent of the formative period.

(8) Form Criticism has unjustifiably assumed that the contexts and settings and chronological details are of no historical or biographical value.

(9) Form Criticism is not justified in assuming that analogy is a guide to the historical truth of their legends and myths.

(10) Form Criticism in evaluating the vital factors does not take account of all the varied interests of the early Church.

(11) Form Criticism gives a wide scope for subjective treatment and to this its supporters are partial.

(12) Form Criticism overlooks the undoubted fact that the primitive Church was

> We have been enabled to penetrate some little way into the mind of the early converts and their teachers, [and] we find that the whole basis of the form criticism theory has been dissolved and has vanished.
>
> —F. J. BABCOCK

willing to suffer and die for its belief in Jesus and the power of His name. Jesus was a real Jesus and their Christ, Who had proved Himself by His deeds and His teaching.

(13) Form Criticism by too great an emphasis on the expected Parousia has lost sight of the normal life which men lived though the Parousia was held to be imminent. (Redlich, FC, 77, 78)

McGinley comments on the defects in form criticism developed by Bultmann and Dibelius, as he states:

It has failed to work out a position in independence of the Two-Source theory [Fascher, DFM, 51]. It has neglected the essential differences between the Gospels and *Kleinliteratur*. It has accepted the discredited theory of collective creation and applied it to a community in which it did not and could not exist. It has mistaken simplicity of style for patchwork compilation. Forms have been too sharply defined and at the price of much excision of the text. A *Sitz im Leben* has been sought in every phase of primitive Christian life except the most important one: the Christian's desire to know the life of Jesus. Throughout, no place is given to historical testimony; substance is neglected in preoccupation with form; the controlling factor of time is disregarded; there is prejudice against the historical value of the whole Gospel story. (McGinley, FCSHN, 154)

One of the peripheral goals of radical form critics has been to establish a historical Jesus authenticated through form analysis.

Form criticism has contributed to the modern evangelical understanding of the Gospels in a negative sense by failing in this quest. As G. E. Ladd summarizes: "Form criticism has failed to discover a purely historical Jesus." (Ladd, NTC, 157)

F. J. Babcock concludes:

But when by using this evidence we have been enabled to penetrate some little way into the mind of the early converts and their teachers, we find that whole basis of the form criticism theory has been dissolved and has vanished. It is ingenious, it is to some extent plausible, there are suggestions that it might contain fragments of truth. So it was with the Tübingen theory, and there is no reason to doubt that in a short time the theory of form criticism will share the same fate. (Babcock, FC, 20)

Rogers states: "The method assumes solutions to questions that are still open, such as the source and synoptic questions. It assumes the validity of the two documentary theory of Mark and Q as the basis for Matthew and Luke. The priority of Mark is also assumed." (Rogers, ULNCNTIET, n.p.)

A general impression by McGinley of form criticism: "At best, much of what is true in form criticism is not new and much of what is new is not true, still, at the worst, there is wheat in the chaff for the winnowing." (McGinley, FCSHN, 154)

McGinley states his opinion of Bultmann's work: "If, as Bultmann contends, Schmidt has destroyed the framework of the Gospel story, then his successor has mutilated the picture itself beyond recognition, and analysis has become annihilation." (McGinley, FCSHN, 68)

In concluding, F. F. Bruce has a suggestion for the form critic: "When this painstaking work has been accomplished and the core of the tradition authenticated as securely as possible, he will do well to stand back among the rank and file of Gospel readers and, listening with them to the witness of the Evangelists, join in acknowledging that this witness has the 'ring of truth' [J. B. Phillips, *Ring of Truth: A Translator's Testimony* (London, 1967)]." (Bruce, TON, 57)

31
MODERN THEOLOGY AND BIBLICAL CRITICISM

by C. S. LEWIS

The undermining of the old orthodoxy has been mainly the work of divines engaged in New Testament criticism. The authority of experts in that discipline is the authority in deference to whom we are asked to give up a huge mass of beliefs shared in common by the early church, the Fathers, the Middle Ages, the Reformers, and even the nineteenth century. I want to explain what it is that makes me skeptical about this authority. Ignorantly skeptical, as you will all too easily see. But the skepticism is the father of the ignorance. It is hard to persevere in a close study when you can work up no *prima facie* confidence in your teachers.

First then, whatever these men may be as biblical critics, I distrust them as critics. They seem to me to lack literary judgement, to be imperceptive about the very quality of the

texts they are reading. It sounds a strange charge to bring against men who have been steeped in those books all their lives. But that might be just the trouble. A man who has spent his youth and manhood in the minute study of New Testament texts and of other people's studies of them, whose literary experiences of those texts lacks any standard of comparison such as can only grow from a wide and deep and genial experience of literature in general, is, I should think, very likely to miss the obvious things about them. If he tells me that something in a Gospel is legend or romance, I want to know how many legends and romances he has read, how well his palate is trained in detecting them by the flavor; not how many years he has spent on that Gospel. But I had better turn to examples.

In what is already a very old commentary,

I read that the Fourth Gospel is regarded by one school as a "spiritual romance," "a poem not a history," to be judged by the same canons as Nathan's parable, the Book of Jonah, *Paradise Lost* "or, more exactly, *Pilgrim's Progress.*" After a man has said that, why need one attend to anything else he says about any book in the world? Note that he regards *Pilgrim's Progress,* a story that professes to be a dream and flaunts its allegorical nature by every single proper name it uses, as the closest parallel. Note that the whole epic panoply of Milton goes for nothing. But even if we leave out the grosser absurdities and keep to *Jonah,* the insensitiveness is crass—*Jonah,* a tale with as few even pretended historical attachments as *Job,* grotesque in incident and surely not without a distinct, though of course edifying, vein of typically Jewish humor.

Then turn to John. Read the dialogues: that with the Samaritan woman at the well, or that which follows the healing of the man born blind. Look at its pictures: Jesus (if I may use the word) doodling with his finger in the dust; the unforgettable ἦν δέ νύξ (xiii, 30). I have been reading poems, romances, vision literature, legends, myths all my life. I know what they are like. I know that not one of them is like this. Of this text there are only two possible views. Either this is reportage—though it may no doubt contain errors—pretty close up to the facts; nearly as close as Boswell. Or else, some unknown writer in the second century, without known predecessors or successors, suddenly anticipated the whole technique of modern, novelistic, realistic narrative. If it is untrue, it must be narrative of that kind. The reader who doesn't see this has simply not learned to read.

Here, from Bultmann's *Theology of the New Testament* (p. 30) is another: "Observe in what unassimilated fashion the prediction of the parousia (Mk. viii, 38) follows upon the prediction of the passion (viii, 31)." What can he mean? Unassimilated? Bultmann believes that predictions of the parousia are older than those of the passion. He therefore wants to believe—and no doubt does believe—that when they occur in the same passage some discrepancy or "unassimilation" must be perceptible between them.

But surely he foists this on the text with shocking lack of perception. Peter has confessed Jesus to be the Anointed One. That flash of glory is hardly over before the dark prophecy begins—that the Son of Man must suffer and die. Then this contrast is repeated. Peter, raised for a moment by his confession, makes his false step; the crushing rebuff "Get thee behind me" follows. Then, across that momentary ruin which Peter (as so often) becomes, the voice of the Master, turning to the crowd, generalizes the moral. All His followers must take up the cross. This avoidance of suffering, this self-preservation, is not what life is really about. Then, more definitely still, the summons to martyrdom. You must stand to your tackling. If you disown Christ here and now, He will disown you later. Logically, emotionally, imaginatively, the sequence is perfect. Only a Bultmann could think otherwise.

Finally, from the same Bultmann: "The personality of Jesus has no importance for the kerygma either of Paul or of John. . . . Indeed the tradition of the earliest Church did not even unconsciously preserve a picture of his personality. Every attempt to reconstruct one remains a play of subjective imagination."

So there is no personality of our Lord presented in the New Testament. Through what strange process has this learned German gone in order to make himself blind to what all men except him see? What evidence have we that he would recognize a personality if it were there? For it is Bultmann *contra mundum.* If anything whatever is common to all believers, and even to many unbelievers, it is the sense that in the Gospels they have met a personality. There are characters whom we know to be historical but of whom we do not feel that we have any personal knowledge—knowledge by acquaintance; such are Alexander, Attila, or William of Orange. There are others who make no claim to historical reality but whom, none the less, we know as we know real people: Falstaff, Uncle Toby, Mr. Pickwick.

But there are only three characters who, claiming the first sort of reality, also actually have the second. And surely everyone knows who they are: Plato's Socrates, the Jesus of the Gospels, and Boswell's Johnson. Our acquaintance with them shows itself in a dozen ways. When we look into the apocryphal gospels, we find ourselves constantly saying of this or that *logion,* "No. It's a fine saying, but not His. That wasn't how He talked."—just as we do with all pseudo-Johnsoniana.

So strong is the flavor of the personality that, even while He says things which, on any other assumption than that of divine incarnation in the fullest sense, would be appallingly arrogant, yet we—and many unbelievers too—accept Him at His own valuation when He says, "I am meek and lowly of heart." Even those passages in the New Testament which superficially, and in intention, are most concerned with the divine, and least with the human nature, bring us face to face with the personality. I am not sure that they don't do this more than any others.

"We beheld His glory, the glory as of the only begotten of the Father, full of graciousness and reality . . . which we have looked upon and our hands have handled." What is gained by trying to evade or dissipate this shattering immediacy of personal contact by talk about "that significance which the early church found that it was impelled to attribute to the Master"? This hits us in the face. Not what they were impelled to do but what I should call impersonality: what you'd get in a D. N. B article or an obituary or a Victorian *Life and Letters of Yeshua Bar-Yosef* in three volumes with photographs.

That then is my first bleat. These men ask me to believe they can read between the lines of the old texts; the evidence is their obvious inability to read (in any sense worth discussing) the lines themselves. They claim to see fern-seed and can't see an elephant ten yards away in broad daylight.

Now for my second bleat. All theology of the liberal type involves at some point—and often involves throughout—the claim that the real behavior and purpose and teaching of Christ came very rapidly to be misunderstood and misrepresented by His followers, and has been recovered or exhumed only by modern scholars. Now long before I became interested in theology I had met this kind of theory elsewhere. The tradition of Jowett still dominated the study of ancient philosophy when I was reading Greats. One was brought up to believe that the real meaning of Plato had been misunderstood by Aristotle and wildly travestied by the new-Platonists, only to be recovered by the moderns. When recovered, it turned out (most fortunately) that Plato had really all along been an English Hegelian, rather like T. H. Green.

I have met it a third time in my own professional studies; every week a clever undergraduate, every quarter a dull American don, discovers for the first time what some Shakespearian play really meant. But in this third instance I am a privileged person. The revolution in thought and sentiment which has occurred in my own lifetime is so great that

I belong, mentally, to Shakespeare's world far more than to that of these recent interpreters. I see—I feel it in my bones—I know beyond argument—that most of their interpretations are merely impossible; they involve a way of looking at things which was not known in 1914, much less in the Jacobean period. This daily confirms my suspicion of the same approach to Plato or the New Testament.

The idea that any man or writer should be opaque to those who lived in the same culture, spoke the same language, shared the same habitual imagery and unconscious assumptions, and yet be transparent to those who have none of these advantages, is in my opinion preposterous. There is an *a priori* improbability in it which almost no argument and no evidence could counterbalance.

Thirdly, I find in these theologians a constant use of the principle that the miraculous does not occur. Thus, any statement put into our Lord's mouth by the old texts, which, if He had really made it, would constitute a prediction of the future, is taken to have been put in after the occurrence that it seemed to predict. This is very sensible if we start by knowing that inspired prediction can never occur. Similarly in general, the rejection as unhistorical of all passages that narrate miracles is sensible if we start by knowing that the miraculous in general never occurs. Now I do not here want to discuss whether the miraculous is possible. I only want to point out that this is a purely philosophical question.

Scholars, as scholars, speak on it with no more authority than anyone else. The canon "If miraculous, unhistorical" is one they bring to their study of the texts, not one they have learned from it. If one is speaking of authority, the united authority of all the biblical critics in the world counts here for nothing. On this they speak simply as men—men obviously influenced by, and perhaps insufficiently critical of, the spirit of the age they grew up in.

But my fourth bleat—which is also my loudest and longest—is still to come.

All this sort of criticism attempts to reconstruct the genesis of the texts it studies; what vanished documents each author used, when and where he wrote, with what purposes, under what influences—the whole *Sitz im Leben* of the text. This is done with immense erudition and great ingenuity. And at first sight it is very convincing. I think I should be convinced by it myself, but that I carry about with me a charm—the herb *moly*—against it. You must excuse me if I now speak for a while of myself. The value of what I say depends on its being first-hand evidence.

What forearms me against all these reconstructions is the fact that I have seen it all from the other end of the stick. I have watched reviewers reconstructing the genesis of my own books in just this way.

Until you come to be reviewed yourself, you would never believe how little of an ordinary review is taken up by criticism in the strict sense: by evaluation, praise, or censure, of the book actually written. Most of it is taken up with imaginary histories of the process by which you wrote it. The very terms thatthe reviewers use in praising or dis-praising often imply such a history. They praise a passage as "spontaneous" and censure another as "labored"; that is, they think they know that you wrote the one *currente calamo* and the other *invita Minerva*.

What the value of such reconstructions is I learned very early in my career. I had published a book of essays; and the one into which I had put most of my heart, the one I really cared about and in which I discharged a keen enthusiasm, was on William Morris.

And in almost the first review I was told that this was obviously the only one in the book in which I had felt no interest. Now don't mistake. The critic was, I now believe, quite right in thinking it the worst essay in the book; at least everyone agreed with him. Where he was totally wrong was in his imaginary history of the causes that produced its dullness.

Well, this made me prick up my ears. Since then I have watched with some care similar imaginary histories both of my own books and of books by friends whose real history I knew. Reviewers, both friendly and hostile, will dash you off such histories with great confidence; will tell you what public events had directed the author's mind to this or that, what other authors had influenced him, what his overall intention was, what sort of audience he principally addressed, why—and when—he did everything.

Now I must first record my impression; then, distinct from it, what I can say with certainty. My impression is that in the whole of my experience not one of these guesses has on any one point been right; that the method shows a record of 100 percent failure. You would expect that by mere chance they would hit as often as they miss. But it is my impression that they do no such thing. I can't remember a single hit. But as I have not kept a careful record, my mere impression may be mistaken. What I think I can say with certainty is that they are usually wrong. . . .

Now this surely ought to give us pause. The reconstruction of the history of a text, when the text is ancient, sounds very convincing. But one is after all sailing by dead reckoning; the results cannot be checked by fact. In order to decide how reliable the method is, what more could you ask for than to be shown an instance where the same method is at work and we have facts to check it by? Well, that is what I have done. And we find that when this check is available, the results are either always, or else nearly always, wrong. The "assured results of modern scholarship," as to the way in which an old book was written, are "assured," we may conclude, only because the men who knew the facts are dead and can't blow the gaff. The huge essays in my own field which reconstruct the history of *Piers Plowman* or *The Faerie Queene* are most unlikely to be anything but sheer illusions.

Am I then venturing to compare every whipster who writes a review in a modern weekly with these great scholars who have devoted their whole lives to the detailed study of the New Testament? If the former are always wrong, does it follow that the latter must fare no better?

There are two answers to this. First, while I respect the learning of the great biblical critics, I am not yet persuaded that their judgment is equally to be respected. But, secondly, consider with what overwhelming advantages the mere reviewers start. They reconstruct the history of a book written by someone whose mother-tongue is the same as theirs; a contemporary, educated like themselves, living in something like the same mental and spiritual climate. They have everything to help them.

The superiority in judgment and diligence that you are going to attribute to the biblical critics will have to be almost superhuman if it is to offset the fact that they are everywhere faced with customs, language, race characteristics, a religious background, habits of composition, and basic assumptions, which no scholarship will ever enable any man now alive to know as surely and intimately and instinctively as the reviewer can know mine. And for the very same reason, remember, the biblical critics, whatever reconstructions they devise, can never be crudely proved wrong. St. Mark is dead. When they meet St. Peter, there will be more pressing matters to discuss.

You may say, of course, that such reviewers are foolish in so far as they guess how a sort of book they never wrote themselves was written by another. They assume that you wrote a story as they would try to write a story; the fact that they would so try, explains why they have not produced any stories. But are the biblical critics in this way much better off? Dr. Bultmann never wrote a gospel. Has the experience of his learned, specialized, and no doubt meritorious, life really given him any power of seeing into the minds of those long-dead men who were caught up into what, on any view, must be regarded as the central religious experience of the whole human race? It is no incivility to say—he himself would admit—that he must in every way be divided from the evangelists by far more formidable barriers—spiritual as well as intellectual—than any that could exist between my reviewers and me.

[*C. S. Lewis was a giant among literary critics, but he came to embrace the Christian faith only after he was well into his adult years. He taught at both Oxford and Cambridge universities and gained prominence as a writer of science fiction and children's stories, as well as scholarly works.*

This essay is from a published collection of Lewis's lectures and articles, Christian Reflections, *edited by Walter Hooper. It is used by permission of the publisher, William B. Eerdmans Publishing Company.*]

Part Four

TRUTH OR CONSEQUENCES

Personal Note from the Author

Some who read chapters 32–40 may feel that the content seems irrelevant or not applicable to "real life." They might not see how it is applicable to one's home, work, family, etc. They may wonder why these issues of truth, history; philosophy are being included in a book on "Evidences" and "why we believe."

The reasons that I've included the following issues, beliefs, and intellectual aspects of truth and history in this work will fall into place or become obvious by keeping in mind this truth: Behind simple phrases and constant accusations against (or about) faith in Christ or becoming a Christian lie some very profound and complicated philosophical and historical issues.

Some readers may wonder, "Why is it necessary to understand the nature of truth?" or "Why is an understanding of history and historical method so crucial?"

The practical reason for their importance is that behind the phrases that constantly confront us and our children there are some very deep profound questions that must be understood. Phrases we hear will seem or appear to be so simplistic. Yet, they are representative of some very profound issues, the implications of which even those who parrot the words may not really understand.

The following are some of those statements:

"Well, it may be true for you, but it's not for me."

"Look, don't force your values on me. Just because they are true for you doesn't mean they're true for me."

"Jesus is the truth!" Reply: "that's wonderful if that's true for you, but it's not true for me."

"Aren't you being a little arrogant by claiming you have the truth? Come on, get real."

"There are so many religions, how can you say yours is the truth."

"Look, all truth is personal. You've got yours and I've got mine."

"You need to determine what is right (true) for you and I need to determine what is right (true) for me. (You need to be tolerant.) Don't impose your values upon me."

"Christianity may be true for you, but it's not for me."

"That's the way you were raised. That's the way your parents brought you up to believe. . . . My parents raised me differently."

The above statements and the answers to them may seem to be obvious, but the following chapters are necessary to logically support what appears to many as "common sense."

Much of this section on truth and certainty is on the level of theory. Some readers may not be accustomed to discussion of truth on this level, and it might sound a bit "out there," or hard to understand or grasp. But it is so crucial to first understand the philosophical foundations which undergird the arguments against faith in Christ or the truth of Christianity.

Some readers who are very philosophical in thinking may feel these chapters are either challenging or may conclude that my treatment of various critical issues is rather unsophisticated. Some may complain that the material is too complicated or hard to understand, while others may feel that the material is too simplistic and not conclusive enough on each issue.

My appeal is this: Please keep in mind that these chapters are designed to initiate thought and the beginning of understanding on a different level for each and every reader.

So please don't give up. If you don't understand, or if it seems too simplistic, don't stop reading. The following chapters will help you see how truth can be more fully applied to our lives in a way that is relevant in today's culture.

Thank you,

Josh D. McDowell

"*Blessed is the man who finds wisdom, the man who gains understanding, for she is more profitable than silver and yields better returns than gold.*" Proverbs 3:13, 14 (NIV)

32
THE NATURE
OF TRUTH

IA. INTRODUCTION

One word we need to explain here is *metaphysics*, since that subject is what we are discussing in this section. Traditionally, metaphysics has referred to the philosophical study of being as being, that is, of reality *as it is in itself*. Metaphysics answers the questions "What really is?" and "What is its nature?"

Another important term is *epistemology*, meaning how we know. The Oxford Dictionary of Philosophy defines epistemology as "the theory of knowledge," or how we came to know what we know. Do we know, for example, that our senses are not fooling us in terms of what they tell us is the reality around us? We turn first to what truth is and then to how we know it.

2A. WHAT IS TRUTH?

Truth is that which corresponds to its referent (that to which it refers). Metaphysical truth is that which *corresponds with reality* or reflects reality—what really is. By "correspondence" we mean agreement with something—in this case, a thought or statement about reality agrees with reality. By "reality" we mean that which is, or exists. (Whether or not we can *know* that they correspond is discussed more fully in the next section, "Is Truth Knowable?")

1B. Truth Is Correspondence with Reality (vs. Subjectivism)

Correspondence describes a situation where there is a fact and there is a belief about that fact. Correspondence means that the belief is true when it accurately reflects the fact.

Subjectivism, on the other hand, is where truth or reality is determined internally by the subject or person.

1C. Truth According to Aristotle

The Greek philosopher, Aristotle, summarizes the difference between true and false: "To say of what is that it is not, or of what is not that it is, is false, while to say of what is that it is, and of what is not that it is not, is true; so that he who says of anything that it is, or that it is not, will say either what is true or what is false; but neither what is nor what is not is said to be or not to be." (Aristotle, M, 4. 7. 1011b25–30)

Aristotle argues that truth relies on the actual existence of the thing which a thought or statement is about: "If there is a man, the statement whereby we say that there is a man is true, and reciprocally—since if the statement whereby we say that there is a man is true, [then in reality] there is a man. And whereas the true statement is in no way the cause of the actual thing's existence, the actual thing does seem in some way the cause of the statement's being true: it is because the actual thing exists or does not that the statement is called true or false." (Aristotle, C, 12. 14b15–22)

Aristotle suggests that a statement or belief can change from true to false only if that to which it refers actually changes:

> Statements and beliefs . . . themselves remain completely unchangeable in every way; it is because the actual thing changes that the contrary comes to belong to them. For the statement that somebody is sitting remains the same; it is because of a change in the actual thing that it comes to be true at one time and false at another. Similarly with beliefs. . . . For it is not because they themselves receive anything that statements and beliefs are said to be able to receive contraries, but because of what has happened to something else. For it is because the actual thing exists or does not exist that the statement is said to be true or false, not because it is able itself to receive contraries. (Aristotle, C, 5. 4a35–4b12)

2C. Truth According to Thomas Aquinas

Thomas Aquinas asserts that "truth is defined by the conformity of intellect and thing; and hence to know this conformity is to know truth." (Aquinas, ST, 1.16.2) Aquinas defines truth as the matching together of both the understanding and the thing understood:

> For all knowledge is achieved by way of some assimilation of the knower to the thing known, an assimilation which causes the knowledge: thus sight is aware of colour because it suffers modification by the kind of the colour. So the first way in which what exists relates to mind understanding it is by harmonizing with it—a harmonizing we call the matching of understanding and thing—and it is in this matching that the formal notion of truth is achieved. (Aquinas, OT, 1.1)

Aquinas again says: "For the meaning of true consists in a matching of thing and understanding, and matching presupposes diversity, not identity. So the notion of truth is first found in understanding when understanding first starts to have something of its own which the external thing doesn't have, yet which corresponds to the thing and can be expected to match it." (Aquinas, OT, 1.3)

3C. Truth According to Contemporary Philosophers

G. E. Moore defines true and false belief: "To say that this belief is true is to say that there is in the Universe a fact to which it corresponds; and that to say that it is false is to say that there is not in the Universe any fact to which it corresponds." (Moore, SMPP, 277)

Moore states again: "When the belief is true, it certainly does correspond to a fact; and when it corresponds to a fact it certainly is true. And similarly when it is false, it certainly does not correspond to any fact; and when it does not correspond to any fact, then certainly it is false." (Moore, SMPP, 279)

Moore suggests that truth is a property thatcan be common to any belief thatcorresponds to the facts:

We have said that to say it is true is merely to say that it does correspond to a fact; and obviously this is a property which may be common to it and other beliefs. The shopman's belief, for instance, that the parcel we ordered this morning has been sent off, may have the property of corresponding to a fact [i.e., that the parcel was actually shipped], just as well as this belief that I have gone away may have it. And the same is true of the property which we have now identified with the falsehood of the belief. The property which we have identified with its falsehood is merely that of not corresponding to any fact [the parcel was not sent off]. (Moore, SMPP, 277–78)

Agnostic Bertrand Russell distinguishes two facts about beliefs: "A mind, which believes, believes truly when there is a corresponding complex not involving the mind, but only its objects. This correspondence ensures truth, and its absence entails falsehood. Hence we account simultaneously for the two facts that beliefs (a) depend on minds for their existence, (b) do not depend on minds for their truth." (Russell, PP, 129)

Russell argues that there is a world of objective facts independent of our minds: "The first truism to which I wish to draw your attention—and I hope you will agree with me that these things that I call truisms are so obvious that it is almost laughable to mention them—is that the world contains facts, which are what they are whatever we may choose to think about them, and that there are also beliefs, which have reference to facts, and by reference to facts are either true or false." (Russell, LK, 182)

Thomistic philosopher Etienne Gilson points out that in order for a correspondence to take place between the knower and

> Each of our beliefs and assertions represents the World as being a certain way, and the belief or assertion is true if the World is that way, and false if the World is not that way. It is, as one might put it, up to our beliefs and assertions to get the World right; if they don't, they're not doing their job, and that's their fault and no fault of the World's.
>
> —PETER VAN INWAGEN

the thing known, there must be a difference between the two:

The definition of truth as an adequation [verification of fulfillment] between the thing and the intellect . . . is a simple expression of the fact that the problem of truth can have no meaning unless the intellect is regarded as distinct from its object. . . . Truth is only the agreement between reason which judges and reality which the judgment affirms. Error, on the other hand, is but their disagreement." Gilson continues: "I say that Peter exists; if this judgment of existence is true, it is because Peter does indeed exist. I say that Peter is a rational animal; if I am speaking truly, it is because indeed Peter is a living being endowed with reason. (Gilson, CPSTA, 231)

F. P. Ramsey illustrates the distinction between minds and facts:

Suppose I am at this moment judging that Caesar was murdered: then it is natural to distinguish in this fact on the one side either my mind, or my present mental state, or words or images in my mind, which we will call the mental factor or factors, and on the other side either Caesar, or Caesar's murder, or Caesar and murder, or the proposition Caesar was murdered, which we will call the objective factor or factors; and to suppose that the fact that I am judging that Caesar was murdered consists in the holding of some relation or relations between these mental and objective factors. (Ramsey, FP as cited in Mellor, PP, 34)

Peter Kreeft and Ronald K. Tacelli of Boston College explain that "truth means the correspondence of what you know or say to what is. Truth means 'telling it like it is.'" They continue,

All theories of truth, once they are expressed clearly and simply, presuppose the commonsensical notion of truth that is enshrined in the wisdom of language and the tradition of usage, namely the correspondence (or identity) theory. For each theory claims that it is really true, that is, that it corresponds to reality, and that the others are really false, that is, that they fail to correspond to reality. (Kreeft, HCA, 364, 366)

J. P. Moreland describes truth as "a relation of correspondence between a thought and the world. If a thought really describes the world accurately, it is true. It stands to the world in a relation of correspondence." (Moreland, SSC, 81–82)

Norman L. Geisler concurs:

Truth is what corresponds to its referent [the idea to which a word refers]. Truth about reality is what corresponds to the way things really are. Truth is "telling it like it is." This correspondence applies to abstract realities as well as actual ones. There are mathematical truths. There are also truths about ideas. In each case there is a reality, and truth accurately expresses it. Falsehood, then, is what does not correspond. It tells it like it is not, misrepresenting the way things are. The intent behind the statement is irrelevant. If it lacks proper correspondence, it is false. (Geisler, BECA, 743)

Mortimer J. Adler states: "Just as the truth of speech consists in the agreement or correspondence between what one says to another and what one thinks or says to oneself, so the truth of thought consists in the agreement or correspondence between what one thinks, believes, or opines and what actually exists or does not exist in the reality that is independent of our minds and of our thinking one thing or another." (Adler, SGI, 34)

Peter van Inwagen explains that

each of our beliefs and assertions represents the World as being a certain way, and the belief or assertion is true if the World is that way, and false if the World is not that way. It is, as one might put it, up to our beliefs and assertions to get the World right; if they don't, they're not doing their job, and that's their fault and no fault of the World's. Our beliefs and assertions are thus related to the World as a map is related to the territory: it is up to the map to get the territory right, and if the map doesn't get the territory right, that's the fault of the map and no fault of the territory. (Van Inwagen, M, 56)

Robert Audi, a leading figure in contemporary epistemology (the study of knowledge), remarks that

> normally, the internal states and processes that justify our beliefs also connect our beliefs with the external facts in virtue of which those beliefs are true. I am thinking of true propositions, whether believed or not, along the lines of a version of the correspondence theory of truth, whose central thesis is that true propositions [or statements of fact] "correspond" [or are identical] with reality. It is usually added that they are true in virtue of that correspondence. Thus, the proposition that there is a green field before me is true provided that in reality there is a green field before me; and it might also be said that it is true in virtue of there really being such a field before me. (Audi, ECITK, 239)

William P. Alston, professor of philosophy at Syracuse University, develops his "realist conception of truth" along similar lines: "A statement (proposition, belief) is true if and only if what the statement says to be the case actually is the case. For example, the statement that gold is malleable is true if and only if gold is malleable. The 'content' of a statement—what it states to be the case—gives us everything we need to specify what it takes for the statement to be true. . . . Nothing more is required for the truth of the statement, and nothing less will suffice." (Alston, RCT, 5–6)

4C. Consequences of Denying the Correspondence View

There are several consequences that must necessarily follow if truth is not that which corresponds to reality.

> Philosophically, lying is impossible without a correspondence to reality. If our words do not need to correspond to the facts, then they can never be factually incorrect. Without a correspondence view of truth, there can be no true or false. There would be no real difference in the accuracy of how a system describes a given fact because we could not appeal to the fact as evidence. Statements could not be judged as true or false, but only more or less cohesive. There has got to be a real difference between our thoughts about things and the things themselves for us to say whether something is true or false. (Geisler and Brooks, WSA, 263)

What is more,

> all factual communication would break down. Statements that inform you of something must correspond to the facts about which they claim to be giving information. But if those facts are not to be used in evaluating the statement, then I really haven't told you anything. I have merely babbled something that you ought to consider and weigh its relevance to you own system of thought. Now this could be quite dangerous if you were crossing the street and my statement was to inform you that a Mack truck was coming. How long should you take to see if that fits into your overall network of beliefs? (Geisler and Brooks, WSA, 263)

2B. Truth Is Absolute (vs. Relativism)

Relativism is the theory that "there is no objective standard by which truth may be determined, so that truth varies with individuals and circumstances." (Trueblood, PR, 348)

1C. Absolute and Relative Truth Contrasted

The fact that absolute and relative truth stand in contrast can be seen in the following two propositions: (1) Truth is not relative to space and time, and (2) truth is not relative to persons.

1D. Truth Is Not Relative to Space and Time

The relativist would say that the statement, "The pencil is to the left of the pad," is relative since it depends on which side of the desk you are standing. Place is always relative to perspective, they say. But truth can be time-bound as well. At one time, it was perfectly true to say, "Reagan is President," but one can hardly say that now. It was true at one time, but not now. The truth of such statements is irrevocably contingent on the time at which they are said. (Geisler and Brooks, WSA, 256)

But that perspective is understood in statements about space and time:

The interpretation of the relativist appears to be misguided. As regards time and place, the perspective of the speaker, temporal and spatial, is understood in the statement. For example, "Reagan is President," when said in 1986 is true and it always will be true. At no time will it cease to be true that Reagan was President in 1986. If someone uses the same words in 1990, then he is making a new and different truth claim, because the present tense is now four years removed from the context of the other statement. The spatial and temporal context of statements is an inherent part of the context which determines the meaning of that assertion. However, if "Reagan is President" (said in 1986) is always true for everyone everywhere, then it is an absolute truth. The same can be said about the pencil on the desk. The perspective of the speaker is understood as part of the context. It is an absolute truth. (Geisler and Brooks, WSA, 256)

Furthermore, Mortimer J. Adler explains that statements such as "That may have been true in the Middle Ages, but it is no longer true," or "That may be true for primitive people, but it is not true for us," are based on two sorts of confusions. Sometimes truth is confused with what a majority of people at a particular time or place think is true, as in the following example:

A portion of the human race some centuries ago held it to be true that the earth is flat. That false opinion has now been generally repudiated. This should not be interpreted to mean that the objective truth has changed—that what once was true is no longer true. . . . What has changed is not the truth of the matter but the prevalence of an opinion that has ceased to be popular.

A second sort of confusion results when the spatial or temporal context of a statement is ignored:

The population of a country changes from time to time, but a statement about the size of a country's population at a given time remains true when, at a later time, it has increased in size. The presence of the date in a statement about the population of the United States in a certain year enables that statement to remain true forever, if it was accurate in the first place. (Adler, SGI, 43)

Adler adds: "The impulse to recoil from what many may be inclined to regard as an outrageous claim can be checked by remembering that the claim does not preclude acknowledging that our judgments about what is true or false change from time to time, as well as differing from place to place. What is mutable and variable with the circumstances of time and place are the opinions we hold concerning the true and false, not what is objectively true and false." (Adler, SGI, 43)

2D. Truth Is Not Relative to Persons

Even agnostic Bertrand Russell argues that truth is not relative to minds: "It will be seen that minds do not create truth or falsehood. They create beliefs, but when once the beliefs are created, the mind cannot make them true or false, except in the special case where they concern future things which are within the power of the person believing, such as catching trains. What makes a belief true is a

> We may differ in our judgment about what is true, but that does not affect the truth of the matter itself.
>
> —MORTIMER J. ADLER

fact, and this fact does not (except in exceptional cases) in any way involve the mind of the person who has the belief." (Russell, PP, 129-30) An "exceptional case" might be the statement "I had a dream," where the mind creates a belief based on a fact which also has to do with the mind. The principle still holds, though. There is a fact and there is a belief, and the belief is true when it accurately reflects the fact.

Philosopher Joseph Owens explains that, "Insofar as existence is incompatible with non-existence at the same time in the same respects, it manifests itself as absolute. To this extent, consequently, it provides an absolute measure for truth. While rain is falling here, that rain is not synthesized existentially with 'not falling.' That is absolute. It is not relative to the observer. From this viewpoint the truth of the judgment has an absolute character, for it is measured by an absolute existence." (Owens, CEI, 208)

Adler observes that the remark "That may be true for you, but not for me" is not mistaken but often misinterpreted. The misinterpretation "arises from the failure to distinguish between the truth or falsity that inheres in a proposition or statement and the judgment that a person makes with regard to the truth or falsity of the statement in question. We may differ in our judgment about what is true, but that does not affect the truth of the matter itself." (Adler, SGI, 41)

"The truth or falsity of a statement," Adler continues,

> derives from its relation to the ascertainable facts, not from its relation to the judgments that human beings make. I may affirm as true a statement that is in fact false. You may deny as false a statement that is in fact true. My affirmation and your denial in no way alter or affect the truth or falsity of the statements that you and I have wrongly judged. We do not make statements true or false by affirming or denying them. They have truth or falsity regardless of what we think, what opinions we hold, what judgments we make. (Adler, SGI, 41)

Adler thus distinguishes between the subjectivity of our judgments about truth and the objectivity of truth itself. He explains: "The subjective aspect of truth lies in the claim that the individual makes for the veracity of his judgment. The objective aspect lies in the agreement or correspondence between what an individual believes or opines and the reality about which he is making a judgment when he holds a certain belief or opinion. The objective aspect is the primary one." (Adler, SGI, 42)

Those who fail to make this distinction, says Adler, have "allowed themselves to fall back into excessive skepticism by their refusal to acknowledge that subjective differences of opinion concerning what is true or false can

> If truth is not mind-dependent and is at least in that sense objective, then we have a version of realism, roughly the view that (external) things are as they are independently of how we take them to be.
>
> —ROBERT AUDI

be resolved by efforts to ascertain what is objectively true or false, remembering that the truth of a statement resides in its relation to reality, not in its relation to the individual's judgment about it." (Adler, SGI, 42)

According to Robert Audi,

> Whether there is a green field before me is not a matter of states of my mind. It seems to be an objective matter independent of anyone's mind and the green seems to be present or not regardless of whether we believe it is. Indeed, whether my belief is true is determined by whether the field is actually there; the truth of such observational beliefs depends on external reality, which does not in turn depend on what we believe. (Audi, ECITK, 239)

External reality or external facts, then, are what they are independent of human minds. Audi concludes: "If truth is not mind-dependent and is at least in that sense objective, then we have a version of realism, roughly the view that (external) things are as they are independently of how we take them to be." (Audi, ECITK, 239)

William P. Alston remarks that the truth of the statement "gold is malleable" is not relative to any person.

> It is not required that any person or any social group, however defined, know that gold is malleable or be justified or rational in believing it. It is not required that science be destined, in that far-off divine event toward which inquiry moves, to arrive at the conclusion that gold is malleable. It is not required that it be accepted by a clear majority of the American Philosophical Association. It is not required that it have been rendered probable by some body of empirical evidence. So long as gold is malleable, then what I said is true, whatever the epistemic status of that proposition for any individual or community. (Alston, RCT, 5–6)

Professor Peter van Inwagen observes that "the World exists and has the features it does in large part independently of our beliefs and our assertions." From this he concludes that "the truth or falsity of our beliefs and assertions is therefore 'objective' in the sense that truth and falsity are conferred on those beliefs and assertions by their objects, by the things they are about." (Van Inwagen, M, 56)

Van Inwagen adds:

> And how do the objects of our beliefs and assertions confer truth on them? . . . If I assert that Albany is the capital of New York State, then what I have asserted is true if and only if Albany is the capital of New York State and is false if and only if Albany is not the capital of New York State. If Berkeley believes that nothing exists independently of the mind, then what he believes is true if and only if nothing exists independently of the mind, and what he believes is false if and only if something exists independently of the mind. If two people, you and I, say, have the same belief about something—perhaps we both believe that Albany is the state capital of New York State—then truth or falsity is conferred on our common belief by the features of that one object. Truth is therefore "one," there is no such thing as a belief or assertion being "true for me" but "not true for you." If your friend Alfred responds to something you have said with the words, "That may be true for you, but it isn't true for me," his words can only be regarded as a rather misleading way of saying, "That may be what you think, but it's not what I think." (Van Inwagen, M, 56–57)

2C. The Self-defeating Nature of Relativism

Michael Jubien, professor of philosophy at the University of California-Davis, offers a similar argument against relativism:

> Either relativism is a genuine theory in which a real assertion is made, or else it isn't. But any attempt to assert relativism without relying on just-plain [absolute] truth would inevitably

fail, because it would generate an infinite regress. And, of course, any assertion of relativism that does rely on just-plain [absolute]

> Most relativists believe that relativism is absolutely true and that everyone should be a relativist. Therein lies the self-destructive nature of relativism. The relativist stands on the pinnacle of an absolute truth and wants to relativize everything else.
>
> —NORMAN L. GEISLER

truth would be self-defeating. So it looks like any apparent assertion of [relativism] is either self-defeating or else is not a real assertion, but something more like an empty slogan. (Jubien, CM, 89)

The "infinite regress" mentioned by Jubien occurs when the relativist claims that the theory of relativism is true. The theory is true either absolutely (for all people, at all times, and all places) or relatively. If the theory is true absolutely, then relativism is false, for at least one truth is true absolutely. But if the theory is only relatively true, the question must be asked, "To whom is it true (relatively)?" Suppose it is true relative to some person named John. The relativist is then asserting that relativism is true for John. But is this claim (that relativism is true for John) true absolutely or relatively? If absolutely, then relativism must be false; but if relatively, then relative to whom? Relative to John? Relative to someone else?

Suppose the claim that relativism is true for John is true relative to some other person named Suzie. Now the relativist will have to explain whether this truth is absolute or relative, and if the latter, for whom it is true. And by now the relativist is well on his way to nowhere. Eventually, the person will either have to admit that at least one

truth is absolutely true, in which case relativism is false, or else he will be unable to say what is really being asserted when he claims that relativism is true. So relativism is either self-defeating (and therefore false) or unassertable.

Geisler comments: "The only way the relativist can avoid the painful dilemma of relativism is to admit that there are at least some absolute truths. As noted, most relativists believe that relativism is absolutely true and that everyone should be a relativist. Therein lies the self-destructive nature of relativism. The relativist stands on the pinnacle of an absolute truth and wants to relativize everything else." (Geisler, BECA, 745)

In a similar vein, Kreeft and Tacelli remark:

> Universal subjectivism is refutable quite quickly, in the same way that universal skepticism is. If truth is only subjective, only true for me but not for you, then that truth too—the "truth" of subjectivism—is not true, but only "true for me" (i.e., true for the subjectivist). So the subjectivist is not saying that subjectivism is really true and objectivism really false, or that the objectivist is mistaken at all. He is not challenging his opponent, not arguing, not debating, only "sharing his feelings." "I feel well" does not contradict or refute your statement "But I feel sick." Subjectivism is not an "ism," not a philosophy. It does not rise to the level of deserving our attention or refutation. Its claim is like "I itch," not "I know." (Kreeft, HCA, 372)

3C. Additional Problems for Relativism

If relativism were true, then the world would be full of contradictory conditions. For if something is true for me but false for you, then opposite conditions exist. For if I say "There is milk in the refrigerator" and you say "there is not any milk in the refrigerator"—and we both are right, then there must both be and not be milk in the refrigerator at the same time and in the same sense. But that is impossible. So, if truth were relative, then an impossible would be actual. (Geisler, BECA, 745)

In a discussion between a Christian and an atheist, it would mean that the Christian is telling the truth when he claims "God exists," and the atheist is telling the truth when he says God does not exist. But it is impossible for God to both exist and not exist at the same time and in the same sense.

Geisler argues that "if truth is relative, then no one is ever wrong—even when they are. As long as something is true to me, then I'm right even when I'm wrong. The drawback is that I could never learn anything either, because learning is moving from a false belief to a true one—that is, from an absolutely false belief to an absolutely true one." (Geisler, BECA, 745)

4C. Moral Relativism

Moral relativism is relativism applied to the morals of a society. J. P. Moreland, in *Love Your God with All Your Mind*, explains that moral relativism "holds that everyone ought to act in accordance with the [individual's] own society's code. . . . It implies that moral propositions are not simply true or false." (Moreland, LYG, 150)

Moreland offers five critical analyses of moral relativism:

(1) It is difficult to define what a society is or to specify in a given case what the relevant society is. If a man from society A has extramarital sex with a woman from society B in a hotel in a third society, C, which holds a different view from either A or B, which is the relevant society for determining whether the act was right or wrong?

(2) A related objection is the fact that we are often simultaneously a member of sev-

eral different societies that may hold different moral values: our nuclear family; our extended family; our neighborhood, school, church, or social clubs; our place of employment; our town, state, country, and the international community. Which society is the relevant one? What if I am simultaneously a member of two societies and one allows but the other forbids a certain moral action? What do I do in this case?

(3) Moral relativism suffers from a problem known as the reformer's dilemma. If normative relativism is true, then it is logically impossible for a society to have a virtuous, moral reformer like Jesus Christ, Gandhi, or Martin Luther King, Jr. Why? Moral reformers are members of a society who stand outside that society's code and pronounce a need for reform and change in that code. However, if an act is right if and only if it is in keeping with a given society's code, *then the moral reformer himself is by definition an immoral person*, for his views are at odds with those of his society. Moral reformers must always be wrong because they go against the code of their society. But any view that implies that moral reformers are impossible is defective because we all know that moral reformers have actually existed! Put differently, moral relativism implies that neither cultures (if conventionalism is in view) nor individuals (if subjectivism is in view) can improve their moral code.

(4) Some acts are wrong regardless of social conventions. Advocates of this criticism usually adopt the standpoint of particularism and claim that all people can know that some things are wrong, such as torturing babies, stealing as such, greed as such, and so forth, without first needing criteria for knowing how it is that they do, in fact, know such things. Thus, an act (torturing babies, for example) can be wrong and known to be wrong even if society says it is

right, and an act can be right and known as such even if society says it is wrong. In fact, an act can be right or wrong even if society says nothing whatever about that act.

(5) If moral relativism is true, it is difficult to see how one society could be justified in morally blaming another society in certain cases. According to moral relativism, I should act in keeping with my society's code and others should act in keeping with their societies' codes. If Smith does an act that is right in his code but wrong in mine, how can I criticize his act as wrong?

One could respond to this objection by pointing out that society A may have in its code the principle that one should criticize acts of, say, murder, regardless of where they occur. So members of A could criticize such acts in other societies. But such a rule further reveals the inconsistency in normative relativism. Given this rule and the fact that normative relativism is true and embraced by members of A, those in A seem to be in the position of holding that members of B ought to murder (since B's code says it is right) and I ought to criticize members of B because my code says I should. Thus, I criticize members of B as immoral and at the same time hold that their acts should have been done. Further, why should members of B care about what members of A think? After all, if normative relativism is true, there is nothing intrinsically right about the moral views of society A or any society for that matter. For these and other reasons, moral relativism must be rejected. (Moreland, LYG, 150-53, emphasis his)

5C. Why Absolute Truth Is Denied

Kreeft and Tacelli comment: "Perhaps the primary origin of subjectivism today, at least in America, is the desire to be accepted, to be 'with it,' fashionable, avant garde, 'in the know,' rather than 'square,' 'hokey' or 'out of it.' We all learned this as children—to be embarrassed is the absolutely primary fear

> [Another source of skepticism] . . . is the fear of radical change—that is, the fear of conversion, being 'born again,' consecrating one's whole life and will to God's will. Subjectivism is much more comfortable, like a womb, or a dream, or a narcissistic fantasy.
>
> —PETER KREEFT AND RONALD TACELLI

of a teenager—but we put more sophisticated, scholarly disguises on it when we become adults." (Kreeft, HCA, 381)

Another source of subjectivism, according to Kreeft and Tacelli, "is the fear of radical change—that is, the fear of conversion, being 'born again,' consecrating one's whole life and will to God's will. Subjectivism is much more comfortable, like a womb, or a dream, or a narcissistic fantasy." (Kreeft, HCA, 381)

According to C. S. Lewis, one source of the "poison of subjectivism," as he called it, is the belief that man is the product of a blind evolutionary process:

> After studying his environment man has begun to study himself. Up to that point, he had assumed his own reason and through it seen all other things. Now, his own reason has become the object: it is as if we took out our eyes to look at them. Thus studied, his own reason appears to him as the epiphenomenon which accompanies chemical or electrical events in a cortex which is itself the by-product of a blind evolutionary process. His own logic, hitherto the king whom events in all possible worlds must obey, becomes merely subjective. There is no reason for supposing that it yields truth. (Lewis, PS, as cited in Hooper, CR, 72)

Van Inwagen muses on the perplexing fact that some people deny the objectivity of truth:

> The most interesting thing about objective truth is that there are people who deny that it exists. One might wonder how anyone could deny that there is such a thing as objective truth. At least I might. In fact, I often have. For some people, I am fairly sure, the explanation is something like this. They are deeply hostile to the thought of anything that in any sense stands in judgment over them. The idea toward which they are most hostile is, of course, the idea of there being a God. But they are almost as hostile to the idea of there being an objective universe that doesn't care what they think and could make their most cherished beliefs false without even consulting them. (But this cannot be the whole story, since there are people who deny that objective truth exists and who also believe in God. What motivates these people is a complete mystery to me.) Let the reader be warned. It must be evident that I am unable to enter into the smallest degree of imaginative sympathy with those who deny that there is such a thing as objective truth. I am therefore probably not a reliable guide to their views. Perhaps, indeed, I do not understand these views. I would prefer to believe this. I would prefer to believe that no one actually believes what, on the surface, at least, it very much looks as if some people believe. (Van Inwagen, M, 59)

33
THE KNOWABILITY
OF TRUTH

1A. INTRODUCTION: IS TRUTH KNOWABLE?

Having defined truth as the correspondence of our thoughts or statements to objective reality, we also must offer evidence defending the fact that it is possible to *know* if they correspond, that is, whether we can *know* truth. This means that in order to know whether our thoughts or statements correspond to reality we have to first be able to know reality.

The field of philosophy that deals with *how we know* is called epistemology. It is enough for our case to give evidence for the fact that *we do know* reality; it is not necessary at this point to fully explain *how* this occurs. Therefore, the evidence we give below is not an answer to the question *How do we know?* but rather *Do* we know?

This is an important distinction, because most of the modern philosophies that deny that we can know reality, and ultimately truth, make the mistake of constructing epistemological systems to explain *how* we know reality without first acknowledging the fact that we *do* know reality. After they begin within the mind and find they can't construct a bridge to reality, they then declare that we can't know reality. It is like drawing a faulty road map *before* looking at the roads, then declaring that we can't know how to get from Chicago to New York!

In this chapter, we will give evidence for the proposition that we do know reality and thus that we can know truth—that which corresponds to reality.

2A. THE KNOWABILITY OF TRUTH

1B. The First Principles of Knowledge

First principles are the basis for all the conclusions drawn in any area of knowledge, whether in science or philosophy.

The philosopher Aristotle noted how evidence relies on first principles. He said that "demonstration must be based on premises prior to and better known than the conclusion." (Aristotle, AP, 1.3.72b.25) "For it is impossible that there should be demonstration of absolutely everything (there would be an infinite regress, so that there would still be no demonstration)." (Aristotle, M, 4.4.1006a)

Thomas Aquinas clarifies what the term *principle* means. "Anything whence something proceeds in any way we call a principle." (Aquinas, ST, 1.33.1). A *first* principle, Aquinas says, "does not signify priority [in time], but origin." (Aquinas, ST, 1.33.1)

James B. Sullivan defines first principles as "the most general judgements conceivable and the most evident, *which presuppose no others in the same order for their proof, and are implicit in every judgement.*" (Sullivan, EFPTB, 33)

Professor Geisler states that a first principle is

the ultimate starting point from which all conclusions may be drawn in a given area of knowledge or reality. First principles are necessary constituents of all knowledge, but they do not supply any content of knowledge.

There are as many first principles as there are orders of knowledge and reality. Since a first principle is that from which everything else in its order follows, first principles of knowledge are those basic premises from which all else follows in the realm of knowing. (Geisler, TA, 72–73)

For someone to come to accurate knowledge, there must be a starting point which is known to be true. This starting point provides the basis for the knowledge and needs no further demonstration this it is true. This is what is meant by first principle.

L. M. Regis states: "A first principle is, therefore, a first among firsts." Regis continues: "The expression *first principles* must therefore be understood to mean a group of judgements by which the intellect observes the existence of necessary bonds between several primary concepts, bonds that oblige it to identify them in affirmation or to separate them by negation." (Regis, E, 378)

2B. First Principles Are the Self-evident Basis of All Knowledge

By "self-evident" we mean that they do not need to be proven. They show themselves to be true. Thus, first principles do not need to be deduced from other principles, and they become the basis of all knowledge.

Thomas Aquinas states that there must be a beginning point of demonstration: "If there were an infinite regress in demonstrations, demonstration would be impossible, because the conclusion of any demonstration is made certain by reducing it to the first principle of demonstration." (Aquinas, CMA, 224)

Aquinas says knowledge must be based on something we are certain of: "Perfect knowledge requires certitude, and this is why we cannot be said to know unless we know what cannot be otherwise."(Aquinas, PH, 1.8)

Geisler restates the point: "If there is to be certainty, then knowledge must be based ultimately on some principles about which there can be no question." (Geisler, TA, 71)

He summarizes: "It is unreasonable to try to get behind them. Hence, one cannot have an 'open mind' about whether they are true. One cannot even have a mind without them." (Geisler, BECA, 259)

George Mavrodes argues that first principles are more basic than argumentation. He concludes that "if there is any knowledge at all then there must be some source of knowledge other than argumentation." (Mavrodes, BG, 49)

C. S. Lewis agrees that "these first principles of Practical Reason are fundamental to all knowledge and argument. To deny them is to deny knowledge itself; it is no use trying to see through first principles. If you see through everything, then everything is transparent. But a wholly transparent world is an invisible world. To 'see through' all things is the same as not to see." (Lewis, AM, 87)

Philosopher James B. Sullivan argues that there cannot be an infinite regress of demonstrations:

As a matter of fact, the very order of reasoning requires that the chain have a beginning. For conclusions are demonstrated through premises which are either self-evident or capable of demonstration through other premises. There can be no regress into infinity, even in the order of logic. If no premise in the chain is self-evident, then the whole chain contains no evidence. For no matter how far back one might go, there would still be a premise left to prove. No; one must come at last to a premise which is self-evident. (Sullivan, EFPTB, 25–26)

3B. First Principles of Knowledge Are Derived from the Most Basic Thing about Reality—Its Being (Existence)

> Our intellect naturally knows being and its properties and in this knowledge is rooted the knowledge of first principles.
>
> —THOMAS AQUINAS

Thomas Aquinas states that the first thing we apprehend is being: "A certain order is to be found in those things that are apprehended universally. For that which, before all else, falls under apprehension, is *being*, the notion of which is included in all things whatsoever a man apprehends." (Aquinas, ST, 1.2.94.2)

Rudolph G. Bandas agrees: "As soon as we come in contact with reality, no matter what the thing that has aroused our senses, the first concept we attain is that of being." (Bandas, CPTP, 60)

Bandas clarifies that what we apprehend is not merely an idea of being, but being itself: "The material world is the only one directly accessible to us, and in it we must discover the metaphysical truths, even the most sublime. It is a real metaphysics because it is the metaphysics of the real, of being as such; its object is not the idea of being (in the Kantian sense), but the being of which we have an idea." (Bandas, CPTP, 34)

Aquinas states that "our intellect naturally knows being and its properties and in this knowledge is rooted the knowledge of first principles."(Aquinas, CG, 2.83)

Mortimer Adler points out that it is the mind that conforms to reality, not reality to the mind:

Underlying [the correspondence] definition of truth and falsity are two assumptions that Aristotle and Aquinas made, which, in my judgment, are philosophically defensible and tenable.

The first is that there exists a reality that is independent of the human mind, to which the mind can either conform or fail to conform. In other words, what we think does not create or in any way affect what we are thinking about. It is what it is, whether we think about it or not and regardless of what we think about it.

The second assumption is that this independent reality is completely determinate. This is Aristotle's metaphysical principle of contradiction. Nothing can both be and not be at the same time. Anything which does exist cannot both have and not have a certain attribute at one and the same time. (Adler, TR, 133)

Rudolph G. Bandas notes that we don't have to "think" about first principles, we perceive them in being: "These fundamental and primary principles the intelligence spontaneously perceives in being." (Bandas, CPTP, 66)

In the next section we will see that other first principles are reducible to the principle of noncontradiction (also called the principle of contradiction). Bandas summarizes that reality, being, the act of knowing, and the principle of noncontradiction are all related:

If the notion of being does not possess ontological value [i.e., real being], the principle of contradiction would be a law of logic but not necessarily of reality. This supposition, however, is even subjectively unthinkable: The idea of being is absolutely simple and nothing can correspond to it only partially. Whatever conforms to it is being; whatever does not, is nonbeing. Our intelligence and act of knowing, then, are essentially intentional and relative to being. If this relation is denied, everything becomes unintelligible. (Bandas, CPTP, 65)

4B. List of First Principles (see Regis, E, 381–403; Sullivan, EFPTB, 51—96; Geisler, BECA, 250–253; and Geisler, TA, 73–74).

Each of the following principles is true in the area of *being* (ontology) and applies to the area of *knowing* (epistemology).

1C. Identity (B Is B)
Being: "A thing must be identical to itself. If it were not, then it would not be itself." (Geisler, BECA, 250)

Knowing (conclusion): Being is intelligible. If it were not we could not conceive of anything. (Regis, E, 395)

2C. Noncontradiction (B Is Not Non-B)
Being: "Being cannot be nonbeing, for they are direct opposites. And opposites cannot be the same." (Geisler, BECA, 251)

Knowing (conclusion): There are at least two ways to express this principle: (1) it is impossible that contradictory statements be simultaneously true; (2) if one contradiction is true, the other is necessarily false. (Regis, E, 388–89)

3C. Excluded Middle (Either B or Non-B)
Being: "Since being and nonbeing are opposites (i. e., contradictory), and opposites cannot be the same, nothing can hide in the 'cracks' between being and non-being. The only choices are being and nonbeing." (Geisler, BECA, 251)

Knowing (conclusion): A proposition

must be either true or false. (Geisler, TA, 73)

4C. Causality (Non-B Cannot Cause B)

Being: "Only being can cause being. Nothing does not exist, and only what exists can cause existence, since the very concept of 'cause' implies an existing thing that has the power to effect another. From absolutely nothing comes absolutely nothing." (Geisler, BECA, 251)

Knowing (conclusion): Not every proposition can depend for its truth on another. Every proposition that is not self-evident depends for its truth on the truth of a self-evident proposition. (Geisler, TA, 74)

5C. Finality (Every Agent Acts for an End)

Being: Every agent acts for an end. (Regis, E, 399)

Knowing (conclusion): "Every proposition has an end in view; it is necessary that every proposition communicate some meaning; and mind communicates what is intelligible." (Geisler, TA, 74)

6C. Other First Principles Are Reducible to the Principle of Noncontradiction

Professor Geisler illustrates how all the above principles are reducible to noncontradiction:

The primacy of the principle of noncontradiction is manifest since the principles of identity and excluded middle are dependent aspects of it. For if contradictions were possible, then a thing would not have to be identical to itself (identity) nor would opposites have to be different from each other (excluded middle). The principle of causality is also reducible to the principle of noncontradiction, for on inspection of the terms it would be a contradiction to affirm that a contingent (dependent) being is uncaused (independent). Likewise, the principle of

finality rests upon the principle of noncontradiction, since otherwise being could communicate something other than being; intelligence would communicate something other than the intelligible. (Geisler, TA, 76)

Aristotle posits two criteria for the most certain principle: "The most certain principle of all is that regarding which it is impossible to be mistaken; for such a principle must be both the best known and nonhypothetical. This, then, is the most certain of all principles, since it answers to the definition given above. *For it is impossible for anyone to believe the same thing to be and not to be. This is naturally the starting point even for all the other axioms.*" (Aristotle, M, 4.3. 1005b, emphasis mine)

Again Aristotle states, "We have now posited [set forth] that it is impossible for anything at the same time to be and not to be, and by this means have shown that this is the most indisputable of all principles." (Aristotle, M, 4.4.1006a)

Thomas Aquinas summarizes the foundational nature of the law of noncontradiction which Aristotle discovered:

"No one can ever conceive," says Aristotle, "one and the same thing can both be and not be." To think thus would be to affirm and deny in the same breath. It would destroy language, it would be to deny all substance, all truth, even all probability and all degrees of probability. It would be the suppression of all desire, all action Even becoming and beginning would disappear, because if contradictories and contraries are identified [i. e., made the same], then the point of departure in motion is identified with the terminus and the thing supposed to be in motion would have arrived before it departed. (Aquinas, M, 4.3)

Aquinas, therefore, agrees that, "the first indemonstrable principle is that *the same thing cannot be affirmed and denied at the same time*, which is based on the notion of *being* and *not-being*: and on this principle all others are based." (Aquinas, ST, 1.2.94.2)

> The logic of truth is the same for all exclusionary claims to truth—claims that something is correctly judged to be true and that all judgments to the contrary are, therefore, incorrect. The proposition may be a theorem in mathematics, a scientific generalization, a conclusion of historical research, a philosophical principle, or an article of religious faith.
>
> —MORTIMER J. ADLER

Mortimer Adler notes that noncontradiction, being, and reality are relative to one another: "Among the first principles of Greek logic is the rule governing truth and falsity of incompatible propositions: either that both cannot be true, though both may be false, or that one must be true and the other must be false. Underlying this rule is an ontological axiom—a truth about reality—that the Greeks thought was self-evident; namely, that nothing can both be and not be at the same time." (Adler, TR, 70,71)

In the list of first principles we saw that they have both an ontological (the state of *being*) aspect and an epistemological (how we know something) aspect. Adler notes the important distinction between them in the law of noncontradiction: "The law of contradiction as a statement about reality itself underlies the law of contradiction as a rule of thought. The law of contradiction as a statement of reality *describes* the way things are. The law of contradiction as a rule of thought *prescribes* the way we should think about things if we wish our thinking about them to conform to the way things are." (Adler, AE, 140)

Reginald Garrigou-Lagrange notes the universality of noncontradiction: "According to traditional realism, as formulated by Aristotle and Aquinas, the universal idea exists in the sense world, not formally, but fundamentally, and of all ideas the most universal is that of being, on which is founded the principle of contradiction." (Garrigou-Lagrange, R, 372373)

Adler concurs: "The logic of truth is the same for all exclusionary claims to truth—claims that something is correctly judged to be true and that all judgments to the contrary are, therefore, incorrect. The proposition may be a theorem in mathematics, a scientific generalization, a conclusion of historical research, a philosophical principle, or an article of religious faith." (Adler, TR, 10)

Adler illustrates the self-evident nature of noncontradiction:

> The law of contradiction, as a statement about reality, says what is immediately obvious to common sense. A thing—whatever it may be—cannot both exist and not exist at the same time. It either exists or it does not exist, but not both at once. A thing cannot have a certain attribute and not have that attribute at the same time. The apple in my hand that I am looking at cannot, at this instance, be both red in color and not red in color.
>
> This is so very obvious that Aristotle calls the law of contradiction self-evident. Its self-evidence, for him, means its undeniability. It is impossible to think that the apple is both red and not red at the same time." (Adler, AE, 140)

5B. Certainty of First Principles

1C. The Self-evident Nature of First Principles

We do not have to contemplate about first principles to know whether they are true; it is obvious to us (self-evident) that they are true as soon as we understand the terms used in the proposition. The five principles above are self-evidently true or reducible to it. Another classic example is the proposition "the whole is greater than the parts." As soon as we understand what "whole" means and what "parts" means, we *immediately* know the proposition is true. Immediately in this sense does not mean quickly, but rather that it *is not mediated* by a reasoning process, that is, we don't have to contemplate about the proposition before knowing it is true.

Thomas Aquinas says the intellect "cannot be in error with respect to those statements that are known as soon as the meaning of the terms is known, as with first principles, from which we proceed to conclusions whose scientific certitude has the infallibility of truth." (Aquinas, ST, 1.85.6)

Aquinas again states: "The intellect is always right as regards first principles; since it is not deceived about them for the same reason that it is not deceived about what a thing is. For self-known principles are such as are known as soon as the terms are understood, from the fact that the predicate is contained in the definition of the subject." (Aquinas, ST, 1.17.3).

First principles are self-evident propositions (i.e., they show themselves to be true). We cannot be mistaken about self-evident propositions; therefore we cannot be mistaken about first principles.

Scott MacDonald comments that immediate propositions depend on reality, they are the factual basis of all inference, and it is impossible to be mistaken about them:

Which propositions are immediate, then, depends solely on what real natures there are and what relations hold among them, that is, on the basic structure of the world, and not on the psychology or belief-structure of any given epistemic subject. Non-inferential justification, then, consists in one's being directly aware of the immediate facts that ground a

proposition's necessary truth. When one sees that a proposition expresses an immediate fact of this sort, one cannot be mistaken in holding it. (MacDonald, TK, as cited in Kretzmann, CCA, 170–171)

MacDonald's point is that immediate propositions are not filtered through any belief system. This point will be important to remember when we begin to critique the self-defeating statements of those who deny that truth is knowable. We will see that, despite their philosophical systems, the philosophers themselves cannot avoid reality and the principle of noncontradiction. They want to filter reality through their system, but, in the case of first principles, reality won't oblige.

2C. The Mind Is Predisposed to Truth

Thomas Aquinas states that the mind is predisposed to truth: "Truth is the intellect's good and the term of its natural ordination; and just as things without knowledge are moved toward their end without knowing it, so sometimes does the human intellect tend toward truth although it does not perceive its nature." (Aquinas, P, 10.5)

Aquinas observes that the mind has a natural appetite for truth. He explains what he means by this: "Natural appetite is that inclination which each thing has, of its own nature, for something; wherefore by its natural appetite each power desires what is suitable to itself." (Aquinas, ST, 1.78.1).

Mortimer Adler clarifies that we do not have certainty about all truth, only self-evident truths:

The human mind has a grasp on the truth to whatever extent the judgments it makes agree with or conform to reality—to the way things are or are not. To say this does not involve us in claiming that the human mind has a firm, final, and incorrigible grasp on any truth, though I personally think that there is a relatively small number of self-evident truths on which our grasp is firm, final, and incorrigible. However that may be, we must acknowledge that truth is *in principle* attainable, even though we may never in fact actually attain it. (Adler, TR, 116–17)

6B. First Principles Are Undeniable and Indemonstrable

1C. Undeniability

We need to be clear on what we are actually saying at this point. By saying that first principles are undeniable, we are not giving a positive evidence for first principles but rather a negative evidence that first principles *cannot* be denied.

James B. Sullivan summarizes Aristotle's argument defending the undeniability of the principle of noncontradiction. He lists eight inevitable results (see chart below).

Avicenna, writes John Duns Scotus, suggested one other undesirable result for anyone who denied first principles. "Those who deny a first principle should be beaten or

exposed to fire until they concede that to burn and not to burn, or to be beaten and not to be beaten, are not identical." (Avicenna, M, as cited in Scotus, PW, 10)

Reginald Garrigou-Lagrange notes this absurd result:

If the principle of contradiction is not absolute, then the formula of Descartes himself ["I think, therefore I am"] loses all real validity and becomes a mere mental phenomenon. If I can deny this principle, then I may say; Perhaps I think and do not think simultaneously, perhaps I exist and do not exist, perhaps I am I and not I, perhaps "I think" is impersonal like "it rains." Without the absoluteness of contradiction I cannot know the objective existence of my own individual person. (Garrigou-Lagrange, R, 372)

One must use a first principle in order to deny a first principle, which is absurd.

First principles are undeniable or reducible to the undeniable. They are either self-evident or reducible to the self-evident. And self-evident principles are either true by their nature or undeniable because the predicate is reducible to the subject. That the predicate is reducible

EIGHT CONSEQUENCES OF DENYING THE LAW OF NONCONTRADICTION

1. To deny the necessity and validity of the Principle of Contradiction would be to deprive words of their fixed meaning and render speech useless.
2. Reality of essences must be abandoned; there would be becoming without anything that becomes; flying without a bird; accidents without subjects in which to inhere.
3. There would be no distinction between things. All would be one. Ship, wall, man would all be the same thing.
4. It would mean the destruction of truth, for truth and falsity would be the same thing.
5. It would destroy all thought, even opinion, for its affirmation would be its negation.
6. Desire and preference would be useless, for there would be no difference between good and evil; there would be no reason to go home, for to go home would not be different from staying where one is.
7. Everything would be equally true and false at the same time, so that no opinion would be more wrong than any other even in degree.
8. It would make impossible all becoming, change, or motion. For all this implies a transition from one state of being to another; but if the Principle of Contradiction is false, all states of being are the same. (Sullivan, EFPTB, 121–22)

to the subject means that one cannot deny the principle without using it. For example the principle of noncontradiction cannot be denied without using it in the very denial. (Geisler, BECA, 250)

Ravi Zacharias agrees: "There is no way to ignore or circumvent these laws of argument, for in effect one is forced to apply them in order to refute them." (Zacharias, CMLWG, 11)

Joseph Owens notes further that neither can noncontradiction be denied in thought: "No matter how much you try to deny it in words, you cannot deny it in thought. Any attempt to deny it involves its affirmation. It is accordingly open to neither doubt nor correction. It is a judgment that expresses universally the being that is immediately known in things perceived through the external senses and in one's own self through consciousness." (Owens, ECM, 269–70)

Mortimer J. Adler explains that common sense finds noncontradiction an undeniable attribute of reality: "Common sense would not hesitate for a moment to assert that at a given time a particular thing either exists or does not exist, that a certain event either occurred or did not occur, that something being considered either does or does not have a certain characteristic or attribute. Far from being an outrageous, not to say erroneous, assumption about the reality to which our beliefs or opinions may or may not correspond, this view of reality seems undeniable to common sense." (Adler, SGI, 36)

2C. Indemonstrability

We need to be clear here that we are not saying indemonstrability (a proposition not subject to proof) is an evidence for first principles; rather, we are only saying that indemonstrability is in fact true of first principles. Remember that there is no other evidence for first principles except themselves—

they are self-evident. They are our basis for all *other* demonstration and argumentation.

Aristotle states what "indemonstrable" means: "Not all knowledge is demonstrative:

> Those who deny a first principle should be beaten or exposed to fire until they concede that to burn and not to burn, or to be beaten and not to be beaten, are not identical.
>
> —AVICENNA

on the contrary, knowledge of the immediate premises is independent of demonstration. (The necessity of this is obvious; for since we must know the prior premises from which the demonstration is drawn, and since the regress must end in immediate truths, those truths must be indemonstrable)." (Aristotle, AP, 1.3.72b)

Aristotle declares: "For it is impossible that there should be demonstration of absolutely everything (there would be an infinite regress, so that there would still be no demonstration)." (Aristotle, M, 4.4.1006a)

Aquinas illustrates the futility of an infinite regress of demonstrations:

Suppose that someone who has a demonstration [for a given conclusion] syllogizes [gives a concise deductive argument] on the basis of demonstrable (or mediate) premises. That person either possesses a demonstration for these premises or he does not. If he does not, then he does not have scientia [i.e., knowledge] with respect to the premises, and so does not have scientia [i.e., knowledge] with respect to the conclusion that he holds on account of the premises either. But if he possesses a demonstration for the premises, he will arrive at some premises that are immediate and indemonstrable, since in the case of demonstrations one cannot go on ad infinitum. . . . And so it must be that demonstration proceeds from immediate premises either directly or indirectly through other mediating [premises]. (Aquinas, PA, 1.4.14)

Alasdair MacIntyre states clearly: "Argument *to* first principles cannot be demonstrative, for demonstration is *from* first principles." (MacIntyre, FP, 35)

Mortimer Adler argues that there is no evidence for a self-evident truth other than itself:

Truths called self-evident provide the most obvious examples of knowledge in the strong sense of that term. They are called self-evident because our affirmation of them does not depend on evidence marshaled in support of them nor upon reasoning designed to show that they are conclusions validly reached by inference. We recognize their truth immediately or directly from our understanding of what they assert. We are convinced—convinced, not persuaded—of their truth because we find it impossible to think the opposite of what they assert. We are in no sense free to think the opposite. (Adler, SGI, 52)

7B. Objections Concerning First Principles

1C. First Principles Are Only a Western Way of Thinking (also see section below on Mysticism)

We must note the self-defeating nature of this objection:

Some say that there is another kind of logic, Eastern logic, which holds to the idea that reality, at its very core, embraces contradictions. However, trying to put geographical limitations on any universal law is logically impossible. According to Eastern logic, reality can be logical and illogical. But if something is both logical and illogical, it is a contradiction and has no meaning. So according to Eastern logic everything is ultimately meaningless. Yet if everything is ultimately meaningless, so is

the distinction between Western and Eastern logic. (Geisler and Bocchino, WSA, n.p.)

Mortimer Adler declares: "The fundamentals of logic should be as transcultural as the mathematics with which the principles of logic are associated. The principles of logic are neither Western nor Eastern, but universal." (Adler, TR, 36)

Adler explains that "Western" thinking underlies all technology—in the East or in the West:

Wherever the fruits of technology are used, the truth of mathematics and natural science are acknowledged. If the underlying mathematics and natural science were not true, the technology would not work successfully. If the underlying mathematics and natural science are true, then the underlying view of reality as free from inherent contradictions must also be true; for if it were not, the conclusions of the empirical natural sciences could not be true by virtue of their correspondence with reality.

Adler concludes, "That there is an independent reality with which the propositions we assert can correspond or fail to correspond is assured by the way in which technologically contrived devices work or fail to work." (Adler, TR, 74)

Ravi Zacharias tells the following story that illuminates the futility of this line of argument:

As the professor waxed eloquent and expounded on the law of non-contradiction, he eventually drew his conclusion: "This [*either/or* logic] is a Western way of looking at reality. The real problem is that you are seeing contradiction as a Westerner when you should be approaching it as an Easterner. The *both/and* is the Eastern way of viewing reality."

After he belabored these two ideas on *either/or* and *both/and* for some time, I finally asked if I could interrupt his unpunctuated train of thought and raise one question.

I said, "Sir, are you telling me that when I am studying Hinduism I *either* use the *both/and* system of logic *or* nothing else?"

There was pin-drop silence for what seemed an eternity. I repeated my question: "Are you telling me that when I am studying Hinduism I *either* use the *both/and* logic *or* nothing else? Have I got that right?"

He threw his head back and said, "The *either/or* does seem to emerge, doesn't it?"

"Indeed, it does emerge," I said. "And as a matter of fact, even in India we look both ways before we cross the street—it is either the bus or me, not both of us."

Do you see the mistake he was making? He was using the *either/or* logic in order to prove the *both/and*. The more you try to hammer the law of non-contradiction, the more it hammers you. (Zacharias, CMLWG, 129)

Zacharias also points out what many don't acknowledge about "Eastern" philosophy:

The whole method of teaching of the greatest Hindu philosopher Shankara was quite Socratic as he debated ideas not in a dialectical mode (*both/and*) but in a noncontradictory mode (*either/or*). He would challenge his antagonists to prove him wrong, and if not, to surrender to his view. The point, then, is not whether we use an Eastern logic or a Western logic. We use the logic that best reflects reality, and the law of noncontradiction is implicitly or explicitly implied by both the East and the West. (Zacharias, CMLWG, 130)

2C. Logical Laws Like Contradiction Are Just Formal Laws for Constructing Symbolic Systems; They Don't Apply to Reality

Ronald Nash answers: "The law of noncontradiction is not simply a law of thought. It is a law of thought because it is first a law of being. Nor is the law something someone can take or leave. The denial of the law of noncontradiction leads to absurdity. It is impossible meaningfully to deny the laws of logic. If the law of noncontradiction is denied, then nothing has meaning. If the laws of logic do not first mean what they say, nothing else can have meaning, including the denial of the laws." (Nash, WVC, 84)

Rudolph G. Bandas concurs:

If the notion of being does not possess ontological value, the principle of contradiction would be a law of logic but not necessarily of reality. This supposition, however, is even subjectively unthinkable: The idea of being is absolutely simple and nothing can correspond to it only partially. Whatever conforms to it is being; whatever does not, is nonbeing. Our intelligence and act of knowing, then, are essentially intentional and relative to being. If this relation is denied, everything becomes unintelligible. (Bandas, CPTP, 65)

3C. To Defend the Principle (Law) of Non-contradiction Using Noncontradiction Is a Circular Argument

Norman Geisler replies that

this objection confuses the issue. For the law of noncontradiction is not used as the *basis* of the indirect proof of its validity; it is simply used in the *process* of defending its validity. Take, for example, the statement "I cannot speak a word in English." This statement is self-destructive, since it does what it says it cannot do. It uses English to deny that it can use English. So it disproves itself. The indirect proof for the law of noncontradiction is similar. We cannot deny the law of noncontradiction without using it in the very sentence that denies it. For the sentence that denies noncontradiction is offered as a noncontradictory sentence. If it is not, then it makes no sense.

In like manner, if I say "I can utter a word in English," it is obvious that I uttered a word in English in the process of doing so. But there is nothing self-defeating about using English to say I can use English. There is only something self-defeating about using English to deny I can use English. Likewise, there is nothing wrong with using the principle of noncontradiction to defend the principle of noncontradiction. There is only something wrong about using the principle of noncontradiction to deny that principle. (Geisler, TA, 79)

4C. We Cannot Know First Principles *A Priori* (i.e., Apart from Experience) Since the Mind Is a *Tabula Rasa* (i.e., Blank Slate) Until It Experiences Something

Thomas Aquinas states: "Sensitive [i.e., experienced] knowledge is not the entire cause of intellectual knowledge. And therefore it is not strange that intellectual knowledge should extend further than sensitive knowledge." (Aquinas, ST, 1.84.6)

Norman Geisler explains that knowledge of first principles is "natural": "Natural knowledge is neither 'infused' a priori nor 'acquired' a posteriori. It is known naturally because we have the natural capacity or 'form' for it." (Geisler, TA, 90)

Peter Hoenen also uses the term "naturally": "Like the other first principles, the principle of contradiction governs both the intellect and being, and the relations between the two. In consequence of the ease with which these principles are known—not always formulated however—they belong to the human mind 'as by nature.'" (Hoenen, RJ, 208)

James Sullivan explains what is meant by "naturally": "The person who makes the sense judgment is not explicitly aware of these principles at the time, but they may be easily and instantly elicited from him by questioning, even though he may never have given them any thought previously. Hence he may be said to possess principles virtually or habitually, from the beginning of his cognitive life. This is what is meant by saying that first principles 'come by nature, and are known naturally.'" (Sullivan, EFPTB, 33)

Aquinas notes that this natural knowledge is had as soon as something is presented to the intellect: "In every man there is a certain principle of knowledge, namely the light of the active intellect, through which certain principles of all the sciences are naturally understood as soon as proposed to the intellect" (Aquinas, ST, 1.117.1).

5C. How Can Knowledge of First Principles Be Both *A Posteriori* (i.e., from Experience) Yet Innate?

Remember that whenever anyone asks a *How?* question regarding knowledge, they are asking about epistemology. We already noted that it is not necessary to answer the *how* questions when giving evidence that something is in fact the case; however, we will offer an answer to this objection.

In answer to this question:

Aquinas makes a significant contribution to epistemology. By a unique synthesis, he unites both the *a priori* and *a posteriori* elements of knowledge. Humans have an innate, natural capacity or form for the truth of first principles that is ingrained into their very nature by God. They have first principles in a kind of virtual and natural way as a precondition of all cognitive activity. And when this innate capacity is filled with the content of sense experience, we are able by conscious reflection to come to a knowledge of the very first principles, which as a fundamental part of our nature, enable us to have a consciousness of them. That is to say, we can only know first principles if we are exercising first principles to know them, otherwise, we would have no means by which they could be known. We have them by way of operation before we know them by way of consciousness. (Geisler, TA, 90)

Etienne Gilson summarizes Aquinas' answer to the *how* question this way:

We find the germs of all knowledge in the intellect itself. These pre-formed germs of which we have natural knowledge are the first principles. What is characteristic of these principles is that they are the first concepts formed by our intellect when we come into contact with the sensible. To say that they preexist, does not mean that the intellect possesses them actually, independently of the action which bodies exercise on our soul; it simply means that they are the first intelligibles which our intellect can reach in starting from sensible experience. The intellection of these principles is no more innate than the conclusions of deductive arguments, but whereas we discover the former naturally, we have to reach the latter by an effort of search. (Gilson, PSTA, 246)

6C. But Logic Doesn't Apply to Reality
In answer to this objection:

There are only three possible views on the relation of logical necessity and reality: (1) logic *can not* apply to reality; (2) logic *may not* apply to reality; (3) logic *must* apply to reality. We argue that the first alternative is self-defeating, the second is meaningless and, therefore the third is the only view which is affirmable. This leaves us with one meaningful alternative, viz, logic *must* apply to reality. For the view that logic *can not* apply to reality affirms that logic does apply to reality in the very attempt to deny that it does. And the position that logic *may not* apply to reality is a meaningless assertion, unless logic does apply to the meanings of the terms "reality" and "possible" in the sentence which claims that logic may not apply to reality. (Geisler, MPOA, 292–93)

Ravi Zacharias asserts: "The laws of logic must apply to reality; else we may as well be living in a madhouse." (Zacharias, CMLWG, 11)

> The laws of logic must apply to reality; else we may as well be living in a madhouse.
>
> —RAVI ZACHARIAS

7C. There Is No Truth that Corresponds to Reality
Ravi Zacharias points out the self-defeating nature of this truth statement: "For anyone to take seriously the statement that there is no truth that corresponds to reality defeats the statement itself by implying that it is not reflective of reality. If a statement is not reflective of reality, why take it seriously? Truth as a category must exist even while one is denying its existence and must also afford the possibility of being known." (Zacharias, CMLWG, 125)

Geisler explains that "even the intentionalist theory depends on the correspondence theory of truth. The intentionalist theory claims something is true if it is accomplishing what it intends. But this means that it is true only if the accomplishments *correspond* to the intentions. So without *correspondence* of intentions and accomplished facts there is no truth." (Geisler, CTID, 335-36)

8C. If All Argumentation Needs a Basis, Then Don't First Principles Need a Basis Also?
Geisler clarifies: "Our argument is not that *everything* needs a basis but that only things that are not self-evident need a foundation. Things that are not evident in themselves must be evident in terms of something else that is self-evident. Once one arrives at the self-evident, it need not be evident in terms of anything else." (Geisler, BECA, 260)

This is a crucial point to remember when discussing this issue with those who demand evidence for first principles; *there is no evi-*

dence for first principles other than themselves—they simply are self-evident.

9C. Not Everyone Sees These Principles as Self-evident

However, "simply because some things are not evident to everyone does not mean they are not self-evident in themselves. The reason a self-evident truth may not be self-evident to someone could be because the person has not analyzed it carefully. But their failure in no way invalidates the self-evident nature of the first principles." (Geisler, BECA, 260)

10C. You Are Just *Assuming* that All Demonstration Depends on a Reduction to First Principles in Order to Prove that There Cannot Be an Infinite Regress of Demonstration

James B. Sullivan replies, "That conclusions are rendered certain by reduction to the first principle of demonstration is not an *a priori* assumption to which infinite regress in demonstration fails to conform; it is rather a conclusion derived from the impossibility of infinite regress." (Sullivan, EFPTB, 26)

11C. Doesn't Heisenberg's Principle of Uncertainty Undercut the Certainty of First Principles?

Mortimer Adler points out the faulty premise hidden in this objection:

The error involved in the Copenhagen interpretation of Heisenberg's principle of uncertainty lies in one extraordinary philosophical mistake made unwittingly or defiantly by twentieth-century physicists. It is the error of restricting reality to what is measurable by physicists, attributing reality only to measurable characteristics. The principle should be understood as attributing uncertainty only to our measurements in quantum mechanics. That uncertainty, which is epistemic, or in the field of knowing, is fallaciously converted into an indeterminacy in the structure of reality, which then becomes ontological, not epistemic. (Adler, TR, 71–72)

34
ANSWERING POSTMODERNISM

1A. INTRODUCTION

At this point we must offer an answer to several of the main philosophical objections to the knowability of truth. The most recent objections are manifested under the guise of "postmodernism." Why is it necessary to answer contemporary philosophers such as Lyotard and Derrida whose philosophies permeate contemporary culture? Because, as C. S. Lewis said, "To be ignorant and simple now—not to be able to meet the enemies on their own ground—would be to throw down

AN OVERVIEW COMPARISON OF ETHICAL THEISM, MODERNISM, AND POSTMODERNISM

	Ethical Theism	Modernism	Postmodernism
Truth	Truth has been revealed to men and women by God.	Truth can be discovered by reason and logical augmentation.	Truth does not exist objectively; it is a product of a person's culture.
Human Identity	Humans are both spiritual and material beings, created in God's image but fallen because of sin.	Humans are rational, not spiritual, beings who can define their existence according to what their senses perceive.	Humans are primarily social beings, products of their culture and environment.
The World	God is the Creator, Preserver, and Governor of His earth and has instructed humans to subdue it and care for it.	Humans can and should conquer the earth and all its mysteries.	Life on earth is fragile, and the "Enlightenment model of the human conquest of nature . . . must quickly give way to a new attitude of cooperation with the earth."
Thought and Language	Reason "can disclose truth about reality, but faith and revelation are needed in addition."	For answers and understanding about life and the world around us, people should rely only on rational discovery through the scientific method and reject belief in the supernatural.	Thinking is a "social contruct," language is arbitrary, and there is no universal truth transcending culture.
Human Progress	Human history is not progressing but awaiting deliverance.	Human progress through the use of science and reason is inevitable.	Things are not getting better; besides, progress is an oppressive Western concept.

(McDowell, NT, 38)

our weapons, and to betray our uneducated brethren who have, under God, no defense, but us against the intellectual attacks of the heathen. Good philosophy must exist, if for no other reason, because bad philosophy needs to be answered." (Lewis, WG, 28)

"Between 1960 and 1990," writes Stanley J. Grenz, in his book *A Primer to Postmodernism*, "postmodernism emerged as a cultural phenomenon," spurred on in many respects by the advent of the information age. Grenz suggests that if the factory is the symbol of the industrial age, which produced modernism, the computer is the symbol of the information age, which parallels the spread of postmodernism" (McDowell & Hostetler, NT, 36–37)

Postmodernism is complex, and its tenets are sometimes contradictory. Still, Lawrence Cahoone, captures its essence in his book *From Modernism to Postmodernism*, "Simply put, they regard it [postmodernism] as rejecting most of the fundamental intellectual pillars of the modern Western civilization . . . At a minimum, postmodernism regards certain important principles, methods, or ideas characteristic of modern Western culture as obsolete or illegitimate." (Cahoone, MPM, 2) Postmodernism represents a rejection of the philosophy that has characterized Western thought since its inception.

2A. THE CHIEF CHARACTERISTICS OF POSTMODERNISM

1B. Truth Does Not Correspond to Reality

Rorty maintains, "For the pragmatist [postmodernist], true sentences are not true because they correspond to reality, and so there is no need to worry what sort of reality, if any, a given sentence corresponds to— no need to worry about what 'makes' it true." (Rorty, CP, xvi)

Rorty denies that truth corresponds to reality:

[The pragmatist] shares with the positivist the Baconian and Hobbesian notion that knowledge is power, a tool for coping with reality. But he carries this Baconian point through to its extreme, as the positivist does not. He

> Kuhn and Dewey suggest we give up the notion of science traveling toward an end called 'correspondence with reality' and instead say merely that a given vocabulary works better than another for a given purpose.
>
> —RICHARD RORTY

drops the notion of truth as correspondence with reality altogether, and says that modern science does not enable us to cope because it corresponds, it just plain enables us to cope. His argument for the view is that several hundred years of effort have failed to make interesting sense of the notion of 'correspondence' (either of thoughts to things or of words to things). (Rorty, CP, xvii)

Rorty, in agreement with Kuhn and Dewey, states, "Kuhn and Dewey suggest we give up the notion of science traveling towards an end called 'correspondence with reality' and instead say merely that a given vocabulary works better than another for a given purpose." (Rorty, CP, 193)

Grenz summarizes, "Richard Rorty, in turn, jettisons the classic conception of truth as either the mind or language mirroring nature. Truth is established neither by the correspondence of an assertion with objective reality nor by the internal coherence of the assertions themselves, says Rorty. He argues that we should simply give up the search for truth and be content with interpretation." (Grenz, PP, 6)

Walter Truett Anderson explains the position of many postmodernists about truth, "Surrounded by so many truths, we can't help but revise our concept of truth itself: our beliefs about belief. More and more people are becoming accustomed with the idea that, as philosopher Richard Rorty puts it, truth is made rather than found." (Anderson, TT, 8).

Richard Tarnas extrapolates on this position, "The mind is not the passive reflector of an external world and its intrinsic order, but is active and creative in the process of perception and cognition. Reality [truth] is in some sense constructed by the mind, not simply perceived by it, and many such constructions are possible, none necessarily sovereign. . . . Hence the nature of truth and reality . . . is radically ambiguous." (Tarnas, PWM, 396–97)

Pauline Marie Rosenau gives a practical example, "while the modern therapist's role might be to help the client sort things out, get below the surface, and achieve a more adequate understanding of reality, the postmodern therapist has no such intent. There is no true reality out there to discover." (Rosenau, PMSS, 89)

Grenz highlights the postmodern position:

Postmodern thinkers no longer find this grand realist ideal [that truth ultimately corresponds to reality] tenable. They reject the fundamental assumption on which it is based— namely, that we live in a world consisting of physical objects that are easily identifiable by their inherent properties. They argue that we do no simply encounter a world that is 'out there' but rather that we construct the world using concepts we bring to it. They contend that we have no fixed vantage point beyond our own structuring of the world from which

to gain a purely objective view of whatever reality might be out there. (Grenz, PP, 41)

Middleton and Walsh summarize the reasoning behind the postmodern rejection of the correspondence theory of truth:

Although modernity has never been simply an intellectual movement, the modern project was predicated on the assumption that the knowing autonomous subject arrived at truth by establishing a correspondence between objectively "given" reality and the thoughts or assertions of the knower. To the postmodern mind, such correspondence is impossible, since we have no access to something called "reality" apart from that which we "represent" as reality in our concepts, language, and discourse. Richard Rorty says that since we never encounter reality "except under a chosen description," we are denied the luxury or pretense of claiming naïve, immediate access to the world. We never get outside of our knowledge to check its accuracy against "objective"reality. Our access is always mediated by our own linguistic and conceptual constructions. (Middleton, FPS, as cited in Phillips, CAPW, 134)

2B. There Is No Metanarrative (Grand Story) that Can Account for All Reality

In 1984 Jean Francois Lyotard, a French philosopher, wrote "The Postmodern Condition: A Report on Knowledge." Not only did he help to popularize the term *postmodernism,* but he gave a definition that is considered to be one of the cornerstones of postmodernism: "Incredulity to Metanarratives" (Lyotard, Jean Francois. *The Postmodern Condition: A Report on Knowledge.* Trans. Geoff Bennington and Brian Massumi. Minneapolis: University of Minnesota Press, 1984).

Anderson explains,

A metanarrative is a story of mythic proportions, a story big enough and meaningful enough to pull together philosophy and research and politics and art, relate them to one another, and—above all—give them a unifying sense of direction. Lyotard cited as examples the Christian religious story of God's will being worked out on Earth, the Marxist political story of class conflict and revolution, and the Enlightenment's intellectual story of rational progress. He proceeded to define the postmodern era as a time of "incredulity toward metanarratives"—all of them.

Lyotard didn't mean that all people have ceased to believe in all stories, but rather that the stories aren't working so well anymore—in part because there are too many, and we all know it. (Anderson, TT, 4)

Albert Mohler takes this definition a step further: "Thus, all great philosophical systems are dead, all cultural accounts are limited, all that remains are little stories accepted as true by different groups and cultures. Claims to universal truth—the metanarratives—are oppressive, 'totalizing' and thus must be resisted." ("Ministry Is Stranger Than It Used To Be: The Challenge of Postmodernism." Southern Seminary, Spring 1997. Vol. 65, #2)

Pauline Marie Rosenau describes this phenomena:

Post-modernism challenges global, all-encompassing world views, be they political, religious, or social. It reduces Marxism, Christianity, Fascism, Stalinism, capitalism, liberal democracy, secular humanism, feminism, Islam, and modern science, to the same order and dismisses them all as logocentric (Derrida's term that is an adjective used to describe systems of thought that claim legitimacy by reference to external, universally truthful propositions), totalizing metanarratives that anticipate all questions and provide predetermined answers. All such systems of thought rest on assumptions no more or no less certain than those of witchcraft, astrology, or primitive cults. The postmodern goal is not to formulate an alternative set of assumptions but to register the impossibility of establishing any such underpinning for knowledge. (Rosenau, PMSS, 6)

Gene Veith says, "In the past, when one framework for knowledge was thought to be inadequate, it was replaced by another framework. The goal of postmodernism is to do without frameworks for knowledge altogether. In postmodernist jargon, 'metanarratives' are stories about stories, 'large-scale theoretical interpretations purportedly of universal application'; that is to say, worldviews. Postmodernism is a worldview that denies all worldviews." (Veith, PT, 49)

Steiner Kvale gives the postmodern perspective: "The Post-Modern Age is a time of incessant choosing. It's an era when no orthodoxy can be adopted without self consciousness and irony, because all traditions seem to have some value." ("Themes of Postmodernity," as cited in Anderson, TT, 27)

Lawrence Cahoone describes this effect on society: "For many irreligious intellectuals, the hope for a utopian socialist future gave badly needed significance to a life lived after the 'death of god.' The loss of this hope struck a sizable portion of this group much as the loss of religion had already struck traditional society: lacking a historical *telos* or goal, it seemed that the world had become centerless and pointless once again. Postmodernism, a wayward child of Marxism, is in this sense a generation's realization that it is orphaned." (Cahoone, MPM, 10)

3B. We Never Epistemologically Encounter the Thing-in-Itself

Grenz says, "Postmoderns conclude that all attempts to describe an objective, unifying center—a single real world—behind the flux of experience are doomed; in the end they produce only fictions, creations of the human mind. In detaching human explanation from the notion of an underlying objective world, the postmodern critique of

> The philosophically pluralistic theories hold that objective truth is inaccessible and that meaning resides not in external reality or texts but in the interpreter.
>
> —CARL F. H. HENRY

modernism cuts us off from things and leaves us only words." (Grenz, PP, 83–84)

Caputo asserts, "The process of uncovering becomes a process of hearsay. We become lost in words and fail to enter into relationships with the things themselves." (Caputo, RH, 75)

Henry concludes, "The philosophically pluralistic theories hold that objective truth is inaccessible and meaning resides not in external reality or texts but in the interpreter." (Henry, PNS, as cited in Dockery, CP, 41)

Richard Tarnas expands on this: "It is recognized that human knowledge is subjectively determined by a multitude of factors; that objective essences, or things-in-themselves, are neither accessible nor positable; and that the value of all truths and assumptions must be continually subjected to direct testing. The critical search for truth is constrained to be tolerant of ambiguity and pluralism, and its outcome will necessarily be knowledge that is relative and fallible rather than absolute or certain." (Cited in Tarnas, PWM, 395–97)

Pauline Marie Rosenau states the postmodern position:

The text itself, not facts, is what counts for the post-modernists. The post-modernists are satisfied to conclude that what is actually going on can never be stated definitively; in any case, it matters little because there is no single meaning for any text, for any political, social, economic event. An infinite number of interpretations of any scenario is possible. (Rosenau, PM & SS, 41)

She goes on to explain, "Language produces and reproduces its own world without reference to reality . . . it is impossible to say anything definite because language is purely an artificial sign system and cannot assure truth." (Rosenau, PM & SS, 79)

Caputo maintains that there is no objective hermeneutic truth: "The point of all this . . . is to concede the elusiveness of the thing itself, to catch on to its play, not to jettison it (whatever that would mean). That is the cold, hermeneutic truth, the truth at there is no truth, no master name which holds things captive." (Caputo, RH, 192)

Grenz summarizes,

Derrida concludes that in the end language is merely "self-referential." A sign, he argues, will always lead to another sign. Thus, a language is a chain of signifiers referring to other signifiers, in which each signifier in turn becomes what is signified by another signifier. And because the textual location in which a signifier is embedded constantly changes, its meaning can never be fully determined. Derrida thus holds that meaning is never static, never given once-for-all. Instead, meaning changes over time and with changing contexts. For this reason, we must continually "defer" or postpone our tendency to attribute meaning. (Grenz, PP, 144)

4B. There Is No Ultimate Foundation upon Which Knowledge or Reality Is Based

Henry claims, "The one epistemic premise shared by all postmodernists is their rejection of foundationalism, the belief that knowledge consists of sets of beliefs that rest assuredly on still other sets of beliefs and that the whole is supported by irreversible foundational beliefs." (Henry, PNS, as cited in Dockery, CP, 42)

Richard Rorty denies certain foundational essences: "My first characterization of pragmatism [postmodernism] is that it is simply antiessentialism applied to notions like 'truth,' 'knowledge,' 'language,' 'morality,' and similar objects of philosophical theorizing." (Rorty, CP, 162; brackets are mine)

Steinar Kvale asserts, "There exists no standard method for measuring and comparing knowledge within different language games and paradigms; they are incommensurable. A postmodern world is characterized by a continual change of perspectives, with no underlying common frame of reference, but rather a manifold of changing horizons." ("Themes of Postmodernity," as cited in Anderson, TT, 21)

Richard Tarnas expounds, "The postmodern paradigm is by its nature fundamentally subversive of all paradigms, for at its core is the awareness of reality as being at once multiple, local, and temporal, and without demonstrable foundation." (Tarnas, PWM, 401)

Veith concludes, "Postmodernism . . . is anti-foundational. It seeks to destroy all such objective foundations and to replace them with nothing." (Veith, PT, 48)

Millard J. Erickson summarizes, "Knowledge is uncertain. Foundationalism, the idea that knowledge can be erected on some sort of bedrock of indubitable first principles, has had to be abandoned." (Erickson, PF, 18)

5B. Objectivity Is an Illusion

Erickson explains the postmodern position on objectivity: "The objectivity of knowledge is denied. Whether the knower is conditioned by the particularities of his or her situation or theories are used oppressively, knowledge is not a neutral means of discovery." (Erickson, PF, 18)

Roy Wagner argues,

Thus the awareness of culture brings about an important qualification of the anthropologist's aim and viewpoint as a scientist: the classical rationalist's pretense of absolute objectivity must be given up in favor of a relative objectivity based on the characteristics of one's own culture. . . . "Absolute" objectivity would require that the anthropologist have no biases, and hence no culture at all.

The idea of culture, in other words, places the researcher in a position of equality with his subjects: each "belongs to a culture." Because every culture can be understood as a specific manifestation, or example, of the phenomenon of man, and because no infallible method has ever been discovered for "grading" different cultures and sorting them into their natural types, we must assume that every culture, as such, is equivalent to every other one. This assumption is called "cultural relativity." (Wagner, "The Idea of Culture," as cited in Anderson, TT, 54–55)

French philosopher Jean Baudrillard captures this perspective in his statement: "The territory no longer precedes the map, nor survives it. Henceforth, it is the map that precedes the territory." ("The Map Precedes the Territory," Baudrillard, as cited in Anderson, TT, 80) In other words, as humans we are unable to objectively approach the world and describe it as it is. We have internal, inescapable biases that determine how we will see reality. Objectivity is an illusion.

Paul Feyerabend states, "To those who look at the rich material provided by history, and who are not intent on impoverishing it in order to please their lower instincts, their craving for intellectual security in the form of clarity, precision, 'objectivity,' 'truth,' it will become clear that there is only one principle that can be defended under all circumstances and in all stages of human development. It is the principle; *anything* goes." ("Anything Goes," Feyerabend, as cited in Anderson, TT, 199)

The *Oxford Dictionary of Philosophy* highlights this postmodern claim, "Objectivity is revealed as a disguise for power or authority in the academy, and often as the last fortress of white male privilege." (Blackburn, ODP, 295)

Michel Foucault argues against objectivity:

> Truth isn't outside power, or lacking in power: contrary to a myth whose history and functions would repay further study, truth isn't the reward of free spirits, the child of protracted solitude, nor the privilege of those who have succeeded in liberating themselves. Truth is a thing of this world: it is produced only by virtue of multiple forms of constraint. And it induces regular effects of power. Each society has its regime of truth, its "general politics" of truth: that is, the types of discourse which it accepts and makes function as true; the mechanisms and instances which enable one to distinguish true and false statements, the means by which each is sanctioned; the techniques and procedures accorded value in the acquisition of truth; the status of those who are charged with saying what counts as true. ("Truth and Power," Foucault, as cited in Cahoone, MPM, 379)

6B. Truth Is Perspectival

Albert Mohler concludes, "Jacques Derrida, the leading literary deconstructionist, described this move in terms of the 'death of the author' and the 'death of the text.' Meaning—made, not found—is created by the reader in the act of reading. The text must be deconstructed in order to get rid of the author and let the text live as a liberating word." (Mohler, "Ministry Is Stranger Than It Used To Be," Southern Seminary, 6)

Rorty indicates, "[The pragmatist] proceeds to argue that there is no pragmatic difference, no difference that makes a difference, between 'it works because it's true' and 'it's true because it works'—any more than

> The postmodern worldview operates with a community-based understanding of truth. It affirms that whatever we accept as truth and even the way we envision truth are dependent on the community in which we participate. Further, and far more radically, the postmodern worldview affirms that this relatively extends beyond our perceptions of truth to its essence: there is no absolute truth; rather, truth is relative to the community in which we participate.
>
> —STANLEY J. GRENZ

between 'it's pious because the gods love it' and 'the gods love it because it's pious.'" (Rorty, CP, xxix)

Rorty applies his pragmatism to both prescriptive and descriptive truth claims: "A second characterization of pragmatism might go like this: there is no epistemological difference between truth about what ought to be and truth about what is, nor any metaphysical difference between facts and values, nor any methodological difference between morality and science." (Rorty, CP, 163)

Rorty concludes, "In the end, the pragmatists tell us, what matters is our loyalty to other human beings clinging together against the dark, not our hope of getting things right." (Rorty, CP, 166)

Rorty, in agreement with James and Dewey, indicates prescriptive and descriptive truth is groundless. As a result, he views both as perspectival: "James and Dewey . . . asked us to liberate our new civilization by giving up the notion of 'grounding' our culture, our moral lives, our politics, our religious beliefs, upon 'philosophical bases'" (Rorty, CP, 161).

Grenz notes, "As nonrepresentationalists,

pragmatists like Rorty do not view knowledge as a matter of 'getting reality right.' They seek instead to acquire habits of action for coping with reality." (Grenz, PP, 153)

Grenz summarizes, "The postmodern worldview operates with a community-based understanding of truth. It affirms that whatever we accept as truth and even the way we envision truth are dependent on the community in which we participate. Further, and far more radically, the postmodern worldview affirms that this relatively extends beyond our *perceptions* of truth to its essence: there is no absolute truth; rather, truth is relative to the community in which we participate." (Grenz, PP, 8)

Middleton and Walsh point out, "One of the defining features of the emerging postmodern culture is our growing awareness, . . . of the perspectival character of human life and knowing." (Middleton, FPS, as cited in Phillips, CAPW, 134)

Grenz indicates postmodernism views truth as subjective only: "Heidegger . . . rejects the common assumption that truth consists in a correspondence between our statements and a fully formed reality that exists outside of us. . . . Truth is not absolute and autonomous, he argues; it is relational. The dominant view is inadmissible simply because the concept of an external world is itself nonsensical. We have only the world of experience in which we are embedded as participants. Consequently, we can speak about truth only insofar as we are 'in' it, not searching for it outside of experience." (Grenz, PP, 106)

Grenz points out, "Postmodern philosophers applied the theories of the literary deconstructionists to the world as a whole. Just as a text will be read differently by each reader, they said, so reality will be 'read' differently by each knowing self that encounters it. This means that there is no one meaning of the world, no transcendent

center to reality as a whole." (Grenz, PP, 6)

Craig illuminates an immediate corollary to postmodernism's notion of perspectival truth:

> Religious diversity requires us to view . . . competing claims as equally true as, or no less true than, or as equally efficacious as, Christian truth claims.

> But why does religious diversity imply *this* sort of openness? The postmodernist is advocating much more than mere intellectual humility here. The postmodernist is not merely saying that we cannot know with certainty which religious worldview is true and we therefore must be open-minded; rather he maintains that *none* of the religious worldviews is objectively true, and therefore none can be excluded in deference to the allegedly one true religion. (Craig, PIS, as cited in Phillips, CAPW, 77)

Grenz concludes, "A denial of the reality of a unified world as the object of our perception is at the heart of postmodernism. Postmoderns reject the possibility of constructing a single correct worldview and are content simply to speak of many views and, by extension, many worlds.

"By replacing the modern worldview with a multiplicity of views and worlds, the postmodern era has in effect replaced knowledge with interpretation." (Grenz, PP, 40)

3A. REPLY TO POSTMODERNISM

1B. Postmodernism Is Self-defeating
Dennis McCallum shares a story:

> A friend of mine told me that when Christian apologist and author Ravi Zacharias visited Columbus to speak at Ohio State University, his hosts took him to visit the Wexner Center for the Arts. The Wexner Center is a citadel of postmodern architecture. It has stairways leading nowhere, columns that come down

but never touch the floor, beams and galleries going everywhere, and a crazy-looking exposed girder system over most of the outside. Like most of postmodernism, it defies every canon of common sense and every law of rationality.

Zacharias looked at the building and cocked his head. With a grin he asked, "I wonder if they used the same techniques when they laid the foundation?"

His point is very good. It's one thing to declare independence from reality when building a monument. It's another thing when we have to come into contact with the real world. (McCallum, "The Real Issue," 1)

McCallum sites two self-destructive aspects of postmodernism:

1. From the postmodern view, postmodernism itself can only be seen as another 'arbitrary social construction' like all other ideologies. As such, we have no compelling reason to accept the theory. We can simply dismiss it as the creative work of extremely cynical people.

2. If Postmodernism can be shown to be true, a world view with objective merit, then Postmodernism's main thesis (rejection of objective truth) is wrong. It ends up teaching that there is at least some objective truth—namely, that Postmodernism is right!

In either case, postmodernism's rejection of rational objectivity is self-defeating. It either denies the plausibility of its own position, or it presumes the reliability of reason and the objectivity of truth. (McCallum, DT, 53)

Craig levels this attack on postmodernism:

To assert that 'the truth is that there is no truth' is both self-refuting and arbitrary. For if this statement is true, it is not true, since there is no truth. So-called deconstructionism thus cannot be halted from deconstructing itself. Moreover, there is also no reason for adopting

the postmodern perspective rather than, say, the outlooks of Western capitalism, male chauvinism, white racism and so forth, since postmodernism has no more truth to it then these perspectives. Caught in this self-defeating trap, some postmodernists have been forced to the same recourse as Buddhist mystics: denying that postmodernism is really a view or position at all. But then, once again, why do they continue to write books and talk about it? They are obviously making some cognitive claims—and if not, then they literally have nothing to say and no objection to our employment of the classical canons of logic. (Craig, PIS, as cited in Phillips, CAPW, 82)

Craig charges postmodernism with an illogical leap: "How does the mere *presence* of religious worldviews incompatible with Christianity show that distinctively Christian claims are not true? Logically, the existence of multiple, incompatible truth claims only implies that *all* of them cannot be (objectively) true; but it would be obviously fallacious to infer that not one of them is (objectively) true." (Craig, PIS, as cited in Phillips, CAPW, 77)

Carson rejects the dilemma posed by postmodernism: "Deconstructionists may insist on *either* absolute knowledge *or* complete relativism. Either we can know something truly and absolutely, or so-called 'knowledge' is nothing more than opinion and thus relativized. The criterion is made rigid and extreme." (Carson, GG, 107) Postmodernism lacks any ground or support for rejecting other possibilities. This is a false dilemma.

Sire points out, "Even relativists can be brought to see that truth is necessary—even to the case for relativism. The truth question, in fact, cannot really be avoided." (Sire, BFCIN, as cited in Phillips, CAPW, 114) Is the postmodernist claiming his philosophy is really true?

Sire concludes, "Let us return to the specific issue at hand: logocentricity. A Christian logocentric approach to the possibility of the knowledge of independent reality is not self-referentially incoherent. The postmodern assumption that we can in principle have no access to the nature of reality is, I think, incoherent." (Sire, BFCIN, as cited in Phillips, CAPW, 115)

Sire unveils another postmodern inconsistency: "Though ultramodernists (postmodernists) ought to say they never met a narrative they didn't like, it is clear that they have. Christian fundamentalist and evangelical stories are often rejected for their exclusivity." (Sire, BFCIN, as cited in Phillips, CAPW, 120)

Gene Veith shows a key inconsistency in postmodernism: "To disbelieve in truth is, of course, self-contradictory. To believe means to think something is true; to say, 'It's true that nothing is true' is intrinsically meaningless nonsense. The very statement—'there is no absolute truth'—is an absolute truth." (Veith, PT, 16)

Diogenes Allen points out the fundamental problem with postmodernism:

The rejection of the meta-narrative of the Enlightenment, however, is not a sufficient reason to reject the possibility of any meta-narrative. In fact, postmodernism is itself a meta-narrative. It has an outlook that applies universally. It thinks that it has established its outlook free of the limitation of a framework. But the only way it can hold its view of human life and of the universe is to forget that the limitations that imprison others to a time and place apply to it as well. To be a postmodernist requires one not to let the left hand know what the right hand is doing. (Allen, "Christianity and the Creed of Postmodernism," *Christian Scholars Review,* 124).

Erickson tells this story to illustrate the impossibility of living postmodernism out consistently:

I believe we must push deconstructionists to the end of their view, to live out consistently that position, believe that no one could actually live on the basis of such a view. . . .

When we do that, we will find some frustration and resistance, but it will also bring to the surface the impossibility of living consistently with a thoroughly radical postmodern view. This was brought out rather dramatically in the case of Derrida. John Searle wrote a response to an article of Derrida's, challenging and criticizing several of his conceptions . . . in his ninety-three page reply, Derrida objected that Searle's statement had been unfair to him, and had at several points misunderstood and misstated his position. He even asserted at one point that what he had meant should have been clear and obvious to Searle. I consider that an incredibly nondeconstructionist, nonpostmodern response for someone who maintains that the meaning of a text is not in the author's intention, but in what the reader finds it saying to him or her. (Erickson, PF, 156)

Pauline Marie Rosenau levels these seven contradictions against postmodernism:

First, post-modernism devalues any pretensions to theory building. But an anti-theory position is itself a theoretical stand. If theory if futile and if every attempt to associate truth with theory must be denied, then such premises must also apply to every "form of theoretical endeavor, including such attempts to discredit other kinds of theory while smuggling one's one back in, so to speak, by the side entrance."

Second, although stressing the importance of the irrational and expressing grave doubts about the Enlightenment's intellectual tools of reason, logic, and rationality, postmodernists employ these latter instruments in their own analysis. Deconstruction, for example, is a highly logical, reasoned, and analytical process.

Third, post-modernists neither judge nor evaluate interpretations as good or bad. But does their suggestion that social science focus on the excluded, the neglected, the marginal, and the silenced, not indicate an internal value structure implicitly favoring certain groups or certain perspectives over others? And does this not fit with their refusal to prioritize? . . . If post-modernists assume, by definition, that their own view is superior to that of the Enlightenment, are they not judging their own interpretations as privileged over any other?

Fourth, post-modernists emphasize inter-textuality, but many of its versions, especially those inspired by Derrida, treat the text in isolation.

Fifth, many post-modernists reject modern criteria for assessing theory. But if post-modernists draw conclusions of any sort, such as the undecidability of questions modern social science seeks to answer, they cannot argue that there are no valid criteria for judging. They themselves must have criteria, implicit perhaps, on which they make such pronouncements. And if such criteria exist, then post-modernists are making a statement to the effect that there is some certainty in the world.

Sixth, although warning of modernity's inconsistencies, they reject being held to consistency norms themselves. They openly deny that they need make any special effort to avoid self-contradiction; this hardly seems fair.

Seventh, post-modernists contend that anything they say or write is itself only a local narrative, relevant only for its own constituency. But very few post-modernists entirely relinquish the truth claims of what they write, and this also makes for self-contradiction. (Rosenau, PMSS, 176–77)

2B. We Can Know the Thing-in-Itself

Gilson writes, "There is knowledge in the world, and that is the fact of the case. The next question to arise is that of the conditions under which knowledge in general is possible." (Gilson, CPSTA, 224)

Gilson maintains, "We do not have to describe a universe and then ask ourselves what our knowledge is like for such a universe to become possible. We must do the

> We do not have to describe a universe and then ask ourselves what our knowledge is like for such a universe to become possible. We must do the reverse. Given that there is knowledge, we have to inquire how things must be made in order to explain how we know them.
>
> —ETIENNE GILSON

reverse. Given that there is knowledge, we have to inquire how things must be made in order to explain how we know them." (Gilson, CPSTA, 225)

Postmodernism demonstrated the modern view of representational correspondence is untenable. Postmodernism is modernity gone to seed. However, the correspondence view of truth set forth previously in this work is not representational. Henry reminds us that postmodernism has not adequately rejected sound medieval metaphysics: "The failed enterprise of modernity left unfulfilled its promise of enlightenment and emancipation. But the medieval heritage is not nearly as discredited as its current critics would have us believe." (Henry, PNS, as cited in Dockery, CP, 50)

"Let us start with the fact that knowledge of an object is the presence of that object in thought." (Gilson, CPSTA, 226)

"If we are to be true to the principles just stated, we must say that the being of the object itself is imposed on the being of the knowing subject." (Gilson, CPSTA, 226)

Gilson goes on to demonstrate that knowledge occurs when the knower and known are one:

The synthesis thus produced involves, therefore, the fusion of two beings which fall together at the moment of their union. The sense differs from the sensible, and the intellect differs from the intelligible; but the sense is not different from the object sensed, nor the intellect from the object which it has actually come to know. Thus it is literally true that the sense, taken in its act of sensing, becomes one with the sensible taken in the act by which it is sensed, and that the intellect taken in its act of knowing is one with the intelligible taken in the act by which it is known. (Gilson, CPSTA, 226)

Gilson adds a corollary to the above notion: "We can regard as an immediate corollary of this fact the Thomistic thesis which states that every act of knowledge supposes that the object known becomes present in the knowing subject." (Gilson, CPSTA, 226)

3B. The Postmodern Rejection of Representational Correspondence Fails to Demonstrate that Truth Does Not Correspond to Reality

Gilson indicates it is an error to consider knowledge as a science of ideas rather than of things:

"If species were beings distinct from their forms, our knowledge would focus upon species, not upon objects. This is unacceptable for two reasons. First, because in this case all our knowledge would cease to deal with exterior realities and would only extend to their representations in our consciousness. Here we should be falling into Plato's error which regards knowledge as a science of ideas instead of a science of things. Secondly, because there would no longer be any criterion of certitude." (Gilson, CPSTA, 228)

Gilson argues from reality, where it is self-evident that knowledge of things takes place, toward a theory of knowing which accounts

for man's experience: "Since, however, there actually is demonstrative knowledge dealing with things, and not with mere opinions, the objects of knowledge must be things in themselves and not individual images distinct from things. . . . In the act of knowledge there is no intermediate being between thought and its object." (Gilson, CPSTA, 228)

Gilson comments, "By rights, and almost always in fact, a human intellect confronted by an oak forms in itself the concept of tree, and confronted with Socrates or Plato forms in itself the concept of man. The intellect conceives essences as infallibly as hearing perceives sounds and sight colors." (Gilson, CPSTA, 230)

Gilson maintains that truth is the correspondence of an affirmation to the thing in reality: "In order that this conformity of the concept to the object become something known and take the form of truth in consciousness, the intellect must add something of its own to the exterior reality which it has just assimilated. Such an addition begins when, not content just to apprehend a thing, it makes a judgment upon it and says: this is a man, this is a tree. Here the intellect brings something new—an affirmation which exists in it alone and not in things. Of such an affirmation we can ask whether it corresponds with reality or not." (Gilson, CPSTA, 231)

Gilson, while discussing the Kantian Critique makes a key point. Namely, the formal presence of things themselves in the mind of the knower solves the epistemological problem Idealism and Postmodernism could not answer:

At our first approach to this doctrine, it is only right to place a criticism of the Critique in order to find out whether the basic Idealist argument does not imply a false position on the problem of knowledge. If we suppose first that things are for themselves and the intellect is for itself, that is, if we suppose that it is impossible for them to meet, then there is no bridge to allow thought to cross over to things, and Idealism is true. It is contradictory to ask whether our ideas conform to things, if things are not known to us save through our ideas.

However,

It becomes possible, contrary to the Idealist thesis, to know whether or not our ideas conform to things, in a doctrine in which the presence of things in us is the very condition of the conception of ideas. (Gilson, CPSTA, 234)

McCallum argues:

Postmodernists hold that since we can't stand outside of ourselves to compare mental image with external reality, we are forced to reject the idea that we can know reality in an objective way. We would answer, to the contrary, that our judgments about the world, while not infallibly accurate, are open to revision by further investigation. Just because we lack absolute *certainty* about the external world doesn't mean we can't know *anything* about what exists apart from us. We don't have to wallow in postmodern skepticism.

The success of scientific technology is a strong argument that our perceptions of the world are relatively accurate. Countless achievements attest to the reliability of human knowledge. (McCallum, DT, 52)

4B. Practical Experience Indicates We Are Able to Extract the Author's Meaning as It Exists Formally in the Text

Howe indicates postmodernists first err in their metaphysics. As a result, they developed a self-destructive hermeneutic:

Contrary to the claims of Derrida, . . . it is possible to articulate the existence of a "transcen-

dental signified" by which the mind apprehends reality apart from any linguistic sign. This is the formal sign, or mental word as presented in a Thomistic Realist epistemology.

Again, it seems that the abandonment of the foundation of a Realist metaphysic leads to a self-destructive conclusion. . . . In his book *Limited Inc*, Derrida asserts, "I shall try to demonstrate why a context is never absolutely determinable, or rather, why its determination can never be entirely certain or saturated." Of course Derrida's own context is determinable, and Derrida is counting on the fact that his linguistic meaning will be determinate in its meaning, that, because a context is never absolutely determinable, linguistic meaning is fundamentally indeterminate. (Howe, TTTM, 99)

Henry distinctively points out, "Cultural baggage can be removed from the text and from the interpreter without forfeiting objective truth . . . Our lack of exhaustive knowledge does not condemn us to intellectual futility." (Henry, PNS, as cited in Dockery, CP, 46)

McCallum illuminates the inadequacy of postmodernism's philosophy of language and meaning to account for man's practical, every-day communication experiences:

Cultures do often approach reality differently. Historians from different cultures sometimes write wildly different accounts of the same event. And pantheists and animists view nature in a radically different way than do naturalistic scientists. But that's not the same as being unable to grasp what the other means. Postmodernists focus on the fringe of the language question—the five percent of language that is hard to translate—and ignore the ninety-five percent that is perfectly clear.

—DENNIS MCCALLUM

Postmodernists miss another important point in their view of language. According to their view, because each language has its own logic (syntax) and meaning (semantics) it should be impossible to communicate meaningfully or to translate accurately from one language to another. To do so would subjugate the unique, culturally contained meaning of one language to another.

But multilingual speakers know that despite differences, sometimes significant ones, between languages, concepts can almost always be meaningfully expressed. Reality isn't divided along language lines in the way many postmodernists have claimed.

Cultures do often approach reality differently. Historians from different cultures sometimes write wildly different accounts of the same event. And pantheists and animists view nature in a radically different way than do naturalistic scientists. But that's not the same as being unable to grasp what the other means. Postmodernists focus on the fringe of the language question—the five percent of language that is hard to translate—and ignore the ninety-five percent that is perfectly clear.

While communicating truth or views of reality across cultures can be difficult, we have no reason to believe it's impossible. The very fact that we are aware of differences proves we can detect and understand our differences if we are careful. Because of our ability to communicate, we can begin to understand one another and think about why we often view things differently. And that communication opens the door to genuine exchange and evaluation of ideas, even concerning abstract concepts such as spirituality and morality. (McCallum, DT, 55)

Carson argues the deconstructionist's philosophy flies in its own face as well as the face of practical experience:

I have never read a deconstructionist who would be pleased if a reviewer misinterpreted his or her work: thus *in practice* deconstructionists implicitly link their own texts with their own intentions. . . .

My point, then, is that in the real world, for all the difficulties there are in communication from person to person and from culture to culture, we still expect people to say more or less what they mean (and if they don't, we chide them for it), and we expect mature people to understand what others say, and represent it fairly. The understanding is doubtless never absolutely exhaustive and perfect, but that does not mean the only alternative is to dissociate text from speaker, and then locate all meaning in the reader or hearer. True knowledge of the meaning *of a text* and even *of the thoughts of the author who wrote it* is possible, even if perfect and exhaustive knowledge is not. That is the way things are in the real world—and that in turn suggests that any theory that flies in the face of these realities needs to be examined again. (Carson, GG, 103)

5B. Truth Is Objective Rather Than Perspectival

A person could not function or live very long if he consistently acted as though truth were perspectival rather than objective. He would bounce checks because his bank account has money "to him," drink poison which "to him" is lemonade, fall through the thin ice that is thick "to him," or get hit by a bus that is not moving "to him." To a person who wants to function effectively and live in the world, Truth's objective correspondence to reality must matter in some sense. Even more dangerous to humanity are those who live by a perspectival view of truth only concerning their moral activities.

McCallum stresses the danger of the perspectival view of truth:

This leads to some alarming conclusions. Recently, for example, a panel of nineteen experts appointed by the National Institutes of Health recommended that federal funding be used for producing and harvesting—and destroying—fetuses for laboratory experimentation. The panel's reasoning is that 'personhood' is a "social construct." Human beings, in other words, aren't born, but defined. According to them, cultural consensus (not always popular, but that of the experts) defines reality.

What happens, however, when culture decides a certain race or gender is non-human, and those non-humans are targeted for extinction? If reality is culture-bound, it would be an act of imperialism for another culture to intervene. Without an absolute standard, there is no basis for judging a Nazi or misogynist any more than there is for defining a human life. (McCallum, DT, 41)

Sire maintains man's imperfect knowledge is not a sufficient condition for us to assume we can have no objective knowledge: "I believe that we can come to grasp some of the truth. We may make mistakes. We may have to change our mind. But our beliefs must not be relegated to the status of private opinion. The only thing worth believing is the truth. When we believe we have apprehended the truth, we must hold it with universal intent." (Sire, BFCIN, as cited in Phillips, CAPW, 119)

Carson makes a similar point: "We may readily concur that human knowing is partial, but not that it is therefore necessarily objectively untrue." (Carson, GG, 349)

Augustine summarizes: "Believers, moreover, trust the report of their bodily senses which subserve the intelligence. If they are at times deceived, they are at least better off than those who maintain that the senses can never be trusted." (Augustine, CG, 466)

Craig contends although some truth may be found in most religions, all religions are not equally true: "While Christians may be open to elements of truth found in non-Christian religions, their minds need not be agape to every religious truth claim, since they are under no obligation to embrace religious relativism, having rejected its *raison d´être*, universalism." (Craig, PIS, as cited in Phillips, CAPW, 97)

35
ANSWERING
SKEPTICISM

(the belief that any reliable or absolute knowledge

is impossible, and any aspects of the supernatural

are unattainable by any individual)

1A. SKEPTICISM ACCORDING TO ITS CHIEF PROPONENT, DAVID HUME

Part of the traditional argument for God's existence is based on the inference of a cause from the observation of effects. The skeptic David Hume said that because we never actually observe (experience) causality (what causes something that happens), we cannot know for certain that any particular cause and effect are connected. Hume did not deny causality, but only that we can infer anything from it. He denied that we can know the truth about a cause from an effect.

1B. All Knowledge Is Derived Through Either the *Senses* or *Reflection* on Ideas

The often-quoted conclusion of Hume's *Enquiry Concerning Human Understanding* summarizes his skepticism: "When we run over libraries, persuaded of these principles, what havoc must we make? If we take in hand any volume; of divinity or school metaphysics, for instance; let us ask, *Does it contain any abstract reasonings concerning quantity or number?* No. *Does it contain any experimental reasonings concerning matters of fact or existence?* No. Commit it to the flames: For it can contain nothing but sophistry [subtle and deceptive reasoning] and illusion." (Hume, ECHU, 12. 3, emphasis his)

Hume makes this categorical statement concerning reason:

All the objects of human reason or inquiry may naturally be divided into two kinds, to wit, *relations of ideas* and *matters of fact.* Of the first kind are the sciences of geometry, algebra, and arithmetic; and in short, every affirmation which is either intuitively or demonstratively certain ... Propositions of this kind are discoverable by the mere operation of thought, without dependence on what is anywhere existent in the universe.

Matters of fact, which are the second objects of human reason, are not ascertained in the same manner [as relations of ideas]; nor is our evidence of their truth, however great, of a like nature with the foregoing. The contrary of every matter of fact is still possible; because it can never imply a contradiction." (Hume, ECHU, 4.1, emphasis his)

Hume says it is indisputable "that all our ideas are nothing but copies of our impressions, or in other words, that 'tis impossible for us to think of any thing, which we have not antecedently felt." (Hume, ECHU, 7. 1)

Jerry Gill summarizes the impact of Hume's skepticism:

Hume put an end to the high hopes of both the continental rationalists and the British empiricists. The former sought and claimed to have found an epistemological [a way of knowing something] foundation for all knowledge in the necessary conclusions deducible from self-evident truths. The latter

sought and claimed to have found such a foundation in the probable conclusions "inducible" from sense impressions. Hume followed the empiricist approach more rigorously than his predecessors and argued a convincing case that neither deduction nor induction can provide an adequate foundation for knowledge. Deduction with its "self-evident" premises, turned out to be definitional (analytic) and empty of factual content, while induction proved to be based upon the indemonstrable assumption that the future must be like the past. Thus Hume thought he had eliminated the possibility of factual truth-claims in mathematics, science, and metaphysics. (Gill, PRK, 73)

2B. Causality Cannot Be Observed but Only Believed Based on Custom

Causality is a condition or situation which brings about a certain effect. It deals with the relationship between a cause and its effect.

Hume exclaims: "There are two principles which I cannot render consistent, nor is it in my power to renounce either of them, namely, that all our distinct perception are distinct existences, and that the mind never perceives any real connection among distinct existences." (Hume, THN, Appendix)

Hume summarizes why he thinks a particular cause cannot be inferred from an effect:

In a word ... every effect is a distinct event from its cause. It could not, therefore, be discovered in the cause, and the first invention or conception of it, a priori, must be entirely arbitrary. And even after it is suggested, the conjunction of it with the cause must appear equally arbitrary; since there are always many other effects, which, to reason, must seem fully as consistent and natural. 'Twould, therefore, be in vain for us to pretend to determine any single event, or infer any cause or effect, without the assistance of observation and experience. (Hume, ECHU, 4.1)

Hume argues that apart from experience we cannot infer any connection between a cause and its effect: "When we reason a priori, and consider merely any object or cause, as it appears to the mind, independent of all observation, it never could suggest to us the notion of any distinct object, such as its effect; much less, show us the inseparable and inviolable connexion betwixt them." (Hume, ECHU, 4.1)

Hume states categorically that "all inferences from experience, therefore, are effects of custom, not of reasoning." (Hume, ECHU, 5.1)

Hume concludes that, because we cannot know, for example, the cause of a rock falling, neither can we know the cause of the world:

While we cannot give a satisfactory reason, why we believe, after a thousand experiments, that a stone will fall, or fire burn; can we ever satisfy ourselves concerning any determinations we may form with regard to the origin of the worlds, and the situation of nature, from, and to eternity? . . . It seems to me, that the only object of the abstract sciences of demonstration is quantity and number, and that all attempts to extend this more perfect species of knowledge beyond these bounds are mere sophistry and illusion. (Hume, ECHU, 12.3)

Ravi Zacharias summarizes Hume on this point: "The principle of causality, then, according to Hume, is nothing but an association of successive impressions. Through habit and custom we expect that the succession will take place; in reality there is no necessary connection. In short, nothing authorizes even science to formulate universal and necessary laws." (Zacharias, CMLWG, 199)

3B. A Capsule of Hume's Skepticism:
Hume "questioned the knowledge claims of all disciplines, i.e., science, mathematics, etc.

He did allow for beliefs based on probability, which transcended our experience. He was deadset against any presuppositions about the uniformity of nature. Because we observe uniformity in nature does not warrant a belief that it will always be uniform. He would argue that induction is not a valid form of reason, but rather a habit of expecting similar results based on a uniformity of experience. Hence, Hume is known as a skeptic." (Dr. William Crouse, personal correspondence, July 14, 1999)

2A. REPLY

1B. Skepticism Is Self-defeating: Should We Be Skeptical of Skepticism?
St. Augustine of Hippo recognized the self-defeating nature of skepticism more than a millennium before Hume expressed his doubts: "Everyone who doubts knows that he is doubting, so that he is certain of this truth at least, namely the fact that he doubts. Thus every one who doubts whether there is such a thing as truth, knows at least one truth, so that his very capacity to doubt should convince him that there is such a thing as truth." (Augustine, TR, 39.73)

Gordon Clark restates the point a bit differently: "Skepticism is the position that nothing can be demonstrated. And how, we ask, can you demonstrate that nothing can be demonstrated? The skeptic asserts that nothing can be known. In his haste he said that truth was impossible. And is it true that truth is impossible? For, if no proposition is true, then at least one proposition is true— the proposition, namely, that no proposition is true. If truth is impossible, therefore, it follows that we have already attained it." (Clark, CVMT, 30)

Norman Geisler offers this critique of skepticism:

The overall skeptical attempt to suspend all judgment about reality is self-defeating, since it implies a judgment about reality. How else could one know that suspending all judgment about reality was the wisest course, unless he knew indeed that reality was unknowable? Skepticism implies agnosticism and, [since it makes a statement about reality] agnosticism implies some knowledge about reality. Unlimited skepticism which commends the suspension of all judgments about reality implies a most sweeping judgment about the knowability of reality. Why discourage all truth attempts, unless one knows in advance that they are futile? And how can one be in possession of this advance information unless he already knows something about reality? (Geisler, CA, 22)

Professor Geisler makes a distinction between partial skepticism (which can be healthy) and complete skepticism: "Complete skepticism is self-defeating. The very affirmation that all truth is unknowable is itself presented as a truth affirmation. As a truth statement purporting that no truth statements can be made it undercuts itself." (Geisler, CA, 133–134)

Scott MacDonald points out that the fact of our knowledge of first principles refutes skepticism: "Our direct acquaintance with the necessary truth of certain immediate propositions constitutes indubitable and infallible access to those truths, and so with respect to those propositions and the propositions we derive from them via strict demonstrations, skepticism is provably false." (MacDonald, TK as cited in Kretzmann, CCA, 187)

St. Augustine, in his treatise *Contra Academicos*, also fell back on the certain knowledge of first principles to refute the skepticism of his day. Frederick Copleston summarizes Augustine in this way: "I am at least certain of the principle of contradiction."(Copleston, HP, 53)

Catholic apologist G. H. Duggan points out the dilemma of the skeptic: "On the one hand the Sceptic holds that there are no certain truths. On the other hand he cannot

> Whenever we find someone saying that no one can know anything, it is only natural to wonder whether [or how] the skeptic knows *that*.
>
> —RONALD NASH

make a statement without admitting that the principle of contradiction is certainly true. According to this principle, being and non-being are not identical. If it is rejected, then in any statement 'is' and 'is not' are interchangeable. It is obvious that on these terms thought and discourse become impossible." (Duggan, BRD, 65)

Mortimer Adler makes the same point: "This principle [of contradiction] provides a complete refutation of the skeptic who declares that no statement is either true or false. For if the skeptic's declaration is true, then there is at least one statement which is true rather than false. And if it is false, then there may be many statements which are either true or false. And if it is neither true nor false, then why should we pay any attention to what the skeptic says?" (Adler, TR, 133–134)

Adler suggests that common sense refutes skepticism:

The commonsense view is the one that all of us embrace when we reject the self-contradictory and self-refuting position of the extreme skeptic as being not only unreasonable, but also impracticable. There is hardly an aspect of our daily lives that would be the same if we were to embrace instead of rejecting the position of the extreme skeptic. We are firmly committed to the view that truth and falsity are ascertainable by us and that, with varying degrees of assurance, we can somehow discriminate between what is true and what is false. Almost everything we do or rely upon is grounded in that commitment. (Adler, SGI, 35)

Ravi Zacharias summarizes: "Hume's skeptical deduction that all judgment about reality be suspended is self-defeating because that call to suspend judgment is in itself a judgment about reality." (Zacharias, CMLWG, 200)

Colin Brown warns us of Hume's categorical statements: "Hume gives the appearance of being disarmingly frank when he acknowledges that 'Nature is always too strong for principle.' At face value it is a salutary warning to both system-builders and system destroyers against being cocksure in either their sweeping affirmations or their sweeping denials. But Hume's observation here is an implicit claim that his approach (difficult though it be) is the only valid one. In fact, Hume's scepticism is suspect at every major point." (Brown, PCF, 71)

Ronald Nash also warns that "whenever we find someone saying that no one can know anything, it is only natural to wonder whether [or how] the skeptic knows *that*." (Nash, WVC, 84)

G. H. Duggan points out another aspect of the self-defeating nature of the skeptical claim: "The skeptical view that the external senses are unreliable can be maintained only if one holds that the external senses are not powers of knowledge but have some other function. For if one holds that the external senses are powers of knowledge, one must hold that they are essentially reliable. If they were unreliable, they would not be powers of knowledge, since they would provide unreliable information; and unreliable information is not knowledge." (Duggan, BRD, 65)

Mortimer Adler notes another dilemma the skeptical claim poses:

In denying that there is any truth or falsity, the extreme skeptic must ultimately either deny that an independent reality exists or deny that it has a determinate character with which our thinking either corresponds or fails to correspond. It should be obvious at once that, in going to this extreme, the skeptic necessarily contradicts himself. Unless he claims truth for his assertion that there is no independent reality or that it does not have a determinate character, his own position vanishes; and if he does claim truth for his denials, he must do so on grounds that ultimately presuppose the definition of truth. (Adler, SGI, 213)

2B. The Statement "All Knowledge Is Derived Through *Senses* or *Reflection* on Ideas" Is Derived from Neither of These

Ravi Zacharias also states: "Hume's contention that, in order to be meaningful, all statements should either be a relation to ideas, i. e., mathematical or quantity, or else should be of experimental reasoning based on questions of facts is itself based neither on mathematical fact nor on experimentally established fact. Therefore, his very definition of a meaningful statement, on his own terms, is meaningless." (Zacharias, CMLWG, 200)

Mortimer Adler observes that in Hume's statement, "two errors are compounded; one is the error of regarding our perceptions and images, miscalled 'ideas,' as the immediate objects of our consciousness; the other is the error of reducing the human mind to a purely sensitive faculty, able to be aware of nothing but what can be perceived through the senses or can be imagined as a result of our sense-perceptions." Adler states the question pointedly, "*Do we or do we not have abstract ideas (i. e., concepts) as well as sense-perceptions and images?...* Hobbes, Berkeley, and Hume flatly say that we do not." (Adler, TPM, 38, 40, emphasis his)

Adler points out the dilemma that results

if we cannot form an abstract idea, or a universal concept of something such as "dog". He suggests the following line of reasoning:

We are, therefore, obliged to ask them whether we are able to apprehend what is common to two or more entities [e. g. the category "dog" is common to both an Airedale and a poodle], or apprehend the respects in which they are the same.

If their answer to this question is negative, they have again completely undercut their own explanation of the meaning of common names as applicable to two or more items *indifferently* (i.e., with respect to some point in which they are *not different*). If we cannot apprehend any respect in which two or more items are the same we cannot apply one and the same name to them indifferently.

The only alternative left open to them is an affirmative answer to the question: Are we able to apprehend what is common to two or more entities, or apprehend respects in which they are the same?

If they give that affirmative answer, because they must either give it or admit that they have no explanation to offer, then the giving of that answer is tantamount to a refutation of their original position. (Adler, TPM, 44, 45)

3B. Radical Empirical Atomism Is Self-defeating and Implies Unity and Connection

The result of Hume's skepticism of causality would be that no events are connected. This is radical empirical atomism (the belief that "the universe consists of innumerable tiny, indivisible pellets of reality" [Geisler/Feinberg, IP, 430]).

Norman Geisler argues that

Hume's radical empirical atomism that all events are "entirely loose and separate" and that even the self is only a bundle of sense impressions is unfeasible. If everything were unconnected there would be no way of even making that particular statement, since some unity and connection are implied in the affirmation that everything is disconnected. Further, to affirm "*I* am nothing but the impressions about myself" is self-defeating, for there is always the assumed unity of the "I (self)" making the assertion. But one cannot assume a unified self in order to deny the same. (Geisler, CA, 22–23)

Ravi Zacharias concurs: "Hume's assertion that all events are entirely loose, separate, and unconnected is unsustainable. His very statement implies a unity and connection, else there would be no way to make that statement. In other words, he assumes a unified self while denying a unity." (Zacharias, CMLWG, 200)

4B. Denial of Causality Is Self-defeating
To clarify Hume's position:

Hume never denied the principle of causality. He admitted it would be absurd to maintain that things arise without a cause. What he did

> A theory which explained everything else in the whole universe but which made it impossible to believe that our thinking was valid, would be utterly out of court. For that theory would itself have been reached by thinking, and if thinking is not valid that theory would, of course, be itself demolished. It would have destroyed its own credentials. It would be an argument which proved that no argument was sound—a proof that there are no such things as proofs—which is nonsense.
>
> —C. S. LEWIS

attempt to deny is that there is any philosophical way of *establishing* the principle of causality. If the causal principle is not a mere analytic relation of ideas but is a belief based on customary conjunction of matter-of-fact events, then there is no necessity in it and one cannot use it with philosophical justification. But we have already seen that dividing all contentful statements into these two classes is self-defeating. Hence, it is possible that the causal principle is both contentful and necessary. In point of fact, the very denial of causal necessity implies some kind of causal necessity in the denial. For unless there is a necessary ground (or cause) for the denial, then the denial does not necessarily stand. And if there is a necessary ground or cause for the denial, then the denial is self-defeating; for in that event it is using a necessary causal connection to deny that there are necessary causal connections. (Geisler, CA, 24–25)

Limiting the principle of causality to the realm of logic is also self-defeating:

Some critics insist that the principle of causality belongs in the realm of logic but does not apply to reality. This is self-defeating. One cannot consistently affirm that the laws of thought cannot be affirmed regarding reality. It is inconsistent to think about reality that it cannot be thought about. Since the principle of causality is a fundamental principle of reason, it must apply to reality. Otherwise, one ends in a self-defeating position that what is known about reality cannot be known. (Geisler, BECA, 122)

C. S. Lewis summarizes: "A theory which explained everything else in the whole universe but which made it impossible to believe that our thinking was valid, would be utterly out of court. For that theory would itself have been reached by thinking, and if thinking is not valid that theory would, of course, be itself demolished. It would have destroyed its own credentials. It would be an argument which proved that no argument was sound—a proof that there are no such things as proofs—which is nonsense." (Lewis, M, 14–15)

Paul Carus notes the connection between the rational and the ontological: "Our belief in causation is after all, although Hume denied it, finally based upon the logical principle of identity A=A. It is an extension of this principle to a state of motion." (Carus, EKP in Kant, PFM, 201)

James B. Sullivan distinguishes between the *notion* of cause and the *principle* of causality: "The *notion* of cause is obtained from intellectual comparison of formalities in one object with those of another and in discovering by induction that one object influences another or produces another by its action. The *Principle* of Causality is established not by induction from experiences, but by an analysis of the notion of contingent being." (Sullivan, EFPTB, 124)

5B. Conclusion

"While skepticism is not defensible as an epistemological position, it is of value. It acts like a burr in the epistemologist's saddle, demanding that any claim to knowledge is based upon adequate evidence and is free from contradiction or absurdity." (Geisler, IP, 100)

36
ANSWERING AGNOSTICISM

(the belief that man "either does not know or cannot know. . . . In theology the theory is that man cannot attain knowledge of God." [Trueblood, PR, 344])

CHAPTER OVERVIEW

The Agnosticism of Immanuel Kant
    The Content of Knowledge Is Structured by the Mind
    There Is an Unbridgeable Gulf Between Our Knowledge and Reality
    A Capsule of Kant's Agnosticism
Reply
    Agnosticism Is Self-defeating
    Categories of the Mind Correspond with Reality: Otherwise Agnosticism Is Unstateable

It Is Not Possible to Affirm *Existence* without Declaring Something of *Essence* (What It Is in Itself)
Kant's Epistemology Cannot Reach Reality Because It Does Not Start with Reality
The Certainty of Kant's *A Priori* Conclusions Are Refuted by Scientific Discoveries

---

1A. THE AGNOSTICISM OF IMMANUEL KANT

Immanuel Kant's philosophy denies that we can know what reality is in itself. This position results in agnosticism; if we can't know reality, then we can't know truth.

1B. The Content of Knowledge Is Structured by the Mind

In order to understand Immanuel Kant's denial of the knowability of truth, we must understand his epistemology. Jerry Gill explains:

Kant's epistemology, set forth in his *Critique of Pure Reason*, is based on the belief that knowledge is composed of two aspects, namely content and form. With the empiricists [those who rely upon sense knowledge] he maintains that the content of knowledge is supplied by sensory experience, but in harmony with rationalism he maintains that the form (or structure) of knowledge is supplied by the mind. Kant asserted that the mind plays an active part in the knowing experience by imposing upon the data of sensation certain fixed "categories." Thus what is known is sensory experience after it has been "filtered through," or organized by, the built-in categories of the understanding. Both of these elements are necessary, but neither is sufficient, for knowledge to exist. (Gill, PRK, 76)

In Kant's own words: "There are two sources of human knowledge (which probably spring from a common, but to us unknown root), namely, sense and understanding. By the former, objects [through our senses] are given to us; by the latter, thought [understanding]." (Kant, CPR, 22)

Kant qualifies the last statement by saying: "But, though all our knowledge begins with experience, it by no means follows that all arises out of experience. For, on the contrary, it is quite possible that our empirical knowledge is a compound of that which we receive through impressions, and that which the faculty of cognition supplies from itself (sensuous impressions giving merely the *occasion*), an addition which we cannot distinguish from the original element given by sense, till long practice has made us attentive to, and skillful in separating it." (Kant, CPR, 14)

Kant argues that the categories by which we understand are in the mind: "Space and time, together with all that they contain, are not things nor qualities in themselves, but belong merely to the appearances of the latter: up to this point I am one in confession with the above idealists. But these . . . regarded space as a mere empirical presentation that . . . is only known to us by means of experience. . . . I, on the contrary, prove . . . that space (and also time) . . . inheres in our sensibility as a pure form before all perception or experience." (Kant, PFM, 152)

Of these built-in categories Kant says, "If the pure concepts of the understanding do not refer to objects of experience but to things in themselves (noumena), they have no signification whatever. They serve, as it were, only to decipher appearances, that we may be able to read them as experience. The principles which arise from their reference to the sensible world, only serve our understanding for empirical use. Beyond this they are arbitrary combinations, without objective reality, and we can neither cognise their possibility a priori, nor verify their reference to objects." (Kant, PFM, 72, 73)

Kant declares that reason alone is not sufficient to know reality: "Reason by all its a priori principles never teaches us anything more than objects of possible experience, and even of these nothing more than can be cognised in experience. . . . Reason does not . . . teach us anything concerning the thing in itself." (Kant, PFM, 134)

In fact, says Kant, reality must conform to reason or we can't know it: "Reason must approach nature with the view, indeed, of receiving information from it, not, however, in the character of a pupil, who listens to all that his master chooses to tell him, but in that of a judge, who compels the witnesses to reply to those questions which he himself thinks fit to propose." (Kant, CPR, 6)

Kant declares: "Understanding does not derive its laws (*a priori*) from, but prescribes them to, nature." (Kant, PFM, 82)

Kant claims to have found a more certain criteria for truth in the a priori forms: "As truth rests on universal and necessary laws as its criteria, experience, according to [Idealism], can have no criteria of truth, because its phenomena . . . have nothing *a priori* at their foundation; whence it follows that they are sheer illusion; whereas with us, space and time (in conjunction with the pure conceptions of the understanding) prescribe their law to all possible experience *a priori*, and at the same time afford the certain criterion for distinguishing truth from illusion therein." (Kant, PFM, 152)

Kant concludes that "things as objects of our senses existing outside us are given, but we know nothing of what they may be in themselves, knowing only their appearances, i. e., the representations which they cause in us by affecting our senses." (Kant, PFM, 43)

Again Kant states categorically that "the senses never and in no manner enable us to know things in themselves." (Kant, PFM, 42)

Mortimer Adler summarizes: "For Kant the only things that are independent of the human mind are, in his words, *'Dinge an sich'*—things in themselves that are intrinsically unknowable. This is tantamount to saying that the real is unknowable, and the knowable is ideal in the sense that it is invested with the ideas that our minds bring to it to make it what it is." (Adler, TPM, 100)

2B. There Is an Unbridgeable Gulf Between Our Knowledge and Reality

Kant's epistemology [way of knowing] draws a limit to our knowledge, and reality is outside that limit.

According to Kant, the mind searches for truth: "But this land is an island, and enclosed by nature herself within unchangeable limits. It is the land of truth . . . surrounded by a wide and stormy ocean, the region of illusion, where many a fog-bank, many an iceberg, seems to the mariner, on his voyage of discovery, a new country, and, while constantly deluding him with vain

hopes, engages him in dangerous adventures, from which he never can desist, and

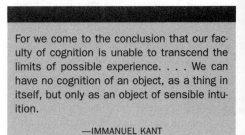

For we come to the conclusion that our faculty of cognition is unable to transcend the limits of possible experience. . . . We can have no cognition of an object, as a thing in itself, but only as an object of sensible intuition.

—IMMANUEL KANT

which yet he never can bring to a termination." (Kant, CPR, 93)

We can't find truth because, according to Kant's epistemology, we can't know reality:

For we come to the conclusion that our faculty of cognition is unable to transcend the limits of possible experience; and yet this is precisely the most essential object of this science. The estimate of our rational cognition a priori at which we arrive is that it has only to do with phenomena, and that things in themselves, while possessing a real existence, lie beyond its sphere. . . . We can have no cognition of an object, as a thing in itself, but only as an object of sensible intuition. (Kant CPR, 8–9)

Kant notes that the mind is not satisfied with knowing the limits [the point beyond which we cannot know truth], but that is all it can know: "The limits pointed out . . . are not enough after we have discovered that beyond them there still lies something (though we can never cognize what it is in itself)." (Kant, PFM, 125)

Kant summarizes: "That which is originally a mere phenomenon, a rose, for example, is taken by the empirical understanding for a thing in itself. . . . On the contrary . . . nothing which is intuited in space is a thing in itself. . . . Objects are quite unknown to us in themselves, and what we call outward objects, are nothing else but mere representations of our sensibility, whose form is space, but whose real correlate, the thing in itself, is not known by means of these representations, nor ever can be." (Kant, CPR, 26)

Kant concludes from his epistemology that metaphysics "is a completely isolated speculative science. . . . It deals with mere conceptions . . . and in it, reason is the pupil of itself alone." (Kant, CPR, 6)

Etienne Gilson notes that Kant does not deny reality but brackets it as unknowable: "In point of fact, Kant never was to speculate on existence as such, but he never was either to deny it or even forget about it. Rather he was to bracket it, so that it would always be present where there was real knowledge, yet would in no way limit the spontaneity of human understanding." (Gilson, BSP, 127–128)

Nicholas Rescher suggests that in Kant's epistemology reality is senseless: "For Kant, the conception of a perceived object freed of the conditions of perception is every bit as senseless as would be that of a view-of-an-object that is freed from any and every point of view, and so regarded in separation from one of the essential conditions of viewability." (Rescher NC, as cited in Beck, KTK, 176)

3B. A Capsule of Kant's Agnosticism
Kant "believed there was a distinction between the real (noumenal) world and the apparent (phenomenal) world of appearance. To understand the phenomenal world one has a set of built-in categories (similar to what we mean by presuppositions). No one comes to data (the phenomenal) without categories (presuppositions). Knowledge, according to Kant, was the joint product of *mind* (the knower) possesses those innate qualities (the ability to organize and categorize) that enable the knower to perceive it as

such." (William Crouse, personal correspondence, July 14, 1999)

2A. REPLY

1B. Agnosticism Is Self-defeating
Kant's epistemology results in agnosticism, the claim that nothing can be known about reality. Norman Geisler comments: "In its unlimited form [agnosticism] claims that all knowledge about reality (i. e. truth) is impossible. But this itself is offered as a truth about reality." (Geisler, CA, 135) He summarizes the self-defeating nature of this claim: "The fundamental flaw in Kant's hard agnostic position is his claim to have knowledge of what he declares to be unknowable. In other words, if it were true that reality cannot be known, no one, including Kant, would know it. Kant's hard agnosticism boils down to the claim: 'I know that reality is unknowable.'" (Geisler and Bocchino, WSA)

Geisler says again,

Complete agnosticism is self-defeating; it reduces to the self-destructing assertion that "one knows enough about reality in order to affirm that nothing can be known about reality." This statement provides within itself all that is necessary to falsify itself. For if one knows something about reality, then he surely cannot affirm in the same breath that *all* of reality is unknowable. And of course if one knows nothing whatsoever about reality, then he has no basis whatsoever for making a statement about reality. It will not suffice to say that his knowledge about reality is purely and completely negative, that is, a knowledge of what reality is not. For every negative presupposes a positive; one cannot meaningfully affirm that something is *not* that if he is totally devoid of a knowledge of the "that." It follows that total agnosticism is self-defeating because it assumes some knowledge about reality in order to deny any knowledge of reality. (Geisler, CA, 20)

This agnosticism is untenable: "The possibility is open that reality can be known. Indeed, this has been one of the most persistent assumptions in the history of philosophy. Men have been and still are in the pursuit of reality. Any reasoning that would eliminate this possibility *a priori* is not only self-defeating but also runs against the major current of the philosophical pursuit." (Geisler, PR, 89)

Mortimer Adler responds to Kant's agnosticism with a question: "And this leads the critic to ask how, if it is possible to know only what lies within the bounds of sense-experience [Kant], [one] can be justified in asserting that real things do not exist beyond, and how can he tell what are the boundaries beyond which the human understanding may not venture, unless he succeeds in passing them himself?" (Ayer, LTL, 34)

Philosopher Ludwig Wittgenstein states: "In order to be able to set a limit to thought, we should have to find both sides of the limit thinkable." (Wittgenstein, TLP, preface)

Etienne Gilson remarks: "The knowledge of what a thing is inasmuch as it is not known is a flat contradiction in Kant's doctrine." (Gilson, BSP, 131)

Ravi Zacharias: "Kant's agnosticism on ultimate reality is self-defeating. It is not possible to posit anything about ultimate reality unless one knows something about ultimate reality. To say, as Kant did, that one cannot cross the line of appearances is to cross the line in order to say it. In other words, it is not possible to know the difference between the appearance and reality unless one knows enough about both to distinguish between them." (Zacharias, CMLWG, 203)

H. A. Pritchard notes any knowledge of reality is inconsistent with idealism in general:

In order to think of the world as dependent on the mind, we have to think of it as consisting only of a succession of appearances. . . . That this is the inevitable result of idealism is not noticed, so long as it is supposed that the essential relation of realities to the mind consists in their being known. . . . [T]he advantage of this [Kant's] form of idealism is really derived from the very fact which it is the aim of idealism in general to deny. For the conclusion that the physical world consists of a succession of appearances is only avoided by taking into account the relation of realities to the mind by way of knowledge, and, then, without being aware of the inconsistency, making use of the independent existence of the reality known. (Pritchard, KTK, 122–123)

2B. Categories of the Mind Correspond with Reality; Otherwise Agnosticism Is Unstateable

Professor Geisler outlines the futility of making categorical statements denying knowledge of reality:

Kant's argument that the categories of thought (such as unity and causality) do not apply to reality is unsuccessful, for unless the categories of reality corresponded to those of the mind no statements could be made about reality, including that very statement Kant made. That is to say, unless the real world

> In other words, knowledge is essentially discovery, or the finding of what already is. If a reality could only be or come to be in virtue of some activity or process on the part of the mind, that activity or process would not be "knowing," but "making" or "creating," and to make and to know must in the end be admitted to be mutually exclusive.
>
> —H. A. PRITCHARD

were intelligible no statement about it would apply. A preformation of the mind to reality is necessary whether one is going to say something positive about it or something negative. We cannot even *think* of reality that it is unthinkable. Now if someone should press the argument that the agnostic need not be making any statement at all about reality but simply defining the necessary limits of what we can know, it can be shown that even this is a self-defeating attempt; for to say that one cannot know any more than the limits of the phenomena or appearance is to draw an unsurpassable line for those limits. But one cannot draw such firm limits without surpassing them. It is not possible to contend that appearance ends here and reality begins there unless one can see at least some distance on the other side. In other words, how can one know the difference between appearance and reality unless he already knows both so as to make the comparison? (Geisler, CA, 21)

H. A. Pritchard responds to the argument that reality is what it is in the knowing of it:

The fundamental objection, however, to this line of thought is that it contradicts the very nature of knowledge. Knowledge unconditionally presupposes that the reality known exists independently of the knowledge of it, and that we know it as it exists in this independence. It is simply *impossible* to think that any reality depends upon our knowledge of it, or upon any knowledge of it. If there is to be knowledge, there must first *be* something to be known. In other words, knowledge is essentially discovery, or the finding of what already is. If a reality could only be or come to be in virtue of some activity or process on the part of the mind, that activity or process would not be "knowing " but "making" or "creating," and to make and to know must in the end be admitted to be mutually exclusive. (Pritchard, KTK, 118)

Etienne Gilson declares that "it is, contrary to the idealist thesis, possible to know whether our ideas are or are not in conformity with things." (Gilson, PSTA, 275)

Paul Carus comments on the problem agnosticism faces when the categories of the mind are not also categories of reality: "When Kant denies that space and time are objective, he becomes confused and self-contradictory. For he would either have to say that space and time are limited within the boundary of the body of the thinking subject, which is nonsense, or he must attribute them to the subject as a thing in itself, which contradicts his own theory according to which time and space do not refer to things in themselves, but to appearances only." (Carus, EKP, in Kant, PFM, 233)

Mortimer Adler notes the error of idealism: "Plato and Descartes, and also later Kant and Hegel, go too far in their separation of the two realms—the sensible and the intelligible. This results from their attributing to the intellect an autonomy that makes its functioning, in some or all respects, independent of sense experience.

"This leads Plato and Descartes to endow the intellect with innate ideas—ideas it in no way derives from sense-experience. Kant's transcendental categories are another version of the same error." (Adler, TPM, 34)

3B. It Is Not Possible to Affirm *Existence* without Declaring Something of *Essence* (What It Is in Itself)

The argument can be stated this way:

Another self-defeating dimension is implied within Kant's admission that he knows *that* the noumena [the real world vs. the appearance of the world] is there but not *what* it is. Is it possible to know that something is without knowing something about what it is? . . . It is not possible to affirm *that* something is without simultaneously declaring something about *what* it is. Even to describe it as the "in-itself" or the "real" is to say something. Furthermore, Kant acknowledged it to be the unknowable "source" of the appearance we are receiving. All of this is informative about the real: namely, it is the real, in-itself source of impressions we have. Even this is something less than complete agnosticism. (Geisler, CA, 21–22)

H. A. Pritchard argues that "since knowledge is essentially of reality as it is apart from its being known, the assertion that a reality is dependent upon the mind is an assertion of the kind of thing which it is in itself, apart from its being known." (Pritchard, KTK, 121)

Etienne Gilson: "That common root from which sensibility and understanding both spring, and of which Kant says that it exists, but that we don't know what it is, should at last be dug out and brought to light. In short, if it is not to remain like a foreign body arbitrarily inserted in the intelligible world of understanding, existence has either to be flatly denied, or else produced *a priori* [conclusion reached independent of experience] like all the rest." (Gilson, BSP, 132)

Gilson continues: "There is too much existence in Kant's criticism, or not enough. Too much, because it is so arbitrarily given, just as in the case of Hume; not enough, because it is so utterly unknowable that there is practically no more of it in the critical idealism of Kant than there was in the absolute idealism of Berkeley." (Gilson, BSP, 134–135)

Paul Carus states: "Therefore, while granting that the sense-begotten world-picture of our intuition is subjective appearance, . . . we claim in contrast to Kant that its formal elements represent a feature that inheres in existence as the form of existence.

"In making form purely subjective, Kant changes—notwithstanding all his protesta-tions—all ideas, all thoughts, all science, into purely subjective conceits. He is more of an idealist than Berkeley. Science can be regarded as an objective method of cognition only if the laws of form are objective features of reality." (Carus, EKP in Kant, PFM, 210)

Carus concludes: "If things in themselves mean objective things, viz., things as they are, independently of our sensibility, we must deny that they are unknowable." (Carus, EKP in Kant, PFM, 236)

Rudolph G. Bandas argues that the idea of being corresponds to reality:

What assurance have we concerning the objectivity of the idea of being? How do we know that it corresponds to reality, since we can not compare it with the extramental thing in itself, the latter being unattainable immedi-

> If our conception of an independent spatiotemporal world is necessarily subjective, then we have no good reason for supposing that there is such a world, especially since it seems self-contradictory to speak of a conception that is independent of our conceptual faculties.
>
> —PANAYOT BUTCHVAROV

ately? This difficulty is by no means new: it was stated and refuted not only by St. Thomas, but before him, by Aristotle. The characteristic tendency of modern thought is to divide and separate. Its fatal mistake in the domain of epistemology is to separate the object known from the thing itself, and then to strive helplessly to bridge the gap between the subject and the object. (Bandas, CPTP, 62)

Bandas further notes the universality of the idea of being.

The idea of being is applicable to all reality, whether actual or possible, present, past, or future. It is applicable to every grade of reality. . . . No affirmation is possible without being. To separate ourselves from the influence of being would be to commit intellectual suicide and to condemn ourselves to eternal silence. Anyone who uses the verb "is" and makes an affirmation—and who is more dogmatic and categorical than most of our moderns—necessarily accepts the philosophy of being with all its consequences, implications, and ramifications. (Bandas, CPTP, 346)

In the *Cambridge Dictionary of Philosophy*, Panayot Butchvarov argues that if the agnostic is not speaking of essence he is faced with two undesirable conclusions:

To accept the objection [that we can form no conception of real objects] seems to imply that we can have no knowledge of real objects as they are in themselves, that that truth must not be understood as correspondence to such objects. But this itself has an even farther reaching consequence; either (i) we should accept the seemingly absurd view that there are no real objects . . . for we should hardly believe in the reality of something of which we can form no conception at all; or (ii) we must face the seemingly hopeless task of a drastic change in what we mean by "reality," "concept," "experience," "knowledge," "truth," and much else. (Butchvarov, MR, as cited in Audi, CDP, 488)

Butchvarov continues: "If our conception of an independent spatiotemporal world is necessarily subjective, then we have no good reason for supposing that there is such a world, especially since it seems self-contradictory to speak of a conception that is independent of our conceptual faculties." (Butchvarov, MR, as cited in Audi, CDP, 490)

4B. Kant's Epistemology Cannot Reach Reality Because It Does Not Start with Reality

As we noted in the introduction to this section, it is wrong to start from within the mind and expect to find a way to reality.

F. H. Parker notes that the proper place to start is with reality: "The realities which are known . . . do not depend on their being known, in either their nature or their existence; the knowledge depends on the realities known." (Parker RAK, as cited in Houde, PK, 48)

Etienne Gilson describes the dilemma this poses for the idealist who makes this error:

The greatest of the differences between the realist and the idealist is that the idealist thinks while the realist knows. For the realist, to think is only to organize some previous acts of knowledge or to reflect on their content. He would never conceive of making thought the point of departure of his reflection, because a thought is possible for him only where there first exists some knowledge. Because the idealist goes from thought to things, he is unable to know if his starting point corresponds or not to an object. When he asks the realist how to rejoin the object in departing from thought, the latter must hasten to answer that it cannot be done and that this indeed is the principal reason for not being an idealist. Realism however departs from knowledge, that is to say from an act of the intellect which consists essentially in seizing an object. Thus, for the realist, the question does not pose an insoluble problem, but a pseudoproblem, which is something entirely different. (Gilson, VMYR, as cited in Houde, PK, 386)

Gilson issues this warning to anyone who argues with an idealist:

One must always remember that the impossibilities in which idealism wishes to corner realism are the work of idealism itself. When it defies us to compare the thing known with the thing itself, it only manifests the internal evil which eats away at it. For the realist, there is no "noumenon"[thing in itself] in the sense in which the idealist understands it. Knowledge presupposes the presence of thing itself to the intellect. There is no need to suppose, behind the thing which is in thought, a duplicate, mysterious and unknowable, which would be the thing of the thing in thought. To know is

> The greatest of the differences between the realist and the idealist is that the idealist thinks while the realist knows. For the realist, to think is only to organize some previous acts of knowledge or to reflect on their content. He would never conceive of making thought the point of departure of his reflection, because a thought is possible for him only where there first exists some knowledge.
>
> —ETIENNE GILSON

not to apprehend a thing as it is in thought, but, in thought, to apprehend a thing as it is. (Gilson, VMYR, as cited in Houde, PK, 388)

5B. The Certainty of Kant's *A Priori* Conclusions Are Refuted by Scientific Discoveries

A priori means "independent of experience." Mortimer Adler explains what Kant did with *a priori* synthetic judgments: "Kant endowed the human mind with transcendental forms of sense-apprehension or intuition (the forms of space and time), and also with the transcendental categories of the understanding." This means that "the mind brings these transcendental forms and categories to experience, thereby constituting the shape and character of the experience we have." (Adler, TPM, 96) In other words, the mind can only know reality according to these *a priori* categories. This means that the only way we judge whether something corresponds to reality (i.e., is true) is according to these *a priori* categories and

not based on our experience of reality itself.

Adler explains that Kant's motive was to establish Euclidean geometry, arithmetic, and Newtonian physics as examples of reality-shaping *a priori* conclusions. However, Adler reminds us that

three historic events suffice to show how illusory is the view that he had succeeded in doing that:

The discovery and development of the non-Euclidean geometries and of modern number theory should suffice to show how utterly factitious was Kant's invention of the transcendental forms of space and time as controlling our sense-apprehensions and giving certitude and reality to Euclidean geometry and simple arithmetic.

Similarly, the replacement of Newtonian physics [The universe is a gigantic machine. God is outside the machine.] by modern relativistic physics, the addition of probabilistic or statistical laws to causal laws, the development of elementary particle physics and of quantum mechanics, should also suffice to show how utterly factitious was Kant's invention of the transcendental categories of the understanding to give Newtonian physics certitude and incorrigibility.

Adler concludes: "How anyone in the twentieth century can take Kant's transcendental philosophy seriously is baffling, even though it may always remain admirable in certain respects as an extraordinarily elaborate and ingenious intellectual invention." (Adler, TPM, 97–98)

Paul Carus argues: "Unless we denounce science as a vagary of the human mind, we must grant that in spite of the shortcomings of the individual scientist, the ideal of science (which consists in describing things in their objective existence) is justified and can be more and more realized." (Carus, EKP, in Kant, PFM, 236)

37
ANSWERING MYSTICISM

("the belief that direct knowledge of God, of spiritual truth or ultimate reality, is attainable 'through immediate intuition or insight [the subjective] and in a way different from ordinary sense perception or the use of logical reasoning' [Webster's New Collegiate Dictionary]" [Anderson, CWR, 37])

1A. MYSTICISM AS EXEMPLIFIED BY D. T. SUZUKI (ZEN BUDDHISM)

There are many forms of mysticism. What distinguishes the mystics is *how* they attain their goal of enlightenment. Remember that *how* we know reality is related to, but different from, whether we *do* know reality. The following example of mysticism reveals the mystics' perception of knowing reality and knowing truth.

1B. Truth Can Entail Contradiction

D. T. Suzuki states plainly: "Zen does not follow the routine of reasoning, and does not mind contradicting itself or being inconsistent." (Suzuki, LZ, 94)

Suzuki: "Zen is decidedly not a system founded upon logic and analysis. If anything it is the antipode to logic, by which I mean the dualistic mode of thinking." (Suzuki, IZB, 38)

Suzuki: "We generally reason: 'A' is 'A' because 'A' is 'A'; or 'A' is 'A,' therefore, 'A' is 'A.' Zen agrees or accepts this way of reasoning, but Zen has its own way which is ordinarily not at all acceptable. Zen would say: 'A' is 'A' because 'A' is not 'A'; or 'A' is not 'A'; therefore, 'A' is 'A.'" (Suzuki, SZ, 152)

Suzuki: "This is the beginning of Zen. For now we realize that 'A is not A' after all, that logic is one-sided, that illogicality so-called is not in the last analysis necessarily illogical; what is superficially irrational has after all its own logic, which is in correspondence with the true state of things.... In other words Zen wants to live from within. Not to be bound by rules, but to be creating one's own rules—this is the kind of life which Zen is trying to have us live. Hence its illogical, or rather superlogical, statements." (Suzuki, IZB, 60, 64)

Suzuki states there is more truth in contradictions than in logic: "However logically impossible or full of contradictions a statement which is made by the Prajnaparamita may be, it is utterly satisfying to the spirit. . . . That they are not at all logical does not mean that they are untrue. As far as truth is concerned, there is more of it in them." (Suzuki, EZB3, 271)

Suzuki says of reality: "The idea is that the ultimate fact of experience must not be enslaved by any artificial or schematic laws of thought, nor by any antithesis of 'yes' and 'no,' nor by any cut and dried formulae of epistemology. Evidently Zen commits absurdities and irrationalities all the time; but this only apparently." (Suzuki, IZB, 55)

Suzuki says of logical categories: "'Ignorance' is another name for logical dualism. . . . If we want to get to the very truth of things, we must see them from the point where this world has not yet been created, where the consciousness of this and that has not yet been awakened." (Suzuki, IZB, 52)

2B. There Are Two Realms of Reality (and Truth) Which Must Be Experienced Differently

D. T. Suzuki gives us the Zen philosophy of knowledge:

I am now ready to present a piece of Zen epistemology. There are two kinds of information we can have of reality; one is knowledge *about* it and the other is that which comes out of reality itself. Using "knowledge" in its broadest sense, the first is what I would describe as knowable knowledge and the second as unknowable knowledge. Knowledge is knowable when it is the relationship between subject and object.... Unknown knowledge is the result of an inner experience; therefore, it is wholly individual and subjective. But the strange thing about this kind of knowledge is that the one who has it is absolutely convinced of its universality in spite of its privacy. (Suzuki, SZ, 146)

Suzuki here describes these as seeing and knowing: "Seeing plays the most important role in Buddhist epistemology, for seeing is at the basis of knowing. Knowing is impossible without seeing; all knowledge has its origin in seeing." (Suzuki, MCB, 46)

Norman Anderson defines mysticism: "In general terms [mysticism] represents the belief that direct knowledge of God, of spiritual truth or ultimate reality, is attainable 'through immediate intuition or insight [the subjective] and in a way different from ordinary sense perception or the use of logical reasoning' (*Webster's New Collegiate Dictionary*)." (Anderson, CWR, 37)

Anderson tells us how Zen reaches this knowledge of ultimate reality: "Zen Buddhists believe that by rigorous self-discipline and a strictly prescribed method of meditation they may attain *satori*, the Japanese term for 'enlightenment'—whether suddenly, as some teach, or gradually, as others hold—by means of a perception which is empirical rather than intellectual." (Anderson, CWR, 88)

Suzuki defines *satori* as completely different than rational knowledge: "Satori may be defined as an intuitive looking into the nature of things in contradistinction to the analytical or logical understanding of it." (Suzuki, EZB1, 230)

Suzuki: "The satori, after all, is not a thing to be gained through the understanding." (Suzuki, EZB1, 243)

Suzuki: "In Zen there must be a satori: there must be a general mental upheaval which destroys the old accumulations of intellectuality and lays down a foundation for a new faith; there must be the awakening of a new sense which will reveal the old things from an angle of perception entirely and most refreshingly new." (Suzuki, EZB1, 262)

Suzuki: "Behind the series of negations offered by the Mahayana [a very diverse sect of Buddhism. Zen is the more popular sect] thinkers there is really the assertion of a higher truth." (Suzuki, AZ, 5)

Suzuki: "In Zen there is an intellectual quest for ultimate truth which the intellect

> It is not the object of Zen to look illogical for its own sake, but to make people know that logical consistency is not final, and that there is a certain transcendental statement that cannot be attained by mere intellectual cleverness. . . . Zen takes us to an absolute realm wherein there are no antitheses of any sort.
>
> —D. T. SUZUKI

fails to satisfy; the subject is urged to dive deeper under the waves of the empirical consciousness." (Suzuki, EZB2, 60)

Suzuki again describes the two forms of knowledge:

In Buddhism generally two forms of knowledge are distinguished; the one is prajna and the other is vijnana. Prajna is all-knowledge (sarvajna), or transcendental knowledge. . . . Vijnana is our relative knowledge in which subject and object are distinguishable. . . . Science and philosophy do not apparently exhaust Reality; Reality contains more things than that which is taken up by our relative knowledge for its investigation. What is left in Reality, according to Buddhism, turns toward Prajna for its recognition. (Suzuki, LZ, 80)

Suzuki: "Prajna is something which our discursive knowledge cannot attain. It belongs to a different category from mere knowledge." (Suzuki, AZ, 22–23)

Suzuki: "Vijnana wants everything to be clear-cut and well-defined, with no mixing of two contradictory statements, which, however, prajna nonchalantly overrides." (Suzuki, SZ, 91)

In Zen illogical and non-sensical statements or questions are employed to jolt a person out of logical thought. One example is: What is the sound of one hand clapping? Suzuki explains the Zen philosophy behind these illogical statements: "It is not the object of Zen to look illogical for its own sake, but to make people know that logical consistency is not final, and that there is a certain transcendental statement that cannot be attained by mere intellectual cleverness. . . . Zen takes us to an absolute realm wherein there are no antitheses of any sort." (Suzuki, IZB, 67–68)

3B. The Reality Which Is This World, Along with Our Experience of It, Are Illusory

Suzuki explains that the material world or reality is illusion (this concept is called Maya):

As has repeatedly been stated, the force of argument adopted in the Prajnaparamita is directed against the fundamental error we all have in regard to the world generally—that is, naïve realism [There is a real, existing, external world]. The chief feature of this realism is to take the world as a reality eternally fixed and externally existing against what is conceived to be an inner world of thoughts, feelings, and sensations. . . . One of the best weapons for destroying the stronghold of naïve realism is to declare that all is Maya and that there is no permanently fixed order in the world, that the dualistic conception of existence, inner and outer, being and non-being, etc., is visionary, and that it is necessary to awaken the Prajna which takes hold of the unattainable. . . . So we are told that the pleasures and pains with which we are affected have no permanent nature as such; and likewise with objects of pleasure and pain, they are transitory and changeable like Maya. They all have no substantial reality. They are mere appearances, and to be regarded as such and of no further value. As far as appearances go, they are there, and this fact will not be ignored; but as for clinging to them thus as finalities, the wise know much better, for their Prajna-eye has penetrated into the rockbed itself of reality. (Suzuki, EZB3, 267–268)

Suzuki says that the more real world lies behind this one: "For this relative world in which we know that we live, and the more real world which lies behind it, form a complete and undivided whole, and neither is more real than the other. . . . The truth is that the world is one." (Suzuki, WIZ, 73)

Suzuki here speaks of reality in the philosophical terms of the West:

Reality, however, is not to be understood in the sense of a kernel or hypostasis or thing-in-itself existing apart from what is known as appearance or phenomenality. It is not an object of intellectual perception to be distinguished as this or that. It is that which remains behind (though we do not like to use this kind of expression) when all the outer skin or casing falls off. This is not to be understood on the plane of intellection. It is symbolic and to be spiritually interpreted; it is the feeling one has while going through what we may call, for lack of proper terminology, Zen experience or satori. (Suzuki, LZ, 30)

Suzuki comments that the use of illogic and nonsense in Zen practice is to free the mind from attachment to an illusory world: "The purpose of the Zen master's flatly contradicting facts of sense-experience is to persuade the psychologist to free himself from undue attachments to concepts which he takes for realities." (Suzuki, LZ, 94)

4B. Mystical Experience Is Ineffable

D. T. Suzuki states categorically that mystical experience is ineffable (unable to be expressed): "Satori is the most intimate individual experience and therefore cannot be expressed in words or described in any manner." (Suzuki, EZB1, 263)

Suzuki: "Reality itself has neither form nor no-form; like space it is beyond knowledge and understanding; it is too subtle to be expressed in words and letters." (Suzuki, EZB2, 21)

2A. REPLY

1B. Zen's Statements Are Self-defeating and *Ad Hoc*

1C. Specific Examples

D. T. Suzuki describes that Zen is beyond criticism: "The Zen master has by his satori attained a vantage-ground from which he sallies out to attack the opponent's camp in any direction. This vantage ground is not located at any definite point of space, and cannot be assailed by concepts or any system based on them. His position, which is not a position in its ordinary sense, therefore, cannot be overtaken by any means born of intellection." (Suzuki, LZ, 95)

Suzuki says that Zen is self-authenticating and not at all concerned about criticism of its contradictions:

> From the logical linguistic point of view the two Zen masters defy each other and there is no way to effect a reconciliation. One says "yes" while the other says "no." As long as the no means an unqualified negation and the "yes" an unqualified affirmation, there is no bridge between the two. And if this is the case, as apparently it is, how can Zen permit the contradiction and continue the claim for its consistent teaching, one may ask. But Zen would serenely go its own way without at all heeding such a criticism. This is because Zen's first concern is about its experience and not its modes of expression. The latter allow a great deal of variation, including paradoxes, contra-

---

If I am asked, then, what Zen teaches, I would answer, Zen teaches nothing.

—D. T. SUZUKI

---

dictions, and ambiguities. According to Zen, the question of "is-ness" (*isticheit*) is settled only by innerly experiencing it and not by merely arguing about it or by linguistically appealing to dialectical subtleties [opposites]. Those who have a genuine Zen experience will all at once recognize in spite of superficial discrepancies what is true and what is not. (Suzuki, MCB, 59)

Finding contradictions in Suzuki's writings is not difficult. He was a prolific and expressive writer, but apparently not at all concerned with contradicting his own statements.

Suzuki writes: "If I am asked, then, what Zen teaches, I would answer, Zen teaches nothing." On a later page he writes: "[This famous gatha (saying) of Jenye] by no means exhausts all that Zen teaches." (Suzuki, IZB, 38, 58)

Suzuki writes this line in a story of a Zen master's reply to a student's desire to be trained in the truth of Zen: "Said the Zen master, 'There is no mind to be framed, nor is there any truth in which to be disciplined.'" On the next page Suzuki comments: "Those who desire to gain an intellectual insight, if possible, into the truth of Zen, must first understand what this stanza really means." (Suzuki, IZB, 57–58)

Suzuki describes the inability to criticize Zen because it is beyond all dualism:

> Zen therefore is not mysticism, although there may be something in it reminding one of the latter. Zen does not teach absorption, identification, or union, for all these ideas are derived from a dualistic conception of life and the world. In Zen there is a wholeness of things, which refuses to be analyzed or separated into antitheses of all kinds. As they say,

it is like an iron bar with no holes or handles to swing it about. You have no way to take hold of it; in other words, it cannot be subsumed under any categories. Thus, Zen must be said to be a unique discipline in the history of human culture, religious and philosophical. (Suzuki, SZ, 146)

2C. Critique

Henry Rosemont, Jr. responds to the denial that Zen is a philosophy:

Zen Buddhism *is* a set of philosophical assumptions, governing the behavioral patterns of its adherents; Suzuki and his colleagues can only ignore this fact by playing with words, with the consequence that readers of Zen commentaries are misled and many fundamental issues are circumvented and obscured. For example, by saying on one page that "In Zen are found systematized, or rather crystallized, all the philosophy, religion and life itself of the Far-Eastern people, especially of the Japanese," Suzuki should know better than to say on the next page that "Zen teaches nothing." The conclusion is obvious. Whether admitting to it explicitly or not, Suzuki is writing philosophy; from the premise that many of the beliefs he espouses in the name of Zen are anti-philosophical, it does not follow that they are non-philosophical. They are one and all philosophical beliefs. (Rosemont, LLZ, 15)

Again, Rosemont says:

It is therefore not begging the question, nor false, nor misleading, but correct to assert that Zen Buddhism is a philosophy, whatever else it might also be. It can be admitted that some of the philosophical beliefs of Zen Buddhism are sufficiently unusual to warrant their being characterized as "anti-philosophical," but such a characterization must not be equated with "non-philosophical." The Zen commentators' statements expressing, elaborating, and defending those beliefs are one and all philosophical statements, hence they are partici-

pants in philosophical enterprises, their assertions to the contrary notwithstanding; and such enterprises thus form a proper subject for philosophical examination and criticism, for anyone reading those statements will be engaged in the study of the philosophy of Zen Buddhism. (Rosemont, LLZ, 32)

Rosemont replies to the ad hoc criticism of logic and Western philosophy found in Zen commentaries: "A thinker cannot charge other thinkers with making fundamental mistakes, and then not allow the accused to examine the charges against them in detail or to reply to them. Such kangaroo-court procedures have no more place in the study of Zen Buddhism than they have in any other field." (Rosemont, LLZ, 7–8)

Rosemont notes that using language to deny logic is contradictory:

Suzuki and the other commentators attack the logical and linguistic framework on which they themselves are required to stand when writing in English, with the result that their attacks are self-defeating enterprises. If, for example, a person believes that logic is somehow highly defective, he certainly is going to find it difficult to induce intelligent people to share his belief by offering supporting arguments which owe whatever conviction they carry to the fact that they are logically valid. . . . If Suzuki's views are taken in their extreme form, it is not possible to advocate them at all without absurdity. (Rosemont, LLZ, 16)

Clark and Geisler point out the logic of Zen's avoidance of logic:

If the Zen masters really were completely illogical, there would be no difficulty in stating explicitly that language always distorts reality and then turning around to use language to describe reality. Of course, this would be a blatant inconsistency. Naturally, it would horrify other philosophers. But if logic really does not matter and inconsistencies really are acceptable, then expressing such contradictions should pose no problem. The masters believe mutism [or a non-sensical answer, or a slap in the face] shows their conviction that rationality has been avoided. But resorting to mutism only shows that logic really does operate in the minds, if not in the words, of the Zen masters. (Clark, ANA, 176)

Rosemont argues that Suzuki's claim is ad hoc:

It is a philosophical belief of Zen Buddhism that we are too much the slaves of words and logic. But from this statement alone we are not entitled to infer immediately, as Suzuki does, that the Zen belief is *correct*, that we *are* slaves to logic and language. It might be true that we are thus fettered, miserable, and go through untold suffering, but it certainly is not true merely because Zen Buddhists believe that it is. Suzuki does not prove, or even attempt to prove, that the belief is correct; he just assumes that it is, and goes on to advocate a number of—in this case implausible—other beliefs about the world which, however, depend for their plausibility on the first belief being true. None of this is an asset to understanding. (Rosemont, LLZ, 39)

Rosemont points out another self-defeating aspect of Zen commentaries: "A significant number of fundamental beliefs of Zen Buddhists have the peculiarity that sentences used to express those beliefs uniformly produce statements that are false, which makes their direct espousal disastrous for a sympathetic interest in and understanding of Zen." (Rosemont, LLZ, 41)

Rosemont concludes:

These authors must be found guilty of logical and linguistic mistakes and abuses which have arisen from their adherence to the metaphilosophical belief and others entailed by it, for such beliefs are inconsistent with beliefs which we know are presupposed by everyone who says or writes anything. Because these authors have obviously written a great deal, they offer *prima facie* evidence of their inconsistencies. The Zen commentators do not, nor can they, give any good reason for exempting their own thoughts and assertions from being judged on the basis of the anti-intellectual, anti-logical, and anti-linguistic beliefs they have attempted to espouse. By attacking ratiocination, logic, and language the commentators surrender the possibility of offering intellectual, logical, and linguistic arguments in support of these Zen beliefs. Indeed, strictly speaking they surrender the possibility of saying anything significant about Zen at all, without being further guilty of, at best, inconsistency, at worst, insincerity. (Rosemont, LLZ, 85)

Norman Geisler notes that

the pantheist's denial that logic applies to reality is self-defeating. Denying that logic applies to reality involves making a logical statement about reality that no such logical statement about reality can be made. For example, when Suzuki says that to comprehend life we must abandon logic, he uses logic in his affirmation

> Now I am inclined to say frankly that such positions are crazy and unintelligible. To say that God is both good and not good in the same sense or that God neither exists nor does not exist is just incomprehensible to me.
>
> —WILLIAM LANE CRAIG

and applies it to reality. Indeed, how can the law of noncontradiction (A cannot be both A and not-A) be denied without using it in the very denial? To deny that logic applies to reality, one must make a logical statement about reality. But if no such logical statements about reality can be made, how can the pantheist even explain his view? (Geisler, WA, 105)

Robert S. Ellwood, Jr. warns:

We must receive with considerable caution the common ideas that if religion became more mystical and less dogmatic it would be better, and that mysticism is the true spiritual core of all religion. While a valid case can be argued for some of the assumptions underlying these propositions, they are highly ambiguous unless we take setting into account. Depending upon setting, what people regard as mystical experience can as well release the demons of war and hate in the name of a spiritual cause. For the self-validating nature of mysticism is a two-edged sword: it might enable the wondrous experience of transcendence, yet validate the separation of its associations from the control of reason. Therein comes the dark side of mysticism. Those who release self-validating experiences from the supervision of reason and social control neglect these controls to the peril of all. The danger may, strictly speaking, lie not in the flash of ecstasy but in the feelings and symbols associated with it. In practice, however, often little separation of the two occurs. The self-validating experience easily becomes the false romanticism of exalting feelings as cognitive and guides to action over reason or tradition. One then is likely to evoke the mood of the Nazi madness or of solipsist fanaticism of Charles Manson. (Ellwood, MR, 186)

In this extended quote William Lane Craig examines several logical problems with the claims of mysticism:

Now under the influence of Eastern mysticism, many people today would deny that systematic consistency is a test for truth. They affirm that reality is ultimately illogical or that logical contradictions correspond to reality. They assert that in Eastern thought the Absolute or God or the Real transcends the logical categories of human thought. They are apt to interpret the demand for logical consistency as a piece of Western imperialism which ought to be rejected along with other vestiges of colonialism.

What such people seem to be saying is that the classical law of thought known as the Law of Excluded Middle is not necessarily true, that is to say, they deny that of a proposition and its negation, necessarily, one is true and the other is false. Such a denial could take two different forms. (1) It could be interpreted on the one hand to mean that a proposition and its negation *both* can be true (or both false). Thus, it is true both that God is love and, in the same sense, that God is not love. Since both are true, the Law of Contradiction, that a proposition and its negation cannot both be true (or both false) at the same time, is also denied. (2) On the other hand, the original denial could be interpreted to mean that of a proposition and its negation *neither* may be true (or neither false). Thus, it is not true that God is good and it is not true that God is not good; there is just no truth value at all for such propositions. In this case it is the classical Principle of Bivalence—that for any proposition, necessarily that proposition is either true or false—that is denied along with the Law of Excluded Middle.

Now I am inclined to say frankly that such positions are crazy and unintelligible. To say that God is both good and not good in the same sense or that God neither exists nor does not exist is just incomprehensible to me. In our politically correct age, there is a tendency to vilify all that is Western and to exalt Eastern modes of thinking as at least equally valid if not superior to Western modes of thought. To assert that Eastern thought is seriously deficient in making such claims is to be a sort of epistemological bigot, blinkered by the constraints of the logic-chopping Western mind.

But this judgment is far too simplistic. In the first place, there are thinkers within the tradition of Western thought who have held the mystical views in question (Plotinus would be a good example), so that there is no warrant for playing off East against West in this matter. Second, the extent to which such thinking represents "the Eastern mind" has been greatly exaggerated. In the East the common man—and the philosopher, too—lives by the Laws of Contradiction and Excluded Middle throughout everyday life; he affirms them every time he walks through a doorway rather than into the wall. It is only at an extremely theoretical level of philosophical speculation that such laws are denied. And even at that level, the situation is not monochromatic: Confucianism, Hinayana Buddhism, pluralistic Hinduism as exemplified in Sankhya-Yoga, Vaishesika-Nyaya and Mimasa schools of thought and even Jainism do not deny the application of the classical laws of thought to ultimate reality. Thus, a critique of Eastern thought from within Eastern thought itself can be—and has been—made. We in the West should not therefore be embarrassed or apologetic about our heritage; on the contrary, it is one of the glories of ancient Greece that its thinkers came to enunciate clearly the principles of logical reasoning, and the triumph of logical reasoning over competing modes of thought in the West has been one of the West's greatest strengths and proudest achievements.

Why think then that such self-evident truths as the principles of logic are in fact invalid for ultimate reality? Such a claim seems to be both self-refuting and arbitrary. For consider a claim like "God cannot be described by propositions governed by the Principle of Bivalence." If such a claim is true, then it is not true, since it itself is a proposition describing God and so has no truth value. Thus, such a claim refutes itself. Of course, if it is not true, then it is not true, as the Eastern mystic alleged, that God cannot be described by propositions governed by the Principle of Bivalence. Thus, if the claim is not true, it is not true, and if it is true, it is not true, so that in either case the claim turns out to be not true.

Or consider the claim that "God cannot be described by propositions governed by the Law of Contradiction." if this proposition is true, then, since it describes God, it is not itself governed by the Law of Contradiction. There-

fore, it is equally true that "God can be described by propositions governed by the Law of Contradiction." But then which propositions are these? There must be some, for the Eastern mystic is committed to the truth of this claim. But if he produces any, then they immediately refute his original claim that there are no such propositions. His claim thus commits him to the existence of counterexamples which serve to refute that very claim.

Furthermore, apart from the issue of self-refutation, the mystic's claim is wholly arbitrary. Indeed, no reason can ever be given to justify denying the validity of logical principles for propositions about God. For the very statement of such reasons, such as "God is too great to be captured by categories of human thought" or "God is wholly other," involves the affirmation of certain propositions about God which are governed by the principles in question. In short, the denial of such principles for propositions about ultimate reality is completely and essentially arbitrary.

Some Eastern thinkers realize that their position, as a position, is ultimately self-refuting and arbitrary, and so they are driven to deny that their position really is a position! They claim rather than their position is just a technique pointing to the transcendent Real beyond all positions. But if this claim is not flatly self-contradictory, as it would appear, if such thinkers literally have no position, then there just is nothing here to assess and they have nothing to say. This stupefied silence is perhaps the most eloquent testimony for the bankruptcy of the denial of the principles of logical reasoning. (Craig, PIS, as cited in Phillips, CAPW, 78–81)

2B. There Are Not Two Contradictory Realms of Reality Which Must Be Experienced Differently

Clark and Geisler make the observation that mysticism is drawn to pantheism in order to maintain that there are two forms of experience:

The mystics' even stronger thrust for unity leads them naturally to pantheism. Ordinary sensuous experience, whether interpreted in naive or in sophisticated form, will not accord

> In the final analysis, most mystics admit that one realm of truth is not really true after all. It is only true from a certain perspective, a perspective that is ultimately false. Despite their denigration of logic, even mystics come hard up against the unavoidable conclusion that truth must be unified—truth cannot contradict itself and still be true.
>
> —DAVID CLARK AND NORMAN GEISLER

with pantheism. Pantheists therefore are driven by an inner logic to posit a form of experience that avoids the apparent implications of sensuous experience, namely, that the world of external objects really exists as it appears to. Thus, they tend to ground their metaphysic on a mode of knowledge that is thought to be somehow superior to empirical knowing. (Clark, ANA, 160–161)

Clark and Geisler ask if the two forms of experience are distinguishable, and if so, is there good reason to abandon one over the other?

Any claim that mystical experience possesses these two qualities, uniqueness and superiority, raises two questions: (1) Can we show that there is a form of experience and knowledge that possesses these characteristics so as to be distinct from ordinary, sensuous experience and knowledge? Obviously, if the two levels of experience and knowledge are not distinguishable, then we should not accept the appeal to the allegedly higher level of knowledge in support of any world view. To reject sensuous knowledge in favor of a different, higher knowledge would be a serious mistake if there were no such different, higher knowledge.

Clark and Geisler continue:

Suppose that pantheists do show that there exists a mode of experience and knowledge distinct from the ordinary. This immediately raises the second question: (2) Were there a distinct form of experience and knowledge, would that experience provide good reason to abandon the sensuous experiences and empirical knowledge that lead us to believe in a real, independent world of objects? To look at it another way, suppose that the pantheists' experiences do possess unique characteristics, features that somehow show them to be different from those that cause most people to believe in a real, independent world. Would those unique characteristics give evidence that the pantheists' experiences are superior? Or would they prove only that those experiences are different?

They conclude,

In sum, it is arbitrary to discount one whole mode or type of experience simply because it differs from another whole class or kind of experience. This applies to the logical positivists when they summarily discount the theological, ethical, or mystical realms. But this could apply equally to the pantheists who reject sensuous experience on the basis of an allegedly "higher" mystical experience. And the mystical pantheist runs into an additional difficulty. How could anyone argue rationally for the allegedly "higher" experience when the pantheist describes this experience as beyond logic and language? If there were indeed two fundamentally different forms of experience, each pointing to different metaphysical conclusions, sorting out the genuine and the illusory would remain an intractably thorny process. (Clark, ANA, 162)

Clark and Geisler answer the Zen theory that posits two independent realms of experience and thought which both possess validity within their own spheres:

The two-truth theory implies a more fundamental distinction. The two realms of truth have no connection. In the two arenas of truth, what counts as a fact, what rules are used to deal with the facts, and the theories that are developed out of those facts are entirely unrelated. The ordinary way of viewing life from the sensuous perspective (and all the scientific ideas, theories, and debates that go along with it) comprises one whole network of truth. In addition, there exists the supraordinary mode of truth, complete with its forms of experience and thought. According to the two-truth theory, the two arenas of truth are unrelated, yet both are "true" within their own realms. . . . But this answer does not really commend itself to us. Rationality impresses us with the need to see reality and truth in a unified way. We all sense the need for a unity of truth so forcefully that the notion of two truths works only as a temporary, stopgap measure. In the final analysis, most mystics admit that one realm of truth is not really true after all. It is only true from a certain perspective, a perspective that is ultimately false. Despite their denigration of logic, even mystics come hard up against the unavoidable conclusion that truth must be unified—truth cannot contradict itself and still be true. (Clark, ANA, 164–165)

One of many examples of the inevitable superiority of one truth can be found in the dogmatic statement of Zen commentator Robert Powell: "It can be shown that *all* dualistic thinking leads to illusion, the conventional ways of describing Reality are 'Maya' (unreal), and the logical outcome of such an enquiry is ultimately the Void. This approach leads thus to the same end as Nagarjuna's Sunyavada, as all true approaches must." (Powell, ZR, 60) Did you notice the *either/or* logic used in making this categorical statement?

Clark and Geisler argue that mystics must finally admit only one mode of experience results in truth: "The result is the same where one form of truth and experience is finally taken as normative. Although initially the two-truth theory allows a greater openness to opposing points of view, that openness is temporary. The problems raised by the reduction of truth to one area of experience are not resolved by the two-truth theory. In the final analysis, when they are forced to get right down to the real issues, mystics admit that one mode of experience breeds illusion and the other truth." (Clark, ANA, 165)

Clark and Geisler point out the impossibility of avoiding rationality entirely:

Any appeal to mystical experience in support of pantheism contains a basic irony. The mystical pantheist rejects empirical knowledge (which points away from pantheism) and acclaims mystical knowledge. He hopes thereby to avoid the logical bifurcations inherent in empirical knowledge and to achieve a supraconceptual knowledge of immediacy and unity. The final irony, however, is that this enterprise succeeds only when it posits the logical distinction between the logically conditioned empirical experience and the allegedly supralogical mystical experience. Thus, the appeal to mysticism, far from overcoming logic altogether, actually requires a basic logical distinction if it ever is to succeed. Once again, there seems to be no way to avoid rationality entirely. (Clark, ANA, 183)

Clark and Geisler give three arguments to support the claim that mystical experiences are understood just as are all other human experiences. First, mystical experience is not self-interpreting, it must be interpreted through the mystic's worldview; second, most mystics claim uniqueness of their mystical experience, but if the experience is unmediated by their worldview, then mystical experiences of one reality cannot differ; third, we inescapably experience the world in terms and categories our philosophy of life provides for us. They comment that "on the issue of immediacy, mysticism is not uniquely unsullied by the philosophical background of the experience. There may be other factors that show the uniqueness of mystical experience. But in the matter of directness of knowledge, mystical experience is not demonstrably different in kind from other modes of experience." (Clark, ANA, 168–170)

Clark and Geisler conclude that "mystical experience does not possess attributes that mark it as completely different from other forms of experience. It has no unique immediacy that bypasses the cognitive. It is not distinctly self-authenticating in a way that needs no external confirmation. It is not strictly ineffable. Mystical experiences do differ from ordinary experiences. But the differences are not so great as to warrant the claims of mystics who say they have a special pipeline to truth." (Clark, ANA, 183)

3B. Reality Is Not Illusory

The argument that reality is not illusory can be stated thus:

You can also show why reality exists by applying the [Law of Identity] to the term illusion. An illusion is defined as a misleading percep-

> Calling our explanation of self, others, and the world an illusion raises another problem: How did this pervasive mistake arise? How did it come about that virtually every human being experiences himself, the world, and their interaction wrongly?
>
> —DAVID CLARK AND NORMAN GEISLER

tion of reality. When someone says that something is an illusion, that person means that the illusion misrepresents that which is real. However, if objective reality does not exist to pro-

vide a contrast for the illusion, there would be no way of knowing about that illusion. In other words, in order to know that you are dreaming you must have some idea of what it means to be awake. Only then can you contrast these two states. Similarly, you only know what an illusion is because you have some idea of what it means to be real. If everything were really an illusion, you would never come to know about it: Absolute illusion is impossible! Therefore, it is only logical to conclude that it is an illusion to believe that reality is an illusion. (Geisler and Bocchino, WSA)

But what is the cause of this illusion? "Calling our explanation of self, others, and the world an illusion raises another problem: How did this pervasive mistake arise? How did it come about that virtually every human being experiences himself, the world, and their interaction wrongly? And note that this pervasive alleged illusion involves not a single experience or even set of experiences embedded in an essentially correct structure or mode of experience. This widespread error concerns the very structure of all possible sensuous experience itself." (Clark, ANA, 153)

Mystics say, for example, that "the whole mode of experience that includes color is essentially and fundamentally misleading." Clark and Geisler respond: "This is an extravagant claim. It burdens the claimant with two tasks: the one who makes it not only must show the different sort of truth that serves as the standard by which the whole color mode of experience is judged misleading, but also must give some explanation as to why most of us miss all truth all the time and why all of us miss most truth most of the time." (Clark, ANA, 153)

They also ask in response to the mystic, why are our perceptions so often wrong?

On the one hand, the minds that supposedly initiate this process of calcification are themselves part of the illusion. . . . [But if] the mind is part of and as such a result of the illusion, it cannot predate the illusion and thus it cannot serve as an explanation for it. On the other hand, if our thoughts are not thoughts of an illusory mind, presumably they are God's thoughts. . . . But this too creates difficulties. C. S. Lewis [in *Miracles*] raised objections to the notion that our thinking is really God thinking precisely because we are sometimes wrong. (Clark, ANA, 154)

Two questions can be asked of the pantheist [mystics are drawn to pantheism as noted above] who says reality is illusory. First,

if we are being deceived about our consciousness of our own individual existence, how do we know that the pantheist is not also being deceived when he claims to be conscious of reality as ultimately one?

Second, if the world is really an illusion—if what we continually perceive to be real is not real—then how can we distinguish between reality and fantasy? Lao-tse puts the question well: "If, when I was asleep I was a man dreaming I was a butterfly, how do I know when I am awake I am not a butterfly dreaming I am a man?" Other examples illustrate this dilemma: When we cross a busy street and see three lanes of traffic coming toward us, should we not even worry about it because it is merely an illusion? Indeed, should we even bother to look for cars when we cross the street, if we, the traffic, and the street do not really exist? If pantheists actually lived out their pantheism consistently, would there be any pantheists left? (Geisler, WA, 102)

The inadequacy of calling a reality such as evil an illusion is manifest. "If evil is not real, then what is the origin of the illusion? Why has man experienced it for so long, and why does it seem so real? Despite the pantheist's claims to the contrary, he, along with the rest of us, experiences pain, suffering, and eventually death. Even pantheists dou-

ble over in pain when they get appendicitis. They also jump out of the way of an oncoming truck so as not to get hurt. If the world is not real, then why, when I sit upon a pin and it punctures my skin, do I dislike what I fancy I feel?" (Geisler, WA, 102–103)

4B. Mystical Experiences Are Not Ineffable (Incapable of Being Expessed)

"Mystics usually assume their words are descriptive, as do their critics and defenders. Thus, the concept of ineffability does not do the logical work that some have hoped for. It does not separate the mystical real, cleanly from other forms of experience. Mysticism cannot provide a unique area of evidence on the basis of which other modes of experience may be summarily ignored." (Clark, ANA, 182)

Henry Rosemont, Jr. suggests: "A Zen commentator cannot advocate the belief, for example, that all language distorts reality, and expect anyone to pay serious attention to him, any more that he could utter the words, 'I am not speaking right now,' and hope to convince anyone that his utterance was a true statement." (Rosemont, LLZ, 134)

Rosemont questions the necessity of the ineffability of Zen:

Is it a *necessary* statement that language cannot convey what is in some sense "seen" in satori? Or is it, as a matter of *fact* the case that the "seer" cannot come up with descriptive statements that he finds satisfactory? If satori is *defined* (necessary) as being "beyond logic and language" then all of the writings on the subject are by definition incapable of giving us any information about it. If, on the other hand, the commentators intend an empirical generalization when they say that satori is beyond logic and language, they are obliged to adduce evidence in support of their generalization, which they cannot do. (Rosemont, LLZ, 19)

Rosemont comments that the claim of ineffability is arbitrary:

We should not be surprised to find the Zen commentators issuing disclaimers, insisting that Zen is beyond the philosopher's scrutiny, it is not subject to the laws of language and logic. . . . In some sense or other Zen might be beyond the laws of language and logic; *but the assertions of the Zen commentators are not, because they are written in the English language.* . . . It is extraordinarily difficult, for example, to induce an intelligent native speaker of English to accept the view that English is a highly defective language; not because he feels a cultural superiority, but because he cannot help wondering how, if English is so highly defective, it was possible to state so clearly the fact that it is defective. It is not possible for him to abandon cognitively [his logical] framework completely on the strength of arguments which must presuppose it; to the extent that the Zen commentators attempt such a task they are doomed to failure. (Rosemont, LLZ, 46, 56)

He argues that "Suzuki's *arguments* are instances of questions, answers, reason, subjects, predicates, negations, and everyday language. If the original beliefs were true, their advocates could not *state* their objections and arguments, and if they seriously hold those beliefs, it is doubtful that they would even attempt to raise these objections and arguments." (Rosemont, LLZ, 66)

Rosemont concludes: "Anyone who must appeal to the principles of logic and language in order to establish as a conclusion that logic and language are fundamentally unsound should immediately suspect not that the conclusion is true, but that he has a *reductio ad absurdum* [absurd conclusion] on his hands, and that therefore not only is his conclusion false, but at least one of the premises as well. What we can't say, we can't say; and we can't whistle it either." (Rosemont, LLZ, 68)

5B. Mystical Experiences Are Not Self-authenticating

Clark and Geisler note that mystical experiences are not even self-interpreting, since "the need for a broader background against

> In some sense or other Zen might be beyond the laws of language and logic; but the assertions of the Zen commentators are not, because they are written in the English language.
>
> —HENRY ROSEMONT, JR.

which to judge experiences is felt both for empirical experiences and for religious experiences. Despite their initial claims, mystics act like empiricists when discussing their experiences. They, too, place their experiences within the context of a world view for interpretation and confirmation." (Clark, ANA, 173)

Geisler and Feinberg note that mysticism is a form of suprarational subjectivism. If there is nothing external against which to measure differing experiences, then it "has difficulty explaining how any of our beliefs can be *wrong*. We know that people have different, incompatible, and even inconsistent beliefs about the world. How can this be, if the knower is in immediate contact with the known through a self-authenticating experience?" (Geisler, IP, 109–110)

6B. Mysticism Results in a Philosophy that Is Unlivable

Below are two stories of the existential inability to interact with reality based on Zen philosophy. Notice the rather quaint and trivial consequences in the first account as told by D. T. Suzuki:

Before I left Japan I read in an English journal

an interesting article by a Russian whose idea was this: "The objective world can exist only in my subjectivity; the objective world does not really exist until it is experienced by this subjectivity or myself." That is something like Berkeley's Idealism. One day this Russian was riding his bicycle and he collided with a lorry; the driver was very angry but the Russian kept on saying, "The world is nothing but my subjectivity." On another occasion when he was thinking in the ordinary way, there was no collision but something else happened and he was awakened to this truth: "There is nothing but my subjectivity." When he experienced this, he had quite an illumination and he said to a friend: "Everything is in everything else." That means that all things are the same but he did not say that; he said, "Everything, each individual object, is in each other individual object. So this world of multitudes is not denied, as each thing is in every other one." This is most significant. When he expressed this to his friend, the friend could not understand but later he attained the same experience. This is Prajna; this is transcendental wisdom, and when this intuition is attained we have Zen. Zen is no other than this intuitive knowledge. (Suzuki, AZ, 24)

Compare the consequences of Suzuki's story with the realistic consequences of the following scenario suggested by Mortimer Adler. Adler illustrates the schizophrenia that results in Far Eastern cultures that segregate the truths of science and technology and the truths of religious faith into logic-tight compartments.

A Buddhist Zen master who lives in Tokyo wishes to fly to Kyoto in a private plane. When he arrives at the airport, he is offered two planes; one that is faster but aeronautically unsound. He is informed by the airport authorities that the faster plane violates some of the basic principles of aeronautical mechanics, and the slower plane does not.

The aeronautical or technological deficiencies of the faster plane represent underlying mistakes in physics. The Zen master, in his teaching, asks his disciples questions the right answers to which require them to embrace contradictions. To do so is the path to wisdom about reality, which has contradictions at its core. But the Zen master does not waver from upholding this teaching about reality while, at the same time, he chooses the slower, aeronautically sounder and safer plane because it accords with a technology and a physics that makes correct judgments about a physical world that abhors contradictions.

If there is scientific truth in technology and physics, then the unity of the truth should require the Zen master to acknowledge that his choice of the slower but safer plane means that he repudiates his Zen doctrine about the wisdom of embracing contradictions.

He does not do so and remains schizophrenic, with the truth of Zen doctrine and the truth of technology and physics in logic-tight compartments. On what grounds or for what reasons does he do this if not for the psychological comfort derived from keeping the incompatible "truths" in logic-tight compartments? Can it be that the Zen master has a different meaning for the word "truth" when he persists in regarding the Zen doctrine as true even though it would appear to be irreconcilable with the truth of technology and physics he has accepted in choosing the slower plane? Can it be that this persistence in retaining the Zen doctrine does not derive from its being true in the logical sense of truth, but rather in a sense of "true" that identifies it with being psychologically "useful" or "therapeutic"?

Adler concludes: "In other words, Zen Buddhism as a religion is believed by this Zen master because of its psychological usefulness in producing in its believers a state of peace or harmony. In my judgment, this view of the matter does not reduce or remove the schizophrenia of Zen Buddhism." (Adler, TR, 72–76)

Henry Rosemont, Jr. points out four

inevitable problems the Zen mystic must face:

> If one accepts Suzuki's claim that satori is devoid of rational content, there are several [resulting problems] which must be examined: (1) How would the student know that he had had the experience? (2) How would he be able to name it? What could possibly count as evidence that his experience was to be called "satori"? (3) How could anyone ever know, or justify the claim, that someone else had had a *similar* experience? (4) How could such an experience, devoid of rational content, verify the metaphysical principles of Mahayana Buddhism, as Suzuki claims that it does? (Rosemont, LLZ, 18–19)

Though the argument of unlivability cannot be built on one anecdotal case, the testimony of ex-Hindu Rabindranath Maharaj illustrates the dilemma facing anyone who adopts the pantheistic mysticism of the East.

> My religion made beautiful theory, but I was having serious trouble applying it in everyday life. Nor was it only a matter of my five senses versus my inner visions. It was a matter of reason also. . . . If there was only One Reality, then Brahman was evil as well as good, death as well as life, hatred as well as love. That made everything meaningless, life an absurdity. . . . It seemed unreasonable: but [I was reminded] that Reason could not be trusted—it was part of the illusion. If reason also was maya—as the Vedas [Hindu religious scripture] taught—then how could I trust any concept, including the idea that all was maya and only Brahman was real? How could I be sure the Bliss I sought was not also an illusion, if none of my perceptions or reasoning were to be trusted? (Maharaj, DG, 104)

Norman Geisler asks this pointed question: "When we cross a busy street and see three lanes of traffic coming toward us, should we not even worry about it because it is merely an illusion? Indeed, should we even bother to look for cars when we cross the street, if we, the traffic, and the street do not really exist? If pantheists actually lived out their pantheism consistently, would there be any pantheists left?" (Geisler, WA, 102)

Francis Schaeffer tells this often-quoted story which illustrates the unlivability of denying logical dualism:

> One day I was talking to a group of people in the room of a young South African in Cambridge University. Among others, there was present a young Indian who was of Sikh background but a Hindu by religion. He started to speak strongly against Christianity, but did not really understand the problems of his own beliefs. So I said, "Am I not correct in saying that on the basis of your system, cruelty and non-cruelty are ultimately equal, that there is no intrinsic difference between them?" He agreed. The student in whose room we met, who had clearly understood the implications of what the Sikh had admitted, picked up his kettle of boiling water with which he was about to make tea, and stood with it steaming over the Indian's head. The man looked up and asked him what he was doing and he said, with a cold yet gentle finality, "There is no difference between cruelty and non-cruelty." Thereupon the Hindu walked out into the night. (Schaeffer, CWFS, 1:110)

38
CERTAINTY VS.
CERTITUDE

How certain can we be about truth? The answer is that we have different degrees of certainty about different truths. In most cases, we have moral or practical certainty about the truths of Christianity.

Frederick. D. Wilhelmsen: "Assent with intellectual certitude is threefold: (a) metaphysical, wherein there is absolutely no possibility for the truth of the opposite; (b) physical; and (c) moral, wherein there is a remote possibility for the truth of the contrary, but we have no sufficient reason to think this possibility will be fulfilled in the situation at hand." (Wilhelmsen, MKR, 171)

Assent to certitude. "Assent is a conscious discernment and commitment to the truth . . . . Assent is the mind's ratification of the proposition it has formed." (Wilhelmsen, MKR, 157)

There are four kinds of natural certainty:

Logical certainty. Logical certainty is found largely in mathematics and pure logic. This kind of certainty is involved where the opposite would be a contradiction. Something is certain in this sense when there is no logical possibility it could be false. Since mathematics is reducible to logic it fits into this category. It is found in statements such as $5 + 4 = 9$. It is also found in tautologies or statements that are true by definition. All circles are round, and no triangle is a square.

Metaphysical certainty. There are, however, some other things of which we can be absolutely certain that are not statements empty of content. For example, I know for certain that I exist. This is undeniably so, since I cannot deny my existence without existing to make the denial. First principles can also be known for certain, since the subject and predicate say the same thing: "Being exists;" "Nonbeing is not Being." "Nonbeing cannot produce Being" is also certain, since *produce* implies an existing producer.

Moral certainty. Moral certainty exists where the evidence is so great that the mind lacks any reason to veto the will to believe it is so. One rests in a moral certainty with complete confidence. Of course, there is a logical possibility that things of which we are morally certain are false. However, the evidence is so great there is no reason to believe it is false. In legal terms this is what is meant by "beyond all reasonable doubt."

Practical certainty (high probability). Practical certainty is not as strong as moral certainty. Persons claim to be "certain" about things they believe have a high probability of truth. One may be certain she had breakfast today, without being able to prove it mathematically or metaphysically. It is true unless something changed her perception, so that she was deluded into thinking she ate breakfast. It is possible to be wrong about these matters. (Geisler, BECA, 122)

39
DEFENDING MIRACLES

1A. MIRACLES ARE POSSIBLE IN A THEISTIC UNIVERSE

If a theistic God exists, then miracles are possible. As C. S. Lewis said, "But if we admit God, must we admit Miracle? Indeed, indeed, you have no security against it. That is the bargain. Theology says to you in effect, 'Admit God and with Him the risk of a few miracles, and I in return will ratify your faith in uniformity as regards the overwhelming majority of events.'" (Lewis, M, 109)

What is meant by the term *miracle*? "The first step in this, as in all other discussions, is to come to a clear understanding as to the meaning of the terms employed. Argumentation about whether miracles are possible and, if possible, credible, is mere beating the air until the arguers have agreed what they mean by the word 'miracle.'" (Huxley, WTHH, 153)

We are defining miracles as special acts of God in the world. Since miracles are special acts of God, they can only exist where there is a theistic God who can perform such acts.

Throughout this book we have provided evidence for the existence of a God who, among His many acts, created the world. If God is able to create the world, then it follows that God is also able to act in it.

It is important to note that we do not use the Bible to confirm the possibility of miracles, but only, as we will see later, to report the historicity of certain miraculous events. That miracles are possible is an inference from the fact that this is a theistic universe, not a conclusion we draw from the Bible. Stephen T. Davis notes that this is, in fact, a presupposition of the Bible: "That God is the world's Creator is claimed in Genesis 1–2, is affirmed or presupposed throughout the Bible, and is the conclusion of any successful cosmological argument for the existence of God. The world is a contingent thing; it exists only because God brought it into existence and sustains it in existence. The claim that God acts in history, attempting to influence human beings and to bring God's purposes to fruition, is a universal presupposition of the entire Bible." (Davis, GA, as cited in Geivett, IDM, 164–65)

William Lane Craig tells how his difficulty with the possibility of a biblical miracle ceased to be a problem once he acknowledged the existence of God: "In my own case, the virgin birth was a stumbling block to my coming to faith—I simply could not believe such a thing. But when I reflected on the fact that God had created the entire universe, it occurred to me that it would not be too difficult for Him to make a woman become pregnant. Once the non-Christian understands who God is, then the problem of miracles should cease to be a problem for him." (Craig, AI, 125)

2A. THE NATURE OF MIRACLES

1B. Miracles Are Supernatural Acts of God

Thomas Aquinas distinguishes between the effects of finite and infinite power:

> When any finite power produces the proper effect to which it is determined, this is not a miracle, though it may be a matter of wonder for some person who does not understand that power. For example, it may seem astonishing to ignorant people that a magnet attracts iron or that some little fish might hold back a ship. But the potency of every creature is limited to some definite effect or to certain effects. So, whatever is done by the power of any creature cannot be called a miracle properly, even though it may be astonishing to one who does not comprehend the power of this creature. But what is done by divine power, which, being infinite, is incomprehensible in itself, is truly miraculous. (Aquinas, SCG, 3.102.3, 83)

Antony Flew states that "miracle" is "a term that has been variously understood, but is most commonly taken to mean an act that manifests divine power through the suspension or alteration of the normal working laws of nature." (Flew, DP, 234)

C. S. Lewis remarks, "I use the word *Miracle* to mean an interference with Nature by supernatural power." (Lewis, M, 5)

Richard L. Purtill notes five characteristics of a miracle: "A miracle is an event (1) brought about by the power of God that is (2) a temporary (3) exception (4) to the ordinary course of nature (5) for the purpose of showing that God has acted in history." (Purtill, DM, as cited in Geivett, IDM, 72)

2B. Miracles Do Not Violate Natural Laws

Some would contend that miracles cannot exist since they would be in violation of the laws of nature. This argument assumes that natural law is a closed system (i.e., that it cannot be acted on from the outside); therefore, a violation of natural law is impossible. However, within a theistic framework, natural law is not a closed system; therefore, a miracle is not necessarily a violation of natural law.

C. S. Lewis illustrates how an open system adapts to intervention:

It is therefore inaccurate to define a miracle as something that breaks the laws of Nature. It doesn't. If I knock out my pipe I alter the position of a great many atoms: in the long run, and to an infinitesimal degree, of all the atoms there are. Nature digests or assimilates this event with perfect ease and harmonizes it in a twinkling with all other events. . . . If God creates a miraculous spermatozoon in the body of a virgin, it does not proceed to break any laws. The laws at once take over. Nature is ready. Pregnancy follows, according to all the normal laws, and nine months later a child is born. . . . If events ever come from beyond nature altogether she will (not) be incommoded by them. Be sure that she will rush to the point where she is invaded as the defensive forces rush to a cut on our finger, and there hasten to accommodate the newcomer. The moment it enters her realm it will obey all her laws. (Lewis, M, 59)

Sir George Stokes suggests that a suspension of natural laws is not the only explanation for a miracle: "It may be that the event

> A man walking through a wall is a miracle. A man both walking and not walking through a wall at the same time and in the same respect is a contradiction. God can perform miracles but not contradictions—not because his power is limited, but because contradictions are meaningless.
>
> —PETER KREEFT AND RONALD TACELLI

which we call a miracle was brought on not by a suspension of the laws in ordinary operation, but by the super addition of something not ordinarily in operation." (Stokes, ISBE, 2036)

Peter Kreeft and Ronald Tacelli note that, in theism, a system of natural law is presupposed:

We begin with a preliminary definition. A miracle is: *a striking and religiously significant intervention of God in the system of natural causes.*

Note two things here: (1) the concept of miracles presupposes, rather than sets aside, the idea that nature is a self-contained system of natural causes. Unless there are regularities, there can be no exceptions to them. (2) A miracle is not a contradiction. A man walking through a wall is a miracle. A man both walking and not walking through a wall at the same time and in the same respect is a contradiction. God can perform miracles but not contradictions—not because his power is limited, but because contradictions are meaningless. (Kreeft, HCA, 109)

Purtill argues: "As an event caused by divine will acting from outside this natural order, a miracle neither confirms nor disconfirms any generalization about the natural order of things. In fact . . . there is good reason in this context to define a miracle as 'a non-repeatable counter-instance to a law of nature.' What this means is that the phenomenon (or event type) is nonrepeatable by us, or by any finite creature, not that God could not repeat the same type of event." (Purtill, DM, as cited in Geivett, IDM, 69)

3B. Miracles Are Immediate

A striking characteristic of a miracle is that it is immediate. There is no progression over a period of time in the occurrence of a miracle. Rather, they are instantaneous. As Norman Geisler observes,

> With specific regard to the healing ministry of Jesus, the results were always immediate. There were no instances of gradual improvement over a few days. Jesus commanded the invalid to "Arise, take up your pallet and walk," and "immediately the man became well" (John 5:8 NASB). In Peter's ministry in Acts 3 we see God healing a lame man instantly at Peter's hand. "Peter said, 'I do not possess silver and gold, but what I do have I give to you: In the name of Jesus Christ the Nazarene— walk!' And seizing him by the right hand, he raised him up; and immediately his feet and ankles were strengthened" (Acts 3:6–7 NASB). There was no lapse of time over which the man gradually improved. The restoration of this man's health was instantaneous and complete. (Geisler, SW, 29)

4B. Miracles Are Always Successful

Furthermore, a true miracle will always be successful. Again, Geisler notes,

> Indeed the Bible records that God is always successful in His efforts. Diseases always vanish at His command, demons always flee at His order, nature is always open to His intervention. This is an important characteristic of the fingerprint of God which bears repeating. *The supernatural acts of God in the Bible were and are always successful.* That is, God always accomplished what He intended to accomplish. If He desired to heal someone, they were

completely healed. There are no exceptions. (Geisler, SW, 28–29, emphasis his)

3A. THE PURPOSE OF MIRACLES

1B. Miracles Can Confirm a Message from God

E. J. Carnell argues that miracles are our only confirmation of a reference point outside the system of natural law: "Miracles are a sign and a seal of the veracity [truthfulness] of special revelation, revelation which assures us exactly how God has elected to dispose of His universe. In this revelation we read that He Who made us, and Who can also destroy us, has graciously chosen to keep the universe regular according to the covenant which He made with Noah and his seed forever. If the scientist rejects miracles to keep his mechanical order, he loses his right to that mechanical order, for, without miracles to guarantee revelation, he can claim no external reference point; and without an external reference point to serve as a fulcrum, the scientist is closed up to the shifting sand of history."

Carnell concludes, "In such a case, then, how can the scientist appeal to the changeless conviction 'that the universe is mechanical,' when from flux and change only flux and change can come? The scientist simply exchanges what he thinks is a 'whim of deity' for what is actually a 'whim of time and space.' Why the latter guarantees perseverance of a mechanical world, when the former seemingly is impotent so to do, is not easy to see." (Carnell, AITCA, 258)

2B. Miracles Can Confirm a Messenger of God

Another purpose of miraculous "signs," as Norman Geisler notes, is

> to be a divine confirmation of a prophet of God. The religious ruler Nicodemus said of

Jesus: "We know that you are a teacher who has come from God. For no one could perform the miraculous signs you are doing if God were not with him" (John 3:2). Many people followed him because they saw the signs he performed on those who were sick (John 6:2). When some rejected Jesus, even though he had cured a blind man, others said, "How can a sinner do such miraculous signs?" (John 9:16). The apostles were confident in proclaiming, "Jesus the Nazarene was a man accredited by God to you by miracles, wonders, and signs, which God did among you through him, as you yourselves know" (Acts 2:22). For his credentials to the Corinthians, the apostle Paul claimed that the signs of a true apostle were performed among them (2 Cor. 12:12). He and Barnabas recounted to the apostles "the miraculous signs and wonders God had done among the Gentiles through them" (Acts 15:12). (Geisler, MMM, 98)

Sproul, Gerstner, and Lindsley argue that a miracle is the only indubitable confirmation God could have used: "Now if God would certify His messengers to us—as we have shown He would do if He intends to send them at all—He would give them credentials that only He could give. Thus, we would know indubitably that they are to be received as the messengers of God.

"What would God give His messengers that all could see could come only from God? Since the power of miracle belongs to God alone, miracles are a suitable and fitting vehicle of attestation." (Sproul, CA, 144)

3A. Miracles Promote Good Alone

A miracle will never promote evil: "Morally, because God is good, miracles only produce and/or promote good." (Geisler and Brooks, WSA, 88)

4B. Miracles Glorify God Alone

A miracle is never merely for show: "[M]iracles are never performed for entertainment, but have the distinct purpose of glorifying God and directing men to Him." (Geisler and Brooks, WSA, 89)

5B. Miracles Form the Framework of Christianity

Peter Kreeft observes that the importance miracles have in Christianity is unique among the world's religions:

The clinching argument for the importance of miracles is that *God* thought they were important enough to use them to found and perpetuate his Church.

In fact, all the essential and distinctive elements of Christianity are miracles: creation, revelation (first to the Jews), the giving of the law, prophesies, the Incarnation, the Resurrection, the Ascension and the Second Coming and Last Judgment.

Subtract miracles from Islam, Buddhism, Confucianism, or Taoism, and you have essentially the same religion left. Subtract miracles from Christianity, and you have nothing but the cliches and platitudes most American Christians get weekly (and weakly) from their pulpits. Nothing *distinctive*, no reason to be a Christian rather than something else. (Kreeft, CMP, 273)

Again Sproul, Gerstner, and Lindsley argue that miracles are also indispensable to the demonstration of the case for Christianity: "Technically . . . miracles are visible and external and perceivable by both converted and unconverted alike, carrying with them the power to convince, if not to convert. Certainly, as far as apologetics is concerned, the visible miracle is indispensable to the case for Christianity, which case would thereby be demonstrated sound whether anyone believed it or not, whether anyone was converted or not, whether anyone experienced an internal 'miracle' or not. The proof would be demonstrative even if all people willfully refused to acquiesce in it." (Sproul, CA, 145)

6B. Miracles Differ from Magic

The following chart emphasizes the differences between a true miracle and a false miracle (magic).

1. Miracles are violations of natural laws.
2. Natural laws are immutable.
3. It is impossible to violate immutable laws.
4. Therefore, miracles are impossible. (Geisler, MMM, 15)

MIRACLE	MAGIC
Under God's control	Under man's control
Done at God's will	Done at man's will
Not naturally repeatable	Naturally repeatable
No deception involved	Deception involved
Occurs in nature	Does not occur in nature
Fits into nature	Does not fit into nature
Unusual but not odd	Unusual and odd
	(Geisler, SW, 73)

4A. ANSWERING OBJECTIONS TO MIRACLES

1B. Benedict Spinoza Claims that Miracles Are Impossible

Benedict Spinoza declares that "nature cannot be contravened, but . . . she preserves a fixed and immutable order." In fact, "If anyone asserted that God acts in contravention to the laws of nature, he, *ipso facto*, would be compelled to assert that God acted against His own nature—an evident absurdity." (Spinoza, ATPT, 82–83)

It is important to note that Spinoza's rational pantheism determined his position on miracles. For Spinoza, transcendence is rejected because nature and God are ontologically identical. God is all; and all is God. Accordingly, if God is immutable and the laws of nature are a modal quality of God, then the laws of nature are immutable. Hence, a miracle is an absurdity, for it would entail a mutation (violation) of an immutable order, namely, God's very essence.

Spinoza's view can be summarized as follows:

A miracle is not a contravention of nature, but an introduction of a new event into nature by a supernatural cause. Nature is not surprised when an event is caused by the supernatural, but hastens to accommodate the new event. As Lewis explains:

If events ever come from beyond Nature altogether, she will be no more incommoded by them. Be sure she will rush to the point where she is invaded, as the defensive forces rush to a cut in our finger, and there hasten to accommodate the newcomer. . . . The divine art of miracle is not an art of suspending the pattern to which events conform but of feeding new events into that pattern. It does not violate the law's proviso, "If A, then B": it says, "But this time instead of A, A2," and Nature, speaking through all her laws, replies, "Then B2" and naturalizes the immigrant, as she well knows how. She is an accomplished hostess. (Lewis, M, 60)

According to C. Stephen Evans, the description of miracle as a "break" or "interruption" with respect to natural law incorrectly presumes God's absence from creation prior to His miraculous activity. But God is constantly present to His creation as the sustaining, necessary Being. Hence, whereas miracles entail special acts of God, nature is still held into being by the normal activity of God. As Evans explains:

> It is however, somewhat incorrect to call such special actions "breaks" or "interruptions" in the natural order. Such terminology implies that God is not normally present in the natural order; but if God exists at all, then he must be regarded as responsible for the whole of that natural order. The contrast, then, is not between "nature" and very unusual divine "interventions" into nature, but between God's normal activity in upholding the natural order and some special activity on God's part. Thus, when God does a miracle, he does not suddenly enter a created order from which he is normally absent. Rather, he acts in a special way in a natural order which he continually upholds and in which he is constantly present. (Evans, WB, 88)

Moreover, Spinoza's argument begs the question. Spinoza's definition of the laws of nature (as immutable) necessarily precludes the possibility of miracles. Based on his rational method, rather than on empirical observation, Spinoza assumed *a priori* that nature is inviolable. As Norman Geisler explains: "Spinoza's Euclidean (deductive) rationalism suffers from an acute case of *petitio principii* (begging the question). For, as David Hume notes, anything validly deducible from premises must have already been present in those premises from the beginning. But if the antisupernatural is already presupposed in Spinoza's rationalistic premises, then it is no surprise to discover him attacking the miracles of the Bible." Geisler adds, "What Spinoza needed to do, but did not, was to provide some sound argument for his rationalistic presuppositions." Spinoza "spins them out in the thin air of rational speculation, but they are never firmly attached to the firm ground of empirical observation." (Geisler, MMM, 18, 21)

2B. David Hume Claims that Miracles Are Incredible

Skeptic David Hume asserts that

> a miracle is a violation of the laws of nature; and as a firm and unalterable experience has established these laws, the proof against a miracle, from the very nature of the fact, is as entire as any argument from experience can possibly be imagined. . . . Nothing is esteemed a miracle, if it ever happened in the common course of nature. It is no miracle that a man, seemingly in good health, should die on a sudden: because such a kind of death, though more unusual than any other, has yet been frequently observed to happen. But it is a miracle, that a dead man should come to life; because that has never been observed in any age or country. There must, therefore, be a uniform experience against every miraculous event, otherwise the event would not merit that appellation. And as a uniform experience amounts to a proof, there is here a direct and full proof, from the nature of the fact, against the existence of any miracle; nor can such a proof be destroyed, or the miracle rendered credible, but by an opposite proof, which is superior. (Hume, ECHU, 144, 145, 146, 148)

Hume is not arguing that miracles are impossible because the laws of nature cannot be broken. That sort of argument, as we discovered with Spinoza, begs the question. Hume, as an empiricist, is limited to an inductive approach to reality, notwithstanding truisms. And induction yields, at best, probability, not absolute certainty. Rather, Hume is utilizing a particular argumentative style known as *reductio ad absurdum*. This form of argument seeks to establish that the opposing view results in an absurdity. Thus, Hume first grants the theistic claim that miracles are rare events, and then he shows how improbable they are in light of the regularity of nature's laws. That is, Hume argues that miracles are deemed highly improbable because the natural laws of which miracles must be exceptions inform us of the greater evidence.

As Philosopher Ronald Nash explains, "First, Hume cleverly manipulates the theist into admitting that he (the theist) must believe in a natural order since without such an order, there cannot be any way of recognizing exceptions to the order. Then, Hume hammers the theist with the obvious fact that the probability for the theist's alleged violations of natural laws must always be much less than the probability that the exception has not occurred." (Nash, FR, 230)

Hume's argument can be summarized as follows:

1. A miracle is by definition a rare occurrence.
2. Natural law is by definition a description of regular occurrence.
3. The evidence for the regular is always greater than that for the rare.
4. Wise individuals always base belief on the greater evidence.
5. Therefore, wise individuals should never believe in miracles. (Geisler, MMM, 27-28)

Hume's notion of uniform experience either begs the question or is guilty of special pleading. As Geisler notes,

Hume speaks of "uniform" experience in his argument against miracles, but this either begs the question or else is special pleading. It begs the question if Hume presumes to know the experience is uniform in advance of looking at the evidence. For how can we know that all possible experience will confirm naturalism, unless we have access to all possible experiences, including those in the future? If, on the other hand, Hume simply means by "uniform" experience the select experiences of *some* persons (who have not encountered a miracle), then this is special pleading. (Geisler, MMM, 28)

Lewis exposes the circular character of Hume's use of "uniform experience" in the following passage: "Now of course we must agree with Hume that if there is absolutely 'uniform experience' against miracles, if in other words they have never happened, why then they never have. Unfortunately we know the experience against them to be uniform only if we know that all the reports of them are false. And we can know all the reports to be false only if we know miracles have never occurred. In fact, we are arguing in a circle." (Lewis, M, 102)

Hume overlooks the importance of indirect evidence in support of miracles. As Nash argues:

Hume was wrong when he suggested that miracles are supported only by direct evidence cited in the testimony of people who claim to have witnessed them. There can also be important indirect evidence for miracles. Even if some person (Jones, let us say) did not observe some alleged miracle (thus making him dependent on the testimony of others who did), Jones may still be able to see abiding effects of the miracle. Suppose the miracle in question concerns the healing of a person who has been blind for years. Jones may be dependent on the testimony of others that they saw the healing occur, but perhaps Jones is now able to discern for himself that the formerly blind person can now see. The situation is analogous to that of someone who hears the testimony that a tornado has ravaged his city. Since he was not an eyewitness to the storm, he is dependent on the testimony of eyewitnesses who were there. But when this person arrives on the scene and sees the incredible devastation—cars on top of houses, other houses blown apart, trees uprooted—all this functions as indirect evidence to confirm the eyewitness testimony of others. In this way, certain effects of a miracle that exist after the

> This argument equates quantity of evidence and probability. It says, in effect, that we should always believe what is most probable (in the sense of 'enjoying the highest odds'). But this is silly. On these grounds a dice player should not believe the dice show three sixes on the first roll, since the odds against it are 1,635,013,559,600 to 1! What Hume seems to overlook is that wise people base their beliefs on facts, not simply on odds.
>
> —NORMAN GEISLER

event can serve as indirect evidence that the event happened. (Nash, FR, 233)

British Philosopher C. D. Broad appealed to indirect evidence to support the cornerstone miracle of the Christian faith—the resurrection of Christ:

We have testimony to the effect that the disciples were exceedingly depressed at the time of the Crucifixion; that they had extremely little faith in the future; and that, after a certain time, this depression disappeared, and they believed that they had evidence that their Master had risen from the dead. Now none of these alleged facts is in the least odd or improbable, and we have therefore little ground for not accepting them on the testimony offered us. But having done this, we are faced with the problem of accounting for the facts which we have accepted. What caused the disciples to believe, contrary to their previous conviction, and in spite of their feeling of depression, that Christ had risen from the dead? Clearly, one explanation is that he actually had arisen. And this explanation accounts

for the facts so well that we may at least say that the indirect evidence for the miracle is far and away stronger than the direct evidence. (Broad, HTCM, 91–92)

Instead of weighing the evidence in favor of miracles, Hume simply adds evidence against them. Geisler puts it this way:

Hume does not really *weigh* evidence for miracles; rather, he *adds* evidence against them. Since death occurs over and over again and resurrection occurs only on rare occasions at best, Hume simply adds up all the deaths against the very few alleged resurrections and rejects the latter . . . But this does not involve weighing evidence to determine whether or not a given person, say Jesus of Nazareth . . . has been raised from the dead. It is simply adding up the evidence of all other occasions where people have died and have not been raised and using it to overwhelm any possible evidence that some person who died was brought back to life . . . . Second, this argument equates quantity of evidence and probability. It says, in effect, that we should always believe what is most probable (in the sense of "enjoying the highest odds"). But this is silly. On these grounds a dice player should not believe the dice show three sixes on the first roll, since the odds against it are 1,635,013,559,600 to 1! What Hume seems to overlook is that wise people base their beliefs on facts, not simply on odds. Sometimes the "odds" against an event are high (based on past observation), but the evidence for the event is otherwise very good (based on current observation or reliable testimony). Hume's argument confuses *quantity* of evidence with the *quality* of evidence. Evidence should be *weighed*, not *added*. (Geisler, MMM, as cited in Geivett, IDM, 78–79)

Moreover, Hume confuses the probability of historical events with the way in which scientists employ probability to formulate scientific law. As Nash explains:

Critics of Hume have complained that his argument is based on a defective view of probability. For one thing, Hume treats the probability of events in history like miracles in the same way he treats the probability of the recurring events that give rise to the formulation of scientific laws. In the case of scientific laws, probability is tied to the frequency of occurrence; the more times scientists observe similar occurrences under similar conditions, the greater the probability that their formulation of a law is correct. But historical events including miracles are different; the events of history are unique and nonrepeatable. Therefore, treating historical events including miracles with the same notion of probability the scientist uses in formulating his laws ignore a fundamental difference between the two subject matters. (Nash, FR, 234)

3B. Patrick Nowell-Smith Claims that "Miracles" Are Simply "Strange" Natural Events that Either Have or Will Have a Strict Scientific Explanation

According to Patrick Nowell-Smith, "No matter how strange an event someone reports, the statement that it must have been due to a supernatural agent cannot be a part of that report." Simply because "no scientist can at present explain certain phenomena," contends Nowell-Smith, "it does not follow that the phenomena are inexplicable by scientific methods, still less that they must be attributed to supernatural agents." In other words, "there is still the possibility that science may be able, in the future, to offer an explanation which, though couched in quite new terms, remains strictly scientific." (Nowell-Smith, M, as cited in Flew, NEPT, 246, 247, 248)

Nowell-Smith's objection to miracles is rooted in a kind of naturalistic faith, not scientific evidence. Norman Geisler exposes the flaws in Nowell-Smith's assertion as follows:

While Nowell-Smith claims that the scientist should keep an open mind and not reject evidence that ruins his preconceived theories, it is clear that he has closed his mind to the possibility of any supernatural explanations. He arbitrarily insists that all explanations must be natural ones or they do not really count. He makes the grand assumption that all events will ultimately have a natural explanation, but doesn't offer any proof for that assumption. The only way he can know this is to know beforehand that miracles cannot occur. It is a leap of naturalistic faith! (Geisler and Brooks, WSA, 81)

According to Lewis, no amount of time will be sufficient to naturalize a legitimate miracle: "When a thing professes from the very outset to be a unique invasion of Nature by something from outside, increasing knowledge of nature can never make it either more or less credible than it was at the beginning. In this sense it is mere confusion of thought to suppose that advancing science has made it harder for us to accept miracles." (Lewis, M, 48)

Nowell-Smith's scientific naturalism confuses natural origin and natural function. As Geisler notes,

One of the problems behind this kind of scientific naturalism is the confusion of naturalistic origin and natural function. Motors function in accordance with physical laws but physical laws do not produce motors; minds do. In like manner, the origin of a miracle is not the physical and chemical laws of the universe, even though the resulting event will operate in accordance with these natural laws. In other words, a miraculous conception will produce a nine-month pregnancy (in accordance with natural law). So, while natural laws regulate the operation of things, they do not account for the origin of all things. (Geisler, MMM, 47)

4B. Nowell-Smith Claims that Miracles Are Unscientific Because They Lack Predictive Value

Of anyone trusting in the possibility of miracles, Nowell-Smith says, "Let him consider the meaning of the word 'explanation' and let him ask himself whether this notion does not involve that of a law or hypothesis capable of predictive expansion. And then let him ask himself whether such an explanation would not be natural, in whatever terms it was couched, and how the notion of 'the supernatural' could play any part in it." (Nowell-Smith, M, as cited in Flew, NEPT, 253)

However, contrary to Nowell-Smith's assertion, there are several natural events that lack predictive value and yet are still within the domain of scientific investigation. As Geisler explains:

Nowell-Smith demands that all explanations have predictive value to qualify as true explanations. And yet there are many events he would call natural that no one can predict. We cannot predict if or when a bachelor will marry. But when he does say, "I do," do we not claim that he was simply "doing what comes naturally"? If naturalists reply, as indeed they must, that they cannot always predict in practice (but only in principle) when natural events occur, then supernaturalists can do likewise. In principle we know that a miracle will occur whenever God deems one necessary. If we knew all the facts (which include the mind of God), then we could predict in practice precisely when this would be. Furthermore, biblical miracles are past singularities that like the origin of the universe or of life are not presently being repeated. But predictions cannot be made from singularities. They can only be projected from patterns. The past is not known by empirical science, but by forensic science. Therefore, it is misdirected to ask for predictions (forward); rather, one is attempting to make a retroduction (backward). (Geisler, MMM, 46–47)

40

IS HISTORY KNOWABLE?

1A. WHAT IS HISTORY AND HISTORIOGRAPHY?

There is no doubt that much of the evidence for the validity of the Christian faith is rooted in history. Christianity is a historically founded faith. Its validity, or credibility, is based on Jesus Christ literally living in history. The resurrection is rooted in time-space history. Every thing that Jesus lived, taught, and died for is dependent upon His literal historical resurrection. This section lays out the task of historiography for the investigation of the Bible's reliability and answers the objectors who claim that history, miraculous or otherwise, is not knowable.

1B. Importance of History and Historiography to Christianity

Dr. William Lane Craig notes that Christianity "is rooted in real events of history." (Craig, RF, 157)

He continues by showing the concern and advantage this gives Christianity: "To some this is scandalous, because it means that the truth of Christianity is bound up with the truth of certain historical facts, such that if those facts should be disproved, so would Christianity. But at the same time, this makes Christianity unique because, unlike most other world religions, we now have a means of verifying its truth by historical evidence." (Craig, RF, 157)

"As people who believe in an objective revelation mediated through historical events, Christians cannot afford to sacrifice the objectivity of history. Otherwise, the events of the life, death, and resurrection of Jesus cannot be said to be part of the objective past because the gospels do not represent objective history." (Craig, RF, 190)

Professor Norman L. Geisler remarks, "In order to verify these truth claims one must first establish the objectivity of historical fact. This leads the discussion naturally into the whole question of . . . whether history is really knowable." (Geisler, CA, 285)

Historian Louis Gottschalk writes in his book *Understanding History*, "By its most common definition, the word *history* now means 'the past of mankind.' Compare the German word of *history*—*Geschichte*, which is derived from *geschehen*, meaning to happen. *Geschichte* is *that which has happened*." (Gottschalk, 41, UH, emphasis his)

Louis Gottschalk states that "the process of critically examining and analyzing the records and survivals of the past is here called *historical method*. The imaginative reconstruction of the past from the data derived by that process is called historiography (the writing of history)." (Gottschalk, 48, UH, emphasis his)

British philosopher-historian Robin G. Collingwood writes, "Every historian would agree, I think, that history is a kind of research or inquiry . . . . The point is that generically it belongs to what we call the sciences: that is, the forms of thought whereby we ask questions and try to answer them." (Collingwood, EPH, 9) Later he extends this by saying, "History, then, is a science, but a science of a special kind. It is a science whose business is to study events not accessible to our observation, and to study these events inferentially, arguing to them from something else which is accessible to our observation, and which the historian calls 'evidence' for the events in which he is interested." (Collingwood, EPH, 252)

He further states that the object of history is "*res gestae*: actions of human beings that have been done in the past." (Collingwood, EPH, 9)

Dr. John Warwick Montgomery presents a more detailed definition of history: "History . . . will here be defined as: An inquiry focusing on past human experience, both individual and societal, with a view towards the production of significant and comprehensive narratives embracing men's actions and reactions in respect to the whole range of natural, rational, and spiritual powers." (Montgomery, SP, 13)

2B. Process and Methodology of Historiography

Fischer, in his book *Historians' Fallacies*, states the nature of historical thought, "It is a process of *adductive* reasoning in the simple sense of adducing answers to specific questions, so that a satisfactory explanatory 'fit' is obtained. The answers may be general or particular, as the questions may require. History is, in short, a problem-solving discipline." (Fischer, HF, xv, emphasis his)

He continues, "A historian is someone (anyone) who asks an open-ended question about past events and answers it with selected facts which are arranged in the form of an explanatory paradigm." (Fischer, HF, xv)

Fischer acknowledges that "historians are likely to agree in principle, but not in practice. Specific canons [test] of historical proof are neither widely observed nor generally agreed upon." Yet, Fischer does think that there are at least seven "simple rules of thumb." (Fischer, HF, 62)

1. "Historical evidence must be a direct answer to the question asked and not some other question."
2. "An historian must not merely provide good relevant evidence but the best relevant evidence. And the best relevant evidence, all things being equal, is evidence which is most nearly immediate to the event itself." (Fischer, HF, 62)
3. "Evidence must always be affirmative. Negative evidence is a contradiction in terms—it is no evidence at all." (Fischer, HF, 62)
4. "The burden of proof, for any historical assertion, always rests upon its author." (Fischer, HF, 63)

5. "All inferences from empirical evidence are probabilistic. . . . A historian must determine, as best he can, the probability of *A* in relation to the probability of alternatives." (Fischer, HF, 63)
6. "The meaning of any empirical statement depends upon the context from which it is taken." (Fischer, HF, 63)
7. "An empirical statement must not be more precise than its evidence warrants." (Fischer, HF, 63)

The article titled "The Study of History" in the *Encyclopaedia Britannica* (15th ed.) states that "the methodology of history does not differ in broadest outline from that of other disciplines in its regard for existing knowledge, its search for new and relevant data, and its creation of hypothesis." (EB,

> Written and oral sources are divided into two kinds: primary and secondary. A primary source is the testimony of an eyewitness. . . . A secondary source is the testimony of anyone who is not an eyewitness—that is, of one who was not present at the events of which he tells.
>
> —LOUIS GOTTSCHALK

635) It further identifies four facets of historiography: "heuristic, knowledge of current interpretation, research, and writing." (EB, 635)

(1) *Heuristic*: "In the case of the historian it embraces such things as knowledge of manuscripts collections, methods of card indexing and classifying material, and knowledge of bibliography." (EB, 635)

(2) "The necessity for *knowledge* of current interpretation is based on the working principle that inquiry proceeds from the known to the unknown; and the historian has to be well acquainted with existing work

in his own field, in contiguous historical fields and in allied disciplines." (EB, 635)

(3) Historical *research* is the term applied to the work necessary for the establishing of occurrences, happenings, or events in the field with which the historian is concerned. Knowledge of these is entirely dependent on the transmission of information from those living at the time, and this information forms what is known as the source material for the particular period or topic. The occurrences themselves can never be experienced by the historian, and what he has at his disposal are either accounts of occurrences as seen by contemporaries or something, be it verbal, written, or material, that is the end product of an occurrence. These accounts or end products have been variously termed relics, tracks, or traces of the occurrences that gave rise to them; and from them the historian can, with varying degrees of certainty, deduce the occurrences. The traces are thus the "facts" of history, the actual occurrences and deductions from the facts; and historical research is concerned with the discovery of relevant traces and with deduction from those traces insofar as this will aid the search for further relevant traces. (EB, 636)

(4) *Writing*: Louis Gottschalk observes four essentials in how to write history:

(a) the collection of the surviving objects and of the printed, written, and oral materials that may be relevant;

(b) the exclusion of those materials (or parts thereof) that are unauthentic;

(c) the extraction from the authentic material of testimony that is credible;

(d) the organization of that reliable testimony into a meaningful narrative or exposition. (Gottschalk, UH, 28)

Gottschalk further identifies the sources of historical analysis:

Written and oral sources are divided into two kinds: primary and secondary. A *primary source* is the testimony of an eyewitness. . . . A *secondary source* is the testimony of anyone who is not an eyewitness—that is, of one who was not present at the events of which he tells. A primary source must thus have been produced by a contemporary of the events it narrates. It does not, however, need to be original in the legal sense of the word original—that is, the very document (usually the first written draft) [authographa] whose contents are the subject of discussion—for quite often a later copy or a printed edition will do just as well; and in the case of the Greek and Roman classics seldom are any but later copies available. (Gottschalk, UH, 53–54, emphasis his)

Gottschalk also asks the two all-important questions that must be investigated: [1] "Was the author of the document *able* to tell the truth; and if able, [2] was he *willing* to do so?" (Gottschalk, UH, 148, emphasis his)

3B. What Is Historical Reliability and Knowability?

Philosopher Mortimer J. Adler identifies the venue of historical knowledge in a discussion of knowledge and opinion.

On the one hand, we have self-evident truths that have certitude and incorrigibility; and we also have truths that are still subject to doubt but that are supported by evidence and reason to a degree that puts them beyond reasonable doubt or at least give them predominance over contrary views. All else is mere opinion—with no claim to being knowledge or having any hold on truth.

There is no question that the findings and conclusions of historical research are knowledge in this sense; no question that the findings and conclusions of the experimental or empirical sciences, both natural and social, are knowledge in this sense. (Adler, TPM, 100–101)

Craig further explains that

an item can be regarded as a piece of historical knowledge when it is related to the evidence in such a way that any reasonable person ought to accept it. This is the situation with all of our inductive knowledge: we accept what has sufficient evidence to render it probable. Similarly, in a court of law, the verdict is awarded to the case that is made most probable by the evidence. The jury is asked to decide if the accused is guilty—not beyond all doubt, which is impossible—but beyond all reasonable doubt. It is exactly the same in history: we should accept the hypothesis that provides the most probable explanation of the evidence. (Craig, RF, 184)

Historian C. Behan McCullagh similarly indicates what in history should be accepted as true, "Why should we hold them [historical descriptions] as true? The reply has been given already: they could be false, but those descriptions which are well supported by evidence are probably true. . . . That is why they should be believed." (McCullagh, TH, 57)

McCullagh further explains that, "If they had not been based upon a careful and fairly exhaustive study of relevant evidence, if they had not been based upon well-established particular and general beliefs about the world, and been arrived at by sound inductive arguments, then they would not deserve to be believed. But those conditions generally do yield reliable beliefs about the world, and the conclusions drawn in accordance with them are generally true." (McCullagh, TH, 57)

He continues, "Methods of historical inquiry are designed to maximize the chance of arriving at the truth. If they do not serve that function, they may as well be abandoned." (McCullagh, TH, 57)

2A. OBJECTIONS TO THE KNOWABILITY OF HISTORY

Most of the following objections to the objectivity, and hence knowability of history, are taken from Charles A. Beard's (1874–1948) essay, "That Noble Dream." His view of historical relativism has influenced many American historians in this century. Beard's critiques of the objectivist's view of history can be classified under six areas.

1B. History Is Not Directly Observable

"The historian is not an observer of the past that lies beyond his own time. He cannot see it *objectively* as the chemist sees his test tubes and compounds. The historian must 'see' the actuality of history through the medium of documentation. That is his sole recourse." (Beard, TND, as cited in Stern, VH, 323, emphasis his)

2B. The Fragmentary Nature of Historical Accounts

"The documentation (including monuments and other relics) with which the historian must work covers only a part of the events and personalities that make up the actuality of history. In other words multitudinous events and personalities escape the recording of documentation." (Beard, TND, as cited in Stern, VH, 323)

3B. The Selective Nature of Historical Methodology and the Interpretive Structuring of the Facts of History

"Not only is the documentation partial, in very few cases can the historian be reasonably sure that he has assembled all the documents of a given period, region, or segment. In most cases he makes a partial selection or a partial reading of the partial record of the multitudinous events and personalities involved in the actuality with which he is dealing." (Beard, TND, as cited in Stern, VH, 324)

"The idea that there was a complete and actual structurization of events in the past, to be discovered through a partial examination of the partial documentation, is pure hypothesis." (Beard, TND, as cited in Stern, VH, 324)

4B. The Historian Cannot Avoid Value Judgments

"The events and personalities of history in their very nature involve ethical and aesthetic considerations. They are not mere events in physics and chemistry inviting neutrality on the part of the 'observer.'" (Beard, TND, as cited in Stern, VH, 324)

5B. Every Historian Is a Product of His Time and Worldview

"The historian seeking to know the past, or about it, does not bring to the partial documentation with which he works a perfect and polished neutral mind. . . . Whatever acts of purification the historian may perform he yet remains human, a creature of time, place, circumstance, interests, predilections, culture." (Beard, TND, as cited in Stern, VH, 324)

6B. The Selection and Arrangement of Materials Is Subjective to the Historian

"Into the selection of topics, the choice and arrangement of materials, the specific historian's 'me' will enter." (Beard, TND, as cited in Stern, VH, 324)

Hence, Beard concludes, "The historian's powers are limited. He may search for, but he cannot find, the 'objective truth' of history, or write it, 'as it actually was.'" (Beard, TND, as cited in Stern, VH, 325)

3A. DEFENSE OF THE KNOWABILITY OF HISTORY

As Craig indicates: "If the historical apologetic for the Christian faith is to be success-ful, the objections of historical relativism need to be overcome. . . . Of course, the subjective elements cannot be eliminated. But the question is whether this subjective element need be so predominant that the study of history is vitiated." (Craig, RF, 169)

1B. Claim: History Is Not Directly Observable

Geisler explains what must be meant by objective: "If by 'objective' one means absolute knowledge, then of course no human historian can be objective. This we will grant. On the other hand, if 'objective' means a *fair but revisable* presentation that reasonable men should accept, then the door is still open to the possibility of objectivity." (Geisler, CA, 290, emphasis his)

In response to the relativist claim that the historian is disadvantaged in comparison to

> While the historian does not have direct access to the past, the residue of the past, things that have really existed, is directly accessible to him. . . . For example, archaeological data furnish direct access to the objects of the historian's investigation.
>
> —WILLIAM LANE CRAIG

the scientist, Craig makes two responses: "First, it is naive to think that the scientist always has direct access to his objects of study. Not only is the scientist largely dependent on the reports of others' research (which, interestingly, constitute for him historical documents) for his own work, but furthermore, the objects of the scientist's research are often only indirectly accessible, especially in the highly theoretical fields like physics." (Craig, RF, 176)

"Second, while the historian does not

have direct access to the past, the residue of the past, things that have really existed, is directly accessible to him. . . . For example, archaeological data furnish direct access to the objects of the historian's investigation." (Craig, RF, 176)

Hence, "the historian, no less than the scientist, has the tools for determining what really happened in the past. The lack of direct access to the original facts or events does not hinder the one more than the other." (Geisler, CA, 291)

2B. Claim: The Fragmentary Nature of Historical Accounts

Fischer indicates the mistaken notion of this argument: "Relativism mistakenly argues that because all historical accounts must be partial, in the sense of incomplete, that they must also be partial in the sense of false. An incomplete account *can* be an objectively true account; it cannot be the whole truth." (Fischer, HF, 42, emphasis his)

In reply:

> The fact that accounts of history are fragmentary does not destroy its objectivity. . . . History need be no less objective than geology simply because it depends on fragmentary accounts. Scientific knowledge is also partial and depends on assumptions and an overall framework which may prove to be inadequate upon the discovery of more facts.
>
> Whatever difficulty there may be, from a strictly scientific point of view, in filling in the gaps between the facts, once one has assumed a philosophical stance toward the world, the problem of objectivity in general is resolved. If there is a God, then the overall picture is already drawn; the facts of history will merely fill in the details of its meaning. (Geisler, CA, 292–93)

3B. Claim: The Selective Nature of Historical Methodology and the Interpretive Structuring of the Facts of History

This may be answered: "The fact that the historian must select his materials does not automatically make history purely subjective. Jurors make judgments 'beyond reasonable doubt' without having all the evidence. If the historian has the relevant and crucial evidence, it will be sufficient to attain objectivity. One need not know everything in order to know something." (Geisler, CA, 293)

Further, we must note the importance of a worldview in answer to these kinds of objections:

> There remains, however, the whole question as to whether the real context and connections of past events are known (or, are knowable). . . . There is really no way to know the original connections without assuming an overall hypothesis or world view by which the events are interpreted. Of course objectivity of bare facts and mere sequence of antecedent and consequent facts are knowable without assuming a world view. But objectivity of the *meaning* of these evens is not possible apart from a meaningful structure such as that provided by an overall hypothesis or world view. Hence, the problem of objective meaning of history, like the problem of objective meaning in science, is dependent on one's *Weltanschauung*. (Geisler, CA, 293–94, emphasis his)

In response, "The argument advanced by some objectivists that past events must be structured or else they are unknowable is faulty. All this argument proves is that it is necessary to understand facts through some structure, otherwise it makes no sense to speak of facts. The question of which structure is correct must be determined on some basis other than the mere facts themselves.

. . . Objective meaning apart from a world view is impossible." (Geisler, CA, 295)

Which worldview, one might ask, is correct Geisler responds, "Granted that there is justification for adopting a theistic world view [see II. above], the objective meaning of history becomes possible. For within the theistic context each fact of history becomes a theistic fact. . . . Within the linear view of events causal concoctions emerge as a result of their context in a theistic universe. Theism provides the sketch on which history paints the complete picture. . . . In this context, objectivity means systematic consistency." (Geisler, CA, 295)

4B. Claim: The Historian Cannot Avoid Value Judgments

It should be noted that:

This by no means makes historical objectivity impossible. Objectivity means to be fair in dealing with the facts. It means to present *what* happened as correctly as possible. Further, objectivity means that when one interprets *why* these events occurred, the language of the historian should ascribe to these events the value which they really had in their original context. . . . Once the world view has been determined, a value judgments are not undesirable or merely subjective; they are in fact essential and objectively demanded. (Geisler, CA, 295–96, emphasis his)

5B. Claim: Every Historian Is a Product of His Time and Worldview

While it is true that every historian is a product of his time, "it does not follow that because the *historian* is a product of his time that his *history* is also a product of the time. . . . The criticism confuses the *content* of knowledge and the *process* of attaining it. It

confuses the *formation* of a view with its *verification*. Where one derives a hypothesis is not essentially related to how he can establish its truth." (Geisler, CA, 296–97, emphasis his)

There can also be "confusion between the way knowledge is acquired and the validity of

> [There is a] confusion between the way knowledge is acquired and the validity of that knowledge. An American historian may chauvinistically assert that the United States declared its independence from England in 1776. That statement is true, *no matter what the motives of its maker may have been.*
>
> —DAVID HACKETT FISCHER

that knowledge. An American historian may chauvinistically assert that the United States declared its independence from England in 1776. That statement is true, *no matter what the motives of its maker may have been.* On the other hand, an English historian may patriotically insist that England declared its independence from the Unites States in 1776. That assertion is false, and always will be." (Fischer, HF, 42, emphasis his)

Further, we note the self-refuting nature of the relativist's argument: "If relativity is unavoidable the position of the historical relativists is self-refuting. For either their view is historically conditioned and, therefore, unobjective or else it is not relative but objective. If the latter, then it thereby admits that it is possible to be objective in viewing history. On the contrary, if the position of historical relativism is itself relative, then it cannot be taken as objectively true." (Geisler, CA, 297)

As already hinted at, the relativist must be granted the point if he insists upon the historian working with a worldview. "Without a world view it makes no sense to talk about objective meaning. Meaning is system-dependent." (Geisler, CA, 296)

But if a theistic universe is granted, as the evidence clearly demonstrates, then objectivity is possible. Geisler argues: "Once one can determine what the facts are and can assign them a meaning in the overall context of the theistic universe by showing that they fit most consistently with a given interpretation, then he may lay claim to having arrived at the objective truth about history. For example, granted that this is a theistic universe and that the corpse of Jesus of Nazareth returned from the grave, then the Christian can argue that this unusual event is a miracle that confirms the associated truth claims of Christ." (Geisler, CA, 296)

6B. Claim: The Selection and Arrangement of Materials is Subjective to the Historian

Concerning the possibility of prejudice, bias, or passion obscuring the objectivity of history, philosopher of history W. H. Walsh has noted: "It is doubtful, all the same, whether we should regard bias of this kind as serious obstacle to the attainment of objective truth in history. It is doubtful for the simple reason that we all know from our own experience that this kind of bias can be corrected or at any rate allowed for. . . . And we do hold that historians ought to be free from personal prejudice and condemn those historians who are not." (Walsh, IPH, 101)

Even Van A. Harvey notes that "it can be questioned, however, whether passion and objectivity are mutually exclusive, if by objectivity one means the capacity to withhold judgment until one has good reason for making it. Might not a judge who is also the father of a son accused of a crime be even more objective in his search for the truth than one who was less interested?" (Harvey, HB, 212)

Harvey further notes that it is wrong to "generally distrust the work of Christian Biblical scholars because *their* deepest convictions are obviously at stake in the inquiry." (Harvey, HB, 213, emphasis his) However, he points out that this should not automatically be one's assumption because it "ignores the distinction between an explanation and the justification of an explanation, between getting in the position to know something and defending what we have come to know, . . . The judge who is also a father may have quite personal and, to that extent, subjective reasons for wanting to find his son innocent, in contrast to his merely being thought to be innocent. But the validity of the reasons he advances for his conclusion, however painful, are logically independent of his desires." (Harvey, HB, 213)

Finally, the notion of total subjectivism or relativism, as indicated by Fischer, is self-refuting. "Relativists all argued that they and their friends were exempt from relativism in some degree." (Fischer, HF, 42) Fischer notes Cushing Strout as observing, "a consistent relativism is a form of intellectual suicide." (Strout, PRAH, as cited in Fischer, HF, 42) Fischer further regards the "idea of subjectivity which the relativists used was literal nonsense. 'Subjective' is a correlative term which cannot be meaningful unless its opposite is also meaningful. To say that all knowledge is subjective is like saying that all things are short. Nothing can be short, unless something is tall." (Fischer, HF, 43)

4A. OBJECTIONS TO THE KNOWABILITY OF MIRACULOUS HISTORY

Even for one who accepts the philosophical possibility of miracles and [that] a theistic worldview provides an essential framework for understanding that historical events can be known objectively, there still remains a question to be answered: Can we actually know the miraculous is a historical way? Can we be assured of the occurrence of miracles through the historical accounts of eyewitnesses?

1B. Philosophical Objections

David Hume presents a historical-criteria argument against miracles by identifying problems with any alleged proof of a miracle from history.

1C. "There is not to be found, in all history, any miracle attested by a sufficient number of men, of such unquestioned good-sense, education, and learning, as to secure us against all delusion in themselves . . . and at the same time, attesting facts performed in such a public manner and in so celebrated a part of the world, as to render the detection unavoidable." (Hume, ECHU, 10.2.92, pp. 116–17)

2C. "The many instances of forged miracles, and prophecies, and supernatural events, which, in all ages have either been detected by contrary evidence, or detect themselves by their absurdity, prove sufficiently the strong propensity of mankind to the extraordinary and the marvellous, and ought reasonably to beget a suspicion against all relations of this kind." (Hume, ECHU, 10.2.93, p. 118)

3C. "It forms a strong presumption against all supernatural and miraculous relations, that they are observed chiefly to abound among ignorant and barbarous nations; or if a civilized people has ever given admission to any of them, that people will be found to have received them from ignorant and barbarous ancestors." (Hume, ECHU, 10.2.93, p. 119)

4C. Other contemporary historiographers have followed Hume in a similar vein.

German theologian and historiographer Ernst Troeltsch argues, "On the analogy of the events known to us we seek by conjecture and sympathetic understanding to explain and reconstruct the past, . . . since we discern the same process of phenomena in operation in the past as in the present, and see, there as here, the various historical

> The critical historian, confronted with some story of a miracle, will usually dismiss it out of hand. . . . To justify his procedure, he will have to appeal to precisely the principle which Hume advanced: the "absolute impossibility of miraculous nature" or the events attested must, "in the eyes of all reasonable people . . . alone be regarded as a sufficient refutation."
>
> —ANTHONY FLEW

cycles of human life influencing and intersecting one another." (Troeltsch, H, as cited in Hastings, ERE, 6:718)

Carl Becker goes so far as to assert that "no amount of testimony is ever permitted to establish as past reality a thing that cannot be found in present reality. . . . [Even if] the witness may have a perfect character—all that goes for nothing." (Becker, DWH, as cited in Snyder, DWH, 12–13)

F. H. Bradley says, "We have seen that history rests in the last resort upon an inference from our experience, a judgment based upon our own present state of things; . . . when we are asked to affirm the existence in past time of events, the effects of cause which confessedly are without analogy in the world in which we live, and which we know—we are at a loss for any answer but this, that . . . we are asked to build a house without a foundation. . . . And how can we attempt this without contradicting ourselves?" (Bradley, PCH, 100)

Contemporary philosopher Antony Flew follows Hume and Troeltsch by asserting, "It is only and precisely by presuming that the laws that hold today held in the past . . . that we can rationally interpret the detritus of the past as evidence and from it construct our account of what actually happened." (Flew, M, as cited in Edwards, EP, 5:351)

"The critical historian, confronted with some story of a miracle, will usually dismiss it out of hand. . . . To justify his procedure, he will have to appeal to precisely the principle which Hume advanced: the 'absolute impossibility of miraculous nature' or the events attested must, 'in the eyes of all reasonable people . . . alone be regarded as a sufficient refutation.'" (Flew, M, as cited in Edwards, EP, 351–52)

2B. Theological Objections

Some have offered objections to the historical knowability of miracles from a theological perspective. Such objections conceivably started with Gothold Lessing: "*Accidental truths of history can never become the proof of necessary truths of reason.*" (Lessing, LTW, 53, emphasis his)

"The problem is . . . that reports of miracles are not miracles. These, . . . the miracles that occur before my eyes, are immediate in their effect. But those—the reports . . . have to work through a medium which takes away all their force." (Lessing, LTW, 52)

"I do not for one moment," explains Lessing, "deny that Christ did miracles. But since the truth of these miracles has completely ceased to be demonstrable by miracles still happening now, since they are no more than reports of miracles (even though they be narratives which have not been, and cannot be, impugned), I deny that they can and should bind me to the very least faith in the

other teachings of Christ." (Lessing, LTW, 55)

Kierkegaard similarly diminished the role of history when it came to faith: "If Christianity is viewed as a historical document, the important thing is to obtain a completely reliable report of what the Christian doctrine really is. If the inquiring subject were infinitely interested in his relation to this truth, he would here despair at once, because nothing is easier to perceive than this, that with regard to the historical the greatest certainty is only an *approximation,* and an approximation is too little to build his happiness on and is so unlike an eternal happiness that no result can ensure." (Kierkegaard, CUPPF, 23)

"Even if the contemporary generation had not left anything behind except these words, 'We have believed that in such and such a year the god appeared in the humble form of a servant, lived and taught among us, and then died'—this is more than enough." (Kierkegaard, PF, 104)

Martin Kahler follows, "For historical facts which first have to be established by science cannot *as such* become experiences of faith. Therefore, Christian faith and a history of Jesus repel each other like oil and water." (Kahler, SHJHBC, 74, emphasis his)

Modern theologians, of both liberal and neo-orthodox persuasion, have echoed these sentiments.

Rudolf Bultmann: "This closedness means that the continuum of historical happenings cannot be rent by the interference of supernatural, transcendent powers and that therefore there is no 'miracle' in this sense of the word. Such a miracle would be an event whose cause did not lie within history. . . . It is in accordance with such a method as this that the science of history goes to work on all historical documents. And there cannot be any exceptions in the case of biblical tests if the latter are at all to be understood historically." (Bultmann, EF, 292)

Paul Tillich believes that it is "a disastrous distortion of the meaning of faith to identify it with the belief in the historical validity of the Biblical stories." (Tillich, DF, 87)

Karl Barth finally asserts: "The resurrection of Christ, or his second coming . . . is not a historical event; the historians may reassure themselves . . . that our concern *here* is with the event which, though it is the only real happening *in* is not a real happening *of* history." (Barth, WGWM, 90, emphasis his)

The influence of Troeltsch's principle of analogy (mentioned above under Philosophical Objections) has also had a great and lasting impact on contemporary theologians and critical-historians. Van A. Harvey, a historian and follower of Troeltsch's historical-critical method, explains the influence:

> I have attempted to show that there was much truth in Ernst Troeltsch's prophetic claim that the emergence of the historical-critical method presupposes a revolution in the consciousness of Western man so profound that it necessarily requires a reappraisal of many of the basic assumptions of Christian belief. . . . I have suggested that this conflict is so profound that much of recent Protestant theology may be regarded as a series of salvage operations, that is, attempts to reconcile the ethic of critical historical inquiry with the apparent demands of Christian faith. (Harvey, HB, 246)

C. Stephen Evans in his book, *The Historical Christ & The Jesus of Faith* (published in 1996), notes how common this contemporary influence is:

> I should also like to note that although Van Harvey's book (1966) may seem somewhat dated, the methodology he defends is still embedded in the practices of a great many

biblical scholars. I do find it remarkable that there are not more recent explicit defenses of this position. . . . The fact that there are so few explicit defences of the Troeltsch-Harvey type of position is not really evidence that the view has been abandoned. Rather, it seems to me that this is due to the fact that the view is so widely held as to appear to its proponents as simply being "common sense" that needs no defense. (Evans, HCJF, 185)

5A. DEFENSE OF THE KNOWABILITY OF MIRACULOUS HISTORY

1B. Critique of Philosophical Objections

Philosopher Frank Beckwith, in his critical analysis of Hume's arguments, responds to Hume's first point: "In many respects this is certainly not an entirely unreasonable criterion put forth by Hume. One would expect when examining any alleged eyewitness tes-

> Few doubt that fact that some allegedly miraculous events are the product of human imagination and the desire to believe the wonderful, but one cannot deduce from this that *all* alleged miracles did not take place. For to do so would be to commit the *fallacy of false analogy.*
>
> —FRANK BECKWITH

timony that the eyewitnesses be of sufficient number and character. However, Hume's criterion demands much more than this." (Beckwith, DHAAM, 49)

Beckwith continues by citing Colin Brown in saying, "the qualifications he demands of such witnesses are such as would preclude the testimony of anyone without a Western university education, who lived outside a major cultural center in Western Europe prior to the sixteenth century, and who was not a public figure." (Brown, MCM as cited in Beckwith, DHAAM, 50)

As Beckwith notes, even this criterion will not work, for "if one succeeds in educating a liar, one only succeeds in making him a better liar." (Beckwith, DHAAM, 50)

"Furthermore," as Beckwith explains, "some of the latest scholarship lends support to the contention that the crowning miracle of Christian theism, the Resurrection of Jesus, seems to fulfill Hume's first criterion." (Beckwith, DHAAM, 50) (See V.B.3. Resurrection from the Dead)

Beckwith indicates the fallacy of Hume's second point, "Few doubt that fact that some allegedly miraculous events are the product of human imagination and the desire to believe the wonderful, but one cannot deduce from this that all alleged miracles did not take place. For to do so would be to commit the *fallacy of false analogy* [an argument that makes an erroneous conclusion]." (Beckwith, DHAAM, 51)

Further, as Beckwith notes, this also just begs the question for naturalism: "After all, you cannot assume that all miracle-claims are involved in exaggeration unless you already know that miracles never occur." (Beckwith, DHAAM, 52)

Philosopher Colin Brown responds, "It is absurd to demand of a witness that he should share the same world view as oneself or have the same level of education and culture." (Brown, MCM, 98) Brown concludes that "the validity of the testimony to a claim *that* something happened depends rather upon the honesty, capacity not to be deceived, and proximity of the witnesses to the alleged event." (Brown, MCM, 98, emphasis his)

Beckwith notes three problems with Hume's third criterion: "(1) Hume does not adequately define what he means by an uneducated and ignorant people; (2) this criterion does not apply to the miracles of Christian theism; and (3) Hume commits the informal fallacy of *argumentum ad hominem* [attacks the person instead of their argument]." (Beckwith, DHAAM, 53)

Geisler responds to Troeltsch's principle of analogy by explaining that it "turns out to be similar to Hume's objection to miracles built on the uniformity of nature." (Geisler, CA, 302)

In response, Geisler first notes: "It begs the question in favor of a naturalistic interpretation of *all* historical events. It is a methodological exclusion of the possibility of accepting the miraculous in history. The testimony for regularity in *general* is in no way testimony against an unusual event in *particular*." (Geisler, CA, 302)

Secondly, "Troeltsch's analogy type argument . . . proves too much. As Richard Whately convincingly argued, on this uniformitarian assumption not only miracles would be excluded but so would many unusual events of the past including those surrounding Napoleon Bonaparte." (Geisler, CA, 302–03)

"It is clearly a mistake to import uniformitarian methods from scientific experimentation into historical research. Repeatability and generality are needed to establish a scientific law or general patterns. . . . But this method does not work at all in history. What is needed to establish historical events is credible testimony that these particular events did indeed occur." (Geisler, CA, 303)

Beckwith similarly responds to the Flew and Troeltsch argument by pointing out that "this argument confuses analogy as a *basis* for studying the past with the *object* of the past that is studied. That is to say, we assume constancy and continuity when studying the past, but it does not follow that what we discover about the past (that is, the object of our inquiry) cannot be a unique singularity." (Beckwith, HM, as cited in Geivett, IDM, 97, emphasis his)

2B. Critique of Theological Objections

Geisler argues to the contrary of this position by stating, "In accordance with the objectivity of history just discussed, there is no good reason why the Christian should yield to the radical existential theologians on the question of the objectivity and historical dimensions of miracles. Miracles may not be *of* the natural historical process but they do

> It is absurd to demand of a witness that he should share the same world view as oneself or have the same level of education and culture. . . . But the validity of the testimony to a claim that something happened depends rather upon the honesty, capacity not to be deceived, and proximity of the witnesses to the alleged event.
>
> —COLLIN BROWN

occur *in* it." (Geisler, CA, 300, emphasis his) He continues,

A miracle can be identified within an empirical or historical context both directly and indirectly, both objectively and subjectively. A miracle possesses several characteristics. It is an event that is both scientifically unusual and theologically and morally relevant. The first characteristic is knowable in a directly empirical way the latter are knowable only indirectly through the empirical in that it is "odd" and "evocative" of something "more" than the mere imperial data of the event. . . . The theological and moral characteristics of a miracle are not empirically objective. In this sense they are experienced subjectively. This does not mean, however, that there is no objective basis for the moral dimensions of a

miracle. If this is a theistic universe, then morality is objectively grounded in God. (Geisler, CA, 301)

Professor Erickson notes that

the theories we are considering do not fit the biblical picture of the relationship between faith and reason, including historical considerations. We could offer several examples. One is the response when the disciples of John the Baptist asked Jesus whether he was the one they had been looking for, or whether they should be looking for someone else (Luke 7:18-23). Jesus called attention to what he was doing: Healing the blind, the lame, lepers, and the deaf; raising the dead; and preaching the good news to the poor (v. 22). There certainly was no separation here of the facts of history from faith. A second example is Paul's emphasis on the reality of Jesus' resurrection (1 Cor. 15). The validity of the Christian experience and message rests upon the genuineness of Christ's resurrection (vv. 12–19). A third consideration is Luke's obvious concern to attain correct information for his writing (Luke 1:1–4; Acts 1:1–5). While our first example might be affected by critical study of the passage, the second and especially the third confirm that the split between faith and historical reason is not a part of the biblical picture. (Erickson, WBF, 131)

Erickson observes the historical assumption and error of Bultmann:

Bultmann in particular has correctly observed that the New Testament believers were committed followers of Jesus, but has then drawn the conclusion that this made them less accurate observers and reporters of what happened. The assumption is that their positive bias toward Jesus and his cause made them less careful in reporting what they observed and in preserving it; they even exaggerated somewhat in the interest of promoting belief in him. Such arguments are usually made with the assistance of an analogy involving courtroom testimonies. But a different analogy, drawn from a classroom setting, may be closer to the situation of the Gospel writers, who were, after all, disciples of the Teacher: In a classroom, who is likelier to catch every word the teacher says and to record correct and complete notes, the casual listener or the student strongly committed to the teacher's view? We would prefer the notes of the latter in virtually every case. They most carefully retain the wisdom of the teacher; because the person writing them down believes they will have value beyond the final examination. As believers in the special value of all that Jesus said, the disciples surely made extra efforts to preserve his teachings accurately. (Erickson, WBF, 131–32)

3B. Conclusion

I would like to conclude this section, as well as this book, with a word, not from my head, but from my heart. Much of the material you've read has been pretty heady stuff. And that's good. God gave us minds to use to evaluate the evidence of His revelation of Himself to us. In Isaiah 1:18, God invites us, "Come now, and let us reason together." (Isa. 1:18). Jesus indicated the importance of reason when He commanded, "You shall love the Lord your God with all your heart, with all your soul, and with all your mind" (Matt. 22:37).

But much more often in the Bible, God speaks on a heart-to-heart level. Again and again He speaks of the importance of humility of the heart. He warns of the danger of developing a hardened heart. Though the Scriptures speak often about the mind, there are approximately five times the number of references to the heart as there are to the mind. God also wants to speak to us on a heart-to-heart level, not just on an intellectual level.

And that's my attitude as I close this book. If you or someone you know is struggling with the issue of giving your life to Christ, I'm imagining myself sitting across the table from you talking heart-to-heart. Perhaps you're struggling with some of the issues mentioned in this chapter. You may be saying, "I've never seen a miracle; how can I put my faith in a message that speaks of the miraculous?"

As we saw earlier in this chapter, David Hume and many other philosophers and educators throughout history have adopted the position that miracles are impossible partially on the basis that it is much more probable that miracles don't occur than that they do occur. But though it may be more probable that miracles do not occur, it is foolish to rule out the possibility of the miraculous simply because of probability. And as we saw in the section on prophecy fulfilled in Jesus, the probability of any one person in history fulfilling all of those nearly three hundred prophecies was literally next to impossible. And yet, the historical records tell us that against all odds, Jesus came and did just that.

I believe the only way to get to the truth is to throw out all preconceived ideas. What if there really is a God, looking down on this earth, observing the pride in the hearts of those in high positions, the ego focus of those climbing the ladder, and the general selfishness of man? What if this God chose in His mind to reveal Himself to certain people? What if He decided that He would reveal Himself, not to the haughty, or the proud, or the arrogant; but to the humble, the downtrodden, and the poor in spirit?

In fact, this is exactly the case if the Bible is true (and we have already seen that the evidence for the reliability of the Bible is staggering). Though many people from all different philosophical and religious backgrounds like to talk about experiences they have had with "God," one of the truths revealed to the prophet Isaiah is that God really is not out to win any popularity contests. Though His desire, as stated by 2 Peter 3:9, is that He is passionately "not willing that any should perish but that all should come to repentance" (NKJV), at the same time, He's not out trying to reveal Himself to everyone who comes along. As Isaiah records, "Truly You are a God, who hide yourself, O God of Israel, the Savior!" (Isa. 45:15).

Isn't that odd? Can you imagine God in hiding? Why would He do that? The answer is: He's waiting. He's waiting for those times in the lives of all people when they will be humble enough in their hearts to hear His voice and respond by opening the door of their lives to allow a personal relationship with Him to begin. As Jesus said in Revelation 3:20, "Behold, I stand at the door and knock. If anyone hears My voice and opens the door, I will come in to him and dine with him, and he with Me."

Three times in the Bible it is explicitly stated (and many more times intimated) that God is opposed to the proud, but gives grace to the humble (Prov. 3:34; James 4:6; 1 Pet. 5:5). I believe God wants us to bring our questions to Him, but there comes a time when He says, "It's time to act on the answers I have given you. Don't wait any longer."

And if we respond to Him at that point, that's when we open ourselves up for the possibility of observing the miraculous. At the beginning of this book I told you about the changed life of my father, the town drunk, who came to Christ late in life and was so dramatically changed that many people came to know Christ in the remaining fourteen months of his life. After what I'd seen and been through, that was a miracle. Nothing but a truly existing God could make that kind of change in a person's life. And as I look at my own life, I would have to say that nothing except a supernatural God could make the kinds of changes I've seen Him make in my life.

If you have never made the decision of trusting Christ, I invite you now to turn to the last pages of this book and read *The Four Spiritual Laws*. It is a very simple explanation for those with a heart that seeks to know Christ. If your heart and mind has been moved towards God's love for you, then I invite you to act upon it.

God bless you in your search,

Josh D. McDowell

BIBLIOGRAPHY

Aalders, G. A. *A Short Introduction to the Penta-teuch.* Chicago: InterVarsity Christian Fellow-ship, n.d. (originally published in 1949).

Abel, E. L. "Psychology of Memory and Rumor Transmission and Their Bearing on Theories of Oral Transmission in Early Christianity," *Journal of Religion.* Vol. 51. October 1971.

Achtemier, Paul J. *Harper's Bible Dictionary.* San Francisco: Harper and Row, Publishers, Inc., 1985.

Adler, Mortimer J. *Aristotle for Everybody: Diffi-cult Thought Made Easy.* New York: Macmillan, 1978.

Adler, Mortimer J. *Six Great Ideas.* New York: Macmillan, 1981.

Adler, Mortimer J. *Ten Philosophical Mistakes.* New York: Macmillan, 1985.

Adler, Mortimer J. *Truth in Religion.* New York: Macmillan, 1990.

Aland, Kurt and Barbara Aland. *The Text of the New Testament.* Trans. by Erroll F. Rhodes.

Grand Rapids: William B. Eerdmans Publish-ing Co., 1987.

Aland, Kurt and Barbara Aland, ed. *Kurzgefasste Liste der grieschen Handschriften des Neuen Tes-taments.* Arbeiten Zurneutestamentlichen Textforschung, Band. 1. Hawthorne, N.Y.: Wal-ter de Gruyter, 1994.

Albright, W. F. *The American Scholar,* n.p., 1941.

Albright, W. F. "Archaeology Confronts Biblical Criticism," *The American Scholar.* April 1938.

Albright, W. F. "Archaeological Discoveries and the Scriptures," *Christianity Today* 12. June 21, 1968.

Albright, W. F. *Archaeology, Historical Analogy and Early Biblical Tradition.* Baton Rouge: Louisiana State University Press, 1966.

Albright, W. F. *The Archaeology of Palestine,* rev. Baltimore: Penguin Books, 1960.

Albright, W. F. *The Archaeology of Palestine and the Bible.* New York: Revell, 1933.

Albright, W. F. *Archaeology and the Religion of*

Israel. Baltimore: John Hopkins Press, 1942.

Albright, W. F. "The Bible after Twenty Years of Archaeology," *Religion in Life.* 1952.

Albright, W. F. *The Biblical Period from Abraham to Ezra.* New York: Harper & Row, 1963.

Albright, W. F. "A Brief History of Judah from the Days of Josiah to Alexander the Great," *Biblical Archaeologist.* Vol. 9. February 1946.

Albright, W. F. *From the Stone Age to Christianity.* Baltimore: John Hopkins Press, 1940.

Albright, W. F. *History, Archaeology, and Christian Humanism.* New York: McGraw-Hill Book Company, 1964.

Albright, William F. "Historical and Mythical Elements in the Story of Joseph," *Journal of Biblical Literature.* Vol. 37. 1918.

Albright, W. F. "The Israelite Conquest of Canaan in the Light of Archaeology," *Bulletin of the American Schools of Oriental Research.* Vol. 74. 1939.

Albright, William F. "King Jehoiachin in Exile," *Biblical Archaeologist* 5, no. 4. December 1942.

Albright, W. F. *New Horizons in Biblical Research.* New York: Oxford University Press, 1966.

Albright, W. F. "New Light on the Early History of Phoenician Colonization," *Bulletin of the American Schools of Oriental Research.* Vol. 83. October 1941.

Albright, W. F. "The Oldest Hebrew Letters: Lachish Ostraca," *Bulletin of the American Schools of Oriental Research.* No. 70. April 1938.

Albright, W. F. "The Old Testament and Archaeology." In *Old Testament Commentary.* Philadelphia: n.p., 1948. Quoted in Merrill R. Unger, *Archaeology and the Old Testament.* Grand Rapids: Zondervan Publishing Co., 1954.

Albright, W. F. "Old Testament and the Archaeology of the Ancient East." In *Old Testament and Modern Study: A Generation of Discovery and Research,* ed. by H. H. Rowley. Oxford: Oxford University, 1956.

Albright, W. F. *Recent Discoveries in Bible Lands.* New York: Funk and Wagnalls, 1955.

Albright, W. F. "Recent Progress in North-Canaanite Research," *Bulletin of the American Schools of Oriental Research.* No. 70, April 1938.

Albright, William F. "Retrospect and Prospect in New Testament Archaeology," *The Teacher's Yoke.* Ed. by E. J. Vardaman and James Leo Garrett. Waco, Tex: Baylor University Press, 1964.

Albright, William F. "The Oldest Hebrew Letters: Lachish Ostraca," *Bulletin of the American Schools of Oriental Research.* No. 70. April 1938.

Alford, Henry. *The Greek Testament: With a Critically Revised Text: A Digest of Various Readings: Marginal References to Verbal and Idiomatic Usage: Prolegomena: And a Critical and Exegetical Commentary.* Vol. I. Sixth edition. Cambridge: Deighton, Bell, and Co., 1868.

Allis, Oswald T. *The Five Books of Moses,* rev. Philadelphia: The Presbyterian and Reformed Publishing Co., 1969.

Allis, Oswald T. *The Old Testament, Its Claims and Its Critics.* Nutley, N.J.: The Presbyterian and Reformed Publishing Company, 1972.

Allnutt, Frank. *Contact* 30:5. May 1972.

Allport, Gordon. "The Roots of Religion," *Pastoral Psychology* V, no. 43. April 1954.

Alston, William P. *A Realist Conception of Truth.* Ithaca, N.Y.: Cornell University, 1996.

Anderson, Bernhard W. "Changing Emphasis in Biblical Scholarship," *Journal of Bible and Religion* 23. April 1955.

Anderson, G. W. *A Critical Introduction to the Old Testament.* London: Gerald Duckworth and Co., Ltd., 1959.

Anderson, J. *The Bible, the Word of God.* Brighton: n.p., 1905.

Anderson, J. N. D. *Christianity: The Witness of History.* London: Tyndale Press, 1969. Reprint, Downers Grove, Ill.: InterVarsity Press, 1970.

Anderson, J. N. D. "The Resurrection of Jesus Christ." *Christianity Today,* March 29, 1968.

Anderson, J. N. D., Wolfhart Pannenberg and Clark Pinnock. "A Dialogue on Christ's Resurrection," *Christianity Today,* 12. April 1968.

Anderson, Norman. *Christianity and World Religions.* rev. ed of *Christianity and Comparative Religion.* Downers Grove, Ill.: InterVarsity, 1984.

Anderson, Norman. *Jesus Christ: The Witness of History.* 2nd ed. Downers Grove, Ill.: InterVarsity Press, 1985.

Anderson, Robert. *The Lord from Heaven.* London: James Nisbet and Co., 1910.

Anderson, Walter Truett (ed.). *The Truth About Truth: De-confusing and Re-constructing the Postmodern World.* New York: G. P. Putnam's Sons, 1995.

Andrus, Hyrum L. *God, Man, and the Universe.* Boston: Beacon, 1947. Quoted in Norman L. Geisler and William D. Watkins, *Worlds Apart.* Grand Rapids: Baker Book House, 1984.

Angus, Joseph. *The Bible Handbook.*

Ankerberg, John, and John Weldon. *Ready with an Answer.* Eugene, Ore: Harvest House Publishers, 1997.

Anselm. *Monologium.* In *St. Anselm: Basic Writing,.* 2d ed. Trans. by S. N. Deane. La Salle, Ill.: Open Court, 1962.

Aquinas, St. Thomas. *Commentary on the Metaphysics of Aristotle.* Trans. by John P. Rowan. Chicago: Henry Regnery, 1961.

Aquinas, St. Thomas. *Contra Gentiles.*

Aquinas, St. Thomas. *Metaphysics.*

Aquinas, St. Thomas. *On Truth.*

Aquinas, St. Thomas. *Peri Hermeneias.*

Aquinas, St. Thomas. *Physics.*

Aquinas, St. Thomas. *Posterior Analytics.*

Aquinas, St. Thomas. *Summa Contra Gentiles.* Book Three: Providence Part II. Trans. with an intro. and notes by Vernon J. Bourke. Notre Dame, Ind.: University of Notre Dame Press, 1975.

Aquinas, St. Thomas. *Summa Contra Gentiles.* 5 volumes. Trans. by Anton C. Pegis. Notre Dame, Ind.: University of Notre Dame, 1975.

Aquinas, St. Thomas. *Summa Contra Gentiles.* In *On the Truth of the Catholic Faith: Book One: God.* Trans. by Anton C. Pegis. New York: Image Books, 1955.

Aquinas, St. Thomas. *Summa Theologica*, vol. 1. Trans. by the Fathers of the English Dominican Province. Allen, Tex: Christian Classics, 1981.

Aquinas, St. Thomas. *Summa Theologica.* In *Great Books of the Western World,* ed. Robert Maynard Hutchins. Chicago: William Benton, 1952.

Archer, Gleason L., Jr. *A Survey of Old Testament Introduction.* Chicago: Moody Press, 1964, 1974.

Archer, Gleason L., Jr. *Encyclopedia of Bible Difficulties.* Grand Rapids: Zondervan, 1982.

Aristides. *The Apology of Aristides.* Translated and ed. by Rendel Harris. London: Cambridge University Press, 1893.

Aristotle. *Analytica Posterioria,* In *The Student's Oxford Aristotle,* ed. by W. D. Ross. London: Oxford, 1942.

Aristotle. *Categories.* In *The Complete Works of Aristotle.* Ed. by Jonathan Barnes. 2 volumes. Princeton, N.J.: Princeton University, 1984.

Aristotle. *Metaphysics.* In *The Complete Works of Aristotle,* rev. Oxford translation. Ed. by Jonathan Barnes. Vol. 2. Princeton, N.J.: Princeton University Press, 1984.

Aristotle. *Metaphysics.* In *Great Books of the Western World.* Ed. by Robert Maynard Hutchins. Chicago: William Benton, 1952.

Armstrong, D. M. *A World of States of Affairs.* Cambridge: Cambridge University, 1997.

Arndt, William F. and F. Wilbur Gingrich. *A Greek-English Lexicon of the New Testament and Other Early Christian Literature.* Chicago: The University of Chicago Press, 1952.

Arrian. *History of Alexander and Indica.* Trans. by Iliff Robson (with an English translation from the Loeb Classical Library, ed. by T. E. Page). 2 vols. Cambridge: Harvard University Press, 1954.

Athanasius. *Letters,* no. 39 (Easter 367). In *A Select Library of the Nicene and Post-Nicene Fathers of the Christian Church.* Ed. by Philip Schaff. Vol. 4. New York: The Christian Literature Company, 1888.

Audi, Robert. *Epistemology: a Contemporary Introduction to the Theory of Knowledge.* New York: Routledge, 1998.

Audi, Robert, ed. *The Cambridge Dictionary of Philosophy.* Cambridge: Cambridge University Press, 1995.

Augustine, St. *City of God.* Trans. by Gerald G. Walsh, S.J., Demetrius B. Zema, S.J., Grace Monahan, O.S.U., and Daniel J. Honan, with a condensation of the original foreword by Etienne Gilson and an introduction by Vernon J. Bourke. New York: Doubleday, 1958.

Augustine, St. *The Confessions, The City of God, On Christian Doctrine.* Trans. by Marcus Dods.

Chicago: The University of Chicago, William Benton, Encyclopaedia Britannica, Inc. 1952, 1984.

Augustine, St. *Of True Religion.* Library of Christian Classics, Ichthus, ed. Philadelphia: Westminster, 1953.

Augustine, St. *Reply to Faustus the Manichaean* 11.5. In *A Select Library of the Nicence and Ante-Nicene Fathers of the Christian Church.* Ed. by Philip Schaff. Vol. 4. Grand Rapids: Eerdmans, 1956.

Avicenna. *Avicenna on Theology.* Ed. by Arthur J. Arberry. Westport, Conn: Hyperion Press, 1979.

Avicenna. *Metaphysics.* In *Philosophical Writings,* John Duns Scotus. Trans. by Allan Wolter. Indianapolis: Bobbs-Merrill, 1962.

Ayer, A. J. *Language, Truth and Logic.* New York: Dover, n.d.

Babcock, F. J. "Form Criticism," *The Expository Times.* Vol. 53. October 1941.

Badger, George Percy. *The Nestorians and Their Rituals.* London: n.d., 1852.

Bahnsen, Greg L. "The Inerrancy of the Autographs," *Inerrancy.* Ed. by Norman L. Geisler. Grand Rapids: Zondervan, 1980.

Baker, Glenn W., William L. Lane, J. Ramsey Michaels. *The New Testament Speaks.* New York: Harper & Row Publishers, 1969.

Ballard, Frank. *The Miracles of Unbelief.* Edinburgh: T & T Clark, 1908.

Bandas, Rudolph G. *Contemporary Philosophy and Thomistic Principles.* New York: Bruce Publishing, 1932.

Banks, Edgar J. *The Bible and the Spade.* New York: Association Press, 1913.

Barker, Glenn W., William L. Lane, J. Ramsey Michaels. *The New Testament Speaks.* New York: Harper & Row Publishers, 1969.

Barnes, W. E. *Gospel Criticism and Form Criticism.* Edinburgh: T. & T. Clark, 1936.

Barnes, William. "Wycliffe Bible Translators," *The Oxford Companion to the Bible.* Ed. by Bruce Metzger and Michael Coogan. New York: Oxford University Press, 1993.

Barnhouse, Donald Grey. *Man's Ruin.* Vol. 1, *Expositions of Bible Doctrines.* Grand Rapids:: Wm. B. Eerdmans, 1952.

Barr, Allan. "Bultmann's Estimate of Jesus," *Scottish Journal of Theology.* Vol. 7. December 1954.

Barr, James. *Fundamentalism.* Philadelphia: Westminster, 1977.

Barrett, C. K. "Myth and the New Testament," *Expository Times.* Vol. 68. September 1957.

Bartsch, Hans-Werner, ed. *Kerygma and Myth.* Trans. by Reginald H. Fuller. London: S P C K, 1962.

Barth, Karl. *The Word of God and the Word of Man.* Trans. by Douglas Horton. London: Hodder & Stoughton, 1928.

Barton, G. A. "Archaeology and the Bible." Philadelphia: American Sunday School Union, 1937.

Barton, George A. *The Religion of Israel.* New York: Macmillan Co., 1918.

Barzun, J. and H. Graff. *The Modern Researcher.* New York: Harcourt, Brace and World, Inc., 1957.

Battenfield, James Richard. *Historicity of Genesis Fourteen.* Unpublished Bachelor of Divinity thesis submitted to Talbot Theological Seminary.

Bauer, Walter, William F. Arndt and F. Wilbur Gingrich, eds. *A Greek-English Lexicon of the New Testament and other Early Christian Literature.* Chicago: The University of Chicago Press, 1957, 1979.

Beard, Charles A. "That Nobel Dream," *Varieties of History: From Voltaire to the Present.* Ed. by Frtiz Stern. New York: Vintage Books, 1973.

Beattie, F. R. *Apologetics.* Richmond: Presbyterian Committee of Publication, 1903.

Beattie, F. R. *Radical Criticism.* New York: Fleming H. Revell Co., 1894.

Beck, John Clark, Jr. *The Fall of Tyre According to Ezekiel's Prophecy.* Unpublished Master's thesis, Dallas Theological Seminary, 1971.

Beck, Lewis White, ed. *Kant's Theory of Knowledge.* Dordrecht, Holland: D. Reidel, 1974.

Becker, Carl. "Detachment and the Writing of History," *Detachment and the Writing of History.* Ed. by Phil L. Snyder. Westport, Conn.: Greenwood, 1972.

Beckwith, Francis J. *David Hume's Argument Against Miracles: A Critical Analysis.* Lanham, Md.: University Press of America, 1989.

Beckwith, Francis J. "History & Miracles," *In Defense of Miracles*. Ed. by R. Douglas Geivett and Gary R. Habermas. Downers Grove, Ill.: InterVarsity Press, 1997.

Beckwith, Roger. *The Old Testament Canon of the New Testament Church and Its Background in Early Judaism*. Grand Rapids: Eerdmans, 1986.

Beecher, Willis J. "The Prophecy of the Virgin Mother," *Classical Evangelical Essays in Old Testament Interpretation*. Ed. by Walter C. Kaiser, Jr. Grand Rapids: Baker Book House, 1972.

Beegle, Dewey M. *The Inspiration of Scripture*. Philadelphia: Westminster, 1963.

Beegle, Dewey M. *Scripture, Tradition, and Infallibility*. Grand Rapids: Eerdmans, 1973.

Begley, Sharon. "Science Finds God," *Newsweek*, July 20, 1998.

Benoit, Pierre. *Jesus and the Gospels*. Vol. I. Trans. by Benet Weatherhead. New York: Herder and Herder, 1973.

Bentzen, A. *Introduction to the Old Testament*. 2 Vols. Copenhagen: G.E.C. Gad, 1948.

Berkouwer, G. C. *Holy Scriptures*. Trans. and ed. by Jack Rogers. Grand Rapids: Eerdmans, 1975.

Bertocci, Peter Anthony. *Introduction to the Philosophy of Religion*. New York: Prentice-Hall, Inc., 1951.

Besant, Annie. "Why I Do Not Believe in God," *An Anthology of Atheism and Rationalism*. Ed. by Gordon Stein. Amherst: Prometheus Books, 1980.

Betz, Otto. *What Do We Know About Jesus?* SCM Press, 1968.

Bewer, Julius A., Lewis Bayles Paton and George Dahl. "The Problem of Deuteronomy: A Symposium," *Journal of Biblical Literature*. Vol. 47. 1929–30.

The Bible Version Debate. Minneapolis: Central Seminary Press, 1997.

Biram, Avaraham. "House of David," *Biblical Archaeology Review*. March/April 1994.

Blackburn, Simon. *The Oxford Dictionary of Philosophy*. New York: Oxford University Press, 1996.

Blackman, E. C. "Jesus Christ Yesterday: The Historical Basis of the Christian Faith," *Canadian Journal of Theology*. Vol. 7. April 1961.

Blaikie, William G. *A Manual of Bible History*. London: Thomas Nelson & Sons, 1904.

Blaiklock, Edward Musgrave. *The Acts of the Apostles*. Grand Rapids: William B. Eerdmans Publishing Co., 1959.

Blaiklock, Edward Musgrave. *Layman's Answer: An Examination of the New Theology*. London: Hodder and Stoughton, 1968.

Blinzler, Josef. *The Trial of Jesus*. Trans. by Isabel and Florence McHugh. Westminster, Md.: The Newman Press, 1959.

Bloesch, Donald G. *Essentials of Evangelical Theology: God, Authority, and Salvation*. San Francisco: Harper and Row, 1978.

Blomberg, Craig L. *The Historical Reliability of the Gospels*. Downers Grove, Ill.: InterVarsity Press, 1987.

Blomberg, Craig L. *Jesus and the Gospels*. Nashville: Broadman & Holman Publishers, 1997.

Blomberg, Craig. "Where Do We Start Studying Jesus?" In *Jesus Under Fire: Modern Scholarship Reinvents the Historical Jesus*, ed. Michael J. Wilkins and J. P. Moreland. Grand Rapids: Zondervan Publishing House, 1995.

Boa, Kenneth, and Larry Moody. *I'm Glad You Asked*. Wheaton, Ill.: Victor Books, 1982.

Bockmuehl, Markus. *This Jesus: Martyr, Lord, Messiah*. Edinburgh: T & T Clark Ltd., 1994.

Boer, Harry R. *Above the Battle? The Bible and Its Critics*. Grand Rapids: Eerdmans, 1975.

Boice, James Montgomery. *Does Inerrancy Matter?* ICBI Foundation Series, International Council of Biblical Inerrancy. Oakland, Calif., 1979.

Boice, James Montgomery. *The Christ of Christmas*. Chicago, Ill.: Moody Press, 1983.

Boring, M. Eugene, Klaus Berger, Carsten Colpe. *Hellenistic Commentary to the New Testament*. Nashville: Abingdon, 1995.

Bornkamm, Günther. *Tradition and Interpretation in Matthew*. Philadelphia: The Westminster Press, 1963.

Bowker, John. *The Targums and Rabbinic Literature*. London: Cambridge University Press, 1969.

Bowman, John Wick. "From Schweitzer to Bultmann," *Theology Today*. Vol. 11. July 1954.

Bowman, Raymond. "Old Testament Research Between the Great Wars." In *The Study of the Bible Today and Tomorrow,* ed. Harold H. Willoughby. Chicago: University of Chicago Press, 1947.

Box, Hubert S. *Miracles and Critics.* London: Faith Press, 1935.

Braaten, Carl E. and Roy A. Harrisville, eds. and trans. *The Historical Jesus and the Kerygmatic Christ.* Nashville: Abingdon Press, 1964.

Braaten, Carl E. and Roy A. Harrisville, ed. *Kerygma and History.* New York: Abingdon Press, 1962.

Bradlaugh, Charles. "A Plea for Atheism." In *An Anthology of Atheism and Rationalism,* ed. Gordon Stein. Amherst: Prometheus Books, 1980.

Bradley, F. H. *The Presuppositions of Critical History.* Chicago: Quadrangle Books, 1968.

Bray, Gerald. *Biblical Interpretation: Past and Present.* Downers Grove, Ill.: InterVarsity Press, 1996.

Briggs, C. A. *The Higher Criticism of the Hexateuch.* New York: Charles Scribner's Sons, 1897.

Bright, John. *A History of Israel.* Philadelphia: The Westminster Press, 1959.

Brightman, Edgar S. *The Sources of the Hexateuch.* New York: Abingdon Press, 1918.

Broad, C. D. "Hume's Theory of the Credibility of Miracles." *Proceedings from the Aristotelian Society* 17. 1916–17.

Broadus, John A. *Jesus of Nazareth.* Grand Rapids: Baker Book House, 1963.

Brotzman, Ellis R. *Old Testament Textual Criticism.* Grand Rapids: Baker Books, 1994.

Brown, Colin. *Miracles and the Critical Mind.* Grand Rapids: William B. Eerdmans, 1984.

Brown, Colin. *Miracles and the Critical Mind.* Grand Rapids: William B. Eerdmans , 1984. Quoted in Francis J. Beckwith, J. *David Hume's Argument Against Miracles: A Critical Analysis.* Lanham, Md.: University Press of America, 1989.

Brown, Colin. *Philosophy and the Christian Faith.* London: Tyndale Press, 1969.

Brown, Lewis, *This Believing World.* New York: Macmillan Company, 1961.

Brown, Raymond E. *The Gospel According to John,* vol. 1. London: Geoffrey Chapman, 1971.

Browning, Iain. *Petra.* Parkridge, N.J.: Noyes Press, 1973.

Bruce, A. B. *The Training of the Twelve.* Grand Rapids: Kregel Publications, 1971.

Bruce, Alexander Balmin. *The Expositor's Greek New Testament.* Vol. I—*The Synoptic Gospels.* London: Hodder and Stoughton, 1903.

Bruce, F. F. "Archaeological Confirmation of the New Testament." In *Revelation and the Bible,* ed. Carl Henry. Grand Rapids: Baker Book House, 1969.

Bruce, F. F. *The Books and the Parchments: How We Got Our English Bible.* Old Tappan, N.J.: Fleming H. Revell Co., 1950. Reprints: 1963, 1984.

Bruce, F. F. *The Canon of Scripture.* Downers Grove, Ill.: InterVarsity Press, 1988.

Bruce, F. F. "Criticism and Faith," *Christianity Today.* Vol. 5. November 21, 1960.

Bruce, F. F. *The Defense of the Gospel in the New Testament.* Rev. ed. Grand Rapids: Wm. B. Eerdmans, 1977.

Bruce, F. F. *The Epistle to the Hebrews,* rev. ed. In *The New International Commentary on the New Testament.* Ed. by Gordon D. Fee. Grand Rapids: William B. Eerdmans Publishing Cmpany, 1990.

Bruce, F. F. "Foreword." In *Scripture, Tradition, and Infallibility,* Dewey M. Beegle. Grand Rapids: Eerdmans, 1973.

Bruce, F. F. *Jesus: Lord and Savior.* Downers Grove, Ill.: InterVarsity Press, 1986.

Bruce, F. F. *Jesus and Christian Origins Outside the New Testament.* Grand Rapids: Zondervan Publishing House, 1970

Bruce, F. F., ed. *The New International Commentary on the New Testament.* Grand Rapids: William B. Eerdmans Publishing Co., 1971.

Bruce, F. F. *The New Testament Documents: Are They Reliable?* Downers Grove; Ill.: InterVarsity Press, 1964.

Bruce, F. F. *The Real Jesus: Who Is He?* In *The Jesus Library.* Ed. by Michael Green. London: Hodder & Stroughton, 1985.

Bruce, F. F. *Tradition Old and New.* Grand Rapids: Zondervan Publishing House, 1970.

Bultmann, Rudolf. *Existence and Faith.* Shorter writings of R. Bultmann. Trans. by Schubert

M. Ogden. New York: Meridian Books—The World Publishing Co., 1960.

Bultmann, Rudolf. *History and Eschatology.* Edinburgh: The Edinburgh University Press, 1957.

Bultmann, Rudolf. *The History of the Synoptic Tradtion.* Trans. by John Marsh. New York: Harper and Row, 1963.

Bultmann, Rudolf. *Jesus and the Word.* New York: Charles Scribner's Sons, 1934.

Bultmann, Rudolf. *Jesus Christ and Mythology.* New York: Charles Scribner's Sons, 1958.

Bultmann, Rudolf. *Kerygma and Myth: A Theological Debate,* Ed. by Hans Werner Bartsch. Trans. by Reginald H. Fuller. London: Billing and Sons, 1954.

Bultmann, Rudolf. "A New Approach to the Synoptic Problem," *Journal of Religion* 6. July 1926.

Bultmann, R. "The Study of the Synoptic Gospels," *Form Criticism.* Ed. by Frederick C. Grant. Chicago: Willett, Clark & Co., 1934.

Bultmann, Rudolf. *Theology of the New Testament.* Vol. 1. Trans. by Kendrick Grobel. New York: Charles Scribner's Sons, 1951.

Bultmann, Rudolf. *Theology of the New Testament.* Vol. 2. Trans. by Kendrick Grobel. New York: Charles Scribner's Sons, 1955.

Bultmann, Rudolf and Karl Kundsin. *Form Criticism.* Trans. by F. C. Grant. Willett, Clark, and Co., 1934. Reprint, Harper and Brothers-Torchbook Edition, 1962.

Burkitt, F. Crawford. *The Gospel History and Its Transmission.* Edinburgh: T. & T. Clark, 1925.

Burkitt, F. C. *Jesus Christ.* London and Glasgow: Blackie and Sons, Ltd., 1932.

Burrill, Donald R., ed. *The Cosmological Arguments: A Spectrum of Opinion.* Anchor Books edition. Garden City, N.Y.: Doubleday, 1967.

Burrows, Millar. "How Archaeology Helps the Student of the Bible," *Workers with Youth.* April 1948.

Burrows, Millar. *What Mean These Stones?* New York: Meridian Books, 1957.

Burtner, Robert W. and Robert E. Chiles. *A Compend of Wesley's Theology.* Nashville: Abingdon, 1954.

Bush, L. Russ. *Classical Readings in Christian Apologetics,* A.D. 100–1800. Grand Rapids: Zondervan, 1983.

Buswell, James Oliver. *A Systematic Theology of the Christian Religion,* 2 vols. Grand Rapids: Zondervan, 1962.

Butchvarov, Panayot. "Metaphysical Realism," *The Cambridge Dictionary of Philosophy.* Gen. ed., Robert Audi. Cambridge: Cambridge University Press, 1995.

Cadbury, Henry J. "Some Foibles of N. T. Scholarship," *Journal of Bible and Religion.* Vol. 26. July 1958.

Cadoux, Arthur Temple. *The Sources of the Second Gospel.* London: James Clarke and Co. Ltd., n.d.

Cahn, Steven M. "The Irrelevance to Religion of Philosophic Proofs for the Existence of God," *Contemporary Perspectives on Religious Epistemology.* Ed. by R. Douglas Geivett and Brendan Sweetman. New York: Oxford University Press, 1992.

Cahoone, Lawrence (ed.). *From Modernism to Postmodernism: An Anthology.* Malden, Mass.: Blackwell Publishers Inc., 1996.

Caiger, S. L. *Bible and Spade.* London: Oxford University Press, 1936.

Cairns, David. *A Gospel Without Myth?* London: SCM Press Ltd., 1960.

Calvin, John, *Commentary on the Book of the Prophet Isaiah,* 2 vols. Trans. by William Pringle. Edinburgh, Scotland: Calvin Translation Society, 1850.

Cambridge Ancient History, The. Vol. XI. Cambridge: at the University Press, 1965.

Campbell, A. Glen. *The Greek Terminology for the Deity of Christ.* Unpublished Th.M. thesis, Dallas Theological Seminary, 1948.

Campbell, E. F., Jr. "The Amarna Letters and the Amarna Period," *The Biblical Archaeologist.* Vol. 23. February 1960.

Campbell, Richard. "History and Bultmann's Structural Inconsistency," *Religious Studies.* Vol. 9. March 1973.

Caputo, John D. *Radical Hermeneutics: Repetition, Deconstruction, and the Hermeneutic Project.* Bloomington and Indianapolis: Indiana University Press, 1987.

Carey, G. L. "Aristides (second century)," *The New International Dictionary of the Christian Church.* Revised ed. Gen. ed., J. D. Douglas. Grand Rapids: Zondervan, 1978.

Carey, G. L. "Justin Martyr," *The New International Dictionary of the Christian Church.* Revised ed. Gen. ed., J. D. Douglas. Grand Rapids: Zondervan, 1978.

Carlson, A. J. *Science and the Supernatural* (pamphlet). Yellow Springs, Ohio: American Humanist Association, n.d.

Carnell, E. J. *Christian Commitment.* New York: Macmillan Company, 1957.

Carnell, E. J. *An Introduction to Christian Apologetics,* 3rd ed. Grand Rapids: Eerdmans, 1950.

Carson, D. A. *The Gagging of God: Christianity Confronts Pluralism.* Grand Rapids: Zondervan, 1996.

Carson, D. A., Douglas J. Moo, and Leon Morris. *An Introduction to the New Testament.* Grand Rapids: Zondervan Publishing House, 1992.

Carus, Paul. "Essay on Kant's Philosophy," *Prolegomena to Any Future Metaphysics.* Immanuel Kant. Trans. by Paul Carus. Illinois: Open Court, 1902.

Cass, T. S. *Secrets from the Caves.* Quoted in Norman L. Geisler, *Baker's Encyclopedia of Christian Apologetics.* Grand Rapids: Baker Book House, 1998.

Cassuto, U. *Commentary on Genesis 1–11.* Jerusalem: Magnes Press, the Hebrew University, 1964.

Cassuto, U. *The Documentary Hypothesis.* Jerusalem: Magnes Press, the Hebrew University, 1941. First English edition, 1961.

Chafer, Lewis Sperry. *Systematic Theology. Dallas:* Dallas Theological Seminary Press, 1947.

Chandler, Samuel. *Witnesses of the Resurrection of Jesus Christ.* London: n.p., 1744.

Chapman, A. T. *An Introduction to the Pentateuch.* Cambridge: The University Press, 1911.

Chase, F. H. *Essays on Some Theological Questions of the Day,* Ed. by H. B. Swelt. London: Macmillan & Co., 1905.

Cheyne, T. K. *Founders of Old Testament Criticism.* London: Methuen & Co., 1893.

Chiera, Edward. *They Wrote on Clay: The Babylonian Tablets Speak Today.* Chicago: University of Chicago Press, 1938.

Chiera, Edward. *They Wrote on Clay: The Babylonian Tablets Speak Today.* Ed. by George C. Cameron. Rev. ed. Chicago: University of Chicago Press, 1966.

Chisti, Yousuf Saleem. *What Is Christianity: Being a Critical Examination of Fundamental Doctrines of the Christian Faith.* Karachi, Pakistan: World Federation of Islamic Missions, 1970.

Chrysostom. *Homilies on the Gospel of Saint Matthew.* In *A Select Library of the Nicene and Post-Nicene Fathers of the Christian Church.* Ed. by Philip Schaff. Vol. X. New York: The Christian Literature Company, 1888.

Clark, David K. and Norman L. Geisler. *Apologetics in the New Age: A Christian Critique of Pantheism.* Grand Rapids: Baker, 1990.

Clark, Gordon H. *A Christian View of Men and Things.* Grand Rapids: Eerdmans, 1951.

Clark, G. W. *The Gospel of Matthew.* Philadelphia: American Baptist Publication Society, 1896.

Clark, Robert E. D. *Science and Christianity: A Partnership.* Mountain View, Calif.: Pacific Press, 1972.

Clemens, Samuel L. (Mark Twain). *Innocents Abroad or The New Pilgrim's Progress.* Vol. II. New York: Harper & Brothers Publishers, 1869.

Cohen, A. *The Teachings of Maimonides.* London: George Routledge & Sons, Ltd., 1927.

Cole, R. Alan. *Exodus.* Downers Grove, Ill.: InterVarsity Press, 1973.

Collett, Sidney. *All About the Bible.* Old Tappan, N.J.: Fleming H. Revell, n.d.

Collingwood, R. G. *Essays in the Philosophy of History* Ed. by William Debbins. Austin, Tex.: Univeristy of Texas Press, 1965.

Comfort, Philip W. *Early Manuscripts and Modern Translations of the New Testament.* Wheaton, Ill.: Tyndale House Publishers, Inc., 1990.

Comfort, Philip Wesley (ed.). *The Origin of the Bible.* Wheaton, Ill.: Tyndale House Publishers, Inc., 1992.

Conzelmann, Hans. *The Theology of St. Luke.* Trans. by Geoffrey Boswell. New York: Harper and Row, Publishers, 1961.

Cook, Frederick Charles, ed. *Commentary on the Holy Bible.* London: John Murray, 1878.

Cooper, David L. "God and Messiah." Los Angeles: Biblical Research Society. n.d.

Copeland, E. Luther. *Christianity and World Religions.* Nashville: Convention Press, 1963.

Copleston, Frederick. *A History of Philosophy.* Volume II, *Medieval Philosophy: From Augustine to Duns Scotus.* New York: Doubleday, 1993.

Copleston, Frederick. *The History of Philosophy.* Vol. 3. Garden City, N.Y.: Image, 1962.

Corduan, Winfried. *No Doubt About It: The Case for Christianity.* Nashville: Broadman & Holman Publishers, 1997.

Cornill, Carl. *Introduction to the Canonical Books of the Old Testament.* New York: G. P. Putnams Sons, 1907.

"Cosmic Designs." *U. S. News and World Report.* July 20, 1998.

Craig, William Lane. *Apologetics: An Introduction.* Chicago: Moody Press, 1984.

Craig, William Lane. "Did Jesus Rise from the Dead?" *Jesus Under Fire: Modern Scholarship Reinvents the Historical Jesus.* Ed. by Michael J. Wilkins and J. P. Moreland. Grand Rapids: Zondervan Publishing House, 1995.

Craig, William Lane. *Knowing the Truth about the Resurrection.* Ann Arbor, Mich.: Servant Books, 1988. Rev. ed. of *The Son Rises.* Chicago: Moody Bible Institute, 1981.

Craig, William Lane. "Politically Incorrect Salvation," *Christian Apologetics in the Postmodern World.* Ed. by Timothy R. Phillips and Dennis L. Okholm. Downers Grove, Ill.: InterVarsity Press, 1995.

Craig, William Lane. *Reasonable Faith: Christian Truth and Apologetics.* Wheaton Ill.: Crossway Books, 1994.

Craig, William Lane and Quentin Smith. *Theism, Atheism, and Big Bang Cosmology.* New York: New York University Press, 1993.

Craige, P. C. "The Book of Deuteronomy," *The New International Commentary on the Old Testament.* Grand Rapids: Eerdmans, 1976. Quoted in Norman L. Geisler, *Inerrancy.* Grand Rapids: Zondervan, 1980.

Criswell, W. A., ed. *The Criswell Study Bible.* Nashville: Thomas Nelson, 1979.

Culpepper, Robert H. "The Problem of Miracles," *Review and Expositor.* Vol. 53. April 1956:

Currie, George. *The Military Discipline of the Romans from the Founding of the City to the Close of the Republic.* An abstract of a thesis published under the auspices of the Graduate Council of Indiana University, 1928.

Curtius, Quintus. *History of Alexander.* Trans. by John C. Rolfe (from the Loeb Classical Library, Ed. by T. E. Page). 2 vols. Cambridge: Harvard University Press, 1946.

Dahood, Michael. "Are the Ebla Tablets Relevant to Biblical Research?" *Biblical Archaeology Review.* September-October 1980.

Dahse, Johannes. "Texkritische Bedenken gegen den Ausgangspunkt der Pentateuchkritik" ("Textual-Critical Doubts about the Initial Premise of Pentateuchal Criticism"), *Archiven fur Religionswissenschaft.* 1903.

Darwin, Charles. *The Origin of Species by Means of Natural Selection or The Preservation of Favored Races in the Struggle for Life* and *The Descent of Man and Selection in Relation to Sex.* New York: The Modern Library, n.d.

Darwin, Francis, ed. "Letter from Darwin to Hooker," *The Life and Letters of Charles Darwin.* Vol. 2. New York: Appleton, 1967. Quoted in Alvin C. Plantiga, "Methodological Naturalism?" *Origins & Design.* Winter, 1997.

Davidson, Samuel. *The Hebrew Text of the Old Testament.* London: 1856. Quoted in Norman L. Geisler and William E. Nix, *General Introduction to the Bible.* Chicago: Moody Press, 1986.

Davies, Paul C. W. *The Accidental Universe.* Cambridge: Cambridge University Press, 1982. Quoted in Alvin C. Plantiga, "Methodological Naturalism?" *Origins & Design.* Winter, 1997.

Davies, Paul C. "The Cosmic Blueprint," *The Creation Hypothesis: Scientific Evidence for an Intelligent Designer.* Ed. by J. P. Moreland. Downers Grove, Ill.: InterVarsity Press, 1994.

Davies, W. D. *Invitation to the New Testament.* New York: Doubleday and Co., Inc., 1966.

Davies, W. D. "Quest to Be Resumed in New Testament Studies," *Union Seminary Quarterly.* Vol. 15. January 1960.

Davis, George T. B. *Bible Prophecies Fulfilled Today.* Philadelphia: The Million Testaments Campaigns, Inc., 1955.

Davis, George T. B. *Fulfilled Prophecies That Prove the Bible.* Philadelphia: The Million Testaments Campaign, 1931.

Davis, H. Grady. "Biblical Literature and Its Cultural Interpretation," *The New Encyclopedia Britannica, Vol. 14, 1994.*

Davis, John J. *Conquest and Crisis.* Grand Rapids: Baker Book House, 1969.

Davis, Stephen T. *The Debate About the Bible: Inerrancy Versus Infallibility.* Philadelphia: Westminster, 1977.

Davis, Stephen T. "God's Actions," *In Defense of Miracles.* Ed. by R. Douglas Geivett and Gary R. Habermas. Downers Grove, Ill.: InterVarsity Press, 1997.

Dawkins, Richard. *The Blind Watchmaker.* London and New York: W. W. Norton & Co., 1986

Day, E. Hermitage. *On the Evidence for the Resurrection.* London: Society for Promoting Christian Knowledge, 1906.

Deere, Jack S., "Song of Songs," *The Bible Knowledge Commentary: Old Testament.* Ed. by John F. Walvoord and Roy B. Zuck. Wheaton, Ill.: Victor Books, 1985.

Deland, Charles Edmund. *The Mis-Trials of Jesus.* Boston, Mass.: Richard G. Badger, 1914.

Delitzsch, Franz. *Biblical Commentary on the Prophecies of Isaiah.* Vol. 1. Trans. by James Martin. Grand Rapids: William B. Eerdmans Publishing Co., 1950.

Delitzsch, Franz. *Biblical Commentary on the Prophecies of Isaiah.* Trans. from the German by James Martin, 2 vols. Grand Rapids: William B. Eerdmans Publishing Co., 1963.

Dembski, William A. "The Intelligent Design Movement," *Cosmic Pursuit* 1, no. 2. Spring, 1998.

Derham, A. Morgan. "Bible Societies," *The New International Dictionary of the Christian Church.* Revised ed. Gen. ed., J. D. Douglas. Grand Rapids: Zondervan, 1978.

Derrida, Jacques. *Of Grammatology.* Trans. by Gayatri Chakravorty Spivak. Baltimore: Johns Hopkins University Press, 1974.

Derrida, Jacques. *Positions.* Trans. by Alan Bass. Chicago: University of Chicago Press, 1981.

Derrida, Jacques. *Writing and Difference.* Trans. by Alan Bass. Chicago: University of Chicago Press, 1978.

Descartes, Rene. *Discourse on Method and The Meditation.* Trans. by F. E. Sutcliffe. London: Penguin Books, 1968.

Dibelius, Martin. "The Contribution of Germany to New Testament Science," *The Expository Times* 42. October 1930.

Dibelius, Martin. *A Fresh Approach to the New Testament and Early Christian Literature.* New York: Charles Scribner's Sons, 1936.

Dibelius, Martin. *From Tradition to Gospel.* Trans. by Bertram Lee Woolf. New York: Charles Scribner's Sons, 1935.

Dibelius, Martin. *Gospel Criticism and Christology.* London: Ivor Nicholson and Watson, Ltd., 1935.

Dibelius, Martin. *Jesus.* Trans. by Charles B. Hedrick and Frederick C. Grant. Philadelphia: The Westminster Press, 1949.

Dibelius, Martin and Hans Conzelmann. *The Pastoral Epistles.* Trans. by Philip Bultolph and Adela Yarbro. Philadelphia: Fortress, 1972.

Diodorus of Sicily, Vol. 1. English translation by C. H. Oldlather. New York: Putnam's, 1933.

Dockery, David. S., ed. *The Challenge of Postmodernism: An Evangelical Engagement.* Wheaton: Victor, 1995.

Dockery, David S., Kenneth A. Mathews and Robert B. Sloan. *Foundations for Biblical Interpretation.* Nashville: Broadman & Holman Publishers, 1994.

Dodd, C. H. *About the Gospels, the Coming of Christ.* Cambridge: at the University Press, 1958.

Dodd, C. H. *The Apostolic Preaching.* London: Hodder and Stoughton Limited, 1936.

Dodd, C. H. "The Framework of the Gospel Narrative," *The Expository Times.* Vol. 43. June 1932.

Dodd, C. H. *History and the Gospel.* New York: Charles Scribner's Sons, 1938.

Dodd, C. H. *More New Testament Studies.* Manchester: University Press, 1968.

Dodd, C. H. *New Testament Studies.* Manchester: Manchester University Press, 1954.

Dodd, C. H. *The Parables of the Kingdom.* London: Nisbet and Co., Ltd., 1935.

Dostoyevsky, Fyodor Mikhailovich. *The Brothers Karamazov.* In *Great Books of the Western*

World. Ed. by Robert Maynard Hutchins. Trans. by Constance Garnett. Chicago: The University of Chicago, Encyclopaedia Britannica, Inc., William Benton, publisher, 1984.

Douglas, J. D., ed. *The New Bible Dictionary.* Grand Rapids: William B. Eerdmans Publishing Co., 1962.

Driver, S. R. "Book of Exodus," *Cambridge Bible for Schools and Colleges.* Cambridge: The University Press, 1911.

Driver, S. R. *The Book of Genesis.* London: Methuen & Co., 1904.

Driver, S. R. "Deuteronomy," *International Critical Commentary.* Edinburgh: T & T Clark, 1896.

Driver, S. R. *An Introduction to the Literature of the Old Testament.* New York: Charles Scribner's Sons, 1913.

Driver, S. R. *Notes on the Hebrew Text and the Topography of the Books of Samuel.* Oxford: Clarendon Press, 1966.

Duggan, G. H. *Beyond Reasonable Doubt.* St. Paul: Boston, 1987.

Duncker, Peter G. "Biblical Criticism," *The Catholic Biblical Quarterly.* Vol. 25. January 1963.

Earle, Ralph. *How We Got Our Bible.* Grand Rapids: Baker Book House, 1971.

Easterbrook, Gregg. "What Came Before Creation?" *U.S. News & World Report,* July 20, 1998.

Easton, Burton Scott. *Christ in the Gospels.* New York: Charles Scribner's Sons, 1930.

Easton, Burton Scott. *The Gospel Before the Gospels.* New York: Charles Scribner's Sons, 1928.

Edersheim, Alfred. *The Life and Times of Jesus the Messiah.* Vol. II. Grand Rapids: William B. Eerdmans Publishing Co., 1962.

Edersheim, Alfred. *The Temple: Its Ministry and Services.* Grand Rapids: William B. Eerdmans Publishing Co., 1958.

Edgar, R. M'Cheyne. *The Gospel of a Risen Savior.* In *Therefore Stand: Christian Apologetics,* Wilbur M. Smith. Grand Rapids: Baker Book House, 1965.

Edwards, O. C. Jr. "Historical-Critical Method's Failure of Nerve and a Prescription for a Tonic: A Review of Some Recent Literature," *Anglican Theological Review.* Vol. 59. April 1977.

Edwards, Paul, ed. *The Encyclopedia of Philosophy.* Vol. V. New York: The Macmillan Co. & The Free Press, 1967, S.v. "Miracles," by Antony Flew.

Edwards, William D., M.D., et al. "On the Physical Death of Jesus Christ," *Journal of the American Medical Association* 255:11. March 21, 1986.

Eerdmans, B. D. *The Religion of Israel.* Leiden: Universitaire Pers Leiden, 1947.

Eichhorn, J. G. *Einleitung in das Alte Testament.* Quoted in S. J. Chapman, *An Introduction to the Pentateuch.* Cambridge: The University Press, 1911.

Eichrodt, Walther. *Ezekiel.* Trans. by Coslett Quin. Philadelphia: The Westminster Press, 1970.

Eissfeldt, Otto. *The Old Testament—An Introduction.* New York: Harper and Row Publishers, 1965.

Elder, John. *Prophets, Idols, and Diggers.* New York: Bobbs Merrill Co., 1960.

Ellwein, Edward. "Rudolf Bultmann's Interpretation of the Kerygma," *Kerygma and History.* Ed. by Carl E. Braaten and Roy A. Harrisville. New York: Abingdon Press, 1962.

Ellwein, Edward. "Rudolf Bultmann's Interpretation of the Kerygma," *The Theology of Rudolf Bultmann.* Ed. by Charles W. Kegley. London: SCM Press, 1966.

Elwell, Walter, ed. *Evangelical Dictionary of Theology.* Grand Rapids: Baker Book House, 1984.

Elwell, Walter, ed. *Evangelical Dictionary of Biblical Theology.* Grand Rapids: Baker Book House, 1996.

Ellwood, Robert S., Jr. *Mysticism and Religion.* Englewood Cliffs, N.J.: Prentice-Hall, 1980.

Encyclopedia Americana. Vol. 8, 16. New York: Americana Corporation, 1960.

Encyclopedia Americana. Vol. 10, 14. New York: Amercana Corporation, 1959.

Encyclopaedia Britannica, 15th ed. New York: University Press, 1970.

Encyclopedia of Religion and Ethics. Ed. by James Hastings. Edinburgh: T. & T. Clark, 1935.

Englishman's Greek Concordance. 9th ed. London: S. Bagster, 1903.

Engnell, Ivan. *A Rigid Scrutiny: Critical Essays on the Old Testament.* Trans. and ed. by John T. Willis. Nashville: Vanderbilt Press, 1969.

Enns, Paul. *The Moody Handbook of Theology.* Chicago: Moody Press, 1989.

Enslin, Morton Scott. *Christian Beginnings.* New York: Harper and Brothers Publishers, 1938.

Erickson, Millard J. *Christian Theology.* 3 vols. Grand Rapids: Baker Book House, 1984.

Erickson, Millard J. *Postmodernizing the Faith: Evangelical Responses to the Challenge of Postmodernism.* Grand Rapids: Baker Books, 1998.

Erickson, Millard J. *The Word Became Flesh: A Contemporary Incarnational Christology.* Grand Rapids: Baker Book House, 1991.

Erlandsson, Seth. Trans. by Harold O. J. Brown. "Is Biblical Scholarship Possible Without Presuppositions?" *Trinity Journal.* Vol. VII. Spring 1978.

Estborn, S. *Gripped by Christ.* London: Lutterworth Press, 1965.

Ethridge, J. W. *The Targums of Onkelos and Jonathan Ben Ussiel on the Pentateuch.* Vols. 1, 2. New York: KTAV Publishing House, Inc., 1968.

Eusebius. *Ecclesiastical History.* Vol. 1. Trans. by Kirsopp Lake. London: William Heinemann Ltd., 1926.

Eusebius. *Ecclesiastical History.* VIII, 2. Loeb. ed., II.

Eusebius. *Ecclesiastical History.* Trans. by C. F. Cruse. Quoted in Norman L. Geisler, *Baker's Encyclopedia of Christian Apologetics.* Grand Rapids:: Baker Book House, 1998.

Eusebius. *The Treatise of Eusebius,* contained in *The Life of Apollonius of Tyana/Philostratus. The Epistles of Apollonius and the Treatise of Eusebius*; with an English translation by F. C. Conybeare. Cambridge, Mass.: Harvard University Press; London: W. Heinemann, 1912.

Evans, C. A. "Jesus in Non-Christian Sources," *Dictionary of Jesus and the Gospels.* Ed. by Joel B. Green, Scot McKnight, I. Howard Marshall. Downers Grove, Ill.: InterVarsity Press, 1992.

Evans, C. Stephen. *The Historical Christ and The Jesus of Faith.* Oxford: Clarendon Press, 1996.

Evans, C. Stephen. *Why Believe?* Grand Rapids: William B. Eerdmans Publishing Co., 1996.

Ewert, David. *From Ancient Tablets to Modern Translations: A General Introduction to the Bible.* Grand Rapids: Zondervan, 1983.

Fairbairn, A. M. *Christ in Modern Theology.* London: Hodder and Stoughton, 1893.

Fairbairn, A.M. *Philosophy of the Christian Religion.* London: Hodder and Stoughton, 1908.

Fairbairn, A.M. *Studies in the Life of Christ.* London: Hodder and Stoughton. 1896.

Fallow, Samuel, ed. *The Popular and Critical Bible Encyclopedia and Scriptural Dictionary.* Vol. III. Chicago: The Howard Severance Co., 1908.

Faris, Murray G. "Disease Free," *Contact,* March 1972. Glen Ellyn: Christian Business Men's Committee, Int.

Farrar, Frederick W. *The Life of Christ.* Dutton, Dovar: Cassell and Co., 1897.

Fascher, E. *Die Forgeschichtliche Methode.* Giessen: Töpelmann, 1924.

Fausset, A. R. *A Commentary Critical, Experimental and Practical on the Old and New Testaments.* Vol. III. Grand Rapids: William B. Eerdmans Publishing Company, 1961.

Feinberg, Charles Lee. *The Prophecy of Ezekiel.* Chicago: Moody Press, 1969.

Feinberg, Charles L. "The Relation of Archaeology to Biblical Criticism," *Bibliotheca Sacra.* June 1947.

Feinberg, Charles Lee. "The Virgin Birth in the Old Testament and Isaiah 7:14,"*Bibliotheca Sacra.* July 1962.

Feinberg, Paul D. "The Doctrine of God in the Pentateuch." Ph.D. dissertation, Dallas Theological Seminary, 1968.

Feinberg, Paul D. "The Meaning of Inerrancy." In *Inerrancy,* ed. Norman L. Geisler. Grand Rapids: Zondervan, 1980.

Felder, Hilarin. *Christ and the Critics.* Trans. by John L. Stoddard. London: Burns Oates and Washburn Ltd., 1924.

Ferm, Robert O. *The Psychology of Christian Conversion.* Westwood, N.J.: Fleming H. Revell-Company, 1959.

Ferré, Nels F. S. "Contemporary Theology in the Light of 100 Years," *Theology Today.* Vol. 15. October 1958.

Feuerbach, Ludwig. *The Essence of Christianity.*

Trans. by George Eliot. New York: Harper Torchbooks, 1957.

Filson, Floyd V. "Form Criticism," *Twentieth Century Encyclopedia of Religious Knowledge.* Vol. 1. Ed. by Lefferts A. Loetscher. Grand Rapids: Baker Book House, 1955.

Filson, Floyd V. *Origins of the Gospels.* New York: Abingdon Press, 1938.

Finegan. Jack. *Light from the Ancient Past.* London: Oxford Press, distributed in the U.S. by Princeton University Press, 1946.

Finkelstein, Louis, editor. *The Jews, Their History, Culture, and Religion.* 3rd ed. Vol. 1. New York: Harper and Brothers, 1960.

Fisch, Harold. "The Bible and Western Literature," *The HarperCollins Bible Dictionary.* Ed. by Paul J. Achtemeier, San Francisco: HarperCollins Publishers, 1996.

Fischer, David Hackett. *Historians' Fallacies: Toward a Logic of Historical Thought.* New York: Harper Torchbooks, 1970.

Fisher, G. P. *The Grounds of Theistic and Christian Belief.* London: Hodder and Stoughton, 1902.

Fisher, J. T., and L. S. Hawley. *A Few Buttons Missing.* Philadelphia, Penn.: Lippincott, 1951.

Fitzmyer, Joseph A. "Memory and Manuscript: The Origins and Transmission of the Gospel Tradition," *Theological Studies.* Vol. 23. September 1962.

Flanders, Henry Jackson, Jr., Robert Wilson Crapps, and David Anthony Smith. *People of the Covenant.* New York: The Ronald Press Company, 1973.

Flew, Antony. "Miracles," *The Encyclopedia of Philosophy.* Ed. by Paul Edwards. Vol. V. New York: The Macmillan Co. & The Free Press, 1967.

Flew, Antony, ed. *A Dictionary of Philosophy,* rev. 2d ed. New York: St. Martin's Press, 1979.

Flew, Antony and Alasdair MacIntyre, eds. *New Essays in Philosophy Theology.* New York: Macmillan, 1955.

Fodor, Eugene. *Fodor's Israel.* New York: David McKay Co., Inc., 1974.

Fohrer, Georg. *Introduction to the Old Testament.* Initiated by Ernst Sellin. Trans. by David Green. Nashville: Abingdon Press, 1965.

Foote, Henry Wilder. *Thomas Jefferson: Champion of Religious Freedom, Advocate of Christian Morals.* Quoted in Norman L. Geisler and William D. Watkins, *Worlds Apart.* Grand Rapids: Baker Book House, 1989.

Frame, Randall. "The Bible: The Year in Review," *Christianity Today.* October 1985.

France, R. T., "Life and Teaching of Christ," *New Bible Dictionary,* 3rd ed. Ed. by I. Howard Marshall, A. R. Millard, J. I. Packer, D. J. Wiseman, Downers Grove, Ill.: InterVarsity Press, 1996.

Frank, Henry Thomas. *Bible, Archaeology and Faith.* Nashville: Abingdon Press, 1971.

Free, Joseph P. "Archaeology and the Bible," *His Magazine.* May 1949.

Free, Joseph P. *Archaeology and Bible History.* Wheaton: Scripture Press, 1950.

Free, Joseph P. *Archaeology and Bible History.* Wheaton: Scripture Press, 1969.

Free, Joseph P. "Archaeology and Higher Criticism." *Bibliotheca Sacra* 114. January 1957.

Free, Joseph P. "Archaeology and the Historical Accuracy of Scripture," *Bibliotheca Sacra* 113. July 1956.

Free, Joseph P. "Archaeology and Liberalism." *Bibliotheca Sacra* 113. July 1956.

Free, Joseph P. "Archaeology and Neo-Orthodoxy." *Bibliotheca Sacra* 114. January 1957.

Freedman, David Noel. "The Real Story of the Ebla Tablets; Ebla, and the Cities of the Plain," *Biblical Archaeologist* 41, no. 4. December 1978.

Freedom, D. N. and J. C. Greenfield, eds. *New Directions in Biblical Archaeology.* Garden City: Doubleday, 1969.

Freud, Sigmund. *The Future of Illusion.* New York: Liveright Publishing Corporation, 1955.

Friedlaender, M. *Essays on the Writings of Abraham Ibn Ezra.* Vol. IV. London: Trubner and Company, n.d.

Frye, Northrop. *Anatomy of Criticism.* Princeton, N.J.: Princeton University Press, 1957.

Frye, Northrop. *The Great Code: The Bible and Literature.* New York: Harcourt Brace & Company, 1982.

Fuller, R. *Interpreting the Miracles.* Philadelphia: Westminster Press, 1963.

Fuller, Reginald H. *The Mission and Achievement of Jesus.* London: SCM Press Ltd., 1967.

Fuller, Reginald H. *The New Testament in Current Study*. New York: Charles Scribner's Sons, 1962.

Fuller, Reginald Horace. "Rudolf Bultmann," *Encyclopedia Britannica*. Vol. 4. Chicago: William Benton, 1962.

Futuyma, Douglas. *Evolumtionary Biology*, 2d ed., 1986, 3. Quoted in Alvin C. Plantinga, "Methodological Naturalism," *Origins & Design*. Winter, 1997.

Gaebelein, Frank E., ed. *The Expositor's Bible Commentary*. Vol. 1, *Introductory Articles: General, Old Testament, New Testament*. Grand Rapids: Zondervan, 1979.

Gaebelein, Frank E., ed. *The Expositor's Bible Commentary*. Vol. 10. Grand Rapids: Zondervan, 1979.

Gallagher, Susan V., and Roger Lundin. *Literature Through the Eyes of Faith*. San Francisco: Harper & Row, Publishers, 1989.

Gardner, James. *The Christian Cyclopedia*. Glasgow: Blackie and Son, 1858.

Gardner, Martin. *The Whys of a Philosophical Scrivener*. New York: Quill, 1983.

Garrigou-Lagrange, Reginald. *Reality: A Synthesis of Thomistic Thought*. St. Louis: B. Herder Book Company, 1950.

Garstang, John. *The Foundations of Bible History; Joshua, Judges*. New York: R. R. Smith, Inc., 1931.

Garvie, A. E. *Handbook of Christian Apologetics*. London: Duckworth and Co., 1923.

Garvie, A. E. *Studies in the Inner Life of Christ*. New York: Hodder and Stoughton, 1907.

Gaussen, L. *The Divine Inspiration of the Bible*. Grand Rapids: Kregel, 1841. Reprint edition, 1971.

Geisler, Norman L. *Baker Encyclopedia of Christian Apologetics*. Grand Rapids: Baker, 1998.

Geisler, Norman L. *The Battle for the Resurrection*. Nashville: Thomas Nelson, 1989.

Geisler, Norman L. *Christ: The Theme of the Bible*. Chicago: Moody Press, 1969.

Geisler, Norman L. *Christian Apologetics*. Grand Rapids: Baker, 1976.

Geisler, Norman L. "The Collapse of Modern Atheism," *The Intellectuals Speak Out About God*. Ed. by Roy Abraham Varghese. Dallas: Lewis and Stanley Publishers, 1984.

Geisler, Norman L. "The Concept of Truth in the Inerrancy Debate," *Bibliotheca Sacra*. Oct.-Dec. 1980.

Geisler, Norman L. "The Inerrancy Debate— What Is It All About?" Oakland, Calif.: International Council on Biblical Inerrancy, 1978.

Geisler, Norman L. *Miracles and the Modern Mind*. Grand Rapids: Baker Book House, 1992.

Geisler, Norman L. "Miracles and the Modern Mind," *In Defense of Miracles*. Ed. by R. Douglas Geivett and Gary R. Habermas. Downers Grove, Ill.: InterVarsity Press, 1997.

Geisler, Norman L. "The Missing Premise in the Ontological Argument," *Religious Studies* l.9 no. 3. 1973.

Geisler, Norman L. *Signs and Wonders*. Wheaton, Ill.: Tyndale House Publishers, 1988.

Geisler, Norman L. *Thomas Aquinas: An Evangelical Appraisal*. With a foreword by Ralph McInerny. Grand Rapids: Baker, 1991.

Geisler, Norman L. *To Understand the Bible Look for Jesus: The Bible Student's Guide to the Bible's Central Theme*. Reprint ed. Grand Rapids: Baker Book House, 1979.

Geisler, Norman L., ed. *Decide for Yourself: How History Reviews the Bible*. Grand Rapids: Zondervan, 1982.

Geisler, Norman L., ed. *Inerrancy*. Grand Rapids: Zondervan, 1980.

Geisler, Norman L. and Abdul Saleeb. *Answering Islam*. Grand Rapids: Baker Books, 1993.

Geisler, Norman L. and J. Kerby Anderson. *Origin Science*. Grand Rapids: Baker Book House, 1987.

Geisler, Norman L. and Peter Bocchino. *When Students Ask: A Handbook on Foundational Truths*. Unpublished manuscript, 1998.

Geisler, Norman L., and Ronald M. Brooks. *When Skeptics Ask*. Wheaton, Ill.: Victor, 1990.

Geisler, Norman and Winfried Corduan. *Philosophy of Religion*. Grand Rapids: Baker, 1988.

Geisler, Norman L. and Paul D. Feinberg. *Introduction to Philosophy*. Grand Rapids: Baker, 1980.

Geisler, Norman L. and Thomas A. Howe. *When Critics Ask*. Wheaton, Ill.: Victor Books, 1992.

Geisler, Norman L. and Ralph E. MacKenzie. *Roman Catholics and Evangelicals: Agreements and Differences.* Grand Rapids: Baker Book House, 1995.

Geisler, Norman L. and Ron Rhodes. *When Cultists Ask: A Popular Handbook on Cultic Misinterpretations.* Grands Rapids: Baker Books, 1997.

Geisler, Norman L. and Frank Turek. *Legislating Morality: Is It Wise? Is It Legal? Is It Possible?* Minneapolis, Minn.: Bethany House, 1998.

Geisler, Norman L. and William D. Watkins. *Worlds Apart: A Handbook on World Views,* 2nd ed. Grand Rapids: Baker, 1989.

Geisler, Norman L. and William E. Nix. *A General Introduction to the Bible.* Chicago: Moody Press, 1968.

Geisler, Norman L. and William E. Nix. *A General Introduction to the Bible.* Chicago: Moody Press, 1986.

Geisler, Norman L. and Yutaka Amano. *The Reincarnation Sensation.* Wheaton, Ill.: Tyndale, 1986.

Geivett, R. Douglas and Gary R. Habermas, ed. *In Defense of Miracles.* Downers Grove, Ill.: InterVarsity Press, 1997.

Genuine Epistles of the Apostolical Fathers. Trans. by William of Canterbury. London: Samuel Bagster, 1840.

The Geography of Strabo, Vol. 8. English translation by Horace Leonard Jones. New York: Putnam's, 1932.

Gerhardsson, Birger. *Tradition and Transmission in Early Christianity.* Trans. by Eric J. Sharpe. Copenhagen: Ejnar Munksgaard, 1964.

Gieser, Ruby Free and Howard F. Vos. *Archaeology and Bible History.* Grand Rapids: Zondervan Publishers, 1992

Gilkey, Langdon B. "Cosmology, Ontology, and the Travail of Biblical Language," *Concordia Theological Monthly* 33. March 1962.

Gill, Jerry H. *The Possibility of Religious Knowledge.* Grand Rapids: Eerdmans, 1971.

Gillett, E. H. *Ancient Cities and Empires.* Philadelphia: Presbyterian Publication Committee, 1867.

Gilson, Etienne. *Being and Some Philosophers,* 2d. ed. cor. and enl. Toronto: Pontifical Institute of Mediaeval Studies, 1952.

Gilson, Etienne. *The Christian Philosophy of St. Thomas Aquinas.* With a catalogue of St.

Thomas's works by I. T. Eschmann, O.P. Trans. by L. K. Shook, C.S.B. New York: Random House, 1956. Reprint, Notre Dame, Ind.: University of Notre Dame Press, 1994.

Gilson, Etienne. *The Philosophy of St. Thomas Aquinas.* New York: Barnes & Noble, 1993.

Gilson, Etienne. "Vade Mecum of a Young Realist," *Philosophy of Knowledge: Selected Readings.* Ed. by Roland Houde and Joseph P. Mullally. Chicago: J. B. Lippincott, 1960.

Glenny, W. Edward. "The Preservation of Scripture," *The Bible Version Debate.* Minneapolis: Central Baptist Theological Seminary, 1997.

Glueck, Nelson. "The Bible as a Divining Rod," *Horizon.* Vol. 2. November 1959.

Glueck, Nelson. *Rivers in the Desert: History of Negev.* New York: Farrar, Straus, and Cadahy, 1959.

Glueck, Nelson. "The Second Campaign at Tell el-Kheleifeh," *Bulletin of the American Schools of Oriental Research.* Vol. 75. October 1939.

Glueck, Nelson. "The Third Season at Tell el-Kheleifeh," *Bulletin of the American Schools of Oriental Research.* Vol. 79. October 1940.

Godet, F. *Commentary on the Gospel of St. John.* Edinburgh: T. & T. Clark, 1892.

Gordon, Cyrus H. " 'Almah' in Isaiah 7:14," *The Journal of Bible and Religion* 21:2. April 1953.

Gordon, Cyrus H. "Biblical Customs and the Nuzu Tablets," *The Biblical Archaeologist.* February 1940.

Gordon, Cyrus H. "Higher Critics and Forbidden Fruit," *Christianity Today.* Vol. 4. November 23, 1959.

Gordon, Cyrus. *Introduction to Old Testament Times.* Ventnor, N.J.: Ventnor Publishers, Inc., 1953.

Gordon, Cyrus H. "The Patriarchal Age," *Journal of Bible and Religion* 21, no. 4. October 1955.

Goshen-Gottstein, Moshe. "Bible Manuscripts in the U. S.," *Textus* 3. 1962.

Gottschalk, Louis. *Understanding History: A Primer of Historical Method,* 2d. ed. New York: Alfred A. Knopf, 1969.

Goguel, M. "Une nouvelle école de critique évangélique: la form-und traditiongeschichliche Schule," *Revue de l'histoire des religions.* Paris: E. Leroux, 1926.

Grant, F. C. "Biblical Studies; Views and Reviews," *Theology Today*. Vol. 14. April 1957.

Grant, Frederick C. *The Growth of the Gospels.* New York: The Abingdon Press, 1933.

Gray, Edward M. *Old Testament Criticism.* New York and London: Harper & Brothers, 1923.

Green, Joel B. and Scot McKnight, ed. *Dictionary of Jesus and the Gospels.* Downers Grove, Ill.: InterVarsity Press, 1992.

Green, Michael. *Man Alive.* Downers Grove, Ill.: InterVarsity Press, 1968.

Green, Michael. *Runaway World.* Downers Grove, Ill.: InterVarsity Press, 1968.

Green, William Henry. *General Introduction to the Old Testament—The Text.* New York: Charles Scribner's Sons, 1899.

Green, William Henry. *The Higher Criticism of the Pentateuch.* New York: Charles Scribner's Sons, 1895.

Greenleaf, Simon. *The Testimony of the Evangelists, Examined by the Rules of Evidence Administered in Courts of Justice.* Grand Rapids: Baker Book House, 1965 (reprinted from 1847 edition).

Greenlee, J. Harold. *Introduction to New Testament Textual Criticism.* Grand Rapids: William B. Eerdmans Publishing Company, 1977.

Greenslade, Stanley Lawrence, ed. *Cambridge History of the Bible.* New York: Cambridge University Press, 1963.

Grenz, Stanley J. *A Primer on Postmodernism.* Grand Rapids: Eerdmans, 1996.

Grinnell, George. "Reexamination of the Foundations," *The Intellectuals Speak Out about God.* Ed. by Roy Abraham Varghese. Dallas: Lewis and Stanley Publishers, 1984.

Groebel, K. "Form Criticism," *The Interpreter's Dictionary of the Bible.* Vol. 1. Ed. by Emory Stevens Bucke. New York: Abingdon Press, 1962.

Grollenberg, Luc H. *Atlas of the Bible.* Trans. and ed. by Joyce M. H. Reid and H. H. Rowley. London: Nelson, 1956.

Gromacki, Robert G. *New Testament Survey.* Grand Rapids: Baker Book House, 1996.

Gromacki, Robert Glenn. *The Virgin Birth.* New York: Thomas Nelson, 1974.

Groothuis, Douglas. *Jesus in an Age of Contro-*versy. Eugene, Ore.: Harvest House Publishers, 1996.

Grounds, Vernon C. *The Reason for Our Hope.* Chicago: Moody Press, 1945.

Gruenler, Royce Gordon. *Jesus, Persons and the Kingdom of God.* St. Louis: United Church Press, 1967.

Guignebert. *Jesus.* Quoted in Wilbur M. Smith, *Therefore Stand: Christian Apologetics.* Grand Rapids: Baker Book House, 1965.

Gundry, Robert H. *A Survey of the New Testament.* Rev. ed. Grand Rapids: Zondervan, 1981.

Gundry, Stanley N. "A Critique of the Fundamental Assumption of Form Criticism, Part I," *Bibliotheca Sacra.* No. 489. April 1966.

Gundry, Stanley N. "A Critique of the Fundamental Assumption of Form Criticism, Part II," *Bibliotheca Sacra.* No. 489. June 1966.

Gundry, Stan. *An Investigation of the Fundamental Assumption of Form Criticism.* A thesis presented to the Department of New Testament Language and Literature at Talbot Theological Seminary, June, 1963.

Gunkel, Hermann. *The Legends of Genesis.* Trans. by W. H. Carruth. Chicago: The Open Court Publishing Co., 1901.

Gunkel, Hermann. *What Remains of the Old Testament?* London: George Allan and Unwin LTD., 1928.

Guthrie, Donald. *New Testament Introduction.* Downers Grove, Ill.: InterVarsity Press, 1990.

Guthrie, Donald. *The Pastoral Epistles.* Grand Rapids: Eerdmans, 1957.

Habel, Norman C. *Literary Criticism of the Old Testament.* Philadelphia: Fortress Press, 1971.

Habermas, Gary R. *The Historical Jesus: Ancient Evidence for the Life of Christ.* Joplin, Mo.: College Press Publishing Company, 1996.

Habermas, Gary R. *The Verdict of History.* Nashville: Thomas Nelson Publishers, 1988.

Hackett, Stuart C. *The Reconstruction of the Christian Revelation Claim: A Philosophical and Critical Apologetic.* Grand Rapids: Baker, 1984.

Hagner, Donald A. "The New Testament, History, and the Historical-Critical Method," *New Testament Criticism and Interpretation.* Ed. by David Alan Black and David S. Dockery. Grand Rapids: Zondervan Publishing House, 1991.

Hahn, Herbert F. *The Old Testament in Modern Research.* Phildelphia: Fortress Press, 1966.

Hall, H. R. *The Ancient History of the Near East.* London: Methuen and Co. Ltd., 1932.

Halverson, Dean. *The Compact Guide to World Religions.* Minneapolis, Minn.: Bethany House, 1996.

Hamilton, Floyd E. *The Basis of Christian Faith.* New York: George H. Doran Company, 1927.

Hamilton, Floyd E. *The Basis of Christian Faith,* rev. ed. New York: Harper and Row, 1964.

Hanson, Anthony, ed. *Vindications: Essays on the Historical Basis of Christianity.* New York: Morehouse-Barlow Co., 1966.

Hanson, George. *The Resurrection and the Life.* London: William Clowes & Sons, Ltd., 1911.

Hardy, G. B. *Countdown.* Chicago: Moody Press, 1970.

Harnack, Adolf. *History of Dogma.* Quoted in E. Hermitage Day, *On the Evidence for the Resurrection.* London: Society for Promoting Christian Knowledge, 1906.

Harper, William R. and W. Henry Green. "The Pentateuchal Question," *Hebraica.* Vol. 5, No. 1. October 1888.

Harris, Murray J. "2 Corinthians," *The Expositor's Bible Commentary.* Ed. by Frank E. Gaebelein. Vol. 10. Grand Rapids: Zondervan, 1976 .

Harris, Murray J. *Jesus as God.* Grand Rapids: Baker Book House, 1992.

Harris, Ralph and Stanley Horton. *The Complete Biblical Library.* Springfield, Mo.: World Library Press, Inc., 1988.

Harris, R. Laird. *Inspiration and Canonicity of the Bible.* Grand Rapids: Zondervan, 1957.

Harrison, Everett F. "Are the Gospels Reliable?" *Moody Monthly.* February 1966.

Harrison, R. K. *The Archaeology of the Old Testament.* New York: Harper and Row Publishers, 1963.

Harrison, R. K. "History and Literary Criticism of the Old Testament," *The Expositor's Bible Commentary.* Ed. by Frank E. Gaebelein. Vol. 1, *Introductory Articles: General, Old Testament, New Testament.* Grand Rapids: Zondervan, 1979.

Harrison, R. K. *Introduction to the Old Testament.* Grand Rapids: William B. Eerdmans Publishing Co., 1969.

Harrison, R. K. *Introduction to the New Testament.* Grand Rapids: William B. Eerdmans Publishing Co., 1971.

Harrison, R. K. "The Old Testament and Its Critics," *Christianity Today,* May 25, 1959.

Harrison, R. K. *Old Testament Times.* Grand Rapids: William B. Eerdmans Publishing Co., 1970.

Harrison, R. K., B. K. Waltke, D. Guthrie, and G. D. Free. *Biblical Criticism: Historical, Literary and Textual.* Grand Rapids: Zondervan Publishing House, 1978.

Hartshorne, Charles E. *Aquinas to Whitehead: Seven Centuries of Metaphysics of Religion.* The Aquinas Lecture, 1976. Milwaukee: Marquette University Publication, 1976.

Hartshorne, Charles E. "The Dipolar Conception of Deity," *The Review of Metaphysics* 21. December 1967.

Hartshorne, Charles E. *A Natural Theology for Our Time.* La Salle: Open Court, 1967.

Hartzler, H. Harold. "Foreword." Cited in *Science Speaks,* Peter W. Stoner. Chicago: Moody Press, 1963.

Harvey, Van A. *The Historian & the Believer.* Chicago: University of Illinois Press, 1996.

Hasel, Gerhard F. "The Polemic Nature of the Genesis Cosmology," *The Evangelical Quarterly.* Vol. 46. April-June 1974.

Hastings, James. *Dictionary of the Apostolic Church.* Vol. II. Edinburgh: T. & T. Clark, 1918.

Hastings, James, ed. *Encyclopedia of Religion and Ethics.* Vol. VI. New York: Charles Scribner's Sons, 1955, S.v. "Historiography," by E. Troeltsch.

Hastings, James, John A. Selbie, and John C. Lambert, eds. *A Dictionary of Christ and the Gospels.* Vol. II . New York: Charles Scribner's Sons, 1909.

Haupert, R. S. "Lachish—Frontier Fortress of Judah," *Biblical Archaeologist* 1, no. 4. December 1938.

Hawking, Stephen. *A Brief History of Time: From the Big Bang to Black Holes.* New York: Bantam Books, 1988.

Hayes, D. A. *The Synoptic Gospels and the Book of*

Acts. New York: The Methodist Book Concern, 1919.

Heeren, Fred. "Does Modern Cosmology Point to a Biblical Creator?" *Cosmic Pursuit.* Spring, 1998.

Heidel, Alexander. *The Babylonian Genesis.* Chicago: University of Chicago Press, 1963.

Heidel, Alexander. *The Gilgamesh Epic and the Old Testament Parallels.* Chicago: University of Chicago Press, 1949.

Heinisch, Paul. *Christ in Prophecy.* The Liturgical Press, 1956.

Hemer, Colin J. *The Book of Acts in the Setting of Hellenistic History.* Winona Lake, Ind.: Eisenbrauns, 1990.

Hendriksen, William. *New Testament Commentary: Exposition of the Gospel According to Matthew.* Grand Rapids: Baker Book House, 1973. Quoted in Norman L. Geisler, *Baker's Encyclopedia of Christian Apologetics.* Grand Rapids: Baker Book House, 1998.

Hengstenberg, E. W. *Christology of the Old Testament and a Commentary on the Messianic Predictions.* Grand Rapids: Kregel Publications, 1970.

Hengstenberg, E. W. *Dissertations on the Genuineness of the Pentateuch.* Vol. 2. Edinburgh: James Nisbet & Co., 1847.

Henry, Carl F. H. *God, Revelation, and Authority.* Vol. 2. Waco: Word, 1976.

Henry, Carl F. H. *God, Revelation, and Authority.* Vol. 4, *God Who Speaks and Shows: Fifteen Theses, Part Three.* Waco: Word, 1976.

Henry, Carl F. H. *The Identity of Jesus of Nazareth.* Nashville: Broadman Press, 1992.

Henry, Carl F. H. "Postmodernism: The New Spectre?" *The Challenge of Postmodernism: An Evangelical Engagement.* Ed. by David S. Dockery. Wheaton: Victor, 1995.

Henry, C. F. H. "The Theological Crisis in Europe: Decline of the Bultmann Era?" *Christianity Today.* Vol. 8. September 25, 1964.

Henry, Carl, ed. *Revelation and the Bible.* Grand Rapids: Baker Book House, 1969.

Henry, Matthew. *Matthew Henry's Commentary on the Whole Bible.* Vols. I, II. Wilmington: Sovereign Grace Publishers, 1972.

Herodotus. Trans. by Henry Cary (from the Bohn's Classical Library). London: George Bell and Sons, 1904.

Hertz, J. H. *The Pentateuch and Haftorahs.* Vol. 2. London: Oxford University Press, 1930, 1951.

Hesiod. *Theogony, Works and Days, Shield.* Trans. by Apostolos N. Athanassakis. Baltimore: The Johns Hopkins University Press, 1983.

Hick, John. *Arguments for the Existence of God.* New York: Herder and Herder, 1971.

Hick, John. *The Existence of God.* New York: The Macmillan Company, 1964.

Higgins, David C. *The Edomites Considered Historically and Prophetically.* Unpublished Master's thesis, Dallas Theological Seminary, 1960.

Hillers, Delbert. *Treaty-Curse and the Old Testament Prophets.* Rome: Pontifical Biblical Institute, 1964.

Hindson, Edward E. "Isaiah's Immanual,'" *Grace Journal* 10. Fall, 1969.

Hinsie, L. E. and J. Shatsky. *Psychiatric Dictionary.* New York: Oxford University Press, 1948.

Hobbes, Thomas. *Leviathan.* New York: Washington Square Press, 1964.

Hobbs, Herschel. *An Exposition of the Gospel of Luke.* Grand Rapids: Baker Book House, 1966.

Hoch, Paul H., Joseph Zubin, and Gerhune Stratton, eds. *Psychopathology of Perception.* New York: n.p., 1965.

Hodge, Charles. *A Commentary on Romans.* Revised reprint ed. London: The Banner of Truth Trust, 1972.

Hodges, Zane C. "Form-Criticism and the Resurrection Accounts," *Bibliotheca Sacra.* Vol. 124. October-December 1967.

Hoehner, Harold. *Chronological Aspects of the Life of Christ.* Grand Rapids: Zondervan Publishing House, 1977.

Hoehner, Harold W. "Jesus the Source or Product of Christianity." Lecture taped at the University of California at San Diego, La Jolla, Calif., January 22, 1976.

Hoehner, Harold W. Unpublished lecture notes from Contemporary New Testament Issues in European Theology 232, Dallas Theological Seminary, Spring, 1975.

Hoenen, Peter. *Reality and Judgment According to St. Thomas.* Chicago: Henry Regnery Company, 1952.

Hofner, Harry A. "The Hittites and the Hurrians," *Peoples of the Old Testament*. Ed. by D. J. Wiseman. London: Oxford Press, 1973.

Holloman, Henry W. *An Exposition of the Post-Resurrection Appearances of Our Lord*. Unpublished Th.M. thesis, Dallas Theological Seminary, May 1967.

Hooper, Walter, ed. *Christian Reflections*. Grand Rapids: Eerdmans, 1967.

Horell, J. Scott. "Trinitarianism," unpublished class notes from Dallas Theological Seminary, 1999.

Horn, Robert M. *The Book That Speaks for Itself*. Downers Grove, Ill.: InterVarsity Press, 1970.

Horn, Siegfried H. "Recent Illumination of the Old Testament," *Christianity Today*. Vol. 12. June 21, 1968.

Hort, Fenton John Anthony and Brooke Foss Westcott. *The New Testament in the Original Greek*. Vol. 1. New York: Macmillan Co., 1881.

Hort, F. J. A. *Way, Truth and the Life*. New York: Macmillan and Co., 1894.

Hoskyns, Sir Edwyn and Noel Davey. *The Riddle of the New Testament*. London: Faber and Faber Ltd., 1947.

Houde, Roland and Joseph P. Mullally, eds. *Philosophy of Knowledge: Selected Readings*. Chicago: J. B. Lippincott, 1960.

Howe, Thomas A. "Toward a Thomistic Theory of Meaning." Master's thesis, Liberty University, 1992.

Hubbard, D. A. "Pentateuch," in *New Bible Dictionary*. 2nd ed. Ed. by J. D. Douglas, et al. Downers Grove, Ill.: InterVarsity Press, 1982.

Huffmon, Herbert B. "The Exodus, Sinai, and the Credo," *Catholic Biblical Quarterly*. Vol. 27. 1965.

Hughes, Philip Edgcumbe. *A Commentary on the Epistle to the Hebrews*. Grand Rapids: Wm. B. Eerdmans, 1977.

Hume, David. *Dialogues Concerning Natural Religion*. Ed. by Henry D. Aiken. New York: Hafner Publishing Company, Inc., 1957.

Hume, David. *An Enquiry Concerning Human Understanding: and Other Essays*. Ed. by Ernest C. Mossner. New York: Washington Square, 1963.

Hume, David. *An Enquiry Concerning Human Understanding*. With an introduction, notes and editorial arrangement by Antony Flew. La Salle, Ill.: Open Court, 1992.

Hume, David. *Enquiries Concerning Human Understanding and Concerning the Principles of Morals*, 3rd. ed. Oxford: Clarendon Press, 1992.

Hume, David. *A Treatise of Human Nature*, 2d. ed. Oxford: Clarendon, 1978.

Hunter, A. M. *Interpreting the New Testament: 1900-1950*. London: SCM Press Ltd., 1951.

Hunter, A. M. "New Testament Survey," *The Expository Times*. Vol. 76. October 1964.

Hunter, A. M. *The Work and Words of Jesus*. Philadelphia: Westminster Press, 1950.

Hutchins, Robert Maynard, ed. *Great Books of the Western World*. Vol. 42. Chicago: William Benton, 1952.

Hutson, Harold H. "Form Criticism of the New Testament," *Journal of Bible and Religion*. Vol. 19. July 1951.

Huxley, T. H. *The Works of T. H. Huxley*. New York: Appleton, 1896.

Ignatius. "Epistle to the Ephesians," *Genuine Epistles of the Apostolical Fathers*. Trans. by William of Canterbury. London: Samuel Bagster, 1840.

Ignatius. "Ignatius' Epistle to Trallians," *Ante-Nicene Christian Library: Translations of the Writings of the Fathers*. Ed. by Alexander Roberts and James Donaldson. Vol. 1. Edinburgh: T & T Clark, 1867.

"The Incomparable Christ." Oradell, N.J.: American Tract Society, n.d.

International Standard Bible Encyclopaedia. 5 vols. Ed. by James Orr, John L. Nielsen, and James Donaldson. Grand Rapids: Wm B. Eerdmans Publishing Co., 1939.

Interpreter's Dictionary of the Bible. Ed. by George A. Buttrick. New York: Abingdon Press: 1962.

The Interpreter's One-Volume Commentary on the Bible. Ed. by Charles Laymon. Nashville: Abingdon Press, 1971.

Irenaeus. *Against the Heresies/St. Irenaeus of Lyons*; translated and annotated by Dominic J. Unger with further revisions by John J. Dillon. New York: Paulist Press, 1992.

Irwin, W. A. "The Modern Approach to the Old Testament." *Journal of Bible and Religion.* 1953.

Jaganay, Leo. *An Introduction to the Textual Criticism of the New Testament.* Trans. by B. V. Miller. London: Sands and Company, 1937.

Jaki, Stanley L. "From Scientific Cosmology to a Created Universe," *The Intellectuals Speak Out about God.* Ed. by Roy Abraham Varghese. Dallas: Lewis and Stanley Publishers, 1984.

James, William. *A Pluralistic Universe.* London: Harvard University Press, 1977.

James, William. *The Varieties of Religious Experience.* London: Harvard University Press, 1985.

Jamieson, Robert, A. R. Fausset, and David Brown, eds. *A Commentary, Critical, Experimental, and Practical on the Old and New Testaments.* Vol. V. Grand Rapids: William B. Eerdmans Publishing Co., 1948.

Jamieson, Robert, A. R. Fausset, and David Brown. *A Commentary, Critical, Experimental, and Practical on the Old and New Testaments.* Grand Rapids: William B. Eerdmans Publishing Co., 1961.

Jastrow, Robert. "The Astronomer and God," *The Intellectuals Speak Out about God.* Ed. by Roy Abraham Varghese. Dallas: Lewis and Stanley Publishers, 1984.

Jastrow, Robert. *God and The Astronomers.* New York: W. W. Norton & Co., 1978.

Jefferson, Charles Edward. *The Character of Jesus.* New York: Thomas Y. Crowell Co., 1908.

Jeremias, Joachim. *The Parables of Jesus.* Trans. by S. H. Hooke. London: SCM Press Ltd., Sixth edition, 1963.

The Jewish Encyclopedia. New York: Funk and Wagnalls Company, n.d.

Jidejian, Nina. *Tyre Through the Ages.* Beirut: Dar El-Mashreq Publishers, 1969.

Johnson, B. C. *The Atheist Debater's Handbook.* Buffalo: Prometheus Books, 1981.

Johnson, Paul H. "Master Plan." Westchester, Ill.: Good News Publishers, n.d.

Johnson, Sherman E. "Bultmann and the Mythology of the New Testament," *Anglican Theological Review.* Vol. 36. January 1954.

Josephus, Flavius. "Against Apion," *The Antiquities of the Jews.* New York: Ward, Lock, Bowden & Co., 1900.

Josephus, Flavius. *The Antiquities of the Jews.* New York: Ward, Lock, Bowden & Co., 1900.

Josephus, Flavius. "Flavius Josephus Against Apion," *Josephus' Complete Works.* Trans. by William Whiston. Grand Rapids: Kregel Publications, 1960.

Josephus, Flavius. *Jewish Antiquities.* Trans. by Ralph Marehus (from the Loeb Classical Library, Ed. by T. E. Page). 5 vols. Cambridge: Harvard University Press, 1963.

Josephus, Flavius. *The Works of Flavius Josephus.* Trans. by William Whiston. Grand Rapids: Associated Publishers and Authors, Inc., 1860.

Journey's End. Oradell, N.J.: American Tract Society.

Jubien, Michael. *Contemporary Metaphysics.* Cambridge, Mass.: Blackwell, 1997.

Kahle, Paul E. *The Cairo Geniza,* 2d ed. Oxford: Oxford University Press, 1959.

Kahler, Martin. *The So-called Historical Jesus and the Historic, Biblical Christ.* Trans. and ed. by C. E. Baraaten. Philadelphia: Fortress Press, 1988.

Kaiser, Walter C., Jr., "The Literary Form of Genesis 1–11," *New Perspectives on the Old Testament.* Ed. by J. Barton Payne. Waco: Word Books, 1970.

Kant, Immanuel. *Critique of Practical Reason.* Trans. by Mary Gregor. Cambridge: Cambridge University Press, 1997.

Kant, Immanuel. *Critique of Pure Reason.* Trans. by Werner S. Pluhar. Indianapolis, Ind.: Hackett Publishing Co., Inc., 1996.

Kant, Immanuel. *Critique of Pure Reason.* In *Great Books of the Western World,* ed. Robert Maynard Hutchins. Vol. 42. Chicago: William Benton, 1952.

Kant, Immanuel. *Prolegomena to Any Future Metaphysics.* Trans. by Paul Carus. 13th printing. Illinois: Open Court, 1902.

Kant, Immanuel. *Religion within the Limits of Reason Alone.* Trans. by Theodore M. Greene and Hoyt H. Hudson. New York: Harper Torchbooks, 1960.

Käsemann, Ernst. *Essays on New Testament Themes.* Naperville, Ill.: Alec R. Allenson, Inc., SCM Press Ltd., 1964.

Käsemann, Ernst. *New Testament Questions of Today.* Philadelphia: Fortress Press, 1969.

Kaufman, Yehezkel. *The Religion of Israel.* Chicago: The University of Chicago, 1960.

Kautzsch, E. *An Outline of the History of the Literature of the Old Testament.* Trans. by John Taylor. Oxford: Williams and Norgate, 1898.

Kee, H. C. "Aretalogy and Gospel," *Journal of Biblical Literature.* Vol. 92. September 1973.

Kee, Howard Clark. *What Can We Know about Jesus?* Cambridge: Cambridge University Press, 1990.

Keener, Craig S. *The IVP Bible Background Commentary: New Testament.* Downers Grove, Ill.: InterVarsity Press. 1993.

Kegley, Charles W., ed. *The Theology of Rudolf Bultmann.* New York: Harper and Row Publishers, 1966.

Keil, C. F. *Biblical Commentary on the Old Testament: The Prophecies of Jeremiah.* Trans. by David Patrick. Vol. I. Grand Rapids: William B. Eerdmans Publishing Co., 1964.

Keith, Alexander. *Evidence of the Truth of the Christian Religion.* London: T. O. Nelson and Sons, 1861.

Keller, Werner. *The Bible as History.* Trans. by William Neil. New York: William and Company, 1956.

Kelso, James. *Archaeology and Our Old Testament Contemporaries.* Grand Rapids: Zondervan, 1966.

Kennedy, D. James and Jerry Newcombe. *What If Jesus Had Never Been Born?* Nashville: Thomas Nelson, 1994.

Kenneson, Philip D. "There's No Such Thing as Objective Truth, and It's a Good Thing, Too," *Christian Apologetics in the Postmodern World.* Ed. by Timothy R. Phillips and Dennis L. Okholm. Downers Grove, Ill.: InterVarsity Press, 1995.

Kenyon, Frederic G. *The Bible and Archaeology.* New York: Harper & Row, 1940.

Kenyon, Frederic G. *The Bible and Modern Scholarship.* London: John Murray, 1948.

Kenyon, Frederic G. *Handbook to the Textual Criticism of the New Testament.* London: Macmillan and Company, 1901.

Kenyon, Frederic. *Our Bible and the Ancient Manuscripts.* London: Eyre and Spottiswoode, 1939.

Kenyon, Sir Frederic. *The Story of the Bible.* London: John Murray, 1936.

Kenyon, Kathleen. *Beginning in Archaeology.* New York: Praeger, 1962.

Kevan, Ernest F. *The Resurrection of Christ.* London: The Campbell Morgan Memorial Bible Lectureship, Westminster Chapel, Buckingham Gate, S. W. I., 14 June 1961.

Kierkegaard, Søren. *Concluding Unscientific Postscript to Philosophical Fragments.* Vol 1. Trans. by Howard V. and Edna H. Hong. Princeton: Princeton University Press, 1985.

Kierkegaard, Søren. *Philosophical Fragments.* Trans. by Howard V. Hong and Edna H. Hong. Princeton, N.J.: Princeton University Press, 1985.

Kim, Chi Syun. *The Mosaic Authorship of the Pentateuch.* Doctoral dissertation, Dallas Theological Seminary, 1935.

Kistemaker, Simon. *The Gospels in Current Study.* Grand Rapids: Baker Book House, 1972.

Kitchen, K. A. *The Ancient Orient and the Old Testament.* Chicago: InterVarsity Press, 1966.

Kitchen, K. A. "Ancient Orient, 'Deuteronism' and the Old Testament," *New Perspectives on the Old Testament.* Ed. by J. Barton Payne. Waco, Tex.: Word, 1970.

Kitchen, K. A. *The Bible in Its World.* Downers Grove, Ill.: InterVarsity Press, 1978.

Kitchen, K. A. "The Old Testament in the Context: 1 from the Origins to the Eve of the Exodus," *TSF Bulletin.* Vol. 59. Spring, 1971.

Kitchen, Kenneth A. "The Patriarchal Age: Myth or History?" *Biblical Archaeology Review,* March/April, 1995.

Kitchen, Kenneth A. "Some Egyptian Background to the Old Testament." *The Tyndale House Bulletins,* Nos. 5 & 6, 1960.

Kittel, Gerhard and Friedrich, Gerhard, eds. *The Theological Dictionary of the New Testament.* Grand Rapids: William B. Eerdmans Publishing Company, 1985.

Kittel, R. *A History of the Hebrews.* Vol. 1. Trans. by John Taylor. Edinburgh: Williams and Norgate, 1895.

Kittel, R. *The Scientific Study of the Old Testament.* Trans. by J. Caleb Hughes. New York: G. P. Putnam's Sons, 1910.

Klausner, Joseph. *Jesus of Nazareth.* New York: Macmillan, 1925.

Klausner, *Yeschu Hanostri,* as quoted by Pinchas Lapide in *Christian Century* 87. Oct., 1970.

Kligerman, Aaron Judah. *Messianic Prophecy in the Old Testament.* Grand Rapids: Zondervan Publishing House, 1957.

Kline, Meredith. "The Concepts of Canon and Covenant," *New Perspectives on the Old Testament.* Ed. by J. Barton Payne. Waco, Tex.: Word, 1970.

Kline, Meredith G. "Dynastic Covenant," *Westminster Theological Journal.* Vol. 23. November 1961.

Kline, Meredith. "Is the History of the Old Testament Accurate?" *Can I Trust My Bible?* Ed. by Howard Vos. Chicago: Moody Press, 1963.

Kline, Meredith G. *Treaty of the Great King.* Grand Rapids: William B. Eerdmans Publishing Co., 1963.

Koldewey, Robert. *The Excavations at Babylon.* Trans. by Agnes S. Johns. London: Macmillan and Company, Ltd., 1914.

Kole, Andre and Al Janssen. *Miracles or Magic?* Eugene, Ore.: Harvest House, 1984.

Kraeling, Emil G., ed. *Rand McNally Bible Atlas.* New York: Rand McNally, 1956.

Kreeft, Peter. *Christianity for Modern Pagans.* Pascal's *Pensees* edited, outlined and explained. San Francisco: Ignatius Press, 1993.

Kreeft, Peter. *Fundamentals of the Faith: Essays in Christian Apologetics.* San Francisco: Ignatius Press, 1988

Kreeft, Peter and Ronald K. Tacelli. *Handbook of Christian Apologetics.* Downers Grove, Ill.: InterVarsity, 1994.

Kretzmann, Norman and Eleonore Stump, ed. *The Cambridge Companion to Aquinas.* Cambridge: Cambridge University Press, 1993.

Kubie, Nora Benjamin. *Road to Nineveh.* New York: Doubleday and Company, 1964.

Kuenen, Abraham. *An Historico-Critical Inquiry into the Origin and Composition of the Hexateuch.* Trans. by P. H. Wicksteed. London: Macmillan & Co., 1886.

Kuenen, A. *The Religion of Israel.* Trans. by Alfred Heath May. Edinburgh: Williams and Norgate, 1874.

Külling, Samuel R. "The Dating of the So-Called 'P-Sections' in Genesis," *Journal of the Evangelical Theological Society.* Vol. 15. Spring, 1972.

Kung, Hans. *Does God Exist?: An Answer for Today.* Trans. by Edward Quinn. New York: Doubleday & Company, Inc., 1980.

Kunneth, Walter. "Dare We Follow Bultmann?" *Christianity Today.* Vol. 6. October 13, 1961.

Kurtz, Paul. *In Defense of Secular Humanism.* Buffalo: Prometheus Books, 1983.

Kushner, Harold S. "How Can Anything Good Come Out of This?" On *Faith & Reason,* Show #9805, aired on 7-30-98. Shreveport, La.: D. L. Dykes, Jr. Foundation.

Kushner, Harold S. *When All You've Ever Wanted Isn't Enough.* New York: Summit Books, 1986.

Kushner, Harold S. *When Bad Things Happen to Good People.* New York: Avon Books, 1983.

Kyle, Melvin G. *The Deciding Voice of the Monuments in Biblical Criticism.* Oberlin, Ohio: Bibliotheca Sacra Company, 1924.

Kyle, Melvin G. *The Problem of the Pentateuch.* Oberlin, Ohio: Bibliotheca Sacra Co., 1920.

Ladd, George E. *The New Testament and Criticism.* Grand Rapids: William B. Eerdmans Publishing Co., 1967.

Ladd, George Eldon. *Rudolf Bultmann.* Chicago: InterVarsity Press, 1964.

Laetsch, Theodore. *Bible Commentary: Jeremiah.* St. Louis: Concordia Publishing House, 1953.

Laetsch, Theodore. *Bible Commentary: The Minor Prophets.* St. Louis: Concordia Publishing House, 1970.

LaHaye, Tim. *Jesus: Who Is He?* Sisters, Ore.: Multnomah Books, 1996.

Lake, Kirsopp. "Caesarean Text of the Gospel of Mark." *Harvard Theological Review* 21, 1928.

Lake, Kirsopp. *The Historical Evidence for the Resurrection of Jesus Christ.* New York: G. P. Putnam's Sons, 1912.

Laney, J. Carl. *John.* In *Moody Gospel Commentary.* Chicago: Moody Press, 1992.

Lapide, Pinchas. *Christian Century* 87. October 1970.

Lapide, Pinchas. *The Resurrection of Jesus: A Jewish Perspective.* Trans. by Wilhelm C. Linss. Minneapolis: Augsburg, 1983.

Lapp, Paul W. *Biblical Archaeology and History.* New York: World Publishing, 1969.

Larue, Gerald A. *Babylon and the Bible.* Grand Rapids: Baker Book House, 1919.

Latham, Henry. *The Risen Master.* Cambridge: Deighton, Bell, and Co., 1904.

Latourette, Kenneth Scott. *American Historical Review* 54, January 1949.

Latourette, Kenneth Scott. *Anno Domini.* New York: Harper and Brothers, 1940.

Latourette, Kenneth Scott. *A History of Christianity.* New York: Harper and Row, 1953.

Layard, Austen H. *Discoveries Among the Ruins of Nineveh and Babylon.* New York: Harper and Brothers, 1953.

Laymon, Charles, ed. *The Interpreter's One-Volume Commentary on the Bible.* New York: Abingdon Press, 1971.

Lea, John W. *The Greatest Book in the World.* Philadelphia: n. p., 1929.

Leach, Charles. *Our Bible. How We Got It.* Chicago: Moody Press, 1898.

Le Camus, E. *The Life of Christ.* Vol. III. New York: The Cathedral Library Association, 1908.

Lecky, William Edward Hatpole. *History of European Morals from Augustus to Charlemagne.* New York: D. Appleton and Co., 1903.

Leemans, W. F. "Foreign Trade in the Old Babylonian Period as Revealed by Texts from Southern Mesopotamia," *Studia et Documenta ad iura Orientis Antiqui Pertinentia.* Vol. 6. 1960.

Leibniz, *The Monadology and Other Philosophical Writings.* Trans. by Robert Latta. New York: Oxford University Press, 1925.

LeMann, M. M. *Jesus Before the Sanhedrin.* Trans. by Julius Magath. Nashville: Southern Methodist Publishing House, 1886.

Lenski, R.C.H. *The Interpretation of St. John's Gospel.* Columbus: Lutheran Book Concern, 1942.

Lenski, R. C. H. *The Interpretation of St. Matthew's Gospel.* Columbus: The Wartburg Press, 1943.

Lessing, Gotthold. *Lessing's Theological Writings.* Stanford, Calif.: Stanford University Press, 1957.

Lewis, Charlton T. and Charles Short, eds. *A Latin Dictionary.* Oxford: Clarendon Press, n.d.

Lewis, C. S. *The Abolition of Man.* New York: Collier, 1947.

Lewis, C. S. *Christian Reflections.* Ed. by Walter Hooper. Grand Rapids: Eerdmans, 1967.

Lewis, C. S. Mere Christianity. New York: Macmillan, 1952.

Lewis, C. S. *Mere Christianity.* New York: Macmillan Publishing Company, Collier Books, 1960.

Lewis, C. S. *Miracles: A Preliminary Study.* New York: Macmillan, 1947.

Lewis, C. S. *Miracles.* New York: Macmillan, 1960.

Lewis, C. S. "Modern Theology and Biblical Criticism," *Christian Reflections.* Grand Rapids: Wm. B. Eerdmans Publishing Co., 1967.

Lewis, C. S. "The Poison of Subjectivism." In *Christian Reflections,* ed. Walter Hooper. Grand Rapids: Eerdmans, 1967.

Lewis, C. S. *The Problem of Pain.* New York: Macmillan Publishing Company, Collier Books, 1962.

Lewis, C. S. *The Weight of Glory and Other Addresses,* rev. exp. New York: Macmillan, 1980.

Lewis, Peter. *The Glory of Christ.* Chicago: Moody Press, 1997.

Liefeld, Walter L. "Luke," in *The Expositor's Bible Commentary,* ed. by Frank E. Gaebelein, vol. 8. Grand Rapids: Zondervan, 1984.

Lightfoot. *Evangelium Matthaei, horoe hebraicoe.* Quoted in M. M. LeMann, *Jesus Before the Sanhedrin.* Trans. by Julius Magath. Nashville: Southern Methodist Publishing House, 1886.

Lightfoot, Robert Henry. *History and Interpretation in the Gospels.* New York: Harper and Brothers Publishers, 1934.

Linnemann, Eta. *Historical Criticism of the Bible.* Trans. by Robert W. Yarbrough. Grand Rapids: Baker Book House, 1995.

Linnemann, Eta. *Is There a Synoptic Problem?* Trans. by Robert W. Yarbrough. Grand Rapids: Baker Book House, 1993.

Linton, Irwin H. *The Sanhedrin Verdict.* New York: Loizeaux Brothers, Bible Truth Depot, 1943.

Liplady, Thomas. *The Influence of the Bible.* New York: Fleming H. Revell, 1924.

Liptzen, Sol. *Biblical Themes in World Literature.*

Hoboken, N.J.: Ktav Publishing House, Inc., 1985.

Little, Paul. *Know What You Believe.* Wheaton: Scripture Press Publications, Inc., 1987.

Little, Paul E. *Know Why You Believe.* Wheaton: Scripture Press, 1987.

Livingston, G. Herbert. *The Pentateuch in Its Cultural Environment.* Grand Rapids: Baker Book House, 1974.

Locke, John. *A Second Vindication of the Reasonableness of Christianity, Works.* Quoted in Wilbur M. Smith, *Therefore Stand: Christian Apologetics.* Grand Rapids: Baker Book House, 1965.

Loetscher, Lefferts A., editor-in-chief. "Pentateuch," *Twentieth Century Encyclopedia of Religious Knowledge.* Grand Rapids: Baker Book House, 1955.

Loetscher, Lefferts A., ed. *Twentieth Century Encyclopedia of Religious Knowledge.* Vol. 1. Grand Rapids: Baker Book House, 1955.

Lucien of Samosata. *"Death of Pelegrine."* In *The Works of Lucian of Samosata*, 4 vols. Trans. by H. W. Fowler and F. G. Fowler. Oxford: The Clarendon Press, 1949.

Luckenbill, Daniel David. *Ancient Record of Assyria and Babylonia.* 2 vols. Chicago: University of Chicago Press, 1926.

MacDill, David, *The Mosaic Authorship of the Pentateuch.* Pittsburgh: United Presbyterian Board of Publication, 1896.

Macdonald, E. M. "Design Argument Fallacies." In *An Anthology of Atheism and Rationalism*, ed. by Gordon Stein. Amherst: Prometheus Books, 1980.

MacDonald, Scott. "Theory of Knowledge." In *The Cambridge Companion to Aquinas,* ed. Norman Kretzmann and Eleonore Stump. Cambridge: Cambridge University Press, 1993.

Machen, J. Gresham. *The Virgin Birth of Christ.* Grand Rapids: Baker Book House, 1965.

MacIntyre, Alasdair. *First Principles, Final Ends and Contemporary Philosophical Issues.* Milwaukee: Marquette University Press, 1990.

Mackay, John. *History and Destiny.* Quoted in Joseph P. Free, "Archaeology and Neo-Orthodoxy," *Bibliotheca Sacra* 114, January 1957.

Mackie, John L. "Evil and Omnipotence." In *The Philosophy of Religion*, ed. Basil Mitchell. London: Oxford University Press, 1972. Quoted in Alvin C. Plantinga, *God, Freedom, and Evil.* Grand Rapids: William B. Eerdmans Publishing Company, 1996.

Mackie, John L. *The Miracle of Theism.* Oxford: Clarendon Press, 1983. Quoted in J. P. Moreland, *Does God Exist?* Amherst: Prometheus Books, 1993.

MacLaine, Shirley. *Out on a Limb.* New York: Bantam, 1983.

Maclean, G. F. *Cambridge Bible for Schools, St. Mark.* London: Cambridge University Press, 1893.

Maharaj, Rabindranath and Dave Hunt. *Death of a Guru.* Nashville: Holman, 1977.

Maier, Walter A. *The Book of Nahum: A Commentary.* St. Louis: Concordia Publishing House, 1959.

Maier, Gerhard. *The End of the Historical-Critical Method.* Trans. by Edwin W. Leverenz and Rudolph F. Norden. St. Louis: Concordia, 1974.

Maier, Paul L. *First Easter: The True and Unfamiliar Story.* New York: Harper and Row, 1973.

Maier, Paul L. *In the Fullness of Time: A Historian Looks at Christmas, Easter, and the Early Church.* San Francisco: Harper San Francisco, 1991.

Maine, Henry Sumner. *Ancient Law.* New York: Henry Holt and Company, 1888.

Malevez, L. *The Christian Message and Myth.* London: SCM Press, Ltd., 1958.

Mallowan, M. E. L. *Numrud and Its Remains.* 3 vols. London: Collins, St. James Place, 1966.

Manley, G. T. *The Book of the Law.* Grand Rapids: Wm. B. Eerdmans Publishing Co., 1957.

Manson, T. W. "Is It Possible to Write a Life of Christ?" *The Expository Times.* Vol. 53. May 1942.

Manson, T. W. *Jesus the Messiah.* Philadelphia: Westminster Press, 1946.

Manson, T. W. "Present Day Research in the Life of Jesus," *The Background of the New Testament and Its Eschatology.* Ed. by W. D. Davies and B. Daube. Cambridge: at the University Press, 1956.

Manson, T. W. "The Quest of the Historical

Jesus—Continues," *Studies in the Gospels and Epistles*. Ed. by Matthew Black. Manchester: Manchester University Press, 1962.

Manson, T. W. *The Sayings of Jesus*. London: SCM Press, Ltd., 1949.

Margenau, Henry. "Modern Physics and Belief in God." In *The Intellectuals Speak Out About God*, ed. Roy Abraham Varghese. Dallas: Lewis and Stanley Publishers, 1984.

Marshall, Alfred. *The Interlinear Greek-English New Testament*. Rev. ed. Grand Rapids: Zondervan Publishing House, 1969.

Marshall, I. Howard. *The Gospel of Luke: A Commentary on the Greek Text*. The New International Greek Testament Commentary Series. Grand Rapids: William B. Eerdmans Publishing Co., 1952.

Marshall, I. Howard. *I Believe in the Historical Jesus*. Grand Rapids: William B. Eerdmans Publishing Co., 1977.

Marshall, I. Howard, ed. *New Testament Interpretation, Essays on Principles and Methods*. Grand Rapids: William B. Eerdmans Publishing Co., 1977.

Martin, J. C. "Converted Catcher." Oradell, N.J.: American Tract Society, n.d.

Martin, J. P. "Beyond Bultmann, What?" *Christianity Today*. Vol. 6. November 24, 1961.

Martin, James. *The Reliability of the Gospels*. London: Hodder and Stoughton, 1959.

Martin, John A. "Isaiah." In *The Bible Knowledge Commentary: Old Testament*, ed. by John F. Walvoord and Roy B. Zuck. Wheaton, Ill., Victor Books, 1985.

Martin, Ralph. *Mark, Evangelist and Theologian*. Grand Rapids: Zondervan Publishing House, 1973.

Martin, W. J. *Stylistic Criteria and the Analysis of the Pentateuch*. London: Tyndale Press, 1955.

Marty, Martin E. "Foreword" to *The Promise of Bultmann* by Norman Perrin. New York: J. B. Lippincott Company, 1969.

Martyr, Justin. "Apology." In *Ante-Nicene Fathers*, ed. Alexander Roberts and James Donaldson. Grand Rapids: Eerdmans, 1989.

Marx, Karl. *Contribution to the Critique of Hegel's Philosophy of Right: Introduction*. In *The Portable Karl Marx*. Trans. by Eugene

Kamenka. New York: Penguin Books, 1983.

Marxsen, Willi. *Mark the Evangelist*. Trans. by Roy A. Harrisville. New York: Abingdon Press, 1969.

Matheson, George. *The Representative Men of the New Testament*. London: Hodder and Stoughton, 1904.

Mattingly, John P. *Crucifixion: Its Origin and Application to Christ*. Unpublished Th.M. thesis, Dallas Theological Seminary, 1961.

Maurice, Thomas. *Observations on the Ruins of Babylon, Recently Visited and Described by Claudius James Rich, Esq*. London: John Murray of Albermarle St., 1816.

Mavrodes, George I. *Belief in God: A Study in the Epistemology of Religion*. New York: Random House, 1970.

McAfee, Cleland B. *The Greatest English Classic*. New York, NY: n.p., 1912.

McCallum, Dennis. *The Death of Truth*. Minneapolis: Bethany House, 1996.

McCarthy, Dennis J. "Covenant in the Old Testament," *Catholic Biblical Quarterly*. Vol. 27. 1954.

McCarthy, Dennis J. *Treaty and Covenant*. Rome: Pontifical Biblical Institute, 1963.

McClain, Alva J. *Daniel's Prophecy of the Seventy Weeks*. Grand Rapids: Zondervan Publishing House, 1972.

McClymont, J. A. *New Testament Criticism*. New York: Hodder and Stoughton, 1913.

McConkie, Bruce R. *Mormon Doctrine—A Compendium of the Gospel*, rev. ed. Salt Lake City: Bookcraft, 1966. Quoted in Norman L. Geisler and William D. Watkins, *Worlds Apart*. Grand Rapids: Baker Book House, 1984.

McCullagh, C. Behan. *The Truth of History*. London: Routledge, 1998.

McDowell, Josh. *Evidence That Demands a Verdict*. Vol. 1. San Bernardino, Calif.: Here's Life Publishers, 1972. Rev. ed., 1979. Reprint, Nashville: Thomas Nelson Publishers, 1993.

McDowell, Josh. *Evidence That Demands a Verdict*. Vol. 2. San Bernardino, Calif.: Here's Life Publishers, 1975. Reprint, Nashville: Thomas Nelson Publishers, 1993.

McDowell, Josh and Bob Hostetler. *The New Tolerance*. Wheaton, Ill.: Tyndale House Pubs., 1998.

McDowell, Josh and Don Stewart, *Handbook of Today's Religions.* Campus Crusade for Christ, Inc., 1983. Reprint, Nashville: Thomas Nelson Publishers, 1996.

McDowell, Josh and Bill Wilson. *He Walked Among Us: Evidence for the Historical Jesus.* San Bernardino, Calif.: Here's Life Publishers, 1988. Reprint, Nashville: Thomas Nelson Publishers, 1993.

McGinley, Laurence J. *Form Criticism of the Synoptic Healing Narratives.* Woodstock, Md.: Woodstock College Press, 1944.

McGrath, Alister. *Christian Theology: An Introduction.* Oxford: Blackwell, 1994.

McGrath, Alister. *Understanding Jesus.* Grand Rapids: Zondervan Publishing House, 1987.

McGrath, Alister E. *What Was God Doing on the Cross?* Grand Rapids: Zondervan, 1992.

McKnight, Edgar V. *What Is Form Criticism?* Philadelphia: Fortress Press, 1969.

McLain, Charles E. "Toward a Theology of Language." *Calvary Baptist Theological Journal.* Spring/Fall 1996.

McNeile, A. H. *An Introduction to the Study of the New Testament.* London: Oxford University Press, 1953.

Mead, Frank, ed. *The Encyclopedia of Religious Quotations.* Westwood, Ill.: Fleming H. Revell, n.d.

Meek, J. T. *Hebrew Origins.* Revised Edition. New York: Harper Brothers, 1950.

Meier, John P. "The Testimonium: Evidence for Jesus Outside the Bible." *Bible Review.* June 1991.

Meisinger, George E. *The Fall of Nineveh.* Unpublished master's thesis, Dallas Theological Seminary, 1968.

Meldau, Fred John. *101 Proofs of the Deity of Christ from the Gospels.* Denver, Colo.: The Christian Victory, 1960.

Mellor, D. H., ed. *Philosophical Papers.* Cambridge: Cambridge University Press, 1990.

Mendenhall, George E. "A Biblical History in Transition." In *The Bible and the Ancient Near East,* ed. G. E. Wright. New York: Doubleday and Company, 1961.

Mendenhall, George E. *Law and Covenant in Israel and the Ancient Near East.* Pittsburgh: Biblical Colloquium, 1955.

Metzger, Bruce. "Circulation of the Bible." In *The Oxford Companion to the Bible,* ed. Bruce Metzger and Michael Coogan, New York: Oxford University Press, 1993.

Metzger, Bruce M. *Lexical Aids for Students of New Testament Greek.* New edition. Princeton, N.J.: Theological Book Agency, 1970.

Metzger, Bruce M. *Manuscripts of the Greek Bible: An Introduction to Paleography.* New York: Oxford University Press, 1981.

Metzger, Bruce M. *The Text of the New Testament.* New York: Oxford University Press, 1968.

Metzger, Bruce M. *The Text of the New Testament: Its Transmission, Corruption, and Restoration.* New York: Oxford University Press, 1992.

Michaud, Joseph Francois. *History of the Crusades.* 2 vols. Philadelphia: George Barrie.

Middleton, J. Richard, and Brian J. Walsh. "Facing the Postmodern Scalpel: Can the Christian Faith Withstand Deconstruction?" In *Christian Apologetics in the Postmodern World,* ed. Timothy R. Phillips and Dennis L. Okholm. Downers Grove, Ill.: InterVarsity Press, 1995.

Miegge, Giovanni. *Gospel and Myth in the Thought of Rudolf Bultmann.* Trans. by Bishop Stephen Neill. Richmond, Va.: John Knox Press, 1960.

Miethe, Terry L. and Antony G. N. Flew. *Does God Exist? A Believer and an Atheist Debate.* San Francisco: Harper, 1991.

Mill, John S. *Three Essays of Religion.* Westport: Greenwood Press, 1970. Reprinted from 1874 edition.

Millard, Alan. "Does the Bible Exaggerate King Solomon's Wealth?" *Biblical Archaeology Review,* May/June 1989.

Miller, David L. *The New Polytheism: Rebirth of the Gods and Goddesses.* New York: Harper and Row Publishers, 1974.

Miller, Ed L. "Plenary Inspiration and 2 Timothy 3:16." *Lutheran Quarterly* XVII. February 1965.

Milligan, William. *The Resurrection of Our Lord.* New York: The Macmillan Company, 1927.

Minkin, Jacob S. *The World of Moses Maimonides.* New York: Thomas Yoseloff, 1957.

The Mishnah. Trans. by Herbert Danby. London: Geoffrey Cumberlege, Oxford University Press, 1933.

Moller, Wilhelm. *Are the Critics Right?* New York: Fleming H. Revell Co., 1899.

Montefiore, C. G. *The Synoptic Gospels.* London: Macmillan and Co., Ltd., 1909, 1927. 2 vols.

Montgomery, John W. *The Altizer-Montgomery Dialogue.* Chicago: InterVarsity Press, 1967.

Montgomery, John W., ed. *Christianity for the Tough Minded.* Minneapolis: Bethany Fellowship, Inc., 1973.

Montgomery, John W. "Evangelicals and Archaeology." *Christianity Today.* August 16, 1968.

Montgomery, John W., ed. *Evidence for Faith.* Dallas, Tex.: Probe Books, 1991.

Montgomery, John W. *Faith Founded on Fact: Essays in Evidential Apologetics.* Nashville: Thomas Nelson, 1978.

Montgomery, John W. *History and Christianity.* Downers Grove, Ill.: InterVarsity Press, 1964.

Montgomery, John W. *History and Christianity.* Downers Grove, Ill.: InterVarsity Press, 1971.

Montgomery, John Warwick. "Is Man His Own God?" *Christianity for the Tough Minded.* Ed. by John Warwick Montgomery. Minneapolis: Bethany Fellowship, Inc., 1973.

Montgomery, John Warwick. *The Shape of the Past.* Ann Arbor: Edwards Brothers, 1962.

Moore, G. E. *Some Main Problems of Philosophy.* New York: Macmillan, 1953.

Moore, James R. "Science and Christianity: Toward Peaceful Coexistence," *Christianity for the Tough Minded.* Ed. by John Warwick Montgomery. Minneapolis: Bethany Fellowship, Inc., 1973.

Moreland, J. P. *An Apologetic Critique of the Major Presuppositions of the New Quest of the Historical Jesus.* Th.M. thesis, Dallas Theological Seminary, 1979.

Moreland, J. P. *The Creation Hypothesis: Scientific Evidence for an Intelligent Designer.* Downers Grove, Ill.: InterVarsity Press, 1994.

Moreland, J. P. *Love Your God with All Your Mind.* Colorado Springs: NavPress, 1997.

Moreland, J. P. *Scaling the Secular City.* Grand Rapids: Baker, 1987.

Moreland, J. P. and Kai Nielsen. *Does God Exist?* Amherst: Prometheus Books, 1993.

Morison, Frank. *Who Moved the Stone?* London: Faber and Faber Ltd., 1958.

Morison, Frank. Who Moved the Stone? London: Faber and Faber , 1967.

Morris, Henry M. *The Bible Has the Answer.* Grand Rapids: Baker Book House, 1971.

Morris, Henry M.. *The Bible and Modern Science.* Rev. ed. Chicago: Moody Press, 1956.

Morris, Henry M. *Many Infallible Proofs.* San Diego: Creation-Life Publishers, 1974.

Morris, Henry, with Henry M. Morris III. *Many Infallible Proofs.* Green Forest, Ark.: Master Books, 1996.

Morris, Leon. *The Gospel According to John.* The New International Commentary series. Grand Rapids: Wm. B. Eerdmans, 1971.

Morris, Leon. *Jesus Is the Christ: Studies in the Theology of John.* Grand Rapids: Eerdmans, 1989.

Morris, Leon. *New International Commentary, the Gospel According to John.* Grand Rapids: William B. Eerdmans Publishing Co., 1971.

Mosely, A. W. "Historical Reporting in the Ancient World," *New Testament Studies* 12. 1965-66.

Motyer, J. A. *The Revelation of the Divine Name.* London: The Tyndale Press, 1959.

Moule, C. F. D. "Form Criticism and Philological Studies," *London Quarterly and Holborn Review.* Vol. 183. April 1958.

Moule, C. F. D. "The Intentions of the Evangelists," *New Testament Essays.* Ed. by A. J. B. Higgins. Manchester: at the University Press, 1959.

Mounce, Robert. Interview, July 2, 1974.

Mounce, Robert H. "Is the New Testament Historically Accurate?" *Can I Trust My Bible?* Ed. by Howard Vos. Chicago: Moody Press, 1963.

Moyer, Elgin S. *Who Was Who in Church History,* rev. ed. Chicago: Moody Press, 1968.

Mueller, Walter, "A Virgin Shall Conceive." *The Evangelical Quarterly* 32. Oct.-Dec. 1960.

Muller, Fredrich. "Bultmann's Relationship to Classical Philology," *The Theology of Rudolf Bultmann.* Ed. by Charles W. Kegley. London: SCM Press, 1966.

Muller, Julius. *The Theory of Myths, in Its Application to the Gospel History, Examined and Confuted.* London: John Chapman, 1844.

Mullins, E.Y. *Why Is Christianity True?* Chicago: Christian Culture Press, 1905.

Murray, John. "The Attestation of Scripture." In *The Infallible Word.* Philadelphia, Pa.: Presbyterian and Reformed, 1946.

Myers, Albert E. "The Use of *Almah* in the Old Testament." *The Lutheran Quarterly* 7 (1955).

Myers, Philip Van Ness. *General History for Colleges and High Schools.* Boston: Ginn and Company, 1889.

Nash, Ronald. *Christianity and the Hellenistic World.* Grand Rapids: Zondervan, 1984.

Nash, Ronald H. *Faith and Reason.* Grand Rapids: Zondervan Publishing House, 1988.

Nash, Ronald. *The Gospel and the Greeks.* Dallas: Probe, 1992.

Nash, Ronald H., ed. *Philosophy of Gordon Clark.* Philadelphia: The Presbyterian and Reformed Publishing Company, 1968.

Nash, Ronald H. *World Views in Conflict.* Grand Rapids: Zondervan, 1992.

Nasir-i-Khurran. *Diary of a Journey Through Syria and Palestine in 1047 A.D.* London: n. p., 1893.

Neatby, T. Millar. *Confirming the Scriptures.* London: Marshall, Morgan and Scott, n.d. Vol. II. Quoted in Joseph P. Free, *Archaeology and Bible History.* Wheaton: Scripture Press, 1969.

Neill, Stephen. *The Interpretation of the New Testament.* London: Oxford University Press, 1964.

Nelson, Nina. *Your Guide to Lebanon.* London: Alvin Redman, Ltd., 1965.

Nettelhorst, R. P. "The Genealogy of Jesus." *Journal of the Evangelical Theological Society* 31, June 1988.

The New Bible Dictionary. Ed. by J. D. Douglas. Grand Rapids: Wm. B. Eerdmans Publishing Co., 1962.

Newton, Benjamin Wills. *Babylon: Its Future History and Doom.* London: Wertheimer, Lea and Co., 1890

Nezikin, Seder. *The Babylonian Talmud.* Trans. by I. Epstein. London: The Soncino Press, 1935.

Ng, David, ed. *Sourcebook.* Philadelphia: Board of Christian Education, The United Presbyterian Church in the U.S.A., 1970.

Niebuhr, Reinhold, ed. *Marx and Engels on Religion.* New York: Schocken, 1964.

Nielsen, Eduard. *Oral Tradition.* London: SCM Press, 1954.

Nielsen, Kai. "Ethics Without God," *Does God Exist?* Ed. by J. P. Moreland and Kai Nielsen. Amherst: Prometheus Books, 1993.

Nielsen, Kai. *Philosophy and Atheism.* Buffalo, N.Y.: Prometheus Books, 1985.

Niessen, Richard, "The Virginity of the 'almah' in Isaiah 7:14." *Bibliotheca Sacra.* April-June 1972.

Nietzsche, Friedrich. *The Antichrist.* In *The Portable Nietzsche.* Trans. by Walter Kaufmann. New York: Viking Press, 1970.

Nietzsche, Friedrich. *Joyful Wisdom.* Trans. by Thomas Common. New York: Frederick Unger Publishing Company, 1971.

Nietzsche, Friedrich. *Thus Spoke Zarathustra.* Trans. by Walter Kaufmann. New York: The Modern Library, 1995.

Nineham, D. E. "Eyewitness Testimony and the Gospel Tradition," *The Journal of Theological Studies.* Vol. 11. October 1960.

Nix, William E. "1 Chronicles," "2 Chronicles," "Joshua." In *The Criswell Study Bible,* ed. by W. A. Criswell. Nashville: Thomas Nelson, 1979.

North, C. R. "Pentateuchal Criticism," *The Old Testament and Modern Study.* Ed. by H. H. Rowley. Oxford: Clarendon Press, 1951.

North, C. R. "Pentateuchal Criticism," *The Old Testament and Modern Study.* Ed. by H. H. Rowley. Oxford: Oxford University Press, 1967.

North, C. R. "Pentateuchal Criticism," *The Old Testament and Modern Study: A Generation of Discovery and Research.* Ed. by H. H. Rowley. Oxford: Oxford University, 1956.

Northrop, F. S. C. and Mason W. Gross. *Alfred North Whitehead: An Anthology.* New York: The Macmillan Company, 1953.

Nowell-Smith, Patrick. "Miracles," *New Essays in Philosophy Theology.* Ed. by Antony Flew and Alasdair MacIntyre. New York: Macmillan, 1955.

Oesterley, W. O. E. and Theodore H. Robinson. *Hebrew Religion: Its Origin and Developments.* London: Society for Promoting Christian Knowledge, 1935.

Ogden, Schubert M. *Christ Without Myth.* New York: Harper and Row Publishers, 1961.

Ogden, S. "Debate on Demythologizing," *Journal of Bible and Religion.* Vol. 27. January 1959.

Ogden, Schubert M. *Faith and Freedom: Toward a Theology of Liberation.* Nashville: Abingdon, 1979.

Ogden, Schubert M. *The Reality of God and Other Essays.* San Francisco: Harper and Row, 1977.

Ogden, Schubert M. "The Significance of Rudolf Bultmann for Contemporary Theology," *The Theology of Rudolf Bultmann.* Ed. by Charles Kegley. London: SCM Press, 1966.

O'Hair, Madalyn Murray. "What on Earth Is an Atheist?" New York: Arno, 1972. Quoted in Ravi Zacharias, *Can Man Live Without God?* Dallas: Word Publishing, 1994.

Olmstead, A. T. "History, Ancient World, and the Bible." *Journal of Near Eastern Studies.* January 1943.

Oman, Sir Charles. *On the Writing of History.* New York: Barnes and Noble, 1939.

Ordonez, Rose Marie. *I Was Blind But Now I See.* Colorado Springs, Colo.: International Students, n.d..

Origen. *Contra Celsum. English Contra Celsum.* Trans. by Henry Chadwick. London: Cambridge University Press, 1953.

Origen. *Contra Celsum. English Contra Celsum.* Trans. and with an introduction and notes by Henry Chadwick. New York: Cambridge University Press, 1965. Reprint, 1980. Quoted in Norman L. Geisler, *Baker's Encyclopedia of Christian Apologetics.* Grand Rapids: Baker Book House, 1998.

Orlinsky. Harry. *Ancient Israel.* Ithaca, N.Y.: Cornell University Press, 1954.

Orr, James. *The Problem of the Old Testament.* New York: Charles Scribner's Sons, written 1905, printed 1917.

Orr, James. *The Resurrection of Jesus.* Quoted in Bernard Ramm, *Protestant Christian Evidences.* Chicago: Moody Press, 1957.

Orr, James. *The Virgin Birth of Christ.* New York: Charles Scribner's Sons, 1907.

Orr, James, John L. Nielson, and James Donalson, eds. *The International Standard Bible Encyclopedia,* Vol. I. Edinburgh: T. & T. Clark, 1867.

Orr, James, ed. *International Standard Bible Encyclopedia,* Grand Rapids: William B. Eerdmans Publishing Co., 1960.

Osborne, Grant R. "Redaction Criticism and the Great Commission: A Case Study Toward a Biblical Understanding of Inerrancy." *Journal of the Evangelical Theological Society* 19. Spring 1976.

Owens, Joseph. *Cognition: an Epistemological Inquiry.* Houston: Center for Thomistic Studies, 1992.

Owens, Joseph. *An Elementary Christian Metaphysics.* Houston: Center for Thomistic Studies, 1963.

Pache, Rene. *Inspiration and Authority of Scripture.* Chicago: Moody, 1969.

Packer, J. I. *Knowing God.* Downers Grove, Ill.: InterVarsity Press, 1973.

Paine, Thomas. *Collected Writings.* Ed. by Eric Foner. New York: The Library of America, 1995.

Palau, Luis. *God Is Relevant.* New York: Doubleday, 1997.

Paley, William. *Natural Theology. God.* Ed. by Frederick Ferre. New York: The Bobbs-Merrill Company Inc., 1963.

Paley, William. *Natural Theology.* In *The Cosmological Arguments: A Spectrum of Opinion.* Ed. by Donald R. Burrill. Anchor Books edition. Garden City, N.Y.: Doubleday, 1967.

Paley, William. *Natural Theology.* In *The Existence of God.* Ed. by John Hick. New York: The Macmillan Company, 1964.

Paley, William. *A View of the Evidences of Christianity.* 14th ed. London: S. Hamilton, Weybridge, 1811.

Palmer, Edwin, ed. *The Encyclopedia of Chrisitianity.* Vol. 1. Delaware: National Foundation of Christian Education, 1964.

Palmer, Humphrey. *The Logic of Gospel Criticism.* London, Melbourne: Macmillan; New York: St. Martin's Press, 1968.

Pannenberg, Wolfhart. *Jesus—God and Man.* Trans. by L. L. Wilkins and D. A. Priche. Philadelphia: Westminster Press, 1968.

Pannenberg, Wolfhart. *Revelation as History.* Trans. by David Granskow. New York: Macmillan, 1968.

Parker, F. H. "A Realistic Appraisal of Knowledge," *Philosophy of Knowledge: Selected Readings.* Ed. by Roland Houde and Joseph P. Mullally. Chicago: J. B. Lippincott, 1960.

Parkin, Vincent. "Bultmann and Demythologizing," *The London Quarterly and Holborn Review.* Vol. 187. October 1962.

Pascal, Blaise. *The Provincial Letters, Pensees, Scientific Treatises.* In *Great Books of the Western World,* ed. Robert Maynard Hutchins. Trans. by W. F. Trotter. Chicago: The University of Chicago, Encyclopaedia Britannica, Inc., 1984.

Patai, Raphael. *The Kingdom of Jordan.* Princeton, N.J.: Princeton University Press, 1958.

Patterson, Bob E. "The Influence of Form-Criticism on Christology," *Encounter.* Vol. 31. Winter, 1970.

Patzia, Arthus G. *The Making of the New Testament.* Downers Grove, Ill.: InterVarsity Press, 1995.

Payne, J. Barton. *Encyclopedia of Biblical Prophecy.* London: Hodder and Stoughton, 1973.

Payne, J. B. *An Outline of Hebrew History.* Grand Rapids: Baker Book House, 1954.

Payne, J. Barton. "The Plank Bridge: Inerrancy and the Biblical Autographs," *United Evangelical Action* 24. December 1965.

Payne, J. Barton. *The Theology of the Older Testament.* Grand Rapids: Zondervan, 1962.

Payne, J. Barton. "The Validity of Numbers in Chronicles," *Bulletin of the Near East Archaeological Society.* New series. 11. 1978.

Peake, W. S. *Christianity, Its Nature and Its Truths.* London: Duckworth and Co., 1908.

Pedersen, J. "Die Auffassung vom Alten Testament." In *Zeitschrift fur die Alttestamentliche Wissenschaft.* Quoted in C. R. North, "Pentateuchal Criticism," in *The Old Testament and Modern Study: A Generation of Discovery and Research.* Ed. by H. H. Rowley. Oxford: Oxford University, 1956.

Pedersen, Johannes and Geoffrey Cumberlege. *Israel, Its Life and Culture.* Vols. 1 and 2. Trans. by Annie I. Fausboll. London: Oxford University Press, 1947.

Peet, T. Eric. *Egypt and the Old Testament.* Liverpool: Univ. Press of Liverpool, 1942.

Pelikan, Jaroslav. *Jesus Through the Centuries: His Place in the History of Culture.* New Haven, Conn.: Yale University Press, 1985.

Peritz, Ismar J. "Form Criticism as an Experiment," *Religion in Life* 10. Spring 1941.

Perrin, Norman. *The Promise of Bultmann.* In the series, The Promise of Theology, ed. by Martin E. Marty. New York: J. P. Lippincott Co., 1969.

Perrin, Norman. *What Is Redaction Criticism?* Philadelphia: Fortress Press, 1969.

Peru, Paul William. *Outline of Psychiatric Case-Study.* New York: Paul B. Hoeger, Inc. 1939.

Pesch, Rudolf. "Form Criticism," *Sacramentum Mundi.* Ed. by Karl Rahner. Vol. 2. New York: Herder and Herder, 1968.

Peters, F. E. *The Harvest of Hellenism.* New York: Simon and Schuster, 1971.

Pettinato, Giovanni, "The Royal Archives of Tell-Mardikh-Ebla," *The Biblical Archaeologist* 39, no. 2. May 1976.

Pfeiffer, Robert H. *Introduction to the Old Testament.* New York: Harper, 1941.

Pfeiffer, R. H. *Introduction to the Old Testament.* New York: Harper and Brothers Publishers, 1948.

Pfeiffer, Charles F. and Everett F. Harrison, ed. *The Wycliffe Bible Commentary.* Chicago: Moody Press, 1962.

Phillips, J. B. *When God Was a Man.* New York: Abingdon Press: 1955.

Phillips, Timothy R. and Dennis L. Okholm, eds. *Christian Apologetics in the Postmodern World.* Downers Grove, Ill.: InterVarsity, 1995.

Philo, Judaeus. *The Works of Philo.* Vol. 4. Trans. by F. H. Colson. Cambridge: Harvard University Press, 1935.

Pickering, Wilbur N. *The Identity of the New Testament Text.* Nashville: Thomas Nelson, 1977. Reprint, 1980.

Pinnock, Clark. *Biblical Revelation.* Chicago: Moody, 1971.

Pinnock, Clark. "The Case Against Form-Criticism," *Christianity Today.* Vol. 9. July 16, 1965.

Pinnock, Clark H. *Set Forth Your Case.* Nutley, N.J.: The Craig Press, 1967.

Piper, Otto A. "Myth in the New Testament," *Twentieth Century Encyclopedia of Religious*

Knowledge. Vol. 2. Ed. by Lefferts A. Loetscher. Grand Rapids: Baker Book House, 1955.

Piper, Otto. "The Origin of the Gospel Pattern," *Journal of Biblical Literature.* Vol. 78. June 1959.

Pittenger, W. Norman. "The Problem of the Historical Jesus," *Anglical Theological Review.* Vol. 36. April 1954.

Plantinga, Alvin C. *God, Freedom, and Evil.* Grand Rapids: William B. Eerdmans Publishing Co., 1996.

Plantinga, Alvin C. "Methodological Naturalism?" *Origins & Design.* Winter, 1997.

Plato. *The Collected Dialogues of Plato.* Ed. by Edith Hamilton and Huntington Cairns. Princeton, N.J.: Princeton University, 1961.

Pliny the Elder. *Natural History.* Trans. by H. Rackham and W. H. S. Jones (from the Loeb Classical Library, ed. by T.E. Page). Cambridge: Harvard University Press, 1951.

Pliny the Younger. *Letters.* Trans. by W. Melmoth. Quoted in Norman L. Geisler, *Baker's Encyclopedia of Christian Apologetics.* Grand Rapids: Baker Book House, 1998.

Polkinghorne, John. *Science and Creation: The Search for Understanding.* Boston: New Science Library; New York: Random House, 1989, 22. Quoted in Alvin C. Plantinga, "Methodological Naturalism?" *Origins & Design,* 23, n. 22. Winter, 1997.

Powell, Robert. *Zen and Reality.* New York: Viking, 1975.

Price, Ira M. *The Monuments and the Old Testament.* 17th edition. Philadelphia: The Judson Press, 1925.

Price, Randall. *Secrets of the Dead Sea Scrolls.* Eugene, Ore.: Harvest House Publishers, 1996.

Pritchard, H. A. *Kant's Theory of Knowledge.* Oxford: Clarendon Press, 1909.

Pritchard, J. B., ed. *Ancient Near East Texts.* Quoted in Norman L. Geisler, *Baker's Encyclopedia of Christian Apologetics.* Grand Rapids: Baker Book House, 1998.

Purtill, Richard L. "Defining Miracles," *In Defense of Miracles.* Ed. by R. Douglas Geivett and Gary R. Habermas. Downers Grove, Ill.: InterVarsity Press, 1997.

Rabast, Karlheinz, as quoted in Edward J. Young, *Genesis 3: A Devotional and Expository Study.* Carlisle, Pa.: The Banner of Truth Trust, 1966.

Rackl, Hans-Wolf. *Archaeology Underwater.* Trans. by Ronald J. Floyd. New York: Charles Scribner's Sons, 1968.

Radmacher, Earl. Personal conversation with Dr. Radmacher in June 1972.

Rahner, Karl, ed. *Sacramentum Mundi.* Vol. 2. New York: Herder and Herder, 1968.

Ramm, Bernard. "Can I Trust My Old Testament?" *The King's Business.* February 1949.

Ramm, Bernard. *Protestant Biblical Interpretation.* Rev. ed. Boston: Wilde, 1956.

Ramm, Bernard. *Protestant Christian Evidences.* Chicago: Moody Press, 1953.

Ramm, Bernard. *Protestant Christian Evidences.* Chicago: Moody Press, 1957.

Ramsay, Sir W. M. *The Bearing of Recent Discovery on the Trustworthiness of the New Testament.* London: Hodder and Stoughton, 1915.

Ramsay, W. M. *St. Paul the Traveller and the Roman Citizen.* Grand Rapids: Baker Book House, 1962.

Ramsey, F. P. "Facts and Propositions." In *Philosophical Papers,* ed. D. H. Mellor. Cambridge: Cambridge University Press, 1990.

Rashdall, Hastings. "The Theory of Good and Evil," *The Existence of God.* Ed. by John Hick, 144–52. New York: The Macmillan Company, 1964.

Rast, Walter E. *Tradition, History and the Old Testament.* Philadelphia: Fortress Press, 1972.

Raven, John Howard. *Old Testament Introduction.* New York: Fleming H. Revell Company, 1906. Revised, 1910.

Redlich, E. Basil. *Form Criticism.* Edinburgh: Thomas Nelson and Sons, Ltd., 1939.

Redlich, E. Basil. *The Student's Introduction to the Synoptic Gospels.* London: Longmans, Green and Co., 1936.

Reed, David A. *Jehovah's Witnesses Answered Verse by Verse.* Grand Rapids: Baker Book House, 1986.

Regis, L. M. *Epistemology.* Trans. by Imelda Choquette Byrne. New York: Macmillan, 1959.

Reichenbach, Bruce R. *The Cosmological Argument: A Reassessment.* Springfield, Ill.: Charles C. Thomas, 1972.

Reid, David R. "Unnaturally Unique." River Forest, Ill.: Devotions for Growing Christians.

[Online]. Available:[http://www.emmaus.edu/dfgc/unique.htm] [1 October 1998].

Reisner, G. A. and W. S. Smith. *A History of the Giza Necropolis,* Vol. 2. Cambridge: Harvard University Press, 1955.

Rescher, Nicholas. "Noumenal Causality." In *Kant's Theory of Knowledge,* ed. Beck, Lewis White. Dordrecht, Holland: D. Reidel, 1974.

Rhodes, Ron. *Reasoning from the Scriptures with the Jehovah's Witnesses.* Eugene, Ore.: Harvest House, 1993

Rice, John R. *Is Jesus God?* 4th rev. ed. Murfreesboro, Tenn.: Sword of the Lord, 1966.

Richardson, Alan. *The Bible in the Age of Science.* Philadelphia: The Westminster Press, 1961.

Ridderbos, Herman N. *Bultmann.* Trans. by David H. Freeman. Grand Rapids: Baker Book House, 1960.

Riddle, Donald Wayne. *Early Christian Life as Reflected in Its Literature.* New York: Willett, Clark and Company, 1936.

Rienecker, Fritz. *A Linguistic Key to the Greek New Testament.* Ed. by Cleon L. Rogers, Jr. Grand Rapids: Zondervan Publishing House, 1980.

Riesenfeld, Harald. *The Gospel Tradition and Its Beginnings: A Study in the Limits of "Formgeschichte".* London: A. R. Mowbray & Co. Limited, 1957.

Roberts, Alexander and James Donaldson, ed. *Ante-Nicene Christian Library: Translations of the Writings of the Fathers.* Vol. 1. Edinburgh: T & T Clark, 1867.

Robertson, A. T. *A New Short Grammar of the Greek Testament.* Part I. New York: Richard R. Smith, Inc., 1931.

Robertson, Archibald Thomas. *Word Pictures in the New Testament.* Vols. I-V. Nashville: Broadman Press, 1930.

Robertson, Archibald Thomas. *Word Pictures in the New Testament.* 5 vols. Nashville: Broadman Press, 1930. Reprint, New York: R. R. Smith, Inc., 1931.

Robinson, George Livingston. *The Sarcophagus of an Ancient Civilization.* New York: Macmillan Company, 1930.

Robinson, James M., ed. *The Nag Hamadi Library.* New York: Harper & Row Publishers, 1981.

Robinson, James M. *A New Quest of the Historical Jesus.* Naperville, Ill.: Alec R. Allenson, Inc., 1959.

Robinson, James M. "The Recent Debate on the New Quest," *Journal of Bible and Religion.* Vol. 30. July 1962.

Robinson, John A. T. *Redating the New Testament.* Philadelphia: Westminster, 1976.

Robinson, William Childs. *Our Lord.* Grand Rapids: Wm. B. Eerdmans, 1937.

Robinson, William Childs, ed. *Who Say Ye That I Am?* Grand Rapids: Wm. B. Eerdmans, 1949.

Rogers, Clement F. *The Case for Miracles.* London: Society for Promoting Christian Knowledge, 1936.

Rogers, Cleon. "Unpublished Lecture Notes from Contemporary New Testament Issues in European Theology 232," Dallas Theological Seminary, Spring, 1979.

Rogers, Jack B. and Donald K. McKim. *The Authority and Interpretation of the Bible: An Historical Approach.* San Francisco: Harper and Row, 1979.

Rohde, Joachim. *Rediscovering the Teaching of the Evangelists.* Philadelphia: The Westminster Press, 1968.

Roper, Albert. *Did Jesus Rise from the Dead?* Grand Rapids: Zondervan Publishing House, 1965.

Ropes, James Hardy. *The Synoptic Gospels.* Cambridge: Harvard University Press, 1934.

Rorty, Richard. *Consequences of Pragmatism.* Minneapolis: University of Minnesota Press, 1982.

Rosche, Theodore R. "The Words of Jesus and the Future of the 'Q' Hypothesis, Part III," *Journal of Biblical Review.* Vol. 79, September 1960.

Rosenau, Pauline Marie. *Post-Modernism and the Social Sciences: Insights, Inroads, Intrusions.* Princeton, N.J.: Princeton University Press, 1992.

Ross, G. A. Johnston. *The Universality of Jesus.* New York: Fleming H. Revell, 1906.

Ross, Hugh. "Astronomical Evidences for a Personal, Transcendent God," *The Creation Hypothesis: Scientific Evidence for an Intelligent Designer.* Ed. by J.P. Moreland. Downers Grove, Ill.: InterVarsity Press, 1994.

Ross, Hugh. *The Fingerprint of God: Recent Scientific Discoveries Reveal The Unmistakable Identity of the Creator*, 2nd ed. Orange, Calif.: Promise, 1991.

Ross, Hugh. "Science in the News," *Facts & Faith* 12, no. 2. Reasons To Believe, 1998.

Rosscup, James. Class Notes. La Mirada, Calif.: Talbot Theological Seminary, 1969.

Rowley, H. H. *The Growth of the Old Testament.* London: Hutchinson's University Library, Hutchinson House, 1950.

Rowley, H. H. *The Old Testament and Modern Study: A Generation of Discovery and Research.* Oxford: Oxford University, 1956.

Rowley, H. H. *Worship in Ancient Israel.* London: S.P.C.K., 1967.

Runia, Klaas. "The Modern Debate Around the Bible," *Christianity Today* 12, no. 20. July 5, 1968.

Russell, Bertrand. *Logic and Knowledge.* New York: The Macmillan Company, 1956.

Russell, Bertrand. *The Problems of Philosophy.* New York: Oxford University, 1959.

Russell, Bertrand. *Why I Am Not a Christian and Other Essays on Religion and Related Subjects.* Ed. by Paul Edwards. New York: Simon and Schuster, A Touchstone Book, 1957.

Ryle, J. C. *Expository Thoughts on the Gospels.* (St. Mark). New York: Robert Carter and Brothers, 1866.

Ryrie, Charles C. *Basic Theology.* Wheaton, Ill.: Victor Books, 1986.

Ryrie, Charles C. *The Ryrie Study Bible, NKJV.* Chicago: Moody Press, 1985.

Sagan, Carl. *Cosmos.* New York: Random House, 1980.

Sanday, William, ed. *Oxford Studies in the Synoptic Problem.* Oxford: at the Clarendon Press, 1911.

Sanders, C. *Introduction to Research in English Literary History.* New York: Macmillan Co., 1952.

Sanders, James A. "Biblical Criticism and the Bible as Canon," *Union Seminary Quarterly Review* 32. Spring and Summer, 1977.

Sarna, Nahum. *Understanding Genesis.* New York: McGraw-Hill Book Co., 1966.

Sartre, Jean-Paul. *Being and Nothingness.* Trans. by Hazel E. Barnes. New York: Gramercy Books, 1994.

Sayce, A. H. *Fresh Light from the Ancient Monuments.* London: The Religious Tract Society, 1895.

Sayce, A. H. *The "Higher Criticism" and the Verdict of the Monuments.* London: Society for Promoting Christian Knowledge, 1895.

Sayce, A. H. *Monument Facts and Higher Critical Fancies.* London: The Religious Tract Society, 1904.

Schaeffer, Francis A. *The Complete Works of Francis A. Schaeffer: A Christian Worldview.* Vol. 1. Westchester, Ill.: Crossway, 1982.

Schaff, Philip. *History of the Christian Church,* Grand Rapids: Wm. B. Eerdmans, 1910.

Schaff, Philip. *History of the Christian Church,* reprint ed. Grand Rapids: Wm. B. Eerdmans, 1962.

Schaff, Philip. *The Person of Christ.* New York: American Tract Society, 1913.

Schaff, Philip. *A Select Library of the Nicence and Ante-Nicene Fathers of the Christian Church.* Vol. 4. Grand Rapids: Eerdmans, 1956.

Schaff, Philip. *A Select Library of the Nicene and Post-Nicene Fathers of the Christian Church.* Vols. IV, X. New York: The Christian Literature Company, 1888.

Scheffrahn, Karl and Henry Kreyssler. *Jesus of Nazareth: Who Did He Claim to Be?* Dallas: Pat Booth, 1968.

Schmidt, K. L. *Der Rahman der Geschichte Jesus.* Berlin: Twowitzsch & Sohn, Limited, 1936.

Schonfield, Hugh. *According to the Hebrews.* London: Gerald Duckworth & Co., 1937.

Schonfield, H. J. *The Passover Plot: New Light on the History of Jesus.* New York: Bantam, 1967.

Schultz, Hermann. *Old Testament Theology.* Trans. from the fourth edition by H. A. Patterson. Edinburgh: T & T Clark, 1898.

Schultz, Thomas. *The Doctrine of the Person of Christ with an Emphasis upon the Hypostatic Union.* Unpublished dissertation. Dallas, Tex.: Dallas Theological Seminary, 1962.

Schwarz, Stephen. "Introduction—Philosophy." In *The Intellectuals Speak Out About God*, ed. Roy Abraham Varghese. Dallas: Lewis and Stanley Publishers, 1984.

Schwarz, Stephen. "Summary Statement." In *The Intellectuals Speak Out About God*, ed. by Roy

Abraham Varghese. Dallas: Lewis and Stanley Publishers, 1984.

Schweitzer, Albert. *Out of My Life and Thought.* Trans. by C. T. Campton. New York: Henry Holt and Company, 1949.

Schweitzer, Albert. *The Psychiatric Study of Jesus.* Trans. by Charles R. Joy. Boston: The Beacon Press, 1948.

Schweitzer, Albert. *The Quest of the Historical Jesus: A Critical Study of Its Progress from Reimarus to Wrede.* Trans. by W. Montgomery. New York: Macmillan, 1960.

Scott, Ernest Findlay. *The Literature of the New Testament.* Morningside Heights, N. Y.: Columbia University Press, 1936.

Scott, Ernest Findlay. *The Validity of the Gospel Record.* New York: Charles Scribner's Sons, 1938.

Scott, Martin J. *Jesus as Men Saw Him.* New York: P. J. Kennedy and Sons, 1940.

Scott, Sir Walter. *The Monastery.* Boston: Houghton Mifflin Co., 1913.

Scotus, John Duns. *Philosophical Writings.* Trans. by Allan Wolter. Indianapolis: Bobbs-Merrill, 1962.

Scroggs, Robin. "Beyond Criticism to Encounter: The Bible in the Post-Critical Age," *Chicago Theological Seminary Register* 68. Fall, 1978.

Segal, M. H. *Grammar of Mishnaic Hebrew.* Oxford: Clarendon Press, 1927.

Segal, M. H. *The Pentateuch—Its Composition and Its Authorship and Other Biblical Studies.* Jerusalem: Magnes Press, Hebrew University, 1967.

Selleck, W. S. *The New Appreciation of the Bible.* Chicago: University of Chicago Press, 1906.

Seneca, Lucius Annaeus, *Letters from a Stoic: Epistulae morales ad Lucilium [by] Seneca.* Selected and Trans. [from the Latin], with an introduction, by Robin Campbell. Harmondsworth, England: Penguin, 1969.

Sheldrake, Robert. "Modern Bio-Chemistry and the Collapse of Mechanism," *The Intellectuals Speak Out About God.* Ed. by Roy Abraham Varghese. Dallas: Lewis and Stanley Publishers, 1984.

Sherwin-White, A. N. *Roman Society and Roman Law in the New Testament.* Oxford: Clarendon Press, 1963.

Sherwin-White, A. N. *Roman Society and Roman Law in the New Testament,* reprint edition. Grand Rapids: Baker Book House, 1978.

Siculus, Diodorus. *Bibliotheca Historica.* Trans. by Francis R. Walton, C. H. Oldfather, C. L. Sherman, C. Bradford Welles, Russel M. Greer (from the Loeb Classical Library, ed. by T. E. Page). Cambridge: Harvard University Press, 1957.

Sider, Ronald. "A Case for Easter," *HIS Magazine.* April 1972.

Sider, Ronald. "The Historian, The Miraculous and Post-Newtonian Man," *Scottish Journal of Theology.* Vol. 25. No. 3. August 1972.

Simon, Herbert. "A Mechanism for Social Selection and Successful Altruism." Quoted in Alvin C. Plantinga, "Methodological Naturalism," *Origins & Design.* Winter, 1997.

Simpson, C. A. *The Early Tradition of Israel.* Oxford: Basil Blackwell, 1948.

Simpson, Carnegie P. *The Fact of Christ.* Sixth edition, n.p., n.d.

Simpson, George Gaylord. "The Meaning of Evolution." Quoted in Alvin C. Plantinga, "Methodological Naturalism," *Origins & Design.* Winter, 1997.

Sire, James W. "On Being a Fool for Christ and an Idiot for Nobody: Logocentricity and Postmodernity," *Christian Apologetics in the Postmodern World.* Ed. by Timothy R. Phillips and Dennis L. Okholm. Downers Grove, Ill.: InterVarsity Press, 1995.

Sivan, Gabriel. *The Bible and Civilization.* Jerusalem: Keter Publishing House Jerusalem, Ltd., 1973.

Skilton, John. "The Transmission of the Scriptures," *Infallible Word.* Ed. by Ned B. Stonehouse and Paul Wooley. Philadelphia: Presbyterian and Reformed, 1946.

Skinner, John. A *Critical and Exegetical Commentary on Genesis.* Edinburgh: T & T Clark, 1930.

Smalley, Stephen S. "Redaction Criticism," *New Testament Interpretation.* Grand Rapids: Eerdmans, 1977.

Smedley, C. Donald. "The Theological Shift of Method and Perspective in Contemporary Biblical Criticism." Th.M. research project, Dallas Theological Seminary, 1980.

Smith, Charles W. F. "Is Jesus Dispensable?" *Anglican Theological Review.* Vol. 44. July 1962.

Smith, George. *The Book of Prophecy.* London: Longmain, Green, Reader, and Dyer, 1865.

Smith, Huston. *The World's Religions.* San Francisco: Harper Collins Publishers, 1991.

Smith, John E. "The Rationality of Belief in God," *The Intellectuals Speak Out About God.* Ed. by Roy Abraham Varghese. Dallas: Lewis and Stanley Publishers, 1984.

Smith, R. W. *The Prophets of Israel.* n.p., 1895.

Smith, W. Robertson. *Lectures on the Religion of the Semites.* London: Adam and Charles Black, 1907.

Smith, Wilbur M. *A Great Certainty in This Hour of World Crises.* Wheaton, Ill.: Van Kampen Press, 1951.

Smith, Wilbur M. *Have You Considered Him?* Downers Grove, Ill.: InterVarsity Press, 1970.

Smith, Wilbur M. *The Incomparable Book.* Minneapolis, Minn.: Beacon Publications, 1961.

Smith, Wilbur M. "The Indisputable Fact of the Empty Tomb." *Moody Monthly,* May 1971.

Smith, Wilbur M. "Scientists and the Resurrection," *Christianity Today.* April 15, 1957.

Smith, Wilbur. *Therefore Stand.* Grand Rapids: Baker Book House, 1945.

Smith, Wilbur M. *Therefore Stand: Christian Apologetics.* Grand Rapids: Baker Book House, 1965.

Smith, William, ed. *Dictionary of Greek and Roman Antiquitie,* rev. ed. London: James Walton and John Murray, 1870.

Snyder, Phil L., ed., *Detachment and the Writing of History.* Westport, Conn.: Greenwood, 1972.

Soulen, Richard N. *Handbook of Biblical Criticism.* Atlanta: John Knox Press, 1976.

Sparrow-Simpson, W. J. "Resurrection and Christ," *A Dictionary of Christ and the Gospels.* Vol. 2. Ed. By James Hastings. Edinburgh: T. & T. Clark, 1908.

Sparrow-Simpson, W. J. *The Resurrection and the Christian Faith.* Grand Rapids: Zondervan Publishing House, 1968. Reprinted from 1911 edition of Langsmans Green, and Co., published under the title, *The Resurrection and Modern Thought.*

Spinoza, Benedict. *A Theologico-Political Treatise.* Trans. by R. H. M. Elwes. New York: Dover Publications, 1951.

Spivey, Robert A. and D. Moody Smith, Jr. *Anatomy of the New Testament.* London: The Macmillan Company-Collier Macmillan Limited, 1969.

Sproul, R. C. *Essential Truths of the Christian Faith.* Wheaton, Ill: Tyndale House Publishers, 1992.

Sproul, R. C. "The Internal Testimony of the Holy Spirit," *Inerrancy.* Ed. by Norman L. Geisler. Grand Rapids: Zondervan, 1980.

Sproul, R. C. *Not A Chance: The Myth of Chance in Modern Science and Cosmology.* Grand Rapids: Baker, 1994.

Sproul, R. C. *Reason To Believe.* Grand Rapids: Zondervan Publishing House, Lamplighter Books, 1982.

Sproul, R. C., John Gerstner, and Arthur Lindsley. *Classical Apologetics.* Grand Rapids: Zondervan Publishing House, 1984.

Spurr, Frederick C. *Jesus Is God.* London: A. H. Stockwell & Co., 1899.

Stallman, Martin. "Contemporary Interpretation of the Gospels as a Challenge to Preaching and Religious Education," *The Theology of Rudolf Bultmann.* Ed. by Charles Kegley. London: SCM Press, 1966.

Stanton, G. N. *Jesus of Nazareth in New Testament Preaching.* London: Cambridge University Press, 1974.

Stanton, Vincent Henry. *The Gospels as Historical Documents.* Vol. 2. Cambridge: at the University Press, 1909.

Stauffer, Ethelbert. *Jesus and His Story.* Trans. by Richard and Clara Winston. New York: Alfred A. Knopf, 1960.

Stearns, M. B. "Biblical Archaeology and the Higher Critics," *Bibliotheca Sacra* 96, no. 383. July 1939.

Steele, Francis. "Lipit-Ishtar Law Code," *American Journal of Archaeology* 51, no. 2. April-June 1947.

Stein, Gordon. *An Anthology of Atheism and Rationalism.* Amherst: Prometheus Books, 1980.

Stein, Robert. H. "Jesus Christ," *Evangelical Dictionary of Theology.* Ed. by Walter Elwell.

Grand Rapids: Baker Book House, 1984.

Stein, Robert H. *Jesus the Messiah: A Survey of the Life of Christ.* Downers Grove, Ill.: InterVarsity Press, 1996.

Stein, Robert H. *The Method and Message of Jesus' Teachings.* Philadelphia: Westminster, 1978.

Stein, Robert H. "The Redaktionsgeschichtliche Investigation of a Markan Seam," *Zeitschrift für die Neutestamentliche Wissenschaft* 61, 1970.

Stein, Robert M. "What Is Redaktiongeschichte?" *Journal of Biblical Literature.* Vol. 88, 1969.

Stenning, J. F., ed. *The Targum of Isaiah.* London: Clarendon Press, 1949.

Stern, Fritz, ed. *The Varieties of History: From Voltaire to the Present.* New York: Vintage Books, 1973.

Stevenson, Herbert F. *Titles of the Triune God.* Westwood, N.J.: Fleming H. Revell, 1956.

Stewart, Herbert. *The Stronghold of Prophecy.* London: Marshall, Morgan and Scott Publications, Ltd., 1941.

Stokes, Sir George. *International Standard Bible Encyclopedia.* Grand Rapids: Eerdmans, 1939.

Stonehouse, Ned B. "The Authority of the New Testament," *The Infallible Word.* Philadelphia: Presbyterian and Reformed, 1946.

Stonehouse, Ned B. *Origins of the Synoptic Gospels.* Grand Rapids: Wm. B. Eerdmans Publishing Co., 1963.

Stonehouse, Ned B. and Paul Wooley, eds. *The Infallible Word.* Philadelphia: Presbyterian and Reformed, 1946.

Stoner, Peter W. *Science Speaks.* Chicago: Moody Press, 1963.

Stott, John R. W. *Basic Christianity.* 2nd ed. Downers Grove, Ill.: InterVarsity Press, 1971.

Strabo. *The Geography of Strabo*, Vol. 8. English translation by Horace Leonard Jones. New York: Putnam's, 1932.

Straton, Hillyer H. "I Believe: Our Lord's Resurrection," *Christianity Today.* March 31, 1968.

Strauss, David Friedrich. *The Life of Jesus for the People,* 2d ed. Vol. I. London: Williams and Norgate, 1879.

Streeter, Brunett Hillman. *The Four Gospels.* London: Macmillan and Co. Fifth Impression, 1936.

Strobel, Lee. *The Case for Christ.* Grand Rapids: Zondervan Publishing House, 1998.

Strong's Exhaustive Concordance of the Bible. New York: Abingdon-Cokesbury Press, 1944.

Strout, Cushing. *The Pragmatic Revolt in American History: Carl Becker and Charles Beard.* Quoted in David Hackett Fischer, *Historians' Fallacies: Toward a Logic of Historical Thought.* New York: Harper Torchbooks, 1970.

Stuart, Douglas. *Old Testament Exegesis.* Philadelphia: The Westminster Press, 1984.

Suetonius. *The Twelve Caesars.* Trans. by Robert Graves. Revised by Michael Grant. New York: Viking Penguin, Inc., 1979.

Sullivan, James Bacon. "An Examination of First Principles in Thought and Being in the Light of Aristotle and Aquinas." Ph.D. dissertation, Catholic University of America. Washington, D.C.: Catholic University of America Press, 1939.

Sullivan, J. W. N. *The Limitations of Science.* New York: Mentor Books, 1963.

Suzuki, D. T. *The Awakening of Zen.* Boulder: Prajna, 1980.

Suzuki, D. T. *Essays in Zen Buddhism: First Series.* New York: Grove Press, 1961.

Suzuki, D. T. *Essays in Zen Buddhism: Second Series.* New York: Samuel Weiser, 1970.

Suzuki, D. T. *Essays in Zen Buddhism: Third Series.* New York: Samuel Weiser, 1970.

Suzuki, D. T. *Introduction to Zen Buddhism.* n.p.: Causeway Books, 1974.

Suzuki, D. T. *Living by Zen.* New York: Samuel Weiser, 1972.

Suzuki, D. T. *Manual of Zen Buddhism.* New York: Grove Press, Inc., 1960.

Suzuki, D. T. *Mysticism: Christian and Buddhist.* New York: Harper & Brothers, 1957.

Suzuki, D. T. *Outlines of Mahayana Buddhism.* New York: Schocken, 1963.

Suzuki, D. T. *Studies in Zen.* New York: Delta, 1955.

Suzuki, D. T. *What Is Zen?* New York: Harper & Row, 1972.

Suzuki, D. T. *Zen Buddhism.* Ed. by William Barrett. Garden City: Doubleday, Anchor Books, 1956.

Swete, Henry Barclay. *The Gospel According to St. Mark.* London: Macmillan and Co., 1898.

Swinburne, Richard. *The Existence of God?* New York: Oxford University Press, 1979.

Swinburne, Richard. *Is There a God?* New York: Oxford University Press, 1996.

Tacitus. *Annals.* In *Great Books of the Western World*, ed. by Robert Maynard Hutchins. Vol. 15, *The Annals and The Histories* by Cornelius Tacitus. Chicago: William Benton, 1952.

Talmage, James E. *A Study of the Articles of Faith*, 13th ed. Salt Lake City: The Church of Jesus Christ of Latter-day Saints, 1924, 466. Quoted in Norman L. Geisler and William D. Watkins, *Worlds Apart*. Grand Rapids: Baker Book House, 1989, 232, n. 48.

Tan, Paul Lee. *A Pictorial Guide to Bible Prophecy.* Hong Kong: Nordica International, 1991.

Tanner, Jerald and Sandra Tanner. *The Changing World of Mormonism.* Chicago: Moody Press, 1980, 1981.

Tarnas, Richard. *The Passion of the Western Mind: Understanding the Ideas That Have Shaped Our World View.* New York: Ballantine Books, 1991.

Taylor, R. O. P. *The Ground Work of the Gospels.* Oxford: B. Blackwall, 1946.

Taylor, Richard. "Metaphysics and God," *The Cosomological Arguments: A Spectrum of Opinion.* Ed. by Donald R. Burrill. Anchor Books edition. Garden City, N.Y.: Doubleday, 1967.

Taylor, Vincent. *The Formation of the Gospel Tradition*, 2d ed. London: Macmillan and Co., Limited, 1935.

Taylor, Vincent. *The Gospels, A Short Introduction.* Fifth edition. London: The Epworth Press, 1945.

Taylor, Vincent. "Modern Issues in Biblical Studies," *The Expository Times.* Vol. 71. December 1959.

Taylor, Vincent. "Second Thoughts—Formgeschichte," *The Expository Times.* Vol. 75. September 1964.

Taylor, Vincent. "State of New Testament Studies Today," *London Quarterly and Holborn Review.* Vol. 183. April 1958.

Taylor, W. S. "Memory and Gospel Tradition." *Theology Today* 15. January 1959.

Ten Scientists Look at Life. Westchester, Ill.: Good News, n.d.

Tenney, Merrill C. *The Genius of the Gospels.* Grand Rapids: Wm. B. Eerdmans Publishing Co., 1951.

Tenney, Merrill C. "The Gospel According to John," *The Expositor's Bible Commentary* series. Gen. ed., Frank E. Gaebelein. Grand Rapids: Zondervan, 1981.

Tenney, Merrill C. *John: The Gospel of Belief.* Grand Rapids: Wm. B. Eerdmans, 1948.

Tenney, Merrill C. *The Reality of the Resurrection.* Chicago: Moody Press, 1963.

Tenney, Merrill C. "Reversals of New Testament Criticism," *Revelation and the Bible.* Ed. by Carl F. H. Henry. Grand Rapids: Baker Book House, 1969.

Tenney, Merrill C., ed. *The Zondervan Pictorial Encyclopedia of the Bible.* Vol. 5. Grand Rapids: Zondervan, 1976.

Tertullian. "Writings of Quintus Sept. Flor. Tertullian," *Ante-Nicene Christian Library: Translations of the Writings of the Fathers.* Ed. by Alexander Roberts and James Donaldson. Vol. XI. Edinburgh: T & T Clark, 1867.

Thaxton, Charles. "A New Design Argument," *Cosmic Pursuit* 1, no. 2. Spring, 1998.

Thiele, E. R. "The Chronology of the Kings of Judah and Israel," *Journal of Near Eastern Studies.* Vol. 3. July 1944.

Thiessen, Henry Clarence. *Introduction to the New Testament.* Grand Rapids: Wm. B. Eerdmans Publishing Co., 1943.

Thomas, Robert L., ed. *New American Standard Exhaustive Concordance of the Bible.* Nashville: Holman, 1981.

Thomas, Robert L. and Stanley N. Gundry. *The NIV Harmony of the Gospels.* San Francisco: Harper San Francisco, 1988.

Thomas, W. H. Griffith. *Christianity Is Christ.* Chicago: Moody Press, 1965.

Thomas, W. H. Griffith. *Christianity's Christ.* Grand Rapids: Zondervan, n.d.

Thorburn, Thomas James. *The Resurrection Narratives and Modern Criticism.* London: Kegan Paul, Trench, Trubner & Co., Ltd., 1910.

Throckmorton, Burton H. Jr. *The New Testament and Mythology.* Philadelphia: The Westminster Press, 1949.

Tillich, Paul. *Dynamics of Faith*. New York: Harper & Row, Harper Torchbooks, 1957.

Toon, Peter. *Our Triune God*. Wheaton, Ill.: BridgePoint Books, 1996.

Torrey, Charles C. *The Composition and Historical Value of Ezra-Nehemiah*. Giessen, Germany: J. Ricker'sche Buchhandlung, 1896.

Torrey, R. A. *The Higher Criticism and the New Theology*. Montrose: Montrose Christian Literature Society, 1911.

Toynbee, Arnold. *Study of History*. Vol. 6. London: Oxford University Press, 1947.

Troeltsch, Ernst. "Historiography," *Encyclopedia of Religion and Ethics*. Ed. by James Hastings. Vol. VI. New York: Charles Scribner's Sons, 1955.

Trueblood, David Elton. *Philosophy of Religion*. New York: Harper & Brothers, 1957.

Tucker, Gene M. *Form Criticism and the Old Testament*. Philadelphia: Fortress Press, 1971.

Tucker, T. G. *Life in the Roman World of Nero and St.Paul*. New York: The Macmillan Company, 1910.

Turner, Steve. "Creed," *Up to Date*. London: Hodder and Stroughton. Quoted in Ravi Zacharias, *Can Man Live Without God?* Dallas: Word Publishing, 1994.

Unger, Merrill F. "Archaeological Discoveries," *Bibliotheca Sacra*. Vol. 112. January 1955.

Unger, Merrill F. "Archaeological Discoveries and Their Bearing on Old Testament." *Bibliotheca Sacra*. Vol. 112. April 1955.

Unger, Merrill F. *Archaeology and the New Testament*. Grand Rapids: Zondervan Publishing House, 1962.

Unger, Merrill. F. *Archaeology and the Old Testament*. Grand Rapids: Zondervan Publishing Co., 1954.

Unger, Merrill F. *Introductory Guide to the Old Testament*. Grand Rapids: Zondervan Publishing House, 1956.

Unger, Merrill F. *The New Unger's Bible Dictionary*. Rev. ed. edited by R. K. Harrison. Chicago: Moody Press, 1988.

Unger, Merrill F. *Unger's Bible Dictionary*. Revised edition. Chicago: Moody Press, 1966.

Unger, Merrill F. *Unger's Bible Dictionary*. Chicago: Moody Press, 1971.

The Upanishads: Katha, Isa, Kena, Mundaka, Svetasvatara, Prasna, Mandukya, Aitareya, Brihadaranyaka, Taittiriya, and Chhandogya. Trans. by Swami Nikhilananda. New York: Bell Publishing Company, 1963.

The Upanishads: Svetasvatara, Prasna, and Mandukya with Gaudapada s Karika. Vol. 2. Trans. by Swami Nikhilananda. New York: Harper & Brothers, 1952.

Urquhart, John. *The Wonders of Prophecy*. New York: C. C. Cook, n.d.

Van Inwagen, Peter. *Metaphysics*. Boulder, Colo.: Westview, 1993.

Van Til, C. Class notes on Apologetics, 1953.

Van Til, C. *The Intellectual Challenge of the Gospel*. London: Tyndale Press, 1950.

Vardaman, E. Jerry. "The Gospel of Mark and 'The Scrolls,'" *Christianity Today*. Vol. 17. September 28, 1973.

Vardaman, E. J. and James Leo Garrett, eds. *The Teacher's Yoke*. Waco, Tex.: Baylor University Press, 1964.

Varghese, Roy Abraham, ed. *The Intellectuals Speak Out About God*. Dallas: Lewis and Stanley Publishers, 1984.

Veith, Gene Edward. *Postmodern Times: A Christian Guide to Contemporary Thought and Culture*. Wheaton, Ill.: Crossway Books, 1994.

Vincent, Marvin R. *Word Studies in the New Testament*. 4 vols. New York: Charles Scribner's Sons, 1924.

Vitz, Paul C. "Modern Psychology and the Turn to Belief in God" *The Intellectuals Speak Out About God*. Ed. by Roy Abraham Varghese. Dallas: Lewis and Stanley Publishers, 1984.

Vokes, F. E. "The Context of Life—*Sitz im Leben*," *Church Quarterly Review*. Vol. 153. July 5, 1952.

Von Rad, Gerhard. *Genesis*. Trans. by John H. Marks (in *The Old Testament Library*. G. Ernest Wright, *et. al.*, eds. Philadelphia: The Westminster Press, 1961.

Von Rad, G. *Old Testament Theology. 2 Vols*. Edinburgh and London: Oliver and Boyd, Ltd, English edition published 1962.

Von Rad, Gerhard. *The Problem of the Hexateuch and Other Essays*. London: Oliver and Boyd, 1966.

Vos, Geerhardus. *Biblical Theology: Old and New Testament.* Grand Rapids: Wm. B. Eerdmans Publishing Co., 1948.

Vos, Geerhardus. *The Mosaic Origin of the Pentateuchal Codes.* London: Hodder and Stoughton, 1886.

Vos, Howard F., ed. *Can I Trust the Bible?* Chicago: Moody Press, 1963.

Vos, Howard F. *Fulfilled Prophecy in Isaiah, Jeremiah, and Ezekiel.* Unpublished doctoral dissertation, Dallas Theological Seminary, 1950.

Vos, Howard F. *Genesis and Archaeology.* Chicago: Moody Press, 1963.

Vos, Howard, ed. *An Introduction to Bible Archaeology.* Chicago: Moody, 1959.

Vos, Johannes G. "Bible," *The Encyclopedia of Christianity.* Ed. by Edwin Palmer. Vol. 1. Delaware: National Foundation of Christian Education, 1964.

Walker, Rollin. *A Study of Genesis and Exodus.* Quoted in Oswald T. Allis, *The Five Books of Moses,* rev. Philadelphia: The Presbyterian and Reformed Publishing Co., 1969.

Wallace, Daniel B. *Greek Grammar Beyond the Basics: An Exegetical Syntax of the New Testament.* Grand Rapids: Zondervan Publishing House, 1996.

Wallace, H. C. "Miracle as a Literary Device," *The Modern Churchman.* Vol. 4. April 27, 1961.

Walsh, W. H. *An Introduction to Philosophy of History.* Key Texts, Classic Studies in the History of Ideas. Bristol, England: Thoemmes Press, 1992.

Waltke, Bruce K. "A Critical Reappraisal of the Literary Analytical Approach," Unpublished paper, Dallas Theological Seminary, 1975.

Walvoord, John F. *Jesus Christ Our Lord.* Chicago: Moody Press, 1969.

Walvoord, John F. and Roy B. Zuck., eds. *The Bible Knowledge Commentary of the New Testament.* Wheaton, Ill.: Scripture Press Publications, Inc., 1985.

Walvoord, John F., and Roy B. Zuck, eds. *The Bible Knowledge Commentary: Old Testament.* Wheaton, Ill.: Victor Books, 1985.

Ward, Philip. *Touring Lebanon.* London: n.p., 1971.

Warfield, B. B. *The Inspiration and Authority of the Bible.* Philadelphia: Presbyterian and Reformed, 1948.

Warfield, Benjamin B. "Introductory Note" in *Apologetics,* vol. 1: *Fundamental Apologetics.* By Francis R. Beattie. Richmond, Va.: Presbyterian Committee of Publication, 1903.

Warfield, Benjamin. "The Resurrection of Christ an Historical Fact, Evinced by Eyewitnesses." Quoted in Wilbur M. Smith, *Therefore Stand: Christian Apologetics.* Grand Rapids: Baker Book House, 1965.

Wedel, T. O. "Bultmann and Next Sunday's Sermon," *Anglican Theological Review.* Vol. 39. January 1957.

Weinfeld, Moshe. *Deuteronomy and The Deuteronomic School.* Oxford: Oxford University Press, 1972.

Weiss, Johannes. *Earliest Christianity.* Trans. by Frederick C. Grant. New York: Harper and Brothers, 1959.

Wellhausen, Julius. *Die Composition des Hexateuchs.* Third Edition. Berlin, 1899.

Wellhausen, J. *Prolegomena to the History of Israel.* Trans. by Black and Menzies. Edinburgh: Adam and Charles Black, 1885. Originally published in 1878 under the title *History of Israel.*

Wellhausen, J. *Sketch of the History of Israel and Judah.* London and Edinburgh: Adam and Charles Black, 1891.

Wells, H. G. *Outline of History.* Garden City, N.Y.: Garden City, 1931.

Wenham, Gordon J., "Bethulah, a Girl of Marriageable Age," *Vetus Testamentum* 22:3. July 1972.

Wenham, John. *Christ and the Bible.* Downers Grove, Ill.: InterVarsity, 1972.

Wenham, John W. "Christ's View of Scripture" *Inerrancy.* Ed. by Norman L. Geisler. Grand Rapids: Zondervan, 1980.

Westcott, B. F. *Gospel of the Resurrection.* London: Macmillan and Co., 1868.

Westcott, Brooke Foss. *Introduction to the Study of the Gospels.* London: SCM Press Ltd., 1951.

Westermann, Claus. *Genesis 1–11: A Commentary.* Trans. by John J. Scullion. Minneapolis: Augsburg, 1984.

Westermann, Claus. *Handbook to the Old Testament*. Trans. by Robert H. Boyd. Minneapolis: Augsburg, 1967.

Westphal, Merald. "The Historian and the Believer," *Religious Studies*. Vol. 2, No. 2, 1967.

Whedon, D. D. *Commentary of the Gospels Matthew–Mark*. Vol. 9. New York: Hunt and Eaton, 1888.

White, W., Jr. "Talmud," *The Zondervan Pictorial Encyclopedia of the Bible*. Gen. ed., Merrill C. Tenney. Vol. 5. Grand Rapids: Zondervan, 1976.

Whitehead, Alfred North. *Process and Reality: an Essay in Cosmology*. Ed. by David Ray Griffin and Donald W. Sherburne. New York: The Free Press, 1978.

Whitehead, Alfred North. *Religion in the Making*. In *Alfred North Whitehead: An Anthology*. Selected by F. S. C. Northrop and Mason W. Gross. New York: The Macmillan Company, 1953.

Whitelaw, Thomas. *Old Testament Critics*. London: Kegan, Paul, Trench, Trubner & Co., Ltd., 1903.

Whitworth, John F. *Legal and Historical Proof of the Resurrection of the Dead*. Harnsburg: Publishing House of the United Evangelical Church, 1912.

Wickramasingha, Chandra. "Science and the Divine Origin of Life," *The Intellectuals Speak Out About God*. Ed. by Roy Abraham Varghese. Dallas: Lewis and Stanley Publishers, 1984.

Wight, Fred H. *Highlights of Archaeology in Bible Lands*. Chicago: Moody Press, 1955.

Wikenhauser, Alfred. *New Testament Introduction*. Trans. by Joseph Cunningham. Freiburg, West Germany: Herder and Herder, 1958.

Wilhelmsen, Frederick. D. *Man's Knowledge of Reality: An Introduction to Thomistic Epistemology*. Englewood Cliffs, N.J.: Prentice-Hall, 1956.

Wilkins, Michael J., and J. P. Moreland, eds. *Jesus Under Fire: Modern Scholarship Reinvents the Historical Jesus*. Grand Rapids: Zondervan Publishing House, 1995.

Willard, Dallas. "The Three-Stage Argument for the Existence of God," *Does God Exist?* J. P. Moreland and Kai Nielsen. Amherst: Prometheus Books, 1993.

Willoughby, Harold R., ed. *The Study of the Bible Today and Tomorrow*. Chicago: University of Chicago Press, 1947.

Wilson, Joseph D. *Did Daniel Write Daniel?* New York: Charles C. Cook, n.d.

Wilson, Robert Dick. "The Meaning of 'Almah' (A.V. "Virgin") in Isaiah VII.14," *Princeton Theological Review* 24. 1926.

Wilson, Robert Dick. *A Scientific Investigation of the Old Testament*. London: Marshall Brothers Limited, 1926.

Wilson, Robert Dick. *A Scientific Investigation of the Old Testament*. Chicago: Moody Press, 1959.

Wilson, R. D. *Studies in the Book of Daniel* (Series II). New York: Fleming H. Revell Company, 1938.

Wilson, Robert Dick. *Which Bible?* ed. by David Otis Fuller. n.p., n.d..

Wilson, Robert M. *The Gnostic Problem*. London: A. R. Mowbray & Co., Limited, 1958.

Wink, Walter. *The Bible in Human Transformation*. Philadelphia: Fortress Press, 1973.

Wiseman, Donald F. "Archaeological Confirmation of the Old Testament," *Revelation and the Bible*. Ed. by Carl Henry. Grand Rapids: Baker Book House, 1969.

Wiseman, D. J., ed. *Peoples of the Old Testament*. London: Oxford Press, 1973.

Witherington, B., III. "The Birth of Jesus," *Dictionary of Jesus and the Gospels*. Ed. by Joel B. Green and Scot McKnight. Downers Grove, Ill: InterVarsity Press, 1992.

Witmer, John A. "The Biblical Evidence for the Verbal-Plenary Inspiration of the Bible," *Bibliotheca Sacra* 121, no. 483. 1964.

Wittgenstein, Ludwig. *The Blue and Brown Books*. New York: Harper & Brothers, 1958.

Wittgenstein, Ludwig. *Tractatus Logico-Philosophicus*. London:Routledge & Kegan Paul, 1961.

Wolff, Richard. *The Son of Man, Is Jesus Christ Unique?* Lincoln, Nebr.: Back to the Bible Broadcast, 1960.

Wood, Bryant G. "Did the Israelites Conquer Jericho?" *Biblical Archaeology Review.* March/April 1990.

Woodward, Kenneth L. "2000 Years of Jesus," *Newsweek.* March 29, 1999.

Woudstra, Marten H. "The Tabernacle in Biblical-Theological Perspective," *New Perspectives on the Old Testament.* Ed. by J. Barton Payne. Waco, Tex.: Word Books, 1970.

Wouk, Herman. *This Is My God.* New York: Doubleday and Co., 1959.

Wrede, W. *Paul.* Trans. by Edward Lummis. London: Elsom and Co., 1907.

Wright, G. Ernest. "Biblical Archaeology Today," *New Directions in Biblical Archaeology.* Ed. by David N. Freedman and J. C. Greenfield. Garden City, N.Y.: Doubleday, 1969.

Wright, G. E. "Archaeology and Old Testament Studies," *Journal of Biblical Literature.* December 1958.

Wright, G. E. *The Bible and the Ancient Near East.* New York: Doubleday & Co., 1961.

Wright, G. E. *Biblical Archaeology.* Philadelphia: Westminster Press, 1957.

Wright, G. E. *God Who Acts.* London: SCM Press, Ltd., 1958.

Wright, G. E. *The Old Testament Against its Environment.* Chicago: Henry Regnery Co., 1950.

Wright, G. E. "The Present State of Biblical Archaeology," *The Study of the Bible Today and Tomorrow.* Ed. by Harold R. Willoughby. Chicago: University of Chicago Press, 1947.

Wright, G. E. "The Terminology of Old Testament Religion and Its Significance," *Journal of Near Eastern Studies.* October 1942.

Wright, G. E. "Two Misunderstood Items in the Exodus Conquest Cycle," *Bulletin of the American Schools of Oriental Research.* No. 86. April 1942.

Wright, G. E., ed. *The Bible and the Ancient Near East.* New York: Doubleday & Company, 1961.

Wright, Thomas. *Early Travels in Palestine.* London: Henry G. Bohn, 1848.

Wurthwein, E. *The Text of the Old Testament: An Introduction to the Biblia Hebraica.* Trans. by Erroll F. Rhodes. Grand Rapids: Eerdmans, 1979.

Xenophon. *The Anabasis of Cyrus.* Trans. by Carleton L. Brownson (from the Loeb Classical Library, ed. by T. E. Page). Cambridge: Harvard University Press, 1950.

Yahuda, Abraham S. *The Language of the Pentateuch in Its Relation to Egyptian.* New York: Oxford, 1933.

Yamauchi, Edwin. "Easter—Myth, Hallucination or History," *Christianity Today.* 2 parts: March 29, 1974; April 15, 1974.

Yamauchi, Edwin. "Jesus Outside the New Testament: What Is the Evidence?" *Jesus Under Fire: Modern Scholarship Reinvents the Historical Jesus.* Ed. by Michael J. Wilkins and J. P. Moreland. Grand Rapids: Zondervan Publishing House, 1995.

Yamauchi, Edwin. *Pre-Christian Gnosticism.* Grand Rapids: Wm. B. Eerdmans Publishing Co. 1973.

Yamauchi, Edwin M. "Stones, Scripts, and Scholars," *Christianity Today.* Vol. 13, No. 10. February 14, 1969.

Yamauchi, Edwin M. *The Stones and the Scriptures.* Philadelphia: J. B. Lippincott Company, 1972.

Yancey, Philip. *The Jesus I Never Knew.* Grand Rapids: Zondervan, 1995.

Yaron, Reunen. *The Laws of Eshnunna.* Jerusalem: Magnes Press, 1969.

Yockey, Hubert P. "Journal of Theoretical Biology." Quoted in Charles Thaxton, "A New Design Argument," *Cosmic Pursuit* 1, no. 2. Spring, 1998.

Yohn, Rick. *What Every Christian Should Know About Prophecy.* Eugene, Ore.: Harvest House Publishers, 1990.

Young. E. J. *An Introduction to the Old Testament.* Grand Rapids: Eerdmans Publishing Co., 1949.

Young. E. J. *An Introduction to the Old Testament.* Grand Rapids: William B. Eerdmans Publishing Co., 1956.

Young, E. J. *Thy Word Is Truth.* Grand Rapids: Eerdmans, 1957.

Young, Edward J. "The Authority of the Old Testament," *Infallible Word.* Ed. by Ned B. Stonehouse and Paul Wooley. Philadelphia: Presbyterian and Reformed, 1946.

Young, Edward J. *Genesis 3: A Devotional and Expository Study*. Carlisle, Pa.: The Banner of Truth Trust, 1966.

Young, John. *Christ of History*. London: Strahan and Company, 1868.

Youngblood, Ronald. *The Heart of the Old Testa-ment*. Grand Rapids: Baker Book House, 1971.

Zacharias, Ravi. *Can Man Live Without God?* Dallas: Word Publishing, 1994.

Zacharias, Ravi K. *A Shattered Visage: The Real Face of Atheism*. Brentwood: Wolgemuth & Hyatt, Publishers, Inc., n.d.

BIOGRAPHICAL SKETCHES OF AUTHORS

Adler, Mortimer Jerome (1902–), B.A., Ph.D., is a philosopher and very influential author. Educated at Columbia College and Columbia University, Adler was a philosophy of law professor at the University of Chicago, and has for many years been the director of the Institute for Philosophical Research and the chairman of the Board of Editors for *Encyclopedia Britannica*. He is the author of *Dialectic, How to Read a Book, How to Think About God, Ten Philosophical Mistakes, Truth in Religion, The Four Dimensions of Philosophy*, and many other works.

Albright, William. F. (1891–1971), Ph.D., Litt.D., was an archeologist and scholar. He was the W. W. Spence Professor of Semitic Languages and chairman, Oriental Seminary at Johns Hopkins University. He taught Semitic languages at Johns Hopkins from 1929 to 1958. He was president of the International Organization of Old Testament Scholars, director of the American School of Oriental Research in Jerusalem, and led a number of archaeological expeditions in the Middle East. He was the author of more than 1,000 publications on archaeological, biblical, and Oriental subjects. He played a prominent role in discrediting the Graf-Wellhausen theory of Pentateuchal origins. In 1933 he described his position as "neither conservative nor radical in the usual sense of the terms" *(Bulletin of the American Schools of Oriental Research,* No. 51, September, 1933, pp. 5, 6).

Allis, Oswald Thompson (1880–1973), was an Old Testament scholar. He graduated from the University of Pennsylvania and Princeton Theological Seminary, then earned his Ph.D. from the University of Berlin. He joined the faculty at Princeton Seminary and became professor of Semitic studies there. Editor of *Princeton Theological Review* for some years, he wrote such books as *The Five Books of Moses, The Unity of Isaiah*, and *The Old Testament: Its Claims and Its Critics.*

Anderson, J. N. D. (1908–1994), OBE, LLD, FBA, lectured in Islamic law for many years. He was professor of Oriental Laws and director of the

Institute of Advanced Legal Studies at the University of London. He was knighted by Queen Elizabeth in 1974.

Archer, Gleason L., Jr., retired former chairman of the division of Old Testament at Trinity Evangelical Divinity School, Deerfield, Ill.; his areas of specialty included archeology, Egyptology, and Semitic languages. He holds a B.A., M.A. and Ph.D. from Harvard; an LLB from Suffolk University Law School, Boston; and a B.D. from Princeton Seminary.

Blaiklock, Edward Musgrave (1903–1983), was a classical scholar and communicator. He graduated from Auckland University in New Zealand and taught there for his entire professional career, retiring as professor of Greek in 1968. He led several tours to archaeological sites in the Middle East and Mediterranean areas and was a prolific writer. He produced works such as *The Acts of the Apostles, The Archaeology of the New Testament,* and *The Pastoral Epistles,* and edited *The Zondervan Pictorial Bible Atlas.*

Bockmuehl, Markus, is a university lecturer in divinity and a fellow and tutor at Fitzwilliam College, Cambridge.

Bright, William Rohl, (1921–), is an evangelist and author, and is founder of Campus Crusade for Christ. He received his B.A. from Northeastern State College in Oklahoma and later studied at Princeton Seminary and Fuller Theological Seminary. In addition to condensing the gospel into four simple points in the evangelistic tool *The Four Spiritual Laws,* he has written many books, tracts, and training materials, such as *Come Help Change the World, The Secret: How to Live with Power and Purpose,* and *Witnessing Without Fear.*

Brown, Raymond E. (1928–1998), B.A., M.A., S.T.B., S.T.L., S.T.D., Ph.D., S.S.B., S.S.L., studied at Catholic University, St. Mary's Seminary, Johns Hopkins University, and the Pontifical Biblical Commission in Rome. Brown served as a professor at St. Mary's Seminary, Union Theological Seminary, the Pontifical Biblical Institute in Rome, Italy, Columbia University, Johns Hopkins University, and Yale Divinity School. His specialty

was New Testament, and he wrote works such as *Biblical Exegesis and Church Doctrine, The Epistles of John,* and many others.

Bruce, Alexander Balmain (1831–1899), M.A., D.D., was professor of theology (apologetics and New Testament exegesis) in the Free Church College, Glasgow (now Trinity College).

Bruce, F. F. (1910–1990), M.A., D.D., was chair of Biblical Studies at Sheffield University and Rylands Professor of Biblical Criticism and Exegesis at the University of Manchester.

Bultmann, Rudolph Karl (1884–1976), was a Protestant theologian and New Testament scholar. He was educated at the universities of Marburg, Tubingen, and Berlin, and held academic appointments at several universities. Bultmann helped pioneer the development of form criticism, a method of examining the Christian scriptures. Bultmann's major works include *Jesus and the World, Jesus Christ and Mythology, Gnosis,* and *Primitive Christianity in its Contemporary Setting.*

Carnell, Edward John (1919–1967), was an Evangelical scholar and theologian. Carnell attended Wheaton College, received Th.B. and Th.M. degrees from Westminster Seminary, and earned a Th.D. at Harvard University. He taught apologetics and philosophy of religion at Gordon College and philosophical apologetics and systematic theology at Fuller Theological Seminary. He also served as president at Fuller and later as professor of ethics and philosophy of religion there. His works include *Introduction to Christian Apologetics, A Philosophy of the Christian Religion,* and *The Case for Orthodox Theology.*

Chafer, Lewis Sperry (1871–1952), was a dispensationalist theologian. He helped C.I. Scofield found the Philadelphia College of the Bible and served on its faculty. He later founded the Evangelical Theological College in Dallas, which became Dallas Theological Seminary, where he later served as president and professor of systematic theology. His major work was *Systematic Theology,* an eight-volume opus.

Corduan, Winfried (1949–), B.S., M.A., Ph.D., is a religious educator and minister. Educated at the

University of Maryland, Trinity Evangelical Divinity School, and Rice University, Corduan is an associate professor of religion and philosophy at Taylor University, Upland, Ind., and has written *Handmaid to Theology* and other works.

Darwin, Charles Robert (1809–82), was a scientist. Educated at the University of Cambridge, Darwin is known for originating the highly influential, yet increasingly discredited, theory of evolution. He was the author of *Origin of Species by Means of Natural Selection* and *The Descent of Man.*

Delitzsch, Franz Julius (1813–1890), studied at the University of Leipzig, professor of theology at Rostock in 1846, at Erlangen in 1850.

Dibelius, Martin Franz (1883–1947), was a German scholar and pioneer of form criticism as a method of examining the Gospels. He earned a Ph.D. at Tubingen, taught at the University of Berlin, and for many years was professor of New Testament at Heidelberg. His major works include *From Tradition to Gospel* and *Studies in the Acts of the Apostles.*

Dockery, David S. (1952–), M.A., M.Div., M.Div., Ph.D., is president and professor of Christian Studies of Union University in Jackson, Tenn. He was formerly vice-president for academic administration and dean of the school of theology at the Southern Baptist Theological Seminary in Louisville, Ky., and professor of theology and New Testament at Criswell College, Dallas, Texas. He studied at the University of Texas-Arlington, Texas Christian University, Southwestern Baptist Seminary, and Grace Theological Seminary. His specialty is the New Testament, and he has written, among others, *The Challenge of Postmodernism: An Evangelical Engagement,* co-edited *New Testament Criticism and Interpretation,* as well as writing numerous articles in theological journals.

Dodd, Charles Harold (1884–1973), was a New Testament scholar and theologian. He studied at Oxford and the University of Berlin, and lectured at Mansfield College, Oxford, where he became professor of New Testament. He later was a professor at Manchester and Cambridge

and authored many books and articles, including *The Bible and its Background, The Gospels as History,* and *Historical Tradition in the Fourth Gospel.*

Dostoyevsky, Fyodor (1821–1881), was a Russian novelist. He is remembered most for authoring *The House of the Dead, Crime and Punishment,* and *The Brothers Karamazov.*

Douglass, Jane Dempsey (1933–), A.B., A.M., Ph.D., is a theology educator. Educated at Syracuse University, University of Geneva, Radcliffe College, and Harvard University, Douglass was a professor at the School of Theology and at Claremont Graduate School (California), and has been Hazel Thompson McCord Professor of History and Theology at Princeton Theological Seminary. She has written *To Confess the Faith Today* and other works.

Earle, Ralph, is head of the department of New Testament at Nazarene Theological Seminary at Kansas City.

Edersheim, Alfred (1825–1889), attended the University of Vienna; a teacher of languages of Pest, Hungary. He was Warbutonian Lecturer at Lincoln's Inn (Oxford); Grinfield Lecturer on the Septuagint.

Evans, Charles Stephen (1948–), B.A., M.Phil., Ph.D., is a philosophy educator. Educated at Wheaton College and Yale University, he was an assistant professor of philosophy at Trinity College, Deerfield, Ill., and was professor of philosophy at Wheaton College and St. Olaf College. He wrote *The Quest for Faith* and *Philosophy of Religion.*

Finegan, Jack (1908–), B.A., M.A., B.D., LL.D., B.D., M.Th., Litt.D., is an archaeology and New Testament specialist. He studied at Drake University, Colgate University Rochester Division, Friedrich Wilhelms University in Berlin, and Chapman College. He was professor and department head of religious education at Iowa State University, Frederick Billings Professor of New Testament History and Archaeology at the Pacific School of Religion, as well as serving as director of its Institute of Biblical Archaeology. Finegan wrote *The Archaeology of the New Testament, Encountering New Testament Manuscripts, Light from the Ancient Past, The Archaeology of World Religions,* and other works.

France, Richard T. (1938–), M.A., B.D., Ph.D., received his education at Balliol College, Oxford University; University of London, and the University of Bristol. He is head of the Biblical Studies department at London Bible College and has served as visiting professor of New Testament at Trinity Evangelical Divinity School, as well as librarian and warden at Tyndale House, Cambridge. France is the author of *A Bibliographical Guide to New Testament Research, Jesus and the Old Testament,* and other works.

Free, Joseph P., Ph.D., is professor of archaeology and history, Bemidji State College; formerly director of archaeological studies, Wheaton College.

Fuller, Reginald H. (1915–), B.A., M.A., is professor of New Testament, emeritus, Episcopal Theological Seminary. Fuller received his education at Peterhouse, Cambridge, and at Tubingen University. He has served as professor at Union Theological Seminary, Seabury-Western Theological Seminary, and St. David's University. Among the many works he has authored is *The Historical Jesus: Some Outstanding Issues.*

Geisler, Norman L., is a graduate of Wheaton College (B.A.) and Wheaton Graduate School (M.A.), majoring in philosophy and theology respectively. He also attended William Tyndale College (Th.B.), Loyola University (Ph.D.), and Detroit Bible College (Th.B.). Dr. Geisler served as chairman of the philosophy and religion department at Trinity Evangelical Divinity School, was professor of systematic theology at Dallas Theological Seminary, and dean of the Liberty Center for Research at Liberty University. He currently serves as dean of Southern Evangelical Seminary, of which he was a co-founder.

Grenz, Stanley J. (1950–), B.A., M.Div., Th.D., is a religion educator. Educated at the University of Colorado, Denver Conservative Theological Seminary, and the University of Munich, Grenz has been a professor at North American Baptist Seminary, and more recently, at Carey Theological College. Grenz is the author of *Prayer: The Cry for the Kingdom, Reason for Hope,* and other works.

Gromacki, Robert G. (1933–), Th.M., Th.D., is a New Testament scholar. Educated at Dallas Theological Seminary and Grace Theological Seminary, Gromacki has been professor of Bible and Greek at Cedarville College, serving as chairman of biblical education there as well. He has authored *The Virgin Birth: Doctrine of Deity* and other books.

Groothuis, Douglas Richard (1957–), B.S., M.A., is a minister. Educated at the Universities of Oregon and Wisconsin, Groothuis is the author of *Unmasking the New Age, The New Age Movement, Jesus in an Age of Controversy,* and *Revealing the New Age Jesus,* and is contributing editor of *Christian Research Journal.*

Gundry, Stanley N. (1937–), B.A., B.D., S.T.M., S.T.D., is a publishing company executive. Educated at L. A. Baptist College, Talbot Theological Seminary, Union College, and the Lutheran School of Theology, Gundry was professor of theology at Moody Bible Institute, adjunct professor of theology at Trinity Evangelical Divinity School, and has since 1980 been vice-president and editor-in-chief of Zondervan Publishing House, Grand Rapids, Mich. Gundry has been co-author and co-editor for many literary projects, including *Tensions in Contemporary Theology* and *Perspectives on Evangelical Theology.*

Guthrie, Donald (1916–), B.D., M.Th., Ph.D., received his education at London Bible College and London University, and was for many years vice-president of London Bible College. Guthrie edited *The New Bible Commentary, The Illustrated Bible Dictionary,* and the *Lion Handbook to the Bible;* and he wrote *New Testament Theology, New Testament Introduction,* and other books.

Harrison, Roland Keith (1920–1993), B.D., M.Th., Ph.D. An Old Testament scholar and theologian, Harrison studied at the University of London, served as head of the Hebrew department at Western Ontario University, and was for many years the chair of Old Testament at Wycliffe

College. Among his writings, which number in the hundreds, were the *International Standard Bible Encyclopedia*, the *New International Commentary on the Old Testament*, and the *Introduction to the Old Testament*. He insisted that biblical criticism should be established only on the foundation of a proper understanding of ancient Near Eastern life and customs.

Harvey, Van A. (1926–), B.A., B.D., Ph.D., is a New Testament scholar who received his education at Occidental College and Yale University. Currently a professor at Stanford University, he was formerly an assistant professor at Princeton University and a professor at Southern Methodist University and the University of Pennsylvania. Among his written works are *Religious Thought in the 19th Century* and *The Historian and the Believer*.

Hengstenberg, Ernst Wilhelm (1802–1869), was qualified at 17 to enter the University of Berlin. There he laid such an excellent foundation in Oriental languages and philosophies that he was able to issue an edition of an Arabic work in German when he was only 21.

Henry, Carl Ferdinand Howard (1913–), is an American Baptist theologian, evangelical leader, and editor. He graduated from Wheaton College, earned his Th.D. from Northern Baptist Theological Seminary, and earned a Ph.D. from Boston University, as well as receiving several honorary doctorates. He was professor of theology and philosophy of religion at Northern Baptist Theological Seminary, and was founding professor of theology and Christian philosophy at Fuller Theological Seminary. He also served as visiting professor at Trinity Evangelical Divinity School. He served as chairman of the World Congress on Evangelism and president of the American Theological Society. Recognized by *Time* magazine as being "the leading theologian of the nation's growing evangelical flank," he earned the respect of many outside Christian circles. Among his works are the six-volume *God, Revelation and Authority*, *Aspects of Christian Social Ethics*, and *The Christian Mindset in a Secular Society*.

Henry, Matthew (1662–1714), was a devotional writer. Henry trained as a lawyer, but became a Presbyterian minister, and is remembered most for his seven-volume *Exposition of the Old and New Testaments*.

Hick, John Harwood (1922–), is a theologian and religious philosopher. Educated at the Universities of Edinburgh and Oxford, he has taught philosophy of religion at Cambridge and Birmingham, and at the Claremont School of Graduate Studies, in California. He has authored books such as *Evil and the God of Love*, *The Second Christianity*, and *The Metaphor of God Incarnate*.

Hoehner, Harold W. (1935–), Th.M., Th.D., Ph.D., is a New Testament scholar and an alumnus of Dallas Theological Seminary and Cambridge University. He has for many years been assistant professor of Bible exposition, and chairman and professor of New Testament literature and exegesis at Dallas Theological Seminary. Among his written works is *Chronological Aspects of the Life of Christ*.

Horn, Siegfried H. (1908–), B.A., M.A., Ph.D., is an archaeology scholar and alumnus of Walla Walla College, Andrews University, and the University of Chicago. He was professor of archaeology at Andrews University and has directed and supervised numerous archaeological excavations. He is the author of *Biblical Archaeology–A Generation of Exploration*, *The Spade Confirms the Book*, and other works.

Hort, Fenton John Anthony (1828–1892), was educated at Rugby and Trinity College, Cambridge. In 1857 he became vicar of St. Ippolyts near Cambridge. Cambridge frequently called upon him to serve as examiner, lecturer, and professor. For six years he lectured on New Testament and patristic subjects at Emmanuel College (Cambridge). In 1878 he was made Hulsean Professor of Divinity.

James, William (1842–1910), was a philosopher. He taught for most of his career at Harvard University. He is remembered most for authoring *The Varieties of Religious Experience*, *The Will to Believe*, and *Pragmatism*.

Jeremias, Joachim (1900–1979), was a theologian and a very influential scholar. Jeremias taught at the Universities of Greifswald and Gottingen and authored *New Testament Theology: The Proclamation of Jesus.*

Josephus, Flavius (c. 37–c. 101 A.D.), was a Jewish historian, author, and member of the Pharisee sect. He studied in the various schools of Judaism, was made a Roman citizen, and devoted himself to studies and literary pursuits. He wrote the seven-volume *History of the Jewish War* and the twenty-volume *Jewish Antiquities.*

Käsemann, Ernst (1906–), is a theologian. A student under Bultmann at Marburg, Käsemann taught at Mainz, Gottingen, and Tubingen. He is a New Testament specialist and is the author of *Exegetische Versuche und Besinnungen.*

Kee, Howard C. (1920–), A.B., Th.M., Ph.D., received his education at Bryan College, Dallas Theological Seminary, and Yale University. Kee has been William Goodwin Aurelio Professor of Biblical Studies at Boston University for many years, and previously taught at Bryn Mawr College and Drew University. A scholar in the areas of archaeology, New Testament, Apocrypha, and post-biblical studies, he has written *Interpreting the Gospels* and other works.

Kenyon, Sir Frederic George, was a British scholar and administrator. He was assistant keeper of manuscripts in The British Museum (1898–1909). He then became director of the museum, an office he held until 1930. He published numerous works including: *The Palaeography of Greek Papyri; Our Bible and Ancient Manuscripts; Handbook to the Textual Criticism of The New Testament;* and *The Bible and Archaeology.*

Kitchen, Kenneth A. (1932–), B.A., Ph.D. Educated at the University of Liverpool, Kitchen is known for his scholarship in the areas of archaeology, Hebrew Bible, New Testament, Egyptology, Mesopotamian studies, Semitic languages, texts and epigraphy, and other subjects. Kitchen is also a veteran of numerous archaeological excavations. Also a prolific writer, Kitchen is the author of *Pharaoh Triumphant (Rameses II)*, *Ramesside Inscriptions*, and more than 100 other books and articles.

Kline, Meredith G. (1922–), Ph.D., is a professor of Old Testament. Educated at Westminster Seminary and the Dropsie College of Hebrew and Cognate Learning, Kline has written such works as *Treaty of the Great King* and *The Structure of Biblical Authority.*

Kung, Hans (1928–), is a Swiss theologian. Kung studied at the German College in Rome, the Gregorian University, at L'Institut Catholique, as well as at universities in Amsterdam, Berlin, London, and Madrid. He became a member of the Catholic theological faculty in Tubingen, and has been professor of dogmatics and director of the Ecumenical Institute of the University of Tubingen. He was also an advisor to Pope John XXIII, and wrote such works as *Infallible?*, *Does God Exist?*, and *The Kung Dialogue.*

Ladd, George Eldon (1911–1982), was a biblical scholar. Ladd graduated from Gordon College of Theology and Missions and completed a Ph.D. in classics at Harvard University. He was a professor at Fuller Theological Seminary and became a major leader among biblical scholars. He sought to be both fully critical and fully orthodox. He wrote *Theology of New Testament*, an alternative to Bultmann's works.

Latourette, Kenneth Scott (1884–1968), was a historian. After graduating from Linfield College, he earned a Ph.D. from Yale University. Latourette taught at Reid College and Denison University, then began a long tenure at Yale, retiring years later as professor of missions and Oriental history. His interests were in East Asian history and missions. Highly regarded as a historian and a churchman, Latourette wrote such works as *The History of the Expansion of Christianity*, *Christianity in a Revolutionary Age*, and *Beyond the Ranges.*

Lewis, C. S. was, until his death in 1963, professor of medieval and Renaissance literature at Cambridge University. A prolific author, his works include the modern classic, *The Chronicles of Narnia*, and other best-sellers: *Mere Christianity*, *The Screwtape Letters*, *Space Trilogy*, *Miracles*, and *The Problem of Pain.*

Little, Paul, was associate director of InterVarsity Christian Fellowship, also serving as its director of evangelism. He spoke on more than 180 college campuses throughout the United States and in 29 countries of Europe and Latin America. Mr. Little served periodically as assistant professor of evangelism at Trinity Evangelical Divinity School, Deerfield, Ill.

Machen, John Gresham (1881–1937), was a New Testament scholar and churchman. Machen graduated from Johns Hopkins University and Princeton Seminary, then studied liberal theology in Germany. He served as a professor at Princeton and wrote, among other books, *The Origin of Paul's Religion, Christianity and Liberalism*, and *The Christian Faith in the Modern World*.

Manson, Thomas Walter (1893–1958), was an English biblical scholar. Educated at Glasgow University and Westminster College, Cambridge, he later served as chair of New Testament Greek at Mansfield College, Oxford, and he eventually taught at Westminster College and Manchester University. Manson was the author of *The Sayings of Jesus* and other works.

Marshall, I. Howard (1934–), B.A., M.A., B.D., Ph.D., was educated at the University of Aberdeen and the University of Cambridge. Marshall has been professor of New Testament exegesis at the University of Aberdeen for many years. He is the longtime editor of *The Evangelical Quarterly*, and has authored *Luke: Historian and Theologian* and *The Origins of New Testament Christology* and other books.

Metzger, Bruce M., was professor of New Testament languages and literature at Princeton Theological Seminary. He holds A.B. and D.D. degrees from Lebanon Valley College, a Th.B. and Th.M. from Princeton Theological Seminary, an A.M. and a Ph.D. from Princeton University, and other advanced degrees from universities in Germany, Scotland, and South Africa. He was president of the Society of Biblical Literature. His area of expertise is New Testament textual criticism.

Miethe, Terry Lee (1948–), A.B., M.A., M.Div., Ph.D., is an educator. Educated at Lincoln Christian College, Trinity Evangelical Divinity School, McCormick Theological Seminary, St. Louis University, and the University of Southern California,

Miethe was assistant professor of theological studies and lectured in philosophy at St. Louis University, and is now professor of philosophy at Liberty University. Miethe is the author of *The Metaphysics of L. J. Eslick, The Philosophy and Ethics of Alexander Campbell, Aristotelian Bibliography, Does God Exist? A Believer and An Atheist Debate*, and other works.

Millard, Alan Ralph (1937–), B.A., M.Phil., was educated at the University of London and the University of Oxford. A veteran of many archaeological excavations, Millard's other areas of specialty are Hebrew Bible, Mesopotamian studies, and Semitic languages, texts and epigraphy. He has written *The Bible B.C.: What Can Archaeology Prove?, Atra-Hasis. The Babylonian Story of the Flood*, and other books and articles.

Montgomery, John Warwick, retired as professor of law and humanities at the University of Luton, England, and previously was professor and chairman, Division of Church History and History of Christian Thought, and director of the library at Trinity Evangelical Divinity School, Deerfield, Ill. He is now at Trinity Seminary, Newburgh, Ind. He also served on the faculty at the University of Chicago, and he studied at Cornell University (A.B.), the University of California at Berkeley (B.L.S. and M.A.), Wittenburg University (B.D. and S.T.M.), University of Sussex, England (M.Phil. in Law), and the University of Chicago (Ph.D.). He is the author of more than 140 books and journal articles.

Morris, Henry M., attended the University of Minnesota (M.S., Ph.D.), Bob Jones University (LL.D.), Liberty University (Litt.D.), and Rice University (B.S.). He was professor of hydraulic engineering and head of the department of civil engineering, Virginia Polytechnic Institute. He serves as president of the Institute of Creation Research, and served as president of Christian Heritage College, San Diego, Calif.

Morris, Leon Lamb (1914–), is an Australian Anglican biblical scholar. He was educated at Sydney University and Sydney Teachers' Training College, and later earned a degree at London and Cambridge (Ph.D.). He served as vice-principal of Ridley College, Melbourne, warden of Tyndale

House, Cambridge, and principal of Ridley College. Morris lectured abroad often and was a prolific author, writing *The Apostolic Preaching of Christ*, *Theology of the New Testament*, and other works.

Moule, Charles F.D. (1908–), B.A., M.A., was educated at Emmanuel College, Cambridge. A New Testament scholar, he was lecturer in divinity at the University of Cambridge, as well as being dean of Clare College, Cambridge. He authored *Essays in New Testament Interpretation*, *The Origin of Christology*, and more than 80 other books and articles.

Nash, Ronald Herman (1936–), B.A., M.A., Ph.D., is a philosophy educator. Educated at Barrington College, Brown University, and Syracuse University, Nash was professor of philosophy at Western Kentucky University and is professor of philosophy and religion at Reformed Theological Seminary. He is the author of more than 20 books, including *Poverty and Wealth*, *Faith and Reason*, and others.

Nix, William, taught at Detroit Bible College and Trinity College. He holds an A.B. from Wayne State University, an A.M. from the University of Michigan, and a Ph.D. from the University of Oklahoma.

O'hair, Madalyn Murray (1919–), B.A., J.D., Ph.D., was litigant in the Murray v. Curlett Supreme Court case that removed prayer from American public schools. She was the founder of the American Atheist Library and author of *Freedom Under Siege*, *What on Earth Is an Atheist?*, *Why I Am an Atheist*, and other works.

Orr, James (1844–1913), was a Scottish theologian and philosopher. He was a graduate of Glasgow University and served as professor of church history at the United Presbyterian Divinity Hall. He also held the chair of systematic theology at the United Free Church College in Glasgow. Orr authored *God's Image in Man*, *The Problem of the Old Testament* (which was an erudite broadside of the Graf-Wellhausen theory of Old Testament origins), *The Virgin Birth of Christ*, *The Resurrection of Jesus*, and other works, and was editor of the *International Standard Bible Encyclopedia*.

Orr, James Edwin (1912–1987), was an evangelist, author, and educator. Orr earned a doctorate at Oxford University and became a professor at Fuller Seminary's School of World Missions. He founded the Oxford Reading and Research Conference on Evangelical Awakenings, and he produced books on faith and scholarly histories of revivals.

Osborn, Grant Richard (1942–), B.A., M.A., Ph.D., is a religion educator and minister. Educated at Ft. Wayne Bible College, Trinity Evangelical Divinity School, and the University of Aberdeen, Scotland, Osborn was professor of New Testament at Winnipeg Theological Seminary, and is associate professor of New Testament at Trinity Evangelical Divinity School. He is the author of *Handbook for Bible Study*, *The Resurrection Narratives: A Reductional Study*, and other works.

Packer, James Innell (1926–), is an Oxford-educated Anglican evangelical theologian. After earning his D.Phil. degree, he served as senior tutor, Tyndale Hall, Bristol, and professor of historical and systematic theology, Regent College. Packer is an influential thinker and Christian apologist whose books include *Knowing God*, *Knowing Man*, *Rediscovering Holiness*, and *Concise Theology: A Guide to Historic Christian Beliefs*.

Palau, Luis (1934–), is an evangelist. He studied at St. Albans College in Argentina and completed a graduate program at Multnomah School of the Bible in Oregon. Palau is the founder of the Luis Palau Evangelistic Team and has written more than thirty books in Spanish and English, including a two-volume commentary on John that he contributed to the *Continente Nuevo* Bible commentary series.

Pascal, Blaise (1623–1662), was a mathematician and theologian. He is remembered chiefly for writing *Pensees*. Pascal believed that God was to be found through faith, not human reason.

Pelikan, Jaroslav Jan (1923–), B.D., M.A., Ph.D., D.D., is a history educator. Educated at Concordia Junior College, Concordia Theological Seminary, and the University of Chicago, Pelikan also received honorary doctorates from dozens of institutions of higher learning. He was a faculty member at Valparaiso University, Concordia Seminary, and the University of Chicago, before starting his long tenure as a faculty member at Yale University. A prodigious author, he has written *From Luther to Kierkegaard, Fools for Christ, The Shape of Death, The Light of the World, The Christian Tradition* (in five volumes), and many other works, and was editor and translator of *Luther's Works* (in twenty-two volumes).

Phillips, John Bertram (1906–1982), was an English Bible translator, writer, and broadcaster. Educated at Emmanuel College, Cambridge, he authored *New Testament in Modern English, Your God Is Too Small, Ring of Truth: A Translator's Testimony*, and other works.

Ramm, Bernard (1916–1992), was professor of theology at Eastern Baptist Theological Seminary and at American Baptist Theological Seminary of the West. He held a Ph.D. from the University of Southern California and authored such books as *An Evangelical Christology, After Fundamentalism, Protestant Christian Evidences, The Christian View of Science and Scripture* and *Protestant Biblical Interpretation*.

Ramsay, Sir William (1851–1939), was a British archaeologist. Educated at Aberdeen, Oxford, and Gottingen, he served as professor of classical archaeology and art at Oxford (1885–1886), and professor of humanity at Aberdeen University (1886–1911). Knighted in 1906, he made discoveries in geography and topography of Asia Minor and its ancient history. He is the author of *The Historical Geography of Asia Minor, The Cities of St. Paul*, and *The Letters to the Seven Churches in Asia*.

Robinson, John Arthur Thomas (1919–1983), was an Anglican bishop and theologian. After earning his Ph.D. from Cambridge, he served as dean of Clare College, Cambridge. Robinson wrote a number of books, including *The Human Face of God* and *The Priority of Man*.

Ryrie, Charles C. (1925–), is a pastor, administrator, and scholar. Ryrie studied at Haveford College and Dallas Theological Seminary, and earned a Ph.D. at the University of Edinburgh. He has

served in professorial and administrative roles at Midwest Bible and Missionary Institute, Westmont College, and Dallas Theological Seminary, and has also been president of Philadelphia College of the Bible. As a fundamentalist scholar, he wrote *New Orthodoxy*, in which he condemned neo-orthodox views as being illogical and unbiblical. He has also written *Biblical Theology of the New Testament, A Survey of Bible Doctrine, Ryrie Study Bible*, and other works.

Russell, Bertrand Arthur William (1872–1970), was a British philosopher, mathematician, and political activist. He taught at Cambridge and at the University of Chicago, and in 1950 was awarded the Nobel prize for literature.

Sagan, Carl Edward (1934–1996), A.B., B.S., M.S., Ph.D., was an astronomer, educator, and author. Educated at the University of Chicago, Sagan received numerous honorary doctorates from prestigious institutions of higher learning. Sagan was a faculty member at Cornell University for more than thirty years and wrote *Cosmos, Intelligent Man in the Universe*, and many other works.

Schaeffer, Francis August (1912–1984), was an American scholar. He was a graduate of Hampden-Sydney College and Faith Theological Seminary, and together with his wife, Edith, founded L'Abri Fellowship, a study center and meeting place for thoughtful Christians. A prolific and influential Christian philosopher, Schaeffer helped broaden evangelical perspectives by urging interest in the arts and culture. Among his books are *Escape From Reason, How Should We Then Live?*, and *Whatever Happened to the Human Race?*

Schweitzer, Albert (1875–1965), was a missionary, musician, physician, and theologian. He studied theology and philosophy at the universities of Strasbourg, Paris, and Berlin, and earned several doctorates. He received the Nobel Peace Prize in 1952. Not an advocate of orthodox Christian views, he was the author of *The Quest for the Historical Jesus, My Life and Thought*, and other books.

Sider, Ronald J. (1939–), is a North American evangelical theologian and social activist. A graduate of Waterloo Lutheran College, he also received a Ph.D. from Yale University. He has taught at the Philadelphia branch of Messiah College and Eastern Baptist Seminary, and is the founder of Evangelicals for Social Action. His most influential literary work is *Rich Christians in an Age of Hunger*.

Smith, John Edwin (1921–), A.B., M.A., B.D., Ph.D., LL.D., is a philosophy educator. Educated at Columbia University, Union Theological Seminary, Yale University, and the University of Notre Dame, Smith has been a faculty member at Yale University for many years, serving as professor of philosophy and also department chairman. Smith has been Clark Professor of Philosophy, Emeritus, since 1991. He is the author of *Reason and God*, *The Philosophy of Religion*, *The Analogy of Experience*, *Quasi-Religions: Humanism, Marxism, Nationalism*, and other works.

Smith, Wilbur, was professor of English Bible at Moody Bible Institute, Fuller Theological Seminary, and Trinity Evangelical Divinity School. His writings include *The Supernaturalness of Jesus* and *Therefore Stand: Christian Apologetics*.

Sparrow-Simpson, W. J., served as chaplain of St. Mary's Hospital of Ilford, England, and was highly respected in Great Britain. He was one of the contributors to the Oxford Library of Practical Theology.

Sproul, Robert Charles (1939–), is a pastor, theologian, broadcaster, and writer. He is a graduate of Westminster College and Pittsburgh Theological Seminary, and he earned a doctorate from the Free University of Amsterdam. He taught at Westminster College, Gordon College, and what is now the Gordon-Conwell School of Theology, before becoming president of Ligonier Ministries. He has also been professor of systematic theology and apologetics at Reformed Theological Seminary, in Mississippi, and is the author of more than thirty books, such as *God's Inerrant Word*, *Classical Apologetics*, *The Holiness of God*, and others.

Stauffer, Ethelbert, was a student and professor at several German universities. He was assistant professor at the Universities of Halle and Bonn

and a professor of New Testament studies and ancient numismatics at Erlangen University. He has also authored six books on Christ and Christian theology.

Stein, Robert H. (1935–), B.D., S.T.M., Ph.D., was educated at Fuller Theological Seminary, Andover-Newton Theological School, and Princeton Theological Seminary. A New Testament scholar, Stein became a professor at Bethel College, and has served for many years as professor of New Testament at Bethel Theological Seminary. Stein is the author of *Difficult Passages in the Gospels*, *An Introduction to the Parables of Jesus*, and other works.

Stonehouse, Ned Bernard (1902–1962), was a New Testament scholar. He graduated from Calvin College and Princeton Theological Seminary and earned a Th.D. from the Free University of Amsterdam. He was a faculty member at Westminster Theological Seminary and taught there for the rest of his career, eventually becoming dean. A vigorous defender of the infallibility of Scripture, he was the editor of the *New International Commentary on the New Testament*.

Stoner, Peter W., M.S., was chairman of the departments of mathematics and astronomy at Pasadena City College until 1953; chairman of the science division, Westmont College, 1953–1957; and professor emeritus of science, Westmont College.

Stott, John R. W., is a graduate of Trinity College, Cambridge. He served for many years as rector of All Souls Church, London. He is the author of books such as *Issues Facing Christians Today* and *The Contemporary Christian*.

Taylor, Vincent (1887–1968), was a New Testament scholar and theologian. Taylor earned a Ph.D. and later a D.D. from London University and taught New Testament at Headingley College, Leeds, where he also served as principal. He wrote *The Formulation of the Gospel Tradition* and *The Life and Ministry of Jesus*.

Tenney, Merrill C. (1904–1985), was dean of the graduate school and professor of Bible and philosophy at Wheaton College, Wheaton, Ill. Noted for his works of rigorous scholarship, he also earned a Ph.D. degree from Harvard University.

Unger, Merrill F. (1909–1980), received A.B. and Ph.D. degrees at Johns Hopkins University and his Th.M. and Th.D. degrees at Dallas Theological Seminary. He was a professor and chairman of the Semitics and Old Testament department at Dallas Theological Seminary.

Van Til, Cornelius (1895–1987), was a reformed theologian and philosopher. He attended Calvin College and Calvin Theological Seminary, then transferred to Princeton Seminary, where he received a Th.M. degree. He also earned a Ph.D. from Princeton University. He later joined the faculty of Westminster Theological Seminary and taught there for the remainder of his career. He authored *The New Modernism, The Defense of the Faith, A Christian Theory of Knowledge,* and other works.

Vos, Howard F., obtained his education at Wheaton College (A.B.), Dallas Theological Seminary (Th.M., Th.D.), Northwestern University (M.A., Ph.D.), Southern Methodist University, and the Oriental Institute of the University of Chicago. He was professor of history at Trinity College, Deerfield, Ill., and The King's College, Briarcliff Manor, N. Y., where he continues as emeritus professor of history and archaeology.

Walvoord, John Flipse (1910–), is an American theologian, pastor, and author. A graduate of Wheaton College and Texas Christian University, he also earned a Th.D. from Dallas Theological Seminary. Walvoord joined the faculty at Dallas Seminary, serving later as its president and, eventually, its chancellor. He is the author of *The Millennial Kingdom, Prophecy Knowledge Handbook,* and other books, and editor of the *Bible Knowledge Commentary.*

Warfield, Benjamin, was an instructor in New Testament language and literature at Western Theological Seminary in Pittsburgh. He studied at Princeton Theological Seminary, and he received the Doctor of Laws from both the College of New Jersey and Davidson College in 1892; Doctor of Letters from Lafayette College in 1911; and Sacrae Theologiae Doctor from the University of Utrecht in 1913. In 1886 he was called to succeed Archibald Alexander Hodge as professor of systematic theology at Princeton Theological Seminary—a position which he occupied with great distinction until his death in 1921.

Wellhausen, Julius (1844–1918), was a biblical scholar. Educated at Gottingen, he later taught in Halle, Marburg, and Gottingen. He is remembered most for authoring *Prolegomena Zur Geschichte Israels,* which contained his theory, known later as the Graf-Wellhausen hypothesis, that the Pentateuch was created from several earlier sources.

Wells, H.G. (1866–1946), was a British novelist. Wells attended Morley's School in Bromley, and earned a B.S. degree, but mainly he was self-educated through extensive reading. For some years he taught in private schools, but moved into a literary career with such influential works as *The Time Machine, The Invisible Man, The War of the Worlds, A Modern Utopia, Outline of History, The Shape of Things to Come,* and other works.

Westcott, Brooke Foss (1825–1901), a theologian and bishop, was educated at King Edward VI's school at Birmingham and at Trinity College, Cambridge, graduating with highest honors. Westcott helped establish the best Greek text of the New Testament, and he helped found the Cambridge Clergy Training School.

Wilson, Robert Dick (1856–1930), was an Old Testament scholar. Wilson was educated at the College of New Jersey (now Princeton University), Western Theological Seminary, and the University of Berlin. He was professor of Semitic philology and Old Testament introduction at Princeton Seminary. He was an advanced linguist, reportedly being fluent in forty-five languages and dialects. He authored *Is the Higher Criticism Scholarly?, Scientific Old Testament Criticism,* and other works.

Wiseman, Donald J., served for many years as assistant keeper of the department of Egyptian and Assyrian (now Western Asiatic) antiquities of the British Museum. Educated at King's College, London, Wadham College, Oxford (M.A.), and the School of Oriental and African Studies (D.Lit.), he excavated at Nimrud, Iraq, and Harran, South Turkey, and served on archaeology survey teams in other Near Eastern countries. He served as professor of Assyriology and is professor emeritus at the University of London. He authored more than 150 books and articles.

Witherington, Ben III (1951–), B.A., M.Div., Ph.D., received his education at the University of North Carolina, Gordon-Conwell Theological Seminary, and the University of Durham. A New Testament scholar, Witherington has been an assistant professor at Ashland Theological Seminary since 1984.

Witmer, John Albert (1920–), A.B., A.M., M.S., Th.M., Th.D., is a librarian. Educated at Wheaton College, Dallas Theological Seminary, and East Texas State University, Witmer was associate professor and later became associate professor, emeritus, at Dallas Theological Seminary. He also served as librarian and archivist there. He has been a frequent contributor of articles to professional journals.

Wright, George Ernest (1909–1974), was a biblical archaeologist. Wright was educated at Wooster College and McCormick Theological Seminary, and he earned a Ph.D. from Johns Hopkins University. He founded *The Biblical Archaeologist* and served as its editor for many years, and he was professor of divinity at Harvard University. He also served as president of the American Schools of Oriental Research, directed several archaeological excavation projects, and authored *Biblical Archaeology, The Old Testament and Theology*, and other works.

Young, E. J. (1907–1968), was a graduate of Stanford University. He received his Ph.D. degree from the Dropsie College for Hebrew and Cognate Learning, Philadelphia. He spent two years in Palestine, Egypt, Italy, and Spain in the study of ancient languages, and studied at the University of Leipzig while in Germany. He served as professor of Old Testament at Westminster Seminary, Philadelphia, until 1968.

Yamauchi, Edwin M., is a graduate of Shelton College (B.A.), and Brandeis University (M.A., Ph.D.). He has been a professor at Miami University (Ohio) for more than 30 years, and his areas of specialty include archeology, Hebrew Bible, and Semitic languages.

Yancey, Philip David (1949–), B.A., M.A., is an author and editor. Educated at Columbia Bible College, Wheaton College, and the University of Chicago, Yancey was for some years the managing editor of *Campus Life* magazine, and is now editor-at-large of *Christianity Today* magazine. He is the author of *In His Image, The Student Bible, Disappointment With God, Reality and the Vision*, and other works.

Youngblood, Ronald F. (1931–), B.D., Ph.D., received his education at Fuller Theological Seminary and Dropsie College. He has been a professor at Wheaton College Graduate School, Trinity Evangelical Divinity School, and at Bethel Theological Seminary, and also served for some years as academic dean at Wheaton College Graduate School. Youngblood's areas of specialty are archaeology, Hebrew Bible, Mesopotamian studies, Semitic languages, texts, and epigraphy. He authored *Evangelicals and Inerrancy, The Living and Active Word of God*, and other works.

Author Index

SUBJECT INDEX

Have You Heard of the Four Spiritual Laws?

Just as there are physical laws that govern the physical universe, so are there spiritual laws that govern your relationship with God.

LAW 1: GOD <u>LOVES</u> YOU, AND OFFERS A WONDERFUL <u>PLAN</u> FOR YOUR LIFE.

God's Love

"For God so loved the world, that He gave His only begotten Son, that whoever believes in Him should not perish but have everlasting life" (John 3:16 NKJV).

God's Plan

(Christ speaking): "I have come that they may have life, and that they may have it more abundantly" (that it may be full and meaningful) (John 10:10 NKJV).

Why is it that most people are not experiencing the abundant life?

Because . . .

LAW 2: MAN IS <u>SINFUL</u> AND <u>SEPARATED</u> FROM GOD. THEREFORE, HE CANNOT KNOW AND EXPERIENCE GOD'S LOVE AND PLAN FOR HIS LIFE.

Man Is Sinful

"For all have sinned and fall short of the glory of God" (Romans 3:23 NKJV).

Man was created to have fellowship with God; but, because of his stubborn self-will, he chose to go his own independent way, and fellowship with God was broken. This self-will, characterized by an attitude of active rebellion or passive indifference, is evidence of what the Bible calls sin.

Man Is Separated

"For the wages of sin is death" (spiritual separation from God) (Romans 6:23 NKJV).

This diagram illustrates that God is holy and man is sinful. A great gulf separates the two. The arrows illustrate that man is continually trying to reach God and the abundant life through his own efforts, such as a good life, philosophy, or religion.

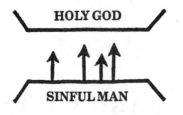

The Third Law explains the only way to bridge this gulf . . .

LAW 3: JESUS CHRIST IS GOD'S <u>ONLY</u> PROVISION FOR MAN'S SIN. THROUGH HIM YOU CAN KNOW AND EXPERIENCE GOD'S LOVE AND PLAN FOR YOUR LIFE.

He Died in Our Place
"But God demonstrates His own love toward us, in that while we were still sinners, Christ died for us" (Romans 5:8 NKJV).

He Rose from the Dead
"Christ died for our sins . . . He was buried . . . He rose again the third day according to the Scriptures . . . He was seen by Cephas, then by the twelve. After that He was seen by over five hundred . . ." (1 Corinthians 15:3–6 NKJV).

He Is the Only Way
"Jesus said to him, 'I am the way, the truth, and the life. No one comes to the Father except through Me'" (John 14:6 NKJV).

This diagram illustrates that God has bridged the gulf that separates us from Him by sending His Son, Jesus Christ, to die on the cross in our place to pay the penalty for our sins.

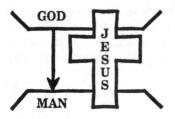

It is not enough just to know these three laws . . .

LAW 4: WE MUST INDIVIDUALLY <u>RECEIVE</u> JESUS CHRIST AS SAVIOR AND LORD; THEN WE CAN KNOW AND EXPERIENCE GOD'S LOVE AND PLAN FOR OUR LIVES.

We Must Receive Christ
"But as many as received Him, to them He gave the right to become children of God, to those who believe in His name" (John 1:12 NKJV).

We Receive Christ Through Faith
"For by grace you have been saved through faith, and that not of yourselves; it is the gift of God, not of works, lest anyone should boast" (Ephesians 2:8, 9 NKJV).

We Receive Christ by Personal Invitation
(Christ is speaking): "Behold, I stand at the door and knock. If anyone hears My voice and opens the door, I will come in to him" (Revelation 3:20 NKJV).

Receiving Christ involves turning to God from self (repentance) and trusting Christ to come into our lives, to forgive our sins and to make us the kind of people He wants us to be. Just to agree intellectually that Jesus Christ is the Son of God and that He died on the cross for our sins is not enough. Nor is it enough to have an emotional experience. We receive Jesus Christ by faith, as an act of the will.

These two circles represent two kinds of lives:

SELF-DIRECTED LIFE

S – Self is on the throne

+ – Christ is outside the life

• – Interests are directed by self, often resulting in discord and frustration

CHRIST-DIRECTED LIFE

+ – Christ is in the life and on the throne

S – Self is yielding to Christ

• – Interests are directed by Christ, resulting in harmony with God's plan

Which circle best represents your life?

Which circle would you like to have represent your life?

The following explains how you can receive Christ:

You Can Receive Christ Right Now Through Prayer

(Prayer is talking with God)

God knows your heart and is not so concerned with your words as He is with the attitude of your heart. The following is a suggested prayer:

"Lord Jesus, I need You. Thank You for dying on the cross for my sins. I open the door of my life and receive You as my Savior and Lord. Thank You for forgiving my sins and giving me eternal life. Take control of the throne of my life. Make me the kind of person You want me to be."

Does this prayer express the desire of your heart?

If it does, pray this prayer right now, and Christ will come into your life, as He promised.

How to Know That Christ Is in Your Life

Did you receive Christ into your life? According to His promise in Revelation 3:20, where is Christ right now in relation to you? Christ said that He would come into your life. Would He mislead you? On what authority do you know that God has answered your prayer? (The trustworthiness of God Himself and His Word)

The Bible Promises Eternal Life to All Who Receive Christ

"And this is the testimony: that God has given us eternal life, and this life is in His Son. He who has the Son has life; he who does not have the Son of God does not have life. These things I have written to you who believe in the name of the Son of God, that you may know that you have eternal life" (1 John 5:11–13 NKJV).

Thank God often that Christ is in your life and that He will never leave you (Hebrews 13:5). You can know on the basis of His promise that Christ lives in you and that you have eternal life, from the very moment you invite Him in. He will not deceive you.

An important reminder . . .

Do Not Depend on Feelings

The promise of God's Word, not our feelings, is our authority. The Christian lives by faith (trust) in the trustworthiness of God Himself and His Word. This train diagram illustrates the relationship between *fact* (God and His Word), *faith* (our trust in God and His Word), and *feeling* (the result of our faith and obedience) (John 14:21).

The train will run with or without the caboose. However, it would be useless to attempt to pull the train by the caboose. In the same way, we, as Christians, do not depend on feelings or emotions, but we place our faith (trust) in the trustworthiness of God and the promises of His Word.

Now That You Have Received Christ

The moment that you received Christ by faith, as an act of the will, many things happened, including the following:

1. Christ came into your life (Revelation 3:20; Colossians 1:27).

2. Your sins were forgiven (Colossians 1:14).

3. You became a child of God (John 1:12).

4. You received eternal life (John 5:24).

5. You began the great adventure for which God created you (John 10:10; 2 Corinthians 5:17; 1 Thessalonians 5:18).

Can you think of anything more wonderful that could happen to you than receiving Christ? Would you like to thank God in prayer right now for what He has done for you? By thanking God, you demonstrate your faith.

Now what?

Suggestions for Christian Growth

Spiritual growth results from trusting Jesus Christ. "The just shall live by faith" (Galatians 3:11 NKJV). A life of faith will enable you to trust God increasingly with every detail of your life, and to practice the following:

G   Go to God in prayer daily (John 15:7).

R   Read God's Word daily (Acts 17:11)— begin with the Gospel of John.

O   Obey God, moment by moment (John 14:21).

W   Witness for Christ by your life and words (Matthew 4:19; John 15:8).

T   Trust God for every detail of your life (1 Peter 5:7).

H   Holy Spirit—allow Him to control and empower your daily life and witness (Galatians 5:16–17; Acts 1:8).

Fellowship in a Good Church

God's Word admonishes us not to forsake " "the assembling of ourselves together . . ." (Hebrews 10:25 NKJV). Several logs burn brightly together; but put one aside on the cold hearth and the fire goes out. So it is with your relationship to other Christians. If you do not belong to a church, do not wait to be invited. Take the initiative; call the pastor of a nearby church where Christ is honored and His Word is preached. Start this week, and make plans to attend regularly.